CW01522672

1 MONTH OF
FREE
READING

at
www.ForgottenBooks.com

By purchasing this book you are
eligible for one month membership to
ForgottenBooks.com, giving you
unlimited access to our entire
collection of over 1,000,000 titles via
our web site and mobile apps.

To claim your free month visit:
www.forgottenbooks.com/free893731

ISBN 978-0-265-81572-4
PIBN 10893731

PART FIRST.

GAZETTEER

AND

BIOGRAPHICAL RECORD

OF

GENESEE COUNTY, N. Y.

1788-1890.

Edited by F. W. BEERS.

"He that hath much to do, will do something wrong, and of that wrong must suffer the consequences; and if it were possible that he should always act rightly, yet when such numbers are to judge of his conduct, the bad will censure and obstruct him by malevolence, and the good sometimes by mistake."—SAMUEL JOHNSON.

SYRACUSE, N. Y.:
J. W. VOSE & CO., PUBLISHERS.
June, 1890.

D. Mason & Co.,
PRINTERS,
SYRACUSE, N. Y.

INTRODUCTION.

IN presenting to the public the GAZETTEER, BIOGRAPHICAL RECORD, AND DIRECTORY OF GENESEE COUNTY we desire to return our sincere thanks to *all* who have kindly aided in obtaining the information it contains, and thus rendered it possible to present it in the brief space of time in which it is essential such work should be completed. Especially are our thanks due to the editors and managers of all the local papers for their uniform kindness, and for granting the use of their files; to Judge Safford E. North for the valuable paper on the Bench and Bar; to Dr. William B. Sprague, of Pavilion, for the paper on the Medical Profession; to D. R. Bacon for history of the town of Le Roy; to J. Lyman Crocker for assistance on the towns of Le Roy and Pavilion; to David Seaver, of New York, for valuable information pertaining to the Masonic history of the county; to John R. Anderson, of Le Roy, for additional Masonic history; to Charles E. Cook, of Byron, for the article on the fruit interests; to the county clerk, Carlos A. Hull, for his assistance in the use of records in his office; and to many others throughout the county, who have rendered valuable aid.

That errors have occurred in so great a number of names is probable, and that names have been omitted which should have been inserted is quite certain. We can only say that we have exercised more than ordinary diligence and care in this difficult and complicated feature of bookmaking. Of such as feel aggrieved in consequence of errors or omissions we beg pardon, and ask the indulgence of the reader in noting such as have been observed in the subsequent reading of the proofs, and which are corrected at the close of this volume.

We would suggest that our patrons observe and become familiar with the explanations at the commencement of the Directory on page 3, part second. The names it embraces, and the information connected therewith, were obtained by actual canvass, and are as correct and reliable as the judgment of those from whom they were solicited renders possible. Each agent is furnished with a map of the town he is expected to canvass, and he is required to pass over every road and call at every dwelling and place of business in the town in order to obtain the facts from the individuals concerned whenever possible.

The map, which has been engraved especially for this work, was compiled from latest existing plans in the county clerk's office, and shows all the new and old railroads, highways, and names of post-offices in the county.

We take this occasion to express the hope that the information found in the book will not prove devoid of interest and value, though we are fully conscious that the brief description of the county the scope of the work enables us to give is by no means an exhaustive one, and can only hope that it may prove an aid to future historians, who will be the better able to do full justice to the subject.

While thanking our patrons and friends generally for the cordiality with which our work has been seconded we leave the work to secure that favor which earnest endeavor ever wins from a discriminating public, hoping they will bear in mind, should errors be noted, that "he who expects a perfect work to see, expects what ne'er was, is, nor yet shall be."

THE PUBLISHERS.

HISTORY

OF

· GENESEE COUNTY.

TO make a history of the importance of a proper one of Genesee County, in the Eden of the Empire State, it would be more complete in itself by introducing, briefly, the early history of the State, the foundation of the title of its territory, its early settlement, and the prominent position this particular county has and does at present sustain in the development of the first State of the Union.

Within the scope of a work of this character the discovery of the continent, and the exploration of its vast territory, need not enter minutely, except so far as relates to our portion of it; the history of its discovery by Columbus, in 1492, is a fact too well known to be repeated, and the discovery of the northern portion by Lief, the son of Eric a Norwegian, who came across the straits from Greenland to Labrador in the year 1000, was only followed by Thorfinn in 1007, who sailed along the same course down the eastern coast to Narragansett Bay, in Rhode Island; this land is called Vinland, and the record of his discoveries is still extant. After quite five centuries had elapsed the intrepid voyager and scholar, Christopher Columbus, by sailing west from Palos, across a then unknown ocean, discovered the Bahama Islands, and was followed by various adventurers from other nations of the Old World who sent them for mercenary motives. In 1497 Henry VII. commissioned John Cabot to sail to this continent, and take possession of it for the Crown of England; and this was successfully accomplished in 1498, on the second voyage by his son, Sebastian Cabot.

In 1524 John Verazzani, in the service of Francis I. of France, sailed along the coast from Georgia to about latitude 41, north, and entered a harbor, which from his description is said to be New York Bay; he remained there 15 days, and is believed to be the first European that landed on the soil of New York; he proceeded northerly as far as Labrador, and, naming the territory New France, took possession for France so far as he could by his rights of discovery. In 1607 Samuel Champlain sailed up the River St. Lawrence in the interest of the French nation; he explored the tributaries of that mighty river, and discovered Lake Champlain, which still bears his name. He also took possession of the "New France," and that nation assumed still greater rights in the new territory.

In 1609 Henry Hudson, an English navigator of note, offered his services to the Dutch East India Company, of Holland, a wealthy corporation formed for trade and colonization, which was accepted; and with a suitable outfit he arrived on the eastern coast of this continent at or near what is now Portland, Me., whence he sailed southward along the coast as far as Chesapeake Bay; from thence he sailed northward again, discovering Delaware Bay, and on the 3d of September anchored off Sandy Hook; he entered New York Bay on the 12th of the same month, and sailed up the river which was given his name, and has been since so called. He anchored just above where the city of Hudson now stands, and sent a boat with a portion of his crew still further up the river on a voyage of exploration; it is supposed, from his description, that the crew ascended above where Albany is now situated. On the 23d of September Hudson descended to the Bay of New York and set sail for home. Holland now claimed the territory from the same right of discovery and exploration, and it will be seen that the three nations mentioned claimed the same; and also that New York State was a part.

It will be no wonder after reading the foregoing that the authority of the different nations should clash somewhat The Dutch sent out other trading vessels in 1612; these were followed by still more, and Manhattan Island was made the chief depot for trade; the States General granted a charter to the merchants for exclusive jurisdiction over "New Netherlands," as it was denominated, and it included all the territory between 40° and 45° north latitude.

In 1621 James I. granted to Ferdinando Gorges and his mercantile associates all lands between the 40th and 48th parallels of latitude, and from ocean to ocean; claim was made of the Dutch for the territory, which was refused, and the subject of title was already becoming important. Both had grants of the territory from the highest authority of their respective nations.

In 1638 William Kieft was made governor of New Amsterdam for the Dutch. He by his acts was plunged into war with the Indians, which lasted till 1645, when a treaty of peace was made, and Peter Stuyvesant was ap_ pointed governor in 1647. To settle the controversy between the Eng_ lish and Dutch settlements arbitrators were appointed to adjust their re_ spective claims; this tribunal assigned the eastern part of Long Island to the English, and a division line specified the boundary between the Dutch New Netherlands and the English Connecticut colonies.

In 1664 Charles II. of England, regardless of the claims of the Dutch or any previous agreement, granted to his brother, Duke of York and Al_ bany,—afterwards James II.,—the whole country from the Connecticut to the Delaware River, which included the entire Dutch possessions. The Duke claimed the territory, which was so strongly to be enforced, if re_ fused, that Governor Stuyvesant surrendered the province September 3, 1664. Thus the possession of New Netherlands passed into the hands of the English, and at once the Duke changed the name to New York, and Fort Orange to Albany. The Dutch attempted to regain the possession of the territory, and nearly succeeded through the treachery of the cap_ tain of the fort at New York. Peace was declared between the rival fac_ tions in 1674, leaving the English in full possession, but the Duke of York, for his own safety, applied for and received from the Crown a new patent.

The French had not been idle, and in the meantime settlements had been made in New France,—the region north of the great lakes and along the St. Lawrence River,—and had allied themselves with the Algonquins in victories against the Iroquois, which embittered the latter against the French; but a peace was concluded in 1667 by the intercession of the Duke of York.

Trade was successfully prosecuted by the French and English in their respective territories for a few years, but artful advantages, instigated by the Catholic missionaries, disrupted the friendly relations between the Iroquois and English, which resulted in a conference, at Albany, of the governors of New York and Virginia and chiefs of the Iroquois, in 1684, and at which harmony was restored. No sooner was peace restored in this direction than discontent arose in another. De la Barre, French gov_ ernor of Canada, made complaint that the Senecas,—a nation of the Iro_ quois,—by their hostilities against the Miamas,—a tribe beyond Lake

Erie, with whom the French were allied,—interrupted their trade. In 1687 the French overrun the country of the Senecas,—Western New York,—and erected a fort at the mouth of Niagara River. The Five Nations flew to arms, descended upon the French, and the settlements south of the lake were abandoned by that nation. This gave the English the government of the territory embraced within the limits of the State of New York.

The revolution in England that placed William and Mary upon the throne was followed in 1669 by war between France and England, which involved, also, their colonies in the New World. Count Frontenac, governor of Canada, endeavored to alienate the fealty of the Iroquois from the English, and in other ways harrassed the latter, even sending an expedition, in February, 1690, to massacre the people at Schenectady. To allay this feeling among the allies Major Schuyler called a council at Albany and secured a renewal of friendship. After several invasions and a long, bloody war the peace of Ryswick, in 1697, terminated the barbarous hostilities between the two nations.

In 1710 it was thought necessary by England to subdue or repay Canada for many depredations and hostilities on the part of the French, and an expedition was sent the following year for her reduction, but failed to make an attack. The treaty of Utrecht, in 1713, terminated the war, and the supremacy of the English over the Iroquois, or Five Nations, was conceded. About this date the Tuscaroras, from the south, joined the Five Nations, and the confederation was thenceforth called the " Six Nations."

A trading post was erected in 1722, at Oswego, by the English, which so displeased the French that they erected one at Niagara to intercept the trade of the western tribes; this led to a chain of forts and trading posts along west and south of the lakes, and the French then claimed possession of the territory west of the Alleghanies. The emmissaries of the French again alienated the Six Nations in their allegiance to the English, and, notwithstanding the existing nominal terms of peace, let loose hordes of Indians on the English frontiers, besides many other overt acts of hostility committed. Early in 1755 England sent over vast armies, and four decisive campaigns were inaugurated against the French in all their possessions, viz.:

First, to subjugate their power in Nova Scotia.

Second, against Fort Duquesne for the recovery of power west of the Alleghanies.

Third, against Fort Niagara.

Fourth, against Crown Point at the head of Lake Champlain.

The varied success of these éxpeditions may be learnèd in more gen_ eral histories, but suffice to say that in 1758 and '59 the French were glad to arrange terms of peace, which was consummated February 10, 1763, by the cession of all possessions in Canada to the English.

During this year the boundary line between the provinces of New York, Massachusetts, and Connecticut was fixed; the line as agreed was to extend north and south, and to be 20 miles east of the Hudson River. The State of New York was now an English province, with no counter claims from the Dutch and French who had so long endeavored to ob_ tain the ascendency on her soil.

The representatives of the provinces now began to remonstrate against various acts of oppression placed upon them by the British Parliament— taxes that abridged their trade and liberties, and the exaction of duties that were unbecoming to a lawful subject. The burden of the late war with France, by which England acquired vast territory, was yet onerous to the provinces, and the arbitrary enforcement of unwholesome collec- tions created a feeling of resistance and revolt. Petitions to King and Parliament were unheeded; the stamp act in 1765 led the colonies to open revolt; its repeal followed in 1767, but in its stead a heavy duty was placed upon tea, glass, lead, paper, etc., that should be brought for the use of their subjects in America; and this led to establishing custom- houses, revenue officers, and arbitrary arrests; collisions occurred be- tween British troops in 1770 in New York and in Boston; blood was shed; the tea act followed; the Crown closed the ports of Boston; public meet- ings were held in all the colonies, and strong resolutions were passed to combine and resist the aggressions of the mother country.

In September, 1774, delegates met in Congress at Philadelphia; a bill of rights was passed and petitions were sent to the Crown for the removal of these grievances; but again they met with disdain. The aggressions of the British troops at Boston in 1775 hastened the call "To arms!" After the British were driven from Boston, in March, 1776, the battle of Long Island was fought, and the British gained the occupancy of New York city.

The Declaration of Independence, July 4, 1776, the long war, the many scenes, and active part assumed by New York are more minutely related in general histories.

The struggle lasted until the surrender of Cornwallis at Yorktown, Va., October 19, 1781; a primitive treaty was signed November 30, 1782; and the final, definite treaty was completed and signed September 3,

1783, by which these colonies were free and independent. On the 25th
of November following the British troops left New York and sailed for
home.

The short, condensed relation of the discovery of the continent; the
several grants of the territory comprising the State of New York; the
gradual condensation of that title into English possession; and their final
quit-claim of all right, title, and interest to the States that gave grants to
the original purchasers, has been concisely shown with dates from the
best authorities. Nations and provinces, as has been demonstrated, by
aggressions in times of peace cause bloodshed; we will mention the last
war between our people and Great Britain, and how the latter again attempted to grapple her lost possessions.

THE SENECA INDIANS.

ALTHOUGH much has previously been said in connection with title
to the Holland Purchase, concerning the Indians denominated the
"Five Nations," it will be well to speak more minutely of the
Senecas—the western tribe of this confederacy, and who, by their simple
rights, occupied the territory of the "Holland Purchase," and particularly
that of Genesee County.

The dim ages of the past offer no rational origin to the aboriginal inhabitants of this territory, and with the shadowy light of their traditions
the enlightened world can only speculate as to the beginning. Indeed,
it is proven by the only records of the Indians—tradition, from generation to generation—that the territory of Genesee County contains works
of which the Indians, who dwelt here when the first white man visited
it, have no tradition, showing that at still earlier periods yet another and
perhaps more enlightened people may have occupied these same lands.
Some mounds seem to have been used as burial-places, and some for defense; they certainly present evidence of no little skill and knowledge of
engineering. Without conjecturing as to any earlier people we will return to the Senecas, as found here by the first Europeans. They were
muscular, reddish brown, black, straight hair, and beardless. They lived
in huts made of barks fastened to poles by withes and thongs, many families often living in one cabin. One of the early Jesuits speaks of finding cabins 40 to 60 feet long "in the Genesee," in which 12 or 14 families were domiciled. They were clothed scantily, with skins; their food
was game and fish, and the corn that was raised by the female portion of

he tribe; their weapons were the bow and arrow, and tomahawk. Their fondness for paints and gaudy ornaments upon their persons was only equalled by their showy rites and ceremonies.

The chiefs seemed to be the law-makers, and their office was inherited or constituted by supreme acts of daring. Polygamy existed, but among the Senecas was not so common as among other tribes. No public pun-ishment for crime seemed to be enforced by their ideas of law, but jus-tice was meted out by private vengeance, and if the ends of justice were met retaliation stopped. Their religious ceremonies were simple and full of reverence; they worshiped a great spirit, feared the evil spirit (which was a less powerful brother of the good spirit), and strove to go to the "Happy Hunting-Grounds" after death; when the burial took place food and weapons were buried with the remains to help the dead on their way.

In war the Senecas were of the bravest, and tradition tells of their con-quests among the Eries, Miamas, and tribes of the southwest; it is thought that the "Five Nations," of which the Senecas held the western door, had carried their conquests to the Gulf of Mexico. They scalped their dead enemies, which was done by seizing the hair on the top of the head with the left hand, cutting the scalp around in a circle with the right, and suddenly jerking the skin from the skull. The greatness of the warrior's exploits was measured by the number of the scalps in his wigwam.

The earthworks, still visible within the limits of the county, are thought to be the fortifications of a race earlier than the Senecas, who held un-disturbed possession of the virgin soil when first visited by the whites; still they may have been thrown up by their ancestors, generations be-fore, and the tradition lost by vicissitudes of war. Oakfield has an an-cient enclosure, and it has been the most distinctly preserved through the lapse of time of any in the county; northeast of this is another called by writers "bone fort," for it seemed to be the receptacle of the bones of their slain; plenty of arrowheads and simple instruments of war and for domestic uses have been found in and around these works. Two miles north of Le Roy, at Fort Hill, upon a peninsula formed by Ford-ham's Brook and Allen's Creek,—high land, and most advantageous for defense,—are the remains of another earthwork of mound and ditch, in-dicating that in generations past the aborigines were necessarily skilled in war. They were implacable in war and generous in friendship, tor-turing by the most barbarous cruelties a portion of their captives, and adopting others with every evidence of family and tribal affection. Mary Jemison, whose history is so familiar to the citizens of the whole Holland Purchase as a captive member of the Senecas, would not return to her white relatives when urged by her brother. The trails of the Senecas were the chosen routes for public roads in later days, evincing undoubted taste in civil engineering.

As is stated in the general history the Senecas quit-claimed their right, title, and interest to the lands of the Holland Purchase and Morris Reserve, and in return received stipulated sums and annuities; they also reserved lands sufficient for their habits of life, which is also mentioned and described, and to these they retired where the remnant of the once powerful tribe resides. What is true of the Senecas applies to other tribes of the confederacy. They have degenerated from their savagery, have become more or less imbued with ideas of civilization, are protected by the laws, and in time will live only in the "white man's written history."

Red Jacket.—"This great orator was always bitter against everything pertaining to the white race, except whisky, and never became reconciled to the criminal law of the white man. He could not understand the justice of the law that would punish an offender by as long an imprisonment for stealing a trifling article as a larger one. It happened that an Indian was indicted at Batavia for burglary in breaking and entering the house of Joseph Ellicott, and stealing some article of trifling value, the punishment for which was a sentence of imprisonment for life. At the same time a white man, who had stolen a larger amount than the Indian, but without the accompaniment of burglary, was sentenced to only a few years imprisonment. Red Jacket with his chiefs attended the trial, for the purpose of rendering what aid he could to his unfortunate brother. The proof was clear and a verdict of guilty followed the trial. When the prisoner was arraigned for sentence, and the usual question propounded, why the sentence of the law should not be pronounced, Red Jacket, who had been watching the proceedings with intense interest, asked permission to speak in behalf of the prisoner. The request being granted, he rose with his usual dignity, and boldly questioned the jurisdiction of the court, and asserted the independence of his nation. He contended that the Senecas were allies, not the subjects, of the whites; that his nation had laws for the punishment of theft; and that the offender in the present case ought to be delivered up to them, to be tried according to the usages and suffer according to the laws of his own people.

"His manner on the occasion was particularly fine for him, but his argument was not sufficiently powerful to avert the sentence, which was pronounced in due form. The orator was dissatisfied with the result. Estimating the measure of delinquency by the pecuniary loss he could not perceive the justice of incarcerating a man for life, who had stolen a few spoons of small value, when another offender, who had stolen a horse, was sentenced to but a few years imprisonment.

"After the proceedings were over, in passing from the court-house to the inn, in company with a group of lawyers, Red Jacket discerned upon the sign of a printing office the arms of the State, with the emblematical representation of Liberty and Justice emblazoned in large figures and characters. The chieftain stopped, and pointing to the figure of Liberty asked in broken English, 'What him call?' He was answered, 'Liberty.' 'Ugh!' was the significant and truly aboriginal response. Then pointing to the other figure he inquired, 'What him call?' He was answered, 'Justice,' to which, with a kindling eye, he instantly replied, by asking, 'Where him live now?'"

One of the highest of the arts of war shown by the Five Nations was the placing of the Mohawks at the east door of their "Long House," as their name *Ho-de-no-saw-nee* implied, and the Senecas at the west—the two strongest tribes of the confederacy.

Indian burial-grounds.—The following is a copy of a letter written July 26, 1845, by D. E. Walker, who was a teacher of a select school in Batavia from about 1840 to 1848. This letter was written to Mr. Schoolcraft, author of Schoolcraft's *Notes on the Iroquois:*

"MR. SCHOOLCRAFT, *Dear Sir:* I have visited the mound on Dr. Nolton's farm (about one and a half miles up Tonnawanda Creek). . . . I think it about 50 yards from the creek, and elevated some eight feet above the general level of the ground. A similar one is found about two miles south of this, upon high ground, of circular form, and has a radius of about one rod. They were discovered about 30 or 40 years since. Nothing has been discovered in them save human bones. . . .

"On some two miles beyond the second was discovered a burial-ground. At that place were ploughed up shell, bone, or quill beads. Near this place was found a brown earthen pot, standing between the roots of a large tree (maple, I think), and with a small sapling grown into it some six inches in diameter. Beads of shell, bone, or porcupine quill have often been found. . . . There is also a ridge at the termination of high ground. I say ridge; it appeared to me a regular fortification. It is, I should judge, from 30 to 45 feet in length. It would appear that the ground was dug down from some distance back and wheeled (?) to the termination of high ground, until a bank is thrown up to a height of some 15 or 20 feet. This ridge some think to be natural; others, from the fact that a smooth stone about the size of a pestle was found in it, think it to be artificial. : . . . All I could learn (and I rode about seven miles out of my way to converse with an old inhabitant) was that this pestle was found in the ridge, and within three or four feet of the surface. We may perhaps infer something from the size of an *under-jaw* found here, which is said to have been so large as to much more than equal that of the largest face in the country.   Respectfully,

"D. E. WALKER."

Ancient works.—This county is peculiarly noted for its ancient earth-works, which remain the most perfect of any in the State. Oakfield township, just west of Caryville, has an enclosure upon which the eye of the white man may gaze and well wonder to what manner of people the architects belonged. It is situated on the western slope of one of those billowy hills so common there, and is washed on the north by a stream making a high bank, showing an artificial grade. The trench surround-ing the works is yet in places visible, showing a vast work and no un-common engineering skill. Ancient lodges have been traceable to those who visited it years ago, and the usual supply of broken pottery. It has gateways plainly visible, and was no doubt the stronghold of the ancient Senecas when the Eries, Miamas, etc., from the southwest, invaded their territory. The "bone fort," a large enclosure a mile or more northeast of the first, was also built up in the customs of the past, and by some ab-original tenants of this territory. Since the settlement of the county by the whites the remains of these enclosures have gradually disappeared; at the present time but little remains to mark the spot of the "bone fort," while during the first years of the present century the enclosure con-tained a mound of bones six feet high, and 30 feet broad at its base.

At Le Roy, three miles north of the village, is other evidence of note. The work occupies a high bank, or table-land, bounded by Fordham's Brook and Allen's Creek, which effect a junction here. The peninsula is now high and with steep banks by the long action of the streams upon the strata of lime and sandstone. The fortification is about 1,300 feet from north to south, and 2,000 feet across its broadest part, narrowing to 1,000 at its neck connecting it with the general table-land. There is a trace of an embankment and ditch about 1,500 feet in length across the broad part, east and west, and either are two or three feet in height or depth. Skeletons and pottery used to be found here; also pipes, beads, arrowheads, etc. Heaps of small stones were discovered in the enclosure, which seemed to indicate they were used by the ancients as missiles of protection. Nothing definite can be concluded as to the ar-chitects of these different forts, whether the Senecas, or another tribe be-fore their occupation of the soil, were the builders. In 1788 Rev. Sam-uel Kirkland, missionary to the Seneca Indians, visited these forts or enclosures, and has left a description of the very perfect condition in which he found them at that date. But no historian has gleaned any evidence from the traditions of the Senecas that the race found here were the builders.

Antiquities of Batavia.[1]—Prior to the advent of Joseph Ellicott, and the survey of the Holland Land Company, what is now Batavia was nothing but a favorite stopping-place and large camp-ground of the Senecas, situated on the *Wa-a-gwen-ne-go*, or great Indian trail, traversing the State from the Hudson River to Lake Erie. The locality of this camping-place was on the north side of the *Ta-na-wun-da* (swift water) *Ga-hun-da* (creek), and in immediate proximity to the bridge at the head of Walnut street. It occupied a space of some two or three acres, extending from the court-house to the old land office. Its area was a grassy plat devoid of trees, and contained a large natural spring opposite the land office, which is still in use. In the Indian dialect this camp-ground was called *De on-go-wah* (the grand hearing-place)

The trail mentioned above was a well-beaten or deeply-trodden path through the forest, about one foot wide, and worn from three to six inches in depth. Crossing the *Gen-nis-ye-ho* (beautiful valley), near Avon, it continued west until it reached the old Roswell Graham farm, about two miles east of the court-house. There, to avoid the Mount Lucy ponds and marsh in that vicinity, it bore off in a southwesterly direction, across the county fair grounds, Levi Otis's farm, etc., and came out on the east bank of the creek near the residence of A. S. Pratt, and within a few rods of the " great bend of the Tonawanda Creek." Circling this bend, and continuing on high ground, it nearly followed the line of what is now part of Jackson and Chestnut streets; then near the banks of the creek *via* the camp-ground, to where the State arsenal now stands. Here the trail bore off northwest, through the oak openings, to the village of Caryville. In addition to this a summer trail, or cut off, was likewise in use when the state of the ground would permit, viz., from the Graham farm, following our present Main street, to the camp-ground and spring. Why is this place called " the bend?" The Tonawanda Creek is a very tortuous stream. Between the villages of Batavia and Alexander, by the highway, is eight miles ; but were a person to follow the meanderings of the creek he would travel nearly 23 miles. Flowing from the south, in a circuitous direction, the stream reaches its extreme easternmost point within the limits of the village plat. Here a large bend, or turn, occurs,

[1] By David Seaver.

and thereafter a westerly course is pursued.   This, also, is the greatest
or longest bend during the entire length of the creek.   Hence the "bend"
was designated for this locality, as is noticed elsewhere.

GENESEE COUNTY, 1795–1800.

THE following extracts are from the pen of the versatile writer,
David Seaver, of New York city, (to whom we are indebted for
favors,) contributing to the columns of *The Spirit of the Times* in
1874; and referring to a work to which he had access, describing the
journey of one Rochefoucauld Liancourt, a Frenchman, in 1795, from
Philadelphia to Niagara Falls, through Western New York, says, after en-
countering the celebrated chief Red Jacket:

"The road from Ontario to Canawago (Canawaugus) is a good one for this country,
but as usual it leads through the midst of the woods, and within a space of 12
miles we saw only one habitation.   In this journey we discovered two Indians lying
under a tree; though we had seen a considerable number of them, yet this meeting
had for us an attraction of novelty, as we found them in a state of intoxication which
scarcely manifested the least symptoms of life.   One wore around his neck a long and
heavy silver chain, from which a large medallion was suspended; on one side whereof
was the image of George Washington, and on the other the motto of Louis XIV., *nec •
pluribus impar*, with the figure of the sun, which was usually displayed with it in the
French army.   This Indian, no doubt, was his excellency in a ditch, out of which we
made repeated efforts to drag him, but in vain.   .   .   .

"Canawago is a small town, the inhabitants few, but Mr. Berry keeps there one of
the best inns we have seen for some time.

"Wednesday, June 17th, 1795.   After remaining half a day at Canawago, we at
length set out to traverse the *desarts*, as they are called.   A journey through uninterrupted forests offers but little matter for speculation or remark; the woods are in general not close, but stand on fruitful soil.   The route is a footpath, tolerably good upon
the whole, but in some places very miry; winding through the forests over a level
ground that rises but seldom into gentle swells.   After a ride of 12 hours, in which
we have crossed several large creeks (Oatka and Black), we arrived at Big Plains (Oakfield), which is 38 miles distant from Canawago.   We breakfasted at Buttermilk Fall (Le
Roy), and dined on the bank of the Tonawaugo (Batavia), and for both these meals
our appetites were so keen that perhaps we never ate anything with a better relish."

Liancourt next describes his visit to the tribe of Indians settled at Tonawaugo.   In another article to the Batavia *Spirit of the Times* Mr. Seaver gives extracts from a work of John Maule, published in London,
wherein the author gives his experiences of a visit in 1800, following
nearly the same route taken by Liancourt in 1795.   The author (Maule)
was an English gentleman.   In August, 1800, Mr. Maule spent several
days in the locality of Genesee Falls (now Rochester).   He speaks of In-

dian Allan's mill at that point, and mentions Colonel Fish (grandfather of the late Eli H. Fish, of Batavia), who at that time was the only resi. dent.   Upon leaving the falls he proceeded to the Indian village of Can. awaugus (then a mile or so west of what is now Avon), where he found the chief ruler to be Hot Bread, or *Ga-kwa da*, who was a warrior be. tween 60 or 70 years of age, and sported a beard two inches long.   His mother was the royal princess *Can-a-wau-gus*, from whom the village was named.   " She can be proved to be at least 120 years old, and yet is able to walk about and plant her own maize."   "She lives surrounded by 40 of her children, grandchildren, etc., and some of the latter old enough to be grandparents."

August 20, 1800, he proceeded on his journey, "accompanied by Hot Bread, who was mounted on a nag, whose ears were rimmed and tipped with silver."   After passing Peterson's Big Spring (Caledonia) he arrived at Ganson's (LeRoy), 297 miles, at 11 A. M., and the following entry is made:

"When my friend L. passed this place last year, Ganson's was a solitary house in the wilderness, but it is now in the midst of a flourishing township, in which 21 families are already settled.   A new tavern and a number of dwelling houses are building.   Two hundred and ninety-eight miles ; recross Allen's Creek ; the bed a flat limestone rock, 15 or 20 rods wide, with three or four inches of water ; a handsome bridge was building This creek is the western terminus of Capt. Williamson's purchase (Pultney tract). A very handsome road four rods wide has been cut, and the whole distance from Gen-esee River to Ganson's being 12 miles in nearly a straight line.   I now entered into what is called the Wilderness, but at 2 P. M. reached the Holland Company's store-house and Frederick Walther's tavern (Stafford), 304½ miles.

"The Holland Company consists of a number of merchants and others, principally residents in Holland, who purchased a very large tract of land of Mr. Morris.   This territory, for such it may be called, is on the east bounded by Williamson's purchase, and on the west by Lake Erie and Niagara River   No part of the land is, I believe, yet settled, but at present under survey for that purpose.   One of the principal surveyors and his gang were at the tavern, and fully occupied the lodging hut ; this, with the ad-ditional circumstance of there being no hay for my horses, and no other feed than oats, cut green in the straw, induced me to give up the design of sleeping here this night, but rather to push on to the next station.   .   .   .   At 4 P. M. we left Walther's, and at 309 miles (Batavia) fell in with the Tonawautee Creek, sluggish, shallow, and broad At 6½ P. M. we reached Garret Davis's tavern, 316 miles (Winan's farm near Dunham's. Corners), near a small run of good water.   This is one of those three stations which the Holland Company has this year established for the accommodation of travelers, who hitherto have been obliged to sleep in the woods.   Davis first began to ply his axe in January last ; he has now a good log house, a field of green oats, sown 18th of June (the only feed I could get for my horses), and a very excellent garden, the most productive of any of its size I have seen since leaving New York.   He had also cleared a pretty exten-sive field for wheat.   On this land the logs were now burning, and I passed a greater part

of the night in making up the fires. This employment I preferred to harbouring with a
number of strangers, one of whom was sick and not expected to live till morning. This,
however, was only the fearful conjecture of Davis. I got some maple sugar for my tea,
and Mr. and Mrs. Davis paid me every possible attention, but I cannot praise them for
neatness. Perhaps I ought not to expect it when the peculiarity of the situation and a
large family of children are taken into account. From Allen's Creek to Walther's was
excellent lands, but miserable roads, at times impassable. and the wagoner would take
his axe to cut a new passage. From Walther's to Davis's the road is better. At Davis's the woods are composed of small tall, saplings, closely crowded. This morning
we experienced a very keen frost with a bright sun, and so late as 11 A. M. I stood
in the sun to warm myself, my hands being benumbed with the cold. Very scorching
sun in the afternoon after leaving Walther's, and troublesome flies and mosquitoes.

"Thursday, August 21, 1800. Start at daylight, 318 miles; we leave the thick woods
and enter upon the Big Plains. These plains (Oakfield) are open groves of oak, in a
light shallow soil on limestone. . . . These plains are many miles in extent, and
it struck me I had seen park grounds in England much like them. At 321 miles the
oaks are smaller and more compact, and at 322 miles we enter woods of beech and
maple. At 7½ A. M. we reached the Indian town of Tonawautee, 330 miles. . This
settlement is on the west bank of the creek, which I now crossed for the second time.
It bore, however, a different character here than at 319 miles (Batavia), being clear and
rapid.

"Left Tonawautee and passed through open plains of oak with less of tamarisk and
more grass to 334 miles, where I fell in with the old road. At 10½ A. M. reached Asa
Ransom's station, distance 344 miles (Clarence, Erie County). I was here greatly surprised with an excellent breakfast of tender chicken and good loaf-sugar for my tea.
Ransom, like Davis, sat down in the woods in January; he has 150 acres, ten acres
cleared and in oats. . . . The Holland Company has laid out a new road from
Ganson's to Buffalo Creek, which passes to the south of Davis's station, but falls in with
the present road at Ransom's, and this new road will make a difference of 10 miles in
42. Ransom informed me that by an account, he had kept, no less than 155 families
with their wagons have passed his house this summer, emigrating from Pennsylvania
and New Jersey to Canada. Sixteen wagons passed in one day."

TITLE TO THE LANDS.

IN a satisfactory manner every shade of the title to the territory of
Genesee County has been given in the general history preceding;
but a few words of summary will here place the link in the chain of
facts.

There are no lands in the State of New York that has or can have
better title to the soil than has the Holland Purchase and Morris Reserve, of which Genesee County is a part. In 1697 a memorial by commissioners of trade and plantations relative to the right of the Crown to
the sovereignty of the Five Nations says:

"Those nations by many acts, acknowledgments, submissions, leagues, and agree-
ments had been united to. or de ended on. the colon of New York."

In 1684, when De la Barre, governor of Canada, commenced an invasion of the territory of the Five Nations, Governor Dongan, of New
York, warned the French official that the Indians were the subjects of the
King of England, who had sent the Duke of York arms to be set up in
every one of the Indians' castles as far as *O-ney-gra* (Niagara). This
was done and the French governor retired. Charles II. granted the
province of New York to the Duke of York after the submission and sub-
jection of the Indians therein — when they were lawful subjects. This
was the foundation of the claim of sovereignty over the Indians.

In 1768 the proper State authorities agreed that a line running north
along the eastern borders of Broome and Chenango counties, to a point
seven miles west of Rome, should be a boundary line over which the
white man should not settle without the consent of the Indian.

In the Revolution the Iroquois espoused the cause of the mother
country, — employed by the British to help subdue the revolting provinces, — and most cruelly did they wage their savage warfare against the
people of their own State who had so often protected them. At the
close of the war, when England quit-claimed all her right and title to the
colonies, the territory belonged to the United States, and the Iroquois
could and should have been dispossessed of all their rights in New York ;
but the proper legal authorities ceded to them all that portion of the
State west of the preëmption line except the mile-strip along Niagara
River. Afterwards Phelps and Gorham and Robert Morris purchased
the lands, obtaining the title from the Indians, also by deed ; Robert
Morris and wife sold to the Holland Land Company, to the Connecticut
School Fund, to Cragie, and others ; and these became the grantors of
the settlers. The wars, encroachments, and full particulars of the title as
related in the general history will be read with additional interest after
this summary.

Previously we have shown the foundation of the English claim to the
sovereignty of the entire territory of the Six Nations, or Iroquois, and
how they maintained and repeatedly asserted it up to the time of the Revolution. The first compromise to be recorded between the whites of the
province of New York and the Iroquois was in 1768. The encroachments
of the settlers upon their hunting-grounds in Central New York caused
uneasiness to the Indians, to allay which a council was held that year at
Fort Stanwix (now Rome, N. Y.) to agree upon a line west of which settlements were not to be permitted. The line defined was along the eastern boundary of Broome and Chenango counties, and the Indians agreed

to surrender to the United States all captives and relinquish all claims to the country lying west of a line starting four miles east of the mouth of Niagara River, following the river by a line four miles east, southerly to Buffalo Creek, thence to the Pennsylvania line, thence to the Ohio River.

The Iroquois, during the Revolution, were more or less the allies of the English,—opposed to the colonies,—and when the struggle ceased were left at the mercy of the United States. In justice, after their hostility, they had forfeited all rights to their territory in New York and could have been driven out; but the magnanimity of the government was shown when, in 1784,—16 years after the other council,—a proper council met at Stanwix (Rome) and recognized the ownership of the Indians to the western part of the State of New York—all the territory between the line mentioned on the east and the line four miles from Niagara River; and it is well to mention here that this last line was afterwards made *one mile* from the river.

The charters given by the Crown to its favorite individuals, and to companies in general terms and from imperfect, unknown ideas of the extent of the territory, often conveyed parts of the same, laying the foundation for conflicting claims. For instance, the grant of the province of New York to the Duke of York—mentioned in former pages—extended to the Connecticut River, covering a portion of Massachusetts; also in the charter to the Plymouth Company was a portion of the same territory, and both charters covered territory extending indefinitely westward.

In 1781 New York relinquished to the United States her claim to all territory west of the western boundaries of the State; and Massachusetts in 1785 relinquished her claim to the same western lands, contenting herself with claiming that part of New York west of the so-called preëmption line. This preëmption line was to be run for the purpose, was to begin on the Pennsylvania line and run due north to Lake Ontario, and is easily found now upon any correct map of the State as forming the east boundary line of Steuben County, running north through Schuyler, through the east edge of Yates, through the foot of Seneca Lake, forming the eastern boundary of Ontario, and through Wayne County to the lake.

New York asserted her claim to this same tract, west of preëmption line, and in December, 1786, commissioners from the two States met at Hartford to settle *this* difference; it was agreed that the ownership of the lands in dispute be with Massachusetts, the sovereignty with New York, and that the Indians hold and possess it as long as they chose. The first right to purchase this land of the Indians was given to Massachusetts; hence this east boundary line was called "preëmption line." New York retained the right to the ownership of the one-mile strip along the Niagara River.

In 1788 Oliver Phelps and Nathaniel Gorham, citizens of that State, bargained with the State of Massachusetts for its preëmption right to all lands west of the preëmption line, for $1,000,000, to which the purchasers must extinguish the Indian title; they were to pay the amount in three annual payments, in certain securities of the State, then worth about one-fifth its face value.   In July, 1788, Mr. Phelps met the Indians in council at Buffalo and purchased their interest in 2,600,000 acres, as estimated, for $5,000 down and a perpetual annuity of $500.   The boundary of the tract which the Indians relinquished to Phelps and Gorham was as follows: on the east by the preëmption line, north by Lake Ontario, south by the State of Pennsylvania, and west by a line that should commence in the north line of Pennsylvania due south of the confluence of Canaseraga Creek with the Genesee River, thence north on that line to the confluence, thence northerly along the Genesee River to a point two miles north of Canawagus (Avon), thence due west 12 miles, thence northerly 12 miles from the river to the lake.   On the 21st of November, following, the tract above described was deeded to Phelps and Gorham, and has been since known as "the Phelps and Gorham purchase."

A land office for the sale of townships and tracts had been opened at Canandaigua, and sales were brisk; many townships were settled in 1788, and the influx of colonies in 1789 and 1790 to this then wilderness region, as given by Turner in his *History of the Holland Purchase*, forms a remarkable page of history.

We hear of the "Pultney estate" lands intermingled; let us explain it. On November 18, 1790, Phelps and Gorham sold to Robert Morris (the financier of the Revolution) the residue of their purchase unsold, amounting to about 1,200,000 acres, reserving two townships; for this Mr. Morris paid £30,000 New York currency, and at once sold the same to Sir William Pultney, John Hornly, and another for £35,000 sterling. These lands were scattered over the original Phelps and Gorham purchase, and the reader will see why the "Pultney estate" had its land offices.

Before Messrs. Phelps and Gorham had half paid for their purchase from Massachusetts the securities of the State had risen to par, and, find-

2

ing they should be unable to fulfill their agreement, they induced the State to resume, its right to that portion of New York which they had not yet obtained from the Indians, which the State of Massachusetts did; this left that State the preëmption right to all Western New York west of the Genesee River and western boundary line of Phelps and Gorham's purchase; and this agreement was consummated March 10, 1791.

In March, 1791, Robert Morris contracted with Massachusetts for the preëmption right to all of the territory of New York west of the purchase of Phelps and Gorham, and it was not until after much difficulty and delay that he completed his title; he met a council of Indians at Geneseo in September, 1797, who surrendered their interest to the entire territory, except 11 reservations for their own use, amounting to about 338 square miles. These, in brief, are the reservations, as it will be of interest to the younger readers of Genesee County: the Tuscarora reservation, of one square mile, east of Lewiston; the Tonawanda, of 17 square miles, both sides of the creek; the Buffalo, of 130, both sides of the Buffalo Creek; the Cattaraugus, of 42 square miles, each side of that creek on Lake Erie; the Allegany, of 42 square miles, on each side of that river; the Oil Spring reservation, of one square mile, between Allegany and Cattaraugus counties; the Canadea reservation, of 16 square miles, along the Genesee River; the Gardeau reservation, of 28 square miles, near Mt. Morris; the Squakie Hill reservation, of two square miles, north of Mt. Morris; Little Beard's and Big Tree reservations, of four square miles, near Geneseo; and the Canawaugus reservation, of two square miles, west of Avon.

On the 11th of May, 1791, the State of Massachusetts deeded to Robert Morris the whole of said land in five deeds, briefly as follows:

1st. A strip 12 miles wide, beginning on the Pennsylvania line 12 miles from Phelps and Gorham's southwest corner, and running north to Lake Ontario, containing about 500,000 acres.

2d. A strip 16 miles wide, beginning and running in the same manner to Lake Ontario.

3d. Another 16-mile strip, next west of the last, and to be run in same way.

4th. All the land contained within another line to be run 16 miles from the last due north to Lake Ontario.

5th. This last deed included all the land owned by Massachusetts, in this State, west of the last described tract.

The last four tracts were estimated to contain 3,300,000 acres, and this concluded the title of all the available lands of Western New York, west of that of Phelps and Gorham, in Robert Morris. Mr. Morris re_ tained the land set forth in the first deed to sell as he chose, and it was called the " Morris Reserve."

On December 24, 1792, Robert Morris and his wife deeded to Hermon Le Roy and John Linklaen 1,500,000 acres west of the strip 12 miles wide that Mr. Morris reserved. February 27, 1793, he gave a deed for 1,000,000 acres to these persons and Gerrit Boon. July 20, 1793, he conveyed to the same three parties 800,000 acres. July 20, 1793, he conveyed to Hermon Le Roy, William Bayard, and Matthew Clarkson 300,- 000 acres, and these four deeds conveyed all the land west of the Morris Reserve, except the reservations previously mentioned. These individ- uals purchased for others who were aliens and could not hold real es- tate in this State; but the legislature of 1798 removed this restriction and the trustees turned over the property to the actual owners. There were several gentlemen who became the owners of this vast tract of ter- ritory, and who were known as the " Holland Land Company." The tract covered the present counties of Niagara (except the mile-strip along the river), Erie, Chautauqua, Cattaraugus, the two western ranges of towns in Allegany, and all of the counties of Wyoming, Genesee, and Orleans except the eastern ranges of towns in each, which are east of the " east transit line," and in the Morris Reserve.

LAND OFFICE NOTES.

OUR younger readers must learn that a land office is a place opened for the sale of the lands of any particular tract, and is called by the name of its territory; there is always found the agent assisted by an efficient corps of clerks; such offices are discontinued when the affairs connected with the tract are completed.

The land office of the Holland Purchase was opened at Batavia in 1801, and discontinued in 1837. It was opened at Ransom's Corners (now in Erie County), and in 1802 an office was built at Batavia, in the forks of the road and facing the east. This spot afterwards became the center of the flourishing village of Batavia, and Joseph Ellicott was its founder.

The first treaty by Robert Morris with the Indians, which was to get their title to the lands he had sold to the Holland Land Company, was in 1797. Joseph Ellicott, the first occupant of the land office, was pres- ent. He came from Philadelphia on horseback, by Wilkesbarre, Tioga

Point, Elmira, Bath, Dansville, and down the Canaseraga Creek and Genesee River to Geneseo, where the treaty was held.   While here in the Genesee country he made all the arrangements for the survey of the vast territory, returning the following February on horseback.

In May, 1798, Joseph Ellicott came into the Purchase to open up the lands and arrange for its sale in parcels; he came on horseback to Avon, thence to Buffalo. The stores for the surveyors' and land office use were sent from Philadelphia in April, 1798, and were sent in bateaux to New York, up to Albany, up the Mohawk to Wood Creek, thence to Oswego River, down to Lake Ontario, thence to the mouth of Genesee River.   Mr. Brisbane, who was in charge, went up the Genesee as far as he could with one load, and the remainder went to Lewiston.   Mr. Ellicott was really the founder of prosperity of Genesee County, and was land office and general agent until 1821, when he was succeeded by Jacob S. Otto.

The original intention was first to divide the Holland Company's lands into townships of 16 sections, each one and one-half miles square, subdividing into lots each three-quarters mile long and one-quarter wide, each lot being 120 acres.   This plan, however, was abandoned, and finally the bulk of the tract was divided into lots three-quarters mile square, or 360 acres each.

The company had a traveling agent named Timothy Backus, who relates the fact that he came upon a man making staves from the company's timber, and to his question, " What are you doing there ? " received the reply, " You will never catch me here again."   About three months afterwards Mr. Backus passed that way again, and discovered the same trespasser, to whom he said, " I thought you told me, some time ago, that I'd never catch you here again."   " Well, now, look here," said the stavemaker, " after you've heard my story you'll never say a word.   In the first place I steal my timber, contract with one man to let him have my staves, receive half pay from *him*, and when done sell them to another man and get full pay, and can't make a living at that ! "   He was left to do the best he could.

In the summer of 1819 two strong men came to the land office armed with very heavy, long-handled axes, and inquired for Mr. Ellicott. Upon stating their business it was learned that they had heard he had offered 100 acres of land to any two men who would cut down Big Tree. They were ready for the job.   They were deeply chagrined to learn that Big Tree was a noted Indian chief at Geneseo, and it was plain that some 'oker had imposed   h

Many laughable scenes transpired that were no part of the land office records, but are handed down as pleasant recollections of the times. An Irishman came one day to purchase a piece of land, but had forgotten the lot and township; as he left the office he said, " Well, Mr. Landlord you will plaze kape it till I find out what land it is, wont you? "

Agencies were established about 1812 to accommodate settlers, where they could deliver wheat and cattle and have the amount endorsed on their debts for land; this was a bad policy for the company, but very pleasing to settlers.

In 1802 a relative of Mr. Ellicott's from Maryland was very solicitous about his social relations, and wrote thus :

" I observe thee says thou art living without society, that thy nearest neighbor is 10 miles. Pray, can a person be justifiable in spending the few years he has to live in a way that is not the most agreeable to him? Think on this and retire from that toilsome life thou hast pursued so long, and enjoy thy few remaining years to the fullest extent."

Mr. Ellicott borrowed a horse to go from Schlosser to Niagara while he was there on business, and in some manner the horse was missing. The owner, knowing he had a good customer, set an exorbitant price on the animal, which Mr. Ellicott had to pay after all efforts to recover the horse had proved ineffectual. He found afterwards that the Tonawanda Indians had need of the animal, and had " confiscated " him.

In February, 1836, a party of anti-renters broke into the land office at Mayville, and purloined the records and burned them. The lands in the southern part of the Holland Purchase had been sold to a trust company, and an office opened there. Word was received at Batavia soon after that the men at Attica and Alexander were about to perpetrate a similar burglary upon the office there. Fifty men were posted in the land office after the records were removed to a place of safety; the bells rang and citizens gathered well armed; the mob several hundred strong appeared in the street near the land office, and halted. The approach of Sheriff Townsend, with 120 men armed with bright, loaded muskets, added to the already formidable force, saved any open attack, and, probably, much bloodshed; for it is a matter of record that if any attempt at violence had been made by the mob they would have been slain by scores at the delivery of the first fire from the sheriff's force and the citizens.

The old stone office is still intact, occupied as a dwelling, and it is hoped sufficient interest will soon be exhibited by the citizens of Bata-

via to purchase it, and preserve it as a pioneer building, devoted to the
storing of relics of bygone days.

ORGANIZATION AND DEVELOPMENT.

IN early colonial days all of Western New York was called Tryon
County, then Montgomery; after 1788, when the preëmption line was
agreed upon, the territory west of that was called Ontario; after the
western bounds of the Phelps and Gorham purchase were determined
the portion of the State west of it was called Genesee County. The county
was established in 1802 as Genesee, embracing what is now eight counties. In 1801 Joseph Ellicott erected the land office of the Holland
Land Company at Batavia, and this became the center; its judicious
selection on the main Indian trail, and in the direct path of emigration,
with its natural advantages and surroundings, has rendered Batavia one
of the wealthiest and most beautiful villages of Western New York.

Counties were erected from the original Genesee as follows:

Allegany, in 1806, with Angelica as capital.

Niagara, in 1808, with Buffalo as shire town; Lockport county seat in
1821.

Chautauqua, in 1811, county seat at Maysville.

Cattaraugus, in 1817, jail and court-house at Ellicottsville.

Erie, in 1821, erected from Niagara with Buffalo for its shire.

Orleans, in 1821, county seat at Albion.

Wyoming, in 1841, with Warsaw for its shire.

Genesee, in its present organization, retains the original county seat,—
Batavia,—with history and importance sufficient to almost render it classical. It has been and is the beehive of industry and facts from which
those counties and colonies have swarmed.

Prior to the erection of the counties named above Genesee was divided
into four townships: Northampton, Leicester, Southampton, and Batavia. Northampton embraced the northern portion of Morris Reserve,
Leicester the central portion, and Southampton the southern; Batavia
embraced the entire Holland Purchase.

PRESENT ORGANIZATION OF THE COUNTY.

THE name Genesee is of Seneca origin, signifying " pleasant valley."
The county is divided into 13 townships bearing the names of Alabama,
Alexander, Batavia, Bergen, Bethany, Byron, Darien, Elba, Le Roy,

Oakfield, Pavilion, Pembroke, and Stafford. The territory embraced in the towns of Byron, Bergen, Le Roy, Pavilion, and the eastern portion of Stafford is east of the "east transit line," consequently from the Morris Reserve; and the greater and remaining western portion of the county is from the Holland Purchase. All previous history concerning title will apply equally to the Morris Reserve and Holland Purchase.

April 11, 1804, the town of Batavia, which, as has been described, included all the Purchase west of east transit line, was divided into four towns. The one farthest east retained the old name, and included all the territory east of a meridian line from the lake southward that passed through the western part of the present Orleans County; the next town was Willink, which included the territory between Batavia and the west transit line (running through Lockport); the next was Erie, which embraced one tier of townships in the present county of Chautauqua; and the next was Chautauqua, which included the remainder of old Batavia. This was Genesee County of that day; but the rapid settlement of its vast territory, and the development of its unlimited resources, soon called for the formation of other counties and centers, so that in about 1825 the county of Genesee was greatly narrowed in its limits, being 36 miles north and south and 26 east and west, with its county site, Batavia, only nine miles from its northern boundary. The removal of the county seat to a geographical center, or the formation of a new county, was urged, and the organization of Wyoming was the result. Its present well-chosen and clearly defined outlines will no doubt remain through many generations. It is now 18 miles by 26 east and west, and its county capital could not be removed in any direction to make it more central. .

The surface is rolling, generally sloping to the north, and lies principally in the second terrace with the south part in the central district. It was originally covered with heavy timber of every variety, and for salubrity of climate from its peculiar position and richness of soil it may be equalled, but not excelled, in the State. It contains about 219,520 acres.

EARLY SETTLERS AND THEIR EXPERIENCE.

PREVIOUS to the war of the Revolution the tide of emigration had commenced its flow from New England, but was arrested by the fear of hostile Indians. After peace was declared the tide again set in for this section. We are told by competent authority that Charles Wilbur settled in Le Roy as early as 1792 and the Gansons in 1798, but the beginning of the present century must be given as the date of the first high tide of immigration.

Perhaps it is some times thought by those living in the older settled sections, where comfort and luxury abounds, where refined society and the best educational advantages are clustered, that the pioneer who would enter the dense wilderness to build himself a home, for a long time depriving himself of the pleasures of life, must be an inferior being; but they were of the most determined, independent class, and such spirits in a few years had for themselves the foundation laid for future wealth and greatness. A small log house in some well-selected spot would be rolled up and made comfortable; the furniture scanty, but sufficient; the fare simple, but wholesome.

The first settlements in Genesee County were along the Indian trails, now the course of the principal thoroughfares; but the more enterprising would strike off into the heavy timber, where the sound of his axe could not be heard. Some had bid adieu for a time to the young wife at home, who watched for the return of the sturdy pioneer; after months of solicitude he returns to spend a short time and the better prepared to occupy the cabin in the wilderness with all its discomforts, but cheered by the presence of the wife. The forest now begins to fall under his blows; a patch is burned off and the crop of corn for the next winter's use is planted.

The improvements must be made in the cabin, also, as necessity and health demand; a door must take the place of a blanket, and with axe, nails, hammer, auger and knife, a rude one is made to swing upon its heavy wooden hinges; the wooden latch, with a leather string attached and hanging outside, has given rise to the homely but hospitable saying; "The latch-string is out." A bedstead must be made, too. Holes were bored into the logs in one corner of the cabin, at sufficient height, one end of a stake or pole placed therein, the other supported by a crotch, then poles cut and placed across these, and then thickly covered with a mattress of hemlock boughs; upon blankets over this soft, fragrant, clean bedding our first pioneers and their wives slept the sleep of health and prosperity. Chairs were composed of blocks hewn from basswood, and the legs added to it by the inevitable axe and auger. Tables were often made in the same manner, and with the axe a floor to the cabin when they needed one. The utensils for cooking were rude and few; plates and trenches of wood often served the early pioneers. The ancient "bake kettle" used by the pioneer, an indispensable article of the time, now forgotten nearly, should be perpetuated through all time, in story at least. It was a shallow iron vessel, with legs to raise it the desired height, so a mass of coals could be put under it ; then with a cover with turned-up edge to hold the hot coals over the food to be cooked ; and it was wonderful how nicely the corn-cake and other bakings could be done. In place of a crane a pole with hooks did service.

This was kitchen, dining room, sitting room, parlor, and bedroom, this one cosy room ; and was very often the workshop for making ox-bows and rude sleds preparatory to the logging and summer fallowing for the first crop of winter wheat, a large patch for which had been felled by the industrious pioneer. The rudy blaze of the fire furnished heat and light for culinary and evening work, and the usual rag in a small dish of oil from some wild animal served upon special occasions. Soon a few sheep could pick their living, and the hand-cards and spinning-wheel were heard preparing the cloth for garments. The barks for coloring cloths were well known to the housewife, and the old " dye-tub " that graced every hearth corner in olden time is not forgotten by some of our elder readers to this day.

Nor were the social enjoyments of life entirely ignored, for soon neighbors a mile away, each with his clearing and his family in the woods learned to visit and assist each other; and the settlement with its little store, a few miles away, situated on some main trail, was to be visited occasionally for simple necessaries, and to learn the news that may have been left by passing emigrants. The anticipations of the future was the incentive for all this seeming hardship.

But the crops of the second year are quite extensive ; the clearings broaden, the stock has increased; the neighbors are plentier; and the deprivations are far less onerous. If the pioneer was a single man he has passed the winter in his old home with parents, brothers, and sisters, and perfected the arrangements for a companion in the new home. An outfit can be taken to the western home now that a road is cut, and the ox-team and a few household utensils to improve the convenience of the the former year. The garden seeds are properly planted, a larger and better prepared piece of corn is planted, many improvements are made, fences are built, and the virgin soil yields abundant harvests. Another cabin has been built for the animals ; a mill to do coarse grinding has been erected on the creek three miles away ; and the settler finds much time to still clear away the forest even during the winter months, to enable his animals to brouse. The pigs and fowls are fed at the door daily by the wife. The echo of the husband's axe during the day, and the hum of the wife's wheel during the evening, was a happy chorus that was

sure to bring prosperity and wealth. Other settlers had come; social
evenings passed; no conventionalities were needed ; more could be present at logging bees and house raisings ; no criticisms ; no jealousies nor
bickerings.

Stick chimnies plastered with mud have been built; a glass window
has taken the place of the greased paper; a log bridge spans the creek
near by ; a better and more spacious log barn has been prepared for the
largely increased stock; the prattle of the first-born gladdens the wife
and mother. Still the forest falls, the fields broaden, and plenty
abounds.

＊　　＊　　＊　　＊　　＊　　＊　　＊　　＊

The tide of immigration has continued ; the curling smoke from the
"clearings" can be seen near together throughout the vast wilderness;
roads have been opened ; fences have appeared around the verdant
fields and meadows ; shouts of merry children are heard ; and the once
pioneer settlement assumes the high niche of a "rural neighborhood."

TWENTY YEARS' CHANGES.

STILL greater changes have taken place in the time. The old house is
the wing of a large, hewed log house, with paneled door and glazed windows. A lawn is in front; a growing, fruitful orchard in the rear; a
large barn occupies the site of the log shanty; forests of waving grain
stand where the forests of trees were. In sight stands the comfortable
log school-house; the peculiar noise of a saw-mill is heard on the stream
above ; a good bridge spans the stream in place of the logs; the first
born in the full vigor of manhood has driven by to the barn with a load
of hay, driving a spirited team in place of the oxen ; the matronly lady
at the well and the middle-aged, strong man coming from the mill are
the young, hopeful couple who dared breast the privations of pioneer life
over 20 years ago.

Another 20 years has passed. An elegant mansion stands on the
site of the old log house. Its entire surroundings show the wealth and
refinement of its owners. The saw-mill has gone; the stream passes un
der a stone-arched bridge. Only patches of wood land can be seen, and
elegant farm houses dot the landscape. In the distance a train of cars
speeds over the plain. A tall spire of a church is plainly discerned in the
little village beyond. An elderly gentleman is busy with the cattle near
the barn ; a motherly lady is knitting and listening to the plays of grand
children. These are the worthy husband and wife, who, over 40 years ago

came to this very spot, and with hopeful hearts engaged to "make the wilderness blossom as the rose." One of the sons manages the farm, and two others have gone West to start in life as their father did.

This, dear reader, is a fair, not overdrawn, painting of the average settler in Genesee County at the commencement of the present century.

CHANGES IN TRADE.

THE vast difference between the trade and value of products from the first settlement to the present should be noted. Now, all products have a cash value and a cash market; then, there was not sufficient money or a market for such ; now, all the necessaries and luxuries of life are based upon the cash value ; then, the potash manufactured from ashes was the only cash article. The little stores of the early day kept only the bare necessaries for the settlers, and at high prices because of transportation : yarn and log chains, pork and tea, tar and molasses, pins and crowbars— everything was kept in a grand chaos. Now, our readers know what a store is without explanation.

Teams hauled the products of this county—after it had been converted into saleable compounds by the old-time asheries and distilleries—to Albany during the first years of trade, bringing in return the goods for the frontier store. In after years the canal opened up new changes, other markets, more and cheaper goods, and better prices for products ; and still greater changes have been produced by the railroads. This change, plain to be seen, has been equally operative and beneficial to all branches of trade, and has only kept contemporaneous with the improvements of the settlers of Genesee as they developed the howling wilderness into fruitful fields and thriving villages. All honor to the pioneer settlers of Genesee County of four-score years ago!

Prices sixty years ago.[1]—"An account book of 1826, or 60 years ago, shows up some of the prices of our ancestors, and gives us food for thought in comparing with the prices of to-day.

"The location was Rochester, N. Y., and the accounts were of a general character. As ladies should always come first I will begin on their goods : Calico, 31 cents per yard ; ginghams, 40 cents ; flannels, 50 cents ; dress silks were from $1 to $3 per yard ; ladies' shoes, $1.50 per pair ; men's boots from $3 to $5 per pair ; ladies' bonnets were then seldom changed in style or fashion, and prices ranged from $1 to $8. Elias Howe, the inventor of sewing machines, was then unheard of, and tailors received for making, coats from 75 cents to $3 each. Pants and vests were each got up in the then prevailing style for from 25 to 50 cents each. The hero of these accounts was then a bachelor some 30 years of age, and several enteries show where 50 cents per dozen

---

[1] From the *National Weekly*.

was the price paid for laundry work. Old folks will remember "dickies," a sort of false shirt front, which are in several places charged 40 cents each.

"Of building material, bricks are quoted at $9 per M.; nails, 12 cents per pound ; glass, 8 x 10 light, 15 cents ; lime per bushel, 15 cents ; hauling with team per day, $.75. Laborers' wages were 40 to 60 cents per day. Stone masons, brick layers, and carpenters are in several places, in the book, credited with work at $1.50 per day Board for workingmen nine cents per meal, or $1.75 per week. Smoked hams were seven cents per pound, fresh beef four cents, fresh pork three and one-half cents ; mutton by the quarter, 22 cents ; butter, 15 cents ; eggs, 12½ cents per dozen ; potatoes, 25 cents per bushel ; coffee, 20 cents; tea, Young Hyson, $1.40 per pound ; rice, six cents ; sugar, seven cents ; molasses, 40 cents per gallon ; maple molasses and sugar were quoted at about the same price ; salt, 70 cents per bushel ; 'locofoco' matches, 25 cents per box, for about as many as are now sold for three cents, and very few appeared to be sold as tinder and steel were relied on for fire. Why the matches were called 'locofoco' I have never understood, but presume some of our old grandsires could tell. Coal for fuel was not then used, and four-foot cord wood is in several places charged for at $1 per cord. Cooking stoves were then just coming in use of the 'horseblock' pattern, and cost $18 each. Corn was 65 cents per bushel. Flour fluctuated from $4 to $10 per barrel, but the average was nearer the former price. Tobacco sold at 40 cents per pound, and cigars appear to have been unknown, at least none are charged. Whisky—not our modern tanglefoot, but good—was 35 cents per gallon. Santa Cruz, Jamaica, Porto Rico, and various kinds of rum were from 50 to $1 per gallon. 'Black strap,' a favorite old-time beverage, commanded $1 per gallon, and was the favorite tipple for 'general training day,' as the day for general muster of State militia was called, and which in those days was a roaring farce. Among the items of the spring of 1827 is one as follows : 'Rev. William Patterson, Cr.: By service at wedding, $5,' and about the same time Mr. Patterson is charged 'One hat, $5,' from which it is presumed that these were the ruling prices for these necessaries of life. Money was of gold, silver, and paper as to-day, but was very scarce, and 'barter' or trade' was mostly used in traffic. Only the larger cities and towns had their own newspapers, and news was stale. Postage on letters was 12½, 18¾, or 55 cents per letter, according to the distance carried, and stamps were unknown for nearly 20 years after. At the option of the sender postage on letters could be prepaid or not ; and right here one of the most highly esteemed old ladies of this country one day received notice of a letter with '25 cents due,' that was held in the postoffice for her. Not having the money she herself killed and skinned a calf, selling the hide to a tanner for 25 cents to redeem the letter."

WAR OF 1812.

THE State of New York, particularly the middle and western portions, after the treaty of peace in 1783 had become settled ; the Indian title had been extinguished ; villages, settlements, and post roads had become established, which will be fully taken up further on. The War of 1812 was of vital importance to the State of New York, for its northern borders were the frontiers, and its settlers were compelled to defend their homes, and especially were the occupants of the Holland Purchase.

The aggressions of Great Britain, for years after peace was declared, was a subject of anxiety to our government, and notwithstanding the strict neutrality observed by the States during the war between England and France the British government was guilty of many overt acts; but not until American vessels were searched by British men-of-war, and American subjects forced into service regardless of law and justice, did the States remonstrate. The continuation of such indignities caused the declaration of war against Great Britain, June 19, 1812. This measure was not fully sanctioned by the people; the Federal party were opposed to it, and but a small portion of the Democratic party favored it; it was not from political prejudice so much, they claimed, but because the country was so poorly prepared.

The invasion of Canada was deemed expedient by the administration, and preparations were made accordingly by posting forces along the frontier from Plattsburgh to Detroit.

The proclamation of President Madison was announced June 19, 1812. Express riders carried the news which reached Gen. Lewis at Fort Niagara and Col. Swift at Black Rock on the 26th of June. The news was not long in reaching the various settlements of the pioneers on the Purchase. Up to this time their struggle to make a home had been a severe one, but now all preparations of clearing the farm and raising crops were suspended; some prepared to leave their homes and bent their faces eastward.

As there were at this time not 1,000 men under arms on the Niagara frontier, in pursuance of an act of Congress the governor of the State ordered a draft of militia, but generally the military force was composed of volunteers. On the 10th of July there were about 3,000 men comprising the force on the frontier. Gen. Amos Hall was placed in command, and in the spring of 1813 the force was augmented somewhat by the assistance of Red Jacket (who for once cast his influence in favor of the United States) and his warriors.

We do not intend to enter into detail all the transactions of this war; only to make such references to it as most directly concerns the territory comprised within the then settlements of the Holland Purchase.

As a result of the disasters to our forces by the capture of Fort Niagara the Niagara frontier was desolated. Those Indians (who had allied themselves with the English) plundered, burned, and massacred without restraint. The towns of Niagara and Lewiston, and the village of the friendly Indians at Tuscarora, were laid in ashes. Governor

Tompkins, on being informed of the removal of the regular troups from the Niagara frontier, on the 27th of November gave orders for the assembling of sufficient bodies of militia to supply the places of those under General McClure, who had charge of the defense of the Niagara frontier. Owing to delays incident to such operations they failed of arriving until after the capture of Niagara, and the destruction of the frontier below the falls. General Hall, commanding the western division of militia, had assembled at Buffalo and Black Rock 2,000 men. The enemy attacked on the night of the 29th ; the militia were ordered out to repel the attack, but they fled at the approach of the enemy without firing a gun. One small regiment alone attempted to cope with the British, but without avail. Thus the flourishing villages of Black Rock and Buffalo, as well as the neighboring settlements, were deserted, and fell a prey to the British and Indians. General Hall retired with the remains of his dispersed militia to Eleven Mile Creek, where he was able to collect only about 300 troups. With these he preserved a show of resistance, to cover the flying inhabitants and check the advances of the enemy. All the flourishing villages and settlements on the Niagara, between the lakes, and to a considerable distance in the rear, were laid in ashes ; the Indians were let loose upon the flying inhabitants, and hundreds of them were overtaken and massacred. The frontier presented one scene of universal desolation. The miserable inhabitants who escaped the Indian tomahawk fled to the interior, without shelter or means of support, in the depth of winter, and subsisted on the charity of their friends. More than 200 houses, with an immense value of property, were pillaged and destroyed, and the wretched inhabitants and owners reduced to poverty. General Hall retired to Batavia 50 miles in the rear of Niagara, where he was enabled to collect 1,800 militia for the protection of the public stores and the defense of those settlements which had escaped desolation.

Turner says :

"Batavia became the headquarters, the final rallying point, of small remnants of a army ; a halting-place for the fleeing, homeless, houseless citizens of the frontier, t the extent of the capacity of all the tenements in the village and neighborhood. Th most valuable effects of the land office were taken beyond the Genesee River ; th house of Mr. Ellicott was converted into quarters for army officers and his office a hos pital ; private houses were thrown open, barns and sheds occupied ; families tha were separated in the hasty departure from Buffalo became united there, their scattere members. male and female, dropping in one after another. All along the Buffalo roa as far as the Genesee River, there had been deserted houses, which did not fail to hav new occupants soon after the flight from the frontier commenced."

Very high credit was given to Gen. Peter B. Porter, who took part in the war, both for his eloquence in engaging the volunteers and his skill and valor in leading them. The press sounded his praises; the citizens of Batavia tendered him a dinner; the governor breveted him a major-general; and Congress voted him a gold medal, he being the only officer of volunteers to whom that honor was awarded during the War of 1812.

Pensioners of 1812 — By reference to records at the court-house we find the following persons were entitled to pensions, recorded in 1819: Lieut. Darius Hówe, $20 per month; Sergt.-Maj. Samuel Huntington, Sergt. Nathan Parker, Privates Jacob Annis, Timothy Baker, Joseph Riddle, Levi Vinton, William Kelly, B. Potts, John Lyman, Nathan Sherwood, Samuel Camp, Peter Truman, and John C. Calhoun (then Secretary of War), each $8 per month.

A treaty of peace was concluded at Ghent, December 24, 1814, but the good news did not reach here until Gen. Jackson had fought and won the battle of New Orleans. **1496986**

We have given a concise history of all the wars that have affected the Holland Purchase except the late Rebellion, which will be given in its proper place. The Holland Purchase, in its settlement and prosperity, was greatly retarded by the War of 1812, as its borders were the scenes of many battles and skirmishes; its pioneer settlers were compelled or volunteered to go "upon the lines" in defense of their homes; constant fear of invasions by the foe, especially Indians, caused many to abandon their settlements and flee east of the Genesee River.

The roads and improvements of the Holland Purchase were of much importance in the success of the war in this part of the State. The population of the tract at this time was about 25,000, and the influx of settlers had made some quite compact settlements, especially along the road to Buffalo.

The noted Ridge road was not in operation until after the War of 1812. Soldiers were marched from Rochester to Clarkson, thence to Le Roy, thence to Buffalo and Lewiston, because there were no other land routes. Batavia was at one time the halting-place—the rallying point—of fleeing soldiers and citizens of Buffalo and the frontier; the back settlements of the Holland Purchase were deserted, and Buffalo and the western frontiers were a blackened ruin of desolation. It is said by historians cotemporary with those times that there were no better soldiers "on the lines" than those from the Holland Purchase.

After peace was declared aid was generously advanced by the legislature of the State, the common councils of New York and Albany, and the subscriptions of individuals in those cities, as well as Canandaigua and other older towns, for the building up and relief of Buffalo and the settlers of the Holland Purchase. The amount of $63,000 was judiciously distributed among the sufferers, and the wilderness commenced "to blossom as the rose."

HOLLAND PURCHASE LAND TITLES.

HAVING shown the absolute title of the colony of New York to the Duke of York, and the severance of all allegiance to the mother country, we will enter minutely into the title of the lands of Western New York, particularly those of the Holland Purchase and of Genesee County.

Prior to the advent of the white man to the State of New York nothing was known of its occupants, but the habits of the aborigines, their customs and history, have been defined since. The present territory of the State was occupied by the "Five Nations," as the English called the confederacy of the five tribes, and "Iroquois," as they were denominated by the French. This confederacy extended through the center of the State, east and west, with the Mohawks at the eastern extremity, the Senecas at the western, and the Oneidas, Onondagas, and Cayugas between. The Senecas occupied the lands of the Holland Purchase, and more especially the lands of the "Genesee."

The superiority of the Iroquois—the confederacy— has been conceded by all writers. It was shown by the original, strong organization of the league, the conception of their campaigns, forms of government, and wisdom and oratory in council. Their origin, or that of any of the Indian races, has not been satisfactorily given, and the opinions are almost as numerous as the tribes. With no written language the traditions of generations past was perverted or lost. The Senecas who occupied the western part of the State,—from Geneva to Buffalo,—and whose moccasined feet had so long trodden the lands of the county of Genesee, were the highest in the confederacy. Red Jacket and other notable braves conducted their councils, but of the origin of the Senecas nothing was known. Their traditions told that the tribe, or its progenitors, issued from the large hill near the head of Canandaigua Lake, called by them *Genundewah*, and that is its present name. The same hill was used for the annual gatherings of the Senecas in some of their rites within the memory of the first settlers. Mary Jemeson, who lived so long on tl Gardeau Reservation of the Holland Purchase, has given the most con plete history of the " great hill " people.

FIRST LANDLORDS AND TAVERNS.

THE original survey of this section, begun by Joseph and Benjamin El cott in 1798, was completed in 1799, so far, at least, as running the townsh and range lines. No settlements having been made, inducements we made to such parties as would locate and erect taverns for accommodatio of would-be settlers. Accordingly three lots were sold, with that end view, first, to Asa Ransom, who settled in what is now the town of Cla ence (Erie County), the condition being " on or before January 1, 180 he should erect on the lot a messuage fit for the habitation of man, n less than 18 feet square, and should live and reside, or cause a family live and reside, therein during the term of five years next ensuing, a that before the 1st day of July next not less than eight acres of la should be cleared and fenced." Asa Ransom died in Buffalo 1835. The second lot sold was to Garret Davis, on the Lewiston roa about five miles from Batavia (now in Oakfield), and was known f years as the old Erastus Wolcott stand, where a tavern was erected ai kept for years. The contract was dated September 16, 1799, located Lot 13, Sec. 5, Tp. 13, Range 2, and called for 150 acres at 120 poun (New York currency), or $2.00 per acre, with like conditions as to Ra som's. Garret Davis died in November, 1801. The third lot was so to Frederick Walther, October 1, 1799, in Tp. 12, Range 1, " beginni in the Transit Meridian line, being the Eastern boundary of the aforesa Township, 13 ch. 38 L., S. of the 68 Mile Stone from the North bounda of Pennsylvania, containing 150 acres " This lot embraced all the pre ent village of Stafford that lies west of the transit line. The tave house was built on the north side of the old Genesee road, near the cre on the west side. Walther only remained a year or two, then we south.

COURT-HOUSE AND JAIL.

MR. ELLICOTT gave his attention to the building of a cou house and jail immediately after the act was passed to form Ge esee County. In May, 1802, Mr. Busti, writing to him, say " I am happy in the promptness with which you have agreed to carry into effect t erection of the court-house and jail, as stipulated to be erected at the expense of t

3

company, by Mr. Ogden and myself. This stipulation was one of the principal inducements towards our effecting the passage of the law establishing the new county."

Isaac Sutherland and Samuel F. Geer were employed as chief architects by Mr. Ellicott to adopt and carry out a building plan sent on by
Mr. Busti. From that plan was created the building now known as Ellicott hall. It is built of heavy oak timbers, and it took three days to
raise the frame work. The workmanship was of a superior order for those
days, and the building remains a monument to the mechanical skill and
energy of its founder, Joseph Ellicott. It was enclosed in the fall of
1802, and finished so far as to permit of holding the first sessions of the
courts in the spring of 1803. The north half was used as a court-room
and jail; the south half for a tavern, and occupied as such until about
1820. The tavern-keeper was then dismissed and the whole upper part
used as a court-room, and the lower part (except the jail) became the residence of the jailor, and so continued until the erection of the new jail in
1850, on West Main street. For several years the old court-room was
used as a place for religious meetings, the gallery being put in for additional seating capacity.

In 1819 Mr. Ellicott addressed "the Honorable the Judges of the
Court of Common Pleas, and the Supervisors of the County," to the effect that the needs of the county (Wyoming County not having been
erected) required an enlargement of the court-room, and proposed, as
agent of the Holland Land Company, to convey to the supervisors the
triangular piece of land (now bounded by Ellicott, Main, and Court
streets), the consideration being for the county to pay $3000; also to
convey to the company the oblong piece of land, 100 feet wide, located
about midway between Genesee (Main) street and Big Tree (Ellicott)
road, and extending from a point on what is now Clark Place, back of
Bieree's store; also a strip about 35 feet wide extending from Genesee street
to the main strip, known as "lot 81." (It was on this lot the first execution by hanging occurred in the county.) The suggestion was accepted, and a few years afterwards a new jail was built (now occupied by
the Hook and Ladder Company); also a county clerk's office was built
in the northeast corner of the triangle. Both were built of brick. This
was occupied until the present court-house was built, in 1842, when the
county clerk's office was moved to the basement of the same; but again
moved to its present location, when it and the surrogate's office was completed in 1873.

The circumstances that led to the building of the new court-house

were, first, a strong effort being made to remove the county seat to At_
tica; second, a movement on foot to divide the county; third, the old
court-room being too small and inconvenient. The supervisors thought
by this stroke they could defeat the removal of the county seat and divi_
sion of the county. The present court-house was built in 1843, and cost
about $17,000.

In 1849 the board of supervisors granted to the village of Batavia the
old court-house, conditioned upon its being repaired. Repairs were made,
and now the building is used for some town meetings, and is known as
Ellicott hall.

POLITICAL AND CIVIL HISTORY.

AT the earliest settlement of the county two political parties ex_
isted—the Federal, opposed to the war and friendly to Great Brit_
ain, and the Republican. The Federalists became quite unpopular
by opposing the War of 1812, and in this part of the State gradually
dropped the name and were stigmatized as "Democrats," which name
was finally adopted. "Bucktails" was a name given to the Republican
party of that day, and their opponents were called "Clintonians." Then
followed the terms "National" and "Democratic" Republicans.

In 1826 the famous Morgan excitement arose to change the political
phase of this section, and its origin was at Batavia. William Morgan
wrote an exposition of the so-called secrets of Free Masonry, and it was
to have been published at Batavia. It was alleged that for this exposure
he was abducted and murdered by the Masons; the details or truth of
the transaction do not belong in this history. The feeling of the people
of Genesee County was so aroused that a party, called the "Anti-Masonic," at once was formed, and was an overwhelming party for a short
time in Western New York. It became fully organized in 1828, and a
coalition was made in 1832 between the Anti-Masons and the National
Republicans of this State in order to carry the State for the Anti-Masons
and elect Henry Clay President of the United States. The scheme
failed and both designs failed. The Anti-Masonic party by this coalition merged into the "Whig" party, and remained until the "Republican" party of 1856 was formed.

In 1833 the agitation of the slavery question commenced and an anti-
slavery party was formed. No issue has wielded a more potent influence
upon national or local politics than this. The legislature of this State
passed an act in 1799 for the gradual extinction of slavery within its

borders.   Although it did not exist in the Holland Purchase, yet it was a legal institution in the older settled portions.   Subsequent enactments entirely obliterated all traces of the dark stain—slavery—from the State of New York on July 4, 1827.   Ten thousand slaves were set free by the act.   Anti-slavery meetings were broken up in the early years of this excitement by the opposition.   Gerrit Smith became the fearless leader of the anti-slavery faction, and it gradually developed into formidable proportions.

Genesee County took an active part in this move.   In 1836 a strong anti-slavery feeling existed here, and was as strongly opposed ; a society was formed and wished to hold a public meeting at Batavia.   The assurance by prominent men, although doubtful as to the justice of the claims of the " Abolitionists," that they should oppose any interference with a meeting in accordance with the right of free speech, that was properly conducted, led to a call for a meeting at the court-house in Batavia, March 12, 1836, at 2 P. M., to take into consideration what measure it was necessary to adopt with reference to the proposed meeting of the Abolitionists in this village ; and the call closed with this appeal : " Let all opposed to fanaticism, and who value the existence and perpetuity of the Union, attend."

This meeting was largely attended and passed strong resolutions against the object of the Abolitionists, that they were opposed to any such meeting in the village of Batavia, and would not be responsible for consequences if the Abolitionists held their meeting as proposed.   (These resolutions and full details can be found in Young's *History of Warsaw*.)   The meeting appointed a committee of 50 to wait upon the Abolition Society, should it meet in Batavia, and inform it of the wishes of the village, etc.

The Anti-Slavery Society met pursuant to notice at the court-house.   Before its organization the committee of 50 entered the hall, and its chairman read the resolutions of their meeting, and also made a short speech.   The Anti-Slavery Society appointed a committee of five to prepare a reply.   This committee was : Henry Brewster and Seth M. Gates, of Le Roy ; Gen. John D. Landon, of Castile ; William Patterson, of Warsaw, and Huntington Lyman.   In the reply they disclaimed a want of respect for the citizens of Batavia, was not appointed without consultation with respectable citizens, asserted the right to peaceably assemble to discuss the interests of their common country, and could not acknowledge the right of any persons or body of men to molest them or require them to cease deliberations.   The long report was made to the committee of 5 and the Anti-Slavery Society proceeded with its organization, but was interrupted with stamping and unusual riotous proceedings, and after an ineffectual expostulation and remonstrance adjourned to Warsaw one week from that day.

The meeting was held pursuant to adjournment, March 22, 1836, declared its sentiments, and pledged $1,000 for the first year's support of a free paper. Such a paper was established (*The American Citizen*) in Warsaw, and was subsequently removed to Perry, then to Rochester.

It was at a convention in Warsaw (then Genesee County) that the first proposition was made to nominate a President of this stripe, and after a stormy debate, in which Myron Holley and William L. Chapin were its advocates, James G. Birney was nominated. A division followed, but the vote was concentrated on the members of Congress who favored the anti-slavery movement. This party was now called the "Liberty party," and numbered about 1,500 in the State. In 1848 they joined the "Free Soil" party. The people of Genesee were divided, and very significantly so, in the campaign of 1848, and were first in the "Hunker" and "Barnburner" division upon the slavery question. The latter division, which opposed the introduction of slavery into new territory, received strong support in Western New York, and gave Martin Van Buren, its candidate, a hearty support in 1848. In 1850, when Horatio Seymour was nominated for governor, the Whig and Democratic parties became divided into the "Hard" and "Soft" factions, the first supporting President Fillmore's administration, the latter led by William H. Seward and opposed. In 1852, on the election of Franklin Pierce by the coalition of the Anti-Slavery or Soft Shell divisions, the Whig Party was practically annihilated, and the Republican party sprang into being, carrying the anti-slavery element with it. In all these movements no section was more active than Genesee County. The "American party," following in 1853, called "Know-Nothing party" from its secrecy, had a brief existence. In 1856 John C. Fremont was the candidate of the Republicans for President, but was defeated. Those opposed were called the Democratic party. In 1860 the choice of Abraham Lincoln was made by the Republicans, and he was elected President. The feeling between the slaveholding States and the North had been growing during these years, and many bitter words and aggressive acts were committed by both sections, which led to the passage of ordinances of secession by the slave States, the inauguration of the civil war of 1861–65, and the extinction of slavery forever.

The Republican and Democratic parties continue to oppose each other on minor issues, alternating the "outs" and "ins," and at this writing the Republicans are in the ascendency, with Benjamin Harrison, President.

Mention should be made of the Prohibition party, which has for the past few years steadily gained in numbers in Genesee as well as in other counties and States. The party advocates the enactment of laws to prohibit the manufacture and sale of intoxicating liquors,—a commendable object,—but many temperance defenders do not sustain the party.

The "Greenback party," of which Genesee County has only a few adherents, has not yet been able to effect a permanent organization.

The increase in parties, and the particular complexion of Genesee County during the past half century,—since the organization of the present county,—will be seen by the aggregate for each presidential election:

	Whig	Dem.	Nat. Am.	Free Soil	Liberty
1844,	3,604	2,111	298		
1848,	2,890	1,180	55	1,201	
1852,	3,358	2,164			323
	Rep.		Am.		
1856,	3,620	1,371	1,166		
1860,	4,464	2,456			
1864,	4,030	2,772			
1868,	4,254	2,847			
1872,	4,034	2,590			
			Greenback	Temp.	
1876,	4,322	3,321	48	2	
1880,	4,815	3,481	72		
				Prohibition	
1884,	4,631	3,643	41	386	
1888,	4,952	3,633		408	

A careful comparison of the vote for governor, each two years, will convey the idea of the local strength of Genesee County:

	Whig	Dem.	Free Soil	Am.	Liberty
1840,	3,650	2,130	20		
1842,	2,765	2,010	116		
1844,	3,590	2,135	345		
1846,	2,910	1,468	231	147	
1848,	2,927	1,217	1,118	53	
1850,	3,049	1,611			
1852,	3,661	2,141			184
			"K.-Nothing."		
1854,	1,597	1,102	2,460		
	Rep.		"K.-Nothing"		
1856,	3,486	1,402	1,218		
1858,	2,840	1,409	584		26
1860,	4,448	2,262	230		
1862,	3,491	2,559			

	Rep.	Dem.	Prohibiton	Greenback
1864.	4,050	2,760		
1866,	3,978	2,495		
1868,	4,239	2,863		
1870,	3,701	2,548		
1872,	4,061	2,604		
1874,	3,088	2,672	82	
1876,	4,328	3,321	33	
1879,	3,735	2,939	43	82
1882,	2,898	3,518	392	52
1885,	3,693.	3,014	382	
1888,	4,835	3,722	418	

Genesee County is the oldest county west of Ontario; its organization is given under the proper title. Its importance in the past and
present in the affairs of the State is evident; its position among the first, its
rapid development, and its admirable local government for a brief century
is directly attributed to the justice and firmness of its rulers and citizens. We append a list of officers from its organization to the present
time, and leave its civil and political status to be felt in the councils of
the State as in former days. Under the first constitution all officers
were appointed in the counties by the governor, and one senator from
each of the four districts into which the State was then divided; this
constituted the appointing power. Under the constitution of 1821
sheriffs and county clerks were elected by the people at the November
elections. In the lists following the years of appointment and election
are given.

SHERIFFS.

Richard M. Stoddard.......... 1803-06
Benjamin Barton............. 1807
Asher Bates................. 1808-09
Nathan Marvin............. . 1810
Aaron Van Cleve............ 1811-14
Parmenio Adams............. 1815
William Sheldon............ .. 1816-17
Parmenio Adams............. 1818-21
Worthy L. Churchill.......... 1822-24
William R. Thompson... 1825-27
John Wilder................. 1828-30
Earl Kidder (app'd *vice* Wilder) 1831
John A. McElwaine.......... . 1831-32
Nathan Townsend............ 1833-36
John Wilder................. 1837-39
Rufus Robertson............. 1840-41

James Long................:.... 1842-44
John Sprague...............'..... 1845-47
Henry Morrell................ 1848-50
Salmon B. Lusk........ 1851-53
James R. Mitchell............ 1854 56
Alvin Pease 1857-59
Ferdinand H. Hull 1860-62
Parley Upton................. 1863-65
Arch. D. McLachlin.......... 1866-68
William L. Parrish............. 1869-71.
George H. Robertson.......... 1872-74
John H. Ward................ 1875-77
George W. Griffis............. 1878-80
Irving D. Southworth.......... 1881-83
Joseph H. Robson............. 1884-86
William J. Reedy............. 1887-89

Addison Foster, under sheriff.

COUNTY CLERKS.

James W. Stevens	1803-09	Timothy Fitch	1831-36
Isaac Babcock	1810	Horace U. Soper	1837-42
Simeon Cummins	1811-15	H. H. Carpenter	1843-45
John Z. Ross	1816-17	Samuel C. Holden	1846-48
Simeon Cummins	1818-21	Merrill G. Soper	1849-54
Chauncey L. Sheldon	1822-24	Hiram W. Haskell	1855-60
Ralph Coffin	1825-27	George H. Holden	1861-66
David C. Miller	1828-30	Carlos A. Hull	1867-75

The present clerk is Carlos A. Hull, who has been kept in the office since 1867, so efficient is he ; his deputy, George H. Holden, has served the office 41 years.

SURROGATES.

PREVIOUS to 1847 surrogates were appointed as were county judges ; by the constitution adopted that year they were elected in counties where the population exceeds 40,000 ; in counties of less population the duties of surrogate devolve on the county judge :

Jeremiah R. Munson	1804	Ebenezer Mix	1821-39
Richard Smith	1805-14	Harvey Putnam	1840
Andrew A. Ellicott	1815-20	Timothy Fitch	1841-44
	Samuel Willett	1845-46	

TREASURERS.

THESE were appointed by the board of supervisors prior to 1847 ; since then elected :

Joseph· Ellicott	1803-09	Pardon C. Sherman	1843-44
James Brisbane	1810	Seth Wakeman	1845
Asa McCracken	1811	Brannan Young	1846-50
William Ramsey	1812	Thomas Yates	1851-53
David McCracken	1813-18	Horace M. Warren	1854-56
James Williams	1819-21	Thomas Yates	1857-59
Ethan B. Allen	1822-24	Oliver P. Clark	1860
George W. Lay	1825-31	Nathan A. Woodward	1861-66
Edgar C. Dibble	1832-33	Andrew D. Tryon	1867-72
William Davis	1834	Hiram K. Buell	1873-75
William S. Mallory	1835-39	Orrin C. Parker	1876-78
Joshua L. Brown	1840-42	Jorome C. Guiteau	1879-81
	John Thomas	1882-91	

FIRST JUDGES, COMMON PLEAS.

PRIOR to 1821 they were appointed by the appointing council ; under the constitution of 1821 the governor appointed for five years ; under the constitution of 1846 they were elected for four years ; the term has been changed to six :

Joseph Ellicott............	1806	William H. Tisdale............	1827–29
Ezra Platt....................	1807–11	Isaac Wilson.................	1830–35
John H. Jones........	1812–20	William Mitchell..............	1836–40
Isaac Wilson.............. .	1821–22	Phineas L. Tracy..............	1841–45
John Z. Ross.............	1823–26	Edgar C. Dibble........	1846

JUDGES AND SURROGATES.

Horace U. Soper..............	1847–50	Randolph Ballard appointed to close the	
Edgar C. Dibble..............	1851–54	term of Charles Henshaw, deceased.	
Joshua L. Brown	1855–58	Lucius N. Bangs............ .	1870–81
Moses Taggart..............	1859–66	Myron H. Peck..............	1882–88
Charles Henshaw.............	1867–70	Safford E. North	1889–96

JUSTICES OF SESSIONS.

THE constitution of 1846 abolished the office of associate judge, and created the office of justice of Sessions—two elected each from among acting justices of the peace of the county :

J. M. Holcomb, William M. Sprague	1847
James S. Stewart, Thomas Riddle.......................................	1849
German Lathrop, Miles Wallace........................	1850
John D. Safford, Charles S. Cone...	1851
John D. Safford, William Barnett....................................... ...	1852
Wheaton S. Miller, John C. Cranston...........................	1853
Abner Hull, Jr., John Munro, Jr........ ......;..................	1854
Augustus Cowdin, Oswald Bond..................................	1855
John G. Bixby, William H. Davis....	1856
John G. Bixby, James Stewart...	1857
William H. Davis, William Barnett.......................................	1858
Oswald Bond, Luther Crosby.	1859
James S. Stewart, Jonathan M. Foreman...............................	1860
William G. Sherwood, William Barnett................................	1861
Halleck Stilwell, John F. Perry...	1862
Halleck Stilwell, William Barnett.......................................	1863
Halleck Stilwell, Samuel Church..........................	1864
Benjamin F. Harris, Samuel Church.......:.....	1865
Nathaniel Reed, Sebastian R. Moore.....................................	1866
Joseph W. Holmes, William Barnett..	1867
Joseph W. Holmes, Lawrence L. Crosby.................................	1868
Charles Sprague, Lawrence L. Crosby..........	1869
Charles W. Rumsey, William L. Rugg.....................................	1870–71
Ansel D. Mills, Thomas J. Dean.............................	1872–73
Ansel D. Mills, Albert H. Perry.........	1874
Philip Cope, Albert H. Perry.....'.	1875

Philip Cope, Henry O. Bostwick.. 1876
Israel M. Peck, Henry O. Bostwick.. 1877-78
Irving D. Southworth, Henry O. Bostwick................................. 1879
William S. Coe, M. Nelson Moulthrop..................................... 1880-81
Alexander Campbell, Roswell C. Curtiss................................... 1882
Roswell C. Curtiss, Alva Babcock... 1883
Israel M. Peck, Roswell C. Curtiss.. 1884
Roswell C. Curtiss, Charles F. Lewis...................................... 1885
Jay W. Stratton, Charles F. Lewis... 1886
Frank E. Vosburg, Jay W. Stratton.. 1887
William G. Pollard, M. N. Moulthrop...................................... 1888-89

DISTRICT ATTORNEYS.

ACT passed in 1801 creating the office; act passed in 1818 made each county a district for one; the officers were appointed by constitution of 1821, and elected after 1846.

Daniel B. Brown..............1818-20
Heman J. Redfield............1821-28
Levi Rumsey.................1829-33
Daniel H. Chandler............1834-37
Isaac A. Verplanck............1838-41
John H. Martindale............1842-44
Moses Taggart...............1845
Isaac A. Verplanck...........1846
John H. Martindale...........1847-49
Seth Wakeman...............1850-55
George Brown...............1856-58
James M. Willett.............1859-61
William Tyrrell..............1862-64
C. Fitch Bissell.............1865-67
William C. Watson...........1868-73
C. Fitch Bissell.............1874-76
Thomas P. Heddon...........1877-79
Safford E. North............1880-82
Safford E. North............1883-85
Frank S. Wood...............1886-92

SCHOOL COMMISSIONERS.

THE office of commissioner for the county was created by law in 1853, and David Ney was appointed by the supervisors for 1854; Mr. Howe was appointed for 1855. The change of 1856 made the election of commissioner for each Assembly district; for the year 1856 Israel M. Peck was appointed for the eastern district, and Homer H. Woodward for the western. In 1857 the county was made one district; then was elected:

Orange S. Throop..............1857-62
D. C. Rumsey.................1863-68
R. L. Selden.................1869-74
William J. Barr..............1887-89
Charles V. Hooper............1875-80
William E. Prentice..........1881-83
Arthur B. Rathbone...........1884-86

MEMBERS OF ASSEMBLY.

Genesee and Ontario Counties.

Thaddeus Chapin, Augustus Porter Polydore B. Wisner.......................1802
Amos Hall, Nathaniel W. Howell Polydore B. Wisner.......................1803

Amos Hall, Daniel W. Lewis... .... ⎫
   Alexander Rea.............................. ⎬ 1804
Ezra Patterson, Daniel W. Lewis............... ⎫
  -Alexander Rea......................... ⎬ .... 1805.

Allegany, Genesee, and Ontario Counties.

Philetus Swift, Asahel Warner................ ⎫
  Alexander Rea....... .... ⎬ 1806-
Philetus Swift, Asahel Warner................ ⎫
  William Rumsey........................ ⎬ 1807

Genesee County.

William Rumsey............. 1808
Zacheus Colby 1811
Chauncey Loomis............. 1809
Chauncey Lewis........ ... .1810
James Gannon..1812
James Gannon........................ 1813
Isaac Sutherland...1814
James Gannon, Elizon Webster............. ..... ⎫ 1815
  John Wilson..................... ⎬
James Gannon, Elizon Webster . ... ⎫ 1816-
  Isaac Wilson........... .... ⎬
Gilbert Howell, Abraham Matteson............ ⎫ 1817
  Isaac Sutherland.... ⎬
Gilbert Howell, Abraham Matteson............ ⎫ ....1818.
  Isaac Sutherland....................... ⎬
Fitch Chipman, Gideon F. Jenkins............. ⎫ 1819
  Robert McKay.... .... ⎬
Fitch Chipman, Jesse Hawley.... .... ⎫ 1820
  Samuel M. Hopkins................... ... ⎬
Robert Anderson, Benedict Brooks.............. ⎫ 1821
  Samuel McWhorter .... ⎬
Apollos P. Auger, William Bristol.............. ⎫ 1822
  Otis Turner, Josiah Churchill............... ⎬
Shubael Dunham, Orin Follett... ..:.... .. .... ⎫ ....1823.
  James Gannon, Horace S. Turner........... ⎬
Jeremiah Brown, Fitch Chipman............... ⎫ 1824
  Shubael Dunham, Gaius B. Rich .... ⎬
Josiah Churchill, David Scott.....:.............. ⎫ 1825
  Phineas Stanton....... .... ⎬
Josiah Churchill, Shubael Dunham............. ⎫ 1826
  John B. Skinner..................... ⎬
Dennis Blakely, Trumbull Cary .... ⎫ 1827
  John B. Skinner.. ... · .... ⎬
Calvin P. Bailey, John Haskell............. ..... ⎫ 1828
  John B. Skinner................. ...... ⎬
Calvin P. Bailey, Timothy Fitch.............. .. ⎫ 1829
  Stephen Griswold.:............. .... ⎬
Robert Earl, Jr., Stephen Griswold.............. ⎫ 1830
  Charles Woodworth.:... .... ⎬
Seth M. Gates, Henry Hawkins................. ⎫ 1831
  James Sprague, 2d..:...................... ⎬

Peter Patterson, Rufus Robertson............... }
    Charles Woodworth... .... } 1832

Truman Lewis, Peter Patterson................ }
    Rufus Robertson............... .... } 1833

Truman Lewis, Samuel Richmond............. }
    Amos Tyrrell, Sr.. . ... } 1834

Charles O. Shepperd, Samuel Richmond .... }
    Amos Tyrrell, Sr....................... } 1835

Charles O. Shepperd, Reuben Benham......... }
    Leverett Seward, John A. McElwaine....... } 1836

Andrew H. Green, Reuben Benham............. }
    John Head, Leverett Seward.............. } 1837

Andrew H. Green, Horace Healey....... .... }
    John Head, Alva Jefferson............... } 1838

George W. Lay, Horace Healey............... }
    John W. Brownson, Alva Jefferson......... } 1839

Samuel Richardson, John W. Brownson......... }
    David Scott, Isaac N. Stoddard.... .... } 1840

Robinson Smiley, Albert Smith...1841
Robinson Smiley, Ira Waite..1842
Charles P. Brown, Chester Hannum...1843
Aaron Long, Chester Hannum...1844
Aaron Long, Heman Blodgett...1845
Alonzo S. Upham, Heman Blodgett...1846
Alonzo S. Upham, Tracey Pardee..1847
Martin C. Ward, Tracey Pardee..1848
Martin C. Ward, John C. Gardiner...1849
Albert Rowe, Levi Fiske..1850
Albert Rowe, Levi Fiske..1851
Theodore C. Peters, Joseph Cook...1852
Theodore C. Peters, Joseph Cook...1853
Ambrose Stevens, David Mallory 1854
Seth Wakeman, David Mallory...1855
Seth Wakeman, John J. McPherson...1856
Frank G. Kingman..1857
Elbridge G. Moulton 1858

Elbridge G. Moulton.	1859	Volney G. Knapp.	1871
George W. Wright	1860	Elbert Townsend	1872
Benjamin Pringle	1861	Elbert Townsend	1873
Loren Green	1862	Newton H. Green	1874
Loren Green	1863	Newton H. Green	1875
John W. Brown	1864	Eli Taylor	1876–77
John W. Brown	1865	John Sanders	1778–79
Henry F. Tarbox	1866	Joseph W. Holmes	1880–81
Henry F. Tarbox	1867	Robert W. Nichol	1882
Edward C. Walker	1868	Lucien R. Bailey	1883–84
Edward C. Walker	1869	Charles A. Seaver	1885–87
Volney G. Knapp	1870	John McKenzie	1888–89
	T. F. Miller		1889–90

STATE SENATORS.

THE following persons have been chosen State senators from the county :

Alexander Rea.... 1808	Trumbull Cary 1831
Isaac Wilson................ 1818	Harvey Putnam...................1843
David E. Evans.. 1820	Alonzo S. Upham................1850
Heman J. Redfield. 1823	George Bowen....................1870
Ethan B. Allen...................1826	Edward C. Walker...............1886

MEMBERS OF CONGRESS.

Samuel M. Hopkins............ ...1813	Seth M. Gates.... 1839
Benjamin Ellicott.................1817	Albert Smith.... 1843
Parmenio Adams..................1825	Harvey Putnam....:.............1847
Phineas L. Tracy 1827	Augustus P. Hascall....... ..... .1851
George W. Lay....................1833	Benjamin Pringle........... 1853
Harvey Putnam....................1837	John Fisher......................1867
Seth Wakeman. 1871	

The coroners now serving the county are Lucius B. Parmelee and Isaac T. Mullen, elected in 1887 ; and Elliott C. Smith and Alpheus Prince, elected in November, 1888.

Present superintendents of the poor : Cortland Crosman, elected in November, 1886 ; Dwight Dimock, elected in November, 1887 ; Richard Pearson, elected in November, 1888 ; Dwight Dimock, Corfu, elected in November, 1886.

Robert A. Maxwell, of Batavia, served as treasurer of the State in 1881, and as superintendent of insurance in 1886–89.

BENCH AND BAR.[1]

THE editors of the *Gazetteer and Biographical Record* have asked for their publication a sketch of the lives of the men who in the past have been representative members of the legal profession in Genesee County. The scope of this article does not include any lawyer now living. It is only of those whose earthly labors are ended that we are to speak. Within the limit of space assigned it will be impossible to give more than an outline of the lives of these men, many of whom have been among the foremost citizens of Genesee County. It is not claimed that mention is made of every lawyer who has practiced here, neither does this sketch include those who have pursued their studies or practiced in this county for a short time, but who have made their reputations elsewhere. In any

---

[1] By Hon. S. E. North.

community the members of the bar are always in a large sense public men. Many important judicial positions are necessarily filled from their ranks, while legislative and other official places are often occupied by lawyers. The bar of Genesee County forms no exception to this rule. There nas never been a time when it did not include many men of recognized ability, and the bar as a whole has always compared favorably with that of any other county of anything like equal size. Of those whose names are here recorded only Martindale, Wakeman, Hewitt, and Taggart were personally known to the writer. The estimates given of the professional characteristics of the men who form the subject of this article have been derived largely from conversation with those who knew them as lawyers and citizens, and partly, of course, from such printed sketches as were available. The historical facts have been gathered from biographies found in many different places, from newspaper files, court records, from recollections of old inhabitants, and in several instances from such meagre statements as are chiseled in marble in the cemetery, or are written down in not less formal phrase in the books of the surrogate's office.

The first judge of the county was Joseph Ellicott, the same man who, as surveyor, blazed his way through the primeval forests of Western New York, and laid out the counties, towns, and villages of the Holland Purchase. Mr. Ellicott was not a lawyer. He resigned the position of judge a short time after his appointment in 1803, and was succeeded by Ezra Platt. Of Judge Platt but little information is available, except that he discharged the few duties of the office until about 1812. His will is recorded in book 1 of Wills in the surrogate's office, at page 11, and is the third will entered in the county records. The first was that of Daniel Totten, recorded January 20, 1808, and the second, that of David Franklin, was recorded March 30, 1809, while the record of Judge Platt's will was made January 9, 1812, making three wills in four years.

The succeeding judges down to 1847 were John H. Jones, Isaac Wilson, John Z. Ross, William H. Tisdale, William Mitchell, Phineas L. Tracy, and Edgar C. Dibble. During the same period the surrogates of the county had been Jeremiah R. Munson,—whose name does not appear in any of the records of the office,—Richard Smith, Andrew A. Ellicott, Ebenezer Mix, Harvey Putnam, Timothy Fitch, and Samuel Willett. Mr. Mix filled the office from 1821 to 1840. Under the law as it has existed since 1847 the functions of county judge and surrogate have been performed by the same official. The duties of surrogate prior to that date were few, as estates were seldom settled.

Richard Smith, whose portrait has for many years hung in the cour
house, over the chair occupied by the presiding judge, was born in Co₁
necticut, February 17, 1779' and died December 31, 1859. He was
graduate of Yale College and removed to Genesee County in 1803.
was at one time a partner of Daniel B. Brown. Judge Smith seldom,
ever, appeared in court. It is not known that any of the other incun
bents of the office up to that time were particularly prominent as lawye₁
neither is much information available as to any county judge prior
Phineas L. Tracy. Judge Ross is spoken favorably of as a citizen a₁
lawyer. He died October 27, 1826, at the age of 40 years.

Few men have been more closely identified with the history of Genes
County than Judge Tracy. He was born December 25, 1786, at No
wich, Conn., and graduated at Yale in 1806. He was admitted to tl
bar at Albany in 1811, and removed to Genesee County in 1813. F
many years he had an extensive and lucrative practice, and was a man
marked force and ability. He was elected to Congress in 1827 and aga
in 1829, and in 1841 was appointed "first judge" of the county
William H. Seward, then governor. After his retirement from tl
bench in 1846 he practiced law but little. He was for many years
member of the vestry of St. James's Church. His death occurred D
cember 22, 1876. An obituary published at that time says: "He wou
have been 90 years old on Christmas day. A good and just man, f₁
of years and ripe for the harvest, has gone to his peaceful rest."

The next county judge was Edgar C. Dibble, who held the office du
ing the year 1846, and again from 1852 to 1856. Judge Dibble was
fairly well-read lawyer, a man of good character, and he discharged t
duties of his office satisfactorily. He died February 28, 1862, at the a
of 57 years. During the period of his professional career he was at di
ferent times in partnership with Timothy Fitch, John H. Martindale, a₁
Martin F. Robertson.

Judge Dibble was succeeded by Horace U. Soper, who served fo
years. Judge Soper is said to have made a good record upon the benc
but was never especially prominent as a practitioner. He was an amiab
and agreeable gentleman, of attractive manners and large general i₁
formation. He died January 15, 1878, at the age of 72 years, leaving ₁
descendants.

Joshua L. Brown became county judge and surrogate in 1856 and he
the office four years. He died at the age of 48, June 19, 1860, a fe
months after the expiration of his official term, at St. Louis, Mo. Jud₹

Brown was a good citizen, and a lawyer of extensive learning and decided ability. He is said to have possessed less aptitude for the trial of
causes before a jury than for the other duties of his profession, although
he tried a large number of cases. Before the court, or as a counselor in
his office, he was a strong, safe man. A member of the bar now living
tells how he had a habit during the trial of criminal causes, where, as
often occurs, the defense was conducted by some yonng man designated
by the court, of taking a seat near the junior thus assigned, when, as the
trial proceeded, he would draw his chair up and make suggestions.
After a little he would be on his feet arguing a law point, and in one
case at the close of the evidence he proceeded at once to sum up to the
jury, much to the discomfiture of the young lawyer who had prepared,
with great care, an address which was to make his reputation. Judge
Brown was for many years a partner of Maj. Henry I. Glowacki, who in
well earned retirement from the active labors of life still survives. The
firm of Brown & Glowacki enjoyed for many years an extensive and
lucrative practice, which was at its full height at the time of Judge
Brown's death.

Moses Taggart, who succeeded Judge Brown, died at his home in Batavia, February 17, 1883, at the ripe age of 82 years. He was the Nes-
tor of our bar, having been in active and continuous practice for about
55 years. During his eventful life he had endeared himself to the profession, of which he was an honored member, and was universally respected in the community where he had so long resided. As a lawyer
he was thoroughly grounded in the elementary principles of legal science.
Throughout his career he was esteemed for his good judgment, safe
counsel, and extensive research rather than for any special ability as a
trial lawyer. He had little liking or aptitude for the work of an advocate. A strong, helpful friend of young men, he had witnessed the career
of every man at the bar at the time of his death, and it is safe to say that
every one of the number felt a sincere attachment for the venerable and
honored father of the fraternity. Judge Taggart was born at Colerain,
Mass., August 21, 1799. At the age of 18 years he left his native town
to find a home in the newer region of Western New York, and traveled
all the way to Byron on foot. His legal studies were pursued in the
office of Phineas L. Tracy. Upon his admission to the bar he became a
partner of Albert Smith, who at that time was an able and noted practitioner. At different periods of his life he was in partnership with
Daniel H. Chandler, Charles Henshaw, Seth Wakeman, and during the

latter years of his life with his son-in-law, W. Harris Day. He was a member of the Constitutional Convention of 1846, and in 1851 was appointed justice of the Supreme Court to fill a vacancy caused by the death of Judge Sill. This position he filled until the close of 1853, and during the last year of his service became, under the then existing provisions of law, a member of the Court of Appeals. In 1860 he was elected county judge and surrogate of this county, and filled the office acceptably for two terms of four years each. In 1871 Judge Taggart was appointed postmaster of Batavia, which position he held for about four years. He maintained his excellent health and vigorous bearing almost to the end of his life, while his intellectual powers remained unimpaired to the last.

Charles Henshaw was born at Java, Wyoming County, and studied law with Gen. L. W. Thayer at Warsaw. He was elected county judge and surrogate in 1868, and died in office September 18, 1870, at the age of 48 years. A man of sterling worth, honest through and through, he possessed qualifications which rendered him in some respects the most remarkable lawyer who has ever practiced at our bar. It is doubtful if any other lawyer of this county has acquired so extended a knowledge of the law itself. His memory was unfailing, and his familiarity with both elementary law and judicial decisions was vast and perfectly at his command. He could always say " on such a book and page you will find the law." He disregarded all forms, and fashioned his papers briefly and accurately to suit himself. Unwilling or unable to try a case before a jury, he seldom if ever appeared in this capacity. His judicial career, upon which he had but fairly entered, gave great promise, and had he lived Charles Henshaw would have filled higher positions upon the bench. The incumbents of the office of county judge and surrogate since Judge Henshaw's death are, in this year 1890, all living.

A sketch of the life of the Hon. Heman J. Redfield, prepared for this article, has been omitted, since an extended notice of his career is printed elsewhere in this volume.

Among the members of the legal profession who have practiced in Le Roy besides Mr. Redfield there may be mentioned Jacob Bartow, Alfred F. Bartow and Charles Bartow, his sons, Seth M. Gates, Charles Danforth, Samuel Skinner, Perrin M. Smith, and Augustus P. Hascall.

Jacob Bartow, although never distinguished as a lawyer, was a man of large attainments and rare scholarly tastes. He was a law student with Aaron Burr. He died about 1845. His son, Alfred F. Bartow, studied law with Heman J. Redfield, and later became his partner. He removed

4

west and died a few years ago in Chicago. Mr. Bartow was an excellent practical business lawyer, and was a prominent and respected citizen of Le Roy. He was for many years a member of the vestry of St. Mark's Church, and took much interest in the work of that society. Charles Bartow studied law with A. P. Hascall, and during the time he practiced in Le Roy was in partnership with Hiram W. Hascall, and afterwards with John R. Olmsted. He removed to New York, where he died. Augustus P. Hascall was for a long time an honored and prominent citizen of Le Roy. He served as presidential elector in 1848, and was a Representative in the 32d Congress. He died June 27, 1872, aged about 76 years. Charles Danforth was a graduate of Williams College, and was at one time judge of Common Pleas in this county. He was a good lawyer and gave satisfaction as a judge. Samuel Skinner was one of the earliest lawyers in Le Roy, and is said to have been an able, well-read member of the bar. He was a graduate of Williams College, and was possessed of scholarly tastes. He died in Le Roy about the year 1853. Perrin M. Smith studied law with Mr. Redfield and became a partner of Mr. Skinner. He removed from Le Roy to the West, where he died many years ago. Seth M. Gates practiced law in LeRoy for many years, and was an able man He was proficient alike as an office lawyer and in the trial and argument of cases. He was elected to Congress in 1839, and soon after completing his term of service removed to Warsaw, where he died about the year 1876. During his residence in Le Roy he was 10 years associated in business with D. R. Bacon, who still resides in Le Roy, an honored citizen of that village. Mr. Bacon was at one time a law partner of James Summerfield, but upon becoming connected with manufacturing interests several years ago retired from active practice of his profession.

A citizen of Le Roy, having at his command sources of information not available to the writer of this sketch, has included in an article prepared for this work much additional information concerning Le Roy lawyers, which might otherwise have been of interest here.

Among the more prominent of the early Batavia lawyers may be mentioned Albert Smith, who in his day had a wide reputation for extensive legal knowledge, and for his power as an advocate. He was a Representative to the 28th and 29th Congresses from this district, and served in the Assembly in 1842. At different times he was associated as a partner with the ablest lawyers of the county. Mr. Smith removed west soon after his service in the State legislature, and has long since been dead.

Daniel B. Brown was born October 18, 1780, and died July 7, 1822, leaving, it is said, no descendants or near kindred. He is reputed to have been one of the most brilliant advocates who ever practiced in this county. He was somewhat intemperate in habits and erratic in disposi_ tion, and consequently never won for himself the position which he other_ wise would have gained. It is hardly probable that he is practicing law in the other world, yet his tombstone bears the inscription, copied quite likely from his sign used while living: " Daniel B. Brown, Attorney and Counselor at Law."

Levi Rumsey was a prominent citizen of this county at an early day, and was intimately concerned in that class of law business connected with the formative period of our history. But little information concerning him is now available, yet an old citizen of Batavia well qualified to know and judge says of him, that in the prime of life he was not only the fore_ most lawyer of this county, but of Western New York. He was unques_ tionably a man of high character and of decided ability. Mr. Rumsey was district attorney of this county from 1829 to 1834. He was born in Connecticut, December 8, 1776, and died December 29, 1833.

Ethan B. Allen was among the most prominent of the early lawyers of the county, and was a man of high character and unusual attainments. In personal bearing he was " a gentleman of the old school." He was born in Columbia County, October 21, 1787, and died April 19, 1835. He was the father-in-law of that distinguished advocate and jurist, Isaac A. Verplanck. Mr. Allen was a State senator from this district from 1826 to 1830. Upon his tombstone are inscribed the words " intelligent, virtuous, and affectionate, he fulfilled the various duties of a legislator, a citizen, and a friend."

Daniel H. Chandler, who was for many years a prominent citizen of this county, was born in 1795 and died March 29, 1864, at Madison, Wis., where he had removed in 1847. He was district attorney of this county from 1834 to 1838. Mr. Chandler was an able and thoroughly equipped lawyer, combining in an unusual degree the characteristics of advocate and counselor. He was a partner at one time of Senator Ethan B. Allen, and later with Hon. Moses Taggart. Mr. Chandler is well re- membered by quite a number of our older residents, all of whom attest his worth as a man and his talents as a lawyer. His ability as a trial lawyer brought him actively into the management of many notable cases, where he won for himself high commendation from bench, bar, and clients. He was the father of the late Rear-Admiral Ralph Chandler, of the United States navy. After his removal to Wisconsin Mr. Chandler acquired a large practice, and fully maintained the reputation he had gained here.

George W. Lay, the fourth son of John Lay, Esq., was born at Catskill, N. Y., July 27, 1798. He graduated at Hamilton College, N. Y., in the class of 1817. He came to Batavia the same year and studied law in the office of Hon. Phineas L. Tracy. After his admission to the bar he became a law partner of Mr. Tracy. The firm of Tracy & Lay did an extensive law business in the territory now embracing the counties of Genesee, Wyoming, and Orleans, and enjoyed a wide reputation and extensive acquaintance throughout the State. At that time the Genesee County bar was composed of lawyers of marked ability and talent. John B. Skinner, Daniel H. Chandler, Ethan B. Allen, Heman J. Redfield, Daniel B. Brown, Moses Taggart, Albert Smith, and many others attended the courts and were in full practice. Mr. Lay was a close practitioner under the old system, and was noted for his skill and dexterity as a pleader. The partnership ended in 1832. Mr. Lay was at that time elected to Congress. He then became a partner with James G. Merrill and Horace U. Soper. In 1840 he was elected to the Assembly of the State of New York, and served as chairman of the canal committee. His canal report was characterized as a document of marked foresight and ability. In 1842 he was appointed Chargé d'Affaires at the court of Norway and Sweden, and resided three years at Stockholm. After his return home his health failed, he became a confirmed invalid, and died October 21, 1860.

Isaac A. Verplanck, who was ranked as one of the of the ablest lawyers in Western New York, practiced for several years in Batavia. He was born October 16, 1812, and came to Genesee County in 1831. For a considerable time he was in partnership with John H. Martindale, the two forming a very strong law firm. Mr. Verplanck lacked the industry and indomitable energy which characterized his distinguished partner, but compensated by his masterly abilities, by his extensive knowledge of the law, and his great forensic power. He was district attorney of this county from 1838 to 1842, and again in 1846. Soon after this he removed to Buffalo. He was elected one of the judges of the Superior Court of that city, and held the position during the remainder of his life. For the last three years he was chief judge. His death occurred October 15, 1873.

Elijah Hurty, whose early death terminated a career of marked promise and usefulness, was a man of scholarly tastes, genial disposition, and excellent character. He was born in Bethany, in this county, and when quite a young man became principal of Union School in Batavia. Soon after his admission to the bar he formed a partnership with Hon. George Bowen, under the firm name of Hurty & Bowen. He died August 10, 1854, at the age of 32 years.

James G. Hoyt spent but a small portion of his professional life in this county, and although a sketch of his career is hardly within the scope of this article, yet so well was he known here that his name cannot properly be omitted. He was born in Camden, January 25, 1806, and removed to Genesee County in 1812. His father died six years later, leaving a widow and nine children in such poverty that the future jurist was at once thrown upon his own resources. In 1830 he was elected a constable, and discharged the duties of his office with so much promptness and intelligence as to attract the attention of leading business men. In 1834 he was elected justice of the peace, and the same year began to read law with Moses Taggart. Shortly after his admission to the bar he removed to Attica, which was then included in Genesee County. He gained almost immediate recognition as a lawyer of unusual industry, thoroughness, and ability. After a few years he removed to Buffalo, and was twice elected justice of the Supreme Court. In the discharge of the exacting duties of that office he gained a high reputation, and is remembered by all our older lawyers as one of the ablest of the many eminent men who have filled the position. He died October 23, 1863. His widow, to whom he was married in 1831, still survives.

Probably no firm of lawyers ever enjoyed so varied and extended a practice in this county as Wakeman & Bryan, who were copartners from 1852 until the death of Mr. Bryan, which occurred in October, 1867. The combination was one of unusual strength. Seth Wakeman was a successful trial lawyer, while William G. Bryan was a counselor of learning and discretion. Mr. Wakeman was born in Vermont, January 15, 1811. His father was a soldier in the War of 1812, and died in the service, leaving a widow and a large family of children in destitute circumstances. They soon removed to this county. When quite a young man Mr. Wakeman was elected a constable of the town of Pembroke, and it was by reason of his occasional duties at justices' courts that he became interested in law. In 1838 he was elected a justice of the peace, and six years later, at the age of 33, he was admitted to the bar. After a brief partnership with Joseph Sleeper the firm of Wakeman & Bryan was formed. After Mr. Bryan's death Mr. Wakeman was for a time a partner of Judge Taggart, and afterwards, and up to his forced retirement on account of failing health in 1875, he was associated with William C. Watson, the firm doing an extensive business. Mr. Wakeman was a Whig until the dissolution of that party, when he became a Republican. He was elected district attorney in 1850 and served two terms. In 1856 and 1857 he was member of Assembly. In 1867 he was a member of the State Constitutional Convention, and in 1870 he was elected to the 42d Congress. As a citizen Mr. Wakeman was generous, companionable, and kind. Distinctively a self-made man, he was always in warmest sympathy with every person whom he found struggling with adverse fortune. While eminently fair as a lawyer his strongest antagonists always found in him "a foeman worthy of their steel." He was an admirable trial lawyer, and gained a splendid practice and reputation as such. Possessed of few of the graces of oratory, Mr. Wakeman was nevertheless a strong, trenchant, and convincing speaker. He died January 4, 1880

William G. Bryan was born January 28, 1822, in Brighton, England. He came to America and settled in Le Roy in 1830. His law studies were pursued with Albert Smith and with Moses Taggart. In 1851 he formed a partnership with John H. Martindale, which was soon dissolved by the removal of the latter to Rochester. In politics Mr. Bryan was an ardent Democrat, and was a trusted adviser in all party matters. He was a lawyer of decided ability, but from choice spent his time inside his office, preparing papers, giving counsel, and examining cases. He was a man of refined tastes, of scholarly attainments, and great personal worth. Between him and Mr. Wakeman the strongest attachment existed. His untimely death, at the age of 45, was the result of an accident. He had gone to Burlington, Iowa, on a visit, and while there, in endeavoring to control a frightened horse, he was thrown from a carriage and killed. A public meeting of the citizens of Batavia was held on the sad occasion. His accomplished and estimable wife, for many years principal of the Bryan Seminary, still survives.

James M. Willett was born October 10, 1831. He graduated at the Albany Law School in 1856. In 1859 he was elected district attorney, being the first Democrat ever elected to that office in this county. He entered the army in 1862 and became major of the famous Eighth New York Heavy Artillery. In the fearful ordeal through which that regiment passed at Cold Harbor he was severely wounded. Upon rejoining his regiment, three months later, he became colonel, and to the close of the war commanded a brigade. After leaving the army he en_gaged in business in New York until 1870, when he removed to Buffalo and formed the well-known law partnership of Laning, Folsom & Wil_lett. The firm were the legal representatives of the New York Central Railroad, and did a large general practice. Colonel Willett continued to suffer from his army wounds, his health gave way, and he died June 6, 1877. He was a strong, well equipped lawyer, a genial and companion_able friend, a Christian gentleman. Few men ever practiced at our bar who had so strong a hold on the affections of his associates and the people at large.

Martin F. Robertson was a native of Genesee County, and passed his life in Batavia. He was possessed of decided ability, fair legal learning, and was a good trial lawyer. As a man he was very companionable and popular. He died March 21, 1868, at the age of 48 years, never having married.

Benjamin Pringle, for many years one of the foremost citizens of this county, was born in the year 1807, at Richfield, in this State. He came to Batavia in 1830 and formed a partnership with Albert Smith, and later became a partner of Heman J. Redfield. He was judge of the county from 1841 to 1846. In 1852, and again in 1854, he was elected to Congress. In 1862 he was member of Assembly, and in 1863 President Lincoln appointed him judge under a treaty between the United States and Great Britain for the suppression of the slave trade. He remained in the discharge of the duties of this office for seven years at Cape of Good Hope. Judge Pringle was a competent equity lawyer, but without special taste for the trial of causes. As a citizen he was public spirited and patriotic. In private life he was exemplary. For many years he was a warden of St. James's Episcopal Church, of which he was a devoted member. During his old age he divided his time between Batavia and Hastings, Minn., where his sons lived. He died at the latter place June 7, 1887. His remains are buried in Batavia.

Marlbro W. Hewitt, though never particularly active as a practitioner, was a respected member of the bar, and an esteemed and well-known citizen of Batavia. He was for a great many years a justice of the peace, and discharged the duties of that office with fidelity and unusul intelligence. Mr. Hewitt died February 23, 1880, at the age of 64 years.

One of the most interesting figures in the history of the bar of Genesee County and of Western New York was Gen. John H. Martindale. Although most of his professional life was passed in Rochester, whither he removed in 1852, he had prior to that time served two terms as district attorney of this county, and had laid the foundation for his brilliant career as an advocate and orator. Having received a military education at West Point he entered the army at the breaking out of the Rebellion. He did active and efficient service in the field quite early in the war, and later served as military governor of the District of Columbia, with the rank of major-general. He was elected attorney general of this State in 1865. General Martindale became famous in his management of actions for damages for personal injuries brought against railroad corporations, particularly the New York Central. His most frequent antagonist was that most brilliant and admirable trial lawyer, the late Albert P. Laning, of Buffalo. They tried a large number of cases opposed to each other in this county, and the memory of those days is an ever recurring delight. The court-house was always filled and the audience always entertained. The limits of this article forbid what might be made an interesting account of this remarkable man. Always eloquent, he had the faculty of being most so in cases otherwise commonplace. The writer has heard many of his addresses to juries, but the most eloquent is remembered as his summing up in the case of Garwood against the New York Central Railroad, an action brought to recover damages for injury to plaintiff's mill-power by pumping water from the Tonawanda Creek into tanks, for the use of locomotive boilers. The theme was certainly not one which would seem to afford opportunity for a display of oratory, yet the speaker proved superior to the occasion, and the result was an address seldom equalled. Although of agreeable disposition General Martindale was rather easily ruffled when engaged in the trial of important cases. His wily opponent learned well his sensitive points, and never failed to take advantage of them. As General Martindale always appeared for the plaintiff in railroad cases he had the advantage of the closing address. He was quite fond, in talking to a Genesee County jury, of indulging in reminiscences, and often referred to his acquaintance with the fathers of some of the younger jurymen, and to old associations connected with Batavia. On one well remembered occasion, when Mr. Laning thought his florid antagonist would be apt to find opportunity for a display of this kind, he turned his weapons against him in that quiet and inimitable manner so strikingly in contrast with the exuberant style of his opponent. He told the jury what the General would shortly proceed to narrate in their hearing, including all that Martindale could possibly say about his early home, his dead partner, "the classic Verplanck," his friends and neighbors, the old church, etc. The result was that the orator was compelled to change his tactics. The contests between Martindale and Laning will always be remembered by those who enjoyed the privilege of listening to and witnessing the efforts of these remarkable but wholly dissimilar men. In private life General Martindale was greatly esteemed. His character was above reproach, and he was a man of sincere piety. His personal appearance and bearing attracted admiration at all times. In 1881 he went to Europe in a vain search for health, but died at Nice, France, on the 13th of December of that year, at the age of 66.

THE MEDICAL PROFESSION.

IN preparing a chapter upon the medical profession of Genesee County the writer, by direction of the publishers, has mentioned only those physicians now dead, or removed to other localities, leaving to the gentlemen canvassing the several towns the furnishing of information concerning those now living and in active practice. The scope of this work must necessarily be limited to little more than a mention of the names of the old physicians, their places of birth and education, the time when they practiced here, the dates of their death or removal, and a few items of special importance concerning them. It has been in some instances impossible to learn all we desired about the early practitioners, but what we have written will, we think, be found reasonably correct.

The modern doctor who drives in an easy carriage, over smooth roads, and with everything needful to protect him from the hot sunshine or the storm, who charges good fees and collects the most of them, who has at his command the elegant and chemically accurate medical preparations of the present day, can have little appreciation of the labors incident to the practice of the pioneer physician, who rode on horseback through the woods, carried his medicines in saddlebags, dug out of the ground almost everything but calomel he prescribed, and did a very great deal of gratuitous work for the early settlers, who were not, as a rule, overstocked with worldly goods. It may be well to state in this place that in the olden time physicians received their diplomas from the medical society of the county in which they intended to practice, and not, as at present, from medical colleges.

THE GENESEE COUNTY MEDICAL SOCIETY.

IT appears that there was an association of physicians in Western New York, then nearly all in the county of Ontario, as early as the year 1801,

for we find the name of Dr. D. McCracken, of Batavia, as member of a
medical society at that time. As, however, Genesee County was not organized until the next year this could not be called in reality the Genesee County Medical Society. Meetings were held each year until 1807,
when a society bearing the above name was established under the law
passed the year before, by which the New York State Medical Society
was legally incorporated.

The first delegate sent from Genesee County to the State society was
Dr. Levi Ward, of Bergen, who attended a meeting held at Albany, Feb-
ruary 6, 1810. No other mention is made in the State *Transactions* of
any delegate from this county until 1828, when Dr. J. A. Billings, of
Batavia, was in attendance. The officers of his society at that time were:
Dr. J. A. Billings, president; Dr. John Cotes, vice-president; Dr. Richard
Dibble, secretary; Dr. O. P. Smith, treasurer; Dr. Frederick Fitch, Dr.
Charles C. Ford, Dr. William H. Webster, Dr. J. K. Barlow, and Dr.
Levant B. Cotes, censors. Several of these names appear in the history
of the several towns, and some of them became famous.

'The County Medical Society was represented by delegates every year
until 1883, when a division of sentiment concerning the counselling
with irregular physicians, nearly broke it up. The new State Medical
Association, formed in 1884, drew away many members, and the old organization gradually died out. The officers of the society at the date of
the last report to the State society (1882) were: Dr. I. V. Mullen, president; Dr. Henry Pamphilon, vice-president; Dr. J. R. Cotes, secretary
and treasurer. The following is a list of the members on the roll at that
time: Dr. S. Barret, Le Roy; Dr. S. C. Bateman, Alabama; Dr. J. F.
Cleveland, Le Roy; Dr. John R. Cotes, Batavia; Dr. F. W. Crane, Corfu;
Dr. G. W. Croff, Bethany; Dr. O. R. Groff, Bethany; Dr. J. C. David-
son, Batavia; Dr. A. G. Ellenwood, Attica, Wyoming County; Dr. B. A.
Fuller, Le Roy; Dr. G. B. Gilbert, Byron; Dr. G. U. Gleason, South
Byron; Dr. A. P. Jackson, Oakfield; Dr. J. M. Lewis, Elba; Dr. H. A.
Morse, Batavia; Dr. I. V. Mullen, Alexander; Dr. John N. Mullen,
Alexander; Dr. Henry Pamphilon, Stafford; Dr. William Pardee, Oak-
field; Dr. C. F. Rand, Batavia; Dr. A. D. Smith, East Pembroke;
Dr. E. C. Smith, East Pembroke; Dr. William B. Sprague, Pavilion;
Dr. M. W. Townsend, Bergen; Dr. L. L. Tozier, Batavia; Dr. J. W.
Warner, Elba; Dr. R. Williams, Le Roy; and Dr. A. F. G. Zurhorst, Ala-
bama. The delegate to the State Medical Society was Dr. A. P. Jack-
son, of Oakfield.

The physicians from Genesee County who became prominent members of the New York State Society were, from Alexander: Dr. John R. Smith, elected in 1854. Batavia: Dr. Charles E. Ford, elected in 1852; Dr. John Cotes, elected in 1855; Dr. Levant B. Cotes, elected in 1860; Dr. John Root, elected in 1864; and Dr. J. R. Cotes, elected in 1873. Bergen: Dr. M. W. Townsend, elected in 1869. Pavilion: Dr. Warren Fay, elected in 1858, and Dr. William B. Sprague, elected in 1874. After a feeble existence of two or three years Dr. B. A. Fuller, of Le Roy, then president of the society, called a special meeting July 27, 1887. Dr. E. C. Smith was chosen secretary. A resolution was offered which rescinded so much of the old code of ethics as forbade the members consulting with irregular practitioners. This was voted on and declared lost, and the meeting adjourned. Dr. Sprague then invited the physicians present to meet for the purpose of organizing a new society, as a voluntary association, with no connection with any other society. This was agreed upon, and Drs. Sprague, Tozier, and Townsend were chosen as a committee to prepare a constitution and by-laws. This committee reported at a meeting held at Batavia, August 9, 1887, Dr. Fuller being chairman, and Dr. Wells, secretary. The report was adopted, and the new organization formed with the following officers: President, Dr. W. B. Sprague; vice-president, Dr. L. L. Tozier; secretary, Dr. W. L. Bolton; treasurer, Dr. E. C. Smith. The meetings of the society are held in January and June, and several valuable papers have been read. At this time (1889) the same officers retain their positions.

The following physicians filed their certificates in the county clerk's office at the dates opposite their names, but we can learn nothing more about them; it is possible they may have resided in places not now within the limits of Genesee County: Dr. Jonah Brown, from Columbia County, 1813; Dr. Robert H. Henderson, from Washington, 1813; Dr. Myron Orton, from Vermont, 1814; and Dr. John W. Bronson, from Vermont, 1814.

ALABAMA.

DR. FLINT L. KEYES joined the County Medical Society in 1829, Guy B. Shepard in 1831, and Alexander H. Cox in 1839. Dr. Samuel C. Bateman came to the town in 1846, and joined the society in 1859. He was killed by the cars at Sanborn, June 15, 1887. Dr. Pettibone came a few years after Dr. Bateman, practiced awhile, and left. Dr. Townsend also practiced in Alabama about 1855, and went to Michigan. Another physician was Dr. Emery, who died in Batavia. Drs. Cox and Tyler lived at South Alabama, and a Dr. Nelson Horning was in practice here a short time. Dr. Horning joined the Medical Society in 1866. He died from an overdose of aconite. Dr. William M. Wallis was a resident about 1870, and Dr. C. R. Pearce about 1872.

ALEXANDER.

DR. CHARLES CHAFFEE came to Alexander (then a part of Batavia) in 1810. It is believed that he was the first physician in that town. A Dr. John Hall died there in 1812. We find no record of any other until Dr. Ammi R. R. Butler, who came from Stafford in 1823. He was for a time associated with Dr. Stephen Martin, about whom little is known. Dr. Butler, however, was in active practice nearly to the date of his death, which occurred at the residence of his daughter, in Buffalo, in 1858. He was an excellent physician, and an exemplary man.

In 1835 Dr. Amos Walker, in 1837, Dr. Erasmus D. Baker, and in 1839 Dr. Lemuel McAlpine practiced in Alexander. In 1860 Dr. H. B. Miller became a member of the County Medical Society, and participated actively it its transactions, being its president in 1867. He removed to Johnsonsburg, Wyoming County, about 1868, and soon after died there.

Dr. Isaac V. Mullen, formerly of Stafford, graduated from the Vermont Medical College in 1850. He served for four years in the war of the Rebellion, and in 1866 located in Alexander. Here he practiced 23 years, and removed to West Bethany, where he now resides. His son, Dr. John R. Mullen, is now at Alexander, and another son, Dr. I. T., was graduated in 1884 at Buffalo, went to Stafford soon afterward, where he remained about six years, and removed to Oakfield, where he now practices.

BATAVIA.

OUR record gives the names of 46 physicians who formerly practiced here, but have died, or removed to other places. It is not at all likely we have them all, for some may have staid but a brief time, and left leaving no sign. It is believed, however, that those most conspicuous by reason of their skill and abilities have been remembered.

In 1801, the year previous to the formation of the town of Batavia, Dr. David McCracken came to "The Bend," as the little settlement on the Tonawanda Creek, now the village of Batavia, was then called. We have no account of his antecedents, but he was evidently a man of good standing in his profession. He moved to Rochester in 1818. Dr. Asa McCracken is recorded in 1805. Whether this related to David is not known. Among the slain in the attack on Lewiston was Dr. Joseph Alvord, who was an early physician (about 1802) from Batavia. In 1811 Dr. John Z. Ross was here. He died in 1826. In 1809 Dr. Ephraim Brown came in. He was quite prominent in medical matters, and practiced here until his death in 1826 or 1829. In 1815 Dr. Orris Crosby, who died in 1862, and in 1816 Drs. Charles S. Rumsey and Winter Hewitt, who died in 1824, are registered. Next came Dr. John Cotes, who was born in 1794, in Eastern New York. He studied medicine in Otsego County, and came to Batavia in 1817. He soon formed a partnership with Dr. Ephraim Brown, above mentioned, whose sister he married two years later (1819). After the death of Dr. Brown Dr. Cotes took as a partner Dr. Levant B. Cotes, his brother ; they were together two years, and he then formed a connection with William Seaver in the drug and medicine business. About this time he took Dr. Truman H. Woodruff as a partner in the practice of medicine. In 1830 he visited Europe, and spent more than a year studying in the schools and hospitals of London and Paris. On his return, in 1831, he resumed his practice here in company with Dr. Woodruff, continuing the partnership until the latter's death. Then Dr. Holton Ganson became his partner, remaining with him until 1855, when Albert Cotes, his youngest son, engaged in business with him, for a short time only, and removed to the West. For 42 years he devoted himself ardently to his profession, and died in 1859, at the age of 65 years.

The year following the advent of Dr. Cotes Dr. James Avery Billings made his appearance in Batavia. He was the eldest son of Perez Billings, of Saratoga County, N. Y., was born in 1795, received a good preliminary education, and was graduated from the University of New York in 1818. He came to this county the same year, and purchased the land upon which he resided until his death. This was the first lot deeded by the Holland Land Co. He was a man of sound judgment, and of more than ordinary ability. Coming as he did to a new country, he was well prepared to sympathize with the early settlers in their varied conditions, their trials and privations, and he became their friend and neighbor. He was at one time a partner with Dr. Winter Hewitt, whose coming in 1816 we have mentioned. He was a member of the Episcopal Church, a loyal supporter of the Democratic party, and one of its chosen leaders. He was twice married. His death occurred August 2, 1858, and at the next annual meeting of the Genesee County Medical Society Dr. R. Williams, of Le Roy, then president, delivered an able and well prepared eulogy upon him.

Dr. Gilbert B. Champlin was here in 1821, Drs. Samuel Z. Ross and Amos Towne (died in 1832) in 1823, and in 1826 we are informed that Dr. H. Thomas delivered a Fourth of July oration. We know nothing more than this about him, but have no doubt his speech was a good one. Dr. E. A. Bigelow was here the same year, and it may be heard Dr. Thomas's oration. The year following (1827) Drs. Richard Dibble and C. Bradford were in company. Dr Bradford had been here previously, for in *The People's Press*, of August 20, 1825, we find an account of the operation of bronchotomy performed by him shortly before.

Dr. Charles E. Ford came in 1826 and remained until his death in 1848. He was also postmaster about 1844. In 1827 came Dr. L. B. Cotes. We copy from the *Transactions* of the New York State Medical Society for 1882 the following obituary notice:

" Levant Ballard Cotes was born in the village of Springfield, Otsego County, N. Y., July 15, 1801, of early English ancestry. His early education was under private tutors and at academies, principally Fairchild Academy, N. Y. He entered the College of Physicians and Surgeons, also located at Fairchild, Herkimer County, N. Y., where he graduated January 21, 1826, his diploma bearing the distinguished names of Westel Willoughby, T. Romeyn Beck, and Jamas McNaughton. He settled in Batavia, after graduation, where, for upwards of 50 years he enjoyed a lucrative and successful practice, largely surgical and obstetrical. He was for more than half a century a member of Genesee County Medical Society, during which time he had occupied its several offices ; was a permanent member of the Medical Society of the State of New York, elected in 1860 ; and of the American Medical Association, elected in 1856. He has contributed papers on medical subjects to the local and State societies, and also reports of cases, among the latter being one on Urethrocele, complicated with diseases of the bladder and kidneys. This case was published in the *Transactions* for 1874. . . . He was curator of the medical department of the University of Buffalo for 25 years ; was formerly postmaster of Batavia ; and for the last 10 years of his life was U. S. examining surgeon for pensions. In 1827 he married Miss Eliza A. Ketcham, who died in 1872. Dr. Cotes continued in the active practice of his profession until about four years prior to his death, when failing health warned him to relinquish the most laborious part of his duties ; he however, still gave the benefit of his large experience and wise judgment, in the way of consultations, up to very near his end, which came quietly and peacefully, at his residence in Batavia, N. Y., September 11, 1880, its immediate cause being apoplexy. He leaves two sons, the eldest, Dr. John R. Cotes, a physician of 30 years' experience, still continuing the practice of medicine at the family residence. [Dr. J. R. Cotes has since died.] Dr. Cotes was a man respected by a large circle of acquaintances, and endeared to the community where he lived so long, as only a man can be who has min... istered tenderly and skillfully to the sufferings of his fellow-men for nearly two generations."

In 1828 appeared Drs Jonathan Hurlburt and William H. Webster, G. B. Worthington, Esq., an old resident of Batavia, speaks highly of Dr. Webster. He practiced here 14 years and died in 1841. Dr. T. H.

Woodruff, whom we have previously mentioned as a partner of Dr. John Cotes, came in 1829, as also did Drs. Eleazer Bingham and Elihu Lee, who seem to have been partners at one time. Then in 1830 Drs. J. V. C. Teller and R. Belden; in 1831 Dr. Zebulon Metcalf; in 1833 Dr. E. H. Rokewood; in 1834 Drs. S. P. Choate, C. V. N. Lent, E. Farnham, and A. F. Dodge, of none of whom can we find much information. Thus it is with the human family: they grow up, become active and useful, and pass away, many of them to fill unremembered graves. Many "mute, inglorious Miltons" of the medical profession have existed, and, it may be, will always exist, only to be soon forgotten.

Dr. Holton Ganson came to Batavia in 1835. He was born in Le Roy in 1810, was a member of the Ganson family of pioneers of that town, and received his early education there. We do not know where he obtained his medical education, but he went to Europe after several years of practice to complete it. He was, as we have seen, for some 20 years a partner with Dr. John Cotes; and the medical firm of "Cotes & Ganson" was known and honored throughout Western New York. Dr. Ganson made a specialty of surgery, and performed with much skill many of the most difficult operations of that department of practice. His practice was large and lucrative, but while still in the prime of active life he received an apoplectic stroke, from which he never fully recovered. He is known as having been the first to use chloroform as an anæsthetic in this region. By the terms of his will his whole estate was to be given to charitable objects in Batavia, viz.: $1,000 to each of the Christian churches, and the remainder to a hospital to be afterwards established. Unfortunately the Doctor wrote his own will, and not being accustomed to that kind of business failed to comply with some legal requirements necessary to its validity. The will was set aside, and the property distributed according to law. There was in the will also a provision for the erection of a monument, at a cost of $550, to General Davis, of Le Roy, who was killed in the War of 1812. His death occurred December 1, 1875, from a second apoplectic seizure.

From 1836 to 1854 there were in Batavia the following: in 1836 Dr. Z. S. Jackson; in 1838 Dr. Thomas E. Everett; in 1841 Dr. Caleb H. Austin; in 1842 Dr. W. B. Slosson; in 1847 Dr. L. D. Stone; in 1848 Dr. C. D. Griswold and Drs. Foote and Baker; and in 1854 Dr. Albert L. Cotes, who was in business with his father (Dr. J. Cotes) a short time, and then removed to the West.

Dr. John Richard Cotes was born in Batavia in 1829. He obtained his

early education in the schools of that village, studied medicine with his
father, Dr. Levant B. Cotes, and received his diploma from the Buffalo
Medical College in 1850. He practiced in Batavia a little while, and
went to Michigan, where he remained four years; then returning he continued in practice seven years until the breaking out of the war. He was
surgeon of the 151st Regiment N. Y. Volunteers, served during the war
then came back to Batavia, where he enjoyed a good practice until his
death in 1884. He was for many years secretary of the Genesee County
Medical Society, was a prominent member of the New York State Medical Society, was for four years physician to the Blind Institution, and was
coroner of the county for one term. Dr. Cotes was a man of ripe
scholarship in medicine, and a thorough and safe practitioner. Disdain-
ing the petty artifices by which lesser men gain notoriety, he kept constantly in mind the honor and dignity of his profession, and observed in
all respects its most trivial as well as its weightier obligations. In his intercourse with other physicians he was strictly honorable, and adhered at
all times implicitly to the code of ethics, which should govern all regular
physicians. He held no truce nor made any terms whatever with quack-
ery either in or out of the profession. His death was occasioned by
"Bright's disease" of the kidneys.

Dr. John Root came to Batavia in 1856 or 1857. He was born in
Sweden, Monroe County, in 1824, was educated in the schools of his
native town, and was graduated at Union College in 1844. He studied
medicine with Dr. Van Ingen, of Schenectady, and received his diploma
from the Buffalo Medical College in 1850. He practiced awhile in Lockport before settling in Batavia. He married Miss Margaret C. Billings
daughter of Dr. James A. Billings, and had five children, three of whom
are now living. Dr. Root was for many years an active member of the
Genesee County Medical Society, and contributed several papers at its
meetings. He was scholarly and courteous, and a strict observer of professional etiquette. His death was from consumption, and occurred
November 29, 1876. The committee which was appointed to draft resolutions concerning his death, in their report to the Medical Society, paid
a most flattering though well deserved tribute to his worth as a physician, and as a man.

During the year 1859 Dr. J. Nolton died, aged 61 years. In 186
Dr. B. H. Benham came to Batavia from Honeoye Falls. He remained
a few years, and returned to his former home. He was esteemed by his
medical associates, and by the community.

. Dr. Norris G. Clark came to Batavia in 1859. He was born at West Bloomfield, Ontario County, in March, 1818, was educated there, and received his diploma from the University of Pennsylvania. He practiced awhile at Clarkson, Monroe County, also at Bloomfield, and came to Batavia to assist his brother, Dr. Oliver P. Clark, whose health had failed. The latter dying soon afterward left Dr. Clark deeply engaged in business. He had a large and profitable practice, which steadily increased until his last sickness. His death occurred July 22, 1876, and was suitably noticed at the next annual meeting of the county society, of which Dr. Clark was a member.

Dr. John L. Curtis was born in Genesee County, and graduated at Philadelphia in 1855 or 1856. He practiced for a time at Elba, and then removed to Batavia. He advertised extensively in the newspapers and otherwise, sold proprietary medicines, and did some other things in violation of the code of ethics of the American Medical Association, so that when, in June, 1870, he applied for admission to the county society his application was rejected. He applied to the Supreme Court for relief, and by a writ of *mandamus* issued by the court the society received him under protest in January, 1872. Charges were soon preferred against him, and he was expelled April 9, 1874, for " gross violation of the Code of Medical Ethics." He did a large business both in the sale of his medicines and by his practice, having at one time offices at Rochester and Buffalo, as well as at Batavia. He died June 5, 1880, of hemorrhage of the lungs.

BERGEN.

OUR researches concerning the early medical history of this town have yielded but scanty results. When the town was formed, in 1812, we learn that Dr. Levi Ward was in practice there, and his name appears upon the roll of the Genesee County Medical Society as early as 1805. The *Transactions* of the New York State Medical Society show that he was a delegate in 1810. He was evidently a good deal of a man, and was recognized as an equal by those prominent in the profession all over the State. The Ward family seems to have been quite prominent among the pioneers as people of character and enterprise. Dr. Ward moved to Rochester about 1817, where he died.

Dr. Apollos P. Auger did business in Bergen in 1818, and the records of the county society show no other physician from that town until 1826, when Dr. Eugene O. Donoghue joined that organization. He practiced here until his death in 1868. At the first meeting of the county society

5

after his death was announced a committee consisting of Drs. L. B. Cotes, Townsend, and O. R. Croff reported resolutions concerning him, in which tribute was paid to his faithful membership of the society and of the profession, and " the courtesy, kindness, and affection manifested in all his professional intercourse, as well as in his private, social, and domestic life." These resolutions were unanimously adopted by the society, and published in the local papers.

In 1836 Dr. Thomas M. Hendry appears to have been in Bergen, but how long a time he remained we are not informed.

Dr. Levi Fay is registered in 1840. He was president of the Genesee County Medical Society in 1853, and excepting those physicians now in practice, with whom this chapter has nothing to do, no other name appears until 1868, when Dr. M. J. Munger joined the society. He atteneded the meetings for a few years, and then appeared no more. His residence was at North Bergen.

In 1868 there were in Bergen Drs. R. Andrews, M. B. Gage, and R. Gay, none of whom joined the county society, and we do not know their present whereabouts. Dr. Andrews advertised as a cancer doctor. Drs. Gilbert Churchill, R. Gay, and Orrin Lee are also mentioned as having practiced at some time.

BETHANY.

IN 1813 Dr. Benjamin Packard, of Bethany, was elected a member of the Genesee County Medical Society. As the town was organized the previous year he may justly be called the pioneer physician. In 1816 Dr. Daniel Spalding and in 1817 Dr. Daniel Rumsey appeared, and in 1818 Dr. Jonathan K. Barlow's name is recorded. It is a somewhat singular circumstance that in the reports of the Genesee County Medical Society to the New York State Medical Society from 1825 to 1841, in each of which the names of the officers are given, Dr. Barlow's name is not given twice alike. It is always Dr. Barlow of Bethany; but it is sometimes James Barlow; next Jotham K. Barlow, again Jonathan A. Barlow, etc., etc. It seems that the secretary either of the county society, or that of the State, thought with the late Josh Billings, " that it was n't much of a man who could n't spell a word but one way." Dr. Barlow stood well in the profession, was a man of scientific attainments, and somewhere in " the forties " procured the necessary apparatus and went about lecturing upon electricity. He explained the magnetic telegraph thunder storms, etc., and gave his audiences an opportunity to be shocked We have no record of him later than 1850 or 1851. It is believed tha he resided and practiced in Bethany more than 30 years. In 1819 Dr. Beriah Douglas was in Bethany. We suppose him to have been the same Dr. Douglas who practiced in Le Roy for a time. Dr. William W. Markham came in 1829, Dr. Theodore C. Hurd in 1835, and another Dr. Hurd (William P.) in 1837. At East Bethany there was for a time Dr. Loomis, and at Linden Dr. John G. Meachern, who afterwards removed to Warsaw, and Dr. John Howard. Old residents speak also of a Dr. Alden, at one time partner of Dr. J. K. Barlow, at Bethany Center.

BYRON.

PRIOR to the formation, in 1820, of this town there were residing within its present limits in 1812 Dr. Silas Taylor, and in 1813 Dr. Samuel Taggart. Of them we know nothing but their names. In 1821 Dr. Oliver Hulett is recorded, and in 1828 Dr. Landon D. Woodruff.

The town of Byron must have been a very healthy place of residence, for no other physician is mentioned as having come there until 1840, when Dr. Emery made his appearance. Sanford Emery, M. D., was born in Vermont, was graduated from the Burlington Medical College in 1838, removed to Byron in 1840, and practiced there about 30 years. He then went to Alabama, doing business there a short time, thence to the northern part of Batavia, where he remained until his death in 1880. He married, first, Elizabeth Warner; his second wife was Chloe Beebee, of Byron. He had four children by his first marriage, and three by the second.

Dr. J. D. Fowler was a son of Deacon David J. Fowler, one of the pioneer settlers of Covington, Wyoming County. He studied medicine with his brother-in-law, Dr. Eben Warner, was graduated, and began the practice of his profession in Byron. He became a member of the Genesee County Medical Society in 1841, and died two years later from the poison received in a *post mortem* examination. He was a young man of great promise, and his early death was much regretted by all who knew him.

Dr. Appleton W. Billings was born in Barre, N. Y., in 1821. When 24 years of age he commenced to study medicine with Dr. Willard Eaton, of Orleans County, and was with him six years. In 1851 he settled to practice his profession at South Byron, and located where he now resides. Until 1888 he faithfully and successfully administered to the sick and afflicted, and is now on the retired list as much as his old patrons will permit him. He married, in 1851, Miss Lavina T. Thatcher, of Orleans County, and they have had seven children. Their son Charles and daughter Hattie reside near their parents.

In 1846 Homer P. Smith, M. D., resided in Byron, and in 1852 Dr. C. C. F. Gay recorded his name on the secretary's book of the Genesee County Medical Society. Dr. Gay was born at Pittsfield, Berkshire County, Mass., January 7, 1821. While a mere lad his parents removed to Lebanon Springs, Columbia County, N. Y. His early education was received at the schools of that vicinity, and at the Collegiate Institute at Brockport, N. Y. In 1844 he began the study of medicine under the preceptorship of Dr. Joseph Bates, of Lebanon Springs. He attended lectures at Woodstock, Vt., and also at the Berkshire Medical College, Massachusetts, from which he was graduated in 1846. He took a course of lectures at the Jefferson Medical College, Philadelphia, after his graduation. He began practice at Bennington, Vt., and afterward removed to Byron, this county. His success here was good, but he desired enlarged opportunities, and in 1853 removed to Buffalo, where he remained until his death. Here he advanced rapidly in professional esteem, and soon took a leading position. He was for many years surgeon to the Buffalo General Hospital, was a prominent member of the Erie County Medical Society, and of the Buffalo Medical and Surgical Association. He was also a permanent member of the New York State Medical Society, and of the American Medical Association. During the last war he was surgeon in charge of Fort Porter. In 1883 he was appointed professor of operative and clinical surgery at Niagara University, Buffalo. Aside from his knowledge of medicine Dr. Gay was an ardent student of the natural sciences, botany being his favorite branch. He died at Buffalo, March 27, 1887.

About 1864 Dr. Earl B. Lounsbury came from East Pembroke to Byron. He was here more than 10 years, when he removed to the West, where, after a further service of 11 years, he died. During Dr. Lounsbury's membership of the county society he was one of its most faithful members. He made several reports of cases, participated actively in its discussions, and was loyal to its requirements. His wife was Miss F. M. Rumsey, of Bethany.

Dr. A. C. Hall, of South Byron, and Dr. Lafayette Carpenter, of Byron Center, are mentioned, but we have no knowledge of the time of their residence here.

In 1873 Dr. B. A. Fuller located at Byron Center, and at about the same time Dr. George U. Gleason was at South Byron. Dr. Fuller removed to Le Roy shortly after the death of his father (Dr. A. W. Fuller) in 1877, where he now resides.

In the year 1868 there were also in Byron (so it is said) Drs. Joseph C. Walker and A. W. Billings.

DARIEN.

THE physicians of this town have been James E. Seaver, 1817; William P. Harris, 1829; Erastus Cross, 1830; John M. Harrington, 1832; Isaiah Rano, 1836; and E. W. Marsh, 1870. Other information concerning a few early physicians may be obtained by referring to the history of the town.

ELBA.

IN the year 1823 Dr. Amasa Briggs had "a local habitation and a name" in the then new town of Elba. He is supposed to have been the first physician in the place, although some claim priority for a Dr. Woodward, of whom we can learn nothing. In 1829 Dr. Benedict practiced there, and in 1830 Dr. J. A. Campbell. Soon after this time Dr. Jonas S. Billings came to Elba. He joined the County Medical Society in 1833, usually attended its meetings, and participated in its discussions. The last meeting he attended was in June, 1869; and we believe his death occurred soon after. Dr. Francis Smiley died at Elba in 1843, aged 86 years. We have no details of his residence there. In 1831 Dr. James H. Smith is registered, and in 1841 Dr. E. B. Benedict. We do not know whether this is the same Dr. Benedict previously mentioned or not; if so, he was somewhat dilatory in joining the county society.

We do not know of any other physicians of Elba excepting those now there.

LE ROY.

THE first physician inhabiting the present town of Le Roy (then Caledonia) was Dr. William Coe, who came in the year 1803. In 1814 he lived on the farm now owned by Mr. Osborn, west of the village. He had the reputation of being an honest, worthy man, and a good physician.

Dr. Ella G. Smith was here in 1805, and Dr. Fred Fitch moved in in 1808. He stood well in the profession, and was very stirring and enterprising. He raised a company of artillery, of which he became captain. While attending with his company a "training" at Stafford he was wounded accidentally in the leg, and suffered amputation in consequence. He built the house where Rev. Samuel Bowden now lives, and also one formerly occupied by R. L. Lawson. We cannot ascertain the date of his death.

Dr. William Sheldon rode into Le Roy on horseback one evening in 1810, and stopped at the famous "Ganson tavern," where is now the residence of H. H. Olmsted. He was looking for a place to practice, and had with him all his earthly possessions, consisting of his horse, saddle and bridle, a pair of saddle-bags, containing a small stock of medicines, with a lancet, and turnkey for extracting teeth. He had ridden from Bennington, Vt., and was wearied with his long journey, and nearly penniless. He, however, turned his horse out to grass, made a supper of bread and milk, and went to bed hoping something might turn up to enable him to pay his bill in the morning. Fortunately for him Mrs. Ganson was taken quite ill during the night, and the young M. D. was called up to prescribe. His efforts were quite successful, and as there was a good deal of sickness in the settlement, and no physician, he was urged by the neighbors to remain there. This he did, and for many years enjoyed an active and lucrative practice. During the War of 1812 he was for a time captain of a militia company, but afterwards became surgeon and *aid-de-camp* upon the staff of General Davis, and was near him when he was killed. He participated in seven battles; was taken prisoner at Black Rock, and carried to Montreal, where he remained for about six months, being discharged in May, 1814. He filled, with much credit, several positions of responsibility, serving as county sheriff two terms.

In June, 1871, Dr. Sheldon, by invitation of the writer, attended the annual meeting of the Genesee County Medical Society. We quote from the secretary's report the following:

"Dr. Sheldon, from Le Roy, one of the pioneers of the society, now old and feeble, whose membership dates back to 1810, by invitation proceeded to make a few remarks concerning the early days of the society. He spoke of the progress made in medicine and surgery since he had ceased to be an active practitioner, and of many other things relating to medicine, which were very interesting, and were listened to with great pleasure.'

Dr. Sheldon died in January, 1874.

Dr. Chauncey P. Smith came in in 1814. He lived for a time on the Woodward farm north of the village, and afterwards built the stone house on Lake street, now occupied by S. Loucks. A popular and hard working man, he saved a large property during the quarter century he practiced here, but investing it in the drug business in company with a dishonest partner, he lost nearly all. His friends made him comfortable in his old age, until his mental powers gave way from brain disease, and h died in the alms house.

Dr. Elizur Butler, of Le Roy, joined the Genesee County Medical Society in 1816, but we can find nothing more about him.

Dr. Ezekiel Kelsey, born in Greenfield, Saratoga County, N. Y., in 1801, came to the Genesee country with his father about 1817, settling one mile south of Le Roy. He taught school a number of years, then studied for a physician, and opened up an office about 1830, and continued a very successful practice till his death in 1840. He was buried in what is known as the Van Allen Cemetery

In 1818 Dr. Lakey moved to Le Roy. He is described as being an active and intelligent practitioner, and with a remarkable memory for incidents. He staid a few years, and went to Palmyra, N. Y.

Dr. Edmund Barnes resided here at about the same time. He married a sister of Henry Olmsted. He built the house just east of Mrs. Bissell's, on West Main street, and died there a few years later. His widow afterwards married Dr. Chauncey Smith, before mentioned.

In March, 1819, Dr. Stephen O. Almy received a license to practice from the board of censors of Genesee County, and began business with Dr. Fitch, his preceptor. Dr. Almy was born in Sterling, Conn., June 18, 1798. His parents soon afterward removed to Vermont, then to Saratoga County, N. Y., and finally to the present town of Pavilion. While still a lad he spent his summers in clearing off timber, and his winters in teaching school. During the summer of 1815 he cleared off 10 acres of land where Roanoke village now stands. After one year's partnership with Dr. Fitch he bought out his little drug store, and went twice on foot to Albany to purchase drugs. In 1821 he attended medical lectures at Yale College, and received a diploma from that institution. In 1823 he married Maria B. Brown, and built a cottage where Ingham University now stands. After about 15 years of active practice he engaged in the lumber business at Olean, in company with Herman Le Roy, sons, and grandsons. He remained at Olean until 1841, when he removed to Cincinnati and engaged still more extensively in the lumber trade. This lasted but a short time, for his many friends, knowing his professional skill, urged him so strongly to resume practice that he finally consented to do so. He practiced about eight years, when his health failed, and forming a partnership with Dr. Alfred Wilcox, a former medical associate in Le Roy, engaged in a private banking business. The financial crash of 1854 nearly ruined them, and Dr. Almy returned to medicine again. He was in Buffalo during 1855 and 1856, and the writer, then a student, remembers well his cheerful face and pleasant smile. He soon returned to Cincinnati, and practiced there until 1866, when the death of his wife, followed soon after by that of his daughter, broke up his household, and as soon as he could settle up matters he returned to Le Roy with the intention of spending the remnant of his days there. In September, 1869, he was attacked with apoplexy, resulting in *hemiplegia*, or paralysis of one side. He lived after this a little more than seven years, in an entirely helpless condition, being an inmate of the home of the late S. C. Kelsey. His death occurred January 2, 1877. We quote the following from a notice of his death which appeared in one of the Le Roy newspapers:

"No man ever enjoyed a fuller measure of popular esteem and affection than did Dr. Almy. He was every man's friend, every man's helper. He had a word of good counsel and cheer for all, and smiles of approval for all who needed them."

Dr. Benjamin Hill, a native of Guilford, Conn., was born April 15, 1765. In 1788 he studied medicine with Dr. Cone, of Pittsfield, Mass. He practiced in Killingworth, Conn., about 40 years. In 1808 he came to Le Roy on horseback, and bought 448 acres of land. In 1819 his son Albert came out and began clearing the land. In 1826 Dr. Hill came again, and in 1828 he brought his family, locating on 160 acres of an additional purchase, residing there until his death in April, 1849, at Pavilion. His practice in Connecticut was very extensive, but limited in this county. Being contemporary with Dr. Sheldon and others he was often called as counsel. He was a self-made man, and respected by all his friends and neighbors.

Of Drs. B. Douglas, who was in Le Roy in 1819 or 1820; Warren A. Cowdery, 1820; Daniel Woodward, 1823; and Nicholas D. Gardner, 1828, we can find nothing more than the record of their names. Dr. Douglas, it is believed, went to Bethany.

In 1830 Dr. Alfred Wilcox, after two years' practice in Pennsylvania, took up his abode here. He was a partner with Dr. Almy, Dr. Pratt, and others during the 20 years he resided here. He resumed partnership with Dr. Almy in Cincinnati, as before mentioned. His health failing he went to California and died there.

Dr. John Codman came to Le Roy when quite young, followed teaching awhile, and studied medicine with Dr. Almy. He practiced here from 1836 to 1840, then removed to Adrian, Mich., and after 10 years to Kalamazoo, where he died in 1870, aged 73. He was an excellent physician, a consistent Christian, and a pronounced temperance man.

In 1830 appears the name of Dr. Prescott Lawrence. He had the faculty of winning the confidence of his patrons in a very marked degree. He lived but a few years and died here. Of Drs. Graham Fitch and

William A. Amy, who resided here in 1830–31, no record except their names is found.

The year 1834 brought to Le Roy Dr. Charles Smith, younger brother of Chauncey Smith, and Dr. Ezekiel Kelsey. The latter died after a few years. Like many others he taught school to enable him to pursue his medical studies.

Dr. Caleb H. Austin was here from 1836 to 1840. Dr. Benjamin Bliss also commenced business here in 1836. He built a house on the present site of Mrs. Barrett's, and followed his calling acceptably to the people until near his death, which took place in 1843.

Dr. Almond Pratt came in 1837. He staid about 15 years, when he removed to Palmyra, and thence to Rochester, where he died.

In 1840 Dr. Joseph Tozier came to Le Roy. He had practiced previously in York, Livingston County. He removed in 1845 to Clarkson, Monroe County, where he died, after many years of successful practice, respected by all who knew him. His son, Dr. L. L. Tozier, has been for many years the leading physician of Batavia.

In 1841 Dr. D. C. Chamberlain made his appearance in Le Roy, where he remained 37 years. We cannot do better than copy a letter written to the present writer by Dr. Chamberlain, in response to some inquiries addressed him concerning his life, etc., omitting some paragraphs of a purely personal character:

"*Dear Sir:* I am in receipt of yours of the 30th ult., and in answer thereto would say: I was born of American parents (emigrants from Vermont), in the parish of Mascouche, in the then province of Lower Canada, now called 'Quebec,' and first saw the light of day January 8, 1815, the day 'Old Hickory' fought the battle of New Orleans, and at the age of eight was sent from the paternal roof to be brought up under the care of a maternal aunt residing in Hubbardton, Rutland County, Vt. Here I passed through boyhood into early manhood, acquiring as good a preparatory education as straitened circumstances and opportunities would allow. In 1833 commenced the study of medicine under the instruction, and with the aid, of Dr. Charles W. Horton, in Sudbury, Vt., and after three courses of lectures in the Vermont Academy of Medicine was graduated in November, 1837.

"I commenced practice in Cuttingsville, Rutland County, Vt., in July, 1838, and remained there until January, 1840; then 'struck tent,' and took a private course of lectures on anatomy and surgery at Castleton under instruction of the late Prof. Robert Nelson, the Canadian patriot and refugee. Soon after, the health of my old preceptor failing, I became associated with him in practice at Sudbury, Vt., and there remained until 1841, when I again packed up for a move, having in mind this time the 'Genesee country,' which was then regarded as quite away West. After debating the pros and cons between Le Roy and Warsaw—the latter place having just been designated by the commissioner appointed as the site of the county buildings of the newly-organized county of Wyoming—I made a choice of Le Roy as my future field of labor, and in

July, 1841, hung out a doctor's 'shingle' and inserted a card in the Le Roy *Gazette.* I was received as a member of the Genesee County Medical Society at its annual meeting in January, 1842.

"For further details of my career in Le Roy I would respectfully refer you to the old inhabitants of that town, adding only that I left Le Roy in September, 1878, since which time I have enjoyed all the blessings and comforts that human life can expect; —more perhaps than I deserve,—but I enjoy them all the same.

"As to the practice of our noble profession, I have been egotistical enough to regard whatever I have done or may do in that line as more of a favor to others than to myself.

"The old partaker of my joys and soother of my sorrows has gone down the hill of life, and sleeps at the foot in Machpelah Cemetery, and I am now also moving down, and by and by we both shall 'sleep thegither at the foot,' like good, old 'John Anderson, my Jo.'

"As regards my military service, I was engaged and interested in 1861, during the fall, in enlisting and recruiting men for the suppression of the Rebellion; was examining surgeon of the recruits that were brought to Le Roy to form the regiment that was finally organized and mustered into the United States service as the 105th Regiment, N. Y. Inf. Vols., and was commissioned as its surgeon. I went with it to the field, and to the front. We were always in the 'Army of the Potomac.' I continued my connection with it until the expiration of my commission, March 26, 1865, and not relishing a falling from a senior to a junior rank, which would occur in case of new commissions, remained an independent volunteer until Lee's surrender at Appomattox."

This concludes what we wish to publish of Dr. Chamberlain's letter, and in addition we can most heartily say that no physician of our acquaintance ever was so universally respected and esteemed as was he. During his 37 years of practice in Le Roy he devoted himself entirely to his patients, and in attending so carefully to their interests greatly neglected his own, so that, although doing a large business, he never accumulated much property. He is now in receipt of a pension, which is sufficient for his needs, and a seat of honor and a warm welcome always await his acceptance in the homes of all his old friends. When, in the years 1852 and 1853, typhoid fever prevailed so extensively in and about Le Roy, Dr. Chamberlain was one of the first physicians to substitute the supporting treatment for the bleeding and purging plan previously in use. He gained a well deserved reputation in the treatment of this disease, and was called often in consultation to neighboring towns.

The Doctor says in his letter that he left Le Roy in September, 1878, but he says nothing of the farewell banquet given in his honor by his fellow physicians of Genesee County at the residence of Dr. Cleveland, in Le Roy, and the presentation to him of a silver tea set. On this occasion Dr. S. Barrett, a neighbor and professional friend of many years standing, made the presentation speech, in the course of which he referred to a time when Dr. Moses Barrett and Dr. Chamberlain occupied adjoining houses, and they were wont to sit with their families of a summer evening upon the back piazzas. Dr. Barrett played the violin, and Dr. Chamberlain was somewhat terpsichorally inclined, which gave rise to a couplet well known in those days:

"Moses and David were neighbors by chance;
Moses did fiddle for David to dance."

In 1842 Dr. Moses Barrett (mentioned above) settled in Le Roy. He was a man of superior scholaiship in his profession and out of it; fond of the study of the sciences, and deeply interested in matters relating to the education of the young. He remained here eight years, then went to Wisconsin, and was appointed superintendent of the State Reform School. He was afterward elected to the chair of chemistry and natural science in the college at Ripon. He died there soon after, aged 58.

In 1849 came Dr. G. Taber, and in 1850 Dr. Solomon Barrett. Dr. Barrett was born at Rowe, Mass., February 23, 1810, received his medical education at Berkshire (Mass.) Medical College, and was graduated from that institution in 1833. He practiced in Buffalo for some time before removing to Le Roy. His specialty was surgery, and he made most of the operations known to that science. The Taliacotian operation for making a new nose was performed by him; also nearly all those pertaining to the eye. He had at one time an eye infirmary at Le Roy. He became nearly blind in his latter years, and died at Le Roy, February 3, 1884. Dr. Barrett was an industrious student, and a very skillful operator. He was also a sincere Christian.

In 1856 Dr. Chauncey M. Smith began medical practice. He was a student of Dr. S. Barrett, and was for a time partner with Dr. Chamberlain. He was, in his younger days, a school teacher, and became town superintendent of schools under the old law. He was possessed of a good medical education, and being personally quite popular soon acquired a large practice. He died of typhoid fever in 1864.

.. In 1864 Dr. Asa W. Fuller made his appearance among Le Roy physicians. Mature in years, with long experience in practice, he at once gained a large clientage. He was born in the town of Lisbon, Conn., in July, 1817, and after having obtained a thorough preliminary education commenced the study of medicine. This he continued until he was graduated from the medical department of Yale College, New Haven, Conn. He was married in 1839, and soon after removed to the State of Rhode Island, where he practiced his profession for nine years, thence removing to the town of Middlebury, Wyoming County, N. Y., where he had a successful practice of 14 years, until 1864, when, against the wishes of the whole community, he removed with his family to Le Roy, and entered at once upon an extensive practice, to which he devoted his whole time and talent, with a determination to overcome all obstacles, and giving excellent satisfaction to his patrons. For the last 13 years of his life, and up to the day of his death, he well sustained in Le Roy the reputation of a faithful, honest, and skillful physician, a genial companion, and a true and tried friend. His death occurred on January 29, 1877.

Dr. O. P. Barber became a member of the Genesee County Medical Society in 1870. He studied medicine with Dr. S. Barrett (whose daughter he afterward married), practiced a short time in Le Roy, and removed to Michigan.

Dr. George Emerson was a student, and afterwards a partner, of Dr. Chamberlain, remained in Le Roy a few years, and went West—we think to Nebraska—in the year 1878. Dr. Emerson made many friends in Le Roy, and did a good business while there.

Dr. George McNaughton came to Le Roy in 1880, but remained a short time, and removed to Brooklyn, where, we believe, he still remains. He was a student of Dr. Menzie, of Caledonia, and was a very promising young man.

There have been several homeopaths and eclectics in Le Roy at different times, but we can find out but little concerning them. Dr. Gage, one of the former class, was there for some time between 1860 and 1870, then removed to the South, and, we believe, died there. It is possible that the names of some early practitioners have been omitted, but any one will recognize the difficulty of finding out about people who died 60 or 70 years ago.

OAKFIELD.

Dr. ANDREW THOMPSON was in Oakfield as early as 1830, at which date he became a member of the County Medical Society. No other physician's name appears upon the roll, from this town, until 1841, when Dr. Horace Clark is recorded. He removed to Bergen in 1876, and died at that place. It is said that as early as 1814 Dr. A. Thompson was living within the present limits of the town, and a Dr. Garret Davis is also mentioned, but no definite accounts of either have been obtained. Dr. William Pardee was in Oakfield in 1868, and for a few years afterward until his death, in 1884, by consumption. He was for a time partner with Dr. A. P. Jackson. He graduated from the Buffalo Medical College.

PAVILION.

WHEN, in the year 1841, the town of Pavilion was formed there were within its present limits in practice Dr. Warren Fay and Dr. Abel Ten. nant. Dr. Fay was at the village of Pavilion, where he had resided for many years, and Dr. Tennant was at South Le Roy, which became, by the organization of the new town, Pavilion Center.

Dr. Fay was born at Walpole, N. H., in 1797. He received a good common school education, was for some time a school teacher, and fi. nally studied medicine under the tutelage of Dr. Daniel White, who seems to have been a prominent practitioner in those early days. He attended lectures at the Castleton (Vt.) Medical Academy, received a diploma from the Livingston County (N. Y.) Medical Society, June 24, 1823, signed by Caleb Chapin, president, and coming to Pavilion soon after began an active practice, which continued for a full half century. He was what is now called a " heroic practitioner," using the lancet very freely, and giving large doses of colomel and jalap. He achieved both fame and fortune, and died February 18, 1875.

" A. Tennant, Botanist," as the sign upon his office read, was a native of Connecticut, but where he received his education we have been un. able to ascertain. He believed that in the plants which nature provides there are all the remedies needful for the cure of disease. He began practice about 1812, and continued it until blindness and rheumatism compelled him to abandon it, some 40 years afterward. He published a work called *Tennant's Botany*, in 1837. This was printed at Batavia by D. D. Waite, for many years editor of the *Republican Advocate*. Dr. Tennant, while in his prime, had a large practice, and an excellent repu- tation for skill and success. He removed to Pennsylvania in 1856, and died soon after.

In 1842 Dr. S. C. Upson came to Pavilion. He was born in Bristol, Conn., March 29, 1792. He received his diploma at Hartford, Conn, in 1816, commenced practice at Fabius, N. Y., and remained there until his removal to Pavilion. He lived here about four years and removed to Nunda, Livingston County, where he died April 20, 1889. Dr. Upson was emphatically a gentleman of the old school, extremely affable, polite, and kind hearted. He is remembered with affection by many of our old res- idents. At one time he made and sold a preparation known as Upson's dandelion syrup, which had a great deal of popularity.

Somewhere about these times Dr. Ira Webb, a root doctor from Ver-

mont, came to Pavilion.   He remained a year or two and went to Le
Roy.   We have not been able to learn much about him, although his
syrups were considered very useful by many people.

In 1849 Dr. William M. Sprague resumed the practice which he had
previously given up to engage in other business.   He was born in New
Marlborough, Mass., in 1803, and came to Covington with his father in
1812.   He attended school at Middlebury Academy, then a noted institution of learning, studied medicine with Drs. Daniel White and Warren
Fay, attended medical lectures at Pittsfield, Mass., and received his
diploma from the Genesee County Medical Society, John Cotes, president, March 9, 1829.   He practiced about three years, and then formed
a partnership with his three brothers in the mercantile, milling, and farming business, which was dissolved in the year above mentioned.   During
his absence from practice he was postmaster, justice of the peace, and
Sessions justice, and was regarded as one of the best informed politicians
of the vicinity as well as an excellent general scholar.   He died August
28, 1868, and it is probable no man's death was more generally mourned
by all his acquaintances than was his.   His professional services, as well
as his friendly counsel, were highly valued by all who knew him.

Some time during the year 1867 Dr. Charles Morgan, a young physician, came to Pavilion.   He remained but a short time, and removed to
Mount Morris, Livingston County.   He is spoken of as a promising
young man.

It is supposed that about the usual number of traveling quacks have
visited Pavilion, and made money out of the credulous and weak-minded
people who believe in such things, but none of them are worthy of record, and we have given all we could ascertain concerning the respectable medical men who lived and practiced here.

PEMBROKE.

DR. ABIJAH W. STODDARD was the pioneer medical man of Pembroke.   He studied medicine with Dr. Sill, of Hartford, Washington
County, N. Y., and soon after receiving his diploma came to Pembroke
(then Batavia).   This was in 1810 or 1811.   He located where the village of Corfu has since been built, and commenced practice among the
first settlers of the surrounding country.   He continued in business here
until about 1854 or 1855, when he removed to Milwaukee, Wis., where
he died at the home of a friend, in 1860.   In the course of his long prac
tice in Pembroke and surrounding towns he accumulated a fair fortune
which was absorbed by his son's business in Rochester.

In 1820 Dr. Elihu Lee was practicing in Pembroke; in 1830 Dr. Aaron Long was registered as residing in Corfu; but previous to this Dr. David Long, with his brother John, had come in as early as 1808, and gave the name Long's Corners to the settlement now called Corfu. Dr. Long resided for many years in a house occupying the site of Dr. Crane's present residence, just north of the principal four corners of the village. He is spoken of as a man of energy and enterprise.

In 1831 Dr. Alanson Owen was in business at Richville, and during the same year somewhere in the town were. Drs. J. S. Dodge, James S. Grout, and Barton Streeter.

In 1833 William E. Brown practiced at East Pembroke; in 1840 Dr. Samuel S. Knight, of Pembroke, joined the County Medical Society; and we find no further mention of physicians coming into the town until 1864, when Dr. Isaiah Rano came from Darien, and remained until his death, in May, 1880.

Sometime in the year 1864 Dr. John Durboraw came in, and lived here two or three years.

Dr. Earl B. Lounsbury was born in the town of Alexander in 1838, was graduated from the Buffalo Medical College, and began practice at East Pembroke in 1864. He remained about one and one-half years, and then removed to Byron Center.

In 1867 Dr. L. B. Parmelee was practicing at East Pembroke. He remained a few years, went to Rochester for a short time, and thence to Batavia, where he still resides.

It is believed that Dr. A. G. Ellinwood, now of Attica, was located for a short time at East Pembroke,—probably about 1860,—but this is uncertain.

In 1868 Dr. Joshua W. Read came to Corfu. He was born in Batavia in 1837. He was a graduate of the State Normal School at Albany, and taught school at Peekskill four years. He studied medicine at that place with Dr. Knight, graduated in 1866, practiced at Bloomington, Ill., two years, and then removed to Corfu. After remaining two years he went to Newark, N. J., where he still remains.

In 1868 Dr. H. W. Cobb was at Indian Falls, but soon removed to the West. Dr. George H. Norton practiced at East Pembroke from 1868 until his death, in 1874 or 1875. A Dr. Lund, now of Medina, N. Y., was at one time in Pembroke.

There have been at different times in Pembroke homeopathic physicians, but none of them seem to have remained long, and we hear only of Drs. Scott and MacPherson.

In 1869 Dr. Absalom Billington was in Corfu. He remained but a short time, and we cannot ascertain where he went.

Dr. Albert Crawford moved to Corfu in 1871. He was born in Darien in 1841, studied medicine with Dr. Milton E. Potter, and received his diploma from the Buffalo Medical College in 1862. He commenced practice at Cairo, Ill., and remained there until his removal to Corfu. He was here 10 years, and then sold out to Dr. William Parker and went to Buffalo, where he still resides.

Dr Parker was born at Clarence, Erie County. He was graduated at Buffalo in 1880, came to Corfu soon after, remained but a short time, then spent one year in Clarence, and finally removed to Buffalo. He is at present attending physician to the Erie County alms house.

The above mentioned are all the physicians we can learn of as formerly practicing in the town of Pembroke. It is quite possible some names may have been omitted, but we have striven industriously to obtain them all. The failure of some to join the County Medical Society has prevented a permanent record of their names, and we have been obliged to rely upon the recollections of old inhabitants for many things.

STAFFORD.

IN 1821 Benjamin Davis hailed from the then yearling town of Stafford as its first *Medicinæ Doctor*. Dr. Ammi R. R. Butler, however, removed to Alexander from Stafford some time prior to 1823, and it may be that he was in the latter place as early as was Dr. Davis. In 1829 Drs. Jonathan G. Abbott and Thomas Blanchard are recorded as residents of Stafford, and about the same time Dr. Elizur Butler and his brother Samuel practiced there.

In 1831 Dr. W. B. Slawson was in business at Morganville. How long he remained we are not informed, but he was a member of the County Medical Society in 1837. Dr. Thomas D. Morrison is registered in 1839 and in 1840 Dr. Lucius M. Haynes. Dr. Haynes married a sister of Stephen Crocker, Esq, who, after the death of Dr. Haynes, married Rev. Richard Radley. He practiced in Stafford until his death, May 19, 1854. In 1851 Dr. Mark W. Tomlinson came to Stafford, and in 1852 Dr. Theophilus S. Loomis. Dr. Loomis removed to East Bethany soon after, and died there.

In 1855 Dr. Henry Pamphilon opened an office in Stafford. He was born in Hackney, near London, Eng., January 14, 1828. He was educated in London, and came to America in 1851, locating in Lancaster,

Erie County. In 1855 he removed to Stafford, remaining there until his death, which occurred March 13, 1884. Dr. Pamphilon was an excellent physician and a most agreeable companion. His knowledge was not confined to medicine, but was extensive on many subjects. He was quite an elocutionist, and read extracts from Dickens remarkably well. He could also dance a hornpipe in good style. He was highly respected by his brother physicians, and by the community at large.

Somewhere about the year 1855 Dr. T. S. King located at Stafford. He was born and educated at Plainfield, N. J., and received his diploma from the University of New York. He remained in Stafford until his death, which took place December 24, 1867, at the age of 42 years.

Dr. Ayer practiced a few years in Stafford. He is highly spoken of as a practitioner, and is also remembered as a man of decided opinions and strong convictions. During his residence at Stafford, in the year 1863, when people were greatly excited over war matters, Dr. Ayer was arrested and taken to the jail at Batavia for the expression of somewhat decided democratic opinions. His imprisonment was, however, of brief duration, but the Doctor never recovered from the sense of oppression and humiliation which that event occasioned. He soon after went to Buffalo, and enjoyed an active and profitable practice there for several years, and until his death. His widow resides in Buffalo, as does also a daughter, the wife of Dr. Rollin L. Banta, one of the most prominent of the younger physicians of that city.

Dr. F. L. Stone was born at Marcy, Oneida County, in 1834. He received an academic education at Whitestown Seminary, studied medicine with Dr. Babcock, of Oriskany, and was graduated at Bellevue College, New York city, in 1865. He remained for a time with Dr. Babcock, and in 1868 came to Stafford. He remained seven years, and removed to Caledonia, Livingston County, where he practiced five years, going thence to Le Roy, where he now resides. Dr. Stone was successful in his practice at Stafford, and made many friends there.

WILLIAM MORGAN.

EXCEPTING, perhaps, the events of the War of 1812 no occurrence in the history of Western New York ever so generally attracted the attention of the country as the disappearance of the Free Mason, Morgan, in the autumn of 1826, with the uprising against the Masonic fraternity which his mysterious fate produced. No other event,

6

therefore, more fairly demands a chapter in the history of the county where the circumstances connected with the affair occurred.

William Morgan was born in Virginia, and was by trade a stone mason. He opened a store in Richmond, in 1819, but in 1821 removed to Canada and went into the brewing business. His brewery having been burnt he moved to Rochester and resumed his trade of mason. While here (living next door to a Dr. Dyer, and also near Thurlow Weed) it is supposed he wrote out his exposure of Masonry. He had a wife and two children. Leaving them he went to Batavia in order to get his book printed. Pretending to be an architect he assisted Thomas McCully in building the Eagle Hotel, and lived for a time in McCully's house (to the east of Eagar's brewery), and also lived where Hewitt's store now is. He also worked on the old stone building back of the postoffice. As near as can be ascertained Morgan was made a Royal Arch Mason at Le Roy. He was represented as being a poor man of indifferent character (which latter fact is suggested as the chief consideration which led him to publish the secrets of the fraternity of which he was a member); was also intemperate and neglected his family; and because of his habits he was expelled from the chapter. Soon after this (presumably in June or July) he began (with the assistance of David C. Miller, editor of the *Republican Advocate*) to publish a book on "Jachin and Boaz," with alterations. The work of publishing was secretly done, Miller at the time occupying the upper part of two buildings on Main street, Batavia.

On July 25th Morgan was taken into custody by the sheriff, for debt, but was soon released. The *Ontario Messenger*, published at Canandaigua, of August 9, 1826, contained the following notice and caution :.

"If a man calling himself Captain William Morgan should intrude himself upon the community, they should be on their guard, particularly the Masonic fraternity. Morgan was in the village in May last, and his conduct here and elsewhere calls forth this notice. . . . Morgan is considered a swindler and a dangerous man."

This notice was also copied in the Batavia papers. September 10th Ebenezer C. Kingsley obtained from Justice Chipman, of Canandaigua, a warrant for the arrest of Morgan on a charge of having stolen a shirt and cravat, which Kingsley had in fact lent him the preceding May. On this warrant Hayward, a constable, proceeded to Le Roy (where he got it endorsed by a justice there), thence to Batavia, where he called at Morgan's, told his errand, and no objections being offered Morgan repaired to Danold's tavern, where he ate breakfast with the constable and his friends. While in custody Miller, his bailor, called at Danold's and objected to Morgan being taken beyond the jail limits, because of liabilities he (Miller) might suffer for. Hayward insisted on carrying out his service, and did so. Arriving at Le Roy Hayward offered to take him before the justice, that he might give bail for appearance at the next term of court. Morgan declined acceptance, saying he could convince Kingsley, the tav‐ ern-keeper at Canandaigua, he did not intend to steal. Morgan's arrest at Batavia was without force. When taken before Justice Chipman he proved his innocence. He was immediately reärrested, on a civil suit for $2, the amount of a tavern bill against him held by one Ackley, which had been assigned to Nicholas G. Cheesebro, the master of the Ma‐ sonic lodge at Canandaigua. Judgment was given against Morgan, to sat‐ isfy which he offered his coat. The offer was refused, and he was lodged in Ontario County jail. (No connection has ever been established between the first persons arresting Morgan and the others who abducted him, ex‐ cept Cheesebro, who was in both actions.)

This was on the evening of the 11th of September, 1826. Twenty‐ four hours later members of the Masonic fraternity called at the jail, and in the absence of the jailor advised his wife to release Morgan, telling her the judgment against him had been paid by one Loton Lawson. The prisoner was liberated, but on reaching the street was suddenly seized, thrust into a close carriage, gagged, bound, and driven rapidly out of the village, westwardly, or to Rochester, and so on to the Ridge road, accompanied by Lawson and two other Masons. Lawson after‐ wards testified "that the Ridge road was followed to Lewiston, and so on down to Fort Niagara, near a grave-yard, where the passengers in the vehicle got out and the coachman dismissed; that none but Masons were allowed to communicate with Morgan; that preparations had pre‐ viously been made for his reception"; and he was taken into the fort, blindfolded, bound, and thrown into the magazine, where he was con‐ fined until the 19th, when he disappeared. In October, 1827, over a year after his abduction, a dead body was found on Lake Ontario beach, and a committee from Batavia and Rochester, deciding after the closest scrutiny that it was that of Morgan, they brought it to Batavia, where it was exposed to view in James Brisbane's yard, and large numbers visited the spot to view the loathsome spectacle. A funeral procession was formed, Mrs. Morgan and D. C. Miller being chief mourners, and the body conveyed to the grave-yard, where in later years the anti-Masons erected a handsome stone to his (?) memory. Later, however, the clothes found on this body were thoroughly identified as belonging to one Timothy Monroe, a man accidentally drowned near the mouth of Niagara. In this connection we state that Mrs. Morgan was supported by the anti-Masons until she joined her fortune afterwards with a Royal Arch Mason's, when she was dropped by the anties.

A tremendous excitement followed the disappearance of Morgan. Investigating committees were everywhere appointed. Governor Clinton offered a reward for the apprehension of those who abducted him. Sir Peregrine Maitland, governor-general of Upper Canada, offered a reward of $200. Lodges and chapters of Masons denounced the deed. The hostility of feeling between Masons and anti-Masons was of the bitterest description. The dividing line ran through families and churches even boys on the streets took sides. The Masonic fraternity throughout a large section of country was threatened with destruction, many lodges being so weakened by withdrawals, expulsions, and lack of applications as to be disbanded for years. The order in 1826 numbered 360 lodges and 22,000 members. Ten years later there were 75 lodges and 4,000 members.

While the several committees were pursuing inquiries the contemplated book, Morgan's *Revelations of Masonry*, appeared. It was in pamphlet form, might have cost 10 cents, but sold for $1, copyright secured. Morgan's partner subscribed under oath not to divulge his secret regarding the publication of the book ; and from letters found it was soon known that avarice, not a love of country or friends, was his principal reason for the undertaking. But a few copies were sold at $1. The price was soon reduced to 50 cents, then to 25 cents, finally to about 10 cents.

As to the trial of the abductors, evidence was given that Cheesebro hired and paid for the carriage, and he with Lawson, Sawyer, and Sheldon were indicted for complicity. The sheriff of Niagara County, Eli Bruce, was fined and imprisoned for the part he took in the matter, and other prominent and respectable men were convicted.

The excitement was kept up. Attempts were made to prevent Masons from meeting as usual. It being the custom to celebrate St. John's day, the Batavia Lodge, in May, 1827, announced their intention to celebrate it in public. Miller endeavored to prevent it, but on June 25th 300 Masons assembled for the purpose. A large concourse of people to the number of several thousand were in Batavia. Some were armed with knives and guns. But the day passed off without any accident. The proceedings were addressed by George Hosmer, of Livingston

County, and the Masons endured the scoffs and jeers of an enraged multitude. The anti-Masons attempted afterwards to exclude Masons from
the jury.

We now return to David C. Miller, who attained almost equal notoriety with Morgan. After the intentions of Morgan and Miller relative
to the book were announced one Daniel Johns, from Canada, came to
Batavia. He had resided in Rochester, and there became acquainted
with Miller's friends, by whom, it is said, he was received as a partner.
Johns had a little money, and offered to make some advances, pecuniary,
as was *desirable* at that time. He was therefore accepted without much
scrutiny as to his motives. It was supposed he wished to procure possession of Morgan's manuscript. Certainly Miller wanted Johns's money;
thus a deception was created in the start. Johns obtained a part of the
manuscript and Miller some of Johns's money, about $30 or $40. This
small sum was of more value to Miller than the manuscript was to Johns,
and so trouble arose between them. A few days before Miller's arrest
(September 12, 1826) a warrant on behalf of Johns was issued by Justice Bartow, of Le Roy, against Miller and one Davids, a partner, to collect moneys advanced by Johns. This warrant was placed in the hands
of Jesse French, of Stafford, the constable (and father of the late J.
Homer French, of French's *Gazetteer of New York*), who, learning that
Miller had determined to resist arrest, employed several assistants, and
on September 12th, followed by Roswell Wilcox and Jesse Hurlburt and
a large party, repaired to Batavia to effect the arrest of Miller and Davids.
The presence of so many strangers in Batavia excited the apprehension of the citizens, many of whom offered their services to resist the attempt to arrest Miller. French, with his assistants, repaired to Miller's
office, where he (Davids) and Miller's son were, and although the office
was fortified with arms none were used. Wilcox arrested Davids, and
French at the same time arrested Miller. Both submitted, and were
taken to Danold's tavern. Davids, being a prisoner within the jail limits,
was soon discharged. Miller was taken to the lodge-room at Stafford,
against the remonstrances of his friends, kept there for two or three
hours, then proceeded to Le Roy, kept at Walbridge's tavern, where he
was discharged, and returned to Batavia. Theodore Talbot was Miller's
lawyer. "It is supposed by some that the main object of Miller's arrest
was to obtain possession of Morgan's manuscript."

The following article appeared in the issue of September 15, 1826, of
the *Republican Advocate* :

"About 2 A. M., Monday morning, September 11, two buildings were set on fire. The same morning Captain William Morgan was seized, as was alleged, by virtue of process and conveyed off no one knows where, by a sett of ruffians. On Tuesday a mob consisting of more than 100 assembled in this village, from various parts of the country, with the openly-avowed intention of destroying our printing establishment, and conveyed the editor of this paper out of town, by ruffian force, in pretence of legal process, to Le Roy, to the magistrate, but no process was exhibited or returned by the office. The constable then disappeared, and the prisoner was discharged.

"Signed : C. W. MILLER, son of D. C. MILLER."

The result of this arrest of Miller was an indictment found against some of the parties for alleged riot, assault, and battery, and false imprisonment. A trial was had before Judges Birdsall, Tisdale, James Taggart, and Simeon Cummings, judges of the Court of Common Pleas, two of whom, as well as a part of the jury, were Masons. French was sentenced to 12 months, Wilcox to six months, and Hurlburt to three months imprisonment.

The most notable effect of the agitation by the anti-Masons was the career of that party, which subdivided and distracted all other political parties, and drew thousands of adherents from them all ; a subject that would require a volume to treat intelligently. .

TEMPERANCE.

OLD people of this and other counties remember distinctly that in their youth the use of spirituous liquors as a beverage was almost universal. Nor was it confined to the laymen. Very many of the settlers of Genesee County had such a habit, and it was thought no harm in those times, for it would be a breach of hospitality to not offer it to visitors. It was the necessary help at the " bees," and the failure of such " bees " and gatherings, from its absence, is well remembered. It was at home, in the field, everywhere, in olden days, and was the universal panacea for wet weather and dry weather, for real and imaginary ailments.

Distilleries sprang up early in many of the towns, and liquor was cheap and pure ; the country stores kept it for sale the same as codfish and molasses ; and its use was sanctioned by all classes—the laborer, the clergy, the bench and bar. Indeed, the words of a modern poet,

> " The power enslaved in yonder cask
> Shall many burdens bear ;
> Shall nerve the toiler at his task,
> The soul at prayer,"

seem very apropos of the customs of former days. With the well founded ideas of the time is it to be wondered that no moves were made for a reform in regard to its use? It is not known definitely when stringent measures were taken in Genesee County; the pulpit always taught temperance, but that was not the temperance—strict prohibition, touch not and handle not—of the present day.

It is known that about 1830 a reform gradually swept over the land in the form of signing a pledge; but this was only a general restriction not to use it to excess, and was not sufficiently effective. In this county, in 1836, a society was formed, and after a discussion of two days, with a negative vote of two (who voted so, fearing the advance was too rapid), the total abstinence pledge was adopted. At the present day it hardly seems credible that a temperance reform could have encountered any opposition. It did receive such opposition in 1836 in Genesee County. There were many earnest, zealous workers in the reform here, but after a half century, with no records, it is impossible to name them. Much good was done, and a check was placed upon the increasing evil, which is felt to the present day.

Like all important reforms it has had its revivals, its new methods of advancing the work, and these waves would sweep over the country animating the friends to good works. The first of these waves that so greatly inundated the country was the "Washingtonian" movement, that started in 1840 at Baltimore. A few confirmed drunkards saw their peril and joined together in a resolution to reform; others joined; and the whole country joined in the good work. Genesee County was remarkably active in the move, but like all superhuman efforts a reaction followed. Still much permanent good is directly traceable to that grand movement. Its restriction by statute was then urged, and in 1846 the first law went into effect: It was termed the "license or no-license" law, and sometimes the "five-gallon" law, but could be consistently called a "local option" law. This, for some reason, was not generally successful; not perhaps so much from any defect in the law, or that the evil cannot be restricted by statute; but having invoked the aid of the law the temperance workers relied too much upon its strong arm and relaxed their efforts in educating the public sentiment to sustaining them.

About 1855 the so-called "Maine law" was enacted, and the friends anticipated good results, but the Court of Appeals decided it to be unconstitutional. This was followed by an act appointing county commissioners to grant licenses, but this was not satisfactory.

The next move was the present local option statute that allows each town to determine, by its votes, if the sale of intoxicating liquors shall be tolerated, and the election of the commissioner gives the decision. The towns of Genesee County are no exception to others, and the excesses of either faction can be held in check by the operation of the law.

Within a few years the Prohibition party has come into existence, which claims total prohibition as its platform. Of its merits it is not our province to speak, and its votes will be found under another head. This fact should be borne in mind by its friends in Genesee County : that all laws are not satisfactory in their results unless the people are educated to a sentiment of their wholesomeness, and a strong majority morally pledged to their fulfillment.

EARLY SCHOOLS.

IT must not be supposed that while the pioneers of this section were so busy in felling the forest, and laying the foundation of future comfort and wealth, they neglected the foundation of those institutions in which they had been reared, and without which no community can prosper. As soon as a sufficient number of children could be gathered the settlers for miles around, by a preconcerted "bee," rolled the logs together that formed the primitive school-house. The desks were slanting shelves of slabs or boards, supported by pins driven into the logs and a brace to the logs below. In front of these was the seat made of a split log, hewn smooth, with legs of proper length for the larger scholars ; in front of these were similar benches for the smaller pupils. If there was a saw-mill within a reasonable distance these rude desks and benches would be made of planks or slabs from the mill. Then the plainest common branches were taught—reading, writing, spelling, arithmetic, and geography. The rude adaptation of the means of instruction in those early days was as primitive, and in the same manner deficient, as were all the means with which the settlers were provided. The books and teaching must be upon the "axe and auger" plan. Not only was there a scarcity of books, but the text books of the time were inefficient ; they would be as much a wonder to the pupil and parents of the present time as would the old-fashioned flax-break ; and the students of the common school of to-day, if such text books were placed before them, would consider them of par value with the rough seats and desks of those primitive days. But these early pioneers provided for their children all that could

be then, and, in fact it was, proportionately, more than parents do un.
der the present uniform and excellent school system. The puritan idea
was " to spare the rod was to spoil the child," and in those primitive
schools were teachers who could ably demonstrate that branch. The
pupil of the present would not tolerate the idea of going from two to
four miles to school, and that, too, along a rough path through a wilderness, his only guide being the marked trees. Is it, then, not a wonder
that the Holland Purchase—the territory of Genesee County—could, in
the early part of the present century, send out into the councils of the
State and Nation men of the highest statesmanship ? To the pioneer
teacher, as well as parents, great credit is due. The teacher must " board
round," and the long walks to the cabins of his patrons, the cheerful hospitality shown, the simple but wholesome food, and social interchange of
thought during the long fire-lit visits of the evening were oases in the
desert of the teacher's life that the present flowery paths of the principals in the same section do not possess. The names of some of the early
pioneer teachers are preserved, and they will generally be noticed in
their respective towns. The school house of hewn logs after a few years,
and of larger proportions and sufficient windows, would follow the 12x14
cabin ; better teachers and more modern text books were introduced ;
and uniformity in methods of teaching was adopted.

"Previous to the year 1828 much difficulty and embarrassment had
occurred throughout the Holland Purchase from a provision in the school
act of the State, ' that sites of school-houses should be secured by deeds
in fee, or by leases from the possessor of the fee, of the land.' In numerous instances there were no deeded lands in the district, or if there were
they were not conveniently located. In the absence of such title or lease
the trustees of the district could not legally levy and collect taxes for
building or repairing school-houses. About this period Mr. Evans, then
land agent of the Holland Land Company, adopted the following plan
to remedy the evil, and prevent the hindrances that were in the way of
a full realization of the benefits of the common school system upon the
Holland Purchase. It was entered upon the books of the office, and the
benefits of it extended whenever asked :

"' In every legally organized School District on the Holland Purchase, where the most
convenient site for a school-house shall fall on land not deeded from the Holland Company, a deed for such site, not exceeding half an acre of land, shall be granted, from
the company to such district, gratis.' Provided that whenever such site shall fall on
lands held under contract, from the Company, by any person or persons, such district
shall procure a relinquishment of the right to such piece of land, by virtue of said contract, to be endorsed thereon by the person or persons holding the same.' "

In 1835 school libraries were established, and every district received
its proportionate quota for such library.   In 1845 institutes for teachers
were considered one of the best means of benefit, and the teachers of
Genesee County eagerly availed themselves of its advantages.

Simultaneously with the advent of the neat, white farm house of the
pioneer the school-house appears, bearing the same advancement that is
warranted by the improvement of the country, and the greatly increased
value of the surroundings.   The growth of the schools can be best
learned from a careful perusal of statistics relating thereto, and which
need not be introduced here.   Our province was to show the early
school ; the present excellent system is realized and familiar to all.   In
the histories of the towns each will have its interesting details.

William E. Prentice, of Batavia, was the school commissioner for the
county in 1885-87, and William J. Barr, of Elba, the present commissioner, to serve until 1891.

The public money apportioned to the towns for 1889 was as follows :
Alabama, $1,415.62; Alexander, $1,352.17; Batavia, $5,368.72; Bergen,
$1,580.30; Byron, $1,294.01 ; Bethany, $1,326.02 ; Darien, $1,523.94 ;
Elba, $1,202.94 ; Le Roy, $2,627.83 ; Oakfield, $1,025.03 ; Pavilion,
$1,187.94; Pembroke, $2,228.26 ; and Stafford, $1,441.79—a total of
$23,574.57.   There are 150 school districts in the county, but 15 of them
are joint districts with the school-houses located in adjoining counties.

THE CIVIL WAR.

GENESEE COUNTY REGIMENTS.

THE bombardment of Sumter aroused the same patriotic feelings in
Genesee County that were manifested throughout the North, and
for the time all partisan feelings were forgotten ; men of all parties
evinced a desire to sustain the government.   At once an enthusiastic
meeting was held at Batavia and 20 volunteers were enrolled ; the same
evening a meeting was held at Le Roy, and soon afterward others in
various parts of the county followed ; the same patriotism prevailed
throughout.

On the 18th of April a call for 500 men was made from the county,
and a meeting called for Saturday afternoon and evening of April 20th, at
Concert Hall, Batavia ; 48 young men were enrolled.   The following

committee was appointed to solicit funds for the support of the families of those who enlisted, and any other expense : Trumbull Cary, John Fisher, Junius A. Smith, Seth Wakeman, and James M. Willett. For a like pur. pose a committee of three was appointed in each of the other towns, as follows :

Alabama.—Chauncey Williams, George H. Potter, Edward Hersey.
Alexander.—Heman Blodgett, Earl Kidder, E. G. Moulton.
Bethany.—Lemuel Lincoln, A. G. Terry, Carlos Huggins.
Bergen.—Horatio Reed, Samuel Richmond, Josiah Pierson.
Byron.—J. T. Boughton, Loren Green, Addison Terry.
Darien.—J. W. Hyde, Col. A. Jefferson, T. C. Peters.
Elba.—Alva Willis, A. T. Hulett, C. H. Monell.
Le Roy.—Hon. A. S. Upham, Walter Gustin, A. O. Comstock.
Oakfield.—C. H. Chamberlain, J. C. Gardner, William Dunlap.
Pavilion.—Oswald Bond, Warren Fay, George Tomlinson.
Pembroke.—G. D. Wright, D. N. Wells, R. F. Thompson.
Stafford.—Cyrus Prentice, Robert Fisher, Perry Randall.

Recruiting went on rapidly. On the 29th of April the first company was formed under the command of A. T. Root, and left the county; it became part of the 12th Regt. N. Y. V. On the 14th of May the com-pany of J. R. Mitchell, and on the 15th that of Capt. William L. Cowan, followed, bearing the adieux and benedictions of all.

The departure of the first volunteers was an occasion of peculiar inter-est, as it was the first time in the history of the county that men had felt the peril of National existence from internal dissension, and was the first call of the present generation for volunteers. The feeling for the first who went out was more poignant than on similar occasions after-wards, for the acuteness was to some extent worn away by frequent ex-ercise, and no idle curiosity was felt. The brave volunteers of Genesee County, who so nobly left the comforts of home to go forth at their country's call, to face death and suffering with no friendly hand to allay, deserve a more minute history than the limits of this work will permit.

In 1861, soon after the outbreak of the Rebellion, the patriotic ladies of Batavia and other parts of Genesee County organized associations for supplying soldiers in the field with comforts and luxuries that the govern-ment did not provide—havelocks, flannels, and articles of clothing, as well as supplies for the sick and wounded, which were sent on, and many a languishing patriot has blessed the ladies of Genesee County. Among those who early and earnestly engaged in this humane work was Mrs.

Gad B. Worthington, Mrs. John Fisher, Mrs. Alva Smith, Mrs. E. R. Pratt, Mrs. Levi Jackson, Mrs. Richard Cotes, Mrs. Wright, Mrs. Dr. N. Clark, Mrs. Putnam, Mrs. Thomas Yates, Miss M. Mallory, Mrs. John Wood, Mrs. George Holden, Miss Parsons, Mrs. Seth Wakeman, Mrs. L. B. Cotes, Miss Carrie Pringle, Mrs. S. C. Holden, Mrs. Junius A. Smith, Mrs. Dean Richmond, Mrs. Macy, and Mrs. H. U. Howard, and many others whose names now cannot be learned.

22D N. Y. IND. BATTERY.

THIS regiment was organized in this county, its rendezvous being at Lockport; was mustered into the U. S. service October 18, 1862; was soon consolidated as Co. M of the 9th N. Y. Heavy Artillery; and participated in the following battles: Cold Harbor, Petersburg, Monocacy, Charleston, Cedar Creek, Petersburg again, and Sailor's Creek. The officers and men when mustered into service were: Captain, John D. Numan; senior 1st lieutenant, Melancthon D. Brown; junior 1st lieutenant, D. D. W. Pringle; senior 2d lieutenant, Robert C. Worthington; junior 2d lieutenant, Edwin F. Clark.

Sergeants.—James M. Waite, Francis N. Parrish, Asahel M. Abbey, Dan E. Waite, William I. Parrish, William E. Wright, John Oldswager, and Josiah T. Crittenden.

Corporals.—Hugh T. Peters, Edward F. Moulton, William H. Maltby, Thomas Walsh, Eugene B. Wing, Robert Fowles, Henry Nulty, Orville Thompson, John Connor, John D. Bartlett, Guy A. Brown, and James G. Hatch.

Musicians.—Charles Foster, Edson H. Pond.

Artificers.—Levi T. Garrett, Henry Wood; guidon, William M. Moulton; stable sergeant, Edwin Lock; company clerk, George Avery.

Privates.—Hezekiah Brown, William T. Barrett, E. J. Benton, John Bower, Seymour S. Brown, Thomas C. Barnard, Curus W. Brown, Charles W. Bradley, Freeman Bailey, Jr., Miles T. Brown, Isaac Bruett, Charles J. Cleveland, George T. Chase, Rowland Champion, John Carmel, John Cox, Alva N. Colt, James W. Case, Michael Carney, James Carney, Thomas Cook, Henry Connelly, Benjamin Cox, Zina W. Carter, Oron H. Conant, William B. Cole, Jerome Canfield, Dioclesian Covey, William H. Chappie, George D. Dodson, James Dunn, Earl A. Dodson, Sylvester Demary, Dennis Dibble, George Edwards, William R. Eddy, Elias Eastwood, James Emory, Orson J. Forbes, Robert Finley, Charles Fairfield, William Faber, Harmon Fitch, Ansel Ford, John E. Field,

John Griffis, George Gann, Cyrus A. Gowing, Charles R. Griffin, Paul Glor, Amos Humphrey, John Harmon, Ira E. Haight, Edward J. Hollenbeck, John Hassett, Archie Hollenbeck, David Hill, Henry Johnson, John L. Kingdon, Albert Knapp, Patrick Keating, Stephen R. King, James Kidder, Silas Knapp, John Kellner, Libbeus King, Henry L. Kreatzer, George B. Lawrence, Henry Lapp, Samuel Lathrop, Benjamin Lewis, Henry Leverington, James M. Lapp, Elias Lyons, Charles Loplow, Thomas McManis, Marion F. Meredith, Jacob Moore, Elias Martin, David Miller, Albert H. Moulton, Archie McMillen, John Munt, Alexander McDonald, Angus McIntosh, Lucius A. Munger, Joseph Marsh, Moses Nichols, Michael O'Donnell, Robert Plant, Thomas W. Paden, James Porter, John J. Peard, Norman M. Putnam, George Rogers, Frederick Reichert, Mortimer Rich, Alonzo Rich, Ambrose Rich, Nathan E. Rumsey, Charles E. Smead, Henry Shafer, Gilbert Shader, David S. Spring, Edwin Shadbolt, John D. Shiller, Edsil Shaw, Charles A. Smith, Wallace M. Smith, Edward B. Smith, Stephen Thompson, Frederick Tanger Homer L. Tisdale, Stephen Taylor, Henry Vishon, Charles VanKuren, Frederick Vickens, Gilbert Wade, Jonah C. Wicker, John J. Warren, Edwin Ward, John Worthington, Warren West, Stephen T. Wing, William Welch, John W. Williams, Walter S. Wright, and Christian Zwetsh. Out of the original 168 only about 65 were in line for discharge at the close of the war and expiration of their three years' service.

CAPT. FENN'S COMPANY, 28TH REGT.

THIS gallant company was mustered into service May 22, 1861, and participated in the following battles : Point of Rocks, Newtown, first Winchester, and Cedar Mountain. In the last engagement the loss was heavy. They were also engaged at Susquehanna Court House and Chancellorsville. The officers and men who enlisted were :

Officers.—Captain, Charles H. Fenn ; 1st lieutenant, William W. Rowley ; 2d lieutenant, George M. Ellicott ; sergeants, Lucian R. Bailey, Charles D. Searles, George W. Sherwood, Edward J. Watts ; corporals, Leander Hamilton, Chandler Gillam, Robert J. Whitney, Darwin Fellows ; musicians, John Prost, Silas Bragg.

Privates.—Calvin Annis, George Hallen, William F. Albro, Edmond Bragdon, Bryon Brinkerhoff, James F. Bennett, Lafayette Barker, Riley Blount, George Barnard, Oscar Barnes, Philip Bittinger, George H. Datton, Henry Baldwin, John S. Barber, William H. Colburn, Roswell Coddington, William Howland, Porter Howard, Truman M. Hawley, George

M. Hamilton, Isaac Hotchkiss, James G. Lawton, Charles G. Liscomb, Joseph Luce, John Moran, Barnard Murray, Lyman B. Miner, William McCracken, Richard Outhoudt, Charles A. Perkins, Edward C. Peck, Robert Chapple, Henry Close, Charles H. Crandall, Alexander Comyns, Henry Dykeman, Joshua T. Davis, Melvin Dodge, Decatur Doty, Irvin H. Ewell, Kirkland Ewell, Theodore Eldridge, Joseph Ennis, George Griffin, Cleveland Gillett, Joseph Gibson, Peter Howland, Erastus Peck, Franklin Peck, Michael Quirck, Charles B. Rapp, Harlow M. Reynolds, Michael Ryan, Howard M. Snell, Henry Scott, William B. Simmons, Stephen Taylor, Riley Thayer, Robert Thompson, Milton Trip, George Thayer, John Van Buren, Francis M. Weatherlow.

CAPT. A. J. ROOT'S COMPANY, 12TH REGT.

THIS was one of the most gallant companies, and first to organize and depart.

Officers.—Captain, A. J. Root; 1st lieutenant, W. P. Town ; 2d lieutenant, Lucius Smith; sergeants, S. Dexter Ludden, Charles F. Rand, James F. Taylor, Thomas Tansley ; corporals, Samuel McChesney, William P. Jones, Joshua P. Taylor, Joseph L. Hunt.

Privates.—William B. Aird, Oscar Allison, John W. Bartlett, Franklin Billings, George D. Baars, John C. Beach, John Briggs, James Braley, Almon G. Bentley, James E. Cross, James Conway, Charles Coppin, Zelotus Colby, James Clifton, Henry R. Casler, Michael Delano, Charles Durant, Martin W. Dean, Robert Dearlove, Charles F. Davenport, William Enwright, Alvin Fox, John B. Foote, Harrison Furguson, Daniel N. Ford, Jasper Gibbs, William Graham, John G. Gardner, Patrick Ganatty, Charles A. Hickox, Jacob Hiber, James F. Hilts, William Johnson, George Keene, John Klansworth, Barney Karker, William H. Leonard, William Lathrop, Francis Lincoln, Frank Murphy, Albert A. Meade, Peter Meschter, William H. Nichols, Cornelius W. Post, Robert Peard, G. W. Reynolds, Michael Ryan, James Shepard, Albert P. Stage, George Smith, John Stone, Frank Seamans, Hiram W. Smith, James Scott, Horace F. Tracey, William Thompson, Timothy Tirney, Alanson Vercillus, William Wheeler, William McGuire, James Preble, Winfield S. Popple, Michael Roach.

105TH REGIMENT NEW YORK VETERANS.

VERY many brave men went out with this regiment, and Company E was largely recruited from Genesee County. Other companies had

Genesee County men, which will be given in the order of the companies. According to the adjutant-general's report the regiment participated in the following battles: Cedar Mountain, Rappahannock Station, Thoroughfare Gap, second Bull Run, Chantilly, South Mountain, Antietam, and Fredericksburg. They saw severe service, and were consolidated with the 94th in 1863.

Officers.—Colonel, James M. Fuller; major, John W. Shedd; quartermaster, Charles Strong; surgeon, Dr. D. C. Chamberlain; chaplain, B. P. Russell; quartermaster-sergeant, Jerome J. Shedd.

COMPANY A.—Andrew Whitney, Abram Van Alstine, Isaiah Thomas, William Thomas, John Thomas, Henry E. Thomas. John Tyrrell, Lewis Skinner, H. H. Ruland, Malcom G. Pettibone, John Nash, Burr Kenyon, John Killen, J. F. Hundredmark, A. D. Harrington, John Free, William Dingman, O. N. Campbell, Alonzo Croft, Lorenzo Croft, Jeff Curtain, Ed Brower, Fred Bramsted, Sam Averry, Lanson R. Chaffee, Lyman T. Miner, George S. Winslow, Clinton Brace, M. Shadbolt, H. Barbet, George H. Smith, George W. Dickey.

COMPANY B.—William Rose, George W. Forster, Philip S. Frost.

COMPANY C.—Edward Thomson, Joseph M. Cook, Charles H. Hodge, Peter A. McIntyre, M. McIntyre, Edward Mercer, Erasmus R. Stephens, William H. Thompson, Orrin Thompson, John B. Way.

COMPANY D.—George W. Griffith, sergeant; John Foster and Emogine Daniels, musicians; Charles H. Miller, James Shine.

COMPANY E.—George Babcock, captain; Willis Benham, and John J. White, lieutenants; Patrick H. Graham, Lucius F. Rolfe, and Edwin J. Hyde, sergeants; Herbert Stacey, Clarence H. McCabe, J. A. Sherwood, George W. Mather, N. J. Hamilton, Taylor Hart, and Edward Brennan, corporals. Privates: Sheldon I. Brown, Fred Eelris, George Fauset, John Johnson, George Schuab, Sylvester Primmer, Oliver B. Olin, Isaac Wakely, Isaac P. Wakely, Franklin Terry, James H. Turner, James P. Thomas, H. Trumball, Joseph Scofield, Michael Strief, William Riley, J. Parshall, David Powell, Robert Odion, William Martin, John Moore, Ezro Maun, J. G. Lawton, John Keenan, Edwin S. Heath, James H. Hogan, Wesley Hawkins, L. Hennesey, Jacob Hagisht, W. H. Heal. O. Gaskin, Thomas Cady, William E. Crane, Herrick C. Crockr, John Barnard, John Blake, Chauncey Bowen, William F. Albro, John F. Armstrong, P. Holden.

CAPT. MOORE'S COMPANY, 100TH REGIMENT.

THIS gallant company was mostly recruited from Genesee County, and stands among the foremost in good work. Its members from this county were: Captain, Walter B. Moore; lieutenants, M. H. Topping, Martin S. Bogart; sergeants, Leonard D. Howell, Edward S. Peck, Peabody Pratt, and Myron P. Pierson; corporals, William Wheeler, W. M. Thompson, and Donald McPherson; musicians, J. O. Price, Samuel Malters, and Willard Joslyn.

Privates.—Robert Brears, Benjamin Bain, Henry C. Bolton, Charles Clough, Henry C. Copeland, M. I. Daniels, Fritz Dato, George Eberhart, George C. Fales, Charles D. Foot, B. Growney, John Golland, Phil Geize, H. M. Haskins, John Jordan, Joseph Maud, Thomas McCann, Charles Meyrer, James McPherson, Mather Moore, William Newton, John B. Ott, A. J. Pervorce, Joseph P. Pierson, John C. Presby, Albert Pursell, Hiram Robison, Philip Ryan, William P. Swift, William Seeley, Chester F. Swift, Peter Freehouse, Sanford C. Thompson, Peter Tracey, Louis H. Todd, Stephen Wakeley, John G. Wicks, Albert U. Ward.

129TH REGT. N. Y. VETERANS.

THIS important regiment was largely recruited from Genesee County, and was worthy of all mention. It was depleted by many decisive battles, and its ranks were refilled from the same patriotic element for which Genesee County was, and still is, noted. In December, 1862, the regiment was changed from infantry to heavy artillery, designated as the 8th N. Y. Heavy Artillery. It belonged to the 2d corps, and participated in all the battles, marches, and duties of the campaign of 1864–65. In the latter part of 1865, being severely depleted by battles and the discharge of men whose time expired, it was transferred to the 4th H. A. to the 4th H. A.

The casualties of this regiment, during the campaign closing with the surrender of Lee, was officially reported at 1,171 officers and men. A greater portion of these valiant men was recruited from Genesee County, and we give them so far as we have been able to obtain their names from many sources.

James M. Willett, of this county, was major.

COMPANY G.—E. G. Sherwin, captain; J. R. Cooper and Orrin C. Parker, lieutenants; John H. Nichols, John F. Hutton, John J. Thomas, James W. Young, and George Ford, sergeants; J. D. Safford, Lewis

Teller, William H. Bennett, M. M. Kendall, Peter Welch, W. W. Burton, M. Manahan, Thomas Cuthbert, James H. Horton, and Peter Barber, corporals; M. McNamara, Joseph H. Horton, musicians; John G. Foster, artificer.

The men who went out with the regiment were: Albert Amidon, John Adams, Nelson F. Bowen, William A. Burris, Charles Brooks, John Bisher, H. L. Bennett, Charles Buell, L. C. Briggs, M. Birmingham, William Brower, Charles Collins, James H Charles, Christopher Cooper, William Cleveland, George A. Cole, J. Cook, J. Donnigan, L. C. Dorman, A. E. Darrow, A. J. Denham, Anthony Davis, Delos Eddy, Nicholas Felter, Harry Fernerstein, Ed. W. Flanders, Charles H. Fuller, George A. Fuller, Peter Fowldin, Frank Gleaser, Warner Howe, Henry Helfman, William Hutton, Christopher Johnson, Henry Johnson, Lyman C. Kendall, William H. Kendall, John Kimmerling, Daniel W. Kinnie, William Morford, Norman Martin, Moses Millington, Peter McDermid, Daniel McDermid, Charles W. McCarthy, Cain Mahaney, Joseph Murdock, Peter Metzler, George Metzler, S Myres, J. McLaughlin, John Munz, George Merlan, Conrad Merlan, Abram Norris, Van A. Pratt, Robert Peard, William J. Pindar, M. S. Parker, F. W. Rice, Fernando Robbins, Charles H. Rice, Nathaniel Rowan, William H Ship, John J. Sherman, William Smith, Devolson Smith, Henry Thomas, Joseph Thompson, George W. Thomas, Lewis Van Dyke, G. H. Van Alstine, Reuben Van Wart, S. A. Wilson, W. W. Wyman, Wash Ward, W. P. Wright, Joseph Willett, Leroy Williams, N. W. Wakeman, William Wood, R. H. Waite, Richard Welch.

The following were recruited and sent on: F. A. Altmeyer, John W. Amlong, N. F. Bowen, William N. Barton, Mark Bossard, Joseph Bongordon, John W. Babcock, A. J. Bennett, M. F. Bowe, John Brown, William Boehme, W. H. Bennett, Peter Barber, P. Colson, Henry Conklin, G. R. Cochran, John Camp, Hibbard Chase, John Collins, James B. Clark, Pat Collins, Dan Dibble, Hugh Duffy, C. M. Dodge, Robert Denham, M. W. Elston, Abram Elston, Robert A. Erwin, Lawrence Flynn, Christopher Follett, K. B. Finley, Matthew Gleaser, J. M. Gilson, Charles C. Gilson, George F. Jones, Ezra Kirby, James Moore, John McNamara, Virgil Marsh, Hiram Marsh, A. J. Mahew, F. B. Maynard, N. A. Mitchell, M Manion, N. Martin, Charles Nichols, R. Ovendan, Thomas E Peard, John Perkins, George W. Parshall, D. M. Pannell, M. W. Parker, George Perry, W. O. Robinson, John Reed, Charles Sanford, J. B. D. Sawtell, Martin Steves, William N. Smith, Jacob M. Smith,

Joseph Steffin, Horatio Thomas, John Thomas, Cassimere Thomas, O. Timmerson, N. Truesdall, Seth J. Thomas, Thomas Wilson, John Waschow, Albert Wilber, Rowley Wilson, Luke White, Edwin Wade, C. M. Whitney, J. Walsh, J. M. Wiggins, F. F. Waterman, E. A. Perrin, Silas Smith.

COMPANY H.—Stephen Connor, captain ; George Wiard, J. H. Robson, W. H. Raymond, and Arch Winnie, lieutenants ; Henry Bickford, W. H. Roberson, William Grant, Louis Mather, Stephen Vail, O. E. Babcock, A. W. Aldrich, R. T. Hunn, sergeants ; E. P. Cowles, Charles Cox, E. J. Winslow, A. M. Allen, C. Chamberlain, William Jones, W. H. Fidinger, W. H. Griffin, E. A. Whitman, Joseph Webber, H. B. Salisbury, L. H. Robinson, corporals ; C. D. Davis, Henry C. Ward, musicians ; F. Krager, W. Cole, artificers ; R. Crosby, wagoner.

Privates.—Orrin Allen, Arthur Allen, Ed. Anthony, Frank Anthony, Thomas Anthony, Henry Anthony, J. O. Aldridge, H. L. Austin, Albert Algo, J. Armidick, D. H. Bailey, F. Burgomaster, J. K. Brown, H. E. Brooks, J. C. Beach, Ira Baker, Henry Britton, James Bush, John S. Barber, W. R. Crook, Eli Cope, J. M. Cook, J. W. Chappel, Joseph Cheney, Robert Caple, P. Carlton, Robert Conroy, Edward Dyer, Alvin Dyer, Ferdinand Dorf, H. E. Duell, Charles Derby, Frank Derson, M. T. Bailey, N. J. Eaton, William Fenner, Daniel Fenner, Irvine Fenner, Leon Feller, N. Frenberger, C. Foster, J. C. Eidinger, A. J. Frayer, J. E. Friesman, W. B. Graham, Jacob Gleaser, R. L. Gumaer, W. J. Gregg, John C. Gray, G. A. Haight, J. E. Haight, Sam Haight, G. Z. Howard, J. B. Hescock, J. D. Henderson, S. B. Holmes, James Heal, Robert Heal, Jonas Holmes, John Hix, J. W. Hildun, Charles Havens, E. G. Havens, F. M. Harden, O. S. Holccmb, F. Johnson, D. V. Johnson, Frank Jones, W. S. Joslyn, H. D. Johns, Thomas Johns, Daniel Johns, F. A. Kenyon, W. P. Kidder, J. W. Kasson, B. R. Lamkins, Fred Lord, C. Lafleur, D. E. Lamphear, William Lewis, James Laighbody, Charles Lilly, J. D. Mason, W. J. Moore, J. K. Merrill, W. A. McMillan, N. N. Morse, Pat Murphy, H. D. Myers, J. McDaniels, J. McAllister, W. H. Mattison, J. Mahannah, A. T. McCracken, Byron Murdock, W. L. Norton, Alfred Riker, G. W. Reynolds, John Radford, A. E. Spaulding, Paul Stevens, D. Sherman, Festus Stone, H. T. Sautell, Moore Smith, W. I. Skidmore, A. V. Simmons, H. F. Snook, Arba Shaw, J Spaulding, H. Suits, Daniel Suits, H. C. Searls, M. Sutfin, Thomas Steele, H. C. Timby, Samuel Throop, George Thomas, M O. Tyrrel, E. Tibbitts, S. D. Tuttle, W. B. Talıman, B. F. Tallman, H. L. Van Dresser, M. L. Watson, J. A. Wall, Robert

Walker, W. M. Walker, John H. Weaver, B. F. Wood, James W. Wood, Julius Wies, Jacob Wies, Thomas Warner, Warren West, J. H. Williamson, Edson Weed, E. G Webster, J. M. Warren, Alpha Warson, N. H. Winslow, A. B. Ward, W. F. Young, Peter Stevens, John Shum, George Walker, J. M.Zimmerman.

COMPANY I.—Alexander Gardner, captain; M. M. Cook, S. R. Stafford, E. R. Loomis, and Ed. Gillis, lieutenants ; Thomas J. Dean, Seth C. Hall, M. Duguid, M. Van Antwerp, J. B. Arnold, N. S. Nier, John P. Thomas, and E. H. Norton, sergeants ; J. R. Perry, J. H. Taggart, L. A. Clark, S. J. Feagles, E. B. Randall, W. H. Elwell, Marcus Wilcox, Thomas Houston, Charles Pindar, Fred Walter, W. L. Benedict, Orville Bannister, corporals; W. F. Osborne, George W. Lower, musicians ; George Kelley, W. F. Perkins, artificers ; W. H. Miller, wagoner.

Privates.—J. D. Ames, James Agett, Jr., James Avery, W. Allen, A. C. Bushman, John Byzn, James Byzn, Leonard Bland, J. F. Bell, J. B. Beardsley, C. Cook, Fred Cook, Joseph Cook, Joseph Cook, 2d, John Cook, Ebenezer Cook, D. Chamberlain, H. A. Church, W. L. Calvert, Elias Chappell, H. T. Clark, Jerome Clark, Charles Carpenter, J. B. Curtis, Thomas Cauffield, G. J. Chandler, Peter Campbell, S. B. Doty, Albert De Wolf, W. H. Dayton, A. K. Damon, F. Eberhardt, Fidelo Eddy, A. Etherefington, John Fulton, W. H. Fuller, W. L. Farr, Sylvester Farr, F. H. Fordham, F. Furey, John Folk, W. H. H. Gillett, C. Gibhartt, Peter Gallagher, Nich. Gossie, W. H. Gordon, G. H. Holmes, George Heath, E. P. Hoyt, Sylvester Hoyt, John Houston, William Houston, E. N. Henderson, James Hunter, W. A. House, E. W. Herrick, D. Y. Hallock, W. H. Howell, Elmer Howell, Daniel Jones, E. M. Kline, John Kelley, Philip Lougle, Joseph Lougle, H. J. W. Lewis, Seymour Lewis, Alonzo Lewis, P. McDonnell, William McGuire, M. H. McNeil, D. McMartin, B. F. McHenry, P. Mingus, Michael Mahan, Alfred Murdock, Dwight Mann, John Monroe, Nicholas Nowe, Alonzo Nichols, F. H. Olmsted, W. D. Perkins, J. B. Palmer, Lewis Payne, S. A. Pease, George Phillips, D. Russell, Robert Reid, Ashley Randall, E. P. Ross, A. J. Reibling, T. C. Rawson, R. E. Roberson, W. W. Stamp, Ed. Stamp, Ed. Sharp, William Sharp, F. A. Shipley, J. A Sherwood, J. M. Sherwood, L. K. Spafford, E. D. Shader, Delos Shattuck, James Sifert, Almon Secor, Ed. Strouch, Riley Stevens, Alexander Shaw, S. L. M. Stafford, Emory M. Tone, J. A. Tone, John Thomas, Amos Topliff, H. W. Trobridge, A. E. Townsend, A. N. Van Antwerp, William Wayman, J. W. Wilson, John Walter, H. A. Williams, Harry Willis, Joel Willis, John Woltz,

Charles Wooliver, E. A. White, F. C. Waltby, E. B. Clark, C. S. Holbrook, J. H. Hoyt, John Shipley, W. H. Thompson, A. R. Terry, G. W. Terry, J. E. Young.

COMPANY L.—S. D. Ludden, captain; H. H. Van Dake, George H. Robertson, W. L Totten, lieutenants; D. L. Fellows, E. T. Forman, W. O. Bartholomew, E. H. Ewell, Joseph Shaw, C. A. Whipple, Edward Bannister, W. H. Hunn, sergeants; D. K. Austin, Allen Buell, J. A. Clark, Robert Chapple, James Drain, Kirk Ewell, Harrison Ferguson, E. F. Ives, G. W. Kendall, George Metzger, William Page, Ed. Williams, corporals; Julius Kassler, William Kisor, musicians; G. A. Barner, Loren Hedger, artificers; Eugene Plumley, wagoner.

Privates.—W. H. Anderson, P. Anthony, N. Armstrong, J. Babcock, Charles G. Bale, Samuel Barnes, William Battersby, Joseph Bloedt, M. Buck, O. S. Burgess, D. W. Burleigh, George Cacner, A. E Carpenter, C. B. Carpenter, J. S. Carpenter, E. L. Carpenter, W. T. Chapman, James H. Childs, O. A. Churchill, W. H. Clancey, Chauncey Clark, Lewis Clark, James Conway, James Courtney, William Craig, I. S. Cross, Orrin Crocker, M. M. Cummings, H. V. Day, D. M. Dean, E. M. Doty, A. J. Drake, Thomas Duffy, Harley Dunham, James Ellis, M. Filkins, James Fluker, G. W. Freelove, W. M. Fuller, Robert Gibson, C. N. Goodenow, G. W. Gould, E. J. Stratton, H. N. Goodenow, D. P. Goodrich, David Greening, Adam Grile, Charles Hale, S. Hamilton, John Hersch, John G. Hersch, John Hewitt, Thomas Hellman, W. H. H. Holden, R. D. Holley, Edwin Hoops, C. A. Howland, Ira Howland, W. R. Howland, Riley Ingaldsbe, Joel B. Jewett, Jeff Judd, W. M. Kendall, Alfred Keyser, Henry Knapp, E. G. Moulton, John Kunst, Lewis Kraft, William Lewis, A. W. Lingfield, Mort Lingfield, Charles Loomis, O. D. Lyman, L. D. Mapes, Morris Marquot, W. C. McCabe, Daniel McMullen, Morris McMullen, Mich Myers, Stephen Myers, Charles Mertz, Caleb Miller, James Morton, William Nixon, Dennis O'Connor, H. Z. Owen, Isaac Page, F. G. Passmore, R. H. Perkins, A. D. Petrie, G. W. R. Pettibone, Harris Phillips, E. P. Pierce, F. Prescott, William Radley, Frank Reinhart, E. H. Rich, E. Robinson, Wesley Robinson, George Rose, E. K. Sage, Frank Sage, I. H. Sanford, Ira Smith, Joseph Sorrell, H. R. Stevens, M. B. Stevens, John Thomas, George Totterdale, D. C. Tracey, C. D. Vickery, George Walker, Tooker Walker, W. H. Walker, H. I. Wallace, H. C. Warner, William Welch, E. Wentworth, L. Whipple, E. G. Wurtz, Charles Youngs.

Many men were enlisted in other regiments, and it is impossible, perhaps, to mention every one.   We find the following in the 49th N. Y. V.: Peter Thomas, Ferdinand Thomas, French Fisher, Joseph Mark, Sergeant Hare, Charles Hayden, Sergeant Slingerland.

CAPT. COWAN'S COMPANY, 14TH N. Y. VETERANS.

THIS company was recruited in Genesee County early in 1861.   It went to Washington, where it remained till early autumn.   Early next spring the company went to Fairfax Court House and Alexandria, thence to Fortress Monroe.   These brave boys did duty at Yorktown, at Cold Harbor, at Gaines Mills; their first open-field fight was at Hanover Court House; they were also engaged at Beaver Meadow, Malvern Hill, etc. The 14th greatly distinguished itself while in service, and Company D was the banner company.   The following are the officers and men who went out: William L. Cowan, captain; Robert H. Ford, 1st lieutenant; George E. Gee, 2d lieutenant; Thomas R. Hardwick, Almon C. Barnard, Jesse R. Decker, I. H. Crosman, sergeants; David W. Manning, Harry Parsons, H. H. Van Dake, Thomas L. Ostrom, corporals; James B. Potter and Gregory Shaver, musicians.

Privates.—O. Aldrich, Charles Archer, Charles Averill, Lucius F. Brown, James Bailey, F. F. Barber, William H. Barnett, M. W. Bliton, Thomas Bowie, John H. Brown, W. F. Burr, A. A. Bagley, George Carpenter, George Chamberlain, Daniel Chamberlain, Martin Coon, Ira S. Cross, William E. Crissey, Ellery I. Delano, James Derrick, George Drain, Stephen Ennis, H. Farnham, George Fisher, D. Glenn, Clark E. Gould, Abram Haner, Bruce Herrington, Henry Hike, N. B. Hopkins, Lowell Howe, Nelson Jenkins, Daniel Johns, Phil Lapp, Andrew Lee, James A. Lewis, John Lyon, Artemas Maxon, R. P. Merrill, James McDermit, Arthur O'Neil, Martin Pilgrim, W. H. Randall, Almon Secore, Robert Scovell, Joseph Shaw, William Shaw, William Smith, F. D. Smith, Andrew Seiber, Andrew Strobel, Paddock L. Tucker, Charles H. S. Tessey, Carmel D. Townsend, Edward Tibbitts, Randolph Tubbs, Arthur Tumalty, Peter Van Valkenburg, Charles B. Vickery, Ira Woodin, Benjamin Winans, Amos B. Wyman, Millard D. York, Menden Young.

THE 25TH IND. BATTERY.

THIS valiant company was recruited in the counties of Orleans, Genesee, and Niagara, and we have taken pains to give the Genesee County men as correctly as possible.   They were mustered in at Lockport, N. Y., in September, 1862, and in December went to New York and became part of the forces of Gen. Banks. They sailed to Fortress Monroe, thence to Ship Island, but were wrecked on the coast of Florida; were picked up by a gunboat and landed at Key West, and in January, 1863, sailed to New Orleans. They were in the siege of Port Hudson, and in the Red River campaign. In the spring of 1865 they went on the expedition to Mobile, and were mustered out at Rochester, N. Y., in July, 1865. The officers and men from Genesee County were: Lieutenant I. D. Southworth, mustered out as captain, then of Byron; Albert Cook, 1st lieutenant, of Alabama; Lieut. James F. Emery and Henry M. Graves, Batavia; Peter Lester, Addison Gates, J. H. Smock, B. F. Ackerson, and Patrick Sage, of Alabama; Aaron Hartwell, J. Madigan, Jacob Miller, William Shelt, Frank McCann, William Wilgin, Frank D. Murdock, Peter Clinch, Paul Nothan, James Darkins, John J. Snyder, Peter Linn, Peter Tharnish, Fred Hartwick, Nathan Leonard, John Oberton, Joseph Brill, and Peter Busser, of Byron; Edgar A. Fisher, William R. Fisher, Charles A. Kendall, Edwin J. Niles, Valentine Riker, Wyman P. Fisk, Byron A. Fisk, and William Jones, of Stafford; William J. Pike, Arthur Little, and Cunningham Primrose, of Elba; William P. Bassett, of Bergen; Freeman Bailey, of Oakfield; and George Conway, Rodney Alexander, Almon R. Blodgett and Levi C. Cleveland, of Pembroke.

SOCIETIES AND ASSOCIATIONS.

GENESEE COUNTY AGRICULTURAL SOCIETY.

IT may not be generally known that this society had its origin in very early years, for June 22, 1819, a meeting was called and met at the house of Hinman Holden. Joseph Ellicott was elected president, and Hon. Samuel M. Hopkins was elected president *pro tem.*, and Parmenio Adams, treasurer *pro tem.* It was agreed to raise $500 for the meeting and exhibition in October, $150 of the amount to be for expenses and $350 for premiums. A committee was also appointed to examine farms, they to be allowed $2 per day each for their time. Col. Green and Col. Touner were appointed marshals The annual fair was ordered held on the second Monday in October. Another record we find in June, 1832, when Jacob Le Roy was chosen president.

The county has shown an uncommon interest in agricultural affairs, establishing a strong, perpetual society very early, and by its continued zeal still sustains large and profitable meetings annually.

In 1839—51 years ago—the present organization was established, and for the first 20 years annual fairs were held at suitable places in and around Batavia. About 30 years ago the formidable proportions of the society called for greater facilities, and the purchase of suitable grounds and erection of adequate buildings was at once effected. A good half-mile track for the development of stock has long been a prominent feature to the grounds. At this writing (spring of 1889) there is a project on foot to sell the present grounds, purchase elsewhere a more commodious site, and erect new and larger buildings.[1] The society is strong and prosperous, and for the past half century has not failed in its meetings and fairs The minutes of meetings prior to 1870 cannot be found, but we give the names of such officers as the books now in use furnish:

1870.—I. A. Todd, president; L. R. Bailey, secretary; Augustus N. Cowdin, treasurer.

1871.—George Burt, president; L. R. Bailey, secretary.

1872.—E. G. Townsend, president; G. H. Robertson, secretary; A. R. Warner, treasurer.

1873.—M. N. Moulthrop, president; F. M. Jameson, secretary; A. R. Warner, treasurer.

1874.—S. B. Lusk, president; J. H. McCulley, secretary; A. R. Warner, treasurer.

1875.—Warren J. Tyler, president; J. H. McCulley, secretary; A. R. Warner, treasurer.

1876.—Cortland Crosman, president; E. R. Hay, secretary; A. R. Warner, treasurer.

1877.—I. S. Durfee, president; E. R. Hay, secretary; A. R Warner, treasurer.

1878.—Albert Parker, president; J. H. Robson, secretary; E. L. Kenyon, treasurer.

1879.— C. W. Van De Bogart, president; N. Bogue, secretary; R. A. Maxwell, treasurer.

1880.—C. W. Van De Bogart, president; N. Bogue, secretary; R. A. Maxwell, treasurer.

1881.—John H. McCulley, president; George W. Pratt, secretary; R. A. Maxwell, treasurer.

1882.—Eli Taylor, president; J. B. Neasmith, secretary; J. Holley Bradish, treasurer.

1883.—D. L. Hodgson, president; Nelson Bogue, secretary; O. Town, Jr., treasurer.

1884.—Nelson Duguid, president; J. M. McKenzie, secretary; B. George Kemp, treasurer.

1885.—N M. Duguid, president; J. M. McKenzie, secretary; B. George Kemp, treasurer.

1886.—B. F. Peck, president; J. M. McKenzie, secretary; B. George Kemp, treasurer.

[1] March 8, 1890, by a vote of 269 to 235, the society decided to purchase what is known as the Redfield site, the price agreed upon being $6,000. This is the old driving park property of 23½ acres and eight and one-half acres additional on the east side of the track, with an eight-rod roadway out to West Main street, and includes the race-track, stables, wells, fences, judges' stand, etc. The eight and one-half acre addition runs east from the driving park 16 rods, and in it there is an oak grove of two and one-half acres. March 19th about two additional acres were purchased of Mr. Redfield for .$200. The society now has nearly 35 acres of land.

1887.—Nelson Bogue, president; J. M. McKenzie, secretary; B. George Kemp, treasurer.

1888.—E. J. Ingalsbe, president; Frank B. Redfield, secretary; William Torrence, treasurer.

1889.—R. R. Losee, president; James Z. Terry, vice-president; Dwight Dimock, second vice-president; L. F. Rolfe, secretary; F. B. Parker, treasurer.

The directors, one from each town, are chosen each year at the January meeting, who, with the officers, have the general management of the fairs. A healthy premium list, prompt payment of awards, and the general interest taken in the affairs of the society have made the Genesee County Agricultural Society a model worthy of imitation, and its long years of prosperity are only an earnest of its stability and usefulness.

The fiftieth annual fair of the society was held on the grounds on Ellicott street in September, 1889. At the regular annual meeting of the officers in January, 1890, it was voted to sell these grounds to the Geneva and Buffalo Railroad Co., who are to build a railroad. At this meeting the following officers were elected: James Z. Terry, president; Dwight Dimock, vice-president; John M. McKenzie, second vice president; L. F. Rolfe, secretary; Fred Parker, treasurer.

GENESEE COUNTY AUXILIARY BIBLE SOCIETY.

THIS society was originally organized in July, 1818, but no record has been found of its meetings prior to 1833. On the 6th of September, 1833, a meeting of the friends of the society and Bible cause was held in Le Roy, and it was resolved to reörganize the Genesee Bible Society under a new constitution. This was done. One of the articles of the constitution adopted was that " the sole object of this institution shall be to encourage a wider circulation of the Holy Scriptures without note or comment.' The officers chosen at that meeting by the society were Colonel Martin O. Coe, president; Deacon Hinds Chamberlain and Samuel Grannis, vice-presidents; Seth M. Gates, secretary; and Colonel S. M. Gates, treasurer.

During the 70 years of its existence the society has made several canvasses of the county for the distribution of the Scriptures, and ample provision has been made for supplying by special agents the inmates of the county-house, jail, and all prisoners leaving the jail with Bibles; also for supplying all hotels in the county and portions of the trains of cars passing through it. The society has kept up its annual contributions to the American Bible Society, to which it is a valuable auxiliary.

The presidents since 1833 have been: Martin O. Coe, who was chosen that year; P. L. Tracy, in 1840; J. E. Tompkins, in 1851; P. L. Tracy, in 1853; John Fisher, in 1864; A. J. Bartow, in 1867; John Fisher, in 1872; A. D. Lord, M. D., in 1873; R. L. Selden, in 1875; Rev. A. D. Wilbur, in 1876; Rev. William Swan, in 1881; Rev. John W. Sanborn, in 1883; Rev. William W. Totherob, in 1884. The officers of 1888–89 were: Rev. A. D. Draper, president; Rev. C. W. Mitchell, Hon. E. C. Walker, Hon. Eli Taylor, and Rev. W. W. Totherob, vice-presidents; James P. Parsons, secretary; F. B. Gleason, treasurer.

AUXILIARY AID SOCIETY.

To the State Charities Aid Association.

IN November, 1883, a number of benevolent ladies and gentlemen of Genesee County organized this society by the adoption of a constitution, the first article of which read as follows:

" The name of this association shall be ' The Local Visiting Committee of the Gene-see County Poor-House, State of New York,' and its object shall be to visit regularly and systematically all the departments of the Genesee County poor-house, with a view to the mental, moral, and physical improvement of its pauper inmates ; and to bring about such reforms as may be practicable."

About 40 members combined in this association, and F. C. Lathrop, of Le Roy, was made the president; J. B. Worthington, of Batavia, vice-president; Mrs. Gardner Fuller, secretary; and S. Massey, treasurer. An executive committee consisting of the officers and Rev. Dr. Hitch-cock, Rev. Mr. Totherob, and Rev. Mr. Zimmer was appointed. The same officers continue, except that Mrs. M. E. Sheffield is the present in-cumbent of the positions of secretary and treasurer. Every member of the society is a committee for the purposes set forth in the first article of their constitution. The society has had committees of three or four each that have made periodical visits to the county house. The society has suggested and assisted in the introduction of many improvements that have greatly ameliorated the condition of the unfortunate inmates.

SUNDAY-SCHOOL ASSOCIATION.

THIS association was organized at a meeting held in the Baptist Church, Batavia, in October, 1857. Its object was to advance the great interest of Sunday-schools by affording a medium of communication among all the schools of the county, and giving facilities for improvements in meth-ods of work by an interchange of ideas and views among the workers, and exercises in these different methods suggested. In furtherance of the object of this society meetings have been held regularly in various parts of the county; addresses have been delivered; discussions and exercises have been successfully engaged in; and the interest in and utility of the cause has been greatly promoted.

The lack of records of the proceedings of the society causes a deficiency in the mention of the names of those who have done efficient work, and of the many improvements and much good service done. The pastors of the churches and many laymen throughout the county have given it their hearty coöperation, and have labored with commendable zeal to aid in the success which has crowned the efforts of the association. The present officers are A. J. Rumsey, of Bethany, president; Rev. C. W. Sweet, of Elba, secretary; and a vice-president from each town in the county.

GENESEE COUNTY PIONEER ASSOCIATION.

THIS county has ever shown more zeal in its early settlement than its neighbors, and has now a large association that bears the name of this heading. On the 25th of August, 1869, a large number of pioneers and citizens met at Union Hall, Batavia, to take into consideration the organization of such a society. Stewart Chamberlain was appointed chairman of the meeting, and Marcus L. Babcock, secretary. The following persons were made a committee to draft a constitution and rules to govern the society: Hon. Moses Taggart, Batavia; Sylvester Willis, Oakfield; Alanson Fisher, Darien; Samuel Scofield, Eden; Stewart Chamberlain, Le Roy; Marcus L. Babcock, Batavia; Augustus P. Hascall, Le Roy. This committee reported at a meeting held October 5th, and a suitable constitution was adopted. A committee was appointed—one from each town—to report a set of officers for the association, who reported the following, and who were elected: Heman J. Redfield, president; Seth Wakeman, vice-president; Phineas Ford, secretary; Augustus P. Hascall, assistant secretary; James R. Mitchell, treasurer. A vice-president from each town was also elected.

At the annual meeting June 13, 1871, eight were reported as having died during the year, and large numbers joined the association. The officers elected were Moses Taggart, president; David Seaver, secretary.

1872.—Alden S. Stevens, president; David Seaver, secretary; 11 reported as having died.

1873.—Benjamin Pringle, president; David Seaver, secretary; 12 reported as having died.

1874.—Benjamin Pringle, president; David Seaver, secretary.

1875.—J. R. Mitchell, president; J. M. Waite, secretary.

1876.—J. R. Mitchell, president; J. N. Beckley, secretary.

1877.—Albert Rowe, president; Safford E. North, secretary.

1878.—Albert Rowe, president; S. E. North, secretary.

1879.—Albert Rowe, president; S. E. North, secretary.

1880.—Israel M. Peck, president; S. E. North, secretary.

1881.—James R. Mitchell, president; Frank S. Wood, secretary.

1882.—Lucius Atwater, president; Frank S. Wood, secretary.

1883.—Lucius Atwater, president; Frank S. Wood, secretary.

1884.—Albert Rowe, president; Frank S. Wood, secretary.

1885.—Lucius Atwater, president; Frank S. Wood, secretary.

1886.—Lucius Atwater, president; Frank S. Wood, secretary.

1887.—Lucius Atwater, president; Frank S. Wood, secretary.

1888.—Hon. E. C. Walker, president; H. F. Peck, vice-president; J. H. Gates, secretary and treasurer; with a vice-president in each town, which are named each year.

The society has accumulated a vast fund of pioneer history, and its annual meetings in June are very interesting. Hon. Norman Seymour, the historian, reported, in an address before the association in 1878, that 53 of the pioneers who settled between 1801 and 1828 in the county were at that date enjoying good health. The officers for 1889 were Rev. L. Atwater, Batavia, president; O. S. Kidder, Alexander, vice-president; J. H. Yates, Batavia, secretary and treasurer.

STATE INSTITUTION FOR THE BLIND.

GENESEE COUNTY was selected for this institution, and its selection shows the good judgment of those having it in charge. It occupies a beautiful site about half a mile north of the court house in Batavia. The law for its establishment was enacted April 27, 1865. The act provided for the appointment of five commissioners to select a site for the institution, three to superintend its building, and a board of trustees to superintend its affairs after its completion. The commissioners to select a site were Hon. E. W. Leavenworth, Syracuse; B. F. Manierre, New York city; James Ferguson, Ovid; O. K. Woods, Chazy; and M. M. Southworth, Lockport. In February, 1866, the board selected Batavia as the site, and that village presented to the State 50 acres of land at a cost of $10,000. In May, 1866, grading commenced; the contract to build was let to Henry T. Rogers, of Rochester; and the corner-stone was laid with appropriate ceremonies on September 6, 1866. A large amount of historical and interesting matter was deposited in the corner-stone : copies of the county papers, programme of the day's proceedings, copy of the act founding it, a continental bank note, a provincial note, a note of the·Bank of Attica and history of the bank, postal currency, his-tory of Batavia, subscribers to the grounds, copy of minutes of first court in Batavia, in 1803, photographs of village trustees, and list of building committee, trustees, and State and federal officers.   In July, 1868, the institution was formally delivered to the trustees.

The building is of brick, three stories high above the basement, which is of limestone quarried from the site ; on this is a broad belt of Lock-port freestone ; the building fronts the south, and consists of four struct-ures—a front and rear center buildings, and two wings connected by corridors.   The length of the entire front is 266 feet, and depth, includ-ing portico, 185.   The basement contains the laundry, bathing-rooms, water-closets, heating apparatus, etc., and the other stories are conven-iently arranged for offices, school-rooms, sleeping-rooms, etc., for 150 pupils or more.   It is heated by steam, and its sanitary arrangements cannot be excelled.   The amount paid for building, stables, cisterns, cooking ranges, engines, etc., was $244,587.24.   In July, 1868, Dr. A. D. Lord took charge of the institution ; school was opened Septem-ber 2, the same year, with 40 pupils during the month..   Seventy-four pupils were enrolled during the first year.   Mrs. E. W. Lord was ap-pointed superintendent in June, 1875.   An efficient corps of teachers is employed, and the institution takes the highest rank.   The annual re-port for 1888 shows the number of pupils for the year 140—75 boys, 65 girls ; the whole number who have received instruction since its founda-tion is 671.

Its annual election of officers occurs in June of each year, and the in-cumbents for 1888—to June, 1889—were Lee R. Sanborn, president ; Levant McIntyre, secretary ; and Gerrit S. Griswold, treasurer.

It is due to the memory of Dr. Lord (the foremost in the organization of the institution, and so long in charge) to give a brief notice of his life.

Asa D. Lord was born in Madrid, St. Lawrence County, N. Y., in 1816.   He taught school at the age of 17, and then pursued a course of study at Potsdam Academy.   In 1837 he went to Willoughby, Ohio, and opened up a private school.   In 1839 he was chosen principal of Western Reserve Teachers Seminary, at Kirtland, Ohio, where he also studied medicine.   In 1846 he started the publication of the *Ohio School Journal,* and continued at journalistic work for 10 years.   In 1847 he

was superintendent of schools in Columbus, Ohio, and in 1856 was appointed superintendent of the Ohio Institution for the Blind   In 1863
he was licensed to preach, and in 1868, after 12 years as instructor for
the blind in Ohio, was invited to take charge of the new institution then
erecting at Batavia, where for nearly seven years he passed a busy, fruitful life.   He died in 1875.   The wife of Dr. Lord succeeded him in the
managment (she had been a teacher in the literary department), and resigned her position in 1877.   She was succeeded by James McLeod, who
served one year, then A. D. Wilbor, D. D., a minister of the Methodist
Episcopal Church, was appointed, who served acceptably for five years,
when the present efficient superinteneent, Arthur G. Clement, M. A.,
took charge, and spares no pains to fully meet the expectations of the
State at large.

Arthur Galette Clement, B. A., M. A., superintendent of the Institution for the Blind, was born in Bethany, December 31, 1854, a son of
Orson J. and Anna J. (Wait) Clement.   His grandfather (Isaac) and
wife came from Vermont at an early day, and resided in Bethany until
their decease.   Ira Wait (his mother's father) was also an early settler of
the same town, living there all his life.   The parents of A. G. Clement
both died in 1876.   The father was a teacher and farmer.

The primary education of Prof. Clement was begun in the district
schools, continued in Batavia, and supplemented by the advantages derived from attendance at Alexander and Wyoming Seminary.   He subsequently entered the University of Rochester, graduating therefrom in
1882, with the degree of B. A., since which has been added that of M. A.
Beginning as teacher in district schools he has always devoted himself
to educational matters, and was principal of the Bergen public schools.
In 1883 he was elected superintendent of the Institution for the Blind, and
has educated himself to a high standard of the requirements of the position, and has held the office longer than any former superintendent
(March, 1890).   At a convention of the American Association for the
Blind he made an able address, which was highly commended, and will
yet achieve a still higher position among educators.   In September,
1883, he was married to Miss Emma C., daughter of Henry Ward,
an old resident of Bergen, and they have two children, Louisa W. and
Edith M.

RAILROAD3.

By the wisdom of its founders the center of Genesee County was
located in the great trail between the East and the West, and the lines of

railways—not leaving a town without such facilities—are numerous. The agitation for railroads began in 1831. The New York Central Railroad was first opened from Rochester to Bergen, and the cars for a time were hauled by horses between those two points. The road was built and opened to Batavia in 1837, and to Buffalo in 1843. This road extends in a southwesterly direction from Bergen, through Byron, Stafford, Batavia, Pembroke, and the northwest corner of Darien. The Canandaigua and Niagara Falls branch of the New York Central Railroad enters the county at Le Roy, passing through Stafford, Batavia, and Pembroke. A branch of this road extends south from Batavia to Attica.

The New York, Lake Erie and Western Railroad, main line, passes through Bethany, Alexander, and Darien to Attica and Buffalo. The Rochester branch of the same corporation, on its line to Buffalo, passes through Le Roy, Stafford, Batavia, and Alexander to Attica.

The "State Line," or Rochester and Pittsburg Railroad, passes through Le Roy and Pavilion in a southeasterly course.

The West Shore Railroad enters the county at Bergen and passes through Bergen, Byron, Elba, Oakfield, and Alabama, thence to Buffalo.

The Delaware, Lackawanna and Western Railroad passes through Pavilion, Bethany, Alexander, and Darien, thence to Buffalo.

The new line called the Geneva and Buffalo Railroad, controlled by the Lehigh Valley Railroad Co., is located through the towns of Le Roy, Stafford, Batavia, Pembroke, and Darien, and the company expects to build and complete the same before 1891.

No county as a whole in New York State has better railroad facilities than Genesee. Its rolling, rich land in every town has a market within its own limits for every product, and the facilities for transportation render the price of products the highest possible to benefit the producers.

FRUIT INTERESTS.

GENESEE COUNTY, located in the territory known as the lake region of Western New York, with its diversity of soil and favorable climatic conditions, has long been recognized as peculiarly adapted to fruit growing. Its products have been eagerly sought in the markets of the country, and the fact that large plantations have been devoted to this industry renders the fruit crop an important item in the material and pecuniary interests of the county. The early history of the industry was mainly the growing of the apple, pear, and peach, and while the labors of the first propagators would now be considered quite insignificant, yet to their efforts and enterprise is the county indebted for much of its past and present progress and success.

About the year 1820 E. Cook, of Byron, started small nurseries, mostly of apples, from which many thrifty bearing orchards are now standing. Then followed that of Col. Pettibone, of Elba, in 1824, who maintained for many years a well kept and, for that period, extensive nursery. Later, Lyman Hollis planted a few acres of fruit and ornamental trees. Following close to these were the diminutive plantings of D. H. Bogue, which furnished the rudimental instruction and training of his sons, the " Bogue Brothers," and which in later years enabled them the more successfully to conduct their extensive business.

Later, somewhere in the forties, A. H. Norris, of Stafford, commenced propagating peaches, for his own setting, and also selling through the county, paying $1 per bushel for the few pits he used, and obtaining buds from Rochester. This proved so profitable that he started other fruits,— apples, cherries, pears, and quinces,— importing quince stock from France for propagating the dwarf pear, and early in the " fifties " sending large quantities to California,—40,000 at one time,—also quantities of stock to Buffalo, where he found market for thousands of cherries. He started a quince orchard, and the product found a ready market at $7 per barrel by the car load. He also started orchards of apple, pear, peach, and plum trees, of which he has, at present, about 100 acres apples, 20 acres dwarf Duchess pears, 5 acres of peaches, and 1,000 yellow-egg plum trees. Following him were Alvirus Loomis, who started a small nursery in Byron, afterwards removing to Batavia, under the firm name of Loomis & Hall, where they continued till about 1864, when both sold out and moved West.

In the fall of 1865 Nelson Bogue made his first planting of a few rods of apple seedlings, on rented ground, near the village of Attica. Here he remained, his business, meanwhile, increasing to the extent that he was not able to obtain available land to warrant extensive business, till in 1872, with his brother, T. Bogue, he bought the farm of W. C. Moreau, three miles north of Batavia, which formed the nucleus of his present extensive nurseries.

But in the early history of fruit raising in the county it was not till centers of population, the cities of the country, became large consumers of fruit, and the establishment of railroads, as a means of transportion, made these markets available, that the production of the larger fruits was of any commercial or pecuniary value. Before this period no value was placed on the apple beyond the home consumption, expecting, perhaps, a few sweet ones for stock, and peaches were allowed to rot in quantities on the ground. Now the thousands of barrels of apples and pears, which are shipped from the county in fruitful years, and the value of the receipts to the farmer and fruit grower, are such that a failure of the crop is a financial calamity. Probably no section of the country is better adapted to the production of long-keeping apples, like the Rox Russet, than the southern towns of Bethany and Pavilion, among whose orchards the "Smeads" and "Pages" have been famous, whose success has been for years attested by the large profits which have been realized from them. In this county, too, the Northern Spy is grown in large quantities, and nowhere more perfectly, and all the finest varieties of winter fruit are here successfully grown and shipped to all parts of the United States and Europe.

The dwarf pear has been quite extensively planted (mostly of the Duchess variety), and probably nowhere grown more successfully, many orchards proving very remunerative, among which are those of "Bishop," of Le Roy, Bond and others, of Pavilion, Eli, Taylor, and Ford, of Elba, William Page, of Bethany, who, for the crop of 1888, from less than five acres, received nearly $2,000; also N. H. Green, of Byron, who, from an orchard of a few acres, received for the last three or four crops a net return of nearly $200, per acre. Among the first dwarf pear orchards planted was that of L. Rathbone, of Oakfield, which produced large quantities of fine fruit, but which finally became unprofitable, and has been removed.

In the year 1862 Elias Cook, of Bryon, commenced the planting of about the first extensive apple orchard in the county, which finally covered about 50 acres, and which contained nearly 2,400 trees in a body, embracing principally the leading varieties of winter fruit grown in Western New York.

Small fruits of all kinds succeed well in nearly all parts of the county, and where properly managed prove fairly profitable, and will undoubtedly continue to do so as the consumption is yearly increasing, besides the demand at the canning factory, now located at Batavia, which uses large quantities.

GAZETTEER OF TOWNS.

ALABAMA.

ALABAMA, the northwest town in Genesee County, was erected from Shelby, Orleans County, April 17, 1826, and originally called "Gerrysville," in honor of Elbridge Gerry, ex-vice-president. The name was changed to Alabama (signifying "here we rest"), April 21, 1828, and in 1832 a portion of the town of Wales, Erie County, was annexed. The Tonawanda Creek flows through the southwest and west portions of the town, from which a feeder of the Erie Canal is taken. This creek also runs through the lands of "the Reservation of the Tonawanda band (or tribe) of the Seneca Indians," occupying a strip of land two miles wide, and comprising about one-fourth of the area of this town. A portion of the well-known Tonawanda swamp also skirts the northwest portion of the town, which by modern drainage has been made some of the most productive land in that section. Oak Orchard Creek is in the northeast portion. The same vein of limestone that runs in Oakfield also forms a portion of the lower part of this town.

"Alabama Sour Springs," also called "Oak Orchard Acid Springs," celebrated for their medicinal purposes, are located on road 7, in the northern part of the town, in the "swamp," on a little elevation two and a half to four feet above the surrounding surface, within a circle of 50 rods, and no two alike; eight in all have been discovered and analyzed, three of which are of an acid nature, one sulphur, one magnesia, one iron, and one of a gaseous nature, affording gas enough to light 50 ordinary gas burners. In one instance three of them issue from one mound within a few feet of each other. An hotel has been erected on road 8, one-half mile from the springs, and the water conducted by pipes to that building.

The earliest settlement in the town of which we have any record is that of James Walsworth, in 1806, who also kept the first tavern, whose

8

children, twins, were the first born in the town.   Other early settlers are
enumerated, as follows, as near in the order of their advent as can be
ascertained:·

In 1814 John and James Richardson, Jr., and Hannah Carr and Samuel
Sheldon ; in 1815 William Daniels ; in 1817 Jones Kinne and Benjamin
Gumaer, and Henry Howard, who taught a school in a log house.   E. F.
Norton located in 1819; Robert Harper, James Peter, and Joseph Holmes
about 1821 ; James Gardner in 1822 ; Elder Samuel Whitcomb in 1824,
who erected the first saw-mill; Samuel Basom in 1825; Selah Vosburgh
in 1826; and Thomas R.Wolcott in 1827.   Jesse Lund, Gideon M. Taylor,
David Webster and brother Leonard, and Nahum Loring, who opened
an early store, came in 1828 ; Sterling Hotchkiss came in 1829; Daniel
Thayer in 1830, and also Ryal Ingalsbe and Elijah Brooks Ingalsbe.
Gideon Howland and Parley V. Ingalsbe came in 1832; Elijah and Ebenezer Ingalsbe in 1834; and Samuel Burr, James Burr, and Isaac Dual
the same year. N. Baker, Jr., was an early merchant, in 1834.   Jacob and
David Martin located in 1835; Anson Norton in 1836; and James Filkins,
George Wight, and Abbott Wight in 1837.   A. Johnson came in 1840,
was a postmaster, kept hotel in one of the old-time taverns at the Center,
and was a prominent man of the town.   He had four daughters, one of
whom married the Hon. Albert Rowe, of Alexander, and one married
Hon. Robert W. Nichols, of Alabama.   Later settlers and business men
were the Piersons; also William Price, who built a steam saw-mill in 1861.
S. C. Bateman, who was a druggist and physician, and Dr. Pettibone
came about 1840, and Rogers Macumber in 1841.

The first annual town meeting was held April 17, 1826, and the following officers chosen: Benjamin Gumaer, supervisor; Chester Wolcott,
town clerk; David Goodrich, Charles P. Brown, and Elijah Craig, assessors.   At this meeting $25 was voted for roads and $50 for schools.
Seven road districts were established, and John S.Wolcott, Joseph Holmes,
and Ephraim Divinny elected commissioners of highways, by whom overseers of roads in the districts were appointed to work them.   The total
number of persons assessed at this meeting were 73.

The supervisors for the town have been as follows: Benjamin Gumaer,
1826–28; Charles P. Brown, 1829–30; George F. Dinsmore, 1831–32;
Guy B. Shepard, 1833–35; Thomas R. Wolcott, 1836–37; Abraham
Bolton, 1838–39; Oren Densmore, 1840–41; Charles P. Brown, 1842;
John Crombie, 1843–44; William McComber, 1845–46; Charles P. Brown,
1847 ; Jacob Winslow, 1848 ; Chester Cabot, 1849–50 ; Jacob Winslow,

1851; Charles P. Brown, 1852–53 ; E. B. Warren, 1854 ; Jacob Winslow, 1855–56; Chauncy Williams, 1857–58 ; B. R. Warren, 1859; Edward Halsey, 1860 ; Chauncy Williams, 1861–64; Aden G. Gage, 1865–67 ; Volney G. Knapp, 1868–69; Joseph W. Holmes, 1870–74; Volney G. Knapp, 1875–76; Sabert H. Basom, 1877–78 ; R. W. Nichols, 1879–81; Charles W. Roberts, 1882–83; Sabert H. Basom, 1884–88; Augustus T. G. Zurhorst, 1889.

About the years 1848 to 1856 Alabama Center was the scene of a crime committed by a woman, Polly Franklin, who married Henry Hoag about 1844. Their children, Rosa and Viola, died suddenly, and soon the father died, then another child, Frances, followed him. After the death of Mr. Hoag his widow married Otto Frisch, but soon was deserted by him. About this time suspicion was aroused, and S. E. Filkins (counselor) caused an investigation to be made, which revealed the fact that some of her family had died from the effects of poison, large quantities of arsenic having been administered to them. She was arrested and tried three times, and being finally found guilty was sentenced to be hung, but eventually was imprisoned for life.

"In 1866 a very large white oak tree was cut down upon the farm of Mr. True, which was evidence of the wonderful strength and fertility of the soil of that section. It measured four feet through at the butt, was straight for 60 feet to the first branch, where it was three feet in diameter. It showed, when cut, 12 circles, or years' growth, to the inch, thus making it about 504 years old. The most remarkable feature on splitting up one of the cuts about 20 feet from the butt was a cavity in the heart, containing about one pint of sound beech nuts. How long they had been deposited there must be left to conjecture. The trunk was split up, and 1,200 fence stakes, 500 other pieces, and eight cords of wood were chopped from the tree."

In the town are the villages of Alabama Center, Wheatville, Smithville, and Basom, a postoffice on the West Shore Railroad.

ALABAMA CENTER, situated north of the center of the town, is a pleasant and enterprising village, on the main road leading from Batavia to Lewiston, one of the earliest laid out roads on the Holland Purchase. Soon after the town organization, in 1826, Hiram Dual opened up a general store, and, though small, it was a great convenience to the settlers in that locality. Soon after James Filkins built the store on the site of Zurhorst Hall. The early blacksmithing was attended to by Samuel Winchell and Shubael Franklin. James Filkins was a shoemaker, and also a tanner and currier for a large section of country.   David Garry kept a tavern about one and one-half miles east of the Center, where the first town meeting was held.   The village contains two churches (Methodist Episcopal and Baptist), one store, one hotel, and postoffice (Alabama), and there is a daily line of stages from Batavia to the Center, and also a line to Medina.   In the vicinity of the Center is a fruit evaporator, operated each year, and a creamery.   There are two steam saw-mills, one three-quarters of a mile west, run by William Price, built in 1861, and burned in 1872 and rebuilt by him the same season, with a capacity of 150,000 feet of lumber annually.   There are also a cheese factory, a heading-mill, two blacksmith shops, one wagon shop, about 50 houses, and 400 inhabitants.   The Model Creamery was built in 1888, by S. S. Parker.   It takes the milk of 400 cows, and makes both butter and cheese.

The Baptist Church was organized in 1832.   Elder Augustus Warren was the first minister in charge, and continued as such nearly all of his long and well-spent life, or until 1876.   The edifice was erected in 1850, at a cost of $2,000, and rebuilt, enlarged, and greatly improved in 1880, the seating capacity being for 200 members.   The valuation of the church property, including parsonage, is about $5,500.   In 1877 Rev. L. L. Stowell was in charge, followed in 1879 by Rev. Merrill Forbes, who served till 1884.   Rev. H. H. Thomas served in 1885–86, and Rev. J. B. Lenion in 1887.   At present the Rev. Increase Child is the minister, and the acting deacons are Ryal Ingalsbe, Charles Bloomingdale, George Hotch-kiss, and Albert P. Tuttle.

Connected with the Baptist Church organization is the Ladies' Home and Foreign Missionary Society.   Flor St. John is president; Sarah Bloomingdale, secretary; and Carrie Dewey, treasurer.

The Methodist Episcopal Church at Alabama Center was rebuilt in 1882.   It is a frame building capable of seating about 200 persons.   They have a membership of 75, and their property has a valuation of about $4,600.   Sunday-school services are held every Sunday.

The Baptist Church of Oakfield and Alabama, located at South Ala-bama, was organized about 1839, when a frame building for worship was erected, seating about 250 persons.   The Rev. J. C. Newman is in charge, with a membership of 50 persons.   The church property is valued at $4,000.

Excelsior Lodge, No. 638, I. O. G. T., was organized in March, 1887. The officers are Allen Norton, Evelyn Eaton, Daniel Ballou, Matie Eaton, William Jones, Minnie Jones, Mrs. S. C. Bateman, Abiah Jones, Anna

Ballou, William Cottringham, Seward Tumalty, and William Phillips. They meet weekly.

The Woman's Christian Temperance Union of Alabama Center was organized in 1886. Its officers are Mrs. Albert Tuttle, president; Mrs. J. P. Willis, vice-president; Mrs. L. Eaton, secretary; Mrs. William Cottringham, corresponding secretary; and Mrs. C. R. Phillips, treasurer. They meet each week.

WHEATVILLE, situated two and one-half miles east of Alabama Center, is located on the Batavia and Lewiston road, in a splendid farming section. There are about 40 houses and 200 inhabitants. Its settlement is co-existent with that of the town. Elder Whitcomb built the first sawmill in this vicinity, which was previous to 1820. Mr. Parrish and Levi Lee were early merchants, and Aaron Lanckton carried on business as a tanner and currier in 1838. John Wolcott kept a tavern here as early as 1822. A Mr. Young was the early blacksmith, Mr. Upton a shoemaker, and a Dr. Shepard looked after the physicial wants of the people and Elder Whitcomb the spiritual. The village contains a store, postoffice, two churches (Freewill Baptist and Roman Catholic), and two blacksmiths.

The Freewill Baptist Church was organized in 1824 by Elder Samuel Whitcomb, who was also its first minister, and for a long time he was the only minister in the town. The valuation of the church property is about $4,000. Rev. S. R. Evans is the present pastor.

St. Patrick's Roman Catholic Church.—There is a small church of this denomination in Wheatville, presided over by Father Connery, who is located at East Pembroke. When Father Barrett was stationed at East Pembroke, about four years ago, he began services in Wheatville, which finally resulted in a building being erected and a continuation of the visits of the priest who may be in charge in several places in the vicinity. The building will seat 150 persons, and cost $2,000.

SMITHVILLE (South Alabama p. o.) contains a Baptist Church, a store, and a postoffice, and is a station on the West Shore Railroad. The station is called Alabama. A hotel was built by Henry Ceder in 1884, who is the present proprietor. He has lately newly refurnished the hotel, and is prepared to accommodate an extensive travel.

The I. O. of O. F. of Alabama, No. 496, was organized several years ago. Its present officers are: L. B. Fisk, M. G.; William Cottringham, V. G.; Frank Vail, R. S; Charles Drake, P. S.; M. Mead, treasurer. They meet weekly.

BASOM postoffice was opened October 25, 1889, by Julius Ingalsbee,

postmaster.   It is a station on the West Shore Railroad, has a hotel, two
stores, Rowley & Eddy's lumber yard, and one blacksmith shop.

THE TONAWANDA RESERVATION is located in Erie and Genesee
counties, and originally contained over 45,000 acres, but has been reduced until now it embraces a tract of 7,547 acres, of which about 3,000
acres are cultivated to some extent, and of this amount one-half is leased
to white men.   The Indians have occupied and owned this land for more
than 100 years; and we quote here an extract from an article furnished
to the *Batavia Times* in 1874 by David Seaver, who had access to an
old work published in London in 1799, written by the Duke Rochefoucauld Liancourt, describing a journey taken by him from Philadelphia to
Niagara Falls in 1795, as follows:

" From Canawango (near Avon, and latterly called Canawaugus) to Buffalo and Niagara Falls the journey was made *via* Tonawango Indian Village, under the guidance of
one Poudrit (Poudry), a Canadian Frenchman, who, deserting from the English Army
at the close of the Revolution, married a squaw, settled at Tonawango, became a trader,
and lived in genuine Indian style."

Extract from the diary of John Maule, a traveler, in 1800 :

" At Tonawautee reside from 15 to 20 families of Seneca Indians, who are well supplied with fish from the creek.   Here also has been settled from the year 1794 Poudrit
(Poudry), a French Canadian ; he very cheerfully gave such refreshments to ourselves
and horses as his slender means would afford.   He converses in very good English, and
is well acquainted with the Seneca language."

Thus is verified the inhabiting of this section by the Indians long before the advent of our early pioneers.

The Indians number at this time about 560 persons, including 32
chiefs.   The population increases slowly.   The tribe has two sources of
revenue: one from the " National farm," the land set apart for the manual labor school, which is leased to individual Indians ; and the other is
rent received from white people for pasture land.   From these two
sources the nation derives about $150 per year.   The individual Indian
also leases land to white men, which is cultivated, but not occupied, by
them.   The nation also receives an annuity of about $6,500 from the
general government.

Politically these Indians have two parties, Pagan and Christian, the
former being largely in the majority and govern the tribe.   The law provides for the election of a president (for the tribe), who must be a chief,
and a clerk, marshal, and peacemakers.   William Parker, a chief, died in
1864.   He was in the War of 1812.   His wife was a niece of Red Jacket.
General Ely S. Parker, one of General Grant's staff, was born on the

Reservation. There are two mission schools upon the Reservation, one a Baptist and one a Presbyterian. There are also district schools taught by competent teachers.

Hon. T. W. Jackson is the Indian agent for the Six Nations. James Paxton is the assistant Indian agent, and William Paxton, superintendent of Indian schools.

In 1825 the Baptists organized a mission church on the Reservation, and built a log chapel. The Rev. Mr. Bingham had charge. At present their denomination has a brick church, which cost $4,000, seating 300 people, and a membership of 32. The Rev. John Griffin is pastor.

The Presbyterians, under Asher Wright, in 1870 started a mission. Their church cost $2,000, will seat 200 persons, and has 40 members, under the charge of Rev. John McMaster. The Rev. S. S. Ballou, of the Methodist Episcopal Church, in 1888 organized a mission under the auspices of the missionary board. Their house of worship, built of wood, will seat 100 persons, cost $400, and they have 18 members, now under the care of Rev. T. C. Bell, who officiates at Alabama Center.

Samuel Basom, son of Peter, born December 12, 1806, came to Alabama about 1825, settling on road 52, on the farm now owned by his son Harrison S. He made the first clearing on the farm and built a log house. About 1834 he married Matilda Piper, who bore him four children, Sabert H., Charles W., Harrison S., all of Alabama, and M. Louise, wife of William B. Chapman, of Ontario County. Mr. Basom died 1875, and his wife (born 1811) March 3, 1880.

Sabert H. Basom was born February 21, 1835, was always a resident here, and married Aramintha Starkweather and has three children, Genevieve, Mabel, and Clare. Mr. Basom has served two terms as justice of the peace, one year as highway commissioner, supervisor of the town nine years, and one year chairman of the board. He has also been a notary public, and since he was 25 years of age has been called upon to settle estates, having the reputation from the county judge of satisfactorily settling more than any other man in this part of the county.

Harrison S Basom was born April 30, 1840, on the farm where his father settled, residing there ever since, and of which he became sole owner in 1880. He married Eleanora Noble, of Alabama. He is a farmer, and has been town assessor since 1884.

Charles W. Basom was born July 8, 1836, and always resided in the town. He married Sarah A. Chamberlain.

Titus Bement, born 1771, married Eunice Lyke in 1795, and they were parents of nine children: Mahala, David, Olive, who married Joel Hill, Delina, Edward, Eunice, William H , who died young, Andrew Z., Philetus, who lives in Chautauqua County, and Edward, who was born in Ontario County and learned the wagon and blacksmith trade. He married Lydia, daughter of John and Deborah (Bates) Bird, located in Mayville, and engaged in business. Their children were Laura A., who married James D. Gregory, of Oakfield, 1851; Sarah M., who married Austin Ingalsbee, 1855, and resides at Elba; William, who died 1839; Emily, who died 1841; and Alpha E., of Alabama. Titus Bement came to Alabama in 1852, and located on the farm now occupied by his son Alpha E. He died March 22, 1866, and his wife March 18, 1874. They were members of the Methodist Episcopal Church.

Alpha E. Bement, born December 16, 1844, learned the carpenter and builders' trade, and married, January 10, 1866, Olive D., daughter of Schuyler and Mary A. (Winchell) Starkweather, of Alabama. Their children are Myron E., born August 8, 1869, who is now assistant cashier and telegraph operator in the W. S. R. R. freight office at Buffalo, and is married; and Emma Elizabeth, born January 12, 1876. Mr. Bement is a justice of the peace and resides at Alabama station.

James Gardner, born in Tompkins County in 1800, a farmer by occupation, came to Alabama in 1822. He married Betsey, daughter of William and Sabara (Adams) Wood, in 1831, and they had one daughter, Sabara Ann. Mr. Gardner was a hard working, industrious man. He died in 1853. His wife died in 1871. Sabara Ann married Jeremiah S. Beals, in 1848. He was the son of Seth and Chloe (Millon) Beals, who was born in Skaneateles, N. Y., in 1826, and came to Alabama in 1847. He taught school several terms. Their children were J. Adelbert, of Alabama; Albert G., also of Alabama; and Grace Anna, born 1868, who died 1879. J. Adelbert Beals was born 1849, married, January 3, 1871, Mary Elizabeth Vosburgh, and they have two sons and three daughters, viz.: Mattie Edith, born September 5, 1872; John A., born September 9, 1874; Daisy Estelle, born December 1, 1876; Lillie May, born June 27, 1882; and Leslie E., born April 21, 1885. Albert G. Beals was born 1857, and married, in 1874, Hannah, daughter of Joseph Safflin, and their children are Nora Inez, born 1876; Arthur G., born 1877; Jeremiah S., born 1879; Estelle, born 1882; Fanny L., born 1884; and May, born 1885. The wife died December 13, 1887. Jeremiah S. Beals is a farmer and resides on road 8. J. Adelbert Beals lives on road 15, and Albert G. resides on the Gardner homestead on road 14.

William F. Bell, M. D., was born in Westfield, Mass., in 1857. He was a graduate of the medical department of the Albany Medical College in 1880. He settled in Alabama in 1881, and died in 1890.

Henry Ceder, son of John and Mary (Block) Ceder, was born in Buffalo, 1856. At the age of 13 years he worked out among the farmers. When 20 years of age he worked a farm in Erie County. He came to Alabama in 1888 and bought the hotel (called Ceder Hotel) at the station, of which he is the proprietor, and also carries on a livery business. He married Augusta C., daughter of John and Elizabeth (Schradier) See, and their children are Belle Mary, born March 30, 1881; Edna, born December 22, 1883; and Henry, Jr., born August 29, 1887.

Rodman Clark was born in Rhode Island, and married Ruth Lemon. Soon after marriage they came to Geneseo, Livingston County, and built a log house, in which most of the family were born. Of the children born there Rodman and Gardner died on their way to Salt Lake City to join the Mormons; Christopher died on the farm; Ruth married David Orton, and died in Illinois; Huldah married William Bryant, and died in 1886; and William resides in Oregon. Rodman, Sr., for his second wife married Rhoda Markham.

Aaron Clark, son of Rodman, was born 1803, and died 1869. He married, in 1821, Mary Jane, daughter of Hugh and Jane (McBride) Gray. He farmed several years in Niagara County, and located in Alabama in 1844 and bought the hotel at the Center. Their children were. Louisa, who married Leander Dutton; Gardner, of Nebraska; William, of Tonawanda; Jane, who married Ezra Dutton, of Shelby; Rodman, who died in Shelby, 1870; Henry, of Nebraska; John, who died in infancy (1840); and Aaron, of Medina. Sarah Jane, wife of Aaron, Sr., died in 1840, and he married for his second wife Sarah Totten, widow of Sylvanus Parker, by whom he had children as follows: Maria, who married Cyrus Hamilton, of Sturgeon Bay, Wis.; Alice, who owns and occupies the homestead in Alabama; and Charles, who married Susie Phillips, of Sturgeon Bay, Wis.

Aaron Clark was born in Geneseo, October 7, 1827, came to Alabama when a young man, and married Elsie Jane, daughter of Gideon and Mary (Snyder) Howland, of Alabama, October 4, 1856. Soon after he located in Medina, and built the hotel which he occupied up to 1884. He was a kind and genial landlord, and justly entitled to the name "Old Sport" given him. There were four children born to them, viz.: Adelbert and Ira, who died in infancy; Carrie E., born 1861, married Robert

McConnell, in 1880, and has a son, Curtis, born November 15, 1882; and Mark, born 1866, who is a noted horse trainer. Aaron Clark's wife died in 1880. He married, second, Belle Lyon, widow of John Montgomery. Mr. Clark is fond of horses, and resides on West street, Medina.

Fred J. Clawson was born in 1857, reared on a farm, and married Mary Elizabeth, daughter of Henry and Bridget (McDermot) Hodges, of Alabama, February 22, 1884. Their children are Dora Emma, born March, 1886, and George Roland, born November 18, 1887. Mr. Clawson is a farmer, leasing the Frary farm, one-half mile east of Alabama Center. The father of Mr. Clawson was John Clawson, of Mecklenburg, and was married to Sophia Dora Tesno. They had four children, viz.: William, born 1853; Augusta, who married August Mehnke, of Alabama; Charles, who died young; and Fred J. They came to Oakfield in 1864, and to Alabama a few years later.

Isaac P. Dual, son of Preserved and Mary (Rice) Dual, was born in St. Lawrence County, N. Y., in 1810. He was a carpenter and builder by trade, and came to Alabama about 1834. He married, in 1836 Florilla, daughter of Amos and Betsey (Benjamin) Starkweather. Their daughter Charlotte L. married Myron St. John 1858, and died 1865. Messrs. Dual and Starkweather, in 1840, built the hotel at the Center. Mr. Dual kept it three years. He also held the office of justice of the peace for more than 30 years. He died 1887, aged 77 years, much respected by all. His wife died 1889.

George W. Dual, born in town March 21, 1843, at the age of 18 learned the trade of blacksmith and wagonmaker, began for himself in 1866, and now is owner of a prosperous business. He married Orril H., daughter of Levi and Susannah (Bixby) Fisk, in October, 1874. Their children are Grace Winfred, born July 11, 1876, and Maud Fisk, born April 28, 1879.

William Fenner, son of William, was a native of New Jersey. He married Lucena Jenks, and they were the parents of John F., Lucy Telithie, Melinda, Joseph, Nathaniel, and William. His wife dying, he married, again, a woman by the name of Salisbury, and they had one son, Calvin, who lives in Herkimer County, N. Y. The father of Nathaniel C. Fenner married Maria, daughter of William and Anna (Palmateer) Grimes, of Fairfield, N. Y. He was a farmer, came to Alabama about 1838, and located on the place where the son now lives. He died in 1860, and his wife in 1888. Both of them were consistent members of the Baptist Church. Their children were Lucy Ann, who married John Stockledger, of Michigan; Adelia, who married John Fishell, of Michigan; Melinda, who married Alvin Fellows, and second, Henry Stevens, of Michigan; Lorena, who married Morrison Jeffers, and died in Monroe County; Filipha, who married Jacob Smith, and died in Monroe County; John, of Michigan; Betsey, who married Levi Morse, of Michigan; Asenath, who married Isaac Horton, and died in Michigan; James W., who died in Darien; Mary, who married Enos Ingalsbe, of Indian Falls; Sophia, who married Emery Ackerson, of Indian Falls; Joseph, who died in childhood; William, who was killed at Cold Harbor, in the late war; Giles, who died in Michigan 1880; and Nathaniel C., who was born in Henrietta, N. Y., April 19, 1822. The latter came to Alabama in 1837, married, in 1840, Eliza, daughter of Gabriel and Clarissa (Dodge) Case, of Alabama, and they were parents of three children, viz.: F. Erwin, born 1845, enlisted in the army in 1862, and was reported missing at Cold Harbor; Clarissa J., who married, first, Daniel McDermott, whose children were Emily, George, Effie, and Bertha, and second, William Marble, by whom she has one son, Irwin, and lives in Dansville; and Rosell, who married Margaret Burg, and their children are Rosalia L., Lawrence, and Ruby. Mr. Fenner's wife died in 1853. His second wife, whom he married in 1881, was Maranda, daughter of Ignatus and Maranda (Marble) Lewis, widow of William Farmer. Their children are Ceneth E. (Mrs. John Wright), of Akron, and Rosabel (Mrs. Charles Moore), of Indian Falls. Mr. Fenner is a farmer, and lives one mile south of Alabama station.

James Filkins, son of Abram and Phebe (Saults) Filkins, settled in Attica, N. Y. He was a farmer, and also learned the curriers' trade. He married, in 1830, Abigail, daughter of Elder Heman and Clarissa (Brown) Jenkins, of Bethany. Elder Jenkins was a Freewill Baptist clergyman; Clarissa Brown was a daughter of Rev. Nathaniel Brown. The Filkins family came to Alabama in 1837, and he engaged in his business as currier at the Center. Their children were Dexter J., born 1831, who resides in Michigan; Augustus R., who died young; Stanley E., of Medina; Emily Cornelia, born 1838, who married Joel Smith, and resides in California (they have one daughter, Jessie); Lorenzo, who died in infancy; Sarah A., born 1844, who married James Stevens, and died 1884; Marion A., of Alabama, born 1842; Ellen M., born 1847, who married, first, Thomas Stevens, in 1865, and second, Ed. Tuttle, of Alabama, in 1887; and James, who died aged three years. Mr. Filkins was an energetic business man. He died in 1849. Stanley E. Filkins was born in Bethany, February 19, 1836, was educated at Austinburg, Ohio, read law with Brown & Glowacki, of Batavia, and was admitted to the bar in 1857 He then began practicing at Medina, where he has a large practice. He was appointed postmaster in 1877, and held the office continuously until 1889. He resides on West street, Medina. He was married, in 1872, to Louise Florence, daughter of Rev. Israel Chamberlain, of Lyndonville, and they have two daughters, Bertha Kate, born January 5, 1874, and Emma Louise, born February, 1877.

George Farnsworth, son of Joseph, born in Scipio, Cayuga County, N. Y., 1815, was brought up on the farm He married Anna Lounsbury, of Scipio, and they had children as follows: Maribath, who married Orville Adams, whose son George resides in Cayuga County (Mrs. Adams died 1889); Laura, who married George Preston, of Fowlerville, Mich.; James, who died in Michigan; Wealthy, who married Alonzo Gilbert, and died in Steuben County; and Philip, who was born in Springwater, N. Y., August 17, 1833, raised a farmer, and married, in 1855, Saraette, daughter of Frederick and Elizabeth (McMann) Westbrook. They lived several years at Springwater, and came to Alabama in the fall of 1864, buying the farm he now occupies. They had three children: Frank W., born 1859; Elizabeth, born 1862, who married William Sparling, of Alabama; and George, born 1872. Mr. Farnsworth owns and occupies the homestead where he first settled, near the railroad station, on road 53.

Benjamin Gumaer, son of Peter, was born in Orange County. When young he located in Onondaga County. He was a contractor, and came to this town in 1817 and built a log house. He was the first supervisor of the town, holding the office several years. He died in 1831, honored and respected by all. He married Patience, daughter of Ephraim Thomas, who survived him many years. Their children were Benjamin, who died in Canada; Lewis, who died in Bethany; Samuel, who went West; Margaret, who married William Lane, and died in Canada; Martha, who married Selah Vosburgh, and died 1849; James, of Alabama; Elizabeth, who married a Mr. Kent, and died in Canada; and Reuben, who died young.

James Gumaer was born in 1814; spent his early years on the farm; and married Elvira, daughter of Inman and Abigail (Thomas) Whipple, in 1841. Their children are Ira J. and Robert L., of Nebraska; Adelbert G., a physician, of Buffalo; Charles H., who went West; and Minnie E. The latter, born 1845, married Jacob Bloomingdale in 1870, whose children are Nellie Belle, born 1871, who is a teacher; Edith E., born 1875; Ralph F. A., born 1878; and Emma Maude, born 1881. The mother, Minnie E., died June 21, 1884; the father, Jacob, died 1887. James Gumaer and wife reside on their farm near Alabama Center.

Joseph Heston, a Quaker, was born in Bucks County, Pa. In 1826 or '27 he came to Batavia from Baltimore County, Md., and settled near Bushville. He died May 19, 1864. He had a family of 11 children, four of whom only are living, viz.: Martha A., widow of W. H. Potter, who resides in Batavia; John E., who resides at Mount Pleasant, Iowa; Rachel L., wife of John Pearson, who resides in Buffalo; and Lewis E. The latter was born November 1, 1812, in Baltimore County, came to Batavia with his parents, and has been a resident of the county since. He married Elizabeth Mason, of Lancaster County, Pa., and has been on the farm where he now resides for about 40 years. Their family were Augusta, who married A. H. Chase, of Philadelphia; Elizabeth (deceased); and Anna E., who married Peter M. Wise, M. D., of the Willard Asylum. Lewis E. commenced breeding Jersey cattle in 1877, and is one of the largest breeders in Genesee County. At one time he was one of the largest breeders of Merino sheep in the county, but has ceased business in that line.

Rev. Philip Houseknecht was born in Lycoming County, Pa., February 6, 1830. He was educated for the ministry, and graduated at Allegheny College, Meadville, in 1853, and has been a resident of this county since. He joined the Methodist Conference in 1853, first preached in Alexander, and has been active in the work, mostly as a local minister. He also has a large farm. His wife, Sarah, is the daughter of Philip Buchanan. They have three children: Philo B., Samuel L., and Isabelle, wife of Alfred Worthington.

Lyman Hitchcock came to Alabama in 1849, from Chautauqua County, and purchased a farm of 48 acres from the Holland Land Company, which proved to be Indian land. After clearing it he was obliged to vacate, losing all he had invested. He was born June 16, 1802, married Sallie Cabot, and raised 10 children, four of whom are living, two in Alabama, Marie, wife of Abel Wight, and W. Q. W. Q. Hichcock was born in Westfield, N. Y., January 2, 1842, came to Alabama with his parents, and married Alice, daughter of Rev. Benjamin Hunt. They had five children, all deceased. One, Walter, lived until four years of age.

Gideon Howland, son of Elisha and Elsie (Dual) Howland, was born in Washington County in 1804, came to Alabama in 1832, followed farming, and in 1827 married Mary Snyder. Their children were Margaret, who married Joseph Palmer, of Michigan; John, who died 1854; Peter, who died 1834; Elisha, of Michigan; Elsie, who married Aaron Clark and died in Medina, 1880; Mary, who died in infancy, 1843; Frances E., who married Peter Craine, of Alabama; and Ira P., who was born 1839, raised on a farm, and married, January 18, 1861, Margaret, daughter of James and Jane (McGowan) Wilson. Their children are Ida May, born December 26, 1861, who married Theodore Stafford, November 2, 1881, and they have a son, Floyd H., born July 30, 1887; and John G., born May 18, 1864, who married Ida Palmer and resides in Michigan. Ira P. Howland owns and occupies the Howland homestead one mile east of Alabama Center.

Hiram Hotchkiss, son of Moses and Lucy (Griswold) Hotchkiss, was born 1815. He married Lucy Sawen, of Bergen, in 1840. He came to Alabama and engaged in sawing lumber, and is a farmer on the Bement place. Their children were Eleanor, born 1843, married, first, Warren Studley, and had a daughter, Dora, and second, Amasa Hills, and has a daughter, Cora, who resides in Michigan; and George E. The latter was born in Alabama, December 3, 1845, reared on the farm, and married, July 3, 1865, Mary Elizabeth, daughter of David and Nancy (Duers) Hescock. Their children are George E., Jr., born May 24, 1872; Nellie Pearl, who died 1881, aged three years; and Frank S., born March 2, 1882. Mr. Hotchkiss is a farmer and does general insurance business, and resides near Alabama station, on road 52.

Sterling Hotchkiss, son of Moses and Lucy (Griswold) Hotchkiss, was born in Connecticut, 1803, and at the age of 14 came to Bergen and worked out among the farmers. He married, April 27, 1826, Anna, daughter of Aaron and Polly (Allen) Jacobs, of Bergen, and located in Alabama in 1829. He built a log house, where most of their children were born. They were parents of six children: Charlotte E., who married William Ingalsbe and died 1874; Charles, born 1829, who died young; Riley, born 1831, who died in Michigan, 1873; Rialto, born 1832, who died young; Almira M., born August 18, 1835, who married William Duers and had a daughter, Victoria E., who married Charles Anthony, and they have a son, Glenn; and Ann E., born January 14, 1847, who married Chester Hitchcock, and had a daughter, Ann E., who married Arthur J. Anthony in 1876, and had two children, Zella Ann and Alson S. Mrs. S. Hotchkiss resides on road 40.

Ebenezer Ingalsbe was a captain in the English army. Desiring to visit America he gave up his commission and secured passage on a ship. Arriving here he settled in Massachusetts, where he remained until his death. His son Ebenezer, born in Massachusetts, moved to Scipio, Cayuga County, where he died in the 70th year of his age. He married Phebe Easterbrooks. Their children were Elijah, born September 12, 1780; Ebenezer, born December 23, 1781; Phebe, born March 28, 1784; Azel, born February 14, 1786; Huldah, born January 4, 1789; Sally, born August 20, 1790; Adna, born January 11, 1793; Emory, born October 24, 1798; and Samuel, born in Hartford, N. Y., August 17, 1796. The latter located in Scipio, Cayuga County, at an early day, and engaged farming. He was a drum-major in the militia. He married, July 15, 1817, Mary, daughter of John and Barbara (Fishell) Bushman, of Scipio, and their children were Sally, born July 15, 1817, who married Ryal Ingalsbe, of Alabama; Ebenezer, born March 5, 1819, who resides in Michigan; John, of Michigan; Mary, who married William N. Walker, and died 1875; Phebe, who married Medad Norton, and died 1848; William, of Alabama; Clarissa, who married Ira Green, of Michigan; Amanda, who married Aaron Green, and died 1879; and Almira, who died May 20, 1855. Mr. Ingalsbe located in Alabama in 1834, on the place now occupied by Alpheus Ingalsbe. He and his wife were active members of the Baptist Church. He died 1848, and she 1879.

Ebenezer Ingalsbe, born in Byron, March 5, 1819, came to Alabama in 1834, and located on the farm where he now lives. He was married, June 14, 1840, to Ann Eliza, daughter of John and Chloe (McBride) Alexander, of Lockport, N. Y. They had children as follows: Sarah, born March 28, 1842, who married Edson Winslow, August 15, 1862, whose children are Ellie and Vervie; Martha, born August 15, 1843, who married Norman H. Winslow, December 1, 1864, whose children are Henry, Warren, and Eben; Charlotte, born April 14, 1845, who married James Gordon, December 1, 1864, whose children are Nora, Albert, Florence, and Tracy; Alfred, born 1847, who married Esther Robinson, September 28, 1868, whose children are Lottie, Ida, Eda, and Florence; Orin, born June 1, 1850, who married Adele Ingalsbe, whose children are Eliza, Lois, and Ebenezer; Eliza Jane, born August 28, 1852, who married Erwin Brown, whose children are Myron, Frank, Clarissa, Manly, Fred, Herbert, and Arthur; and Hattie O, born March 6, 1859, who married Sabert E. Roach, whose children are Moses, Alice, and Adelbert. Mr. Ingalsbe is a prosperous farmer, and resides on road 49.

Elijah Ingalsbe, son of Ebenezer, was born in Boylston, Mass., September 12, 1780, and died in Alabama, 1872. He also located in Scipio about 1814. He married Polly Mitchell, and they were parents of E. Brooks, Ryal E., Polly, Pearley, and Sally. His wife, born 1781, died 1813. He married, second, Nancy, a sister of his first wife. The children by this marriage were Philander, who died in infancy, Phebe, Adna, Andy, and Levi. Elijah Brooks Ingalsbe was born 1805, located in Alabama in 1830, and took up land and built a log house, in which most of his children were born. He married Lucy Eliza, daughter of Jesse and Elizabeth (Streeter) Wright, and their children were Elijah B., Bela W., Lucinda E., Lodeska, Emily A., who married Orimel Saxton, Sarah A., and Riley D. E. B. Ingalsbe's wife died 1849, and he married Barbara Bushman, widow of Thomas Winslow. They had one daughter, Ione, who died in childhood.

Deacon Ryal E. Ingalsbe, son of Elijah, was born 1806, located in Alabama among the early settlers, and married, in 1837, Sally, daughter of Samuel and Polly (Bushman) Ingalsbe. Their children were Warren B., who died 1846, aged four years; Harmon, born 1847, who married Martha Wells, whose children are George C. and Jennie R.; Marion, born 1849, who is a farmer with his father; and Mary Louisa, who married Frank N. Lyday in 1878. Mr. Ingalsbe is a deacon of the Baptist Church, and resides on the homestead he has occupied for over 50 years.

Jacob Martin was born in Rush, N. Y., in 1815. About 1835 he settled in Alabama, on road 85. He married Delilah Fishell, of Rush, and they had a family of eight children. George W., son of Jacob, was born September 15, 1843, married Agnes E. Cameron, and they have four children.

Daniel Martin, born in Rush, N. Y., in 1819, came to Alabama about 1835 or '36. He married Jane M. Thrall, of East Granby, Conn., and they had a family of six children, four of whom are now living. He has always been a farmer, and was at one time assessor. Their children are Wallace H.; Cornelia A., wife of Elmer Reed, who resides in Alabama; Elizabeth, wife of E. C. Selleck; and Emily, wife of James Beckwith, who resides in Quincy, Ill.

Edward Halsey was born December 19, 1809, in Fairfield, Herkimer County, N. Y. He was a wagonmaker by trade, and settled in Alabama in 1847, as a farmer. He married Nancy Goff, of Henrietta, N. Y., and they had two children: Alice, wife of Frank Blackman, who resides in Rockford, Ill., and Henry, who resides in Oakfield. Mr. Halsey's wife was born December 11, 1812. They reside at Smithville.

Deacon William Macomber was born in Kinderhook, N. Y., in 1797. In 1831 he settled in the town of Alabama, on the farm now owned by William Macomber. He married Harriet Cutler, of Alabama, and they had eight children. His second wife was M. M. Roe. Deacon Macomber was a prominent member of the Baptist Church of Smithville, contributing largely to the building up of the same. He was supervisor of the town for many years, and owned a farm of 430 acres in the oak openings. He died December 1, 1861. Only three of his children reside in the county. Amanda M., widow of Julius Reed, resides in Oakfield. Sarah A., wife of P. V. Ingalsbe, also resides in Oakfield. John L. Macomber, a son, was born on the old farm in 1833, and always resided there. He married Helen G. Willis, and they have one child, Alice E. Mr. Macomber is counted as one of the most progressive farmers in the town. He has a fine and large farm, and devotes a portion of it to the breeding of Shropshiredown sheep, having 200 head. Judge Francis A. Macomber, of the Supreme Court at Rochester, is a son of Deacon Macomber. He was born in Alabama, and graduated from the Rochester University. Judson L. Macomber is a lumber merchant in Chattanooga, Tenn., and William Macomber, a son by the second wife of the Deacon, is a graduate of the law school of Rochester University, and is now practicing in Buffalo.

C. M. Mead, son of Charles A., was born in Alabama, May 29, 1850, and has always been a resident of the town. He learned the carpenters' trade of his father. He married Mina Bickford, of Alabama, and they have five children. Mr. Mead has acted as agent of Rowley & Eddy, lumber dealers, since March, 1884. His father came here about 1850, from the eastern part of the State, and died in 1877.

Anson Norton, son of Medad, was born in Goshen, Conn., in 1789, and located in Alabama about 1836, on the farm where Daniel Norton now lives, and engaged in farming. He became possessed of a landed estate of upwards of 700 acres, and was a man of great energy and perseverance. He died August 5, 1838. He married Persis Walker in 1814, and had seven sons: Alonzo, Medad, Moses, Daniel, Benjamin, Theron, and Franklin. Moses Norton was born in 1820, and died November 19, 1886. He was married, in 1845, to Ann, daughter of Jeremiah Lynch, and began housekeeping in a log house, where their children were born. They were Anson, who was accidently drowned in 1847; Albert, a missionary of the Methodist Episcopal Church in India; Heman, late of Alabama; Clara, who married E. J. Fuller, of Batavia; and

9

Joanna, who resides in Batavia.   Moses Norton located on the place now occupied by Mrs. Heman Norton.

Heman Norton was born May 2, 1851, and married, November 1, 1871, Kate L., daughter of Reese and Mary (Jones) Lumley. Their children are Georgia Margery, born February 26, 1874; Moses L., born January 28, 1877; and Izona, born July 27, 1887. Heman Norton died August, 1889. Franklin Norton married Julia F., daughter of Joseph W. and Eliza (Case) Allen, of Alabama. They have one son, Allen E., born April 19, 1870. Mr. Norton has been assessor of his town three terms, was postmaster under President Arthur, holding the office ever since, and is overseer of the poor. He is a farmer and has lived at his present place, Alabama Center, for over 30 years.

The paternal line of ancestors of Anson Norton are as follows: 1, Thomas, who came from Guilford, Eng., to Guilford, Conn., in 1639; 2, Thomas, Jr.; 3, Samuel, who lived in Durham, Conn.; 4, Col. Ebenezer, who lived in Durham and went to Goshen, Conn.; 5, Miles; 6, Medad, born in 1759; 7, Anson, born December 27, 1789, who married Persis Walker; 8, Moses, born January 12, 1820, in Byron. Moses married Ann Lynch, of Wayne County, N. Y., in 1844, the seventh daughter of Susan (McGowan) Lynch. Their children are Anson, Albert, Clara, Heman (deceased), and Joanna. His widow survives him, living in Batavia at the age of 68 years.

Harmon J. Norton, son of Lochlin and Laura A. (Wright) Norton, was born in Elba in 1818, and was reared on a farm. He married Laura C., daughter of Charles P. and Sarah Ann (Driggs) Brown, in 1843, and spent several years West. He located in Alabama about 1854. Their children were Alice L., born in 1844, who married William Ingersoll, of Colorado; Ida B., who married Luman Wilcox, of Dakato; Florence A., who married William Amsden, of Wheatville; Orrella J., who married Oscar Burt, of California; Arthur B., a resident of Idaho; Corabell C., who married Edmund E. Palmer in 1876, and they have children Vivian Clare and Arthur H.; Rosamond Lincoln, who married William Reed in 1884, and their children are Norton R. and Laura Belle; Leoline Clare, who married Asa Pixley, January 22, 1880; and Anna Maria, who married Irwin S. Vincent, whose children are Ivan, Percy, and Catharine, and they live in Shelby. Mr. Norton married for his second wife Mrs. Betsey Crandall, and for his third wife Amanda, daughter of Nathan Graham. The farm now owned by him was taken up by Charles P. Brown, his father-in-law. He was a member of Assembly, justice

of peace 14 years, and supervisor. He married Sarah A. Driggs, daugh_
ter of George, and they had seven children. Mr. Brown died 1859 ; his
wife 1885.

Asa Pixley, son of Joseph and Mary Jane (Jones) Pixley, was born in
Alabama, March 30, 1852, and was reared on the farm. He married
Leoline Clare, daughter of Harmon and Laura (Brown) Norton, Janu_
ary 22, 1880, and their son Jamie L. was born November 18, 1885.
Mr. Pixley is a farmer, and occupies the Norton homestead on road 23.

Jacob Potter, son of Jacob, was born in Cherry Valley, Otsego County,
N. Y., in 1825, and was raised on a farm. He came to Alabama at the
age of 20 years, and bought a farm. For a time he was engaged in
farming in Newstead, Erie County. He married (1850) Margaret,
daughter of Matthew and Eliza (Hart) Burns, of Shelby. He returned
to Alabama in 1860 and bought the farm he now occupies, and by add_
ing to it from time to time he now owns 215 acres. Their children are
Rosella, who died 1851, an infant ; Abbie Jane, a teacher, who lives at
home ; Almeda P., who died 1885 ; and Abel J., born 1856. The latter
married, in 1878, Cora, daughter of William and Elizabeth (Stuffin) Pick_
with, and their children are Edith, born 1879 ; Jennie, born 1882 ; Nora,
born 1884 ; and Jay Eugene, born 1885. He died November 9, 1888.
E. Douglass Potter was born in 1858, and married, in 1884, Emma,
daughter of William and Jane Dorwin. He is a prosperous farmer, and
resides on road 39.

William Donnan was born in Ireland, June 25, 1835. He came to
America when 19 years of age, and settled in Alabama. He married
Margaret J. Leighbody, and has one child, Emma, wife of E. D. Potter.

Charles R. Phillips, son of William H. and Phileta (Pearsons) Phillips,
was born in Wyoming County, N. Y., in 1831. He was reared on a
farm, and married Amelia C., daughter of Jacob and Theresa (Bothwick)
Wheeler, of Erie County, May 6, 1862. He located in Alabama in 1866.
They were parents of four children, viz : Clarence, who died in infancy ;
Ida Augusta, born October 26, 1864, died October, 1866 ; Jennie W.,
who married Albert McVeigh in 1883, and their children are Amelia,
Theresa, Isabella Phileta, and Bertha Adel ; and Willie J., born in Alabama, July 6, 1869, who is a farmer, living on the homestead. Mr.
Phillips is an earnest worker in all temperance movements, is a farmer,
and resides in the village on Railroad street.

William Poodry was of French origin. He married an Indian woman,
by whom he had three sons and one daughter, one of whom, Lewis, was

a soldier in the War of 1812 in the American army. He married Phebe
Jonas, and reared a large family, of whom three only are living. Maria,
a daughter, married Levi Parker, of Alabama.

E. M. Poodry was born on the Tonawanda Reservation, August 15,
1833. He early manifested an aptitude for learning, and, making the best
of advantages within his reach, succeeded in obtaining a good business
education, which enabled him to become one of the chiefs in the councils
of his tribe. He married Amanda Griffin, November 6, 1856, and they
were the parents of 11 children, viz.: Malvina, born February 3, 1858,
married Warren Skye in 1883; Thomas J., born May 5, 1860; Sarah J.,
born April 3, 1862, married Asa Skye; William S., born December 4,
1864, died June 28, 1887; Barnum, born March 30, 1867, married Sarah
C. Brant, February 14, 1889; Anna M., born June 11, 1869, married
Charles Doctor, August 12, 1888; Edward, born July 23, 1871; Stafford, born February 28, 1875; Fanny C., born February 17, 1877; Henrietta, born November 8, 1880; and Dora, born June 26, 1883. Mr.
Poodry is extensively engaged in farming, and occupies about 350 acres
of land on road 38.

Charles W. Roberts was born in Shelby in 1835. He was a son of
Ziba and Susan (Wolcott) Roberts, and grew up on the farm. He married, in 1859, Huldah A., daughter of Jeremiah and Clarissa (Simons)
Loucks, and they had six children, of whom Rolla W., born 1860, was
educated at Medina, Buffalo, and the State Normal School at Brockport,
became a civil engineer, and is now in business at East Saginaw, Mich.
He married Ora A. Tinkham in 1884, and they have three children,
Charles M., Julia H., and Flora. Carrie, Jennie, and Berthella Roberts
live at home. Sarah Elizabeth married E. P. Grennell, of Orleans County,
in 1881, and has two children, Louisa E. and Hugh E., and resides at
East Saginaw, Mich. Jessie O., another child of C. W. Roberts, died
1879. Mrs. C. W. Roberts was educated at East Saginaw, Mich. Mr.
Roberts has held the office of assessor for nine years, supervisor two
years, and is now acting justice of the peace. He is a farmer and resides
on road 11.

Jacob Shoemaker, son of Jacob, was born in Montgomery County, May
19, 1835. He settled in Royalton, N. Y., in 1856, came to Alabama and
married Catherine, widow of Abraham Champlin, and has resided here
since. He is a harnessmaker by trade. They had one child, Mary, who
is the wife of E. H. Miller. Mrs. Shoemaker died March 30, 1875. Mr.
Shoemaker was town clerk of Royalton for several years, justice of the

peace four years, and postmaster four years and nine months. He was appointed under Taylor's administration. He also took the census of district No. 2 of Royalton in 1855.

Orimel Saxton, son of David and Susanna (Spafford) Saxton, was born in Brighton, Ont., in 1828. He engaged as salesman in a store for several years, then took up farming, which he has followed since. He married, May 18, 1858, Emily A., daughter of Elijah B. Ingalsbe, of Alabama, and their children were Gertrude Aramintha, Jennette Eliza, Horatio G, who married Ida M. West in 1886, and has one son, Arthur A., born 1889, Lijetta Irene, Mary Addie, who married, January 6, 1889, Loren Reed, William S., Burhanna, Orimel W., Inez Grace, and Emma Rebecca. Mr. Saxton located in Alabama in the spring of 1883, and engaged in farming on the E. B. Ingalsbe farm, where he died March 25, 1889. Mrs. Saxton and family reside on the homestead near Smithville.

Edward Tuttle, son of Edward and Urana (Orvis) Tuttle, was born in York, Livingston County, in 1820, was reared on the farm, and when of age came to Alabama. He married Lucretia Lynch, a sister of Mrs. Moses Newton, in 1847. Their children were Frances, who married Robert Reynolds; Albert P., of Alabama; and William, who died 1884. For his second wife he married Ella M. Stanley, widow of Thomas Stevens, in 1887. He is a farmer on road 40.

Moses Vail, son of Samuel and Prudence (Vail) Vail, was born in New Jersey in 1797, and was reared on a farm. He was married to his wife, Mercy, September 25, 1816. Their children were Prudence, who married William Gardner, and died in Oakfield in 1842; Samuel, of Canada; Emeline, who died 1840, aged 18 years; Eli P., of Alabama; Susan W., who married Daniel Zanvitz, of Canada; Phebe J., who married James Craft, and died 1880; Sarah E., who married Isaac Zanvitz, of Canada; Jonah, of Iowa; and Ephraim and Stephen, of Elba. Moses Vail located in Oakfield in 1834, and engaged in farming. He belonged to the Society of Friends, and practiced the peaceful doctrines of "Penn." He departed his well-spent life 3d month, 12th day, 1871; his wife died 1st month, 27th day, 1850. For his second wife, in 1853, he married Harriet Wood, who died 1858.

Eli P Vail was born 1824, and raised a farmer. He married Mary D., daughter of Jacob and Rebecca (Runnion) Drake, the 11th month, 30th day, 1853. He located at Alabama Center and engaged in farming. He has been postmaster 11 years, and resides on Railroad street. Their children are Mary Elizabeth, who married Aaron C. Dutton, of Buffalo;

Moses D., of Shelby; Charles A., of Alabama; Eva M. and Eveline, at home; Florence Mabel, who was accidentally killed by a field-roller September 19, 1868, aged three years; Willie, who died 1869, an infant; and Frank D.   The latter was born in 1854, reared on a farm, and learned the carpenters' trade.   He married, January 5, 1875, Nellie Jane, daughter of Orin and Jane (Fisk) White.   Their children are Willie H., born July 5, 1878, and Eudora Maude, born October 9, 1883.   He is a fruit dealer, and resides on Medina street.

Charles A. Vail, born January 5, 1860, married, December 8, 1880, Sarah, daughter of James and Susan (McManus) McCauley, and widow of Oscar L. Lund.   They have two children: Bessie May, born May 28, 1883, and Stanley A., born July 23, 1885.   Mr. Vail is a fruit dealer, has an evaporator, and resides on Main street.

Selah Vosburgh, son of Salem, born in Whitehall, N. Y., in 1807, came to Alabama in 1826.   He was an early settler, and a gunsmith by occupation.   He settled upon a large tract of land and engaged in farming.   He married Martha, daughter of Benjamin Gumaer, and they had children as follows: George H., who studied law and died 1860, aged 24 years; Charlotte A., who died 1863; James O., who married Loduskie Peck, whose children were George W., of California, and Anna M., who died young; John S., a corporal in the army, appointed adjutant with rank of colonel, and was interested with Governor Safford in the Tombstone silver mine, Colorada, now owning a large estate in Los Angeles (he married Kate Slawson, and they have two sons: Royden, born 1887, and Keith, born 1889); Martha A., who married James Peck, of Onondaga County, and they have one daughter, Bertha M.; and Mary E., who married J. A. Beals.   Mr. Vosburgh dealt largely in real estate, and was a successful business man.   He died in 1873.   Mr. Vosburgh's wife died June 11, 1849.   He married for his second wife Maria, daughter of Elijah Hovey.   She died in 1873.   Their children were Charles, who died aged two years; Jennie, who married Lewis M. Phelps, of Michigan; Willie, who died in infancy; and Frank E.   Frank E. Vosburgh was born in 1858, was educated at Medina Academy, and spent his early years on the farm.   March 16, 1880, he married Mary A., daughter of George W. and Phebe (Freeman) Easton, and they have one daughter, Nora Esther, born March 21, 1881, and one son, Orrin J. L, born January 9, 1888.   Mr. Vosburgh was elected justice of the peace in 1885 and justice of Sessions in 1887–88.   He built a stave and heading mill in 1889, and is a farmer, owning the Vosburgh homestead, where he was born.

Nelson Vaughn, a native of Washington County, and son of Francis and Polly (Green) Vaughn, was born in 1815. At the age of 10 years he came to Niagara County and worked on a farm. He was married to Mary Ann Dean, and they had one son, Ula A., of Royalton. His wife died 1853, and he married, second, Marie Clarissa, daughter of Peter and Betsey (Colson) Beamore. Their children are Helen L., who died 1865; Wesley F., who came here in 1865, and bought the farm where he now lives; Oscar D., who married Catherine Hale, and has a daughter, Helen L.; and Freeman S., who married Margaret Smith, and has a son, Artie.

Wesley F. Vaughn was born June 8, 1854' was reared on a farm, and July 3, 1882, was married to M. Maria Joslin. They have two children: Ella May, born September 12, 1883, and William N., born December 24, 1885. They live on road 14.

William Joslin, born in England, came to America at an early age. He married Mary Baker, of Oakfield, and their children are Henry and John, of Alabama; Vienna, Grant, and Frank, of Shelby; Clara, who lives at home; Emma, who married George Bickle, of Wheatville; and M. Maria, who married Wesley F. Vaughn.

Phineas White, born in Massachusetts in 1783, came to Stafford when 27 years of age, taking up land sufficient for farming purposes. In 1810 he married Polly Beswick, and their children were Salma, deceased; Laura, who married James Patterson (deceased); Silas, of Illinois; Alma, who married Thaxter Waterman (deceased), and their daughter was Almira, also deceased, aged 16; Louisa, who married Frederick Barney; Mary A., who married Thaxter Waterman; Orrin, who died in Iowa; Jane, who married Allen Watson, of Michigan; and Phineas B., born 1828, who was reared on the farm. The latter married Harriet N. Graves' in 1850, who died 1853. He then married (1855) Elma S., daughter of Anthony Waterman. Their children were Merton, deceased, aged 14; Arthur P., who married Lottie Huffcut, in 1888, of Alabama; Harriet N. (deceased); and Anna S., who married H. Selden, of Stafford. For his third wife Mr. White married, in 1867, Mrs. Laura Ann (Lawrence) Horning, widow of Eli. They have one daughter, Lillian M. Mr. White located here in 1867, and is a farmer on road 17.

· William Horning, a native of Schoharie County, came to Alabama about 1840, and married Magdelena Wieting. Their children were Anna Maria, who married Amos Crosby (both deceased); Jeremiah, who married Caroline D. Lawrence and had one son, Oscar Lorenzo, who died in Michigan; Dr. Nelson, who practiced medicine in Alabama, and died several years ago; and Eli, born 1828. Eli was reared on the farm, and married Laura Ann, daughter of Richard and Betsey (Barker) Lawrence, in 1855, and began housekeeping in Alabama. Their children were William, born 1858, died 1876; May, who died in infancy; and Nellie Belle, born 1862, who married, in 1878, Moses D. Vail, of Alabama, and their children were Eli H., Bertram N., and Homer D. (died 1886). Eli Horning died October 17, 1864. Mrs. Horning married, second, Phineas B. White.

The paternal ancestor of the Wight family was born on the Isle of Wight. He located in Massachusetts about 1628. Of the family was Ephraim, born 1645, who had two sons, Nathaniel (born 1678) and Daniel. Nathaniel's son Levi was born in 1712, and married Susanna Barstow. They had 10 children, of whom Levi, 2d, was born in Thompson, Conn., in 1761. He married Sarah Corbin in 1782, and they were parents of 11 children. Levi, 2d, died at Centerville, N. Y., in 1830, and his wife died 1852. Of this family was Abbott, born in Oxford in 1787 (died 1863), who married, at Fairfield, N. Y., Alice Cabott, of Dudley, in 1812, and they had nine children, viz.: Lorinda, Emeline, and George, of Alabama; Angeline, who married Benjamin Hunt, of Alabama; Levi, of Pembroke; Roxy, who married Daniel D. Cole, of Michigan; Perry, who died 1862, aged 31 years; and Abbott and Abel, of Alabama.

George Wight was born in Monroe County in 1816, and located here in 1837. He married, in 1846, Esther, daughter of Reuben and Mary (Whitehead) Golden, of Elba. Their son Miles was born in 1855, and in 1877 married Etta E. Clark. Their children are Eliza, Irene, Harry C., George H., Luella Mabel, and Walter C.

Abbott Wight was born in Allegany County in 1825, and came to Alabama in 1837. He was reared on a farm, and married, in 1853, Sarah A., daughter of Ephraim and Minerva (Reed) Hewett. Their daughter Nettie Rosaline married Myron Williams, of Batavia, and their son P. Hewett resides at home. Mr. Wight is a farmer and resides on road 50.

Abel Wight was born in 1828, and in 1850 married Maria, daughter of Lyman and Sally (Cabot) Hitchcock. Their children are Bruce, Hale, and Noah, of Alabama; Cabot, who died in infancy (1859); D. Fay, born 1860, who is a teacher; Grace W., who married Augustus Hunt; Orma, who married John A. Hunt in 1883; Dan, who died in infancy; and Inez, born April 21, 1872. Abel Wight is a farmer and resides on

road 50. Bruce Wight married (1877) Adaline, daughter of Amasa and
Elizabeth (Beecher) Bliss, and their children are Hattie Maria and Effie
Irene. Hale Wight married Christina E., daughter of William and Charlotte (Hotchkiss) Ingalsbe, in 1873, and their children are Dean R., born
November 17, 1878 ; Viola, born November 17, 1881 ; and Owen, who
died in infancy (1886). Noah Wight married Ida May, daughter of John
and Lydia Ann (Aucry) Ackerson, December 20, 1874. They have a
son, Abel J.

Leonard Webster was born in Berlin, Conn., and died in Alabama in
1837. He married Alma Rockwell and had children as follows : Sarah,
who married Zardis Skidmore, of Michigan ; Almira ; Bennett, who died
1847 ; Joseph, who died 1888 ; David, who died 1851 ; Minnie, who
married Luther True, of Batavia ; and Martha, who married Frank Lund,
of Alabama. Mr. Webster came here in 1828, and located where his
granddaughter, Mrs. George E. Stevens, now lives. Of his family Joseph was born in 1815, and in 1844 married Laura Ann, daughter of
Ephraim and Laura (Williams) Hicks. Their children were Ellen A., of
Alabama ; Daniel, who died 1879 ; Emma, who died 1880 ; Hattie, who
married Almon Bristol, and died in Illinois in 1882 ; Laura, who died
in Batavia in 1884 ; and Mary, who died 1880.

Ellen A. Webster married George E. Stevens, November 8, 1868, and
they were parents of four children, viz.: Orpha L., who died 1887, aged
18 years ; Jennie Bertell, born October 25, 1871 ; Stella R., born October 19, 1873 ; and Laura A., who died in infancy (1881). Mrs. Stevens
and family occupy the Webster homestead on road 20, where she was
born.

David Webster, born 1819, came to Alabama in 1828, and was reared
on a farm. He married, in 1846, Mary, daughter of Allen B. and Sarah
(Coleman) Holmes, and their children were Leonard, who died young ;
David M. C., who resides at Rocky Hill, Conn.; and Frances Ella, who
was born 1851. May 27, 1875, she married Frank A. Stevens, and they
have one son, Claude W., born February 10, 1877. David Webster
died in 1851. His widow married Solomon H. Dunham in 1859, and
their children were Anna and Amelia (twins), who died in infancy, and
Jennie Maria, who resides at Rocky Hill, Conn. Mrs. Dunham died in
March, 1889. F. A. Stevens and family reside at Kensington, Conn.
David M. C. Webster married Lumec Ault, and their children are Regi-
nald A., George D., and Alma May, and they reside at Rocky Hill, Conn.

Samuel Winchell, born in Monroe County, N. Y., married Cornelia, daughter of Ashur Merrill, and located in Orleans County. He was a blacksmith, and came to Alabama about 1854. Their children were Mary Ann, who married Schuyler Starkweather; Melissa, who married Lorenzo Horning, and lives in the West; and Lyman W., of Alabama. The father died in 1861, and the mother in 1888.

Lyman W. Winchell was born in 1831, learned the blacksmith trade, and married, November, 1855, Harriet Elizabeth, daughter of Albert and Emma (Davis) Clark, of Oakfield. They located in Alabama. Their sons are Albert S., born January 28, 1857, who married, in 1880, Sarah, daughter of Eleazur R. Underhill, and their children are Nora Cornelia, born 1882, and Frank, born 1885; and Merrill E., born September 4, 1858, who married, in 1880, Eva, daughter of Orin and Jane A. (Fish) White, and lives in Buffalo. Mr. Winchell enlisted in the late war in August, 1862, in the 19th Light Artillery, and was at the battles of the Wilderness, North Anna, Cold Harbor, Weldon Road, and others, serving until the close of the war. He now lives on Medina street in Alabama.

Joseph Waterstreett, a citizen of Mecklenburg, Germany, married Leonora Niendoorf, from the same town. He died there in 1863, aged 61 years. His children were Henry, Christopher, Sophia, Joseph, and Mary. Henry came from Germany to the United States in 1864, settled in Oakfield, and married Minnie, daughter of John and Mary (Burr) Scroger, of Oakfield. Their children are Mary, John, Fred, and George. Mary married Charles Dryer, of Oakfield.

Thomas R. Wolcott was born in Leyden, Lewis County, N. Y., February 2, 1801. About the year 1827 he bought a farm in Alabama from the Holland Land Company. At the time he was engaged in teaching school in Livingston County, which profession he continued until 1829 or '30' when he settled on his farm. He married Aurelia Underwood, and had one child, Sarah, wife of Daniel Inglesbee, of Pontiac, Mich. His wife lived two years. In 1835 he married Orpha Wolverton, daughter of Asher, of Montgomery County, N. Y., and they had 10 children, four of whom are living. He died April 24, 1887. He was supervisor for several years, and justice of the peace for 10 years. His widow resides on the old homestead, which has never been out of the family.

George W. Webb was born in Rochester, N. Y., April 28, 1856. In 1884 he was appointed station agent for the West Shore Railroad at Alabama, which position he has held ever since. He married Mary Zwetsch, of Alexander.

Augustus D. Zurhorst, a practicing physician, son of Frederick William, was born in London, Eng., in 1803. He married Mary Ann
Estell, and came to America in 1836, continuing the practice of medicine. He died 1873, and his wife 1855. His children were Catherine T.,
who married Lorenzo Ely, of Castile, N. Y.; Augusta P., who married John
Pennock and died 1885; Octavia, of Castile; John E., who died 1853,
aged 13 years; Herman S. W., who was a soldier and died 1864, in West
Virginia; Rosina V., who died 1865, aged 17 years; Henry C., who
died young; and Augustus F. G., the subject of this sketch, who was
born September 27, 1847. He was educated at Genesee and Wyoming
Seminary, enlisted in the army in 1863 in Co. G, 21st N. Y. Cavalry,
became quartermaster's sergeant, and served until July, 1866. On his return he studied medicine with his father and with Dr. N. G. Clark, of
Batavia, and graduated at Cleveland Medical College, class of 1869.
He then practiced medicine with Dr. Clark for two years, after which he
located at Alabama Center in 1871. He was postmaster in 1885, justice
of the peace in 1888, and elected supervisor in 1889. Dr. Zurhorst has
a large and growing practice, and resides on Railroad street. He married, in 1878, Emma A., daughter of Frederick A. and Elizabeth (Flanders) Cooley. Their daughters are Iola Jean, born March 9, 1880, and
Kathleen Corinne, born October 10, 1884.

ALEXANDER.

ALEXANDER was one of the very earliest settled towns in the
county, the valuable and productive lands along the Tonawanda
Creek causing the early pioneers to seek homes where the rich soil
awaited their labors; and having that in view it is estimated that over
100 families took up the lands in that township (No. 11) between the
years 1802 and 1815, the greatest influx being prior to the War of
1812. We are informed that the first log house was built near the site
of the present cheese factory. In endeavoring to enumerate their names
and the year of settlement we are unable to be accurate in every instance,
owing to our sources of information being somewhat uncertain as well
as contradictory; but by careful inquiry and verification among the descendants of most of them we are enabled to lay before our readers a

more complete list than has ever heretofore been compiled. A confusion of dates may exist in some cases, arising from the fact that some who signified their intentions of locating did not take possession until sometime after. We will endeavor to present them in their order of date of settlement.

The first record of deed for purchase in the town is that of Alexander Rhea (from whom the town was finally named) in 1802. He was a surveyor of the Holland Co. and founder of Alexander village, erecting a saw-mill in 1804. He was brigadier-general of militia and State Senator for several years. His first deed was for 17 acres of land in the bend of the creek near the present village, and for 11 acres on what was then called the Allegany road (the first cut through, southerly); later, in 1809, he located a larger tract, since known as the Pearson farm. While Mr. Rhea took the first contract for land William Blackman is regarded as the first settler.

In 1803, 1804, and 1805 there came Elijah Root, William Johnson, George Darrow, John Olney, William Blackman, who, it is said, raised the first crop of corn, and whose child was the first born in the town ; William Whitney, whose death was the first, caused by falling from a tree; Lillie Fisher, settling on the farm so-called, and his son Alanson T., who died at the age of 98 years; and Caleb Blodgett, whose large farm stood on higher ground than any place between Batavia and Buffalo. Near his house stood a tall elm tree, the top of which was visible from Bethany and many points in Wyoming County. There also came Lewis Disbrow, Joseph Fellows, Elias and John Lee, Samuel Russel, Elijah Rowe, Solomon Blodgett, Elisha Carver, and Benham Preston, the most of whom took of the land or located in 1804.

In 1806 the following persons signified their intentions of locating, some of whom did, a few, perhaps, failing to make actual settlement : Jonas Blodgett, John Churchill, David Clark, Isaac Chaddock, David Carter, John Chamberlin, Timothy Fay, Aaron Gale, H. Williams, Elnathan Wilcox, Amos Jones (the first school teacher), Capt. Ezekiel T. Lewis, Alexander Little, B. Lyman, J. McCollister, and Henry Rumsey.

In 1807 S. Bradway, Ezekiel Churchill, G. W. Wing, Philo Porter (farmer and pensioner of the War of 1812), Joseph Gladden, and Rudolphus Hawkins, who died in 1849, came in. Mr. Hawkins was the father of Jesse, John, Harvey, Henry, and Van Rensselaer, and they were at one time the largest, if not the most influential, family in town. Timothy Hawkins, who came from Tolland, Conn., was one of the first permanent settlers near the village, on the farm where Ira T. Hawkins now lives, known as the Hawkins farm. He came when only two houses were built between Batavia and Alexander. He died at the age of 84 years. About this time one William Adams erected a saw mill and grist-mill on the site of the present flouring-mill in the village. He was also lieuten-ant of militia, and died in 1810.

. Isaac Parrish was one of the pioneers of Genesee County. He was born in the town of Randolph, Vt His father, William Parrish, moved from Vermont to this county in 1806, and settled in the town of Alex-ander, on a farm just west of the old elm tree. During the War of 1812 his father directed him to go to Batavia and purchase some necessaries for the family. While at Batavia a portion of the army was marching through to Buffalo ; the services of the team and driver were wanted to convey some of their camp equipage to Niagara River ; himself and team were pressed into service, very much to his discomfort, and was com-pelled to proceed with the army to Buffalo, where he was paid for the services rendered, and directed to return home, 30 miles away, through the forest, where anxious friends were waiting his return, as they were very much in want of the articles he was directed to get at Batavia. Soon after the war, and in the employ of his uncle (Alba Blodgett), he drove a seven-horse team for seven years, between Albany and Buffalo, drawing freight for the Western World, before the Erie Canal was in operation. He was employed several months during the construction of the locks at Lockport. He assisted in drawing the machinery and irons from Albany to Buffalo for the second steamboat that ran on Lake Erie. In 1834 he purchased the farm where his son, George B. Parrish, lived. It was at that time a wilderness ; only about 15 acres of the farm were then under cultivation. He was an enterprising and successful farmer ; a resident of the town of Alexander 66 years ; and died in April, 1872.

Harvey Hawkins and Hon. Abel Ensign came in 1808, and kept the first tavern and store, and Thomas Rice, Lyman Riddle (a soldier of 1812), John Squires, Edmund Tracy, and Shubael Wing in 1809. Moses M. Page, from Connecticut, and Levi Thompson came in 1810, when there were only three settlers on the road between Batavia and Alexander. Mr. Page died aged 74 years. The same year Col. Seba Brainard became a neighbor to the few who preceded him. He was held in great esteem by all, and was a zealous Methodist. His son Harris suc-ceeded to his property, and died on the homestead. Harris left two sons, Seba and Charles. John and Samuel Latham, about this time, put up the first framed dwelling. William Waite, Gehial Stanard, and Spencer Waldo were settlers during the year. During 1811 Return B. Cady and John and B. Cady located.

Capt. Elisha Smith was born in Washington County, N. Y., October 19, 1785. In 1807 he united in marriage with Elizabeth Birdsall, of Otsego, Otsego County, N. Y., and in 1812 emigrated to Genesee County and located at Alexander. He performed noble service in the War of 1812, and participated in the memorable battle of "Black Rock." His estimable companion died May 13, 1855, aged 72 years. He never mixed largely in political matters, but his opinions were judiciously formed and fearlessly asserted. He was a faithful and consistent member of the Methodist Church, and that organization lost a valuable member in his demise. A friend, speaking of his death, says:

"Being one of the early pioneers he experienced many of the hardships, privations, and labors of the early settlers, but succeeded well in subduing the forest and bringing the soil to its present productiveness, and supplying his family with the competencies of life. His friends were always welcomed with cordiality at his house, and in his death they lost a much-esteemed and valuable citizen. He was very child-like in his affection for and manner towards his friends, and more than all that can be said of him is that he was a *good man*."

Up to this time settlements upon the Purchase were rapid. Usually the coming of one family would be followed by others from their old homes, but rumors of war and preparations for it about this time (1812) impeded somewhat the increase of pioneers, and while we have no particular names as coming during the year, we note names of some, among whom were Dr. Jonathan Hall, a farmer of genuine worth, and a Presbyterian. He died aged 56. There was also John Riddle (father of Lyman and Thomas), an honored citizen and the first justice of the peace, and supervisor for several years. He died in 1849. Thomas first settled in Darien. He followed mercantile pursuits, was town clerk, postmaster, Sessions justice, and justice of the peace for 28 years. He died in 1889. Lyman Riddle was a soldier of 1812. There were Henry Innis, from Nova Scotia, Rodney Wadsworth, Samuel Favor, who died at the age of 95 years, and during the later period of his life lived in the village, and Timothy Mooers an enterprising mechanic, who was foremost in all movements to build up the village. He built the first grist-mill (now standing), and combined with it a wool-carding and cloth dressing machine, attracting customers to the place. There were also Jerome Dickinson, who died in 1885, and whose daughter taught school for 30 years; and Leverett Seward, a good citizen, a soldier in the war, and wounded, drew a pension, and who was twice elected to the Assembly. He died in 1817, and left two sons, Winfield S. and Charles F.

The Kidder family made their advent in the new settlement sometime during this year or 1813. One authority gives the year 1806; but we can. not verify it. John Kidder came from Massachusetts, and located on the farm now occupied by Earl Kidder. He cleared up his place with the help of a family of sturdy boys, Alvin, Earl, Hosea, and Sidney. Alvin afterwards moved to Boston and engaged in the leather trade. Earl re. mained upon the farm, dying in 1871. He was a justice, supervisor, and loan commissioner. Ruth Kidder is on record as having located a farm about 1813. The Kidder family were quite an element in society in those days.

Gen. Josiah Newton settled at an early day, in 1815, was a large farmer, owned a beautiful place, and died well off. Captain Marcellus Fellows, Josiah Goodrich, Asahel Warner, Stephen Day, Esq., and Wolcott Marsh also located in town, and during the year the Moulton family, consisting of Capt. Royal, Benjamin, and E. C., a full sketch of all of whom will be found further on. Newcombe Demary, Nathaniel Loomis, and Joshua Rix, whose farm was next to the Kidders', were settlers in 1814. It has been stated that Benjamin and Eunice Moulton were the first persons married, but we cannot verify it.

The year 1815 was memorable for a large influx of pioneers in the new settlement. We record the names of Emory and Solomon Blodgett, and Fred Balch, who was a farmer and cooper. He married Harriet Benedict at the old Fargo tavern. Samuel Benedict, a liberal benefactor andc it- izen, was instrumental in founding the seminary, giving $1,000 towards it, and also was an early promoter of the Exchange Bank. He finally moved South. The Chaddocks, Luther (who later built a fine cobble-stone house on his farm), Thomas, and Dennis B., located in the southeast part of the town. There were also C. Williams, Baxter H. Wilmarth, Robert Lounsbury, Emory F. Lincoln, Noah North, who came in 1808, and his sons Noah and James A., Eben North, who came in 1816, and William Parrish, who was a man of integrity and industry. Ae died in 1872, leaving a son, George. He was a commissioner of highways for 18 years.

In 1816 we have Daney Churchill and Cherrick Van De Bogart, of the "Van De Bogart settlement," in the northwest part of the town. Nicholas Van De Bogart, a son, afterwards moved to the village and kept the tavern. He has several sons living. In addition we have

imothy Hoskins, James R. Jackman, Gorama Kelsey, Lyman Brown,
ames Lewis, N. Manson, Ira Newton, who was always at peace with
is fellowmen, and J. G. Tiffany, a handy mechanic, a farmer, and a
vool-carder, who moved to Darien.

The following came in 1817: Silas Southwell, Jonas and James Stimars,
. C. Spring, Ezra W. Osborn, and David Halsted, in the north part of the
own. Philip Cook, Ebenezer Scoville, and Guy Shaw came in 1819. In
820 came S. B. Brainard, Daniel F. Bowen, C. J. Hawkins, Sanford Rid-
le, and S. B. Smith; Horace B. Houghton, Eliphalet Peck, the first settler
n the Peck farm, and John and Benjamin Simonds, in 1824 in the north
art of the town. There were also Philo Porter (a soldier of 1812),
oses Dickinson, and O. T. Fargo, of the famous Fargo tavern, which he
ept for 41 years. It was a favorite place of resort for balls and
arties. A Mr. Austin formerly kept this tavern up to Mr. Fargo's
aking possession in 1825. A Charles Austin was an early school teacher,
n a log house about this time, but it cannot be learned if it is the same
ne.

As we are now coming to an intermediate period, where not a few of
he settlers of that time are still living, we do not deem it best to enu-
erate them all, but will give space to Rufus G. Avery, who came in 1835,
hose son Rufus G. still resides in town. James Day came in the same
ear, whose daughter, Mrs. Hannah H. Lawton, is still a resident. John
irstine, in 1830, married Alice Riddle, and occupies the Riddle farm.
ichard L. Waite was a blacksmith and farmer, and a son, a Methodist
inister, survives him.

The town was organized June 12, 1812, and we will give as we are
ble some names of those identified with it, and the village, who were
nstrumental in advancing its growth. John and Samuel Latham are
upposed to be the first who engaged in mercantile business, and some
ontend that Harvey and Henry Hawkins were in advance of them.
ertainly undue credit cannot be given the latter for their enterprise.
orace B. Houghton was an old resident, a mechanic, and regarded al-
ays as being upright. He was justice for 28 years. James R. Jack-
nan started in life poor, but by hard work became well off. He was
ustice for several years, and was made judge of the County Court by
overnor Seward. George W. Wing, son of Shubael, was a carriage-
aker. The firm of Wing & Willard supplied the country around with
agons of superior make. They also made freight cars, and erected
any dwellings in the village.

Timothy Mooers, who built the present mill, also carried on wool-carding. He made woolen rolls, which were then taken by the women and spun into yarn, and by looms wove into cloth. Mr. Mooers then fulled, dyed, and pressed the same, ready to be made into wearing apparel. This industry he kept up until 1835. He was also in the drug and grocery business, and postmaster for many years. His son Alonzo T. was connected with Judge Rix in the grain and milling business, and kept a drug store in 1869. In 1829 Charles Patterson had a carding and woolen factory. Solomon Cook was a post rider. Ira Earll was postmaster in 1831. W. C. Spaulding was postmaster in 1837, and V. R. Hawkins in 1841. Rix and Blodgett were merchants in 1832, and Hawkins and Blodgett in 1839. E. & E. B. Foote operated a woolen factory in 1841. Blossom & Newton were merchants in 1842, and Heman Blodgett & Co. in 1844. Edward T. Squires was a musician, and also a farmer.

Charles Chaffee was said to be the first physician. Alden Richards was an early tanner. Abner Nichols was a boot and shoe dealer in 1846. Wells, Adams, and Matteson were old-time cabinetmakers. Orlando Fellows, 50 years ago, worked at his trade as blacksmith. Cyrenus Wilbor, an early settler (before 1807), was a tanner and currier. The second couple married by Father Paddock, in 1819, was Mr. Wilbor and wife. He also kept tavern at one time ; during his occupancy it was set fire to and burned, by, it is supposed, the owner of the building. Mr. Wilbor was the father of Rev. A. D. Wilbor, once superintendent of the Blind Asylum, and grandfather of Rev. W. C. Wilbor, now pastor of the Methodist Episcopal Church of Le Roy.

In 1869 the Messrs. Moulton were extensive millers. George Jones was engaged in sash and blind manufacturing. W. L. Dickinson was a merchant, and Horace Hunn had a saw-mill.

The tavern in early times being quite an element of civilization, we wish we were able to devote space to the history of the old stand in Alexander, but can only mention a few of its proprietors after Henry Hawkins opened one in 1807. N. Perry was proprietor for several years, or until about 1837, then a Mr. Lathrop, about 1838, when Nicholas Van De Bogart moved from his farm in 1839, opened up the place on an improved plan, and for 10 years proved he was able to attend to the wants of the traveling public. Alvah Montgomery and Cyrenus Wilbor each kept tavern for a short time. In 1865 C. W. Bowen was pro-

10

prietor, and soon Rufus G. Avery bought the stand and for a long time entertained many guests. At present a Mr. Fancher is in charge.

The unusual fall of water in the Tonawanda at this place was early taken advantage of, and as soon as a mill was built, in 1808, it caused a large business to be done, the products of the soil from a large extent of country finding a market at the village. The Hawkinses, the Blodgetts, Judge Rix, the Moultons, and others, all by their energy and sagacity, aided the farmer to make a sale of his produce, giving an impetus to trade and gradually enabling the pioneers to lead a more comfortable existence.

With this new life came a desire on the part of parents to provide for the education of their children, something beyond what was afforded the first settlers. Preliminary to the move we note the formation of the "Alexandrian Library" as early as 1811, by Alexander Rhea, Henry Hawkins, Colonel Brainard, Samuel Latham, Jr., Harvey Hawkins, Noah North, and Ezra W. Osborn, who were elected trustees. In 1828 a literary society was formed, and in 1837 the citizens raised $6,000 to build a seminary, which cost $7,000, the deficiency being made up by Henry Hawkins. The name was "Genesee and Wyoming Seminary," and E. T. Crooker and E. T. Benedict were the first principals. It was built of stone, and flourished beyond all expectation, there being at one time 300 students in attendance. By a foreclosure of mortgage Henry Hawkins came into possession of the building, and in 1845 obtained a charter from the Regents of the University, gave to it the lands and buildings, and endowed it with $4,000, a large library, and geological specimens. In less than three months after it was in operation he died, of small-pox. Harvey Hawkins died of the same disease soon after.

The building occupied as a union school has now about 100 scholars, and Professor O. Warren is the principal. It is situated on Buffalo street.

The general training day.—In 1807 the military authorities of the State organized a regiment on the Holland Purchase, and one of the companies being located in this town was honored with some of the principal officers. In the fall of 1808 the first regimental or general training was held here, and reviewed by Brigadier-General Alexander Rhea. Colonel William Rumsey was officer of the day. The regiment was formed on the ground east of the village, and on the north side of the road, the right resting near the site of the present stone church, on a line parallel with the road. "Everybody went to general training—men, women, children, and dogs. Some went on foot, some on horseback, and some in ox-wagons. The young fellows wore new 'fine' shirts, about as fine and white as stuff now used for bags, but which cost six shillings per yard, and these were the first fine shirts worn in this town."

The Exchange Bank of Genesee.—The business interests of Alexander and vicinity were so extensive that its enterprising citizens of 1842 de_ termined to have more convenient banking facilities than were accorded them in Batavia; so that, at so early a date, the small village of Alexander became a rival of its larger sister village and county seat. The Hawkins family were instrumental in its organization, and later D. W. Tomlinson became interested in it, and buying up all the stock removed it to Batavia in 1850. Fred Follett and E. S. Warner were cashiers at different times.

The present grist and flouring-mill is owned by C. S. Thompson. For 11 years prior to his ownership Messrs. Moulton and Null conducted the business, buying the same in 1866. E. G. Moulton, the present worthy resident of the village, has the credit of being in business longer than any one person who has ever lived in Alexander. His mercantile life covers a period of 52 years, and his transactions covered a large scope of country, and were as varied as they were extensive. W. G. Pollard is a merchant in the village. D. G. Thomas is manager of the cheese factory, which was built in 1877, by a stock company. They made 272,000 pounds of cheese the first year; their capacity is now 1,200 pounds daily, or the milk from 500 cows.

The village of Alexander was incorporated in 1834. Charles R. Egleston is now the president.

At the depot is an evaporator for drying apples and fruits in their season, which is owned by Charles Benedict, of Attica. Convenient to the railroads is a very extensive storehouse owned by a Mr. Sofsky, of Baltimore, which he uses for storing apples, its capacity being 20,000 barrels.

The Alexander Cemetery, located near the depots, was surveyed in 1813, by Nathan Holmes, and his was the first interment therein. It is beautifully laid out into lots, and the trustees are constantly making improvements in it.

Martin Gray is proprietor of the only saw-mill in town. William Harrington, the dentist, has been a resident for 21 years. Dr. Joel S. Paige came about 1849. He died in 1855, and his widow still resides here. Dr. Edward Smith has lived in town two years, and Dr. E. C. David, a graduate of Ann Arbor (Mich.) University, came in May, 1889.

Alexander has sent out quite a number of men of note, among them being William Tilden Blodgett, who for some time lived in New York

city, and was an influential citizen and a patron of fine arts. He died
in 1875. Henry Martin was at one time president of the Manufacturers'
Bank of Buffalo. He married a sister of Henry Hawkins.

The first religious meeting was held in 1805, Elder Burton presiding.
The first religious society was of the Presbyterian order, in 1807, organized by Harvey Hawkins and Cyrenus Wilbor. A reörganization took
place in 1818, when there were 10 members connected with it. The Rev.
Solomon Hebbard was its first pastor, and the first house of worship was
built of stone in 1828. The present pastor is Rev. McElroy. The church,
built in 1845, will seat about 200 persons, and the property is valued at
$5,000.

The Methodists and Presbyterians used in common a house of worship erected of wood in 1828. Elder Segar aided in organizing a church
as early as 1827, with a very few members. Their present church is
located on Church street, and the property is valued at $8,500. The
building has a seating capacity of 300 persons. There are 35 church
members, and nine teachers and 60 scholars in the Sunday-school.

The Universalist Church in Alexander was begun in 1833, by a few
members, who organized themselves into a society. Their present house
of worship was erected (of wood) June 3, 1833. There are about 30
families connected with the society, and their property is valued at $2,500.
Rev. Herbert W. Carr attends to their spiritual wants.

There is also located in the village a church occupied by the denomination of Free Methodists, but the following is small in numbers.

There is a lodge of the I. O. G. T., No. 796, with the following officers : E. P. Lincoln, C. T. ; Minnie Dart, V. S. ; F. J. Churchill, secretary; John Dart, treasurer; Mrs. M. J. Millington, financial secretary ;
and Mrs. Jennie Webb, chaplain. ·

The Alexander cornet band was organized in 1888. It has now 13
pieces, with Frank Richards as leader, and they meet weekly.

The officers of the Macedonian Lodge, of Alexander, are: George W.
Martin, C. T.; Miss Minnie Dart, V. T.; E. M. Allen, R. S.; Delbert Phelps,
F. S.; Luther Gardner, T.; Mrs. Phelps, C.; R. O. Burt, M.; Mrs. Loren
Pierce, I. G. ; Miss Nettie Zwetsch, sentinel ; Mrs. C. F. Lewis, S. J. T. ;
Emory Lincoln, P. C. T.

Asahel Avery, a Revolutionary soldier, died in New Britain, Conn.,
at an advanced age. His son Rufus G. was born in 1795, came to
Alexander in 1834, and died in 1879, aged 84 years. He drew a pension by reason of service in 1812. He married Keziah G. Goodwill

(who died 1879), daughter of J. Munson Goodwill, of Hartford, Conn., and his children were Sarah, Ruth, John G., Daniel G., Mary J., William C., James M., Julia M., Bradley C., Emma L., Martha E., Charles B., George E., and Rufus G., Jr. The latter was born in Stafford, Conn., October 21, 1824, and came here with his father. He married Helen M., daughter of Capt. Uriah P. B. Monroe, of Batavia, and his children are Florence L. and Walter W. Florence married Ellis R., son of M. W. Hay, of Batavia. She lives on the farm with her father, which place (the Remsen farm) he bought eight years ago, and is now raising improved stock.

George E. Avery came to Alexander in 1848. He served in the late war in Co. M, 9th N. Y. H. A., for three years, and was in the battles of Cold Harbor, Petersburg, Monacacy, Winchester, Charleston Heights, Cedar Creek, Sailor's Run, in front of Petersburg, and in the last battle given to Lee before the surrender, April 9, 1865. He is now a resident of Alexander.

Harvey Andrews, a native of Vermont, came to Middlebury, N. Y., thence removed to Tulare County, Cal., where he died in 1884, aged 84 years. His wife, Annie, bore him three children, Marion, Kirk, and Carlos D. Carlos D. Andrews was born in Middlebury and came to Alexander in 1887, where he died in 1888, aged 51 years. He married Augusta V., daughter of Asa and Clarinda (Alderman) Hogle, and they had one son, Harvey A. Mrs. Andrews lives on the farm owned by her husband, and is 46 years of age.

Fred Burr, son of Joseph, was born in Mecklenburg, Germany, and came to Batavia before his marriage. In 1862 he enlisted in the 27th N. Y. Lt. Art., and died near Richmond, Va., in 1864, aged 30 years. He married Sophia Luplow, and their children were Mary, William, Albert, and Fred E. The latter married Lydia J. White, daughter of Nathan and Sarah (Brothers) White, of Le Roy, and is now a resident of Alexander. His mother married John Munt, of Le Roy, for her second husband.

William Barnett, father of William H., was in the War of 1812. William H. was born April 17, 1833, and moved to Roanoke with his parents when he was nine years of age. He was educated in the common schools. September 28, 1854, he married Mary E. Webber, of Stafford, formerly of England. They have had seven children, two of whom survive, namely: Jennie M. and Jessie C. Mr. Barnett was a soldier in the late war, enlisting twice, first in Co. D, 14 N. Y. Inf. Vols., and second, in Co. M, 2d Mounted Rifles N. Y. Vols. He participated in the battles of Gaines's Mills, Turkey Bend, Malvern Hill, Antietam, Big Bethel, Chancellorsville, second Bull Run, South Mountain, Hanover Court House, White Oak Swamp, Fredericksburg, seige of Yorktown, and Snicker's Gap. Mr. and Mrs. Barnett reside in the village of Alexander.

John Brown, born in the north of Ireland, came to Sandy Hill, N. Y., thence to Clarkson, where he died, aged about 60 years. He married Lucy Barnes, and their chiildren were Phœbe J., David W., George W., Lucy J., David, and John H. The latter, a native of Sandy Hill, was born August 27, 1826, and came to Alexander in 1887, from Attica. He married Salome J. Lyon, and they had one son, Walter N. For his second wife he married Mrs. Amanda M. Donaldson, of Bennington, daughter of John S. and Betsey (Thompson) Lyon, and now resides on road 44, in Alexander. He is a farmer by occupation. He served in the late war in Co. D, 14th N. Y. Vol. Inf., and was discharged August 27, 1862. He was in the seven days' battle of the Wilderness. John S. Lyon (who was in the War of 1812) had 20 brothers and sisters, all of whom attained their majority. Elias Lyon served in Co. M, 9th N. Y. H. A.; John Lyon was in Co. D, 14th N. Y. Vols.; and Moses Lyon went to the war from Oshkosh, Wis.

Nathaniel Baldwin, son of David, a native of Connecticut, died in New Marlboro, Mass., aged 77 years. His wife, Diana, bore him two children, Lucy A. and Dudley. The latter, a native of Massachusetts, came to Alexander in 1861. remaining until his death in 1867, aged 63 years. He married Alta, daughter of Lyman Barber, of Canaan, Conn., and reared children as follows : Exene M., Ellen E., Rose D., Lucy A., John S., and Irwin N. Irwin N. Baldwin was born in Massachusetts, and married Lucy A., daughter of Harrison Cumins, of Bethany, and they have one son, Charles C., who is a hay and grain dealer, and a resident of this town.

Chauncey Cornwell came. from Middletown, Conn., in 1831, and died in 1870, aged 77 years. He served in the War of 1812. He married Mary A., daughter of Thomas and Dolly Church, of Middletown, and their children were Charles, Fidelia, Mary, Jane, John, Shailor, Angeline, Carlos, George, Leonard, and Henry. The latter, also of Connecticut, came here with his father. He married Elizabeth, daughter of David and Mehitable (Frazier) Stark, of Bergen. The children of Henry Cornwell were Chauncey, Carrie, and George (deceased). Mr. Cornwell lives on the farm owned by him the past 12 years ; and his mother survives her husband at the age of 88 years.

Thomas, son of Gideon Garrett, was born in Pennsylvania, and came to Alexander in 1835, where he died in 1861, at the age of 70 years. He married Hannah L. Lewis, of Pennsylvania, who died in 1871. Their children were Gideon, Lydia, Abigail, Penrose, Emma, Jane, Rebecca, Franklin, and Samuel. Samuel Garrett was born in Philadelphia, October 21, 1834, and September 13, 1853, he married Adaline M., daughter of Daniel and Emily (Cooley) Cooley. Their children are Emma and George. The latter married Myrtle Vader, daughter of Cornelius and Azuba (Harrington) Vader, of Linden, N. Y., and their children are Emma M. and Margery L. Mr. Garrett now resides on a farm on road 14, with his father, where he has lived 54 years.

Thomas Chaddock, of Vermont, came to Stafford in 1833, and died in 1834, aged 70 years. He had 14 children, among whom was Luther, who was born in Vermont, and in 1815 came to Alexander, where he died in 1874, aged 76 years. He married Sally, daughter of Capt. Washburn, of Attica, and his children were Rubey, Joseph, Sewell, Luther, Betsey Ann, Mary, Felinda, Benjamin, Pattie A., and Lewis. Lewis Chaddock was born in this town September 17, 1825, and married Laura, daughter of Calvin and Diantha (Burlingame) Underwood. Their children are Sally A., William L., and Julia D. Mrs. Chaddock is 63 years of age, and Mr. Chaddock is 64. He has lived on his place since his birth.

John C. Curtis, a native of Massachusetts, and a son of Edmond who was killed in Canada in the War of 1812, came to Warsaw in 1820, and died in 1878, at the age of 81 years. He also served in the War of 1812, and was in Buffalo when that city was burned. He married Lucy, daughter of Asahel Croft, of Orangeville, N. Y., and their children were Sylvester, Adaline, Edmond, Alfred, Mary Ann, Clarisse, John Harrison, and Marcus L. The latter was born in Warsaw, and came to Alexander in 1886, where he now resides. He married Mary J., daughter of Hiram W. and Rachel (Swan) Davis, of Middlebury, N. Y., and their children are Anson D, Elon J., Noble S., Elzie F., and Arthur E. Mrs. Mary Jane Curtis has one son, Holsa, by her first husband, John B. Smith.

James Day, son of Pelatia, was born in Onondaga Hollow, N. Y., and came to Alexander in 1835, where he died in 1886, aged 82 years. He was the first permanent settler on the farm known as the Day farm, on road 27. He married Amanda Jones, who was born on the Day farm. She died in 1877, aged 69 years. Their children were James H., William H., and Albert H. The latter, born in Pembroke, September 1, 1832, married Hannah H., daughter of Edwin R. and Mary (Hopkins) Greene, and their children were James E. and Mary A. His widow still survives her husband at the age of 60 years. James Elmer Day married Florence, daughter of Jerome B. and Hannah (Clark) Colby, and now resides on the Day homestead. Mrs. Hannah H. Day married George W. Lawton, of Alexander, for her second husband.

George Muchworthy was born in Yarnscombe, Devonshire, Eng., where he lived, and died in 1862, at the age of 65 years. He married Mary Punchard, of England, and his children were Mary, George, Jane, Samuel, William, Henry, Reuben, Susan, Frederick, Elijah, and Mary Ann.

Frederick Muchworthy was born in Devonshire, and in 1872 came to New York city, thence to Stafford. He married for his first wife Eliza Britton, of England, and had four children, Amelia, Susan, William, and Alfred. For his second wife he married Helen, daughter of Thomas and Elizabeth (Newport) Damphier, of Bristol, Eng., and they have three children, viz.: Emily, George, and William H. Mr. Muchworthy resides on road 19, where he has lived three years.

Moses Dickinson, a native of Connecticut, came to Alexander in 1825, where he died September 20, 1868, aged 94 years. He married Rebecca, daughter of Jacob Hart, of Oneida County, who died in 1868, at the age of 87 years. His children were Sophronia, James M., Abbia A., Harriet A., and Moses H. The later was born in Paris, Oneida County, in 1803, and came here at the age of 21 years, remaining until his death, in 1886, aged 83 years. He married Annie, daughter of Gamaliel and Elizabeth (White) Millington, of Shaftsbury, Vt., and their children are Mary L. and Adaline C. Mrs. Annie Dickinson still survives her husband, at the age of 75 years, on the home farm on road 67. Mary L. Dickinson married Eugene B. Wing, of Alexander, son of George W. and Phœbe A. (Bushnell) Wing, and they have a daughter, Minnie D. Adaline C. Dickinson married John Morgan, and his children are Lorraine B. and Moses D.

Schuyler Hindrick was born in Massachusetts and came to Henrietta, N. Y., soon after his marriage, where he died 1860, aged 73 years. He married Abigail Gilman, in Vermont, who died 1851, and their children were Gardner, Melinda, Mary, David, Abigail, Stephen, Warren, Lewis, Byron, and Benjamin F. Benjamin F. Hindrick, born at Sand Lake, Rensselaer County, N. Y., in 1807, came to Alexander in 1863, and married Sally, daughter of Abel and Eunice (Gibbs) Post, of Henrietta. Their children are Francis, Caroline, William, and Lewis. The latter married

Clarissa, daughter of Ira and Ruth (Wood) Armstrong, of Batavia, and lives with his father on the homestead farm.

Thomas Carnes, from Tiperrary, Ireland, lived and died there, aged 51 years. He married Julia Higgins, of the same place, who died at the age of 70 years. Their children were Michael, Patrick, John, Maggie, Nancy, Mary, and Sally. The son Michael was born in Ireland in 1828, came to Quebec in 1879, and to Alexander soon afterwards. He married Nora, daughter of Thomas and Kittie (Taheny) Flinn, and their children are Catherine, Thomas, John, Julia L., and Patrick. Miss Julia L. Carnes lives in Alexander.

Joshua Knight, a native of Massachusetts, came to Bergen in 1815, among the early settlers, and died 1816. He married Hannah White, of Northampton, and their children were Ephraim, Benjamin, Alpheus, Electa, and Silas W. The latter was born in Chesterfield, Mass., May 6, 1821. In 1886 he came to Alexander (from Elba), where he resides. He married Lucy Ann, daughter of Anson and Luranda (Ames) Hulett, of Stafford, and their children are Ann J., Leathy, Theron, and Addie. Ann J. is now Mrs. Thomas Pippin, of Maryland. Leathy married Henry Fellows, of Niagara County, N. Y.

Silas W. Knight served in the late war in Co. H, 78th N. Y. Inf., for three years, and was honorably discharged at Baltimore Hospital for disability in January, 1863. He was in the battles of Harper's Ferry, Winchester, and Cedar Mountain. The grandfather of Mrs. Silas W. Knight (Samuel Ames) served in the war of the Revolution, and her grandfather Hulett was an eminent physician in Connecticut, and was an early practitioner in Byron.

Daniel Lincoln, from Bennington, Vt., was a very early settler—soon after 1800. He located on road 25, remaining there until his death in 1853, aged 91 years. He married, first, Eunice Bragg, of Vermont, and their children were Emory F., Lucius, Appollus, Sophronia, Arathosa, Calvin, and Arial. For his second wife he married Sophronia Tubbs, and for his third wife Susan Tibbals. His son Emory F., at the age of 12 years, came from Vermont with his father, and lived on the homestead until his death in 1884, aged 85 years. He married Janette Nichols, of Alexander, daughter of Thomas and Anna (Duell) Nichols, of Bennington, Vt. Their children were Arial B., Fisher, Franklin, Eveline, Julia A., Warren, Clarissa, and Eunice. Mrs. Janette Nichols survives her husband at the age of 75 years, residing in the village.

Arial B. Lincoln married Emily S. Baker, daughter of Elisha and Mary

Ann (Tisdale) Baker, of Darien, and his children are Otis W. and Merrill
F. . The last mentioned was born in Darien, and married Mary L., daughter of Lewis and Parmelia (West) Munn, and is now living on the old
homestead of his great-great-grandfather.   Elisha and William Baker
served in the War of 1812.   Fisher Lincoln, son of Emory F., a native
of Alexander, married Flavilla, daughter of Leverett and Viola (Sanderson) Peck, of Bennington.   Mr. Lincoln died in 1873, at the age of 36
years.   His children are Lucius D , Belle A. (Mrs. Lewis Johns), of
Beadle County, Dakota, Emory P., and Miles W.   His widow still survives, residing on the home farm, aged 49 years.

The sixth settler among the early pioneers of Alexander was Capt.
Ezekiel T. Lewis, a native of Connecticut, who came in 1806, and died
in 1836, aged 65 years.   He was captain of militia in early days, owned
a large farm on the east side of Tonawanda Creek, was a member of the
Methodist Episcopal Church, and a temperance man.   He was married
three times, first to Phœbe Bushnell, who bore him children as follows:
Sylvester, Betsey, Phœbe, and James.   The latter was born in Oneida
County, came here when 12 years of age, and remained until his death
in 1871, aged 73 years.   He married Phœbe McIntyre, of Vermont,
daughter of Joseph McIntyre, and their children are Cynthia, Ezekiel P.,
Samantha D., Hester A., and Anson.   Anson Lewis was born in Alexander, and married Mary, daughter of Jabez Peck.   Their children are
Jasper B. and James, who were killed at Petersburg, Va., in 1864,
and William W.   For his second wife Mr. Lewis married Hannah,
daughter of Hosea and Lavina Rich, and their children are Charles F.,
Mary J., Cora M., and Jennie A.   The latter married Alexander H.
Webb, a conductor, who was killed on the D., L. & W. Railroad in 1888,
aged 26 years.   Anson Lewis spent all his life on the old homestead.

Loomis Loveridge came from Riga, Monroe County, and located where
he now resides.   He married Emily, daughter of Isaac Butts, of Ogden,
and his children are Charles A., Joel A., George, Emma R., and Fred B.
The latter, a native of Ogden, was born February 27, 1858, and married
Isabel V. Fargo, of Ogden, daughter of John and Abbie (Clark) Fargo.
His children are Judson F., Erva C., Anna B., and Emma R.   Mr. Loveridge is a farmer, residing on road 46, having lived there four years.

Nathaniel Loomis, of Connecticut, came here in 1806, when there were
but a few houses in Batavia.   He moved to Wisconsin, thence to Michigan, and died aged 85 years.   He married Anna Higby (born 1778, died
1834), of Connecticut, and their children were Sylvester, born December

23, 1817; Erastus, born March 21, 1819; Roswell, born June 11, 1810; Mary A., born March 23, 1803; Caroline, born January 17, 1825; Maria, born November 27, 1807; Polly B., born May 30, 1812; Samantha, born March 13, 1814; Francis L., born July 6, 1816; Hanford, born September 6, 1818; and Adaline, born April 20, 1820.   Francis Loomis, born where he now resides, married, first, Fanny Foord, and their children were Irwin and Mary.   His second wife was Olive Southwell, who bore him children as follows: Odell O., Frank A., Sarah J., Scott S., Fred S., Jennie C., Perry A., and Clark.   His third wife was Mrs. Elvira F. Randall, daughter of Norman B. and Lydia (Richards) Raymond.   The children are all living but two.

William Miller came from the vicinity of New York city to Batavia, where he was a farmer for many years.   He finally moved to Alexander, living there 25 years, where he died in 1882, aged 68 years.   His wife, Katherine, bore him children as follows: James, William, and John A. John A. Miller was born in the city of New York, came to Alaxander with his father, and married Annie E., daughter of John and Margaret (Carson) Law.   Their children are George L., Grace A., Elliott J., and Lina A.   Mr. Miller served three years in the late war in Co. C, 151st N. Y. Vols., and was honorably discharged.   He was in the battles of the Wilderness, Fredericksburg, and Cold Harbor.   His wife, Annie E. Miller, lives in Alexander.

Benjamin and Royal Moulton, half brothers, were early settlers, coming in 1810.   The latter was a captain in the Massachusetts militia, and a son of Joseph, who was born in that State.   He married three times and had 19 children.   Capt. Royal Moulton was born near Springfield, in December, 1772, and coming to Genesee County was the first settler on the Batavia road, remaining there until his death, at the age of 93 years.   He was the first Whig supervisor elected in the town.   A man of extended influence, he had not an enemy in the whole country.   He married Betsey Trask, of Springfield, Mass., and his children were Polly, who died in Batavia in 1889, aged 92 years; Lewis, who died aged 82; Lucinda (deceased); Betsey, born 1802, still living at Lancaster, N. Y.; and Marcia, Byram, and Elbridge G.   The latter, born in 1812, has always been a resident of the town.   He married Isabelle M. Clark, of Ohio, by whom he had three children, Frank G., of Batavia, Helen B., and one deceased. For his second wife he married Mary Warren, of Attica, daughter of Pomeroy and Harriet (Buell) Warren, and their children are May E., who died October, 1888, aged 39, Warren E., Hattie C., and Edith A.   Pomeroy Warren served in the War of 1812. To E. G. Moulton is entitled the credit of having done more business in Alexander, in his day, than any other resident. His sales in his store amounted to over $100,000 a year. He was an extensive dealer in every thing raised by the farmer, and had the confidence of the whole community. Mr. Moulton is highly respected and honored by his townsmen. He was supervisor of Alexander several terms, and town clerk a long series of years. In 1859, and again in 1860, he represented Genesee County in the Assembly of the State.

Warren E. Moulton, a native of Alexander, and son of E. G. and Mary Moulton, married Cora A., daughter of David and Betsey (Chaddock) Johnson, and they have one child, Bessie M. He resides on road 59, where he has been for the past 15 years.

The children of Lewis Moulton, son of Capt. Royal, by his wife, Lucy L (Benedict), were Jasper, Orsamond B., Lewis, Jr., Allen J., Lucy L., Josephine, and Olive Loretta. His son, Orsamond B. Moulton, is a native of Alexander, residing on the old Capt. Royal Moulton homestead. He married Emily A., daughter of David and Minerva (Bradway) Thorp, and his children are Elliott C. and Emma F., both of whom were born in Cleveland, Ohio. The latter married C. W. Vrooman. Thomas Bradway was a soldier of the Revolution. Allen J. Moulton, son of Lewis, is also a native of this town, living on his father's farm. He married Annette, daughter of Homer and Elizabeth Nestelle, and they have four daughters, viz.: Flor M., Edna, Grace, and Bessie. Lewis Moulton, Jr., son of Lewis, also a native of Alexander, married Nettie Denslow, and they have one daughter, Minnie, who married Charles, son of James and Anna (Gleason) Lawrence, of Montgomery County, N. Y. Their children are Harry and Marjory, and they reside on the Denslow farm.

Byram Moulton, son of Royal, an early settler, was born here in 1818. He married Corinna L., daughter of Judah and Louise (Adams) Wells. Their children are Edward F., Albert H., Byram, Jr., and Charles W. Mr. Moulton is an iron bridge contractor and builder, and also a farmer and breeder of American and Spanish Merino sheep. He has a flock of 500 head. His sons Edward F. and Albert H. served in the late war in the 9th H. A., and were transferred to the signal corps, being discharged in 1865. Joseph, the grandfather of Byram, served in the Indian and Revolutionary wars. Edward F. Moulton was born in Alexander in 1842. He married Ella E., daughter of Wellington and Phebe (Beardsley) Colby, and they have one son, Albert E., who is now a proprietor of a restaurant on State street, Batavia.

Byram Moulton, Jr., was born in Alexander in 1851, and married Laura Eleanor, daughter of David and Louisa (Beagle) Fleming, of Batavia. He resides on road 12, and is a farmer.

Gamaliel Millington was born in Bennington, Vt. He came from Vermont at the age of 31 years, thence to Alexander, where he died in 1875, at the age of 94 years. By his first wife he had children as follows: Gamaliel, Ann, Deborah, Amie, Esther, and Calvin. By his second wife, Miss Sprague, he had two sons, Quincy and Moses. His son Calvin, now of Alexander, was born in Vermont. He married Martha J., daughter of Gilchrist and Tamma (Towslee) Johnson, of Bethany, and his children are Fred and Arthur, the latter a resident of La Crosse, Wis., and a train dispatcher on the C. & B. Railroad. He married Belle Meader, of Wisconsin. William Johnson (a drum-major) and Gideon Towsley were in the Revolutionary war at Bennington, Vt. Gilchrist Johnson was a native of Connecticut, and came to Bethany at the age of 78, where he died, aged 80 years. He served in the War of 1812. He had one daughter, Martha J. (Johnson) Millington, now living in Alexander.

John Muhs was born in Germany, where he lived, and died at the age of 58 years. He married Mary Morts, and their children were John, Frederica, Morris, Charles, Fritz, Martin, and William. William Muhs was born in Germany and came here in 1886. He married Henrietta Sharnow, of Germany, and their children are Frank, Mattie, and Minnie

John R. Mullen, M. D., was born in St. Lawrence County, N. Y., December 13, 1852. He received a common school and academic education, and in 1871 began to study medicine with his father, Isaac V., and graduated from Buffalo University in 1874. He is a Latin, German, French, and Italian scholar, and writes scientific articles for the leading magazines of the country. In 1870 he married Marion, daughter of Charles Hawkins, of Alexander. He is a practicing physician of this town.

Ira Newton, son of Timothy and Abigail, was born in Barnard, Vt., April 28, 1799. At the age of 17 he came to Alexander, and was employed by his brother Josiah for 14 years. July 4, 1825, he was married to Mary Ann Loomis, and they had two children, Alvira A. and Clark C. His first wife died 1839. His second wife was Betsey Frisbie, who died 1870. The crowning attribute of Ira Newton was that he lived in peace with all men; was never sued, nor never had a lawsuit. His daughter married John King, of Toronto, Can. Clark C. Newton, his only son, was born May 12, 1836, on the farm his father bought soon after marriage. He received a good education. December 29, 1856, he married Sarah E., daughter of H. G. Lincoln, of Bethany. They have two children, Ella M. and Charles Ira. Mr. Newton has been highway commissioner for four years.

Martin North, son of Ebenezer, was a native of Litchfield County, Connecticut, where he died in 1806, aged 86 years. He served in the war of the Revolution for seven years, and drew a pension. He was a wheelwright. He married Mary Agard, daughter of John, who died in 1825. Their son Noah was born in Connecticut, came to Alexander in 1808, and was the first settler on the North farm, so-called, where he lived, and died in 1824, at the age of 39 years. He married Olive, daughter of Reuben and Olive (Gaylord) Hungerford, of Winsted, Conn., and their children were Thetis C., Lot M., Noah, Alcimeda, James A., Olive F., Aurelia N., and Zaxie C. His wife, Olive, died March 11, 1849, in Ohio, aged 61 years. Noah North served as drum-major in the War of 1812. He was a prominent man in the town, and was engaged in so many cases of public trust that on his death a special town meeting was called. Eben North, son of Rufus, came to Alexander in 1816. He died in 1866, aged 76 years. He married, first, Etta Betts, who died in 1841, and second, Mrs. Elizabeth Anderson.

Henry Mitchell, was a native of Massachusetts, where he lived and died. His wife, Elizabeth (now living in Detroit, at the age of 83), bore him five children: Andrew M., Clara, Mary, William, and Nancy L. Nancy L. Mitchell married Henry Banks, of Canandaigua, and had four children who died in infancy, and one still living, viz.: Mary E. Banks, who married Samuel A. Simpson, of Rochester, N. Y., son of Charles and Fanny Simpson. Samuel A. Simpson died in Alexander in 1887, at the age of 53 years. His wife, aged 38 years, survives her husband.

Eliphalet Peck, born in Danbury, Conn., went to Saratoga County, N.Y., and came to Alexander in 1824, settling on the well-known Peck farm, where he died 1840, aged 84 years. By his wife, Abigail, he had children as follows: Nathaniel Eliphalet, Samuel, Benjamin, Asa, Abigail, Rebecca, Ruth, and Eli. The latter was born in Saratoga County, came to Alexander in 1824, and married Nancy, daughter of John and Mary Smith, of Saratoga County. Their children are Walter, Polly M., Priscilla, Adelia, Lois, and Asa. Asa Peck married for his first wife Eliza M.

Van Tassel. For his second wife he married Sultina, daughter of David and Dorcas Root, of Elba, and their children are Emma J., Lucy A., Pamelia, and Charles E. The latter married Mary A., daughter of Herman and Hannah (Green) Day, of Alexander, and they had two sons, Elmer and Harry (deceased). Asa Peck now resides on the homestead farm of his father.

Gehial Stanard was born in New Marlboro, Mass., May 23, 1780, where he died at an advanced age. His son, John Stanard, a native of the above town, came to Alexander in 1810, and was the first settler on the farm known as the "Stanard farm," on road 29, where he lived until his death in 1858, aged 78 years. He married Huldah, daughter of Caleb King, and their children are Mary A., Adaline, Alvira, Eleanora, Huldah, and John P. The latter was born in Alexander, July 3, 1823. He married, January 14, 1847, Ann J., daughter of Zina and Rebecca (Buchanan) Wait, of Darien. Their children are Willis Z., Florence A., Wilber C., Butler R., Nellie M., and Horace A. The latter married Mattie A. Van De Bogart, daughter of George W. and Sarah (Coe) Van De Bogart, of Climax, Mich., and resides with his father on the homestead settled by the grandfather. Butler R. Stanard married Cora M., daughter of Willard and Ellen (Merritt) Pixley, and resides on road 25 corner 26.

Amos Spring was born in Massachusetts, served in the War of 1812, at the burning of Buffalo, and died in Attica, in 1850, aged 71 years. His wife, Reliance Snow, was born in 1780, in Massachusetts, and died in Warsaw, December 3, 1874, aged 94 years. Their children were Erastus, Amos, Harvey, Alpheus, Reliance, Louisa, Rebecca, Olive, and Darius N. The latter was born November 21, 1817, in Le Roy, and is now a resident of Warsaw. He married, April 5, 1840, Angeline, daughter of Alvin and Sally (Terry) Chaddock, of Middlebury, who was born November 14, 1817. Their children are D. Scott, born February 20, 1842, and Sarah J., born March 19, 1850. David Scott Spring married three times. His present wife is Rhoda A., daughter of Azel and Nancy (Melvin) Chaddock, of Bennington, N. Y., and his children by her are Andrew P. and Ruth E. His first wife bore him four children, Stella L., Charles S., Cora A., and Frances H. His second wife was Lucy J. Richardson, who bore him two children, Newton L. and Ernest H. He served in the late war in Co. M, N. Y. H. A., enlisting at the age of 18 years, and was honorably discharged, at Baltimore, in 1865. He was in the battles of Cold Harbor, Petersburg, Winchester (where his blanket was pierced 11 times by the explosion of a shell), Fisher's Gap, and Cedar Creek. Mr. Spring lives in Alexander, and is engaged in farming.

Adam Roth was born on the Rhine, Germany, where he died at the age of 75 years. By marriage with his wife Catherine he had children as follows: Dabolt, Andrew, Philip, Elizabeth, Catherine, Amelia, Sophia, Susanna, Annie, and Adam. The latter was born January 3, 1826, in Germany, and came to New York, August 15, 1849, and to Alexander in 1854, locating on a farm. He married Mena, daughter of Gottifred Bame, of Attica, and their children are Albert, Fred, Hammond, Louis, Charles, and Louise. Mr. Roth lives on a farm on road 66, where he purchased 21 years ago.

Ebenezer Shepard and his son Ebenezer, Jr., were natives of Massachusetts. The latter died in New London, N. H., in 1849, aged 82 years. He married Sarah Burpee, of New London, daughter of Thomas Burpee, and his children were Mary, Daniel, Abigail, Amial, Samuel, Jeremiah, George, Sylvester, Thomas, Benjamin, and James G. The last mentioned was born in New London, N. H., January 4, 1816, came to Alexander in 1851, and settled on a farm on road 33, known as the Nelson farm, which he now owns. He married Mary A., daughter of William and Mary A. (Dudley) Cogswell, of Pittsford, N. Y., and they have one daughter, Mary C., who married Burley, son of Augustus Smith, of Alexander. His children are Florence S., Elizabeth B., Burley, and James A. James G. Shepard is now a retired farmer and publisher, has served as presidential elector in 1858, and is a member of the Grange.

Theodore Schneider was a native of Prussia, where he lived, and died in 1852, at the age of 39 years. He married Mary Dickman, and his children were Gerhard, Henry, and Fred. Fred Schneider, a native of Germany, came to Alexander in 1873. He married Mary, daughter of Constance Bohle, of Rochester, and they have four children, Annie, Augusta, Minnie, and Fred C. Mr. Schneider started the the noted greenhouses located near Attica, in 1881, and has been constantly making additions to them, owing to an increase of business. They are the most extensive in Western New York, outside the cities.

Wilber J. Tallman was born in Wales, Erie County. He served in the late war. He married Cornelia, daughter of William Nichols, of Erie County, and has one son, Adelbert C., who was born in Erie County, and in 1868 came to Alexander. He married Emma E., daughter of Samuel L. and Adaline M. Garrett, and they have one son, Frank G. A. C. Tallman is now a resident of Alexander, and is proprietor of a

saloon and boarding-house on the D., L. & W. Railroad.   Cornelia Tallman died in 1857, aged 22 years.

Cherrick, son of Francis Van De Bogart, a native of Schenectady,
N. Y., came here in 1816, and was the first settler on the present Van De
Bogart farm, bought of the Holland Land Co.   He died in 1835, at the
age of 83 years.   He married Sally Adams, of Schenectady, and his children are Nicholas, Francis, Nancy, Polly, William, James, Margaretta,
John, Cherrick, Abram, and Joseph.   The latter, born in Charleston, Montgomery County, came to Alexander in 1806, where he remained until
his death in 1865, aged 78 years.   He served in the War of 1812.   He
married Lois, daughter of Alexander Knapp (a native of Connecticut), of
Alexander, and his children are Cherrick A., James A., Isaac K., Francis C., Philetus S., Henry I., and Joseph E.   Joseph E. Van De Bogart was
born here June 10, 1824, and married, in 1844, Ann, daughter of Will-
iam and Betsey A. Van De Bogart, of the Black River country, N. Y.
Their children are George F., Henry D., Stephen R., John A., and
Miles H.   The latter married Edith M., daughter of Nial and Josephine
(Moulton) Cooley, of Alexander, and they have one daughter, Alta F.
He is now a resident on the homestead farm of his great-great-grand-
father, on road 19, with his father, Joseph E.   Sarah, a sister of Mrs.
Van De Bogart, is and has been a member of the family for 40 years.
Joseph E. Van De Bogart has served his town as assessor for 18 years
and justice for four years.

Spencer Waldo was a native of New Jersey, but moved to Rutland'
County, Vt.   His children were Loren, Allen, Spencer, and three daugh-
ters.   Allen Waldo came to Batavia (now Alexander) in 1810, and died
in Java, N. Y., in 1858, aged 82 years.   He married Phœbe, daughter of
Thomas Rice, and their children were Catherine, Phœbe A., and Allen
A.   Allen A. Waldo came here at the age of three years, with his father,
in covered wagons, from Vermont.   He married Phœbe A., daughter of
Nicholas and Rebecca (Williams) Van De Bogert, and their children are
Loren C., Mariette, Edward A., Violetta (a widow with one daughter),
Emily P., Ellen E., Nathan P., and Clinton.

David Williams, a native of York County, Pa., came to Rochester, and
died in 1863, at the age of 65 years.   He married Jane Eel, and their children were Mary, James, Joseph, Jane, Susan, Hattie, and David.   David
was born in Pennsylvania, came to Bethany in 1869, located on a farm,
and in 1886 removed to Alexander village.   He married Lucinda Hurlburt, of Naples, N. Y.   David, Hattie, and Charles were their children.

11

For his second wife he married Caroline Scribner, of Victor, N. Y. She is a daughter of Abram and Henrietta Scribner. Mr. Scribner is a retired farmer, living in Alexander village.

John D. Egleston, son of Joseph, was a native of Massachusetts. He moved to Ohio, and died at the age of 65 years. He married Betsey Hoxie, of Marcellus, N. Y., daughter of Rowland and Renhama Hoxie. Their children were Eliza, Louisa, Eveline, Renhama, Jeanette, Jane, Mary, Lavender, Maria B., and Alexander. The latter was born in Marcellus in 1812, and died at the age of 39. He married Ann E., daughter of Ebenezer and Eliza (Snow) Snell, and their children are Jennie E. (Mrs. Lucius Roth); Frank Lewis, of Batavia; and Charles R., of Alexander. Charles R. Egleston lives with his mother, who is 79 years of age. He has been a school teacher eight years, a justice of peace, constable, and president of the village. William Snell and Silas Snow served in the Revolutionary war.

Frank C. Zwetsch, a native of Prussia, came to Alexander in 1852, and died in 1865, aged 68. He married Dora Peck, and had nine children, among whom was Peter, who came here in 1854. He married Christine Woelfley, of Germany, and their children were Emily and John, who reside here. Philip Zwetsch, a native of Prussia, went to Attica in 1852, but now resides in Alexander. He married Margaret Weimar, of Alexander, daughter of George and Margaret, and his children are George, Charles, Philip, Lizzie, James, Maggie, and Harry. Mr. Zwetsch has been a merchant 32 years, a justice of the peace 13 years, was deputy sheriff three years, and notary seven years. John J. Zwetsch served in the late war, and died at the age of 60. Christian also served in the late war.

Daniel Kelsey, son of William, came to this town in 1849, and died in 1861, aged 53 years. He married for his first wife Penninah Van Wart, of Le Roy, and they had eight children. For his second wife he married Sarah Harris, of Le Roy, and had one son, De Forest. Theodore, son of Daniel, is a native of Le Roy, came in 1840, and died in 1889, aged 49 years. He married Lucy Crawford, of Bethany, November 5, 1861. She was a daughter of Daniel and Mary (Fuller) Crawford. Their children are Charles, Mary, and Arthur, with whom their mother resides.

BATAVIA.

BATAVIA.—We here append a list (incomplete as it must be) of early settlers and pioneers of the town of Batavia to 1820, repre_ sented by the present limits of the town.   We have taken great pains to make the list as full as possible, but difficulties are met with in every direction.   Many of the names are taken from the books of the Holland Land Co., which undoubtedly include names of some who took contracts, but never became actual settlers and purchasers.   Where no date is given the inference is that they were here before 1820:

Andrew Adams, 1819 ; Elisha Adams, 1801 ; Joseph Alvord, 1802 ; John Alger, 1805 ; David Anderson, 1804 ; Libbeus Allen,.1817 ; Dr. J. Arnold, 1802 ; Thomas Ashley, 1801 ; James Brisbane, 1798 ; William Blackman, 1801 ; Hiram Blackman, 1801 ; David Bowen, 1803 ; William H. Bush, 1806 ; Benjamin Blodgett, 1808 ; Ephraim Brown, 1809 ; Isaiah Babcock, 1811 ; Guilliam Bartholf, 1815 ; Jeremiah Bennett ; J. I. Bartholf, 1819 ; Ira Boutwell, 1818 ; John Branan, 1800 ; T. Beckwith, 1815 ; James A. Bill_ings, 1818 ; Thomas Bliss, 1819 ; James Cawte ; Samuel Benedict ; Daniel B. Brown ; Richard Buell ; M. Brooks, 1803 ; Clement Carpenter, 1818 ; William Curtis, 1803 ; T. B. Campbell, 1814 ; Russell Crane, 1802 ; E. M. Cook, 1815 ; Benjamin Cary, 1804 ; Ebe_ nezer Cary, 1802 ; Charles Cooley, 1802 ; Silas Chapin, 1802 ; Daniel Curtis, 1802 ; James Clement, 1802 ; Jeremiah Cutler, 1802 ; Elisha Cox, 1803 ; Nathaniel Coleman, 1803 ; Eleazer Cantling, 1811 ; L. L. Clark, 1805 ; Simeon Cummings, 1808 ; John Cotes, 1817 ; Trumbull Cary, 1805 ; James Cochrane, 1802 ; General Worthy L. Churchill ; Daniel H. Chandler ; Gideon Dunham, 1801 ; Garret Davis, 1801 ; Peleg Douglass, 1803 ; Levi Davis, 1804 ; Silas Dibble, Jr., 1805 ; Hugh Duffy, 1805 ; John Dorman, 1808 ; L. Dis_ brow, 1810 ; Andrew Debow, 1813 ; Andrew Dibble, 1816 ; Richard Dibble, 1816 ; John De Wolf, 1805 ; Joseph Ellicott, 1798 ; Andrew A. Ellicott, 1812 ; Gideon Ellicott, 1812 ; John B. Ellicott, 1812 ; Benjamin Ellicott, 1798 ; Dr. C. Chapin, 1801 ; David E. Evans, 1803 ; William Ewing, 1805 ; Seymour Ensign ; Phineas Ford, 1809 ; John Forsyth, 1802 ; Libbeus Fish, 1806 ; Eden Foster, 1805 ; Ezekiel Fox, 1805 ; Othniel Field, 1807 ; Orin Follett, 1816 ; Roswell Graham, 1802 ; E. Gettings, 1802 ; Samuel F. Geer, 1801 ; David Goss, 1804 ; R. Godfrey, 1805 ; Thomas Godfrey, 1805 ; Linus Gunn, 1806 ; Alan_ son Gunn, 1806 ; Horace Gibbs, 1813 ; Thomas Green, 1817 ; Libbeus Graves ; Rufus Hart, 1802 ; James Holden, 1802 ; Paul Hinkley, 1802 ; Paul Hill, 1802 ; Jesse Hurlburt, 1802 ; Hugh Henry, 1803 ; James Henry, 1803 ; John Herring, 1805 ; Hinman Holden, 1805 ; Samuel C. Holden, 1806 ; General Amos Hall, 1809 ; David Hall, 1808 ; R. O. Holden, 1814 ; Winter Hewitt, 1812 ; James G. Hoyt, 1812 ; John Hickox ; Silas Hollister, 1814 ; Joseph Hawks, 1802 ; H. Jerome, 1804 ; Samuel Jacks, 1811 ; Seymour Kell_ ogg, 1807 ; Zenas Keyes, 1804 ; Chauncey Keyes ; William Keyes ; Solomon Kingsley, 1806 ; John Lamberton, 1803 ; John S. Leonard, 1803 ; Henry Lake, 1803 ; William Lu_ cas, 1803 ; John B. Leonard, 1813 ; John Lamberton, 1802 ; Amos Lamberton, 1803 ; Reu_ ben Lamberton, 1805 ; Thomas Layton, 1804 ; David Locke, 1813 ; John Lown, 1813 ;

George W. Lay, 1817 ; P. Lewis, 1801 ; A. Lincoln, 1804 ; ——— Leonard, 1812 ; David McCracken, 1801 ; Asa McCracken, 1803 ; Daniel McCracken, 1802 ; Rufus McCracken, 1802 ; James McKain, 1802 ; Benjamin F. Morgan, 1802 ; David Mather, 1802 ; Elisha Mann, 1802 ; E. Messenger, 1804 ; Azor Marsh, 1804 ; David C. Miller, 1808 ; Thomas McCulley, 1816 ; Ebenezer Mix, 1809 ; Lemon Miller, 1816 ; Wheaton Mason, 1820 ; William McCormick, 1813 ; N. Miner, 1804 ; R. Noble, 1801 ; Zerah Phelps, 1802 ; Peter Powers, 1802 ; William Pierce, 1803 ; Blanchard Powers, 1806 ; Patrick Powers, 1809 ; James Post, 1803 ; Tracy Pardee, 1816 ; Benjamin Porter, 1801 ; William Rumsey. 1801 ; Nathan Rumsey, 1807 ; Stephen Russell, 1801 ; Benjamin Russell, 1802 ; H. Rhodes, 1802 ; Abel Rowe, 1801 ; Amos Ranger, 1802 ; Samuel Ranger, 1810 ; J. Z. Ross, 1811 ; Calvin Rich, 1813 ; Alpheus Reynolds, 1814 ; Daniel Upton, 1818 ; Aaron Van Cleve, 1809 ; Samuel Thomas, 1815 ; Reuben Town, 1803 ; Rowlen Town, 1802 ; I. Norman Town, 1808 ; E. Tillottson, 1802 ; Benjamin Tainter, 1803 ; Joel Tyrrill, 1805 ; P. L. Tracy, 1813 ; Moses Taggart, 1817 ; Ephraim Towner ; Henry Wilder, 1802 ; Aaron White, 1801 ; J. Washburn, 1802 ; William Wood (pioneer blacksmith),1802 ; Jonathan Wood, 1805 ; Reuben W. Wilder, 1805 ; Oswald Williams, 1806 ; Elias Williams, 1807 ; Abel Wheeler, 1807 ; John B. Watkins, 1812 ; Oliver Wilcox, 1813 ; David D. Waite, 1813 ; Joseph Wheaton, 1814 ; Richard Williams, 1815 ; M. Wurts, 1815 ; James Walton, 1817 ; James W. Stevens, 1800 ; Elijah Spencer, 1802 ; Isaac Spencer, 1802 ; Isaac Sutherland,1803 ; Abraham Starks,1803 ; Joshua Sutherland, 1803 ; David Smith, 1804 ; Isaac Smith, 1804 ; Henry Starks, 1806 ; J. P. Smith, 1810 ; Richard Smith, 1817 ; Alva Smith, 1815 ; William Sullings, 1817 ; William Seaver, 1817 ; Erastus Smith ; S. Stoughton, 1809 ; Moses and Aaron Wilcox, 1818 ; William H. Wells ; William Watkins, 1817 ; Seth Wakeman, 1820 ; Benajah Worden ; N. Walker, 1804.

It was under date of February 24, 1802, that Joseph Ellicott applied for the new county of Genesee. It was taken from Ontario, and erected by act of March 30, 1802. Then Mr. Ellicott removed his land office from Ransom's to the new building he had erected in " the forks of the trail," leading from the Genesee to Lewiston and Buffalo. The first land office was really located near where D. E. E. Mix lives. It was only a temporary affair. The early settlers stopped in that section of the place and unpacked their traps. The town of Batavia at this date included the entire Holland Purchase. From this town (or territory) other towns, then counties, were formed, so rapid was the influx of settlers until 1812. In that year Alexander, Bergen, Bethany, and Pembroke were taken off, and Elba and Stafford in 1820, leaving the present town beautifully located in the center of the county. Its surface is level, or gently undulating ; a limestone ridge, forming a terrace from 20 to 50 feet high, extends east and west through the north part of the town. Tonawanda Creek flows slowly northward to Batavia village, and bending westward passes through the town near the center to the west border. The other principal stream is Bowen's Creek, which flows northwesterly across the

southwest corner of the town into the Tonawanda. The soil is a deep
sandy and gravely loam, very fertile, and has a clay subsoil. The town
is rectangular in shape, is nine miles east and west, and six miles north
and south, and contains 34,437 acres of land.

The first settlers in the township were Isaac Sutherland, who erected a
log house on his farm two miles west of the village, and Col. William Rumsey and Gen. Worthy L. Churchill, who settled in the east part. Others
were John Lamberton, Samuel F. Geer, and Benjamin Morgan. The
first town meeting was held at Vandeventer's tavern (now Newstead,
Erie County), March 1, 1803. The following officers were elected:
Supervisor, Peter Vandeventer; town clerk, David Cully; assessors,
Enos Kellogg, Asa Ransom, Alexander Rhea; commissioners of highways, Alexander Rhea, Isaac Sutherland, Suffrenus Maybee; overseers
of the poor, David Cully, Benjamin Porter; collector, Abel Rowe;
constables, John Mudge, Levi Felton, Rufus Hart, Abel Rowe, Seymour
Kellogg, Hugh Howell; overseers of highways, Martin Middaugh, Timothy Hopkins, Orlando Hopkins, Benjamin Morgan, Rufus Hart, Lovell
Churchill, Jabez Warren, William Blackman, Samuel Clark, Gideon Dunham, Jonathan Willard, Thomas Layton, Hugh Howell, Benjamin Porter, and William Walsworth.

The settlement for each year up to 1809 was as follows: in 1801 there
40; 1802, 56; 1803, 230; 1804, 300; 1805, 415; 1806, 524; 1807,
607; 1808, 612; and 1809, 1,160. In 1825 there was a population of
3,352 in the town and village. In 1840 there was 4,000; in 1875 over
7,000; and it is presumed there is now a population of 12,000 in the
town and village, with a sure and steady increase.

James L. Barton, son of Sheriff Barton, in 1807, in commenting on the
early settlement of the town, writes:

"Between Stafford and Batavia were a number of farms taken up by settlers. My
father was sheriff that year (1807), and executed McLean. Governor Tompkins was
circuit judge. The great number attending the trial made it difficult to get lodgings,
and the judge and sheriff slept in the same bed. Near the arsenal in Batavia the road
divides, one branch to Buffalo, the other to Lewiston *via* Lockport. The latter was
called Queenston road. On it, for four or five miles, were only four log houses. The
first house from Dunham's tavern, after crossing the openings and the Indian village, was
Walworth's (tavern), 13 miles."

Gideon Dunham, Sr., a Revolutionary soldier, came in 1804, and kept
a tavern until his death in 1841. He came from Massachusetts, and was
mixed up in Shay's rebellion. He had a noted peach orchard, and it
was a celebrated resort for pleasure parties who went to " Gid's to eat

peaches and hear him swear." His son, Shubael Dunham, succeeded him in tavern-keeping. He was also a member of the State legislature in 1823, and again in 1826, and also a presidential elector. He was a very prominent man in his day, and died in 1848.

We are enabled to give the location of a few of the pioneer settlers. Rufus McCracken, in Jauuary, 1802, bought lot 6, section 10, 168 acres, for $263.37. David McCracken, at the same time, bought lot 8, section 10, 152 acres, for $418. Abel Rowe, in April, 1803, bought lot 8. Samuel F. Geer, in October, 1802, bought lots 5 and 6, sections 7 and 8. Isaac Sutherland, in November, 1803, bought lots 1 and 2, sections 7 and 8. Benjamin Morgan, in November, 1802, bought lot 2, section 6. All the above were in the west part of the town. In the east part Col. William Rumsey bought, in July, 1803, lot 8, section 4.

Turner gives some interesting narratives obtained from personal interviews with the early pioneers, which are worth quoting. That of Mrs. Anna Foster, wife of Eden Foster, is as follows:

"In the year of 1805 we settled upon a farm near Batavia. There were then inhabitants enough to make an agreeable neighborhood. We used to have ox-sleds; occasionally it would be out to Gideon Dunham's, where we used to avail ourselves of the services of the left-handed fiddler, Russell Noble.

"Some of our earliest parties were got up by first designating the log house of some settler, and each one contributing to the entertainment; one would carry some flour, another some sugar, another eggs, another butter; and so on; the aggregate making up a rustic feast. These parties would alternate from house to house. Frolics in the evening; would uniformly attend husking bees, raisings, quiltings, and pumpkin pearings. All were social, friendly, obliging; there was little aristocracy in those primitive days. John Forsyth settled near Dunham's grove in 1802, remaining there until 1807. Joseph Hawks came to Batavia in 1802, and moved to Erie County in 1805. It took him three days with a yoke of oxen and a wagon to go about 18 miles."

In the western part of the town William H. Bush, whose wife was a sister of James Post, who settled in 1803, was the pioneer miller, carder, dresser, distiller, papermaker and farmer, and a narrative of his taken from Turner is well worth reading:

"I moved my family from Bloomfield in May, 1806. The settlers on the Buffalo road between my location and Batavia village were Isaac Sutherland, Levi Davis, Timothy Washburn, Rufus McCracken, Daniel McCracken, Thomas Godfrey, Linus Gunn, Henry Starks, Alanson Gunn, David Bowen, John Lamberton, living on the road west. There was then less than 100 acres cleared on the Buffalo road in the distance of six miles west of Batavia. I built a log house, covered it with elm bark,—could not spare time to build a chimney,—laid a better floor in my house, plastered the cracks, and hired an acre of land cleared—just enough to prevent the trees falling upon my house. When the mill was built I had it paid for, but to accomplish it I had sold some pork

and grain I had produced by working land upon shares in Bloomfield—in fact, every_
thing but my scanty household furniture. My saw-mill proved a good investment ;
boards were much in demand at $7.50 per thousand ; the new settlers stocked the mill
with logs to be sawed on shares. In 1808 I built a machine shop, a carding and cloth.
dressing establishment. These were the first upon the Holland Purchase. On the
10th of June, that year, I carded a sack of wool, first ever carded by a machine on the
Purchase. It belonged to George Lathrop, of Bethany. I also dressed a full piece of
cloth for Theophilus Crocker. There are on my books the names of customers from as
far south as Warsaw and Sheldon ; from the east as far as Stafford ; from the west to
the Niagara River and Lake Erie, including Chautauqua County ; from pretty much all
of the settled portion of the Purchase. I carded in the season of 1818 3,029 lbs. of
wool ; the largest quantity for any one man was 70 lbs., the smallest 4 lbs. The lots
averaged 18 lbs. Allowing three lbs. to a sheep, the average number of sheep then kept
by the new settlers would be six ; though it is presumed that the number was larger,
as in those days much wool was carded by hand.

"The machinists of the present day may be glad to learn how I procured my machinery. I bought my hand-shears of the Shakers at New Lebanon ; my press-plate at
a furnace in Onondaga ; my screw and box at Canaan; Conn.; my dye-kettle, press, papers, etc., at Albany. My transportation bill for these things was over $200. I built a
grist-mill in 1809 ; in 1817 a paper-mill and distillery. I manufactured the first ream
of paper west of the Genesee River. During all the period of my milling operations I
was clearing up the farm where I now reside. Coming into the woods, as I have related, dependent almost wholly upon the labor of my hands, in the first 20 years success had so far attended my efforts that I had accumulated some $15,000 or $16,000."

The above mills were destroyed by fire in 1832. The present mill was
built soon after by Clifford & Bailey. It is now owned by John Garwood, and has a capacity of 50 barrels of flour per day. The saw-mill
built by Mr. Bush in 1806 is now owned by Martin Herbolt.

At Bushville several years ago there was a very extensive canning factory, which made a lively business in its day. But its success was not
of long duration. Some of the plant was moved to Batavia.

In 1850 Charles Cornwall commenced making brick on road 50, and
still·continues the manufacture to the extent of about 100,000 yearly.

In 1875 some 20 members of Friends, at Bushville, built a church. The
first person in charge of the church and society was Mary G. Weaver,
now the president of the W. C. T. U. of the State of New York. W. L.
Dean now attends to the spiritual wants of the society. There are 40
members connected with it. The church is built of wood, at a cost of
about $500, and will comfortably seat 100 persons. They also have a
Sabbath school of 25 scholars and three teachers.

A Dr. Northrup began practice at Bushville about 1840. He died in
1861.

At Dawes Corners, in the, north part of the town, on the Elba town line,

Dr. J. K. Billings settled early. He was a noted physician in his day and practiced over a large scope of country. On the Buffalo road, six miles from Batavia, was located a tavern, at about 1826, kept by Solomon Frisbie. In the southeast corner of the town one Bartholf kept a tavern stand as late as 1854.

One authority tells us that "Batavia" in the Seneca dialect is *Ge-ne-un-da-sais-ka*, the place of mosquitoes, or "Mosquito Town." Another Indian derivation is *Deo-on-go-wa* (the great hearing place).

From best information available we learn that early in 1801 (in January or February) Mr. Ellicott fixed his mind on this location, determining to locate the land office and build up a town. February 17, 1801, he writes to Richard M. Stoddard, at Canandaigua, as follows:

"I expect to make my establishment at or near the Bend of Tonnewauta, and there (or then) let the Genesee Road fork, one to be directed to Buffalo, the other to Queenston, and place my office in the fork looking Eastward. Should you be inclined to improve a 40-acre lot there you can have it."

The fork is where the arsenal stood, opposite the present residence of F. B. Redfield. A post route had previously been established, leading from Canandaigua, by Avon, to the Bend (Batavia), and thence through the "Big Plains," on the Tonnewauta Indian Reservation, to Lewiston. Mr. Ellicott, in writing to Paul Busti, May 30, 1801, says:

"Finding it extremely inconvenient living from the Post Road, I am about making an establishment thereon. I could have wished, however, for a place more central in my district, for the Queenston and Buffalo Road to have forked, but the Tonnewauta Reservation prevented. This establishment will be situate in the 12th Township and 2d Range. The Tonnewauta Creek, a stream of Water 80 feet in breadth, will pass through the Town, at the Western extremity of which the two most public Roads in this Country will fork: one leading to Queenston, in Upper Canada, and the other to New Amsterdam (now Buffalo) at the East end of Lake Erie, Presque Isle, and New Connecticut. The Building Lots will contain 40 acres of land, 20 perches in front, and 320 in depth, being a sufficiency of land, well cultivated, to raise bread, and support a family.

"This place being the first establishment, its local situation cannot otherwise be than always a well situated Village, and probably the next County Town, and a Post Town, as soon as I can have a building erected for an office. I beg leave to compliment this place with the name Bustiville, or Bustia. Several lots are already spoken for, and one house erected."

July 14, 1801, Mr. Ellicott further writes:

"It is with pleasure that I enclose a plan of Bustia, or Bustiville."

Calling the place by that name was opposed by Mr. Busti, as conveying the idea of something ferocious, and Mr. Ellicott yielded to Mr. Busti's wishes. July 18th Mr. Ellicott, writing to John Thompson, directing him to go to Canandaigua, says:

" You can return by Big Tree, and pay Minor for the Pork, and from thence you can explore the road Big Tree to the new town at the Bend. That place is not to be called Bustiville, as I had formally an intention, that gentleman not possessing a wish to have his name perpetuated in that way."

After Mr. Ellicott had abandoned the above name he designed calling it Tonnewauta, as appears by his letter of July 31, 1801 :

" In my last letter I neglected mentioning that I had given over the idea of covering the ' *House* ' at Tonnewauta Town with bark. Indeed, I have ever considered those kind of coverings as money thrown away, when made use of for Dwelling Houses; as all work, done merely temporary, is labor, time, and money lost ; therefore my object is to have everything executed for permancey. Mr. Eggleston has engaged to be at Tonnewauta in two weeks, and make shingles and cover the House in a good and substantial manner. I could have it done sooner, but am of the opinion this is the shortest period. If the roads are not too bad to bring some laths from the saw-mill it would be better to shingle on than split stuff. However, if the laths cannot be procured by the period the shingles are made, I suppose rived laths will do.

" P. S.—The pitch of the roof to be middling flat. I enclose a plan of Tonnewauta, which you will find is at last modified agreeably to my ideas when last there ; that is, to have the Public Square in the forks of the Big Tree and Connewaugus roads."

The precise point of these forks is near where Dellinger avenue intersects Main street, or where the Hon. D. E. Evans built his house (since occupied as a school by Mrs. Bryan), a view being obtained of all the roads in every direction. It will thus be seen that this place was once called " Tonnewauta," for a short time at least, and the " *House* " above noted was important as being the focus of operations of the Holland Land Company.

August 6, 1801, Mr. Busti wrote to Mr. Ellicott as follows :

" By the sketch of the town whose name deriving from mine, I wish you to suppress, and to change to that of its founder, or, if you prefer it, into that of ' *Batavia*.' " [1]

Mr. Busti also says :

" I approve of the cheapness of your prices for the lots, but as it may induce speculation I leave it to you to consider whether it would not be advisable to oblige the purchaser to build a convenient House, in a fixed period, on each Lot. The site of your office is chosen with judgment, and I hope will stop all travelers to the West, to make bargains with you. I suppose that in the neighborhood of the office you will take 500 acres, the half of the 1,000 allowed to you according to contract."

September 8, 1801, Mr. Ellicott, writing from Ransom's, says :

" In respect to the Lots in the Town of Batavia I had anticipated your idea: I dispose of none but to absolute settlers, and only one lot to one man. My intention in laying out the town was for the purpose of forming a compact settlement, and should I dispose of four or five Lots to one man my object would be defeated : and if the place should ever become of much importance the purchaser of a Town Lot will be enabled to

---

[1] In honor of the republic to which the Dutch proprietors belonged.

speculate upon part of his front, which I conceived would be a sufficient inducement to encourage the settlement of the place. In respect to the 500 acres, the half of the 1,000 allowed by contract, I have not as yet fixed its boundaries."

The next allusion to the name of Batavia is in a letter from Mr. Ellicott to Mr. Busti, dated West Genesee, October 3, 1801, and is as follows :

"In my last of Sept. 12th (from Canandaigua) I promised to write you immediately on my return to my office (Ransom's), at which place I expected to arrive in a few days, but on my arrival at *Batavia* I found it necessary to remain there to stimulate the hands employed in the erection of a *Mill-Dam*, at that place ; my Brother, who has that business in charge, being at times, in consequence of indisposition with a slight fever, unable to attend to it. In consequence thereof I was detained so long that I did not reach my quarters here until the 30th *ultimo*."

The first letter written from this place which would seem to settle its name is from Ellicott to Busti dated "Batavia, 7th Nov., 1801," and reads:

"I have delayed writing until this period, with a hope that I should have been enabled to inform you that the Saw-Mill we are erecting at this place, to accommodate the settlement with boards, was in motion, but in this I am disappointed. This season has been extremely unfavorable for business, in this part of the country, as well on account of the continual rains, as that of almost the whole of the people in the infant settlement having been afflicted with the Billious and other Fevers, which circumstance has greatly retarded all our operations, as well as the settlement, and add to the catalogue of our misfortunes.

"The snow commenced falling the night before last, and is now 10 inches deep. I am happy, however, to be enabled to inform you that, amidst all the difficulties we have had to contend with, the Saw-Mill is in such a state of forwardness, that, without something very extraordinary occurs, we shall be able, shortly, to supply the settlement with boards, an article much wanted.

"In regard to the name of this place, it heretofore was called the Bend, from the circumstance of the Bend of the Creek, and is generally known by that name, but I have baptized it by the name of *Batavia*."

The saw mill above alluded to was an object of great solicitude. Its construction was of slow progress, but it was completed in December, as per letter of Ellicott's, dated "Ransom's, Dec. 4, 1801 ":

"The Saw-Mill I have been erecting at Batavia, which has cost a deal of labor, not being a natural seat, but a place where a convenience of this kind is absolutely necessary, will, the millwright informs me, be in motion by the 10th inst., at which period we expect to begin to make ourselves and the settlers comfortable floors, etc."

This saw-mill, operated until about 1822, was situated directly above the grist-mill that stood upon the ground where the present water works building now stands. The pine timber cut up at the mill was brought from the "Pinery" (now Elba, or Pine Hill), six miles distant, and, the demand for lumber being great, Mr. Ellicott employed Isaac Sutherland to cut a road to the "Pinery," and the job was commenced in January,. 1802.

The building designed for the land office appears to have been com-pleted in December, 1801. It was a two-story log building of good size, and situated in front of where D. E. Evans's house stood; and in rear of it was erected a kitchen for the accommodation of Mr. Ellicott and his household. On its completion John Thompson and others in the employ of the company occupied it, but Mr. Ellicott did not remove his office from Ransom's until the spring of 1802.

A road through the village being of vital importance, Mr. Ellicott en-gaged John Lamberton (with the assistance of one Mayo) to cut a road' 100 feet wide and two miles long, from the west bounds of the village, where Mr. Redfield now lives, east, which road is now Main street. The contract price was $12 per acre, the timber to be cut up for logging, sub-sequently to be removed by the owners of the lots living upon the road.

A grist-mill was talked of as early as February, 1802, but was not com-pleted until early in 1804, which event was hailed with delight, for it was sadly needed among even the few residents at that time, who had been obliged to go long distances for flour and meal.

As early as 1801 this place was decided upon for a village and the permanent location of the land office, and several people were attracted here to look around for a residence, among them being Abel Rowe, who arrived in March, 1801. He located on the lot opposite the present land office, raising the first building ever erected in the place. The first frame building was erected on what is now the corner of Main and Church streets, just west of where the old Presbyterian meeting-house stood, and was built by Isaac Sutherland in 1802 as a residence for him-self and family. About the same time he and Mr. Geer put up another frame building, designed for their use as a joiner's shop, east of the dwelling. James Brisbane purchased for $700, in the summer of 1803, the first building from Mr. Sutherland, which was occupied as a dwelling by James W. Stevens. It afterwards became Mr. Brisbane's residence.

During the summer of 1802 William Munger erected the west half of what was known as Keyes House (or tavern), occupied by him, then by Mr. Rowe, and afterwards by Keyes, who enlarged, improved, and kept it as a tavern for many years. It was referred to as "Rowe's Hotel," as appears in a postscript of a letter of Mr. Ellicott's to John M. Minor, of Genesee, in which he says :

"A line forwarded either to the Transit Store House, or Mr. Rowe's Hotel, at the bend of Tonnewauta, will come to hand."

Soon after this Stephen Russell put up a log house on the spot where the old "Genesee House" stood, and where the Genesee Hotel, a brick building, stood, corner of Main and State streets, being the second building erected in the village. In March, 1801, Isaac Sutherland erected a log house on the Lewiston road northeast of the village. In the summer of 1802 Mr. Ellicott erected what was the east wing of the D. E. Evans residence, to which place he moved the land office, and the same year tore down the old two-story land office.

Hotels and taverns.—Abel Rowe was the first tavern-keeper. He located nearly opposite the land office in 1801, but afterwards changed so Mr. Ellicott could locate his tract of 500 acres reserved by him. Rowe founded the "Keyes" stand, afterwards called "Frontier House." Under the administration of Rowe, and afterwards Keyes, the tavern was widely known in early times. It was the *home* of the early settler, whose business was with the land office. About its yard used to be seen the huge covered wagons that transported goods from Albany to Buffalo, and during the War of 1812 was headquarters for officers of the army. This building stood on ground now owned by George Brisbane. A part of it was moved to Church street, and is now used as a dwelling. Keyes occupied it as late as 1829, and during the Morgan excitement announced himself as an anti-Mason. He was also proprietor of a line of stages. He died in 1833. At the court-house (now Ellicott Hall), in 1811, was a place of entertainment, the south portion of the building being used for that purpose. Aaron Van Cleve was sheriff and landlord. John Heacock (or Hickox) kept it in 1815. That portion of the building was so used up to 1820. One Ganson was the proprietor of an hotel in 1823.

Many of the present residents will recollect the "Genesee House," built by C. M. Russell, on the corner of Main and State streets. This was the location of the "Old Snake Den tavern" (one-half log and frame), which was burnt in 1833. C. M. Russell kept this place from 1802 until his death, in 1809, when Horace Gibbs (father of D. D. Gibbs) took possession. Mr. Gibbs married Russell's widow. He was a builder by occupation, and was also a farmer and proprietor of a daily line of stages from Canandaigua to Buffalo, owning 75 horses. Other landlords there were, among whom were Burnham, a partner of Russell, Gifford & Putnam, Belden, Monroe, and Gilbert, between 1825 and 1833. There was also John W. Stewart, brother of the late James W. Stewart, who kept it in 1826, and where William Morgan boarded. The old Eagle tavern was built in 1822, by Gibbs and a company. Erastus Smith, from Buffalo, was its first landlord.   Bissell Humphrey, who had worked for Gibbs, was one of its most noted landlords.   In 1827 he bought the site for $558.75, and put up a new tavern.   This was of brick and painted yellow, and was burned in 1834.   Another tavern or hotel soon took its place, and was called the "Eagle" until 1868, when Collins & Andrews changed the name to St. James.   Some of its proprietors up to that period were Erastus Smith, E. Hall, Tisdale, Wilson (1857), Bradt, Van De Bogart (1863), McLean (1864), and Farnsworth (1866).   O. C. Parker was there in 1886, when it was burned.   A new and handsome brick structure, the Richmond, has been erected on its site, and is under the management of W. J. Mann, of Buffalo.

In 1815 Hinman Holden purchased of James Cochrane a small tavern, which he removed, and upon its site built an old-fashioned three-story framed "inn."   This was about where 112 to 118 Main street is.   Mr. Holden kept the tavern until 1822, when he leased it.   Among its proprietors were James McKain (about 1825), Russell, Ezekiel Hall (1836), A. Smith (1840), J. Chatfield (who kept it as a temperance house in 1842), B. G. Tisdale, and others.   David Danolds kept it in 1826, and it was here that Morgan and Miller were taken during the excitement.   S. D. Green, an anti-Mason, succeeded Danolds.   The American Hotel, a brick edifice, replaced it, which was burnt in 1850.

In 1813 a Mr. Leonard built the house now owned by Solomon Masse, and used it as a tavern.   He died, and Cotton Denio married his widow and assumed the duties of landlord.   Mr. Denio married for his first wife Debby, granddaughter of Benjamin Porter.   At the east end of the village, where the Rochester road forks, a place of entertainment was kept by one Hurd, who was succeeded by a Mr. Johnson.   Lamont Holden kept the West End Hotel at an early day.   It is now under the management of Stephen W. Brown.

The Wilson House was opened in 1869 by one Mossman.   O. C. Parker succeeded him in 1871, and D. Hooper in 1885, and it is now called the Tibbitts House.[1]   The Western Hotel, built a good many years ago by Mr. Gast, was burned in 1889.   On the present site of the Parker House was a tavern called the "Farmers' House," afterwards the "Allen House," and finally the "Western Hotel."   It was kept by a Mr. Tisdale in 1847, by I. Backus in 1848, and by a Mr. Norton in 1859.   John Washburn rebuilt it in 1868, calling it the "Washburn House."   It was run by one

[1] The Tibbitts House has recently been purchased by Eugene H. Stone, who has changed its name to The Arlington.—*Editor.*

Humphrey for a number of years, and L. S. Crocker had it as late as 1886, when it was changed to the " Purdy House," and O. C. Parker, in 1889, renamed it the " Parker House." The "Pioneer House " was next east of the " Eagle tavern," kept by Ezekiel Hall in 1825, E. Parmelee succeeded him in 1826, and Gifford & Putnam in 1831, when it was burned. The East End Hotel, 508 East Main street, was built in 1843, by Anthony Bechtel

The business of tavern-keeping in early days was a remunerative one, and the arrival and departure of stages was atttended with no little curiosity and excitement. Batavia, being on the " Great Bend," was an important trading point ; and being on the " State road " from Canawaugus to Buffalo all travel necessarily tended in this direction. A grant by the legislature was made, in the very early settlement of the place, to Lewis Street for carrying mail from Canandaigua to Buffalo, and to one Beach for carrying mail from Batavia to Lewiston. The stage started from Canandaigua on Monday mornings at 6 o'clock, and, passing through Batavia and Buffalo, reached Niagara on Thursday. The fare was six cents per mile. In 1817 a tri-weekly mail passed through Batavia. The advent of the railroads, in about 1837, caused a great depreciation in tavern and stage values, and the incentive no longer existed for keeping up the old-time hospitality. The stage proprietors continued to run their lines for about six years after the opening of the railroads.

The postoffice.—In early days mail for this village was directed to Genesee court-house, and as early as 1802 it was received and dispatched but once in two weeks, sometimes on foot, or on horseback, Canandaigua being the distributing point. James Brisbane was the first postmaster, his commission being dated July 21, 1802. He holding the office until 1806, when Ebenezer Cary was appointed in his place. Mr. Cary held the office until 1815, when his brother was appointed in his place, retaining the office for 14 years. Trumbull Cary was clerk for Mr. Brisbane, and also for Mr. Cary, and virtually discharged the duties of postmaster from 1805 to 1829, or for 24 years. In 1823 Mr. Cary placed the office in full charge of William Seaver, allowing him the emoluments of the same, which condition was also carried out by Simeon Cummings, who became postmaster in 1829, retaining that position until 1836, when Mr. Seaver was appointed in his place. The latter filled the position until 1842, when, on the accession of Harrison to the Presidency, Dr. Levant B. Cotes was given the commission by President Tyler. Frederick Follett succeeded Mr. Cotes in 1843, who was succeeded by Dr. Charles E. Ford in 1849.

Early merchants.—James Bisbane, the first merchant and postmaster on the Holland Purchase, was born in Philadelphia, October 12, 1776, of Irish parentage. At the the early age of 22 years he embarked from that city with stores for the supply of the large body of men then engaged in the survey of the Purchase, under Joseph Ellicott. Their first destination was Stafford, or the Transit storehouse, so called, where he remained a few months, or until January 2, 1800, when he, in company with Ellicott, returned to Philadelphia. In the spring of 1802 he opened the first stock of goods ever offered for sale in this village. The goods were shipped *via* Albany, the Mohawk, Lewiston, and Buffalo. His commission as postmaster was dated July 21, 1802, by Gideon Granger, P. M. G., and called for an office " in Batavia at the Genesee Court-House." This was the second postoffice west of the Genesee River, Lewiston being the first one. He hired the building erected by Sutherland and Geer, finished it, and opened up his stock. The building was located on the northeast corner of Main and Church streets. He soon afterwards purchased the building for $300. He had for his clerk one Tiffany, who was proficient in the different languages spoken by the Indians, and thus brought trade from them. Rochester was an unknown place at that early day, and Mr. Brisbane's trade covered a large scope of ocuntry from the Genesee to the Niagara rivers and the lakes. Benjamin Dorman, of New Haven, was another clerk of his, and remained in his employ until 1821, when he went to Alabama. In 1806 Mr. Brisbane resigned the office of postmaster, sold his goods, and rented his store to Trumbull 'Cary. Ebenezer Cary was appointed postmaster in his place. Mr. Brisbane went to New York, engaging in the book business for two years, when he returned to Batavia, and resumed business in 1808, upon the spot where he opened his first establishment. He continued his mercantile pursuits there until 1821, when the site was sold for church purposes, when he abandoned them for more lucrative employment. His intimate relations with the Holland Land Co. enabled him to take advantage of the purchase of lands at low prices, and thus became the owner of large tracts of real estate, which in years were greatly enhanced in value by the settlement of the country.

During the agitation of the building of railroads, and particularly in 1833, he associated himself with others and built the Tonawanda Railroad, of which he was the largest shareholder and a director. It was to Mr. Brisbane's house that Gen. Scott (wounded in the battle of Lundy's Lane in 1812) was taken, and where he recovered before going to Geneva.

In 1807 Mr. Brisbane married Mary Lucy Stevens, sister of Hon. James W. Stevens, judge of Genesee County. He died May 29, 1851, and at the time of his death had resided longer on the Holland Purchase than any other man. He left two sons, Albert, born 1809, and George, born March 15, 1812. George Brisbane is the only direct descendant who lives on the original tract, or lot, located by the original settler. The number of the original lot is 16. It was located by James Brisbane in 1809, and has more historic events and interest centered upon it than any other place in Genesee County.

In 1803 Burt & Stoddard put up a small building, using it for a store, it being the second in the new settlement. It was located between Brisbane's and Rowe's (or Keyes's) tavern. When Mr. Brisbane resumed business, in 1808, Trumbull Cary removed his goods and postoffice to the Burt & Stoddard store, until his own store and dwelling were erected in 1809.

Brisbane and Cary continued the only merchants until 1810, when E. Hart built a store, and Clark Heacox managed the business for him. The growth of the village was very rapid from 1808 until the War of 1812. Dr. Dwight, in 1804, passed through the place, and states that "it contained from 20 to 30 houses, most of them built of logs, the rest small, chiefly one story. The court-house has three stories, the second of which is the county jail. When we were there that season so many persons were ill of diseases common to this region that those who remained well were scarcely able to nurse the sick."

The War of 1812 retarded the growth of the village as well as the whole Purchase, so that accessions to the population, and the erection of buildings for business or residential purposes, was not rapid, and this state of things existed up to 1819, at which time, and up to 1830, we are enabled to record a few of the new comers, or merchants, that contributed to the business life of the place. There were in the mercantile trade from 1819 to 1830 James Brisbane, Trumbull Cary & Davis, Jonathan Lay, W. H. Wells, J. P. & A. Smith, W. S. Moore & Co., I. Norman Town, N. Loring, C. L. Swart, W. Davis, Rich & Allen, Finch & Moore, Foot & Ganson, Loring & Palmer, W. R. Thompson, Hanford & Filer, R. Henshaw, Cary & Grant, Platt & Stebbins, Blossom & Swift, H. & E. C. Kimberly, Webster & Reynolds, S. Grant & Co., Hewett & Billings, H. Tisdale, R. Dibble, J. & L. B. Cotes, and Cotes & Seaver. Other trades were represented as follows: Capt. Hull and one Bedford were silversmiths; S. McCain and C. C. Church were watchmak_

ers; and James Cochrane and Cochrane & Fisher were bell founders
Simeon Cummings was a saddler and harnessmaker, and also postmaster,
trustee, and county clerk. In his business he was succeeded by W.
Manley. Ephraim Towner kept a shoe and leather store, and was general
of' militia. O. Williams was a saddler, and located where the present
Catholic Church now is. W. L. Graves kept a leather store, and Stone
& Rice were tanners. Benjamin H. Stevens and N. Follett were hatters,
and James Cawte, H. B. Pierpont, S. Mead, and Samuel Taylor were
tailors. Bush & Pomeroy were millers and sold plows. Oran Follett
kept a book store and started the *Times.* H. Stevenson was agent of
the "old line of stages" to Albany. Thomas Bliss and John De Wolf
were cabinetmakers, Amos P. Parker was a merchant and bookseller,
and Miss Ann Forbes was a milliner and mantuamaker. Philo Sanford made carding machines. A Mr. Folsom kept a meat market in
1819, and a Mr. Hawkins in 1830, for whom Robert Fowler, who came
in 1831, worked. Isaac Joslyn was a blacksmith, and Thomas McCully
was a builder. Bookstores were kept by Abner Pratt, S. C. Steele, and
J. P. & A. Smith, and as lotteries were licensed about the year 1827
drawings were advertised to be made at these stores.

In this connection we give a list of merchants in 1849, compiled from
an article furnished by Col. William Seaver in *The Spirit of the Times:*

Forwarding and commission merchants: J. Foot, L. A. Smith, J. Ganson & Co.
Dry goods; Wells & Son, Smith & Warren, G. A. Lay, N. T. Smith, Thorn & Holden.
Hardware: Belden, Otis & Co., R. Haney. Hotels: American, B. G. Tisdale; Genesee,
S. N. Bierce; Western, I. Backus: Eagle, E. Hall; Railroad Depot, S. Frost; Dutch,
A. Biechel. Livery stable: Ferren & McCormick. Cabinetmakers: C. Kirkham, C. T.
Buxton, J. T. Buxton, O. Griffith. Carpenters: O. Dustin, R. Craig, D. Palmer, J.
Coleman, S. Tuttle, J. Gardner, Lowden, Knapp, Rice, Graham, Hart, and Barner.
Blacksmiths: F. Baxter, A. Tyrrell, M. Kellogg, G. W. Miller, S. Lyon. J. Clark, I. Joslyn,
Trumbull & Son. Gunsmith: I. M. Joslyn. Saddles and harnesses: W. Manley, A. J.
Ensign, J. T. Carr. Masons: T. McCulley, H. Murphey, J. Holton, D. Johnson, A.
Wilcox. Stone cutters: Fellows & Co. Furnaces: T. Hurlburt, J. R. Smith. Bakers:
B. C. & O. Page. Cradlemaker: H. Naramor. Cooper: Z. York. Brewer: E. H. Fish.
Barbers: J. Leonard, D. Leonard. Butchers: R. Fowler, D. Winn. Druggists and
booksellers: W. Seaver & Son, Fellows & Co. Grocers: C. A. Russell, J. C. Wilson,
J. Kenyon, J. McCullant, S. A. Wilson, Wilson & Austin, G Knowles, J. & R. Eager.
Jewelers: J. A. Clark, E. S. Dodge. Hatters: H. & E. McCormick, P. Warner. Boot
and shoe stores: T. Yates, A. Joslyn, H. M. Warren, M. Rupp, Spencer & Merrill,
J. P. Phillips, J. Baker. Milliners: Mrs. Denslow, Blake Griffith, Showerman, and Hal-
bert. Tailors: O. D. Hurlburt, D. Ferguson, J. Jordan, J. M. Royce, H. Smith, J. Allen,
Bissenger & Rebstock. Printers: W. Seaver & Son, D. D. Waite. Bookbinder: Gott-
leib Kiesz. Painters: H. W. Ashling, Howe & Barnard, P. S. Moffett, E. Woolsey,
O. N. Sanford, W. McIntyre. Carriagemakers: J. Clark, G. W. Miller, A. Peck.

12

Physicians.—We give here the names of other than regular physicians, who have been residents of Batavia :

Reuben Town, came 1803, died 1807 ; William L. Horton, came 1803, removed ; Abel Turtlelot, came 1809, removed ; George Anderson, came 1826, died in Ohio, 1834; Abraham Van Tayl and James Winne, came 1835; Sanford Emory, came 1858, died 1880; Richard A. Wells, came 1866, removed to Missouri ; Maxwell G. Walkinshaw, came 1872, died 1887 ; Theron K. Nolton, son of Dr. Josiah, came 1854, died in Oakfield, 1863.

The following were of different schools of practice:

Eleazer Bingham, came 1826, removed ; Charles A. Northrup, came 1850, died 1861 ; S. H. McCall, (had a water cure), came 1854, removed; L. D. Stone (botanic), came 1847, removed; Jacob Delamater (botanic), came 1848, removed ; John C. McKenzie (eclectic), came 1851; Henry W. Wadsworth (eclectic), came 1854 ; J. G. Fross (eclectic) ; Conrad Backer (eclectic) ; Henry R. Foote, came 1848, removed ; Henry Sheffield, came 1852, removed ; J. M. Blakeslee, came 1852, removed ; George F. Foote, came 1852, removed ; Harvey Hutchins, died 1871.

Educational.—The public as well as private education of the young was well attended to, and in addition to the chapter of the "History of Union School District No. 2 " we are enabled to give the names of some of those who opened and taught schools of a private character, with the years engaged in such occupation.

Thomas Layton, who settled in Batavia in 1801, was a teacher of the young prior to 1810. Mrs. Rachel Stevens, wife of Benjamin H. Stevens, a hatter, came in 1822 and taught a private school for 27 years, a part of the time on Liberty street. Her daughter, aged over 80 years, is still living. From that time until 1825 information is meagre regarding times. In that year we learn that the Rev. James Cochran and a Miss Gardner taught private schools. In 1826 Messrs. Nixon and Stearns opened what was termed the "Batavia Academy," and the same year a Mrs. Aikin, Mrs. Winchester, a number of maiden ladies, Miss L. Starr, Plumb, Colton, and Deshon were advertisers; and the query is, where did all the children come from, with the then small population, to furnish a livelihood for so many instructors ?

There were in 1827 M. W. Fletcher and a Mr. Hovey. Horace U. Soper taught in 1828 ; Miss Blanchard (successor to Miss Colton) in 1829; Miss H. H. North and R. Hogue, Jr., in 1831 ; Miss Burnham in 1832–33 ; Mrs. Ford and H. H. Smead in 1833 ; and E. C. Porter and Lester Cross in 1835. A High school was taught in 1836 and 1837 by E. A. Hopkins and C. W. Wilson. S. E. Hollister had a school in 1840, and Mrs. J. F. Ernst a boarding school, at what is now 422 East Main street, in 1841–44. C. N. Chandler taught in 1841 ; Mrs. Rathbun in

1842 ; D. E. Walker in 1843–44 ; and Yound and Oliphant in 1844. A Batavia female seminary was taught by Misses Beardsley and Smith in 1844, and Mrs. William G. Bryan, whom nearly all the present residents will remember, had her noted school in 1848, where David E. Evans used to reside, and conducted it with skill and energy until a very few years ago. Miss E. G. Thrall taught in the same place from 1875 to 1889, and now teaches at East Pembroke. There was a collegiate insti-tute in 1864, taught by E. Wildman, and a Miss McCully taught a school in 1864. This brings us down to the present time. Miss Ellen K. Hooker established, in 1883, " Park Place School," conducting the same for four years, or until about 1887, when the present highly talented and and Christian lady, Miss Mary J. Stephens, took the school and has had charge of it since. There are accommodations for 12 boarding pupils and 50 day scholars. The musical department is under the charge of Herve D. Wilkins, A. M., of Rochester. The rooms are large, airy, and pleasant, heated by furnace, and lighted by gas. The grounds are shady, large, and spacious, with a lawn-tennis court.

Batavia village.—The village of Batavia is 300 feet higher than Buffalo, 400 feet higher than Rochester, and 685 feet above Lake Ontario. The high-est point of-land on the N. Y. C. & H. R. Railroad west of Albany is two miles west of Batavia, called the Summit, it being 923 feet above the ocean. The village is surrounded by a very wealthy agricultural region, and its railroad facilities are being constantly recognized by manufacturers who are seeking locations for pursuing their business. It has, also (more than one ordinarily sees), a tasty and desirable class of residences, built on the finest streets to be seen, and no other village in Western New York can compete with it for beauty and cleanliness.

In 1825, soon after the village was incorporated, there were only about 1,400 inhabitants. At that time land was comparatively cheap. The lot and one adjoining where the Holden store now is was sold for $150 in 1830. The site now occupied by St. James's Episcopal Church was bought in 1820 for $450. In 1811 James Cochrane paid $100 for 18 acres, the land lying on Bank street and fronting on Main street, one-half the distance to State street. In 1802 D. McCracken paid $170 for 34 acres now bounded by Jackson, Main, and Liberty streets. Bank street was called, in old times, " Dingle Alley," it being but a lane, wherein cows were driven to pasture, and the old fashioned cow-bell being at-tached to them in order to find them.

The early settlers of Genesee County were not wanting in patriotism.

Their diversions and holidays were few, and they made much of the return of the only National holiday. The custom then was to listen to the reading of the " Declaration of Independence " and, as many as could, retire to the tavern for dinner, at which toasts were drank. We give herewith the programme in 1826 :

NATIONAL JUBILEE.

"THE following are the regular toasts which were drank at the celebration in this village on Tuesday last (July 4, 1826):

" 1st.—The Fiftieth Anniversary of American Independence! 'And ye shall hallow the fiftieth year and proclaim liberty throughout all the land unto all the inhabitants thereof, and it shall be a Jubilee unto you.'

" 2d.—Our Common Country! 'May the blessings we enjoy under its happy form of government descend unimpaired to the latest posterity.' 3 cheers, 1 gun.

" 3d.—The State of New York ! 'Without an equal in resources and enterprise : may union at home render her respectable abroad.' 3 cheers, 1 gun.

" 4th.—George Washington ! (Drunk standing with solemn music playing.)

" 5th.—The Heroes and Patriots of the two wars of Independence ! 'Honor to the living and tears of gratitude to the memory of the dead.'

" 6th.—The Militia ! 'Bunker Hill and New Orleans, the commencement of the first and the close of the second war of Independence have proved them a sure defense in the hour of trial.' 9 cheers, 1 gun.

" 7th.—The Army and Navy of the United States ! 'The guardians of our National defense and the protectors of our National nights.' 9 cheers, 1 gun.

" 8th.—The youth of our country ! 'Let them remember that virtue and intelligence is the life of liberty.' 3 cheers, 1 gun.

" 9th.—Agriculture, commerce, and manufactures ! 'The true source of a country's glory and happiness : let them have equal encouragement.' 3 cheers, 1 gun.

" 10th.—Party Spirit ! 'Under the dominim of honor and virtue, a ministering spirit in the temple of freemen.' 6 cheers, 1 gun.

" 11th.—Election of President and Vice-President of the United States ! 'Let the people act for themselves ; may the present Congress remember from whom they derived their authority.' 6 cheers, 1 gun.

" 12th.—Greece! 'The votaries of liberty throughout the world behold her sorrows and are afflicted ; may they soon rally to her standard and wrest the iron sceptre from the " mindless Ottoman." '

" 13th.—The Independent States of South America ! 'They followed our example and have triumphed ; with liberty for their object may they reach the goal of their highest ambition.' 5 cheers, 1 gun."

As early as 1827 the traveling showman was around; but we are not informed as to the extent and capacity of the house he drew. The weekly paper of June, 1827, calls attention to a troupe as follows :

" *Theatre.*—Messrs. Gilbert & Trowbridge are now in this village with their theatrical corps. They have already performed three nights to respectable houses. We would recommend the propriety of stationing someone in the back seats to preserve order. We have witnessed it ourselves, and have heard it complained of by others, that the boys on the back seats were too noisy. The bill of fare for this evening is rich and worthy of the attention of those who are fond of the theatrical profession. The pieces consist of 'The Soldier's Daughter' and 'Poor Soldier.'"

Imprisonment for debt was in order, as is shown by a notice taken from a paper dated June 25, 1826:

"A gentleman confined in Batavia jaol, on strong suspicion of debt, offers his services to lawyers, Printers, Merchants, Tavern-keepers, Mechanics, in drafting or copying declarations, making up rolls, *wrighting* deeds, Mortgages, Bonds, &c. Posting books of every description. Apply at this office for further particulars.'

In 1822 a Mr. Farnsworth was convicted of forging United States land warrants, and sentenced to be hanged on the 20th of September. A large crowd assembled to witness the execution, when, to their great disgust, the President granted a reprieve for six months. The murmurings of the disappointed multitude were loud and deep, and before the expiration of the six months' respite he was pardoned, as it appeared that he had committed no crime against the government. The first execution was one McLean, in 1807, who had committed murder in 1807, and was hanged the same year in Batavia. November 5, 1830, James Gray was executed for the murder of Samuel Davis, a tavern-keeper, of Le Roy. It is estimated there were over 5,000 persons present to witness the hanging. The execution took place south of where the railroad is, near the creek.

Batavia library.—In April, 1796, an act was passed by the legislature for the purpose of encouraging the formation of public libraries. Under that act the citizens of the new Genesee country vied with each other in organizing libraries. The first one established on the Holland Purchase was in November, 1804, when a meeting was convened at the house of Abel Rowe (tavern-keeper). Joseph Ellicott was chairman. The trustees were Richard Smith, William Rumsey, John Branan, Reuben Town, and Nathaniel Coleman.

Village incorporation.—Soon after the fire of 1821 a meeting of the citizens was held and a committee appointed to petition the legislature for an act of incorporation, which was granted April 23, 1823. The first meeting (to carry out this act) was held at Ganson's tavern, June 3, 1823. C. Carpenter and D. Tisdale (justices) presided; and the following persons were chosen as trustees: D. H. Chandler, D. E. Evans, N. Follett, S. Cummings, S. Finch, Trumbull Cary, treasurer; and Parley Paine, collector. Subsequently D. H. Chandler was chosen president of the village. The present village officers are George Burt, president; John Quirk, collector; George Roth, treasurer; and John Glade, assessor. Measures were also adopted in regard to fires, but no company was formed until the 20th of April, 1824, composed of the following persons: William Seaver, Jr., captain; Hinman Holden, D. H. Chandler, Frederick Follett, William Purcell, Parley Paine, Oran Follett, William Platt, Daniel Gates, Ralph Stiles, Hezekiah D. Platt, William Dickinson, C. C. Church, Nathan Follett, W. M. Seymour, I. Norman Town, William R. Thompson, Benjamin Allen, Stephen Grant, Nahum, Loring, John S. Moore, Jonathan Lay, Horace Gibbs, David M. Gardiner, and Rufus Burnham. The first engine-house was under the old jail in the court-house. The Holland Land Co. gave the village the lot on Jackson street (now a blacksmith shop), which was to be a fire engine-house. Later they took it back and gave in return the quarters under the jail, the building being raised upon a high foundation, to admit of an engine being run under.

Batavia has had its share of destructive fires. The first one, on the night of December 22, 1821, originated in Mr. Baker's silversmith shop, north side of Main street, destroying buildings owned or occupied by the following persons: Moore & Finch, L. Baker, J. P. Smith, C. C. Church, and D. C. Miller's printing office. The amount of property destroyed was estimated at $10,000.

In April, 1833, fire was discovered in a building nearly opposite the Eagle tavern. It burned nearly the whole row of buildings on Main street, from Jackson to the Arcade block. In 1834 the Eagle tavern was burned, together with all the buildings from the corner of Big Tree (Ellicott) street around upon Genesee (Main) street, involving a loss of $30,000. In 1850 a fire destroyed the north side of Main street, from Bank street west from where the American Hotel stood. In January, 1884, a large portion of the harvester works was burned, involving a loss of over $40,000.

The Genesee County mills were built by Mr. Ellicott in 1803, enlarged to 60 x 150 feet in 1825, and were owned by Ellicott, Evans, Macomber, Jennison, Pierson & Randall, Olmstead, and others. They were destroyed by fire August 22, 1884, after which the land and property was purchased by the village authorities for the purpose of building water works, which purpose was carried out, resulting in the erection of a substantial brick structure, in which is machinery supplying all the power needed for water for fire and village purposes.

Cemeteries.—The Indians had a burial-place on a chestnut knoll on the Dr. Josiah Nolton place, or farm, on Jackson street road, south of the village, as numerous bones and glass beads were found there when the soil was removed to furnish material for a road. The earliest known place for burial within the village was the ground on the bank of the creek, situated nearly back of the brick school-house on West Main street. It was deeded by Benjamin Ellicott, August 10, 1820. Not many interments, however, were made there, owing to the liability of the high water from the creek washing out the soil. The only evidence of burials remaining is the graves of the wives of Oliver Wilcox, one of whom died in 1807, the other in 1824, and the graves of Richard Buell, who died in 1819, and W. T. Stark, who died in 1822, and Wheaton Mason, who died in 1825. Many bodies from this ground were transferred to the new cemetery on Harvester avenue, formerly Cemetery street, between the railroads, on lot 43, purchased October 29, 1823, and laid out by Ebenezer Mix into 88 plats. As is often customary with such enterprises a general apathy and indifference was manifested in caring for the plat, and from 1824 to 1840 it was in a very neglected condition. The latter year a fence was built around the grounds, so that the graves and shrubbery were protected from the invasion of animals. From 1840 to 1867 but little attention was given to the grounds, and the appearance was forbidding. In 1867 a subscription was raised and a large fund directed towards repair of fences and improving the walks and drives, and up to 1875 small subscriptions (under the superintendence of the late William S. Mallory) were devoted to the care of the grounds.

In May, 1880, a number of lot-owners organized under the State laws and the "Batavia Cemetery Association" assumed practical shape, and a systematic effort resulted in plans to purchase land, sell lots, levy and collect assessments on lot-owners for the maintenance and care of the grounds, and the community now has a resting-place for their dead that they may well be proud of. The officers of the association are Gad B. Worthington, president; J. F. Lay, vice-president; L. C. McIntyre, treasurer; J. B. Crosby, secretary; and Jacob Miller, sexton.

Elmwood Cemetery is located on Harvester avenue, south of the Batavia Cemetery. It contains about 12 acres of ground. In the spring of 1872 Edward P. Morse opened up the grounds (having become the owner one year previous), and commenced grading and setting out trees and shrubbery. In the spring of 1889 an organization was formed through the efforts of Mr. Morse, and called the Elmwood Cemetery Association of Batavia. William C. Simpson was president; John B. Crosby, secretary; and Joseph C. Barnes, treasurer. In April, 1890, it was decided to incorporate. The present trustees are T. F. Woodward, J. C. Barnes, George

B. Edwards, J. M. Williams, C. H. Caldwell, W. C. Simpson, E. P. Morse, George Scott, and John M. McKenzie. W. C. Simpson is president; T. F. Woodward, vice-president; and J. C. Barnes, secretary and treasurer.

"Joseph Ellicott, son of Joseph and Judith Ellicott, was born November 1, 1760, in Bucks County, Pa. When 14 years of age his father removed to Maryland. He was partly educated in Bucks County, but at his father's death he was obliged to teach school. He began surveying with his brother Andrew in 1785, locating the western boundary of Pennsylvania. In 1797 he was employed by the Holland Land Company, and came to Geneseo to attend a treaty of the Indians. He came alone in September, on horseback, *via* Wilkesbarre, Tioga Point, Bath, and Dansville, returning to Philadelphia in the following February. In May, 1798, he came again, accompanied by his brother Benjamin, and Ebenezer Cary, arriving in Buffalo in June.

"In March, 1799, Joseph and Benjamin Ellicott went to Philadelphia for the purpose of conferring with Paul Busti, the agent of the company, for a continuance of the surveys. Returning in the spring Joseph Ellicott went to Buffalo, remaining there until the completion of the survey in the fall, and then came to Stafford. In January, 1800, he returned to Philadelphia to report on his surveys. November 1, 1800, when 40 years of age, he was appointed general agent of the company, with liberal salary, a grant of 6,000 acres of land, and five per cent. commission on all sales of lands. He left Philadelphia in November, arriving in Buffalo in January, 1801. He moved from there to Ransom's tavern (now Clarence, Erie County), and opened an office for the sale of lands. In letters written from that place he says he called it 'Ransomville,' 'Pine Grove,' 'Sweetwater Farm,' and 'West Genesee.' At the same time Buffalo was known as New Amsterdam, and also as Buffalo Creek. In 1801, fixing his mind to locate a permanent land office at Batavia, suitable buildings were erected for his occupancy, so that he removed there in the spring of 1802.

"In 1803 David E. Evans, his nephew, came from Maryland to act as clerk in the land office. In November, 1804, Mr. Ellicott was appointed an elector of President and Vice-President. His whole time was taken up in attending to the duties of his office, the place being no sinecure as the records show, and up to the War of 1812 no one was more active. At the close of the war his house was the asylum for sick and wounded soldiers, and all army officers received a hearty welcome. In 1818 he completed the main building of his residence, and by his hospitality was enabled to contribute largely to the social features of the place, and to entertain distinguished travelers on their journey to the Falls. He was a strong advocate of the Erie Canal from its first inception in 1808 to its completion in 1825; was one of the canal commissioners in 1816; and foresaw the great wealth it would bring to the Holland Land Company, proving, as it did, of great assistance to the settlers in paying for their lands.

" Mr. Ellicott's connection with the company enabled him to make fortunate investments in lands, and as he was privileged to take his commissions in lands at low valuations, his possessions eventually became valuable. His great wealth, and his desire to advance the interests of his nieces and nephews, caused their removal from time to time from their different homes in Maryland to new and more desirable homes in Western New York.

"About 1815, and up to 1821, complaints were being made from settlers who were unable to pay for their lands, and through them efforts were made to have Mr. Ellicott resign his agency. But he refused, and was continued until his retirement in October, 1821. He was succeeded by Jacob S. Otto, of Philadelphia, the sub-agents in office being retained. After his retirement Mr. Ellicott went to Philadelphia and Baltimore, and endeavored to interest capitalists in the purchase of unsold lands. In this he was unsuccessful, and returned to Batavia in 1822. His health began to fail him soon after, and he made trips into Pennsylvania and Ohio in order to recruit, but without avail. In November, 1825, he went to New York with two of his nephews, Ebenezer Mix and Joseph Nixon. He was under medical treatment in the city until August, 1826, and on the 19th of that month died in his 66th year. His remains were brought from New York and laid to rest in the cemetery in Batavia, where a monument has been erected to his memory by his sister, Rachel Evans.

"Mr. Ellicott was never married. He was a man of great industry, careful and systematic in all business, and required of all under him a faithful discharge of their duties."

" John B. Ellicott, son of Andrew and Sarah (Brown) Ellicott, was born in 1795, and in early life was in the employ of his uncle, Joseph Ellicott, in Batavia, as clerk in the land office. During the War of 1812 he was a volunteer to defend Fort Erie. In 1817 he was in business in Batavia with his cousin, George Brown, under the firm name of Brown & Ellicott. He married Helen Griffith, niece of his sister's husband. She was born in 1799. Soon after their marriage they resided in Medina. During his residence there he aided in erecting a flouring-mill on Oak Orchard Creek, in company with David E. Evans, to whom he sold his interest in 1828. He afterwards resided on an extensive tract of land in Pembroke, deeded to him by his uncle. His handsome residence on the main road, six miles from Batavia, was admired by all travelers. In the spring of 1851 he moved to Batavia, and died there August 27, 1872, aged 77 years. His wife, Helen, died a few years afterwards. They had seven children, among whom was Mary Jane, born February 9, 1823, who married, first, Nathaniel Pitkin. Their son was Harvey Ellicott Pitkin. She afterwards married Nate T. Smith."

James W. Stevens, the first clerk of Genesee County, was a native of New Jersey and a graduate of Princeton College. He became connected with the Holland Land Co. at the earliest period of its land sales, and remained in the office until the affairs of the company were closed up. He served as county clerk from 1804 to 1810. He was a man of fine literary taste, of quiet habits, of strict business integrity, careful and systematic in his work, and lived a blameless life, respected by all his associates.

Ebenezer Cary was employed by Mr. Ellicott, when he was surveying lands in Pennsylvania, as early as 1795, and came with him to the Holland Purchase, acting as surveyor and clerk, or agent, and was generally useful. He was an early merchant at Batavia, and the founder of the establishment so long continued by his brother, Trumbull Cary.

Trumbull Cary, the founder of the Bank of Genesee, was born August 11, 1787, and was a native of Mansfield, Conn. He came to Batavia in 1805, was clerk for five years with James Brisbane and Ebenezer Cary, and in 1810 bought out that firm, and was in the mercantile business for 30 years. For a time he was of the firm of Cary & Grant, and a part of this time was postmaster. He was an adjutant in the War of 1812; was elected to the Assembly and also served as State Senator; and was a firm friend of Gov. Seward. June 2, 1817, he married Margaret Eleanor, sister of James Brisbane, and they had a son, Walter, who became a prominent physician in Buffalo. Mr. Cary was a very successful man in all his undertakings, and aided materially in establishing the village on the career of growth and prosperity it has ever since maintained. He died June 20, 1869, aged 82 years. His grandson, Trumbull (son of Walter), is now the cashier of the bank founded in 1829.

Ebenezer Mix was born at New Haven, Conn., December 31, 1789.

After learning the masons' trade under his brother, Abiather Mix, he came to Batavia, Genesee County, in the spring of 1809, at which place he worked at his trade during the summer, and taught school in the winter. In March, 1810, he entered the office of Daniel B. Brown as law student, still holding himself ready to do any job of plastering needed in the then small town. In the spring of 1811 Joseph Ellicott, then agent of the Holland Land Co., hired Mr. Mix to plaster a room, with an arched ceiling, by the yard; after the job was done Mr. Mix made out his bill, giving the number of yards and price, and sent it in for payment. Mr. Ellicott, upon examining the bill, sent out to know who made the calculation. Upon being informed that the mason himself did it he sent for Mr. Mix and said: "Young man, I did not suppose that there was another man on the Purchase that could make that calculation correct. The Holland Land Company needs your services." And in March, 1811, Ebenezer Mix went into the employ of the Holland Land Company, where he remained for 27 years as contracting clerk, 21 years of which time he filled the office of surrogate of Genesee County, during which time he codified the laws of New York, as to the descent and distribution of estates, by request of the attorney-general. In the War of 1812, in a crisis of danger with the frontier settlers upon the Holland Purchase, he transferred himself from the land office to the camp and post of danger. He was the volunteer aide of Gen. P. B. Porter at the memorable and successful sortie at Fort Erie, September 17, 1814. He was at one time regarded as the best mathematician in this State, and was the publisher of a work entitled *Practical Mathematics*. He also rendered valuable assistance to Orsamus Turner in the compilation of his book. He was married, March 30, 1815, to Jemima Debow. October 8, 1863, he moved to Cleveland, Ohio, remaining there until his death, January 12, 1869. One of his sons lives in Cleveland, and another, D. E. E. Mix, resides in Batavia, engaged in surveying and engineering.

Aaron Van Cleeve was born in 1768, in New Jersey, and was a coachmaker by trade. He married, in 1791, a daughter of Benjamin Stevens, and a sister to Judge Stevens. He went to Buffalo in 1795, and joined Ellicott later in cutting the west transit line, in 1799. Returning to New Jersey, he resided there 10 years. In 1809 he moved to Batavia, and in September of the same year was appointed sheriff and jailer. In 1810 he was appointed assistant marshal to take the census of all the country west of the Genesee River. He was also a clerk in the land office, and high sheriff in 1811. In 1814 he was appointed by President Madison to take the census of eight westerly counties in New York, and held other important offices.

Orsamus Turner, author of Turner's *History of Phelps and Gorham's Purchase* and *Holland Purchase*, was born in Ontario County. His father, Roswell Turner, came from Connecticut and settled near Honeoye Lake. He moved to Sheldon, Wyoming County, being an early settler of that town. Orsamus was an apprentice in the printing office of the *Ontario Repository* at Canandaigua, and in 1822 became proprietor of a paper in Lockport. He was an editor for 25 years. Chipman P. Turner, a brother of Orsamus, was born in Black Rock, and assisted in the compilation of Turner's *Holland Purchase*. He is now a resident of the town of Elba.

So closely identified are the village, the town, and the whole of Genesee County with each other that it is impossible to separate it, and a perusal of the early event as given in the town and county chapters will aid the reader in connecting the events of the early period. The sketches following this chapter, of some of the prominent individuals that took part in the early settlement, as well as sketches of the residents of the present day, will also be interesting, and connect on important link between the past and present.

Thomas McCully was born in Philadelphia, and came to Genesee County from Schenectady in 1816. He died in 1865, aged 82 years. He was by profession a mechanic, brick mason, and contractor, and built a good many structures in Batavia, among them being the present Episcopal Church. He was a prominent man in the Methodist Episcopal Church, aiding in founding it, and was a trustee until his death. He married Sarah Hollister, daughter of Silas, and they had six children.

James Cochrane settled in 1802 on lot 24, containing four acres, buying the same for $100. He was a bell founder. His foundry was on Bank street, where Mr. Southworth now lives. He made the bells for all the churches. In 1826 he took into partnership with him a Mr. Fisher. Mr. Cochrane built, in 1824, the house where Miss Sarah Stevens now lives. He died in 1846.

Richard Smith, whom Judge North mentions in the Bench and Bar as surrogate, was also clerk of the board of supervisors for 40 years. He lived in a frame house where Baker & Walkinshaw are located. He was a prominent Mason and master of Olive Branch Lodge. In seeking a continuance of his clerkship of the board of supervisors one year the chairman remarked that " it was not necessary for him to ask it, as he should go for him for clerk as long as he was supervisor, and Mr. Smith was alive, and after that would go for Jane, his daughter " (the father's assist_ant).

Dr. David McCracken, located in 1801, took up lot 25, of 34 acres, paying $170. This lot is bounded by Main, Jackson, and Center streets. Shortly after his purchase he erected a log house, on what is now Will_iamson's furniture store, East Main street. He had four brothers, who soon came into the settlement.

Benjamin Blodgett, the early printer and proprietor of the *Times*, and also of the firm of Handford & Blodgett, located on the corner of Main and State streets.' He removed to Richville, and for many years kept a most famous tavern at that place. He died in Illinois in 1857.

David E. Evans, a nephew of Joseph Ellicott, came in 1803, succeed_ing Mr. Otto in the duties of the land agency in 1826. His early life was spent in clerking for his uncle in the land office, so he was familiar with all the responsibilities of the agency. He was elected to the State Senate in 1818, and was there four years. In 1826 he was a member of Congress, but resigned, when he was appointed to the agency of the Holland Land Company, which position he held until the company's affairs were wound up, in 1837. Mr. Evans was an open-hearted, gen_erous man, giving liberally to religious purposes, and for the public wel_fare. He died in 1850.

Rear-Admiral Ralph Chandler was born in Batavia in 1829, in the house where G. B. Worthington now lives. His father, D. H. Chandler, married a daughter of Hon. H. J. Redfield.

In 1814 Libbeus Fish bought lot 44, on East Main street. He came from Vermont in 1806, and died in 1859. He was a man of means, liberal in his investments and in his charities. He was a maltster, and proprietor of the first enterprise of the kind in the county. His son, Eli H. Fish, was born here in 1807, and died in 1879, aged 72 years. He was a grocer and maltster for 50 years. He was captain of the 164th Regiment, and was vice-president of the National Bank of Genesee.

The Cotes homestead, on East Main street, is one of the oldest houses in the place. It was the residence of Dr. Ephraim Brown until 1826, and of Dr. Levant B. Cotes for 30 years after. They were partners for a time.

Roswell Graham, an old-timer, came in 1801, and settled in the east part of the Graham place, on the Le Roy road, residing there until his death, at the age of 95 years. A daughter, Mrs. Nacy P. Coddington, resides in Buffalo, and is in her 83d year.

Isaac Joslyn came in 1828. He was a locksmith and blacksmith for 53 years. His brother, Almiran Joslyn, is still living on East Main street, and is over 90 years of age.

Another old settler still living is John Green Russell (over 90 years of age), on Bank street, son of an early tavern-keeper. Still another old settler, formerly of Elba, is Phineas Howe, 95 years of age, living on East Main street.

Benjamin H. Stevens, brother of Judge J. W. Stevens, and a brother-in-law of James Brisbane, came to Batavia in 1822. He was in New Jersey in 1777. He was the superintendent of a hat factory, and died in 1857. His only daughter, Sarah K., was born September 6, 1810, came to Batavia with her parents, and has resided here since. She has lived since 1824 in the old house on East Main street, built by James Cochrane in 1822. Her mother taught private school for 27 years. She died in 1880, at the age of 97 years. To Miss Sarah K. Stevens we are indebted for many dates and facts connected with the period in which she was a prominent factor.

The old house, 514 East Main street, was built in 1815 by David Locke.

The Rev. Lucius Smith, rector of the Episcopal Church from 1823 to 1833, was a prominent man and minister for those days. He was very decided as well as liberal in his opinion, and took a more than usually active interest in the perpetuation of the Masonic Lodge, of which he was an energetic working member, and an advocate of its doctrines. During the Morgan episode Mr. Smith's attitude was severly criticised by some of his friends, but he stood up unflinchingly in adherence of the course he marked out. Marcus L. Babcock, his half brother, was said to be one of the earliest born children of the village. His son, Junius A. Smith, was a clerk in the land office, and also a representative of the Farmers' Loan and Trust Co., which succeeded the Holland Land Co. He died in 1864.

Kimball Ferren, of Le Roy, was superintendent and proprietor of "the old line coaches" running to Buffalo, Lockport, etc. He was also at one time overseer of the poor, and a member of the Masonic order.

Benjamin C. and Ones Page came in 1838 from New Hampshire, and started a bakery where Baker & Walkinshaw now are. They carried on the business for 30 years. Their business was very extensive, at one time having 12 teams on the road. A son of Benjamin C. is E. B. Page, now, and has been since 1864, engaged in the music business.

Col. William Seaver, one of the most prominent citizens of Genesee County, was born in Berkshire County, Mass., October 10, 1789, and died at Batavia, August 25, 1871, in the 82d year of his age. In early life he taught school, and subsequently embraced the medical profession. This, however, he abandoned for mercantile ventures, and in 1817 emigrated from Albany to Genesee County. For nearly half a century following his removal he was at the head of a large drug, book, and printing establishment. Col. Seaver grew up with the country. He was essentially a "man of affairs," and possessed to an unlimited degree the confidence of the public. His ideas were broad and liberal, his knowledge of men and things was extensive, and during his day and generation his influence was hardly second to any one in Genesee County. For many years he was editor and proprietor of the Batavia *Spirit of the Times*, and aside from being a forcible writer brought dignity to the editorial profession. In public life he was a natural leader, and occupied many local positions. In 1822 he took charge of the Batavia postoffice, first as deputy, but soon thereafter as postmaster. His administration of that office covered a period of 29 years, and was deservedly popular. In 1823, upon the incorporation of the village, he was appointed first captain of the first fire company, and subsequently first chief engineer of the department. Later he was president of the village. He was a man of the highest social standing, and for 40 consecutive years, ending only with his death, was senior warden of St. James's Episcopal Church. With the advance of years he withdrew from active business, grew old gracefully, lived beyond the allotted four-score, and at the conclusion of an honorable and useful life in every sense of the word was held in the highest esteem by his fellow townsmen. Col. Seaver had five sons, all of whom were brought up to practical work and became well known business men, viz.:

1: William A. Seaver removed to Buffalo in 1848, and purchasing the *Daily Courier*, of that city, continued as its editor for the next 10 years. Then disposing of the concern he located himself in New York city. He was a wonderfully versatile writer and prominent in literary circles. For over 20 years he was president of a fire insurance company, and died in New York city, January 7, 1883, aged 68 years. 2: Daniel M. Seaver, for many years U. S. mail agent between Albany and Buffalo, removed to Wisconsin, and was deputy treasurer of that State for some time, but returned to New York and died April 26, 1862, aged 46 years. 3: Lucas Seaver removed to Wisconsin in 1848 and established the Milwaukee

Commercial Advertiser (soon changed to *Daily News*).   In 1850 he was
elected city treasurer of Milwaukee, and held that office for four years.
On accession to office he sold the newspaper, and later on returned to
his native State. He died May 6, 1866, aged 47 years. 4: James F. Seaver began a promising career under adventitious auspices, but died very
suddenly of a bilious attack at Batavia on February 27, 1853, aged 32
years.   5: David Seaver, the youngest and only survivor of the five brothers, was the business partner of his father, and subsequently for a long
time continued the "Seaver establishment" alone. He was a thoroughly
active man and progressive citizen.   Nearly 20 years ago he sold out
and removed to New York city, where he now (1890) resides.

Hon. Heman Judd Redfield's life was a long and useful one, devoted
to the maintenance of Democratic principles, upholding the country in
the days of its peril, and he was in his early manhood, and up to the last
days of his life, a power in the politics of the State and a man whose influence in party affairs was always exerted on the side of integrity and
the good of the public service.   For half a century and more in Western
New York most of his life was spent; he was known and esteemed as one
of the most admirable characters in the State, and has gone to rest with
a fullness of respect that is accorded to few.

Mr. Redfield was born in Connecticut, December 27, 1788.   His father
moving to Western New York, he assisted him on his farm until 1808,
when he entered the Canandaigua Academy.   He remained there two
years, and then read law with the Hon. John C. Spencer.   At the beginning of the War of 1812 he volunteered as a private soldier and served two
campaigns.   He was in the battle of Queenstown Heights, and was with
General Harrison at Fort George, when he received a brevet from the
commanding general for gallant services.   He commenced the practice
of law at Le Roy in 1815, was appointed a justice of the peace and master
in chancery, and soon after district attorney.   He was State Senator during 1823, '24, and '25, during which time he was one of the "seventeen"
Democratic senators who successfully resisted an attempt to change the
law relating to the election of presidential electors.   Prominent among his
associates at this time were Silas Wright and Charles E. Dudley, both of
whom were elected Senators, and Silas Wright, governor.   In 1825 Mr.
Redfield was appointed one of the New York commissioners to settle a
boundary question with New Jersey.   He was postmaster at Le Roy for
more than 20 years.   He soon became distinguished as a lawyer.   When
arrangements were being made for the trial of those accused of abducting

William Morgan he was offered the position of special counsel to assist the attorney-general. He declined the offer and recommended the Hon. John C. Spencer, who accepted and acted as such on the trials. In 1835 he also declined the office of circuit judge tendered him by Governor Marcy. He was also appointed canal commissioner, which he declined. When the Holland Land Company, in 1836, sold out their remaining lands in the five counties he, together with Jacob Le Roy, purchased the same; subsequently the new purchasers appointed him their agent, acting as such for 13 years, for which purpose he removed from Le Roy to Batavia. President Pierce tendered him the appointment of naval officer in New York, which he accepted, but was very soon transferred to the office of collector of the port of New York, which he held until June 30, 1857, when he resigned, although President Buchanan offered to continue him. It was highly creditable to him that, when he rendered his accounts as collector of the port of New York, involving the large sum of $143,493,-957, they were promptly settled exactly as he rendered them. Soon after he returned to his home at Batavia, and settled upon his farm as a cultivator of the soil, which was ever a favorite employment with him.

In all the perils to which our country has been exposed he has ever been on the side of his government. He sustained Mr. Polk through the Mexican war, and exerted himself on the side of the government during the late war. He was a member of the Peace Congress at Albany, which sent delegates to the one at Washington. He presided at meetings, lent his influence to secure the quotas of men called for at different times during the war, contributed largely in raising funds to aid in that purpose, and lent his best energies to sustain our side of the conflict, never doubting the final result. In his intercourse with men he was frank and manly, never misleading; his interests harmonized with those of his neighbors. Although he practiced economy he was not greedy for wealth, either on his own account or for the distinction it often confers; hence the poor were never turned away starving nor the orphans unprotected. He was opposed to all class legislation, and to using the government, State or National, as a means of making one class rich and keeping another poor. It was one of his theories that the less mankind were governed the better for them. He believed the true object of government was to protect men in their person, character, and property, and then leave them to work out their own happiness in their own way.

On Sunday evening, July 22, 1877, he sat with the members of his family on the veranda of his house, enjoying the cool breezes after the heat
13

of the day, appearing in excellent health and spirits. About eight o'clock he complained of a dizziness in his head, entered the house, gradually grew worse, and became unconscious, and about a quarter to 10 o'clock he peacefully, painlessly, breathed his last. Thus closed the earthly career of a good, kind-hearted, and benevolent man, and a true and devout Christian. During his long life he was an active and devout member of St. James's Episcopal Church at Batavia, serving as vestryman and warden. Many citizens attested their respect and esteem for their old neighbor and friend by their attendance at the funeral service Wednesday evening. The procession was one of the longest ever seen in the village. Immediately following the hearse came the venerable roadster, so long the favorite riding horse of Mr. Redfield, saddled and bridled, and led by the groom.

Mr. Redfield was married twice. His first wife was Abby Noyes Gould, whom he married at Canandaigua, Ontario County, January 27, 1817. She died at Batavia on the 11th of February, 1841, in the 44th year of her age. The following children only survive them both: Elizabeth Gould, wife of Robert W. Lowber, of Bald Mountain, Washington County; Mary Judd, wife of Major Henry I. Glowacki, residing at Batavia ; Jane, wife of Lawrence Turnure, of New York city; Cornelia, the widow of Rear-Admiral Ralph Chandler, U. S. N., lately in command of the Asiatic station, at present residing at Yokohama, Japan ; and Anna M., the widow of George Evans, of Albany, N. Y. In 1846 he married for his second wife Constance C. Bolles, of Newark, N. Y., of English and French ancestry, who survives him, and by whom he had four children, as follows : Frank B. Redfield, Abby L. Sunderland, Una Clark (Mrs. Daniel W. Tomlinson), all of whom reside at Batavia, and Martha Evans, wife of Lieut. Samuel Rodman, U. S. A., now stationed at Newport, R. I.   .

Frank B. Redfield, born at Batavia, in 1847, received an academic education, and has followed farming and stock raising. He is now serving his fourth year on the executive committee of the State Agricultural Society. He was president of the Genesee County Agricultural Society, and married, in 1874, Miss Caroline E. Dolbeer, whose people are of New York ancestry. Mr. Redfield lives in the house built by Jacob Otto in 1824.

Peleg Redfield, father of Heman J., was born May 14, 1762, at Killingworth, Conn. He entered the service of the Connecticut troops for the Revolutionary cause in 1778, serving two campaigns, then enlisted in the Continental army for three years, and served his full time. He endured his full share of the privations and sufferings of those who continued steadfast in the Revolutionary cause during its most trying period. The retreat of Washington and his army from Long Island, and from York. town to Valley Forge, and the severe winter of 1780, were often with him a subject of remark. He was present on the memorable occasion of the execution of Major Andre, and always spoke of his fate with sympathy and regret. He was a true Whig of those days, and a true Republican and Democrat in after life. He worshiped his chief, General Washing. ton. After the Revolutionary service, and his discharge from the army, he remained at Suffield, Conn., and soon after married Polly Judd, daugh. ter of Heman Judd, of Farmington, Conn. He exchanged his small prop. erty in Suffield for 200 acres of wild land with Phelps & Gorham, in the then far off "Genesee County," and as early as the winter of 1799–1800 he emigrated to his wild home, now the beautiful and fertile region which surrounds Clifton Springs. With a stout heart, and the help of the willing hands of an excellent pioneer wife and mother, he was fairly un. der way as one of the founders of a settlement and of a numerous family. He died May 26, 1852, in his 91st year. His wife died in 1844, aged 80 years. Both were buried at Manchester, N. Y.

Daniel W. Tomlinson, who died October 5, 1870, aged 57 years, was a native of Middlebury, Vt., where he obtained his education. At the early age of 18 he went to Mobile, Ala., as clerk in a large mercantile house engaged in the cotton trade, where he soon became a partner, ac. quiring a comfortable fortune. He came to Alexander in 1845, pur. chased the large farm of Peter A. Remsen, and took up his residence there. He became a stockholder in the Exchange Bank of Genesee, was made vice-president, and finally took entire charge of the management. Soon after he bought up the whole stock, and removed the bank to Ba. tavia. intending to locate it in a building he had prepared for it adjoin. ing the American Hotel; but that being destroyed by fire (1850) he moved into a building adjoining the old Eagle Hotel. He soon after moved into the quarters occupied by the Farmers' and Mechanics' Bank, now the Bank of Batavia. Mr. Tomlinson was very active in all that tended to develop his town. He was at one time president of the vil. lage, and was instrumental in introducing the present water works, he having secured the ground (from McDonald) where the present pump. house is located. He was one of the organizers of the Batavia Gas Co.

Lucian R. Bailey died in 1886, aged 53 years. He enlisted as a private in 1861 in the 28th Regiment, became lieutenant, and was in many

battles.   After leaving the army he was in Buffalo in the grain business.
He started a clothing store in Batavia with N. Cross, then with D. Jones,
then with J. C. Barnes, was then alone, and finally with Gould & Town.
He was assessor, president of the village, two terms in the legislature, a
prominent Mason, and was treasurer of Western Star Chapter.

Daniel Upton, father of Gen. Emory Upton, came to Batavia in 1817,
and bought the farm in the western part of the town where his daughter,
Sara W. Edwards, now lives, which farm has always been in the possession of the Upton family.   He was the father of 13 children, of whom
Emory was the most celebrated.   The latter was born August 27, 1839,
graduated at West Point, May 6, 1861, and immediately entered into
active service under the government, taking a prominent part in the
war of the Rebellion.   Perhaps no former resident of Batavia has a
name that became so widely known during his short career, for he died in
the prime of life, being only 41 years of age.   His death took place at Pre-
sidio, San Francisco County, Cal., March 14, 1881.   In 1868 he married
Emily Norwood   Martin, of Auburn, N. Y., but left no children.   His
memory is fresh in the minds of all residents, as well as the whole Nation.

The names of a few of the old merchants who are living may not be
out of place.   Joseph C. Wilson came about 1830, and was in the grocery business for 50 years.   H. L. Onderdonk came to Batavia in 1839
and engaged in harnessmaking.   He is still at the same trade, and probably no other man living in the village can make out 51 years of continuous trade in one line of business.   Gad B. Worthington began business for himself about 1845.   M. H. Bierce, the dry goods merchant, has
been in business since about 1850.   Homer Bostwick, the real estate and
insurance agent, came about 1851, and has been engaged in business ever
since.

General training.—" One of the ever-to-be-remembered institutions
in the earlier history of this section was the militia.   There are few incidents of any nature that are recounted with more pleasure by the old
men, or listened to more attentively by the rising generation, than those
of the memorable drills and musters.   The militia consisted of all the
able-bodied white male citizens between the ages of 18 and 45 years.
State officers, clergymen, school teachers, students, and some others were
exempt.   The major-general, brigade inspector, and chief of the staff department, except the adjutant and commissary generals, were appointed
by the State.   Colonels were chosen by the captains and subalterns of
their regiments, and these latter by the written ballots of their respective

regiments and separate battalions. It was the duty of the commanding officer of each company to enroll all military subjects within the limits of his jurisdiction, and they must equip themselves within six months after being notified.

"On the first Monday in September of each year every company of militia was obliged to assemble within its geographical limits for train. ing. One day in each year, between September 1st and October 15th, at a place designated by the brigade officer, the regiment was directed to assemble for a general training. All the officers of each regiment or battalion were required to rendezvous two days in succession, in June, July, or August, for drill under the brigade inspector. Each militiaman was personally notified of an approaching muster by a non-commissioned officer bearing a warrant from the commandant of his company. A fail- ure to appear resulted in a court-martial and a fine, and possibly im- prisonment.

"'General training' was usually regarded as a pleasant occasion to meet friends, and the boys, provided with a few pennies to buy the in- evitable gingerbread, were happier than the lads of to-day with their shillings that are invested in peanuts and a great variety of confections. The place of meeting and the extent of the parade ground were desig- nated by the commanding officer. The sale of intoxicating liquors on the ground could only be carried on by permission of the same officer. Total abstinence was not the rule, however, and an officer who had the right to seize the prohibited article did not always practice self-denial, for often some of it would find its way down his own throat."

Of " general trainings " a veteran of those days writes as follows:

"Although the companies exhibited the *élite* of our regimental splendors, glittering with tinsel and flaunting with feathers, a more unsoldierly parade could scarcely be im- agined. There were the elect from the far-off farms, who sometimes marched to the rendezvous barefoot, carrying their boots and soldier clothes in a bundle—the ambitious cobblers, tailors, and plowboys from cross-road hamlets and remote rural districts, short, tall, fat, skinny, bow-legged, sheep-shanked, cock-eyed, hump-shouldered, and sway-backed—equipped by art as economically, awkward, and variously as they were endowed by nature; uniformed in contempt of all uniformity; armed with old flintlock muskets, horsemen's carbines, long-squirrel rifles, double-barrelled shot-guns, bell-muz- zled blunderbusses, with side arms of as many different patterns, from the old dragoon sabre that had belonged to Harry Lee's Legion to the slim basket-hilted rapier which had probably graced the thigh of some of our French allies in the Revolution.

"The officers of the volunteer companies were generally selected for their handsome appearance and martial bearing, and shone with a certain elegance of equipment each in the uniform pertaining to his company. There was also a sprinkling of ex-veterans of the War of 1812, recognizable by a certain martinet precision in their deportment,

and a shadow of contempt for their crude comrades, but quick to resent any extraneous
comment derogatory to the service. A city dandy who undertook to ridicule the old-
fashioned way in which some officers carried their swords was silenced by the snappish
reply : ' Young man, I 've seen the best troops of Great Britian beaten by men who carried their swords that way.' This harlequinade of equipment, costume, and character
was duly paraded twice a day, marched through the streets, and put through its man-
œuvres on the parade ground adjoining the village, much to the satisfaction of all eman-
cipated school boys, ragamuffins, idlers, tavern-keepers, and cake and beer venders, and
somewhat, perhaps, to the weariness of industrious mechanics, who had apprentices to
manage, and busy housewives, who depended on small boys for help."

The militia history of Genesee County, like other sections, dates back
to an early day. Turner says " there was a general training at Alexander
as early as 1808," but the necessity for its observance grew out of the
War of 1812 ; in fact as early as 1810 or ' 11, when rumors of war began to agitate the country, the State authorities contracted with Ellicott
to build an arsenal. He erected one, of logs, at the forks of the road opposite F. B. Redfield's, 20 feet square. At the close of the war this was
taken down and a stone building put up for the 15th Regt. U. S. A.
This was on the north side of the road, but has within a few years been
demolished. John Baptiste Morris, an old trapper, resided in the old
arsenal for a time.

The " general training " was kept up regularly until about the year
1845. By that time it had become too much of a sham and burlesque,
and the authorities gradually ceased their efforts in maintaining the dis-
cipline provided by the laws for the perpetuation of the old militia system.

The Holland Purchase Insurance Co. was incorporated April 16, 1867,
with 26 persons taking shares. Thirteen directors were chosen, of whom
Hiram Chaddock, George Bowen, and H. T. Cross are the only ones
living. H. J. Redfield was president ; H. M. Warren, secretary; Hiram
Chaddock, general agent and adjuster ; and Tracy Pardee, treasurer.
This company closed up business a few years ago. Hiram Chaddock
was appointed receiver, and closed up the affairs of the company with
great credit to himself and all interested. Besides paying all policies
and expenses (the latter amounting to over $8,000) he paid the stock-
holders $1 20 per share.

The Exchange Bank of Genesee was organized in Alexander in 1838.
Among the stockholders were Samuel Benedict, Jr., Earl Kidder, Henry
Martin, V. R. Hawkins, H. Hawkins, Jesse Hawkins, Stephen King,
Josiah Newton, and Charles Kendall, of Bethany. The capital stock
was $100,000. Heman Blodgett, E. S. Warner, H. T. Cross, J. E.

Pierpont, and others acted as cashiers at various times. D. W. Tomlinson, soon after his coming to Alexander, bought up all the stock and re- moved the bank to Batavia, and it was closed up about 1858.

Farmers' and Mechanics' Bank, of Batavia, was organized November 1, 1838, with a capital of $100,000. . Among the subscribers to the stock were P. P. Kissam, T. Tredwell, John Norton, Jr., D. E. Evans, W. R. Gwinn, H. Holden, John Lowber, and John S. Ganson. The bank con- ducted business until about 1851, when its affairs were wound up.

Newspapers.—Genesee County has had publications of various char- acter, of which the following are worthy of mention. The names of the live papers are printed in SMALL CAPITALS.

The first paper issued here, and the first one west of the Genesee River, was the *Genesee Intelligencer*, in the spring of 1807, by Elias Williams, who purchased an old Ramage printing press from Manlius, N. Y., that had been put aside as useless. He also bought a box of old type in "pi." After much labor he got out his paper, a half sheet, medium size, with a subscription list of 100. It contained two or three columns of advertisements from the Holland Land Company, an account of an elopement, and a runaway apprentice boy, for whose apprehension a bag of bran was offered as a reward. In July, 1807, Benjamin Blodgett with his all ($48.75) joined Williams, and published 13 numbers, when Williams went to a general training in Alexander, and never was heard of more. Blodgett abandoned the enterprise then, but in the spring of 1808 he enlisted Samuel Peck with him, then publishing the *Cornucopia*, an enlarged sheet with new type and a list of 300 subscribers. Peck died in 1811, and the publication ceased. In 1811 Benjamin Blodgett and Col. David C. Miller began the publication of the *Republican Advocate*, Miller continuing the same until 1828 (soon after the Morgan affair), when he dropped out and into politics, and soon moved away. He was succeeded by Charles Sentell and other publishers from time to time, among whom were Charles W. Miller, Edwin Hough, Andrew W. Young (later of the *Warsaw Sentinel*), assisted by Dr. Z. Metcalf in 1832, Lewis & Brown, C. C. Allen, Waite & Cooley, and D. D. Waite, who had charge of the paper more or less for 40 years, and who was first associated with Andrew W. Young in Warsaw. He was a hard worker, and under his management the *Advocate* was for a long time the leading influential Whig and Republican journal of Western New York. He was firm in his political opinions and an honest man. He died in 1878, aged

67 years. About 1854–55 Kimberly & Goodrich, aided by John R. Cooper, a practical printer, who afterwards went to the war, controlled the paper, adding to it the name *Genesee County Whig;* but in 1857 Mr. Waite, on resuming the charge, placed the original name at the head, aided financially by Hon. Benjamin Pringle. In May, 1859, Mr. Waite started the *Daily Advocate,* continuing the same until 1867. Upon the death of Mr. Waite Messrs. Fairman (from Elmira) and Whittle purchased the paper, but they only issued it a few months, when it was discontinued, the publishers making arrangements by which the subscription list of the *Advocate* was merged in that of the BATAVIAN. Messrs. Fairman and Whittle removed to Tioga, Pa., and established an *Advocate* there.

In 1852 (?) or prior a split occurred in the dominant political party in Genesee County, and two factions, known as the " Silver Grays " and " Wooly Heads," came to the surface. The *Republican Advocate* was then allied to the " Silver Gray," or conservative wing, and their opponents had no local organ. The late Trumbull Cary, of Batavia, long a personal friend of Hon. William H. Seward, then furnished the means to establish a paper named the *Genesee County Whig,* and intended it to further the interests of what soon became the Republican party. This paper appeared in 1852, with Kimberly & Tyrrell as editors, and its columns were constantly filled with the well written and spicy editorials of John H. Kimberly and William Tyrrell. It was a pronounced political success, and in two years (1854) the proprietors, having purchased the *Advocate,* consolidated the two papers.

The PROGRESSIVE BATAVIAN is a weekly newspaper published at Batavia by R. S. Lewis, its editor and proprietor. It was established by him in 1868, and succeeded the *Genesee Democrat,* which he acquired by purchase. It is Republican in politics, and has been, almost since its establishment, the leading paper of that party in the county. It has a circulation of over 2,000. It is a firm friend and advocate of temperance and good morals, and is, as its motto expresses it, " Firm in the Right, as God gives us to see the Right." Local news is one of its strong features. In each town in the county it has bright, active correspondents, who furnish it, weekly, with the local happenings in their respective towns and localities, and thus the BATAVIAN is enabled each week to furnish its readers with a very complete report of the local news of the whole county. It is an influential and prosperous newspaper.

The *People's Press* was published in 1825 by Benjamin Blodgett, who carried it on, with the assistance of several gentlemen, for about one year, when it passed into the hands of Martin, Adams & Thorp, and was merged into the SPIRIT OF THE TIMES. The Morgan episode, occurring in the fall of 1826, was the occasion of numerous publications being started for and against Masonry. The *Advocate*, published by Miller, not being able to hold all the invectives directed against the Masons, he supplemented it by the issue of the *Morgan Investigator*, which was published from his office until 1827. During this excitement, and for about one year, the *Masonic Intelligencer* was issued from the office of the *People's Press*, and it is to be inferred that the whole subject was pretty thoroughly ventilated. In September, 1830, the *People's Press* was united with the SPIRIT OF THE TIMES.

In 1837 Peter Lawrence, a jolly, witty, smart, and shiftless Irish printer, went to Alexander and stared the *Farmers' and Mechanics' Journal*. That village was then very small, and though Lawrence was bubbling over with Hibernian humor, he could not make the thing pay. In 1840 Frederick Follett purchased an interest in the concern, and it was then removed to Batavia and called the *Batavia Times and Farmers' and Mechanics' Journal*. Its removal, however, brought no profit to the owners, and Peter Lawrence, who soon left, established a paper at Perry, N. Y. Mr. Follett continued until August 6, 1843, when he sold the establishment to William Seaver and his son Lucas, who merged it into the SPIRIT OF THE TIMES.

In 1842, when a phenomenal temperance *furor* prevailed, the *Temperance Herald*, a small monthly quarto newspaper, was published by Lucas Seaver from the SPIRIT OF THE TIMES office. Branon Young, a lawyer, of Batavia, was its editor, and, although the subscription price was only 50 cents a year, it had a wonderfully large circulation for two years, and was then discontinued.

The first number of the SPIRIT OF THE TIMES was issued at Batavia, February 3, 1819, by Oran Follett, a young printer from Canandaigua. He was assisted by Daniel P. Adams, also a young printer, and Frederick Follett, apprentice. Oran Follett continued as proprietor until January, 1825, when he sold out to his brother and went to Buffalo. Adams also went away, but returned a year later. In 1826 Frederick Follett added the name *Batavia Advertiser*, but soon dropped it. In 1830 the *People's Press* was united with it, both names being used, and published by Follett & Adams. Follett run the paper for five years, when it was sold to a " Democratic " syndicate, D. E. Evans, William Seaver, H. J. Redfield, Stephen Grant, D. H. Chandler, E. Mix, S. Cummings, J. B.

Skinner, W. B. Collar, and R. H. Smith, William Seaver being sole editor, and N. D. Wood the publisher. In 1837 Mr. Follett returned and issued the paper for three years, when Col. William Seaver bought out the interests of all the proprietors for his son Lucas, a practical printer. He issued the paper for five years, when Col. Seaver and his other sons continued the paper until September, 1853, when it was sold to C. S. Hurley, who tried to publish it (but unsuccessfully) as a " Know-Nothing" paper. It was sold (in 1856) under the hammer, and most all the material shipped to Central America. Andrew J. McWain, an apprentice with Col. Seaver, in 1856 purchased the *Genesee Herald* (then printed at Le Roy), moved all the material to Batavia, and in January, 1857, continued its publication under the title of *Genesee County Herald and Spirit of the Times.* The late Dr. Chauncy D. Griswold was its editor, and a *Daily Herald* was published in 1858, '59' and '60' and then dropped. Mr. McWain died June 29, 1860, aged 25 years, and for a few months his administrators carried on the paper, when, in 1860, Henry Todd bought out the establishment and dropped the *Herald* designation, retaining the familiar name of the SPIRIT OF THE TIMES, and once more made it the Democratic organ of Genesee County.

Henry Todd, a practical printer, came from England in 1852, and was for several months employed as a compositor on the *Buffalo Courier,* then owned by William G. Seaver. In 1852, with the assistance of Messrs. Redfield and Richmond, he went to Le Roy and began the publication of the *Le Roy Democrat.* In 1853 he removed the establishment to Batavia, and called his paper the *Batavia Democrat,* continuing the publication as such for two or three years, when H. Wilber and his brother-in-law became proprietors, and changed the name to *Genesee Democrat,* but it soon was a non-paying investment, so that the press and type were sold to R. S. Lewis, who began the issue of the PROGRESSIVE BATAVIAN. Henry Todd published the SPIRIT OF THE TIMES from 1860 until January 1, 1886, when his son, Charles E. Todd, and A. H. Thomas leased the plant, continuing the the arrangement for one year, when Mr. Thomas became owner and conducted the office alone until April 15, 1889, when the present proprietors, Messrs. Thomas & Hall, took up the work so long pursued by Mr. Todd. They are giving the citizens of the county an ably edited, newsy, Democratic journal.

A. H. Thomas was born in Tarrytown, N. Y., November 8, 1855. He learned the trade of printer in the office of the *Phelps's Citizen,* and for a time was with the *Newark Courier,* after which he published the *Clifton*

Springs News, at Clifton Springs, N. Y. For two years he was engaged in business at Cincinnati, Ohio, when he came to Batavia, and was local editor of the PROGRESSIVE BATAVIAN for three years when he became connected with the SPIRIT OF THE TIMES.

Joseph F. Hall was born in Rochester, N. Y, September 26, 1865. After completing his education he became connected with the Joseph Hall Manufacturing Co., of Rochester. N. Y., and Oshawa, Ont. He came to Batavia in 1885, and was in the employ of the Johnston Harvester Co. for two years. Since attaining his majority Mr. Hall has taken an interest in politics, and now occupies a position of considerable prominence in the Genesee County Democracy. Mr. Hall was married to Miss Frances Holden Seaver, daughter of David Seaver, in September, 1889.

The Batavia DAILY NEWS was established June 25, 1878, by M. D. & S. P. Mix. W. H. Bradish was the editor, remaining about three months, when G. S. Griswold succeeded him. It was a small four-column sheet, but being sold for one cent a copy it soon reached a circulation of 1,000 copies a day. The paper was enlarged in 1879 and the price raised to two cents per copy. G. S. Griswold, who had before retired from the paper, formed a copartnership with A. J. McWain, and together they bought out the business, which had never reached a solid foundation, the circulation having dwindled down to 500 copies. Under the new management of Griswold & McWain they have continued to publish the NEWS, enlarging and improving it as their means would allow, and the business has increased until at the present day it is one of the most successful village dailies in the State, printing the United Press dispatches, having a circulation averaging 3,000 copies daily, and enjoying a large advertising patronage as well as doing a job printing business. The editor is A. J. McWain; the business manager is G. S. Griswold; the parents of both were engaged in newspaper work many years ago in Batavia.

For a short time from October, 1888, the *Morning Advertiser* was issued by George B. Herrick, an active, go-ahead man. There were 33 numbers published. In February, 1890, L. C. Parmer and M. A. Weed started the SUN, a weekly issued every Saturday.

Union School District, No. 2.— In 1811 a deed was executed conveying to Simeon Cummings and Libbeus Fish the premises which afterwards came to be known as the "old brick school-house," standing upon the northwest corner of what is now Main and Ross streets. This building was torn down in 1873, upon the widening of Ross street, after the erection of the present High School building. The earliest official school record of the district extant is dated November 25, 1813, and is as follows :

TOWN OF BATAVIA.

" School District No. 2 includes all that part of the village of Batavia East of an alley on the East side of Lot No. 16, and a line running South from the South end of Said alley to the Southern boundary of said village ; the North half of Lots No. 7, 9, and 11. Section 8, North third of Lot No. 1, Section 12; Lots No. 8, 10, and 12, Section 8; Lots No. 7, 8, 9, 10, 11, and 12, Section 9; Lots No. 2, 4, and 6, Section 13' T. 12, R. 1,

" To Simeon Cummings, Esquire : You are hereby required and directed to warn all the freeholders or taxable inhabitants of District No. 2, a description whereof is above given, to meet at the Brick School-House in said District, on Wednesday the first day of December next, at One O'clock, P. M., by virtue of an act entitled : An act for the establishment of Common Schools.

"JOHN Z. ROSS,
"EBEN'R MIX,   } Com. of Schools for Town
"ISAIAH BABCOCK.   of Batavia.

" Batavia, November 25, 1813."

Following this is a list of 43 freeholders, or taxable inhabitants, warned in accordance with the above notice. At this meeting, held on the first day of December, 1813, Simeon Cummings, Libbeus Fish, and Daniel B. Brown were chosen trustees of the district; Richard Smith, clerk ; and James Cochrane, collector. This marks the formation and the election of the first officers of school district No. 2.

By a report of the trustees to the school commissioners of the town dated March 26, 1822, it appears that 155 children had been taught in the school during the school year closing at that date ; and that the number of children between the ages of five and 15 years residing in the district on the first day of January preceding was 121. At the annual school meeting held October 12, 1829, school district No. 2 was divided. All that portion of the district west of Center and Bank streets was set off and designated as district No. 12 ; the portion of the district east of said streets retained the original title of school district No. 2. The school records of the preceding and the following years are very meagre and unsatisfactory, as they contain little else than the recital of the election of certain persons as officers of the district, and the levying of certain small taxes, usually less than $50 annually. In the autumn of 1846 districts No. 2 and 12 were reunited under the title of " Consolidated School District No. 2."

At a meeting of the inhabitants of the new consolidated district, held December 28, 1846, a committee was appointed to ascertain where a suitable site could be obtained for the erection of a new school building. This committee reported at an adjourned meeting, held January 19, 1847, in favor of the lot now occupied by the Baker Gun Company. The recommendation of the committee was adopted at the meeting by a vote of 36 yeas to 12 noes. April 6, 1847, the trustees were authorized to borrow $5,500 for the purpose of purchasing the site and building a school-house. With the money thus voted the two-story brick building on Liberty street (now occupied by the Gun Company) was erected, and made ready for occupancy in the fall of 1848. In November, 1853, at a special meeting, it was decided by a vote of 102 to 34 to establish a Union Free School. At the same meeting, and by reason of the decision to establish a Union Free School, a board of education consisting of six members was elected. This board at its first meeting elected L. W. Hart principal of the Union School just established. The board, also at this meeting, passed the following resolution :

" Resolved, That we do not deem it expedient, at present, to establish an Academic Department."

In April, 1854, G. W. Starkweather was employed as principal, the records leaving us in mystery as to the fate of his predecessor (L. W. Hart), employed the November previous. At the annual meeting, September 29, 1857, the following action was taken:

"Resolved, That the trustees, if they deem it proper, establish an Academic Department in the school."

No action on the part of the trustees, so far as the records show, resulted from this resolution. In January, 1861, the board of education made application to the Regents of the University of the State of New York for the establishment of an academic department in connection with the Union School. This request was granted, and in October of the same year the first "Report to the Regents" from school district No. 2 was adopted by the board of education and forwarded to them at Albany.

In the year 1871 it was found necessary to provide additional room for pupils, as the school building on Liberty street could not accommodate those seeking admission. A dilapidated tenement house in the vicinity was rented and fitted up with school furniture. It was soon crowded with from 60 to 70 pupils. As the number of those attending school continued to increase the subject of additional room forced itself upon the attention both of the board of education and the patrons of the school. In April, 1872, at an adjourned school meeting held in Ellicott

Hall, the site of the present school building on Ross street was adopted, and $50,000 appropriated for the purpose of erecting a school building thereon. The State superintendent of public instruction, upon appeal, set aside the action of this meeting.

Pending the appeal to the State superintendent of schools the trustees purchased the present site for the school, there being no stay of proceedings, and the vote of the district meeting in April, 1872, having authorized it. On the first day of August following this decision the district, by a decisive vote, authorized the raising of $40,000, together with whatever money should accrue from the sale of the old school building and lot, for the payment of the new site and the erection of a new school building thereon. At the annual meeting in October, 1873, $25,000 additional was voted for the completion of the building.

On the first day of September, 1874, dedicatory exercises were held in the completed building, which was pronounced at that time by competent judges one of the finest and best equipped school buildings in the State. In October, 1874, the district voted the further sum of $5,000 for the furnishing of the building, grading of the grounds, etc. Although two rooms (one each upon the first and second floors) were not required for school purposes when the new building was first occupied, and the remark was by no means uncommon that provision for the wants of the district had been made for 50 years to come, yet within five years the building was crowded to its utmost capacity.

October 10, 1882, the annual school meeting voted $10,000 for the erection of a school building for the accommodation of the younger children living south of the railroads. With this appropriation a site was purchased and the Pringle Avenue school building erected. School was opened in two rooms of this building in September, 1884, but in November following it was found necessary to open the two additional rooms to meet the wants of the school. A special meeting of the district was called by the board of education July 21, 1884, to take into consideration the subject of providing still further accommodations for the children seeking admission to the schools. At this meeting the site of the Washington Avenue School was selected, and $8,000 voted for its purchase and the erection of a school building. The house was completed and occupied for school purposes in September, 1885. School district No. 4 (now West Main Street School) was united with Union School District No. 2 in June, 1883, and the district formerly known as district No. 15 (now Pearl Street School) in January, 1887. The area of the Union

School District No. 2, as now constituted, is some 15 square miles. The number of children of school age (over five and under 21), according to the census of June, 1889, is 2,116.

Principals of the Batavia Union School from its formation in 1853 to 1889 are: G. W. Starkweather, 1853-54; George Babcock, 1855-59; George H. Stowilts, 1859-60; N. F. Wright, 1860-67; Gardner Fuller, 1867-89.

Table showing the average number of pupils registered during the month of September in periods of five years for the last 20 years:

September, 1868, average number registered 216
" 1873, " " " 280
" 1878, " " " 420
" 1883, " " " 720
" 1888, " " " 890

Table showing amount of money appropriated by the Regents of the University for academic scholars in periods of five years for the last 20 years:

In January, 1868, money appropriated .... $ 179 00
" 1873, " " 252 53
" 1878, " " 296 07
" 1883, " " 317 96
" 1888, " " 890 79
" 1889, " " 1,049 48

An event, perhaps the most worthy of commemoration of any in the history of the district, occurred March 12, 1889. Mrs. Mary E. Richmond had erected a beautiful library building and reading room as a memorial of her son, Dean Richmond, Jr. This she deeded, on that day, to the trustees of the Batavia Union School District No. 2, and their successors, for the accommodation of the school library, and to provide a free reading room for all the inhabitants of the district. This most munificent gift will doubtless prove through all the future an ever widening influence for good. At the same time the trustees of the Batavia Library Association conveyed to the trustees of the Union School District their library of upwards of 3,000 volumes and nearly $4,000 in invested funds; the library to be consolidated with the Union School Library, and the income of the invested funds to be used for the support of a free reading room in connection with the Richmond Memorial Library.

Professor Gardner Fuller, who is at present the superintendent of schools of Batavia, was born in Fullerville, St. Lawrence County, N. Y., and prepared for college at Falley Seminary, Fulton, and Cazenovia Seminary,

Cazenovia, N. Y.   He was graduated from Wesleyan University, Middletown, Conn., in 1858.   After leaving college he taught for a time at
Great Barrington, Mass., and also at Newtown and Bridgeport, Conn., and
was principal of Macedon Academy, at Macedon, N. Y., from 1865 to
1867.   In 1867 he was employed as principal of the Union Free School
at Batavia, to succeed Prof. N. F. Wright.   Professsor Fuller took charge
of the school, teaching as principal in the academic department, which
had been established 10 years before.   Soon after entering upon his duties he reörganized every department.; classes were more thoroughly
drilled ; more attention was paid to the classics and higher branches of
mathematics; and a greater thoroughness in all the branches was insisted
upon.   The course pursued by Professor Fuller drew in many pupils from
surrounding districts, and people began to move into the village to educate their children.   In 1871 it was found that additional room was required for the pupils, and school meetings were held in 1872, which resulted in the erection and completion of the large and elegant school
building on Ross street.   Upon moving into the new building the school
was regraded under his supervision.   The number of pupils has been on
the increase ever since, and several private schools have been abandoned
for the reason that they could not compete with the public school.   Large
additions to the population of the village have been made, and the prices
of real estate have been kept up by the fact that it was everywhere well
known that the village had an excellent Union Free School.   By his thorough drill and management a great impetus has been given to the study
of the classics and higher branches of an English education.   A large
number of students have been prepared for college, and wherever they
have applied for admission they have been readily received, and in every
instance have been found fully qualified for the classes they have entered.   Others have prepared for the learned professions and are successful.   These things operate as a great stimulus to those in the lower
classes, who are stretching forward with eagerness to reach the academic
department and complete the full course adopted in the school.

It is now over 22 years since Professor Fuller took charge of the school,
and notwithstanding its multitude of pupils it was never more efficient
or prosperous than at the present time.   As a teacher and organizer of
schools he has proved a very decided success.   This of course requires
great ability, a large amount of intelligence, and untiring energy and
perseverance, all of which qualities he fully possesses.   He is not only
an excellent classical scholar and well versed in mathematics, but is well

DEAN RICHMOND.

Caze... N. ... graduated from W
dleto... C... After leaving colleg
Grea... also at Newtown a
was ... ademy, at Mace...
1867 ... d as principal ...
at B... Wright. Pro
of th ... in the aca
had l. ... Soon at
ties ... classe
drilled, ... attention was ... classi
math...mati... and a greater thoroughne... in all
upon. The ...rse pursued by Professor Fuller
surroundi... ... ...s, ...ople began to mov
cate ... ... was found tha
quire... ... meetings were
sulte... ... ...pletion of the
build.. ... ...n moving into th
was ... ...pervision. The num
the in... ... ...several private sch...
for th... ... ...d not compete with
addit... ... ...of the village have ...
of real ... ...kept up by the fact th...
know... ... ...on excellent Union F
ough ... ...nd a great impetus ha
of the ... ...branch... ...t an Eng
numb... ...been prepared for c...
have ... ...n they ha... been read
insta... ...d fully qualified for t
tered ... ...ed for the learned
cessf... ...as a great stim...
class... ... ...d with eagern
depa
    It ... ...essor Fuller
and ... ...of pupils i...
or prost ... ...time. As ...
schoo's h...
great ...ty,
perse ... ...tion by ...ff...
an ex ... ...ed ...sol...

Atlantic Publishing & Engraving Co. N.Y.

DEAN RICHMOND.

read and keeps up his acquaintance with the literature of the day, as may be seen by the well selected library connected with the school, a large portion of its volumes having been selected at his suggestion.

The school is an institution the citizens of Batavia may well be proud of, and by their continuance of Professor Fuller in charge of it for nearly a quarter of a century they have shown their appreciation of his work. When he came here only four teachers were required to conduct the school. Now it requires upwards of 20. There were then four school-rooms occupied. Now 17 are in use besides the recitation rooms, and more school rooms are needed, and yet the utmost harmony pervades every department. The success of the school is due to an intelligent, liberal minded public, to its efficient board of education, to its energetic, self-sacrificing corps of teachers, and, most of all, to its able and energetic principal and superintendent, Gardner Fuller.

Dean Richmond, who for a long series of years was recognized as a vital force in the financial, political, and railroad world of New York State, won his way to the front rank of his generation by sheer energy, hard work, and a genius for overcoming obstacles and making circumstances the servants of his will. He possessed also the keen vision that enabled him to read the signs of the times, and shape his course in accordance therewith. He was truly the architect of his own fortune, inheriting nothing from the generations before him but an honored family name and the high qualities of character for which the Richmonds of New England were noted. He was a native of Vermont, and was born March 31, 1804, in the town of Barnard. His parents were Hatheway and Rachel Dean Richmond, who early immigrated to that portion of New York State now embraced in the corporate limits of Syracuse, where his father was engaged in the early salt industry of that region. His father, being unfortunate in business, removed to Mobile, where he died, leaving a widow, two daughters, and a son, the latter only 14 years of age, dependent upon their own exertions. It was at this early age that young Richmond showed the material of which he was made, resolutely taking up the business abandoned by his father, and with little else save the debts of the old concern, and a capital composed of health and energy, began his active life. A year later the death of his mother left him an orphan.

The market for salt had heretofore been limited, but the energy with which the young man pushed the sale soon extended it to new districts, and ere long the business began to yield a satisfactory income. He soon

14

after began to interest himself in various other enterprises, in which he also commanded success. In 1842 he removed to Buffalo, where he engaged in the commission and transporting business, dealing principally with the products of the great West. Bringing to his business operations the wise foresight and judgment which ever characterized him, he became, in the course of a few years, one of the wealthiest and most influential men of the lake region.

In the midst of this active career he formed his first connection with railroad affairs, becoming a director of the Utica and Buffalo Railroad Company. When the direct line to Batavia was completed he became a resident of that village, which continued to be his home for the remainder of his life, although his business headquarters were still retained at Buffalo. His connection with the New York Central Company was one of the great events of his railroad career. When competition of rival roads forced the consolidation of the seven distinct companies into the New York Central, in 1853, Mr. Richmond was foremost in the determined struggle, and his sagacity, address, and perseverance alone carried the measure in the State legislature. He was the first vice-president of the company, which position he held until he was elected president on the retirement of Mr. Corning in 1864. He also served as president of the L. S. & M. S. Railroad for a number of years. While connected with the Central the company relied most implicitly upon his judgment, and never undertook any enterprise of importance without first submitting it to him for advice and approbation. He was the first American railroad man to advocate the laying of steel rails, and after trial, his judgment proving correct, a large order was sent to England, but they did not reach this country until after his death.

It is needless to mention in particular all of the various business enterprises with which he was connected through a long an active career ; he was eminently successful in all. His private business always possessed a charm to him superior to the allurements of office or public life. Esteeming it a duty, however, that each man owed to his country he gave close attention to politics. His political convictions were very strong, and were steadfastly maintained. His views were broad, and he grasped National affairs with no more difficulty than matters purely local. While a resident of Onondaga County, early in life, he was one of the Democratic leaders, and he always enjoyed the unlimited confidence of his political associates, and exerted a greater influence in the Democratic party of the State than any other man of his time. He served as chairman of the Democratic party from about 1857 until his death in 1866.

From a speech upon the life-work of Mr. Richmond, in the Democratic State convention of September, 1866, by Hon. S. J. Tilden, we
quote the following:

"I remember very well in 1864. when the Nation was anxiously looking for a candidate for the highest office in its gift, public opinion turned very generally to this gentleman. . . . Mr. Richmond firmly and persistently refused to entertain the idea. It
is my firm conviction that except for that refusal his nomination was entirely possible,
and his election extremely probable. . . . I think he was one of the best informed
and ablest men whom I have ever had the opportunity to know."

While Mr. Richmond's mental qualities were all the foregoing describes, they were even excelled by his goodness of heart. Many noble
deeds of his benevolence might be related. His acts of philanthrophy were
so numerous, and so disinterested and generous, that they defied attempts
at concealment, and his name became as well known in the State for goodness of heart as it was for business astuteness and political sagacity. In
his social relations he was kindly and genial, while in the privacy of the
family circle his noble qualities shone with lustre.

In the summer of 1866, after attending the Saratoga convention, he,
in company with Mr. Tilden, made a trip to Washington and Philadelphia, returning to New York, August 18th. The following day, while calling upon Mr. Tilden at his residence, he was taken seriously ill, and
August 27th death relieved him from his sufferings. The marks of respect
paid his memory by high and low, and the words of sympathy and sorrow that came from all sections, voiced the world's appreciation of the
greatness and goodness of the departed. Mr. Richmond was laid to rest
in the cemetery at Batavia, where a magnificent mausoleum marks his
final resting-place.

The Richmond Memorial Library, of which we present an engraving,
was erected by Mrs. Mary E. Richmond in memory of her son, Dean
Richmond, Jr., who died in 1885. The building stands on the west side
of Ross street, in close proximity to the Union School. The site has a
frontage of 179 feet on the street. The building was carefully planned
by James G. Cutler, of Rochester, to afford the necessary accommodation
for a combined reference and lending library, and is so arranged that the
books are housed in a fire-proof building. It is of a monumental and
elaborate character, befitting its memorial object, and care has been taken
to so fit the library as not to incur a heavy expense in its maintenance.
All of the structure as seen from the street is of light gray Fredonia
sandstone and red Albion stone, which, combined, make two of the finest
building materials in this section. The style is Romanesque, and is re-

garded as best adapted to the United States, and in which style most of the fine modern buildings erected within a few years past have been designed. A liberal amount of handsome carving gives a sense of completeness and richness to the structure, and a warm and agreeable color effect is produced by the orange red of the roof and crestings. The gutters and metal work are of copper. The dimensions are 87 feet across the front, and an extreme depth of 87 feet, the plan being in the form of the letter T; the reading room, hall, librarian's room, and toilet rooms being in front, and the stock rooms projecting from the center to the rear of the main building. Ascending the low, broad flight of stone steps near the center of the front, the visitor stands first in a wide vestibule, with a handsome tile floor, and under the large half-circle arch which forms the principal entrance. From the vestibule a massive oak door gives entrance to the hall, 14 feet wide, at the end of which is the window communicating with the stock room. At the right of the hall on entering is the toilet and cloak rooms for ladies and gentlemen, and the door which connects with the office of the librarian. To the left of the hall a large pair of folding doors open into the reading room, which is the most attractive feature of the interior. This magnificent room is 24 feet wide by 42 feet long, with a height of 15 feet. At the end of the room, opposite the entrance, in a recess formed by the half-circle arch, is a great fire-place finished in red brick tile and surmounted by a handsome oak mantel with rich carving, and above the shelf is a large oak frame, on which is a bronze tablet bearing this inscription : "This building, erected A. D. 1887, as a memorial of Dean Richmond, Jr., by his mother, Mary Richmond." This tablet is oblong in shape, and fits in the wood work over the fire-place. A large and very elaborate pair of wrought-iron andirons complete the fire-place, which has a brick tile hearth. The room is furnished with handsome oak tables and chairs of beautiful design ; a handsome outfit of gas fixtures of wrought-iron, including a 24-light central chandelier, which hangs from the ceiling, between the heavy oak beams with which this part of the room is finished; and bracket lights, with Argand burners, over each table. The room is panelled in antique oak for a height of $7\frac{1}{2}$ feet from the floor, on a line with the bottom of the high windows, which have plate glass in suitable patterns in the transoms. The interior finish of all the rooms in the library is of antique oak. An extra room, for the storage of pamphlets, etc., has been arranged over the librarian's and toilet rooms, access to which is by a winding stair in the octagonal tower, which is a striking

feature of the exterior. This fire-proof building was commenced in 1887, and completed and presented to the village March 12, 1889. The capacity is for 40,000 volumes; the cost was about $35,000.

Mrs. Mary Elizabeth (Mead) Richmond, whose many acts of charity and benevolence, and whose generous aid to every enterprise to build up Batavia and advance its moral and material growth, deserves especial mention in the history of Genesee County; was born in Troy, N. Y., in June, 1813, her ancestry being of English and French extraction. Her father was a ship chandler, and for many years navigated the Hudson River. Her mother died when she was nine years of age, and three years later the death of her father left her an orphan. Finding a home with her grandparents, in Troy, her early education was commenced in Mrs. Willard's Academy. Subsequently she found a home with her only sister, the wife of Brig.-Gen. Enos D. Hopping, who died while in the Mexican war. In 1849 her sister died, leaving no children. While residing with her sister she met Dean Richmond, and February 19, 1833, they were united in marriage. Nine children were born to them, namely: Alfred William, who died in New York in 1881 ; Harriet, who died in infancy ; Henry A., the head of the Richmond Lithographic Co., of Buffalo ; Charles, who died in infancy ; Adelaide R. Kenny ; W. Eugene, a resident of Buffalo ; Edgar and Edward (twins); the former deceased, and the latter a resident of Chattanooga, Tenn.; and Dean, Jr. Dean Richmond, Jr., was a young man of promise, and died in 1885. He was a resident of Kansas City, Mo. Since 1853 Mrs. Richmond has resided in Batavia, and here we find her enjoying the autumn of her life, in her beautiful home, in a community in which she has done so much to advance its welfare and elevate its social and moral life.

The Richmond Memorial Library, erected by her to the memory of her son, Dean Richmond, Jr., will carry to posterity a grateful remembrance of her noble and generous nature.

Mrs. Adelaide R. Kenny has, since her residence in Batavia, been an able assistant and promoter of the good works of her mother, and has also been conspicuous in charitable, educational, and progressive business movements. She was born in Syracuse, but received her elementary education in the schools of Batavia, being also under the charge of a private governess. February 2, 1869, she was united in marriage with Dr. William J. C. Kenny, of New York city. He died in June, 1873, while serving as treasurer of the Buffalo Courier Co., of which he was the largest stockholder. Since 1873 Mrs. Kenny has resided with her mother in Batavia. She is now serving her second term as a member of the school board of education, and is also a director of the Genesee County Bank, of which her brother, Dean Richmond, Jr., was one of the founders Mrs. Kenny and her mother were instrumental in advancing the interests of the new Hotel Richmond.

The First Presbyterian Society of Batavia.—The first organization of a society was September 19, 1809. A meeting was held at the Center school-house, presided over by Rev. Royal Phelps, of the Hampshire Missionary Society of Massachusetts, and a Congregational Church was formed. The original membership was as follows: Silas Chapin, David Anderson, Ezekiel Fox, Solomon Kingsley, Mrs. Solomon Kingsley, Patience Kingsley, Eleanor Smith, Elizabeth Mathers, Mrs. Esther Kellogg, Elizabeth Peck, Huldah Wright, and Mrs. Polly Branard. The church became Presbyterian, October 2, 1818. Its present corporate name was legally acquired in 1822. A sacramental service was next held in September in Jesse Rumsey's barn, and in June, 1810, a regular meeting was held in Abel Wheeler's barn, a sermon being preached by Rev. Reuben Parmelee. Subsequently other meetings were held at Phelps's inn, Phelps school-house, Clark's settlement, and the houses of Ezekiel Fox and Samuel Ranger. Benjamin Porter (of the Revolutionary war) was a trustee and deacon. In 1813 services were held in the court-house, and continued there until the completion of the "meeting-house" on Main street in 1824. The Presbyterian form of government was adopted October 2, 1818, The following are the names of the missionaries officiating at intervals up to 1818: Rev. Reuben Parmelee, Rev. John Spencer, Rev. John Alexander, Rev. Messrs. Ames, Bliss, Swift, Hanning, Sweezy, Squires,. Colton, Duvel, and Chapin. In 1818 Rev. Ephraim Chapin was regularly settled, and officiated until 1822, and others succeeded as follows : Rev. Ephraim Chapin, 1817–22 ; Rev. Calvin Colton, 1823–26; Rev. Charles Whitehead, 1827–28; Rev. Russell Whiting, 1829–31; Rev. Erastus J. Gillett, 1837–39; Rev. William. H. Beecher, 1839–43; Rev. Byron Sunderland, 1843–51; Rev. William Lusk, 1852–55; Rev. Isaac O. Fillmore, 1855–58; Rev. Charles F. Mussey, 1861–69; Rev. Chester W. Hawley, 1871–74; Rev. Thomas B. McLeod, 1875–77; Rev. William Swan, 1878–87; Rev. Allan D. Draper, 1887.

The first edifice was constructed of wood, at a cost of $3,574, and occupied by the society up to the opening of the present beautiful stone church edifice, dedicated February 20, 1856. The present church has been improved from time to time, and especially made more commodi-ous by the addition of the Sunday-school rooms in 1882; by a new gal-lery in 1888; and a complete renovation and decoration of the inside walls in 1889. The old bell, cast in town in very early days by Coch-ran, did duty in its wooden tower until dashed to the ground on the night of election in November, 1856. In 1886 a new bell was purchased. The board of trustees of the society are Henry F. Tarbox, president; Levant C. McIntyre, secretary; Theron F. Woodward, treasurer; Leon-ard Travis and W. Harris Day. The total membership of the society is 677. The Sabbath-school has 504 members upon the roll, with 29 classes, under the superintendence of L. C. McIntyre. The value of the property of the society is between $50,000 and $60,000, and the seating capacity of the church is 900.

Rev. Allan D. Draper, the pastor of the First Presbyterian Church of Batavia, was born in Phelps, N. Y. His parents were V. V. and Eliza-beth Draper. He graduated from the Iowa State University (classical department) in 1876, and while there served one year as captain of Co. B, Iowa State Militia, University Battalion. In 1879 he was graduated from the Union Theological Seminary, New York city. He then served a pastorate of nearly six years at Red Creek, Wayne County, when he came to Bergen in 1884, remaining until July, 1887, when he was called to Batavia. December 29, 1881, he married Bertha F. Stoutenburgh, of Phelps, N. Y.

St. James's Protestant Episcopal Church.—The parish of St. James's Church is one of the oldest in this section of the State. The church stands to-day upon the same ground it has occupied from the beginning. The parish was established chiefly through the labors of the Rev. Alan-son W. Welton, a clergyman of the church residing in Ontario County. For several years prior to 1815 he had been invited and officiated in this and the neighboring towns, though of necessity but few times each year. His labors were rewarded by the organization of the parish at Batavia, at a meeting held in the court-house, or Heacock's inn, on Tuesday, June 6, 1815. A committee was appointed to wait upon Joseph Ellicott, who agreed to give $1,500 if the new structure would be of brick. No record has been kept as to the number of members at that time, but enough certainly to comply with the law. At this meeting the following persons were elected members of the vestry: John Heacock and Sam-uel Benedict, wardens; Richard Smith, Isaac Sutherland, Isaac Spencer, John Z. Ross, Chauncey Keyes, David C. Miller, Aaron Van Cleve, Os-wald Williams, vestrymen.

Steps were taken as early as 1815 for the building of a house of worship, but the first (brick) building was not completed so as to be occupied until eight years after, and was consecrated by Bishop Hobart, September 22, 1826. The sum of $5,100 was subscribed towards the debt of the church, the parties so contributing owning the pews occupied by them. Among the contributors we find the names of Libbeus Fish, $500; D. E. Evans, Trumbull Cary, and Joseph Ellicott, $350 each; J. Z. Ross and O. Williams, $300 each; J. Brisbane, $200; R. Smith and E. Mix, $150 each; and many others. James Cochran donated the bell at present in use, costing $300, and also $75. The majority of the subscribers mentioned above agreed to a transfer of their privileges in pews on the building of the present edifice. The second or present church building, of stone, was erected in 1835–36; at the same time the main part of the old rectory was built. The lot was given by D. E. Evans, who also gave $1,500 and the chandelier. Trinity Church of New York gave $1,000. Services were continued from the organization of the parish by the Revs. Samuel Johnston and L. B. Ives. The list of rectors is as follows: Rev. Lucius Smith, 1823–33; James A. Bolles, D. D., 1833–54; Thomas A. Tyler, D. D., 1854–62; Rev. Morelle Fowler, 1863–68; Rt. Rev. C. F. Robertson, Bishop of Missouri, a few months; Rev. George F. Plummer, 1868–75; George S. Baker, 1875–77; Rev. H. L. Everest, 1878–82; Rev. William A. Hitchcock, D. D., 1883–87; Rev. A. M. Sherman, 1887.

The church has a seating capacity of 700; number of families 180; number of communicants 330. The Sunday-school has 19 teachers and 150 scholars, with C. W. Stickle, superintendent. The estimated value of church property is $39,200. The windows in the present church are all memorial, that of the chancel being presented as a gift by Bishop De Lancey in 1854, in gratitude for his recovery from an accident while on his annual visitation, and for the kindness of the congregation during his illness. The parish records denote long service on the part of some of its wardens and vestrymen. Among them were William Seaver, 40 years; Phineas L. Tracy, 25 years; Judge Pringle, 30 years; Trumbull Cary, 46 years; H. J. Redfield, 18 years; Junius A. Smith, 26 years; G. B. Worthington, 27 years, and now serving.

St. John's Methodist Episcopal Church of Batavia.[1]—No religious organization of any denomination took formal shape in Genesee County

---

[1] Adapted from an article written by David Seaver, Esq., July 19, 1889, and published in the *Batavian*.

until about 1809, and prior to that time the region was only visited by an occasional missionary. Prominent among them was Glezen Fillmore, a young man who received a license to preach in 1809, and during that year emigrated from Vermont to what is now Clarence, Erie County. For a long time he was known as one of the "Fathers of the Church" in Western New York. The history of Methodist denomination begins with the formation of the Genesee Conference, organized at Lyons, N. Y., July 20, 1810, by Bishops Francis Asbury and William McKendree. The region west of the Genesee River was designated as the "Holland Purchase Mission," and connected with the "Susquehanna district," then in charge of Rev. Gideon Draper as presiding elder. For the next two years John Kimberlin, William Brown, Loring Grant, Elijah Metcalf, Marmaduke Pease, and Anning Owen were the only itinerant preachers whose names are mentioned on the records. In 1813 the name of "New Amsterdam Circuit and Genesee District" was given to all of the territory extending from Batavia to Niagara River, and from the mouth of Tonawanda Creek to 20 miles south of Buffalo, and comprised 28 or 30 stations, or appointments, which were each to be filled once in about every two weeks. In 1813–14 Rev. Gideon Lanning was the only traveling preacher on the circuit. As is well known no church edifice of any kind was built until about 1823, and the services in Batavia were held either in the court-house or a frame school-house, which formerly stood a short distance west of the old land office, on Main street. The itinerant system of course necessitated a yearly change of ministers, and in 1814–15 Rev. James S. Lent succeeded Elder Lanning. In 1815–16 Rev. Robert Minshall took charge of the circuit. In 1816–17 Revs. James H. Harris and William Jones officiated at Batavia and vicinity, and in 1817–18 they were replaced by Elders Alpheus Davis and John Hamilton. In 1818–19 Rev. Aurora Seager and Rev. Peter Foster succeeded them, and about the same time Rev. Elisha House became a brief resident of Batavia. In 1819–20 Elder Ara Williams succeeded to the circuit, but Rev. Elisha House remained in the village.

At this juncture an organization was formed, called the First Methodist Episcopal Church of Batavia, and efforts were made to build a church. In 1820–21 Rev. James Hall and Rev. Zachariah Paddock governed the circuit and officiated at Batavia. In due time, 1821–22, they were succeeded by Elders James Gilmore and Jasper Bennett. These in regular rotation were followed in 1822–23 by Rev. John Arnold and Rev. Asa Orcutt. On the 16th of May, 1823, a subscription paper was drawn up

and a sufficient amount raised to warrant the undertaking.   Hon. Joseph
Ellicott made the largest subscription, which was $250 in cash and a lot
upon which to erect the church, valued at $250, making $500 in all.
On June 23, 1823, the board of trustees contracted with Thomas McCulley, Joseph Shaw, and Seymour Ensign for the building of a stone church
to be 40x45 feet.   McCulley was to do the mason work for $762, Shaw
the outside carpenter and joiner work for $511, and Ensign the inside
joiner work for $400.   On its completion, at a cost of about $2,800, the
church was dedicated June 13, 1824.   The location (corner of Main and
Lyon streets) was never, however, considered a good one, and after about
16 years' occupancy the society, desiring a more central location, sold the
structure in 1839 to the " First Freewill Baptist Church of Batavia," by
whom it was later occupied.

Continuing the names of " preachers in charge " I append a list of
the various ministers who officiated at Batavia from 1822 to 1841 : John
Arnold, Asa Orcutt, John Beggarly, Andrew Prindel, J. B. Roach, Be-
najah Williams, Jonathan Huestis, Asa Abell, John Cosart, Ira Bronson,
Micah Seager, Glezen Fillmore, Chester V. Adgate, S. W. D. Chase,
Levi B. Castle, John H. Wallace, Gideon Lanning, Richard L. Waite,
John B. Alverson, William Fowler, G. B. Benedict, Daniel M. Murphy,
Wesley Cochran, Darius Williams, and D. Nutter.

After the sale of the " West End " or Lyon street church the society
regularly assembled, and for about two years held services in the " Nixon
building," later a district school-house, which stood (now torn down) on
the easterly side of the Episcopal Church on Ellicott street.   On January 28, 1841, a subscription was opened and a sufficient amount raised to
build a new church on the east side of Jackson street.   The lot was donated by John Lomber, and Thomas McCulley contributed the stone
foundation walls at a cost of $150.   The entire cost, which included the
donations of lot and foundation walls by Messrs. Lomber and McCulley,
was about $3,000.   Rev. Allen Steele was then the " preacher in charge,"
and the structure was dedicated on December 3, 1841, under the name
of St. John's Church.   In this condition it was occupied until February,
1866, when the property was sold to William M. Terry, then converted
into a feed store, tenement, and temple of dramatic art, which was destroyed by fire on Sunday, July 15, 1888.

On leaving the Jackson street church the congregation worshiped about
a year in Concert Hall, on the corner of Main and State streets, but previously had purchased the lot adjoining the then residence of David Seaver,

on Main street. Upon this site the society erected an elegant edifice at an expense of about $20,000. This church, built of brick, is in the Norman style of architecture, 50x90 feet, with a lecture room in the rear. The spire on the corner is 160 feet in height, and contains a town clock. Its interior appointments and arrangements are of the most substantial kind, and reflect great credit, not only upon the trustees and congregation, but upon Rev. Sandford Hunt, D. D., then (1868–70) preacher in charge, under whose supervision the edifice was built. The corner-stone was laid June 30, 1868, by Rev. E. E. Chambers, then presiding elder, with appropriate ceremonies. The first service in the session room was held on Sunday, August 1, 1869, and the edifice solemnly dedicated September 14, 1869.

The following is a list of the various ministers who officiated from 1841 to 1870: Allen Steele, five years; Philo E. Brown, one year; Joseph Cross, one year; John Parker, one year; William R. Babcock, one year; Daniel C. Houghton, one year; Philo Woodworth, one year; J. K. Cheeseman, one year; William M. Ferguson, one year; Charles Shelling, one year; E. Everett Chambers, one year; James M. Fuller, two years; John B. Wentworth, two years; De Forest Parsons, one year; King David Nettleton, two years; Joseph H. Knowles, two years; George G. Lyon, one year; Schuyler Seager, two years; Charles R. Pomeroy, two years; Sandford Hunt, two years.

To complete the history to the present time we add the names of those who have been pastors of this church since Rev. Allen Steele, who last served the society in 1870–71 : 1871–73, R. C. Brownlee, two years; 1873–76, James E. Bills, three years; 1876–78, A. D. Wilbor, two years; 1878–81, T. H. Youngman, three years; 1881–82, O. S. Chamberlain, one year; 1882–85, John W. Sanborn, three years; 1885–88, C. W. Winchester, three years; 1888, S. W. Lloyd (now acting). During the pastorate of Rev. C. W. Winchester the church was re-frescoed, the seats elevated in amphitheater style, and a new organ purchased, the improvements costing about $3,000.

The First Baptist Church of Batavia.—On July 8, 1834, a council of delegates from Wyoming, Middlebury, La Grange, Bethany, and Batavia met, with Elder B. N. Leach, of Middlebury, for moderator, and William Smith, of Bethany, as clerk. Resolutions were passed "to give fellowship to the brethren and sisters — 24 in number — as a sister church in the gospel." Elder Leach preached from Phil. 1, 27 : "Only let your conversation be as becometh the gospel of Christ;

that whether I come and see you, or else be absent, I may hear of your affairs, that ye stand fast in one spirit, with one mind striving together for the faith of the gospel." After the sermon Elder Clark, of La Grange, gave the right-hand of fellowship to the members of the new church, and the First Baptist Church of Batavia started out upon its mission of salvation. On the 9th of November, 1835, due notice having been given, the members met at the court-house in Batavia for the purpose of organizing a society according to law. Gideon Kendrick and P. S. Moffat were called upon to preside at the meeting. It was voted that the organization be called the "Baptist Society of Batavia village." The following trustees were then elected: Richard Coville, Jr., John Dorman, William Blossom, William D Popple, and Calvin Foster. A special meeting was called in January, 1836, to take into consideration the purchasing of a lot and the building of a house of worship. Calvin Foster, John Dorman, William Blossom, and Richard Coville were appointed a committee for that purpose. The lot now occupied by the society was purchased March 17, 1836, of William D. Popple, of Elba, for $400, and the deed was recorded in the clerk's office by the late Benjamin Pringle, then a deputy clerk here. The church building was erected soon after the purchase of the lot, and the prayer room was located in the front of the church, upstairs, where the gallery now is. About 25 years ago it was remodeled at a cost of $10,000. The edifice was as it now stands. In 1877 the society reörganized under the new State law, and took its present name.

Since its organization the church has had 12 pastors. The following are their names and the date of the commencement of their work: 1834, Ichabod Clark; 1837, William W. Smith; 1840, L A. Esta; 1844, Gideon Williams; 1845, S. M. Stimpson; 1852, W. Harrington; 1855, J. B. Vrooman; 1859, L. J. Huntley; 1861, S. M. Stimpson; 1865, O. E. Mallory; 1875, D. D. Brown; 1877, William C. Learned; 1882, C. A. Johnson. In 1843 Isaac Fargo was granted a letter and a license to preach. William Putnam and H. P. Brotherton were also sent forth to declare the glad tidings of salvation, the former in 1844 and the latter in 1869. Two ladies from this church are now working in the missionary field, viz.: Mrs. Alice Buell Roberts and Mrs. Lillian Clark Chase.

The Sunday-school was organized in 1837, with 13 teachers and 60 scholars. The school now numbers six officers, 21 teachers, and 280 scholars. The membership has grown from 24 to 327, and during the past year, for the support of the church, they gave $2,200 and $460 for benevolences. The new lot on East Main street was purchased December 10, 1883, of Miss Mary L. Douglass, and cost $4,500, and a new church, of stone, in process of construction, will cost over $30,000, and will seat about 500 persons. The church was never more united and prosperous than at present.

Rev. Cyrus A. Johnson, the pastor of the First Baptist Church of Batavia for the past eight years, was brought up in Connecticut, graduating from the Wesleyan University there in 1865, and from the Union Theological Seminary of New York in 1868. His first pastorate was at Cohoes, but his health failing he traveled for two years. On his return he went to Whitehall, N. Y., and preached in that section for 12 years. In 1882 he accepted his present charge, and through his labors the church society has largely increased. The new edifice now being erected was made possible through his efforts and the harmony of the entire society. He was married, in 1872, to Miss Sarah Scott, who died in 1884, leaving two children, Bertha and Lester. In 1886 he was united in marriage to Mrs. Anna Potter, of New York, who shares with him the labors of his field.

The First Freewill Baptist Church, on Bank street, was organized in January, 1885, with about 25 members. The church was built and completed in 1889, at a total cost for the whole property of $10,000. It will seat 450 persons, is a neat wood structure of churchly design, and in a quiet neighborhood. There are about 60 members belonging to the church and 70 to the Sunday-school. The pastor is Rev. J. H. Durkee, the superintendent is Charles J. Stanley, and the secretary is George Redshaw. The church's trustees are Calvin S. Loomis, E. A. Rial, and Albert B. Crary. Jacob H. Durkee, the pastor, is a native of Yarmouth, Nova Scotia. He was born in 1847, educated at New Hampton, N. H., and took a collegiate course at Bates Theological College. His first pastorate was in Meredith village and New Market, N. H. From there he came to Phœnix, N. Y., where he remained four years, when he went to Pike, N. Y., for four years, and in 1885 located in Batavia. He was married, in 1876, to Miss Susan T. Douglass, a native of Maine, whose father was a clergyman there. They have one child, Harold K., and their residence is at 159 Bank street. Rev. Mr. Durkee is also the editor and publisher of the *Welcome*, a monthly newspaper published in the interest of his church and congregation. By his superior executive abilities he has organized several church societies and erected three new churches.

Evangelical Association of Batavia is located at 27 Center street, with the Rev. G. H. Gelser in charge. It was organized in 1862, by M. Pfitzinger and Adolph Miller, the first pastor being Jacob Seigrist. The first house of worship was built of wood in 1862. The present house is of brick, and was built in 1871, at a cost of $6,000. There are 14 members.

St. Paul's German United Evangelical Church was organized April 20, 1873, by John Friedley, president; Martin Wolfley, treasurer; and Louis Uebele, secretary. The first pastor was Rev. George Field. The church is located on Ellicott street. Rev. J. Bank, who has been pastor for about seven years, has recently resigned. He intends to retire from the ministry and will reside in Buffalo.

St. Joseph's Roman Catholic Church.—From 1840 to 1843 the few Catholics who had settled around Batavia (perhaps not more than 12 or 14 in all) were occasionally visited by Rev. Father Gannon. No written record of his visits remains, but he is yet remembered by some of the oldest Catholic residents. Rev. Bernard O'Reilly, subsequently bishop of Hartford, Conn., and his brother, Rev. William O'Reilly, both at the time stationed at Rochester, attended the settlement from 1843 to 1847. These gentlemen officiated at the house of James Ronan, and sometimes at the residence of Edward O'Connor. Soon the number of Catholics had so increased that a private dwelling could no longer afford them sufficient room to assemble for divine worship, and then, through the kindness of Messrs. Otis & Worthington, they were allowed, free of rent, the use of a large room in the second story of the building still used by G. B. Worthington as a hardware store. Rev. Thomas McEvoy attended the mission in 1848. April 4, 1849, Rt. Rev. Bishop Timon appointed Rev. Edward Dillon to the pastoral charge of Batavia, and on the following Sunday, April 8th, which was Easter day, Father Dillon officiated in the brick school-house on the corner of Main and Eagle streets. At this time the number of Catholics was about 75. Encouraged by the presence of their resident pastor they immediately went to work raising a fund for the erection of a church. But it was difficult to find a suitable lot that would be sold to them for that purpose. In May following Bishop Timon lectured in a small hall near the Eagle tavern, now the Hotel Richmond, and a few days afterwards Benjamin Pringle sold to the Catholics of Batavia a two-story stone building on Jackson street for $1,200. This building had been erected for a select school. The Catholics worshiped in it for several years, and it is now the parochial school

of St. Joseph's Church, where 300 children are taught in all the branches
of a practical English education.   Mr. Pringle donated $25 towards the
purchase of the building and lot; Messrs. Redfield, Cary, Smith, Rowan,
Glowacki, Haney, Ganson, Knowles, and Holden also contributed liberally.   In November, 1850, Father Dillon resigned the pastoral charge,
and was succeeded by Rev. Thomas Fitzgerald.   Rev. Francis O'Farrell
succeeded Father Fitzgerald on the 5th of September, 1852.   On the 10th
of December, 1855, Father O'Farrell was appointed vicar-general of the
diocese of Buffalo, and rector of St. Joseph's Cathedral.   Rev. Peter
Brown succeeded him in Batavia.   September 28, 1856, Father Brown resigned, and was succeeded by Rev. James McGlew, who resigned on the
10th of December, 1860, and was succeeded by Rev. Thomas Cunningham, with Rev. John Castaldi as his assistant.   September 15,1862, Father
Cunningham purchased the present site of St. Joseph's Church, on the
site where in early days one Williams owned a tannery, on the corner of
Main and Summit streets, from Lawrence Timmons, for $2,500, and in
1864 the edifice was erected at a cost of $45,000.   Father Cunningham,
having retained the pastoral charge for nearly 13 years, was succeeded
on the 23d of August, 1873, by Rev. P. A. Moloy.   On the 22d of August,
1874, Father Moloy resigned to Rev. Martin McDonnell, who left in April,
1880.   His charge at that time numbered about 2,200 Catholics.   Attica was also made a mission.   He was succeeded by Father James Mc-
Manus in January, 1882.   He died in Batavia at the age of 40 years.   During his sickness Father Walsh, an assistant, was in charge until February,
1882, when Father T. P. Brougham, the present priest, was called to preside over the spiritual wants of the parish.   Father Brougham came from
Java.   He had been previously at Somerset, Niagara County, in charge
there of three churches for a period of 10 years.   During his incumbency
here great changes in the parish have taken place.   The old convent,
located on Jackson street, was sold in 1882, and the new one erected on
Summit street the same year, as was also a parochial school adjacent,
which accommodates 400 pupils.   Sister Felice is in charge of the school.
St. Joseph's Convent of Mercy is built of brick, and is a house for sisters,
called the Mother house, or Novitiate, novices being taken in here and
sent to all parts of the State.
   Father Brougham was also instrumental in acquiring additional
grounds east of the church, where in time will be erected a new priest's
house.   The church also has been completely renovated and newly dec-
orated inside, making a very attractive edifice.   The first convent (on

Jackson street) was built in 1862, where they remained until 1880, when a building on Ross street was leased for two years, until the present edifice was completed.

The Bank of Genesee was incorporated under that name about 1829, and March 23, 1830, the first by-laws were adopted. The bank began business with a capital stock of $100,000, which was subsequently increased.the same year to $150,000. Trumbull Cary was elected the first president, and William M. Vermilye, cashier. For many years it was the only bank in this section, and its business extended all over Western New York. The old bank building, corner East Main and Bank streets, is one of the old landmarks of Batavia, and is now occupied by the Batavia Club. The bank was reörganized in 1851, as a State bank, and in March, 1865, it became the National Bank of Genesee, with a capital stock of $114,400. Previous to this period the capital stock had been changed several times, and for some years was $500,000. The charter to the bank was renewed in 1885, and it continued business as a National bank until June, 1888, when their charter was surrendered and it was reörganized under the State laws, with a capital of $75,000. The business office of the bank was removed to its present place, 98 East Main street, in September, 1887.

The officers of the bank from its organization have been as follows: Presidents: Trumbull Cary from organization until March 31, 1840; Phineas L. Tracy from 1840 to December, 1851; Benjamin Pringle from 1851 to June 12, 1855; H. U. Howard from 1855 to July, 1885; and A. N. Cowdin from 1885 (still serving). Vice-presidents: P. L. Tracy from 1834 to 1840; J. C. Ferris from 1840 to 1844; J. B. Skinner from 1844 to 1849; Benjamin Pringle from 1849 to 1851; Alva Smith from 1851 to 1853; H. U. Howard from 1853 to 1855; Alva Smith from 1855 to 1857; J. B. Skinner from 1857 to 1870; E. H. Fish from 1870 to 1874; Walter Cary from 1874 to 1880. Cashiers: William M. Vermilye from organization to May, 1830; J. S. Ganson from 1830 to January, 1838; J. E. Robinson from 1838 to 1851; T. C. Kimberly from 1851 to 1858; M. L. Babcock from 1858 to 1859; A. N. Cowdin from July, 1859, to July, 1885; Trumbull Cary from July, 1885 (still in office). It is impossible to give a full list of directors who have served this venerable and noted corporation, but we subjoin a list of some of them whose names will be familiar to old-time residents. The directors elected June 8, 1830, 13 in number, were Jacob Le Roy, Oliver Benton, Alva Smith, James C. Ferris, Henry Hawkins, Gaius B. Rich, T. Cary, Rufus H. King,

Jonathan Lay, R. S. Burrows, Israel Rathbone, P. L. Tracy, and Joseph Fellows. The following were elected subsequently: John Foot, David E. Evans, G. W. Lay, John S. Ganson, James Wadsworth, Horatio Stev. ens, Samuel Skinner, C. M. Lee, John B. Skinner, Benedict Brooks, Ho. ratio Averhill, Thomas Otis, William M. Sprague, J. E. Robinson, B. Pringle, S. Grant, A. D. Patchen, W. Cary, J. S. Wadsworth, and T. H. Newbold. When the bank became a National one, in 1865, the first directors were Trumbull Cary, Miles P Lampson, Thomas Brown, Walter Cary, Alva Smith, William Lampson, H. U. Howard, E. H. Fish and R. T. Howard. The present board consists of five members, viz.: A. N. Cowdin, T. Cary, H. F. Tarbox, Dr. Charles Cary, and J. N. Scatcherd

Augustus Cowdin, the father of Augustus N., was born in New Hampshire in 1803. At the age of 30 years he came to Batavia and engaged in the boot and shoe trade. He immediately identified himself with the Presbyterian Church, was for 50 years a teacher in the Sabbath school, and was ever a willing and valued helper in church work. He always proved himself worthy of the respect and esteem of the whole community, and held positions of trust at various times. He was justice of the peace, supervisor, superintendent of the poor, and a trustee of the Union School. He died February 25, 1884 His wife was Jane G. Getty, a native of this State. The son, Augustus N., born here in 1840, was reared and educated in the schools of his native place, and at the age of 17 years entered the bank (of which he is now the head) as a clerk. He filled all the intermediate positions, and is now its trusted and honored president. For one-third of a century he has been connected with the oldest and staunchest monetary institution of Genesee County, and has rounded out this long period with a reputation of unsullied honor and integrity. He has served as town clerk, as treasurer of the village, and is secretary and treasurer of the Gas and Electric Light Company. He is also a Knight Templar.

The First National Bank was established in 1864, with a capital stock of $50,000, and its number was 340. The first trustees were R. H. Farnham, C. H. Monell, George Bowen, Tracy Pardee, and Henry Monell, and the first officers elected were R. H. Farnham, president, and C. H. Monell, cashier. The latter never acted, and subsequently, in June, 1864, Marcus L. Babcock was appointed to the office and served over one year. May 31, 1865, the capital stock was increased to $75,000, and January 9, 1883, was made $100,000, which still continues. The officers have been as follows: Presidents: R. H. Farnham from March 21, 1864,

15

to June 29, 1865; Tracy Pardee from June 29' 1865, to January 10, 1884; Levant C. McIntyre from January 10, 1884 (still in office). Cashiers: C. H. Monell, appointed March 21, 1864; M. L. Babcock from June 4, 1864, to February 8, 1865; Daniel E. Waite from February 8, 1865, to August 13, 1866; L. C. McIntyre from August 13, 1866, to January 16, 1884; J. L. Bigelow, appointed January 16, 1884 (still in office.)   The office of vice-president was created in 1883, and Gad B. Worthington was elected, serving in that capacity ever since.   The first board consisted of five directors, and in 1869 the number was increased to seven.   The directors have been R. H. Farnham, C. H. Monell, George Bowen, Tracy Pardee, Henry Monell, John McKay, Leonidas Doty, John Fisher, Gad B. Worthington, and Cyrenus Walker.   Since 1884 the board has consisted of the following members: L. C. McIntyre, D. W. Tomlinson, Samuel Parker, E. C. Walker, G. B. Worthington, and George Bowen.   In 1874 the directors were Leonidas Doty, Tracy Pardee, John Fisher, George Bowen, Edward C. Walker, and Gad B. Worthington.

Gad B. Worthington, the vice-president of the First National Bank, was born in Lenox, Mass., in 1815, where he was educated in part, and at Owego, to which place the family moved, remaining there until 1836, when our subject came to Batavia, and was a clerk in the hardware store of Belden & Otis.   Later he became a partner with them, and finally controlled the business, in which he has since been engaged.   Mr. Worthington was one of the organizers of the Batavia Gas Light Co., and is now a director.   He and family are members of the Episcopal Church. His children are Gad D., a partner in the hardware business; Edward W., an Episcopalian minister at Cleveland, Ohio; Amanda C., living with her parents; and Sarah, wife of E. De L. Palmer, of Albany, N. Y.

Tracy Pardee, at one time president of the First National Bank, was a man of prominence in the village.   He was born in Steuben County, and came to Batavia in 1852, where he lived until his death in 1883   He was at one time a member of the legislature.   His father was in the War of 1812, and died in Elba in 1858.

Levant C. McIntyre, president of the First National Bank, is a native of Genesee County, and was born in 1829.   His father, Eden McIntyre, was an early magistrate of the town.   His mother was Harriet Dunham, a daughter of Col. Shubael Dunham, a very early tavern-keeper, from whom Dunham's Corners was named.   Mr. McIntyre received good educational advantages, attending Cary Collegiate Seminary, and commenced business as a druggist, pursuing the same for eight years in Batavia. He then went to Romeo, Mich., in the dry goods business, and assisted in the organization of the First National Bank of that place, being cashier of the same. He remained there until 1865, when he returned to Batavia, and became identified with its banking and business interests. Mr. McIntyre is conservative in the business management of his bank, yet withal progressive in spirit. He enjoys the confidence and esteem of the entire community. He is a member of the board of education, trustee of the Johnston Harvester Co. and the Cemetery Association, president of the Y. M. C. A., and is foremost in acts of charity and benevolence. In 1852 he united in marriage with Miss Marietta Fellows, and they are parents of four children, viz.: Allan F., Mary L., Nellie G., and Grove E. The family are members of the Presbyterian Church, of which Mr. McIntyre is an elder and superintendent of the Sunday-school.

The Genesee County Bank was organized as the Genesee County National Bank, No. 2,421, April 4, 1879, with a capital stock of $50,000. The first officers were S. Masse, president; Dean Richmond, Jr., vice-president; and William F. Merriman, cashier. The first board of directors consisted of 11 members, viz.: Solomon Masse, Dean Richmond, Jr., Dr. H. S. Hutchins, Charles R. Gould, Henry Craft, William C. Watson, W. F. Merriman, J. C. Guiteau, Edwin Darrow, H. A. Huntington, and F. C. Lathrop. The officers have been as follows: Presidents: Solomon Masse from organization until July 14, 1885; Royal T. Howard from July 14, 1885 (still serving). Vice-presidents: Dean Richmond, Jr., from organization until January 12, 1882; Dr. H. S. Hutchins from January 12, 1882, until January 9, 1883; William C. Watson from January 9, 1883 (still serving). Cashiers: William F. Merriman from organization until June 22, 1880; Charles R. Gould from June 22, 1880, until August 28, 1882; Jerome L. Bigelow from August 28, 1882, until January 18, 1884; John W. Smith from January, 1884 (still in office). H. K. Buell succeeded W. F. Merriman as a director January 12, 1881, and Alvin Pease succeeded Dean Richmond, in May, 1882. January 9, 1883, the by-laws were amended, and the board was reduced from 11 to seven members. The present board consists of R. T. Howard, Mrs. A. R. Kenny, H. A. Huntington, William C. Watson, R. A. Maxwell, Henry Craft, and J. C. Guiteau. The charter of the bank was surrendered to the government December 31, 1884, and the bank was at that time reorganized under the State laws as the Genesee County Bank. The place of business is 103 East Main street.

Royal T. Howard, president of the Genesee County Bank, is a native of Wyoming County, and a son of Samuel and Roxa (Carpenter) Howard, both from Connecticut. Samuel Howard came to Perry in 1811, where he married and resided until his death. Royal T. began business as a lumberman in Allegany County, pursuing this business for 18 years, and was also engaged in the manufacture of staves and heading in Warsaw and interested in pine lands in Michigan. Mr. Howard removed to Batavia in 1871, purchasing a lumber yard and planing-mill, and soon after organized the firm of Howard & Olmsted, which continued business three years. The firm then became R. T. Howard & Co., and was such until 1882. Mr. Howard engaged in various business enterprises until 1885, when he became president of the bank. He is also vice-president of the Genesee County Permanent Loan and Building Association.

John W. Smith, cashier of the Genesee County Bank, is a native of Batavia, where he was born April 23, 1850, and is a son of George W. and Mary A. (Baldwin) Smith. His father was a native of Vermont, and his mother of Connecticut. They have been residents of Batavia many years. John W. was educated in the schools of his native town, and early in life began his business career as recording clerk in the office of County Clerk Holden, where he was engaged six years. He began his banking life as book keeper in the First National Bank, where he was employed over one year, and subsequently entered the Bank of Batavia, with which institution he served as book-keeper until April, 1879, when, upon the organization of the Genesee County National Bank, he became identified with that corporation. In January, 1884, he succeeded J. L. Bigelow as cashier, which position he has creditably filled, and is still serving in that capacity. Mr. Smith was married, August 30, 1871, to Miss Emma Fillmore, of Batavia, and resides at 112 Ellicott street. He and his wife are members of the First Baptist Church, of which he is clerk and a leading working member. He is also a member of the K. of P. and the Empire Order of Mutual Aid. He is a young man of ability, enterprise, and promise.

The Farmers' Bank of Batavia was established in 1860 by Leonidas Doty, who came from Attica, where he had been engaged in the banking business with the late Dean Richmond. Mr. Doty came from Greene County, where he was born in 1812. He was in the mercantile business at Attica for 20 years, then engaged in banking, and was also identified in other business measures in that village. He was also one of the founders of the National Bank of Batavia, and a member of the vestry of St.

James's Episcopal Church, being a liberal contributor to its support. He died in 1888, at Buffalo, where he had resided for 12 years after leaving Batavia. The Farmers' Bank has lately erected and is now occupying an elegant and commodious structure on the corner of Main and Jackson streets, having the best facilities for transacting its large and increasing business of any bank in Western New York outside of Buffalo. A few years since John H. Ward was admitted as a partner in the business of the bank, and he is now sole manager of the concern. He was born in Bergen in 1846, a son of Henry M. and Adelia C. (Curtis) Ward, who are natives of Bergen, and descendants of the earliest pioneers of that town. His father, Henry M. Ward, was a merchant, and died in 1857. His mother died in 1882. Their children were Emma C., wife of Prof. A. G. Clement, and John H., who began his business career at the age of 13 years as a clerk in Bergen. He was afterwards a member of the firm of Green & Ward until 1875, when he was elected sheriff of Genesee County, and removed to Batavia. At the expiration of his term of office (three years) he entered the Farmers' Bank. Mr. Ward is the U. S. loan commissioner, and is a 32d degree Mason. He was united in marriage, in 1871, with Isabella D. Mann, of Syracuse, and they have one child, E. Gertrude.

The Bank of Batavia was incorporated July 11, 1876, with a capital of $50,000, the late D. W. Tomlinson being the leading man in its formation. In March, 1883, the capital stock was increased to $100,000. D. W. Tomlinson, son of D. W., is now president; H. F. Tarbox, vice-president; and H. T. Miller, cashier. The bank is located in a fine brick building at 71 East Main street.

Olive Branch Lodge, No. 39, was chartered in 1811, and held its first meeting May 11th at the public tavern of William Keyes. The first master was Ezra Platt; senior warden, Richard Smith; secretary, I. Babcock, who acted as such for four years. Richard Smith acted in the capacity of warden three years. L. Foster was warden in 1814 and master in 1815. Blanchard Powers was master in 1816–17, J. Z. Ross in 1818, and Powers again in 1819–20, when sessions were held at his house in Bethany. The meetings in Batavia were generally held at the taverns, for want of regular lodge rooms, and after holding two meetings at Keyes tavern an arrangement was made with Aaron Van Cleve, sheriff and landlord at the court-house, for their meetings in his tavern. On September 2, 1811, a plat of ground was bought by the trustees of the school district, acting in conjunction with the Free Masons, the sum of

$5 being paid for the same. The location was on lot 32, north side of Main street, on the corner of an alley, and contained 1,500 feet of ground, being where 315 Main corner of Ross streets now is. This was sold by Nathan Rumsey, conditioned upon there being a two-story brick building erected on the site within one and a half years, the lower portion to be occupied as a school, the upper portion for lodge uses. The Masons subscribed funds toward the erection of the building (as was understood). The War of 1812 prevented the completion of the building until the winter of 1813–14, when it was finished and ready for occupancy. The first meeting in their new rooms was held February 28, 1814, and subsequent meetings were continued there until 1816, when they tired of the location and tried to sell their interests to the school trustees, but failed. Other meetings continued to be held at the taverns until about 1819, when trouble arose among its members and the lodge was removed, and meetings were held at Bethany in Powers's and Huggins's houses and C. J. Lincoln's inn. From Bethany it was moved to Le Roy, where it is now located.

A new lodge was again formed in 1824, called " Batavia Lodge, No. 433," and a charter was granted that year. It was installed December, 13, 1825, at St. James's Church. William Seaver was the presiding officer for 10 years, and Blanchard Powers, senior warden. Richard Dibble was junior warden; and Richard Smith, secretary and treasurer. Meetings were held at Bissell Humphrey's "Eagle tavern" until it was burnt in 1833, and in 1839 the warrant was surrendered. The Morgan excitement, beginning in 1826, interfered seriously with the cause of Free Masonry, and for 16 years, or until 1842, meetings were held only at rare intervals. In 1842 the charter was revived, and for 18 months the lodge met at O. T. Fargo's tavern, midway between Batavia and Alexander. Ebenezer Mix was master for three years, Joel Allen two years, and G. B. Shepard one year. D. M. Seaver was junior warden, and H. Humphrey, treasurer. In January, 1844, they moved from Fargo's tavern to the " Cobble-stone block," and held regular meetings until 1847, when the charter was again surrendered. In the course of a year or so a new lodge, No. 88, was formed, but did not long survive. The records of this lodge were destroyed by fire, so names of officers cannot be given. In the winter of 1850–51 the fraternity again organized under the name of "Fisher's Lodge, No. 212" (named after Lillie Fisher, a very early settler of Alexander). They met for about one year at the old lodge rooms in the "Cobble-stone block." For masters until 1859 (when its charter was surrendered) there were Cyrus Pond, Horace M. Warren, E. C. Dibble, K. Ferren, Gad Worthington, and S. A. Wilson. H. T. Cross was treasurer for a few years, and John Eager and D. Seaver, secretaries. Meetings were also held at the corner of Main and Jackson streets, in the new hall occupied by the Odd Fellows.

In 1859 the charter of this lodge was surrendered, and what remained of Fisher's Lodge was reörganized April 7th into "Batavia Lodge, No. 475," the charter being granted July 4th. In 1860 or 1861 the Masonic fraternity desired more independent quarters, and they leased rooms in the Champion block, owned by Joseph C. Wilson. Again, in 1865, it was decided to make another change, and a spacious series of apartments were leased on the corner of Main and State streets, and about $2,000 expended in fitting up the same. The dedication of these rooms was the occasion of drawing together a large assemblage of the fraternity from all parts of the county, lodges from Le Roy, Canandaigna, Pembroke, and Akron being represented. A delegation of Knights Templars from Buffalo Commandery, led by Captain Lockwood, and another from Pen Yan, by Hon. Darius A. Ogden, in full regalia, gave splendid effect to the scene. The dedication was made by John L. Lewis, P. G. M., who delivered a brief address to the fraternity and citizens assembled in the park. The brethren, accompanied by the ladies, passed from labor to refreshment in the dining-room of the lodge. The meetings are now held in elegant rooms in the Walker block, which were dedicated in 1880. The officers are as follows: A. Hays, W. M.; B. F. Showerman, S. W., George E. Perrin, J. W.; Wilber Smith, treasurer; Charles W. Stickle; secretary; W. D. Sanford, S. D.; A. W. Tyler, J. D.; S. E. North, S. M. C.; A. J. McWain, J. M. C.; H. S. Morse, organist; and W. H. Brown, tiler.

Batavia Commandery, No. 34, *K. T.,* was organized September 27, 1865, with the following officers: W. D. Sanford, E. C.; A. W. Caney, G.; W. P. Simpson, C. G.; Rev. Pierre Cushing, prelate; F. M. Jameson, rec.; I. D. Southworth, treasurer; A. Hays, S. W.; A. J. McWain, J. W.; A. T. Miller, W.; John M. Kurtz, standard bearer; C. B. Austin, sword bearer; H. S. Morse, organist; W. H. Brown, sentinel. The present officers are: W. D. Sanford, E. C.; A. W. Caney, G.; W. P. Simpson, C. G.; I. D. Southworth, treasurer; F. M. Jameson, recorder; Charles Pratt, trustee; Alexander Hays, S. W., A. J. McWain, J. W., A. T. Miller, T.; John F. Kurtz, standard bearer; C. B. Austin, sword bearer; W. H. Brown, S.; J. M. Hamilton, Andrew Hiller, and E. N. Stone, guards.

Western Star Chapter, No. 35, *R. A. M.,* was organized March 29, 1813. The officers of the chapter are A. W. Caney, H. P.; Alexander Hays, K.; George P. Bowen, S.; F. M. Jameson, secretary; E. N. Stone, treasurer; A. J. McWain, C. of H.; C. B. Austin, P. S.; George E. Perrin, R. A. C.; Andrew Hiller, 3d V.; Dr. H. A. Morse, 2d V.; A. T. Miller, 1st V.; W. H. Brown, tiler.

The Order of I. O. O. F., No. 197, was instituted in Batavia in August, 1868, by H. S. Andrews, D. G. M., with five original charter members, to wit : Weeden T. Bliss (deceased), formerly an attorney of Batavia ; William Hoyt, since moved to New York ; Simeon Lothiem, who now resides in Germany; and Thomas Yates and B. P. Fonda, who are now living, the oldest members of the fraternity in the county. The present officers are Oscar Netzen, N. G.; Fred Gardner, V. G.; Frank Snyder, R. S.; Ira Howe, F. S.; Frank A. Moreau, treasurer. The lodge meets every Wednesday evening at their hall in Jackson street.

Richmond Encampment, No. 67, *I. O. O. F.,* was instituted August 21, 1872. The chief patriarch is D. B. Pratt, of Alabama, L. B. Fisk is H. P., William Toulson is S. W., and E. W. Davis is scribe.

Batavia Rebekah Degree Lodge, No. 37, meets in the rooms of the Richmond Encampment.

Security Lodge, No. 21, *A. O. U. W.,* has now 121 members. It was chartered April 20, 1876, when its officers were C. F. Starks, C. M.; L. L. Crosby, M. W.; J. L. Foster, G. F.; A. J. Fox, O. C.; C. O. Frost, rec.; F. T. Schlick, fin.; James Jones, rec.; W. C. Mann, G.; M. E. True, I. W.; J. B. Neasmith, O. W. The officers for 1889 were A. B. Clark, P. M. W.; H. G. Buisch, M. W.; E. A. Perrin, G. F.; Thomas Johnson, O. C.; J. O. Griffith, rec.; L. F. Rolfe, fin.; A. E. Brown, rec.; David Byum, G.; C. J. Crabb, I. W.; M. C Schrader, O. W.

Batavia Council, No. 14, *Royal Templars of Temperance.*—The officers are Mrs. A. F. Lawrence, S. C.; Mrs. M. A. McWain, V. C.; George W. Pratt, P. C.; Mrs. G. H. Ferren, chaplain; Byron Orendorf, recording secretary ; Miss Vantia Smith, financial secretary; Mrs. Anna L. Torrey, treasurer ; Miss Jessie Tallman, her.; Mrs. Hannah Delbridge, sentinel.

Upton Post, No. 299, *G. A. R.,* was organized October 25, 1882, with 30 members. The commander was W. J. Reedy. W. H. Raymond was S. V. C.; George Thayer, J. V. C.; John O. Griffis, Q. M.; M. McMullen, officer of guard ; C. R. Nichols, chaplain ; Peter Thomas, adjutant; O. C. Parker, officer of day; L. L. Crosby, S. M.; Russell Crosby, Q. M. sergeant. There were 91 members in 1889, with the following officers :

E. A. Perrin, P. C.; E. J. Benton, S. V. C.; J. R. Colt, J. V. C.; A. M. Weed, adjutant; R. E. Churchill, Q. M.; H. J. Patton, sergeant; A. Benchley, chaplain; John Thomas, O. of D.; R. Senate, O. of G.; R. C. Odion, S. M.; D. H. Wheeler, Q. M. S.

The Equitable Aid Union, No. 396, has 19 members, who meet bi-monthly. Thomas Capp is president; William Wescott, V. P.; I. V. Dibble, treasurer; and William Udritz, secretary.

Batavia Farmers' Club was organized in 1872, with P. P. Bradish as president; J. G. Fargo, secretary; and Henry Ives, treasurer. The present officers are Sylvanus Ford, of Elba, president, and John B. Crosby, secretary. It is one of the oldest clubs in the State.

The Young Men's Christian Association was organized in the spring of 1889. L. C. McIntyre was elected president; Safford E. North, vice-president; C. H. Harrington, general secretary; A. H. Thomas, recording secretary; and John M. McKenzie, treasurer. The rooms are located on Main street, corner of Jackson, being elegantly fitted up for recreation for the young men, making an attractive and desirable place in which to spend their evenings, with no restraint so far as pleasant games and amusement are concerned. Tables of choice serials, magazines, and daily papers are at hand for those inclined to a literary taste, and a spacious gymnasium, fitted up with all necessary appliances for healthful exercise, make this an inviting place for those interested in the moral and religious welfare of the young men of Batavia.

The Philharmonic Society has been organized about six years. The officers for 1889 were S. J. Lawrence, president; F. A. Lewis, vice-president; L. D. Collins, secretary; C. C. Bradley, treasurer; and E. G. Hartshorn, librarian.

Batavia Lodge, No. 50, *Empire Order of Mutual Aid.*—This lodge meets the first and third Tuesday evenings of each month in Empire Hall, 84 East Main street. It was instituted March 15, 1879, with 33 charter members. Of this number are R. A. Maxwell, L. C. McIntyre, W. C. Simpson, E. L. Kenyon, N. J. Nobles, M. H. Peck, Jr., E. H. Wood, and E. P. Morse. This lodge has lost during its 10 years' existence but two members by death, viz.: Edwin Darrow and H. B. Ferrin, both of whom were charter members. The present officers are: President, Whiting C. Woolsey; vice-president, William Hoffman; secretary and treasurer, John W. Smith; trustee, L. C. McIntyre; representative to Grand Lodge, Whiting C. Woolsey.

The Batavia Gun Club's officers are: President, Dr. Harry Sutterby;

vice-president, John McNish; secretary, A. Wyness; treasurer, Philip
Hensner; captain, John Stein; directors, Charles Herbold, Dr. Patten,
and L. F. McLean.

The Genesee County Loan and Building Association was incorporated
April 21, 1879, the object of the association being to encourage the saving of small sums of money weekly, thus accumulating a fund to be
loaned to other members in such manner that they can repay the loan in
easy weekly payments, or the amount of ordinary rent, thus helping
them to secure a home. Its first officers were : President, Wilber Smith;
vice-president, C. H. Howard; secretary, F. M. Sheffield; treasurer,
F. S. Wood; attorney, S. E. North. There are at present 560 members, with the following officers : George Wiard, president; M. B. Adams,
vice-president; B. F. Hamilton, secretary; John W. Pratt, treasurer;
and S. E. North, attorney.

Batavia Athletic Association was organized in 1887, with 40 members.
M. F. Cross was president; W. S. Wakeman, secretary and treasurer.
The officers for 1889 were A. E. Brown, president; S. J. Lawrence, secretary; and B. G. Tallman, treasurer. Their rooms are in the Ross
block.

Batavia cornet band.—The earliest record we have of any band was
one led by Phineas Todd and a Mr. Hunt in 1820. This was disbanded
after six years. The present one was organized about 1856, with A. W.
Gardner as leader, and consisted of 14 members, among whom were Dr.
Showerman, A. Bowen, E. Locke, W. Locke, and R. B. Pease, who
loaned the band money to purchase instruments. The present officers
are : Leader, C. Klimitz; treasurer, L. M. Smith; secretary, —— Leonard; and there are 15 pieces.

The Batavia Club was organized July 28, 1882, under the management of nine directors. The first ones elected were L. R. Bailey, D. W.
Tomlinson, J. H. Bradish, A. E. Clark, F. S. Wood, A. N. Cowdin, J. H.
Ward, A. T. Miller, and W. L. Otis. The first officers were D. W. Tomlinson, president; J. H. Bradish, vice-president; A. T. Miller, secretary;
F. S. Wood, treasurer; L. R. Bailey, W. L. Otis, and A. E Clark, house
committee. The club-house, situated on Main street near the opera
house, was opened January 4, 1883. This building was destroyed by
fire February 16, 1886. On the 17th of April, 1886, the club was removed to its present building, on the corner of Main and Bank streets.
This desirable building with location are the former quarters of the Bank
of Genesee. The club was incorporated April 7, 1888, and shortly af-

terward they purchased the present property. They have now 58 resi-
dent members and 31 non-resident members. The present directors are
Henry Todd, D. W. Tomlinson, R. D. Dewey, J. H. Bradish, F. S.
Wood, A. N. Cowdin, George P. Bowen, Trumbull Cary, and H. B.
Fisher. The officers are Henry Todd, president; George P. Bowen,
vice-president; F. S. Wood, secretary and treasurer; D. W. Tomlinson,.
J. H. Bradish, and R. D. Dewey, house committee.

Batavia Business University was established by W. W. Whitcomb in
1867, at 92 East Main street. In 1885 the Hon. John M. McKenzie
became associated with Mr. Whitcomb in the reëstablishment of the
school, with all the later improved methods, Mr. McKenzie acting as
secretary and treasurer. The school was then located at its present
quarters, Main corner of Jackson streets. The school has graduated over
800 pupils since it was established. Many of the young business men of
Batavia are among its graduates. The " business practice " course of
about two months is made to cover all possible transactions that may
ever occur.

To a limited extent Mr. Whitcomb has become quite proficient in the
subject of astronomy, having published an *Illustrated Solar Chart*, which
gives at one view the relative positions of the planets; their orbital speed
per hour; length of years; length of days; amount of light and heat on
each; distance of each from the sun, also from the earth; inclination of
orbits; diameter of each; density; gravity; eclipses of the sun and
moon; phases of moon; inclination of axis of earth; Saturn and moon,
from photographs; Saturn's rings and moons; annual parallax; sun
spots and faculæ; moon, Saturn, and Mars, from photographs; the three
motions of the sun explained; tide waves; transit of Mercury and Venus.
The contents of several books are all before the eye, and in a plain, com-
prehensible manner. Mr. Whitcomb has also invented and procured letters patent on a *Lunar Globe*. The earth globe is confined in a groove
forming an eclipse, thus showing the sun at the *foci* and the earth at a
corresponding greater distance in June than in December; also the radius
vector for each day in the year. The moon ball is so arranged as to follow the exact path of the moon, climbing in her course for 173 days and
descending in same length of time, and in passing her nodes will show
plainly *when* and how an eclipse is caused. Also how we may have
seven eclipses in one year and only four in another, and will also pass
accurately through the Chaldean period, or *saros*, and repeat the eclipses
once in about 18 years. The " orbit band " is so arranged that the

higher part indicates at a glance where, and in what months, the aphelion part of the moon's orbit is located—and careful study proves that wherever this is found the weather is under its influence : warmer, when between the earth and sun in winter, and cooler when *from* the sun in summer ; or, to state it again, when the "orbit band" is *toward* the sun in summer we have extremes of heat, and, as when it is *to* the sun in summer, it is *from* the sun in winter, we have extreme cold. This is proved by dates covering over 60 years.

The Johnston Harvester Company.—In 1868 Johnston, Huntley & Co. established at Brockport, N. Y., a manufactory of harvesters, having had the machines built on contract for 1867. The principal member of the firm was Byron E. Huntley. They first manufactured what was known as the Johnston sweepstakes. After a few years the manufacture of these machines was abandoned, being supplanted by the present Johnston harvester. In 1870 a joint stock company was organized for the manufacture of these machines, with Samuel Johnston, president, and Byron E. Huntley, secretary and treasurer. In 1874 Mr. Johnston withdrew from the company, although the name of the corporation was not changed. In June, 1882, the works at Brockport were burned, and the company at once determined to remove to a place offering greater facilities for transportation, and accordingly they were located here. The works now consist of seven large buildings, occupying 17 acres of ground on Harvester avenue, between the N. Y. C. & H. R. Railroad and the N. Y., L. E. & W. Railroad. Steam engines of 300 horse-power furnish the propelling force for the machinery, and from 400 to 500 skilled mechanics are employed. The original cost of the plant was $300,000. The fact that Batavia is a good manufacturing point has been fully demonstrated, and a number of new manufacturing concerns have recently located there; none, however, are equal in magnitude to the Johnston harvester works.

In November, 1888, the company was reörganized by the election of the following directors : George E. Dana, of Syracuse ; C. C. Briggs, of Pittsburg; L. C. McIntyre, B. E. Huntley, and A. J. Glass, of Batavia. The officers are A. J. Glass, president and treasurer ; Byron E. Huntley, vice-president; and E. J. Mockford, secretary and superintendent. In January, 1889, there was added the manufacturing of the " Continental rotary disk pulverizer and corn cultivator," representing about 40 patents. They manufacture four styles of mowers, two styles of reapers, and two styles of self-binders.

Albert J. Glass, president and treasurer of the Johnston Harvester Co., is a native of Livingston County, and was born in 1841. Receiving an academic education in his native county upon attaining his majority he went to McGregor, Iowa, and became engaged in selling farming machinery and agricultural implements. In 1867 he was appointed the agent for the sale of Johnston harvesters, and in 1871 was made the manager of the Western business of the company, with offices located at Chicago. In 1882 he left the service of the company, and was for six years the manager of the Janesville Machine Co, at Janesville, Wis. In January, 1888, he came to Batavia at the request of Mr. Huntley, and was active in the reörganization of the present company. Mr. Glass is a man of superior executive ability, and under his supervision the affairs of the works are flattering and prospering.

Byron E. Huntley is the vice-president and European manager of the Johnston Harvester Company. His native home was Mexico, Oswego County. He moved to Fairport, Monroe County, with his parents, when 12 years of age, and in 1844 to Brockport. He prepared for college at Brockport Collegiate Institute, and subsequently attended the Madison University, at Hamilton, Madison County. Owing to failing health, however, he was compelled to give up his college course, and soon after he took a position as office boy in the factory of Fitch, Barry & Co. About 1845 an arrangement was made by Fitch, Barry & Co. with McCormick (who had come up from Virginia to Brockport to get his reaper built) to manufacture his machines under a license. The McCormick machine was built for a few years at this factory, which was one of the earliest in this line of work. Mr. Huntley spent about five years here as employee, and at the expiration of that time he secured an interest in the business, the firm being then known as Ganson, Huntley & Co. But few machines had been turned out up to this time ; and the records show that Huntley, Bowman & Co. commenced work on the Palmer & Williams self-rake in 1853, that 50 machines were made that season, that in 1854 the number was increased to 325, and in the following years to 825 machines. In 1871 failing health compelled Mr. Huntley to seek a change, and he spent that year in Colorado, a rest that was of great benefit to him, and one of the best investments he ever made, he thinks ; but prior to this he had established a market for their machines in Europe, and had opened an office there. As the Franco-Prussian war was in progress he did not go over in 1871, but he went the next year, and has gone regularly ever since. Mr. Huntley has crossed the Atlan-

tic 38 times, and is, perhaps, better posted on the European harvester
and mower trade than any man living; and the aim of the Johnston
Harvester Company, influenced by his practical suggestions, has not
been to lead in numbers of machines turned out, but to regularly make
the best; and it is this course that has gained for them a world-wide
reputation.

Edward J. Mockford was born in England in 1853, and came so this
country in 1866. He entered the employ of Johnston, Huntley & Co. at
Brockport in 1869, and has remained with the company ever since through
all the changes of management. He has filled the positions of book-
keeper and cashier, and is now the very efficient secretary and superintendent of the large factory of the Johnston Harvester Co.

The Wiard Plow Company.—Thomas Wiard was a blacksmith and
farmer in East Avon, N. Y. In 1806 he was engaged in the manufacture of the old-fashioned " bull plow " that was used by the pioneer farmers. In 1815 he began to purchase from Jethro Wood (the inventor of
the first successful cast-iron plow) the necessary castings, and these he
wooded and completed in his shop. Thus he continued until 1819, when
he erected a foundry, made patterns for improved plows, and manufactured all the parts himself. He continued the manufacture of plows at
East Avon, in connection with his sons William, Seth, Thomas, Henry,
and Matthew, till about 1830, and one or more of his sons were manufacturing there until 1871. During this period improvements were being
made in the Wiard plows till they had acquired a reputation above those
of any other pattern in use. It is worthy of note that all the numerous
members of the Wiard family from the grandfather down were men of
superior practical ingenuity.

In 1865 George Wiard, son of William, and president of the present
company in Batavia, purchased a half interest in the establishment at
East Avon, and in 1871 Charles W. Hough, treasurer of the company,
purchased the interest of Matthew Wiard, the firm being Wiard & Hough.
The firm continued at East Avon until 1876. During its existence at
East Avon the works were several times burned. In 1876 the business
had so increased as to necessitate better facilities for transportation, and
a removal was determined on. The village of Batavia offered better railroad facilities than any other place, and the citizens saw fit to donate a
site for the works as a further inducement to the company to locate here.
The works, located on Swan street, between the Erie and Central railroads, were erected by Wiard & Hough, and on their completion in Sep-

tember, 1876, the present company was organized. The capital stock was originally $70,000, but was subsequently increased to $100,000. George Wiard was the president and general superintendent, and C. W. Hough the secretary and treasurer. The present officers are the same, except that J. J. Washburn is now the secretary. Since the establishment of the works here the business has been mainly the manufacture of plows, of which the company makes an endless variety, adapted to all kinds of soils and circumstances, and the more important parts of which are covered by letters patent in the United States and Canada. These consist of one, two, and three-horse plows, with chilled and steel mold-boards, wood, malleable, and cast-iron beams, sulky and walking, flatland and side-hill, and particularly swivel plows for level land. The original capacity of the works has been about doubled; the establishment now covers about four acres of ground, and an average of 125 hands are employed. The machinery is driven by an engine of 100 horse-power, and the shops are heated by steam and lighted by the Edison system of incandescent electric light, and are provided in all parts with automatic sprinklers. One feature, rare in manufactories of agricultural implements, is that these works have never, since the company was organized in Batavia, for one day been closed for want of something to do. The company has also invented important improvements in sulky hay rakes, for which patents are pending, and having added this class of implements to their business are now engaged in the extensive manufacture and distribution of the same.

George Wiard, the organizer and head of the Wiard Plow Company, is a self-made and representative business man of Western New York. His parents were William and Lucinda (McLaughlin) Wiard, early settlers of Western New York, and for several years in East Avon, where his father engaged in manufacturing. In 1820 he removed to Canada, and was the first to manufacture cast-iron plows in that country. He resided there until his death in 1841; his wife also died there in 1864.

George Wiard was born in Canada in 1833. When 15 years of age he went to Buffalo and learned the trade of molder, and thus gained a practical knowledge of the requirements of the business he was to follow, and has so successfully developed. He has been a resident of Genesee or Livingston counties since 1854. Losses from fire, several times, have only resulted in renewed energy and perseverance, until at last a model establishment is the result. Mr. Wiard is also closely identified with the growth and developement of the village. He has been an active and

influential member of the board of education for many years, serving as
its president for four terms.   He was one of the organizers of the Genesee
County Permanent Loan and Building Association, serving as president
for 10 years.   He was one of the commissioners appointed to build the
water works.   To religion, charity, and works of benovelence Mr. Wiard
is a cheerful giver, he and his family being connected with the Baptist
Church.

Mr. Wiard has an honorable record of service during the late war.
He enlisted in the 129th Regt. N. Y. Vols. in 1862.   This regiment subsequently was changed to the 8th N. Y. H. A.   In a battle before Petersburg Mr. Wiard received a wound by which he was confined to the
hospital, from where he was ordered to Washington to instruct fresh
troops.   He was on the staff of Gen. Hardin and Gen. Haskins, commanding defences of Washington.   He was inspector of artillery until
the close of the war, after which he had charge of dismantling forts south
of the Potomac, and was finally transferred to the 4th N. Y. H. A., being
a captain in that regiment when mustered out in October, 1865.   In 1856
Mr. Wiard married Miss Emeline Warren, of East Avon.   She died in
1870, and in 1872 he was married to Miss Isabella Warren, also of East
Avon, and they are parents of five children, viz.: May, Louis, Ernest,
Henry, and Harry.

Charles W. Hough, treasurer of the Wiard Plow Company, is a native
of Cayuga County, N. Y., where his father was engaged in agricultural
pursuits.   He was born in 1836.   Receiving a business education he
early in life became a clerk in a store.   In 1855 he went to Iowa, and
while there was an assistant in a store, taught school, and served as deputy county treasurer of Boone County one year.   In August, 1862, he
enlisted in Co. E, 138th Regt. N. Y. Vols., which was afterwards changed
to the 9th N. Y. H. A.   This regiment was assigned to the defence of
Washington, remaining there for 18 months.   Mr. Hough served on the
staff of Gen. Haskins as ordnance officer of the defences north of the
Potomac.   He was also on the staff of Gen. Hardin and Gen. Wilcox,
was promoted to first lieutenant, and commissioned captain on the
mustering out of the regiment.   After the close of the war he had charge
of dismantling the forts around Washington, north of the Potomac, and
was mustered out in October, 1865.   He then resumed his business life,
engaging in mercantile trade in his native county, but removed to Minnesota, engaging in the manufacture of farming implements until he became a member of the Wiard Plow Co. in 1871, where his knowledge of

the requirements essential to the sale of farming implements has redounded to the benefit of the company. He has been largely interested in real estate operations; has opened up an addition to Batavia on Central av. enue, Pringle and Wood streets, and the section where the new Union School is located. He is also a large owner of plantation property in Florida, where he is engaged in cultivating orange and lemon groves. In all the enterprises to promote the growth of Batavia he is a valued counselor and a liberal contributor.

Mr. Hough formed a matrimonial alliance, in 1866, with Miss Jennie Young, of Cayuga County, and they have two children, Arthur G. and Edward W.

Julian J. Washburn, secretary of the Wiard Plow Company, was born in Randolph, Vt., in 1842. He came of old Puritan stock, being a direct descendant of the Rev. Robert Cushman, who first obtained the charter of the ship *Mayflower*, and of his son, Thomas Cushman, and Mary Allerton, both of whom came to Plymouth on the first voyage. Mr. Washburn was educated in the grammar schools of his native State, and became a teacher, pursuing that vocation until September, 1862, when he joined the 15th Regt. Vt. Vols. (Col. Redfield Proctor), and served during its term of enlistment. He was then employed as clerk in the U. S Hospital Department until the close of the war, when he engaged in agricultural pursuits and teaching until 1870, being officially connected with various agricultural and literary associations during the time. He next engaged in commercial pursuits, going to Boston, Mass., in October, 1870, and spending most of the time in traveling for the seven succeeding years. In 1877 he became a resident of Batavia, and has ever since been connected with the Wiard Plow Co., of which he has been a trustee, and the secretary since May, 1880. In this time he has also served both as trustee and president of the village of Batavia. Mr. Washburn is a genial and cultivated gentleman, and an honored and respected addition to the social and business element of the county.

He was married, in 1866, to Martha K. Bigelow, daughter of the late Hon. Abel Bigelow, of Brookfield, Vt. They have two children, Edward A., a counselor at law, and Mary V., at present a pupil in the Union School of Batavia. The family attends the Presbyterian church, and takes the greatest interest in all that pertains to the moral and intellectual advancement of the community.

The Batavia Wheel Company was organized May 13, 1887, by Frank Richardson, William W. Leavenworth, Dr. W. C. Gardiner, A. M. Colt,

16

E. E. Leavenworth, Mrs. Mary E. Richmond, Mrs. A. R. Kenny, Moses E. True, John M. Sweet, and James R. Colt. The capital stock was placed at $50,000, and the following officers were elected: Frank Richardson, president; Dr. W. C. Gardiner, vice-president; William W. Leavenworth, secretary; A. M. Colt, treasurer; and John M. Sweet, superintendent. The business was originally inaugurated in 1880, by Colt Brothers & .True. In 1885 Mr. Sweet became associated with the old firm, manufacturing hardware specialties and subsequently the Sweet wheels. The works were located at Exchange Place, and were burned in January, 1886. Upon the organization of the present company grounds were secured on Walnut street, adjoining the Central Railroad tracks, consisting of 254 feet on Walnut street and 478 feet on the railroad. Upon these grounds spacious buildings were erected, consisting of a main building 40x150 feet, three stories in height, with brick engine and boiler rooms, and other buildings consisting of a hub room 40x20 feet, storage and coal sheds, etc., and a handsome office building. A switch from the Central tracks connects the manufactory with ample transportation facilities. The machinery is propelled by a 60-horsepower engine, and the firm employs an average of 40 workmen, and turns out from 50 to 75 sets of wheels per day. The wheels manufactured by the firm are Sweet's concealed band and the True shell band, which rank as the best in the world and find a ready sale all over the United States and Australia. The firm also manufactures various other hardware specialties. The plant is a model of its kind, and cost, with machinery, about $40,000.

Frank Richardson, the president of the Batavia Wheel Co., is a native of Saratoga County, where he was born in 1851. His father was a railroad contractor, and this business was followed by the son, who was connected with the construction of various lines of road in this country. He next engaged in the hardware trade in Watertown, and in October, 1886, purchased the stock of Volz Brothers, hardware merchants, of Batavia. Three months later he lost his stock of goods by fire. He then organized the company of which he is president, and is devoting his exclusive attention to the management of this progressive manufactory. Mr. Richardson was united in marriage, in 1883, with Miss Emma P. Johnson, who died October 25, 1888, leaving one child, Rufus J.

William W. Leavenworth is a native of Darien, and was born in 1855, a son to Rev. Hobart and Nancy (Gridley) Leavenworth, of English descent and of New England nativity. His father was a Baptist clergyman, and had charge of many pastorates in the State. William W. was reared in this county, educated in its schools, and had also the advantage of Lima Seminary. His business career began as a drug clerk in Batavia, and for the past five years he has been a member of the well-known drug firm of his name. Since entering the service of the Batavia Wheel Company he has served as secretary. His wife's maiden name was Miss Ida Barber.

Alva M. Colt, treasurer of the Batavia Wheel Co., was born in Warsaw, N. Y., in 1842, and is a son of Joseph R. and Sarah A. (Phelps) Colt, who moved to Darien in 1853. Learning the trade of blacksmith in Warsaw Alva W. followed this calling from 1859 to 1880, in Erie and Genesee counties. In 1869 he came to Batavia, where he has since resided. He was a member of the firm of Foster & Colt, and in 1880 a partner of the Batavia Clamp Co. He was one of the original members of the company to start the manufacture of wheels in Batavia, and was instrumental in the erection of the plant of the Batavia Wheel Co. He married a Miss Hicks, of Erie County, in 1867.

John M. Sweet, general superintendent of the Batavia Wheel Co., and an inventor, is a Canadian by birth, but has been a resident of the United States since he was 11 years of age. He is a carriagemaker by trade, but possesses a talent for general mechanics. He has taken patents on four hubs, and is the inventor of various useful labor-saving machines. In 1872 he was united in marriage with Mrs. Julia A. Griswold, of Batavia.

William C. Gardiner, the vice-president of the Batavia Wheel Co., is a descendant of Roger who came to America in the *Mayflower*. He was born in 1842, in Madison County, N. Y., and went to the war in 1861, remaining about two years. In 1864 he began to practice dentistry in Wauseon, Ohio, and after visiting several places in the West he settled in Batavia, where he is now engaged in practice. He is a Republican, a member of the Masonic order, and a member of the Presbyterian Church. He married Elizabeth C. Wheeler, of Hamilton, N. Y., and they have one son, Charles.

The New York Lumber and Wood Working Company is now one of the leading manufacturing industries of Batavia. In 1884 the Batavia Manufacturing Company was formed, with a capital stock of $200,000. This firm was soon changed to the Batavia Sewing Machine Company, the capital stock authorized to be increased to $300,000, and they contracted to manufacture the Post combination sewing machine. During the summer of 1884 the company erected, near the eastern boundary line of the village, a brick building, 60x300 feet, three stories in height, with an engine-house attached. The cost was about $40,000. Financial embarrassment prevented the execution of the plans of the company, and in 1885 the building became the property of the New York Lumber and Wood Working Co., formerly the New York Wood Turning Co., of New York city. This company has a capital stock of $100,000, all owned by New York parties, where the principal office is located—173 Broadway. The officers of the company are W. C. Andrews, president; George P. Smith, vice-president; Lewis Coon, secretary; and O. P. Shaffer, treasurer. C. Honeck is superintendent of the manufactory, and W. H. Sidway is the local financial representative. The company employs on an average 150 workmen, and its principal market is New York city. The work produced by the company consists of all kinds of decorative and cabinet work for house finishing, besides a vast variety of fancy furniture, wood turning, molding, carving, etc. The machinery is of the latest improved pattern, and the establishment is a model of its kind. The building is protected from fire by the automatic water system. The business of the firm is fast increasing, and their force is now working 10 hours per day throughout the year.

W. H. Sidway, who is the financial manager of the Batavia office of the New York Lumber and Wood Working Co., is a native of Buffalo. His business experience began as a reporter for the *Express* of his native city. In 1886 he became a clerk in the New York office of his present company, and was subsequently promoted to his present position. Mr. Sidway is a young man possessing fine business qualities, and represents his corporation with energy and fidelity.

Charles H. Honeck, superintendent of the New York Lumber and Wood Working Co., is a native of Prussia, and immigrated to America in 1856. He learned the trade of cabinetmaker in New York, and evincing an aptitude for art designing entered the Plassman School of Art in New York city, and was graduated therefrom. He subsequently became the superintendent for Brooks & Co., of Brooklyn, retaining that position three years, and also had charge of the establishment of R. W. Myers, cabinetmaker and interior decorator, for three years. He was then placed in charge of the works of his present employers, in New York city, and since 1887 has been superintendent of the Batavia works.

The Syracuse Forging and Gun Company removed their plant from Syracuse to Batavia in the spring of 1889. This company began business in the manufacturing of an improved fifth wheel for wagons, and finally added the manufacture of the new Baker gun. They are located in the old brick school building on Liberty street, and with additions made by them have in use about 20,000 square feet of flooring, and one and one-half acres of ground. The motive power is supplied by three engines aggregating 75 horse-power, and an average of 100 men are regularly employed. An electric light plant furnishes 150 lights for their use. The fifth wheel manufactured by them is a combination of valuable patents, and ranks as a leader in the trade. The new Baker gun is the invention of W. H. Baker, the general superintendent of the company. It is a breech-loading, double barrelled shot gun, manufactured in many different weights, and about 5,000 are sold annually at a list price of $30 each. The market for the gun extends all over the United States. The business of the company will exceed $175,000 annually. Dr. E. L. Baker is the president of the company; Ralph Helm, of Syracuse, vice-president; W. T. Mylcrane, secretary and treasurer; and W. H. Baker, general superintendent. The capital stock is $60,000.

The Batavia Preserving Company was orignally started by John Pierson in 1879, who began canning fruits and vegetables at Bushville. He supplied himself with all the modern appliances of the trade, but owing to want of attention to the details was not pecuniarily successful. In 1881 the Bank of Batavia became the owner of the establishment, and the business was conducted by it one season at Bushville. In 1882 Sprague, Warner & Co., of Chicago, the present proprietors, purchased the establishment and conducted the business. In the spring of 1883 they removed to the corner of School and Liberty streets, in the old schoolhouse, then a manufactory of engines. The business as conducted by the present company is very successful. All kinds of fruits and vegetables common to this locality are put up in glass or tin, the latter being manufactured on the premises. From 175 to 350 hands are employed, and 1,350,000 cans are put up in a season. The business increased so rapidly that the company was forced to erect larger and more convenient buildings, and in May, 1888, they moved to the new quarters on Mill street. The main building is 50x209 feet, with wings 80x35 and 40x60 feet. The motive power is furnished by a 70-horse-power engine. This company has also a branch at Spencerport, Monroe County, where 200 persons are employed during the busy season, producing about 500,000 cans.

W. E. Flynn, the manager of these works, was born in Newark, N. Y., in 1860.   He became connected with the firm in 1884, and in 1886 was appointed to his present position.   He is deserving of the confidence reposed in him.

Breweries and malt-houses.—In 1827 a brewery and malt-house was built by Libbeus Fish on what is now Elm street, on the present site of A. H. King's malt-house.   It was a wooden building of small capacity, though sufficient for the demands of the place and vicinity at that time. From time to time the capacity of the establishment was increased to meet the demands of the trade, till in 1860 it was capable of turning out 8,000 barrels annually.   It was conducted by Libbeus Fish until 1835, when Eli H. Fish, his son, became proprietor, and he continued the business till 1862.   In that year he disposed of the establishment to Boyle & Smith, who carried it on as a brewery till the autumn of 1864, when it reverted to Mr. Fish.   In January, 1865, it was burned.   In the summer of the same year a malt-house was erected on the site by Mr. Fish, who conducted it till 1871, when R. A. Maxwell (now State superintendent of insurance) became a partner.   In a year's time that firm was succeeded by Maxwell & Ensign.   In December, 1872, the buildings were again burned, and in 1873 again rebuilt by Mr. Fish.   Soon afterwards A. H. King became a partner with Mr. Fish.   The firm continued until 1876, when the interest of Mr. Fish was purchased by King & Son. In May, 1883, the establishment was again burned, but was at once rebuilt by King & Son, with about double its previous capacity, and with all modern improvements.   About 80,000 bushels of barley are annually converted into malt in this establishment, and the barley crop of the county is the principal one.   Mr. King became sole owner in 1886.   Upton & Warner have conducted the business since.   The cost of the building is $26,000.   New York and Boston are the principal ports of sale.

A. H. King, a native of Monroe County, was reared upon a farm, and has always been engaged in handling agricultural productions.   He was for many years a large dealer in grain and wool in his native county, and during the late war was an extensive dealer in oats, which he furnished the government.   He has served as supervisor in Monroe County for eight years, and for five years was superintendent and weighmaster on the Erie Canal.

In 1857 Eli H. Fish built spacious ale vaults on the site of the brewery above noted, which were used as such till 1870, when they were converted into a brewery, which was conducted by different parties from time to time till 1880, when William Gamble purchased the property and successfully operated it till 1887, when the buildings were burned. Their capacity was 4,500 barrels annually. Mr. Gamble now confines his attention to bottling beer, handling ale, and retailing liquors, at 508 East Main street.

In 1850 John Eagar purchased the old stone church (built in 1827 by the Methodists) on West Main street. This he converted into a brewery, using it as such till 1862, when it was burned out. He then erected, on the south side of the street (opposite), a large brick building, which has been used as a brewery and wholesale liquor store from that time. The size of the building is 50x125 feet, three stories high, with basement. After the burning out of the old stone building it was re-roofed and fitted up as a malt-house. Mr. Eagar died in 1869, but the business is still carried on under the firm name of Eagar & Co., composed of John F. V., H. B., and W. T. Eagar, and Mrs. Emily M. Whitcomb, and they are agents for Syracuse ale. After the destruction by fire of the Fish malt-house, on Elm street, in 1872, R. A. Maxwell and H. J. Ensign erected a new malt-house on Union street, near West Main street. It was of concrete, three stories high, 100x140 feet. They conducted a malting business until 1881, when Craft & Caldwell purchased the business and have carried it on since, malting 35,000 bushels of barley per year.

The Batavia Brewing Company was organized November 1, 1889, with William Hooker, president, and William Gamble, manager. A building 40x60 feet, three stories in height, and an extension, will be used for the business. It is expected that 10,000 barrels of ale and porter will be manufactured annually.

House's bottling works are located on West Main street.

Callender's crayon factory was started in 1887, on Jackson street. Oil, lithographic, and lumber crayons are manufactured.

Giddings's cigar factory is located on Main street and employs four hands.

J. F. Garnier's cigar factory is located over 90 Main street. It was started in 1884, and now makes 15,000 cigars per month.

The Batavia Steam Laundry, located at 202 East Main street, was established by Mrs. Nettie Showerman, October 7, 1889. It has all the modern appliances for doing first-class work.

Ellicott street roller-mills, of Batavia, were erected by Frank G Moulton in the summer of 1889. The structure is 60x40 feet, five stories high, and from foundation to roof is symmetrically and substantially built. The motive power is furnished by a 60-horse-power steam engine. All the machinery is of the latest patents and the best manufactured. A requirement in the contract between Mr. Moulton and the builder was that the mills should be capable of doing as good work as any on the American continent. These mills have a capacity of 100 barrels of flour per day. They were constructed with anticipations of doubling their capacity. The business is now conducted under the firm name of Parsons & Co., with Mr. Moulton as the chief proprietor and factor in the firm.

The Batavia Gas and Electric Light Company was organized as the Batavia Gas Light Company in 1855, with a capital of $32,500. The first directors were George Brisbane, D. W. Tomlinson, G. B. Worthington, S. C. Holden, Alva Smith, Frank Chamberlin, and R. Merrifield. D. W. Tomlinson was president, secretary, and treasurer, and W. H. Tompkins, superintendent. The works, located on Ellicott street, near the Erie Railroad freight depot, were completed in the autumn. The gas holder at that time had a capacity of 13,500 feet. There were 150 consumers and 20 street lamps. In 1878 a new holder, with a capacity of 35,000 feet, was built. From the first construction of the works the consumption of gas has steadily increased, till now over 400 consumers and 124 street lamps are supplied. The mains have been extended from two miles to seven miles. Early in 1885 new works were erected for the manufacture of gas from crude petroleum. The gas so manufactured is of a better quality and cheaper in price. In 1886 the company augmented their plant by introducing a dynamo for electric light, using both the Jenny and Brush systems. The present officers are Wilber Smith, president; A. N. Cowdin, secretary and treasurer; and Alexander Wyness, superintendent, he succeeding Mr. Tompkins.

Consumers' Electric Light and Power Company was organized in 1889, with a capital of $25,000, with Henry Craft, president; C. H. Caldwell, secretary; R. L. Kinsey, treasurer. The works are located off Evans street on the Erie Railroad, and the company will furnish light for stores, residences, and factories, and power for all who want it.[1]

Schad Wheel Company was organized in December, 1889, with J. J. Ellis as president; Bernard Schad, vice-president; Henry S. Allis, secretary; and Frank J. Shultz, treasurer. The capital stock is $40,000.

---

[1] A new company has recently been formed called the "Consumers' Electric Light and Power Co.," the directors of the same having bought out the two above named companies. The parties interested are S. D. Purdy, H. D. Rhodes, Henry Craft, Charles H. Caldwell, R. C. Garhart, and R. L. Kinsey.—*Editor.*

They manufacture the Schad and other carriage wheels. The superiority of the Schad wheel consists of its locked spoke in an iron jacket, with its heavy shoulder resting wholly on the wooden hub, making it especially desirable for stone pavements. The company contemplates manufacturing on a large scale this superior wheel.

In September, 1888, D. K. Chaddock opened up a spacious livery stable at No. 8 State street. He keeps from 15 to 20 horses. He is also owner and proprietor of the Pratt mills at Indian Falls, and is a dealer in horses. He resides on the corner of Ellicott avenue and Mix Place.

E. N. Rowell & Co. manufacture paper boxes in every style, their heaviest output going to the drug trade. This factory is an offshoot of one started by Dr. A. S. Palmer in Utica, N. Y., prior to 1860. The Doctor made his own pill-boxes, and invented his machinery and tools. After Dr. Palmer's death the business was carried on by his children in a small way until 1883, when it was moved to Batavia. In 1889 E. N. Rowell, finding the old plant inadequate to his business, took in E. G. Buell, and they purchased a new outfit of machinery and moved into larger quarters, using both plants, to which they are constantly adding new machinery for further enlargement of the business. E. N. Rowell has invented many new boxes for the drug trade, some of which are now made and quoted by every box factory in the United States and Canada. So many new things are being made that it is often called the Novelty Manufacturing Company. Their goods are shipped into every State in the Union and to Canada.

The Batavia roller flouring-mills, on Evans street, were established in 1884, by N. D. Nobles. They have a capacity of 65 barrels of flour per day. The building is 36x48 feet.

Cope & Son's pump works, on Harvester avenue, were established in 1825, by Simon Cope. The business is now in the hands of Orville G. and Philip Cope.

The West End Hotel, located on West Main street, is owned and conducted by S. W. Brown, he having been in possession for six years. The house is 40x40 feet, and has about 25 rooms for transient guests.

The Cottage restaurant is located at 1 State street. It is run as a first-class restaurant under the management of Burt Moulton.

William T. Palmer's box factory is located at 56-60 Main street. It was moved from Utica in 1881 by Palmer & Rowell. Since 1883 Mr. Palmer has conducted the business. He has about 15 hands at work making paper boxes.

Watson Bullock manufactures the People's liquid bluing at 39 Liberty street. The concern was established in 1882. The bluing has no superior for laundry work. Mr. Bullock also has a dyeing and scouring establishment, and has been 18 years in business.

Calvin Armstrong, born in New London, Conn., came to Batavia in 1853, and settled near Bushville, where he remained until his death in 1857, aged 73 years. His wife was Clarissa, daughter of Amos and Edna (Smith) Armstrong, and their children were Mary, Ira, and Edna. Ira was born in Wheatland, N. Y., in 1843. He married Ruth A., daughter of Jacob and Huldah (Washburn) Wood, of Attica, and their children were Nancy L., Ira L., and Clara A. His widow is still living in Batavia, at the age of 72 years. Ira died July 9, 1886, at the age of 72 years. Nancy L. married Charles A. Snell, of Batavia, son of Charles and Elizabeth (Seamans) Snell, and their children are Charles I., Frank A., and Nettie L. They now reside on the Snell homestead farm. Calvin Armstrong served in the War of 1812, and was at the burning of Buffalo.

Egbert A. Bigelow, son of William R., married Lillian F., daughter of George and Eliza (Knickerbocker) Kellogg, of Batavia, and their children were George E. and Winifried. For his second wife he married, January 13, 1889, Eugenie M., daughter of Lorenzo D. and Julia S. (Strong) Langmade, of Oberlin, Kansas, natives of New York State. Mr. Langmade was of Scotch and French ancestry; his wife was of Holland and English descent, and was the daughter of George and Julia (Dingman) Strong. Mr. Bigelow is a farmer, residing on road 76.

Elisha Bigelow was born in Guilford, Vt., and came to Onondaga County, thence to Batavia in 1830, where he died in 1883, aged 89 years. His first wife was Maria Reed ; his second wife was Harriet Jerome. The children were Horace E., James R., Jerome L , Mary, Sarah, Mariah, and William R. The latter was born in Hastings, N. Y., and married Jennie A., daughter of John D. and Abigail R. (Wolcott) Safford, of Pembroke. Their children were Egbert A., Gertrude S., Florence J., and Luella E. · Gertrude S. is a missionary in Japan, where she has been three years under the auspices of the Presbyterian board. William R. Bigelow is a farmer on road 76.

. Andrew J. Andrews was born in Attica, May 15, 1830. In April, 1846, he commenced driving stage between Warsaw and Batavia for J. A. McElwain, being thus employed by him two years, when he bought the line and run it until July 1, 1852. He also had charge of a livery stable for one year in Warsaw for Mr. McElwain. In 1853 he purchased the stable, and Andrews & Kinney run it for four years. He was out of business for one year, when he again engaged in the livery business for one year in Warsaw. He afterwards bought a livery business in Rochester, moved it to Warsaw, and was with his former partner (Kinney) until 1860, when he moved to Batavia and opened a stable, keeping in the business since. In 1864 he engaged in the rear of St. James Hotel, where he has since been located. In 1885 he built a brick stable, 56x82 feet, with basement and accommodations for 75 horses. He keeps from 10 to 15 horses for livery use. At one time he was in company with A. G. Collins, under the firm name of A. G. Collins & Co., proprietors of the old St. James Hotel.

Edward W. Atwater, at 212 East Main street, is the business manager of the Dean Richmond estate. He is a native of Rochester, was born in 1842, educated in Providence, R. I., enlisted in the war of the Rebellion, served nine months, and became connected with the American Wood Paper Co., at Rogersford, Pa. He was there eight years, and was then secretary and treasurer of a manufacturing concern until 1874. He was engaged in business at Palmyra and Fairport, came to Batavia in 1886, and connected himself with the Johnston harvester works for two years. Mr. Atwater is trustee of the Railway Register Manufacturing Co. and Batavia Wheel Co., and treasurer of Batavia Hotel Co. He was married, in 1872, to Miss Fannie A. Langworthy, and they have four children.

Rev. Lucius Atwater is president of the Pioneer Association, a position he has filled for many years. He has been instrumental also in building up many churches. He was at Middlebury for four years, at Elba seven years, and has preached to the Tonawanda Indians.

Libbeus Allen came to Batavia in 1817 from Otsego County, N. Y., and settled in the northwest part of the town. He had a family of seven children. His son William was born November 7, 1819, and has always resided in the county. He married Rebecca Carr, and they have two children, Franklin W., who resides in Oakfield, and Jennie, wife of Alexander Clark, who resides at Lakeville, Livingston County.

Henry Agar was born in Seneca County, N. Y., April 22, 1829. He worked in his father's (John) shop at Ovid, N. Y., and learned the carriage painting trade. In 1854 he came to Le Roy, working at his trade until 1857, when his health failed. He then acted as mail agent on the railroad until 1860, and was conductor from Batavia to Canandaigua until 1870, since which time he has worked at his trade, and has been en-

gaged in other business. He has always been in politics and is a Democrat. He married Elizabeth Hazen, and has a family of three children.

Miles B. Adams, a successful business man, was born in Saratoga County
in 1829, a son of Arial and Anna (Dennis) Adams. The father died in
1848, and the mother is now living in Wisconsin, over 90 years of age.
At the age of 19 Miles B. Adams began for himself, learning the machinists' trade, working at it 11 years. He next engaged in business in York,
Livingston County, remaining there seven years. In 1869 he became a
resident of Batavia, and was for seven years located at 98 Main street,
and nine years at 99 Main street, during which time he established a
large grocery trade. He finally moved to Jackson street. After many
years of active business he decided to abandon the grocery trade and
market, and established a coal and wood yard on School street, which
now occupies his attention, and to which he devotes the same progressive methods that characterized his former business relations. He has
also been active in interests to better the condition of Batavia, both materially and morally, is one of the directors of the loan association, and a
staunch Prohibitionist. In 1850 he was united in marriage with Miss
Polly Dowd, daughter of Joseph and Polly (Dutton) Dowd, of this
county. Joseph Dowd was a farmer of Stafford, residing there until his
death. His son, William Dowd, is president of the Bank of North
America of New York, and prominent in business and political life. The
Dutton family were among the earliest pioneers, and have been prominent in the history of the Presbyterian Church of the county.

Peter Bater, son of Peter, was a native of Canada, and is now a resident of Franklin County, N. Y. He married Mary Sampson, of Canada.
Their daughter Mary married Joseph, son of Peter and Olive Votrey, of
Franklin County, N. Y. Joseph Votrey died in Batavia in 1888, at the
age of 64 years. His children were Ezra, Joseph, Olive, Helen, Peter,
Annie, John, Hettie, Mary, Walter, and Frank. His widow, Mary, survives her husband, and resides on road 61, in Batavia, at the age of 66
years.

John Brown was a native of County Limerick, Ireland. In 1847 he
came to Batavia, and now resides on Cedar street. His brothers and
sisters are Margaret, Ellen, Stephen, and Michael. John Brown married
Ellen Sexton, of Ireland, and his children are John, Johanna, Mary J.,
Kittie, and Stephen W. The latter was born in Batavia, and married
Sarah Francis, daughter of William and Johanna (Monion) Francis, of
Bethany. He is now proprietor of the West End Hotel on West Main
street, Batavia, where he has been four years.

Asa Burr, a native of Connecticut, moved to Otsego County, thence to Henrietta about 1810, where he died in 1835, aged 86 years. He married Melinda Hoskins, of Connecticut, and their children were Asa, James, Warren, Doras, Emily, Melinda, and Maria. James was born in Granby, Conn., in 1791, and died in Alabama in 1882, aged 91 years. He served in the War of 1812. He married Lorinda, daughter of Thomas and Phœbe Norris, of Richfield, N. Y. Lorinda Norris was born in 1798. Her parents were from Connecticut. James Burr's children were Alcinda, Asa, Fidelia, Mary T., and Norris T. The latter was born in Henrietta, October 25, 1819, and married Marietta A., daughter of David and Nancy (Clark) Gill, of Barre, N. Y., and they have one daughter, Alcinda C., who married Luther H., son of Levi and Mary E. (Harmon) Townsend, of Batavia, and their children are Olive G. and Ada R. Mr. Burr has lived 22 years on his farm. Mr. Townsend resides with him.

Rice Baldwin, of Connecticut, came to Elba in 1825, where he died in 1874, aged 72 years. He married Phebe McCrillus, and their children were Milton, Aaron, Elvira, Eunice, Janette, Eleanor, Joanna, and William H. He married for his second wife Lucy Wheelock, of Batavia, and their children were Henry, Adelbert, Charity, Albert, Francis, Freedus, and Belle. William H. Baldwin was born in Elba, January 28, 1828, and came to Batavia in 1883. He married Mrs. Jane M. Storms, daughter of Henry and Jane (West) Edgerton. Their children are Phebe J. and Lillian E. The first husband of Mrs. Storms was John C. Storms, and their children were Mary E. and John C., Jr. Mr. Baldwin has been engaged in farming, but is now retired and lives in Batavia village. His age is 62 years, and that of his wife is 60 years. Mary E. Storms married John M. McKenzie, of Wisconsin, son of John and Eunice (Baldwin) McKenzie. They live in Batavia and have one daughter, Bessie L.

Herbert B. Booth, the present efficient overseer of the poor in Batavia, has been in office several years. He was married, in 1865, to the daughter of Homer Bostwick.

Garry Brinckerhoff was a native of the eastern part of the State, served in the War of the Revolution, drew a pension, and died in 1840 at Fishkill-on-the-Hudson, at the age of 99 years. His wife, Phebe, bore him five children, viz.: Stephen, Daniel, Maria, Emeline, and Cornelius. The latter, a native of Dutchess County, came to Batavia in 1840, and died in Rochester in 1881, aged 69 years. He was a master mechanic in wood, iron, and steel, was an inventor and manufacturer of agricultural implements, built the plow factory in Batavia, and was well known in Western New York. His wife was Catherine, daughter of William Russell, of Poughkeepsie. Their children were Alonzo, Emma, Byron, Phebe, Horace, and Garry R. Garry R. Brinckerhoff was born in Fishkill, N. Y., and married Olive A Moulton, of Alexander, daughter of Lewis and Melvina (Benedict) Moulton. Their children are Elsie L., Ralph M., Mabel, Lewis C., and Mary M. (deceased). Mr. Brinckerhoff is a farmer and resides on road 48, where he has lived for three years. Cornelius Brinckerhoff built the first successful mowing machine in use in Western New York, and is the inventor of the rake for reaping machines, and also of the self-holding furrow guage plow, having a diploma awarded for the same from the American Institute in 1853. He was the owner and captain for 20 years of the vessel *Samuel Coddington*, which run from New York, and was the inventor of the augur that bores a a square hole, the patent of which is now owned by Mayor Parsons, of Rochester, N. Y.

H. H. Benjamin, the oldest practicing dentist in Batavia, is a native of Orleans County, where he was born in 1835. He commenced the study of his profession in Albion with John A. Straight, remaining with him three years. In 1863 he came to Batavia and entered the office of Nelson Stevens, the first dentist in the county. Dr. Benjamin soon after began practice alone, and is now widely known throughout the county. He served as treasurer of the village three years, and is a member of the present board of health.

Joseph C. Barnes, a merchant tailor of Batavia, is a native of England, and when 11 years of age came to America, locating in Canada. He learned his trade there, and in 1865 came to Batavia. In 1872 he formed a partnership with L. R. Bailey, which lasted eight years. Since that period he has conducted his business alone. Mr. Barnes is an artistic cutter, and carries a large stock of imported and domestic cloths. He also has a large line of clothing and gents' furnishing goods. For the past 16 years his place of business has been at 96 East Main street, where he has spacious salesrooms. He has served as a member of the board of trustees of the village, and is foremost in all enterprises. He was married, in 1869, to Miss Clara Hawken, of Canada, and they have two children, William A. and Eva J., and belong to the Methodist Episcopal Church.

Dr. Elmina H. Benedict was born in Bath, Steuben County, and married Dr. H. S. Benedict, of Corning. She studied medicine with him and has practiced for the last 25 years. She located in Batavia in 1885, and has been a member of the Steuben County Medical Society since 1877. Her specialties are female diseases. She also spent one year at Geneva studying medicine.

William H. Burns was born in Utica, September 25, 1834. In June, 1852, he began work for the N. Y. C. & H. R. Railroad Co., and has been in their employ since. In April, 1873, he settled in Batavia, and has been roadmaster since for the Rochester, Canandaigua, and Attica division.

M. C. Bergman started a barber shop in Batavia in 1878, and has been in business here since. In May, 1888, he opened up a first-class shop in the Parker House, with three assistants.

Albert E. Bloomfield was born in Shelbyville, Ky., September 19, 1831, came to Batavia August 24, 1856, and was a cutter for William Mann for two years. In 1868 he opened a merchant tailoring store for himself, carrying on the same ever since, having been located at 50 Main street since March, 1876. He has a full line of goods connected with his trade, and also deals in gents' furnishing goods.

Martinas S. Badgerow, son of Justin, a native of Markham, 14 miles from Toronto, Ont., came to Lockport in 1860, and died in 1871, aged 55 years. He was a carpenter. He married Phœbe A., daughter of William H. and Sarah Smith, of Whitby, Ont., and their children were Melinda A., William H., Isaac B., Joseph A., Mary J., Carey E., and Isaac B. The last mentioned was born in Mona, Ont., and married Helena, daughter of August and Adelle (Boult) Begue, of Buffalo. Their children are Howard E. and Elma E. He is now a resident of the village of Batavia, and proprietor of a meat market on Jackson street. Anson and Weston Badgerow served in the late war and were honorably discharged. Weston is in Oregon on a cattle ranch, and Anson is in Dallas, Texas.

William Briggs, a soldier of the Revolution, of Rhode Island, moved to Rensselaer County and died aged 70 years. By his wife, Sarah, he had children as follows: William, Alexander, Thomas, Nancy (Mosher), Amy (Briggs), Mrs. Justus Aiken, and one deceased. William Briggs, a native of Nova Scotia, at the age of three years went to Hoosick, N. Y., thence to Batavia in 1826, where he died on the Briggs farm in 1860, aged 76 years. He married Christiana, daughter of James and Margaret McGowan, of Scotch origin, who immigrated in 1772 to Easton, N. Y.

Their children were William, James. John, Sarah, Emily, Margaret, and George A. George A. Briggs was born in Hoosick, N. Y., February 18, 1816, came to Batavia in 1826, and married Harriet M., daughter of Dr. Amos and Hannah Town, of Batavia. Mr. Briggs, at the age of 74 years, resides on the Briggs homestead. His wife died in 1879, aged 55 years.

John Brown, a native of Canada, was accidentally drowned at the age of 36 years. He married Betsey Thomas, of Cook's Mills, Canada, and their children were John and Joseph. The latter, a native of Canada, came to Batavia at the age of 18 years. He married, first, Thetus Kennedy, by whom he had children as follows: George, Sarah, Mary A., Amidon, Henry W., and John. His second wife was Mary Ann, daughter of Jacob and Anna (Merrill) Lown, of Batavia. He is now a merchant at West Batavia. Mary A. married Cyrus Amidon, and they have a daughter, Nellie L. Mr. Brown's first wife, Thetus, was born in Otsego County, and died in Batavia, May 13, 1888, aged 68 years

Charles M. Bosworth is manager for W. R. Bosworth, dealer in boots and shoes, 69 East Main street. This business was started in 1877 by the present manager, in the Opera House block, and was subsequently removed to its present location, where a full and attractive line of goods are constantly in stock. Charles M. Bosworth, son of William R. and Susan (Wilcox) Bosworth, a native of Vermont, was born in Stafford. His mother's father came from Otsego County, at an early day, and was a tanner and currier. William R. Bosworth followed farming until he retired from active business. Charles M. was educated in the schools of Batavia and Rochester, and began business as clerk in the postoffice, where he remained six years. He then established his present business. He was married, in 1874, to Miss Fannie Smith, and they have three children, Clara L., C. Merton, and Susie L. They are members of the Presbyterian Church.

George P. Bowen, a well-known business man of Batavia, and a native of Darien, was born in 1841, a son of Portica Bowen, of Easton, N. Y., who came here in 1812 and resided until his death in 1860. George P. is the youngest of a family of eight children, all of whom are now living, viz.: David, a farmer, of Darien, Rufus, Mrs. Olive Dunbar, Mrs. Flora Major, Mrs Betsey Curtis, Richard, and Mrs. Myra Burk. He began business in Batavia in 1865, engaging in the grocery trade, subsequently in the crockery trade, which he has since continued. Mr. Bowen has been located at 107 East Main street since 1877, where he has attractive and commodious salesrooms, and has secured a large and extended trade.

His stock is the largest carried in his line in the county. He is a member of Batavia Commandery, No. 34.

Albert E. Brown was born in Batavia in 1860, a son of William H. and Ann (Caple) Brown, from Bristol, Eng. They came to America and located in Skaneateles, subsequently removing to this county. William H. Brown was a merchant in the furniture trade for 20 years. Albert was reared and educated in the Batavia schools, and entered the book and stationery business for four years. He then worked for C. M. Bosworth in the boot and shoe business for nine years. In 1885 he started in business for himself, at 82 East Main street, where he is at present located, and has an extensive trade. He was elected town clerk in 1886, and is now serving his third term. He is a K. of P., an A. O. U. W., president of the Athletic Association, and a member of the Alert Hose Company. He was married, in 1884, to Miss Frank E., daughter of Joseph M. Parker, of Elba

Martin Brown, an attorney in Batavia, was born in Montgomery County, in 1850, and in 1863 enlisted in Co. B, 25th Ohio Vols., serving until the close of the war. He was wounded in 1864 during the engagement at Grahamsville, S. C. After the close of the war he came to Genesee County, learned the carpenters' trade, following it for 10 years, and teaching district school in the winters. Entering the office of Judge M. H. Peck he studied law two years, subsequently graduated from the Albany Law School, class of 1882, and the same year was admitted to practice. He served as justice of the peace in Pembroke six years, and in Batavia two years. He was married, in 1882, to Miss Mary J. Mattison. They have one son, Allen G.

John F. Baker, M. D., is a native of Delaware County, N. Y., where he was born in September, 1815. His parents, Joseph and Eunice (Follett) Baker, from New England, were farmers. Dr. Baker commenced the study of medicine in the office of Dr. Jonathan L. Cowles, and graduated from the Geneva Medical College in 1840. His practice began at Otselic, Chenango County, as an allopath, and continued for about four years, when he was converted to homeopathy. He moved then to Lebanon, Madison County, living there about four years, when he came to Batavia, November 18, 1848, being the first practitioner in his school in the county and the fifth in the State. In a few weeks after he came here Dr. Foote came and was his partner for nearly a year; when Dr. Foote left Dr. C. C. Baker, a younger brother, was taken into partnership, about 1851, and continued for about one year, when they separated,

17

and again became partners in 1862, continuing so for three years. Dr. Baker's health failing at this time, he went to Delaware and remained five years, returning with improved health, and located in Le Roy for a short time, when he finally settled again in this place, where, at the age of 74 years, we find him in the full vigor of health and earnestly pursuing his profession, with a practice extended over a large section of country. He is a member of the New York Central Homeopathic Association, and of the Western Homeopathic Medical Society, in the latter of which he has served as vice-president, and is now serving as secretary. He is also a member of the Masonic order of the 32d degree. Dr. Baker is the author of a long article on rupture and hernia, for which he has received high econiums from celebrated surgeons in this country and Europe. His son, John W. Baker, a native of Batavia, was under the instruction of his father from his youth. He graduated from Pulte Homeopathic College of Cincinnati in 1887, and is associated in business with his father.

 Dr. C. C. Baker came here in 1851, was associated with Dr. J. F. Baker for about one year, when he went to Albion, where he remained about one year, and then returned as partner with his brother, continuing so until 1865. He died in 1887.

Very prominent among the physicians of Batavia, though young in the profession and practice, is Dr. William T. Bolton, who, by his indefatigable energy and devotion to the responsibilities assumed by him, has succeeded in establishing a business second to none in the community. Dr. Bolton is a native of Wallingford, New Haven County, Conn., and son of William and Harriet (Self) Bolton, residents of New England, but of English ancestry. He was born March 21, 1859. Receiving the superior primary education afforded by the schools of his native town (so well known throughout New England), he prepared for Yale College at Hopkins's Grammar School, New Haven, and studied with Dr. Paul C. Skiff, of the same place. In 1877 he entered the medical department of Yale College, graduating therefrom and receiving his diploma in 1879. He commenced the practice of his profession in Braidwood, Ill., and in 1881 entered Jefferson Medical College of Philadelphia, from which institution he graduated in 1882. He was immediately appointed resident physician of Charity Hospital on Blackwell's Island pursuing the superior advantages which that position afforded him for nearly two years. In 1883 he moved to Batavia, depending only upon his own native energy to gain the esteem and confidence in a com-

W. T. Bolton, M. D.

and again became partners in 1862, continuing so for three years. Dr.
Baker's health failing at this time, he went to Delaware and remained
five years, returning with improved health, and located in Le Roy for a
short time, when he finally settl   ...n in this place, where, at the age
of 74 years, we find h·   ..il vigor of health and earnestly pursuing his ·   ...actice extended over a large section of
country.   .... of the New ...... Central Homeopathic Association,   ... Medical Society, in the
latter of v ...   ..at, and is now serving as
secretary.   1.   ... rder of the 32d degree.
Dr. Baker is ...   ..pture and hernia, for which
he has receive ·   ... l surgeons in this country
and Europe. ::   ... ve of Batavia, was under
the instruction ... :   ... :i· graduated from Pulte
Homeopathic Co..   Xc/, ...! is associated in business
with his fath...
. Dr. C. ...   ... associated with Dr. J. F
Baker for ...   vent to Albion, where he remained
about one .... artu.. with his brother, continuing
so until 1×∂.
  Very peopr...   Batavia, though young in
the prof ...en ·   Bolton, who, by his indefatigable ..rg. ·   ...nsibilities assumed by him,
has suc   ... d to none in the community. ... Bo...   ...ord, New Haven County,
Conn., :   ...t ol ·   ... of) Bolton, residents of New
Englan ... ·... En   .., born March 21, 1859. Receiving   rded by the schools of his native tow   ... know'   ...ngland), he prepared for Yale
College   .. t   ...v Haven and studied with
Dr. Pa   7 ...ated the medical
departi   :erc ... .nd receiving his
diplom   ... .. the   ...re of his profession in Braidwood,   ... ente   ...cal C... ... Philadelphia,
from v   ... in 1.. He ... i. .ediately ap-
pointe   ... ...y the   ... on the well's Island
pursui   ..ich 1· ... tion a ...ed him for
nearly   ... Eu ...vend. only upon
his ow   ... ... cem ... viden... in a com-

munity so necessary to the building up of a successful practice. That he has succeeded goes without saying ; for he ranks among the profession as a popular and successful practitioner ; being studious in his nature he keeps well up with the advance of his profession. Dr. Bolton is a member of the Genesee County Medical Society, being elected such in 1884, and also as secretary of the society in 1866, and still holds that office. He was united in marriage, November 14, 1884, to Alice J. Brooks, of Watkins, Schuyler County, N. Y., and they have two children, Robert W. and Elsie B. The family are members of the Baptist Society in Batavia, and the Doctor is one of its board of trustees.

Peter Broadbooks was born in Alsace, France, (now Germany,) in 1840. He came to America in 1854, settled at Rome, N. Y., and learned his trade. He remained there about four years, when he came to Attica, working at his trade three years, and thence removed to Pine Hill (Elba), where he lived for three years. He finally removed to Batavia, where he has been in business for 12 years as a carriage ironer. He is a mechanical genius, and has invented shears for cutting iron, a metal punching machine, nippers and pliers, and a tire shrinker, all of which are placed on royalty. He has been located at 37 and 39 Ellicott street for 10 years, and owns his property. Mr. Broadbooks has manufactured carriages, but now devotes his time to general repairing, and has succeeded to the business of the Batavia Iron Co.

The firm of Beck & Salway was formed in 1888, by William Beck and John E. Salway. Their place of business is in the Exchange building on Court street, where they keep a large stock of flour, feed, grain, hay, and fertilizers. William Beck, the senior member of the firm, is an Englishman, and came here in 1870, and for 10 years was engaged in raising hops, having charge of the yards of C. D. Lane, of Batavia. He was finally employed in Parsons's flour and feed store, and became a partner under the firm name of Beck & Parsons. They dissolved in 1888, and Mr. Beck became a partner of John E. Salway, who is also a native of England. He came to America in 1872, and in 1875 to this county. For 10 years he was with John Garwood, the miller of Bushville, and subsequently in the employment of Mr. Parsons, until the above firm was established. The firm has excellent facilities for the prosecution of its business, and handles reliable brands of goods only.

O. R. Clark, an insurance, real estate, and loan agent, is a native of Stafford, and was born in 1821, a son of Benjamin and Lucy (Lee) Clark. The father was from Vermont, coming at an early day from Madison

County, where he was married, and came with his wife to Stafford about 1812. He was in the War of 1812. He moved to Elba and engaged in farming until his death in 1864. The mother died in 1867. Of a family of six children O. R. Clark is the only one living. He remained upon the home farm until 23 years of age, when he engaged in farming for eight years, and then removed to Elba village, engaging in the real estate and loan business. In 1865 he removed to Batavia, conducting the same line of business, and is now at 110 East Main street. Mr. Clark has served upon the board of village trustees, and is a Knight Templar. He married Cynthia L., daughter of George King, of Stafford. She died leaving one child, Alice, the wife of Samuel Parker, of Elba. In 1874 Mr. Clark married Miss Hattie Fisher, and they have three children, viz.: Cynthia M., Orlo R., Jr., and Le Roy F.

Chauncey Cornwell, a native of Middletown, Conn., came to Alexander in 1820. He served in the War of 1812, and died in 1869, aged 81 years. He was married to Mary A. Church, of Connecticut, and their children were Henry, Cordelia, Mary, Jane, John, Shaler B , Corliss, George, Leonard, Charles B , and Angela. Charles B. Cornwell was born in Connecticut, March 31, 1820, came to Batavia in 1851, and married, first, Eveline Starges, and they had one daughter, Frances. In 1862 he married for his second wife Isabella, daughter of Robert and Elizabeth (Town) Burgess, of Scotch descent, and their children are Agnes E. and Mattie C. They now reside in Batavia.

Joseph Campbell, son of Daniel, of Scotch origin, was born in Johnstown, N. Y., in 1810, and died in 1869, aged 59 years. He came to Caledonia at the age of eight years, where he remained until his death. He married Margaret, daughter of Daniel and Catherine (McLaren) Mc-Vane, of Caledonia, and their children were Harriet E , Catherine A., Donald, John J., Duncan, Malcolm, of Kansas City, and Peter C. The latter, with John J. and Harriet E., reside on the farm on road 76, where they have lived for eight years. The wife of Daniel was Catharine St. Clair, and their children were Daniel, John (the first minister that preached in the Presbyterian Church in Caledonia, being there four years), Catherine, Harriet, Elizabeth, and Janette.

William Crary, a native of Connecticut, went to Cattaraugus County, thence to Arcade, where he died at the age of 80 years. His children were Benjamin and Sophia. Benjamin was born in Wallingford, Conn., July 29, 1811, and came to Cattaraugus County, where he now resides. He married Rhoda, daughter of John Howe, of Groton, N. Y., and their children are Lemi, Marianna, and Albert B. Albert B. Crary, a native of Humphrey, Cattaraugus County, came to Batavia in 1887, where he now resides. He married Ella Roberts, daughter of Joel and Hannah (Wight) Roberts, and his children are Alta E. and Mildred. Mr. Crary's ancestor was a captain in the War of 1812, and was of Scotch origin.

Craft & Caldwell.—C. H. Caldwell started the coal business April 1, 1878, and carried it on one year, when W. F. Merriman joined the firm, under the name of Caldwell & Co. In 1880 Henry Craft was admitted, the firm then doing business as Henry Craft & Co. Thomas H. Combs joined in 1881, and the firm was called Craft, Combs & Co., continuing as such until 1886, when Combs retired, and Craft & Caldwell have since conducted the business. They also conduct a malting business on Union street, and are general agents for Armour & Co in the Chicago dressed beef business, using one car load of beef every 10 days.

Abram Coupland was a native of and died in Lincolnshire, England. By his wife, Fanny, he had children as follows: John, Joseph, William, Edward, Betsey, Jane, Mary, Fanny, and John, the latter of whom was a native of England, where he died in 1866, aged 73 years. He married, and his children were Edward, Elizabeth, Mary, Jane, Abram, and Joseph. Joseph Coupland, a native of Gayton, England (1826), came to Batavia in 1878, and settled on the farm he now occupies, on road 66. He married Martha, daughter of James and Sarah (Madison) Clark, of Gayton, Eng., who died in 1858, at the age of 28 years. Abram Coupland, a native of England, came to Batavia in 1883, and died in 1889, aged 48 years. He married Ann, daughter of John and Mary (Jubb) Smith, of Branston, Eng., and their children were Annie, Louisa, Rose E., Kate S., John W., and Esther J. His widow still survives at the age of 49 years.

Center Street Laundry, located at 15 Center street, was established in May, 1889, by Mary J. Brockway. It is fitted up with modern machinery, and is prepared to do all kinds of first-class laundry work.

Samuel Cooper was born September 15, 1818, in Syracuse, N. Y. When 17 years old he went to Holley, Orleans County, and learned the harnessmakers' trade. In 1837 he came to Batavia and worked a few months, and in 1840 started a shop in Lockport, N. Y., where he remained 12 years. He came to Batavia in 1852 and formed a partnership with Henry Ensign, under the firm name of Ensign & Co., continuing nine years. In 1861 he began business for himself, and has been burned out three times. He was appointed village collector in 1888

Mr. Cooper married Mary Chamberlain, and they had one child, Charles, who died at the age of 22 years.

Robert Clark came to Batavia in 1839, from Pennsylvania. He died in 1847. Only two children are living here: Mrs. H. Colby, wife of Jerome Colby, and Mary Clark. Rachel Spencer lives in Mahomet, Ill.

Francis B. Comiskey, born in Ireland in 1846, came to America in 1866. He learned the tailoring trade at home and the art of cutting in New York in 1871. He came to Batavia and was cutter for S. Masse for three years, when he moved to Canton, St. Lawrence County, N. Y., and was cutter for R. B. Ellsworth five and one-half years. He then returned to Batavia and opened up a merchant tailoring establishment, carrying on the business since, being now located at 110 Main street. He was in business in New York city for five years previous to coming here.

J. M. Chapin, wholesale and retail lumber dealer at 22 Evans street, took charge of the business in 1888. He has a coal trestle with a capacity of 1,000 tons, the only one in town. He has the best of facilities for furnishing any kind of lumber, giving his attention to all kinds of manufactured work for houses complete. The yards are under the management of C. N. Dwight, who has been connected with the business since 1879. The sales for 1889 were over 2,000,000 feet in this vicinity, and are constantly increasing. Mr. Chapin also has two large saw-mills at Three Rivers, Ont., and owns timber lands in Michigan and Pennsylvania.

Dr. N. G. Clark, father of Arthur E. Clark, was a well-known physician, whose counsels were of great service to the Democratic party. The son, Arthur E. Clark, was born at Clarkson, Monroe County, N. Y, in 1854. When the father moved to Batavia the son was six years old, and the place has been his home ever since. He was a student in the public schools, and having fitted for college he entered Yale. There he graduated in 1875. He took a course of legal study with W. C. Watson, of Batavia, and gained admission to the bar in 1878. He associated with Mr. Watson, which connection lasted until three years ago, when he started out alone on the opposite side of Main street. Mr. Clark is not a young lawyer in a legal sense. He has been engaged for some time in important railroad business, and managed the right-of way work for the D., L. & W. and the Buffalo and Geneva roads through Genesee and adjoining counties. His business is largely railroad and land business, and his opinion in these matters has unusual weight. Mr. Clark resides with his mother at the old homestead in Batavia, and is one of the most prominent members of the Batavia Club.

Caney & Bradley, the most enterprising watchmakers and jewelers in Batavia, are located on the site of the oldest established jewelry firm in the place, on the southwest corner of Main and Jackson streets, for over 50 years being associated in that line. C. C. Church began the business here in 1830, and was succeeded by G. W. Allen in 1835. Others followed him until Homer Kelsey located there. In 1887 Messrs. Caney & Bradley bought out Mr. Kelsey. Ashton W. Caney, the head of the firm, came from New York city, possessing a large experience of many years' practice as a watchmaker and jeweler, which qualifies him to largely control the trade of this section, an evidence of which is shown by the full and complete line of goods, and varied assortment of fancy articles, carried by the firm. C. C. Bradley, who came from Palmyra, N. Y., is a young man of integrity, and a worthy aid to Mr. Caney in maintaining the position held by the firm.

Lawrence L. Crosby, attorney, was born in Bergen in 1835. His grandfather, Jedediah, came from Connecticut in 1805, settling on lots 9 and 10, section 7, of the Triangle tract, about one mile north of the village. His wife was Mabel Austin, also from Connecticut. The father of Lawrence L. (Luther), born in 1806, was the first white child born in Bergen. He married Mary Ann Avery, and resided in Bergen all his life, being justice of the peace for 20 years, supervisor several terms, and a colonel of dragoons of the old uniformed militia. He died in 1864, and his wife in 1857. Of a family of five children Lawrence L. is the only one now living. He commenced the study of law in Iowa, and continued it in the office of Wakeman & Bryan, of Batavia, being admitted to practice in 1860. In 1862 he enlisted in Co. I, 5th Mich. Cavalry, and served with them 20 months. He was then transferred to the Signal Corps, serving there until the close of the war. He commenced practice in Bergen, and since 1874 has continued it in Batavia. He served as clerk of the village five years, and is now serving as police justice. He is adjutant of Upton Post, G. A. R., and second lieutenant in the National Guard. Mr. Crosby was married, in 1866, to Miss Joan, daughter of Briggs Loring, an old resident of Bergen They have one child, Harriet D.

Chaddock & Hickox, grain and produce dealers on Ellicott street, was established in 1886, by John B. Chaddock and George W. Hickox. In 1889 they had about 500 acres of seed wheat under cultivation. They are also largely engaged in raising and handling oats and potatoes, and in buying wool. Mr. Chaddock came to Batavia from Wyoming County in 1882, and was successfully engaged in the coal business until the present partnership was formed. He is a young man with good executive abilities, and has established an honorable record in the short period of his residence in Batavia. George W. Hickox was born in Orleans County in 1848, but his parents, Edwin and Caroline (Smith) Hickox, moved to Alexander in 1850, where they still reside. George W. was reared on the farm, and continued that business until 1882, when he engaged in selling agricultural implements. Two years later he became a resident of Batavia and engaged in his present trade. The firm has been very successful and will extend their business to meet their growing trade. Mr. Hickox married, in 1877, Miss Sarah Dean, daughter of Rev. D. S. Dean, a Baptist clergyman of Rochester. Three children have been born to them, viz.: Edwin Dear, Raymond V., and Ethel May.

Hiram Chaddock, son of Dennis B. and Lydia (Thompson) Chaddock, was born in Alexander in 1826. His father was a native of Worcester, Mass., and when 20 years of age came from Vermont to Alexander with a younger brother, Luther. The father was married in 1820. Levi Thompson, the grandfather of Hiram, came from Washington County in 1810. Dennis and Luther took up about 400 acres of land in the southeast part of the town. Dennis died in 1868, aged 54 years, and his wife in 1834. His second wife died in 1881. Hiram was reared upon the farm and had the advantage of a seminary education. He made a study of the insurance business, and for a number of years traveled throughout the State. Ill health caused him to abandon the business, and, having purchased a farm in Bethany, he followed farming for 21 years. In 1852 he married Harriet A., daughter of Rev. Josiah Keyes, a Methodist divine and presiding elder. In 1873 he came to Batavia, purchased the Ellicott property of about 40 acres, and opened up streets and laid out lots, donating land for Prospect and Richmond avenues and Mix Place. He has erected seven dwellings, and lives in one of the best in town. Mr. Chaddock was one of the organizers of the Holland Purchase Fire Insurance Co., which was conducted successfully for 17 years. He served the company as general superintendent, agent, and adjuster for 13 years, and was appointed receiver of the concern and settled up its affairs. By his prudent management he paid to the stockholders a premium of 20 per cent. on their stock. Mr. Chaddock is the owner of over 1,000 acres of land, having given 500 acres to his children. He has three children: Walter H., a farmer of Batavia; Dennis K., a liveryman and farmer; and Hattie L., who married the only son of Rev. Dr. Paddock, of Rochester. Mrs. Chaddock is a member of the First Methodist Episcopal Church of Batavia.

William Drake lived and died in Greene County, N. Y. His son Samuel, of Greene County, came to Elba in 1813, and died at the age of 90 years. He was one of the pioneers and cleared the farm where he died. He married Sylvia Thorn, of Greene County, and his children were Edward, Orin, William, Moses, Mary A., Jane, Stephen, Elvira, and Samuel O. Samuel O. Drake, born in Elba, September 7, 1818, married Almira, daughter of Stephen and Rebecca (Palmer) Johnson, of Batavia, and they have two children, Sarah A. (Chamberlin), of Buffalo, and Charles O., of Dakota.

John A. Eggleston was born in Rush, N. Y., November 15, 1830. About the year 1865, while engaged in farming, he discovered he had magnetic powers, and has been practicing that profession since, meeting with good success. He married Azubah Mann, who is also a magnetic healer, and assists her husband in his practice. They have been permanently located at Batavia since 1880.

John Dellinger was born in Lorraine, France, August 14, 1826, and came to America with his father, Peter, in 1840, settling in Wyoming County. In 1855 he came to Batavia, where he worked at the carpenters' trade one year, when he began building and contracting on his own account. He had previously worked four years at Capt. Scott's distillery on carpenter work. He has erected more structures in Batavia than any other man. He built and owns the Dellinger block and Dellinger Opera House block, and is a member of the firms of Dellinger & Glade, Haitz & Dellinger, and Schad, Dellinger & Glade. He married Clara Demon, of Sheldon, and they had eight children, six of whom are living.

John Glade, born in Westphalia, Prussia, in 1843, came to America in 1868, and settled in Batavia. He married Minnie Gizer, and they have five children. Mr. Glade has been a contractor and builder since 1874, and is a member of the firm of Dellinger & Glade, who employ about 20 men. They have built the convent on Summit street, the Masonic block, Bank of Batavia, Hotel Richmond, etc

Bernard Schad was born in Darien, February 10, 1855. In 1877 he settled in Batavia, and in 1879 opened a carriage shop on State street, where he carried on the business four years. In 1884 he invented the Schad bicycle wheel and began manufacturing the same. In 1887 he invented improvements on it, and it is now used in every State in the Union. In 1888 he invented a novel carriage wheel, which he has been manufacturing since. He also, in 1888, invented the Schad broom-holder, which he manufactures.

William Didget, a native of England, came to Batavia in 1852, where he now resides. He married Charlotte, daughter of John and Elizabeth Wilkey, of England, and they had one son, John, who married Jemima, daughter of Archibald and Eleanor (Jacoby) Primmer, of Bethany, and their children were Frank, who was killed on the railroad in 1889, Ella, Lottie M., Minnie, Fred, Walter E., and Albert, the latter of whom is now a resident of Batavia, on road 66. Archibald Primmer died in Troy, N. Y., in 1877, at the age of 77 years, and his wife, Eleanor, the same year, aged 68 years.

Lemuel Dean, a native of Vermont, and a soldier of the Revolution, moved to Ohio in 1840, where he died in 1859, aged 75 years. His wife, Emeline, bore him children as follows : Rockwell, Carl, Abram P., Fordyce, and Corbin. Abram P. Dean, a native of Vermont, came to Orleans County, thence moved to Ohio, and finally to Buffalo, where he died in 1862, aged 64 years. He married Patty Winchell, daughter of Martin, of Pompey, N. Y., and his children were Mary Wood, Lucia Birch, Caroline A., and Fordyce O. The latter was born in Moriah, Essex County, N. Y., November 9, 1833, and married Myra M., daughter of Reuben P. Hauser. Their children are Abram P., Kate M., and Myra M. For his second wife he married Mrs Elizabeth M. Hinchey, daughter of R. P. Hauser, and now resides on road 10 in Batavia.

Michael Dailey was born in County Clare, Ireland, in April, 1843. When about eight years of age he came to Batavia with his father, Michael. He attended public schools only a short time, and being obliged to earn his own living he clerked for Joseph Wilson, and when 17 years of age started a small grocery store. After paying for his first bill of goods he had less than 50 cents left. Being active he prospered, and was soon able to purchase the store he occupied, and soon after the adjoining building, opening up a grocery and crockery store on Main street, opposite the Hotel Richmond. In 1871 failing health caused him to abandon the business, but in the following spring he opened two stores on the west side of State street, devoted to the furniture business. Increasing trade necessitated an extension of the business, and he bought a store on the east side of the street. He built up a large trade, engaged in the undertaking business, and finally erected three new stores on State street. He died March 13, 1883. At the time of his death he was chairman of the Democratic County Committee ; was the first Irishman elected trustee of the village ; and was also one of the trustees of the Blind Asylum, holding the position two terms, or until his decease. He took an active part in politics. He married Anna Prindle, of Batavia, and they had a family of eight children, five of whom are living with his widow, who survives him, at 307 East Main street.

Fred H. Dunham, of Batavia, was born in Orangeville, Wyoming County, October 20, 1861. He was educated at Attica Union School, and was graduated at Cornell University. He studied law with Judge North, of Batavia, and was admitted to the bar in June, 1889. He is now engaged in practice in Batavia.

Edna V. Dyer was born in Darien in 1850, and has been a clairvoyant physician and magnetic healer since 1881. Her practice is principally in Genesee County, though she has many patients from other States as well as from this vicinity.

Ferdinand Dorf was born in Germany and came to America about 1852, settling in Elba, and engaged at farming. He enlisted in Co. H, 8th N. Y. H. A., and was killed at Cold Harbor, June 3, 1864. He had four children, three sons and a daughter. Frank, son of Ferdinand, has been in the dry goods business for seven years, six years in a general store. August 26, 1889, he opened a dry goods store at 107 Main street, and keeps a full line of dry goods, carpets, etc. He was born August 8, 1856.

Stephen A. Dustin, son of Stephen, was born in Buffalo in 1851. He came to Batavia about 1856, learned the drug business, and opened a store December 20, 1880, at 108 Main street. His present store, at 57 Main street, was opened March 1, 1888. He carries a full line of drugs and school books, and manufactures sarsaparilla compound and mandrake pills.

Isaac V. Dibble was born in Schoharie County, July 1, 1845. He married Mary Conway, of Lima, N. Y., and they had 10 children, seven of whom are living. In 1867 he moved to Avon and entered the employ of M. & G. Wiard, remaining with them until they came to Batavia, when the firm name was changed to Wiard Plow Co. He was foreman for the company until June 1, 1889, since which time he has been a contractor, and now employs eight to 12 men.

James H. Dewey, son of Otis W., was born in Geneseo, N. Y., May 3, 1839. When eight years of age he moved with his parents to Batavia. He learned the carpenters' trade in Rochester. In 1833 he settled in Batavia, and has been building and contracting since, and now employs from 10 to 15 hands. He married Mary P. Bowe, and they have three children. He and his family are Christadelphian in their religious belief.

Dudley & Cooley, dealers in drugs, medicines, school books, etc., are at 92 Main street. This firm was organized August 1, 1888, on the site of the oldest drug store in the county, which was started by David Seaver. Hall & Co. were Seaver's successors, then E. G. Elmore, Shaw & Stiles, then W. Stiles, Stiles & Dudley (1886), and now the present firm.

O. Cooley, son of Levi, was born in Sweden, Monroe County, July 31, 1839. He is the inventor for most of the machinery for the Johnston Harvester Co. In 1873 he went to Europe and set up the first reaper that was exhibited in France. He has been to Europe eight times in the interest of the Johnston Harvester Co. He operated a machine at the Vienna Exposition in 1873, at Paris in 1878, and at Philadelphia in 1876.

Henry J. Ensign. whose portrait appears in connection with this sketch. was born in Alexander, this county, August 14, 1821. His parents, Hon. Abial and Abbie (Higley) Ensign, of English descent, were natives of Hartford, Conn. His father was a printer, and early in life settled in Utica, N. Y., where he owned, edited, and published the *Utica Democrat* several years, and also represented his district two terms in the State legislature. Later he removed to Alexander, where, by his integrity, intelligence, and fine abilities, he soon gained the confidence and respect of his party in Genesee County, who sent him to represent it in the legislature three terms. He was also postmaster of Alexander, which office, with the office of justice of the peace, he was holding at the time of his death.

Mr. Ensign was liberal in his religious views, and he and his worthy wife were members of the Universalist Church. Their children were Louis, deceased ; Clara, who married John Parish, and resides in Nevada; Emily, who married Robert Kenyon (both deceased); Parmelia, who married George Slayton, and resides in Liberty, N. Y.; Horace, who resides in Illinois; Charles, who lives in Albion, Mich.; and Henry J., the subject of this sketch. Henry J. Ensign received an academic education in Alexander Seminary. After completing his school days he commenced his business life in Batavia by engaging in the manufacture and sale of harnesses and harnessmakers' goods. In 1865 he became the partner of Hon. R. A. Maxwell (ex-State treasurer and present State superintendent of insurance) in the business of malting. Mr. Ensign continued his harness business until about six years before his death, and was a member of the malting firm at his decease, November 30, 1881.

H. J. Ensign

Dudley & Cooley, dealers in drugs, medicines, school books, etc., are at 92 Main street. This fir— ฟ̣a- ˙ ฺanized August 1, 1888, on the site of the oldest dr— ฺ ฺ ฺ ฺ , which was started by David Sea\ ฺ ฺ ฺ ฺ ฺ ssors, then E. G. Elmore, Shaw & St ฺ ฺ ฺ ฺ ฺ y (1886), and now the present firm.

O. ฺooiey. s n ฺ ฺ ฺ ฺ ฺ ฺ en, Monroe County, July 31, 1839. He is the invento, ฺ ฺ ฺ of ฺ ฺ ฺachinery for the Johnston Harvester ฺo ฺ In 1873 ฺ ฺ ฺ ฺ Europe and set up the first reaper that ฺa- ฺ ฺ ฺ ฺ France ฺ ฺ ฺ has been to Europe eight times in the in ฺ ฺ ฺ the Johnston ฺ ฺ ฺ ฺ ฺ ฺ Co. He operated a machine at the Vฺ ฺ ฺ ฺ ฺ ฺ in 1873, ฺ ฺaris in 1878, and at Philadelphia in 1876.

He ฺ ฺ ฺ ฺ ฺ whose portrait appears in connection with this sketch ฺ ฺ ฺ ฺ ฺ this county, August 14, 1821. His parents, ฺ ฺ ฺ ฺ (ฺ ฺ ฺ) Ensign, of English descent, were native ฺ ฺ ฺ ฺ ฺ. ฺ ฺther was a printer, and early in life settle ฺ ฺ ฺ ฺ where ฺ ฺ ฺ ฺ, edited, and published the *Utica Democ* ฺ ฺ ฺ ฺ also represented his district two terms in the State ฺ ฺ ฺ ฺ removed to Alexander, where, by his integrity, ii ฺ ฺ ฺ es, he soon gained the confidence and respec ฺ ฺ ฺ ฺ ฺ ฺty, who sent him to represent it in the leg ฺ ฺ ฺ postmaster of Alexander, which office, ฺ ฺ ฺ ฺ ฺ he was holding at the time of his ฺ

Mr. ฺ ฺ ฺ his religious views, and he and his worthy wife we ฺ ฺ Uni ฺ ฺ ฺ Church. Their children were Louis, ฺ ฺ ฺ ฺ ฺ d John Parish, and resides in Nevada: Emily, ฺ ฺ ฺ ฺ Kenyon (both deceased); Parmelia, who married ฺ ฺ ฺ ฺ ฺ ฺ ฺ, N. Y.; Horace, who resides in ฺ ฺ ฺ ฺ ฺ Albion, Mich., and Henry J., the subject ฺ ฺ ฺ ฺ ฺ ฺ ved an academic education ฺ ฺ ฺ ฺ completing his school days he commei ฺ ฺ ฺ ฺ by engaging in the manufacture of and sal ฺ ฺ ฺmakers goods. In 1895 he became the part ฺ ฺ ฺ ฺ the treasurer and present Stat superint ฺ ฺ ฺ ฺ ฺ ฺusiness of making Mr. Ensig continue ฺ ฺ ฺ ฺ ut six years before his death was a m ฺ ฺ ฺ ฺ at his death. November 30, 18

Eng by H.B.Halls Sons New York

H. J. Ensign

He was a prominent, earnest, and unswerving Democrat, who gave the weight of his great influence to further, strengthen, and build up the great party of which he was an acknowledged leader in Genesee County. To accomplish this he served as chairman of the State, county, and local committees of the Democratic party. He was also an active and liberal supporter of the educational, religious, and benevolent interests of the community in which he lived and the country which he loved. He served as president of the board of aldermen of Batavia, and as director of the First National Bank.

July 12, 1854, he united in marriage with Miss Elizabeth Lee, a native of Hammondsport, N. Y., and daughter of Benjamin and Cynthia (Wardsworth) Lee, natives of Connecticut, and descendants of Puritans who came to America in the *Mayflower*. Mrs. Ensign is a lady of culture, and has traveled quite extensively in the West. She has spent a year in California, visited Nevada, Colorado, and Salt Lake City, and now resides in a beautiful home in Batavia, where she is most liberal in every worthy cause of benevolence. She is a prominent member of the Episcopal Church.

Richard Edgerton, a native of Massachusetts, came to Elba, accompanied by his wife, very early in the first settlement of the town. He died in Batavia at an advanced age. He taught school most of the time after 18 years of age. His wife was Judith Graves, of Massachusetts, and his children were Henry and Richard. Henry was born in Massachusetts, November 26, 1788, and died in 1873, aged 85 years. He came to Barre, N. Y., when 29 years of age, with but $7.50 in his pocket. He married Jane, daughter of John and Betsey (Miller) West, of Massachusetts, who died in 1886, aged 87 years. Their children were Betsey J., Henry G., Savilla A., Jane M., Philo A., Rodney R., Mary F., and Eva L., all of whom grew to maturity. The sons, men of integrity, are residents of the county. One daughter is a resident of this county, one of Orleans County, and two of Michigan. Eva L. Edgerton married Eben Noyes, grandson of Rev. John Noyes, of Connecticut. Their children are Philo E., Allie E., and Hattie E., now residents of Batavia village. Jane M. Edgerton married William H. Baldwin, of Elba (now Oakfield). In the early days of the settlement it was very hard to procure enough food for families. Henry Edgerton and family suffered many privations, and often times his family were without sufficient food, so that the approach of the teams coming from the mill was the scene of much rejoicing and anxious waiting.

Farrar & Farrar, attorneys at law, Batavia :

Alonzo H. Farrar was born in Middletown, Vt., in 1843. He was educated at Burr & Burton's Seminary, Manchester, Vt., and also at Fort Edward Collegiate Institute. He graduated at the University of Law, Albany, N. Y., and went to Kinderhook, Columbia County, in 1866, to practice law, continuing there until 1889. He was elected member of Assembly for two years from Columbia County, and was for 10 years director and vice-president of the National Bank of Kinderhook. He moved to Batavia in 1889, and commenced the practice of law, where he now resides.

Elbert Olaf Farrar, born in Middletown Springs, Vt., June 17, 1846, was educated at Burr & Burton's Seminary, Manchester, Vt., and also at Fort Edward Collegiate Institute. He was admitted to the bar in 1872 in Dayton, Ohio. He went to Syracuse in the fall of 1874, living there until 1889, when he removed to Batavia. He was judge advocate in the 10th Brigade Staff, N. G. N. Y., with the rank of major, and was member of Assembly from the second Onondaga County district for the years 1882 and 1883.

J. B. Fonda, an energetic business man of Batavia, was born here in 1855, the son of B. P. Fonda. He was educated in the public schools, and began business as clerk for the grocery house of Griswold & Pendill, being in their employ three years. He was then in the employ of Worthington & Son, hardware merchants, for 13 years, obtaining a knowledge of the business, and such an extensive acquaintance with the community as warranted him in 1885 in establishing his present business at 70 East Main street, where he is engaged in handling all kinds of hardware, stoves, furnaces, and house furnishing goods, having built up a good trade. In 1877 Mr. Fonda married Miss Nellie A. Sheldon, daughter of F. G. Sheldon, of Monroe County, and they have three children, Maud, Roy, and Ethel. The family are Presbyterians.

George W. Griffis was elected sheriff of Genesee County in 1879, and served three years. He was under sheriff for six years previous to that time. He died April 1, 1882. Mr. Griffis married Anna Alpangle and had four children. He was born in Niagara County, October 8, 1839.

The Green family came to America in 1750. The descendants are John, James, Jabez, Rufus, David, and Edwin R. Jonathan David Green, a native of Rhode Island, and a sea captain, married Eunice Hopkins, and his children are Martha, Edwin R., Mary, and Phœbe. Edwin R., of Conanicut Island, R. I., born January 12, 1788, came to

Batavia in 1846, and settled the place known as the Green farm, where he died in 1869, aged 82 years. He married Mary Hopkins, of Rhode Island, and his children were David, Eunice, Joseph, Demaris, Mary, Edwin, Hannah, and Jonathan. Jonathan Green, born in Laurens, Otsego County, January 17, 1821, came to Batavia in 1847. His first wife was Minerva Nash, of Butternuts, N. Y. They had one daughter, Minerva. His second wife was Eliza A., daughter of Charles and Olive Gould, of Batavia, and their children were Estella, Alice, Nathaniel, Edwin, and Mary. For his third wife he married Mary J., daughter of Joseph and Sarah (Underhill) Gurney, of New Baltimore, N. Y., and they reside on the Green homestead. Mr. Green is a breeder of American registered Merino sheep.

Richard Grice, a native of Griffield, Yorkshire, Eng., came to Batavia in 1851, and died in 1885, aged 55 years. He married Margaret, daughter of John and Jane Thompson, and their children were Charles, Jennie, Helen, Ida, Eugene, Nettie, Alice, and Richard S. The latter married Alice, daughter of William and Betsey Harris, of Batavia, and their children are Charles and Walter. Mrs. Margaret Grice survives her husband, and is 60 years of age.

John C. Greene, a real estate dealer and a native of Batavia, was born in 1856, a son of Edwin and Marietta (Ellsworth) Greene, from Eastern, N. Y. He was raised here and followed farming for some years. In 1884 he commenced dealing in real estate, establishing loans, and representing insurance companies, to all of which he gives his attention, and has secured a large patronage. He represents the Glens Falls, Girard of Philadelphia, the Milwaukee Mechanics' and Employers', the Liability Assurance Corporate, and the Limited of London, and does a large loan and real estate business, at 61 East Main street. He is a member of the K. of P. and A. O. U. W.

Henry P. Gast, born in Germany in 1826, came to America in 1847, and to Batavia in 1854, engaging in the business of making caps. He also kept hotel and saloon, and built the Western and West End hotels, the latter of which was burned in 1889 and rebuilt. F. J. Gast, son of Henry P., established a bakery at 119 Main street, in 1884, and carried it on until January, 1890, when he sold out to David McKeown, of Toronto, Ont., who now conducts it and a confectionery store. The firm of H. P. & J. E. Gast was formed in March, 1890. They deal in fine groceries and confectionery.

The Griffis family are of Welsh descent. Daniel N. Griffis was born in Vermont about 1803, and came with his parents to Cambria, Niagara County, N. Y., and to Batavia in 1861. About 1833 he married Belinda Croy, of Troy, N. Y., and they had five children, of whom John J. died in infancy, and four grew to adult age, viz.: Charlotte E., George W., Daniel W., and John O. Daniel W. was born in Cambria, Niagara County, August 22, 1844, and was educated in the public schools. August 2, 1862, he enlisted 'in Co. C, 151st Inf. N. Y. Vols., was made corporal, sergeant, and first sergeant of his company, was discharged at the close of the war, and returned to Batavia. November 21, 1867, he married Harriet C., oldest daughter of Hiram P. Flanders, of Batavia. They have four children, namely: Guy E., born October 30, 1868; Florence E., born February 23, 1872; Raymond, born March 19, 1873; and May E., born April 22, 1876.

Henry I. Glowacki has for 50 years been a resident of Batavia. He was born in Poland in 1816, a son of a prominent general of the Polish war of 1812. At the time of the Revolution, in 1830, Mr. Glowacki, then a youth, was imprisoned for two years in Trieste on account of his sentiments. Subsequently, with 300 com-patriots, he was exiled by the Austrian government and found refuge with the U. S. Minister to Ghent (Albert Gallatin), who was an acquaintance of his father. He was met by David E. Evans, of Batavia, while in Ghent, who offered the young man a position in the land office. In 1834 he came to Batavia, was asso-. ciated with H. J. Redfield in the land office for four years, with whom he read law, and was admitted to the bar in 1840. He was appointed master in chancery by Gov. Bouck, holding the office until 1846. He then practiced law until his retirement in 1879, being a partner of Joshua L. Brown for a time. Maj. Glowacki has been chairman of the county committee of the Democratic party, has attended four National Democratic conventions as delegate, has taken an active interest in local affairs for the improvement of the village, and has served as president of the board of education for nine years. He was trustee for many years of the Institution for the Blind, and was instrumental in the introduction of stone sidewalks for the village. In 1847 he was married to Miss Mary J. Redfield. They have an adopted daughter, Elizabeth, the wife of Le Roy Parker, an attorney, of Buffalo, N. Y. The family are members of the Episcopal Church.

Seth M. Hinman, lately the genial manager of the Hotel Richmond, began his life in Cattaraugus County, where he was born in 1844. He enlisted in 1861 in Co. C, 64th N. Y. Inf., as a private, and served nearly

four years. In 1863 he received a commission as first lieutenant of Co.
D, and had command of his company until the close of the war. He
participated in 15 battles with the Army of the Potomac, and at the battle of Spottsylvania was severely wounded. After the close of the war
he engaged in the dry goods business at Ellicottville for about five years,
and then became a commercial traveler. This engaged his attention for
10 years; subsequently he engaged in the hotel business at Attica for
three years, and then went to Warsaw, where he leased the Purdy House,
and conducted it about 18 months. He then came to Batavia and was
connected with the management of the Purdy House until April, 1889,
when he became manager of the Hotel Richmond. He was well qualified
to fill that responsible position, having a wide acquaintance among the
traveling public. He is a Mason and a member of the G. A. R. In
1867 he was united in marriage with Miss Mary Miller, daughter of
Dr. H. B. Miller, of Alexander. They have two children, Edward M.
and Blanche A.

John Godey, a native of Massachusetts, served in the Revolutionary
war, and moved to Illinois, where he died about 1840, aged 94 years.
His children were Libbeus, Aruna, Eliphalet, Anna Elaine, and Asenath.
His son Aruna, also a native of Massachusetts, at the age of 15 years
moved to Madison County, and in 1818 came to Pembroke, where he
died in 1859, aged 75 years. He married Mercy, daughter of Samuel
Record, of Morrisville, and his children were Levi and E. Ward. The
latter, born in Pembroke, December 21, 1819, married Fannie E.,
daughter of Jacob and Harriet (Hitchcock) Brinstool, of Henrietta, N. Y.
Their children are Marian E. and Maynard A., the latter of whom married Harriet, daughter of John H. and Mary (Bescoby) Stuffins, of Lincolnshire, Eng., and they have a son, Fred B. Marian E. Godey married Martha E., daughter of George Spensley, and they have one son, E.
Ward.

James Gowen, a native of Massachusetts, served in the war of the
Revolution, and died at the age of 60 years. His wife was Lydia Well-
mann, who bore him 12 children, viz.: Lydia, Samuel, Benjamin, Simeon
Tirzah, Levi, James, Joseph, Esther, William, Asal, and Rosanna. Joseph Gowen was born in Jaffrey, and died in Dublin, N. H., aged 60
years. He married Hephzibah, daughter of Asa and Hephzibah Fair-
banks, and their children were Asa F., Joseph M., Zaman A., Louisa H.,
Amna A., Charles W., Lavater L., and Lydia R. Joseph M. Gowen,
who was born in Dublin, N. H., came to Batavia in 1840. He married
18

Harriet M., daughter of Cyrus and Milla (Lawrence) Brown, of East Pembroke. Their children are Adelbert C., who served in the 6th Art., and died at Camp Barry, in the late war; Ida M., who married Oliver C. Uphill, of England, and has two children; Harriet P.; Anna L.; Joseph D., of Clifton Springs; and Willis C., of Batavia.

Gurdon Hartshorn was born in Franklin, New London County, Conn., May 31, 1798. He married Almira Coats, of Stonington, and in 1824 came to Genesee County and settled in Darien. He was a farmer, and died May 13, 1861. He had two children, namely: Uri, born in 1833, died in 1865, and Nelson, born April 12, 1828. Nelson married Helen McVean, daughter of John, and they have two children, Eugene G. and Cora B. He was justice of the peace in Darien for 16 years. He owns the farm his father settled in 1824. Cora married B. H. Re Qua, and they reside at Sioux Falls, Dakota. Eugene G. resides in Batavia.

O. D. Hammond was born in 1836, in Sheldon, N. Y. He learned harnessmaking in Attica, N. Y., and carried on business there 15 years. In 1870 he located in Batavia, where he has since resided. In 1888 his son L. W. was taken into partnership, the firm name being Hammond & Son, located at 108 West Main street. They employ several hands. O. D. Hammond enlisted in Co. G, 160th N. Y. V., in 1862, and served three years and four months, being honorably discharged.

Franklin Hartshorn, a native of New London County, Conn., died there at the age of 87 years. His children were Uri, Elijah, David, Isaac, Gurdon, and Jerusha. Isaac, a native of Franklin, Conn., served in the War of 1812, came to Darien, thence to Batavia in 1821, and died in 1875, aged 80 years. He married Delia, daughter of Samuel Ellis, of Connecticut, and his children are Asher, Franklin, Samuel, Elijah, now of Indiana, Delia, and Andrew. Andrew Hartshorn, born in Connecticut, January 23, 1821, married Caroline, daughter of William and Caroline (Mather) Brownell, of Batavia, and now resides on the Brownell homestead on road 41.

Claudius Hay, born in Rupert, Vt., was a soldier of the War of 1812. He came to Cortland, N. Y., married Fannie Wallace, and in the fall of 1820 moved to Pembroke. In 1837 he went to Guilford, Ohio, and died there in 1850, aged 60 years. He had a family of six children, four of whom are living. Michael W., born March 21, 1820, learned the wagonmakers' trade, and was also a farmer in Pembroke. He has been constable and deputy sheriff four years. In 1863 he opened up a grocery store in Batavia and was in business 15 years. He was mail agent two years, from Batavia to Buffalo *via* Tonawanda, and was keeper of the county alms-house three years and one month. He has held the office of superintendent of streets for three years, or since April, 1887, and has been an F. & A. M. since 1855. He married Lurania Waite, and they have four children, Ellis R., Walter H., Charles F., and Fannie L.

Anson Higley.—The pioneer settlers of Genesee County and their children are rapidly passing away, and in a few years all will have been gathered to their fathers. But they have a no more worthy representative living in this county than Anson Higley.

John Higley, the eldest child of Jonathan Higley and Katherine Brewster, his wife, was born in Surrey, England, 30 miles southwest of London, July 22, 1649. When of suitable age he was apprenticed to a glover in London for the period of his minority. Family tradition says that, in his seventeenth year, he incurred the displeasure of his master, who promised him a severe flogging the next morning. To escape the lash, and perhaps to satisfy a longing for adventure, or actuated by the worthier motive of becoming a free citizen of the new and promising land which he no doubt had read and heard of much, he hastily bundled up his scanty wardrobe, and concealed himself in a vessel which was about to sail for America. In due time he landed at the trading post of Windsor, on the Connecticut River, and there he found employment. In 1671 he married Hannah Drake, daughter of a prominent citizen of the place; soon after purchased a home, and became in time one of the most prominent in the colony. In 1690 he was commissioned a lieutenant, and was afterward promoted to the post of captain. He was elected to the General Assembly of Connecticut in 1689, and afterwards elected to 28 of the 37 sessions of that body. He was the father of 16 children. This runaway boy, John Higley, is the sole ancestor of all who bear the name in America.

In 1808 Isaac Higley, Sr., (the grandfather of Anson,) with his brother Eber, (who was in the War of 1812, taken prisoner, and died in Halifax,) and Isaac, Jr., came to Elba and settled on Spring Creek. There were seven children, of whom Isaac, Jr., was the eldest and the only son. The daughters were Abbie, wife of Elias Pettibone, the father of Col. Elias J.; Ruth, wife of 'Squire Daniel Mills, an old justice of Elba; Adah, wife of Zebulon Woodruff, of Elba; Anna, wife of Samuel Lampson, of Onondaga County; Hannah, wife of William Knapp; and Candace, wife of John Hawkins, of Alexander. The grandfather died in 1810, and was the first person buried in the old burying-ground in the southeast part of Elba.

Isaac Higley, the father of Anson, married, in Connecticut, Dorothy Killburn, and reared seven children, namely: Emily (Mrs. W. Holbrook), who died in Ohio; Horace, who died in Elba; Maria (Mrs. Isaac Tinkham), who also died in Ohio; Eber, who died in 1887 in Wisconsin; Isaac N., who died in Elba; Elvira (Mrs. Charles Ames), now of Seneca County, Ohio; and Anson. The father was a farmer in Elba from his settlement in 1808 until his death in 1829.

Anson Higley was born in Elba in 1811, and is one of the oldest living natives of the county. He followed farming in his native town for nearly 70 years, and has obtained by hard work and steady application a handsome property, which he has generously divided among his children. Since 1881 he has been a resident of Batavia, where he is enjoying a well earned rest from active labor. While a resident of Elba Mr. Higley was for several terms assessor and supervisor of his town, and was always in favor of improvements to the benefit of town and county. He was one of the first highway commissioners, and labored assiduously in establishing the roads of his section. He united in marriage, in 1837, with Lydia Newkirk, of Orange County, who died in 1858. They had six children, viz.: Mary, wife of M. M. Brown, a leading attorney of Osage, Mitchell County, Iowa; Sarah E., wife of F. P. Terry, of Batavia; Isaac A., a leading farmer of Elba; Elizabeth W.; Humphrey (deceased); John O., a farmer of Batavia; and Emma, wife of William Robe, a prominent farmer of Elba. In 1875 Mr. Higley was united in marriage with Lizzie Cassidy, a native of Vermont. They are active members of the Baptist Church, and are liberal contributors to its support. Mr. Higley is still interested in farming, and in all the relations of life has borne himself conscientiously, uprightly, and honorably. He is a man of genial personality, of superior mental attributes, and a kindly, Christian gentleman.

Philip Houseknecht, a native of Pennsylvania, is a Methodist minister, and resides in Alabama. He married Sarah A., daughter of Philip and Margaret Buchanan, and his children are Isabella, Samuel L., and Philos B. Philos B. Houseknecht, born in Alabama, married Ada F., daughter of James A. and Lydia A. (Fonda) Gibbs, and they have one son, Joshua L. Mr. Houseknecht is a photographer in Batavia.

James Hopkins was born in Londonderry, N. H., served in the war of the Revolution, and died in Erie County, N. Y., aged 82 years. He was a farmer and a tailor. He married Mary A., daughter of Rev. David McGregor, of Londonderry, and their children were Thomas N., Polly,

Isaac Higley
Killburn and
brook)
Isaac
consi
of Se
from

An
ing n
nearl
a ha
dre
ing
H
w
F
it
v
s

McGregor,

David M., James, Margaret, and Robert. Thomas N. was also a native of Londonderry, N. H., but went to a place of the same name in Vermont, where he lived several years, when he moved to Sardinia, N. Y., where he died in 1870, aged 94 years. He married Sally Howe, of Londonderry, Vt., daughter of Nehemiah Howe, and their children were Thomas, Eliza, Dudley, James M., Nehemiah, Nelson, Mary A., Clarissa, and Robert N. The last named was born in Vermont, June 10, 1812, came to Batavia from Erie County in 1860, and married Sarah A., daughter of Aaron and Serephina Carnahan, of Picton, Canada. His children are Thomas M., William S., Eliza A., and Jesse B. Mrs. Sarah A. Hopkins died in Batavia, October 12, 1878, aged 62 years. Mr. Hopkins, grandfather of James, was of the old Puritan stock, and at the time of the French and Indian war suffered for the necessaries of life. It is told of him that prices for inferior provisions at that time were enormous: for one-quarter of a dog five shillings and sixpence were paid; for a dog's head two shillings and sixpence; horse flesh was nearly two shillings per pound; even cats, rats, and mice were used for food. A pound of tallow was worth four shillings. William S. Hopkins married Prudence E. Jones, of Batavia, and they have two children, Robert J. and Eliza. He is now a resident of Buffalo, being engaged in the malleable iron works at Black Rock. Robert N. Hopkins is a farmer on road 63, where he has lived for 29 years.

Hector Humphrey was born in Marcellus, Onondaga County, N. Y., December 25, 1809. When a young man he came to Batavia with his brother Bissell, who was proprietor of the old Eagle tavern. He assisted his brother in the hotel and stage business. He married Hannah M. Patterson in 1838, and engaged in the livery business, carrying a large stock of horses and vehicles until his health failed. He died June 5, 1855. Two sons and one daughter were born to him, all of whom are deceased but Frances, wife of Reuben H. Farnham, of Attica. His widow resides in Batavia.

Henry W. Homelius was born in Buffalo, N. Y., in 1850. He was the first and is now the only architect in Genesee County. Since 1875 he has been engaged in contracting and building, and now employs from 10 to 12 men, making a speciality of fine house building. He has built many of the finest residences in the county, and also does work in Rochester, Buffalo, and surrounding towns. Henry B. Homelius, son of Henry B., was born 1830, and came to America when six years of age. He married Catherine Knight, settled in Batavia in 1856, and is engaged in contracting and building.

Dr. Horace S. Hutchins, son of Asa and Lydia (Willis) Hutchins, was born in the village of Manlius, Onondaga County, N. Y., January 5, 1829. The father, a descendant of sturdy New England stock, was one of the early and efficient pioneers in the early settlement of the central part of this State. He died in Genesee County, October 1, 1871. The mother is from a long-lived family, and the oldest of a family of children each of whom lived to the age of 80 years. She married successively two brothers, and by each husband reared two sons and one daughter: Oramel, Loren, and Lure Ann; Sophia, Horace S., and Harvey. Dr. Hutchins's early life was spent upon the farm and in attending the district school winters, receiving such knowledge as they afforded a half century past. At the age of 16 he commenced his academic work in Hamilton Academy in Madison County, N. Y., pursuing a four years' course of preparatory study, which enabled him to enter Madison University, from which institution he graduated and secured the degrees of A. B. and M. A. in course. He was teacher of mathematics in the Ladies' Seminary of Hamilton two years, and principal of Peterboro Academy one year, during which time, having formed a taste for the study of medicine, and obtaining from many able physicians a good practical knowledge of therapeutics, he naturally developed the faculties necessary for the course he marked out for himself, and to which profession he has since devoted his energies and life. At the age of 25, seeking to restore his health and to learn something of the world, he set out on an ocean voyage to the West Indies, Central America, across the Isthmus, along the route of the Nicaragua Canal, up the San Juan River from Greytown to Castillo rapids; thence across Lake Nicaragua and the highlands of Gautemala to the Pacific Ocean; thence with the Coast Survey along the coasts of Mexico and California to San Francisco, landing there in the early years of the gold fever. For three years, and during his stay in Nevada City, he had charge of its school work, and also pursued the study and practice of medicine. He held various official positions in that city, whose foundations were laid in gold. It was during his visit and stay in California that he was one of many who engaged in that terrible struggle for supremacy between law and order, and the minions of overt criminality, when the famous Vigilance Committee assembled in hosts sufficient to awe and overpower the workers of crime. The powers of State were restored, society purified, and an example for good was inaugurated which has left its impress upon the whole Nation. It may not be out of place here to state, for a comparison, that the last

Horace S. Hutchins M.D.

Dr. Horace S. Hutchins, son of Asa and Lydia (Willis) Hutchins, was born in the village of Manlius, Ononda. County, N. Y. January 5, 1829. The father, a descendant of sturdy New England stock, was one of the early and efficient pioneers in the early settlement of the central part of this State. He died in Genesee County, October ., 187 . The mother is from a long-lived family, and the oldest of a family of children each of whom lived to the age of 80 years. She married successively two brothers, and by each husband reared two sons and one daughter: Oramel, Loren, and Lure Ann; Sophia, Horace S., nd Harvey. Dr. Hutchins's early life was spent upon the farm and in attending the district school winters, receiving such knowledge as they afforded a half century past. At the age of 16 he commenced his academic work in Hamilton Academy in Madison County, N. Y., pursuing a four years' course of preparatory study, which enabled him to enter Madison University, from which institution he graduated and secured the degrees of A. B. and M. A. in course. He was teacher of mathematics in the Ladies' Seminary of Hamilton two years, and principal of Peterboro Academy one year, during which time, having formed a taste for the study of medicine, and obtaining from many able physicians a good practical knowledge of therapeutics, he naturally developed the faculties necessary for the course he marked out for himself, and to which profession he has since devoted his energies and life. At the age of 25, seeking to restore his health and to learn something of the world, he set out on an ocean voyage to the West Indies, Central America, across the Isthmus, along the route of the Nicaragua Canal, up the San Juan River from Greytown to Castillo rapids; thence across Lake Nicaragua and the highlands of Gautemala to the Pacific Ocean; thence with the Coast Survey along the coasts of Mexico and California to San Francisco, landing there in the early years of the gold fever. For three years, and during his stay in Nevada City, he had charge of its school work, and also pursued the study and practice of medicine. He held various official positions in that city, whose foundations were laid in gold. It was during his visit and stay in California that he was one of many who engaged in that terrible struggle for supremacy between law and order, and the minions of overt criminality, when the famous Vigilance Committee assembled in hosts sufficient to awe and overpower the workers of crime. The powers of State were restored, society purified, and an example for good was inaugurated which has left its impress upon the whole Nation. It may not be out of place here to state, for a comparison, that the last

Horace S. Hutchins M.D.

professional act of Dr. Hutchins on the coast brought him the sum of $40 in gold, he being the recipient of that amount for a simple prescription, unsolicited on his part.

In June, 1857, he returned from California to Buffalo, N. Y., engaging in active business relations with his brother Harvey, and in September of the same year was married to Harriet M., daughter of Corrington Babcock, of Madison County, N. Y. In May, 1859, he moved to Batavia, taking up his old work—the practice of medicine. Visiting New York city the next year, and spending many months in review and study in the old and new schools of medicine, he graduated and returned to Batavia, where for the past 30 years he has faithfully and successfully labored, obtaining a rank in the profession possessed only by the few, gaining the respect and confidence of those who are the recipients of his ministrations, and by his consistent conduct and steadfastness of purpose has gained the respect of the whole community. He has been one of the vice-presidents of the New York State Homeopathic Medical Society, and one of the censors of the same society for years; a member of the American Institute of Homeopathy 23 years; a member of the Western New York Medical Society since its formation; an alumnus of the New York Homeopathic Medical College Hospital Association; and a director and active worker in the banking interests of the village. For nearly 10 years he was president of the board of education, and an active and zealous promoter of the cause of education. Dr. Hutchins's children are Fanny A. and Eleanora, the latter the wife of Dr. John W. Le Seur. The family are earnest and devoted members of the Baptist Church, contributing generously to its growth and support.

Dr. John Wesley Le Seur (son of John Le Seur, now in his 85th year, and a minister of the Methodist Church in Vermont) was born in Hartland, Vt., in 1857. He was graduated in turn from the Fort Edward (N. Y.) Collegiate Institute, class of '77; Rochester University, class of '81; Rochester Theological Seminary, class of '84; and the Hahnemann Medical College of Philadelphia, class of '86· In 1885 he founded the *Medical Institute* of Philadelphia, to which he still contributes articles. He began to practice with Dr. Hutchins at Batavia in the spring of 1886. In 1887 he was appointed by Governor Hill one of the trustees of the Institution for the Blind at Batavia. During the same year and the succeeding one he was town physician, and is now jail physician. Dr. Le Seur for three years has been president of the Philharmonic Club in Batavia. He is a member of the American Institute of Homeopathy and the Western New York Homeopathic Medical Society. His family consists of a wife, formerly Miss Eleanora Hutchins, daughter of Dr. Hutchins, and two children. He belongs to the Baptist Church, and is also an active member of the Young Men's Christian Association. Dr. Le Seur is regarded as one of the most skilled physicians in the place, and commands a lucrative practice.

Hinman Holden was born in Adams, Mass., in 1787, and came to Batavia in 1805, and thus was closely identified with the early history of this village and county. He was a man of good sound judgment, one to be relied upon to help and succor a just cause. In the War of 1812 he took his sled and oxen and drew flour to Buffalo to supply the soldiers, traveling night and day, which, in the state of the roads at that time, was no light task. At one time (about 1825) he kept the American Hotel. He died in 1871, aged 84 years. He was father to Richard O. Holden, who was born March 5, 1814, in a log house on the farm owned by W. H. G. Post. Richard O. Holden was a clerk in New York for five years, and on his return went into business with G. A. Lay, in a store where the Masse block now is. In 1847 the firm was Holden & Thorn, corner of Main and Jackson streets. In 1859 he built the large store now occupied by his son, and had as partners Messrs. Glover and Foote. Other (branch) stores were operated in Alabama and Warsaw. In five years' time Glover and Foote retired, and in 1880 Mr. Holden took his son Hinman into partnership, under the title of R. O. Holden & Son. He died May 29, 1887, aged 73. During his long residence here he made many friends. He enjoyed the fullest confidence of all his neighbors, was ever fair, and scrupulously honest. His judgment was often sought in matters of public interest, and he took a kindly welfare in the efforts of others to succeed. He married Miss Hannah Wells. Hinman Holden, the eldest son of R. O. Holden, was born here in 1852. He was educated in the schools in this section, and finished his studies in Hamden, Conn. In 1869 he entered his father's store, and in 1880 became his partner, but since 1872 has had the care and responsibility of the business. He possesses the rare executive ability which so marked the life of his father, and is a worthy successor. He was married, in 1886, to Miss Eva O. Smith, daughter of Wilber Smith, and they have one son, Richard O. The family are Episcopalians.

Samuel C. Holden was born in Otsego County, N. Y., August 8, 1794, and died in December, 1881, aged 87 years. He came here in 1806, and thus spent 75 years of his life in this village. He was a brother of Hinman Holden, and they were sons of James Holden. Samuel C. Holden was at one time U. S. loan commissioner, was county clerk in 1846, and was in the mercantile business as early as 1822 under the firm name of Rich & Holden. His son, George H. Holden, held the office of county clerk for six years from 1861, and is now the deputy, having given his valuable assistance to the office for 30 years.

Hayden U. Howard, for many years identified with the banking and business interests of this county, was born in 1821 in Livingston County. His parents, Talcott and Sally (Tufts) Howard, came from New England to Perry, where Hayden was reared. He began life as a clerk, and in 1840 entered the bank at Le Roy as clerk. For nearly 50 years he has been identified with the banking interests of the county. He became cashier of the Bank of Le Roy in 1845, serving until 1852. The two years following he conducted a private bank in Buffalo, and then returned to Genesee County as vice-president of the Bank of Genesee. In 1855 he became president, serving until 1885, since which time he has conducted a loan office. He has been active in educational matters, serving as trustee in the school board and of the Institution of the Blind. He was also president of the Western New York Life Insurance Company. He married Lucy L., daughter of Erastus Bailey, of Le Roy, an old resident. They have three children, Charles H., William E., and Mary M., and are members of the Presbyterian Church.

Joseph Hamilton has been a resident of Batavia since 1852. He inherited a taste for engraving, and learned the trade of cutting marble in Rochester, and since coming here has established a large trade in the marble and granite line. He erected the brick block on East Main street in 1872, where he has spacious salesrooms. In March, 1877, he admitted his son John M. as a partner, and the business is now conducted under the firm name of Joseph Hamilton & Son.

Ezekiel Hackley, a son of Simeon, of Connecticut, was born in Columbia County, in 1794, and came to Batavia in 1819, settling on the farm in the north part of the town, where he now resides with his son Orlando D. Mr. Hackley married Sarah Smiley, daughter of Dr. Francis Smiley, of Herkimer County, N Y., and they had six children. He is the oldest settler in the town, being now over 96 years of age.

Samuel Jacks, a native of Londonderry, N. H., came to Batavia in 1811. He was a blacksmith, but settled on a farm where he died in 1866, aged 74 years. He came when but few settlers had located, and had a shop at the corner of Bank and Main streets. He married Betsey, daughter of Ephraim Husted, of Elba, and his children were James C., John, Mary, Samuel, John, Ephraim, and Betsey.   James C. Jacks, born in Batavia, married Josephine B., daughter of John C. and Eunice (McCrillus) Wilford, and their children are J. Wilford; Mary E., Julia W., Josephine, and J. Corwin.   The latter married Emma, daughter of Joseph and Eliza (Staples) Haviland, of Glens Falls, N. Y., and they have one daughter, Elma H.   Mr. Jacks is a farmer, residing on road 13.   J. Wilford Jacks. is a Presbyterian minister at Romulus, N. Y.   Mary E. Jacks married Rev. H. H. Kellogg, pastor of the Presbyterian Church at Windham, N. Y.   Josephine Jacks married Rev. Frank L. Silliman, now a merchant of Little Falls, N. Y.   Julia W. Jacks married William T. Bradley, a farmer in Batavia.

Alva Jones was born February 23, 1820, in Stafford, was a farmer, and always resided there.   He married Amelia C. Hull, and they had four children, viz.: Edwin R., George F., Mary A., and Frances C., all deceased.   Mr. Jones died February 5, 1873, and his widow resides in Batavia.   The son George F. enlisted in Co. G, 8th N. Y. H. A., in 1863, and August 25, 1864, he was captured by the rebels and taken to Libby prison, from there to Belle Isle, thence to Salisbury, N. C., where he died November 2, 1864.   Edwin R. Jones died in Nebraska, November 8, 1888.

Obadiah Johnson was a native of Berkshire County, Mass , and a soldier in the war of the Revolution.   He had six children, viz. : Horace, Obadiah, Gordon, Anna, Sallie, and John R.   John R. Johnson, also a native of Massachusetts, came to Monroe County in 1813, and died at Riga in 1870, aged 84 years.   He married Lucy, daughter of David Tuttle, of Byron, and their children were Rufus, Azubette, Ira, Jane, Lucy, Lucinda, Spencer, Sarah, Eunice, and Horace.   The latter was born in Riga, July 16, 1827, settled in Byron in 1876, and came to Batavia in 1882, locating on a farm.   He married Mary E., daughter of Ephraim and Nancy (Hults) Johnson, of Nunda, N. Y., and their children are Lewis M., Ernest H., William H., Morris W., Julia E., Cora B., and Mary E.   Lewis M. Johnson married Martha Judd.   Their children are Charles J., Cora B., Lena L., and Ilma M.   He resides with his father on road 13.

Prof. Charles A. Klimitz was born September 23, 1826, in Pomerania, Prussia.   He received a musical education in the city of Stettin.   In 1855 he came to America, and was a resident of Rochester one year, and came to Batavia in 1856.   He has taught music in the Young Ladies'

Seminary 11 years, and has since been a private music teacher. He was married to Emily .E. Brussow, and they have had six children, four of whom are living.

John Kenyon in 1836 opened a grocery and general store in Batavia. After carrying on the business for years he sold out to his sons Edward L. and George D. In 1886 Edward L. bought out George D., carrying on the business until 1888, when he sold out the store and retired. In May, 1889, his son, E. Porter Kenyon, opened a store at No. 80 Main street, and is now carrying a full line of groceries. He also controls the ice business of Batavia.

Darius King was born in Pompey, N. Y., April 30, 1819. When six years of age his father, Hiram, settled in the northern part of Batavia, where he resided until he moved to Oakfield in 1860. He was a farmer and building mover, and was supervisor two years and assessor nine years. He married Cornelia Showerman, and they had a family of three children, two of whom, F. D. and W. E., are living. He died December 9, 1885. His widow lives in Batavia. F. D. King was born March 6, 1846, and s a contractor and builder. He married Miss C. Bowers, of Victor, N. Y., and they have one child, Everett D.

Paul Knowlton lived and died in Grafton, Mass. His children were Paul, Levi, Daniel, Ruth, and Annie. Daniel was born in Massachusetts, and came to Pavilion in 1816, remaining there until his death in 1847, aged 72 years. He married Polly Hemmingway, of Massachusetts, and their children were Mary, Pamelia, Adaline, Venus D., Hephzibah, Levi P., and Thaddeus J. The last mentioned was born in Bethany, March 30, 1822, and came to Batavia in 1885. He now lives in Batavia village at 24 Wood street. He married, May 28, 1845, Phœbe, daughter of Joseph and Sarah (Buckbee) Stewart, of Warsaw, N. Y. She was born January 16, 1820. Their children are Daniel S., Eva F., and Frank J. Daniel S. married Nellie Vernon, of Perry, N. Y. They have three children, and reside at La Grange. Joseph Stewart served in the War of 1812. Richard Buckbee, father of Sarah, died in Saratoga County at the age of 82 years, and his wife, Phœbe, in Dutchess County at the age of 52 years. Mr. Knowlton also owns a farm of 69 acres in Pavilion.

Kenny & Rourke, grocers and wholesale and retail liquor dealers, are located at 152 Ellicott street. They started in business in 1884, renting the store, and since then have bought the property. They are doing a large business, which is increasing each year.

Charles A. Kibbe, of " Kibbe's farm advertising agency," established in 1875, is a native of Fulton County, N. Y., and son of Nathaniel S. Kibbe, who came to Batavia in 1870. Previous to living here Charles A. was engaged in the glove and mitten business at Gloversville, N. Y. He has made a great success of his real estate business, his sales the past three years amounting to $2,000,000, and a total of $8,000,000. He handles property all over the United States. He makes a specialty of advertising, having spent in all over $26,000 for that purpose, or about $2,000 per year. He has about 500 coöperative agents in the United States. Mr. Kibbe has opened a branch office in room 1, No. 8 State street, Rochester, with W. P. Hawkins as manager. His work is strictly a commission one. He originated this "new idea" of dealing in farm properties, and has proved it to be a success. Mr. Kibbe is one of the energetic business men of the town ; an active mover in all enterprises to build up the place by the introduction of new manufactures.

Martin L. Kempton in 1888 commenced the manufacture of the Batavia combination fence at Elba. In 1889 he located in Batavia at 117 Harvester avenue, and is now using from 10 to 12 tons of wire and 300,-000 pickets per year. He also makes ordinary farm fence and fancy picket fence of different varieties.

Lawrence & Lane, attorneys at law.—This association was formed in 1889 by Spencer J. Lawrence and Louis B. Lane. Mr. Lawrence was born in 1864, a son of James and Alida (Chase) Lawrence, a farmer who died in 1880. After completing his preliminary education Mr. Lawrence entered the office of William C. Watson and began the study of law. He was admitted to practice in the spring of 1889. Mr. Lane, a native of Allegany County, was born in 1862, son of Rev. John W. and Mary E. (Watson) Lane. His father was a Presbyterian minister of over 30 years of service in Allegany County, and died December 25, 1881. Louis was educated under the care of his father, and was also a law student in Mr. Watson's office. He was admitted to practice in 1889.

G. W. Lefler, V. S., was born in Seneca County, N. Y., August 6, 1834. He graduated at Boston Veterinary College in 1858, was appointed chief veterinary surgeon of the Army of the Potomac in 1863, and remained there until 1866. He enlisted as farrier in the 30th N. Y. Engineer Corps, and was discharged on special order 515 to receive the appointment of chief veterinary surgeon. After the close of the war he practiced in several cities in the West, and located in Batavia in 1884. He has his office and hospital at Exchange Place.

James A. Le Seur, the efficient clerk and assistant of Judge North in the surrogate's office, is a native of Brattleboro, Vt, where he was born November 18, 1861. He was married, December 31, 1884, to Miss Carrie Eckler, of Pittsford, N. Y., and came to Batavia in September, 1887, from Boston, Mass.

Harry Lathrop, born in 1804, is a native of Rutland, Vt., and came to Stafford in 1816. He is now a resident of Medina, N. Y. He married Olive, daughter of Moses Chapin, of Massachusetts, and their children are Elsie E., Edward F., James E., and Harry E. Harry E. Lathrop, who was born in Stafford, married Mary E., daughter of William and Eliza (Wilcox) Russell, of Rocky Hill, Conn., and their children are Frank E., born February 11, 1873, and Mary E., born November 18, 1876. They now reside in Batavia, where they have lived for eight years. The father of Harry (Abigal) was a soldier of the War of 1812, and was at the burning of Buffalo. Anson Lathrop came to Darien from Connecticut in 1818, and settled in the southeastern part of the town. He was a farmer. He married Elizabeth Bertram, and had born to him eight children, Samuel, son of Aaron, was born March 28, 1834, and married Sarah E. Salisbury. He enlisted in Co. M, 9th N. Y. H. A., was taken prisoner at Mononacy Junction in July, 1863, taken to Danville prison, and died November 9, 1863. Henry Salisbury, born in Columbia County, N. Y., married Sallie Owen, of Massachusetts, and settled in Darien in 1810. They had eight children. He was a large farmer, and died September 26, 1869. He was in the War of 1812, and was stationed at Fort Erie.

Samuel Lusk, a native of Wethersfield, Conn., moved to Poultney, Vt., and died in 1828, aged 76 years. He served in the war of the Revolution. He married Naomi Bryant, of Connecticut, and their children were Samuel, Irena, Alvin, Salmon, Sally, and William. The latter, of Castleton, Vt., came to Batavia in 1835, and died in Newstead, Erie County, in 1870, aged 84 years. He served in the War of 1812. He married Althea Sanford, of Poultney, Vt., daughter of Oliver Sanford, and his children were William H., Reuben S., Marcus, Caroline, Clarissa, Ann E., and Salmon. Salmon B. Lusk was born in Poultney, August 28, 1815, came to Batavia and married Sally, daughter of Jabez and Relief (Wheelock) Howe, and their children are Althea, Elizabeth, Helen, Mary, Frank R., Clara E., and William B. Mr. Lusk has resided at his present place 24 years. He was elected sheriff in 1851, and served three years in the late war; was deputy provost-marshal, and held many offices of trust in the county. He was jailer seven years, and deputy sheriff three years. He is a breeder of thoroughbred American Merino shee

Philip Luckel was born in Germany and came to America in 1854, settling in Batavia in 1855, where he has since resided. He is a tailor by trade, and has carried on that business most of the time. Charles W. Luckel, son of Philip, was born in Batavia, April 8, 1858. He learned the tailors' trade with his father, finishing in New York city. In 1884 he started in business for himself. He has been in the store at 30 Jackson street since 1889, carrying on merchant tailoring. He carries a good line of foreign and domestic goods, giving employment to from 12 to 15 hands.

Andrew Lape was born in Germany, and when a young man came to Batavia. He married Catherine Michel, and they had two children. He enlisted in Co. H, 148th N. Y. Regt., served two years and six months, and died from wounds received in service. His only son, Joseph, was born near Buffalo, N. Y., October 21, 1848, and resides in Batavia. Joseph Lape was elected constable in February, 1889. He married Hattie I. Johnson, of Shortsville, Ontario County, and they have one child, Pearl P.

Robert A. Maxwell, State superintendent of insurance, is a native of Washington County, where he was born in 1840. He is a son of Alexander and Jane (Alexander) Maxwell, both of Scotch lineage. Robert was educated in the schools of his native county, and received the advantage of a course of study in the State Normal School of Albany. He then taught for two years in the schools of Greenwich. Deciding upon a larger field of operation he went to Chicago and engaged in mercantile pursuits, but was forced to return east on account of ill health, and in 1869 he became a permanent resident of Batavia. Mr. Maxwell was actively engaged in the malting business for 10 years, first forming an association with E. H. Fish in 1871, and later with Henry J. Ensign, in the brewery and malt business. He was appointed one of the early trustees of the Institution for the Blind, and also served one year as village trustee. In 1881 he was nominated on the Democratic ticket for State treasurer, and was elected by 22,000 majority, the balance of the ticket being defeated. In 1883 he was reëlected by over 5,000 in advance of the rest of the ticket. In January, 1886, Gov. Hill appointed him State superintendent of insurance, which office he now holds. He was married to Mary McLean, of Washington County. Two children have been born to them, viz.: William A. and Marion Grace (deceased, aged nine years).

John M. McKenzie, of the firm of McKenzie, Ryan & Storms, was born in Lockport in 1846. He was educated in the public schools of that place, and learned the trade of cabinetmaker. He moved to Wisconsin and there worked at his trade, but came to Batavia in 1868, and was engaged at farming four years, when he entered the employ of R. O. Holden, with whom he studied the business of general merchandising for nine years, attaining the position of head clerk and buyer. In 1881 he opened up business on his own account, when there were eight competing stores in the line of clothiers and gents' furnishing goods, while at the present time only three survive. His strict attention to business, fidelity to friends, and thorough regard for his word caused him to be brought forward as a candidate for the Assembly in 1887. Such was his popularity that he was elected by a majority of nearly 1,200, being far in advance of the rest of the ticket, and by a greater majority than his predecessors. Again, in 1888, he was placed in nomination for the same place, which resulted in an increased majority (1,311), keeping up with that for the presidential ticket. The fact of his being a member of the Ways and Means Committee is an honor not often given to Genesee County. Mr. McKenzie was married to Mary E. Storms, daughter of the late John C. Storms. They have one girl, Bessie L.

Timothy Lynch, proprietor of the Genesee House, was born in Ireland, and came with his parents to America in 1847. His father, Daniel Lynch, came to Batavia about 1850, and resided there until his death. Timothy Lynch was reared and educated in the schools of Batavia, and early in 1861 enlisted in Co. E, 100th N. Y. Vet. Inf., as a private. Before going to the front he was commissioned second lieutenant of his company. He was in active service about three and one-half years. His regiment saw severe service, and participated in the engagements at Yorktown, Williamsburg, Seven Pines, and Fair Oaks, where Lieut. Lynch was taken prisoner and confined for five months in Libby and Salisbury prisons. After rejoining the regiment he was promoted to first lieutenant to date from the battle of Fair Oakes, having command of Co. B. He was finally made captain of his company, and served until November, 1864, when he resigned. The latter part of his service he was in the engagements at Folly, James, and Morris islands, and before Charleston, Richmond, Petersburg, and Fort Darling, where one-half of his regiment was lost and he was wounded, Weldon Railroad, Bermuda Hundred, etc. Returning to Genesee County Mr. Lynch farmed for two years, and in 1867 became owner of the Genesee House on Jackson street, Batavia, which he has since conducted, with the exception of two years. Mr. Lynch is post commander of Upton Post, G. A. R., and is now serving as one of the Grant treasurers of the State for the C. M. B. A., a benevolent organization of which he is one of the oldest members. He has served as a member of the board of trustees of Batavia, and is one of the enterprising men of the town, as well as a genial and deserving host.

Allen D. Lincoln, youngest son of Sylvester, who was the fourth settler in the town of Bethany, was born in Bethany, December 6, 1821. He received a public school and academic education, and until recently was a farmer by occupation. He is now a retired farmer, residing on Jackson street, Batavia., March 28, 1855, he married Sarah E., oldest daughter of Morris Garton, of Wyoming County, N. Y. They have two children, viz.: Wallis G., born January 3, 1862, and Kate F., born October 1, 1871. November 2, 1884, Wallis G. married Monica McNerhany, of Washington, D. C., and they have two children, Harry G. and Margaret. He is a telegraph operator in the Western Union office in Chicago, Ill. Kate F. is a music teacher and resides at home with her parents.

Harry M. Lay, successor to Blake & Lay, is the young but progressive proprietor of a leading business enterprise of Batavia. The business was started by John H. Blake, and subsequently became, in 1887, Blake & Lay. During the continuance of the firm extensive buildings were erected, and the business assumed large proportions. Mr. Lay assumed the entire charge and ownership in 1889. The office and yards are on Liberty street, convenient to railroad transportation, and consist of lumber yard, coal sheds, a planing-mill 40x80 feet, two stories in height, and a hay barn 40x120 feet and 50 feet high, with a capacity for 2,000 tons of hay, which is shipped to eastern markets. - Mr. Lay employs about 20 assistants, and has a promising future. He is a native of Chicago, and a son of George W. Lay, Esq., an attorney and descendant of old Genesee County families. Mr. Lay received an excellent education, graduating from Williams College in 1887. The same year he began his business career.

John Moore, a native of Columbia County, N. Y., came to Batavia in 1847, where he died at the age of 72 years. He married Cherry Sparks, daughter of Benjamin, of Massachusetts, and their children were Abigail, Betsey, Louisa, Clarissa, Sabery, John, Benjamin, Andrew, George, and Michael. The latter came to Batavia in 1836, from Lima, N. Y. He married, first, Sarah Ward, and second, Nancy Ward. His children by his second wife are Franklin, Charles, Elmer, Newton, Herbert, Watson, and

Libbie L. They now reside near East Pembroke in the town of Batavia. Herbert Moore is a merchant at East Pembroke. Libbie L. married Cash M., son of Edwin and Lucinda (Curtis) Durham, of Batavia, and is now a resident of East Pembroke.

William Martin, son of William, a native of Orange County, N. Y., came to Shelby, N. Y., in 1816, and now resides there. He married Sarah, daughter of Daniel Ross, of Shelby, and their children are William A., Wallace, Mary, Harriet, Alice, Frances, Albert R., Elizabeth, and Charles T. Charles T. Martin was born in Barre, N. Y., March 3, 1843, and now resides in Batavia on road 7. William Martin, Sr., was a native of County Down, Ireland. He came to New York city in 1801, and thence to Barre, where he died in 1848, aged 82 years. He was a linen weaver by trade. His wife was Mary Trumbull, who died in Barre in 1844, aged 72 years. Charles T. Martin married Augusta S., daughter of Robert Balmer, of Porter, Niagara County, N. Y., and they had one daughter, Maude Snow, now deceased.

William J. Mann, proprietor of the Hotel Richmond, is a native of Buffalo. He was born in 1844, a son of William B. and Aurelia (Armstrong) Mann. His father, an Englishman by birth, came to America when a youth, and has been a prominent grain and shipping merchant in Buffalo, with an experience of 40 years, and is the oldest member of the board of trade in that city. William J. began his business career with his father, for a time the firm being William B. Mann & Son, and was subsequently interested in other enterprises in the city. He finally embarked in the hotel business as a member of the well-known firm of Stafford & Co., proprietors of the Tifft House and Mansion Hotel. He soon became proprietor of the Hotel Richmond in his native village, which was destroyed by fire March 8, 1887, in which he lost his wife and only child, and nearly perished himself, being severely burned and disabled for a long time. Mr. Mann became proprietor of the Hotel Richmond upon its completion in May, 1889. He is endowed with a genial personality, which, with business attributes of a high order, fit him for presiding over one of the neatest and best equipped hotels in the Empire State.

Sidney U. Main, a retired merchant, was an active business man for many years. He was born in Cazenovia, N. Y., in 1811, a son of William and Sophia (Briggs) Main, of New England stock. They were married there and settled in Madison County in 1829, whence they removed to Bennington, Wyoming County. The father was a merchant and

19

farmer there until his death in 1838. The mother died in 1877, at the home of her son in Batavia. There were eight children, six of whom are living, viz.: Mrs. Jane C. Bride, Mrs. Lucy A. Studley, Mrs. Caroline L. Dorman, Mrs. Margaret Hulett, Mrs. Louisa Shadbolt, and Sidney U. Main. The latter began his business career when a youth, and pursued it untiringly until he retired from active labor. He was for some time a traveling salesman. In 1837 he began business in Bergen, continuing there until he came to Batavia. In 1854 he formed a co-partnership with Dr O. P. Clark in the drug and book trade, and was afterwards associated with A. D. Tryon. He was also in business in Randolph, N. Y., for 20 years, and was a large real estate dealer. Throughout his entire business life he sustained a reputation for honorable dealing. In 1837 he married Miss Ophelia Beecher, of Bergen, who died in 1844. In 1849 he married Adeline E Botsford, who died in 1851. In 1854 he was married to Adeline E., daughter of Aaron and Betsey (Bent) Pingrey, of Mount Holly, Vermont, who were early settlers of Cattaraugus County, N. Y.

Rufus Monger, a native of Vermont, came to Bethany in the very early days of the settlement of that town, and cleared the farm where he remained until his death in 1870, at the age of 92 years. He was often times obliged to carry wheat to mill to Attica upon his back. He served in the War of 1812. He married Lydia Everest, of Bethany, and their children were Rufus, Lydia, Luman, Deliverance, Israel. Sally, Ephraim, Lavina, and Orange. Luman Monger was born in Bethany, near Linden, November 22, 1815. He married Amanda, daughter of Daniel Barnes, of Iowa, and they have one son, Charles, now a station agent on the Illinois Central Railroad. Mrs. Monger died in 1875, aged 70 years. Mr. Monger went to Dubuque, Iowa, in 1845, but now resides in Batavia village, and is a gunsmith.

Prof. Humphrey D. Maddock was born September 25, 1839, in Taunton, England. In 1857 he came to America and settled in Buffalo, where he did such work as a boy could find to do. About 1860 he moved to Pavilion, and there learned the broom manufacturing business, and was there 12 years. He then opened a broom factory, which he carried on until 1882. In October of that year he came to the New York State Blind Institution and taught broommaking. He also has charge of the gymnasium. He married Susan M. Buck, of Buffalo.

John Myers, born in Switzerland, came to Batavia in 1849, where he died in 1881, aged 75 years. His children were John, Alonzo, Theresa,

Elizabeth, Frank, who served in the 49th Regt. of Buffalo, and died in hospital at Fort Monroe at the age of 35 years, John, 2d, who also served in the 49th Buffalo Regt., Sefarie, who served in the 8th N. Y. H. A., Sophronia, and Peter. The latter was born in Switzerland and came to Batavia with his father, John, where he now resides. He married Amelia, daughter of Frederick and Wilhelmina (Schultz) Darrow, and they have three children, viz.: Wilhelm (deceased), Herman, and Estella. Frederick and Wilhelmina Darrow were born in Berlin, Prussia, and in 1853 came to Richville, N. Y. Frederick was killed at that place by an accident in a saw-mill, in 1857, at the age of 38 years. His wife was 58 years of age at the time of her death. Their children were William, Amelia, Augusta, Minnie, Henry, and Annie R.

Thomas Mogridge's carriage shops are located at 2 Seaver Place. In 1877 he started the business here, but previous to that, in 1875, he was located for two years on Clark Place. He employs from five to seven men, manufacturing all kinds of wagons and carriages, and has a black-smith shop connected with his business. Mr. Mogridge was born in England, April 18, 1835. In 1852 he came to Batavia and worked at his trade, which he had learned in England. He married Sarah Lyons, and they have three children.

M. Moynihan, a merchant tailor and dealer in ready-made clothing, was born in Ireland in 1840, and came to Batavia with his parents when 10 years of age. He entered the clothing store of S. Masse in 1862, where he was employed for 14 years, when he engaged in business for himself, opening a clothing store in the Opera House block, where he did a prosperous business for three years. He then purchased a lot on East Main street, 41x100 feet, and erected the Moynihan block, which contains three stores. He occupies No. 47, where he has a large stock of clothing and gents' furnishing goods. Mr. Moynihan has established the *one price* system, and has built up a lucrative and prosperous trade.

Benjamin F. Morgan, a native of Amboy, N. J., born in 1768, came to Batavia, N. Y., in 1802, and settled on a farm. His was the first deed of land in the town for 80 acres, and was given to him by the Holland Purchase. He remained on the farm until his death, February 12, 1840, aged 72 years. His wife, born in 1773, was Sarah, daughter of Ebenezer Mary, of Kinderhook, Washington County, N. Y. She died in 1856, aged 83 years. They had nine children—seven daughters and two sons. Ebenezer B. Morgan, born in Batavia, January 16, 1817, died November 3, 1882, in the 66th year of his age. He was poormaster for a time and supervisor for two years. He married Sarah B., daughter of John and Hannah Janson, and his children were Martha, Allen J., Kittie E., George E., and William E. George E. Morgan, a native of Batavia, moved to Oakfield in 1885, and engaged in the business of buying grain and produce. He married Laura E., daughter of James P. and Clara (Rich) Parsons, and they have one daughter, Laura P. Mr. Morgan now lives in Batavia.

Sylvanus M. Nestell was a native of Montgomery County, N. Y., where he lived, and died in 1874, at the age of 65 years. His wife, Harriet Ellis, bore him seven children, as follows: Daniel, Lorenzo, Amenzo, Amelia, Jane, Martha, and Homer. For his second wife he married Catherine Ellis, and they had three children, viz.: George, Harriet, and Mary. Homer Nestell was born in Pike, N. Y., in February, 1832. He married Mary E. Case, December 12, 1854, daughter of Daniel and Dolly (Moore) Case, and his children are Annette Frank, Jennie Edna, and Fred. Mr. Nestell served in the late war in Co. F, 2d N. Y. H. A., for three years, or during the war, and was honorably discharged in 1865. He was engaged in the battles of Cold Harbor, Petersburg, North Anna, Kolopotomy Creek, Reams's Station, and Hatcher's Run, and was in the 2d Corps near Petersburg. He is now drawing a pension, and lives on road 61 in the town of Batavia.

Hon. Safford E. North, judge and surrogate of Genesee County, is a native of Alexander, having been born in that town January 27, 1852. His father, James A., was a resident of Alexander for 70 years, but is now living at Attica. Judge North received his early education in the district schools, later attended the Genesee and Wyoming Seminary at Alexander, and was also one year at Cornell University, entering at the opening exercises of that institution as a member of the first class. At the early age of 17 he began teaching school, and during the winter months was an instructor of the young. In the spring of 1873 he went to Le Roy and entered upon the study of the law in the office of Hon. L. N. Bangs, remaining there less than a year, being compelled by failing eyesight to give up his studies for a period of two years. In March, 1876, he came to Batavia and resumed his law studies with William C. Watson. January 4, 1878, he was admitted to practice at Syracuse, and in May following opened an office in Batavia. He was elected clerk of the village in 1879 and '80, and district attorney in 1880–81. He has always been successful in his practice, and having been honored with the nomination for county judge and surrogate, against one of the ablest lawyers in the county, was elected to that office in 1888, and which he now holds. He is a member of the Presbyterian Church.

William O'Brien, a native of Tipperary, Ireland, came to Canada in 1850, and to Batavia in 1852. He died in Illinois in 1877, aged 70 years. His wife was Annie Enestie, of Ireland, and their children were William, Michael, John, Ellen, Mary, and Dennis. Dennis O'Brien, who came here in 1853, married Margaret, daughter of James and Mary (Carroll) Carey, and they have one son, William. He is a farmer.

Chester Orcutt, son of Moses, a soldier of the Revolution, was born in Great Barrington, Mass., and came to West Bloomfield, thence to Riga in 1808, and then went to Summit County, Ohio, where he died at the age of 77 years. He married Nancy, daughter of John Phillips, of Richmond, N. Y. Their children were Olive, Parnell, Elizabeth, and Chester E. For his second wife he married Jerusha Chamberlain, and their children were Esther, Elmira, and Chester E. Chester E. Orcutt was born in Richmond, N. Y., March 1, 1818. In April 1848, he came to Batavia, where he now resides. He married, first, Amelia Howell, of Chili, and their children were Burdette, Louisa A., Jane A., and Frank H. His second wife, Mary A., daughter of Danforth and Olive (Sprague) Tounsley, of Gates, N. Y., bore him children as follows: J. Elwood, Willis T., Ida, Martha, Charles, Arthur, and George. Mr. Orcutt has lived on his farm 41 years.

Henry L. Onderdonk was born in Monticello, N. Y., April 26, 1818. When 13 years of age he came to Genesee County with his mother. In 1839 he opened a harness store and shop, and has been engaged in that business most of the time since, being one of the oldest business men in Batavia. His mother, who was born October 7, 1779, resides with him. He was trustee of the village two terms and overseer of the poor six years. He married Elmira S. Godfrey, of Geneva, N. Y.

Owen O'Hara was born in County Lathram, Ireland, June 24, 1828. He married twice, first, Catherine McCloughlin, March 17, 1851, and started for America the same day. They had two children, Mary and James A. For his second wife Mr. O'Hara married Jane Shean, by whom he had three children, of whom two survive, namely: Patrick and Kate. James A. O'Hara was born May 10, 1859, in Alabama, was educated in the public schools, and began work on the railroad when he was 14 years old. He was promoted conductor June 1, 1887, on the N. Y. C. & H. R. Railroad. February 3, 1886, he married Nellie Skahen, of Batavia, and they have two sons: Charles, born November 9, 1886, and

James V., born July 28, 1889. Mr. and Mrs. O'Hara reside at No. 18 Robinson street, Batavia.

Albert C. Olmsted, a native of Le Roy, was born in 1847, a son of Chauncey L. and Marietta (Bailey) Olmsted (both of Le Roy). The paternal and maternal grandparents, Stephen Olmsted and Erastus Bailey, were natives of Connecticut and early settlers in Le Roy. Mr. Bailey was a miller, and built many of the first mills in the Genesee country. Bailey's mills, so long and well known, were the result of his energy, and were operated by him and subsequently by his son. Chauncey L. Olmsted was a prominent builder; he erected the Oriental mills of Chicago, and Orchard City mills, of Burlington, Ia. His lumber interests caused him to spend much time in the Saginaw valley. He was also a banker at Burlington, and president of the Orchard City Savings Bank from June, 1868, to 1872, when he sold out on account of ill health. His son Henry B. was cashier, and died in 1872, and the father died the same year. Mr. Olmsted also built the Red flouring-mills of Le Roy, and the Batavia and Le Roy planing-mills. In 1873 A. C. Olmsted came to Batavia and has since resided here. He started in the coal and lumber business in 1878, locating at 43 Center street, his present location. He is a stockholder of the Le Roy Gas Co. and a prominent member of the Masonic order. Mr. Olmsted has always been identified with the milling interests, and is interested in lumber and coal. He graduated at Poughkeepsie in 1865, when he went to Iowa, in charge of the Orchard City mills, where he was for seven years. He was married, in 1874, to Grace Clark, daughter of the well known Dr. Norris G. Clark, of Batavia, and they have one child, Henry B.

Lucius B. Parmele, A. M., M. D., is a native of Erie County, N. Y., where he was born in 1840. He is a son of John J. and Joanna (Baker) Parmele, both natives of Connecticut. Dr. Parmele commenced the study of medicine in 1864, with Dr. Barrett, of Le Roy, having graduated from the University of Rochester the same year. He subsequently entered the medical department of the University of Buffalo and was graduated therefrom in 1867. He commenced his practice in East Pembroke, where he continued for 15 years. After a short residence in Rochester he located in Batavia, in 1883, where we find him in active practice. Dr. Parmele received the degree of A. M. from the Rochester University in 1872. He was elected supervisor of Pembroke three years, and in 1884 was elected coroner of the county. He was reëlected in 1887, and is now serving. Dr. Parmele is a member of the Genesee County Medical Association, and also of the Masonic fraternity. He was married, in 1868, to Susan A. Allen, daughter of Ebenezer Allen, an old settler of the county. Three children have been born to them, viz.: Alice L., Lucius A , and Porter L. S. The family are members of the Baptist Church.

Capt. Orrin C. Parker, proprietor of the Parker House, was born in Stafford in 1838, a son of Rev. Aaron C. and Alvina (Watson) Parker, both natives of Vermont. His grandfather, James Parker, came from Vermont to this county about 1815. He served in the War of 1812, as captain, and was a farmer. His mother's father also came from Vermont to Stafford. Rev. Aaron Parker was a clergyman of the Christian denomination, and was also a farmer. Capt. Parker enlisted in Co. G, 129th N. Y. Inf., afterwards in the 8th H. A., and won a commission as captain. He was wounded three times, and served until the close of the war. On his return home he engaged in various business enterprises, and was an active and successful business man. While conducting the St. James Hotel it was destroyed by fire in 1886, leaving him with but little property, and several obligations, but he successfully discharged all his indebtedness and is again prosperous. In June, 1889, he leased of C. G. Purdy the well known Purdy House, changed the name to Parker House, and is now conducting the same. He is also an extensive real estate dealer in Western New York. In 1875 he was elected treasurer of the county, serving three years. While captain of the 14th Separate Co. N. G. he participated in the railroad riots of 1877, and was aid-de-camp to Gen. Rogers. He is a 32d degree member of the Masonic fraternity. Mr. Parker was united in marriage, in 1862, with Miss A. Pember, daughter of Leander U. Pember, a native and old resident of Batavia. .

James P. Parsons, a native of Springfield, Mass., was born in 1824, a son of David and Cynthia (Comstock) Parsons, natives of Connecticut. He came to Batavia in 1844, and finally went to Albion. The father was a farmer and machinist, and was in the government employ for 24 years in the Springfield rifle works, and six years at Harper's Ferry. James P. was reared as a farmer, following the same 18 years. He has been engaged in shipping grain, flour, and feed for many years. He was married, in 1849, to Clara, daughter of Calvin Rich, of Batavia, and their children are James R., a member of the produce exchange, Laura, Morgan, Clara A., and David L. The family are Presbyterians.

Robert D. Pease, a leading merchant and honored citizen of Batavia, and son of Alvin and Caroline (Chase) Pease, is a native of Avon. In 1843 they came to Batavia, where the father still lives. Alvin was a

farmer, and in 1857 was elected sheriff   Robert B. became a clerk for
Otis & Worthington, hardware merchants, remaining with them 12 years,
thoroughly learning the business.   He then became a partner of Hiram
K. Buell in 1865, under the firm name of Pease & Buell, hardware merchants, remaining thus 21 years.   Since 1886 Mr. Pease has conducted
the business alone at 54 East Main street.   He served as deputy sheriff
under his father, was trustee for five years, and has served on the board
of education six years.   He married Mary Bainbridge, of Wyoming
County, and their children are Francis C., Fred A., and Maud E.   The
family are members of the Presbyterian Church.

· The first known of the Perrin family was one John Peryn, who came
from London, England, on the ship *Safety*, and landed at South Shore,
Braintree, Mass. He was born in 1614.   Edward A. Perrin, a lineal descendant of John Peryn, was born in Woodstock, Windham County, Conn.,
August 10, 1836, and was educated in the public schools with several
terms at Woodstock Academy.   In 1858 he came to Batavia, and July
28, 1859, married Jane M., second daughter of Daniel Carpenter, of Rome,
N. Y.   They have three children, viz.: George E., born July 28, 1861;
Florence M., born October 13, 1870; and Charles N., born January 27,
1873. ' September 6, 1864, Mr. Perrin enlisted in Co. G, 8th N. Y. H. A.
Vols, and in June, 1865, was transferred to Co. F, 4th H. A., and was
discharged as corporal in September, 1865.   He is a member of Upton
Post, No. 299, G. A. R., and is its present commander.

Blanchard Powers, a native of Bennington, Vt., came to Batavia about
1806.   He was a civil engineer and school teacher, a prominent Mason,
and at one time master of the Olive Branch Lodge, meetings being held
at his house quite frequently during and after the Morgan troubles.   And
for the intense interest taken by him to keep up the meetings he was
presented with a medal.   IIis son, E. P. Powers, was born in Bennington,
Vt., in 1803, and came here with his father.   He was a farmer, and helped
to build the Tonawanda Railroad and worked for the railroad company
around the depot.   He married Harriet Case and reared a family of seven
children, only two of whom are living, viz.: Charles, who has been a stationary engineer for the N. Y. C. & H. R. R. R. Co. since 1861, and John
R., who is a baggagemaster.

George Prescott was born in Devonshire, England, about 1817, and
married Mary Clark of the same place, by whom he had two sons, Francis, and Thomas F.   Francis Prescott was born in England, June 25,
1843, was educated in the public schools, came to America with his par-

ents in 1855, and located in Stafford. He subsequently learned the blacksmiths' trade. He married twice, first, in 1870, Lydia Passmore, formerly of England. They had three children, Mary J., Nettie E., and Lydia A. Mrs. Prescott died October 17, 1875, and for his second wife he married, in November, 1876, Lucy A Simpson. They had five children, viz: Myrtia V., Olive A., Alice P, Ralph T., and Frank S. She died September 15, 1889. December 29, 1863, he enlisted in Co. L, 8th N. Y. H. A. Vols., and was afterwards transferred to Co. I, 3d Regt. Vet. Reserve Corps, and was discharged at the close of the war. Mr. Prescott is now in the employ of the Wiard Plow Co. as general blacksmith.

William E. Prentice, an attorney in the Walker block, Batavia, is descended from Stephen Randall (a great-grandfather) and Elisha Prentice (grandfather), the earliest pioneers of Le Roy and Stafford. William E. is a son of John and Sarah (Randall) Prentice, and was born February 22, 1859. He was a pupil in the district school and later in Le Roy Academy, commenced teaching at the age of 16, and entered college at 19, but was obliged to leave to provide for his younger brothers and sisters. Later he completed a college and post-graduate course, receiving degrees from Yale University and Rochester University, and has also done special work in Columbia. He was elected school superintendent of the county in 1881 and again in 1884, each time running ahead of his ticket, during which terms the systems were greatly extended and benefited. He then became a law student with William C. Watson, and also with Judge North, and was admitted to the bar in 1885. His practice is a lucrative one, and by fortunate investments in the West he has shown an unlimited capacity for work and honest devotion to duty.

Aaron Perry was born in Reading, Conn. He served in the War of 1812, and died in Fairfield, Conn., aged 76 years. His wife was Esther Sanford, of Reading, of English ancestry, and his children were David and Andrew S. David was born in Reading, and came to Riga, N. Y., in 1840, where he died in 1886. He married Lydia, daughter of Joshua Richmond, and his children are Truman A., a farmer of Churchville, N. Y., and Frank D., who was born in Churchville, May 15, 1849, and came to Batavia, April 1, 1885. Frank D. married Jennie E., daughter of Jeremiah and Lucy (Kelsey) Sibley, of Rush, N. Y., and they have children as follows: Lydia F., Richmond D., and Lucy K. Mr. Perry is a farmer on road 46.

John Parsons, a native of Lyme, Conn., died there in 1813, aged 60 years. He married Lois Waite, of the same place, and they had 13 children, among whom was Marshfield, who was born in Lyme, and came to Le Roy in 1815, settling upon a farm. He was a carpenter, and died in 1881, at the age of 83 years. He married Betsey, daughter of Joseph and Mary Keeney. Their children were Mary E., Anna S., Ezra K., Emma L., and Thomas G. Thomas G. Parsons, a native of Le Roy, was born August 3, 1828, and married Mary, daughter of Hiram and Maria (Fowle) Pratt, of Buffalo. Their children are Hiram P., Charles F., Bessie M., Jennie L., and Howard M. Mr. Parsons resides on road 7, where he has lived seven years. Hiram Pratt, one of the pioneers of Buffalo who settled there in 1804, from Westminister, Vt., was elected mayor in 1836 and 1839. He died in 1840, aged 40 years.

John B. Peckes, born in Belgium in 1852, came to America in 1872, and has been a resident of Batavia since 1874. He married Mary Clark, of Batavia, and they have three children.

W. S. & J. J. Patterson's drug store is located at 102 Main street. The business was established by them in 1886, and they carry a full line of drugs, books, and medicines.

Henry J. Patten, M. D. is a native of Oswego County, where he was born in 1838. His father, George Patten, was a native of Vermont, and his mother, whose maiden name was Moot, was a native of the Empire State. Henry J. enlisted as a private in Co. H, 122d Regt. Veterans, participated in 18 battles, and served until the close of the war. He practiced dentistry in Syracuse for 16 years, then became a medical student in the office of Dr. E. L. Baker, of Syracuse, and subsequently graduated from the Cincinnati Eclectic College. He is also a graduate of the Poulte Medical College of Cincinnati, class of 1883. Dr. Patten has been a resident of Batavia since 1883, and devotes his practice principally to the special treatment of the eye, ear, and throat. He is now serving his second term as health officer of the village. He married Sarah Wilder, of Syracuse, and they have one child, Carrie B. The family are Presbyterians.

George Redshaw was born in Derbyshire, England, November 27, 1822. He married Martha Robinson, of his native town, emigrated to America, and arrived in Batavia, June 3. 1850, where he still resides. He served an apprenticeship to the trade of carpenter and joiner in England, and followed that calling until 1855, when he increased his business and became quite an extensive contractor and builder. He continued in the business until 1882. Mr. and Mrs. Redshaw are parents of three sons and four daughters, all of whom reside in Batavia. His son, John T. Red_shaw, was born in Batavia, February 6, 1851, where he was raised and educated. He learned his father's trade, and has been engaged in the business from early boyhood, and on his own account for the past 16 years. In 1882 he formed a partnership with Asa King, under the firm name of King & Redshaw, contractors and builders, which continues. They now employ from four to 12 men. Mr. Redshaw is a staunch Republican, and although his ward is Democratic by more than 50, such is his popularity that he now holds the position of alderman. In 1873 he united in marriage with Evelyn Johnson, of Batavia, and they have two sons and one daughter.

William J. Reedy, sheriff of Genesee County, is a native of Kent County, Delaware, where his father still resides. He was born in 1841, and in 1862 entered the U. S. service as first lieutenant of the 1st Delaware Cavalry, serving until the close of the war. He was promoted to captain, then to major, and was wounded at the battle of the Wilderness. He was then transferred to the regular army, and February 23, 1866, secured a commission as second lieutenant of the 13th U. S. Inf., and was sent to the West. In 1867 he was made quartermaster and commissary. Upon the reörganization of the army in 1868 he was assigned to the 22d Infantry, with commission as first lieutenant. He served several years in the West, and was transferred to Brooklyn, N. Y., upon recruiting service. He was next sent to New Orleans, and participated in the election and legislative troubles of 1873–74. In June, 1874, Capt. Reedy came to Buffalo with his regiment and served as quartermaster and commissary until he came to Batavia in 1877. Since then he has been a resident of this county. In the fall of 1887 he was elected to his present position, which he fills efficiently and creditably In July, 1877, he was married to Mrs. Amelia E. Dewey, widow of Henry Dewey, and daughter of Addison Foster, an old resident of Batavia.

Charles F. Rand, M. D., was born in 1839, a son of James and Angeline (Rutland) Rand. His grandfather Rand was killed in the war of the Revolution, and his grandfather Rutland was a soldier of 1812. His parents came to Genesee County at an early day, residing here until their deaths. Dr. Rand was born in the house he now occupies. He was educated in the schools of the county, and April 16, 1861, he entered the Union service, being the first volunteer in the county. He served as private in Co. K, 12th Regt., until June 27, 1862, when he was shot at Gaines's Mills, taken prisoner, and sent to Libby prison. His wound resulted in the loss of his right arm. In 1863 he was commissioned lieutenant, and subsequently captain. He served during the war, and in the regular army until 1869. He had made a study of medicine, and during his confinement in the hospital, and in leisure hours, gave further attention to it. After leaving the service he entered the University of Georgetown and graduated in March, 1873. For six years he practiced in Washington, and in 1879 returned to his native place, where he has since been in active service. He is a member of the Masonic order, and is a learned and cultivated gentleman.

Meredith Ross, wholesale dealer in tobacco, cigars, and grocers' sundries, Park Place, and who resides at 57 Ellicott avenue, has been a resident of Batavia since 1884. He built the Ross block on Main street in 1886, and in 1888 opened a wholesale store at Park Place. His teas, coffees, syrups, and molasses are shipped from first hands direct to his customers, and no money is invested only as his sales are made, thus enabling him to sell on a small margin, giving his customers the benefit of the profits to middle men. He employs three traveling salesmen, who travel over Western New York and Pennsylvania.

Ross Brothers (George and Edwin), carriage manufacturers and painters, are located in the rear of the Parker House. They started in business April 1, 1888. They are practical carriage manufacturers, prepared to do any work in that line.

George M. Rupp was born in Baden, Germany, and came to Batavia, July 4, 1836. He was a shoemaker by trade, and in 1847 he opened a shoe store and carried on the business until 1879, when he was succeeded by his son Ernst. He died May 22, 1884, and his wife died June 30, 1876. Six children out of a family of 11 are living in Batavia. Ernst was born in Baden, October 12, 1834, and came here in 1836. He married Margaret Gress, of New York city, and they have five children. Andrew Rupp was born May 14, 1840. He is a tinsmith and deals in real estate.

Ephraim Rolfe, a Revolutionary soldier, was a native of Vermont, where he died. His wife, Lucy, bore him 12 children, viz.: Ephraim, Jonathan, Nathan, Benjamin, Hazen, Charles, Manasses, William, Ira, Sally, Lucy, and Sophia. Jonathan, born in Vermont, came to Bethany in 1809, thence to Batavia, where he was an early settler, and lived many years before he moved to Ellington, N. Y., where he died in 1858, aged 76 years. He married Esther Brown, of Strafford, Orange County, Vt., and his children are Heman, Mary, Lucy, Mariann, Sarah, and Walker P.

Walker P. Rolfe, born in Orange County, Vt., February 15, 1807, came to Bethany with his father, and married Mary, daughter of Eleazer and Tamzy (Godfrey) Crocker, of Pembroke, and they have one son, Lucius F., who married Jennie Egleston, and has one daughter, Amy P. Mrs. Mary Rolfe died March 6, 1880, in Bethany, on the homestead farm, at the age of 70 years. Walker P. Rolfe is still a resident of Batavia, aged 83 years.

William E. Richardson, a popular and enterprising dentist of Batavia, a native of Michigan, was born in 1858, son of Rev. C. C. and Ann E. (Rahl) Richardson, of Pennsylvania. His father, a Universalist clergyman, preached for many years in Corfu, Alexander, and Indian Falls, organizing the societies and building the churches at the latter place and at Corfu. He also labored in other places in Western New York. William E. began the study of dentistry with Dr. Whitcomb, of Buffalo, and also pursued it in Pennsylvania. He began practice in 1877, in Alexander, and in 1880 removed to Batavia, where he has successfully practiced since. He is a skillful and able operator, and has all the latest appliances for doing all kinds of work in his line. His office is at 101 East Main street. He was married, in 1878, to Hattie, daughter of E. G. Moulton, of Alexander, and they have one child, Elbridge M.

Isaac Quance, a native of Southampton, Mass., came to Genesee County in 1808, living in Batavia until his death in 1851, at the age of 61 years. He married Mehitable Powers, of Phelps, N. Y., who came here when there were but two houses built. She was a daughter of Peter and Sally Powers. Their children were Sarah, Lyman, Israel, and James M. The latter was born in Batavia, October 5, 1824, and January 18, 1849, married Lucy, daughter of Nichols and Lucy Barnea. Their children were Rose C. and Roselle, both deceased. Mr. Quance resides on road 63.

Henry Speyer, a native of Bavaria, Germany, lived and died there. He had four children, namely: Frederick, Louis, Michael, and Catherine. Frederick, a native of Bavaria, died there, aged 55 years. He married Christine Coonrad, and their children were Julia, Michael, Margaret, and Conrad. Conrad Speyer came to Batavia in 1859, and married Barbara, daughter of Michael Surieker, of Attica. Their children are Frank, Fred, Charles, George, Elizabeth, and Julia. Mr. Speyer is postmaster and general merchant at Dawes Corners.

Ebenezer Shepard, a native of Dedham, Mass., moved to London, N. H., where he died. He was a soldier in the Revolutionary war. He had seven children, viz.: Ebenezer, Jr., Jesse, John, Susan, Abigail, Elizabeth, and Hannah. Ebenezer Shepard, Jr., died in London, N. H., aged 83 years. He was a farmer. His wife, Sallie Burpee, bore him children as follows: Abigail, Mary, Daniel, Amial, Sylvester, Thomas, James, and Benjamin. Thomas Shepard, a native of London, N. H., came to Batavia in 1868. He married, first, Eleanor Shelden, and their children were Helen and Isabella. For his second wife he married Mrs. Hannah Hubbard, daughter of Lysander Smith. He now resides in Batavia, on road 6, where he has lived 20 years.

B. F. Showerman, M. D., is a native of Genesee County, and son of Dr. J. M. Showerman. He was a medical student in the office of Dr. L. L. Tozier, and graduated in medicine in 1886. Since that time he has been in practice at Batavia. Dr. Showerman is a Royal Arch Mason.

Bradley S. Smith is the proprietor of the only news room in Batavia. He bought, April 1, 1885, the establishment of Mackey Brothers, and has since enlarged his facilities for business and extended his trade, so he is now able to supply the wants of a large community in the line of newspapers, periodicals, and stationery generally. He is ably assisted by his brother, Lewis E. Smith. The news-room is at 67 East Main street.

Joseph C. Shults was born March 17, 1832, in Europe. Aspiring to live under a republic he came to America in 1848, on account of the condition of the government of France. He spent 25 years in trade in Rochester, came to Batavia in 1872, and has been in the mercantile business most of the time since. He has been a member of the board of excise for six years and a trustee of the village for two years. He is a Democrat, and takes an active part in the politics of the county. He married Margaret Hagan, of Rochester, and they have a family of five sons and four daughters. Mr. Shults has made a close study of his present business, and imports the choicest teas to be found in the market.

Gottleib Scheuing, a florist and vegetable gardener of Batavia, is a native of Stuttgart, Germany, where he was born February 1, 1833. In 1852 he came to Le Roy and was engaged in the Le Roy mills until 1889, with the exception of five years, during which time he was traveling in the West. He married for his first wife Rosa Frank; for his second he married Rosa Stoll, and they have five children. In the fall of 1889 Mr. Scheuing entered into partnership with Elizabeth Bleyler, under the firm name of Bleyler & Co. They have three greenhouses and about 10 acres of ground on West Main street.

Willis D. Sanford, a native of Jackson, Mich., was born in 1854. He is the son of O. D. and Susan (Baker) Sanford, the father being a resident of this county. Willis D. learned the tinners' trade at Pease & Buell's, and commenced clerking for O. W. Lord, a dealer in hats, caps, and furs, remaining with him five years. He then traveled for R. D. Kellogg in the tobacco and cigar line for four years. In 1883 he started his present business at 76 East Main street, where he has secured a large and profitable trade in the line of hats, gloves, trunks, caps, and furs. Mr. Sanford is a member of the Masonic order, the Philharmonics, the Alert Hose Company, and I. O. O. F. fraternity. He was married, in 1876, to Ella Dulmage.

Charles A. Snell, a native of Connecticut, was born in 1839. He was son of a Baptist clergyman, who came to Pembroke in 1851, and died in Bethany in 1875. Mr. Snell was first engaged in farming, but subsequently engaged in business at Churchville for seven years. In 1881 he went to Darien, resumed farming for five years, when he came to Batavia and formed a partnership with John C. Greene, they remaining together two years, and in 1886 he embarked alone in the general insurance business. He represents the Ætna Life, American, Fire of New York, and Geneva Accident. He also deals in real estate and loans, representing the Western Trust Co., of Kansas. He has a farm of 25 acres on the Lewiston road, where he lives. He does a large business throughout the State and Union. He married, in 1860, Nancy L. Armstrong, daughter of Ira, of Batavia. Their children are Charles I. (a teacher), Frank A., and Nettie L.

Alva Smith came to Batavia in 1815, from Connecticut, and was in business here for 55 years. He was at first clerk for his brother, J. P. Smith, five years, then started for himself as A. Smith & Co., then with J. P. Smith for a few years, when J. P. withdrew (in 1827). D. P. Warren was his partner for four years from 1845. He was then alone until 1856, when his son Wilber was taken in as partner, and the firm was continued for 10 years as A. Smith & Son. Alva Smith's business was indeed an extensive one ; he had branches at Albion, Holley, Alabama, Oakfield, and Pine Hill, and started many young men in mercantile life. Nathan Townsend, sheriff of the county in 1834, was the father of Mrs. Alva Smith, and a very early settler. Wilber Smith was in the dry goods business from 1868 to 1880, in the present "Stone" block, now occupied by E. N. Stone. He was born in this village in 1835. Besides devoting his life to active business he has taken an active part in the progress and growth of the village. He has been president and trustee for a number of years, was president of the Loan Association, and also of the Batavia Gas Co., He is a member of the Episcopal Church, and is connected with the Masonic order. He married Eva A. Dolbeer, of Perry, Wyoming County, daughter of Col. William Dolbeer.

James S. Stewart was born in Orange County, N. Y., April 25, 1810. When 13 years of age he came to Batavia and finally learned the carriagemaking business. In 1831 he went to Elba and opened a carriage shop, and carried on the business about 20 years. He was elected justice of the peace in 1840, and held that office for 20 years and the office of justice of Sessions for two years. He was also license commissioner for six years, and assistant revenue assessor for nine years. In 1854 he settled in Batavia, where he had an insurance office from 1857 until 1889. He died October 8, 1889.

Horace K. Smith, son of Orr, was born in Wells, Bradford County, Pa., April 13, 1847. When seven years of age he moved to Cooper's Station, Steuben County. Through an illnes she lost his sight when four years of age. He lived on the farm with his father, came to Batavia in 1872, entered the Institution for the Blind, and in 1879 commenced teaching piano tuning, which he has since pursued. He married Minnie E. Newton, of Akron, N. Y., and they have one child, Orr N.

Schellenger's restaurant, located at 49 Main street, was opened September 1, 1883, by the present proprietor, William L. Schellenger, who conducts it as a first-class restaurant.

John Schaefer was born in Prussia in 1834. In 1852 he came to America and settled in Batavia. . He married Theresa Todt, and they have a family of nine children. He is a mason, has been a contractor for 25 years, and helped to build many of the best buildings in Batavia, among which are the Opera House block, Union School, Walker block, Washburn House, Wilson House, Richmond Library, and Richmond Hotel.

James Short, born in Dublin, Ireland, came to Batavia about 1846. He was a maltster, and followed that business for years. He married Margaret O'Brien, and they had a family of eight children, six of whom are living. He died March 27, 1889. His widow resides at 320 West Main street. James, son of James, was born July 9, 1857, and is a harnessmaker, a member of the firm of Short & Roth. He was elected trustee of the village in 1886, and served two years, and was elected excise commissioner in 1888–89.

Herman Schafer was born in Hessen, Germany, in 1848, and came to America in 1871. He opened a wholesale and retail liquor store in Batavia in 1872, being located at 15 Jackson street since 1885.

E. N. Stone, one of the leading merchants of the county, was born in Wyoming County in 1841. His parents, Harry and Mary (Williams) Stone, were descendants of New England ancestry. His father, for many years a merchant, resides in Pembroke. Mr. Stone began business life when a youth in his father's store, remaining in Pembroke until 1865, when he moved to Batavia, where for three years he was associated with George P. Bowen in the crockery trade, and subsequently with John Thomas. He finally purchased the interest of Mr. Thomas, and conducted the business until 1878. In that year he purchased the stocks of Wilber Smith and E. B. McCormick. Since 1878 Mr. Stone has devoted his attention to the dry goods and notion trade, and has secured a large and increasing patronage. His store at 94 East Main street is filled with a choice assortment of goods pertaining to his line. Mr. Stone served four years as town clerk. He is a Mason and a member of the I.O.O.F. In 1868 he was united in marriage with Elizabeth McCann, of Batavia, and their children are Norine R. and Harry.

Isaac Southworth came to Genesee County in 1820 from Cayuga County, and resided here until his death. He was born in 1794, served in the War of 1812, settled in Bergen, and served as justice of the peace for many years. He was twice married. His first wife, Rachel Tone, died in 1836, leaving seven children, viz.: Mrs. E. Miller, Mrs. Luranda Case, Andrew J., Mrs. Clara R. Shaw, Edwin M., Samuel, and Irving D. His second wife was Elizabeth Bower, who died in 1888, leaving a son, John B., now a resident of Michigan.

Irving D. Southworth was born in Bergen in 1832, and learned the carpenters' trade, which he followed for 30 years. In 1862 he enlisted and served as captain in the 25th N. Y. Lt. Art. for three years. He was elected sheriff of the county in 1881, serving three years, and has resided in Batavia since 1881. He served as justice of the peace for many years, one term as justice of Sessions, and is now a member of the board of trustees. He married, in 1866, Maria A. Prentice, of Stafford, and they have four children, viz.: Dollie E., George P., Pear A., and Irving D., Jr.

Daniel Swezey, of German ancestry, was born in Suffolk County, L. I., in 1753. He went to Herkimer County and died October 26, 1825, at the age of 72 years. He married Sarah Beal, of Connecticut, daughter of a celebrated music teacher, and their children were Daniel, George, John, Samuel, Sarah, Mary, Eunice, and Matthew B. George Swezey was born at Middle Island, Suffolk County, N. Y., August 9, 1780. His

20

death, in 1851, at the age of 71 years, in the town of Russia, Herkimer County, was occasioned by an accident. He married Elizabeth Wood, of Orange County, N. Y., and their children were William. W., Jane, Elizabeth A., Achsah, Harriet, Hiram, and Franklin. Hiram Swezey, a native of Russia, N. Y., born October 6, 1824, came to Victor, N. Y., in 1858, and to Batavia, where he now resides, in 1882. He married Mary, daughter of Daniel and Catherine (Sherwood) Silliman, of Salisbury, N. Y. Their children are Annie E., George S., Cora J., Edward H., May G., H. Eugene, and Carrie L. George S. Swezey is pastor of the First Presbyterian Church at Peabody, Kan. Samuel Swezey visited Batavia in 1814 and '15 as a missionary from Herkimer County. Daniel, upon the death of his father, took upon himself the care of the family. In 1796, with his father, he purchased land in Norway, Herkimer County, erected a cabin, and made improvements, so that in the spring the whole family left Long Island in a boat, coming to Albany, where they purchased a cart and oxen, and continued their journey to Norway. They were three weeks on the road, enduring many hardships. With native energy and perseverance they performed the duties of pioneer life, and exerted an influence for good that extended to their children as well as to the community around. They were prominent in school and church matters, and aided in building up both for the benefit of all concerned.

George Scheer was born in Germany in 1838, came to America in 1840, with his parents, and located in Buffalo. In April, 1882, he came to Batavia and started a store on Ellicott street. In 1884 he built his present store at 202 Ellicott street, and has since carried on business there. In 1857 he went to Cincinnati, O., as foreman of the Kentucky Central Railroad shops, and in 1861 enlisted in Co. B, 9th Ohio Vols., served three years and three months, and afterwards returned to Cincinnati, remaining there until 1882, working in the shops until he came to Batavia.

Harry Sutterby, a veterinary surgeon, was born May 31, 1855, in Cambridgeshire, Eng., and came to America with his parents in 1861, He graduated from the Ontario Veterinary College of Toronto in 1878, and located in Batavia, practicing his profession since that time. He is located at 20 West Main street, and has a veterinary hospital and pharmacy.

Isaac Stringham, born in Dutchess County, came to Oakfield, and died in 1862, aged 70 years. By his wife, Anna, he had children as follows: Daniel, Albert, Cora, Peter, Eliza, and Anna. Peter Stringham, a native of Oakfield, died in Rochester in 1886, age 65 years. He married Eliza Sodo, of West Bloomfield, N. Y., and their children are Charles A., Clara M., Isaac W., Cara A., and Alonzo H. The latter, a native of Oakfield, married Lois L. Quance, of Batavia, daughter of Israel and Elizabeth Quance. She died in 1884, aged 28 years. They had one son, Mortimer E. He is now foreman for H. M. Lay, of Batavia.

John Sullings, of Cogshall, Eng., came to Rutland in 1775, and died there. By his wife, Ruth, he had children as follows: Charles, Harvey, David, Henry, William, Phœbe, Elizabeth, Ruth, and John. William was born in New Bedford, Mass., and moved to Vermont with his father. He came to Batavia in 1817, and settled on the farm where he died in 1873, aged 82 years. He married Temperance, daughter of Benjamin and Cloil (Branch) Hulbert, of Rutland Vt., and their children are Ruth Adelia, F. Julius, Harvey, and David. The last named is now a resident on the home farm with his sister Ruth. He married Augusta, daughter of Aaron and Sarah Rogers, of Pembroke. She died in 1885, aged 50 years. Their children were Cora, Georgiana, Alice, and William B.

Thomas Strong, a native of England, came to New York city about 1800, and engaged in the brewing business. He died in 1828, aged 42 years. His wife, Maria, bore him two children, John and James. John Strong, born in New York city, now resides in Turin, Lewis County, N. Y., and is a farmer. He married Elizabeth, daughter of Sylvester Foster, of Turin, and their children are Amelia, Fanny, John, Maria, and Sylvester. Sylvester F. Strong, a native of Turin, came to Batavia in 1882, and married Louisa M., daughter of Eli H. and Elizabeth (Rosecranz) Fish. He now resides in Batavia on road 7.

William Tyrrell, of the law firm of Tyrrell & Ballard, was born in Darien, October 24, 1823, a son of Amos and Salome (Harroun) Tyrrell, early settlers of the county. Amos, a grandfather, came in 1816 with his wife and eight children, and subsequently located in Darien. The father of William, a member of the Assembly in 1834 and '35, lived on the old homestead until his death in 1860. The mother died in 1872. When 21 years of age William Tyrrell began to study law with Timothy Fitch and Henry Glowacki, and afterwards studied with Verplanck & Martindale. In 1849 he was admitted to practice, and since 1852 has followed his profession in Batavia. He has served the county as district attorney, and in 1866 was appointed postmaster of Batavia. In 1873 he was again appointed to that office, serving until 1885.

Frank W. Ballard, an attorney, was born in Allegany County, in 1860. He is a son of John D. and Cynthia (Bingham) Ballard, now residents of Batavia. James, a grandfather, came from New England to Monroe County in 1814, and finally moved to Allegany County. Frank W. Ballard received a good education and graduated from Pike Seminary in 1881. He studied law with Richardson & Smith, of his native county, and graduated from the Albany Law School in May, 1884. The same month he was admitted to practice. In the fall of 1844 he became a partner with William Tyrrell, and has become prominent in the legal fraternity of the county.

Charles W. Tallman, the oldest photographer in Batavia, is a native of Wyoming County. He was born in 1833, and learned the rudimentary details of his art in Buffalo. His life has been devoted to this valuable and pleasant profession, and he has kept pace with its marvelous advances and improvements. Mr. Tallman located in Batavia in 1869, and has since occupied the third floor over 80 and 82 East Main street. He has the latest facilities for all kinds of photographic, stereoscopic, and portrait work, and has established a reputation, for superior work and finish. His studio is centrally located and admirably adapted for his business.

John Thomas, dealer in hats, caps, trunks, robes, gloves, and mittens, a native of France, was born in 1848, a son of Peter P. and Dorothy (Schimpf) Thomas, who came to America when he was seven years old (1854), locating in Wyoming County, where he was reared. At the age of 13 he became a clerk for Porter Brothers, of Corfu, remaining two years. When he was 18 years old he enlisted in Co. G, 8th N. Y. H. A., serving until the close of the war. He then came to Batavia, clerked for R. O. Holden for four years, and became a partner with E. N. Stone, under the firm name of Stone & Thomas, dry goods dealers, at 78 Main street, continuing thus for eight years. For the past 10 years he has been in his present quarters, doing a successful and extensive business. He has served as village collector and town clerk ; was elected county treasurer in 1885, and reëlected in 1888, and is still holding that office. He belongs to the F. & A. M., K. of P., and G. A. R. In 1881 he married Mary, daughter of Charles Holden, of Le Roy, and they have two children, John F. and James B.

Dr. Lemuel L. Tozier, M. D., now engaged in the practice of medicine in the village of Batavia, located in this town shortly after the close of the war, in the summer of 1865. He comes of a family of physicians,

Yours Truly
L. D. Vigin

Frank   . . born . . 'egany County, in 186o
He is a   . (Bio . . .) Ballard, now residents of
Batavi   came .   New England to Monroe
Count   moved   g. ny County. Frank W.
Ballar   ion an   ua: d from Pike Seminary in
1881.   . Rich   . S ith, of his native county,
and g1   any f   oo in May, 1884. The sam
month   . .   . fall of 1844 he became a
partne   rrell,   b. . prominent in the legal
fraterr
Cha   he olde   og ther . Batavia, is a native of
Wyom   was b   3? . d learned the rudimentary
details   lato. H   ia . cu devoted to this valuable
and pl   and h   t ce with its marvelous advances
and in   r. Tal   at in Batavia in 1869, and ha
since   . d   r . and 82 East Main street.
He ha   .   . . hoto raphic, stereoscopic, and
portrai   r nation, for superior work and
finish.   .   ed d admirably adapted for his
busines
John   .   tr nk , robes, gloves, and mitten ,
a nativ   .8, son of Peter P. and Dorothy
(Schim   e . when he was seven years old
(1854),   w re he was reared. At the age
of 13 h   he . of Corfu, remaining two years.
When   i . o. G, 8th N. Y. H. A., serving
until tl   i   ar to Batavia, clerked for R. O.
Holde   o .ner with E. N. Stone, under
the firi   vo. s dealers, at 78 Main street.
contin   the ast 10 years he has been in
his pre   nd xtensive business. He ha
served   ; w s elected county treasurer
in 188   u .   le ding that office. He be
longs   . P.   A. R. In 1881 he married
Mary,   m, o . y, and they have two chil
dren,]
Dr. . . . . ozier, M : . w eng g : o the practice of medicine
in the . . e . . Batavia, lo te . . this p n hortly after the close of
the wa . . . . . mner of 1865. He comes o a family of physicians,

as both his father, Joseph C. Tozier, of Bangor, Me., and his maternal grandfather, Joseph Allen, of Buckland, Mass., followed this profession as their calling. Doubtless the unconscious influence of their bent of mind, and their lives, tended to intensify his taste, and decide his fitness for this department of professional life. It cannot be questioned that Dr. Tozier is serving in his proper vocation. He was born in York, Livingston County, March 16, 1839, and is therefore now in the full strength of natural life. Receiving the benefits of an academic education, he began active work as a teacher at 18 years of age, and many will recall him while laboring in this capacity. But the study of medicine was his objective, and so, after completing the prescribed course of study with the late Dr. Norris Clark, of Batavia, he entered Bellevue Medical College of New York city, graduating from that institution in March, 1864. Previous to receiving his degree as Doctor of Medicine he had passed his examination before the U. S. army medical board and had been appointed to service in the U. S. A. Hospital in New York city under Surgeon Alexander B Mott,—in charge of that institution,—where he remained until the close of the war. During his term of service there he graduated as an oculist and aurist, and served as a member of the medical army board for the enlistment of recruits.

Upon the closing of the hospital, in June following the close of the war, being ordered to distant service, and preferring private practice, Dr. Tozier resigned his commission and returned to Batavia, where he had previously married his wife, Miss Emily A. Putnam, and began the practice of his profession. He served as county coroner from 1869 to 1884, and has been president and secretary of the County Medical Society. He has always been an indefatigable worker in his profession, studiously devoted to its interests, its progress, and its dignity, and has built up an extensive and lucrative practice. A daughter and two sons have been born to him, the elder of whom came to an untimely death by drowning in the summer of 1881. Although belonging to what is called the "old school," he readily recognizes the merits of other systems of medicine, and is keenly alive to all that is progressive and valuable in professional investigation.

Joseph Thompson, a native of Vermont, came to Aurora, N. Y., in 1811, and died at the age of 83 years. He married Martha Bemis, who died in Aurora, aged 76 years. Mr. Thompson was a farmer. His children were Albert, Perry, Sarah, Joseph, Adaline, Mary, Aurelia, Susan, Fernando C., and Sylvanus B. Sylvanus B. Thompson was born in Aurora, and June 4, 1854, married Emeline, daughter of Eben and Phila (Washford) Salisbury, of Aurora. Their children are Cicero H., Newton K., Seymour B., Lottie M., Myrtle E., J. Minelle, and Charlie S. Mr. Thompson has been a merchant 46 years, and owns the Almonarch stock farm, where he resides. He is also the proprietor of the stock horse "Almonarch," from Paris, Ky.

Moses E. True, the inventor of the True shell band wheel and other ingenious contrivances, is a native of Genesee County, born in 1845, and is a son of Luther and Minerva (Webster) True, natives of Connecticut. His grandfather, Moses, was one of the early settlers of Genesee County. Mr. True was reared upon a farm, but his inclinations led him to mechanical pursuits. He is the inventor of several valuable patents.

William C. Taggart, a native of Schoharie County, settled in Niagara County for a few years, then came to Bethany, where he resided a few years, when he went to Wyoming County for a short time, and finally removed to Pembroke, where he died November 17, 1886. His son, Earl W. Taggart, was born in Bethany, August 5, 1841. He has been a farmer most of the time. In April, 1883, he started a livery stable on Russell Place, and in April, 1888, formed a partnership with his son Fred E., under the firm name of Earl W. Taggart & Son. They keep nine horses. Mr. Taggart married Emma Strong, and they have four children.

Benjamin Throop, son of Orange, came to Bergen in 1806, from Middlebury, Vt. He was a farmer and settled in the north part of the town on Black Creek. He married Anna Shedd, and they have had four children, two of whom are living. O. S. Throop, the only one living in this county, was born March 28, 1825. He married Hannah A. Gillett, and they had two children. Mr. Throop attended the common schools and several private schools, finishing his education at the State Normal School in Albany in 1846. He was principal of public school No. 33 in Buffalo for 13 years, and taught in Genesee and Monroe counties several years. He was school commissioner for six years and town superintendent of schools in Bergen for three years.

William M. Tompkins, who was born in County Wicklow, Ireland, came to America when young. He entered the employ of the Batavia Gas Co., being the first man to lay gas pipes in the village, and remained with that firm until his death, June 19, 1889. He married Sarah Hull, of Niagara County, and they had two children, viz.: Walter H., a student at Cornell University, and Abbie, who resides with her mother on Jackson street.   Mr. Tompkins was a member of the Masonic Lodge and a Knight Templar.   The family are members of the Episcopal Church.

Among the very early settlers of Batavia were Dr. Town, who came in 1803 and died in 1807, and I. Norman Town, a son, who was in business in 1827.   Both came from Palmyra, N. Y.   The latter died in Elba. Dr. Town built the house now owned by Mr. McMillan.   Orlando Town bought a farm in 1822, and engaged at farming for 55 years.   Orlando, son of Orlando, was born in Elba in 1845.   He was educated at Caryville, Canandaigua, and Detroit.   He was in business in New York for three years, was on the farm for three years, and was supervisor of Elba at one time.   In 1883 Orlando Town bought out the late Hon. L. R. Bailey, and engaged in the clothing business.   In a few years the firm was composed of Gould & Town, continuing such until February 13, 1888, when it became O. Town & Son.   They have a complete assortment of ready-made clothing and gents' furnishing goods.

William Tozer's brick yard is located in the rear of 538 East Main street. It was started by Mr. Tozer in 1882.   He makes about 400,000 brick per year, employing nine hands.   Mr. Tozer was born in Devonshire, Eng., in 1825, and came to America in 1850, settling in Batavia in 1876, where he has since been engaged in his present business.

Richard Torrance was born in Starkey, N. Y., and moved to Avon, where he died at the age of 66 years.   He married Betsey Dann, of Mendon, N. Y., and their children were Charles G., Lucinda P., Underhill, Louisa P., Phœbe Ann, Lucy, Henrietta, and Floyd.   Charles G. was born in Yates County, came to Batavia in 1869, and died in 1876, aged 62 years.   He married, first, Harriet Chapel, of Avon, by whom he had two children, Charles F. and Ella.   His second wife was Eunice, daughter of Ezra and Marietta Sherwood, of Avon, and their children were William M. and John G.   His widow still resides on the home farm in Batavia.   William M. Torrance married Isabella Harris, November 13, 1889.   Ella Torrance married William Andrew Martin, of Batavia, December 11, 1889.   John G. married Lulu Burke, of Alexander, September 12, 1889.   Charles F. is a resident of Portland, Mich.

Henry Uebele was born in Wurtemberg, Germany, where he lived, and died about 1866, aged 60 years.   He married Sophia Elba, of Wurtemberg, and they had one son, Jacob L., who was born in Germany, July 17, 1833, and came to Batavia in March, 1855, at the age of 22 years. He married Elizabeth Burckhardt, of Germany, daughter of Jacob Burckhardt, and their children are William C., Ida E., and Lewis A.   The latter was for sometime the valuable assistant in the Purdy and Parker houses. Jacob L. Uebele built a handsome brick block on the north side of Main street in 1886, known as the Uebele block, and is the proprietor of the bakery in the same building.

Underhill & Bean, dealers in ready-made clothing and gents' furnishing goods, opened their store March 27, 1889. They carry a full line of choice goods, making a specialty of fine ready-made clothing. They are located at No. 88 Main street.

Union Coal Co. was established in May, 1883, by J. B. Chaddock. It was conducted by him until 1885, when Ferrin Brothers rented the yard and carried on the business one year. The Union Coal Co. (J. H. Tanner and Sarah F. Lincoln) bought the stock in 1889, and August 5th of the same year George F. Weaver & Co. purchased the business. They handle 3,500 tons of coal a year. Their yard is at 28 Swan street.

William E. Webster, attorney at law, a native of Ontario County, born in 1859, was educated at Canandaigua Academy, and in 1879 became a teacher at Cary Seminary, where he remained three years. Deciding upon the profession of law he entered upon a course of study in the office of William C. Watson, and was admitted to the bar in January, 1883. He commenced practice in company with William Tyrrell, continuing two years. He was in the West one year, and returned to Batavia, where he is building up a successful practice. He was married, in 1886, to Miss Jennie Ward, of this county.

N. A. Woodward was born in Vermont and came to this State in 1834. He prepared for college at Canandaigua Academy under Dr. Howe, graduated from Union College in 1845, and taught school at Honeoye Falls and Geneseo Academy. He read law in the meantime, and was admitted to the bar in 1848, after which he taught school three years at Scottsville. In December, 1851, he came to Batavia and opened a law office. He was a partner with George Bowen for four years, and with H. F. Tarbox a few years. He has held the offices of town superintendent of schools, loan commissioner five or six years, and county treasurer two terms, during the war. Mr. Woodward has been twice married. He has two daughters and two sons. He was the active attorney for defendant in the great Lent litigation, which was in the courts for several years, and won the case.

Ward Beecher Whitcomb, M. D., is one of the progressive and rising young physicians of Western New York. He is a native of Windham County, Vt., and was born in 1858. He commenced the study of med-

latter was for sometime the valuable assistant in the Purdy and Parker houses.   Jacob L. Uebele built a handsome brick block on the north side of Main street in 1886, known as the Uebele block, and is the proprietor of th

l   ...ing and gents' furnishing   They carry a full line
of c   ..... made clothing.   They
are

U.   ..y, 1883, by ; B Chaddock.   It
was   ..... Brothers rented the yard
and   . Union Co ii Co. (J. H. Tanner   .. 1889, and August 5th of
the same   .... the business.   They
handle   it 28 Swan street.

William Webste   native of Ontario County, born
in 18 , was educate   ...demy, nd in 1879 became a
teach of ary Sch   .. three years.   Deciding
upon the profession   .. course of study in the office William W.   ., the bar in January, 1883.
He   commence   William Tyrrell, continuing
two years   year, and returned to Batavia,
whei   ..tice. He was married, in 1886,
to M

N   ... came to this State in 1834.
He   ... J   y under Dr. Howe. graduate   .. .. hool at Honeoye Falls
and   .. the meantime, and was admitted t   ..ght school three years at Scottsville.   .. Batav.. . opened a law office.
He   ..wen for   years, and with H. F.
Tarb   ..   town superintendent of
scho   ommiss   .. ..ty treasurer two
term   .. twice married   He
has t   .. attorney for defendant i   ic   ..ats   several years,
and

W.   ...ce and rising
youn   n   .... of Windham
Coun   .... study of med-

Edward C. Walker

icine with Dr. Tozier, and under his excellent tutelage and care remained four years. He graduated from the medical department of the University of New York in 1881, since which time he has practiced in Batavia, a small portion of the time with Dr. Tozier. He has in a short period established a large practice and secured the confidence of all who know him. He is untiring in the advancement of his chosen profession. Dr. Whitcomb is an Episcopalian and a member of the K. of P. He married Miss Eagar, of Batavia.

Hon. Edward C. Walker, son of Cyrus, was born in Byron, June 14, 1837. His grandfather, Amasa Walker, who was born in Ashford, Conn., in 1767, came to Byron with his family in 1811, when Cyrus was but 12 years of age. Genesee County at this time was mainly a dense and heavy forest. Here this hardy pioneer located, and by thrift and industry a good home was secured in the new Genesee country. Their unmistakable English ancestry can be clearly traced to Plymouth Colony, Mass., and is distinguished for strength of mind, high aims and purposes, industry, and unyielding perseverance. Cyrus Walker united in marriage with Anna Hulette, of Byron, in December, 1822. They were industrious, economical, hardy, possessed sound judgment, sterling integrity, and were very successful.

Senator E. C. Walker, their fifth and youngest child, was a studious youth, and fortunately had the very best early advantages to acquire a thorough literary and business education, which he wisely improved. At an early age Mr. Walker was a student at the Cary Seminary of Oakfield, and later pursued his studies at Wilson Academy, Niagara County, and graduated in June, 1861, at Genesee College, in Lima, N. Y., now Syracuse University. He studied law and was admitted to the bar in 1862. His large and varied business interests have demanded a great portion of his time, and left but little for the practice of his profession. He has been an extensive traveler through both America and foreign countries. Senator Walker has been a citizen of Batavia since 1862, and has been active in promoting the general interest and improvements of the town. He has responded nobly to the cause of benevolence and charity, and is especially generous to home and foreign missions. He has served some years as trustee of the New York Institution for the Blind at Batavia, and trustee of Syracuse University; is now a trustee of Ingham University at Le Roy, and of the Y. M. C. A. of Batavia. He has also been commissioner of Auburn Theological Seminary. Later he was a delegate to the General Assembly of the Presbyterian Church of the United States. He has been a director of the Bank of Batavia most of the time since 1870, and was also a director of the Holland Purchase Fire Insurance Company. His political life began with his election to the Assembly of the State of New York in 1868, which position he held two years, and was chairman of the important committee of public education, which reported many bills that became laws that improved the State system of public instruction. In 1885 he was elected State Senator from the 30th senatorial district, composed of the counties of Genesee, Livingston, Niagara, and Wyoming. He was honorably recognized by being appointed chairman of the important committees of banks and the manufacture of salt, and was also a member of the committees of railroads, insurance, and engrossed bills. He was reëlected in 1887 by an increased plurality of 859 over the previous election in 1885. In the last Senate (1889) he was chairman of the committee on railroads, a member of the committee on general laws, and of several others. It also fell to the lot of Senator Walker to be placed on the committee to investigate the corrupt ring that procured the franchise of the Broadway Surface Railway Company of the city of New York. This committee did good work. In doing their whole duty they built for themselves a monument for integrity and virtue that will endure in history when granite and marble will have crumbled to dust. The committee relentlessly pursued and shattered the corrupt ring, exposed the gigantic fraud, and brought the guilty perpetrators to condign punishment.

As a legislator Senator Walker is industrious, and his object is always " the best interests of the people." Among the bills that he introduced which became laws were a number improving the banking system of the State; the motor power bill, authorizing street service railroads to change from horse to any other power, after obtaining the consent of the majority of the property owners along the line of the roads, and the consent of the railroad commissioners ; and the bill which prevents assignees from giving to preferred creditors more than one third of the estate. He also introduced the marriage license bill, which would prevent ill-timed marriages, protect the clergy, and provide a more perfect record for tracing the estates of children. This bill passed the Senate twice, and it is hoped that the day is not far distant when it will become a law in this State. For this Mr. Walker has received complimentary letters from Bishop Doane and other prominent clergymen, and also from prominent judges and attorneys throughout the State, who appreciate the importance of such a law. Senator Walker is known throughout his State, and is highly respected as a gentleman of sterling integrity, and as a safe and careful law-maker. He is a good organizer, and a forcible and logical speaker who goes direct to the issue and "hews to the line." In January, 1890, he was selected by the Hon. William Windom, Secretary of the Treasury, one of three commissioners to locate the government and postoffice building at Buffalo. He wears his honors modestly, which his character and mind richly deserve ; and as a Christian gentleman and representative man he is widely known and highly respected.

January 14, 1861, he was united in marriage with Martha Marsh, of Lockport, N. Y., a highly cultivated lady of a cultivated family, and a sister of the eminent scientist, Prof. O. C. Marsh, of Yale College. Mr. and Mrs. Walker are parents of two sons, Edward C., Jr., and Raymond Marsh. This Christian family are members of the Presbyterian Church.

James M. Walkinshaw, a popular druggist and baker, is a native of Batavia, and was born in 1840, a son of James and Isabella (Pattison) Walkinshaw, natives of Scotland, who came to America in 1839. They located in Batavia, where he pursued his trade as a baker until his death in 1851. He was employed by B. C. Page, who started the bakery now owned by Baker & Walkinshaw, in 1835. James M. learned the trade, and in 1869, with Lucius Baker, purchased the business, and they have conducted it since under the firm name of Baker & Walkinshaw. In 1874 Mr. Walkinshaw added to his business interests a full line of drugs, medicines, and fancy toilet goods, and in this branch has secured a large trade. The prescription department is under the charge of a competent pharmacist. His place of business, at 63 East Main street, is central and attractive. Mr. Walkinshaw has served as alderman from his ward, and as chief engineer of the fire department. He was married, in 1861, to Martha Winn, of Batavia. Their only child, Onis, is deceased.

William C. Watson is a gentleman of fine physique and commanding presence. His life has been that of a leader, and his face bears the impression of his character. He has gone down to the very substratum of the principles of the law, and his opinion has almost judicial weight. The year 1837 marked the opening of his career in the little village of Pembroke, in Genesee County. He is not a college-trained man. His early opportunities were limited. His father tried cases in justices' courts, and from him the son imbibed a love for the profession. A short period was spent at the seminary at Alexander, and Col. James M. Willett gave him a start in law study. Next he is found in the office of Wakeman & Bryan, and in 1865 he was admitted to the bar. He practiced for a short time with Mr. Tyrrell and later with Hon. Seth Wakeman. For some 15 years he

has done business alone. Mr. Watson was the only Republican supervisor elected in many years. He was twice district attorney, and in 1882
was candidate for member of Congress. He frequently goes to State
conventions. Mr. Watson has been on the board of education a number
of times, and has contributed largely to manufacturing industries
locating in Batavia. His family consists of a wife and three children.

Simeon Wheeler was a colonel in the Revolutionary war from Massachusetts. One of his sons, George, was born in Rehoboth, Mass.,
November 4, 1815, was educated in the public schools, and came with
his parents to Monroe County, N. Y., when he was seven years old, and
to Genesee County when he was 20. February 18, 1838, he married
Hannah S., second daughter of George Burton, of Byron, and they had
one son, George H., who was born March 14, 1841, and received a common
school and academic education. March 22, 1866, he married Lovina,
third daughter of John Fishill, of Rush, Monroe County, and they had
one daughter. August 8, 1862, he enlisted in Co. K, 12th Inf. N. Y.
Vols.; March 8, 1863, he was transferred to the 5th Vet. Fire Zouaves,
N. Y. Vols.; and was honorably discharged May 7, 1865. Mr. Wheeler
is a breeder of Royal George horses, and is a farmer by occupation.

Whiting C. Woolsey, president of the village of Batavia, was born in
1834. His parents were Whiting R. and Alvalina (Post) Woolsey, the
former a native of Columbia County. The mother was born in Batavia
in 1811, and her parents were early settlers of the town, about 1803.
She is still living. The father, a farmer for 50 years, died in 1884, aged
81 years. Three of the children are living, viz.: Henry H., Martha, and
Whiting C. The latter when a young man went to Galena, Ill., and
learned the trade of carpenter and builder, which occupation he has since
pursued. He is the proprietor of the limekiln and stone quarries on
road 13, in the north part of the town. In 1862 he enlisted and served
as private in the 96th Ill. Regt. In 1863 he returned to Batavia, where
he has since been engaged in business. He served on the board of trustees, and was elected president of the village in 1888–89. He is a member of the I. O. O. F. and commander of Upton Post G. A. R. In 1852
he was united in marriage with Sarah E. Worth, of Oakfield. They
have one daughter, Mrs. Martha E. Nobles.

David E. Wescott, a native of Massachusetts, moved to Monroe,
Mich., and died in 1867, aged 68 years. He married Thyrza, daughter
of John and Deborah A. Bird, of Manchester, N. Y., and their children
are Jane, Deborah A., E. Myra, Eliza, Elizabeth, Laura, Helen, and

James R. The latter was born in Manchester, March 5, 1824. He married Mary Ann, daughter of William and Charity (Cook) Hickey, of Arcadia, and their children are George E., Lucy J., Hattie A., and Margaret E. Mr. Wescott lives in Batavia on road 13.

Theron F. Woodward, proprietor of the old and reliable boot and shoe store, for the past 18 years at 74 Main street, is a native of Orleans County, where he was born 1838, a son of Rev. Franklin and Elizabeth (Ross) Woodward. His father was a Baptist clergyman and organized the first church at Fairport, N. Y., where he was pastor until his death. Mr. Woodward was reared in Fairport, was a clerk in a dry goods store, and at the age of 21 years engaged with his brother-in-law in the coal and lumber business. Afterwards, and until 1867, he was engaged in the manufacture of staves and headings. He then came to Batavia and bought the stock of Thomas Yates, and has since been in the boot and shoe trade. He carries a large line of goods. He has been a member of the board of trustees, was treasurer for a number of years, and is a trustee of the Loan Association and of Elmwood Cemetery. He married n 1865, Emma C. Adams, of Riga, N. Y., daughter of Asa Adams, and they have three children, Grace E., Louis A., and Mabel E. The family are members of the Presbyterian Church.

Frank S. Wood, the present district attorney for Genesee County, was born in Detroit, Mich., September 14, 1856. His father was for a long time in the employ of an express company. Mr. Wood came to this county with his parents from Detroit in 1859, and became a resident of the village in April, 1864. His tastes and inclinations caused him to prepare for the study of law, in which pursuit he has been engaged since January, 1877, when he became the clerk of the surrogate's court in Batavia, remaining there until 1883, when he engaged in the active practice of his profession, following the same ever since. In 1887 he was nominated and elected to the office of district attorney for the county, giving such satisfaction that at the end of the term he was again elected to serve until 1893. September 4, 1884, he united in marriage with Harriet G. Holden, of Batavia.

Joseph Weed, of Cheshire County, N. H., died at the age of 40 years. His wife, Susan Farnsworth, bore him children as follows: Sally, Abigail, Susan, James, Elijah, and Joseph. The latter, a native of New Hampshire, served in the War of 1812, and came to Kendall, N. Y., in 1816, thence to Batavia, where he died in 1862, at the age of 80 years. He married Polly, daughter of Benjamin Clough. She died in 1877, aged

93 years. Their children were Joseph, Willis, Johanna, Sally, Mary, and Harvey. Harvey Weed was born in Kendall in 1817. In 1843 he came to Batavia and married Sarah B. Sawdey, daughter of Henry and Rhoda, of this town. He has been a resident on the home farm since 1843. His sister Mary resides with him.

Daniel Wood, son of Ephraim a Revolutionary soldier, was born in 1760, and died in 1844, at the age of 84 years. He married Hannah Barrett, and their children were James, Ephraim, Mary, Elijah, Milly, and William. Elijah Wood was born in Concord, Mass., September 18, 1790, and died there November 26, 1861, aged 71 years. He married Elizabeth Farmer in September, 1815. Their children were Elijah, John, Augustus, William, Henry, Charles, George, and Edward F. · The last named was born in Concord, Mass., November 26, 1821, and came to Batavia in 1859, settling on a farm, where he remained four years. He is now a resident of Batavia village. He married Mary, daughter of Ezekiel N. and Mary (Bryan) Humphrey, of Hillsdale, Mich., and his children are Charles E., Edward, William, Frank S., George F, Mary E., John H., Augustus, and Robert E. He lived 12 years in Detroit, and was one of the first four men who had charge of the United States mail to Chicago.

Matthias Whiting, a native of Massachusetts, moved to Fort Ann, N. Y., and died in 1846, aged 96 years. He married a Miss Vaughn, of Massachusetts, and their children were Willard, Sarah, Sylvester, Lucy, John, Matthias, Susan, Silas D., Laura, and Mary. Sylvester, born in Hancock, Mass., came to Riga, thence to Oakfield in 1815, and died there in 1856, aged 70 years. He married Laura, daughter of Joel and Rachel (Moss) Yale, of Granville, N. Y. His children were Mary Almira, Celestia, Laura, Matilda, Silas, Nelson, and Sylvester. The latter was born in Fort Ann, February 13, 1813, and in 1831 settled in Batavia, where he now resides, on road 30. Only three of his children survive. Nelson Whiting, a native of Riga, married Ellen F. Miller, daughter of George W. Miller, of Batavia, and they have one son, George M.

George D. Williamson, proprietor of the leading furniture manufactory and salesrooms in Genesee County, is a native of Wayne County, where he was born in 1856. His parents were W. H. and Anna (Cottrell) Williamson, also natives of Genesee County. Mr. Williamson has been engaged in business since his youth; in 1887 he came to Batavia, and was of the firm of Weeks & Williamson for one year. He then pur chased the entire interest, and is now successfully conducting the same. His salesrooms and factory are at 111 East Main street, where he occupies three floors, with a fine display of furniture and house furnishing goods. The factory is located in the rear, where several men are employed. Mr. Williamson devotes special attention to undertaking. In 1879 he was united in marriage with Emma E. Hine, of Palmyra, and they are parents of two. children, May A. and Roy H. They are members of the Methodist Episcopal Church.

C. A. Weaver, of 104 Main street, commenced business January 1, 1889, where he was clerk for two years previous. He now carries a full line of boots, shoes, and rubbers.

Frank Wagner was born in Wurtemberg, Germany, September 16, 1828, and came to the United States in 1854. In May, 1856, he married Catherine Myers, formerly of Byrnes, Germany. They have five children, viż.: Louisa, Charles, Emogene, Mary, and Henry. August 11, 1862, he enlisted in Co. C, 151st Inf. N. Y. Vols., and was honorably discharged at the close of the war.

William Ward was a native of Merton, Devonshire, Eng. By his wife, Ann, he had children as follows : John, Thomas, Hugh, and William. The latter came to Stafford in 1854, was a blacksmith, and died in 1854. He married Ann Horden, of Barnstable, Eng., and their children were John, Richard, Thomas, Sarah, Elizabeth, Ann, and William. William Ward, a native of Merton, in 1851 came to Stafford, and in 1888 to Batavia. He married Eliza, daughter of Francis and Sarah (Rice) Broadmead, of England, and they have an adopted daughter, Eliza A. Ward, who married Augustus Hammer, and now resides on road 65. Mr. Ward is a farmer, but was formerly a blacksmith.

Sylvanus Young, of German ancestry, came from Chenango County, N. Y., to Pavilion in 1811. He removed to Michigan, where he died, aged 70 years. His wife was Ruth Burgess, who bore him children as follows: Almira, Josiah, Lucy, Rachel, Sylvanus, Melissa, William, Henry, and Clarissa. William, born in Pavilion, came to Batavia in 1860, where he still resides. He married, January 20, 1847, Betsey, daughter of John and Clarissa (Sparks) Moore, of Massachusetts. Their children are John E. and William H. John E. married Clara L. Calkins, and they have a daughter, Edith. William H. married Harriet C., daughter of Nathaniel K. and Adeline (Brewer) Cone, and their children are Ruth A. and Hobart Cone, all residents of Batavia, on road 65.

The name of John H. Yates, for the past few years, has appeared in connection with a class of homely, popular ballads, which fairly entitles him to a prominent place among American poets. He was born November 21, 1837. He is a native of Batavia, of English parentage, and therefore possesses the simplicity of manners common to that class of people. His mother was a schoolmistress, and from her he inherited his literary taste. His education was not very extensive, taking in only the common English branches, and much of his time since early boyhood has been spent as clerk, yet he is well informed on general subjects, and does good service as licensed preacher of the Methodist Church, of which he is a member. His active work as assistant editor of the *Progressive Batavian*, with which he has been connected for four years, brings him in contact with all classes of men, the better fitting him for the exercise of his excellent taste in subjects for poetry. He has written for the Rochester *Sunday Morning Times*, the *Batavian*, *Harper's Weekly*, and *Harper's Bazaar*, and his " Old Man Ballads" (as they are called), " The Old Man in the New Church," " The Old Man in the Stylish Church," " The Old Man in the Model Church," and " Goin' West to Die " will ever appeal to the finer feelings and sympathies of all who inherit the love and respect of the aged.

Park Place School.[1]—Among the leavening influences of the village of Batavia, and, in fact, of the county, must be prominently included the Park Place School, whose incipient steps were so faithfully watched and cared for by its founder, Mrs. Ellen A. K. Hooker, who has so happily impressed her influence on all its pupils and students whose good fortune it has been to be under her guidance; and who now is in charge of the lady students of Cornell University; and to whom, being so prominently connected with Sage College as principal, those interested in the higher education of women look with great confidence. The school was founded September 11, 1884, and was organized with a college graduate in each position in its faculty; and its design was to prepare young ladies for entrance into the most advanced colleges for ladies in the country. It is now presided over by Miss Mary J. Stephens, who maintains its high standing, and who is a lady of culture and refinement.

---

[1] This article was furnished us too late to be printed earlier in the history of Batavia.—*Editor.*

BERGEN.

BERGEN is situated in the northeastern part of the county, is the eastern town of the northern tier, and contains 17,289 acres of land. It is a portion of the triangular tract, described as sold to Le Roy and others from the Morris Reserve; it also has two tiers of lots from the Connecticut tract, on the west side of the town. The town was erected from Batavia, June 8, 1812, then including the present town of Byron, which was set off in 1820, leaving Bergen in its present form.

The soil is a very rich, fertile, and level farming land, with slight undulations and inclinations towards the north, and is gravelly with clayey loam. Black Creek flows easterly through the town, just north of the center, which, with its tributaries flowing from every direction, renders the entire territory of the town a well-watered, desirable section, and to its abundance, excellence may be added. Its agricultural interests excel, because of its advantages, and wheat, barley, beans, and potatoes are its main products in the order named.

The first settler in the town was Samuel Lincoln, who took articles for land in 1801. In the same year Mr. Lincoln received the following neighbors: George and William Letson, Benajah Worden, Richard Abbey, Solomon Levi, Jesse Leach, James Letson, Gideon Elliott, and David Scott. These were the pioneers who first built cabins and made clearings in the town. Between 1801 and 1810 the following pioneers settled: John Landon, Abram Davis, Alexander White, Captain James Austin. David Potter, Esq., Levi, Aaron, and Alexander Bissell, Amos Hewitt, Jedediah Crosby (died in 1834), Samuel Gleason, Esq., Captain William Peters, Aaron and Eben Arnold, Oliver Avery, Samuel Butler, Jesse Barber, John Gifford, Wheaton Southworth, Orange and Joseph Throop, Isaac Wallace, James Landon, and A. E. Wilcox. The following actual settlers came to Bergen between 1806 and 1810 from East Guilford, Conn.: Dea. Benjamin Wright, James Munger, Esq., Joarab and Wickham Field, Dea. Timothy Hill, Joel Wright, Stephen R. Evarts, David H. Evarts, Capt. Phineas Parmelee, Nathan Field, Uriah Crampton, Capt. Samuel Bassett, Selah M. Wright, Bela Munger, T. Wilcox, William H. Munger, Harvey Field, Joshua Field, Esq., Dea. Levi Ward, Dea. John Ward, Dr. Levi Ward, Col. W. H. Ward, Dea. Pitman Wilcox, Hamilton Wilcox, M. C. Ward, and Gen. Daniel Hurlburt.

Those who came from Killingworth, Conn., prior to 1810 settled between Bergen Corners and Fort Hill. They were Josiah Pierson and his five brothers,—Simeon, John, Philo, Linus, and Russell,—David Franklin and his four brothers,—Ishi, Sylvanus, Daniel, and Reuben,— Harvey Kelsey, Capt. Daniel Kelsey, Uriah, Martin, and Charles Kelsey, Josiah Buell, Jesse Griswold, Thomas Stevens, Daniel Stevens, Job

21

Seward, Abner Hull, Sr., Ebbie Hull, Roswell and Ebenezer Parmelee, Samuel and John Smith, Phineas Nettleton, Maj. Nathan Wilcox, Dea. Selden, Augustus Buell, Jonathan Wright, and Calvin Seward. Others, in 1814–16, were William Gorton, Willian P. Munger, Alvah Stevens, and Lathrop Farnham. Lines Beecher settled in West Bergen in 1816.

The first church organization was established in December, 1807. The first Congregational religious society was organized January 25, 1808, at the house of Dea. John Ward. The first temperance society was established in 1826, with only six members—Rev. Josiah Pierson, Rev. Heman Halsey, Dea. Pitman Wilcox, Dea. John Spencer, H. H. Evarts, and Henry D. Gifford. The first religious meeting on the Sabbath was at the log house of David Franklin, and the first sermon preached in the town was in Mr. Franklin's barn by Rev. Calvin Ingalls, a missionary. The first school was taught by Harvey Kelsey, a graduate of Yale College. Titus Wilcox taught the second school, and Joshua Field the third. Chloe Wright, daughter of Dea. Benjamin Wright, was the first female teacher, Lucy Hill was the second, and Betsey Pierson was the third. The first marriage was that of Isaac Wallace and Susannah Brooks, at the house of Dr. Levi Ward, and by Judge Ezra Platt, of Le Roy. Luther, son of Jedediah Crosby, was the first male child born in the town. The first female born was Louisa, daughter of Orange Throop, who became the wife of David Fancher. The first death was the child of Capt. Daniel Kelsey; the first death of an adult was Mr. Kelsey's wife, both dying the same year. The first frame house in the town was erected by Dr. Levi Ward, the second by Dea. Benjamin Wright. The first frame barn was built by David Franklin, the second by Dea. Wright. The first saw-mill in the town was erected by Jared Merrill, the second by Levi Bissell The first store in Bergen was opened in 1808, by Dr. Levi Ward; the second in 1811, by Josiah Pierson; the third in 1812, by Titus Wilcox. The first inn opened in the town was in 1809, by Samuel Butler, and the first postmaster was Col. W. H. Ward. The first supervisor was Dr. Levi Ward, who held the office seven years. He died January 4, 1861, in his 90th year. The first road was opened in 1801, when the Lake road was surveyed and opened four rods wide from Le Roy to the lake. This road is now a very important one, upon which is the stone church, and is the principal street of Bergen village.

Hamilton Wilcox came to the town in 1808 from East Guilford, Conn. He taught school here at the age of 16, and was a successful teacher. When the call for troops was made in the winter of 1813–14 he left his school to take command of a company, to report at Buffalo, where he was when that "village" was burned. He was ordered to Black Rock in the night of December 30, 1813, as the enemy were crossing the river at that point. In the affray he received a bullet through his chest, lodging in his arm. Several days after he was brought back to Bergen. It was soon necessary to amputate his arm, from which he died January 25, 1814, aged 28 years.

This town has been devoted to the cause of religion, and can point with pride to 12 of its citizens who have been leaders of flocks in the cause of the Master. They are Revs. Josiah Pierson, A. C. Ward, F. De Ward, H. M. Ward, William H. Spencer, H. W. Pierson, D. D. H. Parmelee, Bela Fancher, Franklin Howe, William H. Evarts, C. Dibble, and W. Pierson.

Solomon and Levi Leach, brothers, whose names are among the early settlers, traded wives, Levi giving Solomon five gallons of whisky "to boot." In two weeks, being sick of his bargain, he gave Levi a horse to trade back. It is just to presume that the whisky in those "hard" days was the great incentive to this unusual occurrence.

Bergen's town officers for 1889–90 are: Supervisor, Samuel E. Bower; town clerk, E. L. Fisher; justices of peace, J. W. Stratton, S. E. Parker, J. Dean, E. H. Parmelee; commissioner of highways, A. A. Sands; collector, George W. Sackett; overseer of poor, M. Seeley; assessors, D. McPherson, E. T. Stephens, James Templeton.

The Presbyterian Church at North Bergen was organized November 18, 1823, by the following persons, who assembled at the home of Jonah Gurthrie: Rev. A. Darwin, Josiah Pierson, John T. Bliss, and David Fancher. It was denominated the Congregational Church of Bergen, Byron, and Clarendon. Its original membership was 21, and at a meeting held April 11, 1827, at the stone school-house, it was resolved to become a Presbyterian society and unite with the Rochester Presbytery. D. Fancher, Milton Bird, Thomas Templeton, and Daniel Robinson were elected the first ruling elders, and Milton Bird was ordained deacon. The first regular pastor was Rev. N. Clapp, who was ordained and installed February 25, 1827. On the 2d of April, 1829, the society was called after the postoffice of that time,—Lyme,— but in 1840 with the postoffice the name of North Bergen was appended to its religious title. In 1832 a framed church edifice was erected, neat and commodious, with a seating capacity of about 250, at a cost of nearly $10,000. The society numbers over 100 members, and Rev. Lindsey C. Rutter was the pastor as late as 1887. Rev. John R. Lewis is the present pastor.

NORTH BERGEN is a postoffice in the northwest corner of the town, containing a church, a store, two manufactories, and about 150 inhabitants.

STONE CHURCH (p. o.) is in the southeastern portion of the town, on the Lake road, in direct line with Le Roy and Bergen villages. Good postoffice facilities are enjoyed by its inhabitants, who number about fourscore, and it contains one church, one store, and one manufactory. In 1828 Col. Norton S. Davis built a stone tavern, and kept it for some time.

WEST BERGEN is still another postoffice in the west part of the town, on the Central Railroad, and has a store and shop, with a good community around it.

The Cold Spring Creamery, on road 8, is owned by a stock company, and managed by B. A. Walker. It uses the cream from 900 cows, making 400 pounds of butter per day in summer, which is sold in Buffalo, Rochester, and New York.

BERGEN is a pretty, flourishing, incorporated village, pleasantly situated on the N. Y. C. & H. R. Railroad between Rochester and Buffalo, and is the principal village in the town, with a population of about 1,000 —a trifle more than one-third of the town. It contains four churches, two hotels, 14 stores, one machine shop, two grain elevators, eight manufactories of different kinds, three blacksmith shops, one saw and planing-mill, two feed-mills, etc., and is one of the most healthy and pleasant hamlets of Western New York, enjoying all the facilities of daily mails and the advantages of the best of thoroughfares. This village has been unfortunate in being partially burned at two several times—January 16, 1866, and March 1, 1880; the last fire covered an area of five acres in the business portion, consuming elevators, stores, shops, offices, halls, hotel, dwellings, and barns, to the amount of over $120,000. Bert E. Hall, A. L. Green, and George H. Church were severely burned in their endeavors to stay the progress of the fire and save property. The burned district was at once built up with substantial brick buildings, with a vigor and perseverance peculiar to the enterprise of the place, and the pride of the citizens in their neat village is commendable. The Bergen village officers are as follows: George H. Church, president; A. T. Southworth, treasurer; D. J. McPherson, clerk; trustees, T. J. Tone, two years, James Miller, one year, T. D. Richardson, one year. The board of education is composed as follows : George H. Church, president ; L. D. Arnold, H. S. White ; G. N. Buell, collector. The officers of the fire department are : James R. McKenzie, chief engineer; G. O. Emerson, president; M. F. Bergin, vice-president ; D. S. Thompson, secretary; Michael Bower, treasurer; trustees, J. J. Snyder, D. A. Ide, James Whalen. Bergen Hose Company No. 1, 10 men, headquarters in Buell block : E. C. Snyder, foreman ; E. D. Snyder, assistant foreman; equipments, hose cart and 400 feet hose. Bergen Engine Company No. 1, 30 men, headquarters in Buell block: Irving Ide, foreman ; G. W. Sackett, assistant foreman ; equipment, hand engine. The postoffice is located in the Southworth block on Lake street. M. H. Parmelee is the postmaster. He was appointed under the present administration and took charge of the office June 10, 1889. E. H. Parmelee is assistant postmaster and W. G. Woodworth, clerk.

The First Congregational Church of Bergen was organized in December, 1807, by Rev. John Lindsley and 13 others. At this time Bergen was Northampton. Levi Ward, Sr., and Benjamin Wright were the first deacons, and Levi Ward, Jr., the first clerk. The present church organization was perfected January 25, 1808, by the following persons, at the house of John Ward: Alexander White, John Gifford, Levi Ward, Sr., Benjamin Wright, Josiah Pierson, Simon Pierson, John Ward, Selah Wright, W. H. Munger, and Levi Ward, Jr. The first trustees were Alexander White, Simon Pierson, and Levi Ward, Jr. This church, excepting a Scotch church at Caledonia, is the oldest one west of the Genesee River. Rev. Allen Hollister was its first ordained minister, and was installed July 4, 1810. The church edifice was first situated on Cemetery

Hill, one mile south of its present location, where it was removed in the spring of 1854 Rev. A. O. Whiteman was pastor at the time of its removal. Although a Congregational Church strictly, it placed itself in the Presbytery on the accommodation plan soon after its organization, and so it remains to-day. It has a fine frame building that seats about 400 people, and its property is worth $10,000. It has never had missionary aid in support of its ministry. Its present pastor is Rev. J. R. Lewis.

The Second Congregational Church of Le Roy and Bergen is in the southeast part of Bergen, which has originated the postoffice " Stone Church " in the town. Sixteen persons in 1828, March 18th, met and organized the society. They chose S. Dibble and J. Ward, deacons, and Russell Pierson, David Byam, and Luther C. Pierson as assistants, and the five were to be a standing committee. Quite a number from the First Congregational Church united with this society by letter early in its existence. On September 24, 1828, a stone edifice was erected, which has perpetuated the name "Stone Church" to the present time, although in 1864 a fine frame edifice was built upon the site, which was dedicated in 1865. The first pastor was Rev. Elisha Mason, who accepted the call October 20, 1828. The church property is worth $4,000, its seating capacity about 250, and its membership about 65.

The First Roman Catholic Church of Bergen was erected in 1859. An organization had been effected prior to that date (about 1850), and meetings held from house to house. Rev. Father McGowan was mainly instrumental in the erection of the church, and for several years had the pastoral charge of the society. It is under the diocese of Buffalo, Bishop Ryan presiding. In 1883 the old church was torn down and the present edifice, more commodious and better, was erected, under the supervision of Father Maloy. It has a seating capacity of 400, cost $7,000, and is a fine frame edifice. It has not had a resident pastor during all these years, until Father O'Riley came in 1886. He was there 15 months. The Rev. Father H. H. Connery came in September, 1888, and now presides over the spiritual wants of the parish. He was born May 15, 1853, in County Derry, Ireland, and came to America July 22, 1875. He was educated at the Seminary of our Lady of the Angels, and placed in charge of the parish at Limestone, N. Y. He was there two years, at East Pembroke two years, and at Rexville, Steuben County, three years.

In June, 1872, a mission was organized in 'this town by Rev. E. L. Wilson, holding services in the M. E. Church and in David Hooper's hall. In March, 1874, Mrs. Cynthia L. Richmond presented the trustees of the parochial fund of the diocese a deed of lot No. 65, as a memorial gift to her late husband, upon which the ceremony of laying the corner-stone was held June 6, 1874, by the Rt. Rev. Bishop Coxe, who conducted the dedicatory services January 6, 1875. The building, which was consecrated June 15, 1880, is a frame one, with a seating capacity of about 200. The society is small, and is supplied by Rev. A. A.

Brockway, of Attica, N. Y.   It is called St. John's Church, and is situated on Rochester street.   They have no settled rector.

The First Methodist Episcopal Church was organized April 5, 1831. The records of the society show that Rev. Reeder Smith founded a society prior to this date, which was called the "First Society of the M. E. Church of Bergen." A small plat of land, located on lot 120, in the town of Le Roy, on the 100,000-acre tract, was deeded to the society. It is said that the society was born in a revival meeting by itinerants, and was made part of the Scottsville circuit.   The first place of worship was at the stone school-house, Bergen Corners, but the meetings were changed to the town-line school-house.   A profitable season of meetings gave courage to build a church, and in 1838 an edifice, costing $1,000, was erected.   In 1853 the society removed to the present site the former edifice, and beautified and enlarged it at a cost of over $2,000.   In 1873 the society numbered 45 members and was a part of the Churchville circuit, but under the labors of Rev. T. E. Bell the membership in that year was swelled to 118 and 60 probationers, and a separate existence was created.   In 1876 a parsonage was erected at a cost of $1,500, and August 3, 1882, the present elegant brick edifice, built in gothic style, was dedicated, with Rev. J. B. Countryman, pastor.   Its value in dollars is at least $10,000, seating capacity 400, and the membership on January 1, 1887, was 132.   It has two endowments—the Doolittle fund of $500, and that of Wickham Fields of 17 acres of his town-line farm. The present pastor is Rev. J. A. Smith.   The Sunday-school numbers 200 members.

Wardville Lodge, No. 198, *I. O. O. F.,*—originally No. 412,—was organized September 19, 1849.   Its founders were Dr. Andrews, Sr., F. T. Moseley, John Norton, E. B. Andrews, and H. S. Andrews.   Fourteen members were initiated at the first regular meeting of the lodge.   It is the oldest of its order in the county, having been sustained for 40 years, and is still strong in its old age.   The first N. G. of this lodge was the elder Robert Andrews, M. D.   Its books, regalia, furniture, etc., were lost in the fire of 1866, and again in the great fire of 1880, when Bergen suffered so greatly, its property was destroyed; still phenix-like, it has flourished, and has not missed any meetings during its adversity.   The elegant rooms are now in the Carpenter block, and nearly 100 members enjoy the benefits of the fraternity.   When the territory of Bergen was a wilderness Levi Ward, one of the pioneers, prepared a map of the land where Bergen is, and purposed to call it "Wardville."   It somehow lost his adopted name as to the town, but it is kept in memoriam by the oldest and most prosperous order of the county.   The lodge has a membership of about 40.   The officers are: E. C. Snyder, N. G.; J. J. Snyder, V. G.; G. W. Grimes, recording secretary; Fred Lewellyn, permanent secretary; N. J. Davis, treasurer.

Bergen Lodge, No. 187, *I. O. of G. T.,* was organized July 18, 1885, by the installment of the following officers: G. W. Parkerson, W. C. T.;

Mrs. Lizzie Murray, W. V. T.; Richard Bassett, W. chaplain; William Gillett, W. secretary; Miss Clara Peck, W. A. secretary; Fremont Peck, W. F. secretary; Miss Stella Butler, W. treasurer; Samuel Bassett, W. marshal; Miss Rena Gordon, W. A. marshal; John Langham, W. O. guard; Bert Sackett, W. I. guard; Miss Ella Fenn, W. R. H. S.; Miss Emma Snyder, W. L. H. S.; Mrs. C. Clothier, P. W. C. T. The number of charter members was 29, and George E. Whittaker was elected lodge deputy for the first year. The lodge has been a very active and successful one, and numbers now nearly 100 members. Its influence for good is felt and respected. The place of meeting is in the Carpenter & McKenzie block.

Wilbur Fuller Post, No. 412, G. A. R., was organized October 13, 1883, with a charter membership of 16. The post occupies a fine suite of rooms in the Carpenter block, over Carpenter & Son's store. The charter members were William H. Randolph, H. C. Matoon, John Byrne, M. McFarlane, Jerry Feathers, William C. Kneale, Isaac Bristol, James A. Miller, Patrick Kerivan, H. W. Thompson, A. L. Preston, Benjamin Coxe, Murray Johnson, A. E. Wilbur, James A. Cooper, and Sidney Richmond. The post is a very strong and flourishing one for its age, and will hold its place with any other in the county. The present officers are as follows: H. F. Fordham, commander; E. M. Wilcox, S. V. C.; E. C. Day, J. V. C.; J. A. Miller, adjutant; J. D. Richard, Q. M.; M. W. Townsend, surgeon; J. T. Crittenden, chaplain; G. E. Wilber, O. D.; M. W. Lyman, O. G.; J. R. Emerson, S. M.; E. Howell, Q. M. S.

Bergen Grange, No. 163, was organized in March, 1873. It had a charter membership of about 18 members. N. C. Johnson was its first master. For a few years they used the Odd Fellows hall. In 1878 they had one of their own, but were burned out at the big fire of 1880. After the Carpenter block was rebuilt they had their lodge room overhead until the fall of 1885, when they sold out to the G. A. R. Since then they have held their meetings at the homes of different members throughout the town. Its present membership is about 60.

The schools of the town are excellent, and 13 teachers are constantly employed in each school year. There are nine districts in the town, with a fine graded school in the village. The Union School building, which was erected in 1868, is located on Rochester street. The school is in a flourishing condition. The average daily attendance is about 140. Four instructors are employed, as follows: E. M. Crocker, principal; Miss Mary J. Russell, second grade; Miss Ella Wood, intermediate; Miss Maud Meyers, primary.

The early settlers were desirous of keeping abreast of the times, and took measures to foster their literary taste by organizing libraries, one such, called "Bergen Moral Library," being organized in 1815.

Doran's cider-mill was built in 1886 by Michael Doran. It is run by steam-power, and has a capacity of 30 barrels of cider per day. It is located on Munger street.

Aaron Arnold, eldest son of Enoch Arnold, of Berkshire County, Mass., was born November 3, 1781. He engaged in farming till of age, when he was a foreman for three years on the turnpike then being constructed between New York and Philadelphia. In 1806 he was married to Eliza, daughter of Amos Allen, of Caanan, Conn. In 1807 he came with his wife to this town—then Northampton—and began farming. He died March 28, 1843, and his wife survived till June 1, 1855. He filled in his day many offices of trust, being supervisor, etc., for a number of years. Three children were the result of the marriage, viz.: Charles G., born August 12, 1809, died April 17, 1841 ; Harriet, born July 18, 1816, married Alson Ostrander, of Poughkeepsie, N. Y., and died April 20, 1853 ; and George W., born July 18, 1822, who is the only survivor. He married Martha G., daughter of Aaron and Harriet Gifford, October 19, 1843, and is a resident of the village. They had one child, who was born February 12, 1848, is a resident of the town, and is a carpenter and joiner by vocation. George W. Arnold has given much attention to stock dealing in connection with his farming, and has been very successful. At the big fire in 1880 he lost nearly all his village property, and indeed has often been a sufferer by fire. Amos Allen, father of Mrs. Aaron Arnold, was a Revolutionary soldier, and at his death, in 1845, was the oldest pensioner in Genesee County.

Robert Andrews, M. D., third son of Robert Andrews, Sr., was born in Wheatland, Monroe County, N. Y., in 1836, and removed to Bergen in 1843 with his father. He received the advantages of a common school education. His father was a physician of large practice, which he retained till one year before his decease, in 1862. Dr. Andrews carried on the practice of his father, as a general practitioner, but has been very successful as a specialist in curing cancers. He is now in the midst of a profitable and wide-spread practice, and is 53 years old. He married Julia A., daughter of Joseph Beardsley, and they have four children now living—Lewis B., Charles H., Fred E., and Robert M. The eldest, Lewis B., is a practicing physician and surgeon. The entire family are members of the First Congregational Church. The second son, Charles H., is a graduate of the Buffalo Medical University, and Fred E. graduated in the classical course of the Brockport Normal School in 1887.

Dea. Ebenezer Arnold, youngest son of Daniel Arnold, came with his parents from East Haddam, Conn., in 1802, to this town—then Northampton and afterwards Ogden. Here the father died in 1813, leaving the Deacon a lad only 12 years old. At the age of 18 he came to Bergen, and purchased the farm now in part owned by James Barr. He purchased the farm now owned by him in 1854. He first married Chloe, daughter of Captain Austin Wilcox, in 1824, who died in 1836, leaving two children, of whom Henry W. is the only one living. In 1839 he married, second, A. Jannette Cushman, by whom four children were born to him, three of whom survive, viz.: Linden D. and Irving R., who reside here, and Rose (Mrs. Nelson F. Holman), of the State of Washington. Mr. Arnold acquired the title of deacon from long years of service as such in the First Congregational Church. In 1882 he was compelled to retire from active life. Linden D. Arnold, the third son of Deacon Arnold, was born in this town, January 16, 1843. He has followed farming from choice, but makes a specialty of stock, notably the breeding of Chester White and Poland China swine. His farm is a fine one of 81 acres, situated on the Lake road one-half mile south of Bergen village ; he also has a farm of 90 acres on the town line road west of the village. On the two farms, during the seasons of 1885–86, he produced 3,950 bushels of wheat and 1,920 bushels of barley. November 5, 1874, he was married to Nellie A., daughter of Abel E. and Elizabeth S. Wilcox, of Bergen, and they have three children, namely : Clara A., born November 14, 1877 ; Percy L., born January 6, 1883 ; and Rose E., born May 25, 1885.

Philo P. Bassett, the youngest son of Samuel and Betsey Bassett, was born in Bergen, August 26, 1834, and at the age of 20 began life for himself, choosing the occupations of carpenter, joiner, and painter, which he followed successfully till 1877. February 25, 1859, he married Harriet W., daughter of William H. and Frances E. Keytes, of Owosso, Mich. In 1877 he commenced the undertaking business in this town, being located then one block south of his present place of business. . Just before the big fire of March 1, 1880, he had removed to the building just south of the Bergen Hotel, and thus escaped The latter part of 1885 he removed his business to the Carpenter & McKenzie block. He deals in funeral furniture, artists' materials, pictures and frames, stationery, etc., and is a funeral director. As an undertaker he is successful and worthily very popular, and his business is largely extended to neighboring towns.

Jacob Baird was a resident of Richmondville, Schoharie County, N. Y., where John Baird was born February 13, 1827. Although reared to farming John learned the art of brickmaking when he attained his majority, and has followed that business the most of the time since. He was two years at Batavia, and made the brick for the Blind Asylum and M. E. Church there. Soon after the fire of 1880 he came to this town and started a brick yard, from which he has furnished brick for all the business places except two hotels, manufacturing in a single year as many as 1,000,000 He is well and favorably known as an upright, reliable dealer. Mr. Baird was married, October 7, 1853, to Agnes Doland, of Rochester, N. Y., and one child, Lydia, was born to them, August 7, 1854, now the wife of Frank Jones, of Darien.

John Bergin, son of Michael Bergin, born in 1837 in Kilkenny, Ireland, came to this country February 5, 1865, and located first at Hartford, Conn. After two years he went to Brooklyn, N. Y., and for one year engaged in the cotton business. He then went to South Amboy, N. J., thence to Genesee County, locating at South Byron, where he spent two years in farming and work for the N. Y. C. & H. R. R. R. In 1870 he removed to

Bergen, and has since made his home here. He is baggagemaster at the Bergen depot. He married Hanorah Welch, of his native country, in 1858, and of their eight children only one is living, a son, M. F. Bergen, born in Ireland, December 10, 1859. Up to 20 years he was employed on a farm, and then began business in this town as proprietor of a first-class restaurant and saloon. He married Mary A., daughter of Philip and Mary Whalen, of this town, January 15, 1884, by whom he has one child, Gregory, born January 2, 1885. In February, 1881, Mr. Bergin opened an extensive grocery and wholesale liquor store, of which he is still the proprietor.

Aaron M. Bissell, the third son of Aaron and Lucinda Bissell, of Hebron, Conn., was born in Bergen, August 10, 1818. He followed farming, carrying on 265 acres of land which he owned, and was a breeder of fine horses and sheep. On April 29, 1845, he married Avis Mitchell, of this town, and died August 24, 1862, leaving, besides his wife, six children, namely: James A., born January 27, 1846; Emily L. (Mrs. John R. Emerson), born October 24, 1847; Franc A. (Mrs. Andrew Gifford), born July 26, 1849; Frederick M., born July 29, 1851; William A., born August 24, 1857; and George A., born September 9, 1859. Frederick M. Bissell, the fourth son of Aaron M., was born in this town and remained on the farm till of age, when he engaged in the occupation of house painting, which he has followed since. He married, April 24, 1872, a daughter of Malden and Rhoda C. Gifford, of Bergen. They had five children, as follows: George R., born August 6, 1873; Carrie A., born August 16, 1875; Clarence G., born January 3, 1880; Earl C., born February 19, 1881; and Bert L., born September 15, 1883. Mr. Bissell is a professor of music, having led the Bergen cornet band for years, and has given instructions upon the violin and cornet, of which he is master. He is also leader of Bissell's orchestra. William A. Bissell, the fifth child of Aaron M. and Avis Bissell, was born here August 24, 1857. He, with George A., his brother, owns 218 acres of land one mile north of Bergen village. They are partners not only in farming, but in the produce and coal business, with warerooms at the West Shore freight house. William A. was married, November 30, 1880, to Nellie, daughter of Alexander and Lois Miller, of Caledonia, N. Y., and they have one daughter, Jennie, born September 15, 1885. One remarkable fact worthy of mention is that 208 acres of the 218 belonging to these brothers was the original homestead taken up by Aaron Bissell in 1807. James A. Bissell, the eldest child of Aaron M., born January 27, 1846, was married, January 8, 1880, to Loretta E., daughter of George and Catherine Wrightmeyer, of Baraboo, Wis. They have one child, Avis M., born July 8, 1883. Mr. Bissell is a farmer, owning a valuable farm of 42 acres just east of the corporation line, and makes a specialty of furnishing fresh milk to the residents of the village.

William A. Bower, eldest son of Michael and C. Caroline Bower, was born in Bergen, October 26, 1855. His grandfather, Jacob Bower, was an old resident and pioneer of Bergen, from Cayuga County, N. Y., and followed farming till his death in 1871. William A. Bower, also a farmer, in 1878 purchased a farm in Byron, where he resided until March 6, 1886, when he removed to Bergen village, into his residence on Buffalo street. He married, November 8, 1876, Florence L., daughter of Andrew Y. and Harriet A. Weeks, of Bergen, and they have three children. Michael Bower, father of William A., was a farmer until 1881, when he removed to Bergen village, on Clinton street, where he now resides.

Benjamin Bower, one of the early settlers, came from Cayuga County to Bergen in 1834. His wife and six children located on the town-line road west of the village. His wife died in August of the same year. Mr. Bower followed farming, renting, until his death September 2, 1864. Three of his children survive him, viz.: Mary Ann (Mrs. Ai S. Chase) of Byron; Susan (Mrs. J. D. Gifford), of North Bergen; and Abner, who lives on the old homestead. The latter was born in Springport, Cayuga County, October 23, 1825. He was three years old when his father came here, and has always remained on the farm. He was married to Mary E. Huff, of Canadice, Ontario County, February 27, 1845. They have had three children, only one of whom is living, Mary A., wife of Chester Adams. She was born in 1845.

Jacob Bower came to this town from Aurelius, Cayuga County, N. Y., in 1833. He located in the western part of the town, on what is known as the "town-line road," and lived there until his death, April 21, 1871. One of his two children was Michael, who was born in Cayuga County, May 19, 1831, and was reared a farmer, following that occupation to the present time. He married, January 1, 1855, Cynthia C. Billings, of Byron, and their three children were William A., born October 26, 1855; Rosanna E., born December 25, 1857; and Charles M., born February 27, 1875. The daughter died April 26, 1875, and his wife February 2, 1878. He married for his second wife Eliza E. Berry, relict of James Berry, by whom he had two children, namely: Ella F., born August 15, 1881, and Joseph L., born July 16, 1886. Mr. Bower still owns the old home farm, but resides in the village, though still actively interested in farming, and has been master of the Bergen Grange for several years.

Samuel Carpenter, the fourth son of James and Sarah Carpenter, was born in Somersetshire, Eng., February 22, 1826, and was one of a family of 13 children,—seven daughters and six sons,—all born in England. Samuel was bound out to the tailor trade when 10 years old, and this is his business at the present time. In December, 1849, he came to America with only $5 in his pocket, but as an expert at his trade he was soon in the employ of James Moore, of Rochester. He moved about some, and came to this county, stopping a short time in Bergen, where he was married to Anna A., daughter of Samuel and Betsey Bassett, November 1, 1851. He then went to Oakfield in the employ of Chamberlain & Parmelee, where in six months he saved up $60, with which he returned to Bergen and "opened shop" for himself. Benjamin Wright assisted him to put in a comfortable stock for those days, and he soon was able to buy out and pay off his interest. After two other partnerships, which lasted about four years, he continued alone till 1863, when he formed a partnership with Wolfe & Bachman, of Rochester, who purchased the Doolittle block of Bergen village. Shipping goods to Canada proved a successful venture and resulted in the accumulation of quite a sum. His stock and the Doolittle block were afterwards carried away in smoke and flames. He at once commenced to rebuild, doing business in the meantime in the building just south of where the Bergen Hotel now stands, and in the autumn of 1866 opened in the new store. After three years he leased to Fisher and Murdock, on a three years' lease, but he had built two other stores, one of which he moved into, and here he was when the big fire of 1880 occurred, which destroyed again all of his real property. In 1880 he built the Carpenter block, and in 1882 built the block occupied by Oathout & Gage as a hardware store. This block, costing $2,800, he gave to his youngest son on his 17th birthday. He has three children, viz.: George A., born March 2, 1852; Carlos N., born August 6, 1859; and Burton W., born October 9, 1866. The elder sons are now in partnership with the father, carrying on an extensive business in ready-made clothing, hats, caps, machines, wall paper, trunks, etc., and keeping about 20 employees in the business. Mr. Carpenter is a model business man, as his beginning in life and present high standing will attest.

Thomas Jefferson Dean was the son of Ephraim Dean, and was born at Mansfield, Conn , July 7. 1800. In early days he learned the blacksmiths' trade, which he followed till two years before his death, which occurred August 5, 1848. May 4, 1824, he married Fanny F. Gurley, of Mansfield, Conn., and came to Genesee County in the spring of 1835, to Pine Hill, in Elba. Here he lived most of the time until he died, leaving seven children, of whom only one is living — Thomas Jasper Dean, born October 29, 1836. The latter learned the shoe trade, which he followed for 10 years, when he engaged in farming and its kindred duties, which suited better his taste. He was in the civil war, enlisting as a private in Co. B, 129th N. Y. V., and was mustered, August 22, 1862, into the U. S. service. His regiment was transferred to the 8th N. Y. H. A., and Mr. Dean was in all the battles of that valiant regiment, serving until the close of the war. A shell-wound on his left shoulder was the only injury he received during the entire list of battles. He received a commission as second lieutenant July 1, 1864, dated June 3d. He was mustered out of service at the expiration of his term, June 22, 1865. On January 30, 1866, he married Celestia M., daughter of S H. and Sarah K. Reed, of Bergen. Three children were born to them, viz.: Minnie C , born January 6, 1868; Charles R., born January 25, 1870; and Calvin N., born June 15, 1874. He has filled the offices of justice of peace seven terms and justice of Sessions two.

John W. Davy, third son of John and Margarette Davy, was born in Canada, November 22, 1845, and at the age of 17 commenced the trade of blacksmithing. In April, 1866, he came to this town, and for eight years he worked for other parties, but for the past 15 years has carried on the business himself. He married Anna B. Gordon, of Kingston, Canada, September 30, 1867, and has a family of three children, one of whom, Ethel E., is an adopted daughter. Willie J. was born December 6, 1869, and Grace G. July 9, 1876. Mr. Davy has been very successful in business, and is able to reap the reward of industry by doing business in his own brick block on Buffalo street. He enjoys the confidence of his townsmen, as is attested by his success in business and the offices of trust he fills in the school and other corporations of the village.

Erastus Emerson, eldest son of Joseph Emerson, was born in Riga, N. Y., July 27, 1810. He followed farming till 1854, when he was compelled to retire by reason of injuries received. Four children were born to him, as follows: Joseph T., John R., Jerome E., and George E., all of whom are living except the first named. John R. Emerson, the second child, of Bergen village, was born in Riga, February 9, 1844, and at the age of 15 he went to Colchester, Conn., to learn the trade of tanner and currier, remaining there about three years. He enlisted in Co. H, 21st Conn. Vols., for three years, or during the war. He was mustered into service at Norwich, Conn., August 22, 1862, and left for the seat of war September 11th. He was attached to the Army of the Potomac, in the 9th Corps; was at the battle of Fredericksburg, was marched the length of the peninsula to Hampton, July 12th, and on the 15th was marched to Portsmouth to act as provost-guard for the city. On the 15th of May he joined Butler's army, on the James River, and was assigned to the 18th Corps. He was at the battle of Drury's Bluff, joined Grant's army at Cold Harbor, June 1st, and was at the surrender of Lee. He arrived at Richmond, June 15, 1865, and embarked for home. Arriving at New Haven on the 18th he was mustered out July 1st, making the term of service 34 months. Five battles and three skirmishes were participated in without a scratch. He then attended Eastman's Commercial College at Rochester, from which he received a diploma in 1866. March 18, 1868, he married Emma L., daughter of Aaron and Avis Bissell, of Bergen. He followed farming till 1883, when he entered the mercantile business as partner of A. B. Enoch. They carried on a general store for several years. Mr. Emerson has two children—Clayton B., born December 28, 1870, and Bessie E., born July 1, 1879.

Abraham Enoch was born in Wood County (now Wirt), West Virginia, January 16, 1804. His father, Isaac, was one of the earliest settlers in the "Old Dominion." Abraham married Mary Gibbrus, October 14, 1830, and to them were born eight children, of whom six are living, viz.: I. L., M. V., J. T., A. F., J. G., and A. B. The first four named are now residents of Virginia. I. L. Enoch has served four years in the West Virginia legislature. Mr. Enoch was a farmer and lumberman, and at the breaking out of the civil war was a Union man—and a Democrat. He was the first county judge of Wirt County in the new State of West Virginia, and held court contrary to the order of the rebel governor, who subsequently offered a reward for his person delivered at Richmond. Wirt County was near the borders, and furnished men for each army, but pronounced Union men had to suffer from the repeated raids and injuries of the rebel bushwhackers. It was nothing to be stripped of horses and stock, and also sleep in well-guarded quarters. The last eight years Mr. Enoch spent in Henrietta, Monroe County, N. Y., where he died in November, 1883. His youngest son, A. B. Enoch, was born in Wirt County, as above, February 6, 1849. Although a boy he belonged to the home guard during the war, and had considerable army experience while protecting property. He had one brother who served in the 6th W. Va. Regt., and another who raised a company for the 11th Regt. A. B. Enoch was married, January 12, 1871, to Mary, daughter of Cornelius S. Dewitt, of Henrietta, N. Y. They have one child, Sherman D., born September 25, 1873. Mr. Enoch came to this town April 18, 1880, and engaged in the mercantile business. He was appointed postmaster March 16, 1886.

Wickum Field, one of the pioneers of the county, came to Bergen from Killingworth, Conn., in June, 1809, and located on what is now known as "the town line road," about two miles west of Bergen village. Here, until his death, August 11, 1853, he lived, rearing a family of seven children, two of whom survive, viz.: Nathan and Charles. Charles Field was born in the town April 20, 1819, and has passed his entire life here. He married, November 20, 1849, Abigail J., daughter of Nat and Cynthia Spafford, of Byron, and three children were born to them, two of whom survive, viz.: Mary E., born September 25, 1857, now the wife of George W. Sackett, of Bergen; and Jennie Estelle, born May 27, 1860, now the wife of Henry A Arnold, of Le Roy. Mr. Field is now 69 years old, and is still an active man. He remembers the early days of the county and has witnessed its rapid development. Mrs. Elizabeth Field, wife of Wickum Field, died January 22, 1848, aged 69 years.

Lathrop Farnham, a native of Connecticut, came to Bergen (then Le Roy) in 1816, where his sons Joseph N. and Stephen L. now reside. He died in 1880, aged 84 years. He married Zeurah Tiffany, of Byron, by whom he had four sons and five daughters. One son died in infancy. William D. died in his 21st year. Joseph N. and Stephen L. live in the town on lot 96. The daughters were Mary, Lorinda, Ora Lovina and Ora Louisa (twins), and Jane. The latter died June 20, 1888. Mary and Lorinda reside in Chicago, Ill. Ora Lovina and Ora Louisa reside in Bergen.

Francis Fordham, born in Vermont, October 31, 1800, came with his father to Genesee County about 1806, settling in Le Roy, and followed farming. He married Caroline Woodward, of Le Roy, and eight children were born to them, five of whom survive, namely: Gideon, of Le Roy; Mariette (Mrs A. S. Westlake), of Le Roy; Esther (Mrs. James P. Quackenbush), also of Le Roy; Harlan F, of Bergen; and Sabrina (Mrs. Henry Rowe), of Kansas. Mr. Fordham, the father, died in 1885, and was really a pioneer of four-score years. His wife survives him, and resides with her daughter, Mrs. Quackenbush. Harlan F. Fordham, the younger son, born August 4, 1837, is a farmer on the Lake road about two miles south of Bergen village. He enlisted in Co. I, 129th Regt. N. Y. V., August 9, 1862, serving to the close of the war. He participated in the battles of Spottsylvania, Cold Harbor, Hatcher's Run, Petersburg, and several minor engagements. He was severely wounded at Cold Harbor, and was honorably discharged June 25, 1865. He was married, January 5, 1869, to Sarah, daughter of John D. and Sibyl Seely, of Leon, Cattaraugus County, N. Y. They have two children, Ruth L., born July 24, 1871, and Orwell S., born January 2, 1877. Mr. Fordham has served his town as justice. The father, Francis, was employed as a messenger in the War of 1812, when 12 years old, and passed through many hairbreadth escapes.

Abner Gay was born in Pittsfield, Mass., June 12, 1806. He learned the trade of carriagemaker, but the latter part of his life was spent in farming. He moved from his native town to Lebanon Springs, where he lived till 1837, and came to Byron, this county, in 1856. September 9, 1830, he married Rachel M. Rowley, of Lebanon Springs, and died July 15, 1875. His son, G. Rowley, was born in Byron, December 26, 1838, and is a farmer. He is also agent for Lister Brothers, dealers in standard and chemical fertilizers, and agent for the Western New York Hedge Company. He married, first, Aggie A. Grey, December 26, 1865, who died June 4, 1866, and second, Emma A., daughter of Jonas and Mary Shaffer, of Clarkson, N. Y., November 16, 1872, by whom he has a daughter, Hattie J., born March 4, 1873.

Moses M. Gillette came with his family from Kinderhook, N. Y., in 1830, to this town. He was born in Connecticut, July 30, 1772, and had a family of eight children, nearly all of whom died in the prime of life. He was a schoolmate with Martin Van Buren, and served in the War of 1812, holding the commission of captain. He died September 17, 1847, and his wife in June 1854. Sylvester Gillette, the only surviving son, was born at Kinderhook, January 16, 1816, and came here in 1830, when 14 years old. He is a farmer and has resided on the same farm over 50 years. November 4, 1852, he married Mary A. Hoag, of Ridgway, Orleans County, and three children were born to them, viz.: Miller S., now residing at Livonia Station, born April 29, 1854; Mary O. (Mrs. A. G. Holdridge), born February 11, 1857; and Luella A. (Mrs. George M. Gillette), born August 16, 1865, who now resides with her father. The mother died March 18, 1886. Mr. Gillette has filled prominent places in the gift of his townsmen, and was postmaster under President Johnson.

Zalmon Green was born in Lisle, Broome County, N. Y., October 19, 1795. He married Eliza Patten, of Cayuga County, in 1818, and in 1824, with his family, he permanently located in Bergen as a farmer. His farm was on the Swamp road, and a part of the 100,000-acre tract. He purchased 50 acres in 1825, and subsequently increased his farm to

102 acres.   In 1867 he sold the farm to Jerome Spafford, removing to
the village of Bergen, where he died June 29, 1886, aged nearly 91
years.   He served in the War of 1812, and passed through the hottest
of the battle of Fort Erie without injury.   His wife died October 14,
1865.   Seven of their 10 children are now living.   Elias P. Green, one
of the sons, was born September 17, 1835, and married Elizabeth H.,
daughter of A. M. and Eunice C. Stewart, of Bergen, July 4, 1857.   Mr.
Green has followed the vocation of teaching, and has taught successfully
nearly 60 terms, being for years the principal of a graded school in Ohio.
He has resided in Bergen village since 1866.   He has two children,
viz.: W. S., born December 27, 1860, and Alice E., born November 5,
1865.   W. S. was educated at the Brockport Normal School.

Seth Hopkins, son of Joseph, was born near St. Albans, Vt., in 1823,
and at the age of 11 years came to this town with his parents.   He was
a farmer, and died August 13, 1859, leaving one living child, Bruce.
Bruce Hopkins was a farmer, but began teaching school winters at the
age of 20 years, continuing for 34 terms.   He was married, August 20,
1856, to Ora P., daughter of Loren H. Stevens, of Bergen, and they
have two children living, Frank, born September 12, 1860, and Millicent B., born October 31, 1871.   Frank is engaged in the Western
Union Telegraph office at Mansfield, Pa.   Bruce Hopkins was a soldier
in the civil war, enlisting June 13, 1861, in Co. A, 3d N. Y. Cav.   He
participated in the battles of White Hall, Kingston, Goldsboro, Stony
Creek, Charles Station, Little Washington, Reams's Station, Petersburg,
and other minor engagements.   After three years of service he received
an honorable discharge July 17, 1864.

Abner Hull, a native of Killingworth, Conn., came to Genesee County
in 1808.   He arrived in the North Woods (so-called) after a journey of
400 miles, in 21 days, with the family.   They had two yoke of oxen and
a cart.   He was justice of the peace for many years, and his reputation
for honesty and integrity was such that he had to perform the duties of
executor for many estates.   He served as supervisor for many years.
One of his sons, Ferdinand H., was sheriff of the county in 1860;
another, Carlos A., was elected county clerk in 1867, and has held the
office since.   Abner Hull married Rachel Parmalee, and died in 1882.
They lived where their son Eugene D. now resides.

Marcena B. Hewes, son of Ralph, was born in Oneida County, N. Y.,
March 7, 1822.   He came to Genesee County when about 20 years old,
locating in the town of Le Roy, where he resided till 1879, when he
moved to Bergen.   He has a fine, large farm of 290 acres, about four
miles northwest of Bergen village, and also owns 30 acres in Riga.   He
married Cordelia Banister, October 10, 1848, and 10 of their 11 children
are living.   Dayton Hewes, the fourth son, was born in Le Roy, April 3,
1862, and by occupation is a farmer.   He was educated for a teacher,
and taught a few terms, but the farm duties predominated and he drifted
to farming exclusively.   October 27, 1886, he was married to Cora,

daughter of George and Amelia Snyder, of Bergen. He and his brother Otis now work the farm of their father.

Daniel Ide, Jr., the first son of Daniel Ide, was born at Sand Lake, Rensselaer County, N. Y., October 9, 1829, and during his entire life has been a farmer. He resided at Sweden, Monroe County, from 1866 to 1875, when he moved to Irondequoit, same county, where he still resides. He married Geraldine Horton, February 9, 1849, and has five children. Dorwin A. Ide, the third child, was born in Milton, Saratoga County, March 4, 1853, and began the occupation of saddlery and harnessmaking at the age of 20. In December, 1877, he came to Bergen and began business for himself in the Parrish block. By the fire of 1880 he lost most of his stock, but soon opened up at another place. He is now on Lake street, north of the N. Y. C. & H. R. Railroad tracks, where a full line of horse furnishing goods are kept. He also manufactures harnesses. He was married, December 22, 1880, to Anna A., daughter of William and Jane Sands, of Sweden, N. Y., and they have one child, George I., born March 28, 1882.

Hiram Knickerbocker, eldest son of Cornelius and Elizabeth B. Knickerbocker, was born at Northeast, Dutchess County, N, Y., October 22, 1815. His father moved to Elba, Genesee County, in 1820, and after three years removed to Riga, thence to Avon, where he hired 280 acres of land of James Wadsworth for seven years. At the expiration of the lease he removed to Wilson, N. Y., thence to Gates, Monroe County, where he died March 27, 1844. The father, of whom mention has been made, was a soldier of 1812, and was honorably discharged at the close of that war. Hiram Knickerbocker came to Bergen in 1840, where he still resides, and is by occupation a farmer. February 16, 1842, he married Polly, daughter of Charles S. and Amy Wilcox, Sr., who were originally from East Guilford, Conn. Mr. Knickerbocker has been prominently connected with the Methodist Episcopal Church for over 40 years, filling the position of class leader in the Sunday-school and in the district.

Fred Lewellyn, youngest son of Frederick and Mary Lewellyn, was born in Bergen, August 18, 1849. He followed farming till the spring of 1885, when he removed to the village, where he now resides, still retaining his fine farm of 100 acres three miles west of the village. He is a dealer in agricultural implements. April 7. 1874, he married Minnie E., daughter of Barney and Harriet Sprague, of Batavia, and three children have been born to them, namely : Dean, born January 8, 1878 ; George, born October 31, 1881 ; and Roy, born September 13, 1884. The father, Frederick, was an early settler, coming to the town in 1827, and followed farming till his death, May 20, 1881. He was much respected by the entire community.

James Miller, second son of John and Mary Miller, was born in County Cumberland, Eng., June 6, 1813. He was but little over two years old when Bonaparte was defeated at Waterloo, but such was the rejoicing throughout England, and the circumstances were of that impressive char-

22

acter, that he remembers it to this day. He has always been a farmer. In 1846 he emigrated to this country, coming directly to Genesee County, where he has since resided. He married, February 28, 1849, Ann, daughter of James and Ann McDonald, of Scotland, who died September 30, 1884. They adopted a niece, Nettie, when she was only two weeks old, who is now the wife of John Menzie, of Riga, N. Y. She was born August 6, 1854. Mr. Miller is now 76 years of age, yet is active and cares for his farm of 46 acres. He has been prominent in politics, by faith a Republican, and has filled many representative offices and places of trust. He and his wife were connected with the First Congregational Church here in 1852, and have been very prominent in its workings and support since. In 1880 he was appointed to take the census of the town, which, with his daughter's assistance, was very efficiently completed.

James A. Miller, son of Henry and Evaline Miller, was born in Cooperstown, N. Y., August 3, 1830. He early learned the carriagemaking trade, and followed it. At the age of 22 he went to Binghamton, N. Y., worked there nine years, marrying in the meantime Sarah A., daughter of Joseph and Sally Chalker, of that city. In 1861 he enlisted in the 16th Bat. N. Y. V. He removed to Bergen in 1867, engaging at his trade. Their four children now living are Orville J., born October 19, 1858 ; Lewis J., born October 26, 1863 ; Albion J., born October 6, 1869 ; and Bertha E., born March 26, 1874. The first two sons are now engaged in business in the town, and both sustain a high reputation for their mechanical ingenuity. Orville has three distinct trades—machinist, brass molder, and pattermaker. His accomplishments seem miraculous when considered in the light of circumstances. At present the manufacture of brass cylinder force-pumps is his specialty. Lewis J. is engaged at his trade—carriage and cuttermaker. He is considered an expert in mechanism, is only 23 years old, and yet has plenty of the best of work to do. The remaining children are yet being educated.

Daniel Merrill was born December 25, 1791, and died August 12, 1818. Daniel F., his son, was born May 1, 1818, in this town, and was a merchant at North Bergen 18 years. He married Elvira, daughter of Joshua S. Hudson, of Byron, March 17, 1841. He removed to Bergen village in the spring of 1862. He has filled the offices of supervisor and justice of his town for several terms, and also the position of assistant assessor of internal revenue for many years In 1872 he received the appointment of a position in the New York custom house, where he has been engaged for many years, being promoted three different times. He resides at Brooklyn, N. Y. Mr. Merrill has seven children, namely: Frank M., of Bergen; Edwin H., of Dell Rapids, Dak ; Sarah J. (Mrs. W. H. Torry), of Tonawanda, N. Y.; J. C. Fremont. of Chicago, Ill ; Rosa E. and Hattie C., at home ; and Zella S. (Mrs. Lafayette Briggs), of Chicago. Frank M. Merrill, the eldest son, was born at Clarendon, N. Y., February 9, 1848. At the age of 15 years he entered his father's store as clerk, when, after four years' service, he was made deputy postmaster, and in 1869 was appointed postmaster, a position he held over 16 years, and added the office of notary to it for three terms. He started the Bergen *Herald*, but the promised support not appearing he discontinued it after a few months. He married Sophia A., daughter of Horatio and Betsey Graves, of Wethersfield Springs, December 31, 1868. Mr. and Mrs. Merrill have four children, viz.: Clinton S., born May 24, 1870; Bertram G., born March 15, 1873; Lillian S., born October 11, 1874; and Daniel H., born December 3, 1878. Mr. Merrill's grandfather, Joshua S. Hudson, was a veteran of 1812–15.

A very prominent firm, and one of long standing, is composed of William and Thomas Morton, twin brothers. They were born on the Isle of Man, Eng., September 3, 1827, and engaged in the tailors' trade at the age of 12 years. When only 18 years old they came to America, locating and working at Rochester a short time. In the fall of 1846 they removed to Bergen, where they have since carried on a successful business, and can justly be called "old settlers." William Morton married Olive, daughter of Mr. Fosket, of Bergen, June 5, 1856, who died May 15, 1886, leaving one daughter, Harriet A., now Mrs. E. L. Snyder. Thomas Morton was married, October 26, 1856, to Charlotte L., daughter of John and Electa Tone, of Bergen, who died January 15, 1866, leaving one daughter, Charlotte E., now Mrs. E. G. Callister, of Byron. Thomas married, second, August 14, 1874, Susan Callister. These brothers have continued in business and have lived together except about nine years.

David McKenzie, a native of Inverness-shire, Scotland, was born February 2, 1806. He was bound out at the age of 14 to the carpenter and joiner trade. This apprenticeship was completed at the age of 21, when he came to America and worked in New York city three years, and in 1831 went to Hamilton, Canada. In 1833 he removed to Franklinville, Cattaraugus County, N. Y., where he took up 130 acres of wild land, and built a house. While here he, with Lansing Crosly, built several houses, mills, etc. In 1843 he came to Bergen, where he lived 40 years, and removed to Michigan, where he died April 11, 1886. In 1830 he married Anna, daughter of Nathan and Anna Cochrane, who died July 26, 1880, leaving six children, now living, viz.: Thomas, born August 15, 1833; James R., born July 12, 1837; Nathan, born December 27, 1839; Anna, born December 29, 1841, now Mrs. Jerome Spafford; Mary (Mrs. George Rathbone), born June 10, 1844; and William, born November 29, 1846. James R. McKenzie has resided in Bergen village since his majority. December 22, 1864, he married Anna, daughter of John and Mary Menzie, of Riga, N. Y., and six children were born to them, of whom only four are living, namely: Mary, born February 1, 1866; Roy, born November 29, 1870; Anna C., born January 17, 1877; Kenneth, born August 10, 1879; Jennie, born July 26, 1868, died December 29, 1875; and David, born March 4, 1872, died December 17, 1875. James R. McKenzie built the first planing-mill and started the first lumber yard in the town, in 1867. A large portion of the buildings in the village have been erected under his supervision, and after the large fire he erected 10 of the fine brick blocks on Lake street.

William Johnson Mansfield was born in the town of Manchester, Vt., March 22, 1819, and the most of his life has been spent in farming, although in 1857–58 he was in the grocery business near the site occupied by S. E. Spencer. He married Anna, daughter of Harvey and Polly Field, March 26, 1846, who died April 2, 1864, leaving three children, as follows: Mary J , now the widow of Thomas J. Thompson, of Bergen; Sarah A., of this village; and George W., also of Bergen. He afterwards moved to Wisconsin, where he still resides. He served with honor in the civil war. George W. Mansfield, his only son, is now a resident of Bergen, and a farmer by occupation. He married, December 17, 1879, Ada L., daughter of Asa and Catharine Clothier, of Mexico, N. Y. Two children were born to them, viz : Onnolu W., December 3, 1880, and Dayton H , September 22, 1886.

In the parish of Lagan, Scotland, August 16, 1814, Donald McPherson, the fifth son of John McPherson, was born, and in 1837 he came to this State, settling at Riga, Monroe County. He followed farming till 1840, when he came to Bergen, purchased a warehouse, and has since followed the produce and coal business. In January, 1840, he married Jane, daughter of Duncan and Isabel McPherson, of Wheatland, Monroe County, who died in 1845. January 1, 1847, he married, second, Margery, daughter of John and Catharine Gordon, of Caledonia, Livingston County, and Daniel J., their only surviving child, is engaged in business with his father and resides in the village. Donald McPherson is a prominent member of the First Congregational Church, which he joined in early life, and has filled its offices with fidelity and ability for more than a score of years.

Harvey Parmelee, son of Capt. Phineas Parmelee, was born at East Guilford, now Madison, Conn , in 1794. He came with his father to this town in 1809, when it was a wilderness, where he took up land near what is now known as "Stone Church." The father died in 1810, but Harvey remained on the farm until 1886—a period of 77 years. February 9, 1825, he married Lucinda B. Ward, of Bergen, who died July 1, 1852, leaving three children, as follows: Edward H., born November 13, 1825 ; Lucinda E., born June 26, 1831 ; and Myron H., born May 12, 1835. All are living in Genesee County. Myron H., the youngest, resided with his father on the farm until 1886. He married Mary J., daughter of Jared and Nancy Atwater, of Riga, N. Y., March 31, 1860. He has filled many prominent positions among his townsmen, and among others has been supervisor of his town three terms.

Samuel Parker removed from Peru, Mass., at an early day, with his son, Eleazer, then only eight years old, locating in Byron. The grandson of Samuel, Sylvester E. Parker, was born in the town of Elba in 1827, and has spent his life in Genesee County. He married Sophia S. Gifford, of Bergen, in 1848, and removed to this town in 1871. He followed farming for many years, and still owns the farm of 150 acres that was taken up by his grandfather in 1811. He makes the breeding of fine-wooled sheep a specialty. He has filled the office of justice of the peace for several years.

Hon. Horatio Reed was born in Tolland, Conn., June 13, 1798, and removed to Otsego County, N. Y., in 1815, to Orleans County in 1825, and to Bergen, January 1, 1845. He is a farmer, but has been very prominent in the affairs of the county. He was inspector of schools in Clarendon 16 years, served several years as supervisor, assessor, and justice, and served Orleans County in the Assembly during 1838–39. He has spent a long life as an active Sabbath-school and Christian worker, and has ever acknowledged the guiding hand of Providence to lead him in his ways. He married Jane Green, May 22, 1828, daughter of Joshua Green, who was also a settler in this town in 1809. Jane Green, his wife, was born May 22, 1808, at Rome, N. Y., and died at North Bergen, September 13, 1883, after residing in Genesee County 74 years. Their family consisted of three sons and one daughter, viz.: Andrew H., born November 26, 1829, died August 13, 1849; Herbert, born April 19, 1832, was killed while serving as captain in the 3d Mo. Cav., at Little Rock, Ark., September 10, 1863; Mrs. Harriet S. Lewis, born October 4, 1834, now residing at Brockport, N. Y.; and Charles N., born May 9, 1837. The latter attended Cary Academy and Monroe Institute, and came to Bergen, January 1, 1845. His occupation is farming. September 25, 1860, he married Charlotte A., daughter of Nathan B. and Mary Church Griffin, of Bergen, and their family consists of two sons—Herbert Griffin Reed, born December 2, 1864, and Charles Louie Reed, born February 2, 1872.

Isaac Southworth, the second son of Samuel Southworth, was born in Cayuga County, N. Y., December 15, 1794, and early learned the trade of carpenter and joiner, which for 20 years he closely followed. He was twice married, first, to Rachel, daughter of John and Margeret Tone, January 11, 1820, and second, to Elizabeth B , daughter of John and Mary Bower, who died April 12, 1836. Eight children were born to him by the first and one by the second marriage. Seven of the eight are living. Isaac Southworth came here in 1821 and died August 17, 1872. He was a soldier in the War of 1812–15, although young, and received an honorable discharge. Andrew T. Southworth, the eldest son, was born in this town August 12, 1824, and remained on his father's farm until 18 years of age. He then hired out for six months on a farm for $10 a month, which he drew at the end of that time, placing $50 of it at interest, which was the foundation of his future financial success. He was married, September 23, 1853, to Eliza A., widow of Marlin Mosier, of this town, who died September 2, 1885, leaving no children. Mr. Southworth soon became a speculator, buying stock for several years, then grain and produce till 1880, when his warehouse and dwelling were burned with his barns, furniture, etc. In 1881 he built a large brick block, 50x84 feet, the lower floor containing four stores, in one of which he opened a flour and feed store. He also engaged in the manufacture and sale of harnesses, agricultural implements, etc. He has filled honorably and ably the offices of justice, assessor, trustee of the village, clerk of trustees of the Methodist Episcopal Church, etc. He married for his second wife, December 22, 1886, Mrs. Amy A. Gifford, a resident of this village.

John B. Southworth, the only son of Isaac Southworth by his second wife, was born July 25, 1841, in Bergen, on the home farm. He has always been a farmer here except one year that he was employed by the N. Y. C.& H. R. R. R. February 22, 1862, he married Mary J., daughter Malden and Electa Gifford, who died January 27, 1882, leaving seven children, viz.: Esther M., born August 26, 1862 ; Mary E., born October 23, 1864 ; Isaac, born February 17, 1866 ; Minnie A., born April 23, 1868 ; Rosannah L., born December 13, 1869 ; Catharine, born August 8, 1871 ; and Ellen A., born May 26, 1874. He married, second, Almira J. Moore, widow of George Moore, July 24, 1883. Although he owns other farms he still retains and works the home farm on which he was born. He has filled offices of trust and honor in his town for many years.

William Storer came to this town from Killingworth, Conn., in 1828. His family consisted of a wife and six children, two of whom only now survive, viz.: Eben, who lives in Flint, Mich., and Danford, of Bergen. William Storer died here in 1886, aged 90 years. Danford, the youngest son, born February 2, 1820, was about seven years old when he came to this town with his father. He has been a farmer since he has resided here. He married Emily A., daughter of William Ellis, Jr., of Norwich, Conn., whose family consisted of eight children, who are still living, the eldest being over 72 years old. Danford Storer has two children by adoption—Charles S. Mills, in Michigan, and Julia, now Mrs. Gilbert Briggs, of Ovid, Mich. Mr. Storer sold his farm at West Bergen (part of which was his father's homestead since 1830), and now lives a retired life, enjoying the fruits of his industry.

Jay W. Stratton was born at Roxbury, Delaware County, N. Y., November 21, 1832. He was the youngest son of Walter and Esther Stratton, was educated at the Binghamton Academy, and engaged in farming till he was about 25 years old, when he taught a few terms, but finally learned the trade of carpenter and joiner, which he followed for 15 years. He has been twice married, first, to Emma, daughter of Jesse D. Minkler, of Binghamton, who died April 3, 1882, leaving three children, viz.: Edward E., born January 3, 1863, who has long been the station agent of the West Shore depot in this town ; Jessie E., born October 25, 1865, now Mrs. Charles Patterson, of Rochester, N. Y.; and Nellie E., born October 18, 1873, who has been attending school at Gilboa, N. Y. He married, second, Eva, daughter of John H. Hilyer, of New Hudson, N. Y. At the age of 33 Mr. Stratton enlisted in the 193d Regt. N. Y. V., as sergeant, and was honorably discharged January 18, 1866. He came to Bergen in 1874, and has been engaged in the coal business for 10 years, and also as insurance and real estate agent. While he was acting justice he was elected as associate justice of the county courts. Mr. Stratton was a schoolmate with Jay Gould at Roxbury, N. Y.

Eugene L. Seely, the fourth son of Thaddeus and Susannah Seely, was born in Orange County, N. Y., November 4, 1804. He was a farmer, and married Sally Gilmore, of Churchville, N. Y., who bore him 13 children, nine of whom survive. He died January 6, 1883. Harriet, now the wife of Vincent Brown, and Laura, wife of Charles Birge, live in Michigan; Elizabeth, wife of John McPherson, lives in Le Roy; Sarah, wife of Joseph Farnham, lives in Bergen; Homer and Eugene L., live in Bergen, on the Lake road; and Maurice lives at Stone Church. The latter is a grocer and postmaster at that place, and was born February 25, 1841. He married, February 10, 1884, Mary, daughter of Frederick Gearing, of Riga, N. Y. He has been a resident of this town his entire life except eight years spent in Michigan. Homer Seely, the eldest son of Eugene L., was born August 24, 1833, and has followed farming, now residing on the home farm of his father. · He was married, December 3, 1877, to Lovina Orra, daughter of L. Farnham, of Bergen, and they have two children, namely: Sarah, born August 10, 1865, and Homer L., born December 3, 1870. His grandfather on his mother's side served in the War of 1812.

John Tone, the fourth son of John A. Tone, was born in Scipio, Cayuga County, N. Y., October 17, 1799. In 1820 he came with his father to this town, locating on the farm now known as the Elijah Loomis place, which was owned by the Tone family for 46 consecutive years. John A. Tone died September 29, 1825. John Tone married Electa E. Hubbard, of Oneida County, N. Y., in May, 1824. He was a builder and contractor, and many of the buildings of Bergen, Byron, Sweden, etc., are the witnesses of his skill. He had a family of 11 children, six of whom survive. He was a prominent member of the Methodist Episcopal Church, acting as trustee and leader for many years. He died February 27, 1861, and his wife November 2, 1872. Thomas J. Tone, the eldest son of John A., was born in Bergen, June 5, 1830, and received his education at the district school of the town and at the Brockport Collegiate Institute. At the age of 22 he went to Claysville, Kentucky, where he taught school, thence to Cincinnati, O., where he taught 12 years, and then resigned and went into the commission business for a year and a half He afterwards returned to Bergen, where he has remained, engaged in the business of dealer in grain, produce, and coal, and proprietor of Tone's elevator. October 18, 1858, he married Catharine D., daughter of Sumner Spafford, of this town, and has three children, viz.: S. La Rue, born November 1, 1864; Frank D., born October 16, 1868; and Florence M, born January 3, 1871. Mr Tone has been a prominent member of the First Congregational Church, leading the Sunday-school, and acting as trustee and clerk of the society. He is also largely interested in all matters of public interest, so much so that he has long been one of the board of trustees of the public school.

Dr. W. M. Townsend, born in Mendon, Monroe County, in 1827, was educated at Philadelphia and graduated at Jefferson Medical College in 1853. He married, June 22, 1849, Sarah Lamphier, of Lima, N. Y., and came to Bergen in 1859 from Riga, N. Y. He was surgeon in the 44th and 47th N. Y. Vols. from New York, from 1861 to 1864, and is now engaged in a successful and extended practice in Genesee and Monroe counties.

Samuel C. Tulley, the second son of Francis S. and Adaline Tulley, was born September 22, 1837, in the city of New York. His father was a well-known dealer in stoves, gas fixtures, etc., in Rochester, where he came in 1840, and died there in 1884. Samuel C. Tulley began business for himself in this town in 1859, and has followed the hardware business since. February 21, 1865, he married Mary I., daughter of James R. and Mary Thompson, of Philadelphia, Pa., and three children have been born to them, as follows: Loa Belle, December 20, 1865, died April 16, 1867; James F., January 4, 1868; and Harry L., January 8, 1870. Mr. Tulley is a general and extensive hardware dealer. In 1886 he erected a fine building, of brick, corner of Lake and Buffalo streets, 50x157 feet, and occupies the entire front for his large business.

Nelson D. Wright was born in the town of Bergen, January 22, 1826. His father, Alfred Wright, came to this town from Guilford, Conn., in 1807, with his father, who was an early settler of the town, one of the founders of the Congregational Church, and a prominent citizen of those early days. Nelson married Mary F. Green, of Bergen, in 1851. He was a farmer for 30 years, and then engaged in the produce business. His life has been spent in Bergen with the exception of a few years.

Hon. Samuel Church, an old resident of Bergen, was born in Sangersfield, Oneida County, N. Y., December 16, 1809. He was one of 11 children. One brother, George H., survives him, and lives in Waterville, Oneida County—a prominent man politically and religiously.

Mr. Church came to Bergen at the age of 16, in 1825, on a packet boat, the year the Erie Canal was opened, and walked from Brockport to Bergen. He attended the village school during the winter. In the spring he chose the trade of a blacksmith, entering the shop of C. B. Bigelow, his half brother, giving attention to his studies during the winter seasons until he attained his majority. He made great progress in learning as well as in business. His earlier days were those of earnest toil and struggle. He had no aid of money, only as he earned it by his own labor. He soon mastered the trade, hired the shop, and commenced business for himself, which he managed successfully until his health began to fail He then followed the business of broker. Mr. Church never recovered his health, but battled with disease periodically during a life of only 56 years. May 17, 1835, he married Harriet A., youngest daughter of Capt. Austin Wilcox, a pioneer of the town. She still lives in Bergen.

Samuel Church

Their children are Mrs. B. F. Taber, of Buffalo ; George H., a lumber dealer, of Bergen ; and Charles Samuel, who died in 1875, at the age of 17 years.

Of Samuel Church, Ebenezer Scofield, his cotemporary, said :

"Mr. Church has resided here since 1825, where he was so favorably known and highly esteemed for his many virtues and pleasing social qualities. He will long be remembered by his numerous friends and associates, who ever took pleasure in his society. He was a man of more than ordinary mental faculties, whose opinion was looked up to in matters of public interest by all who knew him. He had filled many public positions with honor to himself and credit to his town and county. His loss will be deeply felt by the community, and by his family who are sorely afflicted by the bereavement."

The Rochester *Union and Advertiser* of April 14, 1866, had the following :

"At the session of Genesee County Court, on Tuesday last, the following resolutions on the death of Samuel Church, Sessions justice, were presented by William G. Bryan, Esq., and ordered by the court entered at large in the minutes :

"'*Resolved*, That the members of the bar of Genesee County have heard with regret of the sad and unexpected intelligence of the sudden death of Samuel Church, Esq., one of the justices of Sessions of Genesee County ; that as a magistrate of large experience, clear and forcible mind, rare good sense, unquestioned uprightness, and integrity of purpose and purity of character, he will be favorably remembered by the community in which he has so long resided ; and that we shall miss and lament his absence from the bench to which he has twice been chosen by the people of this county. ·

"'*Resolved*, That, with the permission of the court, these resolutions be entered in the minutes, and a copy transmitted to the widow of the deceased.'

"District-Attorney Bissell seconded the resolutions, adding some remarks referring to his long acquaintance with deceased, and the loss the county has sustained in the death of so excellent a magistrate. The county judge, in directing the entry of the resolutions, spoke at length of the dilligence and aptitude of Mr. Church, both as a Sessions judge, magistrate, and business man ; and it being suggested that the funeral would take place to-morrow, the court ordered, as a mark of respect to the memory of deceased, that the jury be discharged, and the Court of Sessions adjourned until Thursday morning."

Capt. Austin Wilcox, a pioneer of Western New York, was born in Madison, Conn., October 28, 1779, and married Clarissa, daughter of Ezra Nettleton and Damaris Seward, of Killingworth, Conn., March 27, 1805. They lived in Westbrook, Conn., he following the business of a blacksmith, spiking vessels, till May 20, 1815, when they emigrated to Bergen, where he had previously been to explore the country and make a purchase in 1813. Their journey of 400 miles was made with two yoke of oxen and a covered wagon, containing their necessary valuables, and a one-horse covered wagon, in which the family, consisting of the mother and five children, rode. All the children were under 10 years of age. Three more children were added to this family in after years. Mrs. Wilcox's life in this new settlement, with her growing family, was one of hardship and toil, like that of all the pioneers, a life she was not calculated for. She was reared tenderly, in affluence, and possessed a slender constitution, predisposed to consumption. At an early age, after an illness of 18 months, she fell a victim, with many others of the pioneer mothers, to the prevailing malady of the pioneer settlement,—consumption,—leaving her little family of eight children to the care of a tender husband. Her death occurred in June, 1828, at the age of 49 years. The Congregational Church on the hill was just completed, and hers was the first funeral held there.

Chloe B., the oldest daughter, married Ebenezer Arnold in 1825, and died aged 31, leaving two sons, H. Windsor, now living in Bergen, and Homer W., deceased. Polly N. married William Carey, and removed to Fond du Lac, Wis., in 1845. Mr. Carey died in March following their removal, and Mrs. Carey in 1866. Their children numbered eight, three of whom are now living in Fond du Lac, prominent and useful citizens. Clarissa married Ira Bidwell. They removed to Adrian, Mich., in 1836. She died at the age of 54. They had five children. Austin Scranton, the oldest, married Hannah Bodwell, of Bergen, and removed to Adrian, Mich., in 1837. He purchased 80 acres of land west of the village, then an unbroken forest. His highest ambition seemed to be to excel in his calling, and he was able to look out upon over 200 acres of splendid farming land changed from a wilderness to fruitful fields by his own industry. He always declined office and notoriety. He is deceased. He had born to him six children. Elizabeth A. married Josiah Pierson, Jr., of Bergen, where they resided during her short life of 31 years. They had one son and one daughter. Harriet A., born January 31, 1817, married, May 17, 1835, Samuel Church, of Bergen, where she still resides. Their children are Mrs. B. F. Taber, of Buffalo; George H., of Bergen; and Charles Samuel (deceased). William Seward, born April 25, 1819, lived in Bergen until September, 1836, when he went to Michigan in the employ of his brother-in-law, Ira Bidwell. He afterwards became a partner in the business, and soon after started the hardware store and continued the business alone until 1867, when his brother H. H. became his partner. After five years the firm was changed to Wilcox Brothers & Co., when George A., son of W. S., became a partner. This is the name of the firm at the present time.

In 1848 W S. Wilcox was elected treasurer of the village of Adrian, and held the office one year. In 1864 he was elected to the legislature of Michigan, which office he held two terms, and was chosen a member of the ways and means committee, and during the second term acted as its chairman. In the spring of 1865 he was elected mayor of the city of Adrian. In the fall of 1870 he was chosen State Senator, which office he held one term, and was chairman of the finance committee. In 1869 he was appointed State prison inspector by Governor Baldwin, and was immediately chosen president of the board of inspectors, which he held for 12 years. In 1866 he was elected president of the Michigan State Insurance Co., which position he still holds. In 1884 he was elected one of the presidential electors on the Republican ticket In 1879 he became partner in the firm of Whitney & Wilcox, Commercial Exchange Bank, giving his time and attention to the institution. For 50 years successively he has been superintendent of the Baptist Sunday-school. Mr. Wilcox was first married at Benton, Ind.,

Captain Austin Wilcox

May 10, 1842, to Sarah Frances, daughter of Rev. Bradbury Clay. Mrs. Wilcox died February 12, 1852. His second marriage was, August 17, 1854, to Miss Josephine Southworth, daughter of Dr. William Southworth, of Avon Springs, N. Y.

Henry Hamilton Wilcox reached his majority in the fall of 1843. He went West to seek his fortune, and found employment in the hardware store of George L. Bidwell. In the spring of 1844 he received a letter from his father expressing feelings of sadness that his boys had all left him in his old age. The next morning found his youngest boy, H. H. W., homeward bound, that he might be a comfort to his father in his declining years. He remained at Bergen until after the death of his father, and in the fall of 1858 he started with his family for Adrian, Mich., again with a view of purchasing a farm. He was induced to take a place in his brother's hardware store and give his children the benefit of the Adrian schools until a favorable opportunity presented for the purchase of a farm. Although fresh from the fields, and unaccustomed to business, he very soon became master of the situation and the leading salesman in one of the largest hardware houses in Southern Michigan. In 1867 he became one of the firm of Wilcox & Brothers, contributing largely to its successful management. Mr. Wilcox was married, in Northampton, Mass., in 1844, to Eunice J., daughter of Hervey Smith, by whom he had five children

The pioneers of Bergen, who laid at the same time the foundations of the church and town, were a noble race of men. Unlike most early settlements the population was not mixed, but homogeneous. Nearly all of them came from Connecticut and Massachusetts, and brought with them the sturdy New England virtues of industry, integrity, and high moral aim Among them was Capt. Austin Wilcox. We wish we could present him to the present and future residents of the town exactly as he appeared to his cotemporaries; but that is a difficult matter. His portrait shows that his was a very strong and original character. Mr. Lincoln, in preparing a brief sketch of his own life for the *Congressional Directory*, wrote: " Education limited." This describes Capt. Wilcox ; but his natural ability and quick wit largely overcame this disadvantage.

He was a man of stalwart frame and untiring industry. Settling in this county before the time of railroads, he soon saw a place was needed where man and beast could find refreshment and rest as they sought a market for products of Genesee's rich fields, and he soon built up a hotel business, showing tact and ability in that line that in these days would make a railroad magnate. When he began hotel life it was in his own house on his farm at Bergen Corners. To this building he made various additions as his patronage increased It is impossible for those of the present day to understand the enormous travel of those days to Rochester and Brockport, when all the produce of the farmers, and all the merchandise sold over a large extent of country, passed over these roads. At the same time Capt. Wilcox ran a line of stages from Le Roy to Brockport and

Clarkson, carrying the mails, and also kept the postoffice. But large as his patronage was it is difficult to understand how he could have made such vast improvements with the very small charges of those days : sixpence for lodging; 18 and 20 cents for the best of meals. Most of the farmers carried their own dinner, a box and oats for their teams, with them, and if they paid for a pint of cider and hay to bait their horses, that was all it cost them for shed-room and a warm fire before which to eat their meals from the ample dinner-pail.

A close observer of men, united with a natural detective ability, made him an acute reader of human nature. Quick to detect guilt, and fearless in exposing it, many a rogue has quailed beneath the keen glance of his eye, and has been betrayed into a confession of his guilt by his apt questions. On one occasion, as a man on horseback rode up to his platform, he took his horse by the bridle and said to him, in the most abrupt manner, "You have stolen this horse!" The man was so startled he could only say, " What makes you think so ? " He replied, " If it was your horse you would not be riding him with this blind bridle ; he is a valuable horse ; if you owned him you would not be riding him so hard as you are." The men in pursuit soon rode up and captured the thief. At another time some men in pursuit of a thief, who was escaping to Canada, stopped at his house to dine and feed their horses. At he listened to their conversation he found they were in trouble because they did not know the name of the thief and could not insert it in the warrant for his arrest. He asked to see the warrant, took his pen, and, after filling the blank, handed it back, saying, " What I have written will read any man's name that ever lived." Many other acts might be told illustrating his ready detective wit. His manner of expressing himself was so striking and original as to draw around him a crowd of listeners, not only at home, but wherever he traveled. At a meeting of the pioneers in Rochester he was called upon to relate his experience as a pioneer. He began : " I was born in Madison, Conn. I remember the day just as well [great laughter] as any other man remembers his birthday." With this beginning he did not lack attention to the close of his strikingly original address.

He was ever foremost in promoting public good and spared neither his time or means. The church and its interests were ever dear to him, and when, in mature years, he gave to the subject of personal religion, thought and study, that same sense of right that ever governed him was acted upon, and he became a true, consistent member of the church, making a public profession in 1836. This consecration was largely due to the power of religious instruction and example of his mother, who was a woman whose peculiarities were more strongly marked than his own. His peculiar traits of character were chiefly inherited from her. Her religion was simple, earnest, genial, and hence influential with her children and others. At the age of 60 she came to Genesee County to visit her children. Here she died and is buried in beautiful Mount Rest Cemetery, where many of her decendants lie. , He ever took a deep interest in religious society, and was for many years one of its trustees and burden bearers. The burying-ground was also his pride, he giving his particular attention to any matters of interest connected with it. This interest increased with his years, and was also a family trait for generations.

His hospitality to ministers of the gospel, who, in his time, nearly all traveled in their own conveyances, and who, in the capacity of agents or missionaries, were far more numerous than now, was ever unstinted. His house was always open to old friends from Connecticut, and his journal records many such visits.

From the *Genesee Evangelist*, written by his pastor, Rev. Sabine McKinney, now of Binghamton, N. Y.:

"Died in Bergen, Genesee County, New York, Capt. Austin Wilcox, aged 77 years, August 18, 1856.

"Capt. Wilcox was a native of Madison. Conn., from whence he removed to Bergen in the year 1815. He was widely known as a man of great influence, energy, and decision of character. He took a hearty interest in everything which he regarded as of public utility, and was especially remarkable for kind attention to and sympathy for the sick, and for his attendance at the house of mourning, which won for him the gratitude of many. Both as a member of the First Congregational Society of Bergen, and for many years one of its trustees. he was liberal and efficient, and the society is largely indebted to his efforts for their beautiful church edifice. He ever welcomed ministers of the gospel to the hospitalities of his house, in that respect setting an example worthy of all imitation, and while in health was a constant attendant upon divine service. Hopefully converted after he was 50 years of age, he made a public profession of his faith in 1836. During the past spring and summer he frequently expressed it as his conviction that his days on earth were nearly numbered, and though he had not that full assurance which God is pleased to give to some of his children, yet he indulged the hope that, through grace in the Lord Jesus Christ, his name was written the Book of Life."

Dea. Pitman Wilcox, one of the pioneer settlers of Genesee County, came from East Guilford, Conn., in 1810. He was married to Eliza Wilcox, and they reared a family of five sons, viz.: Thomas F, Abel E., Edmund, Harmon, and Pitman, Jr. He died July 13, 1828. The second son, Abel E., was born August 12, 1801, and came to this county with his father when about eight years old. He followed farming, and had necessarily received, from the early condition of the new country, a limited education. He married Clara Richmond, of Cayuga County, N. Y., November 7, 1825, who died December 25, 1826, leaving no children. Mr. Wilcox married, second, Elizabeth, daughter of Deacon John and Elizabeth Spencer, of Bergen, by whom he had 10 children, seven of whom survive, viz.: Clara. A., widow of Reynold Curtiss of Cambdride, Eng.; Edwin M.; Jane E. (Mrs. John Birdsall), of South Evanston, Ill.; J. Spencer; H. Halsey ; Ellen A. (Mrs. Linden D. Arnold) ; and Charles J., of Vicksburg, Mich. Abel E. Wilcox became a member of the First Congregational Church of Bergen in 1834, with which he was prominently connected for years as deacon. He died October 2, 1879, aged 76 years. Edwin M., the eldest, born March 5, 1836, was married, December 19, 1865, to Ella A. Dudley, of Guilford, Conn , and their children are Hamilton, born February 27, 1867 ; L. Dudley, born May 25, 1870 ; William S., born May 14, 1875 ; and Edwin E., born June 23, 1880. Edwin M.

Wilcox enlisted in Co. G, 14th Conn. Inf., July 27, 1862, and continued in the service to the close of the war, participating in the battles of Fredericksburg, Chancellorsville, Wilderness, Petersburg, and several minor engagements.   He was wounded at Fredericksburg and again at the Wilderness, and was twice a prisoner, being once in Libby and once in Belle Isle.   After the war he returned to farming.   J. Spencer Wilcox, second son of Abel E., was born in Bergen, November 25, 1842, and has followed farming   April 11, 1872, he married Hermoione, daughter of William Patten, of Bergen, by whom he had four children, as follows: Clarence E., born March 4. 1873 ; Mary E., born December 8, 1875 ; Nellie G., born September 25, 1877 ; and Russell H., born March 11, 1882.   H. Halsey, third son of Abel E., now living, was born in this town November 23, 1847   He has always lived in Bergen as a farmer and breeder of thoroughbred sheep.   He was married, October 10, 1878, to Anna M., daughter of William P. Squiers, of Churchville, N. Y., and they have three children, as follows: Anna Mabel, born August 19, 1879; Roscoe S., born June 14, 1882; and Marion H., born April 15, 1884.

Charles J. Wilcox, youngest son of Abel E. Wilcox, was born in Bergen, January 7, 1856, and in his early years worked with his father on the farm.   At the age of 20 he graduated from Eastman's Commercial College.   In the spring of 1879 he went to Kalamazoo, Mich., and remained there, farming, seven years, when he removed to Vicksburg, Mich., where he now resides.   He married Elizabeth Adams, of Kalamazoo County, Mich., February 13, 1882, and they have one child, Ina Belle, born February 14, 1883.

Thomas J. Wilcox, fourth son of Elias and Rachel Wilcox, was born in Sweden, Monroe County, N. Y., January 26, 1835, removing to Bergen with his parents when quite young, where his younger days were spent in work on the farm and attending the common schools.   At the age of 17 he began apprenticeship with Carmine Martin; at carpentering, where he was employed seven years.   In 1859 he married Eleanor, daughter of Carmine and Caroline Martin, at Avon, Livingston County, N. Y.   He enlisted in the service of his country October 5, 1861, in the 27th N. Y. Vols.   He was a member of Scott's cornet band of Rochester.   From Washington, D. C., he was ordered to Western Virginia, where he was taken sick with typhoid fever, and died at the 7th Brigade Hospital, January 26, 1862.   His remains were at once brought to Bergen, and now rest in Mount Rest Cemetery.   He left, surviving him, his wife and one son, Sanford H. Wilcox, who is now engaged in the carpenter and joiner business. · Mrs. Eleanor Wilcox, his widow, still resides here, and is a dressmaker.

The third child of John and Betsey Walker, born April 30, 1832, was William C. Walker.   He was from Gates, Monroe County, N. Y., whence he was removed to Ogden, on the town line of Riga, at the tender age of two years.   Here the father died in 1881.   William C., at the age of 22, purchased a farm in Riga, one mile east of Bergen village, where he lived till 1882, when he removed to the village. The year previous he had built a fine brick building on Lake street, corner of Rochester, for a hotel, which he opened to the public in the spring as the "Walker House." This is first-class in all its appointments and enjoys the favor of the public. He married, April 4, 1857, Candace, daughter of Rhoderick and Mary Gooding, who died January 5, 1858, leaving no children. August 21, 1861, he married Elizabeth A., daughter of Leander and Lavia Hitchcock, of Eagle Harbor, Orleans County, and they have five children— Gertrude E., Sidney E., Dewitt C., and Lewis E. Mr. Walker, as a farmer, made a specialty of hops, which proved very successful under his management. The genealogy of the family is extensive, extending back to 1620, and has been published down to 1861. W. C Walker, grandfather of the present William C., was born at West Becket, Mass , in 1761, and died October 8, 1841. John Walker was also born at West Becket, November 18, 1795, married Betsey Sprague in 1823, and died in 1881.

Dr. Levi Ward, son of Levi, and a native of Connecticut, emigrated to Bergen in 1807, accompanied by his brother, John Ward. At Le Roy they met R. M. Stoddard, agent of the Triangle tract, and were induced to locate in what was then called the North Woods (now Bergen village). Finding temporary quarters in the newly erected log house of Daniel Kelsey, Dr. Ward erected a small frame house and covered it with cedar shingles, which were then deemed aristocratic for the new country. His brother erected a log house, and both began clearing off the land. It was on Saturday that they arrived at their new home in the wilderness. Accustomed to regular attendance at public worship their first thought was to provide for religious exercises. A meeting was agreed upon at the house of the new settler, and 14 or 15 persons assembled from the scattered settlements. Prayers were offered, a sermon read, and hymns were sung. For nine years Dr. Ward was one of the most active of the early pioneers He was an efficient helper in all that was to be done in the back woods : in opening new roads, establishing schools, organizing religious societies. He came to the new country to find a home for himself and family rather than to practice his profession. In 1811 he was appointed agent to settle the accounts of the commissioners who built the bridge over the river at Rochester. In 1812 he was the means of getting mail routes established. At the time of the War of 1812 he collected all the muskets, rifles, etc., with what ammunition could be found, for the use of Gen. Davis. He was supervisor for six years, and judge of the county at one time. In 1817 he moved to Rochester. His eldest son, W. H , was postmaster of Bergen.

BETHANY.

BETHANY, as will be seen by the list of the early settlers, was among the earliest towns which invited the pioneers to its rich lands. The most of the settlements were made before the War of 1812 On June 8th of that year the town was formed, being taken from Batavia. The land is rolling in the upper half, and somewhat hilly as the lower bounds are reached. It is a well watered section, Black Creek, Tonawanda Creek, and White Creek being the principal streams.

In 1803 John Torrey, Orsamus Kellogg (who had a child born that year), Charles Culver, John Dewey, L. D. and Samuel Prindle, Nathaniel Pinney, Jedediah Riggs. M. Scott, Horace Shepard, O. Fletcher, David Hall, Capt. George Lathrop, and Richard Pearson either settled on lands in the town or declared their intention so to do ; and in 1804 many others came ; the sound of the axe was daily heard in the forests, and a musical and welcome sound it must have been in those days to all those who had determined to deny themselves so many comforts in order to make a home in the new Genesee country. Capt. Lathrop, who located in the center of the town, is said to be the third person who came. He was a captain in the War of 1812, and died on his farm, aged 92 years. Solomon Lathrop, who came in 1804, lost his wife about 1816. He went on a visit (soon after) to Cattaraugus County, and was never heard from. Henry Lathrop located in 1804, and died on his place, aged 85 years. Richard Pearson, Sr., came from Lyme, Conn., to Genesee County about 1803, bought 155 acres of land for $426.25, and returned to Connecticut, coming again to the county in 1806. He returned to Connecticut again in 1807, and finally came to the county in 1812, in which year he bought 50 acres in the Craigie tract for $200. He married and settled on his land in 1815, coming with a neighbor with an ox-team and one horse, each family having one child. He died on his farm in 1853, aged 71 years. His son lives on the old homestead. Richard Peck, among the earliest settlers (1806), was a lieutenant in Col. Rumsey's regiment in the War of 1812 ; he was at Chestnut Ridge and Black Rock. The old commission signed by Gov. Tompkins is in the possession of his son, who lives in Stafford. Another son, Benjamin F., lives on the old homestead.

The Lincoln family were very prominent in the early settlement. Jedediah, who came in 1805, when last heard from was over 96 years of age. He was living in Illinois with a son. Peter Putnam located in the northwestern part of the town in 1805 or 1806

Because of the valuable water privileges on the Little Tonawanda, in the southwest part of the town, there was greater activity there than elsewhere This locality (now Linden) was first called Gad-Pouch, because it is supposed " gadding women " were more numerous than elsewhere.

The name "Linden" was first suggested by a clerk in the store at that place, and the first sign was put up over the mill, Judge Isaac Wilson being the postmaster and a justice. John Wilder, a pioneer of Attica, built many mills, among which was one, in 1810, for Judge Wilson at this place. This mill was enlarged in 1833 by Daniel Calkins. It was the first grist-mill that served the inhabitants of the northern part of Wyoming County, and a great portion of the towns of Darien, Alexander, and Bethany. About the year 1809 Calvin Barrows came in, and made the pioneers glad by fitting up a carding and woolen mill. He came from Massachusetts, and lived in the town 60 years. He built a log house in the same year (which was burned), and lived in it six years. He rebuilt about 1817 where Sexturs, a son, now lives. Mr. Barrows was a Master Mason and a member of Olive Branch Lodge, which met at Huggins's tavern after the troubles in Batavia.

One Coles built a saw-mill in Linden about 1808. There was a fall of 24 feet to the dam, and owing to insecure foundation this mill tumbled over that distance and hurt some of the operatives. Another saw mill was built, which was burned. Several fires have occurred in the place from time to time, among which have been the stone distillery (started by Nathaniel Eastman), which had also been used as a cooper shop by Collins; the old store built by Wilson & Dewey; the railroad depot in 1860; the flour-mill in 1879; and the W. H. Barrows house. After the stone distillery was destroyed a wooden one was built in 1825, and a stone one in 1838. Some of the owners of the old (Wilson) mill site have been George Perry (an old settler), Collins, Remer & Tuttle, Remer & Barrows, and W. H. Barrows. The latter also started a cabinet shop in 1837, continuing it for 15 years, when he kept a store for four years, and then moved to Attica.

Among the store-keepers were Judge Wilson, Horace Tripman, Webster (who also had an ashery), and Collins. One Gardner also had a store and ashery in 1820. The first tavern there was kept by Joseph Chamberlain, in a house built by Mr. Lusk. E. and Jeduthan Faunce in 1835 kept a tavern in the house owned by Myron Kemp.

The first settlers who arrived at Linden were Calvin Barrows, Samuel Jolls, Alexander Grimes, Jacob Grimes, Andrew Grimes, Rufus Munger, Jesse Fay, Matthew Alger, Sanford Bowers, Israel Everest, Nathan Blood, and a few others. A Mr. Towner was an early miller. At the time of the advent of the railroad, about 1850 or 1852, business was not very brisk in the place, there being only a grist-mill, cider and shingle-mill, and a cooper shop. In 1869 one Bunce had a tannery here. Durgy & Huggins and Faunce & Whaley had stores, W. E. Kemp a barrel factory, S. Metcalf a saw-mill, and Quale Brothers a flour and saw-mill. It is supposed Aaron Bailey, in 1828, taught the first school in Linden, but Matilda Wedge, in 1808, is credited with being the first teacher in the town.

CANADA, a small hamlet on Black Creek, in the eastern part of the

23

town, claims to have had a mill erected in 1808, by one Bennett, one of
a family who came in 1805, and for some time the place was called
" Bennett's Mills." There was a tavern here in early times.   No business
of importance is transacted at the locality at present.

Sylvester Lincoln, in 1805, had a tavern, said to be the first in town;
the same one, it is presumed, which, in 1821, was kept by C. J Lincoln,
who was also postmaster and colonel of militia, and where the Masonic
meetings of Olive Branch Lodge were frequently held after their removal
from Batavia.   B. R. Brown also had a tavern about 1825, and one
L. Brown, in 1828, kept an inn on the new State road.   Nathaniel Huggins also kept a tavern, built in 1828, and kept by him until his death in
1852, where the Masons met.   This is now the residence of Thomas J.
Harding.   Mr. Huggins was a postmaster in 1832.   W. H. Rumsey
had a tavern in 1841.   Nelson Blood had one in 1859, and very early
Buell Brown kept an inn.   R. A. Taylor, in 1864, kept the hotel at East
Bethany, and Davis Gray kept the same place in 1869.   Elisha Hurlburt opened a store in 1808, the same year Sylvester Lincoln opened his
tavern, each in a log house.

The postoffice at Bethany was established in 1825 by Orange Allen.
Phineas Smith was postmaster in 1826; E. C. Dibble in 1829; C. J.
Lincoln in 1831; and Harvey Prindle later.   The firm of Chipman &
Lusk was in business in 1830, Owen & Prindle in 1844, and Carlos A.
Huggins in 1869.

A prominent early settler was Richard Powers, a Mason, who died in
1849, aged 80 years.   His son Blanchard was also an active and prominent man, especially in Masonic matters.   The old lodge often met at
his house.

The Genesee Manual Labor Seminary was chartered in 1832, with a
capital of $20,000.   Subscriptions to the amount of $5,516 enabled the
organizers to erect the building.   R. Whiting was the principal from
1834 to 1841, and Joseph Hurty until 1844.

The Genesee County alms-house is located in the south part of the
town, on roads 40 and 41.   It has room for 100 inmates, and is a well
managed institution.   The superintendents are C. Crosman, of Alexander; Dwight Dimock, of Pembroke; and H. O. Bostwick, of Batavia.
Benjamin W. Hartwell, of Pavilion, is the keeper, and Dr. Ganson W.
Croff the resident physician.   Connected with the house is a farm of 200
acres in a fine state of cultivation, and is valued at $11,500.   An inven-
tory taken in 1889 showed a total value of $18,000.   In 1890 there were
73 inmates, the estimated cost of keeping which was 15 cents per day,
exclusive of the products of the farm.   This includes salaries, excepting
that of superintendent.   Wheat, corn, oats, and pork are raised on the
place.   The value of the products raised in 1889 was $2,587.   In 1832
James Thayer, aged 84 years, and Anny Danforth, aged 86, were married here.

LINDEN, the first village of importance, is located on the N. Y., L. E.

& W. Railroad, has 35 houses, one school, three stores, one wagon shop, one blacksmith shop, a grist-mill (built by George Perry in 1881), with three runs of stones, one saw-mill, with a capacity of 3,000 feet of lumber per day, one cooper shop, built by Daniel Merritt, with a capacity of 10,000 barrels, and one cider-mill, with a capacity of 4,000 barrels annually. The village is without church privileges.

EAST BETHANY, the next village of importance, is located on the D., L. & W. Railroad, in the northeastern part of the town. There are 24 houses with about 108 inhabitants. It is a post village, has a Presbyterian Church, a school, one hotel, two stores, a harness shop, a blacksmith shop, and a cider-mill, the latter having a capacity of 400 barrels per year. There is now building (May, 1890) a fine school-house, which will cost about $1,500.

BETHANY CENTER, also a post village, is south of the center of the town, and has a Presbyterian and Baptist church, two stores, a blacksmith shop, a town hall, a school, two dressmakers, about 25 houses, and 85 inhabitants.

LITTLE CANADA (formerly Bennett's), in the northeastern part of the town, has a Free Methodist Church, a school, a grist-mill, with a capacity of 150 bushels of grain per day, a saw-mill, with a capacity of 2,000 feet of lumber per day, and a wagon shop.

WEST BETHANY (p. o.) is a hamlet in the west part of the town. It has a grist mill, located on road 29, built by Nathaniel Brown in 1811, and now owned by Joseph Crawford, having a capacity of 50 bushels of wheat and 200 bushels of feed per day. The village has also a grocery store, a Freewill Baptist Church, a blacksmith shop, and six houses.

Bethany was the only town in Genesee County but what received a donation from the Holland Land Co. of 100 acres of land for religious purposes. The earliest record we have of religious services is that of the Freewill Baptists, the Rev. Nathaniel Brown being instrumental in organizing a church in 1809. In 1839 they put up a wooden edifice. They now have 82 members in the society, which is presided over by Hiram G. Schoonover. Their property is valued at $1,000.

The Methodists held camp-meetings at "Bennett's," or Little Canada, as early as 1810, and Benjamin Barlow, a local preacher, held services in the town in 1811, as did also Father Waller and Brother Howe, who came from Wyoming County. They also built the church now owned by the Free Methodists. This society was organized by Jonathan K. Barlow, the pioneer physician, and held its meetings in the same building with the Presbyterians, which was afterwards used as an academy. A society was organized in 1820, and one January 7, 1832, but soon became extinct. A Bethany Union Church Society was organized in 1828.

At Little Canada a Free Methodist Society was organized and the church, formerly built by the regular Methodists, was purchased, but we cannot learn when. The church is small in membership, there being now only about 17 persons, with C. W. Bacon, pastor.

The first regular Baptist Church, located at Bethany Center, was organized May 7, 1820, with 26 members, and John Blain was its pastor. In 1826 a building was erected, and the same is still occupied by the society. They now have 58 members, and Rev. T. M. Scarff is the pastor. Their property is valued at $2,000. The Sunday-school, organized in 1829, now has about 75 members.

October 20, 1829, a Presbyterian Church was organized at Bethany Center by Messrs. Whiting, Watts, Bliss, and a few others. Rev W. Whiting was the first pastor. They built a structure, of wood, in 1839. At present they have 50 members, and about 60 scholars in the Sunday-school.

On June 17, 1817, a Congregational church was organized at East Bethany by John Bliss, a missionary from Connecticut, with 11 members. Their first pastor was Rev. Reuben Hard, who came in 1823. The society built a brick edifice in 1824, costing about $3,000. The same year they adopted the Presbyterian form of government. In 1825 there were 23 members; in 1834, 58; in 1843, 65; and in 1846, 35. The ministers have been Revs. Wilcox, Kniffen, Miles, Smaller, Clark, Barris, and others. The membership is now only 16, and the Sunday-school has about 70 scholars. The Rev. W. M. Modestti is pastor.

A protestant Episcopal church was built about 1826 called Zion church. At the laying of the corner-stone, July 4th, Judge Mitchell delivered the oration, and Masonic ceremonies aided in making the occasion interesting. In 1845 Bishop Delancey visited the church, at which time Rev. M Oaks was the minister. A Rev. Mr. Atwater was a minister at one time, but we fail to learn but little about the society.

The following are names of some of the early settlers of Bethany, with the date of settlement:

In 1803: Charles Culver, John Dewey, O. Fletcher, David Hall, Orsamus Kellogg, Solomon Kingsley, Capt. G. Lathrop, L. D. and Samuel Prindle, Richard Pearson, Sr., Nathaniel Pinney, Jedediah Riggs, M. Scott, Horace Shepard, and John Torrey. In 1804 : Peter Adley, John Boynton, William and W. B. Coggeshall, James and Jerry Cowdrey, Lewis Disbrow, Peleg Douglass, N. Eastman, Elisha Giddings, John Grimes, C. Glass, Joseph Hawks, Thomas Harding, John Halstead, Alanson Jones, Henry and Solomon Lathrop, Sylvester Lincoln, Sr., John Roberts, John and Phineas Smith, Israel Shearer, David Tyrrill, Joel S. Wilkinson, and Isaac R. and William Williams. In 1805 : David Anderson, Patrick Alvin, Israel and Abel Buell, Erastus, James, and Jeremiah Bennett, Joseph Bartlett, Eli Bristol, Jonathan and Jason Bixby, John Chambers, Ezekiel Fay, John Greenough, John Huntington, Thomas Halstead, Jedediah Lincoln, Asher Lamberton, Gershom Orvis, Peter Putnam, Jr., Eli Perry, A. Robbins, Alfred Rose, Richard Stiles, Josiah Southard, Elisha Wallace, Peter Wilkinson, Isaac Wilson, and Philo Whitcomb. In 1806 : Joseph Adgate, Elisha Andrews, Lewis Barney, D. W. Bannister, Peter and Chester Davidson, Eben Eggleston, Moses Goodrich, Liberty Judd, David Ingersoll, David Morgan, Henry Miller, F. Putnam, Richard and Mather Peck, Henry Rumsey, Thomas Starkweather, David Stewart, Joseph Shedd, and Eben Wilson. In 1807: Heman and Buell Brown, and Sylvester Lincoln, Jr. In 1808 : ——— Cole, Elisha Hurlburt, Moses Page, and Eliza Peck. In 1809 : Elder Nathaniel Brown, Calvin Barrows, and Eleazer Faunce. In 1810: Patience Kingsley, O. Walker and W. Waite, Sr. In 1811: Israel Cook, Alexander Grimes, Daniel Marsh, Jesse, Rumsey, Charles Smead, and Judge Wilson. In 1812: Israel Fay and Robert Lounsbury. In 1813: Abner Ashley, S. Bowers, Josiah Churchill, Capt. Lodowick Champlin, W. R. Dixon, John Eastland, I. Everest, John Metcalf, William Odiorne, Harvey Prindle, John Page, and Nathan Rumsey. In 1814: Thomas Adgate, Charles Dixon, T. Fay, Alanson D. Lord, Rufus Munger, and W. F. Norton. In 1815: James Bennett, Jr., Charles Brisbee, Richard B. French, John Green, John Lincoln, A. Parsons, J. Saunders, James Stewart, and Benjamin Smith. In 1816: G. Cottrell, J. Rolfe, and Asahel and James Shepard. In 1817: B. Barlow and Daniel Hyde. In 1818: David Merritt and Jared S. Lord. In 1819; S. Debow and ——— Gardner. In 1824: James Baker. In 1825: Orange Allen and R. R. Brown. In 1828: Aaron Bailey. In 1829: E. C. Dibble. In 1832: Nathaniel Huggins. The following came prior to 1825: Richard Powers, Ira Waite, Matilda Wedge, Samuel Jolles, and C. J. Lincoln.

Our readers will find some interesting facts connected with the following sketches of the present prominent living residents and their ancestors, the early pioneers.

The late Martin Armbrewster was born November 24, 1819, in Baden-Baden, Germany. About 1846 or '47 he married Frances Snneeff, of the same place, and in 1854 they came to the United States, locating first in Buffalo, then in Batavia, and finally in the town of Bethany. They had 15 children, of whom three died in infancy, Louisa died aged about 22 years, and 11 survive, namely: Caroline, Mary, Francis, Ezra, Elizabeth, Sophia, Fred, Frank, Jennie, John, and Ella M. Mr. Armbrewster died September 26, 1879. Mrs. Armbrewster is living on road 31, in this town.

Robert Benington, father of John R., was born in England, and was a resident of Yorkshire and Lancaster. January 14, 1822, when 21 years old, he came to America and located in New Lisbon, Otsego County, N. Y. In 1847 he married Eliza Kenyon, of Edmeston, Otsego County. They had 10 children, namely: Charles, Henry G., William, John R., Edwin, Harriet, Phebe, Alfred, Agnes E., and Mary L. John R. was born in the town of New Lisbon, Otsego County, September 28, 1852. He was educated in the public schools until he was 20 years of age. He is a farmer and breeder of grade sheep, and at present is superintendent of the James H. Hume farm, on road 2, of 411 acres. February 11, 1880, he married Jane E., only daughter of Thomas Rathbone, of Burlington, Otsego County, and they have one girl, Ethel H., born February 23, 1882.

John Boyle was born in Tipperary County, Ireland, in 1846, and came to America in 1863. In 1867 he married Kate Dower, of County Waterford, Ireland. They were married in New York city, and soon after returned to Ireland, where they remained five years, when they came to this country and located in this town. They have nine children, viz.: Patrick W, John R., Lawrence, Mary, Thomas, Kate, Robert, Julia, and Edwin. They reside on road 16 corner of 15. Mrs. Kate Boyle is a thrifty business woman.

Rev. Nathaniel Brown, grandfather of Wilder and Walter, came from Strafford, Orange County, Vt., in 1809, and located at West Bethany, on the place now owned by John S. Baldwin. He was the first Freewill Baptist minister west of the Genesee River. He organized the first church of that denomination there in 1809. He was a pensioner of the

Revolution. Rev. Mr. Brown, after coming to West Bethany, preached for the people there the remainder of his life without compensation. On one occasion he was induced to take one dollar, and before he arrived home he gave it away to a poor man. Col. Daniel Brown, his youngest son, was born at the old home in Orange County, Vt., August 10, 1806, and came in 1810 with his parents to the home his father had located in 1809. He received a fair education for that early day, and was a man well versed in all matters concerning the welfare of his country and county. He was a fluent public speaker, and was colonel of the 16th N. Y. Cav. He first married Julia Lounsbury, by whom he had three children, Jane, Laura, and Marquis. For his second wife he married Elanora A. Cook, and they had nine children, viz.: Wilder, Julia, Emerette, Cassius, Walter, Sarah, Abigail, Marquis, 2d, and Alice. Wilder, born May 28, 1841, received a common school education, and is a carpenter and farmer by occupation. November 29, 1865, he married Frances E., youngest daughter of Charles Lorish, of Linden. They have one son, Cassius Stanley, born April 3, 1875. Col. Daniel Brown died March 31, 1879. Walter Brown was born February 13, 1847, and received a good education. He has a good intellect with perceptive faculties well developed, and is a farmer and general dealer. December 31, 1872, he married H. Jenne, youngest daughter of the late Harry G. Lincoln, of Bethany. They have one son, Leon H. D., born May 14, 1884. Mr. and Mrs. Brown are living on road 19, adjoining the Col. Brown homestead.

Heman Brown, Sr., grandfather of Benjamin R., was a soldier in the Revolutionary war. Heman, Jr., came with his parents from Strafford, Vt., to this town when he was 13 years old. He was born May 30, 1794. He was in the War of 1812. They located at Brown's Corners, road 17 corner 19. He married twice, first, Maria Huntington, formerly of Litchfield, Conn. They had four children, of whom two sons are deceased, and two daughters survive, namely: Mary and Harriet. For his second wife Mr. Brown married, February 10, 1842, Sophia Ann Conklin, formerly of Steuben County, N. Y. They had four children, of whom two daughters are deceased, and the sons survive, viz.: Lee E. and Benjamin R. Benjamin R. was born November 13, 1848. He received a good education. September 24, 1874, he married Celia S., second daughter of Charles and Elizabeth Snell, of his native town. They have had six children, four of whom survive, namely: Charles H., Fernie E., Jesse R., and Bessie M. Mr. and Mrs. Brown reside on land which his father bought in 1821, on road 19 corner 27. Mr. Brown's mother resides with him, being a pensioner of the War of 1812, aged 80 years.

Calvin Barrows, father of Sexturs T., was born near Worcester, Mass., in 1783, and came to Seneca Falls, N. Y., in 1808. He married Olive Patterson, of Waterloo, Seneca County, and soon after moved to Bushville, in this town, where he remained two years, and was in charge of the cloth factory there for Mr. Bush. In 1809 he came to Linden, when there were only three houses in the place. He built a dam for the purpose of utilizing the water-power of Little Tonawanda Creek, and erected a wool-carding and cloth-dressing factory, which was completed in 1810. They had seven children, namely: John, Volney, William, Franklin, Sexturs T., Jeanett, and Evander H. Sexturs T., born in Linden, December 25, 1819, was educated in the common schools, and worked in the carding-mill 10 years. December 21, 1842, he married Rachel, third daughter of John Merritt, of Middlebury, Wyoming County. They have four children, viz.: Margaretta J., Olive R., George N., and Charles C. Margaretta J. married Hiram O. Reddish, of Wyoming village; Olive R. married Buel Rogers, of Linden, now of Attica; Charles C. married Aurelia J. Richardson, also of Linden. Mr. Barrows has lived on the old homestead 70 years.

Amos Blood, grandfather of Oscar W., was born March 11, 1763, and his father was killed in the Revolutionary war. One of Amos's sons, Nason, was born November 4, 1796, at Haverhill Corners, Grafton County, N. H. He received a good education, and was a farmer by occupation. He came with his father to Alexander, this county, when 15 years old, and February 28, 1822, he married, first, Rhoda Everest, of Bethany. He served in the War of 1812. They had six children, as follows: Nelson, Niles, Warren, Obed, Luman, and Amos. For his second wife he married Mrs. Eunice (Knowlton) West, October 1, 1840.. They had one son, Oscar W., born December 17, 1843, on the farm upon which he resides and owns. Oscar W. received a common school and academic education, until he was 21 years of age. May 9, 1867, he married Mary L., oldest daughter of Robert Eastland, of Bethany, and they have six children, viz.: Eunice E., Jessie L., Charles R., Walter E., Mary J., and Monroe T. Eunice E. is a student at the Geneseo Normal School, and is also a school teacher. The family all reside at home. Mr. Blood is a successful fruit grower and breeder of thoroughbred Merino sheep, and is one of Bethany's enterprising farmers, residing on road 33.

Mark Bassert, born in Baden, Germany, April 22, 1829, came with his mother to America in 1847, and located at Batavia, N. Y. December 3, 1853, he married Catherine Miller, of Germany. They have three children, Louis, George, and Ursilla. Louis married Anna M. Dennis, of Stafford; George married Lydia Worst, also of Stafford; and Ursilla married Urbon Botmer, of Batavia. Mr. Bassert served his adopted country in Co. G, 8th N. Y. H. A. Vols., and was discharged at the close of the war. He was wounded in the right shoulder June 16, 1864. in front of Petersburg, while charging the enemy's works. Mr. and Mrs. Bassert reside in the village of East Bethany.

Michael Burns, father of James, was born in Wicklow, on the east coast of Ireland, about 1833. and married Elizabeth Duffy, of the same place. They had 10 children. He came to America in 1852 to prepare a home for his family; his wife and three of his children followed in 1854. James, who was born at the old home June 25, 1843, came to America about

1856, and located in the town of Bethany. About November 1, 1872, he married May Frolicker, of East Bethany, and they had one son, Frank M., born October 23, 1873. Mrs. Burns died October 24, 1887. Mr. Burns and his son reside on road 14 in this town.

John Burkel, born in Arlin County, Belgium, October 15, 1850, came to America in 1870, landing in New York, February 22d. He finally located in Byron, Genesee County. May 10, 1874, he married Barbara, oldest daughter of John and Kate Coltax, of Sheldon, Wyoming County. They have had three children, namely: John, Jr., born May 20, 1875 ; Lizzie, who died aged one year and nine months; and Sylvester, born September 29, 1882. Mrs. Burkel's parents are of French extraction. Her father, John Coltax, came to America from France in 1846, when he was 21 years old, and located in Wyoming County, N. Y. He married Kate Coltax, of his native country, and they had seven children, viz.: John, Michael, Barbara, Mary, Libbie, Anna, and Margaret. Mr. and Mrs. Burkel reside on road 6, in Bethany.

James Baker, father of Thomas S., was born in Butternut, Otsego County, N. Y., in September, 1804, and came to Stafford, Genesee County, in 1824. About 1828 or '29 he married Betsey R. Shedd, of Bethany. They had four children, viz.: Joseph R., Thomas S., Sarah P., and James P. Thomas S. was educated in the common schools. November 10, 1854, he married Hannah R., youngest daughter of John Reed, of Pavilion, and they have one son, John A., born February 14, 1857. John A. was educated in the common schools, and March 9, 1880, he married Libbie A. Smith, of Le Roy. They have had two sons and one daughter, of whom the latter died in infancy. Edgar T. and Clarence S. survive. Mr. and Mrs. Baker reside on road 36.

Ambrose Booth, father of Fred A., was born in Steuben County, N. Y., January 24, 1834. He was educated in the public schools, and is a farmer by occupation. April 6, 1857, he married Charity G. Hovey, of Cattaraugus County. They have three children, namely : Adna J., Frank D., and Fred A. The latter was born in Dale, Wyoming County, March 14, 1865. He received a good education, and is a farmer. August 9, 1888, he married Sadie L. youngest daughter of Philip Moyer, of Alexander. They reside near the village of Linden.

Adam Cacner was born in Hesse-Darmstadt, Germany, about 1776. He married Mary A. Winterman, and they had seven children, three of whom were born in Germany. George, born December 25, 1841, came to Bethany when he was 12 years old, and made his home with Israel E. Judd. December 18, 1863; he enlisted in Co. L, 8th N. Y. H. A. Vols., and was discharged from Zekel's General Hospital, May 27, 1865. He was in the battles of the Wilderness, Cold Harbor, and in front of Petersburg, where he was disabled June 23, 1864, by a gun-shot wound in the leg. December 25, 1865, he married Sarah Jane, oldest daughter of Edward Smith, formerly of Canada. They have six children, namely : Mary O., Kattie M., Frank J., Emily S., Clary A., and Charles W. Mr. and Mrs. Cacner are residing in this town on road 20.

John Covey, born in Saratoga County, N. Y., in 1787, of English ancestry, married Betsey Althouse in 1809. Alvah Covey, his eldest son, was born at Half Moon, Saratoga County, July 22, 1810, and married, February 6, 1837, Jane, daughter of John Hardick. She was born September 3, 1816. Her father was born in Athens, Greene County, in 1783. Ten children were born to Alvah and Jane (Hardick) Covey, five of whom survive, namely : Alvah S., Charlotte I., Eugene, Emma J., and Frank H. The latter, born April 9, 1861, in Penfield, Monroe County, received a common school and commercial education, and was associated in business with his father, who came to Penfield about 1838 and was a successful nurseryman there. By energy, perseverance, and strict integrity he laid the foundation for his afterwards ample fortune. July 13, 1882, Frank H. Covey married Minnie J., third daughter of Henry and Louisa (Groom) Palmer, of Glenville, N. Y. She was born in Clifton Park, Saratoga County, December 18, 1860. They have a daughter, Minnie Ethel, born September 20, 1883. Mr. Covey came to Bethany in the spring of 1888.

Elisha Chadwick, born in Lyme, Conn., June 2, 1788, married Betsey Russell, of the same place, February 15, 1815. They came to Bethany about 1823, with an ox-team and cart. They had eight children, namely: Nancy M., Daniel R., Israel M., Mary E., Harriet. Joseph H., J. Edward, and David R   J. Edward was born April 1, 1829, in this town. He received a public school and academic education, and September 9, 1857, married Emeline M. Dutton, of Pavilion, who was born August 6, 1830. Mr. Chadwick is doing a general insurance business in the adjoining towns and counties, and resides on road 24 in the town of Bethany.

Patrick H. Cannon was born in Galway, Ireland, March 17, 1836. March 4, 1863, he married Mary Galman, of his native place, and April 3, 1864, they landed in New York, and located at Roxbury, Mass. They have had nine children, one of whom died in infancy, and eight survive, namely : Mary A., Patrick H , Jr., John J., Kattie T., Fannie E., Nellie M., Thomas E., and James. Mr. and Mrs. Cannon are living on road 22.

Joseph Crawford was born October 10, 1833, in Rochester, N. Y., received a practical education, and in early life was a farmer. He moved with his parents to Attica, Wyoming County, in 1841. In 1854 they moved to the town of Bethany, and located on road 17 corner 19   April 10, 1861, he married Julia, oldest daughter of Col. Daniel and Eleanora Brown, of Bethany. She was born February 7, 1840. Mr. Crawford learned the milling business about 1873, and is now proprietor of the grist-mill and grocery store at West Bethany. He was appointed postmaster, during President Grant's second term, in 1876, which office he still holds.

Stewart Copeland was born in County Down, Ireland, in December, 1807. He married Agnes Fennon, of his native place, and came to America in 1833, first locating in Rochester, and finally came to Bethany, Genesee County. They had nine children, as follows: Thomas Robert, John, Elizabeth, Stewart, Jr., Agnes, James, Marion, and William W., of whom Thomas, Robert, James, Agnes, and Marion are deceased. Stewart, Jr., a bachelor, is a fruit grower and farmer, and his father resides with him. John Copeland married Nellie Neff, of Liecester, Livingston County, and they had seven children, as follows : Thomas, Katie, Everett, Fennon, Nancy, James, and John, Jr. Thomas and Nancy are deceased. He enlisted in 1861 in Co. E, 9th Inf. N. Y. Vols., and was discharged in August, 1863. Both John and Stewart, Jr., reside on road 34, in this town.

Calvin Curtis was born in Berkshire County, Mass., July 25, 1778. He was married three times, first to Jemima Thompson, and second to Polly Clapp, and five children were born to him. For his third wife he married Mrs. Nancy (Hibbard) Storrs, of Wyoming County, by whom he had four children, namely : Samantha, Martha, Daniel S., and Roger H. Daniel S., born September 5, 1829, was educated in the public schools until he was 16 years old. January 10, 1850, he married Amanda H., fifth daughter of Clark Eldridge, of Canandaigua, Ontario County. They have three children, of whom Calvin died at the age of three years, and two survive, namely : Frank R., born January 3, 1857, and Lottie B., born July 3, 1858, who married Andrew B. Morris, of Middlebury, Wyoming County. Frank R. married Sarah Boyce, of Wyoming village. Mr. and Mrs. Curtis reside on road 14, in the hamlet of Little Canada.

Dr. Orlando R. Croff was born three miles west of Warsaw village, August 10, 1817, *at two o'clock in the afternoon.* He received a common school and academic education, studied medicine with Dr. Jonathan K. Barlow, of Bethany Center, graduated in 1843, and has practiced medicine since (46 years). April 14, 1844. he married Mary E., second daughter of Dea. Elisha Chadwick, of Warsaw. They have two children, namely : Ganson W., born April 1, 1845, and Nella M., born May 28, 1866, who resides at home with her parents. Ganson W. is a practicing physician. He studied medicine with his father, attended lectures at Ann Arbor, Mich., and graduated from the University of Buffalo in 1867. He married Clara S., fifth daughter of Edmond Brainard, of this town, and they have had 10 children, viz.: Orlando W , James B., R. D., Belle, Effie M., Betsey, Lois, Ganson W., Jr., Clara M., and D. Olive. They all reside at Bethany Center.

Samuel Dye, born in the town of Mayfield, Montgomery County, N. Y., June 20, 1818, came with his parents to Springwater when 13 years of age. In 1841 he married Sarah Bevins, of Springwater. They had eight children, now living: Samuel H., William R., Jennie M., Julia A., Ada M., Eudora H., and George E. Samuel H. owns a fruit farm on road 20. In the war of the Rebellion he enlisted, August 30, 1862 in Co. I, 136th Inf. N. Y. Vols., and was discharged on surgeon's certificate of disability by loss of use of left leg, from a gun-shot wound received in the battle of Gettysburg, from the hospital at Philadelphia, Pa. At the same time he was shot in the right arm near the shoulder, which was broken, and also through the third finger of the right hand, the ball passing through the fleshy part of the hand, under the thumb, into the wrist.

Charles Dixon came from Chatham, Conn., to Bethany, and located on road 23 in 1814, leaving his family at home while he built a log house. In 'the spring of 1815 he returned for his wife and 12 children. Their conveyance was an ox-team and cart and a one-horse wagon. Two children were born to them in their new home, two also died, and 12 survived. One of them, William R., who was born on the old homestead in Bethany, May 13, 1822, was educated in the public schools, and was a farmer by occupation. December 24, 1863, he married Sophia, oldest daughter of Nicholas Chilson, of Pavilion. They have had five children, three of whom died in infancy, and two survive, namely : W. Walter, born September 21, 1866, and Charles A., born December 24, 1871. Mrs. Sophia Dixon and her two sons reside on the Dixon estate in this town.

Caleb Ellison was born in Orange County, N. Y., in 1803, and after his father's death went to Canada with his mother, where he remained 40 years. He married Jane Wilkins, of Ancaster, County Wentworth, Canada, and they had seven children, as follows : Nelson C., Eleanor, Matilda, Louisa, Jane, John, and William. Nelson C. was born in Canada, August 2, 1828. He received a common school education, and August 23, 1859, married Caroline, second daughter of Aaron Taylor, formerly of England. They have eight children, namly : Roenna, Mary J., Delila V., Florence, Milton, Robert, Courtney J., and Lilly B. Mr. and Mrs. Ellison reside on road 28.

Daniel Edwards, who was born in Rutland, Vt., March 27, 1807, came to New York State when a young man. He crossed the Genesee River at Rochester before any bridges were built, and located in Monroe County. December 22, 1836, he married Abby M. Conlee, of Stillwater, and they had two children, Sylvester C. and Charles D. The latter was born in Sweden, Monroe County, November 21, 1840. He received a public and Normal school education, began teaching school when he was 16 years old, and taught 17 terms August 11, 1862, he enlisted in Co. A, 140th Inf. N. Y. Vols; and was discharged December 18, 1864, for physical disability. He acted as company commissary-sergeant. January 1, 1865, he married Caroline, third daughter of Lawrence Cooper, of Clarkson, Monroe County. They have had eight children, viz.: Arthur Alger, who died in 1873, aged 19 months ; Sheridan, born November 25, 1865; Ida M., born June 1, 1868 ; Belle J., born May 8, 1870 ; Henry C., born April 12, 1874; Lillie E., born August 21, 1878 ; Erwin B., born August 13, 1883 ; and Carrie, born May 24, 1887. Mr. and Mrs. Edwards reside on road 3 in this town.

The first known of the Elliott family was in East Cocker, Somersetshire, England. One Andrew Elliott came to Beverly, Mass., about the year 1668, joined the first church there in 1670, and died in 1703 or '04. The Rev. Jesse Elliott was born in Mason, N. H., in 1799, was educated in the theological college of Hamilton, N. Y., graduated in the class of June, 1826, and afterwards taught in the Oneida Indian Mission

Station. For 54 years he was a faithful minister of the gospel in the Baptist denomination. He married twice, first, June 21, 1827, Phebe, daughter of Nathaniel and Betsey Yeomans, of Greenville, N. Y., by whom he had five children, of whom one son died in infancy, and four survive, namely: Emily R., Elizabeth, William, and Nathaniel. His first wife died October 22, 1840, and May 16, 1841, he married, second, Mary C., seventh daughter of Hezekiah Willis, of Western, Oneida County, who bore him one daughter, now Mrs. Jerome H. Filkins, of Bethany Center, and one son, S Willis, born April 17, 1848, in Middlebury, Wyoming County The latter received a good common school and academic education until he was 16 years old. He was engaged in mercantile business 11 years, has taught school several terms, and is a farmer by occupation. September 28, 1869, he married Angela A., seventh daughter of Edmund Brainard. They have had five children, three of whom are deceased, and two survive, namely: A. Grace, born September 17, 1874, and Brainard W., born September 21, 1879. Rev. Jesse Elliott died March 24, 1880. S. Willis Elliott has been actively engaged in purchasing and helping to survey land for the new line of railroad from Geneva to Buffalo during the fall and winter of 1889–90.

David Filkins was born in Dutchess County, N. Y., in 1807, and came with his parents to Pavilion in 1809. About 1834 he married Jemima Peck, who was born in Lyme, Conn. They had five children, namely: Angeline M., Caroline P., Sarah E., Jerome H., and Albert D. Jerome H. was born in this town November 7, 1839 He was educated in the public schools and is a farmer by occupation. He married twice, first, April 14, 1864, Emily O. Stevens, who died December 24, 1865, and second, June 23, 1868, Mary C., third daughter of the late Rev. Jesse Elliott, formerly of Churchville, Monroe County. They had two children, viz.: Jessie M., born October 25, 1869, and Angela E., born August 30, 1877, both of whom are deceased. Mr. and Mrs. Filkins reside in the village of Bethany Center.

John Folk, who was born in Germany, June 17, 1812, married Catherine Shelabarger, also of Germany, and they had five children, as follows: Casper, John (who was killed in the late war), Catherine, Michael, and Mary. Casper Folk, eldest son of John, was born in Germany, January 24, 1849, and came with his parents to America in 1853, locating in Bennington, Wyoming County, N. Y. November 17, 1868, he married Mary Crouse, of Lancaster, Erie County. They have 10 children, namely: Kate, George, John, Mary, Sarah, Lizzie, Clara, Michael, Frank, and Julia.

The French family came from England on the ship *Mayflower*, and first located in the East. Richard B. French was born in the northwest part of the town of Bethany in 1815. He received a common school and academic education, was a farmer, school teacher by occupation, and July 4, 1843, he married Esther, only daughter of Nehemiah Tracy, of Alexander, and they had three children: Carson F., W. Cary, and Ernie.

W. Cary, born November 20, 1847, was educated in the common schools and in Pike Seminary, Wyoming County. Mr. French has held the office of highway commissioner of his town. June 25, 1874, he married Zorada, seventh daughter of Edmund Brainard, of Middlebury, Wyoming County. They have had three children, of whom one son is deceased, and two survive, namely: Irma E., born June 30, 1875, and C. Tracy, born December 23, 1881. Mr. and Mrs. French reside on road 35, on the old Brainard place.

Caleb Gifford was born in Lyme, Grafton County, N. H., April 10, 1805, and came to Genesee County with his parents when he was two years old. They located in Warsaw (old Genesee County), and their mode of conveyance was an ox-team and cart. He married Julia, second daughter of William Raymond, of Warsaw, and they had four children, viz.: William R., James H., Mary E., and Frances J. James H. was born in Bethany, June 22, 1835, and received a common school and academic education. He is a farmer and fruit grower. February 28, 1872, he married Martha A , oldest daughter of Edmund Stebbins, of his native town. They have two children, William C., born January 8, 1879, and Mabel, born September 23, 1881. They reside near East Bethany, on road 22.

Seba Granger, grandfather of Byron, was a resident of Cherry Valley, Otsego County. One of his sons, John, married Elizabeth Cleaveland, formerly of Vermont. They had eight children, as follows: Chester, Seba, Jr., Byron, Elizabeth, Mary, Chloe A., Almira, and Abigail. They located in Monroe County about 1815. Byron, born in Penfield, Monroe County, August 28, 1819, was a carpenter and joiner by trade. February 19, 1852, he married Lucetta S. Disboro, of Stafford, and they had five children, only two of whom, Sanford B. and Charles D., survive. Charles D. married Barbara Harsch, of Le Roy. Byron Granger served in Co A, 1st Dist. Columbia Cav. Vols., and now resides on road 6 in Bethany.

James Gillard, who was born in Devonshire, England, in 1820, married Ann Warren, of the same place, and they had children as follows: Mary A., William, Ellen, Edward. Emma, John, Walter A., and Jessie. Walter A. Gillard was born in North Devon, May 1, 1859. He was educated in the common schools, and in 1879 came to America, locating in Stafford, this county. October 7, 1884, he married Mary L., second daughter of Hiram Porter, of Bethany. Mr. Porter was a native of Vermont. He resides in Little Canada in the town of Bethany.

John Gartner, born in Wurtemberg, Germany, about 1789, married Catherine Bessinger, and they had 10 children, only three of whom are living, namely: Jacob, Barbara, and George. They came to America and located in Lancaster, Erie County, where Jacob was born October 3, 1839. He received a common school education, and is a farmer by occupation. May 8, 1861, he married Elizabeth, second daughter of Alexander Lewis, of Clarence, Erie County. Her father was born in Vermont, of Scotch ancestry. They reside on road 31.

John Harper was born in Devonshire, England, June 22, 1824. He married Susan Holland, of his native place, came to America in 1852, and located in the town of Stafford. They have five children, viz.: Emma, Charles W., Kate, George. and Elizabeth. Charles W. Harper was born in Stafford, August 4, 1855, received a common school education, and is a carpenter and joiner by occupation. September 18, 1884, he married Ellen R., oldest daughter of Elias Lyon, of Attica, by whom he has two children, Edna A. and Charles.L. Mr. and Mrs. Harper reside on road 24.

Ephraim Harding, grandfather of Erastus D., served from Connecticut as a soldier in the Revolutionary war under General Putnam. Alfred Harding served in the War of 1812. Erastus D Harding was born in Lyme, Conn., February 14, 1815, and when 10 years of age came with his parents to Genesee County, where they arrived October 5, 1824, and located three-quarters af a mile north of Bethany village. February 22, 1838, he married Mary H., oldest daughter of William Nott, formerly of Devonshire, England, but now of Bethany. They have had 10 children, of whom eight survive, namely: Eveline B., Mary E., Erastus G, Jennie M., Estella A., Flora C., William E, and Herbert H. Erastus G. Harding is a physician and surgeon in Wyoming County; William E. is professor in the literary department of the Institution for the Blind in Batavia; Jennie M. resides with her parents; and Herbert H. is married and takes charge of the farm. Mr. Harding has been deacon in the Baptist Church for many years.

David Hyde was born in Essex, Vt., in 1792. He learned the cabinet-makers' trade, went to Boston, Mass, at the age of 21 years, and worked at his trade, and also carpentering. He left Boston in 1817 and located on the Little Tonawanda, on road 27½, in the town of Bethany. About 1826 he married Theirsy Alger, of Bethany, and they had two children, Edgar and Edwin J. The latter was born June 6, 1830, on the old homestead, where he spent his boyhood, alternately on the farm, in the saw-mill, and in school. 'July 5, 1851, he married Jane E., oldest daughter of Erastus L. Norton, of Alexander. They have had five children, of whom three are deceased, and two survive, namely: Charley E. D. and Lillian E., the latter a graduate of the New England Conservatory of Music, in Boston. Mr. Hyde served as first sergeant in Co. E, 105th Inf. N. Y. Vols., and was discharged for disability. He is a teacher of vocal music and leader of the Genesee and Wyoming Musical Association. His grandfather, Ephraim, served in the Revolutionary war, and his father in the War of 1812.

John Jenne was born in Rutland, Vt., in 1791, and when a boy came with 'his parents to Cayuga County, N. Y. He married Sarah F., oldest daughter of William Freeman, and soon after located one-half mile south of Bethany Center. They had three children, namely: Lansing K., William N., and Jerusha F., the latter of whom married Harry G. Lincoln. William N. was born on the old homestead, August 19, 1831, received a common school and academic education, and is a progressive farmer. January 1, 1855, he married, first, Sophia, N., daughter of Henry W. Gardiner, of Attica, Wyoming County, and they had one son, Charles G., born October 16, 1857. He, too, received a good education, and is a farmer and speculator. April 15, 1886, Mrs. Jenne died, and October 5, 1887, Mr. Jenne married for his second wife Mrs. Hattie L (Stewart) Norton, who died February 1, 1889. February 15, 1882, Charles G. Jenne married Nellie, only daughter of Charles W. Cone. She died November 17, 1885.

Israel E. Judd was a soldier in the Revolution, and very likely was killed, as he was never heard of again. His son was born at the close of the war, and was named Liberty in honor of the victory achieved by the colonies. He was a soldier of the War of 1812. He was born August 27, 1775, and was married twice, first to Miss Hannah Thompson, and second to Abigail Everest, October 4, 1807. He had born to him seven children, namely: Hannah, 1st., Israel E., Abigail, Anna M., Rhoda, Philip, and Hannah W. Israel E. Judd was born February 8, 1811, in the town of Bethany, and is now living on the farm his father located in 1806. He received a common school education. January 29, 1852, he married Mary, sixth daughter of Reuben Wright, of Alexander, and they have one son, Franklin I., born June 20, 1853. who received a common school and academic education. September 3, 1879, he married Sarah J., third daughter of A. D. Waldo, of Elba. They have four children, namely: Everest A, Mark W., Florence M, and Franklin H. Israel Everest, grandfather of Israel E. Judd on his mother's side, was captured by the Indians, and suffered untold hardships during his prison life in Montreal, Canada, and during his escape.

John Kemp was born in New Hampshire, December 20, 1786, and came to Marcellus, Onondaga County, N. Y., when a young man. He married Charity Barrows, of Skaneateles, and in 1832 they came to Middlebury, Wyoming County (old Genesee) They had eight children, namely: Harriet, Milo M., Emily, Maria L., George B., Myron J., William E., and Caroline A. Myron J. Kemp was born in Marcellus, May 6, 1822, and came with his parents to the Genesee country when 10 years of age. He received a common school education, and has been a farmer by occupation. May 17, 1848, he married Louisa M., second daughter of Jonathan Gates, formerly of New Hampshire. They have no children. Mr. Kemp is now a gentleman of leisure, and resides on East Main street, in the village of Linden.

Sylvester Lincoln, Jr., walked from Castleton, Vt., to Batavia in 1803, and helped to survey lands in what is now the town of Elba. He returned to Vermont in 1803 or '04 and married Eleanor Wallace, of Hubbard ton, Vt., and came with his young wife and his father's family to Bethany. They were the fourth family that located in the town, and one of his sons, Harry G., was the second child born in the town. Charles F., late husband of M. Jennie Lincoln, and son of Sylvester, was born August 29, 1833, in Middlebury, Wyoming County. He came with his parents to Bethany when very young, and received a liberal education. February 25, 1862, he married M. Jennie, only daughter of Thomas Cathcart, of Corfu. They had four children, namely: Harry T., who is a farmer with his mother; John S., a graduate of the Normal School of Geneseo, N. Y., who is now teaching as principal of a High school in Steuben County; Florence M., also a teacher, who resides at home with her mother; and Anna L., who also resides at home. After his marriage Mr. Lincoln united with Presbyterian Church at Bethany Center, was always a consistent Christian, and for many years was an elder until his decease, May 29, 1886. He left a widow and family and a large circle of friends to mourn his death.

The first known of the Lounsbury family was three brothers who came from England at an early day. One of them had a son by the name of Robert, who married Elizabeth Pinkney, of Dutchess County, N. Y., and went to Canada, being tempted by liberal offers of land which he secured by settling there. One of their nine children was John, who was born in Canada, May 10, 1802, and in 1812 came with his parents to the United States. His father incurred the enmity of the Canadians for his unflinching loyalty to the United States. His 800 acres of land they confiscated, and he barely got away alive. He purchased 300 acres of land situated mostly in the town of Alexander. Very little of this land was cleared at this time. Deer and bears were plentiful. John's father died before he attained his majority, and the care of the family early devolved upon him. In 1826 he married Abigail Hayes, of Bethany, and they had eight children, of whom four survive, namely: Cordelia, Edwin, Henry, and Emily. Edwin Lounsbury was born March 18, 1828, on the old homestead in Alexander. He worked on the farm and attended school, and has always been a farmer. March 22, 1860, he married Nora, daughter of John Welch, and they have two children, viz.: Thomas E., a farmer with his father, and M. Isabel, who married Frank J. Prue, of Alexander. Mr. and Mrs. Lounsbury reside on a part of the original purchase in the town of Bethany.

Cordelia Lounsbury was born in the east part of the town of Alexander, November 27, 1826, and received a good education. She has been twice married, first to Permina A. Cogswell, of Alexander, April 11, 1843, and second to Thomas Hoyle, formerly of England, in November, 1860. Both are deceased. Mrs. Cordelia Hoyle resides on road 29, near the old homestead.

Shadrack Lent was born in Montgomery County, N. Y., June 2, 1802, and came to Genesee County with his parents when 10 years old. He heard distinctly the reports of the guns of the contending armies at the battle of Buffalo, in the War of 1812. They first located in Pavilion. He married Prudence A. Dixon, of Bethany, formerly of Chatham, Conn. They had five children, namely: Lucy A., Charles H., William B., George V. N., and Charlotte E. George V. N., born August 10, 1841, was educated in the public schools, and is a fruit grower and farmer. January 29, 1879, he married Minnie O. Burton, of Cambridge, Mass., by whom he had one daughter, Harriet A., born January 6, 1883. Mrs. Lent died February 14, 1887. Mr. Lent's sister, Charlotte E., is keeping house for him. He resides on road 21.

Frederick Leitz was born in Germany, April 21, 1817. He received a good education, and in 1852 came to America, landed in New York city, and first located at Lancaster, Erie County, and finally in Wyoming County. November 8, 1858, he married Bridget Haley. In August, 1862, he enlisted in Co. E, 136th Inf. N. Y. Vols., and participated in the battles of Chancellorsville and Gettysburg. On the third day of the latter battle, at 3 P. M., he was wounded in the left wrist by a minie-ball, was sent to Jarvis Hospital, Baltimore, and was transferred to West Building Hospital, being in both 15 months. After leaving the hospital he served in the Veteran Reserve Corps until his discharge, October 1, 1864, for disability. He came to Bethany in 1871. Mr. Leitz's wrist is much disfigured and entirely useless. He resides on road 35 in this town.

Alanson D. Lord was born in 1806, in Herkimer County, N. Y., and about 1814 he came with his brother, Smith Lord, to Bethany. February 4, 1835, he married Mary M., fifth daughter of James Stoughton, of Bethany, and they have had six children, of whom three survive, viz.: Laura M. (Mrs. David Denton); Ann M. (Mrs. Luin L Munger); and James S., born October 27, 1844, in Wheatland, Monroe County. In early life he was a mechanic, but is now a fruit tree jobber, apiarist, and farmer. June 19, 1873, he married Laura A., second daughter of Ira Wait, Jr. They have had six children, namely: Frank J. and Minnie L., deceased; and Mary E., Mark D., Anna L., and Tracy T., who survive. Mrs. J. S. Lord is a breeder of thoroughbred Wyandotte and Java fowls.

Jared S. Lord was born in Durham, Greene County, N. Y., May 17, 1798. and died December 15, 1885. When he was 20 years old he came to Western New York, and finally located in Bethany. He married twice, first, in April, 1821, Polly Everest, by whom he had two children. September 16, 1828, he married, second, Hannah Curtis, formerly of Plymouth, Chenango County, and they had three children, namely: Jared C., Mary J., and Hattie C., the latter of whom resides in the village of Linden.

James Millerick was born in Ireland in 1838, came to America in 1856, and located in Bethany. March 5, 1866, he married Ann, fourth daughter of Thomas Benson, of this town. They had five children, as follows: Fannie A., Richard, Mary, John, and Nellie C. Mr. Millerick died in February, 1888. Ann Millerick, his widow, resides on road 34 in Bethany

Isaac V. Mullen, M. D., was born in Hector, Tompkins County, February 16, 1827, and spent his boyhood days on the farm and in the store. In 1848 he began to study medicine with Hon. Charles D. Robinson, of Hornellsville, Steuben County, and graduated from the Castleton (Vt.)

24

Medical College, June 18, 1851. He married Laura D., youngest daughter of Royal Aldrich, of Castleton, and they have four children. He began the practice of medicine in St. Lawrence County, N. Y., where he remained until he went into the army as assistant surgeon of the 13th Inf. N. Y. Vols. When the 14th H. A. was organized he became its surgeon, and was retained in hospital service six months after the war closed. He has a good practice in the towns of Alexander and Bethany.

Salmon Munger, grandfather of Luin L., was a soldier in the War of 1812. He went from Connecticut and served on the frontier near Buffalo. His son Anson was born in Schoharie County, N. Y., and in 1844 married Lydia, eighth daughter of Asa Thompson. They had two children. Luin L. Munger, born July 28, 1845, in Bethany, received a liberal education, and February 15, 1862, he enlisted in Co. E, 105th Inf. N. Y. Vols. He was engaged in the battles of Cedar Mountain, second Bull Run, and Antietam. At the latter battle, which occurred September 17, 1862, he was wounded in the left leg, with a 12-pound solid shot, which caused its amputation, which operation was performed in the Smoke Town Field Hospital, where he remained until he was discharged, April 2, 1863. July 4, 1865, he married Ann M., second daughter of Alanson D. Lord, of this town, but formerly of Herkimer County. Mr. and Mrs. Munger reside on road 28.

Benjamin F. Norton was born in the town of Bethany, October 1, 1816. His parents came from Vermont He received a good education, and in 1832 he married Edna Frary, who died March 8, 1848. He married for his second wife Elizabeth, second daughter of David Locke, of Batavia, and they have had four children, namely: Charles, Walter Frank, Fred L., and William. The last two named are deceased. Walter Frank, born January 3, 1851, received a common school and academic education, and January 23, 1872, he married Mattie K., oldest daughter of Erastus Wood, of Little Canada, in the town of Bethany. Mr. and Mrs. Norton have adopted two children, namely: Cora L. (Wood) and Arthur. They are living on road 27, on the old Ira Waite place.

George Prescott was born in Devonshire, England, in 1819. He married Mary Clark, of the same place, and they have two children, Frank and Thomas. In 1834 they came to America, and first located in Stafford, Genesee County. Thomas Prescott was born January 6, 1850, was educated in the public schools, and is a farmer and fruit grower. March 21, 1881, he married Mary, oldest daughter of Richard Watson, of Dunkirk, N. Y. They have three children, namely: George F., born February 19, 1882; Ruth W., born June 2, 1883; and Charles F., born December 27, 1888. They reside on road 7 in this town.

Seth M. Peck, who was born in Lyme, Conn., January 4, 1800, served as waiter for Major Lord in the War of 1812. September 9, 1824, he married Sarah Pierson, of his native place, and came to Bethany and located where his son now resides, on road 24, corner 35. They had six children, namely: Sarah E., Phebe, Laura, S. Marvin, Almira, and Henry.

S. Marvin was born April 14, 1831, received a liberal education, and is a farmer by occupation. May 17, 1860, he married, and has had born to him two children: a daughter who died in infancy, and Robert C., born July 12, 1861, who survives. Robert C. Peck married Mary Bolt, of this town, January 8, 1889.

Richard Peck, who was born in Lyme, New London County, Conn., February 5, 1786, came to this town in 1806, and located where Benjamin F. Peck now resides. He returned to Connecticut the following spring, and returned with his grandmother and mother, with a two-horse wagon. About 1815 he married Catherine Hope Comstock, of Bethany, formerly of Haddam, Conn. They had 12 children, 10 of whom grew to maturity, viz.: Elizabeth M., Maria L., Nathaniel, Richard, Israel M., Catherine H., Mary A., Benjamin F., Lucy J., and Charles A. Benjamin F. Peck was born on the homestead July 16, 1829, and received a public school and academic education until he was 18 years of age. February 24, 1853, he married Phebe R., second daughter of S. Marvin Peck, of Bethany. They have three children, namely: Florence, born July 17, 1855; Richard, born October 12, 1857; and Mary A., born July 15, 1869. Richard Peck was educated in the public schools and an academy, and is farming for his father, Benjamin F. October 25, 1883, he married Helen C., second daughter of Freeman M. Sanford, of Jackson County, Mich., and they have two children, Franklin H. and Helen S.

The first known of the Putnam family was three brothers who came from Holland to America, and located in Vermont. Peter Putnam, grandfather of Orrin, served in the Revolutionary war and held the position of major. Peter Putnam, Jr., was born October 21, 1785, and came to Bethany in 1805 or '06 February 26, 1809, he married Prudence Johnson, who was born in Connecticut, November 15, 1784. They had seven children, namely: Orrin, Warren, David, Philotheta, Osgood, Seymour, and Emeline. Orrin Putnam, born February 21, 1810, married, April 4, 1831, Sophia Huntington, and they had six children, namely: Edmond, Alfred, Emogene, Hartson O., Lewis V., and Marion. Lewis V. is in Red Canon, Wyoming Territory; Edmund resides in Rossville, Ill.; and Emogene is in Albion, Mich., the wife of Joseph Shepard. Hartson O. Putnam was born December 12, 1849, in Batavia. He received a common school education, and is a farmer and fruit grower. About 1870 he married Rozelle Quance, of Batavia, by whom he had one son, Herbert D. Mrs. Putnam died when they had been married five years, and February 22, 1882, he married, second, Alice, third daughter of John C. Kinney, of Albion, Mich. They have three children, viz.: Lester O., born June 8, 1883: Persis A., born May 15, 1886; and Mary L., born February 10, 1888. They reside on road 1.

Elijah Rogers was born at Lyme, Conn, in 1785. He married Maria Beckweth, of the same place, and they had four children. They came to Genesee County in 1811, and located in Stafford. William E., born April 9, 1809, in Lyme, received a pioneer education. May 13, 1834, he married Mehetabal P. Banning, of his native place, and they have no children. Her father, Calvin Banning, was also born in Lyme, January 22, 1785. William E. Rogers and wife have been married 56 years, and have resided on road 24 for 54 years.

Bethel Stavely was born in Yorkshire, England, in 1817, and in early life married Ann Clayton, of the same place. They had four children, namely: Eliza J., Sarah A., Jonathan, and Henry C. In November, 1856, they came to the United States, and located near Geneva, Ontario County. Jonathan was born in England, March 1, 1843, and when 15 years of age, at Geneva, he enlisted in Co. E, 1st Vet. Cav. N. Y. Vols. He was discharged at the close of the war at Rochester, N. Y. Mr. Stavely was a brave soldier. He located at East Bethany, this county, and September 12, 1869, married Annie E., youngest daughter of Edward Fullerton, of Buffalo. They have had five children, of whom Charles W. and Sarah A. survive. Mr. and Mrs. Stavely reside in the village of East Bethany.

Andrew Showerman was born in Alexander about 1846, and when 18 years old he became a railroad man, first as brakeman on the N. Y. C. & H. R. Railroad, and afterwards on N. Y., L. E. & W. Railroad, where he was conductor for 20 years He is now baggage and express agent on the same road. He married twice, first, Lucy Vandebogart, by whom he had four children, of whom two died in infancy, and two survive, viz.: Frank C. and John. For his second wife Mr. Showerman married Agnes Carl. Frank C. was born June 20, 1866, and received a good academic education until he was 17 years old. He is now station agent, telegraph operator, and express agent at Linden.

· George South was born in the village of Stratton, Warwickshire, England, October 10, 1830. At the age of 13 he was apprenticed for seven years to learn the trade of a carpenter and joiner. There are now few men who equal him as a carpenter and builder. He has a good education for the short time he attended school. Mr. South married twice, first, Mary Wyatt, of London, England, about 1855. They had two children, Mary and Julia. In 1869 he came to America, and located in Rochester, N. Y. His wife died in 1872, and for his second wife he married Mrs. Emerett (Brown) Judd, of Bethany. They have one daughter, Clara E., born April 16, 1883. Mrs. South had three children by her first husband, viz.: Thomas, Oscar D., and Walter E. Mr. and Mrs. South reside on the Col. Daniel Brown homestead, on road 19.

James Shepard was born in Otsego County, N. Y., November 29, 1804, came with his father, John, to this town in 1816, and married Amanda Putnam, January 2, 1827. She was born October 2, 1806. They had 10 children, all of whom grew to maturity, viz.: Debora C. (deceased), Phebe M., Maria, Franklin P., Daniel, Harlan J., Ransom A., Ordelia A., David M., and Ellen. Daniel Shepard, born in Batavia, April 10, 1835, received a common and Normal school education, and is a farmer and speculator. March 2, 1859, he married Carrie, second daughter of David Filkins, and they have had two children, namely: Effie, born February 22, 1862, died December 13, 1885 ; and Dwight D., born April 10, 1865. The latter was educated in the public schools, also in the high schools of Batavia, and August 26, 1886, he married Rubie E., second daughter of Augustus Woodworth, of this town. They reside on the farm he purchased on his wedding day, on road 4.

Thomas Squires was born in Barnstable, England, in 1819, and married Ann Ward, of the same place. They came to America in 1854, and located in Stafford, this county. They had seven children, namely : Lizzie, George, Susan, William, Charles, Emma, and Frank. George Squires was born in England, January 27, 1849, and came with his parents to America in 1854. November 23, 1870, he married Clara H., oldest daughter of Hiram Porter, of Bethany, and they have four children, viz.: Frank H., born April 21, 1874; Albert J. and Alfred B. (twins), born December 20, 1875 ; and Flora I., born June 4, 1872. The latter attends a select school at Alexander. Mr. and Mrs. Squires reside on road 28 in this town.

John Staub, who was born in Alsace, Germany, in 1814, came to America when he was 16 years old, and first located in Buffalo, N. Y. He married Elizabeth Wrestle, of Alsace, and they had 12 children, seven of whom survive. One of his sons, John Jr., was born in Lancaster, Erie County, February 6, 1844, and was educated in the common schools. April 28, 1868, he married Anna M., youngest daughter of John Kelley, of New York city. They have six children, namely : William, Libbie, John R., Anna M., Kattie, and George. They reside on road 25.

Orlando M. Smiley was born in Oneida County, near Utica, N. Y., received a good education, and when a boy moved with his parents to the town of Elba. He married Eunice Knickerbocker and they had two children, Frank J. and Mary Eunice. Frank J. Smiley was born in Elba, and received a common school and academic education. He is a farmer and a traveling man. May 14, 1867, he married Mary I., oldest daughter of Edward T. Squires, of Alexander. They had three children, of whom two survive, namely : Earl F., born March 27, 1878, and Ruth M., born August 7, 1884. The family reside on road 31.

Norman G. Thomas was born in Williamstown, Mass., of Welsh ancestry, and June 6, 1809, he came with his parents to Cazenovia, N. Y. He was a carriagemaker by trade, and in his latter years a farmer. January 14, 1835, he married Lucy E., oldest daughter of Alexander Patterson, of Livonia. They had two children, of whom the daughter died in infancy. Mr. Thomas died December 17, 1878. George R. Thomas was born October 24, 1839 In 1841 he moved with his parents to Genesee County, and in 1866 he engaged in mercantile business October 21, 1866, he married Emogene McKay, of Groveland, Livingston County, and they have seven children living, viz.: Heman S , Norman G., Irene H., Lesley, Cecil R., Adelbert, and Grover.

Samuel J. Toll, born in Schenectady, N. Y., August 24, 1829, was educated in the common schools, and when 20 years old he went to Ohio, Indiana, Michigan, Illinois, and finally located at Lyons, Iowa, where he followed the occupation of auctioneer. August 10 1861, he enlisted in the 1st Iowa Cav. Vols.; was discharged October 10, 1862 ; and was then mustered into the United States service as mustering officer with the rank of second lieutenant. January 31, 1863, he received his commission as second lieutenant of Co. A, 6th Iowa Cav. Vols., and was in command of the company one year and six months. He was discharged at the close of the war, and resided in Chicago, Ill., and Nashville, Tenn., each four years. He then returned to Bethany, where he is now a farmer on road 12½, near East Bethany village.

Frederick F. Wilson was born in County Kent, England, March 4, 1811, and came to America in 1830, locating in Phelps, Ontario County, N. Y. About 1832 he married Harriet Price, and they had eight children, viz.: Charles, Jane, Ellen, Franklin S., Emma, Harlo, Mary, and George V. The latter was born in East Bloomfield, Ontario County, November 27, 1854. He received a common school education until he was 14 years of age, and in his boyhood worked on a farm. At the age of 18 he began to learn the blacksmith trade, and is a first-class mechanic. March 21, 1874, he married Alice J., oldest daughter of William H. Hedger, of Attica, Wyoming County. They have one son, William F., born January 10, 1875. They reside at West Bethany village.

Harry Woolf was born in Rochester, Kent, England, August 23, 1861. He received a commercial education, and in 1884 came to America, and located in New York city as a book-keeper. He finally came to Linden, Genesee County, where he began his career as a merchant by peddling goods through the several towns of this and adjoining counties. January 9, 1888, he married Irma M., youngest daughter of Capt. William Grant, of Darien, and they have one son, William A., born December 13, 1888. Mr. Woolf located in Bethany Center as a general merchant February 9, 1889.

Guy Wheeler was born in Lanesborough, Mass., July 30, 1782, and removed to Vermont. March 12, 1804, he married Clarissa Kimball, in Springfield, Vt. They had 10 children, all deceased but two, namely: Mary J. and Guy, Jr. The latter was born in Benson, Vt., May 2, 1825, and came with his father's family to Middlebury, Wyoming County, in 1836. He received a liberal education, and May 30, 1870, he married Mrs. Melinda M. (Gould) Emery, who had one son, Clark H., a telegraph operator, who died in Mexico of yellow fever. They have four children, namely: Nora G., Maud M., Guy E., and Margie C. Nora G. is a school teacher. Mrs. Wheeler's maternal grandmother lived to be 104 years of age.

Constant Webster was born in Rensselaer County, N. Y., in November, 1792. About 1818 or '19 he married, first, Miss Fanny Spring, of his native place, and they had four children, namely: James H., John M.,

Almira, and Ebenezer. He married, second, Miss Ann Dusenbury, of the same county, by whom he also had four children, viz.: Alfred, Oren S., Aaron B., and Helen. John M. Webster was born July 1, 1822, in Rensselaer County. He received a good education, and married, April 22, 1847, first, Miss Sarah J. Smith, of Attica. They had children as follows: Cassius M., Henry P., Eulelia J., Cora A., Helmer J., Grant S., and Flora J., of whom Eulelia J., Helmer J., and Grant S. are deceased. For his second wife Mr. Webster married Mrs. Mary (Read) Lincoln, of Bethany, second daughter of the late Henry and Laura Read. Mr. Webster is a retired farmer, and has been justice of the peace for 16 years.

Erastus Wood was born in Lyme, Conn , July 26, 1803, and came to Little Canada, this county, in 1823. March 21, 1837, he married Jane Halleck, of Orange County, N. Y., and they had five children, namely: William J., Henry H., Leonard D., Mattie J., and Phebe A. William J. Wood was born in Little Canada, January 29, 1838, and received à public school education. He is a carriagemaker and blacksmith by occupation. He married twice, first, September 18, 1867, Mary A. Knowlton, by whom he had four children, namely: Jennie A., Charles F., Ella A., and Carrie M. His first wife died April 12, 1882, and for his second wife he married, January 1, 1886, Mrs. Fannie (Brooks) Barnes, of Ross, Kalamazoo County, Mich., who bore him two sons, Cleon K. and Frank R. She had one son, Chester A., by her first husband. The family resides in Little Canada in the town of Bethany.

Ira Wait, better known as Judge Wait, was born March 2, 1793, and came with his father, William Wait, to Batavia from Washington County, N. Y., at a very early date in the history of Genesee County. In early life he united in marriage with Anna Brown, who bore him nine children. He married, second, January 3, 1837. Phebe Hotchkiss Rumsey, daughter of Jimmy Rumsey. She was born in Hubbardton, Vt., March 15, 1808. They had a daughter and a son, Leonora V. and Addison. Mr. Wait settled in Bethany, and was a farmer and surveyor. He was called upon to survey lands until he was 70 years of age. He received the appointment of associate judge of Genesee County courts, under the old State constitution, from Gov. William H. Seward, and held the position several years. He represented Genesee County in the Assembly of 1842, and was a magistrate of his town. These positions of honor are conclusive evidence that he was a man of superior abilities. He was also a man of sterling integrity, and had a mind and will of his own. He began his political life an "Old Line" Whig, and joined the Republican party at its organization. Mr. Wait died of paralysis, at the home of his son-in-law, Oscar W. Lord, in Batavia, May 31, 1875, while there for a visit. Mrs. Wait survived until June 24, 1884.

Leonora V. Wait, daughter of Ira and Phebe H. (Rumsey) Wait, was born in Bethany, February 27, 1839, and married Oscar W. Lord, September 28, 1870. Oscar W. Lord was born in Bethany, July 25, 1825, the son of Jared S. Lord, who emigrated from Connecticut. He graduated from the State Normal. School at Albany and taught a few terms, and then settled permanently in Batavia as a dealer in hats, caps, and furs. He died of apoplexy January 25, 1879.

Robert Walker, born in Yorkshire, England, October 14, 1806, came to America in 1839. He married Mary Ellis, of his native place, and they had eight children, viz.: William M., Robert, Matthew, Sarah, Hannah, John, Frank, and Ellen. Robert Walker was killed in the battle of Cold Harbor. William M. was born in England, and came with his parents and located in Onondaga County, N. Y. September 27, 1858, he married Mary L. Archer, of Bennington, Wyoming County, and they have had seven children, as follows: Mary L., Hannah F., Robert J., William L., Charles E. (deceased), John E., and Raymond M. William M. Walker enlisted December 30, 1863, in Co. H, 8th H. A. N. Y. Vols. He was in the battles of the Wilderness, Cold Harbor, Hatcher's Run, and the three days' battle before Petersburg, and was discharged at the close of the war.

Joseph Wellert was born in Prussia, Germany, March 3, 1824. In 1862 he married Mary Burdger, of the same place, and in 1862 came to America and located first in Batavia, afterwards in Stafford, and finally in Bethany. They had five children, namely : Charles, who married Minnie Lee, of Aurora, Ill.; Minnie, who married Christian Etter, of Le Roy, Lewis, who resides with his parents; Henry, who also resides in Aurora, Ill.; and Eliza, who resides in Le Roy.

John Weber was born in Germany and died when his son George P. was five years of age. George P. Weber was born October 9, 1827, came to America in 1852, and first located in Cincinnati, O., where he remained two years, when he came to Western, N. Y. He married twice, first, Catherine Spring, in Canada, formerly of Switzerland, and second, February 15, 1882, Wilimina Hart, who was also born in Germany. Mr. Weber served in the late war, enlisting, first, in September, 1861, in Co. A, 9th Cav. N. Y. Vols., and second in Co. K, 2d Mounted Rifles N. Y. Vols. He was wounded by a minie-ball in his left arm, near the shoulder, at the battle of Cold Harbor, and was discharged as duty sergeant at the close of the war.

BYRON.

BYRON was formed from Bergen, April 4, 1820, and named in honor of Lord Byron. It lies in the north border of the county, and is bounded on the north by Orleans County, east by Bergen, south by Le Roy and Stafford, and west by Batavia and Elba. The surface is gently undulating, and the soil a fine gravelly and sandy loam. The streams are Black, Silver, and Bigelow creeks. On Black Creek, a short distance north of Byron, is found a remarkable sulphur spring, emitting carbureted hydrogen gas. In the southwest part of the town is found an acid spring, known as the " Sour Spring." This spring issues from an elevation four or five feet above the plain, and is about 200 feet long by 100 feet broad. Beck, in his *Mineralogy*, says : " The strength of the acid is increased by drought, and in some places it is quite concentrated and nearly dry in its combination with the charred, vegetable coat, which everywhere covers the hillock to a depth of from five to forty inches."

This town is a portion of the Connecticut tract (of the Morris Reserve) and the Pultney estate or tract. A portion of these tracts is also included in the town of Bergen. There are in all 200 original lots or subdivisions of these tracts in this town, and they average about 100 acres each.

Among the first happenings was the settlement of Benham Preston, on lot 197, in 1807 or 1808. A Mr. Hoskins and Elisha Taylor, from Otsego County, settled on lot 186, in 1808. Elisha Miller, from Pennsylvania, and Wheaton Carpenter, from Rhode Island, located on lot 2, in 1809. Nathan Holt came from Otsego County, and located in 1810. Asa Merrill emigrated from Oneida County, and located in 1811. The first child born was a son of Elisha Taylor, in 1809. The first marriage was that of Samuel Montgomery and Polly Parks, in 1811 ; and the first death that of Mr. Hoskins. Chester T. Holbrook taught the first school, in 1810 or 1811. Ira Newburg kept the first inn, in 1815, and Amos Hewitt the first store, in 1813. William Shepherd erected the first saw-mill, in 1813, and Asa Williams the first grist-mill, in 1814. It is claimed that the first tangible spirit manifestation on record, of what is now called modern spiritualism, was had in this township. A " Byron Library Society " was organized May 9, 1824, by the literary pioneers of that period. Miles G. White, with his father, came in 1828, and kept an hotel at Pumpkin Hill, or North Byron, for five years He lived here 52 years. Samuel Parker built the first mill in town, about 1809.

We here note the names, with dates of settlement, of many of those who located in Byron prior to 1820, as follows :

In 1806, Samuel and Sherrard Parker. In 1807, Benoni Gaines and Benham Preston. In 1808, Wheaton Carpenter, Elijah Loomis, and Elisha Miller. In 1809, Asahel

Cook. In 1810, Richard G. Moses, Elijah Brown, Elkanah Humphrey, Nathan Holt, and E. Taylor. In 1811, John Bean, David Cook, Andrew Dibble. Benajah Griswold, and Amasa Walker. In 1812, Paul Bullard, David Shedd, Ezra Sanford, and Zeno and William Terry. In 1813, Abner Thompson, Andrew Hunter Green, and William Shepherd. In 1814, Ira Newburg, John Searls, and Asa Williams. In 1815, Jason Adams, Seth C. Langdon, Asa Merrill, and James Tillotson. In 1816, Abner Chase, Chester Mann, A. Norton, and William, Lyman, and Milo Warn. In 1817, Andrew Adams, Joseph and Marcus Barker, Charles Beswick, David Mann, William Peckham, and Jonathan Wright. In 1818, Levi Fish, Moses Gillett, and Calvin Wells. In 1819, W. S. Miller and Harmon and Erastus Norton. James H. Sherwood, date unknown.

NORTH BYRON is a hamlet situated one mile north of Byron Center, and was of some little importance before the railroad passed through, as there was business for an hotel in early times. It now contains only a few houses. For some time it went by the name of "Pumpkin Hill," so-named by Moses Gillian, from the fact that a tavern sign, at that place, in shape and color resembled a pumpkin.

SOUTH BYRON is a post village in the southern part of the town, on the N. Y. C. & H. R. Railroad. It has a flourishing grain market, where Boynton, Prentice & Co. do an extensive produce business, two or three stores, one hotel, one church (Methodist Episcopal), a good school, and a population of about 300 inhabitants. Erastus Cash was the first postmaster. The place was for some time called "Brusselville," named from the fact that an early settler, Elijah Shumway, had a "brussel head."

BYRON CENTER (Byron p. o.) is located near the center of the township, on Black Creek, and on the West Shore Railroad. This little village has mainly sprung into existence since the advent of the railroad. It is especially noted as the principal and largest pork market in Genesee County, and also as a leading grain market. The village contains a population of about 300, six or eight stores of all kinds, an iron foundry and manufactory of agricultural implements, two flouring-mills, one hotel, two church edifices (Presbyterian and German), a well sustained school, and the usual complement of mechanics and artisans.

McElver & Sons' agricultural works are located at Byron Center. Their machinery is driven by steam-power. The firm manufactures agricultural implements, and do a general job and repairing work in castings, etc.

Genesee mills, originally built by James Taggart, are located on Black Creek, about half a mile east of Byron Center. McKenzie & Bennett are the present proprietors. The creek, with steam as auxiliary, furnishes ample power to turn all the machinery. The mills are furnished with seven sets of rolls for flouring and five runs of stones, and have a capacity of 50 barrels of flour and 500 bushels of provender per day. These mills were built by Rowley H. Douglass in 1880, and furnished with new and improved machinery for stone mills only. Since then rollers have been added, and, thus equipped, McKenzie & Bennett now turn out work of superior quality. Mr. Bennett is a practical miller and gives his whole attention to the business.

Byron cheese factory, the first erected in the county, was built in 1867 by a stock company. It receives the milk from 224 cows, and manufactures cheese for the English market. The property is now owned by Erastus H. Norton, of Byron Center, with H. C. Norton as salesman, and Alfred Stevens, cheesemaker. The factory is located about three-quarters of a mile west and south of Byron Center.

In 1868 there were in business in the town of Byron the following persons: Lafayette Carpenter, a physician, miller, and farmer; Earl B. Lounsbury, a physician and surgeon; Seaver, Hall & Co., merchants; J. W. Seaver, postmaster; Holden T. Miller, supervisor and proprietor of a general store; C. Leonard, hotel and stage proprietor; Dr. A. C. Hall, an eclectic physician and surgeon, at South Byron; Cooper & McCracken, harness dealers; W. Coward, a dealer in boots and shoes; J. B. House, hotel-keeper; John Rambo, a justice of the peace and dealer in stoves; B. J. Spafford, store-keeper, and also postmaster; and Loren N. Green, at North Byron, proprietor of the flouring-mills.

John W. Goodliffe is a carpenter and joiner, builder of all kinds of wooden cisterns, and a cidermaker. He has a 30x50 three story building, where he makes 10 barrels per day. He has all the latest improvements for manufacturing refined cider and vinegar, and has also a feed-mill.

Religion.—The first religious services were held in 1809 by Rev. Royal Phelps, of the Presbyterian Church, from Cayuga County. The First Congregational Church of Byron was organized in 1818, by Rev. Herman Halsey, with 11 members. A church was built, of wood, in 1830, and later was enlarged by additions. Rev. Mr. Halsey was the stated supply until 1826. In 1830 there were 27 members; in 1831, 162; and up to this time Revs. W. P. Kendrick, Lot B. Sullivan, and Lewis Cheeseman were the different pastors. Rev. B. B. Gray then supplied the pulpit for three and one-half years, Abelyn Sedgwick for one year, Ebor Child for four years, F. Danforth for one year, and J. B. Preston from 1844 to 1846, when there were 186 members. The society was afterwards called Presbyterian, and still remains of that faith. The number of members now is 90. They have no pastor. The church property is valued at about $8,000. Harry C. Norton is the superintendent of the Sunday-school, which has about 150 members.

The First Methodist Episcopal Church was first established at Byron Center, but they have no organization at that place at present.

The Second Methodist Episcopal Church is located at South Byron. The first meeting was September 26, 1842, when John Cook and others were present. Alva Wright was the first pastor. The church was erected in 1853 at a cost of about $2,500; the present value of the property is $4,200. There are about 43 members, and Rev. Edward W. Harnel is the pastor. They have a Sunday-school of about 300 scholars.

A Baptist Church at Byron Center was organized in 1810, but was long since disbanded.

The Freewill Baptist Church at North Byron was organized in 1820 by Rev. Nathaniel Brown and Harmon Jenkins, and a church erected in 1833, of wood. They now have 100 members, and about 100 scholars in the Sunday school. Rev. A. B. Loomis is the pastor. Their church property is worth about $4,500.

The Concordia German Evangelical Lutheran Church, in the eastern part of the town, was organized September 25, 1889, by Rev. L. Gross. There are 33 members, and they have just erected a beautiful house of worship at a cost of $1,200.

For a number of years a Grange was in successful operation in Byron, but after a time the interest died out, and the organization was finally abandoned In March, 1890, the matter was revived, and the 20th of that month the old lodge was reörganized with the following officers : W. S. Green, master ; J. C. Walker, overseer ; J. G. Todd, treasurer ; I. W. White, secretary ; and J. G. Terry, chaplain.

Nearly every pioneer has his " bear stories," and were all these to be repeated here they would, like Mark Twain's misfortunes, " be somewhat monotonous " One, however, may be related. George Batcheller, about 40 years ago, went some distance into Tonawanda swamp with a neighbor, to assist in bringing out a bear which he had killed. On his way the nails of his boot-heels grated upon something which gave forth a metallic sound. On examination he found that some moss had been scraped from what proved to be a large bear-trap. It was lying with its jaws downward, nearly covered with muck, and the roots of trees had grown through the jaws and springs in all directions. One of these, a black ash root, was nearly as large as a man's wrist The trap was but very little corroded. Some years afterwards Mr. Batcheller learned from a man who assisted the owner of the trap in his hunt that, 22 years previous to the finding of it, it was set in the usual way, with a clog attached, in this town (Byron) ; that a bear was caught in it ; that they followed his trail through a light snow seven or eight miles to within 80 rods of where the trap was found ; and that they here abandoned the pursuit because night was approaching, and the melting of the snow rendered the trail indistinct. Mr. Batcheller still has the trap in his possession.

Wheaton Carpenter was born in Scituate, R. I., in 1788. At mature age he went to Scranton, Pa., then a wilderness. and resided a few years, and married there Nancy Dickerson. In 1808 he, in company with Elisha Miller, came to Byron on foot, with knapsacks on their backs, in which they carried their provisions for the long and tiresome journey. Mr. Carpenter located a farm of 100 acres about one-half mile southwest of Byron Center. He then returned to Scranton, and two years later came with his wife and two infant daughters to the wilderness of Byron. In the meantime his claim was forfeited, and he procured another of 100 acres, 80 rods west of a log tavern kept by Ben Hall, on Black Creek, where he resided until the ensuing spring (1811), when a freshet swept away his pig, fowls, and all movable property, and left only his cow and horse. Thus warned off he never returned, and never again owned real estate in Byron. He participated in the War of 1812, and went with the militia to Buffalo when they were called out. He was a miller and resided in " Sodom," a location in Byron, and in the cold season of 1816 found his increased family destitute. On a Monday morning he wended his way to where A. W. Graves's flouring-mill is now located, and where was one of the most primitive grist-mills, con structed of logs and without an iron cog wheel in it; in fact nothing but wooden trundle-heads to drive the stones, which were made of a rock from an adjacent field. He turned the bolt with one hand and fed it with the other. This mill was built by one Williams and was the first in town. He engaged to run this complicated machine for half the toll, and at once went to work, remaining until Saturday, when he returned to his family with meal, who all this time knew nothing of his where-abouts. He found his wife roasting a few beans for her children's sup-per. the last edible morsel in the house. On Monday he removed his family to the vicinity of the mill, and fortunately placed them beyond want the remainder of their lives. He continued a miller for 40 years, in different parts of Genesee County, and died in Byron, at the house of his daughter, Mrs. Nancy Gaines, in the fall of 1876, aged 88 years. His son, M. D. L. Carpenter, born in 1827, resides one-fourth of a mile from North Byron.

Jacob Bushman, son of John, a native of Pennsylvania, was born in Cayuga County, April 1, 1795. He married Martha Halstead, and in 1823 came to Byron, settling on the Bushman farm, so-called, near South Byron. He first had 50 acres, which was finally increased to 250. He was a good financier, honest, and upright. They were members of the Christian Church, and gave liberally to its support. He held several town offices. Mr. Bushman's wife died May 17, 1843. They were par-ents of 13 children, nine of whom are now living, viz.: Mary, in Wis-consin; Henry; Lany, who married Henry S. Philleo, a farmer; Andrew, who married Rachel M. Jones; Harriet, who married John Brainard, and is now a widow; Angeline (Mrs. Humphrey); Winslow J., in Wisconsin; Byron, a mechanic; and Martha J. (Mrs. C. L Benham), of Le Roy. Henry Bushman, born in Scipio, January 18, 1821, came to Byron with his par-ents when three years old. He was reared a farmer, was educated at the district schools, and October 1, 1846, married Sarah J. Mills, of Coving-ton, N. Y., and settled in Perry, N. Y., where he resided two years. He returned to Byron to the Bushman homestead in 1854, where he resided until 1872, when he retired to his pleasant home in South Byron, where he now resides. He is an influential and respected citizen, and has served as assessor for nine years. The family are active members of the Metho-dist Episcopal Church, and Mr. Bushman is an earnest Republican. Of their children Mary E. (Mrs. Charles Kellogg) resides with her husband on the homestead, and Nettie A. married J. F. Rose, a mechanic, of South Byron.

John Bean, a native of Vermont, came to Stafford in 1810, resided there a few years, and finally settled in Byron. He was an extensive trader, owned much live stock and real estate near South Byron, and was engaged in dealing in live stock for the Boston market. After the completion of the railroad he built a store house and dealt largely in grain and general merchandise. With all his large transactions he was regarded as being strictly honest, liberal to the poor, and a strict observer of the Sabbath. He died in 1883, aged 84 years. His son has been a station agent since 1858, and was also a merchant at one time.

Milton Allen is on old resident of Byron. He came in 1822, married Betsey Strong, and followed the masons' trade and farming. He has held several public offices, and aided in building up the town by his labors and influence for good. He is now living, aged 85 years.

James M. Bower, son of Francis and Catharine (Manahan) Bower, was born May 11, 1826, and was reared on his father's farm and educated in the common school. In 1850 he married, first, Parnell, daughter of Erastus Cash and settled on a farm about a mile east of Byron Center, where he resided to the close of his life, December 23, 1884. His wife died February 22, 1859, and October 8, 1863 he married Celinda Cash, a sister of his first wife, who survives him, and resides on the farm where he first settled. His first wife bore him one son, who died in early childhood. The children by the second marriage are twins, Albert C. and Arthur E., who are students at Cary Seminary, Oakfield. Mr. Bower was an enterprising, industrious, and progressive farmer, who gave close attention to his farm and made it better year by year. He was a man of sterling integrity, strictly honest, and highly respected, a thorough temperance man, a genial companion, and kind and generous to the poor and needy.

Pierpont E. Bull came from Stephentown in 1826, settling on the farm where his daughter, Rebecca W. Bull, now lives. He was a farmer and had two daughters, Rebecca W. and Mrs. Elizabeth M. Barker, of Clarendon, Orleans County. He died in Byron in 1868.

Richard G. Brown, born in Massachusetts in 1799, removed to Verona, N. Y., with his father's family as early as 1804, or earlier. In 1813 the family again moved westward, and settled in the woods near the Rock school house. His father built a log cabin, and resided in Byron until 1839, when the spirit of adventure took him to the far West again, and he settled in Oakland County, Mich., where he died in 1857, aged 82 years. Mr. Brown was reared a farmer, and had a limited common school education. In 1824 he married Laura, daughter of Samuel Searls, of Byron, and moved his bride and her effects to his log house in the woods, on lot 124, which he had previously built. In 1829 he sold his first "pitch," and removed to a log house, and a larger and better farm, on lot 110, where he resided until 1850, when he built a fine farm house which is now the home of his son, M. B. C Brown. Here he resided the remainder of his business life. He sold the homestead to his son in 1877, and died at North Byron, February 2, 1885, aged nearly 86 years. He was a man of medium stature, active and hardy, and a great worker. Besides clearing his own farm he felled the timber, and cut it up in lengths for logging, on 100 acres for his neighbors. Mr. Brown was a worthy member of the Methodist Church of Byron Center as long as it existed. Later united with the Free Baptist Church at North Byron, and gave to it his hearty support. He was a man who, when he had formed an opinion, seldom changed, but always strove to pursue the right.

William F. Brown, third child of Richard G. and Laura (Searls) Brown, was born in the log cabin on lot 110, in June, 1829, and was brought up at hard labor and educated in the common schools. December 18, 1851, he married Hannah S. Benton, of Byron, and settled on a part of lot 122. He has always been a farmer. In the spring of 1871 he removed to the farm of 170 acres, on lots 99 and 111, where he now resides. Mr. Brown is a pushing, enterprising, business manager and farmer. He has built a fine set of buildings on each of the farms that he has owned, and an especially elegant set at his present pleasant home. As a man he is courteous and affable, an obliging neighbor, and a kind, indulgent husband and father. He is a staunch Republican, but not an office-seeker. He has the confidence of his townsmen, and has consented to act as their assessor four years. Mr. and Mrs. Brown have had two children, Mary E. and Edwin B. Edwin B. married Mary E. Swan, is a farmer adjoining his father, and has two daughters. Mary E. died in 1879, at the early age of 16 years and six months.

Melville B. C. Brown, son of Richard G Brown, was also born in the log cabin on lot 110, November 7, 1833, and was educated in the common schools and early taught industrious habits. January 25, 1877, he married Mrs Amy (Merrill) Brown, widow of his brother George C., and brought his wife to the homestead, which he was conducting. In April, 1877, he purchased the farm of his father, which has been his home from his birth. Mr. Brown is a good farmer, and gives his whole attention to the cultivation of his fine farm of 155 acres. He is an extensive reader, a close observer, and has acquired a fund of practical information. In influence and excellence of character he well sustains the high reputation of the Brown family of Byron. Mr. and Mrs. Brown are parents of one son, Searls G. Mr. Brown was raised a Democrat, voted for Millard Fillmore in 1856 and for Abraham Lincoln in 1860, and remained a thorough Republican until 1888, when his temperance principles induced him to join the ranks of the Prohibitionists.

Abner Chase was born November 9, 1777. He married and settled in Oneida County, and about 1816 removed to Byron and settled in the woods where his grandson now lives. He first lived in a log house, and later he built a stone residence, which was taken down about 1856. The present framed house was then erected by his son, Ai S. Chase. It is claimed that he owned the first team of horses in the neighborhood, and hauled wheat to Rochester when it brought only two shillings and sixpence per bushel. He was many years a magistrate and the trial justice, and held court in the kitchen of his log cabin and officiated at numerous weddings   He was a Mason until the Morgan excitement, when he left the order. Mr. Chase was a man highly respected and prominent in all town affairs. He died June 2, 1844, aged 66 years. His wife, Matilda C. Chase, died December 26, 1855, aged 77 years. They had four sons and three daughters, all deceased. His youngest child, Ai S., was reared on the home farm, married Mary A., daughter of Benjamin Bower, and always resided on the Chase homestead. He was an industrious, quiet man, and gave his whole attention to his farm and the care of his family   He never enjoyed robust health, but by good management and the aid of his oldest son he kept his farm in good condition. He died May 24, 18;0, aged 54 years. His widow still survives and resides with her youngest child, H. B. Chase, on the homestead. They had born to them three daughters, all deceased, and two sons, Charles O. und Heber Burdett. Charles O. Chase is a farmer in Byron.

Asahel Cook, in the summer of 1809, started from his home in the town of Marcellus, Onondaga County, to go to the then '' far West,'' to find for himself and family a new home. He came to Western New York, passing through what is now the city of Rochester, and selected a location in what is now the town of Byron. He bought a farm of 87 acres of the Holland Land Co., paying, or agreeing to pay, $4.50 per acre, the same price for which he could have purchased as he passed through Rochester, but considered that district too low and wet. There was only about one acre cleared on this lot, or on the territory of several hundred acres adjoining. He contracted, before returning home, with Elijah Loomis for the erection of a cheap building for a temporary home, and later for a more substantial log house. In the winter of 1810, with his wife and three sons, Elias, David, and Reuben, and two daughters, and all his effects, he moved by ox-team and sled to his new home, the eldest boy, Elias, being in his 11th year, and Reuben, the youngest, only six.

In the War of 1812 their nearness to the frontier, and their unprotected condition, rendered them naturally fearful and watchful, and when the report came that the Indians were on the "war path" and coming from Buffalo they were panic stricken, and with almost the entire neighborhood started for places of more security. He and his family, by ox-team and sled, went by Stafford, main road, as far as a hotel, between Le Roy and Caledonia, where they found soldiers quartered. They staid there until the next morning, when the good news came that they were in no immediate danger, and the third day found them again at home, there being about 18 inches of snow on the ground. Here, under these circumstances, in an almost unbroken forest, with few and scattered neighbors, he commenced the establishment of a Christian home, and the efforts toward a living or a fortune. Being a shoemaker by trade, as neighbors appeared he found employment and opportunity to earn something toward his support, and by industry and economy secured his home.

Mr. Cook and his wife became members of the First Congregational Church of the town, thus identifying themselves with the religious interests of the community. He was born in 1760, and died in 1834, aged 74 years. The three brothers, on reaching maturity, associated together in the manufacture of potash quite extensively, on the lot on which they lived, using the ashes they made in clearing their own property, and also gathering them from the country surrounding, finding a market for the potash in Batavia and at the canal The two brothers, David and Reuben, finally located on lots adjoining the eldest, retaining the original lot and also adding another of about the same size.

Elias Cook started about the first—if not the first—nursery (mostly apple stock) grown in the county, from which many thrifty bearing trees are now standing in different parts of the county. He also, in 1862, commenced the planting of one of the largest apple orchards in the county, on the original farm which 50 years before was covered by dense forests. His second marriage was to Elizabeth Holmes, in 1833. Three children were born to them, two of whom are now living, viz.: Mrs. Dr. G. U. Gleason and Charles E. The latter still retains the homestead, on which he resides. Besides regular farming Mr. Cook is engaged quite extensively in the cultivation of standard fruits, having about 50 acres, 2,000 bearing apple trees, 2,000 dwarf and standard pears, and quince and other fruits. Mr. Cook is also the inventor of a fruit gatherer.

Irving D. Cook, son of David and Tabiatha (Ballard) Cook, was born in Byron, May 5, 1829, in the house where he now resides, and where he has always lived. He was reared a farmer, and was educated in the common schools and the academy of Alexander. November 10, 1859, he married Julia A. Holmes, of Illinois. Mr. Cook's father died when he was but four years old, and his mother, a lady of great energy and a fine manager, kept her family together and educated them. He was her oldest son, and at the early age of 18 years the management of the farm was placed in his hands. When Mr. Cook was about 21 years of age he, in company with his brother, Marshall N., bought the interest of their sisters in the farm, and conducted it and another farm, which they had purchased in company, until the close of the war in 1865, when he bought his brother's interest in the homestead, and is now its sole owner. Mr. Cook is a thorough farmer and a close thinker. He has contributed to the *New York Tribune*, the *Cultivator*, the *Rural New Yorker*, and the *Ohio Farmer*. He is one of the reliable and trusted citizens of Byron, and has a large acquaintance with leading citizens and agriculturists in Genesee County, by whom he is highly respected. Mr. and Mrs. Cook are parents of five children, viz.: Edwin I., who has been in the employ of the U. S. postal service the past six years; Clara H., who married William S. Greene, a farmer in Byron ; Ella F., a music teacher in Cottage Seminary, Clinton, N. Y.; Julia E., who resides with

25

her parents; and Irving C. H., a student at Oberlin College, Ohio, where his brother and all of his sisters have been educated.

Capt. Marshall N. Cook, son of David, was born in Byron in 1833, and was educated in the common schools with a few terms in the academies. His youth was spent on the farm in Byron and at the old home until August, 1862, when he enlisted in Co. I, 129th N. Y. Inf., and went to the front as first lieutenant of his company. He was promoted captain June 3, 1864, led his command until the close of the war, and was mustered out of service and honorably discharged June 12, 1865. In the winter of 1862 and '63 the 129th Regiment was transferred from the infantry to the artillery service, and became the 8th N. Y. H. A., and remained in Baltimore until May 15, 1864, when the regiment joined the Army of the Potomac. Capt Cook led his company in the battles of Spottsylvania, North Anna, Cold Harbor, and Hatcher's Run, was at the siege of Petersburg, followed the retreating army of Gen. Lee until his surrender, and was nine consecutive days under fire in a severe engagement at Clover Hill. Capt. Cook received a severe wound at the battle of Cold Harbor, and barely escaped with his life. At the same engagement his captain and seven men of his company were killed and 30 wounded. At the close of the war he returned to Byron, engaged in farming four years, was a general merchant the ensuing five years, was in Albany 14 months as assistant superintendent of tool boys, was a general agent and traveling salesman for agricultural implements, and has for the last two years given his attention to fruit growing and gardening on his fine place in South Byron, which he has owned the past 12 years. February 13, 1867, he married E. Maria Clark, by whom he has two daughters.

Capt. Nathan Cash, son of Daniel and Mary (Tracy) Cash, was born in Orange County, N. Y. His father was from Pittston, Pa., a survivor of the celebrated Wyoming massacre. He had volunteered to go to Connecticut, and was thus saved, as were also his family. Nathan Cash married Parnell Southworth, came to the Holland Purchase about 1812, and settled in the north part of Stafford and engaged in farming. Being a carpenter he erected his own buildings. He lived there until his death in 1856. His granddaughter, Mrs. Bennett Waterman, occupies the old homestead. He was a public-spirited man, was a promoter of schools and churches, and was trusted to offices of responsibility. A daughter, Mrs. Phœbe Bassett, lives in Stafford, aged 83 years. Erastus, a son, born in 1798, came with his parents to this town, and frequently had as high as 100 acres of wheat harvested with sickles and cradles. He married Achsah Deming, of Livingston County, whose father settled here in 1805. Mr. Cash settled in Stafford in 1826, and in 1836 located in South Byron, where his daughter Ella (Mrs. George G. Chick) now lives. He died in 1875, and his wife in 1887. Their daughter Anna married John H. Rapp, of Byron, and Celinda, widow of James M. Bower, lives in Byron. Mr. Cash, besides cultivating over 400 acres of land, was engaged in the manufacture of fertilizing plaster. In 1847 he built a large stone flouring-mill in South Byron, which was soon burnt. He was the first postmaster of South Byron, was a temperance man, and an anti-slavery Democrat, but joined the Republican party and supported all war measures. He was a man of great weight in all benevolent and worthy enterprises, and a member of the Presbyterian Church, as was also his family. Andrew, D. Cash, a son, married Sally F. Ward, and died in 1858, aged 32 years. She died in 1885. Parnell, a daughter of Andrew, married James Bower, and died in 1859.

William H. Deming was born November 6, 1804, in Berkshire County, Mass., and emigrated to Monroe County, N. Y., with his parents in 1812. He learned the trade of building fanning-mills of his brother-in-law. About 1827 or 1828 he married Sally Costelin, and settled in Byron Center, engaging in wagonmaking. He finally enaged in farming in connection with wagonmaking, and removed to the farm now owned by Mrs. George McDaniels, where he built the farm buildings. Here he spent the most of his business life. He again sold out, and removed to a farm north of Byron Center, where he resided until his death in May, ·1889, aged 84 years. Mr. Deming was one of the prominent men in the society where he resided, and commanded the respect of all who knew him. He held the office of assessor several years, was a consistent member of the Presbyterian Church, and for years was one its trustees. Three of his six children are living, viz.: Henry D., Sophronia, and Sarah Helen. Henry D. married Delia A., daughter of Nat Spafford, who died in 1864. She bore him one son, William H., who resides with his father. In 1866 Mr. Deming married, second, Marion L. Hume, who bore him a daughter, Fanny Edith, and a son, Charles Hume, both of whom reside with their father. Mrs. Deming, second, died June 30, 1887. Mr. Deming has always given his attention to cultivating and improving his farm.

Andrew Dibble, born in Massachusetts, March 23, 1777, married Piercy Dodge, October 24, 1799, who was born May 20, 1783. He settled on a farm, where he resided until 1816, when he removed to Byron and located on a farm three-quarters of a mile east of Byron Center, where he resided until about 1833, when he built a comfortable house for the Andrew brothers, who were Thompsonian doctors who practiced on a contract for him by the year. Mr. Dibble learned their system of practice, received a diploma, practiced with and succeeded them, and continued in practice over 40 years. He died at the great age of 98 years, February 6, 1875. He possessed great physical vigor, energy, and courage, and led an active life. His wife died November 6, 1864, after a married life of 65 years. They had born to them 17 children, 11 of whom grew to maturity, and only Joseph D., born February 13, 1817, resides in Byron, on a part of the old homestead.

Silvanus Dillingham, of English descent, son of John, was born June 6, 1771. He was twice married, and was the father of 12 children. In 1824 he went " West " from Saratoga County, N. Y., and settled on a new farm in Caledonia, where he resided until his death, October 17, 1830, aged 59 years. He was a member of the Society of Friends, was a worthy citizen, and carried on the dual occupation of farmer and carpenter. His son, Stephen Dillingham, was but 15 years old when he settled in Caledonia. He remained with his father, and at his death he assumed the debts against the farm, which he paid off and gave a home to his mother and younger brothers and sisters. He married Mrs. Anna (Shotwell) Hoag, a few years after which he sold the homestead and settled on a farm in Elba. Several years later he sold a portion of the farm, including the buildings, and built a new set on the remaining 100 acres, where he resided until he died, April 9, 1881, aged over 72 years. Mr. Dillingham was an exemplary member of the Society of Friends. Mrs. Dillingham survived her husband about six months. They were parents of nine children, six of whom lived to mature age, viz.: Mary J. (Mrs. Lewis Genung), of Orleans County ; Maria L. (Mrs. L. B. King), of Lockport, Niagara County ; Isaac Oscar, who married Miss Sarah Thistlethwaite, and is a farmer in the east part of Elba ; Stephen, who married Emeline E. Porter, and is a farmer in Oakfield ; and Rosetta, who married Wilbur F. Curtis, and resides at Independence, Iowa. Isaac Dillingham is a farmer in Byron. He married Martha Hosmer, of Elba, and they have one son, George. Mr. Dillingham is a staunch Republican, and is now serving his town as supervisor. He is a progressive and enterprising farmer, and a worthy citizen.

Levi Fisk came to Byron from Shelburne, Mass., in 1818, and settled where John S now lives. He carried on the business of wool-carding and cloth-dressing, and was a farmer. He married Cynthia Coleman, of Buckland, Mass., in 1819, and reared six children, viz.: John S., Clarissa, Cynthia, Abigail, Euseba, and P. B., all of whom are living except Euseba. Levi took an active part in public affairs, was supervisor of the town, and was an active member of the church and assisted in its organization. John S. Fisk has always resided in the town, and for a time was engaged at wool-carding. He is a farmer.

Benoni Gaines came to Byron from Connecticut about 1807, settling in the north part of the town. About 1826 he built the house where his son Solomon now lives. He was a millwright and made the first threshing machine used in this vicinity. He died in Canada.

Jesse Goodwin, born April 22, 1781, married Dolly Watkins, of Canandaigua, who was born April 14, 1790. Mr. Goodwin emigrated from New England as early as 1812, and drove the first stage coach through from Canandaigua to Buffalo, loaded with army officers, just before Buffalo was burned. He was in the employ of Mr. Powell, proprietor of the stage line, as a driver several years. In 1817 he settled in Riga, where he made himself and family a good home. In 1850 he and his son James M. sold the homestead in Riga and removed to the northwest part of the town of Byron, where he spent the remainder of his long life. He died March 18, 1867, aged 86 years. His son, James M. Goodwin, has added to the farm of 190 acres from time to time, until he now has one of the best farms in Genesee County, of about 400 acres. October 28, 1858, he married Ellen M., daughter of Zeno S. Terry, and they have a son, Charles T., and a daughter, Jenny L., who reside with their parents.

Galette B. Gilbert, M. D., was born in Darien, July 24, 1845, and received his education in the common schools and at Alden Academy, with two years at Ann Arbor University. He then studied medicine at the Buffalo Medical College, where he graduated in 1868. He began practice in Wyoming County, where he remained three years, and practiced in Rochester in 1872–73, where he also conducted a drug store. In the fall of 1873 he located in Marilla, and in 1877 came to Byron Center, where he has built up an extensive and successful practice. He is a progressive man in his profession, giving all his spare time to study, and is well up in the improved methods of practice. He is a member of the Genesee County Medical Society. In 1868 he married Mary M. Moore, of Wyoming County, and they have two sons.

Andrew Hunter Green, a native of Montgomery County, was born in 1797, and came to Genesee County in 1809 with his father, Joshua. The year previous Joshua had purchased 3,000 acres of land at 22 shillings per acre, in the towns of Bergen and Sweden. Andrew attended school in 1811, which was distant seven miles. In 1812 he hauled flour from Le Roy to Buffalo. His father shortly after moved to Byron. Andrew H. returned East and lived with his maternal grandfather, near New Lebanon. In 1821 he married Lavina Gould. His father died in 1822, leaving a family, and he moved to Byron and resided with his mother until his death in 1875. He was owner of a grist and saw-mill, was a land surveyor, assisted in running the first line of the N. Y. C. Railroad, was active in public affairs, and represented his county in the legislature of 1838–39. Loren, the oldest son of Andrew, was born in New Lebanon in 1822. While a young man he took charge of his father's farm and property, and resided here all his life. In 1852 he married Abigail, daughter of Hon. Levi Fisk. He served as supervisor for several years, and was a member of Assembly in 1863–64. He died February 12, 1879, on the old homestead. A daughter of Andrew H. married John H. Steel, of Byron.

Moses Gillett was born in Connecticut in 1799, and came with his father from Ovid, N. Y., to Byron in 1818, settling on a new farm in a log house about a mile west of the village of South Byron, where he resided until his death, December 17, 1860. February 28, 1828, he married Polly Gillett, a native of Connecticut, who was born October 27, 1803, and died on the homestead October 6, 1865. Their children were Seth, born December 4, 1828; Silva A., born June 18, 1830; Jerome, born September 2, 1833; John, born May 26, 1835; Cleaveland, born June 16, 1838; and William H. H., born April 16, 1840. Mr. Gillett was an industrious man, and gave his attention to his own business. In politics he was a staunch Whig, but declined office. His son Jerome was reared on the homestead, and learned the trade of mason, which he followed some years. He also dealt in fruit and live stock, made a trip to the " West " with the intention of settling there, but returned to his native town, and for five years he engaged in dealing in live stock and country produce. In 1873 he bought the hotel which bears his name, and which he is still conducting, being also engaged in farming and dealing in horses and all kinds of marketable property. March 13, 1862, he married Hattie M. Gardner, of Stafford, who was born in Batavia, June 14, 1841. They have had four children, of whom three sons are now living. Their only daughter died in early childhood. Their oldest son, Cleveland M., born December 19, 1862, has been a general merchant a year or two, has conducted a meat market one winter, and traveled one year in the West. He is now a farmer with his father.

Andrew J. Hall was born in Sodus, N. Y., about 1826. His father, Joseph Hall, settled in Rochester about 1828, and there invented the first cylinder threshing machine, the first one being a cylinder of hard wood, with hickory teeth. The concave was only a four-inch scantling, with teeth of the same kind, and driven by a rope that passed over a grooved pully attached to the cylinder. He continued improvements until he perfected his machines, and erected the Joseph Hall works in Rochester, and for 50 years his machine was the standard model for all implements of this kind built in the United States and Canada. Andrew J. Hall learned the trade of machinist in his father's manufactory, and remained there until the latter's death in 1865. In the spring of 1866 he removed to the farm, about a mile and a-half east of South Byron, where he now resides. In 1842 Mr. Hall married Mary A. Fitzpatrick, a native of Ennismon, Ontario, Canada, and they have three children, viz.: Minnie, (Mrs. Newman Culross), a widow, whose husband was of the firm of J. R. Culross & Co., manufacturers of the celebrated Culross cracker; William T., a farmer with his father; and Joseph E., who also resides with his father.

Seth C. Langdon, born in Berkshire County, Mass., moved to Verona, N. Y., with his parents, where he married Elizabeth Avery, and settled on a farm. He was a captain of militia in the War of 1812. In 1815 he emigrated to this town, bought the improvements of three acres of Joseph Barker, and took a contract for the farm where he spent the remainder of his life, and where his son Gordon now lives. He lived in a log cabin until 1826, when he built a frame house. He lived plain and wore clothes which were spun and woven by his wife. He gave his influence to build school-houses and churches, and was a member of the Presbyterian Church and did his share towards its support. His wife became a member at its organization. He died in March, 1862, aged 77 years, and his wife in August, 1863, aged 81 years. They had nine children, three of whom are living. His youngest son, Gordon, was born on the homestead, February 26, 1826, and received his education in the common schools. March 21, 1849, he married Sarah Hudson, of Byron.

He has always resided on the old homestead, but has found time to fill some of the offices of his town. Mr. and Mrs. Langdon are members of the Presbyterian Church of North Bergen. Their children are Guil ford A., who is married and resides in Des Moines, Iowa; Mary E., who lives with her parents; Estelle S., who married D. Sheldon and resides in Rochester; Herbert E., a carpenter in Byron; William H., who married Anna Frear, and works the home farm; and Carrie E., who resides with her parents.

Gottlieb Mayback, a native of Germany, came to Buffalo in 1845, and in 1863 he removed to Oakfield, where he now resides. He married Christina Donerwort, of Pine Hill, Erie County, and their children were Charles W., Caroline, Jacob H., Julia, and Emma. Charles W., who was born in Buffalo and came to Oakfield with his father, married Rose, daughter of Nelson K. and Julia (Dikeman) Reed, of Knowlesville, N.Y., and is now a resident of Byron. Jacob H. Mayback was born in Alabama in 1859, and married Cora Haxton, by whom he had two children, Ernest and Harry, both deceased. Ernest was run over by a land-roller and killed April 13, 1889. Mr. Mayback is a general merchant and keeps the East Oakfield postoffice. He also carries the mail from Oakfield to East Oakfield. His wife is assistant postmaster.

Aaron Miller about 1759 moved from Weathersfield, Conn., to Pittsfield, Mass. He had a son, Aaron, who fought at Bunker Hill, German Flats, and Stillwater, and was at the siege of Yorktown. After leaving the army he became a Methodist preacher, a blacksmith, and an edge-tool maker. He was the father of Dewey Miller, whose narrative of his life, in his own words, is as follows:

"I was born October 8, 1787, at Pittsfield, Berkshire County, Mass. My father was born in Connecticut and was brought up in Pittsfield when there were no schools. His mother taught him to read in words of two syllables, which was his only schooling. He was a blacksmith by trade and a maker of edge tools. I helped him when quite young, and we made the hoes and some other tools which I afterwards used on my farm here in Byron. When I was between five and six years of age we came to Burlington, Otsego County, and after eight years removed to Brookfield, Madison County. It was from there, in 1811, that I started with an ox-team and sled, and after a two weeks' journey reached this town. I purchased from a man named Gillam land, which is now a part of the Warboys farm, for $50. While grinding my axe at Asa Merrill's a young man named Sanford, from Vermont, came along and I sold him my land for $50. I sold because I found that the land was not crossed by Black Creek, as I had supposed when I bought it. In March, 1812, I took up the land upon which I am now living.

"There are many things that occurred at about that time which I well remember. A man named Shepherd, living about where James Mills does now, wished me to go in with him and build a new mill. I refused, as I did not think it would pay. He built it himself, and the mill cleared expenses and paid for itself the first year. Our nearest grist-mill then was Churchville, and the nearest market Rochester, where we had to take two shillings sixpence per bushel for our wheat and $2.50 per hundred for pork. The cotton cloth which we brought home cost us 50 cents per yard, cotton yarn a dollar a pound, salt $5 a barrel, and other things in proportion. When I came here there were no roads marked out; only paths here and there. There was no church service about here. When I went back to Brookfield I attended the Methodist Conference, about 20 miles from father's. There I fell in with a circuit preacher named Loren Grant, who came here to preach for us. The first store that I can remember was in the building which Mr. Knapp now uses for a barn. In 1813 I fenced off a piece of land

and planted a peach pit in every corner of the fence. I recollect a scare which we had here during the War of 1812. A neighbor who came from Batavia brought home the report that 1,500 Indians were at Black Rock, and would come down through here to butcher us all. The people gathered and took measures for defense. It was afterwards found that the 1,500 Indians were awaiting their revenue from the British government and had no intention of coming this way. I was married, August 1, 1813, to Miss Electa Sanford, of Pownell, Vt. I lived with her, with never a cross word, for seven years, seven months, and seven days. I had two children by this wife—Aaron, now a machinist in Brockport, and Lucy. One year after the death of my first wife I married her sister, Mrs. Merrill, by whom I had four children, three of whom—Albert, John, and Emily—are now living. The fourth, Electa, is dead. I lived four years with my daughter Electa, who married Benjamin Squires, of Wyoming County. My daughter Emily married Mr. Agard, who was then a clerk in Rochester, but removed soon after marriage to Rockford. Ill., where they now live. I was converted 90 years ago, and four years later joined the Methodist Church. After marrying my second wife I became a Freewill Baptist, in which church I have since remained. I have always been a Republican."

Dewey Miller died November 20, 1887, aged 100 years and one month, at the home of his son, A. D. Miller, who lives in the northeastern part of Byron.

Elisha Miller came to Byron (then included in the town of Bergen) on foot, with a knapsack on his back, from Providence, Lucerne County, Pa., in the spring of 1809, and selected a farm about two miles west of Byron Center. He cleared a field, built a log house, and in the fall returned to Pennsylvania. He married Martha Tripp, and in 1810 brought his bride to his cabin in the woods. On this farm these pioneers spent the remainder of their lives. For a long time they were guided in their short and necessary journeys by marked trees. They worked hard, lived prudent, and wore homespun, which Mrs. Miller spun and wove. In addition she wove for her neighbors. They owned a farm of 236 acres, and in 1817 they built a frame house, which is still in good preservation, and occupied. Their children were Hamilton, a farmer, who married Jennette Culver, settled on 50 acres adjoining his father, and died in December, 1885; Nancy, who married Lavinus A. Dibble, settled near her father, and died in November, 1853; and Wheaton S., born December 28, 1817, who was raised on his father's farm, obtained an academic education, and chose the profession of law, and prepared for admission to the bar, but on account of defective eyes declined to be admitted. He was a safe and able adviser in law matters, and often practiced in the lower courts. February 13, 1840, he married Emarett Southworth, of Bergen, daughter of Isaac and Rachel (Tone) Southworth, and settled on the Miller homestead, which is still owned by his heirs. Mr. Miller was a man of comprehensive business ability, and in addition to conducting his farm he was early a large and successful dealer in live stock and farmers' produce. Before the construction of the railroad he drove his cattle and hogs to Albany. He served his town as supervisor and magistrate, and also settled several large estates. He was a peacemaker and advised his neighbors to settle disputes rather than resort to law. At the time of his death he was the largest land owner in Byron. He died May 28, 1864, at the age of 46. In politics he was an old line Whig, and joined

the' Republican party at its organization. During the war he was enthusiastic in the support of the government. Mr. and Mrs Miller were parents of 10 children, of whom nine are now living, and all reside in Genesee County, viz.: Holden T., cashier of the Bank of Batavia; Elisha H.,
of the firm of F. T. & E. H. Miller, insurance agents and produce and coal
dealers; Edwin S., a farmer, and produce and coal dealer in Bergen;
Hon. Francis T., of the firm F: T. & E. H. Miller, and an extensive farmer
and member of the State legislature of 1890; Martha N. (Mrs. George
W. Prentice), of South Byron; Arietta L. (Mrs. W. H. Adams), of Byron
Center; Mary J. (Mrs. George G. Humphrey), of South Byron; Rachel
E. (Mrs. Charles H. Coward), whose husband is a successful farmer near
Byron Center; and Andrew T., assistant cashier of the Bank of Batavia.
Elisha H. Miller, born January 3, 1844, married Lydia L., daughter of
George W. Peckham, of Byron, and they have three children. Mr. Miller
has served his town as supervisor four consecutive years, and was chairman
of the board two years. He has also officiated as justice of the peace the
last seven years. Hon. Francis T. Miller, born October 16, 1847, married
Julia A., daughter of James D. Benham, by whom he has seven children,
now living. He is deservedly popular with the people of Genesee County.
He has been honored with the office of supervisor three terms, assessor
three years, and is now the representative of his county in the State legislature. He and his four brothers, and three of his four brothers-in-law,
are staunch Republicans, and all are doing their party good and active
service.

Asa Merrill, son of Jared, came to Byron in 1809, on foot, with a
knapsack on his back, in company with his brother. They traveled
about 35 miles a day. Loren O. Merrill, son of Asa, the pioneer, was
born August 7, 1829, married Ermina J. Holbrook, of Byron, and settled on the homestead where he resided until after the death of his father.
In 1875 he removed to Wheatland, Monroe County, where he is now
engaged in farming. His son, Maj. H. W. Merrill, was born on the
Merrill homestead, September 25, 1854, was reared a farmer, and married Nettie Warboys, February 21, 1878. He settled in his native town,
and engaged in farming, where he still resides. They have a daughter
and son, Georgiana and Walter J.

Maj. Hamilton Wilcox Merrill was born in Byron, February 14. 1814,
became a cadet in the U. S. Military Academy in June, 1834, and graduated in June, 1838. He was in the Seminole Indian war in 1839,
1840, and 1841, and in the Mexican war in 1846–47.

Daniel Merrill, son Jared and Abigail (Phelps) Merrill, came from Connecticut to Whitestown in 1790, the year of his birth. He married Sally
Sanford, of Vermont, and settled in Bergen, where he died, aged 28
years, leaving two sons, Ezra S. and Daniel F. Ezra S. being but three
years old at his father's death, he made his home with an uncle, Arzy.
He had a limited education, taught school, and April 22, 1847, married
Mary, daughter of Abner and Irene (Miller) Hitchcock. They settled

on the farm he had bought, where his son Abner J. now lives, and where he resided until his death, August 25, 1881, aged 66 years. Mrs. Merrill died November 3, 1878. Mr. Merrill was a prominent man in his town, a Republican, but not an office-seeker. He was always a farmer, and was enterprising, economical, and industrious, and quite successful. He was a man of sterling integrity, and was highly respected. The children of Mr. and Mrs. Merrill are Milan Daniel, a fruit grower and florist residing in South Haven, Mich., who married Mary I. Main, of Michigan; Ellen I., who lives with her brother on the homestead; and Abner J., who married Mary L. Munger, February 18, 1885, and who, soon after his father's death, bought the homestead of the heirs and lives on the place where he and his brother and sister were born, and where he has always resided.

Ony Merrill, son of Jared and Abigail Merrill, came to Byron and bought the Sawyer farm and the saw-mill, and afterwards 100 acres northwest of Byron, known as the Green farm, where he lived over 30 years. He built a saw-mill on Spring Creek, which was a great convenience to the early pioneers. In 1860 he moved to Orleans County and died there, aged 77 years. He was three times married. Nelson, one of his sons, bought the Asa Merrill place (settled in 1811), where he now resides.

Robert Merriman, a native of Connecticut, married Lucina Woodruff, and in 1826 settled in the northwestern part of Byron, where he died. His father was a soldier in the Revolution. Robert worked hard to establish himself on his farm, and being a cooper as well as a farmer succeeded in business. Their children were Harry, Josiah, Lucina M., Marietta, and Lydia. Josiah was born in Massachusetts, January 8, 1811, came to Byron with his parents at the age of 15 years, and resided with them until 26 years of age. He married Mary Wheeler, of Ogden, N. Y., January 5, 1837, and about a year later settled on a farm of his own. He now owns 231 acres in Elba, and about 700 acres in this town. He is very successful, possesses more than ordinary ability, and is universally respected. His son Harry W. married Lillian A. Benham, December 23, 1868, and owns a farm of 282 acres east of Byron Center. Sheldon J., another son, was born January 8, 1851, married Minnie E. Harris, of Batavia, and now lives in Elba on the farm with his father.

Harry Merriman, son of Robert and Lucina Merriman, was born in Saratoga County, July 18, 1809, and came to Byron with his parents in 1826. He married Sally Torpy, of Elba, April 30, 1834. She was born in 1810 He settled on a portion of the old homestead, and resided in a log house until he built his present dwelling. Besides being a farmer he has, since 1870, been engaged in the sale of the Johnston harvester, and by his engaging manners he made a success. He is a Republican, has been highway commissioner 15 years, and assessor and overseer of the poor six years. He is now over 80 years of age. Mrs. Merriman died in 1861. Their children are Lucina, who lives with her father; Robert

E., a farmer, who owns 100 acres of the homestead and 63 acres near by; and Juliette, whose husband, James Knickerbocker, is a farmer in Elba. Lucina M., daughter of Robert and Lucina Merriman, was born in 1811, and married Nelson Tuttle, a farmer. Suffering from a tumor, in 1845 she had it removed while under mesmeric influence, and afterwards was licensed to practice as a clairvoyant, making many wonderful cures. She died in 1888.

Harmon Norton, son of Medad Norton, of Connecticut, married Selina Gillett, came to Byron in 1818, and settled on the farm now owned by his son Erastus H. He died in 1865. Erastus H. served in the war of the Rebellion, in the 129th N. Y. Regt. He is the proprietor of a cheese factory.

Charles Leonard was born in Sangerfield, Oneida County, where he lived until 1852, when he came to South Byron, and kept a livery stable and saloon for three years. He was a farmer for three years in Le Roy. In April, 1865, he came to Byron Center, and has kept the hotel there since that time, and has also carried the mail from South Byron to Byron Center.

John Rambo came from Brockport to Byron in 1857. He embarked in the hardware trade at South Byron, in which business he is still engaged.

Rev. Robert E. Nesbitt, born at Hamlin, Monroe County, was educated at the district schools and the State Normal School at Brockport. He taught the school at Hamlin for six terms, and was ordained as a Freewill Baptist minister April 15, 1884. He has preached at North Byron three years. He was first licensed June 3, 1882, and preached at East Hamlin his first year, then at Hamlin, and came to North Byron, where he preached until April 1, 1887, when he moved to North Scriba to take pastoral charge of the First Freewill Baptist Church at that place.

David Mann, who had married Phœbe Parker, came to the Holland Purchase from Manlius, N. Y., and settled in Byron on a farm in 1817, now owned by his granddaughter, Mrs. Benton, where he spent the remainder of his long life. He died in August, 1850, aged 77 years. His wife died in 1830. He was the father of nine children, seven of whom lived and married. His youngest son, Reuben, was born January 28, 1810, and was seven years of age when his father settled in Byron. He was reared on the homestead, and received his education in the common schools. In 1835 he married Betsey Hall, of Byron, a native of Peru, Mass., and settled on a farm of 25 acres adjoining his father's. In 1854 he removed to the farm where his only daughter now resides. He built a residence and buildings, and added to his farm from time to time, until it now contains 115 acres. He died October 25, 1889, aged 79 years. Mrs. Mann died August 2, 1886. Their daughter Livilla, born February 15, 1840, married Edward B. Clark, December 28, 1860, who was a farmer and mechanic. In 1863 he enlisted in the Union army, served 11 months, received a gun-shot wound in his left arm, near Peterburg, and was confined in the hospital at Alexandria six months, when he was discharged. This wound caused him much suffering until 1875, when he was relieved by amputation. He eventually died of blood poisoning, April 21, 1887, aged 55 years. Mr. and Mrs. Clark had one daughter, Evelyn, born May 4, 1868, who resides on the homestead with her mother.

William Mann, son of David, was born in 1804, and came with his parents to Byron in 1817. In February, 1832, he married Azubah, daughter of Nathan and Lois (Tuttle) Hall, who were also early pioneers of Byron. He had previously purchased the homestead, where they lived to the close of his life in 1851. His widow still survives (1890), and resides with her youngest son, Lucius, in the village of South Byron. William Mann was an enterprising farmer, a man of integrity, and highly respected. Alfred, son of William, was born February 8, 1834, was reared a farmer, and was educated in the common schools. He married Sima Feagles, and settled permanently on the farm where he now resides, about two miles from South Byron. He is a respected citizen, and in politics is a Republican. His children are Earl W., who married Estelle Dunn and resides in South Byron, and Willie E., Charles, Nettie, and Alma L., who reside with their parents. Elvira Mann married Thomas H. Benton, a farmer, and resides in Clarendon, Orleans County. Ezra Mann, a farmer, married Diantha Wood. He served in the Union army, received a serious gun shot wound at the battle of Fredericksburg, and was discharged for disability. He now resides at North Byron, and receives a pension. Lucius Mann, also a farmer, married Helen Perkins, and settled on the old homestead, where they resided 10 years, when they removed to the village of South Byron, where they now reside, and with whom his aged mother has a home. Chester Mann, son of David, was born August 15, 1800, in Connecticut, and came to Byron when 16 years of age, with his father. He married Eunice Hall and had a family of six children. He was a farmer, and died May 22, 1884. His widow resides in Batavia, with her daughter, Mrs. J. A. Eggleston, aged 86 years. She was born September 10, 1803.

Joel Philleo, of Scipio, N. Y., married Clarissa Lathrop, and was at Auburn when the State prison was built there, engaged as a teamster, and drew the first load of iron used in its construction. In 1818 he removed to Stafford, about a mile and a quarter from where the village of South Byron is now located, and where he resided until 1847. In 1847 he emigrated to Somerset, Niagara County, and engaged in farming. He died in 1857, aged about 63 years. His wife died about 1879, aged nearly 96 years He was a man of the old school, and carved out a home in the wilderness. Of his nine children four are now living. Melissa married Alfred Rutty, a farmer in Michigan, who enlisted in the Union army, and died in the service. His widow resides with her children in Michigan. Henry S., born in Scipio, N. Y., in 1816, came with his parents to Stafford in 1818, and remained with his father until he was 27 years of age. February 10, 1842, he married Lany Bushman, and 12 days later commenced housekeeping on a small farm adjoining his father. In 1844 he went to Michigan, where he remained about four years, and was quite prosperous financially, but were not healthy, in consequence of which he returned to his native State. They resided in Niagara and Orleans counties, and eventually settled on a farm near the village of South Byron, where they have resided the past 31 years. Mr. and Mrs. Philleo are parents of two daughters, and two sons, viz.: Martha, who married James E. Mills, a farmer, of Byron; Emma R., who married William R. Mills, also a farmer, of Byron; Winslow H., a farmer in Hanson County, Dakota; and Charles Edgar, a farmer with his parents. Alonzo Philleo, son of Joel, is a fruit grower in Ridgeway, Orleans County, and Edgar resides in Lockport, N. Y.

Elisha Prentice, of Massachusetts, born in 1771, married Sally Howard, of Oneida County, N. Y. He came on foot in 1812 to Stafford, secured 100 acres of land, built a cabin, cleared two acres, and planted it with corn, "Indian style." He returned to Massachusetts, and came again in the fall with a pair of oxen, and found a good crop of corn ready to harvest. Here he remained and died in 1859, aged 88 years. Mrs. Prentice died in 1858. Their seventh child, Cyrus Prentice, was born in Massachusetts, June 20, 1812, came to Stafford in his mother's arms, and has always resided in Genesee County near the old home. He had more days at work than days at school. In October, 1835, he married Dolly Clapp, of Stafford, daughter of Paul Clapp, a pioneer, and took his bride to the Prentice homestead, cleared off the indebtedness on the farm, built a comfortable house for his parents, and administered to their comfort the remainder of their long lives. Cyrus Prentice has been a successful financier, gaining an enviable reputation for economy, industry, and fair dealing. He added to his real estate until he owned 400 acres. In 1871 he moved to South Byron, where he still resides, having sold his homestead to his son George W., of the firm of Boynton, Prentice & Co. He has been an old line Whig, but now votes with the Republican party, and has held all the important town offices. Mrs. Prentice, a worthy member of the Methodist Church, died June 2, 1886. They reared seven children, six of whom are now living, viz.: Mary (Mrs. James Bean); Imogene (Mrs. M. D. Bean); Adelbert, a collegiate, who resides in South Byron; Marion (Mrs. Irving D. Southworth), of Batavia; Eva (Mrs. Edward Lapp), of Buffalo; and George W, a merchant in South Byron.

Elkanah Humphrey, of Rhode Island, came to Byron in 1813, and bought 100 acres of land at South Byron, where his son Erastus now lives, but did not settle on it until 1828. He died in 1846. He was a man of strict integrity, a good Methodist, and a Whig in politics.

Rev. D. M. Rollin was born in New Sharon, Me, August 11, 1804. He married Mary Carey, of Boston, Erie County, N. Y., and they had four children. He was pastor of the Freewill Baptist Church, of Byron, for many years. He commenced preaching in 1825, and has been in service since. Rev. Mr. Rollin·studied Greek while riding over the country on horseback. He was ordained when 23 years of age, and has been a resident of Byron for many years. He has the respect of all who know him.

David Shedd, born October 16, 1774, married Jane Brewer, and they had 13 children. He came from Oneida County about 1813, and settled where his granddaughter, daughter of the late Milo W. Shedd, now lives. He was a large farmer, cleared up his farm of 160 acres, and lived to see his large family all married and settled in life. He died in 1848 Milo W. was born in 1808, bought the homestead in 1844, and died in 1887. He was a useful man in Byron, was magistrate 35 years, was a man of exemplary habits, and widely respected. In 1830 he married Wealthy Sanderson, who died in 1832. They had one daughter, now Mrs. William Osborne, of Iowa. In 1834 he married Abigal Phelps, with whom he lived 53 years. They celebrated their golden wedding January 8, 1885. Their children are Mrs. S. J. Arnold, of Rochester, and Mary, wife of Thomas Close, and who resides on the homestead with her mother.

Thomas Close was born in Poughkeepsie, N. Y., November 14, 1840. His parents went to Buffalo when he was young, At the age of 12 years he was induced to go to Byron and live in the family of Milo W. Shedd, where he remained until 1859, when he learned the trade of mason. In 1862 he enlisted in Co. F, 105th N. Y. Vols., which was consolidated with the 94th Regt. He served honorably until 1865. January 6, 1866, he married Mary Shedd, and, settling in Byron, worked at his trade. He has lived three years in Batavia. Latterly they have resided on the Shedd homestead. Mr. Close has been collector of taxes for three years. When in the army he was in 26 regular battles, among them being Antietam, Gettysburg, and Fredericksburg. He was twice wounded.

John Searls, son of Isaiah, was born in Westchester County, August 23, 1792, moved with his parents to Schoharie County, and came to Byron with his older brother, Isaiah, who was born June 17, 1790. They made their first location April 14, 1814. Very soon after Isaiah was drafted in the War of 1812-15, and John enlisted, At the battle of Lundy's Lane Isaiah was wounded, and was carried a prisoner to Montreal, where he died of fever. At the close of the war John was discharged and returned to Byron. September 14, 1815, he married Hannah (Stocking), his brother's widow, and settled on the farm where his son Isaiah now lives, and where he resided 61 years. He died December 3, 1875, aged over 83 years. In 1818 he bought the homestead and moved into a planked house, and in 1840 he built the farm house now occupied by his son Isaiah. Mrs. Searls died in June, 1875. Their children were Stephen D., of the State of Washington; Charles C., a builder, of Grand Rapids, Mich.; and Isaiah, who resides in Byron, on the old homestead, and who is an enterprising farmer, and a highly respected citizen. Mr. Searls has paid off the heirs and added to the homestead of 125 acres, until it now contains 253 acres. In 1853 he married Eliza T. Hall, of Elba, by whom he has had two sons, viz.: Horace H., who married Anna Brainard, of Barre, N. Y., and resides on a farm adjoining his father's; and Charles C., a farmer with his father, who married Clara Potter, of Clarendon, N. Y.

James W. Seaver, of Byron, second son of Dr. James Everett Seaver, was born in Hebron, N. Y., June 29, 1812. His father was the eldest son of William Seaver and Mary Everett, the latter a first cousin of Edward Everett, of Massachusetts. Dr. James E. Seaver died at Darien, January 25, 1827. He came to Darien (then Pembroke) in 1816, a very poor man, but had a stock of medicine in his pill-bags. His first outlay was $2.50 for a bushel of wheat. From overwork and exposure he became ill and had to give up work. His family was left almost destitute. James W., at the age of 16, began clerking, and followed a mercantile life for 60 years. He came to Byron in 1832, and was a clerk in the store of C. Jenks & Co. He married, in 1839, Mrs. J. W. Bennett. In 1844 Mr. Seaver and his brother John purchased of Zeno S. Terry the stock of goods formerly belonging to Loren Clark, a pioneer merchant of Byron. In 1845 James W. Seaver was appointed postmaster, which position he held for about 40 years. In 1858 he was elected justice of the peace, holding the position for 20 years. He has three daughters: Mrs. J. A. Moore, whose husband is Mr. Seaver's partner in the mercantile business; Mrs. Julia A. Stone, who for 12 years has been a teacher in the Blind Institution at Batavia; and Mary M., the wife of Rev. H. C. Woods, now pastor of the Methodist Episcopal Church at Victor, N. Y. Mr. Seaver is an active and pronounced spiritualist.

Zeno, son of Zeno and Tabitha (Abbey) Terry, was born in Connecticut in 1779, married Polly Griswold, and came to Oneida County, thence to Byron about 1811, where he passed the rest of his life. He died in 1864, and his wife in 1851. In 1827 he bought the place where his daughter, Mrs. M. H. Crocker, now lives. He served at one time as supervisor, and was also a magistrate. Zeno S, a son, was born in 1809, was a farmer, and always resided in Byron. William, son of Zeno, came to Byron about 1811. He married Phœbe Morse, settled on a farm, and died aged 69 years. They had five children. Addison, a son, was born in 1812, married Lucetta Hurd, of Stafford, in 1836, and lives south of Byron Center. He is and has been an extensive dealer in live stock, particularly before the advent of the railroad.

James B. Todd, son of John and Rachel (Duncan) Todd, was born November 25, 1787, on the Todd homestead, in Peterboro, N. H., where his father settled in early life. He married Sarah Appleton, March 8, 1816, who was born in Dublin, N. H., March 5, 1790. They settled on the homestead, where they remained until 1828, when they went West, with a team of horses and a wagon as far as Troy, N. Y., where they took a canal boat, and afterwards their own conveyance, arriving at their future home in the west part of Byron, May 27, 1828, where they spent the remainder of their lives. Mr. Todd was a man of fine physique, six feet in height, strong, robust, and a great worker. He occupied a log house four years, and in 1832 built a fine framed residence, now the home of his son Isaac. Mr. Todd died May 29, 1862. He was a man of integrity, upright, and honorable. Mrs. Todd died March 28, 1884, aged 94 years. Mr. Todd was a captain of militia in the War of 1812, and was stationed with his command at Portsmouth, N H. His father, John Todd, was a private soldier in the Revolutionary war, and was present at the surrender of Burgoyne at Saratoga. His grandson Isaac has in his possession the musket which he captured from a Hessian soldier. Mr. and Mrs. Todd reared six children. Their oldest son, Isaac Todd, was born in Peterboro, N. H., December 18, 1816, and came with his parents to Byron in 1828. He was educated in the common schools, supplemented by a few terms in the academies. November 3, 1847, he married Frances H. Dewey, of Byron, and settled near Byron Center. In 1870 he removed to the old homestead. Besides conducting a farm of 300 acres he deals in fine horses and live stock. He is a Democrat and has served as justice eight years. His children are James G., a farmer and dealer in stock; Sarah (Mrs. S. C. Hall), of Rochester; William G., a farmer in Elba; and Ida J., John D., and Emily, who reside with their parents. Their youngest child, Joe D., died in 1887, aged 22 years.

William Warn, a native of Massachusetts, came in 1816 to Byron. He served in the Revolution, and died at the home of his son Warren, in Byron, aged over 90 years. His four sons, William, Warren, Lyman, and Milo, came to the Holland Purchase as early or before the "cold season" of 1816, and were all farmers. Lyman Warn was born in Massachusetts in 1797, came to Byron in 1816, married Jane Gillam, a native of New Jersey, and settled on a farm in Byron. In early life he cut stone for the construction of the locks in the Erie Canal. In 1838 he removed to the farm where his son Horatio now lives, on road 6, where he died in 1871, aged 74 years. He was a Democrat. He was honest and industrious. His only son, Horatio, born in 1829, was educated in the common schools, and married Sarah E. Green, January 12, 1859, a native of Massachusetts, who was born in 1839. He settled with his father where he still resides. Mr. Warn is much like his respected father, a man of sterling integrity. They have two sons and a daughter, viz.: Francis G., born in 1861; Charles L., born in 1868; and Fannie J., born in 1873. All reside at home with their parents. Mandana Warn, the only daughter of Lyman Warn, was born in 1831. She married M. D. L. Carpenter in 1877, who resides at North Byron, and is a farmer.

Amasa Walker, son of Ebenezer, of Ashford, Conn., was born in 1767, and died in 1828. He married Martha Smith, and they came from Massachusetts to Byron in 1811. He had 12 children. Achsah, a daughter, married Simeon Hosmer, a farmer, of Byron. Amasa, a son, married, first, Lydia Dwight, and second, in 1813, Lydia Nichols. He settled in Byron with his father. Asahel C., son of Amasa and Lydia (Dwight) Walker, was born in 1823. He bought the old homestead, married Sarah Ford, and resided there until 1868. He died in 1870.

Alpha M. Wh ton, M. D., was born in Royalton, Niagara County, in 1857. He entered the Hahnemann Medical College of Philadelphia, and graduated from that institution in 1881. He also attended a course of special lectures at Jefferson College for two years, and passed an examination of the medical faculty of the Homeopathic College of New York city. In July, 1883, he settled in South Byron, where he has since practiced his profession. In the short time that he has been there he has gained the confidence of the people, and has, by his ability, industry, and close attention to his professional duties, built up a fair and successful practice. Although he graduated with honor he thinks it essential to be a close student, and strives to keep pace with the improvements and discoveries in medical science.

DARIEN.

DARIEN was formed from Pembroke, February 10, 1832, and lies in the southwest corner of the county. The surface is hilly in the south and rolling in the north. Murder Creek flows through the town from south to north, in the eastern part. Crooked and Eleven Mile creeks are the other principal streams. The soil in the north is a sandy and gravelly loam, and in the south a clayey loam underlaid by limestone. The Buffalo, New York & Erie Railroad extends through the town from east to west, a little south of the center. The N. Y. C. & H. R. Railroad extends through the northwest corner. The Delaware, Lackawanna & Western Railroad runs through the center of the town from east to west, and the Geneva & Buffalo road will soon have its line built in the northern part of the town. There are four postoffices.

DARIEN CENTER (formerly called King's Corners) is a post village situated three-quarters of a mile north of the Erie Railroad, which affords easy transit from the place, good facilities for transporting produce to market, and enabling the farmers to send milk daily to Buffalo. There are at this place four stores of various kinds, an hotel, a school-house, a Methodist Episcopal Church, the usual complement of mechanics, and in all about 50 dwellings.

DARIEN village, or Darien City, as it is sometimes called, the name given it by some eccentric individual when there were only a few houses

26

built, is situated towards the southeast part of the town, on Murder Creek (so-called from the supposition that a murder had been committed near it at an early day), and near Griswold station (named from B. Griswold) on the Erie Railroad. The village contains a Methodist Episcopal Church, postoffice, school-house, blacksmith shop, saw and feed-mills, a wagon shop, and about 30 dwellings. Before the advent of the railroads it was a place of more active local trade and manufacturing than at present.

SAWENS (p. o.), so named in honor of the Sawens family in the near neighborhood, is situated on Murder Creek, in the northeast part of the town. This little hamlet contains a general store where the postoffice is kept, a saw mill and cider-mill, blacksmith shop, and about 10 houses.

FARGO (p. o.), on the Delaware & Lackawanna Railroad, in the northwest part of the town, contains a general store, cheese factory, blacksmith shop, and about 10 dwellings.

The first town meeting was held at Stephen King's inn (this being the first tavern reported in the town), April 3, 1832, and the following officers chosen: Hugh Long, supervisor; Thomas Riddle, town clerk; Jonathan Durkee, James Sutherland, Adna Tenney, justices of the peace; William Thayer, William Williams, Thomas Miller, assessors; Chilson Mullet, Price Mattison, overseers of the poor; Lyman H. Seaver, Lewis Clark, William Kidder, commissioners of highways; Daniel Carter, Constantine Gilman, Newton Haws, commissioners of schools; Daniel Kendrick, collector. When the division of the county was made, in 1840, the citizens of Darien were not disposed to submit to the new measure without resistance. The following resolution was unanimously adopted at a meeting of the citizens held in 1840:

"That we, the legal voters of the town of Darien, do most earnestly remonstrate against any division of the county of Genesee, and that our representative in the Assembly be, and is hereby, requested to use his utmost endeavors to prevent any division of the said county."

Religion.—The earliest account we have of any religious services in Darien is by a Baptist minister, Elder William Throop, in 1820, who held services until about 1840. The First Congregational Society is on record as organizing May 9, 1823, at Darien Center, with 12 members, with Hugh Wallace as minister. In 1825 there were 18 members; in 1834, 13, with Rev. T. Baldwin, minister; in 1840, 76, with Rev. L. A. Skinner, minister; and in 1846, 40. They built a wooden building about 1839, which is still standing. The church edifice was sold about 1880 for a small sum, and there has been no preaching since 1860.

There is upon record a society of the first Methodist Episcopal Church organized March 18, 1833, but we can find no other information concerning it. The present church was organized in 1848, by J. W. Vaughan. Its first pastor was Rev. K. D. Nettleton, and there were 35 members. There are two churches: one in Darien, built of wood in 1848, and one in Darien Center, built in 1874, having a combined membership of 84 members, under the pastoral charge of Rev. H. A. Slingerland. The valuation of the properties is $7,500.

The Advent Church of God was organized in North Darien, January 16, 1864, by Elder C. W. Low, with a membership of 40. The first pastor was A. C. Newell, and the church edifice was built in 1867. There are at present 50 members, with Elder George A. Streeter in charge. The house and grounds are valued at nearly $2,000. The Sunday-school has 40 scholars.

Laban H. Robinson's feed and saw-mills are located at the village of Darien, on Murder Creek, which furnishes the motive power. These mills were built by Mr. Robinson in 1881, on the site of the mills built in 1854 by Stephen Douglas. His mills and a succeeding set were destroyed by fire. Mr. Robinson does custom grinding, and deals in feed and grain. He also does custom sawing. His saw-mill is furnished with a circular saw and has a capacity for sawing from 5,000 to 8,000 feet of lumber per day. He grinds about 5,000 bushels of grain annually.

Harlow Brothers (Henry L., Jefferson P., and Charles J.) were extensive manufacturers of carriages at Harlow's Corners. The older brother, Henry L. Harlow, began business in a small way about 1844, and as his brothers became of legal age he admitted them to partnership. This firm had a wide reputation, and had not only a market in this State, but in Michigan, Ohio, Illinois, Wisconsin, Indiana, and California. In the busiest season they sometimes employed as many as 35 men. The business was continued in Darien and Lancaster about 40 years.

Zeno Griswola's grist, saw, and cider-mills are located at the little hamlet of Sawens, on Murder Creek, which furnishes the power, with steam as auxiliary. He does custom grinding, sawing, and cidermaking.

In the sketches and reminiscences following will be found a complete history of the town as made up from the lives of its earliest and most prominent pioneers and families. When settlements were made several families, or members of the same families, would locate in a neighborhood. Hence we have in Darien the Colby settlement, the Wait settlement, and many others, so that the neighborhoods, with their appropriate names, retain their early designations to the present time.

The first settlement was made near Darien City by Orange Carter, from Vermont, in 1803. Isaac Chaddock, from Vermont, settled near Darien City in 1804. The first birth was that of Harriet Carter, in 1805. Stephen Parker kept the first inn, in 1808, at Darien City, and Stephen King the first store, at Darien Center, in 1815. The first saw-mill was erected by Amos Humphrey, in 1809, on Eleven Mile Creek.

In addition to the mercantile and other business interests that are noted in the biographical sketches we here group the business that was done in the town in 1869. At Darien Morganstern & Garegan were carriagemakers, and Theodore Young was postmaster and merchant. M. D. Bartlett kept an hotel and was a carriagemaker at Darien City. Amos B. Humphrey had a grist-mill, Kensie Brothers were grocers and proprietors of a cheese factory, R. O. Lewis had a grist and saw-mill,

J. Nichols was a merchant, and H. N. Vickery was a physician at Darien Center.

The following is a list of many of the principal settlers prior to 1820, in what is now Darien and Pembroke:

Benjamin C. Adams, Selah Carpenter, Alanson T. Fisher, Lott K. Griswold, William and Dexter Humphrey, Selvy Kidder, ——— Mullett, David Nay, Jesse Tubbs, Zina Wait, Capt. Jonathan Woodward, and George Wright. In 1804, Isaac Chaddock and David Goss. In 1806, Rufus Kidder, Orange Carter, Saxton Bailey, Israel Doane, and James Day. In 1807, Capt. Jonathan Bailey, Benjamin and David Carter, and John and David Long. In 1808, John Lamberton, Abraham Matteson, Stephen Parker, Joseph Peters, and Samuel Carr. In 1809, S. D. Cleveland, A. L. Clemens, Owen Curtis, Amos Humphrey, Samuel Matteson, John Sumner, James G., H. G., and D. Tiffany, Maj. William Thayer, and Jonathan Vaughan. In 1810, Anna Horton, Daniel and Levi Jones, Jotham Sumner, Sally and Henry Salisbury, Dexter Bordwell, Orris and E. N. Boughton, Maj. Jonathan Durkee, and John Jr., and Russell Waite. In 1811, John Ball, Peleg Brown, Nathaniel Jones, John Murray, Jerome Sumner, Joel Sutherland, and Harry Stone. In 1812, Ichabod and Alva Jefferson, Jonas Kinne, Winslow and Tyler Sumner, David and John Sutherland, John Stickney, Daniel and Barzilla Carter, Frank Chapin, Abner C., Reuben, and Daniel Colby, and Ira J. Tisdale. In 1813, Anson Ackley, Harvey Butler, Hiram Hedges, Jonathan Hastings, John A. Lathrop, Josiah Lee, William and Thomas Vickery, John McCollister, and Thorp Wildman. In 1814, Daniel Marsh, William B. Garfield, Horace Sloan, Jonathan Vickery, and John Webb. In 1815, Ezra Clark, Baxter Gilbert, A. Hutchinson, Shadrach Harmon, Obadiah Jenks, Quartus and D. J. Lee, Elijah Lamb, Joshua Peters, Jr., Ephraim Sumner, and David Salisbury. In 1816, Col. Jesse Safford, D. Anderson, William Cole, Benajah Griswold, John L. Hoyle, Daniel C. Stoddard, John Seaver, and Julius Wildman. In 1817, John W. Brown, C. Dodge, Davis Huntley, Elisha H. Lathrop, Noah Winslow, and Hugh Wallis. In 1818, Elijah Lee, Philo Farnham, Lemuel Stickney, and Silas and Adna Tiffany. In 1819, James Booth, L. H. Colby, Justus Fales, Oliver Harper, Samuel Harroun, Zebulon Jones, Stephen King, Anson and Caroline Lathrop, William Shumway, Benjamin Sloan, and John W. Willett.

Saxton Bailey came to Darien in 1806, with his son Joshua, and bought 600 acres of land where Charles C. Magry now lives. His family came in 1808. His son Daniel came in 1808, and served as a captain in the War of 1812. He was a Presbyterian, and built the church at the Center. Joshua Bailey was also an early settler. He was a farmer of much industry and accumulated a great deal of property. He sold his farm and started a school at the Center.

Benjamin C. Adams was a very early store-keeper at Darien City, and had the business all to himself for a number of years, or until about 1832.

Dexter Bordwell, son of John and Mary (Edson) Bordwell, of Orange County, Vt., was born March 24, 1801. With his father he came to Darien in 1810, residing with him until 22 years of age. The labors of clearing the farm were so great that all were obliged to assist. The first school-house, of logs, Mr. Bordwell assisted in erecting. At this school he was educated, and proved himself a master of the spelling book. He purchased, in 1825, the farm where his only son, Aaron Bordwell, now lives, and borrowed $1 to pay for making out the contract. He married Tirzah, daughter of Sullivan and Lucy Russ, in 1829, and by close economy, industry, and perseverance succeeded in paying for his place. He was an "old line Whig" and a staunch supporter of the Republican party. He died in 1885, and his wife in 1873. Their only daughter, an amiable lady of culture, came to her death by being thrown from a carriage, January 7, 1850. Aaron, the only son, was born October 26, 1836, received an academic education, and September 28, 1872, married Libbie Bordwell, of Alden, Ill., and settled on the old homestead. Their only son, Clarence H., was born March 11, 1880. Mr. Bordwell is engaged in breeding fine stock, having a large flock of Oxforddown sheep, reported to be the best in the State, and upon which he has obtained many first premiums at State and international shows. He is also a breeder of fine high grade Holstein cattle. Mr Bordwell is a genial, courteous gentleman, a lover of home and its surroundings.

Cyrus Brown, son of John and Abigail (Wright) Brown, was born in New Ipswich, Hillsborough County, N. H., May 20, 1785. In his boyhood he removed with his father's family to Sharon, N. H. In December, 1810, he married Milla Lawrence, and settled with his father in Sharon. In 1817 he removed to Pembroke, this county, and settled on the farm (then unimproved) where he resided the remainder of his life. He was three times elected to the chief office of the town of Sharon, and he held the office of supervisor of Pembroke seven years. Mrs. Brown, daughter of Benjamin and Rebecca (Woods) Lawrence, was born in Jaffrey, Cheshire County, N. H., September 18, 1791. Mr. and Mrs. Brown had six sons and four daughters, and all but one lived to adult age. He died in 1846, and she in 1849.

Peleg Bowen, son of Peleg and Lenty Bowen, was born in Galway, Saratoga County, N. Y., May 26, 1790, and about 1811 came to Darien, then included in Batavia, and selected a home on the town line, where F. Timms now lives. He lived there till his death. He spent a year or two. inclosing and building, and married Eleanor Green. He was one of the sturdy pioneers who cleared out of the forest a good farm and made himself a comfortable home. In the War of 1812 he was a militiaman, and went for the defense of Buffalo when that city was attacked and burned. He was always a farmer, and a man of strict integrity, industrious, honest, a good neighbor, and a reliable citizen. He died in March, 1861. Mrs Bowen died in December, 1858. They had eight children : David, a farmer residing in Alexander ; Rufus, a retired farmer residing in the village of Attica ; Olive (Mrs J. Dunbar), whose husband is a farmer residing in Attica ; Florania, who married William Major, and is now a widow residing in Amsterdam, N. Y.; and Richard, who is the only one residing in Darien. Betsey M. married F. Curtis; is a widow, and resides in Wisconsin; Myra married Fernando Burk, and is a widow living in Meridian, Cayuga County; and George P. is a merchant in Batavia. Richard was born December 18, 1828, and has a good practical education, which he received, not in the common schools, but by a course of reading and observation. In October, 1853, he married Susan Curtis, of Alexander. They had three children, of whom Ellen and Flora are living and reside, unmarried, in Attica. Mrs. Bowen died December 9, 1864, and March 8, 1866, Mr. Bowen married Janette M. Lathrop, by whom he has a son, Charles B., born June 3, 1868, and a daughter, Nettie E., born May 7, 1872. Mr. Bowen is a Democrat, but not an " offensive partisan." He is giving his attention to the cultivation of his large farm, and the breeding of pure blood Oxforddown sheep and imported and registered pure blood Durham cattle. He is well and favorably known throughout the county.

Francis J. Bauer, born in Wurtemberg, Germany, October 8, 1837, emigrated to America in 1853, and in 1865 married Elizabeth Bauer. They had four children: Edward C., Frank J., Helen M. (Mrs. Milo Langworthy), of Pembroke, and Ida H. In 1876 they settled on a farm at Darien Center, where they now reside.

Charles F. Chick, son of George and Jane (Percy) Chick, who came from England in 1852, was born in Buffalo at the Cold Springs, December 21, 1856. May 3, 1881, he married Carrie Welker, and in 1884 settled on the farm of 247 acres where he now resides, near the southeast corner of the town. Mr. Chick is an extensive dealer in half-breed Percheron horses and roadsters, mostly brought from Iowa. He also deals in cows from Canada, and in fertilizers, besides conducting his large farm and dairy of 35 cows.

Owen Curtis, a pioneer settler, was born in Warren, Conn., in 1789. He came to Genesee County in 1808, and selected a farm in the wilderness of Batavia, now Darien, on which he lived over 70 years. In 1815 he married Abigail Wait, of Washington County, and reared eight children. Mrs. Curtis died in 1848, and a few years after he married Mrs. Abel, who survived him. Mr. Curtis died in 1879, in his 90th year. He was not a man of forms and ceremonies, but lived within himself and minded his own business, conceding the same rights to others that he claimed and stubbornly maintained for himself. He was a man for home and peace, and made no effort for show or popularity. He was proverbial for his integrity, and was kind and neighborly. By fair dealing and prudence he accumulated a good property.

Orange Carter, born December 23, 1774, in Connecticut, married Betsey Rumsey, of Vermont, and settled on a farm in St. Albans. In 1806 he came to Darian (then Batavia), being the first settler in the north part of the town, near the Baptist Church. Harriet, his daughter, was ths first child born in 1806. Mr. Carter had previously spent several yeart assisting the surveyors on the Purchase. He received the deed of his farm in 1805, and in February, 1806, came with his family, occupying, until June, when his own cabin was completed, the log school-house at Stafford. His nearest neighbor in Alexander was three and one-half miles and the grist-mill six miles distant. Being robust, hearty, and courageous, pioneer life suited him. The next year his brother David came, and after that the settlement was increased by the arrival of Williams, Ackley, Clark, McCollister, Doane, Lathrop, and other families. Mr. Carter was a volunteer in the War of 1812. In 1838 he sold his farm, and in 1840 went to Wisconsin with his sons Ackley, Orange, and

William, living with the latter until his death in 1855, aged 81 years. Mrs. Carter was born in 1777, and died in 1847. They were the parents of 10 children, all of whom married. Daniel Carter, a son living in Corfu, is the only one remaining in the county. He was born in St. Albans, Vt., October 4, 1802, and married, first, Maria Matteson, by whom he had two children, both deceased. He married, second, Mrs. Martha Williams. Mr. Carter was always interested in the welfare of his town. He held the office of supervisor, and others. A gentleman of the old school, he is a man of sterling integrity and respected by all his acquaintances. He has always been a farmer, a great reader, well up on all the current topics, and a Democrat since 1840. He has resided in Corfu for 25 years, and has been street commissioner all the time but three years. In the exercise of his office he has given great satisfaction, giving the citizens an excellent roadway by using gravel from an acre of ground to the depth of eight feet. At the advanced age of 87 years he cultivates his own garden. He has been trustee of the Presbyterian Church for many years, and is a liberal contributor to its needs.

Brazilla Carter, born in Connecticut, married there, and in 1812 came to the Holland Purchase and settled in the woods in the town of Darien, then included in Pembroke, on the place where his grandson, Riley Carter, now lives. He built his log cabin in the field, near a spring, about 80 rods north of the highway. He came from Connecticut with an ox-sled and cart, loading the cart when he found sleighing, and *vice versa* when the ground was bare. He was six weeks on the road. Five of his children were born in Connecticut and two in Darien. He died on the farm where he first settled, at about the age of 86 years. His son William, born in Connecticut in 1804, came with his parents to Darien. When 21 years of age he took charge of the farm, cleared it up, paid for his first 100 acres, and later added another 100 of cleared land. He was a stalwart man, six feet in height, and weighed over 200 pounds; honest and industrious. Mr. Carter was a clear-headed man, of good judgment, and accumulated a good fortune. He died in April, 1880, aged 76 years, highly respected by a multitude of friends. He married Harriet Hannan, who bore him six children. She died and he married Hannah Finch, of Wyoming County, who bore him one child. His son Riley, before mentioned, bought the original 100 acres at the death of his father, and is now an enterprising and successful farmer on the old homestead. He married Frances Crossman, and they have a son and a daughter. Mr. Carter is a decided Democrat and is doing his party good service. He is now assessor.

Abner C., Reuben, and Daniel Colby, sons of Daniel, came from Canaan, N. H., and settled in Darien in 1812. Their brother Aaron came in 1816. All took contracts for land at $3 per acre, with 10 years for payment. Their farms were contiguous and the settlement was known as the Colby neighborhood. With no roads, the nearest mill at Batavia, and with wild animals abundant, these pioneers were able to clear off their land, and convert the forests into cultivated fields. All died where they first settled, and the same farms are still occupied by Colbys.

Abner C. Colby, born May 2, 1776' settled where his son, Levi H. Colby, now lives. November 9, 1816, he married Nancy (Steward) Cutler. He died August 1, 1856, aged 80 years, and his wife in 1862. Their children were Levi H., Abner C., Hiram, and George. Levi H., the eldest, was born on the homestead January 6, 1819. He purchased the homestead from the heirs, and December 25, 1846, married Susan A. Root, by whom he had four children, three of whom died in childhood. The survivor, Dexter D, was born August 14, 1852, and is a farmer in Michigan. Mrs Colby died June 12, 1859, and Mr. Colby married, March 29, 1860, Elizabeth D. Lincoln, by whom he had children as follows: John L., born December 27, 1860, who is a farmer in Michigan; Libbie G., born October 27, 1867; and Levi Henry, born November 8, 1869. The last two live at home. Mr. Colby is a Republican in politics, devotes his time to his farm, and is a highly respected friend and neighbor.

Joshua Colby, son of Reuben, was born in New Hampshire in 1808, and married Elizabeth Town in 1827. In early life he carried on an ashery, collecting in one winter 3,000 bushels of ashes. He now lives on the Daniel Colby homestead.

Aaron H. Colby, son of Reuben, was born in New Hampshire in 1811, spent his boyhood in Darien, and went to the district school. He married Ellen Beardsley, and settled on the place where he now resides. He is a mason as well as a farmer, but leads a retired life, residing with his son Darius H.

Horace H. Chapin, son of Ralph and Betsey (Otis) Chapin, was born in Massachusetts in 1813, and when three years of age came with his parents to Batavia. He began clerking in 1832, with Stephen King, and later became his partner. He was also in business with 'Squire Riddle for 10 years from 1841. He sold his store to Theodore Young in 1864, and has since cultivated his farm of 65 acres. Mr. Chapin is a Republican, and belongs and gives liberally to the Methodist Episcopal Church. In 1836 he married Louisa C. Walker, and their daughter, Mrs. James Matteson, resides in Rochester. Mrs Chapin died in 1838, and in 1851 he married Sarah M. Church, by whom he has two children, Hattie E. (Mrs. Frank L Harris) and Ralph E., who married Florence Heal. Mr. Harris and Ralph E. Chapin are partners in business in Oakfield. In June, 1866, Mr. Chapin married his present wife, Selinda L. Munger.

Jonathan Durkee, son of Thomas and Abiah (Smith) Durkee, was educated in the common schools and at Dartmouth College. He married, first, Chloe Gleason, January 3, 1798, and settled in Hanover, N. H., caring for his parents until their decease. He came to Darien in 1810, bought 400 acres of land where his daughter, Mary Ann Wilson, Frank Chapin and his son Albert F., now live. He put in two acres of wheat, returned to New Hampshire, and the next spring brought his wife and six children to share his pioneer life. He erected the set of buildings now standing. Mr. Durkee died in 1856, aged 82 years, and his wife in 1841. They had 12 children. In 1843 he married Betsey Felton, who died about 1857. He was known as major ; was a prominent man in his town, and held the offices of supervisor, justice of the peace, and trial justice. His only daughter married Frank Chapin, August 30, 1838, and settled near her father. At his death Mr. Chapin bought the old homestead, residing there until his decease in 1887.

Albert F. Chapin, son of Frank and Mary Ann (Durkee) Chapin, was born in Darien, January 20, 1841, and was educated at the academy. At the age of 18 he was a clerk in Buffalo, became a partner, and was in trade 30 years. In 1884 he returned to the homestead, and is now a worthy citizen and an enterprising farmer. He married Sarah Bostwick, of Newark, N. Y., September 18, 1872.

John J. Ellis, son of Chester and Elizabeth (Smith) Ellis, was born in Bath, Steuben County, August 24, 1854, received his education in the common schools and at the academy, and taught school when 17 years of age. He then went into the railroad office at Bath, and has been in the employ of the Erie Railroad since. In 1874 he was placed in charge of Darien station. He also deals in farm produce and agricultural impiements. In politics he is a Republican, and has the confidence of his townsmen, who elected him supervisor in 1885–86. He is a man of excellent business ability. October 20, 1875, he married Matilda J. Spann, of Attica, a lady of culture and refinement.

James Kinsey was born in the town of Huntington, County Hereford, England, in 1783. He married Elizabeth Gwillen, and came to America with his family in 1832, landing in New York. He set out for Ohio, but on hearing that his destination was an unhealthy region he remained in the vicinity of Utica about two years, and in 1834 settled on a farm in Darien, where he lived till his death. His son, James Kinsey, Jr., was born in England, came to Darien with his father in 1834, and married Grizilda Freeman in 1847. He first settled on the homestead, but now owns an extensive farm one mile west of Darien Center. Mr. Kinsey and his brother Stephen have been the largest dealers in cattle, horses, sheep, and swine of any in their town, and among the largest in the county. Mr. Kinsey is a staunch Democrat, and has been very popular with his townsmen. He was elected supervisor of his town in 1887, and reëlected in 1888, and has also served as magistrate. He is a man of influence, energy, and enterprise, and is widely known. He and his brother Stephen erected the first steam cheese factory in Genesee County, and aided with their influence and money the building of a steam saw-mill at the depot. An overwhelming sorrow befell Mr. and Mrs. Kinsey at the burning of their home, February 11, 1861, when their sons Frank, aged nine years, and Stephen, aged seven, perished in the flames. Their surviving children are James H., born May 3, 1849, who is an extensive grain merchant at St. Croix, Wis.; Russell L., born June 8, 1858, a lawyer in Buffalo;

and William E., born May 24, 1863, a dealer in farm produce in Darien.

Stephen Kinsey, son of James K., Sr., was born in England, July 7, 1827, came to Darien with his parents in 1834, and was educated in the common school of Darien Center. In February, 1869, he married Sophia Champany, by whom he has one child, a daughter, born October 28, 1882. Mr. Kinsey and his brother succeeded their father on the homestead, which Mr. Kinsey now owns. He, like his brother James, is a decided Democrat, and has served his town as highway commissioner and tax collector. Mrs. Kinsey was an expert cheesemaker in the aforementioned factory and took the first premium for cheese at the State fair held in Buffalo in 1866.

Alanson T. Fisher, son of Lillie, was born in Boonville, N. Y., September 20, 1800. His father came from Boonville to the Holland Purchase, in Alexander, in 1804, and settled on what is still known as the " Lillie Fisher farm." There he spent the remainder of his long life and died at the age of 98. He was a man of influence and highly respected, was a leader in the Masonic order, held the honorable position of Master of the lodge, and was buried with Masonic honors. Alanson T. Fisher, February 27, 1844, married Sophia Monroe, of Batavia, who was born November 4, 1815. He settled at Darien Center, where he remained until his death, March 6, 1886. Mr. Fisher was a man of great financial ability, and his great diversity of business (stage driver and proprietor, hotel-keeper, merchant, dealer in live stock, and town officer) was managed with consummate skill and success. He was clear-headed, far-sighted, and amassed the largest fortune of any one in Darien. As a man he was honorable, a fair dealer, a reliable citizen, and a kind neighbor. Charles M., only son of Mr. and Mrs. Fisher, was born November 28, 1845, married Alice M. Granniss, August 1, 1866, and their children are Monroe L., who married Clara Harrington, and Carlton G.

Owen Frink, son of Israel, was born in Peru, Mass., March 31, 1807. In August, 1814, he came with his father to Alexander and located where his grandson, Wilbur Frink, now lives, and where he resided till his death, November 22, 1866. He was also a carpenter and a skillful joiner, and helped in constructing some of the fine buildings in Rochester and Batavia. Owen, his only son, was educated in the common schools, and was always a farmer. He married Sally, daughter of Nicholas Van De Bogart, in 1828, and resided on the homestead till his death, September 17, 1872, at the age of 65. His wife died May 12, 1867, aged 58 years. Mr. Frink was an honest and fair dealing man. As a neighbor he was proverbially accommodating, and the poor and needy had his aid and sympathy. Mr. and Mrs. Frink were parents of five sons, all of whom lived to mature age. Wilson, their oldest son living, was born January 31, 1831, and remained on the homestead with his parents until he was of age. He married Eliza Edson, of Darien, and settled as a farmer in Marilla, Erie County, where they resided for 24 years. They still own the place. For the last six years they have been farming in Darien. They have had two sons, John, born December 3, 1862, who died May 28, 1885; and Earl, born February 28, 1869, who is studying telegraphy, and resides with his parents.

John Griswold, son of Lott K., was born in Bennington, N. Y., and was early taught industrious habits on his father's farm, and had only a common school education. November 17, 1846, he married Rachel Osborne, and settled on a farm in the south part of Darien. In 1870 he removed to the place where he now resides, near the village of Darien. He has always been a farmer. He cast his first vote with the Whig party, and in 1856 voted for John C. Fremont for President. Since then he has served the Republican party. Like his brother he commenced poor and has earned what he has, both in property and reputation. He has filled acceptably the office of overseer of the poor 11 years, and now, at about the age of 70, has an excellent character for integrity and fair dealing. He has three sons and one daughter.

The Griswold family in America descended from Sir Humphrey Griswold, of Malvern Hall, England. The first in this country of whom we have any record were Edward and Matthew, brothers, who came from England about 1645, and settled in Connecticut, Edward at Windsor and Matthew at Lyme. Edward afterward moved to Killingworth. Matthew was the first magistrate of Saybrook colony, and married Anna, daughter of Henry Wolcott. The seat or manor of the Griswolds at Lyme was a large feudal grant of some eight miles square, bounded on the west by the Connecticut River, and on the south by Long Island Sound. The buildings were situated upon the height of land overlooking the Sound. The name of the place was "Black Hall." This grant was given to Matthew in 1645.—[From genealogical sketch furnished by Benajah Griswold, of Darien.]

Lott K. Griswold, son of Benajah and Hannah (Kilham) Griswold, was born in Enfield, Hartford County, Conn., July 23, 1792, and, as near as can be ascertained, was a descendant of Matthew The family removed to Sangerfield, Oneida County, where the father, Benajah, died. About 1811 or 1812 they settled in Byron. In 1815 Lott K. Griswold married Phebe Tucker, and settled on a wood land farm; but, to avoid fever and ague, he removed to Bennington and commenced anew by cutting the first tree on his "pitch." He moved to his location with a pair of three-year-old steers attached to a cart that carried his goods, and a single cow two years old. This property and a single shilling was his entire fortune. His habitation was a low log cabin covered with boughs; one window without glass, but covered with oiled paper; and not a sawed board in the whole structure. The floor was made of split basswood and hewn with an axe; the door was of the same material, and held together with pegs, swung on wooden hinges. In this primitive abode this pioneer family resided nine years. The nearest mill was at Batavia, 17 miles distant. Mr. Griswold remained on this farm to see it transformed into a good home, which, in 1852, he sold to his oldest son,

Benajah, and removed to Darien and engaged again in farming. He died January 9, 1870, in his 78th year, on the farm of 22 acres where his son John now lives. Mrs. Griswold died June 28, 1874. Their children were born as follows : Benajah, February 14, 1816; Mary, January 19, 1818; John, January 17, 1820; Harriet, October 2, 1821 ; Sophia, March 17, 1827; Nancy, January 30, 1831 ; William, August 30, 1833; and Julia, December 26, 1836.

Benajah Griswold, son of Lott K. and Phebe (Tucker) Griswold, spent his boyhood on his father's farm and in attendance at the common school. When he attained his majority he engaged in teaching district school for seven winter seasons, working for the farmers the remainder of each year, until he married Polly Seaver, January 1, 1840, and engaged in farming. In 1852 he purchased his father's farm of 75 acres, which he added to from time to time until it contained 242 acres. In 1860 he sold it and removed to his present house near the depot, which, in honor of him, and for his generosity in giving the railroad company the grounds, bears his name. Mr. Griswold began his political life a Democrat, and so remained until after the formation of the Republican party in 1856, when he cast his lot with it, and has done it good service ever since. He has held the offices of superintendent of the poor for Genesee County nine consecutive years, has been supervisor of his town five years, and early in life was many years town superintendent of schools. He commenced his active life with no capital, except his correct habits of strict honesty, sterling integrity, and continued persevering industry. He has acquired a competency, and has the respect and confidence of a large circle of acquaintances. Mr. and Mrs. Griswold had three children. Eugene, born February 22, 1841, married Laura Cowan, who died in January, 1888. He was a soldier from 1862 till the close of the war in 1865, and is a farmer and resides with his father. His son Charles C., born February 9, 1867, is conducting his grandfather's farm. De Witt Clinton, born October 30, 1847, married Lizzie, daughter of Dr. Evans, with whom he studied medicine, and is now a druggist at Shullsburg, Wis. Flora (Mrs. George W. Peck) resides in Prattsburg, Steuben County, N. Y. Mr. Peck is a dealer in hardware.

Henry W. Harmon, son of Asaph and Mary A. (Curtis) Harmon, and grandson of Owen Curtis, an early pioneer, was born in Darien, January 21, 1859, was reared on the farm, educated in the common schools, and began an academic course at Batavia, but ill health prevented its completion. He then went to the Pennsylvania oil regions, but soon returned, and went to Dakota in 1882 and engaged in the real estate business. In 1883 he was appointed postmaster at Harold, Dakota, which office he held two years, and was county commissioner of Campbell County one year. In 1885–86 he went South, visited the Arkansas Hot Springs and the New Orleans Exposition, and returned to Darien in June, 1887. In April, 1889, he was appointed station agent and telegraph operator at the D., L. & W. Railroad office in Darien. He married, July 21, 1889, Ellen L. Burr, of Darien.

Davis Huntley, of Lyme, Conn., settled in Darien about 1817. He was a millwright and carpenter, and built many structures in the town. He died in 1843. His sons were E. M. and Allen J., the latter a carpenter.

Dexter Humphrey, an early settler, lived near the gulf, was a conscientious and noble Christian gentleman, and had two sons, Linus and Wallace. William Humphrey, his brother, came at the same time, and reared a large family. Amos Humphrey, a settler in 1807 on a tract of 350 acres where Hiram Tullar now lives, erected the first saw-mill on Eleven Mile Creek, in 1809. He was justice of the peace for some time.

Aaron P. Hutchinson, son of Aaron, came in 1815 from Vermont with his parents. He found it serious business tiding over the next year, 1816, so memorable as the "cold season." He recollects going to school in a log shanty, roofed with bark, and taking the teacher's dinner, consisting of hulled corn and milk.

Samuel C. Higgins was born in Elizabeth, N. J., September 9, 1809, and received an academic education. In 1830 he came to Rochester and followed the occupations of cordwainer and weighmaster. October 16, 1831, he married Mary Godby, of Massachusetts. In 1844 the family came to the northwest part of Darien, to the farm where they now reside. Mr. Higgins, though an octogenarian, has devoted himself to his farm, and even now assists his son Robert S. on the place. Mrs. Higgins died November 13, 1885. They were the parents of five children, of whom three sons and one daughter are now living, viz.: J. Morris, who married Jenette Schuyler, of Attica, is a well-to-do farmer in Macon, Ill., and has three children; Mary J. (Mrs. Harvey Richards), also of Macon, Ill.; Luke C., who married Louie Weed, and is a graduate of the Buffalo Medical College, now practicing in Naples, Ill.; and Robert S., who married Jessie L. Nott, in January, 1878, has two sons, and is a farmer on the homestead with his aged father.

Alva Jefferson, a pioneer in 1812, was a very prominent man 60 years ago. He was a farmer and a mechanic, and was of the firm of Horton & Jefferson in Darien City. When he gave up business he settled on a farm on the Buffalo road. He built a store in 1832, was a member of the Assembly, and a firm friend of Gov. Seward. He had two sons and two daughters.

Among the early settlers of Darien was Ichabod Jefferson, who arrived in 1812, settling in the south part of the town. For a few years before his death, in 1848, he made his home with his daughter Betsey, the wife of Elijah Robinson. Mr. Robinson was a blacksmith, and came from Vermont to Darien in 1822. He died in 1889, and his wife in 1884. They resided in the village. Alva, a son, is a blacksmith occupying the shop of his father.

Stephen King was the earliest merchant at Darien Center, and was a well-to-do, substantial, energetic, and successful business man. He also owned a farm, built a brick house upon it, and kept a good hotel, and was at one time a partner of Thomas Riddle and Alanson Fisher. He married a daughter of Lillie Fisher, of Alexander.

Elijah Lamb came about 1815 from Canada, and settled where his son John E now resides. He brought with him a team of horses, but had to sell one in order to make payment on his purchase of land. He made his own household furniture, worked hard at cleaning off the land, planted orchards, and was soon able to put up good buildings. He built a tannery, and tanned on shares the few hides he obtained from the farmers. From the flax raised on the place, and the wool from the sheep, Mrs. Lamb clothed the family. He was one of the prosperous citizens of the town when he died in 1869.

David Harroun, son of David and Elizabeth (Anderson) Harroun, was born in Brattleboro, Vt., in 1771. He married Margery Wilder, and settled in Hebron, Washington County. About 1819 he came with his family and settled on the north line of the town of Darien, then included in the town of Pembroke. This family encountered the hardships incident to a life in the woods, and in a few years they had replaced the log cabin with a comfortable house and had transformed their wood land into cultivated fields. Mrs. Harroun was a woman of great energy and industry. She spun and wove cloth, not only to clothe her own family, but also for her neighbors. They resided where they first settled till they died. Mr. Harroun died in 1857, aged 86 years, and Mrs. Harroun aged 93 years. They were parents of 11 children, all of whom lived to adult age. Their son James A. was born in Hebron, N. Y., January 3, 1813, received a limited education, and married Harriet Crawford, of Darien. He succeeded his father on the homestead, where he had been the manager after he was 18 years of age, in consequence of his father's disability from rheumatism, and administered to the wants of his parents till their deaths. Mr. Harroun has always been a farmer, Mrs. Harroun died in 1876. They had three children, only one of whom, George W., lived to maturity, and died February 6, 1889, aged 49 years. Mr. Harroun has been a member of the Presbyterian Church since 1830, and is a staunch Republican.

Elisha H. Lathrop, son of Samuel and Lucy Lathrop, of New London County, Conn., was born September 15, 1800. His education was received in district schools, and by strict attention to his studies he was subsequently qualified to teach, which he did. At the age of 16 he and a brother, three years younger, managed their father's farm of 60 acres. He had a strong constitution, and at an early age could swing a scythe with the best of men. In 1819 he moved with his father's family to Genesee County, and settled on the eastern line of the town of Darien, then Pembroke. Here he remained till 22 years of age, when he began business for himself. In April, 1830, he purchased the farm of 100 acres upon which he now resides, paying $1,200 for the same. The same year and month he married Marcia Moulton, of Alexander, by whom he had three children, two of whom are dead, and perhaps all, as one has not been heard from since 1872, when he was in the mining regions of the far West. Mrs. Lathrop died February 1, 1858,

and June 22, 1860, Mr. Lathrop married Euseba, daughter of Abram
and Fanny Sharick, of Darien, who bore him five children, three of
whom are living. Mr. Lathrop began life poor, but by industry and
good management succeeded in obtaining a competency, and owned one
of the finest farms in the town. He cast his first vote for Andrew Jackson, and always voted with the Democratic party. He held various
offices within the gift of his townsmen. Mr. Lathrop died January 15,
1879, retaining his mental faculties in a remarkable degree to the last.
He was highly prized by his neighbors and considered a man of good
judgment. Mrs. Euseba Lathrop was born February 6, 1828, in Columbia County, Pa., came with her father's family to Genesee County in
1844, and settled on the farm adjoining Mr. Lathrop's. James C. Lathrop, son of Elisha H., was born August 19, 1861, was educated in the
common schools with a few terms in the academy at Batavia, and married Minnie Usher, of Pulaski, N. Y., February 24, 1887. Andrew J.,
his brother, born February 19, 1865, received a similar education, and
they now jointly conduct the homestead farm. Fanny A. married,
October 2, 1888, E. C. Dearstyn, who is a telegraph operator at Newark,
N. Y.

Anson Lathrop, son of Samuel and Lucy (Pendleton) Lathrop, was
born November 23, 1803, in Bozrah, Conn., and removed to Darien with
his parents in 1819. His father was a mechanic and farmer. Mr. Lathrop remained with his parents until he was 21. He settled on the
farm where he now resides a year or two before his marriage, and has
always been a farmer. In June, 1834, he married Elizabeth Bartram,
whose father was a sea captain. She died February 24, 1880. Their
children were Samuel, born March 28, 1835, who enlisted in the war,
was taken prisoner at Knoxville, and died of starvation in a rebel prison
in North Carolina; Henry, born February 15, 1837, who also enlisted in
the army in Pennsylvania, and participated in the battles of Gettysburg
and the Wilderness, in the latter of which he received a wound in his
left lung, and died at Fredericksburg 13 days after; Burr B., born June
3, 1843, who was drafted at the age of 18, entered a company from the
town of Mexico, Oswego County, and died in the service, but how or
just when we cannot now ascertain; Edmund P. G., born March 28,
1847, a farmer, who died on the homestead at the age of 17 ; Janette M.,
born August 24, 1840, who married Richard Bowen, a farmer, and
resides near her father; Caroline C., born November 15, 1841, who married A. McCall Stickney and resides at Fargo station; Charles, born November 1, 1849, who died October 2, 1866; and George W., born January
28, 1851, who died September 20, 1852.

Ebenezer Losee was born in Saratoga County, N. Y., June 8, 1797.
About 1820 he came to Darien, and began to improve the farm of 50
acres where Daniel McVean now lives. January 3, 1826, he married
Diana Dean, of Pompey, N. Y., where Mr. Losee was raised. She died
in March, 1865. He soon added to his farm until he had 200 acres.

About 1833 he bought the farm where his son, Richard M. Losee, lives, and where he died March 20, 1880. By his perseverance and hard work he had at one time in his possession 400 acres. He was supervisor of the town at one time. He had four children: Almon D., who died at the age of seven years; Hannah J, who died at the age of 18; Frank E., born July 11, 1837, who married Sarah Dirstine, May 25, 1865, who was born July 3, 1843, and their children are Fred R., and Marie Louise; and Richard M. Frank E. is a farmer living one mile east of Darien village.

Richard M. Losee was born June 29, 1834, and received an academic education, but chose to be a farmer, which vocation he has always followed. January 1, 1857, he married Helen L. Lincoln, of Pembroke. He gives his attention to the breeding of and dealing in full blooded registered American Merino sheep, through New Mexico and Colorado. He is a decided Democrat, but such is his popularity he has been elected twice to the office of supervisor in a Republican town. He is a man of good financial ability and well off. His children are Frank D., a farmer, born October 25, 1857, who married Mary Grant, and lives adjoining his father; Nellie H., born December 11, 1859, who married Andrew Meinweiser, a farmer, who conducts the Losee homestead; Clara A., born June 26, 1863, who married Eugene W. Harrington, station agent at Alden; and Royal R., born October 27, 1870, who is now in the telegraph office of the superintendent of the D., L. & W. Railroad at Buffalo.

Philip W. Morgan, of Canada, born September 23, 1841, came to Buffalo when young, and resided there 12 years. His father came to Darien and located on the farm where Mr. Morgan now lives. In 1861 he enlisted in Co. I, 100th N. Y. Vols., serving three years and a half, and received an honorable discharge. He was in the battle of Fair Oaks, was captured and sent to Libby prison, thence to Salisbury and Belle Isle, being confined in all four months, when he was exchanged. He was at Fort Wagner during the siege, and from there was sent home on recruiting service for four months, in 1863. He joined his regiment the next spring, was in the engagement at Drury's Bluff, was captured and taken to Libby, thence to Dansville, Andersonville, and Florence prisons, when he was paroled. His seven months' sufferings while a prisoner were mittigated in part, and his life spared, by his shrewdness as a trader, and his aptness in gaining the confidence of his guards. An imitation chain, made of bogus gold dollars, when polished up furnished him additional food supplies, the last dollar bringing him in a porker of 90 pounds. His imprisonment caused him to be in service six months beyond his term, and he returned home with poor health. December 26, 1865, he married Sarah Dyer, of Darien. The next three years were spent in the Pennsylvania oil regions. His wife died November 4, 1869, being the mother of his sons Walter E., a mechanic in Buffalo, and Endell N., who lives at home. Mr. Morgan spent three years in Kansas, and then returned to Darien. January 14, 1873, he married Ella Burns, of Pembroke, and she is the mother of his son George M., and daughters Winnie and Jennie, who live at home. Mr. Morgan has been highway commission and collector of taxes.

Col. Abraham Matteson, son of Abraham and Lydia (Hopkins) Matteson, was born in Bennington Vt., in 1781. He married Betsey Woodard, of the same town, and came to Onondaga County, thence to Darien with an ox-team with a horse ahead, in 1808, and settled in the woods north of Darien, where he built a log cabin. Having little means he took the land on contract. He was a private in the War of 1812, and was mustered out as colonel. He was prominent in civil affairs, was a member of Assembly, a magistrate for 16 years, and held other offices. He died in 1831. Mrs. Matteson died in 1870. They had nine children. The father, Abraham, Sr., came to Darien soon after his son, and resided near him. He died in 1819. His wife died in 1829. Norman, fourth son of Abraham, was born in Darien, May 21, 1810, and has always lived in the county. He had a common school education, married Sarah Ann Smith, and has always been a farmer. In addition he has been for about 15 years an extensive dealer in cattle and hogs, shipping from his vicinity and Chicago to Albany, New York, and Boston. He has been supervisor two terms. Their only son was accidentally killed by a pistol-shot at the age of 26 years.

David Nay was for many years a resident of Darien. He was a poor boy, and worked hard as a farmer. He taught school winters, and married into the North family, of Alexander. He was the first superintendent of common schools. His son Bruce was with Gen. Butler at New Orleans, and received the thanks of President Lincoln for his bravery in some hazardous undertakings.

Joseph Peters, one of the first settlers, in 1808, purchased land on the Buffalo road, west of the village, and was a hard working man. He was twice elected to the Assembly, and was influential in the interests of the Agricultural Society. His son, T. C. Peters, was educated for the law, but followed farming, and has been a prominent and influential man in the western part of the State.

The Riddle family of Genesee County are of Irish and Scotch descent. Thomas Riddle, of Ireland, came to New England when a child, married Rebecca Moulton, of Massachusetts, and died in 1807. John Riddle, his oldest son, born in Massachusetts in 1761, married Olive Blodgett, and came to Alexander in 1807. He was a justice of the peace and supervisor many years. He died in 1849, aged 88 years. Thomas Riddle, third son of John, was born in Vermont in 1804, married Elois A. Johnson in 1834, and settled in Darien. In early life he followed mercantile pursuits; was postmaster, town clerk, and justice of the peace for 28 years He was a man highly respected in his community, and died at his home in Darien, September 3, 1889.

Henry Saulsbury's father emigrated from Holland and settled in Scho-

27

dack, Rensselaer County, N. Y., where Henry was born in 1790, as near as can be ascertained. He married in Connecticut, and removed to Darien (then included in Batavia) in 1810, where he remained to the close of his life. Mrs. Saulsbury survived him. Mr. Saulsbury, besides carrying on his farm of 114 acres, was engaged in buying cattle and sheep for the Buffalo market. He was a Whig until the organization of the Republican party, which he at once joined. He held the offices of highway commissioner, overseer of the poor, and town clerk. In religion he was a Methodist, and many years was a consistent member of that church. Mr. and Mrs. Saulsbury reared eight children, all of whom resided in their native town, and four are living, viz.: Samantha (Mrs. Tuttle), David, Sylvia, and Sarah (Mrs. Samuel Lathrop), of Batavia. David Saulsbury was born in Darien, December 12, 1815, and spent his youth on his father's farm and in attendance at the district school. After his ninth year he only had the winter season for schooling. February 11, 1846, he married Mariah H. Adams, of Darien, and settled on lot 9, in the southeast part of the town, which he sold in the spring of 1889. In 1869 he removed to his present location in the village of Darien. He has always been a farmer, although he has sometimes been engaged in selling specialties, and was one season, like his father, a drover. Mr. Saulsbury left the Democrats in Buchanan's administration and joined the Republican party. Mrs. Saulsbury died in April, 1856, and in October following Mr. Saulsbury married Phebe A. Hickox, who died in October, 1863. His first wife was the mother of two sons: Nelson L., born January 11, 1847, who married Alice Shaw, and is a grower of small fruit in Batavia; and Charles F., born August 4, 1850, who married Sarah Grant, and resides with his father. He has three daughters.

Arunah Sawens, born in Massachusetts in 1784, married Sarah Mahen in Washington County, N. Y., and a few years later removed to the Holland Purchase and worked at shoemaking in Le Roy. He located in Darien, where his son Hiram now lives, and cleared quite a portion of the farm before removing his family to it in 1818. He died January 20, 1835. He was an enterprising man, and accumulated property rapidly. Mrs. Sawens died July 20, 1843. The postoffice there is named "Sawens" in honor of this family. They had 10 children, five of whom are now living. Hiram Sawens was born in the house where he now lives, June 28, 1825. He was educated in the common school of his district; and December 31, 1847, married Euphemia Sutherland. They have an only daughter, Florence H. Sawens, who resides with her parents. Mr. Sawens has always been a farmer. He is a man of sterling integrity, industrious, honest, upright. In politics he is a Republican, and has the confidence of the voters of his town and county who have elected him to the offices of county superintendent of the poor six years, town assessor six years, and collector one year. He is now over 60 years of age, and has so carefully conducted all his business relations that he has never been sued nor sued any man. His son William, born on the homestead April 17, 1827, received a common school education, and December 15, 1847, married Atassa Foster. He inherited and purchased the west 110 acres of the original farm, and built a new set of buildings. Here he has always resided as a farmer. They have four children living: Flora A. (Mrs. Asher Graves), of Kansas; Mary I., wife of Charles Johns, of Nebraska; Hattie E. (Mrs. Henry J. Cleveland), of Illinois; and Dora, the youngest, who lives at home.

Eben P. Strong was born in Warren, Conn., January 28, 1794. He served in the War of 1812 and went from his native town with a detachment of soldiers to Sackets Harbor. After his discharge in 1813 he came to Darien, then a part of Pembroke, and located a farm of 160 acres, and obtained for it a contract, or "article," from the Holland Purchase land office. January 16, 1822, he married Margaret Johns, who was born in Lancashire, Eng., January 11, 1799. He immediately removed his bride to his humble home. He was highly respected as a man of sterling integrity, honest, and industrious. He died on the place where he first settled, March 23, 1843 Mrs. Strong survived him until October 7, 1888.

John Simonds, born in Williamstown, Mass., in 1779, was well educated, and taught school several seasons. He then read law one year, but abandoned that profession for surveying, which was more to his taste, as he had a natural gift and desire for the study of mathematics. He began surveying in Jefferson County, N. Y., and was at one time six weeks in the woods without seeing a house. In 1807 he married Sabra Cole, and in 1814 moved to the Genesee country with his wife and three children. He purchased a small farm in Leicester, Livingston County, which he cultivated until 1824, when he moved to Genesee County and located on a farm in North Alexander. This was the commencement of his prosperity, which was largely due to the industry and economy of his family. He was quite negligent in looking after the odds and ends of his business affairs, being too credulous for his own interest. He was a man of sterling integrity, a firm believer in the teachings of the scriptures, but not a member of any sect. His children obtained as good an education as his means would allow. He resided in Alexander until his death, September 4, 1862. His wife survived him 10 years, and died at the home of her oldest daughter, Mrs. Warner, in Dane County, Wis., with whom she resided. She was the mother of 11 children.

Benjamin C. Simonds, son of John and Sabra (Cole) Simonds, was born in Geneseo, Livingston County, N. Y., April 7, 1817. He came to Alexander in 1824 with his parents, spent his boyhood on his father's farm, and attended the common schools and academy in Alexander. At the age of 18 he began teaching district school and followed it six winters. In 1839 and '40 he traveled three times over the State of Ohio, and made in all a journey of more than 10,000 miles with a pair of horses and carriage. He returned home and in 1843 married Almira H. Wait, of North Darien, and soon after purchased 100 acres of his father's farm. In 1854 Mrs. Simonds's father, Russel Wait, was killed by the cars, and Mr. Simonds purchased his farm in North Darien, where he removed and now resides. Mr. Simonds has been a great reader. Early in life he was a thorough temperance worker. In the anti-slavery movement he was a pioneer worker, when it cost a man his popularity and sometimes the respect of his best friends. He remained with the . Liberty party until the organization of the Republican party, when he became a Republican, and so remained till the Prohibition party was organized, when he at once gave it his hearty support. In 1841 he united with the Baptist Church, with which he remained until 1849. After several years' careful investigation of the scriptures he and Mrs. Simonds became convinced that immortality is conditional and obtained only through Christ at the resurrection. Mr. Simonds has been instrumental in organizing a church which is in accord with his views. With his influence and his means he has for 40 years labored to sustain it. He is a natural leader of men, of great intelligente, decidedly radical, and has many sharp points and keen edges, but is not aggressive. He is always able to give a good reason for the faith within him, and is also a noted peacemaker.

John Sutherland came from Onondaga County to the Holland Purchase in 1812, and settled in Darien on the farm where J. Beck now lives, and where he lived until his death, and was buried there. He was a practical surveyor as well as a farmer, and took a prominent part in the affairs of his town. He reared four sons: John, James, Amaziah, and David. John resided with his father, unmarried. James married and settled in the village of Darien, was for a long time a magistrate, conducted a harness shop, and reared seven children. About 1843 he removed with his family to Green County, Wis. Amaziah was always a farmer, not a politician, but he possessed the confidence of his townsmen, and served as overseer of the poor 10 or 12 years. He married Lucy Horr about 1823, and settled on the homestead, where he resided until 1833, when he removed to a farm across the road, and later sold the homestead. He died March 7, 1882, and Mrs. Sutherland September 27, 1877, both at the home of their son James H. They had three sons and three daughters, viz.: William, James H., Mary, Adaline, George, and Helen. David went to Florida, and while returning died at Lancaster, Pa. William, son of Amaziah, married Cytheria Dimock, settled in Darien, and died in June, 1863.

James H. Sutherland was born on the homestead December 16, 1827, was educated in the common schools, and at the age of 19 began teaching, which he continued four winter seasons. He was engaged in general mercantile business at Darien village from 1852 to 1867, when he became station agent at Griswold depot, and was also engaged in the coal, grain, and lumber trade. In the spring of 1887 he resigned his position as station agent, and is now continuing his other business with the aid of his son-in-law, Giles Ranger. They are also building a factory for cutting bar—

rel headings. In politics Mr. Sutherland has been a life-long Democrat, and though his town is Republican by a small majority he has held the offices of supervisor four years and justice of the peace 12 years, which latter position he now fills. He has been postmaster eight years and notary public four years. In all these positions he has given his attention to the interests of all concerned. July 4, 1853, he married Emma Carter, by whom he has had two children, viz.: Charles L., who died March 15, 1879, in his 24th year, and May L. (Mrs. G. Ranger).

John and Ephraim Sumner came from Vermont with a team of horses in 1810, settling where Winslow now lives. They had to cut their way through the woods from Batavia on the old Buffalo road. In a few years Ephraim sold his farm to his brother and moved to Olean   John Winslow cleared his farm, planted orchards, erected the building where his son now lives, aided in school enterprises, and was prominent in town affairs. He married Clarissa Winslow, of Halifax, Vt., and died in 1836, aged 50 years. His wife died 15 years later.

Jerome Sumner, son of John, was born January 9, 1811, had a meagre schooling, and with his brother Winslow settled on the homestead. April 20, 1843, he married Clarissa, daughter of James and Esther Bentley, of Steuben County. In 1846 he exchanged his interest in the homestead with his brother Tyler, and settled where his nephew, John W. Sumner, now lives. He built a saw-mill, and was a lumberman and farmer until 1864, when he moved to Corfu, where he died June 7, 1887, and where Mrs. Sumner still resides. He was highly respected and held several town offices. Winslow Sumner was born October 30, 1812, received a common school education, and worked in his father's mill and on the farm. He married Phila Freeman, of Darien, in 1839, and settled on the farm where he was born and always resided. He is a progressive farmer, honest and upright, and at the age of 77 is mentally and physically well preserved, and with the aid of his son, Dallas A. Sumner, still conducts his fine farm of 150 acres. Their children are John W., a farmer adjoining his father, who married Clara Kimball, and his three sons ; Lewis, a farmer, who married Anne Barney, and has three daughters ; Wilder E., who resides in Corfu and deals in produce, and who married Augusta Kinsey and has one daughter, Phila (Mrs. A. K. Carrier), whose husband is a large farmer near Corfu ; and Alice D., who resides with her father.

John Sumner, son of John the pioneer, was born November 3, 1814, on the homestead, had a limited education, and September 15, 1836, married Emeline Hughes and settled in the neighborhood, where he remained until 1841, when he sold out and bought where he now lives. Mrs. Sumner died December 31, 1876. Their children were Cecilia (Mrs. J. W. Dunbar), of Attica ; Clara P. (Mrs. H. R. Dunbar), of Alexander ; and Emeline O. (Mrs. C. S. Pettibone), Mr. Pettibone is joint owner with Mr. Sumner in the farm whereon they live. Mr. and Mrs. Pettibone have one son. Mr. Sumner has been elected supervisor two terms, assessor 19 years, and has been constable and collector. His son Horace, born on the homestead, married Almira Marsh, of Alexander, settled in Darien, and now lives in Batavia.

Tyler Sumner, another son of John the pioneer, was born on the homestead March 19, 1821, and received a common school education. October 20, 1850, he married Mary Reed, who died December 24, 1877. He married, second, in 1879, Mrs. Jane Anthony, who died June 28, 1886. He settled on a portion of the homestead, where his son Charles now lives. He died May 22, 1888. His surviving children by his first wife are Elsie, wife of L. B. Cadugan, the proprietor of a flouring-mill in Osceola, Pa.; Charles, who was born on the place where he now resides, and married Emma Shaw, January 23, 1878, and has a son and a daughter; and Jerome, a farmer, who married Hattie Anthony, has two daughters, and settled opposite his brother Charles.

Ephraim Sumner, youngest son of John the pioneer, was born on the homestead March 23, 1825, received a common school education, and at the age of 21 received a portion of the homestead. June 2, 1852, he married Flora A. Kendall, who died in July, 1853. In November, 1855, he married Mary M. Lamb, who died two weeks later. November 11, 1857, he married, third, Julia A. Way, of Michigan, and their children are Emmett E., born September 9, 1858, who owns a farm in the northwest part of Darien, but resides in Corfu, where he has a meat market, and who married Maggie Bennett; and Ernest T., born March 19, 1870, a student, who resides with his parents. Ephraim Sumner has been a successful farmer, raises good stock, has all the improved implements, and is an influential, kind, and obliging friend and neighbor. His sister Delphia W. was born on the homestead October 20, 1878, and married Calvin Topliff (deceased). She resides with her brother.

Jotham Sumner (son of Daniel, of Massachusetts) came to Darien in 1810, and died in 1847. He settled where Earl Sumner now lives. He was a carpenter and built many barns in the neighborhood. He had six children, among whom was Seth, who died in 1882. He was a prominent contractor and builder.

John Seaver was born in Hebron, N. Y., in 1810, and came to Darien in 1816. He was an apprentice in the harness business from 1825 to 1830, when he moved to Byron.

Henry Schrader was born in Germany, June 24, 1820, married Charlotte Miller, and emigrated to America in 1857, first settling in Erie County, but removed to Darien in 1859. In 1875 he settled on the farm in the southwest part of the town where his son, Fred A. Schrader, now lives. He died June 7, 1888. Mrs. Schrader still survives and lives with her son. They were parents of three sons. Fred A., born in Alden, N. Y., November 11, 1857, received a good common school education, and became a farmer. He married Tracy Shaffer, May 8, 1889. Mr. Schrader is a Democrat He was elected collector in 1882 and assessor in 1886, filling both offices acceptably to the people.

Jonas Stickney came to Alden, N. Y., in 1812, clearing a place where that village is located. He removed to the Sumner settlement, Darien, soon after, engaged in farming, raised a large family, and died aged about 65 years. His son, A. McCall Stickney, was born in Darien, June 13, 1824, and married Sarah Marvin, who was the mother of three of his children. She died about 1864. In 1866 he married Caroline Lathrop, his present wife, by whom he has three children. Mr. Stickney has been a trader, and is now engaged in farming and carrying the mail from Fargo postoffice to Corfu.

Warren Stiles, son of Warren, was born in Hawley, Mass., in 1804, and received a common school education. He began his business life early selling watches and jewelry through New England. He married Betsey E. Holcomb, of Granby, Conn., and soon after came to Darien, settling on a farm now owned by N. Hartshorn, where he resided until 1860, when he moved to the place now occupied by his son, John F. Stiles. He died August 14, 1875. He was a decided Republican, and did his share to promote the welfare of society. His wife died December 31, 1879. Three of their five children are living, viz.: Mary E., who resides with her niece, Mrs. Orlando Reed, in Pembroke; Cornelia (Mrs. Charles Jones), of Pembroke ; and John F., who resides on the homestead. John F. Stiles received a good education, and enlisted in the army at the age of 18 years, but being in poor health was soon honorably discharged for disability, and was brought home an invalid. He is a staunch Republican, is liberal in his religious views, and contributes liberally to his society. November 29, 1877, he married Mary E. Boyce, of Pembroke, and they have four children. Henry Stiles, son of Warren, was born in Darien, and responded to the first call of 75,000 troops, but finally enlisted August 14, 1862, in Co. K, 127th Ill Vols., and served until January 27, 1863, when he died of disease contracted in the army. In 1859 he went on foot and drove a team to the gold regions of Pike's Peak.

Ira J. Tisdale, son of William and Clarissa (Goodwill) Tisdale, was born in Willington, Conn., January 21, 1812. His parents (the father of Welsh and mother of Irish descent) came from Connecticut to the Holland Purchase in the cold season of 1816, and settled in the northwest part of Darien, then included in Pembroke. They suffered the hardships and privations incident to pioneer settlements. Mr. Tisdale died in 1819, leaving Mrs. Tisdale with seven children. She was born July 12, 1786, and died December 10, 1873. Ira, after his father's death, and at the age of 16, learned the carpenters' trade, which he followed as his chief occupation until his 75th year. He also owned and cultivated a farm. April 26, 1840, he married Rhoda M. Williams, and they had two sons. Mrs. Tisdale was born December 11, 1812, and died October 9, 1885. Their son Homer L., born February 19, 1841, married Julia A. Robinson, October 25, 1870. He served in the war in Capt. J. D. Newman's Independent Battery, and died September 20, 1878. His wife died May 22, 1873. Their only child, Bertha R. Tisdale, now resides with her aged grandfather. William T. was born August 22, 1843,

and died‚April 22, 1848.   Mr. Tisdale commenced his political life an
"old line Whig" and is now a Republican.   He held the offices of
magistrate and school superintendent.

Major Amos Tyrrell and his son Amos, Jr , emigrated from Washington County, N. Y., to Newstead, Erie County, in 1816. About 1823 they removed to Darien (then Pembroke), settling on the north line of the town, now the south line of Corfu village.   The homestead is still in the Tyrrell name.   Amos Tyrrell was an active partisan.   He was a prominent Anti-Mason during the existence of that party, and was afterwards a Whig.   He was elected a representative to the legislature of 1834–35.   Upon the organization of the Republican party he became one of its staunch and decided supporters.   He was an independent thinker, a hard worker, and a natural leader.   During the years of the old State militia he was appointed a major, hence his appellation.   He married Salome Harroun, and they reared five sons and three daughters, all of whom are living.   One son, William Tyrrell, is an attorney of Batavia, and a recognized leader in the affairs of the Republican party of Western New York   Maj. Tyrrell died in 1860, and his wife in 1872.

James G. Tiffany, son of James and Ruth (Durkus) Tiffany, was born in Randolph, Vt., October 2, 1794, and came with his parents to the Holland Purchase, June 26, 1809, settling on what is known as the "Tiffany farm," about half a mile east of Darien Center, then a part of the town of Batavia.   The year preceding his father came from Vermont.   Mr. Tiffany was a mechanic as well as a farmer, and built carts, wagons, sleds, and wooden plows for his pioneer neighbors.   He met an untimely death in June, 1830, by being thrown from his wagon, while hauling goods from Brockport to Darien.   James G. Tiffany married Martha Matteson in 1815, located in Alexander, and engaged in wool-carding about two years,when he removed to a farm of 120 acres, a mile and a half north of Darien City, where he resided until after his father's death, when he sold out and purchased the old homestead, where he resided till his death, April 5, 1874, in his 80th year.   He was a man of sterling integrity, trusted and honored by his townsmen, and his good judgment was sought to settle many difficulties.   His children were Sarah Ann, Juliette, Delieu, Richelieu, James D., Harriet, Ruth, Laura, Maria, and Mary.   Of these only five are living, and Delieu alone in this town   He married Elizabeth C. Babcock, of Delevan, Wis., settled on the homestead with his father, and there resided until 1880.   He now resides with his son.   Mrs. Tiffany died March 7, 1884.   Their children were Henry C. and Frances A. (Mrs. James H. Kinsey).   The latter died November 25, 1886, in her 30th year.   Henry C. Tiffany married Ella Smith in 1879, and is now an enterprising merchant and the postmaster of Darien Center.

Abram Thomas, son of Simmons and Lucy (Felton) Thomas, was born in Lafayette, N. Y., April 29, 1821, and moved to Alden in 1832 with his parents, settling on a portion of the Indian Reservation.   His parents lived and died there. His mother died aged 66, and his father 91. His brother Ephraim still lives on the homestead. Abram married, first, Mary Law-rence, who died six years after marriage. He married, a few years later, Nancy J. Roy, who is the mother of two of his daughters. She died in July, 1874. He first settled in Alden on the old homestead, moved to Pem-broke, and finally to Darien, where he now lives. George W. Thomas, oldest son of Abram and Mary, was born in Alden (now Marilla), March 27, 1844. July 28, 1862, he enlisted in Co. G, 129th N. Y. Vols , was transferred to the 8th N. Y. H. A., and served until the close of the war, being honorably discharged June 9, 1865. He returned home and taught school 11 terms. March 8, 1870, he married Elvira J. Stiles, of Darien, and settled on the farm where he now resides. Mrs. Thomas died No-vember 19, 1885, leaving an only daughter, Bertha M., and March 15, 1887, Mr. Thomas married M. Amelia Taylor. He is now serving his sec-ond year as assessor, is secretary of the Patrons' Mutual Fire Relief As-sociation of Genesee County, and is master of Corfu Grange, No. 142. In politics he is a Democrat, is liberal in his religious views, and is super-intendent of the Union Sunday-school. Wesley L., second son of Abram and Mary Thomas, was born in Alden, August 16, 1846. He enlisted in the 3d N. Y. Cav., in February, 1864, was taken prisoner the ensuing summer, and died of starvation in Andersonville, September 17, 1864. Julia M. (Mrs. H. J. Brown), daughter of Abram and Nancy Thomas, re-sides in Corfu ; and Jennie N. (Mrs. Charles Schwartz) resides near her father.

Major William Thayer, son of Barach, a native of Vermont, came here in 1808, and settled on a farm next north of where his son William now lives. He held the office of major in the War of 1812, and was appointed by the governor a commissioner of highways in 1826. He located several roads on the Purchase, and placed mile-stones on them. He was also supervisor, magistrate, and overseer. He died in 1844.

Samuel N. Vickery, son of Benjamin and Catherine (Waterbury) Vick-ery, was born in Nassau, N. Y., September 14, 1821. May 8, 1833, he came with his parents to Yates, Orleans County, and spent his boyhood on his father's farm and at the common schools, with a few terms at Yates Academy. August 29, 1847, he married Jane E. Lombard, of Yates, where they settled on a farm, and remained six years He became ill with neuralgia, and because of failing to receive any benefit from the phy-sicians he investigated for himself, and commenced a course of self treat-ment, with so good results that he read further and commenced practice as an eclectic physician. In 1855 he removed to Darien, where he now resides, and where he is a successful practitioner and an enterprising farmer. His youngest son, Howard H., resides with him. His other chil-dren are Meritt E., an engineer in the West Avenue mills, at Attica ; Charles H., one of the proprietors ; and Albert E., a farmer, residing in the village of Alexander. Dr. Vickery has successfully passed the legal ex-amination required, is a registered physician, and a graduate of Physio

Eclectic Medical College of Cincinnati, O.   He is liberal in religion, and in politics is a decided Democrat.

Jonathan Vaughan, born in Lebanon, Conn., April 15, 1784, came to Darien from Westmoreland, Oneida County, N. Y., in 1809, and settled where his daughter Emma S. and her husband, James R. Langworthy, now live.   He cut the first tree and cleared the first acre on his farm, and in 1812 married Sophia Weston and brought her to his log cabin.   In February, 1814, the pioneers were disturbed by the report that the Indians in the employ of the British were on their way from the lake region to burn and destroy this infant settlement.   Dea. William B. Garfield, cousin of the late President Garfield, with his family, and Mr. Vaughan with his, all loaded into an old sled hitched to a pair of horses, retreated two and a half miles in the night, and broke the sled near the cabin of their neighbor, Mr. Peck.   They remained there and soon got news from Batavia that the Indians were not on the "war path."   The party returned to their deserted houses.   They suffered all the privations incident to pioneer life.   In 1829 he built his pleasant and comfortable residence, which is now in a good state of preservation ; from time to time he has built nearly all the farm buildings now standing on the place. Mr. Vaughan had an original and clear intellect, was somewhat eccentric, a great reader, and was proverbially kind and generous to the poor and needy.   In 1816 he and his wife united with the Baptist Church.   The meetings were held at the school-house located on his farm, and his house was familiarly called the "Baptist tavern."   Sometimes they had a pastor, but in the absence of a minister Mr. Vaughan, assisted by others, conducted the services.   He was foremost in influence and in contributing to the financial interest of the church.   Mr. and Mrs. Vaughan were always in sympathy with their neighbors when any were sick, and went miles to attend them and administer to their comfort.   Mr. Vaughan died December 17, 1857, aged 73, and Mrs Vaughan August 6, 1876.   They had nine children, of whom only Mrs. A. A. Williams, of Attica, and Mrs. J. R. Langworthy, who resides on the old homestead, are now living.

Zina Waite, a native of Washington County, N. Y., was born in March, 1800.   In 1823 he married Rebecca Buchanan, and in 1826 came to Darien, where he lived, and died March 2, 1843.   Mrs. Wait died in 1868.   He was a large farmer, having at one time 325 acres.   He was elected supervisor three terms, and held other town offices.   He was an old line Whig, and a delegate to the convention that nominated Harrison in 1840.   They had a son, Horace, who married Almira Wyman, of Pembroke, and who was keeper of the county poor-house 10 years.   Cyrus Waite, son of Zina, was born on the Waite homestead, April 6, 1831, was educated in the district school and in the Wyoming and Genesee Seminary, and married, in 1856, Amaretta, daughter of John Lincoln, of Darien.   She was born in May, 1831.   He settled on the homestead, which is still owned by him, where he resided until 1880, when he removed to Corfu village, where he now resides. Inheriting much of the native energy and spirit of his father Mr. Waite, besides attending to his farm, conducts an extensive business in wool, in which he has been successful. He takes an active interest in municipal affairs, is a promoter of the cause of education, and aids in the furtherance of religious matters. He has been supervisor two terms and a magistrate four years. Their only son, Charles, is in mercantile business in Buffalo. Mrs. Waite died January 6, 1885, lamented by a large circle of acquaintances.

Russel Wait was born in Cambridge, Washington County, N. Y., in 1787. He came to Genesee County in 1810, and located on a farm in Darien, then included in Batavia. In 1811 he married Mercy Booth, of his native town, and they resided on the farm in Darien until his death in 1854, the result of an injury received by being run over by the cars. He was strong and healthy, and a hard worker. He was noted for his honesty and fair dealing, was generous to the poor and needy, and was especially liberal to the Baptist Church, of which he was a member. His first wife was the mother of his 15 children, and died in 1835. He married, second, Mrs. Polly Aplin, who died in 1842. For his third wife he married Mrs. Clark, who survived until January 1, 1879. Four sons and six daughters survived their father, all of whom were married.

Michael Warner was born in Alsace, France, emigrated to America in 1830, lived in Orangeville and Attica, and died in 1885, at the home of his son Peter, in Darien, where he lived for 18 years. He was a farmer, and married Barbara Broadbrooks, who died in March, 1885. They were the parents of seven children. Peter was born in Orangeville, February 26, 1838. In February, 1867, he married Mina Giese, of Darien, and in 1868 settled on the farm where he now resides. Mr. Warner is an enterprising and industrious farmer. A Republican in politics, he has been honored by his townsmen with the office of highway commissioner for four years, and is still holding the same. He is a kind, worthy, and intelligent citizen. The family consists of eight children, all of whom are living with their parents.

Theodore Young, son of Jacob, was born in Germany, January 14, 1841, and came to America with his parents in 1852, living with them until 14 years old, working on the farm summers and attending school winters. He was engaged as clerk in a grocery store for three years, after which he spent a short time at school. From 1858 to 1862 he clerked for H. H. Chapin, of Darien, when he was a partner until 1864, after which he purchased Mr. Chapin's interest, and has since conducted the business alone. By his management he has more than doubled the former business of the firm. By economy, industry, and perseverance Mr. Young has secured a competency. February 3, 1870, he married Fanny E. Fisk, who was born in Akron, N. Y., September 25, 1847. She has been of great assistance to him in his social and business relations. Their children are Leonard E., Arthur L., Delevan C., and Floyd T.

Mrs. Aurelia (Lapping) Lee came from Willington, Conn., to Darien in 1824, and married David J. Lee the same year. He was the son of Quartus Lee, a pioneer of Connecticut, who came to Darien in 1815. Mrs. Lee reared three adopted children, of whom Mrs. Theodore Young was the youngest. Says Mrs. Lee: "She was a good friend, and a true mother." Mrs. Lee is now 82 years of age, and one of the few old settlers left. Mr. Lee died in 1866.

ELBA.

ELBA was erected from the town of Batavia, March 14, 1820, and at that time included the present town of Oakfield, covering an area of 38,000 acres. The early settlement of Elba will, to a considerable extent, also include that of Oakfield, as it was not until April 11, 1842, that that town was erected and Elba assumed its present area of 22,631 acres. The act of March 14, 1820, was:

"That all that part of the town of Batavia known as the 13th township in the first and second ranges, including that part of the Tonawanda Reservation lying east of the division line between the second and third ranges, and north of the division line between the 12th and 13th tiers of townships in the Holland Company's Purchase, be and is hereby erected into a separate town by the name of ELBA."

Another section of the act provided for the election of town officers at the tavern of Nehemiah Ingersoll, on the Oak Orchard road, one and a half miles south of the village, on the 14th of April, 1820; and that the supervisor and overseers of the poor of Batavia act as a board of canvassers for the election, all of which was done according to the act.

It has been found, by improving the soil, that the early predictions of its productiveness have not failed. The surface is undulating, with gently rising slopes without obstruction to easy cultivation. The composition of the soil is a mixture of clay and loam with perceptible calcarious properties. Various crops are successfully raised, and wheat has been formerly its staple crop. Limestone deeply underlies the soil, but pebbles of it are everywhere perceptible.

The never-failing supply of pure water is an indispensable characteristic of this healthy town. The principal source of the Oak Orchard Creek is an outlet of an ever-flowing spring, near what has long been known as "Dunham's Corners," called the "Hackley spring." It passes northeast through the center of the town to the northeast corner, thence west through the north part; and this is the general direction of the tributaries that combine to swell Oak Orchard Creek. Spring Creek is formed from springs in the southeast corner of the town, and flows northeasterly into the town of Byron. These streams furnish pure spring water to the inhabitants and ample power for the flouring and custom mills of George

W. Mather. The " Scott spring," strongly impregnated with sulphur, rises a mile away, which, with its accumulations, furnishes power for a woolen-mill and saw-mill located on the "Transit" (owned by Mason Fuller), and uniting with Spring Creek gives ample power for the "Transit flouring mills." To the abundant supply of pure water from springs, and the wells so easily sunk in every part, is attributed the healthfulness of this beautiful town. A strip of the average width of one-half mile is occupied along the north edge by the Tonawanda Swamp.

ELBA (p. o.) village is located a short distance south of the center of the town, and is most beautifully situated. It was called " Pine Hill " at an early day, and by many " The Pinery"; and it is written by some historians that Joseph Ellicott contracted with Isaac Sutherland to cut a road from where he had located his land office, Batavia, to "The Pinery," in 1802. The term " rural retreat " cannot be more applicable than to this. A sufficiently dense farming population has vigorously made and sustained one of the enterprising villages of Western New York. Other sister villages have had natural advantages, as well as artificial, to aid their advance; but this has had only the confiding support of a wealthy farming community, and the personal, well-applied energy of those who are engaged in its mercantile and mechanical pursuits, to bring it to its present important position. The advent of the West Shore Railroad has given the village an impetus for more rapid prosperity, and its permanence is assured by the background of rich and fertile farm lands of an area of over 40 square miles. The village has a population of about 500, settled in lucrative business and in homes of their own. The school and church advantages compare with sister villages of greater pretensions; a commodious school building for primary and advanced departments accommodates the public, and a private seminary, established by Miss Mary Hollister in 1883, is receiving a support that promises a permanent and useful institution. Its places of business are, mainly, three dry goods stores, one hardware store, a drug store, two wagon shops, three blacksmiths, one millinery store, barber shop, meat market, a well-kept hotel, and no saloons. There are located here two of the largest stave and heading factories in the country, producing large quantities annually ; also saw-mills and feed-mills with their peculiar advantages.

The land from which the village plat was taken was originally the farming lands of Asa Babcock, John Willis, Charles Woodworth, and Thomas Davis. Messrs. Babcock and Willis settled their lands in 1817, and the remaining portions were purchased of their descendants. For use on public occasions there are two well provided public halls, namely, Willit and Shepard's. The business of the place is provided with telephonic and telegraphic communication with all principal villages and cities.

An organization, of which the citizens may well be proud, is represented by the cornet band. Organizing in 1874, they have built on the public park a stand or *pagoda*. Unlike many others, attempting to sustain like voluntary efforts to amuse the public, this remains popular and in a flourishing condition.

At the earliest effort of concentrating the business of the town at this point a postoffice was established, called "Elba," with Mason Turner first postmaster. Previous a wide spread settlement had to endure the burdens of obtaining their mail from Batavia. A daily mail arrives and departs. The only other postoffice in town is East Elba, established in 1857, from which is received two mails a week.

Early settlers.—John Young and wife came from Virginia in 1804, on horseback, and after innumerable dangers and hardships settled on the eastern part of the premises now owned by Albert Parker, south of Elba village. He received the first deed of farming lands issued by the Holland Land Co., July 11, 1803, in what is now Elba. For a bed they obtained a large cotton bag of Mr. Brisbane, at the "Transit store house," which, filled with the down of the cat-tail flag, certainly afforded them a downy bed, if not one of ease.

John Roraback settled at "Pine Hill," now Elba village, in 1804, and was the weaver for the entire section for many years. Thomas Turner settled on the premises now occupied by Mrs. Wilford, and Ephraim Husted settled on the adjoining lot, both of which were afterwards purchased by Mr. Wilford. Bannan Clark came upon the place latterly owned by Orlando Town, who also was an early settler, and is now owned by Edwin Parker, in the north part of the town. Ephraim Wortman early located upon the farm now owned by William Maltby. A story is told of Mr. Wortman that will bear repetition here. He went to the War of 1812 under Capt. White (who was killed at the burning of Buffalo), and poor Wortman had endured pioneer hardship so practically that, when he arrived in fort where there seemed such plenty, he suggested to the captain, " so much being on hand they might lunch 'tween meals."

Samuel, John, Jesse, and James Drake came about 1811. John settled in the southwest part of the town, on the farm now owned by Aaron Drake, and Norman Drake resides on the premises taken up by his father, James. Lemuel Foster settled on the farm afterwards owned by his son Eden, who also came to the town early. Eleazur Southworth settled in 1808 on the farm now owned by Albert Parker; Asa Sawtell located the farm now owned by Watson Bradley ; and Sherrard Parker settled a short distance north of the present village. Daniel Mills, in 1808, located on the farm now owned by his son-in-law, Horace B. Norton, in the southeast part of the town. Mr. Mills was the first Sunday-school superintendent of the first Sabbath-school established in the town. Joel Mills, a brother of Daniel, settled on the premises now owned by his son Daniel D. There were also George Mills and John Mills, and the " Mills neighborhood " remains as a memento of this worthy family, of whom much could be said. The primitive residence of the pioneers, with its old fire-place, yet remains, and is preserved on the premises to remind the present generation that its proverbial hospitality is yet extant in the family. Locklin Norton settled near the " Mills neighborhood," and the death of his wife the first year was a serious event of that day. Isaac Higley settled in the eastern part of the town in 1808, and John Taylor located in the southeast part of the town in 1814, and was long noted for his enterprise and model farming.

Borden Wilcox became a resident in 1812, and we will mention the settlers of his neighborhood as he said he found them : Dudley Sawyer, Dea. Seymour, Enos Kellogg, and Sylvanus Humphrey. Mr. Wilcox also mentions Chester Scott, who came about 1817. He was a valuable man for the new settlement. Mr. Scott taught the first school in the town, assisted Comfort Smith in perfecting the first grist.mill, becoming the owner, and completing the carding works started by Solomon Smith, and rebuilding an old log distillery to enable the pioneers to realize some cash for their grain. The raising of the mill, Mr. Wilcox said, was a memorable event for the town, and took the settlers for miles around to a jubilee. Col. Kellogg mounted the highest part of the frame, with the bottle, as was the custom of the day, and announced " another addition to the population of Pleasant Valley." The usefulness and enterprise of Capt. Scott is gratefully remembered by the elder and middle-aged citizens of the county as well as the town. He carried on the distillery for 10 years, and then moved to Batavia. Whisky in those days was only 15 cents per gallon for new.

Andrew B. Jones purchased 20 acres on the Transit line, early, and a saw-mill of Horace Gibbs (also an early pioneer), in which was a set of native stones for grinding feed. He at once erected a distillery, in 1820 rebuilt the saw-mill, in 1822 built the mill known as the " Transit mill," and in 1836 completed a flouring-mill below. Mr. Jones proved himself a benefactor to the new and prosperous country. Nathaniel Ford, in 1820, located in the north part of the town, leaving descendants to perpetuate the name.

The settlers of the northwest portion of the town are not definitely known, but Ambrose Douglass gives a list of those who had settled prior to 1822, the time he became acquainted with the locality, viz.: John Wilson, Washington Gardner, Elisha Buck, James Fuller, Abraham Sleeper, Smith Lane, Israel Hoag, Miles Britton, Wanton Aldrich, James Harris, Richard and Isaac Shotwell, and Robert Irwin.

Patrick O'Fling settled in the town very early, and he, with three sons and a son-in-law, enlisted in the War of 1812. At Fort George, in 1813, Gen. Dearborn, then in command, was attracted by the soldier-like bearing of the old man, and asked him where *he* had seen service, to which he replied, " in the Revolution under *Captain* Dearborn." This led to a recognition by the General, who afterwards took much interest in this family of soldiers.

Besides those mentioned previously as pioneers in the town of Elba we find from Turner's *History* of the early days of the Holland Purchase, and from other reliable sources, that the following were settlers at an early date : Archibald Whitten, David Kingsley, Thomas Parker, Nathaniel Johnson, Hiram Smith. Col. Samuel Hall, Horace Carr, Benjamin Chase, Elisha Kellogg, Dudley Sawyer, Samuel Cumings, Nathan Miner, Silas Torrey, Edmund Burgess, Joel and Horace Jerome, Joseph Mills, Aaron White, Sylvanus Eldridge, Stephen Harmon, Mason Turner, Samuel Laing, Col. E. J. Pettibone, Asa Babcock. John Willis (an early tavern-keeper, the second in town), Mark Turner, Nelson Parker, Phineas and Loren Barr, John Lamberton, Isaac Barber, Ira Howe, Phineas and John Howe, Simeon Hosmer, Peter H. Knickerbocker, Cornelius Barr, I. Barlow, Richard Edgerton (1806), Nathaniel Ford (1820), S. Eldridge, Thomas Griffin (1820), Reuben Perry (1810), Daniel Woodward (a physician), and C. Woodworth, the greater portion of whom have left worthy descendants to perpetuate their memories and enjoy the fruits of their enterprise.

The first birth in the town was that of Betsey White in 1802, and the first death was David Kingsley in 1804 Stephen Harmon opened the first inn in 1815, and Samuel Laing the first store in 1819, at the place called Pine Hill. The first saw-mill and grist-mill were on Spring Creek, erected by Horace Gibbs and Comfort Smith, in 1810, as mentioned previously; and the first school was taught by Mason Turner in 1811, on "Gifford Hill," at the house of J. W. Gardner. Daniel Woodward was the first physician who settled in the town, and the first justice of the peace appointed for the newly organized town was Charles Woodworth. Dr. James A. Billings was an early physician who located at Dawes Corners, where he died. His brother was at Pine Hill.

The first town meeting held, as was provided by the act, was March 14, 1820, at which the board of canvassers declared the following persons elected : supervisor, Lemuel Foster ; town clerk and collector, Mason Turner ; assessors, George Mills, Charles Woodworth, and John Underhill ; overseers of the poor, Erastus Wolcott and Isaac Benedict ; commissioners of highways, Jeremiah Wilford, Mark Turner, and Dudley Sawyer ; commissioners of schools, Lemuel Foster, Jeremiah Wilford, and Isaac Higley ; constables, Eleazur D. Davis, Ichabod Hinckley, Jr., and Jessemin Drake ; school inspectors, E. D. Davis, Samuel White, and Martin Wilson ; poundmaster, Nehemiah Ingersoll.

The number of votes cast in the town was 166 It would be well for the reader to remember that in 1820, at this election, there were only the 166 voters, and the territory embraced was all that comprises the present towns of Elba and Oakfield. The number given in by the proper board for jury duty, as " fit and eligible " at the time, was 118. Eighteen road districts were organized in the spring of 1820, and the respective pathmasters appointed. In 1821 it was enacted by the town that every pathmaster destroy Canada thistles, tory weeds, and burdocks on his district three times during the year—a commendable law, and far in advance of the State at large at the present day.

Shubael Dunham, Isaac Benedict, Lemuel Foster, Simeon Hosmer, and Nathaniel Ingersoll were constituted a committee to draft "by-laws for the town." The school committee formed seven full school districts and five joint with surrounding towns.

The development of the town was more rapid as the facilities of surrounding towns and its own were improved, and on the 11th of April, 1842, it was found necessary to form Oakfield from the territory, thus leaving the present town of Elba about six miles square.

Religious organizations.—About 1820 there was a strong feeling in favor of a sect called " Friends," and those prevailed upon the Farmington quarterly meeting to authorize a meeting for "preparation and worship " in the town of Elba. There were 48 members, heads of families, in this town, and more in adjoining towns. During January, 1821, the " Hartland monthly " was established, the members residing in Elba, Hartland, and Royalton. The visiting committee appointed by the quarterly meeting was: Elijah Pond, Ira Lapham, Jonathan Ramsdale, Joseph Jones, William Cromwell, and Abraham Gifford. The first house of worship was erected in 1820, of logs. The society prospered, obtained four acres of land of Joseph Ellicott, erected a substantial stone church, and numbered 138 members in 1838. The property of the organization is located about one mile north of Elba village and includes a cemetery. The society is still in a prosperous condition and has stated meetings. The present pastor is Charles W. Sweet.

East Elba Methodist Episcopal Church, located in the southeast part of the town, commenced its existence by the association of a few fervent friends of that faith at private dwellings, for worship, as early as 1810, by Elder Grant, John Howe, and Brother Seth. A local preacher, with his wife and mother, settled in the town in 1811. At the same time Joseph Walter, an exhorter, with his wife and sister and two brothers—Zalmon and Fayette Luttington—with their families, came in, which enabled the formation of a class of 11 by Rev. Ralph Lanning, and Joseph Walter was appointed leader. The first pastor was Marmaduke Pierce. The first house of worship was built in 1814 The Sunday-school was organized in 1827, and the same year an effort was made to erect a church edifice to accommodate the increasing numbers, and Levi Barnes, John Taylor, Phineas Howe, William Knapp, Isaac Barber, and Locklin Norton were made trustees of the society. Pledges were obtained sufficient to erect the church on the present site, which was dedicated in 1830. The building is plain and substantial, free from decoration outside or in and without a dome—a memento of the simplicity of the earlier Methodists. The present membership is 64, and Rev. Edward L. Graves is the minister in charge. The church will seat about 300, and the property is valued at $2,500.

The society called the Second Baptist Church of Elba, consisting of 16 members, was formed September 13, 1822, and the first church was erected in 1824. They received the donation of land from the Holland

28

Land Company, according to the rule of that company. The Rev. John Miner was the first pastor. The lot upon which the first edifice was erected was conveyed to the society in 1837 by Perez Billings, the consideration being $100; another deed was given April 13, 1849, by Stephen Selleck. The first church was burned in 1837, and rebuilt in 1849–50. The present membership is 70, and Rev. D. D. Bailey is in charge.

The Presbyterian Church of Elba was organized as a Congregational Church, October 8, 1822, Solomon Hibbard being its first pastor and influential in its organization. There were 16 members. In 1840 it had about 50 members, in 1843, 76, and in 1846 about 80. The first church was built of wood in 1822. Rev. E. H. Stratton was pastor in 1835, R. Whiting in 1838, and G. S. Corwin in 1842. The society adopted the Presbyterian form of government. In 1875 they built a commodious edifice, costing $7,000, and seating 300 persons, which, with parsonage and grounds, is now valued at $10,000. This church possesses the only bell in the town. The membership is about 75 and 125 attend the Sabbath-school.

The Methodist Protestant Church, located on Chapel street, was organized in 1833 by Rev. Isaac Foster, with about 25 members, and a church building was erected of wood in 1834. A new edifice was built in 1878, also of wood, and capable of seating 300 persons. This and the grounds are valued at about $4,300. The membership is about 55, with 13 officers and teachers in the Sunday-school. Rev. A. Smith is pastor.

The weak condition of both the Methodist and Congregational societies, named above, was such, at that early day, that it was necessary to join interests in the erection of an edifice. In 1829, by an agreement adopted by both, each society had a joint ownership in the edifice erected, and to alternately have worship; but not many years elapsed before the Congregational Society gained strength sufficiently to become the sole proprietors. Both societies are now self-sustaining and enjoy modern built places of worship.

A German Evangelical Church has lately been erected through the energy of Rev. Mr. Lange.

The Elba cornet band on January 1, 1889, consisted of 13 pieces. The active members were Charles W. Moore, Benjamin F. Moore, Edward J. Strauts, and Robert Calkins. They meet weekly for practice, and in the season discourse music from the band stand in the public park.

Elba Tent, No. 25, K. O. T. M.—The senior commander of this order is William H. Hunn, and Dr. J. M. Lewis is physician.

Elba Lodge, No. 357, I. O. G. T., was organized in June, 1883, and is a worthy organization managed by the young people of the community.

Cemeteries.—The well provided resting places for the dead should not be passed as least worthy of notice. The first ground, one acre, was conveyed for a nominal consideration by Asa Babcock. The new cemetery, located at the west bounds of the village, was originated by the public enterprises of the late Sherrard Parker, in 1870. It contains two and one-fourth acres, located on a sand and gravel deposit, appropriate for interment, and desirable as a picturesque location.

In 1868 the following were some of the industries in operation : Phineas Barr, Jr., was proprietor of a saw mill and shop ; Edward Bateman kept the Pine Hill Hotel ; E. Murphy operated a stave and barrel factory; Jonas S. Billings was a prominent physician and surgeon; French & Co. had a stave and heading-mill, and were coopers ; Thomas Griffin had a saw-mill ; Hall & Grimes were proprietors of the Spring Creek woolen-mill ; Maltby & Barton were in the grocery and provision business ; W. C. Raymond was postmaster and kept a general store ; Southwick & Staples were stave manufacturers ; Israel W. Warner was a physician and surgeon ; and E. M. Witney was proprietor of the flouring-mills. At East Elba A. Crocker was postmaster, and James Bray and Frank Kurtz had woolen mills. Dr. Francis Smiley was a prominent physician of the town about 50 years ago. He died at the age of 86 years.

Some of the present active business men of the village of Elba are Larrck-ton Harris & Co., dealers in lumber, produce, coal, etc., with an office on South Main street; John H. Dorman, a dealer in produce and agricultural implements, with an office also on South Main street; and William A. Hundredmark, a general merchant.

Phineas Barr, grandfather of William J., was born January 10, 1794, in Deerfield, Mass. He served in the War of 1812, while his father (Cornelius) came and located their new home (about 1811) in Elba. Upon his discharge Phineas joined his parents. He married and had five children, one of whom, Julius J., was born January 15, 1826, and is a farmer. He married, April 9, 1861, Mary A., daughter of Freeman D. Lake, of Batavia, and they have had three childreen, viz.: one deceased ; Freeman P.; and William J., who was born January 12, 1862, received a common school education and attended boarding school in Batavia, and taught several terms. He went to the Normal School in Owego, from which he graduated in 1885. He has devoted his entire attention to teaching and educational interests, and has achieved an honorable position among the educators of the State. In the fall of 1887 he was elected school commissioner of the county for three years.

Daniel Booth was born in Charlemont, Mass. In 1759 he married Lucinda Allis, and they were parents of 10 children, of whom but two urvive, namely : Martha M. and Joel A. The latter was born in Massachusetts, September 29, 1808, and when about 20 years of age came to Nunda, N. Y. He married, first, Emeret E. Jackman, of Livonia, by whom he had eight children, of whom two are deceased, and six are living, viz.: Cyrus M., Eliza, Emily E., George A., Charles W., and Frank S For his second wife he married, January 24, 1858, Mrs. Laura T. (Colburn) Hannah, and reared two children, Parlemon J. and Lola G. Mr. and Mrs. Booth have lived on road 56 for 31 years.

William Butcher was born in Cambridgeshire, Eng., March 3, 1829, came to Clarendon, Orleans County, in 1850, and afterwards to Elba. September 26, 1856, he married Eunice L. Van Dusen, of Elba. She was born in Byron. They have two children, viz.: Laura, born May 5, 1857, who married Thomas Barber; and Mattie A., born May 1, 1866. The family resides on road 16.

Carl Berk and Fred, his son, were born in Germany, the latter November 1, 1850. Fred received a common school education, came to America in 1865, and May 5, 1871, he married Rachel Shoultz, formerly of Germany. Their children were twins, one of whom is deceased, and the other, Annie, married Albert Burr, April 5, 1887. They have one son, George, born May 12, 1888. Mr. and Mrs. Berk live on road 9.

Thomas Bradway was born in Massachusetts, in 1782, and was twice married, first, to Miss Moulton, who bore him children Lester, William, and Louisa. His second wife was Rebecca Riddle, of Massachusetts, who came to Alexander in 1809, by whom he had nine children, viz.: Rebecca, Emily, Minerva, Polly, James M., George W., Lavina, Alvira, and Warren. George W. Bradway, born in Alexander, January 25, 1819, received a fair education for the times, and was a woolen manufacturer by occupation. In 1847 he came to Byron Center. October 11, 1843, he married Polly Rose, who was born in Monroe County in 1817. They have four children, viz : a son who died aged 13 years, and Frederick, Emily, and Ella D. Frederick married twce, first, Catharine Fonda, of Batavia, and second, Bertha Gould, of Elba. Emily married Charles Adams, of North Java, N. Y., and Ella D. married John W. Roach, of Byron.

Robert Caple was born near Bristol, Somersetshire, Eng., September 26, 1819, and came to Onondaga County, N. Y, in 1836. Two years later he returned to England, and remained there 10 years. May 23, 1840, he married Sarah Saynsbury, and a few years after returned to this country with his wife and four children. They had eight children in all, viz.: Henry, Maria, Alfred, Mary A., John, Sarah, Emma L., and Martha. Emma L. is a dressmaker, with two of her sisters as assistants. September 11, 1861, Mr. Caple enlisted in Co D, 49th Inf. N. Y. V., and was discharged for disability. His wife was born July 22, 1818, and died December 4, 1886. Henry, Alfred, and John Caple are merchant tailors in Oakfield.

Elias M. Chapell was born in New London, Conn., and came to Orleans County with an ox-sled at an early day. David, his son, was born in Clarendon, and August 14, 1818, married Amy A. Haskins, of Byron. They have six children, viz.: James B., Morris D., Amy A., Ida, Frank, and Edgar H. Frank Chapell was born June 24, 1861. He received a common education, and married, November 11, 1883, Mary A., daughter of John W. Parnell, of Elba.

William J. Crawford was born in County Antrim, Ireland, in 1820, and came with his parents to America when he was seven years of age.

locating in Buffalo. January 1, 1850, he married Frances E., oldest daughter of John A. Brown, of Elba, who was born November 20, 1826. They have had a son, George, who died when four years of age, and a daughter, Mary E., who married Corydon Barber, by whom she has a son, Glen. Mrs. Crawford died October 30, 1878. Mr. Crawford has been a resident of this country for 62 years.

Amasa E. Dorman was born in Batavia, December 12, 1832, and was an engineer and conductor on the railroad. February 19, 1851, he married Sarah, oldest daughter of Samuel Churchill. They had one son, George E., born March 29, 1854. George E. received a common school and academic education, until he was 22 years old. March 29, 1879, he married Nettie, oldest daughter of Alfron W. Howe, of Elba. She was born October 31, 1856. Mr. Dorman is a farmer by occupation, and now resides on road 43. His grandfather, Ira Howe, was a soldier of the War of 1812.

John Drake, born in Dutchess County, August 3, 1781, about 1806 married Clarissa Worth, of Dutchess County, who was born March 12, 1791. They had seven children, viz.: Sarah, born January 27, 1808; Moses and Aaron (twins), born August 13, 1809, the former of whom died when two years old; Catherine, born August 3, 1811; Emeline, born April 20, 1813; Malinda, born September 9, 1815; and Eunice, born January 7, 1819. Aaron Drake came to Batavia with his parents in 1811, when two years old, and has always lived on the homestead with the exception of nine years spent in Rush. He married, first, Pauline Bullock, of Elba, who died in June, 1871. April 30, 1879, he married, second, Mrs. Margaret (Knapp) Shaw. The Drake family have been identified with the history of the county since 1811.

Peter Dies, father of Henry, 1st, was born in Germany in 1809. He married Marguerette Hoffman. He located in Elba, and six children were born to them, viz.: Henry, 1st, Henry, 2d, John, 1st, Philip, John, 2d, and Barbara E. Henry Dies, 1st, was born October 20, 1863, and married Catherine Motz, of Germany. They landed at Castle Garden September 7, 1864, and came to Elba. Their children are George, Henry, John, Otto, William, Kate C., and Charles Mr. and Mrs. Dies have lived in Elba 26 years.

Eli Atwater, the first husband of Martha M. Gardner, was born in Danbury, Conn., in 1849, and when young moved with his parents to Western New York. December 25, 1868, he married Martha M., third daughter of Chauncey P. Turner, of Livonia, N. Y., and they had two children, Lucius B. and Minnie M., both of whom reside with their mother. Their father died July 10, 1873. For her second husband Mrs. Atwater married Jeffrey W. Gardner, July 11, 1875, and their children were Jeffrey T., born October 2, 1876, died March 21, 1877; and Grace F., born December 28, 1878. Mr. Gardner died May 1, 1882. Mrs. Gardner's married life with her first husband was spent in Wisconsin.

George W. Graham, Sr., was married, twice, first, to Minnie Annis, by whom he'had 13 children, viz.: Roswell, Benjamin, George W., Jr., Albert, Oliver, Elmer, Hannah, Lydia, Jane, and Eliza, and three deceased. George W. Graham, Jr., was born in East Batavia, February 5, 1848. He went to district school until he attained the age of 15. October 31, 1867, he married Elva J., daughter of Orrell Whipple, of Byron, who was born September 3, 1851, in Addison, N. Y. They have had four children, one of whom died in infancy. The others are Charles A., born June 1, 1869; Llewellyn H., born August 21, 1872; and Ella M., born June 8, 1874. Mr. and Mrs. Graham reside on road 56, between Byron ♦ and Elba.

Thomas Edds was born in Marcellus, N. Y., February 28, 1842. He enlisted in Co. F, 122d N. Y. V., and was discharged May 17, 1865. July 27, 1862, he married Mary A., daughter of John Case, of his native place, and they have five children, viz.: Willie F., Frederick S., Cora S., Alvin J., and Leuella M. The oldest son is a minister of the gospel at Corfu, this county.

Sebastian Eckert was born in Baden-Baden, Germany. He married Helena Keubler, and they had seven children, one of whom, Lewis, was born February 11, 1827, in Baden Baden, and there received a fair education. He came to Oneida County in May, 1852, and August 29th married Mary A., third daughter of Francis Smilkling, of Oneida County. They have nine children, viz.: George A., Lucy, Lewis, Jr., Franklin C., Fred, Fannie S., Mary E., Cora B., and John W. Mr. Eckert is a farmer and shoemaker, and with his family lives on road 26.

Nathan S. Godfrey was born August 15, 1809, in Orange County, N. Y., of English ancestry on his father's side and Welsh on his mother's. He came to the town of Benton, and to Stafford in 1826. His education was derived from the common schools, and he has always been a farmer until he retired. In September, 1831, he moved to Elba. January 30, 1831, he married Alvira, second daughter of Andrew B. Jones, of Elba, and they have four children, viz.: Oscar E., Malvina E., Eli N., and Andrew B. Oscar E. Godfrey was born September 10, 1833, in Elba. His education was liberal, and he is a farmer. March 1, 1883, he married Anna E., oldest daughter of Stephen A. Shepard. Malvina E. married Charles L. Pease, of Batavia. Eli N. Godfrey, born September 25, 1839, received an academic education, and April 16, 1863, married Caroline L., fourth daughter of Seymour P. Hunn, of Elba. They have one son, Charles A., born August 2, 1869, who lives at home with his parents, on road 49.

Phineas Howe, now aged 95 years and living with his son on East Main street, Batavia, moved to Elba from Pennsylvania with his parents in 1810. He went to school only two winters, with Moses McIntyre as his teacher, in the old school house on the Howe farm. He was assessor for 10 years. Over 68 years ago he built the first house where liquor was not used in the raising, and is to-day still firm in his temperance principles. He is a well preserved old man.

Moses Hoffman, born in Herkimer County in 1823, about 1842 married Caroline Lawton, of the same county, and they had three sons, viz.: Elias, Roswell, and Razell. Elias Hoffman was born in Clarendon, N. Y., December 12, 1844, and was educated at the district schools until he was 19 years old. February 7, 1863, he enlisted in Co. G, 194th N. Y. V., as corporal, and was discharged June 3. 1865. October 8, 1886, he married Annie M., oldest daughter of John L. Farnsworth, of Nunda, N. Y., and their children are William M., George E., and Elmira B. The family lives on road 59.

Robert Joslin was born in Devonshire, England, September 15, 1846, and was educated at the parish school. He came to America in 1874, located in Stafford, and in 1880 came to Elba. April 9, 1880, he married Elizabeth Squires, who was born in the parish of Sornbridge, Devonshire, Eng., July 24, 1846. They have two children, viz.: William, born November 10, 1882, and Grace A., born December 23, 1885. The family lives on road 59.

George Kern was born in Baden-Baden, Germany, February 22, 1838. He came to Lancaster, Erie County, in 1855, thence to Darien, and after a year or so to Elba. October 1, 1856, he married Elizabeth Darsm, of Hesse-Darmstadt, Germany, and their children are Mary, born October 29, 1857, who married Jacob Wiedrich, of Elba; Kate, born January 16, 1869, who married Patrick McNarney, of Elba; and Libbie K., born November 5, 1870, who married Charles Wiedrich. Mr. and Mrs Kern are living on Mechanic street in the village of Elba.

John Jones, born in Devonshire, Eng., in 1844, located in Batavia in 1870, where he remained seven years. March 9, 1877, he married Susan, second daughter of James White, of Elba. Their children are William J., born January 18, 1878, and Fred D., born October 23, 1880.

Eli M. Jones was born February 12, 1822. His education was derived from the district schools, and by occupation he was a farmer and miller. July 4, 1844, he married Roxania S. Reynolds, of Phelps, N. Y., and his children were Ellen L., Esther A., Jasper B., Andrew E., Fanny A., Henry C., Charles W., and Nancy L. Eli M. Jones died June 1, 1881. Mrs. Roxania S. Jones carries on the farm on road 25.

Dr. Joseph M. Lewis was born in York County, Canada, July 7, 1851. His father died February 18, 1851. The family on both sides are of Welsh ancestry, his father being born in North Wales, County Montgomeryshire, and his mother in York County, Canada. Dr. Lewis was educated at Victoria Square, and at the age of 18 he attended the Collegiate Institute of Toronto, and studied medicine at Victoria in connection with his collegiate work. In 1873 he went to Jefferson College, and in 1874 was at Philadelphia University, from which he graduated. May 26, 1874, he married Elizabeth, youngest daughter of Abraham Steckley, of Bethseda, York County, Canada. They have three children, namely: Bertha L., Mary G., and Joseph Lister. Dr. Lewis first located at Clarence Center, Erie County, and came to Elba in 1877.

Col. Elias J. Pettibone died in February, 1890. He was born in Connecticut in 1799, and started in life as a peddler of Yankee clocks. He received his title of colonel in the old State militia. He was postmaster at Elba many years. His children are A. E. Pettibone, Mrs. Barton, and Mrs. Willis.

William Maltby, born May 4, 1809, in 1818 moved with his parents to Oneida County, N. Y. He was a member of a rifle regiment in the State militia for three years. He married, first, Cynthia Carr, of Canandaigua, who died May 16, 1835. September 1, 1835, he married for his second wife Delia W. Chapin, of the same place, who was born in Gorham, November 19, 1813. They had three children, namely: Cynthia J., William H., and John C. The latter was born October 24, 1842, in Hopewell, N. Y., and November 11, 1863, he married Cornelia E., youngest daughter of Uri Norton, of Elba. They have two children, Delia E. and Mary S., both school teachers. Mr. and Mrs. Maltby are living on the Maltby homestead on road 48.

Thomas Moore was born in Canisteo, August 19, 1838. He married Diana B., oldest daughter of W. B. Upson, by whom he had children as follows: John L., Charles W., and Benjamin F. John L., a baggage-master, married Emma J. Staples. Charles W. Moore is station agent on the West Shore Railroad, and Benjamin F. is engaged with John H. Dorman in the produce business.

Joel Mills was born in Vermont, came to Cayuga County, N. Y., and in 1808 located in Elba, on road 42. Ansel D. Mills (one of a pair of twins) was born March 17, 1825, in Elba, in the southeast part of the town. He was educated at the district schools and reared a farmer. November 9, 1848, he married Amanda M., oldest daughter of John Taylor. Three of their five children survive, viz.: Elon T., Olin J., and Ansel D., Jr. Olin J. Mills was born May 5, 1857. He received a common school and commercial education, and March 20, 1880, he married Ella M., second daughter of Alfron W. Howe Their children are Amanda M., Frances E., John H., Sarah A., and Marjorie E. Mrs. Olin J. Mills was born May 2, 1859.

Samuel Parker; a native of Massachusetts, served in the Revolutionary war. Sherrard, his son, was born in Massachusetts, August 4, 1794, and came with his parents to Byron in 1806. He was educated at the district schools, and taught several terms. He was a farmer and millwright by occupation, and built the first mill in the town of Byron. In 1817 he married Sarah, daughter of William Williams, of that town, and the same year located on road 23, in Elba. They had eight children, viz.: Harlow E., Sarah D., Mary E., Clara, Albert, Edward, Amanda M., and Samuel. Samuel Parker was born on the old homestead, where his father located in 1818, and where he still resides, September 22, 1834. His education was derived from the district schools and an academy. He has been supervisor of the town, justice of the peace, and president of the Genesee County Agricultural Society. April 10, 1861, he married

Alice L., only daughter of O. R. Clark, and they have children as follows:
B. Clark, who married Mary C. Fuller, of Oakfield; Carrie A., who married Lewis H. Chase, of Philadelphia; and Bert H., who lives at home with his parents.

Fred B. Parker, the only son of Edwin, was born November 4, 1863, in this town, and received a common school and academic education. He is a farmer. February 27, 1889, he married Alice E., only daughter of John McComber, of Alabama. Mr. and Mrs. Parker reside north of the village of Elba.

The history of the Raymond family dates back to the third century, and we find them among the Romans, the Germans, English, Scotch, Irish, and Americans. Ferguson, an authority on names, says "that the name Raymond is derived from the old German name *Raginmund.*" This was in the eighth century. The modern German name is Raimund. There was a long line of Counts of Toulouse of Southern France called Raymonds. The present form of the name was, in all probability, from the above mentioned counts, and translated as follows: *Rai* (a beam of light) and *monde* (*i. e.* world). Coming down the pages of history we find one Simeon Raymond, 9th, great-great-grandfather to William H.; and Walter H., who was born at Old Well, Norwalk, Connecticut, in 1711. He held a commission as captain under the Crown of England. At the breaking out of the Revolutionary war he resigned his command, and joined the rebels (as they were then called). For this act the tories burned all his property. At the time of his death he had 10 children, one of whom, William (24), was born at Old Well, Conn., January 11, 1747, and moved to Granville, N. Y., about the beginning of the present century. From there he came to Western New York in 1824. He married Ruth, daughter of Nathan Hoyt, of Norwalk, Conn., who was born January 22, 1749. One of their children, William (68), was born August 10, 1779, at Granville, N. Y. He married Mary Kellogg, June 20, 1805, and died at Elba, May 15, 1847. One of his sons, William C. (177), was born March 7, 1808, and July 11, 1837, married Sarah Aspinwall Southworth, daughter of Eleazer and Mary, who was born in Elba, March 8, 1815. [From *Grafton County (N. H.) History:* "The first known of the Southworths in the United States was a mistress Alice Southworth, a widow with three children, who came from England in the good ship *Mayflower* and landed at Plymouth Rock, Mass. She was a lady preëminent for her many good qualities, and afterwards became the wife of Governor William Bradford, of Colonial fame. From her children sprang the Southworths, Southards, and Southers, some of whom went West and South."]

William C., father of William H. Raymond, settled in Elba, in October, 1831, and at once engaged in the mercantile business on Main street. He had eight children, two of whom are in Elba, who succeeded their father in business. William Henry (352), born December 16, 1839, received a commercial education, and August 2, 1862, he enlisted for the defence of his country in Co. H, 129th N. Y. V. Inf., which was changed afterwards to the 8th N. Y. H. A. He was promoted to sergeant, 1st sergeant, 2d lieutenant, and 1st lieutenant, and was honorably discharged at the close of the war. He was a prisoner of war for many months. September 1, 1878, he married Miss Waite, fourth daughter of Christopher and Rahama (Larkins), of Elba. Their children are George L., born July 14, 1879, and Winifred S., born June 14, 1887. Walter Hyde (353) was born July 25, 1845. He also received a commercial education, and July 18, 1872, married Flora A., daughter of John Wilder, of Elba. They have two children, Maude E., born July 19, 1874, and Grace, born December 28, 1887. Their father, William C. (177), died June 7, 1873. He had been in business in Elba for 42 years.

Elisha Reynolds was a soldier of the Revolution. His father, Jacob, was a soldier in the War of 1812. Martin Reynolds was born in Vermont, February 21, 1814, and received a good education. In 1840 or '41 he was a member of the State legislature from St. Lawrence County, N. Y., and also served as judge of the county. He married, first, in 1838, Lucia Hall, by whom he had children as follows: George M., Gerry W., and Sarah L. March 3, 1851, he married Videlia Hogan, of North Hill, Vt. They came from St Lawrence County to Elba in 1877, and now live on road 26.

Luther Shepard was born in Vermont, August 10, 1789, and came to Augusta, Oneida County, when a lad, and thence to Hopewell, Ontario County, in 1814. He served in the War of 1812. He married Anna, oldest daughter of Stephen L. Maltby, formerly of Vermont, by whom he had seven children, of whom four grew to maturity, viz.: Nancy J., Sarah A., Stephen A., and Stilson A. Nancy J. died aged 23 years. Stephen A. Shepard was born in Hopewell, N. Y., October 11, 1824. He received a common school education, and at an early age had to earn his own living. He is a farmer. October 4, 1848, he married Jane, second daughter of Enos Cook, of Byron. She was born November 17, 1824. They have three children, viz.: Anna E., Emeline M., and Clara J. Anna E. married Oscar E. Godfrey. Clara J. married Philo E. Noyes. Emeline M. married Charles Spencer, and they have a son, Stephen S., who is living with his grandparents in the village of Elba.

William E. Strouts, born in Essex County, Eng., May 3, 1845, came to Le Roy in 1855 with his parents, and married Mary Bangs, of Ogden, N. Y., by whom he has five children, viz.: Edward J., Herbert W., Eveline M., Mabel L., and Byron D. Mr. and Mrs. Strouts came to Elba in 1868, and located where they now reside, on road 12.

John A. Swartz was born near Hazelton, Pa., September 16, 1843. His opportunities for education were limited, and he had to work when he was seven years old. January 15, 1864, he enlisted in Co. K, 3d N. Y. Cav., and was discharged April 26, 1865, on account of wounds received in the battle of Cold Harbor, which necessitated an amputation of the leg six inches above the knee. April 12, 1868, he married, at

Hazelton, Pa., Anna A. Fasnacht, of Neverell, Switzerland. They lived 11 years in Pennsylvania. They have had five children, of whom one, a son, died in infancy; the others are Lizzie W., John, George, and Charles J. Mr. Swartz died from the effects of his wound June 8, 1887, beloved and respected by all of his friends and neighbors.

Sebastian Schurz, born in Germany, came to America and located in Genesee County in 1858. He married Miss Caslerine, of his native place, and they had one son, George F., who was born in Elba, October 3, 1860, and is a farmer by occupation. March 19, 1884, he married Eliza J., third daughter of Alexander Fowles, of Elba. Mr. Fowles was from County Down, Ireland; his father was from Scotland. Mr. Schurz has lived in Elba for 53 years.

George W. Steele was born in Patterson, N. J. He received a liberal education, came to New York State when young, and was a machinist in early life, and afterwards a printer. October 20, 1859, he married Mary R.; oldest daughter of John and Lois Fuller, by whom he had three children, viz: Emma R., born January 3, 1861; Herbert J., born August 22, 1862; and Mary R., born June 29, 1866. For his second wife Mr. Steele married Martha Barr, by whom he had three children, viz.: Edward (died young), George, and Mertie. Herbert J. Steele was educated in the district schools and at the academy, and is a farmer. January 1, 1885, he married Lottie M. Joiner, of Barre, and they have two children, namely: Marvin F., born March 16, 1887, and Clarence F., born November 29, 1888. Mr. and Mrs. Steele are living on road 8.

Ephraim Smith was born in Vermont in 1803. He married Abigail Hall, and they had 12 children, viz.: Hamilton H., Julius D., Mary J., Abigail H., Riley E , Gordon, Alonzo, Emily, Truman, Lawrence, Erwin, and one who died in infancy. About 1828 he came to Amboy, Oswego County. Alonzo Smith was born September 9, 1844, in Oswego County. His education was secured at the district school and the academy. September 10, 1861, he enlisted in Co. G, 1st Lt. Art , and reënlisted December 17, 1863. He served on the staff of Gen. Hassert, with the rank of 2d lieutenant. January 28, 1864, he married Nettie, youngest daughter of John Dunn, of his native county. They have three children, viz.: Herbert M., born November 24, 1868, who is a merchant in Corfu; Pearl, born September 6, 1876; and Mabel E., born February 8, 1881. Mr. Smith was discharged from the army, on account of wounds, March 17, 1865. He has been a minister of the Methodist Protestant Church.

Gilbert Shelley was born in Westchester County, December 23, 1804, and was a cattle driver for many years. He married, first, Catherine Braw, in 1829, by whom he had six children, viz.: William B., Phœbe J., Anna, Sarah, and two deceased. His wife died when his youngest child was seven months old, and for his second wife he married, in 1842, Mary Dove Their children are Kate, Joseph, Frank, and Adelia. Kate married Zebulon Crosby, of this town. Mr. Shelley has been a member of the Methodist Protestant Church 65 years, and a class-leader 45 years.

William B. Shelley was born in Westchester County, March 24, 1832. His education was limited, being confined to the public schools. He is now a farmer. In April, 1860, he married Adelia Shelley, of Delaware County, N. Y., and they have five children, viz.: Margarette, born June 20, 1866; Ella F., born January 26, 1869; William H., born April 7, 1868; John, born January 28, 1871; and Myrta, born May 28, 1879. Mr. and Mrs. Shelley are living on road 20, in Elba.

Lyman Staples, a native of South Adams, Berkshire County, Mass., came to Elba in 1847, where he died at the age of 52 years. He was a farmer, and married Susan, daughter of Jacob Harkness. His children were George F., Nathan H., Ruth (deceased), Lyman D. (deceased), Henry M., Ruth H., and Job A. The latter came to Elba in 1847, and served as supervisor of the town two terms. Henry M. Staples was born in South Adams, Mass., September 24, 1862, and married Rachel A. Van Alstine, of Oakfield, by whom he has two children, Carrie C. and Loren H., the latter a student at the Buffalo Medical College. Carrie C. married Walter Brockway.

Joseph Wilford, a native of Connecticut, was a soldier in the Revolutionary army. The British offered a bounty of 300 sovereigns for his body. He spent $40,000 of his private fortune to aid our government. He afterwards went to Vermont, and from there came to Batavia (now Oakfield). John C. Wilford, his son, was born in Rutland, Vt., in 1787, and came to Oakfield in 1811. His education was liberal, and he taught several terms. He was a soldier of 1812, was wounded in the battle preceding the burning of Buffalo, and his wound was not dressed until he arrived at Batavia. January 1, 1823, he married Eunice McCrillus, of Oakfield, and their children were Josephine B., Eugene B., Janet C., Julia E., William C., John B., Joseph E., and Sarah E. Eugene B. was born in Oakfield, September 8, 1826. He is a farmer and speculator. January 3, 1861, he married Catharine Sutphin, of Sweden, N. Y., and their children are Joseph S. and Arthur C. One son died aged 19 years, and one child in infancy. The family resides on road 45.

James Watson, born in Fifeshire, Scotland, about 1793, was a ship carpenter. He married Helen Ross, of his native place, and they came to Herkimer County in 1839, and had six children. David Watson was born in Scotland, December 17, 1831, and is a farmer by occupation. He enlisted in Co. B, 3d N. Y. Art., and afterwards in Co. A, 80th N. Y. Inf., and was discharged as corporal at the close of the war. February 25, 1866, he married Elizabeth Zeiter, of his native place, and they have six children, viz: Lottie H., Hattie M., David J., Lizzie A., Helen G., and Maggie M.

Joseph Wheat, born in Concord, N. H., December 9, 1793, was cast upon his own resources at the age of nine years. His education was limited, but he acquired much by keen observation and close application. When 12 years of age he came to Phelps, N. Y., with Benjamin, his brother, and a carpenter by trade. July 23, 1815, he married Caroline

D. Andrews, of New Hampshire, and their children were Albert F., Elias A., Julia A., Lucinda A., Laura A., Benjamin A., Eliza J., and Caroline A. Elias A. Wheat was born in Barre, N. Y., October 20, 1818, was raised on the farm, and was educated in Chautauqua County, but by association with men of learning and piety was fitted for the ministry, which vocation he entered in 1839 in the Methodist Protestant Church, continuing in its service 44 years. November 25, 1847, he married Hannah M., oldest daughter of Josiah Rich (by his second marriage), of Ogden, N. Y. Of their five children two survive, viz.: Mary L., who married Albert E. Blood, of Elba, and Frank, who resides with his parents.

LE ROY.

L E ROY.—The narrator of to-day labors under the disadvantage of being unable to derive materials from original sources of its first settlement, the actors in the scene having passed away, and from their descendants or tradition local facts are mainly to be derived. Historical societies, patient and industrious antiquarians, and county historians have indeed rescued many interesting events from oblivion, but much has perished and will from neglect now be lost. But from what has been preserved, particularly from the careful and industrious researches of the late Mr. Turner, a fair picture of the life of the pioneer settler upon the Holland Purchase may be obtained, which in all the salient features were throughout substantially the same. Western New York, it is seen, was peopled by a hardy race,—strong of limb and stout of heart, with that patience in toil, power of endurance, enterprise, thrift, and moral stamina which make men fit to found a State.

This is a centennial period, so far as to mark the beginning of emigration and the settlement of this fair country of the Genesee. The first main cause history distinctly traces. It was to the campaign of Maj.-Gen. Sullivan against the Iroquois that we chiefly owe the opening to the world at large of this magnificent domain, and the complete subjugation of the war-like tribe that had here their home. Previous to the war of the Revolution white settlements did not advance beyond the lower Mohawk Valley. At its close and the declaration of peace in 1783 the spirit of emigration revived and became almost universal. No field was more inviting than the rich, alluvial soil, broad plains, and picturesque scenes which had been revealed to the army of General Sullivan in the conquest of the Senecas. How complete this was, a brief extract from a dispatch of Sullivan's to General Washington will show, as well as furnish a glimpse of the fertility of the country, even under savage and barbarous rule.   Under date of October 17, 1779, he writes, announcing his victory :

"Forty of their towns have been reduced to ashes, some of them large and commodious, that of Genesee alone containing 128 houses. Their crops have been entirely destroyed, which by estimation it was said would have produced 160,000 bushels of corn, besides large quantities of vegetables of several kinds. Their whole country has been overrun and laid waste, and they themselves were compelled to take precipitate flight to Niagara "

Suffice it to say that this subjugation of the Seneca-Iroquois was final, and was the last rising they ever made against the white man.   But to us it was something more than a victory and punishment of the red man for his atrocities during the war of the Revolution.   To the invading army it opened, as it were, a new world, and became at once an inspiration and revelation.   In the tide of emigration which flowed thither, after peace was declared, it proved the truth that " peace has its victories not less renowned than war."   It was the beginning of that onward march and progress which has ever since continued, and in its grand results the marvel of the age we live in.   But to note this advance and change, which has developed into an empire of itself, is outside of our present purpose.

In this army of General Sullivan's was a soldier who, captivated with the beauty and fertility of the country through which the army passed, resolved as early as practicable to select from thence a spot for his future home.   It was Capt John Ganson.   He was born in Bennington, Vt., in 1750, and entered the army of the Revolution at the beginning of the war ; was wounded in the battle of Bunker Hill by the loss of a finger, which was shot off in that battle ; received the commission of captain ; served honorably through the war, and retired at its close to his home in Bennington.   It was only to make preparation for his final removal.   In 1789 or '90 he started with two of his sons, James and John, of the respective ages of 12 and 14 years, on a prospecting tour to these western wilds.   They continued their journey until they reached the Genesee River, late in the autumn, two miles below what is now the village of Avon, where he made a purchase for a future home, and returned to Bennington for the remainder of his family.   Not wishing to expose his boys to the hardships of another journey he made an arrangement with a friendly Seneca to receive and take care of them in his absence, which he supposed would not be long delayed.   In this he was disappointed. On his return to Bennington he found his wife prostrated by a serious illness, which, after lingering for several months, proved fatal, and it was late in the following spring before he, with his family and effects, was on his way westward, for his new possession.   We have a pen and ink portrait of a portion of the country as it then was.   It purports to be from the pen of an English traveler, but presumably written by Colonel Williamson, the then agent for the " Pultney & Hornby tract " ; but as it gives a glimpse of what this part of Western New York then was we extract a passage.   He had left New York on this route, and writes :

"On the evening of the third day's journey from Whitestown (a village of a few straggling huts) we were agreeably surprised to find ourselves on the east side of Seneca Lake. . . . We forded the outlet of the lake and arrived safe at Geneva--only consisting of a few log houses. From Geneva to Canandaigua the road is only an Indian path, a little improved the first five miles over gentle swellings of land, interspersed with bottoms seemingly very rich. The remainder of the road to Canandaigua, the county town, for six miles, was the greatest part of the distance through a rich, heavy timbered land. On this road there were only two families settled. Canandaigua consisted of only two small frame houses, and a few huts surrounded by thick woods. . . . From Canandaigua to the Genesee River, twenty-six miles, it is almost totally uninhabited, only few families residing on the road. The country is beautiful and very open. In many places the openings are free of any timber, appearing to contain 200 or 300 acres beautifully variegated with hill and dale. Enclosing any one of them with a proportionable quantity of timbered land an enclosure might be made not inferior to an English park."

Such was the outlook of the face of the country when Captain Ganson passed over it, and on his arrival at the Genesee River (1790) there was scarce a white settler to greet him. As he stood before the door of the Indian's wigwam, in whose charge he had left his boys, what was his surprise to witness their perfect transformation. In everything but color they were veritable natives. In manners, language, unkempt locks,—not to omit vermin,—their pale-face origin was barely discernible. But their greeting with the returned parent, whom they had supposed lost, from his long absence, was not the less cordial, and they were quite content to abandon the Indian life, which they had expected to be permanent. This early experience of the Gansons with the Senecas was not without its future use in their intercourse with the tribe, who in large numbers still made this part their camping-ground and "council fires." They were always after on a friendly footing with the tribe, and from their knowledge of the language were often called upon as interpreters. The following from a daughter of Captain Ganson, who married, first, a Mr. Forsyth and afterwards a Mr. Warren, and settled and died on the Ridge road in the county of Niagara, contains a brief note of the early life of her father:

"After my father moved from Avon to the west side of the river (now Le Roy), and opened a public house, other settlers came in. The Indians were frequent visitors at my father's. I used to see them often; the chiefs Red Jacket, Hot Bread, Jack Berry, and Little Beard. Sometimes the Indians were turbulent—they would become a terror to the new settlement. My father was a stout athletic man, and had great influence over them, and would quell them in their worst drunken frolics."

When settled upon the Genesee the Gansons put up the first grist-mill erected upon the river. It was made of logs, the stones of the native rock, and was mainly useful in grinding corn. It was a primitive structure, and in but a limited way could supply the necessities of the settlers. It was quite a common practice to break the first crop of corn in a mortar. A cotemporary settler of the period (1790) speaks of his carrying his buckwheat (brought from Connecticut) 20 miles on horseback to Ganson's mill. But this distance was comparatively small. "Going to mill" was the great family event, when days were consumed in the journey, and was like the fitting out of an expedition. Of the one erected at a

later period, at the mill site in Mumford, John McKay, Esq., in speaking
of it, says :

"I came to Caledonia in 1803. There was then but two houses at the springs. I
purchased two hundred acres of land, including the Big spring and the mill site. Captain Williamson had built a small grist-mill, with one run of stones, to accommodate
the Scotch settlers about eighteen months before I came. . . . My customers for
some time were from the settled portions of the Holland Purchase; they came from as
far as Buffalo when they could not cross the river to Canada on account of the ice.
In fact, at times from all the region west of me."

The want of mills was a privation from which they were soon relieved
by the above mill erected at Mumford and one by Stoddard & Platt, in
1803, at Le Roy, and soon after one by the Holland Land Co. at Batavia. The primitive milling of the Gansons having soon been abandoned,
they decided, in 1797, upon a removal on the west side of the river.
Charles Wilbur had preceded them in 1793, and opened the first farm
west of the Genesee and erected a small log dwelling for a tavern. This
Captain Ganson purchased. It was the beginning of what was afterwards known as the "Ganson settlement," which was to develop and ex-
pand into the present village of Le Roy. The farm purchased and occupied by the Gansons, ever since known by that name, is the same now
owned and cultivated (but in somewhat shorn proportions) by Henry H.
Olmsted, at the east boundary of the village. Hinds Chamberlin, about
the same time, commenced his improvements upon what was subsequently known as the Sheldon farm, which he later sold to Asher Bates,
who came in from Canandaigua. Chamberlin then opened the farm east
in the village, which is owned by the estate of Widow Osborn, and on
which he lived until his decease. Of Deacon Chamberlin we would add
a few particulars, as he was literally the first pioneer and an enterprising
and useful settler, and prominent in all works of improvement. He
opened the first road (previously nothing but an Indian trail) from the
river to Ganson's tavern, under Richard M. Stoddard as road commissioner, but made at the expense of the Holland Land Co. If not the first
white man who saw, he was the first who bore record of, the Oatka, and
the beauty and future promise of this locality. It was in midsummer of
1792 that with two companions he started on an exploring tour westward, and they made their first halting-place on the banks of the Oatka,
at or about the site of the present Episcopal Church. It was a beautiful
Indian camping-ground. The stream was clear ; full and flowing over a
rapid of 60 feet in extent and a fall of 11 feet. The practical mind of the
Deacon foresaw and did not forget its value and importance as a future
water-power. Whether, in their bivouacking, "buttermilk" formed a
part of the luxury of the haversack tradition does not affirm, but is not
a construction improbable, for the name was attached to the falls from
the earliest period, but of which it has since been ruthlessly robbed and
applied to the "big fall" two miles below. As unromantic as this sob-
riquet is it should at least historically be restored to where it belongs.
The Seneca name for the falls was not quite so pronounceable—*Te-car-*

no-wan-no, signifying "many rapids." There is, it may be remarked, everything in a name. It is to us a source of pride that to the beautiful Oatka has been given back its Indian name, which signifies "opening," from the "oak opening" at its junction with the Genesee in place of "Allan's" Creek. It took its name from Allan becoming the owner of a large tract upon the stream.

Ebenezer Allan was a noted character in his day,.and one not uncommon in border life, and would in some particulars answer to that of "border ruffian." A brief digression may be pardoned in speaking of him, since his name in common parlance is still a prefix to our beautiful and more euphonious Oatka, and is now found upon our title records. He was a bold, bad man, of much energy and force of character, and at one time the owner of the Genesee Falls at Rochester, where he erected the first grist mill, with 100 acres embracing the heart of the city, and in other sections was a large property holder. He was familiarly called "Injun Allan," doubtless from the fact that he had married two squaws, —Millie and Lucy,—the first bearing six children and the latter two daughters. Mr. McKay, before mentioned, of Caledonia, said of him:

"I knew Allan well He was about 50 years of age when I first came to the Genesee River. He was tall and straight, light complexion, genteel in appearance, and of good address."

He enlarged his domestic household by marrying at intervals two white women, probably to console himself for the earlier *mesalliance;* the one by captivating the daughter of a passing emigrant, the other a widow, whom it was said and believed he made such by "making way" with an inconvenient husband. How far this blending of domestic colors tended to harmonize the picture is not left upon record.

A word, however, may be added of this à la Mormon household, the first of the kind upon the Genesee,—of the two half-breed daughters who were destined to a higher career. In 1791, from the law and custom of the Senecas in regard to the division of the avails of their land sales and land, they deeded to Allan four square miles lying upon the Genesee and covering the present village of Mt. Morris, on the condition in the deed of trust that out of the proceeds he should cause the girls to be instructed in reading, writing, and sewing, and other useful arts, according to the custom of the white people. Allan took pride in carrying out to more than the letter this trust. He placed his girls in Philadelphia in the best schools the city afforded, and took pains that they should be wanting in no accomplishment money could supply. On attaining womanhood they returned, it is said, highly educated, and in manners and refinement, as well as in beauty of person, commanded admiration from all with whom they came in contact. This may be inferred from the fact that, soon after their "coming out," Allan, having an offer of 3,000 acres from Governor Sinclair of the province, removed with them to Canada, where he died in 1814. He took with him but one wife, and that a white one; where his daughters shortly formed marriage alliances from the best soci

29

ety, and their descendants are now found among the first families of the
province.   So that at the last, in his devotion to his daughters, it may
be said of this graceful but graceless corsair,

> " That linked with one virtue was a thousand crimes."

But to return from the digression.   Deacon Chamberlin extended his
travel west, following the Indian trail, over unbridged streams and miry
swamps, and finding *en route* but a solitary settler until he reached Buffalo
(then Erie).   It had not yet received the name of New Amsterdam,
which it was later christened by Joseph Ellicott.   Here, too, there was
but a solitary white man,—Cornelius Winne, a Hudson River Dutchman,
—who, in 1789, had been tempted into their wilds to open trade with
the Indians that, since the treaty for the sale of their lands to Phelps &
Gorham, congregated here in large numbers.   His log store was on the
site of the present Mansion House in the city, and his goods consisted of
rum, whisky, knives, trinkets, etc.   Here he entertained Chamberlin, if
being in close quarters, in a house filled with drunken Indians, could be
called "entertainment."   It was afterwards confessed by him to be
"rather a poor night's rest."   His adventures on this trip, which was as
far as Presque Isle (now Erie), it is not our purpose to relate, only so far
as to show the general condition of this virgin soil before the white man
peopled it, when as such he was the object of great curiosity both to
squaw and Indian, who in straggling bands peopled the route.   His return to the Genesee followed, finding no country more inviting for improvement and tillage than the one he had left behind, a characteristic
which it retains to this day.

But what a world of change it was permitted the Deacon in the space
of a single life to witness !   A transformation more wonderful than any of
Aladdin's creation on every spot on which his eye had rested !   Upon the
spot where in this first adventure he had traveled, where the Iroquois
were its undisturbed lords, he was to see a city to spring up and spread
in ever increasing magnitude, and destined to rank in the near future
with the great capitals of the western world.   And over all the broad
domain, which he had traversed by an Indian trail, he was to see arise
populous villages, smiling fields, and homes indicating prosperity, plenty,
and content.   An empire "born in a day ! "

Deacon Chamberlin died in Le Roy, in 1848, at the advanced age of
85, "like a shock of corn fully ripe," as was aptly said at his funeral.   He
was one of the organizers of the first Baptist Church in Le Roy, and for
this purpose granted a lot from his farm at the east of the village, on
which the building was erected   As population increased, and business
centered near the Oatka, the church location was considered too remote,
and it was removed to its present site on Church street, on the convincing
and analogous argument of its then pastor, that " if one would catch rabbits he must set his trap where rabbits run."   Mr. Chamberlin left a
family of three sons and one daughter, none of whom now survive.
Stewart, the eldest, was for many years the leading grocer in the village.

He built the present Central Hall, and contributed otherwise largely to village improvements. The children that survive him are George, Henry, 'and Spencer, and Mary, the wife of Mr. Cole, all residents of Chicago.

The Ganson settlement.—Upon the opening of new roads, and the completion of the surveys of the Holland Land Co. under Joseph Ellicott, in 1802, the whole section became alive with immigrants. It was during this period that the Ganson settlement received many accessions. The "Ganson tavern," its chief landmark, required to be enlarged, the log tavern razed to the ground, and a frame building erected in its place as a necessity from the the increased travel. John Ganson, Jr., was its proprietor, and under him the hostelry became one of the most noted for the accommodation of the traveler between Albany and the lakes, a reputation which it retained for the whole period it was used as a public house.

It is not within our limit, neither is it our purpose, to give detailed items of personal history. For this a volume would not suffice, and save in exceptional instances of interest, and where the descendants are among us, a brief mention is all that so condensed a history will permit. It must suffice to group names as far as they can be recalled, and this will probably be chiefly conspicuous for its omissions. But by far the greater number, all, indeed, of those first-comers, will be found reposing in honored graves in our own or in contiguous cemeteries. The first of these, opened about 1801, was on a lot donated for this purpose by Capt. Jotham Curtis, one of the early settlers and a tavern-keeper, on his farm two miles east of the village; and where a Mr. Wiley, the first person whose death is recorded, was buried, subsequently sold to Capt. Daniel Buel, and since known as the Buel farm. This for many years was the sole burying-ground. The Episcopal and Presbyterian yards were opened on the organization of their respective societies. And it is at quite a modern period that a company was formed for laying out the Machpelah Cemetery, which has become one of the most beautiful in the country, and to which many of the remains of these pioneers have been removed. It is from these moss-covered stones in the old and new grounds that their names may be found, with a brief record of their birth, their age, their death. But this is not all. They live in their fruits. The smiling plenty of to-day attests to their sturdy virtues, their patient and hardy toil.

> "Oft did the harvest to their sickle yield ;
> The furrow oft the sturdy glebe has broke.
> How jocund did they drive their team afield !
> How bow'd the woods beneath their sturdy stroke !"

The first bridge over the Oatka was built in 1802. It was a memorable event. James Ganson was the contractor, and Charles Wilbur and Jotham Curtis the commissioners. Two hundred dollars in addition to $50 voted by the town had been raised for its construction. Laborers and a derrick, etc., had been obtained from Canandaigua, and a general "bee" raised for the work of laying the timbers over the stream, made of split chestnut logs. A shanty for the men, and for providing entertainment for the occasion, was erected on the bank of the Oatka, and the great work was commenced and finished in five days. Mrs. James Ganson, in her old age, informed the writer that she was the hostess that made provision for the entertainment, which was abundant in substantials, and not wanting in doughnuts and gingerbread, and of the liquids " old rye " was not without a fair representation. It was before the day of temperance agitation. The second grand occasion at this spot was when the first dam for the grist mill was finished, and the hour had come for the gate to be raised. For this honor, among the crowd of maids and matrons assembled to witness it, Mrs. Stoddard, Mrs. Wolcott, and Mrs. James Ganson were selected, and when they had lifted the gate and the waters rushed through a shout went up from the waiting crowd, upon so memorable an event, which was the first triumph over the waters of the Oatka, and all joined in the festivities which followed.

It is not to be supposed that the new settlement was without its recreations and amusements. From the earliest period of its history general training was the great annual event, that brought from far and near all the settlers to enjoy its display and partake of its festivities. The first was held on the Ganson farm in 1801. At the meeting to organize the first company, after choosing Joseph Hewitt, captain ; Daniel Davis, lieutenant ; James Ganson, ensign ; and eight subalterns, there were but 10 men left for privates. But the general training took in the wide circuit of all the outlying settlements. It was held sometimes on the Ganson and Davis farms, and sometimes on the bank of the Oatka. It usually closed with a sham fight and often with a real one, particularly among the Indians, who were always out in " full feather " to imbibe the " fire water " and enjoy the sights. In the proper season for such gatherings " paring bees " for both sexes and raisings for the men was the hospitable custom, and good cheer and social enjoyment abounded. But terpsichore was by no means neglected. The fiddler of the period was Chapman Hawley, who made his first settlement on what is now the Vary farm, east of the village, and discoursed the music of the dance to the waiting and expectant company assembled for the purpose. This was usually in the ball room of the old Ganson tavern, the present residence, as has been stated, of Mr. Olmsted, where it can still be seen in its primitive state. If its walls could but speak what festive times would they reveal !

Northampton was the first name given to the township, and it embraced all of the territory west of the Genesee River. It has often been called by the early pioneers the town of "two rivers," from the fact of its being bounded on the east by the Genesee River and on the west by the Niagara. It had Lake Ontario for its northern boundry, and extended south to the Pennsylvania line. It is this broad extent of Northampton that gives interest to the infant settlement, of which this is but an imperfect outline. Its history begins when Buffalo was not, when Rochester was not, and when no intervening homestead had been planted in all of the territory. In 1789 a few adventurers had crossed the Genesee River and settled upon its border. Peter Shaefer opened a farm at the mouth of the

Oatka, bought of Ebenezer Allan before mentioned. He was soon followed by Isaac Scott, the beginner of Scottsville, and from whom it took its name. A Mr. Schoonover settled near the mouth of Dugan's Creek. Gilbert Berry was the first to establish a ferry over the Genesee at the site of the present bridge, and built a log house, where he opened trade with the Indian village of Canawaugus.

The first town meeting of this "empire" township was held at Big Springs (Caledonia), on April 4. 1797. The following were its officers: Gad Wadsworth, presided ; Josiah Fish, supervisor ; Eli Granger, town clerk ; Peter Shaefer, road commissioner and poormaster ; Isaac Scott, fence viewer ; and Hinds Chamberlin, constable. At a town meeting at the same place the following year $50 was voted for building the bridge over the Oatka, at a point which thus early was termed the "Buttermilk Falls," and the name here first appeared upon record. It was not until 1800 that the first tax was levied, for literally there was nothing previous subject to taxation. The roll contained 142 names, and of these 85 were assessed less than 50 cents each. The burden of the taxes was laid upon non-residents, there being but $200 assessed upon the settlers. Of these John Ganson, Sr., paid the largest, $2.10. and his son James the smallest, two cents, on a personality of $12. The "bloated capitalist" had not yet found his way in these parts. The total tax raised was $8,387. Contrast this with the millions now annually assessed and collected from the cities and counties which cover the territory.

In 1800 a census was taken (which was the first) by Gen. Amos Hall, the United States deputy marshal, under the census law of 1790. In the list is found the names of all the settlers from a mile west of Seneca Lake. The list shows from what small beginnings this large and populous district has sprung. The census enumeration was made soon after the act, and in it the only name found belonging to this section is that of John Ganson. The total of males in the enumeration was 728; females, 340; free blacks, 7 ; slaves, 9 ; total, 1,084.

In 1802 the county of Genesee was erected from the county of Ontario, and Batavia made the county seat. The office of the Holland Land Co. (which had completed its surveys) was also established there. By the same act which erected the county Northampton was divided, and this part took the name of Southampton.

Southampton.—The first meeting of the new township was held in March, 1802. Although shorn of its grand proportions it still embraced all there now is of Caledonia, Wheatland, and the territory south to the Pennsylvania line. At this meeting Christopher Layburn was chosen supervisor. Among the names of officers chosen from the Ganson settlement we find there James and John Ganson, Hinds Chamberlin, and Ezra Platt. Coming down as late as 1808 we find the following as justices of the peace in the new township: Richard M. Stoddard, Joseph Hewitt, Ezra Platt, John and James Ganson, who served early ; and later Amos Hall, Robert Nesbitt, Samuel Davis, Jeremiah Hascall, Asher Bates, S. Bates, David Davis, and G. H. and J. Fox.

Ezra Platt came into the settlement from Canandaigua in 1801–02. It was about the same period that Richard M. Stoddard accompanied him. He had married the daughter of Dudley Saltonstall. In May, 1801, Joseph Ellicott, acting as the special agent of Messrs. Le Roy and Bayard, employed Mr. Stoddard to survey the Triangular tract, giving minute directions, especially as to the laying off of 500 acres at "Buttermilk Falls." This same tract of 500 acres was in 1802 bought by Platt and Stoddard, which is now all covered by the village of Le Roy. The interest of Saltonstall in the purchase was sold to Ezra Platt, and Stoddard and Platt formed a copartnership and erected on the Oatka the first grist-mill west of the Genesee River. Mr. Platt was a popular and influential man in the rising community, and took a leading part in its improvement. He donated to the public the land for the park, christened by the Rev. Dr. Samuel Hanson Cox "Trigon," from its triangular shape, and built at his own expense a frame school-house on the site of the present Methodist parsonage. He was a lay-reader in the Sunday services held in the school-house before a church was organized. In his church relations he was an Episcopalian, and the first Episcopal baptism was of a child of his, by the Rev. Davenport Phelps, who was the first officiating minister of this church this side of the Genesee River.

Judge Platt was the first to receive the appointment of judge in the new Genesee County, from Governor Tompkins, and appointed with him were Judges John H. Jones and Benjamin Ellicott. Ezra Platt's original commission for judge is now in the possession of Walter H. Smith, a lawyer, of Le Roy. He died at an early age, in 1811, and left three sons, Elijah, Ezra, and George, and one daughter, the consort of Stephen A. Wolcott, all deceased. Mr. Wolcott came into the settlement from Geneva in 1802, and settled upon the present site of Ingham University. He was a builder, the first cabinetmaker, and put up a frame house for Samuel B. Walley—the oldest frame now standing in the village of Le Roy. It was removed by Mr. Austin, the first miller in Le Roy, to its present site, and now is the west wing of A. O. Comstock's residence on Trigon Park, in the village. Mr. Wolcott died in 1857 and left one son and three daughters, of whom but two survive, Mrs. Clarenda Buel, from whose reminiscences many facts herein narrated are obtained, and Miss Anne Wolcott. Both reside on the old homestead.

Richard M. Stoddard, in 1802, opened the first land office. He was the local agent of the "Triangle" tract. He erected the first building on the west side of the Oatka. It was built of logs, and its site was on the corner of Main and Mill streets, the site of Steuber's furniture store. He also erected a frame building on the site of the present Wiss House. Rufus Robertson and Samuel Deveaux occupied it first as a store, and afterwards Robertson as a public house. The house was enlarged by a Mr. Walbridge, and called the Globe and Eagle Hotel, so-called from the brazen sign of an eagle standing on a globe. Many now remember this glittering and conspicuous sign, which was the first to arrest attention in an approach to the village Among the early landlords succeeding Walbridge was Elisha Stanley, who was as noted as a good landlord as later in life as a good churchman. His nephew, John H. Stanley, was its landlord on the occasion of the first great State convention of the Anti Masons, held in Le Roy in 1827. It was presided over by Gen. William Wadsworth, and it was the beginning of the great party which spread over the State and Nation, and to which further allusion will be made. On this occasion there were three stands erected for the display of oratory, on which Solomon Southwick, afterwards nominated as the Anti-Masonic candidate for governor, held forth on the evils of Masonry in a speech of three hours.

Richard M. Stoddard was elected the first sheriff of Genesee County, and a wide jurisdiction was his for the service of a writ, and from which to summon a jury. As an illustration of the experience of the pioneer, from his Indian surroundings, an incident may be related of the Stoddard family while living upon the bank of the Oatka. Mrs. Stoddard, the wife of Richard, remembered as a woman of culture as well as of courage and resolution, was awakened at midnight by the sudden entrance into her house of a party of intoxicated Indians. Her husband at the time was absent at his mill. They entered her kitchen, made a large fire, and commenced a pow-wow as if they were masters of the premises. Mrs. Stoddard, who was in bed in another room, managed to get a little girl out of the window, who ran to the mill and gave the alarm. As Mr. Stoddard came into the house the Indians attacked him and a severe fight ensued. Mr. Stoddard was, however, the victor, and succeeded in expelling the intruders. Turner, in speaking of Stoddard, says that he was fearless and determined, and had seen much of frontier life, and few were better adapted to the work of settling a new country and becoming its chief executive officer. Notwithstanding the above conflict he was much esteemed by the Indians, and was often consulted by the chiefs. Mrs. Stoddard, too, redeems the Indian character from the disgrace of the drunken frolic by bearing witness to their interest and kindness in cases of sickness, particularly where it was required to administer the Indian "sweat." She related an occasion when her family were sick with a prevailing influenza. They dug holes in the ground, put in hot stones, over which they poured hot water, then placed the patients where they would receive the steam, and covering them with blankets suffered them to remain until the "sweating," of which there can be but little doubt was certain to effect the cure.

Mr. Stoddard continued his work of improvement and built a tavern on the site of the present Eagle Hotel. He died in 1810, and was greatly missed in the rising community for his public spirit and enterprise. His widow, with her son Thomas B., a lawyer, who is remembered by early residents now living, removed to Irving, Chautauqua County, where they resided until their decease. The only other surviving child at the time was a daughter, who married Hon. John B. Skinner, then a resident of Middlebury, and one of the most distinguished at the bar as an advocate and lawyer. He subsequently removed to Buffalo. He and his wife are since both deceased, and their remains rest in Forest Lawn of that city.

Graham Newell was the first lawyer settled in the place, and he succeeded Mr. Stoddard in the land office, his residence and office being the same as at present occupied by F. C. Lathrop

Daniel Davis was among the earliest of the pioneers. He, soon after his arrival, married Naomi Le Barron, who had emigrated to the settlement with the family of Philemon Nettleton from Killingworth, Conn., and it was the first marriage in the settlement, if not the first this side of the Genesee, and their daughter Naomi was the first child born in the settlement (1797). The marriage ceremony was performed by Charles Wilbur, the first justice of the peace. His commission was granted by Gov. Clinton, who, in the first State constitution, had the appointing power. Davis opened a farm two miles east of the Gansons. He had a passion for military life. As we have before remarked, in the first military organization, in 1801, on the Ganson place, he was chosen lieutenant. His military taste was destined to be displayed on a wider field. On the first declaration of war in 1812 he was among the first to enlist, and entering upon the field he was rapidly promoted for his coolness and bravery, until he obtained the rank of brigadier-general. It was in this capacity he acted in the command of the force at the sortie of Fort Erie, September 14, 1814. It was one of the bravest and most desperate encounters of the war. His coolness and courage were here especially conspicuous. He led in advance of his division with sword in hand ; and when warned not to ascend the parapet, did so, and was instantly and fatally shot in the neck and fell in the arms of his aid-de-camp. He was borne from the field and thence to his home for burial, where his remains now rest in the old cemetery east of the village. Thus ended a brilliant and promising career, at the early age of 37. His widow subsequently removed to Ypsilanti, Mich., where she survived him many years, and died there in a good old age

In the same ground are also found the remains of several who, in this desperate encounter on the frontier, offered their lives for their country. They deserve to be held in honored remembrance,—Capt. Daniel Buel, Nathan E Wilcox, Aaron Scribner, Nathaniel King John Sweatland, Darius Spring, Orange Judd, Orrin Datus Olds, William Olds. To these might be added others who lost their lives in the war by exposure : Ensign Platt, Pierson, Hubbard, Todd, and Porter Buell.

The honor of precedence in the first marriage in the Ganson settlement has to be divided with Gardner Carver and Lydia Davis, who, on the same occasion as the above, were joined in matrimony by the same justice.

Among a few of these earliest pioneers, of whom some will be further mentioned under the head of the different professions, was Asher Bates, who came from Canandaigua and settled here in 1801, on the farm opened by Hinds Chamberlin, known as the Sheldon farm. He died in 1810, and his widow became the wife of Dr. Sheldon. His son Asher, Jr., was a lawyer and became the attorney-general of the Sandwich Islands, and afterwards a judge in San Francisco, where some of his descendants are still living. Friend Hall was among the earliest comers, and opened the Murphy farm. Gilbert Hall had preceded him, in 1799, and opened a farm known as the Phelps farm adjoining the Buel place. At this period Mrs. Hall related that, in removing to her new home, but two white settlers were found at Big Spring. She said her heart failed her when she reached her rude cabin at the close of the day ; she had not even a door with which to protect her from the Indian intruders, with which the country was filled. She was, however, hospitably entertained by the first comer, Charles Wilbur. She died in 1825. Jabez Fox was among these early settlers, on what is known as the Cornell Williams place. And about the same time James Davis, Jr., came into the settlement. Among these early beginners on West Main street was Lyman Prindle, who built a dwelling on the present site of Dr. Barret's house ; on West Main street, in 1802, Richard Waite came in from Canandaigua and built and settled upon the Brewster place, now owned by F. C Lathrop. He was an exemplary Christian, and after the erection of his cabin opened it for Sunday worship whenever a supply could be found for its occupancy. He was the father of the late Daniel D. Waite, the sometime editor of the *Advocate* at Batavia, and his son, Elder Waite, has for a long time had charge of a Methodist Church at Alexander. Richard Waite died there in 1857. Capt. James Austin came into the place in the capacity of a miller, and removed the Walley house from the bank of the creek to the present site of A. O. Comstock's dwelling, and opened a public house. Thaddeus Keyes, the first tanner, settled at about the same time, on Trigon Park. Ebenezer Fox soon followed and opened here the first singing school, where it is said the first tune learned was " Concord." Aaron Scribner was an early resident, on what was afterwards the Hurlburt place. Among these early settlers was Samuel Davis, who owned and opened the Abial Robertson farm east of the village, and where his tragic end occured at a later period, and which many of our older residents will recall. He opened a tavern—as was almost every dwelling upon the road—for the accommodation of the incoming emigrant. This tragedy was upon the person of the landlord himself, who was killed in a brawl by Elijah Gray, Sr., and James, his son. Both were tried and convicted of the murder, the former sentenced for life (afterwards commuted), and the latter suffered the extreme penalty of the law, and was hung in Batavia, the last public execution witnessed in the county. This occurred in 1829 The remains of the murdered man were buried in a lot upon his own farm. One other trial for murder had preceded it in the county as early as 1807. It was that of the murder of William Orr by James McLean, who was tried before Daniel

D. Tompkins, then the presiding judge, when McLean was convicted and expia°ed his offence upon the gallows.°

There was at a somewhat later period another influx of immigrants. Jeremiah Hascall emigrated from Connecticut, and settled here in 1805, upon the farm east of the village, now known as "Dreamland," and owned and occupied by S. C. Wells. He had four sons, Jeremiah, Amasa, John, and Augustus P. (noticed more at length in "Bench and Bar"), and two daughters. Gen. Milo Hascall, now of Indiana, was a son of Amasa, a graduate of West Point, and a distinguished officer in in the late war. Herbert, a son of Augustus P., was also a graduate of West Point, and gallantly served in the civil war.

Major Simon Pierson, subsequently an officer in the War of 1812, came in 1808 and settled near Fort Hill, where he explored and exhumed the mysteries of the fort, which brought to light many Indian relics, found often below the largest trees, showing that it was of remote antiquity when "live" Indians occupied it as a fort. He died in 1864. He was in direct line of descent from Rev. Abraham Pierson, the first president of Yale College. Many of these relics are in the possession of Mr. Huftelen, a fancy florist of the town, and of F. C. Lathrop. The first blacksmith was Mr. Brown, opposite the Sheldon farm. There was, a little later, the advent of John Gilbert, also a blacksmith and axemaker, who settled upon the hill on West Main street. His son became in after life a distinguished portrait painter, whose work ranked high with artists, and who was settled in Rochester. It was with this blacksmith that the late Thomas C. Ladd came to serve as an apprentice, and learned his trade and settled here. His hospital for disabled and broken down vehicles was a conspicuous ornament for the east end of the village. But notwithstanding those standing monuments of "incapables" he was a good and faithful poormaster, and served the public and the poor in that capacity for many years to the satisfaction of both. George W. Blodgett was the pioneer saddler and harnessmaker, and settled the tract now occupied by his daughter, Mrs J. R. Anderson. Levi Farnham established the the first clothing business, and Thaddeus Keyes was the first tanner. Capt. Isaac Marsh built the first saw-mill. His son removed to Rochester and acquired eminence as a physician, especially as an oculist. In 1806 William Whiting came from Canandaigua and located on Main street, on the tract now occupied by a block of stores and the present Lampson House. About the same period Isaac Perry bought on the hill, which he sold to Jason Munn. John Hay was a pioneer stone mason, and evidences of his labor exist in the present stone structures (stuccoed): one, the first building west of the Oatka. north side of Main street, formerly occupied by John Champion, Sr., and one by Daniel Foster as a shoe store. He also built the first Episcopal Church. William Olmsted emigrated from Williamstown, Mass., in 1806. He married a widow Pierson, whose maiden name was Cynthia Franklin, said to have been related to the philosopher and patriot, Benjamin Franklin. Her first marriage was to John Pierson, who came in 1806 with what was called the Bergen colony, consisting of the Wards, Wilcoxes, Kelseys, Halls, Parmelees, and others. John Pierson died in 1812 from exposure on the frontier at the beginning of the war. The widow afterwards married Col. William Olmsted and died on his farm near Fort Hill, in her 89th year. His only surviving children are John R., a lawyer of this village, who married Elizabeth, the daughter of Oliver Allen, of Mumford ; and Charles and Egbert, residents upon the old homestead.

There was quite an accession of immigrants to the settlement from 1808 to the close of the war, but which space will allow of but casual mention. The names of many of them, during the earlier as well as the later period, will be found on another page. They will be found to cover what was then a single township ; but since the division a portion of the names will appear in what is now the towns of Pavilion, Bergen, and Stafford.

There was soon after the close of the war among the settlers in the town Dea. Clark Selden, upon the farm still occupied by his descendants. His sons that survived him were Edmond (since deceased), Stephen M., and Richard L. The latter has been conspicuous as a useful and efficient officer in' the town in various capacities. He served for a time with great acceptability in the office of school commissioner, and for repeated terms has been elected as its supervisor, where he served with ability and with the single aim of the interest of the town.

Libbeus Graves at about this time opened the farm afterwards sold by him to Isaac Crocker, three miles south and now in Pavilion. Mr. Crocker was from Colchester, Conn., and was a first-class farmer and highly esteemed as a citizen. His son. J. Lyman Crocker, who survives him, is an antiquarian, and zealous and industrious in preserving the records and traditions of our early settlement, and to whom the present writer is much indebted.

In general it may be remarked of the early settlers, although in scattered communities and miles apart, they were all neighbors, and in social intercourse all on the same footing, and were never wanting in acts of mutual kindness and hospitality. While the luxuries of modern life were few, the comforts were not wanting, and the average happiness of the rising community, it may be reasonably supposed, would compare favorably with the older portions of the East. It was, however, no asylum for drones or tramps (of which even the name was then unknown) to doze, and repose, and depredate.

The experience of Captain Daniel Ward, on his first advent to the settlement in 1810, was so similar to that of most of the earlier settlers of the period that it might, as an illustration, be briefly stated. Mr. Ward with his family came from Keene, N. H. His journey, with all his household effects, was with an ox-team. His point of location was on the farm, about 140 acres (three miles southeast of the village), on which he continued to reside until his decease in 1856, and which in his hands was converted from a wilderness into one of the finest farms in the county. What it was when he reached it is described by a descendant :

"The South Woods, so-called, was an almost impenetrable forest, and it was with great difficulty that a loaded team could be driven through it ; starting in the morning from Davis's tavern, in the settlement, they made slow progress, often stopping to clear logs out of the road, or pry up a wagon out of the mud, and they came to the end of their journey at 10 o'clock at night, consuming the whole day in traversing a distance of three miles, which was characteristic of the condition of the paths (so-called roads) at that time. Here the only improvement upon the place was a log house, without roof or floor, and one acre chopped ready for logging. In this skeleton of a house was spent the first night, the stars of heaven looking down upon them, their only canopy. The captain's first income was from the ashes sold from their log heap, and was 75 cents, as he often said, "the best and most prized of any money that I ever had." It may be remarked that at this period the only products that brought in money were black salts and potash, which were transported to Eastern markets *via* Lake Ontario, the St. Lawrence, and Montreal. Capt. Ward was a man of the strictest integrity, was highly esteemed for his Christian virtues, and lived to enjoy an ample reward for his persever-ance and toil, not only by the acquisition of a competence, but the satisfaction of con-verting the wilderness into one of the finest and most productive farms in the country."

Capt. Ward died on his place in 1856 at the age of 74 years.

Capt. John Ganson, Sr., died in 1813, at the home of his son John, Jr., at the age of 63 years, leaving three sons and a daughter before men-tioned. The following quaint epitaph was at the time engraved upon his tombstone (transported from Albany), now in Maplewood Cemetery, where his remains have been removed :

" In trackless climes he bent his weary way,
Where perils prowled, and wild beasts lurked for prey ;
By perseverance and industrious toil
Laid low the forests and made the desert smile,
Till low in death he laid his weary head—
Beloved while living, and revered now dead."

His grandson, Dr. Holton Ganson, by a provision in his will, caused a beautiful monument to be erected to his memory in the Machpelah Ceme-tery. James, the eldest of the Captain's sons, figured conspicuously in the early settlement. He married Luseba Scott, a daughter of the Isaac Scott before mentioned, and by her he was the father of nine children, six sons (John S., Joseph, Hiram, Corneal, Cornelius, and William) and three daughters. The widow survived to her 85th year. She removed to Buffalo, and died at the home of her eldest son, John S. Ganson, a prominent banker of that city. The sons were active business men in their respective callings, and none of his children now survive.

In 1819 he built and kept the present Eagle (on the site of the old) Hotel on Main street, from brick furnished by Uni Hurlburt, the first brickmaker. The tavern on this site had been previously kept by Auntie Wemple, who afterwards kept a boarding-house in the dwelling occupied by A. O. Comstock. He also built a tavern on the corner of Main and North streets, now the residence of Mrs. R. L. Sampson, and sold it to Mr Hosmer, of Avon. He was during his life a prominent and active politician, and became conspicuous as one of the defendants in the Masonic trials for the abduction of Morgan, in 1826, in which trial he was acquitted. He subsequently removed to Jackson, Mich., and died at an advanced age.

John Ganson, Jr., the keeper of the Ganson tavern, married, in 1808, Lucy, a daughter of David Anderson, who had the year previous come into the settlement from Northampton, Mass., and who made his first home in Middlebury. He afterwards settled here on what was known as the Deming farm. Deacon Anderson was of Scotch descent, of the true "Kirk and Covenant stamp," and brought his influence and example to tell largely upon the new community. He conducted the first religious services held in Middlebury,—then in a barn,—and the settlers for miles around would gather in to hear the good Deacon exhort, and sing, and pray. He was one of the nine who, in 1812, organized the First Presbyterian Church Society in this village. The Deacon was the father of the late Dea. Seneca Anderson, of Le Roy, who was the father of the Rev. Dr. Galusha Anderson, who holds a distinguished place in the Baptist denomination. Deacon Anderson subsequently removed to Chautauqua County, where he died at an advanced age, always respected for his exemplary Christian character and great moral worth. John Ganson, Jr., died in 1819, at the age of 43, leaving a widow and three sons, Holton, James, and John, whom she survived to see arrive at men's estate and occupy honorable places in the world. The widow married, in 1821, Israel Rathbone, a former resident and merchant of Lewiston, N. Y. Dr. Holton Ganson became a leading practitioner in Batavia, of whom a fuller notice will be found under the head of physicians of the county. James M. Ganson was, until his decease, the president of one of the leading banks of Buffalo. He died in that city in 1883.

Of the youngest son, John, it will not be out of place to speak more at length, as he in after life became a public man of position and influence in the State. At the age of 17 he entered Harvard University, where he graduated at the age of 22, and commenced his law studies in the law office of Mark H. Sibley, in Canandaigua. Soon after his admission to the bar he removed to Buffalo and entered upon the practice of the law, and rose rapidly in his profession, and as an industrious, conscientious, and able lawyer attained the first rank among his compeers Mr. Ganson was elected State Senator in 1861 and again in 1873. He was elected to the 68th Congress in 1863, where he became conspicuous among the few who placed their country before party. Although a Democrat he supported with ability every war measure of President Lincoln's, even his Emancipation Proclamation, and in all of his votes was for a vigorous prosecution of the war until the Rebellion was suppressed and the Union restored. At the time of his death he had been prominently named as the Democratic candidate for governor, a nomination which he would doubtless have received, possibly followed by higher honors, had he lived. Mr. Ganson died suddenly in September, 1874, from a paralytic stroke which he received while trying a case in the court-house at Buffalo. His wife, the daughter of the Hon. Mark H. Sibley, of Canandaigua, and a daughter Emily survived him.

The only remaining son of John Ganson, Jr., was Benjamin, who took part in the War of 1812. On his decease he left a son Chandler, also a daughter who married the late Col. J. W. Shedd, neither of whom now survive. The only living representative here of Captain Ganson, Sr., is a daughter, Mrs. Luseba Ballard, the mother of Randolph Ballard, Esq., a lawyer in the village.

Game, etc —The country abounded in game. The deer was at their very doors. The more dreaded bear was a frequent but not so welcome a visitor. It is related that on an occasion soon after the removal of Joseph Annin from East to West Main street, to his store (burnt in the great fire of 1854), that a bear with two cubs made an unceremonious call. A clerk seized a musket, pursued the intruders, and brought back with him a cub which he had shot down in the encounter. It is not recorded whether these grizzly customers returned for another charge.

More destructive and a greater enemy to the settler was the large number of wolves which abounded. Their hides were quite a source of income to the hunter. A bounty of $1 per hide was first offered, which was increased until it reached, in 1810, $10 per hide, such was the havoc of the wolves among the herds. Among the pestilential intruders, into even the cabins and cellars of the settlers, was the rattle snake. An innocuous instance is given of one of the intruders which shows that, as venomous as it is, it has the power to charm. It was in the family of a Mr. Douglass, whose little daughter, accustomed to go out in the field to play, was on one occasion forbidden by her mother, but who yielded to the importunity of the child, who said she had a kitten she wished to play with. The mother's curiosity induced her to watch the child, when to her alarm and horror she saw a " rattler " partaking of milk from the same dish with the daughter. The little one was cautiously called away and the species of a " pet kitten " quietly disposed of.

The following is a list, as accurate as we are able to make it, of the early settlers of Le Roy, up to 1820:

Alexander Anderson, Joseph Austin, David Anderson, Joel Butler, Thankful Buell, Edmund Beach, Jonas Bartlett, Christopher Cadman, Joseph Cook, Amasa Clapp (lot 141), Lee Comstock, Augustus H. Ely, Henry Goodenow, Ezekiel Hall, Israel Herrick, William Holbrook, John Hoy, Asenath Judd, George Laramy, Moses McCollum, Alfred Morehouse, Zalmon Owen, David W. Parmalee, Ebenezer Parmalee, Russel Pierson, Daniel Pierson, Elias Peck, Martha Richardson, Heman J. Redfield, James Roberts, Thomas Severance, Thomas Studley, Stephen Stillwell, Samuel Skinner, Orange Scott, Capt. William Thomas, Joy Ward, Benjamin Webb, Auntie Wemple, Jonathan Wright, Daniel Woodward. In 1797, Charles Wilbur. In 1798, Daniel Buell, Hinds Chamberlin, John Ganson. In 1799, Gen. Daniel Davis, Gilbert Hall, Joseph Hewitt, Philemon Nettleton. In 1800, Jesse Beach, Philip Beach, Capt. Jotham Curtis, Gardner Carver, Col. Norton S. Davis, David Le Barron, Francis Le Barron. In 1801, Dudley Saltonstall, Richard M. Stoddard. In 1802, Phineas Bates (justice), Asher Bates, S. Bates, David Davis, Cyrus Douglass, Dr. David Fairchild, Jabez Fox, E. Green, Amos Hall, Friend Hall, Chapman Hawley (fiddler), Nathan Harvey, A. McPherson, Abel Nettleton, Ezra Platt, Lyman Prindle, —— Scofield, Amzi Stoughton, Richard Waite, Stephen A. Wolcott. In 1803, Capt. James Austin (first miller), Dr. William Coe, Calvin Davis, Samuel Davis, James Davis, Jr., Thaddeus Keyes, John McPherson, Aaron Scribner, Samuel B. Walley, Daniel White, David White. In 1804, G. Fox, Allen and Alexander McPherson. In 1805, Gideon Fordham, John Franklin, Jeremiah Hascall, Jacob McCollum, Robert Nesbit, Dr. Ella Smith, Capt. David Scott. In 1806, Asa Buell, Moses Lilly, Col. William Olmsted, Isaac Perry, John Pierson, William Whiting, George A. Tiffany. In 1807, G. W. Blodgett (harnessmaker), David Emmons, Jason Munn, Philo Pierson, Simon Pierson (author). In 1808, Abram Butterfield, Ithamar Coe, John Elliott, Dr. Fred Fitch, Dr. Benjamin Hill, Capt. Theo. Joy, H. Johnson, Silas Lawrence, D. P. Mirl, Hugh Murphy, Maj. Simon Pierson, R. Sinclair, Stephen P. Wilcox, Maj. Nathan Wilcox. In 1809, Harry and Timothy Backus, James Goble, Ebenezer Niles. In 1810, Salmon Butler, Chester Barrows, Willis Buell, Ward Beckley, Jacob Coe, Silas Fordham, William Harris, Seth Harris, Martin Kelsey, Uriah Kelsey, James McPherson, Jr., Capt. Isaac Marsh, Graham Newell, Stephen Olmsted (taught school at Fort Hill), Elias Parmalee, Harvey Prindle, Dr. Chauncey P. Smith Dr. William Sheldon, Thaddeus Stanley, Alanson Stanley, J. Harlow Stanley, Thomas Tufts, Thomas Warner, Chester Waite, Capt. John Webb, Washington Weld. In 1811, Joseph Annin, Abraham Buckley, Nathan Bannister, Joseph Curtis, Levi Farnham, Julius Griswold, Samuel Gilbert, Ebenezer Lawrence, Pliny Sanderson, Elisha Stanley, Dea. John Thwing, Stephen Taylor, Stephen Walkley. In 1812, Azor Curtis, F. Campbell, Martin O. Coe, David Gustin, Ebbe Hull, Abner Hull, Daniel Huggins, C. Kelsey, Lyman Mills, William Morgan, Preserved Richmond, Rufus Robertson, G. Terry, Zalmon Turrell, Charles Warren, Elijah Warner, Daniel Waite, J. Wheeler. In 1813, L. Fowler, John Lent, Henry Prindle, Orange Risdon, Moses Todd, Benoni Webb. In 1814, Levi Beardsley, William Le Roy Bishop, Manley Colton, Paul E. Day, John Gilbert, P. McVane, Abel Noyes, John Richards, Elisha Severance, A. Williams. In 1815, Jeremiah Buell, James Ballard, James Campbell, John Deming, Daniel Foster, Timothy Fitch, W. G. Gustin, Harry Holmes, Timothy Hatch, Joseph Keeney, Marshfield Parsons, Joseph Tompkins. In 1816, Versal Bannister, Isaac Crocker, Elijah Crocker, Jacob Gallup, Daniel Harris, Timothy Judd, Harry Lathrop, Solomon Root, Dea Clark Selden, Elliott L. Stanley, Joel White, Parker Weld. In 1817, C. Butler, Nathaniel Farnham, E. Hart. Uni Hurlburt, A. Perry. In 1818, Samuel Bishop, Silas Jones, Miles P. Lampson, Thomas C. Ladd, Charles Morgan S. Tiffany, Levi Ward, Jr. In 1819, Dr. S. O. Almy, Albert Hill. In 1820, S. M. Gates, Daniel Le Barron.

LE ROY village was incorporated in May, 1834. The first meeting was held to take action on incorporation at the Eagle Hotel, Theodore Dwight, proprietor; Hinds Chamberlin presided Seth M. Gates was acting clerk. They adjourned to July 12th, when an election was held and the following trustees chosen: Joshua Lathrop, John Lent, Rufus Robertson, Theodore Dwight, and Dennis Blakely. S. M. Gates was chosen clerk, H. J. Redfield, treasurer. The trustees for 1890 are Isaac G. Mason, George M. Howe, Reuben Glass, Frank E. Gooding, and Thomas B. Tuttle. S. D. Gilbert is clerk, and John Wiss, treasurer.

Postoffices.—A word may be added of the early postoffices and post-masters. Previous to 1804 there was no mail service in the settlement, and no postoffice nearer than Canandaigua, and letters and papers were sent and delivered by private hands. Asher Bates was the first post-master. R. M. Stoddard succeeded in 1808; James Ganson in 1809; and he by Samuel Deveaux, who held the office until 1815. Mr. De-veaux was in trade with Rufus Robertson. Their place of business was on the corner of Main and Lake streets. He removed from here in 1815 to Niagara Falls, where he accumulated a large estate, the whole of which he devised for the foundation and support of the present Deveaux College, at the Falls, under the trusteeship of the Episcopal Church of the diocese. Hon. H. J. Redfield was his successor, and held it until his removal to Batavia.

The Erie Canal.—This was finally accomplished and the first boat launched on the first day of October, 1825. It was a memorable day for the State and Nation. It was literally " a dayspring from on high " which had visited the people, giving life and light to a vast country virtually shut out from commercial intercourse with Eastern markets. Before this great event from 25 to 35 cents per bushel was all that wheat would command to the producer here, and transportation to Eastern markets was so slow and costly that it was practically excluded. The ordinary mode was, as has been said, by "big teams," made up from five to seven horses, and a night and day line, which in the round trip occupied from three to four weeks. The old State road, built in 1820, was the principal thoroughfare. The teamsters were a hardy race, and camped and lived in their " schooners," and knew the route as " seamen know the sea." No wonder that the opening of the Erie Canal was an auspicious day for this secluded garden of the West. It was a literal " boom." The cannon on the morn of its opening, beginning at Black Rock, commenced the boom, which, planted along the line, continued the joyful sound until its last echo was lost at the ocean tide, which evermore was to be enriched by the commerce which it brought to its bosom. It was during this revival season from 1826 on, and for a few years following, that many business firms were established in the place, of which but brief notices can here be made. A half a century ago there were in active business the following, in their several branches, in Le Roy, and others are necessarily omitted.

Merchants.—Of the early merchants R. M. Stoddard was the first to introduce a few goods, but no regular store was opened in the settlement until 1806. George F. Tiffany was the first regular merchant. He commenced trade on the east side of the Oatka, near or on the present university grounds. Philo Pierson was also an early merchant, on the corner of Main and North streets. He died in 1820, leaving five children. His widow afterwards married Capt. Hatch, one of the first wardens of St. Mark's Church. Daniel, his second son, married a daughter of Joshua Lathrop, and moved to Cincinnati, where he died about 1888. He was a very prominent lumber merchant, noted for great business capacity and integrity. His widow still resides there. About the same time a store was opened by David Emmons. It was but a short time after that Capt. Theodore Joy settled and entered into trade, and became the most noted of the early merchants. It was the day of "big teams," and was the only mode of land transportation between the East and this outlying West. Turner says of him that thus early his teams were known on the whole route to Albany. He built here the first brick store, a part of the present dwelling of the late C. B. Thomson, on the corner of East Main and Church streets. He subsequently removed to Albany, where he became prominent in the transportation business, and was succeeded by Lay & Co. (Hart & Lay), whose large and conspicuous sign upon the side of the building remained long after it was disused as a store. M. & B. Murphy built a store near the corner of East Main and Wolcott streets, and became among the early merchants. James Annin came into the town from West Bloomfield in 1811, and commenced trade near the same locality, but these latter merchants removed their business to the west side of Main street when it was discovered that business was to abandon the east and center upon the west side of the Oatka. Mr. Annin continued in the mercantile trade until his decease. His place of business was on the north side of West Main street, on the site of the present store of S. Loucks. He was a veritable Isaak Walton in his skill and taste in capturing the trout of the "Big Springs." Those who have belief in heredity will find it illustrated in his descendants, particularly in that skillful angler, his son James, and in his grandson James, Jr., who holds domain and dispenses the "beauties" to grateful guests at the world-noted springs. The game was not quite so abundant and tame as in 1803 if we credit what Mr. McKay says of them:

"They [the trout] were frequently so tame we caught them with our hands as they lay under the cedar trees. There would be occasionally one weighing three pounds."

Mr. Annin died in 1835, and of the children who survive are William L., George, Joseph, James, and Catharine, wife of the late Mr. Bryant, of Washington, D. C. William L. was the first child born in Le Roy after its incorporation. Lewis M. Gates and William Bradley (Gates & Bradley) were the last to continue business on the east side of Main street. It was in the brick store, corner of Wolcott and Main streets, which at a later period was abandoned and converted at first into a land office, next into schools, and last into a blacksmith shop, which was finally demolished to open a more extensive western vista from the university grounds. Thomas Tufts came into the settlement to reside in 1810, as land agent for the Craigie tract. He built and opened a store and a tavern on West Main street, nearly opposite the Lent place. He also built a dwelling house near by, now occupied by Mr. Walker. He continued in business for several years, and on his decease left but one son, Thomas, who now survives.

It would be an imperfect sketch of Le Roy if no mention was made of that intermediate class of merchants and business men, who occupied conspicuous places and made Le Roy what it is, between the pioneer and the present period of its history. The beginning of its prosperity, like that of this whole Western domain, takes its date from the completion of the Erie Canal.

Dry goods and general merchants.—Lampson & Co. (the Co.: Samuel Skinner and John Lent), L. S. Bacon & Co. (the Co.: John P. Mitchell and J. G. Bixby), Comstock & Co. (the Co.: Deacon Comstock and his son Otis A.; later A. O. Comstock and Chauncey L. Olmsted), S. W. Carpenter & Co., A. L. Stevens & Co., A. B. Murphy & J. Whitney (afterwards I. B. Browning & S. C. Kelsey), Thomas & Parks, Barron & Kneeland, Champion Brothers, Tompkins, Morgan & Co. (the successors of Lampson & Co.); later Morgan & Jackson, succeeded by Charles Morgan, who for 50 years was in continuous mercantile business, and justly

30

won on his retirement the reputation of an honorable and capable merchant. Following later was Adam Pratt and William P. Rathbone. The only survivors of the above, still residents here, are A. O. Comstock and Charles Morgan. Samuel F. Comstock might be added, as at one time he was partner with his brother A. Otis. Among later firms was one established by the late Jonathan M. Foreman, who came in 1854. He was partner of Henry Starr. The business was then carried on by F. W. Foreman (a son) and Washington Tryon (now of Toledo), and afterwards by Foreman & Rider. Mr. Foreman, Sr., died in January, 1890, at the age of 86. He was a prominent and useful citizen, and held many offices of public trust, which he discharged with ability and integrity. For 16 years he was justice of the peace, and also held other offices.

Grocers.—S. Chamberlin,—afterwards Chamberlin & Henry Starr,—Ralph Lord, Elijah Gray, and F. W. & G. W. Drake.

Hardware.—Bacon & Mitchell, succeeded by Frank W. Drake, who became the successful railroad millionaire, now of Corning, N. Y.; E. Walker & Co., succeeded by J. G. Bixby and A. G. Carpenter ; and Darling & Grannis.

Harness and saddlers. — Newman & Dodge (succeeded by Jacob Newman) and B. R. Crane.

Shoemaker.—Capt. Daniel Foster.

Leather.—Shedd & Ganson (J. W. Shedd and Chandler Ganson).

Jewelers.—Horatio Stanley and Russel & Sampson.

Carriagemakers.—A. S. Upham and Thomas Ladd.

Plows, etc.—Azor Curtis and Webb & Cowan.

Cabinetware.—Howard Bosworth, Loring Pratt, and Steuber Brothers.

Landlords.—Isaac Dwight, succeeded by Powell Carpenter, in the Eagle ; J. H. Stanley and Elisha Stanley, and later Lyman Ballard, in the Globe and Eagle.

Druggist —J. G. Barbor.

Of the above names, who contributed largely to build up the business of the town during this intermediate period, many had marked characteristics, but in the limits here assigned but a few only can be noted.

Miles P. Lampson was born in New Haven, Vt., came to Le Roy when a young man, and engaged, first, as a school teacher and afterwards as clerk in the store of Thomas Tufts. He early entered into mercantile business with Capt. John Lent, and afterwards was associated with Samuel Skinner (a lawyer of the village), which from the beginning was a successful firm. Mr. Lampson possessed those natural qualities which commanded success. He was of sound judgment, industrious and persevering, prudent and frugal, and of strict integrity and honor in all of his business intercourse. He was at the same time sagacious in embracing opportunities for the increase of his estate, and in this he was successful. Retiring from the mercantile business he organized the first bank in Le Roy, in 1838 (the Genesee County Bank), of which he was the first cashier, soon after its president, and its sole financial officer. A full account of this bank will be found under its proper head. His connection with the bank under its different forms continued during the remainder of his life, as president, and under his chief control and management, with the satisfaction that no losses of moment ever occurred ; and in the change of the same to the " First National " the capital was all restored to the stockholders. Mr. Lampson died in March, 1869, at the age of 75, leaving a widow, since deceased, and three sons, only two of whom, William and Miles, still live.

Capt. John Lent was a man of less education, but of natural abilities of a superior order and of great force of character. He came into the village from Easton, Washington County, in 1813, and commenced keeping a public house, built by Thomas Tufts, the present homestead of the Lent estate, and engaged at once in land and other enterprises with such sagacity and judgment as soon to accumulate a handsome estate for the period. He was somewhat eccentric, and although eminently social in his nature cared little for the amenities or usages of society, but more for accumulation, of which he was proficient in whatever enterprise he engaged. He prided himself upon his just dealing, and that his " word was always as good as his bond." He died, and was buried in a private vault on his own grounds, in 1861, at the age af 78, and left a son John, since deceased, whose widow is now the consort of Gen. C F. Bissell, who resides on the old homestead at the west end of the village.

Lathrop S. Bacon, during his entire business career, was always termed a " live " man, from his activity and enterprise. He was born in Hamilton, N. Y., in 1810, and from thence removed with his father, Rufus Bacon, to Le Roy, in 1830, and entered at once into the business of general merchandise. This was soon known, for he gave extensive publicity to his business and soon commanded a large trade from surrounding and even distant towns. He literally gave a " boom " to the business of the village, which did not subside until his final retirement. He was subsequently associated with John P. Mitchell, and later with J. G. Bixby, under the firm name of L. S. Bacon & Co. In 1840 he commenced the establishment of a stove foundry in the village, which he continued to extend and enlarge until it became the most extensive industry in the county. The cook stove known as the Clinton Elevated, and the self-regulating sheet-iron parlor stove, were of his invention, and they became leading and popular and commanded a large sale in this and the Western States. Mr. Mitchell became associated with him in the manufacture, and later D. R. Bacon, under the firm name of L. S. Bacon & Co. The sudden death of his two children, by a camphine lamp explosion, rendered his residence in Le Roy distasteful, and he removed to Rochester, where he built up the present iron works in Ontario, and in 1850 closed his connection with the foundry at Le Roy by a sale to Harry Backus, and the business for a few years longer was carried on by the firm name of Backus & Bacon, when in 1854 it was closed, and this industry here has not since been revived. L. S. Bacon was for a time president of the Eagle Bank in Rochester, but he soon left for England to establish the manufacture of India rubber goods, which business proved a marked success. Owing to the misuse of the firm's name by a partner, after Mr. Bacon's retirement, he suffered a financial reverse, from which he did not fully recover. He retired and spent the closing period of his life in Florence, Italy, where he became prostrated by a stroke of paralysis, which, being repeated by a second attack, permanently disabled him both in mind and body. He returned to this country with his wife and retired to Michigan, where he died in his 68th year; and in all his relations of life he was held in high regard for his superior qualities of head and heart. His wife did not long survive him, and they both rest by the side of their children in Machpelah Cemetery.

Chauncey L. Olmsted, a partner of A. O. Comstock in the days of the most lively boom in the trade of the villages, of which they were not behind in giving it an impetus, on his retirement from the firm became noted for his enterprise and business energy. He established and built up the planing and lumber business now owned and conducted by Murdock Brothers, on Mill street. Two disastrous fires of his mill and works did not quell his energy. They were rebuilt on an extended scale and became the largest of the class in the county. The works were continued under his brother William, while he engaged largely in the lumber trade West. Mr Olmsted took a lively interest in all of the improvements of the town, toward which he always was a liberal contributor, whether in church or schools. Of the latter he showed his generous intentions by making for them liberal provision, of which the subsequent change in times rendered it unavailable. At his decease he left a widow, and a son, Albert C., now a resident of Batavia, and a daughter, Mary, who still survive him.

· There was Dea. Samuel Comstock, who removed with his family from Colchester, Conn , in 1834, and engaged in the mercantile business with his son Otis A. Their enterprise soon secured a large trade, and it soon became one of the leading business firms of the community. The Deacon was an honorable competitor and justly merited the soubriquet always accorded to him of the "honest deacon." He was always scrupulously just, and foremost in every good and benevolent work. He was the organizer and founder of the Congregational Church in the village, subsequently merged in the Presbyterian, and was a deacon until his decease, at the age of 79. His children that survive him are Otis A , Samuel F., and a daughter Elizabeth.

As the Hon. Alonzo S. Upham filled a conspicuous place in the village, and subsequently in the State, a brief reference to him will not be out of place. It was in 1832 that he removed from Onondaga County, where he had recently married Mary, daughter of Deacon Monroe, and commenced here the business of carriagemaking on a scale hitherto unknown in this section. He soon obtained a wide reputation through the county as a skilled and tasteful workman, and with a fine address became a popular citizen. He early was identified with the Whig party, and was during its life an ardent supporter of Henry Clay. When the Whig became merged into the Republican party he followed its fortunes, and his first political honor was in his election to the Assembly by that party in 1847, and again in 1848, where, by his address, he soon ingratiated himself into the favor of the Weed-Seward branch of the party, and became one of their trusted leaders This was increased upon his nomination and election to the State Senate in 1850, and again in 1854, when he was a recognized leader of the party in the State, and influential in its counsels. He was an adroit politician and skilled in the management of caucuses and conventions. In his later senatorial career he became an important and efficient aid in carrying measures favorable to the interests of the N. Y. C. & H. R. Railroad, by which he received from the company his reward in obtaining contracts for building cars for the road. This led to the establishment and construction of the stone buildings for his works in the village, since converted into the present malt-houses. Failing in an election for a third term in the Senate, in consequence of the popular prejudice against railroad influence in legislation, the further construction of cars for the road was withdrawn, and in consequence the business and the works collapsed. Mr. Upham thus became financially embarrassed, from which he failed to recover. In his prosperity he was noted for his geniality, his open-handed liberality, and his devotion to his friends, as well as his public spirit and diffuse hospitality. He obtained a situation in the custom-house in New York, where he remained until his decease.

Physicians.—We pass to a brief notice of the first physicians. Dr. William Coe was the first settled practitioner. He came in 1803. He was not so wholly engrossed in professional duties but that he could devote a portion of his time, particularly evenings, in teaching some of the higher branches of instruction. Dr. Ella Smith came in soon after and settled on the now Blodgett farm. Dr. Frederick Fitch commenced practice in 1808. He was of an eccentric character, and fond of military display. On an occasion of general training, wishing to display his skill in sword exercise, he wounded himself in the leg, which resulted in requiring an amputation of the limb. He was a skillful practitioner, and he built the house where Jacob Newman formerly and now Rev. Mr. Bowden resides. He formed a copartnership with Dr. Sheldon in the practice in the village, and subsequently removed to Ypsilanti, Mich., where he died. His son, Newell Fitch, remained, but subsequently removed to Logansport, Ind , and had in his adopted State a distinguished career. He took for his wife, before his departure, Hattie Satterlee, of this village. He was elected U. S. Senator from Indiana, served also in the war of the Rebellion, and attained the rank of major-general. Their son married a daughter of Gen. W. T. Sherman. Dr. Chauncey P Smith came into the place early in 1810.

Dr. William Sheldon removed from Rupert, Benningtom County, Vt., and traveled on horseback until he reached the Ganson tavern, where he stopped for the night, designing to pursue his journey westward in the morning. His last dollar was exhausted. During the night a sickness occurred in the family which he was called upon to treat, and by their importunity was prevailed upon to remain and settle here, and enter upon his practice. The following year he married the widow of Asher Bates, and soon became a successful practitioner. When in 1812 the war with Great Britian was declared he entered into the service and received the commission of captain of a volunteer company, and left for the frontier for service. He was made aid-de-camp of Gen. Daniel Davis, his fellow townsman, and was by his side, as before stated, in the gallant sortie at Fort Erie. The Doctor himself, in the skirmish at Black Rock, was wounded and taken prisoner, and carried to Montreal, where he was kept six months in prison, and his treatment was not such as to mollify his feeling toward the redcoats, which was decidedly anti-English during his life-time. He served during the whole war and was in seven different engagements. On the organization of the town of Le Roy Dr. Sheldon was chosen the first supervisor, and again in 1818. He was appointed by Governor Tompkins sheriff of the new county of Genesee, and was subsequently reäppointed, an evidence of his ability and fidelity. He died at the age of 85, and left three sons, Lucius, William, and Horatio, all of whom are still living

The name of S. O. Almy, associated in practice with Dr. Alfred Wilcox, calls up one of the most genial, kind-hearted, as well as capable, physicians of the medical profession. He had a large practice until his retirement, temporarily to Cincinnati, from which place he returned under a mental cloud. His host of friends were saddened from his prostration by a paralytic stroke, from which he never recovered, but lived many years, his mind and body both shattered by its effects, until his decease a few years ago. Among the cotemporary practitioners, and a little later, there were Bliss and Pratt, and Tozier, and the Barretts, and Dr. Smith, of whom full notice appears under the county head of the profession.

Lawyers.—Of the early members of the legal profession the name of Graham Newell has been mentioned as the first practitioner. Hon. Heman J. Redfield early opened a law office in Le Roy, on the corner of East Main and North streets, and continued in the practice here until his removal to Batavia, in 1835, as law counsel of the Holland Land Co. He was an active and prominent politician of the Democratic faith, and in 1823, '24, and '25 was a State Senator from the old Eighth District. His popularity was temporarily impaired by his vote on the electoral law of the State, giving to the people the election of their electors, and by his vote for the postponement of the law became one of the immortal 17 senators. He, however, continued to be a leading member of his party, and in 1853 was appointed by President Pierce collector of the port of New York. Samuel B. Skinner, Seth M. Gates (who later and after his election to Congress formed a law partnership with D. R. Bacon under the firm name of Gates & Bacon), Hon. Augustus P. Hascall (who served one term in Congress), Alfred F. Bartow, Charles Danforth, Perrin M. Smith (who, after his removal to Michigan, was a prominent judge), and James Sumerfield were all practitioners in Le Roy, and have all passed away except Mr. Bacon, who retired from the profession. Of the present living members of the profession there will be found full notices under the appropriate head.

In 1807 the name of the town was changed to Caledonia, which it retained until 1811, when it received the name of Bellona, so-called from the goddess of war, and not inappropriately, as every able-bodied man had, with musket on shoulder, gone to the war, leaving the women-folk alone to tend the farms, and to guard and protect the homes.

The War of 1812.—It is at this day impossible to conceive the panic which pervaded this whole border region on the news of the declaration of war in the summer of 1812. It was first feared that the Senecas would side with the British as they had in the war of the Revolution. This was allayed by the influence and eloquence of Red Jacket and Cornplanter, first by a promise of neutrality, followed by an alliance of the tribe with the American forces, and who afterwards rendered to our arms important and effectual aid But the special dread was of an invasion from Canada, where the British were in large force upon the border. But the invasion never came. The fear of it was equally great on the Canada side. This singular apprehension of mutual invasion was at once our safeguard and protection. And it was one of these instances, often recorded in the history of wars both great and small, where "one was afraid and the other durst n't." But there was enough of war excitement to keep alive the sharpest watchfulness and interest in what was transpiring on the border where the hostile forces were arrayed face to face. This was greatly intensified by the ill-timed and censurable surrender of Fort Niagara and the burning of Newark, now the village of Niagara Falls, by General McClure, of the New York militia. Its retaliation was at once followed by the successful attack upon Black Rock and the burning of the village of Buffalo by the British force. It was a wanton and cowardly act, for it was committed in violation of a flag of truce, after General Riel, the commandant of the English, had accepted the surrender and promised protection to the feeble colony. But the destruction was complete, only one house, that of Mrs. Jones, remained standing. This occurred in midwinter, December 31, 1813, and the defenceless inhabitants, including delicate women and young children, were driven into the snow-bound forests to find home and shelter in the outlying settlements of the interior. These were cheerfully given, and the rites of hospitality to the houseless sufferers were in no place more cheerfully accorded than to those who reached Le Roy.

Never was hospitality more general or more needed. It was extended to the Tuscaroras, whose cabins had not escaped the British torch. They came to the Ganson settlement, where they were provided with camping-ground, on what is now Lime Rock, three miles east, and were supplied with provisions by the settlers and in part by the commissary of the public stores.

But it was not always adverse news. The settlement had its days of rejoicing. The achievements and success of Commodore Perry upon the lakes created a thrill of joy. This was greatly enhanced when the signal success of our arms at the battle of Lundy's Lane, sometimes called the Niagara Falls battle and Chippewa, under the command of General Brown and the late Gen. Winfield Scott, was here proclaimed. It was here General Scott won his spurs. He received a wound in the battle, from which he never fully recovered, and was borne in a litter to the Ganson tavern, where all turned out to do him honor, and those who came never forgot his manly form and martial bearing, characteristics which distinguished him through life.

The war of the Rebellion belongs to general history, and is too modern for any extended notice in this sketch of our early annals. It should not be entirely passed over, as Le Roy was made conspicious by its being designated as a point for a recruiting camp by the military authority of the State. In March, 1861, Governor Morgan ordered its organization here, and it was opened for this purpose under the designation of Camp Upham, in one of his abandoned car shops. Immediately over the whole western district the most active efforts were put forth by our patriotic citizens for enlistments to fill up and complete the regiment. The camp was under the immediate charge of Rev. J. M. Fuller, an earnest and eloquent platform orator on the Union's cause, who earnestly engaged in enlistments, assisted by Maj. J. W. Shedd, Col. Grey, and the captains of the several companies. It was stirring times in Le Roy during the season of its formation. The music of the fife and of the spirit-stirring drum was ever rife in the streets, and the frequent public speeches and addresses kept active this patriotic enthusiasm until the formation of the regiment was complete. The full complement of men was at length attained, and March 26, 1862, the regiment was ordered to the front under the designation of the 105th Regiment of the State, and the camp broken up. The first regimental officers were Rev. James M. Fuller, colonel; Howard Carroll, of Rochester, lieutenant-colonel; and J W. Shedd, major. Dr. D. C. Chamberlin received the commission of surgeon of the regiment. The following were captains of the respective companies when they left Camp Upham: Richard Whiteside, James B. Delong, H. E. Smith, Isaac S. Tichenor, George Babcock, Abraham Moore, John McMahon, Patrick W. Bradley, and S. J. Wilber .

Previous to the departure of the regiment for the front a grand ovation was given it by the citizens of Le Roy, and Central Hall was literally packed for the occasion. Miles P. Lampson was chosen president, who made an appropriate and patriotic speech, and L. N. Bangs was chosen secretary. It was the chief purpose of the meeting to present from our citizens an elegant sword and revolver to Col. Fuller prior to his departure. D. R. Bacon was appointed to make the presentation of them to the Colonel, which he did in an address suited to occasion, which was replied to by the recipient in an eloquent speech, followed by other patriotic speeches, in which the departing regiment received a most hearty godspeed, commending it to the "God of Battles." On other occasions previous to the departure a sword presentation was made to our townsmen, Major (afterwards Lieut.-Col.) Shedd and to Dr. D. C. Chamberlin of a sword, belt, and cap, the presentation, in behalf of the donors, being made by Gen. C. F. Bissell in appropriate and fitting terms, and accepted by the recipient in a grateful acknowledgement. Of the reverses and sad depletion of the regiment, and the changes of its officers after it entered upon active service, it is not the purpose of this brief sketch of its organization to mention. It belongs to the general history of the war. Arriving at Washington the regiment was placed in Gen. Duryea's brigade with that of the 97th and 104th N. Y. and 107th Pa. regiments. When the campaign opened Col. Fuller led his regiment to the front and into the field, following Stonewall Jackson across Blue Ridge to Thoroughfare Gap, and returning pitched their tents on the Orange & Alexandria Railroad. They moved across the Rappahannock, where they were first engaged in the battle of Cedar Mountain, August 9, 1862, and acted gallantly. For reasons unexplained two days after this battle Col. Fuller tendered his resignation, which was thrice repeated before its acceptance; and Lieut.-Col. Carroll, a brave and capable officer, was promoted to the colonelcy, J. W. Shedd to that of lieutenant-colonel, and Capt. Whiteside to major. By order of the division commander, Gen. Ricketts, the regiment retraced its steps across the Rappahannock. Gen Pope was in command of the Army of the Potomac. The regiment was engaged in the second battle of Bull Run (or Manasses), South Mountain, and Antietam, where Col. Carroll was wounded and soon died at the hospital in Washington. Lieut.-Col. Shedd was also severely wounded, and Lieut. Buckley was killed. The death of Col. Carroll led to another change of officers, resulting in promoting Lieut.-Col. Shedd to the colonelcy, Whiteside, lieutenant-colonel, and Adjutant Sharp, major The regiment was in the first battle of Fredericksburg, December 13th, and in the famous march under Gen. Burnside in the winter of 1863, when many officers and privates were taken prisoners. It had become so depleted by these engagements and other causes that in March, 1863, it was consolidated with the 94th N. Y., Col. Root (now of Buffalo) commanding. The 94th, being the senior regiment, retained its numerical designation, and the field officers and staff of the 105th were all mustered out except the surgeon, Dr. D. C. Chamberlin, and the quartermaster.

But it is due to the brave hearts who went from our town to the war, never to return, that at least brief mention should be made of their honored names Some perished on the bloody field; some in the more terrible and slower death of the southern prison. "They died that the country might live." There was Olmsted at Andersonville, and either

by shock of battle or wasted by disease there were added to this roll of
honor a Hazelton, Thomas, Calvert, Hascall, Hoffman, Swift, Graves,
Tyrrell, Bell, Clark, Rose, Gladden, Frasier, Avery, O'Connor, Stamp,
Houston, Darrow, McLochlan, King, Moody, Rogers, and the Kinnes.
Though no monumental stone has been erected to their memory, they
will ever be held by a grateful people in lasting remembrance.

> " How sleep the brave who sink to rest
> By all their country's wishes blest!
> * * * * * *
> There Honor comes a pilgrim gray
> To bless the turf that wraps their clay;
> And Freedom shall awhile repair
> To dwell a weeping hermit there."

Le Roy.—It was not until 1813 that the name of the town was changed
and received the name of Le Roy. The following were the first town
officers: Dr. William Sheldon, supervisor; Thomas Tufts, town clerk.
The other town officers were Benjamin Ganson, Asa Buell, David Le
Barron, Philo Pierson, Salmon Turrell, David Biddlecom, Richard Waite,
Henry Prindle, G. Newell, L. Fowler, G. Terry, A. Hascall, and J. Hascall. The town took its name from Herman Le Roy, who was an afflu-
ent gentleman of French descent of the old school at the beginning of the
present century, residing in the city of New York. His connection with
the land tracts of Western New York had commenced in behalf of certain
residents in Amsterdam, Holland, known afterwards as the Holland Purchase Being aliens the company could not hold the fee of lands in this
country, which disability was afterwards removed by the legislature of
New York. The purchase was made in several conveyances of Robert
Morris, the distinguished patriot and financial officer of the Revolution,
who was tendered the place of Secretary of the Treasury in Washington's
first cabinet, and whose large fortune was freely contributed in the support of the war. The tract was bought of the State of Massachusetts, on-
the failure of Phelps & Gorham to perform their contract, and consisted
of 3,300,000 acres, reserving the Indian title, which was gradually, by
several treaties, extinguished, the first at Buffalo in 1788 and the second
at Big Tree (Geneseo), at less than one cent an acre By later councils
these reservations were further reduced, and the last of the once powerful
Senecas are now found in the small reservations of Cattaraugus and Tonawanda.

In all these concessions Red Jacket, whom our older citizens remember when he made his home with his people, the Senecas, upon the Genesee, and on the camping-grounds on Wolcott street and Ganson's Brook,
was an eloquent and uncompromising opponent. He was *facile princeps*
of his tribe and race. It was displayed when a young man in the first
treaty between the Six Nations and the U. S. commissioners, after the
close of the Revolutionary war, at Fort Stanwix in October, 1784, where
his marvelous eloquence in opposition gave him his Indian name of power,
Sagowatha, the "keeper awake." General La Fayette, who was present

at this council, was so fascinated with his power that it was not forgotten
40 years after, on his visit to America, when, in an interview with Red
Jacket at Buffalo, he inquired for the young Cicero who had so captivated
the council, and was surprised to receive answer from the chief himself
that he was the man. He had subsequently frequent occasions for the
display of his indignant eloquence against the further surrender by his
people of their hunting-grounds and council fires; but all in vain. By
one treaty after another he saw his own tribe, the Senecas, surrender them
for a bare pittance to the white man. He stood firmly and boldly against
it in the treaty at Buffalo Creek in July, 1788; again in the council held
at Canandaigua in October, 1794, followed by the one at Big Tree (Geneseo) in 1797, when still greater concessions by his tribe were made, until
at last he lived to see it dwindled to the present narrow reservations from
the vast territory it once possessed. It was the old story of the Indians,
fate when in conflict with the pale face and civilization, which no eloquence
or logic of theirs have yet been able wholly to resist. But with Red
Jacket it embittered the close of his life, and he persistently refused to use
the speech or the dress of the white man, or conform to his habits, except
as the unfortunate victim of the vice it had introduced among his people.
So uncompromising was his bitterness toward his conquerors that Gen.
Ely S. Parker, a Seneca and one of Gen. Grant's staff, said that among
Red Jacket's last requests was that " white men should not dig his grave
or bury him." Notwithstanding this hostility Buffalo has done him honor,
in admiration of his genius and his eminent service in the War of 1812,
by the removal of his remains to Forest Lawn, and erecting in 1883 a
noble monument to his memory, with impressive ceremonies, conducted
by its historical society. It was a merited honor. Did a William Tell or
a Brutus ever display a loftier patriotism ? As justly might it be said of
Red Jacket as of the latter, " This was the noblest Roman of them all."

It is a sad instance that these and other land speculations, of which
there was a mania at the close of the Revolutionary war, should have
proved late in life the financial ruin of the patient Morris. So great was
the reverse of this opulent merchant prince, who, unaided and alone,
sustained the army of Washington during the trying period of 1781, that
he was, in the crisis which followed, actually imprisoned for debt, and
for a time became the tenant of a prison. We have the testimony of his
son, Thomas Morris, that his advances to the government were reim-
bursed. But he died poor, and his widow was sustained by a dower interest of $1,500 from the Holland Purchase.

The parceling out of these several tracts to different companies has
more of an historical than local interest, as the title of the owner and occupant has long been fixed and settled, and each settler now reposes under
his own vine and fig tree.

The final sales of the Holland Land Co. were made and the office
closed in 1835. Among the early subdivisions of the original Morris
tract was what was termed the " Triangle," consisting of 85,000 acres, of
which Le Roy, Bayard, and McIvers became the purchasers.

The Le Roy family naturally took a lively interest in the town, where a large landed interest was centered, and from whom it had derived its name. Jacob Le Roy, the son of Herman, came to the village to reside in 1821, having then recently married Charlotte Otis, of Massachusetts. He came as successor of Egbert Benson as land agent of the "Triangle." His brothers, Edward and Daniel Le Roy, followed. The former removed to Canawaugus, where he occupied and cultivated a large farm, which he subsequently sold to Gen. James Wadsworth. Daniel opened a store in Le Roy in 1822, under the firm name of Le Roy & Co., previously occupied by Mr. Annin, on the site of the present store of S. Loucks. Trade had now centered and become fixed on the west side of the Oatka. Daniel did not continue long in business before he returned to New York. In the year 1826 Jacob Le Roy built the grist-mill upon the site of the Stoddard & Platt mill, and commenced flouring on a scale hitherto unknown in the West. It is the present mill of C. F. Prentice. He enlarged the Egbert Benson office to a spacious dwelling, on the east side of the Oatka, known as the Le Roy mansion, now occupied by William Sheldon and the grounds by the Le Roy Academic Institute His grounds were beautifully laid out, with the choicest fruits and flowers, and he was noted for his wide and generous hospitality. He was a brother-in-law of Daniel Webster, the great orator and statesman, whose visits here are remembered by many of our oldest citizens. In one of the volumes of his published speeches there is a dedication by him to the Le Roy family, highly appreciative and laudatory. It was in one of these visits that Mr. Webster had a reception, which drew a large number of his admirers from the country round, with whom he had free and cordial intercourse, who were not a little surprised that the Marshfield farmer was as much at home in agriculture as in affairs of State, and in advance of all in knowledge of stock. Mr. Le Roy, during his residence in the village, was highly respected and esteemed for his uniform courtesy and liberality. He donated the lot on which the old Episcopal Church and rectory stood, and was one of its principal supporters. This was continued after his removal to the East, to New York, in 1838, where he resided many years, until his decease. He subsequently donated $1,500 to the church. But one of his children, Otis Le Roy, survives him, who is a resident of New York city.

Joshua Lathrop and family removed to Le Roy from Norwich, Vt., in 1824, and he became the successor of Jacob Le Roy in the agency of the land office. His office was in the present brick dwelling of Mrs. Elizabeth Brown, daughter of the late C. B. Thomson, after its use as a store had been abandoned, and his dwelling was on the same premises, still occupied by his son, F. C. Lathrop. Mr. Lathrop continued as agent of the company until its final close, when he became the owner and proprietor of the present Le Roy flouring-mills, and conducted an extensive milling business until his decease. In all of his business relations Mr. Lathrop bore the highest character for strict probity and honor, and he was also noted for his urbanity and courteous manner in his business and social intercourse. He was a member and liberal supporter of the Episcopal Church of the place for a period of 25 years and a continuous member of the vestry. Mr. Lathrop was a man of but few words, but of exemplary deeds, and through life maintained the reputation of a public spirited and useful citizen. He died in August, 1856, aged 69 years, leaving a widow, since deceased. His present surviving children are Mary, the widow of A. F. Bartow, Esq., Ruth, and Frank C. (the private banker of the village), all residents of Le Roy; Joshua, a produce dealer of New York; and Lydia, the widow of Daniel Pierson, of Cincinnati, O. His daughter Rebecca (since deceased) was married to Rev. G. D. Gillespie, the present bishop of Western Michigan.

The following is a list of the supervisors and town clerks of Le Roy from its organization in 1813 to 1890:

SUPERVISORS.

William Sheldon	1813	Dr. David C. Chamberlin	1857–58
David Le Barron	1814–15	Hon. A. P. Hascall	1859–60
Ella Smith	1816	Walter G. Gustin	1861–62
Thomas Tufts	1817	John H. Lent (died)	1863
William Sheldon	1818–19	Abial Robertson	1863–64
Thaddeus Joy	1820–22	Walter G. Gustin	1865–68
Willis Buell	1823	Richard L. Selden }	
Daniel Le Barron	1824	W. Le Roy Bishop }	1869
Harry Backus	1825	Samuel Gillette	1870
——— Gates	1826–27	W. Le Roy Bishop	1871
John Hascall	1828	William S. Brown	1872
Seth M. Gates	1829–30	Samuel Gillette	1873
Dennis Blakely	1831–35	Walter G. Gustin	1874
John Tomlinson	1836–39	Samuel Gillette	1875
Knowlton Rich	1840–41	Richard L. Selden	1876
Elijah Platt	1842–46	Samuel Gillette	1877
Abial Robertson	1847–48	Walter G. Gustin	1878–79
William Morgan	1849–52	Samuel Gillette	1880
John G. Bixby	1853	Richard L. Selden	1881–86
John Tomlinson	1854	Melvin D. Pratt	1887–90
John J. McPherson	1855–56		

TOWN CLERKS.

Thomas Tufts	1813–15	M. Gates	1824–25
Heman J. Redfield	1816–17	A. P. Hascall	1826
Willis Buell	1818–20	J. H. Stanley	1827–78
M. Gates	1821	James B. Gillett	1879
Timothy Fitch	1822–23	Samuel F. Comstock	1880–90

Early industries. — Among the early tavern-keepers was Charles Wilber, in 1797, who was also a justice of the peace. He was succeeded by Capt. John Ganson in 1798. Samuel Davis, C. H. Thomas, and Gen. Daniel Davis were tavern-keepers east of the village.

The Eagle Hotel was built in 1825, and was on the site of Auntie Wemple, kept by Maj. James Ganson, who died in Michigan, Ebenezer Hall, Theodore Dwight, Lewis Jackson, and Powell Carpenter, Jr., who was proprietor for 25 years, and died in 1885, aged 82 years. J. W.

Lyon was proprietor in 1868, and Edward Search succeeded him. A Mr. Wilcox was landlord in 1875. W. C. Reed, the present proprietor, succeeded him.

The old Globe and Eagle, which had a sign of a large globe, was kept by Rufus Robertson in 1816, a Mr. Walbridge in 1827, Elisha Stanley, J. H. Stanley, Sornberger, Spencer, Lyman Ballard, and A. G. Collins, who sold to Wiss, when the name was changed.

John Lent kept tavern in the house now occupied by Gen. Bissell, on the hill. His store was also in the same locality. It may be mentioned here that in the "tavern days," before the railroads, stage travel was a large item; for 10 or more stages, with four horses, and six horse freight teams passed Le Roy daily. Freight to Albany was $10 to $30 per ton. Whisky was three cents per drink.

Before the Erie Canal there were over a dozen distilleries in this vicinity. Corn would not pay for transportation; whisky would; and many farmers had their corn made into whisky on shares, and at the distillery hogs and cattle were fattened. The foremost in the business was Thomas Tufts, who was also the last one to close up. Elisha Stanley built one on Fort Hill, on lot 8, in 1812, and a grist-mill near by in 1841. William Morgan had one above Coe's brick yard; J. & M. Colton had one on the hill; and J. H. Lent, who run a mill as well as a hotel. Lampson and Lent were his successors. Dickey had one on the west side of Prentice's mill race. W. Merry had one on the brook near Roanoke road. Fred Foot run one on the flat southeast of Mrs. Johnson's. Joseph Annin had a distillery in 1822, and Jonathan Le Barron had one near the paper-mill on the same ground where Jacob Le Roy owned one. It was the largest west of the Genesee River, and was devoted to the manufacture of proof spirits for the Albany market. There was one also on the Beechnut lot, at the head of the pond.

Elijah Warner built an ashery in 1817, and made potash for five or six years. Thaddeus Joy also had an ashery, and north of the Episcopal Church was one owned by a Mr. Sherman.

Martin O. Coe started an oil-mill as early as 1816. It was afterwards purchased by L. C. Morgan, and in later years was owned by Foreman, Starr & Co., and I. M. Foreman, who sold to a Mr. Rogers. He now makes about 25 barrels per day. The seed was mostly raised in Wyoming County. Martin O. Coe and Uni Hurlburt operated brick yards. About 1812 J. & A. Nobles had a carding factory where Haskins's mill now is, and one Stewart run one where Tomlinson's mill was. Samuel Clifford also run one in 1833. Luther Newton made bed-cord and kept hotel on the road between here and South Le Roy. James Ballard made hats from 1820 to 1831. A. E. Hutchins and D. Sevey made chairs. Richard Waite was the first blacksmith, and Stephen Stillwell was a shoemaker.

Tomlinson's mill, on the Oatka, two miles southwest of Le Roy, was first built in 1831, by John Tomlinson. It was a frame building with three burrs. Formerly a large business was transacted. Thomas Tufts also operated a mill on the same site. Now only a small feed business is located on the spot.

D. &. W. Graves operated a tannery below the mill on the flat. Shedd and Ganson were workmen under them, and they afterwards carried on the business in that locality. Jacob Le Roy built a flouring-mill about 1832, about one mile north of the village. In 1869 it was sold to W. F. Jones, who manufactured wrapping-paper there until it was burned in the spring of 1887. Before and after the year 1835 threshing machines were being built at Deacon Webb's foundry, which was located on the bank of the creek near where the Episcopal Church is now located.

Schools.—Like all early settlements of New England stock in the institution of schools Le Roy was not behind. The log school-house followed closely upon the log cabin. As early as 1801 a log school-house was built opposite the old Dr. Sheldon farm, and the first teacher was Luseba Scott, afterwards the wife of James Ganson. She was succeeded by Phœbe Bates, sister of Asher Bates, and in 1803 by Mrs. Stephen Wolcott. The first framed school-house west of Genesee River was erected in 1804, by a joint stock company organized at a meeting where Daniel Davis was chairman and William Coe, secretary. It was formed by a company, of which there were 30 shares at $4 each, of which one-half could be paid in labor, produce, or building materials. The bachelors evinced their interest in the cause of education and the rising generation by taking one share each. The first teacher called was a Mr. Pomeroy, of Albany. He was succeeded by David Hascall. It was located a little east of the primitive log one. On the advent of Thomas Tufts, on West Main street, a school-house was erected opposite the Lent tavern, where religious services were often held, as were also meetings of the Masonic fraternity. Dr. William Coe gave evening instruction in the higher branches after his settlement. Later Rev. Calvin Colton, the first settled pastor of the Presbyterian Church, also gave instruction in the classics.

The Round-house in fact became an educational institution instead of a Masonic lodge, for which it was originally designed. This somewhat noted building in its day had its origin with the Masonic fraternity here in the year 1825. The order had its existence here from the commencement of the settlement, and its meetings had been in the school-house, partly built by it, on the Tufts lot on the corner of Craigie street; also meetings were held in the ball-room of the Ganson tavern. The building was of a circular form, from which it took its name as the Round-house; was 40 feet in diameter, and built of brick. The ceiling on the first floor was 16 feet in height; the second was not as high, but of the same circular form. The mystery of mysteries was designed to be conducted in an upper room, called "the sounding room," from the echoes that followed any sound in it. The square tower in front had also three stories, and above them a belfry of 20 or 24 feet, and the whole height of the imposing Masonic pantheon was 70 feet. But its use for the purpose of its construction was never demanded. The popular excitement, which grew out of the taking off of Morgan in the autumn of 1826, who was spirited through Le Roy, arrested its purpose. The printer Miller, of the Masonic book, was arraigned on a bogus charge before Jacob Bartow, then a justice of peace here ; made this the central point of agitation from whence sprung the Anti-Masonic party, destined to spread over the Union. It was, from the circumstances of its origin, and the mystery which veiled the deep damnation of the taking off, the cause of bitter party feeling, which divided families, churches, and communities. Political aspirants soon took advantage of the excitement and made " down with Masonry " the banner cry of the Anti-Masonic party in the State. The first convention was held in Le Roy, of which mention has before been made. It brought many new men to the surface, and the party organization spread into the adjoining states, and it became a National party which nominated William Wirt for president. But it was a meteor party which had its day, and like the baseless fabric of vision passed away. It, too, achieved its good, in exposing the danger of secret societies and binding oaths—which conflict with the safety of the person or the State, and which none more than the present Masonic fraternity now repudiate and denounce.

But it is in its educational use that the Round-house has a conspicuous place. It was never finished by the projectors for the purpose designed. The lower room was used for religious purposes by the Congregational Church, and for public meetings and lectures. The second story was finished off for a school room in 1828, and occupied as a select school until its demolition in 1859, and the erection of the Universalist Church on its site. It was rented to Mr. Hatch and afterwards to a Mr. Bradley. In 1834 the school passed into the hands of William Le Roy Annin, who still lives, and from his " reminiscences " the present writer is indebted for many of the foregoing items. He gives his personal experience and says in this connection :

"I had been to the Wadsworth school in Geneseo at its opening in October, 1827, and had remained about two years. Not then being prepared to enter Harvard College, I spent most of the two other years in teaching and studying privately, and then joined the Sophomore class of that institution and graduated in 1834."

On his graduation he rented the Round-house and opened a classical school, which was a success. William Le Roy Annin is an accomplished scholar, especially in the Greek and Latin classics, and at an advanced age still pursues his favorite reading and studies. He is usually selected by the Regents of the State in the examination of the schools here previous to the award by the board to them of the public moneys. He was the first child born after the organization of the town.

Afterwards Messrs Daniels and Olmsted had a flourishing school in the building, and still later Joel Whiting, Messrs. Brooks, Reed, McCall, Beckley, and others. The demolition of the Round-house rendered the erection of another and more commodious edifice for school purpose as necessity.

It will revive this period of our early history by giving an extract from a letter written by an intelligent lady of the village, on the 26th of June, 1826, cotemporaneous with the laying of the corner-stone of this Masonic temple. She thus graphically writes:

. . . "The site of the building is nearly opposite the church, and is to unite taste and elegance in an uncommon degree. Its cost is to be $7,000, $4,000 of which is to be supplied by the different lodges in the State and the remainder by the village. The spirit of Masonry is excessively prevalent in these parts, as the display on Saturday clearly evinced. Among the novelties of the scene I was particularly struck with the ladies and babies walking in procession; the latter of course in the arms of the parent, whose turn it might be to bear the lovely burden. The procession of Masons, headed by a band of music, marched to the base of the temple, halted, parted to the right and left, while the ladies from youth to age, two by two, marched through the lines to the spot where the ceremony of laying the corner-stone was performed; . . . from thence in like order to the church, where an oration was pronounced (it being St. John's Day), thence to Ganson's tavern, where 250 females took dinner, and double that number of men—the former within doors, the latter in a bower made for the occasion. The company dispersed, without accident, in vehicles of various form and size, chiefly drawn by mares with colts in train. The whole was a rare exhibition."

The trustees into whose hands the Round-house fell were John Lent, I. M. Murphy, Israel Rathbone, William Sheldon, John Jackson, John Clifford, Marshall Smead, James Ganson, Ezekiel Hall, and Jonathan Barron, all of the Masonic order. It was disposed of by them to J. G. Barbor, who held it until the time of its sale to the Universalist Society, when it was demolished.

The Le Roy Academic Institute grew out of this necessity. It was designed from its origin for a first class institution for English and classical instruction for both sexes. It was started by its friends by a stock subscription, which was promptly filled, and the requisite amount raised for an organization which was completed, and in 1864 an incorporation obtained from the legislature of the State. D. R. Bacon was the first president; L. N. Bangs, secretary; and J. R. Olmsted, treasurer. The first term commenced January 5, 1865. Its first principal was J. K. Lombard, from 1863 to 1865, and on the resignation of Mr. Lombard, E. Harlow Russell succeeded him as principal, remaining until 1874. In recognition of the high character of the school the town of Le Roy, by a decisive vote, appropriated $10,000 for the institute. Since its first organization it has maintained, without any diminution, its high standard of instruction in the classical and modern languages, and in the natural sciences as well as in music. The several principals who succeeded Mr. Russell (who resigned to accept the headship of the Normal School at Worcester, Mass.) are as follows: Alvin P. Chapin, 1875; Prof. W. H. Munroe, 1875 to 1879, called from here to the presidency of Deveaux College; and the present principal, F. C. Comstock, who took charge in 1880. The academy was never more flourishing in number of pupils than under the present principal. The officers of the board of trustees for 1890 consist of John Maloney, president; Fred A. Steuber, vice-

31

president ; John P. Sampson, secretary ; and Augustus E. Miller, treasurer.   The value of the grounds, buildings, and other property connected with the institute exceeds $25,000.   Seven teachers are employed,
and there is an average attendance of over 200 scholars.

Ingham University, for the education of young ladies, has survived
under different corporations over a half century of growth, and has attained a National reputation.   It was established in Le Roy by Misses
Mariette and Emily E. Ingham, who were born in Saybrook, Conn., and
who first located in Attica, and after a two years' residence there removed and opened the school as the Le Roy Female Seminary in 1835.
The founders at its commencement purchased the fine residence and
grounds of Robert Bayard, on the corner of Wolcott and East Main
streets, which property (greatly enlarged) the institution has ever since
retained.   In this purchase the sisters were aided and supported by Albert Brewster, Seth M. Gates, A. P. Hascall, Samuel Comstock, Jonathan P. Darling, A. S. Upham, Enos Bacheler, Lee Comstock, Israel
Rathbone, Richard Hollister, and William S. Bradley, none of whom or
of the founders now survive.   It was first chartered in 1841, with the
above as corporators.   The school, by the energy, ability, and superior
attainments and adaptability of the founders for the work, sprang at once
into the first rank of this class of institutions in the State.   Miss Mariette,
the eldest of the sisters, was a lady of remarkable energy and business
capacity ; and the younger, then at the head of the school, was equally
distinguished for her culture and scholarly attainments. and especially for
her tact and skill in the management and securing the confidence of the
pupils in the school under her charge.   Aside from its advanced curriculum at this period of female institutions it adopted, as a rule, ever
since rigidly maintained, that " no teacher will be employed who will not
conscientiously make continued efforts for the highest moral and spiritual
good of the pupils."   Under such a guidance, and with so high a standard, the success of the school was assured from the first.   But Mrs. Emily
Staunton, the guiding and controlling spirit which directed the institution, was never satisfied with present attainments.   After several years
of marked growth and prosperity, in which they had seen other similar
institutions arise, flourish, and, at last, perish for the want of support,
in order to avoid such a catastrophe, they resolved to relinquish their
private interests in the institution and the large addition that had been
made to the school buildings, and the estate, real and personal, of the
founders, and enter upon a novel and radical change.   It was the volunteer surrender of this large property, owned and acquired by them, to
the Synod of Genesee, who accepted the gift made upon the sole condition that a full collegiate course should be established in the school, and
a permanent fund raised for its support.   The trust and responsibility
was thus placed upon the Synod, and the first charter as a collegiate institute was obtained April 6, 1852, its title being the " Ingham Collegiate Institute," located at Le Roy, N. Y.   The corporation thus created

consisted of Rev. Charles N. Mattoon, Samuel Skinner, A. P. Hascall, J. B. Skinner, C. Danforth, Moses Taggart, Samuel Comstock, C. Comstock, M. O. Coe, A. F. Bartow, Israel Rathbone, J. G. Bixby, J. P. Darling, Albert Brewster, Phineas Staunton, and Mariette Ingham. Twenty-four trustees were appointed, nine of whom constituted a quorum to do business. The trustees mostly consisted of the same persons, and the corporation was vested with the power to create a Normal school, a seminary, and collegiate departments, to appoint professors and teachers, and to grant diplomas. It will be observed that this institution was thus in advance of all female institutions in the provisions of its charter, in that it was the first to introduce a college curriculum into the education of young ladies, and a charter with power to confer degrees and grant diplomas. In this it preceded South Hadley, Elmira, Farmington, Wells, Packer, and Vassar.

Notwithstanding this material advance it made an effort for a still higher rank in the scale of an educational institution, and asked of the legislature of the State a charter for a university. This was at first refused, on the ground assumed of its inadaptability to a female institution for learning, and a rank hitherto unknown in this or any other State. In the following session of the legislature the charter was persistently urged and finally granted with university privileges, and in April, 1857, the name of the trustees was changed to that of counselors. The Rev. Samuel Hanson Cox, a distinguished clergyman of New York city, was installed in 1857, under imposing ceremonies at the Presbyterian Church, as its first chancellor. His high attainments, as a scholar and divine, were at once applied to elevate the standard of education and make it a university worthy of the name—indeed, a model institution, unique of its kind, for the perfect intellectual training of woman for her preëminent duties and responsibilities. In this, during his many years of active devotion to the duties of his chancellorship, he was eminently successfuls and gave to the institution a reputation and preëminence which filled it, halls and gained for it a wide and merited popularity.

Colonel Phineas Staunton was temporarily elected vice-chancellor. He was an artist of high merit, and made his branch a specialty in the university. He was the son of General Staunton, a distinguished officer in the War of 1812; was born in Wyoming, N. Y.; was married to Miss Emily E. Ingham in 1847; and from that period became connected with the institution either as professor or as one of its officers. By his own pencil, or by selection as a connoisseur, he made a fine collection of paintings still preserved in the art gallery of the institution. His life-work became devoted to the interests of the university, which was only interrupted by the call of his country in its crisis at the opening of the civil war. This call caused him to drop the pencil and enlist in its service, and on the organization of the 100th Regiment in Buffalo he was chosen lieutenant-colonel, and immediately went with it to the front. At the battle of Fair Oaks, which soon followed, he was prostrated by a spent-ball, wounded, and in consequence returned to his home at the university, and there resumed his art work. At a later period he became a member of the scientific expedition organized at Williams College, which proved his last work. He was taken suddenly ill at Quito, South America, from which he did not recover, and there died, and was buried in that city. The expedition was not without its value to the university, for Mrs. Staunton became the purchaser of the large and rare collection of birds and natural objects secured by Prof. Orton, at the head of the expedition, and which now adorn and enrich the collection of the art building. It may be here added that this fine structure (the art gallery and hall) is the best in the State for the purpose of its construction ; was erected in 1870, at the cost of some $15,000, by Mrs. Staunton, as a memorial to her husband, and which now stands a noble monument of her devotion to his memory as well as a most valuable accession to the university buildings. These latter have at different periods all been greatly improved and enlarged.

The property valuation of Ingham University (the voluntary surrender by the founders to the corporation), as reported by it to the Regents of the University of New York, in 1875 was $101,000. Times may have affected and reduced somewhat the valuation, but a recent addition of a large brick dormitory, largely the gift of the Alumni Association (an incorporated body), would in great degree offset that diminution. Space will also fail to speak at length of the several chancellors who have succeeded Dr. Cox after his resignation in 1863. There was the Rev. Dr. Samuel D. Burchard, who served until 1872 ; then Dr. Edward B. Wadsworth, elected in 1883 ; and the last, Dr. W. W. Totherob. All gave efficient aid in maintaining the university up to that high plane upon which it was founded. On the resignation of the latter, by his removal to Chicago, the chancellorship became vacant and has not yet been filled. It is due here to make brief mention of a few of the able professors in the different departments, who under these several administrations aided in maintaining this high standard and giving to the university its wide-spread popularity. There was in the art department Prof. L. M. Wiles, of New York, who, as a landscape painter, acquired a National reputation, aided by his son Irving. There was in music the accomplished Henri Appi and Mrs. C. S. Cory. There was the able divine, the late Rev. William L. Parsons, in moral philosophy, and his cultured consort, Mrs. Lucy A. C., in the same department and in history, which position she still retains, and whose liberal benefactions to the university, often repeated, merit grateful acknowledgment and recognition. There was Prof. H. J. Schmitz, at one period at the head of the institution, and who was called as principal of the State Normal School at Geneseo. There was the late Rev. Dr. Henry J. Van Lennep, unsurpassed as an oriental scholar, and a voluminous author upon the " Land of the East," the place of his nativity, and whose merited reputation drew pupils from that remote portion of the globe.

By a careful estimate made by Prof. Van Lennep, in 1875, at that period (40 years from its origin) above 5,000 persons in all had here enjoyed the benefits of the institution, and now the number is over 8,000. It is but due to its liberal founder; who then alone survived, Mrs. Emily Ingham Staunton, that during this period more than $30,000 had been given to indigent but well deserving students, and many of these beneficiaries are now occupying positions of great honor and usefulness.

After the granting of the university charter, in 1861, aid to the extent of $25,000 was asked from the legislature, but only $5,000 was obtained, and further appeals to the public resulted in securing only the small sum of $1,400   The Synod of Genesee then relinquished its trust, and in 1883 a new charter was granted, and a new and the present board of trustees organized, as follows: Hon. James H. Loomis, Hon. Henry N. Page, Charles F. Prentice, Schuyler C. Wells, William Lampson, Rev. W. W. Totherob, Butler Ward, Rev. Edward B. Walsworth, Nicholas B. Keeney, Hon. Augustus Frank, Rev. Herman C. Riggs, Augustus E. Miller, Hon. Edward C. Walker, Rev. Samuel Bowden, and Rev. Amasa S. Freeman. When Mrs Staunton retired from the institution the new board granted her an annuity for life.   Its real head is the highly cultivated and endowed lady principal, Miss R. N. Webster, whose experience and executive ability well qualify her for the place, and give her a deserved popularity with the pupils as well as with the officers of the university.   There are 18 instructors under her, and the institution for instruction in all branches is maintaining its high standard.

The present faculty of Ingham University consists of Rev. W. W. Totherob, chancellor; Miss R. N. Webster, Mrs. Lucy A. S. Parsons, Miss Ella M. Arnold, Miss E. P. Ballantine, Miss F. L. Beach, Miss J. Dawman, Miss C. A. McPherson, Miss A. Harkort, Mrs. R. W. Bellamy, Miss M. E. Samson, Miss Rose M. Shave, Miss Edith Innis (Reg.), Prof. Herman Dossenbach, Miss E. S Peeke, Miss M. M. Pomeroy, and Sarah A. Innis, matron.

This article should not close without notice of the recent death of the last of its early founders—Mrs. Emily Ingham Staunton.   This estimable lady, whose name must ever be associated with the university which bears it, closed her long and useful life in November, 1889, at the advanced age of 78 years and eight months, at the home of her brother Albert, at Oil City, Pa.   Here is no place or space for her life or extended enconium. Her works do follow her.   She was the first in the country to conceive and carry out to a successful issue a university charter for female education.   Her life-long labor and all of her estate were cheerfully bestowed on this cherished idea.   This alone should place her name among the great benefactors of the age.   Her remains were brought for burial to the spot she had loved so well, and where all of her life's labor had been unselfishly devoted.   Appropriate honors were here paid to her memory in the University Hall, where a crowded audience assembled to give evidence of their respect and sense of the great loss the community had experienced by her decease. Her remains rest in the university grounds (as she had requested) by the side of the noble cenotaph erected by her to her husband, whose remains repose in a foreign land.

Churches.—The beginning of religious service was coincident with the beginning of the settlement. The primitive barn, the settler's cabin, and the log school-house had their Sabbath gatherings, so that the spiritual wants were not neglected—whenever an itinerant pastor appeared to conduct the service. The Rev. David Perry, a missionary from Massachusetts, was the first preacher, in 1800. There was no organized church, as such, west of the Genesee River until 1803, and this was of the Presbyterian order, at Big Springs (Mumford). It was of Scotch emigrants, of the true "kirk and covenant" stamp, who had in 1799 emigrated and settled there from the old country, and consisted of but five families : John McVean, Hugh McDermott, Donald McPherson, James McLean, and John Anderson. Their first minister was Jedediah Chapman, who occasionally served the Ganson settlement, as did also his successor, Rev. A. Denoon, who came in 1805. The first church service of the Episcopal order was held here in 1802, by the Rev. Davenport Phelps, and who thereafter occasionally officiated, of which mention is made in the notice of that society. Transient visits were made by ministers of other denominations, but mostly of the Presbyterian order. Among the latter were the Rev. Isaiah B. Andrews and John Lindsley. In 1808 the Rev. Mr. Coleman was sent out by the Missionary Society of Connecticut, who spent several months in this and the adjoining settlements. He was succeeded by the Revs. Mr. Phelps, Reuben Parmalee, and Lemuel Parker, the latter pursuing his missionary march westward, it is said to Oregon, but whether thus early in the century this heroic purpose was accomplished the record does not appear.

It was not until February 7, 1812, that the Presbyterian Church was first organized in Le Roy, and it was followed by a union with it of the Congregationalists. They were merged into one society. It was organized by the Revs. Oliver Ayer and Reuben Parmalee, and David Anderson was chosen and ordained deacon. Rev. David Fuller was the first resident clergyman, and its first pastor was the Rev. Calvin Colton. The present church edifice was built in 1826. Mr. Colton built the brick dwelling on the Oatka, now occupied by Dr. Taylor. He subsequently left the ministry and gave his attention to literary pursuits and became an author of some note, of which his *Four Years in Great Britain* gave him wide reputation. Many of the pastors that followed were distinguished for their zeal, piety, and earnest work in building up the church and society to its present standard of growth and strength. It is here designed to present but the early beginnings, which were quite as favorable for religious advantages as in other new communities. They were indeed greater than could have been expected, when in 1803 there were but four Presbyterian ministers west of Oneida County : Revs. Jedediah Chapman, J Lindsley, Samuel Leacock, and Jabez Chadwick.

The first services of the Episcopal Church here were conducted by the Rev. Davenport Phelps, a missionary of the church in Western New York. He again officiated in 1804 in the school-house erected by Ezra Platt, on the south side of Trigon Park, on which occasion he performed the rite of baptism in his family. One of these, it is presumed, was Elijah, his son, who, in his manhood, became a prominent member of the society, and was, until his death, one of its vestrymen and wardens. In 1817, under the Rev. Samuel Johnson, a parish was organized with the present name of "St. Mark's Church." Its first officers were: Timothy Hatch and Hugh Murphy, wardens; Abel Noyes, Solomon Root, George A. Tiffany, Ezra Platt, Thaddeus Stanley, Elisha Stanley, Manly Colton, and Graham Newell, vestrymen.

It is due in this connection to note briefly the name and character of one of the officers of the church, elected at its first organization. Elisha Stanley came to this village in 1811, from Goshen, Conn., and continued his residence until his decease, in his 89th year. During his long residence here he was held in high esteem, for his strict integrity, high sense of honor, and exemplary character. He was never behind or faltered in any good work, whether of church, community, or State. Of this estimate of his character the society gave ample testimony by continuing him in his office from its organization in 1817 until the day of his decease, a period of 61 years, 55 of which as a warden of the church. He died in 1888. His son, the Rev. Henry Stanley, rector of the Episcopal Church at Little Falls, preceded him in his decease, in 1870, the latter leaving two daughters who reside here, one the wife of Harry H. Falkner, an insurance agent of the village. Elisha Stanley left but one surviving child, Mrs. Taylor, the wife of Dr. Taylor.

Hugh Murphy, one of the first wardens, was born in Ireland, in 1760, was drafted in the British army, and came to America during the Revolutionary war. He entered our army and was wounded near Philadelphia. In 1785 he married Eunice Botsford, of Newtown, Conn. Mr. Murphy came to Le Roy in 1810, and purchased the farm on which his descendants have ever since lived, on East Main street. He died in 1826, leaving seven children: Amarilla, Joseph, Barnabas, Sarah, Mary, Amos B., and Charlotte. Mary, the only one surviving, now in her 93d year, was in the first class for confirmation, in 1817, by Bishop Hobart. The service was held in the school-house opposite Captain Lent's.

In 1826, while the Rev. Seth W. Beardsley was rector, a stone church, 40x60 feet, was erected on Church street (its site the present cemetery on the street), and was finished and consecrated by Bishop Hobart, August 7, 1827. Of this edifice not "one stone has been left upon another which has not been cast down." The land was the gift of Jacob Le Roy, and also $1,000 toward the completion of the building, and in 1844 he gave $1,500 additional. The rectors who followed the Rev. Mr Beardsley in the service of the church were as follows, to the period of the erection of the present church edifice: In 1830 the Rev. J. M. Rogers was called to the rectorship, who was followed by the Rev. Dr. F. H. Cummings, in 1831, who subsequently removed to Grand Rapids, Mich., where he died after a long and useful pastorate. Rev. Dr. Kendrick Metcalf became the rector of the parish in 1833, where he continued for eight years. He was a learned divine, and a polished writer, as well as an earnest Christian worker, and was called to the professorship of languages in Hobart College, where he remained until his decease. In 1841 Rev. George D. Gillespie took charge of the parish. He married the daughter of Joshua Lathrop, of Le Roy; his wife has since died. He served the parish until 1846, when he was called to Cincinnati, and to the parishes of Palmyra and Ann Arbor; was subsequently elected and yet remains bishop of Western Michigan. The rectors who followed were the Rev. T. D. Chipman, in 1846, since deceased; in 1850 the Rev. George H. McKnight, the present rector of Trinity Church, Elmira, who continued in the rectorship until 1855, and was succeeded in 1856 to 1860 by the Rev. R. J. Parvin. The sad catastrophe of the burning of a steamboat on the Ohio River, in 1866, brought to a sudden close the life of a most zealous and able Christian churchman. Then followed a brief pastorate of Rev. A. M. Wylie, and his successor was Rev. A. H Gesner, who served the parish for four years, when, in 1868, the Rev. J. H. Waterbury took the charge. It was under his pastorate that the present church edifice was designed and completed. The corner-stone was laid April 24, 1869, with appropriate church ceremonies. The edifice was formally opened December 22, 1870, and its consecration was on November 23, 1876 by Bishop Coxe, the late Rev. Dr. T. M. Bishop being the rector. Other rectors were L. D. Ferguson, J. H. Weibel (until 1885), Arthur W. Sloan in 1886, and the present rector, Rev. Pierre Cushing. The church has benefitted by a legacy of $2,000 from Albert Hill, and the Sunday-school of $1,000 from Mrs. D. P. Mirl. The number of communicants is 169; Sunday-school scholars 70, with nine teachers. The valuation of their property is $28,000. The rectory is located on Church street, corner of St. Mark. The present vestry is as follows: Wardens, D. R. Bacon and A. O. Comstock; vestrymen, H. H. Falkner, John Eyres, A. E. Miller, S. F. Curtiss, W. H. Smith, William Lampson, T. B. Tuttle, John Wiss, and E. H. Martin, clerk.

The First Presbyterian Church of Le Roy was organized February 7, 1812. The Congregationalists afterwards united with it, and the two societies were merged into one, under the Presbyterian form of government. The early history of this church has already been given. Services were held in the school building on Craigie street, which was used in turn by the Episcopal and Baptist churches, until the completion of a church in 1826. During that year Mrs Colton organized the first Sunday-school. The first members of the church were Moses McCollum, Joel Butler, Nathan Wilcox, David Anderson, Mehitable Judd, Eunice Farnham, Sarah Parmalee, Elizabeth Chamberlin, Sally Seymour, Mercy Buell, Mary Butler, Elizabeth McCollum, and Elizabeth Wilcox. Moses

McCollum and Edmund Beach were ruling elders. The present church was remodeled in 1850, and renovated in 1888. It, with the parsonage, has a valuation of $25,000. The church seats about 750 and now has 475 members. The Sunday-school has 300 members. The present officers of the church are C. K. Ward, clerk; S. T. Howard, J. L. Crocker, W. R. Halbert, S. Gillette, M. D. Pratt, ruling elders; M. A. Ladd, C. L. Olmsted, E. L. Miller, and John Hager, deacons; L. J. Bovee, M. D. Pratt, W. C. Donnan, J. P. Sampson, and F. D. Ward, trustees. The pastors have been as follows: 1820, Calvin Colton; 1828, Joseph Myers; 1835, B. B. Stockton; 1843, Ebenezer Mead; 1855, Charles A. Mattoon, D. D.; 1863, E. Whittlesey; 1878, C. H. Taylor, D. D.; 1888, William W. Totherob, D. D.; Rev. James A. Anderson, the present pastor, took charge May 1, 1889.

The First Baptist Church of Le Roy.—In 1806 Elder Peck, a missionary of the Baptist Church, visited the settlement and preached in the school-house. In 1807 Elder Bennett preached a sermon. In 1810 Elder Witherell spent a Sabbath here, and preached in Hines Chamberlain's barn. Rev. Donald Mann, of Caledonia, often preached, walking from his home in the morning and returning at night, a distance of about 20 miles. Elder Leonard Anson was an early preacher, and assisted in the organization of the church. The council which gave fellowship to the church met June 25, 1818, at the school-house near Oliver Langworthy's. Rev. E. Vining was moderator, and Henry Slayton, clerk. The number of members when constituted was 26. Elder Amos Lampson was their first pastor. Services were held alternately at this school-house and one in the village. Hines Chamberlain was chosen deacon. In September following they were received into the association at its annual meeting in Sweden. The present house of worship was erected on Main street, on the eastern limits of the corporation, on land now owned by E. P. Branch. It was commenced in 1823 and completed in 1829. In 1835 it was removed to Church street and located on land purchased of Joshua Lathrop. In May, 1841, the Baptist Society became a corporate body in accordance with the provisions of the statute, under the name of " The First Baptist Society in Le Roy."· The trustees were elected and Austin Phelps made president of the board, and P. M. Smith, clerk. In June of this year the land was deeded by John Lathrop to the board of trustees. A parsonage was built on Wolcott street in 1858, at a cost of about $1,800. This was subsequently exchanged for a house on Church street, near the church. In 1881 this was rebuilt. The church property, including parsonage, is valued at $10,500. The names of pastors in the order of their service are Amos Lampson, E. M. Spencer, David Morris, John Minor, Barach Beckwith, Ely Stone, A. Willey, John Miller, W. I. Cram, Ichabod Clark, William Hutchinson, H. Daniels, A. C. Barrell, D. Moore, O. A. F. Spinning, I. Clark, W. F. Basten, E. P. Brigham, D. D. Reed, A. L. Wilkinson, C. M. Rupe, and O. C. Kirkham, the latter of whom came in 1885. The present number of members is 217.

The Methodist Episcopal Church.—The most reliable information we are able to secure points to the fact that Rev. James Mitchell was the first Methodist minister who crossed the Genesee, in 1809. In 1813 the Clarence circuit included Clarence, Batavia, Alexander, Attica, westerly to Buffalo, and Bethany, Warsaw, and adjoining country. Rev. Zachariah Paddock came to this circuit in 1819. He preached at Batavia,. then came to Alexander, and put up at Father Hawkins's. The first class of the First Methodist Episcopal Church of Le Roy was formed early in 1823, by Alfred Morehouse, who came here from New Rochelle late in 1822 The members of the class were Alfred Morehouse and his wife, Orange Scott and wife, Asenath Judd, John Hoy, Julia Herrick, Mr. and Mrs. I. Herrick, Mrs. Stanley, Alanson Stanley, and Henry Goodenow. The church was legally organized in 1828. It was included in Caledonia. circuit. The first preacher was Micah Seager, and Goodwin Stoddard, presiding elder. Services were held once in two weeks in the school-house east of the village, and so continued until 1829, when the first brick church was built and occupied, being dedicated by Bishop Roberts. The cost of the building was $950. In 1882 efforts began towards additional church facilities, and Rev. M. C. Dean, with the aid of George W. Dutton, secured financial aid toward purchasing the present parsonage, it being a necessary step for room for the proposed new church. The interior of the old church was burned out by fire in 1884, which hastened the movement for a new building, and in 1885 pledges were obtained sufficient to warrant contracts being made. The corner-stone was laid in May of the same year. The beautiful stone edifice, the finest in Western New York outside of the cities, was completed in 1886, at a cost of over $25,000, by the diligent and faithful efforts of the pastor, Rev. G. H. Dryer. It has a seating capacity of 450 persons, and the Sunday-school of 400, and is heated by steam. The handsome rose window is a memorial to Rev. Daniel Anderson, who was born in 1795 and died in 1886. He received a license to exhort in 1817, and to preach in 1827. He moved to Le Roy in 1823, and was for over 60 years a devoted worker in the church. Another window is a memorial to William Le Roy Bishop, a true friend and generous benefactor. The pastors have been as follows: 1823, Micah Seager; 1824, J. Hustes; 1825 C. V. Adgate; 1827, W. Hoag; 1829, S. Madison; 1830, R. Parker; 1831, M. Seager; 1832, S. Mattison; 1833, R. L. Waite; 1834, L. B. Castle; 1835, I. Chamberlyne; 1836, G. Osband; 1837–38, J. Latimer; 1839–40, P. E. Brown; 1841, D. D. Buck; 1842, M. Seager; 1843, P. Woodworth; 1844–45, A. Steele; 1846–47, C. C. Houghton; 1848–49, R. L. Waite; 1850, H. R. Smith; 1851–52, J. M. Fuller; 1853–54, A. P. Ripley; 1855, S. C. Clark; 1856–57, J. McEwen; 1858, G. De Lamatyr; 1859–60, P. R. Stover; 1861–62, E. A. Rice; 1863, C. Shelling; 1864–66, K. D. Nettleton; 1867–69, P. R. Stover; 1870–71, W. S. Tuttle; 1872, J. Hartwell; 1873, J. Morrow; 1874–75. J. B. Wentworth; 1876, R. F. Kay; 1877–78, R. C. Brownlee; 1879, K. P.

Jervis; 1880–82, M. C. Dean; 1883–85, G. H. Dryer; 1886–89, W. C. Wilbor.

St. Peter's Catholic Church.—Early in the spring of 1849 Rev. Father Edward Dillon came to the village, finding but few families within its limits, but in the town quite a number desiring the ministrations of the church. The nucleus of a congregation was thus obtained and mass was said in the old "Round-house," on the site of the present Universalist Church. Services were held monthly thereafter at the house of Dennis Butler. Bishop Timon made his first visit in July of the same year. In September Father Dillon purchased a lot on Pleasant street and erected a wooden church thereon, in which mass was celebrated on the Christmas night following. Father Dillon continued his ministrations until October, 1850. From the time of his leaving till the coming of Rev. Francis O'Farrell the congregation was served by Rev. Fathers Fitzpatrick and Moloney. Rev. Francis O'Farrell was in charge from October, 1852, to 1856. He gave the congregation two services a month, and enlarged the church to meet the increased attendance. Batavia and Attica churches were also under Father O'Farrell's charge. Father Brown succeeded him for a short period. He was followed by Father F. McGlew, who was here from 1857 to 1860. He officiated three Sundays instead of two, and opened a school in the basement of the church. To meet the increased attendance he bought a lot on Myrtle street (now owned by the Free Methodist Church). In 1860 Rev. Father Thomas Cunningham took charge. He gave service every Sunday, paid for the property on Myrtle street, bought eight acres of ground on Exchange street, and laid out what is known as St. Francis's Cemetery, and greatly enlarged the church accommodations, besides starting a fund for a new church, that being necessary owing to the rapid growth of his congregation. In December, 1868, the congregation was raised to the status of a parish, and Rev. Daniel De Lacy Moore was appointed the first resident pastor. He took up the work of his predecessor, in preparing for increased accommodations, by purchasing a lot on Lake street and preparing plans for a church, which has resulted in the present large edifice, 60x148 feet, built at a total cost of $29,000. Father Moore was not permitted to witness the result of his efforts, for he died in January, 1871. Father L. Vanderpool, who was assistant to Father Cunningham in 1866–67, came here in December, 1870, and after two years of earnest, devoted work, aided by a hard working and generous congregation, finished the beautiful stone edifice in which they now worship. It was dedicated in December, 1873, by Rt. Rev. St. V. Ryan, bishop of Buffalo. To the cost of the church edifice is to be added an outlay of nearly $9,000 to furnish it with the necessary apparatus. There remains an indebtedness of $7,000 on the church. In addition to their church and parsonage the congregation of St. Peter's own a cemetery, which is steadily enlarged and improved in keeping with their needs and means. On Monday, September 2, 1889, the new parochial school-house was opened, under the charge of three teachers, with an attendance of 120 scholars. The congregation numbers 1,300 souls.

The Universalist Society was organized in 1831. They held meetings in the "Round-house," which many citizens will remember as an old landmark of the village for a number of years. The first services preached by any clergyman of this denomination was by Rev. Nathaniel Stacy, in 1812, who died in Pennsylvania. Among the early ministers after the formation of the society were Tomlinson, Knapp, Kelsey, Peck, Brayton, and others. In 1858 Rev. Charles Cravens was chosen pastor and reörganized the society. Under his ministration they purchased the old "Round-house" and caused to be erected on its site the present commodious edifice at a cost of $8,000. Twenty-six members participated in this organization, the officers being H. A. Olmsted, G. D. Crofoot, John Thwing, Alba Paul, and Henry Steuber; A. T. Drake was treasurer, and S. F. Gibbs, clerk. The number of members at this time is 51, under the pastorship of Rev. C. L. Haskell. The present valuation of the property is $5,000. The seating capacity of the church is 250. Mrs. Olive Haaze, who died in 1881, left a legacy of $6,700 to the church, on condition that services are held regularly for 10 years from the time of her death. Rev. F. M. Gibbs succeeded Rev. Cravens, and he was followed by Revs. C. H. Dutton, G. W. Powell, E. W. Fuller, M. L. Hewitt, H. B. Howell, J. F. Gates, De W. Lamphere, M. D. Shumway, and C. L. Haskell.

Machpelah Cemetery [1] is the name bestowed upon a beautiful plat of ground, of about 25 acres in extent, on North street, north of the railroads. The ground was originally bought by Messrs. George W. Blodgett, Abial Robertson, and Chauncey L. Olmsted, who held it for several years and sold lots enough to reimburse them for their outlay. It was transferred to the Cemetery Association at the time of its incorporation, April 30, 1873, by Francis C. Lathrop, Lucius N. Bangs, Henry H. Olmsted, Augustus L. Tryon, William D. Olmsted and Abial Robertson. The grounds are upon an elevation, and are beautifully laid out with an excellent taste displayed in adapting new ideas to the laying-out and beautifying of burial plots, which is worthy of imitation. It is pleasant to note the affectionate regard bestowed in finding room for the remains of so many old and honored residents of the village, thus associating their memories with those of later days. Attention is being attracted and encouragement given to the endowment of lots, whereby the plots can be assured of perpetual care and attention. Some $800 in such funds have already been invested in good mortgage securities, and it is hoped that an increased interest will be manifested in this direction. The chapel fund has the sum of $900 securely invested, of which the sum of $800 was the legacy of Mrs. D. P. Mirl. The endowment fund of the cemetery is to be augmented by a legacy from Mrs. Olive Haaze. The present officers are William Huyck, president; F. C. Lathrop, secretary and treasurer. The trustees are William Huyck, N. B. Keeney, L. G. Paul, E. Rogerson, George W. Cook, and F. C. Lathrop.

Of the other places of interment in and about Le Roy the old bury-

---

[1] By Rev. Samuel Hanson Cox.

ing-ground east of the village is worthy of mention. It was opened in 1801. Most of the early pioneers were buried there. That on Clay street, called the Presbyterian burying-ground, is the next oldest, and the Episcopal burying-ground on Church street is next. The one at Fort Hill also contains the remains of many old residents.

Free Masonry.[1]—On January 7, 1815, a dispensation was granted to Orange Risdon, James Ganson, Levi Farnham, Hugh Murphy, Salmon Butler, Levi Beardsley, Elisha Severance, Thomas Tufts, John Gilbert, Frederick Fitch, Daniel Biddlecome, John Richards, and Paul E. Day to organize and open a lodge of Free Masons under the name of "Le Roy Lodge." Orange Risdon was the first worshipful master; James Ganson, senior warden; and Levi Farnham, junior warden. The first meeting was held February 16, 1815, and on March 8, 1815, Daniel Le Barron was the first candidate initiated. A charter or warrant was subsequently granted by the Grand Lodge of the State June 11, 1816, under the style and number of Le Roy Lodge, No. 260. For the succeeding 11 years it maintained a prosperous career, and during that time acquired a membership of about 150 Masons. The unfortunate "Morgan episode" then occurred, and produced a local explosion of public and private opinion. The village of Le Roy was in the vortex. Some of the best citizens, who were also members of the fraternity, were divided in sentiment as to the perpetrators of the alleged outrages, and quite a number of them openly renounced further continuance with the institution. Several public meetings and antagonistic conventions were subsequently held, and the culmination of circumstances resulted in the complete collapse of Le Roy Lodge, No. 260, by the surrender of its warrant to the Grand Lodge on September 19, 1827.

For nearly a score of years Le Roy then enjoyed an uninterrupted Masonic slumber, and no attempt whatever was made towards any sort of fraternal assemblage or reörganization. Every cycle of time, however, always brings more or less change in public opinion. Many pronounced opponents had either removed elsewhere or died. The crisis was over, and a healthy reäction followed and wiped out the previous antipathy against secret societies. In the adjoining towns of Bethany and Attica Olive Branch Lodge, No. 39, had maintained only a nominal existence. Its condition was paralytic, sickly, and intensely feeble; in fact a mere skeleton; but at this juncture Lucius Parks, William Sheldon, Azor Curtis, Thomas C. Ladd, Consider Warner, Orator H. Kendall, Daniel Biddlecome, and one or two others, who had always adhered to the fraternity, succeeded in having it removed from Attica to Le Roy, and this change of climate and membership brought both health and life to Masonry in this town.

On January 27, 1847, Olive Branch Lodge, No. 39, held its first meeting in the village of Le Roy, under the mastership of Wor. Bro. Lucius Parks, and at the next meeting (February 24, 1847) Patrick Hassett was

---

[1] By David Seaver.

the first candidate initiated. Following that date for more than 42 years the membership has been increased by the healthy addition of several hundred of the very best residents of Le Roy and vicinity. Of course many changes have occurred by deaths, removals, etc., and the limits of a gazetteer sketch preclude entering into a detailed account of the various public ceremonials incident to its history. Its activity, however, has been continuous. Its charities have been bountiful, and with its present good sized membership and healthy treasury no reasonable doubt can exist that Olive Branch Lodge will ever cease in the work of brotherly benevolence. The following are the officers of Olive Branch Lodge for 1890: W. M., Harry H. Falkner; S. W., Walter H. Smith; J. W., Frank Darrow; treasurer, Charles N. Vicary; secretary, Henry Steuber; S. D., Rev. Pierre Cushing; J. D., John N. Champion; S. M. C., Fred T. Wilcox; J. M. C., John C. Ross; marshal, Dr. S. W. Skinner; tiler, Cyrus W. Walker; finance committee, S. F. Curtiss, William Huyck, and C. F. Bissell.

Any résumé of Masonry in Le Roy would be incomplete without mention of R. W. John R. Anderson. To that gentleman more than any other living resident of Le Roy belongs the credit of its present prosperity. As the immediate successor of Lucius Parks be brought brains, zeal, and administrative ability to Olive Branch Lodge, and for 18 years (16 continuously, the longest service of any Mason in the State) Brother Anderson was its W. M. and presiding officer, having initiated, passed, and raised 328 members therein during the time. His life-long love for the brotherhood has been unabated. His many public addresses and contributions to the literature of Free Masonry have always been of a high order and rank among the ablest contributions to Masonry, and his official services to the craft produced good results everywhere. His various terms of office outnumber any one in Western New York. His well-known administrative ability brought Olive Branch Lodge from obscurity to prominence, and gave it a fame as extended as are the limits of the State, and he was second to none in his devotion to the fraternity. As district deputy grand master he exercised supervision over Genesee, Wyoming, Monroe, Orleans, and Livingston counties for six years; as past junior grand warden of the Grand Lodge of the State of New York his well earned reputation is widely known throughout the commonwealth; as grand steward of the Grand Lodge his work was most efficient and equally compensating to the craft; as deputy grand lecturer his work has been of the highest order and benefit to the brethren. He has also acceptably filled the office of assistant grand lecturer of the Grand Chapter of the State of New York. He revived Royal Arch Masonry at Le Roy after a struggle of seven years, and restored it to its pristine eminence by organizing Le Roy Chapter, No. 183, and was appointed its first high priest and served continuously for nine years. He was petitioning member of Batavia Encampment of Knights Templars, and was appointed its first generalissimo. As sovereign grand inspector of 33 in the Scottish Rite he has acquired the highest Masonic distinction ever obtained by any resident of Genesee County; and "that long may he live" is the earnest desire of his many friends.

The semi-centennial celebration of Olive Branch Lodge was celebrated at Starr Hall, June 22, 1870, followed by a banquet at Central Hall, where 1,000 persons were fed at the tables. Visiting brethren from different parts of the State took part in the ceremonies. W. S. Brown, the worshipful master of the lodge, delivered the historical sketch, and R. W. John R. Anderson the principal address. A poem, written for the occasion by William H. C. Hosmer, of Avon, was also delivered by that gentleman.

Le Roy Chapter, Royal Arch Masons, No. 183, was organized pursuant to and by virtue of a dispensation duly issued under the hand and seal of the most excellent Royal Arch Chapter of the State of New York, for that purpose, bearing date of the 12th day of December, A. D. 1864, and granted upon the petition of and directed to companions. John R. Anderson was to be first high priest; Comp. C. Fitch Bissell, first king; and Comp. Marcus L. Babcock, first scribe; and to companions John Butterfield, William Sheldon, Lucius Parks, Consider Warner, Orator H. Kendall, Albert Brewster, William Barnett, Nelson Thayer, William M. Irish, Charles Cravens, Thomas C. Ladd, William M. Tompkins, Robert F. Stage, and Robert McKay, petitioners. Of these petitioners companions Anderson and Bissell are the only ones left in Le Roy. Henry Moody, D. J. Bissell, and Frank Darrow are the principal officers for 1890.

Royal Arcanum received its charter in April, 1882, with 20 charter members. There are at present 33 members, and it is in a flourishing condition. The present officers are Dr. Skinner, regent; G. Strobel, V. R.; E. J. Rumsey, secretary; John Anderson, col.; and T. B. Tuttle, treasurer.

Hope Lodge, No. 76, A. O. U. W., was opened in Le Roy in March, 1877, with about 30 charter members. The present number is 57, showing a steady increase. Its officers are I. C. Mason, P. M.; L. Sellinger, M. W.; M. A. Merritt, fin.; R. M. Dillon, O.; A. K. Drury, recording secretary; A. Harsch, financial secretary; D. E. Curtiss, recorder.

Charity Lodge, No. 53, E. Q. M. A., was organized in 1879. The first officers were A. L. Tompkins, president; L. G. Paul, P. P.; E. D. Shepard, V. P.; S. A. Ball, treasurer; F. A. Steuber, financial secretary; and John Wiss, recording secretary. There were about 35 charter members; there are now about 40 members. The present officers are Harry H. Falkner, P. P.; L. Sellinger, V. P.; F. A. Steuber, treasurer; E. D. Shepard, secretary; and Rev. Pierre Cushing, trustee.

Knights of Labor, No. 9,647, was first started here about 1886. It has had a membership of over 100, but now has only 40.

St. Patrick's T. A. S., No. 275, incorporated in 1869, has 55 active members. Its officers are F. J. Kemp, president; O. Foughey, V. P.; F. Hoy, recording secretary; F. Tulley, financial secretary; H. Coyle, corresponding secretary; W. H. Brown, treasurer; C. Leahy, marshal.

Branch 72, C. M. B. A.—The present officers are as follows: President, Owen Foughey; first vice-president, W. H. Brown; second vice-president, Richard Holland; secretary, Thomas M. Burns; assistant secretary, Thomas H. Linsler; financial secretary, John Martin; treasurer, John Maloney; marshal, Peter Coleman; guard, Peter Cain; trustees, Thomas H. Murnan, M. Muller; representative to Grand Council, James L. Morris; alternate, William Elmore; spiritual adviser, Rev. L. W. Vandepoel.

Staunton Post, No. 396, G. A. R., was organized September 6, 1883, by the resident surviving members of the late war. The present officers are M. P. Pierson, commander; D. E. Curtis, S. V. C.; W. H. Brown, J. V. C.; James Morton, Y. M.; Louis Barr, surgeon; E. J. Niles, chaplain.

Royal Templars of Temperance.—The present officers are S. H. Murdock, counsel; Mrs. A. Paul, vice-counsel; and C. L. Carlton, chaplain.

The Le Roy Gas Light Company was organized in July, 1860, with a paid in capital of $25,000. Nathan Randall was chosen president; P. H. Agan, treasurer; and C. M. Randall, secretary and superintendent. L. M. Bangs and C. L. Olmsted were among the first organizers. At first only 12 street lamps were put up; five years ago there were 48; now there are 122. There are about five and a-half miles of pipe laid. The same company controls the electric light plant now in operation. The officers of the company are D. J. Bissell, president; M. P. Lampson, secretary and treasurer; John C. Bissell, superintendent.

The fire department.— The old method of extinguishing fires by means of buckets, distributed among the villagers, who kept them on hand for use, was superseded in 1834 by a veritable (piano) engine, operated by two cranks, one on either side, turned by hand; this in turn was succeeded by a Silsby (break) engine, costing perhaps $250. Up to this time, about 1850, there was a semblance of organization; but on February 8, 1851, the department was formed and organized, with John W. Shedd, chief; John G. Barber, first assistant; and A. O. Comstock, secretary. The department at present consists of three companies: one chemical, one hose, and one hook and ladder company, whose chief is John Wiss; first assistant, T. W. Larkin; second assistant, W. P. Randall; secretary, S. F. Comstock.

The Firemen's Benevolent Association was chartered in 1851, and consists of the active members of the fire department. Its first officers were John W. Shedd, president; A. D. Lampkins, vice-president; J. H. Lent, secretary; and J. J. Tompkins, treasurer. This association is supported by a two per cent. tax, authorized by the legislature, upon non-resident insurance companies doing business in the State. The association has a fund of over $4,000 invested in bonds and mortgages, and a contingent fund of $300 in the bank. In February, 1889, the sum of

$160 was given to each company. The present officers are S. P. Hooker, president; F. L. B. Taft, vice-president; John Wiss, treasurer; and F. M. Comstock, secretary.

The chief engineer of the fire department is John Wiss; first assistant, Frank Seiz; second assistant, W. P. Randall; and there are about 70 active members.

Fires.—There is scarcely a business house in Le Roy village that is not reared over the ashes of its predecessor. In an old file of the *Gazette* is this startling announcement: " Destructive Fire in Le Roy—all the Business Portions in Ruins." At 3 o'clock in the morning of January 17, 1855, a fire broke out in an old wooden building occupied by Grummon and Pinney, by the former as the printing office of the *Genesee Herald.* Mr. Pinney was a tobacconist. The fire spread both ways till everything between Drake's grocery and Mill street was consumed. The loss was estimated at $100,000, and among the sufferers were Barton & Olmsted, Browning & Kelsey, Samson & Elmore, Foreman & Sons, James Annin, Hascall & Bangs, Olmsted and Adams. This was the largest fire that has ever visited Le Roy. It was 14 years before another really large one occurred. In 1869 a fire broke out in the rear part of Mr. Steuber's cabinet shop. Eighteen buildings in all were destroyed, all those between the old town hall and Mr. Maloney's grocery being burned. The latter was afterwards torn down to make room for new buildings. Le Roy has lost few of its dwelling places by fire. The Bacon Place and the Shayer house are recalled. In the summer of 1875 the Starr block was burned, and with an adjacent block, stores, offices, the public library, which cost so much noble labor, and old Starr Hall with its host of memories.

Newspapers.—In the early settlement the first newspapers published were the *Ontario Gazette* and *Western Repository,* and were issued from Canandaigua in 1804. The mail was brought on horseback once a fortnight by Phineas P. Bates, the mail carrier between Canandaigua and Fort Niagara. His horn was hailed with great delight by the settlers. Previous to the establishment of the mail route letters had to be sent by private hands. John Metcalf succeeded Mr. Bates.

The *Le Roy Gazette* was commenced in 1826 by I. O. Balch. It was a four-page (13x21) sheet, with four columns to the page. At that time the village was very small, and while business was brisk the merchants had not been initiated into the benefits of advertising, and consequently the income from a paper was limited. Mr. Balch's successors in the paper were in the following order: Starr & Hotchkiss, D. D. Ward, Richard Hollister, Rufus Robertson, F. Goodrich, Hon. S. M. Gates, Martin O. Coe, and Cyrus Thompson. The latter, in 1840, sold to C B. Thomson, who was editor and proprietor for 44 years. In May, 1885, Messrs. Marcellus & Hand bought out Mr. Thomson, and in September, 1887, G. E. Marcellus became, and is now, sole owner.

George E. Marcellus was born in Monroe County, and came to Le

32

Roy in 1877. His father, George W. Marcellus, was a minister. Desiring to engage in newspaper work George E. entered the office of the *Courier*, and was for some time local editor of that paper. Upon the retirement of Mr. Thomson from the *Gazette* he, in company with Mr. Hand, assumed control of that paper, enlarged it one column, introduced new features, and notably increased the circulation. For the past two years Mr. Marcellus has been the sole proprietor of the paper. He has enlarged his facilities for job and press work, and fitted up a tasty and convenient office, thus making his a model establishment.

Charles Bartell Thomson, the fourth son of Joseph and Sarah Thomson, was born in Cohocton, N. Y., in 1815. At the age of 15 years he entered Judge Hovey's office, at Mount Morris, to learn the printers' trade. After a time he was publisher of the *Livingston County Journal*. In 1840 he came to Le Roy from Washington, D. C., purchased the *Le Roy Gazette*, and at the time of his decease was the oldest continual editor in Western New York. Mr. Thomson was a man of decided opinions. For 50 years he was a strong supporter, first of the Whig party and then of the Republican party, from which his paper never swerved or changed. During this period he was ever a strong advocate of temperance and good order, as well as of all improvements for the growth and prosperity of the place. He died at Le Roy in 1887, at the age of 72 years, leaving a widow, Sarah H., who survived him only a few months, and a daughter, Elizabeth, who was married to a Mr. Brown, a lawyer, formerly of Binghamton, N. Y., and now a resident of Le Roy, on the Thomson homestead. Mr. Brown is a practitioner in the city of Buffalo.

There were other papers which had a short life. O. A. Brownson, afterwards in high repute among the Roman Catholics for his religious journal, published in Boston, was the editor of the *Genesee Republican and Herald of Reform* in 1829, an agrarian and infidel paper. In 1844 Edward Bliss established, and for two or three years conducted, the *Le Roy Courier*. In 1854 William C. Grummond commenced the *Genesee Herald*, and in April, 1857, Thomas B. Tufts the *Le Roy Advertiser*, discontinuing it in July, 1858. All of the latter had but a brief existence.

The *Le Roy Times* was established in Le Roy in June, 1881, by Charles Morgan and his son, Frank H. Morgan, the latter having since that time managed both newspaper and job office. The paper is a weekly of eight-page form, and 48 columns, pasted and trimmed, and the job department has a city equipment of type, with steam-power presses. In 1886 the Le Roy Times Company, with a capital stock of $10,000, was incorporated, Charles Morgan being made president, and F. H. Morgan, secretary and manager of the office. Manager Morgan was born in Le Roy in 1852, prepared for college at Phillips Academy, Exeter, N. H., and graduated in 1876 from Harvard College, Mass. During the next year he was an editorial writer for various papers, was one of the editorial staff of the *Buffalo Courier*, but giving up this position, owing to impaired health, he, in 1878, bought an interest in the *Index* at Meadville, Pa., where he remained over three years. He came thence to Le Roy to establish the *Times*, in a field then already covered by two newspapers. He succeeded in creating a demand for such a live weekly chronicle of news as has been developed by his excellent tact and management.

The *Genesee Courier*, published by George M. Howe, and now completing its 20th volume, was started in 1870 as a straight out and out Democrat organ for the people in this and Livingston County. The issuing of this publication at that time was rendered possible by an ardent admirer of the editor and proprietor ; thus a beginning was made under very favorable circumstances, and the publication has been kept up to this time without any diminution in the spirit which prompted it, nor loss in circulation. George M. Howe, the editor and proprietor, was born in Yorkshire, Cattaraugus County, N. Y., March 15, 1833, and came here in 1849. He learned the trade of printer with Col. William Seaver (long editor of the *Spirit of the Times* of Batavia), and then assisted in the office of the *Le Roy Gazette*, while C. B Thomson was in charge of that paper. From that office he gained an experience which fully qualified him in becoming the editor and proprietor of the *Courier*. Mr. Howe has identified himself with the growth and prosperity of the village ; has held the office of trustee for five years, and president of the board for two years. During the recent agitation regarding the introduction of the electric light in the village, and when all the members but he resigned, he was elected president, which office he held for seven months, and was the only member during that time, carrying alone the responsibilities of disbursements for the corporation, the like of which had never been done before in any town in the State. Mr. Howe married Isabella Walker, daughter of Andrew Walker, of Scotch ancestry,

The Bank of Le Roy.—The first bank organized in Le Roy was December 28, 1838, under the name of the Genesee County Bank. Its first board of directors was Israel Rathbone, M. P. Lampson, John Lent, Elisha Stanley, Samuel Skinner, I. N. Stage, A. Wilcox, Marshall Smead, Lucius Parks, J. C. Ferris, and Noah Starr. Its first officers were Israel Rathbone, president; John Lent, vice-president; M. P. Lampson, cashier. Subsequently M. P. Lampson became and remained for several years the president of the bank, and S. T. Howard, cashier. On the decease of Mr. Rathbone D. R. Bacon was chosen a director to represent his estate. Other changes occurred among the directors, among them being S. B. Skinner, T. Brown, Warren Fay, and R. H. Smith. The bank continued to do a successful banking business under the supervision of its president, Mr. Lampson, until it was closed and merged in the First National Bank of Le Roy, in January, 1864. D. R. Bacon is the sole survivor of the old bank directors. On the death of M. P. Lampson his son William succeeded him as president, and has since remained at the head of the institution, now called the Bank of Le Roy, which was chartered July 1, 1889, under the State law. Its present officers are William Lampson, president ; Butler Ward, cashier ; W. C. Dorman, assistant cashier ; and William and M. P. Lampson, R. Ballard, Butler Ward, and John Maloney, directors.

F. C. Lathrop is a private banker of Le Roy, where he has been engaged in that business for many years.

Salt interests —During the period of the early settlement of this section, up to about 1815, when the hard working pioneers were striving to make homes for themselves, when no luxuries were to be thought of, and their means limited, one of the necessities then (as always) was salt, which was not attainable without an effort. At that time, with wheat only about three shillings per bushel, and salt from $10 to $12 per barrel, it took 30 bushels of wheat to pay for one barrel of salt, that commodity being hauled from " Onondaga Salt Springs," attended with great expense. Little did the settlers in early times dream of having such an immense store of salt beneath them as to make the value of one bushel of wheat equivalent to a barrel of salt. And yet for a period of 75 or 80 years, during the rapid increase in growth of the Genesee country, all this immense wealth has laid dormant, and from its first inception in 1878 has only attained its present status by slow, hard stages, with periods of great discouragements, ending with a well-earned measure of success.

Salt having been discovered at Wyoming in 1878 some of the leading citizens of Le Roy, believing it could be found here, were induced, through the active efforts of N. B. Keeney, to contribute a fund of $1,500 to test the enterprise. The above named gentleman was enabled to interest C. M. Everest, of Rochester, in the undertaking, and with the guarantee of the sum just mentioned Mr. Everest assumed the responsibility of the work, agreeing to bore for salt to the Niagara formation, or not to exceed 1,000 feet in depth. Mr. Everest, on his part, was anxious to discover oil. C. B. Matthews, of Wyoming, was engaged by Mr. Everest to look after his interests. He secured Mr. Higley, of Bradford, Pa., who contracted to drill for salt or oil. A beginning was made December 4, 1878. In February, 1879, such progress had been made that gas was reached at a depth of 500 feet, and also brine, which came up with such force as to cover the derrick with water, and, freezing, presented a grand sight. At this stage of the work, for some unknown reason, Matthews ceased operations, and, abandoning the work, demanded payment for his labors, by the advice of Mr. Everest. The citizens refused to accede to their claims, on the ground that the contract had not been carried out. A long litigation ensued, extending to the fall of 1881, when Mr. Everest, ascertaining he had been deceived by Matthews, made a proposition to the citizens to put down another (No. 2) well. This was begun, under the superintendence of A. E. Miller, by Curtis & Whitaker, with John Eyres representing the citizens. In this venture four citizens guaranteed to Mr. Everest the sum of $1,300 if he would assume all other risks. This second test-well developed brine at the depth of 615 feet and a salt vein of

20 to 25 feet, and so satisfied the four citizens that they desired to make other tests with Mr. Everest, but, his other engagements not permitting it, he declined; and turned over his interests to the other parties, who began cleaning out the first well, which they found to be plugged with iron obstructions. So difficult an undertaking did this prove that the summer of 1882 was occupied in that work, which proved very expensive. The idea, up to this time, was to demonstrate to the citizens the presence of salt in this locality, seeing that the Warsaw experiments had proved successful.

Work was practically abandoned until the spring of 1883, when, under the auspices of the American Chemical Co., of West Bay City, Mich., a small plant, equal to an output of 100 barrels per day, was started, and the first salt made and shipped in September, amounting to one car load. The process of the above company proving a failure, the works were remodeled in May and June, 1884, and the grainer process adopted. At this juncture, and after the failure of the American Chemical Co., it became necessary for the parties interested in the enterprise to determine whether future business warranted an increase of capital sufficient to enter upon the manufacture of salt on an enlarged scale. To this end it was decided to put down another well, this time at the junction of the R. & P. and D., L. & W. railroads in Pavilion, on the Gilmore farm, three miles south of Le Roy. A well drilled there, to the depth of 840 feet, developed a vein of salt 51 feet thick, a strata of limestone rock being found above and below the salt. This experiment decided the planning for a permanent business, and to locate the future plant at Le Roy, where the railroads offered unusual facilities for shipment. In the fall of 1884 C. F. Prentice, S. C. Wells, A. E. Miller, and N. B. Keeney organized the Le Roy Salt Company, and Mr. Miller was put in full charge of the works. Two grainers were put in with four boilers, so that it resulted in 14,000 barrels of salt being shipped that fall with the aid of 14 workmen.

While this result was fairly satisfactory for a new business, with a small force, it was clearly evident the output could be increased, and good results follow, if an addition could be made to the plant. Grasping the situation in a broad and comprehensive manner additions were made to the buildings, new grainers erected, boilers introduced, and a capital of $30,000 employed, all proving a success. Changes, however, have been made constantly for a more economical production, until, by the energy and enterprise of the company, under the careful superintendence of A. E. Miller, the production has reached 600 barrels per day. The force employed is now 75 hands. Ten boilers of 80 horse-power each furnish the steam and motive power; 11 grainers are in operation night and day; a storage capacity of over 100,000 bushels is crowded to its limits; and a capital of $150,000 is employed. The first block erected was 36x300 feet. The main building is now 136x300 feet, with an addition 40x136 feet. The company has eight wells from which to pump brine. In January, 1889, S. C. Wells disposed of his interest, which is now owned by the other members.

To the members of the Le Roy Salt Co. this community is largely in-debted for such an enterprise in their midst, which has brought prosperity to the town, produced a more active business in all lines of trade, caused the building of many new houses, and the improvement of many more. The pay-roll, aggregating $32,000 per year, turns $600 cash into the channels of trade every Monday.

A. E. Miller, superintendent and general manager of the Le Roy Salt Co., was born August 4, 1840, in Chesterfield, Mass., a son of Lawrence and Alzada (Clapp) Miller. Lawrence Miller, a native of Bavaria, and a graduate of Berlin College, came to the United States in 1835, settling in Massachusetts. In 1841 the family came to Byron, where Mr. Miller died in 1847. He had one son, A. E. Miller, and two daughters. A. E. Miller received only a common school education, but began teaching at the early age of 16 years, and so continued until 28 years of age, when he engaged in farming for a few years. In 1872 he began the drug business, associated with T. B Tuttle, which he carried on until 1884, when he was called upon to take charge of the extensive interests of the Le Roy Salt Co., since which time he has given his whole attention to that industry, and, by his active business management and judgment, has created a business second to none in this locality. Through the respect and confidence of his townsmen Mr. Miller has been placed in offices of trust, having been a member five years, and president three years, of the board of trustees of the village. He married Louise, daughter of John Burden, and they have two children, Maud L. and Jessie B. The family are members of St. Mark's Episcopal Church.

Malt-houses.—The present malt-houses were originally built for car shops by A. S. Upham, where 100 men were employed. They are stone buildings, 50 feet wide and 300 and 312 feet long. After their use as car shops was abandoned they were idle for some time, when they came into the possession of Hugel & Co., who fitted them up into malt-houses. They carried on the business for a time, and then sold to Bergdell & Co. After a time William Huyck & Co. (in 1872) took charge, from whom the present owners, W. D. Matthews & Co, bought in 1878. They employ from October 1st to June 1st about 75 hands, and malt in that time from 600,000 to 700,000 bushels of barley, principally that which is grown in Canada. The superintendent of the business, Edward Rogerson, was born in Yorkshire, Eng., January 27, 1850, where he was educated. He came to Toronto with an uncle, was engaged in the dry goods and hat and cap business for a while, and then became interested in the malting industry. He married Marian R. Matthews, and they have four children: Marian I., Edward A., Vida S., and Wheeler D. His wife died in January, 1888. The family are members of the Methodist Church, and have contributed most liberally to the erection of the new edifice.

The Le Roy roller flour-mills were erected in 1822 by Jacob Le Roy. On his removal to New York Joshua Lathrop continued the manufacture of flour for some time. The present owner, C. F. Prentice, with J. D. Cam-

eron, came into possession of them in 1866. In a few years Mr. Prentice purchased Mr. Cameron's interest. It was a seven-burr mill, but has
been changed to a roller-mill, using the Stevens process, and has a capacity of 200 barrels per day, as well as ample facilities for grinding feed.
The building is very capacious, being five stories in height, and has a
storage capacity of 15,000 bushels.

John Brown's cooper shop is a busy place in the season of fruit. He
makes from 5,000 to 25,000 barrels per year. He has been in the business here since 1853, and is now located on Myrtle street.

L. Sellinger's cider and vinegar works are located on Myrtle street. In
1865 the building was used as a brewery, and operated as such until
1883. There are two vaults for storage.

N. B. Keeney & Son.—The present extensive produce business of N. B.
Keeney & Son was started in 1864 by N. B. Keeney, who purchased of
I. B. Phelps a building on Lake street, near the railroad, designing to do
a general produce business. His warehouse being destroyed by fire, in
1874, he rebuilt the following year on a larger scale and with better facilities to accommodate a rapidly increasing trade. In 1888 the firm
erected a six story iron-clad building west of the old one, in which they
placed all the modern appliances for conducting their business. The are
extensive growers and contractors of seeds, principally peas and beans, of
which they have over 2,500 acres under contract. They also have
branch houses at Pearl Creek, N. Y., Traverse City, Mich., Valley Springs,
Dak., and Oshawa, Ont. In their Le Roy establishment are employed
about 75 persons, among whom are distributed annually wages to the
amount of $10,000, thus greatly benefitting many persons, and advanc-
ing the growth and welfare of the place.

N. B. Keeney was born October 4, 1820, one mile west of Le Roy. He
was a son of Joseph and Mary (Bishop) Keeney, natives of New London,
Conn. Joseph Keeney, son of William, and a farmer, came to Genesee
County in the spring of 1815, and in June of the same year he settled on
95 acres one mile west of Le Roy village. He died in 1846, aged 66
years. He and his wife, Mary, were of the 26 constitutent members of
the First Baptist Church organized at Roanoke in 1816. Mrs. Keeney
died in 1877, at the age of 94 years, having been a worthy and consistent member of the Le Roy Baptist Church 61 years. Joseph and Mary
Keeney had 10 children, of whom Allen, J. Bishop, Nicholas B., and Mrs.
Emma L. Bixby are living. Of N. B. Keeney it can truly be said he is
the architect of his own fortunes. Receiving as good education as the
schools of his early day offered he commenced work for himself at the
age of 18 years, and lived on a farm till 1862, when he moved to Stafford,
where he commenced the produce business, and in 1864 removed to Le
Roy, where he has since resided Mr. Keeney married Mary M., daugh
ter of Calvin Ely, of Lancaster, N. Y., by whom he had two children, Calvin
N. and Martha J. His wife died in 1877. He afterward married Hor-
tense A. Murdock, who was a daughter of Rawson Harmon, of Wheat-

land.   The family are members of the Baptist Church.   Calvin N. Keeney, the present energetic member and manager of the firm of N. B. Keeney & Son, was born in Le Roy, February 6, 1849.   He was educated at Le Roy Academy, and at the age of 18 years began assisting his father in his business, and in 1870 was admitted as partner.   In 1880 he married Charlotte, daughter of Rev. Dr. A. S. Freeman, of Haverstraw, N. Y., and they have two children, Ruth Mary and Charlotte Freeman.

Shiloh's Family Remedies. — These celebrated proprietory articles are manufactured by S. C. Wells & Co., in a capacious four-story brick building, at No. 1 Church street, in Le Roy village.   The arrangement of the building upon the banks of the Oatka River ensures well lighted rooms in every part.   The structure is 45x60 feet in size, and is supplied with an elevator and all the modern improvements to aid in simplifying and lessen the labor of the manufacturers.   It was built in 1877 and enlarged in 1882, and it is again becoming too small for the firm's constantly increasing business.   Being among the first manufacturing interests established here it has contributed largely to the growth of the village, and by extensive advertising in every county in the Union Messrs. Wells & Co. have undoubtedly made the name of Le Roy more familiar to the public than all other local interests combined.   The firm is composed of Schuyler C. and George H. Wells.

Decker & Titman's fruit distillery was established in 1872, on the bank of the creek opposite Haskins's mill, on Munson street, with a capacity of 500 bushels of fruit per day.   This is the only one in the county.   The cider building is 40x50, and the still building 45x50 feet.

John H. Haskins's grist-mill, located on Gilbert street, on the site of an old carding-mill built as early as 1812, is noted for the excellent quality of the flour produced.   This property has been in the Haskins family for upwards of 45 years.

M. A. Ladd's carriage and wagon shop was established in 1854.   The building is 26x80 feet in size, two stories, and built of stone.   Mr. Ladd employs eight or 10 men throughout the year.   Thomas Ladd, father of M. A., came here in 1818 and opened a wagon shop on the opposite side of the street from the present works, and worked at his trade about 40 years.

There have been several fruit evaporators established in Le Roy, but the business is not conducted as extensively as formerly.

Lawson & Houston's new livery stable is located in the rear of the Ross block.   It was started January 12, 1890.   They keep a first-class establishment.

W. S. Brown, a manufacturer of and dealer in all kinds of wagons and carriages, is located at 60 Main street.   He is also an extensive dealer in lime and stone, handling over 85,000 bushels of lime in this vicinity each year.   In his carriage establishment about 15 hands are employed.   The factory was established in 1857.

The Genesee Steam Laundry, the first and only one in Le Roy, was established December 25, 1888, by Edward A. Robbins, at 4 Main street. This is a model establishment, having modern machinery and appliances, and turns out a fine class of work.

Jerome French's broom factory is located on Union street, where he has been in the manufacturing business for over 20 years. He makes about 75 dozen brooms and 50 dozen brush brooms per month. He first began the business at the old Rockwell Hotel, two and one-half miles south of Le Roy, about 1850, and has since been engaged in the broom trade, manufacturing and selling for other people. He also has a farm of 51 acres, and resides at 6 Union street. His first work on brooms was done by hand.

Thomas Gallagher & Son's broom factory, located on Exchange street, was started about 1875. They do a business of about 50 dozen brooms and brushes per week.

Stone quarries.—The stone quarries of Le Roy have been noted for the excellent quality of product, as well as the large quantities shipped. At one time George H. Holmes employed as many as 135 men and 40 stonecutters, shipping 50 car loads per day, fully one-half being used in Buffalo. He has also been a large manufacturer of lime, running two kilns, or about 700 bushels per day. The lime from these kilns is remarkable for its strength. Livingston D. Howell now operates a quarry opened by him in 1873, shipping 25 to 30 carloads per week, the stone being used on all the railroad bridges in this part of the State.

Morris & Strobel's stone quarries are located one-half mile north of Le Roy village, on the Oatka Creek. The firm employs from 50 to 60 hands in getting out building material of blue limestone and stone for railroad bridges.

. W. M. Wattles has extensive monumental works on East Main street. They were started about 45 years ago by a Mr. Kenfield. A Mr. Starr afterwards obtained possession, and was succeeded by Starr & Gordon, and afterwards by James & Morrison. About 1864 C. Strobel took charge, and in March, 1889, W. M. Wattles purchased the works. He handles all kinds of marble and granite.

The Le Roy planing mill was established by Chauncey Olmsted, and was the first of the kind in the county. It was burned, then rebuilt, and again destroyed by fire. William Olmsted then owned the mill for a time, and was succeeded by Laramee & Smith. Olmsted & McKenzie built the present mill in 1872. The owners after this were McKenzie, King & Sage, Hartwell & Sage, and King. In 1879 Frost & Murdoch bought it and continued until 1885, when S. H. Murdoch, the present proprietor, obtained possession.

J. T. Warren's foundry and machine shop is situated on Mill street. He established it in 1878, by purchasing the old Catholic Church. This is the only shop of the kind in the village, and the principal business is model and novelty work.

Elias O. Albee was born June 7, 1841, in Norfolk, St. Lawrence County.

He was a son of Isaac and Sophia (Lincoln) Albee, natives of Vermont, who, after marriage, came to St. Lawrence County.   Mr Albee was a contractor and builder, a farmer, and a leading member of the Methodist Episcopal Church.   He reared seven children.   In 1852 he came to Wyoming County.   His first wife died in 1876.   He then married Nancy (Griswold) Dimock, and is now 84 years of age.   Elias O. Albee was reared on the farm.   When 11 years of age he earned $1.50 per day, and at the age of 16 finished his first house alone.   He went to Buffalo and worked three years in Dart Brothers' planing-mill, and later was three years on the Erie Railroad as brakeman   He was foreman for one year for Holmes Brothers, was contractor and builder eight years in Buffalo, lived at Attica and Darien three years each, spent five years in Batavia, and came to Le Roy in 1880, where he has since resided.   He married for his first wife Jennie Austin, and for his second wife Anna E., daughter of Francis and Mary (Seymour) Pinder, of English descent, who settled in Le Roy in 1849. Mr. and Mrs. Albee had six children, three of whom are now living. They are members of the Methodist Episcopal Church.

Rev. James A. Anderson was born in Ohio County, W. Va., March 1, 1854, a son of James and Rhoda (Thomas) Anderson, who were natives of North Ireland and Washington County, rspectively.   James Anderson came to West Virginia with his parents in 1820, was a farmer, and reared two sons and five daughters.   James A., the youngest, was raised on the farm, was educated at the district schools, and at 16 years of age went to the West Alexander Academy, preparing for the Westminster College at New Wilmington, Pa., where he graduated as A. B. in the class of 1877. He then entered the United Presbyterian Seminary at Allegheny, graduating in the class of 1880.   He was ordained by the Mansfield Presbytery, November 9, 1880.   He taught at Atwood Academy, Armstrong County, Pa.   His first charge was at Mansfield, Ohio, where he remained over six years, and was in Beulah, Monroe County, for two years.   In May, 1889, he came to Le Roy.   December 30. 1879, he married Julia M., daughter of Hon. William M. Francis, of Wilmington, Pa.   He has three children, James F , Joseph Junkin, and William.

James Annin was born July 29, 1828, in Le Roy.   His parents, Joseph and Melinda (Wells) Annin, were born in New Jersey and Milford, Conn., respectively.   Joseph Annin came to Cayuga County, thence to Le Roy, and engaged in the mercantile business, being one of the earliest in the village.   They had children as follows: William Le Roy, the first male child born in the town after the name was changed from Bellona to Le Roy, George W., Joseph W., Catharine, James, Charles, and Sarah. Joseph Annin died in 1835, aged 45 years.   He was a son of William Annin, who was an early pioneer of Cayuga County, and was one of the earliest pioneer teachers of that section   James Annin, son of Joseph, was reared in Le Roy village.   After his mother's death, and at the age of 11 years, he began to earn his own livelihood.   He entered a dry goods store at Mount Morris.   In the fall of 1840 he returned to Le Roy, and with Russels & Sampson began the trade of jeweler. After three years' experience he went to Boston and finished his trade. Six years later he returned to Le Roy and opened a store near the Eagle Hotel, where he remained one year, after which he carried on business at various places until the Lampson House was complete, when he entered the room he now occupies. Mr. Annin is the oldest merhant now doing business in Le Roy. He has since beginning business repaired over 65,000 watches, engraved over 4,000 coffin plates, and has made over $80,000. He married, August 30, 1849, Priscilla W., daughter of William Keith, of Boston, by whom he had seven children, viz: James, Jr., Charles H., of Grand Rapids, Mich.; Elizabeth W., Hattie K., also of Grand Rapids; Frank, of Toledo, O.; Herbert E., of Grand Rapids; and Lillian G. Mrs. Annin died in September, 1879.

Rev. Samuel Bowden, A. M., S. T. D., was born in the city of New York, August 26, 1822. His parents, Andrew Bowden and Rose With-erspoon, were both Scotch-Irish Presbyterians, a race from which our country has derived so many of its most valued and useful citizens. His mother was a relative of John Witherspoon, the well-known signer of the Declaration of Independence. She came to New York city with her parents when she was a young child, and always remained a resident of that city. His father was born January 12, 1786. When 26 years of age he left his father's house and sailed for America, expecting a pios-perous passage; but while he was on the ocean war was declared between Great Britain and the United States. In those days news traveled slowly. As the ship neared the American shores a British war vessel approached, stopped, and boarded the merchantman. The able-bodied men were taken away and pressed into the British service. A few days afterward they were landed at Halifax Mr. Bowden was offered a good position in the British cavalry, as he was a man of unusual power and a superior horseman.

But it was not his object in leaving his native land to become a British soldier. His mind was made up from the first to become a merchant in the city of New York, and that object he lost not sight of for a moment. At the earliest opportunity he escaped from Halifax, boarded a smug-gling boat, with the captain of which he had made the necessary arrange-ments, crossed the Bay of Fundy, narrowly escaping death by drown-ing, and landed in Maine, then a part of Massachusetts, and almost entirely a trackless wilderness. Ignorant of the country, with nothing to sustain him but his unfaltering trust in God and a stout heart, he started on his long journey. It was nearly all prosecuted on foot, through the most of Maine, Massachusetts, and Connecticut. Yet with all these hardships he used to say, "Within a little over three months after leav-ing my father's house I was seated at a communion table, in Dr. Mc Leod's church, in the city of New York." His long journey had almost exhausted his means; still, in about three years, he commenced business as a merchant in the same building where he and his sons prosecuted it for nearly half a century. He retired from active mercantile life at the age of 62, and devoted himself to the care of his invalid wife, and to works of active beneficence. In 1876 came his great sorrow, the death of his wife, after a singularly happy union of 62 years. After her death he lived six years, and died August 17, 1882, at the advanced age of nearly 97 years. To the last he was strong of body, and his mental powers were absolutely unimpaired ; with scarcely a day's illness he quietly closed his eyes and passed within the vail.

Samuel Bowden, the subject of this sketch, was the fifth child in a family of six sons and one daughter. Four of his five brothers still survive. All the family attended private schools in the city, and the sons with one exception went into the father's business. Samuel Bowden entered Columbia College, N. Y., and graduated in 1840, with the degree of A. B. In 1843 he received the degree of A. M. from his Alma Mater. Meanwhile he had devoted himself to the work of the Christian ministry, and after a four years' course of theological study, chiefly prosecuted in the city of Allegheny, Pa., he was licensed to preach October 29, 1844. His health having become impaired by so long and constant study he then spent one year in European travel, and another year in travel through our own country. While he was traveling he was called to the pastorate of the Reformed Presbyterian Church of York, Livingston County, N. Y. This call he accepted, and he was ordained and installed as pastor December 31, 1846. In this pastorate he remained until 1876, when his health again broke down through excessive study and labor. He was obliged again, as in 1844, to obtain relief in travel ; after spending some months in Florida and South Carolina he spent the summer among the mountains of Switzerland. Upon his return, not finding his health sufficiently reëstablished, he resigned his pastoral charge. For three or four years he preached occasionally as strength permitted.

In 1882 he removed to Le Roy, for the purpose of educating his daughters in Ingham University. Finding that his health would probably permit the resumption of regular work he has now been for seven years the stated supply of the Tonawanda Valley Presbyterian Church at Johnsonsburg, Wyoming County, making his home, however, in Le Roy.

Mr. Bowden has been twice married, first, to Maria, daughter of James Beattie, of Orange County, N. Y., her surviving children being Charlotte Jane and Margaret I. His first wife died in 1858. In 1864 he married his second wife, Mary E., daughter of John Donnan, of York. She died in 1873, leaving three daughters, Mary R., Elizabeth D , and Emma S. The trustees of Columbia College, New York, this year conferred on Mr. Bowden the honorary degree of S. T. D.

D. R. Bacon, an old resident of Le Roy, came here in 1839, and formed a law partnership with the Hon. Seth M. Gates, then member of Congress from this distirct. This partnership was continued through Mr. Gates's

Samuel Bowden

for   a cen··   He retired from a
the   himself to the care of
wor   In 1876 c·me his
of h   happy union of 62 ·
he   · ·   August 17, 1882, ·
near·   ·   last he was strong o
pow··· ··   ··· unimpaired · with scar
quie·· ··   ··· ···ed within the vai
    S····   ··· s·· ·r ·· this sketch, ·
fami·· ··   ··· one ··· ···· four of h
vive   A··   ···ly atte··d ···· schools h
with   ··· ···nt ···· ···· busines
tere·
of A   ···· e of A.
ter.   ···· he had ·   ··n·elf to the
mini · ··· ···· a f··· ··· · ·· of theolog
ecute· ·· ··· ···· of ··· · · he was lice·
29, 1844. H·· health ·· ·   ···e impaired ·
study he the ··· ··· ve· ·· ··opean trav
travel through ··· ·· ·· ··   While he was
to the pastorat· ·· ···· ··· ·esbyterian C
ston County, N··· ·   ···ented, and ·
stalled ·· ···· ····· ··   ··· In this
until ··· ·· ···· ··· ·····
and ···· ··· ··· ···· ·
after ·· ···· ·· ·· ·· ·· ·· ·· ·ida and Sout
sumr ·· ····   ·witzerland.
findin· h·· ·· ··· ···· ··· blished, he
charg· ··· ·· ··· yea· ·· preached ·
perm ·ed
    In ··82 ··· ·   to L·· ·· · ·or the pu
daug ····   ·versity. ·· ·ding that
bly p   ·· of ··gu·· ·ork he ·
years   · the Ton··· ·nda Vall·
at Jo   ··· County, making hi·
Roy.
    Mr   ·· ···· first, to M
Beatt   ·· · ·viving ·
Jane ·   ··· ···r·t L· ·l·· ··· wife ·· ··· in 185
his se   Mary E., dau··ter of ··· Don·
in 18·   ···re daug····· ·· Mary · ·, Eliza·
The t·   ··· New· ···k, th·
Bowd·
    D. ··
a law ··· ·   ·eth M. Gates, t·
from t··

Samuel Bowden

second term in Congress, and until the latter's permanent removal from the village to Warsaw, N. Y. Mr. Bacon was born in Hamilton, Madison County, N. Y., April 19, 1812. His residence here had been preceded by his father, Rufus Bacon, and his brother, L. S. Bacon, in 1831. His father purchased a farm at the west end of the village, adjoining that of Capt. Lent, where he built his home and occupied it as a family mansion until his removal to Rochester in 1850. D. R. Bacon's early education was at Hamilton Academy, where he prepared for college, and was graduated at Union College in 1831. His law studies were pursued in the offices of Hon. Joshua A. Spencer, of Utica, and Judge Philo Gridley, and he was admitted to the bar in 1835. For a brief period after his admission he was engaged in the office of Stephen G. Austin, of Buffalo. In 1836 the N. Y. & E. Railroad Co. was constructing the western division of its road, and Mr. Bacon was employed by the company in obtaining the right of way from Olean to Dunkirk. In consequence of this employment he removed to Olean, where he remained until, from want of State aid, the work was temporarily suspended, when he removed to and settled in Le Roy. Mr. Bacon married, in 1844, Elizabeth, eldest daughter of Israel Rathbone, of Le Roy, and Lucy Anderson, neé Ganson. He was elected secretary of the Genesee Mutual Insurance Co., which he held until his temporary removal to New York city. He also formed a law partnership with James Summerfield. His residence in New York was but for two or three years, when, by a sudden affliction in the family of his brother, L. S. Bacon, (resulting in the death of his children,) he returned to Le Roy to engage in his brother's extensive stove manufacturing business, in which he became a partner, and resulted in the relinquishment of his law business, which was never afterwards fully resumed. On the removal of his brother to Rochester Mr. Bacon continued the business in company with Harry Backus until its final discontinuance in 1853. His father also removed to Rochester, where he died in 1854, at the age of 74 years, and was buried in Mount Hope Cemetery. Mr. Bacon purchased the homestead, which was destroyed by fire in 1854, and rebuilt by him. He sold it to the late Rufus Palmer, and it is now owned by Gen. Bissell. Mr. Bacon's present residence is on Trigon Prak, the former residence of Stewart Chamberlin.

In politics Mr. Bacon was an earnest and active supporter, by pen and otherwise, of the Whig party, and of the Republican party from its organization, but was no seeker for political honors. He was appointed postmaster by President Lincoln, which office he held during the war. Liberal and public spirited, Mr. Bacon is always ready to promote social order and morality, contributing within his means to churches and schools. His tastes and pursuits are essentially literary, and contributions from his pen in the public press for the past 30 years unfold a style that is concise and vigorous, the result of careful study and preparation. Mr. Bacon early united with the Episcopal Church in the village, and from his first residence here, except at brief intervals, has been chosen one of its officers, and is at present one of its wardens. He has a family of four sons and one daughter. His eldest son, Walter, has for the last 10 years been a resident of London, Eng., where he is president of one of the tramway railroad companies. Edward is a leading railroad lawyer of New York city, and is the recently elected president of the Baltimore and Ohio Southwestern Railroad. His son Lathrop is a stock broker, and John is at the head of the Meriden Brittania Co's house in New York city. His daughter Mary married Oliver Allen, Jr., of the woolen manufacturing firm of O. Allen & Son, of Mumford, N. Y. It is with his daughter that Mr. Bacon and his wife have their residence in Le Roy.

Frank W. Ball, an enterprising young merchant of Le Roy, was born November 7, 1862, in Le Roy village, a son of Samuel A. and Falla M. (Sherman) Ball, who were born in Bloomfield and Ogden, N. Y., respectively. Samuel A. Ball was reared on a farm and received a common English education. He came from Adams Basin to Le Roy in 1852. About 1863 he entered the grocery store of A. T. Drake as a salesman, and later formed a partnership with Mr. Estee, and afterwards with Mr. Pratt. He was in Churchville two years, and in 1873 returned to Le Roy and engaged in business alone, which he continued until his death in 1887. He was a successful business man, and had the largest trade of any grocer in Le Roy. He reared a family of three children, viz.: Jennie M., Frank W., and Charles H. Mr. Ball was an active and consistent member of the Masonic fraternity, and he and his wife were leading members of the Presbyterian Church. He was a son of Isaac Ball, who came from Massachusetts to Bloomfield, and died at Adams Basin. He had been twice married. By his first wife he had two sons and four daughters. His second wife was Lucinda Adams, by whom he had one child, Samuel A., father of Frank W., the subject of this sketch. Frank W. Ball received a good English education, and at the age of 16 entered his father's store. Since the death of his father he has had sole charge of the large business, and has succeeded in managing it with excellent results. He married Mary R., daughter of Samuel B. Gillett, and they have one child, Helen. He and his wife are members of the Presbyterian Church.

Alexander Baxter was born in Dundee, Scotland, July 6, 1832. He came to the United States, and after reaching his majority he settled in Le Roy. He worked for 21 years for Mrs. Lent (now Mrs. Bissell) as a florist, and at the same time managed a garden of his own for 28 years. He died in November, 1882. He married Mary, daughter of Patrick and Ellen (Donavan) Elwood, who came from County Tipperary, Ireland, in November, 1847, and settled in Batavia. His children were John, who enlisted in the army from Michigan and died in Minnesota, from the effects of two wounds received in the war, and William, who served in the 6th U. S. Cav., and was killed at Brandy Station. Mr. and Mrs.

Elwood died in Batavia. Mr. and Mrs. Baxter had nine children, viz.: Ellen (Mrs. Blair), George (deceased), Jennie (Mrs. Rogers), William, John (deceased), Mary, Maggie, Annie, and Robert. Mrs. A. Baxter has a beautiful house in Le Roy, and deals in all kinds of flowers

Frank J. Bissell was born at Montville, Conn., October 4, 1828, a son of Abel and Mary (Vallett) Bissell, of Hebron and Montville, Conn., respectively. Abel Bissell, born in 1785, was a clothier by trade. In early life he run a carding and woolen factory. In 1848 he came to Bergen being 18 days coming by canal from New York. He reared children as follows: John, Calvin, Jeremiah, Frank, Lucy A., Phebe, and Rachel. He died August 30, 1861, aged 75 years. His wife was born April 1, 1786, and died January 14, 1879, and was a daughter of Jeremiah Vallett, a farmer of Connecticut, whose children were John, William, Jeremiah, Mary, and Nancy. Frank J. Bissell was reared in Connecticut, worked in a carding-mill and a tannery, and after coming to Genesee County became a farmer. He came to Le Roy in April, 1863, locating where he now resides, and where he owns a fine farm. He married, April 18, 1854, Mary Ann Constantine, a native of Java, Wyoming County, and a daughter of Dennis and Honora (Gilligan) Constantine, who were born in Ennis and Durah, County Clare, Ireland, and came to the United States in 1811, with two sons and a daughter, locating first in Rochester, and finally in Java, where he settled on a farm of 100 acres. His children were John, Patrick, Bridget, Margaret, Mary A., Ellen, Catharine, and Elizabeth. Mr. Constantine died in 1861, aged 74 years. He was a son of Dennis Constantine, of Ireland. Mr. and Mrs. Bissell's children are Mary L., now of Wichita, Kan., Francis E., and Catharine G. They have liberally contributed to the erection of the Roman Catholic Church for which he purchased the bell at a cost of $500.

Levi Bissell was born in Hebron, Tolland County, Conn., April 12, 1819, and was a son of Ira and Aseneth (Mann) Bissell, natives of Hebron, Conn. Ira Bissell, son of Levi, was a leading and prominent farmer of Connecticut. He served in the State Senate, as did also his son and grandson, and in the Assembly. He reared two sons and two daughters. Levi Bissell, the subject of this sketch, came to Bergen, where he purchased 167 acres of land which his widow now owns. In May, 1868, he moved to Le Roy, where he resided until his death. He married Bellona A. Anderson, daughter of Seneca and Lucy (Webb) Anderson, who were born respectively July 17, 1798, and February 12, 1804, in Massachusetts. Seneca Anderson came with his parents to Middlebury, Wyoming County, N. Y., in 1805. About 1807 or '08 he came to Le Roy and settled about one mile southwest of the village. He reared eight children, viz.: Bellona A., who was named after the village before it became Le Roy; Col. David, of Van Buren County, Mich.; Harmony Whelan, of Rochester; Lucy Whelan, of Brockport; Orphana Wilbur, of Oklahoma Territory; Holton D., of Belle Plaine, Kan.; Galusha, of Granville, O.; and Dell H. Whelan, of Hillsdale, Mich.

Seneca Anderson died March 27, 1882. He was a son of David, who came from Westchester,. Mass., and who was a farmer, a deacon of the Presbyterian Church for 25 years, one of the organizers of the Presbyterian Church at Le Roy, served as justice of his town, and married Sarah Ewell, who bore him three sons and six daughters. David Anderson was a son of Jonathan, of Ingham. Mass., who came from Edinburgh, Scotland. Levi Bissell and his wife had one daughter, who died at the age of 22. They have an adopted daughter, Bell Bissell.

Fordyce Bannister, born November 8, 1800, in Windsor, Mass., is a son of Versal and Hannah (Packard) Bannister, of Windsor and Goshen, Mass., respectively. His parents came to Genesee County in 1816, with two yoke of oxen and one horse and wagon. Their family consisted of one son and three daughters. He erected a log house (20x36) on lot 156. A roof was put on one end. Fire was built in the center on the ground, and the cabin had neither door nor window. He lived here until his death. He arrived at his new home March 12th with only $1.37 in money. Being in want of bread for his family he went to Mr. McPherson, who had considerable wheat, and arranged to cut one acre of heavy timber, piling brush and cutting rails, and for seven days' work received in pay one and a half bushels of wheat, which he carried on his back to Stanley's mill and returned home with flour. Mr. Bannister reared one son and four daughters. He was a plain, practical man, and died in 1852, aged 87; his wife died in May, 1851, aged 54. He was a son of Christopher Bannister, of Massachusetts. Fordyce Bannister married Charlotte, daughter of Alvah and Hannah (Case) Utley. They had children as follows: Gaston D., of Dakota; Ellen M.; Cora (Mrs. Wright), of Michigan (deceased). who left two children, Versal B. and Harry M.; Evans, of Dakota; Mary; and Jasper, of Dakota. Fordyce Bannister died in 1883, and his wife in 1852.

Luther Bannister was born November 20, 1819, four miles northwest of Le Roy village, on the Stafford line. His parents, Nathan and Thankful (Thwing) Bannister, came from Massachusetts to Genesee County with an ox-team about 1811, and settled on 50 acres. Nathan Bannister served in the War of 1812. He reared a family of five children, namely: Christopher C., Nahum, Luther, Lucinda, and Cordelia. He died in Yates, Orleans County, and his wife in Le Roy. Nathan was a son of William Banister, who was twice married, his wives dying in Massachusetts and he in Roanoke. Luther Bannister was reared on a farm, and at the age of 14 began life for himself, working by the month. He located in Byron, afterwards in Bergen, and settled where he now resides in 1873. He married Mary L., daughter of Uri and Mahala (Utley) Kelsey, natives of Killingworth, Conn., and Bridgewater, N. Y., respectively. Uri Kelsey was one of the earliest shoemakers of Le Roy. His latter days were spent on a farm. His children were Charles D., Mary L., Lodoiska S., and Dorliska A. Luther Bannister has 10 children, as follows: Alice G. (Mrs. Rapp), Carrie M., Adolphus D., Myran N., Mary C. (Mrs. Crittenden), E. Lucinda (Mrs. Brodie), Effice M. (Mrs. Coffey), Carl L, Dwight N., and Delia G. Adolphus Bannister was born June 15, 1853, three and a half miles northwest of Le Roy village.

William Le Roy Bishop, son of William and Laura (Castle) Bishop, was born June 15, 1814, in the town of Le Roy. William Bishop was born in Schoharie County, and his wife in Oneida County, N. Y. He came to Genesee County in 1812, with an ox-team, and settled on 50 acres where his son William L. now resides He served in the War of 1812. He reared three children, Leman C., Harriet, and William L., and was a son of John Bishop, who raised a large family of children. William L. Bishop, having received a fair English education, engaged a few terms in teaching. He has taken great interest in farming, is energetic and ambitious, and has done much to improve the stock of the farmers in his locality. He has been especially interested in breeding and improving Merino sheep, Shorthorn cattle, and Wilkes horses, and is now breeding Holstein cattle. He married Juline, daughter of Abner Ward, of Bergen, and they have had four children: Theron C., Wilber (deceased), Ella (deceased), and Florence. Mr. and Mrs. Bishop are active and prominent members of the Methodist Episcopal Church.

W. S. Brown, a prominent manufacturer and long a resident of Le Roy, was born in Palmyra, Wayne County, June 22, 1828. In 1857 he came to Le Roy and commenced manufacturing wagons and carriages, in which business he is still engaged. In 1866 he located at 60 Main street, where he employs from 12 to 15 hands. He was married to Harriet E. Thompson, of Bethany, and their only child, Louise D., is the wife of Prof. F. M. Comstock, of the Le Roy Academy. Mr. Brown has been supervisor of the town one term, was corporation assessor, and is a worthy member of Olive Branch Lodge, having served as its master in 1868 and 1870. The latter year was the semi-centennial of the lodge, upon the anniversary of which Mr. Brown delivered an historical sketch.

Chauncy E. Bowen, an only child, was born July 25, 1833, in Saratoga County, N. Y. His parents dying when he was but a child, he lived with his grandfather Bowen, on a farm. At the age of 10 years he came to Le Roy and lived with an uncle He received a common school education, and was a painter by trade. December 24, 1861, he enlisted in the 105th N. Y. Regt, which afterward became the 94th Regiment, and participated in the battles of Bull Run, Fredricksburg, Antietam, Gettysburg, and others, and was discharged in December, 1864. He married, January 1, 1856, Emeline J. M, daughter of Julius C. and Hannah M. (Widdifield) Kellogg. Julius C. Kellogg, born in 1811, came with his parents to Le Roy when young. He was a good swordsman, and during the Patriot war in 1837 received a commission as lieutenant for the purpose of drilling troops. He was a regimental drill master, and a prominent Mason. In 1870 he moved to Iowa, where he remained two years, when he returned to New York, but in 1878 went again to Iowa and located in Cedar County, where he died January 21, 1882. He

33

reared two children, Emeline J. M. and Julius F.   The latter was killed in May, 1889, at Trenton, Tenn., while assisting the marshal of the village in making an arrest.   Julius C. Kellogg was a son of Elijah, who was born in Vermont, and was a paper manufacturer.   His wife was Hannah Herrick, who bore four sons and three daughters.   He moved to Bethany in 1856, where he died, aged 88 years.   Chauncy E. Bowen, for a time after his marriage, lived in Bethany, and after the war he located in Le Roy, where he resided until his death, January 4, 1888. He reared four children, viz.: Julius F., Lewis C., Emma M., and Leon W.

James A. Collins, born in Le Roy, August 7, 1841, is a son of Dewey and Anna (Rich) Collins, natives respectively of Massachusetts and Genesee County.   Dewey Collins, born in 1802, was a farmer and brick-maker, and came with his parents to Wyoming County in 1813.   After his marriage he located in Le Roy, where he worked a quarry for plaster, and reared four sons.   He was a son of William Collins, who was an early settler of Wyoming, where he kept hotel for some years.   He had three sons and two daughters, Dewey being the youngest.   James A. Collins received a good English education, and taught school one term.   After attaining his majority he clerked in a grocery store one year, when he returned to the farm near Le Roy.   He has been engaged in selling farm implements and phosphates, and operated a bakery one year.   Since January, 1889, he has been engaged in the shoe trade.   He married Bell, daughter of William Calvert, of Le Roy, and they have one child, Ada G. Mr. and Mrs. Collins are members of the Presbyterian Church.

Archibald D. Campbell, born August 6, 1856, where he now lives, is a son of Duncan and Margaret (Campbell) Campbell.   Duncan, son of Archibald and Catherine (McDermott), was born in Le Roy in 1817, where he always lived.   He married when 33 years of age, located where Archibald D now resides, and died at the age of 66 years.   His children were John (deceased), Anna (deceased), Archibald D., and Peter D.   His parents came from Scotland to Johnstown, and thence to Le Roy in its early settlement.   They reared four sons and eight daughters, and died in Wheatland.   His wife died in 1876.   He received a common school education, and married Jennie, daughter of John and Christie (Campbell) Tyrrell, natives of Vermont, who came to Le Roy when young.   Mr. Tyrrell was killed in battle.   Archibald D. Campbell has four children, Duncan G., Christie A., Florence M., and Jane A., and the family are members of the Presbyterian Church.

Samuel Comstock, a captain in the War of 1812, was born June 17, 1790, in Montville, Conn., and married Elizabeth Turner Comstock, of Connecticut.   His family came to this town in 1834.   The children were Asahel O., Elizabeth A., Amy, and Samuel F.   He engaged in the mercantile business, which he pursued till 10 years before his death, May 16, 1870.   His wife died February 8, 1871.   The daughter Amy died at the age of 16 years.   He was a prominent member of the Presbyterian

Church, holding the office of deacon for nearly 40 years. Asahel Otis Comstock, son of Samuel, was born August 6, 1813, in Montville, Conn., was clerk in a store at Colchester, Conn., came to Le Roy in 1834 with his father, and engaged in mercantile business under the firm name of A. O. Comstock & Co. Their trade was very extensive, having branch stores at Mumford, Warsaw, and other places, the sales in a single year amounting to $80,000. In 1856 the business was changed so as to include the purchase of produce, which he pursued for 30 years. Mr. Comstock was a progressive and enterprising business man. He served as treasurer of the Buffalo, Corning & New York Railroad for several years, was a director for 20 years, and was well posted in all its affairs. He was also a director of the Rochester & Genesee Valley Railroad. He married Fannie, daughter of Zacheus Wheeler, of Connecticut, and their children are Fannie (Mrs. F. C. Lathrop); O. W., a banker in New York; Isaac T., a member of the produce exchange; and Annie, a teacher of music. The family are members of the Episcopal Church.

Samuel F. Comstock, born in Connecticut, March 29, 1825, was nine years of age when he came here. He was educated at the district schools, and entered his father's store when 16 years old, where he remained until 21 years of age, when he entered into partnership with his father and older brother, Asahel O., continuing until 1855, when, in the great fire of that year, their goods and store were burned. He next engaged in the merchant tailoring business for six years, or until 1861, when he took up the general insurance business, which he has followed to the present time. In this line of work he has been very successful, being considered one of the best agents in the county, representing, as he does, a line of old established companies for over 25 years. He has been town clerk for 10 years. He married N. M. Turner, daughter of Peter and Mary Turner, of New London, Conn., and they have two children: Frank M., born May 20, 1855, and Mary T., born October 6, 1865. Frank M. graduated from Union College, N. Y., in 1876, and for the past of 11 years has been principal of Le Roy Academic Institute,

Rev. Pierre Cushing was born in Speedsville, Tompkins County, N Y., May 4, 1855, a son of John and Hannah (Curtis) Cushing. His father was a native of Scituate, Mass., a graduate of Trinity College, Hartford, Conn., and a minister of the Protestant Episcopal Church. His ancestors came from England about 1640 Rev. Pierre Cushing, the third son and fourth child of five children, was educated at Oxford Academy, from which he graduated in the class of 1877, and at Hobart College, where he graduated in 1881 as B. A. He then went to the General Theological Seminary in New York, from which he graduated in 1884, and was ordained a deacon in St. Paul's Church, Rochester, in June, 1884. He was assistant at St. Paul's Church in New York, where he was ordained a priest May 16, 1886, and came to Le Roy in November, 1886, being called to the rectorship of St. Mark's Church. He married Kate B., daughter of George W. Nichols, of Hammondsport, N. Y.

Dr. J. Fred Cleveland, the youngest son of John and Sarah Cleveland, was born at St. Catherine, Ontario, February 25, 1837. When 19 years of age he went to Chicago, and remained there nearly two years, being engaged in the railroad business. About 1862 he went to New York and entered Bellevue Hospital, graduating therefrom in the spring of 1865. He then entered the United States service as acting assistant hospital surgeon, remaining until the close of the war. He afterwards located at Wyoming, N. Y., to practice his profession, where he lived but two or three years, when he came to this town, where he has since resided, enjoying the fruits of an extensive practice and an honorable profession. He was married, April 20, 1870, to Fannie V., daughter of M. B. and Ellen M. Fisher of Wyoming. He has one child, Harold F., born May 3, 1880. Dr. Cleveland's medical career has been, from the first, one of continued prosperity. When only a first-year student he was selected by the faculty of the college, out of a class of over 100, as house physician of Charity Hospital, Blackwell's Island. He was soon promoted to Bellevue Hospital, taking charge of the female wards, over which he presided until the date of his graduation.

John N. Champion, only child of John N. and Amanda A. (Boyer) Champion, was born May 21, 1849, in Le Roy village. Receiving a good academic education he, at the age of 19, entered the hardware store of A. G Carpenter & Co , as salesman, and later was with M. F. Bixby. In October, 1873, he started the Le Roy livery and sale stable, and September 1, 1878, he took charge of the same as agent for H. W. Hascall. January 1, 1890, he purchased the entire business, and has handled more fine horses than any other man in Genesee County, making his purchases in nearly every part of the United States and Canada. His shipments of horses have been mostly from the Western States. Mr. Champion has to a considerable extent engaged in contracting earth work. He is an honored and respected member and officer of Olive Branch Lodge, F. & A. M., of Le Roy, and also a member of Batavia Commandery. He married Carrie E., daughter of H. H. Olmsted, of Le Roy, and they have four children, John O., Henry H., Carrie E., and Albert N. John N. Champion, Sr., born in Lebanon, Conn., was one of two sons and two daughters born to John and Rhoda (Rockwell) Champion. He came to Le Roy with his parents about 1825, and was a leading dry goods merchant for about 25 years, which business was established by his father. His wife was born in New York city, a daughter of Capt. Joseph Boyer, who was born on Bermuda Island, and was a sea captain during his life. He married Mrs Emma (Maghee) Lewis, who bore him two sons and five daughters, and who had one son and one daughter by her former husband, Richard Lewis, of Lown Island. She lived in the old Somerindyke house, which was the last of the old relics torn down. After Mr. Boyer was lost at sea his widow and family, in April, 1831, came to Le Roy.

Alexander Clark, son of William, was born May 28, 1819, in County

Monaghan, Ireland, a son of William and Ann (Anderson) Clark, natives of the same place. They had three sons and three daughters, as follows: Alexander, William, David, Martha, Mary A., and Sarah. William, Sr., with his family, came to the United States in 1849, and located in Mumford. In 1868 he located where Alexander now resides, where he died, aged about 80 years. He was an Episcopalian. Ann (Anderson) Clark was a daughter of John Anderson, a farmer, who had three sons and three daughters, and came to the United States and settled in Genesee County. Alexander Clark, who was reared on a farm, came to the United States in November, 1847, and settled in Mumford, and located where he now resides in 1868. He married, June 19, 1872, Jane, daughter of James and Elizabeth (Wood) Wilson, all of whom came from County Down, Ireland, in 1851, and settled in Wheatland Center. The children were Robert and John, of Nebraska, and Jane. Mr. and Mrs. Clark's children are William J., Libbie A., Jennie D., Martha G., and Alexander E. David Clark, brother of Alexander, served in the 8th N. Y. Cav., and was wounded by a ball entering the right side of his mouth, which was taken out at the back of his head.

Willard M. Chapman, born November 22, 1855, in Le Roy village, is a son of William J., who was born in England and came to the United States about 1830. The latter lived in New York until about 1852, when he came to Le Roy, where he resided till his death in 1886. By occupation he was a butcher. Perhaps no man in Le Roy was better informed in ancient and modern, sacred and profane, history than he. Mr. Chapman was a great lover of Shakespeare, and was a ready and interesting talker upon almost any topic. Willard M. Chapman is self-educated. When but 10 years of age he began as errand boy in the grocery store of A. T. Drake. At the age of 12 he began working by the month, which he continued until 1877, when he entered the postoffice as a clerk. In 1883 he opened a real estate agency. By his indomitable will, energy, and perseverance he has built up a good trade. Honorable in all the relations of life, pleasant and courteous to all, he is respected and esteemed by all who know him. Mr. Chapman was married, in April, 1879, to Elizabeth, daughter of Russell Robbins. They are the parents of two sons, Carlos and Theodore R.

Charles L. Carlton, son of George W. and Sarah (Annas) Carlton, was born May 7, 1833, in Piscataquis County, Maine. He received a good English education and at the age of 16 began working by the month on a farm. When 18 years of age he came to Le Roy, where he learned the wagonmakers' trade with W. S. Brown. In 1866 he opened a shop for himself, on Mill street, which he has since continued, doing mostly custom work. He was burned out in 1869. He married Sarah M., daughter of Aruna and Margaret (Howland) Fosket, old settlers of Bergen. George W. Carlton and his wife were born in Orono, Maine. He was a drummer in the War of 1812, was a farmer, and came to Riga, Monroe County, in 1846, where he resided till within a few years of his

death, which occurred in Iowa City in 1870, aged 71. He had four sons
and seven daughters, of whom three sons grew to manhood, viz.:
Charles L., Thaddeus S., and James A. The latter served in a New
York cavalry regiment during the war, and died in Iowa City. Charles
L. Carlton was a farmer and came to Monroe County about 1830. He
reared a family of four sons and four daughters His sons were Barney,
George W., Elijah, and William.

George W. Chaddock, born in Lockport, August 4, 1826, is a son of
Thomas and Sallie (Bow) Chaddock, who came from New England,
Thomas was a blacksmith and had four children, namely : James, Thomas,
Elizabeth, and George W. Thomas died in Bethany. George W. lived
with an aunt in Stafford, secured a limited education, and at the age of
15 years began to learn his father's trade at Pine Hill. At the age of 20
he learned the tailors' trade at Barre Center. He came to Le Roy and
worked in Upham's car and carriage works two years, was four years at
Pavilion, and then moved to Batavia. In 1861 he returned to Le Roy,
where he has since resided with the exception of four years spent in Rochester. By his wife, Frances L., whom he married January 1, 1851, he
has one son, George W., of Los Angeles, Cal. They are Presbyterians.

Matthew Conlin, a native of Ireland, was born in 1820. His father
died in 1823. At the age of 12 years he came to Clifton, thence to
Wheatland, and finally to Le Roy in 1869. He married Ann Fox, of
County Westmeath, Ireland, and they have three sons, Michael, Matthew,
and William. They are members of the Catholic Chuch.

David E. Curtis was born June 19, 1842, in Le Roy. His parents,
Joseph and Tirzah K. (Hulburt) Curtis, were born in Vermont, the
former April 22, 1806, and the latter May 13, 1807. Joseph came to
Genesee County with his parents, who were among the first settlers of
the county. He was a farmer and an axe helvemaker. In 1854 he
moved to Wyoming, Stark County, Ill. where he remained one year.
He returned to Illinois, and died October 21, 1886. His wife died in
August, 1878, in Genesee County. He reared eight children : Laura
Havens, of Illinois; Sabrina (deceased); Daniel J., of Panora, Ia.; Betsey
J. (Mrs. Eddy), of Michigan ; Morley ; Anson H., of Davis County, Mo.;
David E.; and John C., of Illinois. Joseph Curtis was a son of Joseph
and Betsey Curtis, who came from Vermont in 1811, making the trip in
an ox cart. They located on 100 acres of land where David E. now resides. He was a soldier of 1812, and moved to Wyoming County and
died there. His wife died in Genesee County, May 17, 1854, aged over
90 years. They had 13 children One of his sons Stowell, served in
the War of 1812, and died in Allegany County. Mrs. Tirzah K. Curtis
was a daughter of Daniel Hulburt, who was born December 29, 1779.
Mr. Hulburt married Kezia Byam, and they were early settlers of Stone
Church. He served as captain in the War of 1812, had three sons and
three daughters, and died in Genesee County, February 12, 1818. His
father was Gen. Daniel Hulburt, of Revolutionary fame, who died Febru-

ary 16, 1816, in Genesee County. David E. Curtis was reared in Genesee County. November 3, 1861, he enlisted in Co. D, 104th N. Y. Regt., and participated in the battles of Cedar Mountain, second Bull Run, Antietam, Brandy Station, Chantilly, Seven Days' Fight, Thoroughfare Gap, Manassas Junction, the two battles of Fredericksburg, Gettysburg, second Brandy Station, and the Wilderness. At Gettysburg he was wounded in the left foot, and at the Wilderness he lost his right jaw. He participated in 17 battles and skirmishes, and was discharged, after being in the hospital nine months, in February, 1865. He had been made sergeant in the fall of 1862, and after the battle of Gettysburg was made color-sergeant. After his discharge he returned to Genesee County, where he has since been engaged in farming. He purchased his first 26 acres where Mr. Stoppelbine now lives, and in 1876 located where he now resides. He has served as constable and deputy sheriff, the latter position of which he now holds. Mr. Curtis married, March 9, 1864, Laura, daughter of Daniel and Ora (Harris) White, and their children are William E., Franklin H., and Nellie L.

Alexander A. Douglass was born in Madison County, N. Y., in May, 1815, a son of Alexander and Elizabeth (McBeth) Douglass, natives of Scotland, who came to Peoria about 1829, where he resided until his death. He was a soldier of the War of 1812. He reared two sons and three daughters, and in 1859 settled where his widow now resides. He was twice married. His second wife was Margaret C., daughter of Archibald and Catherine (McDermott) Campbell, natives of Scotland, who came to York, Livingston County, in 1813, and later to Le Roy, settling on 160 acres of land. They reared 11 children. He was 78 years old at the time of his death. His wife died in 1876, aged 82. She was a daughter of John and Epheriah McDermott, who were among the first settlers in Wheatland. Mr. Douglass was a United Presbyterian, and died July 3, 1878.

C. N. Dibble, son of Henry B. and Pamela (Pierson), was born June 1, 1838, where he now resides. His parents were from Massachusetts and Connecticut. Henry B. came to Bloomfield, and thence to Stone Church about 1820, where he lived until his death in 1875. He was a son of Linus Dibble, who married Vienna Kellogg, who came to Stone Church about 1820. The children of Henry B. were Vienna, C. N., and Harlan. C. N. Dibble has always been a successful and prosperous farmer.

Morris C. Decker was born April 12, 1850, in Sparta, Sussex County, N. J., where he was raised and received his education. On reaching his majority he engaged as a street car conductor in Newark, N. J., for one year, when he came to Watkins, N. Y., where he had a meat market until the spring of 1873, when he came to Le Roy, where he has since operated and managed a fruit distillery for Decker & Titman He also owns and successfully operates a large wholesale and retail liquor and cigar store in Le Roy village. He is a son of James L and Ellen (McCoy) Decker, of Sussex County. James L. Decker is a prominent citizen of Sussex County,

N. J., both in politics and business. He has been sheriff of his county, represented his county two terms in the Assembly of his State, and is largely engaged in manufacturing interests and farming. He reared four sons and one daughter, of whom Morris C. is the second child. He is a son of James Decker, who was a son of Henry, a descendant of Peter Decker, of Holland parents, and the first white man who, in 1740, settled where Deckertown, N. J., now is. Some of the most distinguished and wealthiest families of New Jersey are the descendants of the Decker family. Gen. Judson Kilpatrick's grandmother, Fametje Kilpatrick, was a daughter of Josiah, son of Peter Decker, of Deckertown. Morris C. Decker married Mary, daughter of William and Elenore Smith, of Unionville, Orange County, N. Y. William Smith came from England, and was the patentee of rubber webbing, which became very valuable to the owners. Mr and Mrs Decker have one child, Percy C. He is an active and leading Mason, and one of the active and progressive business men of Le Roy.

Ira C. Davis, son of Powell C. and Ann (Scribner) Davis, was born July 7, 1856, in Newstead, Erie County. Powell C. Davis was born in Erie County, and his wife near Toronto, Canada. Their children were Ira C., William, Jennie, and Porter. Mr. Davis moved to near Batavia, and thence, in 1879, to Perry, Wyoming County. Powell C. was a son of Eden Davis, who was born in Genesee County, and reared six children, as follows: Lewis, Gehana, who married a Mr. Brown, Lyman, James, Powell, and Caroline, who married John McPherson. Eden Davis was a son of James and Johanah (Wilcox) Davis, who came from Killingworth, Conn. with an ox-team, and first settled about three miles east of Ganson's (now Le Roy), on a farm taken up by Gen. Daniel Davis about 1800 James Davis reared four sons and two daughters: Lewis, Eden, Ezra, Hamlet, Sarah, and Betsey. Ira C. Davis was reared on a farm and received a common school education. May 6, 1885, he married Margaret, daughter of James C. and Ann (Cunningham) Williams, of Geneseo. Mr. Williams was raised near Dublin, Ireland, and came to the United States about 1849. He moved to Livingston County, and is a molder by trade. He has been twice married. His first wife was Kate Baugardner

Samuel L. Dix, son of Leonard and Dorothy (Johnson) Dix, was born June 4, 1809, in Wilmington, Vt The family moved to Jefferson County, N. Y. They had 10 children, of whom Samuel was the sixth. He came to Monroe County about 1831, and in April, 1842, married Julia A., daughter of William and Sarah (Widner) Wooden, who were born April 1, 1780, and February, 1782, respectively. William Wooden, of Newburg, came to Ontario County, thence to Chili, Monroe County, where he resided and accumulated much property. He was an influential and leading citizen of his town, a liberal giver to all improvements, was justice several terms, and held other positions with honor and credit. He died aged 83 years. His father was James, who was born in New

York, and whose father was from England James Dix served in the French and Indian wars. In 1795 he came to Geneva, and in 1811 to Chili, where he died. Sarah (Widner) Wooden, born in 1782, came to Geneva at the age of six years with her parents. Her father was an early ferryman. She was the mother of 14 children. Samuel L. Dix was a farmer. In 1865 he came to Le Roy, and died in 1872. He reared five children: Harriet N., Wallace R., James M., Julia A., and Sarah M. Mrs. Dix still survives.

John Eyres, son of John and Eleanor (Whitmore) Eyres, was born May 13, 1836, in County Leeds, Canada. He received a good English education, has been a farmer and a shoemaker, and came to Le Roy about 30 years ago. He has carried on shoemaking for about 20 years. Mr. Eyres was one of the first movers in developing the salt interests of Le Roy, representing the citizens in superintending and looking after their interests at the test-well, which was begun January 4, 1882, and has been connected with the Le Roy Salt Co for one year. For the past three years he has been associated with Mr. Kidd, who started May 28, 1886, and now has four wells. Mr. Eyres gives his entire attention to the salt industry, and is well posted in the geology of this section. He has been twice married, first, to Margaret Wright, by whom he had one daughter, now deceased For his second wife he married Mary E., daughter of Matthew Shaw, of Le Roy, who has also borne him one daughter.

William Elmore, son of Richard and Elizabeth (Aylward) Elmore, natives of County Kilkenny, of Ireland, was born September 10, 1830, and was educated in Ireland. He came to Quebec, September 9, 1854, where he worked until 1855, when he came to Dunkirk and worked in a tannery, and afterwards removed to Buffalo, and thence to Pennsylvania. In 1857 he came to Alexander, where he has since worked on the railroad, except four years which he spent on a farm, and four years in the oil regions. He has been connected with the N. Y. C. & H. R. Railroad since 1861. By his wife, Catherine, he has 10 children living: Richard J., Thomas F., William J., John B., Elizabeth C., Catherine L., Michael J., Mary, Frances, and Ellen G The family are Roman Catholics.

Charles E. Edson, son of Dr. Galen K. and Lucy (Hudson) Edson, was born September 6, 1839, in Rutland, Vt With his parents he came to Le Roy, and received a common school education. In 1870, with a colony of 100, he went to Blue Rapids, Kan., where he lived five years, when he returned to Le Roy, where he has resided since, and for the past five years has been engaged in gardening. He married Martha E., daughter of Ward and Eliza (Trimbell) Beckley, who were born in Connecticut and Johnstown, N. Y., respectively, and who reared one son and four daughters. Mr. and Mrs. Beckley came to Le Roy in 1810, and settled where Mrs. Rumsey now resides. Mr. Beckley died in 1880. He was a son of David Beckley, of Connecticut, was an early pioneer of

Genesee County, and was a soldier of 1812. Mr. and Mrs. Edson's children are Archie N., Frank C., Charles L., and Hattie.

Dr. Galen K. Edson was born in Maine, June 13, 1815, a son of Cyrus and Hannah (Hudson) Edson, who were both born at Bridgewater, Mass., in 1777. Dr. Galen K. came to Le Roy in 1842, and practiced his profession until 1878. His parents located at Rutland Vt., about 1817. Cyrus Edson was a son of Ezra, who was born at Bridgewater, Mass. His wife was Rebecca D. Johnson, and he was grandfather of ex-Mayor Edson, of New York city. Ezra Edson was a son of Samuel, who was the fifth generation from Samuel Edson, who settled at Bridgewater, Mass., in 1692, and who built the first mill in the place.

Felix Falkner, son of Jeremiah, was born in Leicestershire, England, May 26, 1804. He was a banker. With his wife and two children he came to this country in 1853, locating at Utica, N. Y , where he died in 1887. His wife died in 1880. His eldest son, Joseph G., resides in Utica, and is engaged in the auction and commission business. The second son, Harry H. Falkner, was born in Leicestershire, England, September 7, 1838, and was 15 years of age when he came to the United States. He married, June 16, 1875, Rebecca W. C., daughter of Rev. Henry Stanley, of Le Roy, and they have three children, viz.: Henry S., born March 13, 1876; Rebecca W. C., born October 13, 1878; and Catharine D., born February 22, 1886. All are members of St. Mark's Church. For the past 10 years Mr. Falkner has been engaged in the real estate and fire, life, and accident insurance business, in the latter of which he has been associated with S. F. Comstock. He represents five large fire insurance companies, one life, and one accident (the Travelers).

Benjamin A. Fuller, M. D., born in Providence, R. I., November 17, 1845, was a son of Asa W. and Nancy A. (Woodworth) Fuller. At the age of five years he came to Middlebury with his parents, and received his education at the academy there. In 1862 he came to Le Roy, entered the office of Gen. F. C. Bissell, read law for three years, and entered and graduated in 1865 from the Albany Law School. He was in a law office in New York for three months, but the business not suiting his taste he traveled for five years for George W. Bassett & Co. In 1870 he came to Le Roy, studied medicine with his father, and attended the Buffalo Medical College, from which he graduated in 1873. He began practice at Le Roy and Byron Center. In 1877, after his father's death, he succeeded him in his profession, and has since been a successful practitioner here. He married, July 16, 1873, Alice I., daughter of H. O. and Jennie Cowan, who came from England. Mr Cowan was a merchant tailor. Dr. Fuller has a daughter, Clara Louise.

William W. Faunce was born September 29, 1831, in Wheeling, W. Va., a son of Jeduthan L. and Abigail (Davis) Faunce, natives of Vermont and Pennsylvania, respectively. Jeduthan L. came with his parents to Bethany about 1809 or '11. When a young man he went to Wheeling, where he married his wife. He was a molder by trade. In

1832 he returned to Bethany, where he was engaged at farming, running a hotel, and working at his trade. He died in Pennsylvania. He was a son of Eleazer and Melinda (Kendall) Faunce, both of Vermont. Eleazer Faunce was a blacksmith and settled three miles east of Linden, where he worked at his trade, his wife often assisting him. He served as a drummer in the War of 1812. Mr. Faunce had two sons, Halsey K. and Eleazer, and one daughter, Fannie E. Roe, of Attica. He died in Linden. He also run a hotel for many years, and was engaged in hauling lumber from Pennsylvania, which he put into buildings. His father was a Frenchman. William W. Faunce lived in the hotel with his grandparents until 13 years of age, when he went on a farm, and at the age of 15 he entered the store of George Dimond, of Batavia. Returning to Bethany he attended Bethany Academy, and afterwards learned the trade of wagonmaking. When 19 years of age he came to Le Roy and worked for A. S. Upham and Charles Brindsmade, after which he entered the Eagle Hotel, where he remained two years, when he began business for himself. In 1861 he began the livery business, and soon after purchased the barn where he is now engaged. This was formerly the old stage barn, and is the oldest livery stand in the place. Mr. Faunce served nine years as deputy sheriff, beginning in 1875, and has been constable 15 years. He married Ann M., daughter of Charles Brow, of Dresden, Yates County, and they have one son, George E.

William H. Graham was born in London, Eng., January 10, 1855, a son of William H. and Mary (Grant) Graham, who had three sons and two daughters, of whom William H. was the second. He received his education in private schools, came to the United States in 1883, and lived in New York and Rochester, where he was engaged as a veterinary surgeon. In April, 1887, he came to Le Roy, where he has resided since, giving his entire attention to his profession. His wife was Florence Tidy, of near London, Eng., and they have two sons and two daughters.

Jerome French, son of Elijah and grandson of Gen. French, of Vermont, was born October 17, 1825. His father died when he was three years of age, and he lived with John Deming until 21 years old, when he worked for farmers about one year, after which he learned the broom trade. He married Abbey M., daughter of Samuel Bishop, and they have one child, Grace B. Elijah French married Sallie Flint, of Randolph, Vt. He died about 1828, and his wife October 10, 1873, aged 76 years. Samuel Bishop came to Le Roy in 1811, served in the War of 1812, and was the first settler in what is now Pavilion, on the farm now owned by J. R. Bliss and Jay Bishop. The first night of his arrival he slept on a rock. He cleared the farm, lived a bachelor's life for nine years, and finally married Electa Allen, and they had a family of four children, three of whom are living, viz.: Willard W., of California; Caroline (Mrs. George Roberts); and Abbey (Mrs. Jerome French), of Le Roy. Mr. Bishop died April 14, 1870, aged 85 years, and his wife

April 8, 1871, aged 70 years.   He took an active part in politics, and was a Whig and Republican.

Samuel Gillett, born August 6, 1823, in Orange County, N. Y., is a son of Isaac and Eleanor (Vail) Gillett, who were born in Orange County, he in 1796 and his wife in 1799.   In 1843 they removed to Avon, and thence to Stafford, where they resided till their deaths.   Isaac Gillett was a man of sterling worth and integrity, and filled several responsible local positions.   He reared a family of four sons and two daughters, viz.: Caroline, Samuel, Alsop V., Charles, Frances (Mrs. Van Vleeck), of Shiloh, Ill., and William, an attorney, who died at East Saginaw, Mich. Isaac Gillett died in 1869 and his wife in 1867.   His father, Charles Gillett, was born on the Hudson River, and was a farmer in Orange County, N. Y.   His wife was Sarah Godfrey, who bore him two sons and four daughters.   Samuel Gillett was raised on a farm and received his education at Montgomery and Chester, N. Y.   He began teaching school when but 16, receiving $13 per month.   On reaching his majority he began life on a farm, and made his first purchase of 80 acres in 1848, in Stafford.   In 1867 he came to Le Roy so that he might better educate his children, and located on the farm where he now resides, about one mile northwest of Le Roy village.   Mr. Gillett is an intelligent and substantial farmer, courteous and hospitable, and commands the respect of all who know him.   He was married to Susan, daughter of James J. and Huldah (Hudson) Board, and their children are Emily, William, Hudson (deceased), H. M., an attorney at Bay City, Mich., James B., Nellie, Charles, of Sioux City, Ia., S. Frank, Elmer, also of Sioux City, May (Mrs. Ball), Bertha, Gaylord C., and Jesse O.   Mr. and Mrs. Gillett are leading and consistent members of the Presbyterian Church.

James B. Gillett, son of Samuel and Susan (Board) Gillett, was born January 26, 1854, in Stafford, was reared on a farm, and received a good common school and academic education.   At the age of 18 he began teaching school, which lasted three terms, and at the age of 21 entered the hardware store of Pease & Buell, of Batavia, where he remained three years.   In the fall of 1877 he formed a partnership with James McKenzie, and opened a hardware store the first door east of his present place of business, with about $2,500 in stock.   Four years later he moved into the store he now occupies, with Mr. McKenzie.   Mr. Gillett is a first-class business man and has made his business a success.   The concern is carried on under the firm name of James B. Gillett & Co. He married Louise, daughter of John and Anna K. Wiss, and has two children, Marian L. and Anna K.   Mr. Gillett is a member of the I. O. O. F.

John W. Grumiaux was born January 17, 1861, in Le Roy, a son of Lewis and Louisa E., who came from France and England, respectively. He received his education in the village of Le Roy, and in December, 1880, engaged as agent for the *Buffalo News*.   Three years later he received the agency for the *Rochester Union*, and worked one year in the

Western Union Telegraph office. He then entered in succession the employ of Chapman & Boak, newsdealers, of J. K. Boak, and of H. J. Goodyear, tobacconist, who occupied a store in the Maloney block. In June, 1885, his father bought out H. J. Goodyear, and conducted the business as Grumiaux & Son until April, 1887, when John W. became the sole owner. He also purchased the news business of J. K. Boak, April 1, 1888, and opened the store where he is now located, and where he has worked up a successful trade. He has a reading room and a circulating library connected with his store, and is the agent for Butterick's patterns.

Patrick Gleason, born in Le Roy, June 18, 1859, is a son of Michael and Mary (Mackey) Gleason, of Tipperary, Ireland, who came to Le Roy in 1848, and lived here until their deaths. The father died in 1872, and the mother in 1889. Their children were Thomas, Catherine, and Patrick. The latter received a common school education, and at nine years of age began work in Keeney & Son's warehouse, continuing there until 1886, when he purchased the business of H. E. Walker and began dealing in coal, fruits, beans, and all kinds of produce, doing a very extensive business. He married Mary, daughter of Robert and Bridget Flinn.

Bernard Growney, son of Barney and Rose (Fagan) Growney, natives of Ireland, and farmers, was born in September, 1834. Barney died in Ireland, and left five children, viz.: Mary, James, Ann, Bernard, and July. Bernard came to Bergen in 1852 with his mother and the children, and settled on a farm where the mother died. He received a limited education, and October 14, 1861, enlisted at Fort Hill School in Co. B, 100th N. Y. Inf, and was in the battles of Williamsburg, Fair Oaks, Charleston, and at the siege of Fort Wagner, where he was wounded ; was taken prisoner at Deep Bottom, Va., in 1864, was taken to Belle Isle, Libby, and Salisbury prisons, and was released in March, 1865. He was sent to Wilmington, N. C., thence to Annapolis, and was discharged at Rochester, May 25, 1865. He was also wounded in 1864, when tearing up the Petersburg & Richmond Railroad, and at Salisbury in attempting to escape from the prison. Since the close of the war he has been engaged in farming, and in 1869 purchased his present place. He married Bridget, daughter of Miles O. and Maria Finn, of Le Roy, who bore him children as follows : James M , Mary L., and Willie (deceased). His present wife is Bridget Carroll, of Wyoming. · The family are Roman Catholics.

John H. Haskins was born in Londonderry, Vt., January 13, 1823, a son of Solon and Sophia (Hasey) Haskins, natives of New Hampshire and Bennington, Vt., respectively. Solon was a farmer, and served in the War of 1812. He came to Le Roy, Genesee County, in 1830, and settled on a farm of 86 acres. In 1838 he located where John H. now resides, and in 1844 purchased Clifford's mill, now known as Haskins's mill, which his sons have since operated. His children were Sophia, Warren P., Mary A. (deceased), John H., Rhoda M., and Orville R. (deceased). Solon Haskins died April 14, 1865, aged 79. His father, David, came from Eng-

land and settled in New Hampshire.   John H. Haskins received an academic education, and at the age of 21 he began farming, and with his
brother operated the mill for a time.   From 1865 to July, 1887, Rufus
Bartlett was interested in the mill, and since then Mr. Haskins has had
full control.   Mr. Haskins has served in several town offices.   In February, 1863, he married Marion Latham, daughter of William, an Episcopal minister, who came from England.   By this marriage he had one
son, now deceased.   His second wife was Catharine L., daughter of Andrew Clifford, of Le Roy.   They have two children, Frank J. and Mary
E.   Mrs. Sophia Haskins was a daughter of John Hasey, a Revolutionary soldier.

Hiram W. Hascall, a leading and influential lawyer and a politician,
was born December 18. 1812, in Le Roy village.   His parents, David
and Sarah (Walden) Hascall, came from New England to Genesee
County in 1808, and located one mile north of the village, and latter settled on 100 acres one-half mile west of Le Roy, where they resided for
many years.   They afterwards moved to the village, residing on Clay
street until their deaths, at the age of 85 and 89, respectively.   David
Hascall in early life was a school teacher.   He served in the War of
1812.   Being a man possessed of more than ordinary intelligence and influence, he was an honored and respected citizen, and always took an
active and prominent part in all movements for the advancement
and improvement of his community.   He served in several responsible local positions for many years.   He reared three sons and two
daughters.   David was a son of Jeremiah Hascall, who was born in Connecticut and came to Genesee County in 1805, locating on 100 acres
where S. C. Wells now resides.   He served as justice for many years, and
died here at the age of 96 years.   He married Hannah (Nichols) Nichols,
who bore him five sons and five daughters, the sons being Jeremiah, David,
Amasa, John, and Augustus P., all of whom were men of considerable
prominence, and some attained considerable distinction in the State and Nation.   John served in the Assembly ; Augustus P. served as judge and
represented his district in Congress.   Gen. Milo Hascall, of Goshen, Ind.,
was a son of Amasa.   Hiram W. Hascall was reared on a farm and received a good common school and academic education.   At the age of 20
he began the study of law in the office of Gates & Hascall, of Le Roy,
and was admitted to all the courts of the State.   In 1855 he was elected
clerk of Genesee County, which position he filled for two terms, and in
1864 he was appointed collector of internal revenue.   Three years later
he was appointed postmaster at Le Roy, serving as such for 16 years.
During the war he was appointed by President Lincoln commissary of sub-
sistance, with rank of captain.   Mr. Hascall is a man of strong convictions.   He has always taken an active and prominent part in the political affairs of his county and State, and has always wielded a powerful
influence in shaping and molding the work of his party.   Energetic
and unflinching in his zeal for the success of Republicanism, he has al-

ways commanded the confidence and respect of his party. Mr. Hascall has been twice married, first to Harriet Hinsdale, of Le Roy, by whom he had two children, Alice C. and Laurence H. He married for his second wife Mrs. Amanda A. Champion. The mother of Mr. Hascall was a daughter of Nathan Walden, a native of Connecticut, who was a soldier in the war for independence. He was captured, and imprisoned in an old church in New York city for nearly a year. He was a prominent farmer near Bloomfield for many years, and died in Le Roy, aged about 90 years. His wife was Mercy Egleston, who lived to about the same age.

George H. Holmes, born May 7, 1840, where Mr. Vary now resides, is a son of Harry and Susan (Cole) Holmes, who were born in 1799 and 1803, respectively. Harry Holmes was a farmer in early life, and during his latter years was engaged in the stone business in this county, where he was one of the early pioneers, settling in Le Roy in 1815. George H. Holmes, one of a family of four sons and four daughters, received a common school education, and worked at the stone business until 27 years of age, since which time he has been extensively engaged in the stone trade for himself, having at times as high as 90 men at work quarrying and 40 men cutting. During the busy season he has shipped as many as 50 car loads per week, about 25 car loads going to Buffalo. He was doing all the heavy stone business in this section for about five years. He is now, and has been for a number of years, extensively engaged in lime burning, operating two kilns and making about 700 bushels per day. Mr. Holmes enlisted in August, 1862, in Co. I, 129th N. Y. Inf., and at Baltimore the regiment was transferred to the 8th N. Y. H. A. and garrisoned for many months at Forts McHenry, Federal Hill, Carroll, and Marshall. He was detailed to remain at Baltimore six months, and later joined his regiment at Petersburg, Va. He participated in the engagements at Deep Bottom and Weldon Railroad, and thenceforth in all the battles in which his regiment was engaged to the close of the war. He became noted in his regiment for his accuracy in directing and landing mortar shells. In February, 1865, he was promoted sergeant, and in June following received his discharge at Rochester, N. Y., as commissary sergeant. He located where he now resides in July, 1882. November 28, 1861, he married Caroline M., daughter of John and Lorana (Payne) Buckley, who were born in Mendon, Monroe County, and Turin, Lewis County, respectively, and who were among the early settlers of Stafford and Le Roy. Abraham Buckley was a soldier in the War of 1812, and reared six sons and five daughters. Mr. and Mrs. Holmes have three children, Eva, Frank H., and Parley M. Mr. Holmes is related to Thurlow Weed.

William R. Halbert was born in Glasgow, Scotland, September 14, 1819. His parents, William and Elizabeth (Russell) Halbert, were born in Edinburgh and Glasgow, respectively. William Halbert was a stonecutter by trade. In May, 1827, he came to America, landing at Quebec, and shortly after came to Utica, N. Y., where he was employed in the New York mills as a weaver.   His wife and six children left Scotland in May, 1828, and were eight weeks on the ocean and six days coming from New York city to Utica.   About 1840 with his family he moved to Middlesex County, Canada, and located on a farm of 100 acres.   He was a leading member of the Presbyterian Church, and was an elder for many years.   He died at Ailsa Craig, Canada, aged 86 years.   He had nine children, viz.: a son who died at Albany when the family was on their way to Utica, William R., Mary (Mrs. Alexander Henderson), deceased, Margaret (Mrs. Ross), Elizabeth (Mrs. Henderson), Jane (Mrs. Hover), Bethiah (Mrs. Wyllie), Caroline (Mrs. Menzie), and Isabella (Mrs. Forbes). William R. Halbert received a common school education, and lived three years in Canada.   In 1843 he came to Le Roy, and worked two and one-half years by the month.   He married, March 17, 1852, Ellen E., daughter of Linus and Nancy (Wilcox) Pierson, who came from Killingworth, Conn., to Genesee County about 1808, and first settled in Bergen, and later at Churchville, where he died.   He was a soldier of 1812, and a farmer.   Mr. Halbert's first wife died at the age of 53.   He located where he now resides in 1853, and where he has a beautiful and pleasant home.   He is a good neighbor and citizen, and respected by all who know him.   He and his wife are active members of the Presbyterian Church.

Thomas P. Hedden, born in Stafford, December 2, 1839, is a son of Thomas and Ann (Perryman) Hedden, of Devonshire, Eng., who came to Stafford about 1828, and settled where he resided until his death, in 1845.   His wife died in 1870.   They had eight children.   Thomas P. was educated at Genesee and Wyoming Seminary (Alexander).   At the age of 21 he studied law with R. Ballard, and taught school three winters.   In 1867 he was admitted to practice, and in 1877 was elected district attorney of Genesee County for one term.   He has been justice of the peace ever since his admission to the bar, except while serving as district attorney.   He married Emily M. Hill, who bore him two children, Cornelia A. and Thomas P.   His second wife was Mrs. Henrietta Kenyon.

Livingston D. Howell, son of Leonard D. and Elizabeth A. (Wells) Howell, was born in Bethany, February 28, 1853.   His father, a farmer and quarryman, came to Le Roy in 1854.   About 1873 he opened the quarry now operated by L. D., and shipped stone quite extensively, at times as many as 30 car loads per week.   In 1862 he enlisted in Co. B, 100th N. Y. Vols., as sergeant, participating in all the battles with his regiment.   He was with Gen. Butler on the peninsula, received two wounds, and was made lieutenant, when he resigned.   He creditably filled several town offices, was successful in all business transactions, and died in 1888, aged 60 years.   He was a son of John M., an early settler of York, and the father of eight children, and whose father came from New Jersey.   Livingston D. Howell was reared on the farm, received a common and academic education, and assisted his father in his business. He married Elizabeth, daughter of Jerome and Fannie (Howell) Wheelock, of Cuylerville, N. Y., and their children are Fannie B. (deceased) and William L.

Andrew Harsch, of Wurtemberg, Germany, was born August 3, 1842, a son of Andrew and Barbara (Hensler) Harsch, who came in 1854 to Syracuse, where they resided until their deaths. He enlisted in Co. B, 149th N. Y. Inf., and was discharged on account of ill health soon after the battle of Gettysburg. He reared four sons and four daughters. Jacob enlisted in a regiment of cavalry and was killed at the battle of Silver Springs, Va. His other sons were Andrew, Gottlieb, of Syracuse, and John (deceased). Andrew was raised in Syracuse, began work at the age of 13 years in a cigar factory, and came to Le Roy in 1870 and worked for Moses Yale on Bank street. In 1872 he opened a cigar factory in the Starr block, and in 1873 located in his present store and factory. October 7, 1863, he married Sophia, daughter of Joseph Obermiller, of Syracuse, and they have 10 children living, viz.: Sophia, Barbara, Libbie A., Andrew F., Lana, Tillie, Clara, Ida, Hubbard H., and William F. He is a member of the A. O. U. W., of the Stafford Benefit Association, and of the Southern Tier Masonic Association

Mrs. Huldah Hubbell, born in New York, was a daughter of Thomas and Christina Burgess. He was a farmer in Western New York, and had two sons and eight daughters. Mrs. Hubbell first married Porter, son of James T. and Delilah (Robinson) Burroughs, who was born in Hannibal, N. Y., and came to Pembroke with his parents. He moved to Steuben County, Ind., where he resided a few years, and died there, when Mrs. Burroughs, with her children, returned to this county. Her children are Alonzo, of Michigan; William A., of New York; and Anna M., who married Lucius Loomis. William A , who enlisted in the 8th N. Y. Art., lives in Pembroke, and married Frances Madison. For her second husband she married James Hubbell, a farmer, who came to Le Roy in 1873; and died in 1876.

William Heaman, a native of Devonshire, Eng., was born November 8, 1856, a son of Richard and Sarah Heaman. He came to Le Roy in 1880, and has since resided here. He is engaged in the manufacture of custom boots and shoes. He married Mary Garrish, of Devonshire, and they have two children, Willie and Annie.

Thomas Heaman, son of Richard, was born in Devonshire. Eng., October 17, 1865, came to America in 1882, and settled in Le Roy as a blacksmith. He opened a shop on Mill street, January 1, 1890, where he is doing a successful business. He married Jane Mooney, of Le Roy.

Charles Hogan, born May 11, 1826, in County Carlow, Ireland, was reared on a farm and had a common education. In July, 1849, he landed in New York city, came to Auburn, and engaged in farming a short time, when he went to Ohio. In April, 1850, he came to Le Roy, and in 1853 began work for the N. Y. C. & H. R. Railroad, where he was

34

soon made track superintendent, which position he has faithfully filled ever since. His first wife was Ann Wolf, of Ireland, whose children were Charles H., a railway engineer at Buffalo, and Mary Thomas. His second wife was Mary Lawler, and their sons are John, of Niagara Falls, and Edward, of Batavia. His daughter, Kittie, aged 10 years, is by his last wife.

Seth Harris, son of Daniel and Mary (Paddock) Harris, was born April 9, 1815, in Le Roy. He received a common school education, was a lieutenant of militia, and was one of the substantial and leading farmers of the town. He married Elsie, daughter of Elijah and Dimmis (Kneeland) Crocker, and their children were Mary (Mrs. Ward), Elijah, Emeline C. (Mrs. Bulkley), Jane (Mrs. Kingdon), and Phebe. Elijah Crocker (son of Simeon) and his wife were born in Norwich, Conn., came to Le Roy in 1816, and located on 140 acres where the widow of Seth Harris now resides. Mr. Crocker died lacking 13 days of being 90 years of age. He had three children, viz.: Eliza, who married, first, a Mr. Van Allen, by whom she had one son, Edward W., and second, a Mr. Elderkin, by whom she has one daughter, Eunice (Mrs. Phillips); Emeline, who died at the age of 12 years; and Elsie, now the widow of Seth Harris. William Harris was born May 14, 1825, where he now resides. He received a good common school education, and at the age of 23 began business for himself at Lime Rock. After his father's death he returned to the homestead, where he now resides. He has been thrice married. His first wife was Aseneth Crouch, who died without issue. His second wife was Emeline, daughter of James Chase, of Pavilion, and their two children were William H. and Carrie R. James Chase was born in Albany County, N. Y., and moved to Allegany County, thence to this county. The third wife of Mr. Harris was Mary, daughter of Froman Winnie, by whom he has three children: Emma, Nellie, and Daniel. Mr. Harris has served three years as excise commissioner, and for the past three years has served as assessor. He is a son of Daniel and Mary J. (Paddock) Harris, natives of Middletown, Conn , who came to Genesee County in 1810, and settled on 100 acres where William now resides. When Daniel first came to the county he exchanged one bushel of wheat for a yard of factory cloth, and continued this until he had enough to make a suit of clothes—the finest he had ever worn. This was made from flax and wool, which was spun by his family. He had 14 children, and raised five sons and seven daughters, the sons being Daniel, Seth, William, James, of Cleveland, and Elijah, the latter of whom is a professor in Amherst College.

Albert N. Jones was born March 6, 1844, in England, a son of William and Eliza (Fisher) Jones, natives of Cookham and Branford, England, respectively. William Jones was one of four sons and five daughters who grew to maturity, and born of William and Martha (Mason) Jones He was a papermaker and came to the United States with a sister in 1849, and settled at Rochester, N. Y., where he was engaged in paper manufacturing. He went to Shortsville, thence to Mount Morris, and in 1868 located in Le Roy. He purchased the mill north of the village and converted it into a paper-mill, which he operated until it was destroyed by fire. He had five children: Albert N., Lizzie, Walter S., Frank E., and George H. Mrs. Jones died in 1886. Albert N. Jones received a good English education when he came to Le Roy, and soon after began growing seeds. He went to Steuben County, where he spent five years, when he returned to Le Roy and at once gave his entire attention to novelty seed growing, in which he is meeting with success. He cultivates and produces new varieties of grain and beans, and ships to all parts of the country. Mr. Jones is industrious and applies himself closely to his business. He has succeeded in producing several varieties of seeds for different climates. He married Marietta Crofut, who was born in Canandaigua, N. Y., a daughter of Joel B. and Lucinda (Coy) Crofut, natives of Connecticut and Vermont, respectively. Mr. and Mrs. Jones have one child, Ida S. They are members of the Baptist Church.

Ezra S. Janes, a substantial and successful farmer, was born October 15, 1835, in Lyme, Conn., and is a son of Ezra and Mary (Haines) Janes, who were born in Brimfield, Mass., and Connecticut, respectively. Ezra Janes was a farmer, and his children were all born in Connecticut. He came to Genesee County in 1828, and settled one mile north of Le Roy village. In the fall of the same year he located two miles west of Le Roy, just over the line in Stafford, on 80 acres of land which he improved. He had five children: Israel D., Elizabeth H., Ryland E., Mary, who died young, and Ezra S. Ezra Janes died in 1869, aged 88 years, and his wife five years prior. He was a son of Israel Janes, of Massachusetts. Ezra S. received his education in the common schools and Le Roy and Middlebury academies, and spent several terms in teaching. He was married, May 22, 1866, to Margaret J. Kinner, of this county, and their children are Mary E. and Herbert S. He located where he now resides immediately after his marriage. He is a leading and influential member of the Baptist Church.

Richard M. Kellogg, born in Le Roy village, December 28, 1842, was a son of Smith and Susan (Manwaring) Kellogg, who were early pioneers of Genesee County. Mr. Kellogg received a liberal English education. He was engaged in farming for a few years, and at the age of 29 embarked in the insurance business, in which he was very successful, and which he continued till his death, in May, 1882. He married Frances, daughter of Elisha and Alice (Oatman) Parks, who came from Wells, Rutland County, Vt., about 60 years ago. Mr. and Mrs. Kellogg had born to them five children: Charles F., Walter P., Mary S., Harry S., and Alice H. Elisha Parks was for some years engaged in the furniture business, and afterward in the dry goods trade. He was an active and honored member of the Masonic fraternity, and died about 25 years ago. He reared one son and two daughters, the latter of whom are living.

John Johnson was born August 1, 1826, in Richmondville, Schoharie County, N. Y., a son of Peter and Abigail (Crane) Johnson, natives of Schoharie County and Connecticut, respectively. Peter, a farmer, who has been living for 35 years in Onondaga County, was born in 1795, and was a son of John, who was born near Schenectady. Peter was twice married. His children by his first wife were William C., Mary A., and John, and he had three children by his second wife (Ann Eliza Perry). John, at eight years of age, began driving horses on the canal. He lived 10 years in Madison and Onondaga counties, and in March, 1859, he located on 94 acres where he now resides. He married, December 21, 1854, Margaret E., daughter of William and Juliana (Dewey) Rogers, of Madison County, and they have five children, viz : Ina A. (Mrs. McVean), Luella, Olena C., William D., and Bertha.

John M. Kelley, of County West Meath, Ireland, was born July 20, 1845. His parents were James and Mary (Murray) Kelley, and their children were Ann, John M., Dennis, and Mary. John M. came to Springfield, Mass., in 1866, thence to Worcester, and then to New York city. In 1867 he went to Port Henry and worked in the iron mines until 1874, when he came to Le Roy. In 1883 he was placed in charge of Machpelah Cemetery, of which he now has control. July 7, 1874, he married Katie, daughter of Hugh and Rose O'Neil. They have eight children: Mary R., Elizabeth, Catherine C., Mark, Eugene V , Hugh E., Frances T., and George C., and belong to the Roman Catholic Church. He has served as constable.

Melvin N. King, born in Stafford, March 7, 1832, is a son of Merritt and Lucinda (Smith) King. Merritt King was born in Bennington, Vt., December 30, 1796, and was a teamster in the War of 1812. With his parents he came to Genesee County in 1813, moving with an ox-team and sled, and settled on 100 acres two miles west of Le Roy village, which had been located by a brother, Nathaniel King, who was killed in the battle of Lewiston. Here Merritt married and then sold the farm, and in 1841 he located in Le Roy village, where he ran a dray the remainder of his life. He was thrice married. By his first wife he had two sons and three daughters. One son, Willard, was a sutler in a New York regiment. His second wife was Eliza Howard, and his third Maria Lord, by whom he had three sons and three daughters. He died aged 81 years. His father was Zedediah King, who came to Genesee County with a son, and died. He reared three sons and three daughters, the sons being Ezekiel, Nathaniel, and Merritt. Melvin N. King was reared in Le Roy village, received his education at the old Round house, and has earned his own living since 10 years of age. He learned the trade of painter, and August 30, 1862, enlisted in Co. I, 151st N. Y. V. His first duty was as special guard on the B. & O. Railroad. He participated in the battles of the Wilderness, Spottsylvania, Cold Harbor, first battle of Petersburg, and several others, and was taken prisoner at the battle of Monocacy Bridge, July 9, 1864, and served seven months and 13 days at

Danville and one month in Libby, receiving his discharge in August, 1865, at Rochester. He was engaged in the produce business 10 years. In 1867 he was elected constable, which position he has since filled, except one year. In January, 1873, he was appointed deputy sheriff, and has filled the position three terms. He married Helen M., daughter of Leander and Rachel Stevens, of Bergen, and they have two children, Willard M. and Alice.

Rev. O. C. Kirkham, son of Joshua and Ruth (Witherell) Kirkham, was born January 21, 1837, at Glens Falls, and was reared on a farm. He graduated at Glens Falls Academy and Fort Edward Institute, and began theological study with his pastor, Rev. R. F. Parshall, which he continued for two years. He was licensed to preach by the Baptist Church at Sandy Hill, Washington County, April 3, 1858, and was ordained at Pittstown, near Troy, October 19, 1859, where he had a charge one year. He was called to Hoosick Falls, N. Y., to Patterson, to Connecticut, and then to Newark, Wayne County. In 1885 he was called to Le Roy, where he has since been engaged. He married, October 24, 1860, Sarah E., daughter of James Pagan, of Hoosick Falls, and their children are Ruth E., Walter A., James E., and Mary G. Joshua Kirkham was born near Glens Falls, June 19, 1780, and was a soldier in the War of 1812. He was twice married. His first wife bore him one son and four daughters, and his second wife, the mother of Rev. O. C., had four sons and two daughters. He served as justice several terms, and was a cousin of Prof. Samuel Kirkham, author of *Kirkham's Grammar.* Joshua's father came from Scotland during colonial days, and participated in the war for independence. Ruth (Witherell) Kirkham was born in Rupert, Vt.

S. Loucks, son of Benjamin and Elsie (Lake) Loucks, was born October 31, 1829, in Montgomery County, N. Y. Benjamin Loucks was born in Montgomery County, and his wife in Oswego County. He had for many years acted as superintendent of public works, was employed on canal construction, and was also a merchant. About 1836 he came to Rochester, thence to Scottsville, and later to Livingston County, and died in Steuben County. He had been twice married. His first wife was a Miss Wagoner, who bore him two sons and two daughters. By his second wife he had three sons and two daughters. His father came from Germany. S. Loucks received a common school education, and at the age of 14 years began life as a clerk in a grocery store; at the age of 15 he entered a general store at Fowlerville as salesman, and in 1856 became a partner. In 1858 he sold his interest and began business alone at Caledonia. In 1868 he came to Le Roy and began business at 16 Main street, where he and his son are now engaged. Mr. Loucks has been remarkably successful; starting at the age of 17, without a dollar, he has succeeded, by perseverance, industry, and economy, in accumulating a fortune. Besides his store he owns two large farms, one of 200 and another of 150 acres, east of Le Roy. Mr. Loucks is a liberal giver to any public enterprise that tends to promote the welfare and better the con-

dition of his community.   He married, first, Clara, daughter of Silas B.
Whitcomb, of Fowlerville, and their children were Walter F., Fred B , and
Flora B., who died in infancy.   He married, second, Elizabeth Hardy,
whose parents come from Lincolnshire, Eng.

Archibald McEwen, born in Johnstown N. Y., in February, 1823,
was a son of Peter and Helen (McNab) McEwen, natives of Scotland.
Peter McEwen, at the age of 19, came to the United States with his parents, who settled in Fulton County on a farm.   They reared five sons
and one daughter.   Archibald McEwen married Margaret J., daughter
of Gideon G. W. and Margaret (McKinley) Green, natives of Johnstown
and Mayfield, N. Y., respectively.   They raised two sons and six daughters.   Gideon G. W. was a son of James Green, who was born in Wales
and came to America in colonial days, and was a soldier of the Revolution.   He married Margaret Crowley, of Ireland, and reared five sons and
and three daughters.   Archibald came to Le Roy in 1852, and settled
where his widow now resides.   Mr. and Mrs. McEwen reared two children, J. William and George S.   J. William married Elizabeth, daughter of Henry W. Veghte, and they have three children: Archibald H.,
Edith M., and Helen.

Frederick J. Millener, ticket agent and telegraph operator at the Erie
depot, was born in Corning, N. Y., February 18, 1866, where he attended
school and received an academic education.   He married, January 13,
1888, Lizzie A., daughter of Andrew and Catherine Sawtell, of Mount
Morris, and they have a son, Harry, born October 15, 1888.   Mr. Millener comes from a noted family, numbering among his ancestors many
who have lived to the age of 100 years and over, among whom were his
great-great-grandfather (a soldier of 1776) and grandmother.   Many of
their children lived to be nearly 90 years of age.   The father of Frederick J., Alexander H., is living in Rochester, and has been connected
with the Erie Railroad for 32 years.   Alexander H., son of James C.,
has brothers and sisters living as follows: Sarah, of Missouri; Lucy, of
Cayuga County; Eugenie, an experienced and practical nurse; Eliza,
widow of G. C. Stone, of Auburn ; and Isaac B., a noted sculptor and
manager of the business of John Matthews, of Melbourne, Australia.
Three of his brothers died young.   The trade of boat building is a prominent feature of the Millener family, Alexander H. and his sons, at Port
Byron and Rochester, having been extensively engaged in that business,
Joel P., one of the sons, having built 53 canal boats in 52 weeks at Rochester.   He was buried at Rochester, where a monument in Mount Hope
marks his grave.

Samuel H. Murdoch was born near Belfast, Ireland, March 22, 1845,
a son of Samuel and Mary (Hutton) Murdoch, of Irish and Scotch descent.   They came to Port Hope, Canada, in 1848, and he was a farmer.
In 1854 he came to York, Livingston County, where he resided until his
death in 1889; his wife died the same year.   Their children were Archibald, Samuel, William J., John, Ann, and Jane.   Samuel had an aca-

demic education at Le Roy, taught school in Berry County, Mich., one winter, and in March, 1865, he enlisted in Co. K, 6th Mich. Cav. He returned to Le Roy, July 6, 1865, and was engaged in farming one year, when he learned the carpenters' and joiners' trade. In 1873 he erected and run a planing-mill at Caledonia for two years, and in 1879 came to Le Roy and erected the house of George Wells. He married, January 1, 1872, Martha, daughter of Hugh Simpson, and their children are Nellie L., Wilber E., Clarence G., and Samuel. Mr. Murdoch is a member of the Masonic fraternity.

Patrick Marion, of County Louth, Ireland, born February 9, 1821, is a son of Francis and Mary (Kelley) Marion, who had 11 sons and one daughter, all of whom came to the United States. James and Owen came in 1837 to Rochester; Patrick and Peter in 1841; and Thomas, Francis, Lawrence, Barney, John, and Mary in 1838. Patrick received a common school education, was reared a farmer, and first located in Wheatland, but came to Le Roy in 1849, where he now resides on a farm of 116 acres. He married Mary, daughter of Nicholas and Mary (Carney) Wood, who came from Ireland in 1830, settled in Wheatland, and reared two children, Nicholas and Mary. Mr. and Mrs. Marion have had children as follows: Francis (deceased); Margaret (Mrs. Ottnet); Mary (deceased); Nicholas, of Detroit; Thomas, of Michigan; Edward, Clara, Frank, and Anna. They are Roman Catholics.

Henry Moody, son of William and Martha (Bayley) Moody, natives of County Carlow, Ireland, was born January 14, 1846. They were farmers, and came to Le Roy in 1850. The father worked at carpentering until his death in 1862. His wife died in 1888. They raised six children: Henry; Richard, who enlisted in the 100th N. Y. Regt., was taken prisoner in 1863, and died at Andersonville; William, of Warsaw; Mary; George, of Wethersfield; and Martha. The family are Episcopalians. William, Thomas, and Robert, sons of Henry, all settled and died in Le Roy, and left families. Henry Moody received a common school education, and at the age of 17 he learned the carpenters' trade, which he has since followed, except one and a half years which he spent in Chicago after the fire Since 1874 he has been a contractor. He has served as excise commissioner for six years, and is a leading member of the Masonic fraternity. He married, October 28, 1874, Maria E., daughter of Daniel N. and Elizabeth Eddy, of Bergen, and they have had two children, Ida L. and Bertha (deceased).

Nelson Meyette, son of Anthony and Libbie (Strong) Meyette, was born February 14, 1853, in Richmond, Vt. Anthony was born in France, and his wife in Canada. He came to Canada when a young man, thence to Boston, and was at sea a few years. when he settled in Vermont. At one time he was a merchant in Montreal. Of 16 children they raised three sons and six daughters. The grandmother of Nelson died at the age of 100 years. Nelson was reared on a farm, received a common school education, and attended Middlebury Academy. At the age of 11 he began to learn a trade. He was at Fort Edward Institute for three years, and came to Le Roy in 1879, where he has since resided, working at his trade of painter and decorator. December 16, 1879, he married Flora A., daughter of Joseph R. and Matilda I. (Ingram) Eddy, and they have one son, J. Eddy. Joseph R. Eddy was born in Wyoming County, and his wife in Erie County. He died December 2, 1889, aged 71. His daughter Anna I. married a Mr. Woodard. Another daughter is Flora A. He came to Le Roy in 1825, was interested in a stone quarry for many years, and was a builder and contractor. He built the Roman Catholic Church and Lampson House. Between 1844 and 1850 he spent seven years at sea, and had some thrilling experiences.

John Maloney, a prominent business man of Le Roy, was born June 24, 1841, in County Clare, Ireland, a son of Simon and Catharine (McDonnell) Maloney, who were born and raised in County Clare. In 1843 Simon came to America, landing in Canada. He soon after came to Batavia, where he died in 1863, aged 63, leaving a widow, who is still living, and three sons and one daughter. John Maloney received a common school education. When his parents came to Batavia there was but one other Irish Catholic family in the place—Patrick Dailey's. There were two or three German Catholic families. Father Dillon built the first Catholic Church, which was situated on Jackson street. Our subject was the first Irish boy who assisted at mass in Genesee County. Mr. Maloney is a self-made man. At the age of 16 he entered the grocery store of Frank Maloney, of Batavia, and in 1858 came to Le Roy and entered the store of Andrew Elliott, where he remained two years, when he became a partner, which continued two years, and has since successfully carried on the business alone. He does a large and extensive business. In 1876 he erected a handsome brick block on the corner of Main and Bank streets, and occupies the second store on Main street. He married, in August, 1865, Ellen, daughter of John Fitzgibbons, of Rochester, by whom he has four children : Francis E, John A., Joseph W., and Maud I. Mr. and Mrs. Maloney are active and influential members of the Roman Catholic Church.

John Munt was born in Bertroff, Mecklenburg, Germany, and came to the United States in 1850, with a brother, who died on the way of smallpox. He was over seven weeks on the ocean. He settled in Oakfield, and September 4, 1862, at Lockport, N. Y., he enlisted in the 22d Independent Art., which was afterward attached to the 9th N. Y. H. A. He participated in the battles of Cold Harbor and Fredricksburg, and served two years and 10 months. He purchased his first land in Oakfield about 1865. In April, 1875, he located where he now resides. He married Sophia, daughter of John and Sophia (Krohn) Luplow, and they have children as follows : Frank J., George E, Eddie H, and Sophia A. Mrs. Munt's first husband was Fred Burr, by whom she had four children : Fred, Mary, William (who died leaving a son and a daughter), and Albert. With her parents she came from Mecklenburg, Germany, in 1856, and settled in Oakfield.

Michael Murray, son of Patrick and Margaret (Davine) Murray, was born September 18, 1828, in Kildalkay Parish, County Meath, Ireland. With his youngest brother he came to New York city in 1854, and was five weeks on the ocean. He came direct to Le Roy, where he began work in the Le Roy limestone quarry, with which he has since been connected, except one season. His parents, who were born in County Meath, Ireland, reared four sons, as follows : Patrick, who came to the United States in 1851, and lived and died in Caledonia; Hugh, of Ireland; Michael; and Thomas. Michael Murray married, January 9, 1859, Christine, daughter of Thomas and Mary (Farley) Roe, of Ireland, who raised one son and five daughters, of whom only Bridget, Maggie, and Christine came to the United States. Mr. and Mrs. Murray have six children, viz.: Patrick H., Mary J., Maggie T., Thomas F., Kittie C., and Michael John.

Alexander McPherson, Jr., was born October 21, 1827, one half mile west of where he now resides, and is a son of Alexander and Jane (McVean) McPherson. Alexander was born July 1, 1803, in Le Roy, where his father had first settled. He was second lieutenant of militia, held several responsible positions in his town, and had 10 chilnren, eight of whom grew to maturity, viz.: Alexander, Jr., Sarah, Eliza, Jane, Helen, Donald, John A., and Margaret C. He died in May, 1879 His father, Alexander McPherson, was born in Scotland, and was a shepherd by occupation. He married Nellie McPherson, and had five children born in Scotland, as follows : Nellie, John, Angus, Nancy, and James. They came to the United States in 1800, after which six more were born, namely: Donald, Allen, Alexander, Mary, Isabell, and Margaret. Alexander McPherson lived in the eastern part of the State until 1801, when he located one mile below Oatka Falls, on the north bank of the creek, when he erected his first cabin. He was $7 in debt when he landed in Genesee County. He was a hard worker and accumulated 1,500 acres, most of which he improved. In early days he hauled wheat to Rochester and sold it at 25 cents per bushel, taking in exchange a barrel of salt worth $14. Alexander McPherson, Jr., received a common school and academic education, and taught school four winters. He married, first, Eliza Ann, daughter of Phycle Monroe and Julia (Howard) Ward, of Perry, Livingston County. Their children were Ward H., Archibald H., and Mary E. His second wife was Mary Elizabeth, daughter of David and Jane (Milroy) Donnan, of Leicester, Livingston County. Mr. and Mrs. McPherson and children are members of the Presbyterian Church.

Mathias Müller, son of Peter and Anna (Morgan) Muller, natives of Treves, Germany, was born October 15, 1847. He was the oldest of three sons and three daughters, and came to Le Roy in 1870 and worked for an uncle in a liquor store. In 1886 he opened a grocery store at 36 Main street, which he has successfully conducted. His first wife, a daughter of John McSparrow, a native of Scotland, bore him five children : John P., Joseph H., Ambrose M., Elizabeth M., and Victor. His second wife is a sister to the first wife. They belong to the Roman Catholic Church.

John A. McPherson, son of Alexander and Jane (McVean) McPherson, was born September 28, 1845, where he now resides. He was reared on a farm, received a common school and academic education, and at the age of 19 began farming for himself. He has always lived on his present place, except five years spent in Wheatland. He was drafted into the State militia. March 15, 1871, he married Sarah E., daughter of Philo L. and Sarah (Hull) Pierson. John A. McPherson has five children: Jean L., Roy P., Hobert P., Sarah F., and Ethel H., and all are members of the Presbyterian Church.

Thomas Murnan, son of Michael and Mary (O'Connell) Murnan, was born in Le Roy, December 23, 1856, and was reared on a farm. He was educated at Le Roy Academy, and at the age of 17 years learned the blacksmiths' trade of W. S Brown, with whom he worked for 10 years, when he spent a year each at Brockport and Medina, and returned to Le Roy, where he has since resided. In 1885 he opened a wholesale and retail liquor and cigar store. He takes an active interest in politics. Michael Murnan was born in Limerick, Ireland, and his wife in County Clare. He is a farmer and came to the United States in 1846, lived a short time at Bath, when he removed to Corning and entered the employ of the Erie Railroad, and in 1855 came to Le Roy, settling on nine acres where he now lives, which he has since increased to 50 acres. He has eight children: Thomas, William, John, George M., Katie, James, Frank T., and Arthur. The grandfather of Thomas (Michael) died young. He had five sons and one daughter (Mary, who went to Australia). Two sons, Michael and William, live in Genesee County.

Edwin J. Niles was born in Le Roy, June 30, 1836, a son of Ebenezer and Eliza (Sprague) Niles, natives of Vermont. Ebenezer was born in 1806, and came with his parents to Le Roy about 1809. He was a farmer, had three children, and died in September, 1852. His father, Ephraim, of Vermont, and of English descent, married Mary Hill, came to Le Roy on sleds, and settled on 50 acres of land adjoining Perry Randall's. He was a member of the Christian Church, and reared 12 children The mother of Edwin J. was a daughter of Eli A. Sprague, of Vermont, a soldier of 1812, who served at the battle of Plattsburgh. Edwin J. Niles was raised on a farm, had an academic education, and taught school one term at the age of 16 years. After his father's death he lived on the homestead until 1885, when he moved to the village. He enlisted in the 25th Ind. N. Y. Battery, under Capt. Grow, and was discharged from University Hospital, New Orleans, in 1864. He married, August 29, 1867, Elizabeth, daughter of John and Eliza (Huyck) Austin, of Buffalo, and their children are Daisy E., Henry C., and Edwin John Mr. Niles is a member of the I. O. O. F.

Charles L. Olmsted was born August 19, 1827, across the road from where he now resides. He received a good academic education, and has been twice married. His first wife was Mary A., daughter of Solon and Sophia Haskins, and their child was Fred C   For his second wife he married Carrie M., daughter of William and Eliza (Grosvenor) Calvert, natives of New York and Pittsfield, Mass., respectively, by whom he has had one daughter, Mary Edna.   Mr. and Mrs. Olmsted are Presbyterians. At the age of 16 he and his brother purchased a farm of 50 acres.   In November, 1857, he purchased his brother's interest.   For six years he has dealt in agricultural implements.   In 1870 he was in Rochester engaged in the flour and feed business.   He is a son of William and Cynthia (Franklin) Olmsted, natives of Rutland, Vt., and Killingworth, Conn., respectively.   William Olmsted came from Vermont to Genesee County in 1812, locating on 150 acres of land.   He was a teacher, and married the widow of John Pierson, who came from Connecticut in 1808, and located first near Stone Church, and later where Charles L. now resides.   Mr. Pierson lost his life in the War of 1812.   He left a widow and two children, viz.: Harlow W., who was drowned on Lake Erie from the steamboat *Washington*, and Louisa C.   William Olmsted and wife had four sons and two daughters: William H., Florilla F., John R., Ursula M., Egbert S , and Charles L.   Egbert S. and Roxanna (Brown) Olmsted had a daughter, May, who now lives with her uncle, John R.

Dwight H. Pierson, son of Philo L. and Sarah M. (Hull) Pierson, was born November 5, 1844, in Le Roy, was reared and educated on a farm, and spent 10 years in teaching.   With the exception of three years in Hardin County, Ia., he has always lived in Le Roy.   In the spring of 1889 he was elected assessor.   He married Catharine, daughter of Alexander McPherson, of Le Roy, and they are members of the Presbyterian Church. Philo L. Pierson, born at Stone Church in 1810, was a carpenter and builder.   He built the Ingham University building in Le Roy, and his latter days were spent on a farm.   He served as assessor several terms. He had born to him 10 children, seven of whom attained maturity, viz.: Cordelia M , Helen E., Myron P., who served as lieutenant in the 100th N. Y. Regt., and was in Libby and Columbia prisons, Halbert M., Dwight H., Daniel M., and Sarah M. (Mrs. McPherson).   Philo Pierson died about 1875, and his wife in 1856.   He married for his second wife Lydia Pratt. His father, Simon Pierson, born in Killingworth, Conn., was an officer in the War of 1812.   He married Sylvia Kelsey, of Connecticut, came in 1807 to Genesee County with an ox-team and cart, being about 25 days on the road, and located at Stone Church.   The lid of his chest, which he used for a table, is now in the possession of Dwight H.   He reared a family of two sons and five daughters, and died in the spring of 1864, aged 85.   He was a son of Samuel Pierson, of Killingworth, who was a Revolutionary soldier and a son of Samuel, a son of Abraham Pierson. Rev. Abraham Pierson came from Yorkshire, Eng , in 1640, and was pastor of the church at South Hampton, Long Island.   He had a son, Abraham, who graduated from Harvard College in 1668, and became the first rector of Yale College.   He had three sons, Abraham, James, and

John. Abraham died in Killingworth. Abraham, 3d, was justice for about 40 years at Killingworth, and died in January, 1852.

George Platt, one of the earliest pioneers of Le Roy, was born July 27, 1804, across the street from the Episcopal Church. He had a limited education, was a farmer during his early life, and served as colonel of militia. He was twice married, first to Rachel Lyman, by whom he had three children, one of whom attained maturity—George G., now of Rochester. He died April 2, 1888. Mr. Platt spent his latter life on Summit street. He was a youth when the ground on this street was cleared, and he cut the top out of a small elm tree, which he could bend over by his weight. He trained this from year to year, till now it is a most beautiful and magnificent shade tree, whose branches reach from 75 to 80 feet in all directions. Miss Harriet J. Farnsworth now occupies the lot upon which this tree stands. George Platt was a son of Judge Ezra Platt, who was one of the earliest settlers of Le Roy. He erected a house on the corner of Main and Church streets in 1803, which he occupied until his death in 1811. He left seven children: Mrs. L. Wolcott, Ezra, Oliver, Elijah, Margaret, Ira, and George. He was one of the earliest judges of the county, and built and run the first grist-mill in the town. He owned all the land on the east bank of the creek. Miss Farnsworth, who cared for Mr. Platt in his declining years, occupies a neat cottage which was left her for her kindness to him.

Lyman G. Paul, born December 16, 1844, on Lake street, received a common school and academic education, and at the age of 21 entered the employ of the N. Y. Central Railroad, at Le Roy, as agent, which position he held for 14 years. In 1878 he became agent for the B., R. & P. Railway. He is also agent for the American Express Co. He was one of the charter members of the R. A. and E. O. M. A. He married Mary J., daughter of Henry H. Olmsted, and they had two children, Dean R. and Mary O. By his second wife, Kittie S. Goff, of Rochester, he has one child, Maud G. Mr. Paul is a son of Alba and Sarah (Gould) Paul, who were born at Hartland, Vt., and came to Genesee County in 1841. They kept the Arsenal Hotel, Batavia, for a time, and in 1843 came to Le Roy, where he was engaged in selling fanning-mills for two years and stoves for 18 years, after which he engaged in farming west of Le Roy village. He reared four sons and one daughter. He was one of the founders and a leading member of the Universalist Church at Le Roy, and was a son of Hale Paul, of Vermont.

Hubert Ponce was born in Belgium, September 15, 1843, a son of Nicholas and Elizabeth (Feltun) Ponce, who had three children. At the age of seven years he began to assist his father, who was a mason and weaver, and at the age of 25, in 1867, he came to Stafford and worked on a farm for two seasons, when he came to Le Roy and assisted in building the Episcopal Church and the art gallery of Ingham University. In 1874 he opened the Capitol restaurant and saloon, and has been proprietor of the Franklin House since the fall of 1881. He is also a dealer in real estate and live stock. He married Barbara Rider, of Sheldon, but a native of Belgium, and they have three children, Peter, Mary, and Lena. All are members of the Roman Catholic Church.

Melvin D. Pratt, son of David and Electa (Gibbs) Pratt, was born January 21, 1830, in Livonia, Livingston County, and since six years of age he has lived where he now resides, except four years, two years of which he spent in Flint, Mich., engaged in the agricultural furnace business. He has filled several responsible positions in his town : has been 12 years assessor, one year clerk, and three terms supervisor. He married, first, Cornelia L., daughter of Robert and Dolly (Warner) Adams, by whom he had one daughter, Cornelia L. His second wife was Mary A., daughter of Peabody Pratt, of Flint, Mich. David Pratt was born in Greenville, Albany County, N. Y., June 11, 1791, and his wife in Litchfield, Conn. He came to Livonia in 1810, served in the War of 1812, was a shoemaker in early life, and in 1816 moved to Aurora, Erie County, where he resided six years, when he returned to Livonia. In 1836 he located on 50 acres about one mile east of Le Roy. He served in several responsible positions of trust. His children were Augustus G., Melvin D., Peabody W., and Lydia A. He was a son of Peabody Pratt, a soldier in the war for independence, from Connecticut, who married Sarah Buckingham, of Saybrook, Conn., who was a relative of Governor Buckingham. They had five sons and two daughters. He died in Livonia and his wife in Mount Morris, over 80 years of age. The Pratt family sprung from Lieut. William Pratt, who came to Cambridge, Mass., in 1633, and settled in Saybrook. Electa (Gibbs) Pratt was a daughter of Philo and Lydia (Lindsley) Gibbs, who came from Litchfield, Conn., and settled in Livonia in 1803, where they resided. He was a soldier in the Revolution, and had three sons and one daughter.

Albion D. Richmond, son of Preserved and Lucinda (Stiles) Richmond, was born December 17, 1829, one mile east of where he now resides. His father, Preserved, was born in Fairfield, N. Y., July 25, 1799, and his mother, Lucinda, in Danville, Vt., December 25, 1803. Preserved came to Genesee County with his parents and lived on the homestead nearly all his life. He was commissioned lieutenant of militia in 1829, and September 10, 1830, as captain. He had 11 children, and died in September, 1878, and his wife in June of the same year. His father, Preserved, was born June 25, 1764, and was twice married, first to Mary Olin, who bore him children as follows : Ezra, who was killed at the battle of Fort Erie, Adam, David, Simeon, Preserved, George, Alva, Polly, and Sarah. His second wife was Mary Luther, by whom he had nine children, eight of whom grew to maturity, as follows : Hiram H., Electa, Simoon L., Hazzard, William H., Angeline, Sanford L., and Caroline. They settled in Le Roy in October, 1812, where Albion D. now resides. About 1844, with a daughter, they moved to Clinton County, Mich., where he died, aged 85. He was a staunch and devoted member of the F. & A. M., and stood by the order during the exciting times after the Morgan affair. It is stated the order met in his house on several occasions. He was a son of Adam Richmond, who was born in 1739, and who was twice married, first to Molly Hazzard, and second to Molly Hall. He reared four sons and five daughters. Adam Richmond was a son of Stephen, who also had four sons and five daughters. Stephen was a son of John Richmond, who had two sons, Cyrus and Stephen. Albion D. was reared where he now resides. He went to Michigan and worked for an uncle two years. He married Margaret, daughter of Duncan Campbell, of York, Livingston County, N. Y., and they had five children, four of whom attained adult age, viz.: George C., Mary L., of Montana, Franklin D., and Cora E. After his marriage he moved to De Kalb County, Ind., where he resided 10 years, when he returned to Le Roy, and has since lived where he now resides. His wife died June 18, 1886. He is a respected member of the F. & A. M.

E. B. Rawson, son of Sanford and Caroline (Boyd) Rawson, of Shelburne, Mass., was born in Essex County, N. Y., March 14, 1829, was raised on a farm, and received a good academic education. At the age of 16 years he began teaching school, and when 21 went to New York city, where he was a book-keeper for 10 years, and was a member of the 7th N. Y. Regt., which defended Washington, and which was the first full regiment in the capital In February, 1862, he went to Key West on business, where he continued after the war, and started the first cigar manufactory there. The town now has 30 or 40 cigar establishments. For the past four years he has been in Le Roy. He married in Key West. Mr. Rawson has filled several positions of responsibility, and has been one of the most active and prominent men of the village. Sanford Rawson and wife were married in Massachusetts. He was an active man in business, and was one of the leading tanners who used hemlock. In 1848 he settled in Le Roy. He has served as postmaster and supervisor. He reared three sons and three daughters. December 9, 1889, he was 95 years old, and in good health. He is a son of Simeon Rawson, of Massachusetts, who was also a tanner, and who served in the Revolutionary war, and was an early settler of Essex County, N. Y., to which he came in 1792, where he died, aged over 80 years. His wife was Anna Holden, of Barre, Mass. They had five sons and seven daughters, and moved to Shrewsbury, Vt., thence to Essex County, N. Y., and were successful in business. Simeon Rawson was a son of Josiah, who was a son of William, who was a son of Edward, who came from England in 1636, and settled in Newbury, Mass. Edward was an Episcopal minister, and was a very prominent man in his adopted place for many years; he was also a member of the colonial Assembly.

Orange F. Randall, son of Perry and Mary E. (Bachelder) Randall, was born January 3, 1850, in Stafford. He was reared on a farm and received his education in the common schools and at Brockport, N. Y. October 17, 1871, he married Sarah F., daughter of John S. and Mary (Rapp) Traver, of Stafford. They have one child, Perry T. Since his marriage he has been actively engaged in farming. In 1880 he located where he now resides.

William Chauncey Reed, born in the town of Hickory, Pa., is a son of Joseph N. and Maria (Goodrich) Reed, of Hartland, Conn. The father was born in 1816 and died in 1882. The mother was from Washington County, N. Y., and died in 1882. Joseph N. was a farmer and broom-maker, spent some time in Ohio, was a conductor on the Erie Railroad, and lived in Attica. They died in Groveland, Livingston County. Their children were William C.; Dwight T.; Frank J. (deceased); David A., of Duluth; and Mary L., widow of David A. Abell, of Duluth. Dwight T., born in Ohio, at the age of 16 was a messenger in the Assembly at Albany, and later received an appointment in the State department at Washington, under President Hayes. He was sent as Secretary of Legation to Madrid, Spain, but resigned on the election of President Cleveland, and began work for the New York Life Insurance Company. In 1889 he was appointed secretary of the company in Spain. William C. Reed lived with his parents until he attained the age of 20. He was on a farm until 1871, when he came to Le Roy and conducted a restaurant two years, when he took possession of the Eagle Hotel, where he has attained the reputation of a courteous and obliging landlord. October 29, 1874, he married Jennie Livingston, of Batavia, daughter of Arthur and Margaret (McMahon) Livingston, natives of Ireland, who were married in the Eagle Hotel in Le Roy. They reared five sons and four daughters. Mrs. Livingston died in West Sparta, and he married again in Michigan, where he died.

Caspar Renner, born August 25, 1855, in Bamsberg, Germany, is a son of John and Barbara Renner. He learned the tailors' trade with his father, and served in the army six years, until 1879, when he married Veronica Schoenhoefer. January 1, 1881, he came to New York, and after residing at Lancaster and Philadelphia, Pa., he removed to Le Roy, in June, 1882, where he worked for Rose & Everhart one year. He worked three years for C. Vicary, and in October, 1886, entered into partnership with T. H. Ross, as merchant tailors. In September, 1889, he assumed control of the business, which he is now conducting at 29 Main street. His family attends the Roman Catholic Church.

Joseph Sutterby was born July 31, 1866, in Seneca County, a son of Henry and Elizabeth (Norris) Sutterby, and was reared on a farm, received an academic education at Seneca Falls, and at the age of 19 came to Batavia to study veterinary with his brother Harry. He entered Ontario Veterinary College, Toronto, in 1887, and graduated from that institution in 1889, when he located in Le Roy village.

Philo J. Sperry was born in Pavilion, May 22, 1848, and is a son of Cyrus and Olive (Coe) Sperry, natives of Massachusetts and Pavilion, respectively. Philo J. was reared on a farm, received a common school and academic education, and taught school one term. He located where he now resides in 1868, and married Emma, daughter of Martin and

Phœbe (Mills) Seekins, of Le Roy. Mr. and Mrs. Sperry have one child, Wilber M.

Gottleib Strobel was born in Wurtemberg, Germany, in 1842. He came to Le Roy in July, 1866, where he has since resided. He married, first, Elizabeth Ruchty, and second, Rosa M. Sauer, both of Rochester. Of his seven children three are living. Mr Strobel is a member of the firm of Morris & Strobel, stone contractors.

Richard L. Selden, son of Clark and Eliza (Wilcox) Selden, was born where he now resides September 18, 1827. Clark Selden, from Haddam, Conn., was a carpenter and joiner, and visited the Genesee country in 1811. In 1816 he settled on 200 acres and erected his cabin where Richard L. now lives. He had 14 children, 11 of whom attained maturity. He died in 1863, aged 86 years. His father, Thomas, a farmer, of Connecticut, and of English descent, married a daughter of Nathan Wilcox, who married Elizabeth Elliott, a descendant of John Elliott. Mr. and Mrs. Wilcox came to Le Roy in 1808, and he was one of the early magistrates. He died in 1813. Two sons served in the War of 1812. Richard L. Selden, a farmer, received a thorough education, and by close application fitted himself for engineering and surveying. He taught 37 years in common schools, and in the Le Roy Academy. About 1867 he began breeding Berkshire swine, and in 1880 Jersey cattle. In 1853 he was elected town superintendent for three years, served as justice one term, as supervisor nine years, and as school commissioner six years. He married Eunice Wilcox, daughter of Stephen P., and their children are C. Virginia, C. Hubert, Mary E., and William A.

Stephen M. Selden, born September 16, 1836, on the farm where his brother R. L. now resides, is a son of Clark and Eliza (Wilcox) Selden. He was reared a farmer, and had a common school education. He is a member of the Presbyterian Church, and has three sisters and a brother living with him on the old homestead.

Ephraim L. Snow was born June 18, 1828, in Le Roy. His parents, Jesse and Lucinda (Royce) Snow, who were born in Berkshire County, Mass., October 24, 1786, and July 4, 1796, respectively, came to Genesee County in 1816 and settled on 200 acres where Ephraim L. was born. In 1866 he moved on a farm west of Le Roy, where he died July 15, 1867. His widow is still living, on Lake street, in Le Roy village. His children were Jerome, Carlos, Marcius, of Minnesota, Ephraim L., Homer, James O., Emeline R., Sylvia E, and Sarah J. Jesse Snow was a son of Ephraim and Martha Snow, who moved from Cape Cod to Berkshire County, Mass. Lucinda Snow was a daughter of Francis and Rebecca (Spring) Royce, who came from Massachusetts to Genesee County in 1816 and settled in Pavilion. Ephraim L. Snow was reared on a farm, received a common school and academic education, and at the age of 20 left the farm. In 1856 he went to Ohio, and the same year removed to Montgomery, Ala., where he was engaged in hulling and shipping cotton seed. At the commencement of the war he went to Medina, Orleans

County, where he was connected with the N. Y. Central Railroad for two years, when he engaged in the produce business for two years, after which he was located for two years at Lockport. He returned to Le Roy and has since continued in the produce business more or less. He has served five years as collector, and has taken an active interest in politics. Mr. Snow was a delegate to the State convention that nominated Gov. Robinson, and was appointed postmaster of Le Roy in April, 1887. He married Eliza, daughter of Wait B. Arms, of Pavilion, and they have three children, Rosa, Henry P., and Harriet B.

Dr. F. L. Stone, born in 1834, in Marcy, Oneida County, N. Y., prepared for college at Oriskany Seminary, and graduated in 1865 from the medical department of Bellevue College Hospital, New York. He was also one year at Ann Arbor, Mich. He studied medicine with Dr. W. H. Babcock, of Oriskany, and practiced with him one year after his graduation. Mr. Stone came to this county 22 years ago, was at Stafford in active practice for seven years, during which time he was town clerk, and moved to Caledonia, where he practiced five years, when he came to Le Roy, where he has done active work in his profession for 10 years. He married a Miss Brierly, of Le Roy.

Walter H. Smith, an attorney and counselor of Le Roy, was born in West Bloomfield, N. Y., July 25, 1852, attended common schools, and entered the Le Roy Academy under the efficient and careful tutelage of Prof. Russell, now of Worcester, Mass. He then attended Williston Seminary, East Hampton, Mass., after which he studied law with Judge L. N. Bangs in 1873, and graduated at the Albany Law School in 1876. Mr. Smith soon commenced practice in this village, and for a time was aided by the intimacy and experience of Judge Bangs in establishing a profession and practice, which has resulted in building up a lucrative business. He has been elected a trustee of the village, yet he is no aspirant for politcal privileges.

Rev. M. D. Shumway, born June 17, 1855, at East Pembroke, is a son of William and Emeline (Elliott) Shumway. William was a son of Cyril and Hannah (Hannum) Shumway, who came from Massachusetts, and were among the earliest settlers southeast of Pavilion Center. Dr. M. D. was reared on the farm, received his education in the common schools and East Pembroke Academy, and entered the store of Jacob Arnold, of East Pembroke, where he was a clerk for four years. He then became a book-keeper for Rathburn Brothers, of the same place, and in the fall of 1879 he began studying for the ministry with Rev. G. W. Powell. In 1881 he settled in Alexander, and in 1882 was called to Mount Gilead, Ohio, where he took charge of two parishes. Here he was ordained by Rev. G. W. Powell, in June, 1882, and after two years removed to North Bloomfield, where he remained one year, when he was called to Le Roy, occupying the pulpit three years. On account of failing health he retired from active ministerial work, and in March, 1888, engaged in the drug trade. In January, 1889, in company with Rev.

35

G. W. Powell, he engaged in the manufacture of a patent buggy dash at Le Roy, their shop being in the old foundry on Mill street, formerly the old Catholic Church. Rev. Mr. Shumway is held in high esteem as an eloquent and popular minister, a ready and pleasing talker, and as a citizen is beloved by all. He married Harriet E., daughter of John D. and Althea E. (Munson) Rogers, of Le Roy. Mr. and Mrs. Rogers were natives of New London County, Conn., and Dutchess County, N. Y., respectively. John D. Rogers came to Avon in 1832, where he was a farmer and broker. In 1871 he came to Le Roy, where he died in 1880. His wife still survives.

Henry Steuber was born June 5, 1828, in Munden, Hanover, Germany. His father, a glazier by trade, was born in Swarbaack, and his mother, Catharine (Devis), in Hanover, Germany. Mr. Steuber, after receiving such an education as the common schools of Germany afforded, served his apprenticeship as a cabinetmaker, and in January, 1849, landed in New York city, after a voyage of 10 weeks. He went to Hamilton, Madison County, where he remained until June, 1850, when he came to Le Loy. Here he worked for A. & C. Burpee for three years, when, with his brother, George G., he opened business where Gillett & McKenzie are now located. Here they carried on a large and successful business. In 1859 they opened a branch shop and store in Batavia, which was destroyed by fire in 1862, when they abandoned the Batavia branch, but continued in operation at Le Roy until 1868, when a destructive fire destroyed their business. With undaunted spirit they immediately rebuilt a large and commodious brick store, now occupied as a hardware store. They continued one year, when they sold to R. Miller, who sold to Joy & Williams. Mr. Steuber worked for this firm about two years, when he formed a partnership with A. F. Drake, which continued until 1872, since which he has been alone. In October, 1888, he moved to the store he now occupies, corner of Main and Mill streets, where he carries on a flourishing business. Honest and upright in all his dealings with his fellow men, he has the respect of all. Mr. Steuber is an active member of the Masonic fraternity. In April, 1853, he married Charlotte, daughter of James Caple, of Le Roy, who came from Somerset County, England. Mr. and Mrs. Steuber have had born to them six children: Frederick A., Charles H. (deceased), Frank G., Lewis W., Harvey J., and Minnie (deceased).

Andrew J. Sanderson, born March 8, 1841, in Byron, is a son of Richard and Ann (Beebe) Sanderson, natives of Oneida County, N. Y. Richard Sanderson was born November 13, 1801, came to Byron in September, 1828, and settled on a farm. He reared children as follows: Reuben H., of Minnesota, Lyman L., of North Carolina, Anson T., Welthy A., of Oneida County, Levi L., Andrew J., and Laura, of Orleans County. He died in June, 1875. His father, Levi Sanderson, was born September 7, 1775, and died in Springfield, N. Y. He had three sons and three daughters. His widow married John Brown. Levi's ancestors from

England were Joseph [5], the great-grandfather of our subject, Joseph [4], Joseph [3], William [2], and Robert [1], the latter of whom came from England in 1638 with his wife and two children. The next year he took the Freeman's oath, and moved to Watertown, Mass., in 1642, and to Boston about 1658. Andrew J. Sanderson was reared on a farm, received a good English education, and January 1, 1874, married Addie, daughter of Luke and Fannie (Knight) Wilder, who were born in Northampton, Mass. Luke Wilder came to Byron as early as 1820. His children were Luke Sylvester, of Dakota, Henry, of Eaton County, Mich., Dwight, of Crawford County, Kan., Alvin (deceased), Laura, Martha, Sarah A., Emily, and Addie. Luke was a son of Lot Wilder. Mr. and Mrs. Sanderson have two children, Ada R. and Bertha A. In 1880 they located on a farm of 75 acres two miles west of Le Roy village, and in 1882 removed to where they now reside. They are devoted members of the Presbyterian Church.

Samuel Steiner, son of John and Magdaline (Strahn) Steiner, natives of Switzerland, was born in July, 1829. His parents came to Churchville in 1848, where they died. They reared nine sons. Samuel had a limited education, and came to where he now resides in 1873, where he purchased 125 acres of land. For 10 years he has been a breeder of fine horses. He married Catharine Maran. They are members of the Presbyterian Church.

Matthias M. Stevens, son of John and Charlotte E. (Walfrom) Stevens, natives of England, was born October 17, 1860, in Stafford. John Stevens came to Stafford, and has always lived there. His children are Matthias M. and Sarah K. His wife was first married to Levi K. Williams, by whom she had four children. Mr. Stevens is a carpenter and joiner.

William H. Smith, son of Leonard, was born in Monroe County, N. Y., April 27, 1850, and came to Le Roy when about five years of age. He learned the harnessmakers' trade of M. D. Brown, and opened a shop at 70 Main street in 1887, where he has since carried on a thriving business.

Dennis Scanlan, son of Michael and Margaret (Mullin) Scanlan, was born in 1828, in County Kerry, Ireland. January 10, 1850, he landed in New York city, where he remained until May, when he went to Skaneateles and engaged in farming. He removed to South Byron, and in 1853 came to Le Roy and engaged in farming until 1854, when he entered the Upham car works, where, after a brief experience, he received an injury, which disabled him for some time. In 1855 he became a salesman in the grocery store of Foreman, Starr & Co., where he remained until 1863, when he opened a general store in a frame building on the site now occupied by Lampson Hotel. In April, 1877, he moved into the store which he now occupies, and where he is meeting with success. Mr. Scanlan has increased his stock from time to time, until now he carries a choice line of clothing, boots, shoes, hats, caps, and gents' furnishing goods. Starting in life without a dollar he has succeeded in accumulating a competency. Honorable in all the relations of life he has won for himself the confidence and esteem of all who know him, and he has been honored with several responsible positions. He has served as tax collector several terms and trustee for seven years. He married Bridget, daughter of Nicholas Kehoe, of Rochester. His wife was born in County Wexford, Ireland, 'and with her parents came to the United States about 1845. Mr. and Mrs. Scanlan have seven children, viz.: Anna J., Margaret, Mary, Theresa, Gertrude, James E., and Loretto J.

George F. Sprague, a prominent and substantial farmer, was born in Middlebury, Wyoming County, N. Y., April 30, 1825, a son of Jesse and Irena (Goddard) Sprague, natives of Massachusetts, who came from Poultney, Vt., in 1812. Jesse Sprague in 1811 came to Wyoming County, where he took up a farm. He sent a substitute to the War of 1812. He had 10 children, eight of whom attained maturity. Mr. Sprague used to go to Perry to mill, 12 miles distant. He hauled wheat to Rochester and sold it for 31 cents; it took nearly a load of wheat to buy a hat. He died in 1864, aged 85, and left a fine property. His father was William Sprague. George F. Sprague received a common school and academic education at Wyoming and Perry academies, and at the age of 18 he purchased a farm. He has been a farmer all his life except three years spent in Dansville. In 1867 he located where he now resides. He has been twice married, first to Susan, daughter of John Tomlinson, of Le Roy, who was an early pioneer of this town. They had seven children, of whom four are living, viz.: Jennie L., George F., of Lawrence, Kan., Susan L., and Jessie R., also of Lawrence, Kan. Mr. Sprague's second wife was Mary L., daughter of Isaac and Jane E. (Whitbeck) Baker.

Erastus Spring, born August 20, 1805, in Berkshire County, Mass., is a son of Amos and Reliance (Snow) Spring, natives of Massachusetts, who came to Genesee County in September, 1810, with an ox-team and one horse. They settled on 100 acres of land four miles south of Le Roy, on what is known as the State road. Their first cabin was of rough logs, with a puncheon floor. Amos was three times called out in the War of 1812, under Capt. Buell and Gen. Davis. He had a brother with him, who was a fife-major, and who was killed in Canada. Amos Spring, one of the early justices, had five sons and five daughters. In 1833 he sold his farm and moved to Attica, where he died in 1849, aged over 70 years. His wife died at the age of 94. His father was Amos Spring. Erastus Spring received his education in the common schools, and was married in March, after he became of age, to Eliza, daughter of B. Webb, of Pavilion, and they have three sons and two daughters, all of whom are living. About 1832 he went to Geneva, where he lived two years, when he returned to Pavilion, and afterwards moved to Niagara County, where he resided 10 years, after which he lived in Attica, Wyoming County, about 40 years, where he owned a fine farm of 619 acres. He came to

Le Roy in 1887. His children are Sylvester P., Sidney S., George W., Helen, and Art. E.

L. K. Stowell was born in Cazenovia, Madison County, October 18, 1826, a son of Calvan B. and Mary (Southwell) Stowell, natives respectively of Vermont and Madison County, N. Y. Calvan B. Stowell, a blacksmith by trade, in 1843 located in East Pavilion, and engaged in farming. His children were Oscar P., of Nebraska, Lucian, L. K., John, of Kansas, Martin, of Ohio, George R. (deceased), Franklin, and Ralph, who died in the army. Calvan B. was a son of Calvan Stowell, a tailor by trade, who came from Vermont to Madison County, and reared four sons and one daughter. The sons were all blacksmiths. L. K. Stowell received a good English education, and at the age of 19 began life as a farmer, in which occupation he has since continued. He purchased his first farm, near Asbury Church, in 1853, and in January, 1858, located where he now resides, and where he has a pleasant home. His first wife was Genette, daughter of John McGregor, of Le Roy, by whom he had one son, William H., of Richardson County, Neb. He married, second, Sarah A., daughter of Capt. William Thomas, who was a sea captain. By this marriage he had one child, Ernest C. Mrs. Stowell died in 1873. He is a member of the Methodist Episcopal Church.

Thomas B. Tuttle was born in Yates County, N. Y., September 30, 1844. At the age of two years his parents moved to Hillsdale County, Mich., where he was reared and received his elementary education in the common schools, suplemented by a thorough business education in the High School, from which he graduated. He spent two years in Hillsdale College. He early evinced a marked taste for the drug trade, and when but 17 years of age entered a drug store in Hillsdale, where he remained until he attained his majority, when he went to Dubuque, Ia., where he was actively and successfully engaged in the drug business until 1871, when he sold out and came East, in order to recuperate his health, which had been somewhat broken by his energetic and untiring efforts to succeed in his chosen profession. Having spent an active and industrious life he could not be content to remain idle, and in August, 1872, he came to Le Roy, where he purchased the drug store of J. M. Parker, at No. 18 Main street, an old and long established business. His thorough knowledge of drugs has drawn to him a large and substantial trade. Mr. Tuttle is a self-made man. Besides his business in Le Roy he has considerable interest with F. H. Mott in Washington (D. C.) real estate. Possessing a fine intellect, and good, clear judgment, his townsmen have honored him by electing him a member of the board of trustees, of which he has served as president. He has always taken an active interest in politics, and was a delegate to the Chicago convention in 1884. Mr. Tuttle married, in August, 1869, Henrietta, daughter of George Crocker, of Stafford, by whom he has one son, George. They are Episcopalians. Thomas Tuttle, grandfather of Thomas B., was born on Reade street, New York city, and when a young man emigrated to Yates County. Later he removed to Michigan, where he died, aged 90 years. His ancestors came from England about 1640. The name was then spelled Tuthill. Thomas Tuttle reared three sons and three daughters, one of whom was Henry, the father of Thomas B. Henry Tuttle, born in Yates County, married Elmira Wells, of the same county, and they had three sons and two daughters. In 1846 they moved to Hillsdale County, Mich., where he died in 1869, aged 54. He was a substantial farmer.

Angus A. Tompkins, a prominent politician, and only child of Jerome J. J. and Eliza M. (Hulbert) Tompkins, was born October 16, 1835, in Le Roy village. Jerome J. J. Tompkins was born in 1805 in Easton, Washington County, and his wife in Bergen, this county. He came to Le Roy in 1815 with his uncle, John Lent, and entered a store as a salesman in 1820. Having been a salesman and merchant all his active life he retired from business in 1852, and died in 1875. He filled several responsible local offices. His father, Joseph Tompkins, an early settler of Washington County, N. Y., was a sea captain and ran a vessel on the Hudson River. He married a Miss Lent, and had one son and two daughters, as follows: Jerome J. J., Julia Graves, and Catharine Bennett. Eliza M. Tompkins was a daughter of Unni and Julia C. (Elmore) Hulbert, who came from Hartford, Conn., to Bergen in 1816, and a few years later removed to Le Roy. They had two daughters. Mr. Hulbert worked in a woolen factory while in Hartford, and after coming to Genesee County was engaged in the manufacture of brick and in farming. Angus A. Tompkins was reared and received his education in Le Roy. In 1853 he began his career as a clerk in a store, and in 1856 entered the law office of John R. Olmsted and began the study of law. One year later he entered the office of Bissell & Ballard, was admitted to the bar, and in 1862 went to California, thence to Central America. In 1866 he was appointed Secretary of Legation to the American Consul to Central America. He returned to his home in Le Roy in 1872 and practiced law till 1886, when he was appointed assistant secretary to superintendent of State insurance at Albany. Mr. Tompkins is a staunch Democrat, has always taken an active interest in political affairs of his county and State, and aimed to promote the best interests of his party. He is well informed on all general topics of the day, and is an honored and respected citizen.

Timothy Toomey, born in Cork, Ireland, when a young man came to the United States and first settled in Vermont. He later removed to Utica, N. Y., where he married Mary Kennan, who was born in County Louth, Ireland, and came to the United States in 1854. They have had seven children, viz.: John, of Wisconsin, Michael (deceased), Kate, Tim, Anna, Pat W., and Mary. About three years after their marriage they came to Le Roy, where they resided until his death in January, 1888. Mr. Toomey while in Utica followed railroading, and after his removal to Le Roy engaged in farming.

Charles N. Vicary, son of William N. and Charlotte (Cook) Vicary, was born in Morgansville, N. Y., June 15, 1858. At the age of 14 he entered the store of S. C. Kelsey, of Le Roy, to learn the tailors' trade. Upon the death of Mr. Kelsey, in 1878, Mr. Vicary purchased the merchant tailoring branch of the trade, and in 1881 he bought the whole stock of goods, and has since carried on a successful business. Mr. Vicary, by energy, perseverance, and close application to business, has succeeded in building up a substantial and flourishing trade. He is courteous and genial, and an honored member of the F. & A. M. In August, 1881, he married Louise H., daughter of E. N. Bailey, of Le Roy, and they have three children: Arthur C., Grace L., and Marguerite B. The family are active members of the Presbyterian Church. William Vicary, born in Devonshire, Eng., came to Stafford in 1849, and worked on a farm for a short time, when he engaged in the mercantile business. About 1862 he became an agent for the Erie Railroad, and continued in that capacity until 1882, since which he resided upon a farm until his death, April 7, 1889. He was a prominent member of the Episcopal Church, and was at the time of his death one of the wardens. He had eight children, four of whom were born in England, viz.: Charlotte, Thomas C , Margaret, and Carrie. All came to the United States except Margaret. Of the children born in this country three are living, namely: Annie, George, and Charles N. In January, 1890, Mr. Vicary took as partner in his business L. W. Steuber, who had been in his employ for the past eight years, and the firm name became Vicary & Steuber.

John H. Van Valkenburgh, a prominent farmer of Genesee County, was born at Lyons, Wayne County, November 10, 1830, and received his education in the common schools. At the age of 16 he started in life at $4 per month, and afterwards received $120 per year. In 1856 he came to Le Roy and worked in the car works for a time. He then followed butchering for 20 years, and in 1868 purchased the farm where he now resides, and upon which he located in 1873. He has filled various local offices in the village. He married Mary P., daughter of Thomas P. Hedden, and they have one child, Effie (Mrs. Townsend). Mr. Van Valkenburgh is an honored and respected member of the F. & A. M. His parents, Abraham and Deborah (Craft) Van Valkenburgh, were born at Kinderhook and Peekskill, respectively, and were early settlers of Lyons. Abraham was a stage driver in his early life until after the canal was built. In the war he enlisted a regiment, made up exclusively of old men, for the purpose of defending Washington, D. C., but instead was sent to New Orleans and was killed in the battle of Baton Rouge, La. He had four sons and four daughters, and all but one reared families. His wife died in 1883. Abram Van Valkenburgh, grandfather of John H., was born in Holland, came to America during colonial days, and settled at Kinderhook. He was a farmer for a time, and later ran a vessel on the Hudson. He raised five sons and three daughters.

Peleg G. Vary was born December 1, 1818, in Greenbush, Rensselaer County, N. Y. His grandfather, Samuel L. Vary, of Welsh ancestry, reared a family of four sons and eight daughters, and died in Kinderhook. His sons all came to Pittsford, Monroe County. Samuel T., the father of Peleg G., was born in Berlin, Rensselaer County, October 11, 1791, and moved to Kinderhook and thence to Monroe County. He lived in Lima for a time, and died in Rochester, October 26, 1864. His wife, Mehetable Thomas, bore him five sons and three daughters, and died in Le Roy, September 7, 1882, aged 88. Peleg G., a retired farmer, received a common school education, and began life for himself at the age of 21. When 28 years of age he moved onto a farm near Avon, and in March, 1853, located on a farm about two miles east of Le Roy village. In 1874 he retired from farming and located in the village, where he has a beautiful and pleasant home. He married Lucinda, daughter of Luther and Rachel Landon, of Avon, who bore him children as follows: George P., Caroline (Mrs. Hollenbeck), Emma J., Hattie (Mrs. Clark), Jennie (Mrs. Johnson), and India. His wife died in December, 1883.

Schuyler C. Wells, for 20 years past numbered among the most successful business men of Genesee County, was born in Poultney, Vt., February 6, 1840. Reared upon his father's extensive farm he had ample opportunity for developing a naturally ambitious and persevering spirit. From the age of 15 years he took the lead in the management of the farm when not engaged in his studies at Troy Conference Academy, one of the most noted educational institutions of Vermont, which is located in his native town, and where he received a thorough business education. By judicious management of the opportunities afforded him he had accumulated, of his own earnings, when 25 years of age, a sum sufficient to enable him to enter business for himself.

From boyhood up he had always had a natural fondness for drugs and medicines, and only refrained from preparing himself for a physician, not being content with the limited opportunities to make a financial success out of the legitimate fields of the profession. In the fall of 1866 he decided to enter the drug trade at Le Roy, and with that end in view negotiated for the purchase of Medical Hall. Dr. L. S. Hooker, his brother-in-law, then a practicing physician in Wisconsin, was sought, to whom he divulged his plans, the result being a copartnership under the firm name of Hooker & Wells. This partnership existed for three years, during which time Mr. Wells applied himself to the study of medicine, and the building up of their drug trade. His restless and inquiring mind led him to devote his attention closely to the observation of the immediate results of certain formulas in respect to their favorable action upon various diseases that afflict the human system. The unusual success of these formulas ultimately created a great demand for them. During this time Mr. Wells had other projects in view, and was successful in securing the sole right to manufacture and sell "McLea's Patent Pail Ear" and "Eave Trough

Former"— articles of merit and usefulness. Having confidence in the merits of these articles, and believing there was money to be made out of them, he sold out his interest in the drug business, and formed a co-partnership for three years with James P. Kneeland, for their manufacture and sale, under the firm name of Wells & Kneeland. Through his energy and push they built a large factory, and equipped it with steam-power and stamping presses, and built up an extensive business, being compelled to run night and day to fill their orders. Many men lost their heads and judgment over the success of the entprise, and numerous were the applicants anxious to purchase an interest in the concern. A favorable proposition to purchase Mr. Wells's interest having been made to him, he sold out a two-thirds interest at a handsome profit, after which a stock company was organized, but after it went out of his control the business soon went to pieces. He now again engaged in the drug trade alone, and with increased capital and facilities laid the foundation for his greater success. Taking up his formulas where he left off, two years before, he brought out the several products now known as "Shiloh's Family Remedies," and which, from a small beginning in his own store in 1871, has grown to be the most important and successful business enterprise of the county. In 1873 he sold his interest in the store and devoted his whole attention to the introduction of his popular Remedies, which are now known and sold in every part of the United States, and in many foreign countries.

In 1877, to keep pace with his growing trade, Mr. Wells was obliged to seek enlarged quarters, which resulted in his building the commodious four story brick block on Church street, a few rods below Main street bridge. to which, in 1882, he erected an addition, doubling its capacity, the whole being now occupied by the business of the firm. His phenomenal success stimulated many imitators who sprung up throughout the county like mushrooms, but their feeble breath scarcely disturbed the autumn leaves, and one by one they soon became extinct, with perhaps a single exception. In 1882 he sold to his brother, George H. Wells, a one-third interest in his Shiloh's Family Remedies, and the business is carried on under the firm name of S. C. Wells & Co.

In September, 1865, Mr. Wells married Anna E., daughter of S. P. Hooker, then president of the bank at Poultney, Vt., and a prominent manufacturer there. Their children are Josephine H., Anna E., and Schuyler C., Jr.

In 1880 he purchased "Dreamland," a villa property on the elevation of East Main street, just within the corporate limits of the village. This fine property Mr. Wells has greatly improved, and having bought adjoining lands now has a stock farm of 200 acres. The residence has been remodeled, and is now, with its beautiful surroundings, considered one of the most elegant homes in Genesee County.

Always an active man, and never satisfied unless with business enough to keep two men occupied, Mr. Wells, who had been fond of a horse from boyhood, determined to go into the breeding of fashionable trotters and roadsters for recreation and pleasure. With him to wish is to act, and going to Kentucky he purchased, as his pioneer stallion, "St. Gothard," a son of "George Wilkes," which he brought back to "Dreamland," paying what was considered at that time an extravagant price. To-day no horse in the State stands higher in the estimation of Kentucky breeders than "St. Gothard." The breeding of fashionable horses, and the training incident thereto, demanded barns and buildings of large proportions; hence Mr. Wells built one of the most complete, largest, and commodious stock barns in the State, with room for 125 horses, a fast half mile track, and an eighth-mile track, the latter entirely under cover His stallions, brood mares, and colts number about 100 head. Dreamland, with its equipments, buildings, and stock, is one of the most complete enterprises of its kind in the United States. He organized the New York State Trotting Horse Breeders' Association, and was elected president of the organization, and served one term.

At the reörganization of Ingham University he was chosen one of the 15 incorporators and trustees. To him more than to any one else is due the magnificent Methodist Episcopal Church, of which he is a trustee, as not only being the largest contributor to it, but also giving much of his time and executive ability, which was of even more importance than his purse. He was one of the original incorporators of the Le Roy Salt Co., going into it as much for the benefit of the village as for personal gain.

Mr. Wells is a very successful man, and there are few whose abilities are as varied. Yet in the prime of life, he is constantly looking for new fields for investment, and finds a real pleasure in work which to the average man would be too exhaustive. His wealth has been accumulated from many counties, and to that extent has enriched this county.

Mr. Wells's grandfather was Noah Wells, a native of Colchester, Conn., who settled in Poultney, Vt., in 1795. He married Lucy Broughton, and their children were Abbie L., Anna R., and Pomeroy. The latter, the father of Schuyler C., was born in Poultney, December 3, 1810, on the Wells farm, where he also died. He married Rebecca Ann Blossom. Four children were born to them, namely: Helen (Mrs. George W. Gibson), of Schenectady, now deceased; Schuyler C.; Adelbert, who was drowned in 1856; and George H., who is the junior member of the present firm of S. C. Wells & Co.

George H. Wells, son of Pomeroy and Rebecca Ann (Blossom) Wells, was born June 12, 1848, in Poultney, Vt., and received his education in the common schools and Linsley Commercial College. At the age of 17 he went to Rutland, Vt., and entered a dry goods store as salesman Upon reaching his majority he embarked in the flour and grain business at Poultney, which he sold in 1876, and came to Le Roy, where he has since been engaged with his brother S. C. in the manufacture and sale of the celebrated "Shiloh's Remedies," having charge of the correspondence. Mr. Wells is one of the substantial and wealthy citizens of Le Roy. He has a pleasant home, and in his domestic and social relations he is kind and genial. Strangers always find him courteous and pleasant. He is liberal and public-spirited, and a free and cheerful giver to public enterprises that tend to promote the best interests of his community. Mr. Wells has been twice married, first to Alice C., daughter of Robert Bull. She died April 21, 1874, leaving one child, Helen. He married for his second wife Mary B., daughter of John R. and Sophia G. (Blodgett) Anderson, of Le Roy, by whom he has one child, Mary Blossom

Rosman L. Walkley, born October 30, 1838, in Pavilion, on the corner opposite and east of Asbury Church, is a son of Richard and Juliette (Mills) Walkley. His grandfather, Stephen Walkley, a soldier of 1812, was born March 1, 1778, in Haddam, Conn., and September 10, 1806, married Hannah Lawrence, who was born October 12, 1785, in Middletown, Conn. In 1807 Stephen first came to Genesee County and settled on 200 acres four miles southeast of Le Roy village. Here he cleared two acres and erected a cabin, and in March, 1808, purchased this tract for $600. This same year he brought his wife and resided on this farm for the rest of his life. His family consisted of nine children, as follows : Asahel, Daniel, Richard, Emeline, Stephen, Jr., Harry, Harriet, William Rosman, and Eunice, all of whom were born on this farm. He died April 26, 1869. His wife died June 13, 1863. He was a son of Gurden Walkley, of Haddam, Conn., and a soldier in the Revolutionary war. Gurden had three sons and two daughters, Stephen being the only one who came to Genesee County. Gurden was a son of Richard Walkley, who was born November 8, 1812, and after his marriage moved to Pavilion. About 1844 he purchased 100 acres one-half mile south of Asbury Church, and in 1866 moved to Le Roy village, where he died February 24, 1887. He reared two sons, Miller M. and Rosman L. The latter received his education in the common schools and Lima Academy, and also spent two years in Genesee College. At the age of 24 he began life for himself, residing in Pavilion until 1884, when he located on the old homestead, which he now owns. He married, October 18, 1865, Mary E., daughter of Benjamin F. and Elizabeth Peck, of Alden, Erie County, and they have one son, Franklin L. They are all active and leading members of the Presbyterian Church.

Frederick T. Wilcox, the third son of Pitman and Anna (Parish) Wilcox, was born in Bergen, July 10, 1849. His early education was obtained at the district schools, and finished at Le Roy Academic Institute. At the age of 17 years he began the study of pharmacy with A. S. Fisher, of Bergen, with whom he remained until 21 years of age, when he engaged in the drug business at Corfu for three years. In October, 1874, he removed to this town. March 19, 1872, he married Genevieve A., daughter of Henry D. Thurston, of Livonia, N. Y. He has had four children, viz.: Ralph T., Fred T., Dean A., and Marion, three of whom survive. Mr. Wilcox has been a resident of this town for the

past 15 years.   By presistent work and close attention to business he has
built up a fine trade.   The stock he carries, consisting of drugs, chemicals, trusses, fancy goods, and stationery, is complete and attractive.

The present proprietor of the Wiss House is the widow of John Wiss,
who was born in Landau, Bavaria.   He came to this country and settled in
New York city in 1847, where he carried on business as tailor.   In 1856
he came to Batavia, and in 1858 to Le Roy, and opened a hotel on the
site of the Lampson House.   In 1869 he bought out the proprietor of
the Collins House (formerly the Globe and Eagle), and named it the
"Wiss House."   He died in March, 1873.   He was a member of the
Presbyterian Church.   Mr. Wiss reared a family of seven children, viz.:
John, a prominent business man of Batavia, Carrie, Louisa A., Frank,
George, Lute, and Joseph.   Mrs. Anna K. Wiss was born in Etzlelwang,
Berne, Germany.   She has conducted the prosperous business left by
her late husband with a fidelity and attention to its cares that is seldom
equalled, and has caused this hostelry to become one of the three well-
known hotels of Le Roy.

John Wiss, son of John and Anna (Barr) Wiss, was born in Williamsburg (now Brooklyn), N. Y., January 2, 1852.   Receiving his education
at Le Roy Academy at the early age of 14 he began clerking in a drug
store at Schenectady, where he remained one year, when he was
with Smith & Co., of Churchville, for one year, and for seven years
was with Foreman & Rider and F. W. Foreman, of Le Roy.   At his
father's death he assumed charge of the Wiss House, and in 1873 he
purchased the store of F. W. Foreman, a business of 30 years standing.
Mr. Wiss has a fine and elegant stock of goods.   He has been chief of
the fire department for three years, treasurer of the village for 12 years,
is treasurer of the Firemen's Benevolent Association, and one of the vestrymen of St. Mark's Episcopal Church.   He married, first, Mary E.,
daughter of Lucian A. Hascall, by whom he had one son, John H.   His
second wife is Millicent N., daughter of M. A. Dix.

W. M. Wattles is a son of William P. and Sarah F. (Sweeting) Wattles, who were born in Geneseo and Connecticut, respectively.   William
P. Wattles was a graduate of Temple Hill Academy, and a prominent
and influential farmer.   He filled various positions of honor and responsibility.   Prior to the war he moved to Greenville, Ill., where he was actively engaged in farming.   In 1862 he enlisted in an Illinois regiment
and served as clerk in the quartermaster's department, with rank of lieutenant.   At the close of the war he returned to Geneseo, where he resided at the time of his death, in March, 1877.   His children were W. M.,
Allen H., and Mary A. W.   His father, David, married Sarah Smith, and
reared two sons and one daughter.   The father of David was Roger
Wattles, who was one of the first settlers of Geneseo, and of Scotch extraction.   Sarah F. Wattles was a daughter of Nathaniel and Catharine
(Waldo) Sweeting.   His mother was a daughter of Gen. Israel Putnam,
of Revolutionary fame.   W. M. Wattles is one of the active and pro-

progressive young men of Le Roy. He was born in Geneseo, November 14, 1866, received his education in the common schools and Starkey Seminary, and at the age of 15 went to Missouri Valley Junction, Ia., where he was connected with the C. & N. W. Railway for over a year. In 1884 he returned to this county and was connected with the Warsaw Salt Co. for two years, and for two years with John Henegan's monumental works. He was one year in the Glenwood granite works, of Lockport, and in May, 1889, located in Le Roy, having purchased the marble works of C. Strobel. He married Eva A., daughter of John Henegan, and they are members of the Presbyterian Church.

Henry L. Wingate, born August 30, 1811, in Charleston, S. C., is a son of Joseph and M. Ann (Wingate) Wingate, natives of Maryland. Joseph Wingate served as lieutenant in the War of 1812. He lived in Charleston, was a trader in slaves, and in 1819 returned to Maryland, where he died. He had 10 children, as follows: William, Joseph, Henry L., John. F., Rebecca M., Mary, Elizabeth, Millicent, and two who died in childhood. Joseph was a son of John, who was born in Massachusetts, and was a farmer. He emigrated to Dover, Delaware, with his brother and two sisters, and thence moved to Maryland. He served in the Revolutionary war. John Wingate was a descendant of Rev. Mr. Wingate, of Amesbury, Mass., where he was born September 10, 1703. He died February 19, 1784. Many of his descendants ranked among the most influential and prominent men of Massachusetts. One, Moses Wingate, of Haverhill, Mass., was a very prominent Mason, and his 101st birthday was celebrated by the Masonic fraternity October 25, 1869. Henry L. Wingate is self educated, having attended school but little. At the age of 14 he went to sea, being gone about three and one-half years. After an absence of seven years he returned home. He was for a time connected with the Baltimore & Susquehanna Railroad, and in February, 1833, came to New York city, and in October of the same year to Le Roy, where he has since resided. He has followed painting for 60 years. April 13, 1836, he married Mrs. Mary Ferren, who was born in Cazenovia, March 2, 1805, and was a daughter of John and Esther (Clark) Plato, of Batavia. John Plato and family came in 1810 and settled in Stafford as a farmer. Mr and Mrs. Wingate had three sons and two daughters: John F., William H., and Francis M., all of whom died in childhood, and Henrietta L. and Harriet I. Haskins. The latter has one child, Mary P. W. Mr. Wingate's wife had one son and two daughters by her first husband, Thomas Ferren, as follows: Charles K., Mary J., and Sarah. Mr. Ferren carried on the crockery business in Le Roy.

Charles A. Walton, son of Robert B. and Elizabeth (West) Walton, was born near Port Gibson, Ontario County, in January, 1859, and received his education in the common schools and on the farm. He came to Le Roy in 1881, and married Adelaide M., daughter of Samuel P. and Mary (Harris) Weld, natives of Genesee County, who reared two sons and three daughters. Mr. and Mrs. Walton have two children,

Mary H. and Phebe E. They are members of the Baptist Church. Robert B. Walton was born in the city of York, England, and with his parents, James and Louisa (Bollins) Walton, came to the United States about 1838, and settled in Palmyra, N. Y. He had 13 children. James Walton was a sailor, and had two sons and two daughters.

Casey Williams was born March 5, 1833, in Almond, Allegany County, only child of William and Esther (Wallace) Williams, who were both born in Allegany County. William Williams was a son of William, who was one of the early pioneers of Genoa, Allegany County, and who raised 11 children. Casey Williams was reared by his grandfather, having lost his father when a babe. At the age of 20 he began life on the farm, and married, July 4, 1857, Jane, daughter of George and Hannah (Wetherbee) Allen, of Allegany County, by whom he had three children, all of whom died in infancy. In March, 1871, he located where he now resides. He enlisted February 4, 1863, in Co. G, 16th H. A. His first battle was Chapin's Farm, Va. He participated in all the engagements in which the regiment was in, and was discharged in August, 1865, at Hart Island.

James White, born April 6, 1847, where he now resides, has always been a farmer. He married Delia, daughter of Ransom and Sarah (Corson) Auffman, of Pavilion, and they have three children, James H., Alice, and Fannie C. Daniel White, the father of James, was born in Massachusetts, and came with his parents to Pompey, Onondaga County, thence to Genesee County about 1803 or '04, locating where James now resides. Here he lived until his death, February 12, 1881, aged 84. His wife, Orra (Harris) White, died June 24, 1884, aged about 73. His father, who about 1803 settled on 60 acres and afterward added 20 more, was a soldier in the War of 1812. The night before starting to Buffalo the men in his regiment slept on the floor of the old Eagle Hotel. He had three sons, Daniel, John, and Nathan.

Albert S. Westlake, son of John S. and Louisa (Hancock) Westlake, was born July 10, 1837, at Skaneateles, N. Y. John S. Westlake and wife were born near Bristol, England, and in 1837 came to the United States and settled at Skaneateles. The same year they moved to Venice, Cayuga County, where they resided until 1848, when they moved to Perry, Wyoming County, where they now reside. They had seven children, viz.: a son who was lost at sea; Albert S.; Alfred S., a leading merchant in Marquette, Mich.; Mary Anna, who resides with her parents; Elizabeth L. Washburn, who, with her husband, died in Cairo, Mich., and left two sons, John and Fred; Priscilla M. (Mrs. Fiske), of Rochester; and Lucy Chapin, of Cairo, Mich., whose husband was an editor. John S. Westlake was a merchant tailor and a leading member of the Baptist Church, in which he always lead the choir, and was one of the deacons for many years. His uncle, William Westlake, was a prominent minister in England, where he built his own church, in which he preached, asking no assistance from the public. The mother of Albert S. was a lineal descendant of the John Hancock family. Albert S. received his education in the common schools and Perry Academy. At the age of 18 he went to Mount Vernon, Ia., and spent three years with an uncle. After his return home, in 1859, he began the study of dentistry with Dr. Scranton, of Perry, and in 1862 came to Le Roy, where he has since successfully practiced his profession. His social and genial qualities, for which he is distinguished, have endeared him to all who know him. He married, November 29, 1866, Marietta, daughter of Francis and Caroline (Woodard) Fordham, who were born in Vermont, and had eight children. Francis Fordham was a son of Silas. They were among the very earliest settlers of Genesee County, settling four miles north of Le Roy prior to the War of 1812. Dr. and Mrs. Westlake have one child, Caroline Louise. Mrs. Westlake and daughter are members of the Presbyterian Church.

Daniel Woodard, born July 18, 1781, in Dorset, Bennington County, Vt., was a son of Ebenezer and Betsey (Curtis) Woodard, of Vermont. He was reared on the farm, was self educated, and married Sarah Hastings, a native of Colchester, Conn., and daughter of Paine and Mary Hastings, of Connecticut. Mr. Woodard, after his marriage in 1803, located in Jennings, Seneca County, whence he emigrated to Phelps, Ontario County, and about 1811 removed to Chili, Monroe County. He came to Genesee County about 1835, locating at Cary's Mills for three years, and then removed two miles north of Le Roy village, on 225 acres, where he resided until his death, June 18, 1863. His wife died July 2, 1871, aged 86. He was drafted in the War of 1812, hauled provisions, and later hired a substitute. He had four sons and six daughters, viz.: Mary A., Eliza, Joseph, Orson, Jane, Solomon, Betsey, Cornelia, George, and Sarah. Ebenezer Woodard was a soldier in the war of the Revolution, was at the battle of Bennington, and was a farmer. He emigrated to Phelps, Ontario County, and reared five sons and five daughters. He and his wife died in New Fain, Niagara County, and were both upward of 90 years of age. Ebenezer Woodard's father came from Wales with a brother, one locating in Vermont, the other in Virginia.

O. F. Woodward, born in Bergen, July 26, 1856, is a son of Abner T. and Phœbe J. (Lyman) Woodward, natives of Genesee County. His father was a carriagemaker. O. F. came to Le Roy in 1860, was educated at the common schools, and the age of 12 began to earn his own living. In 1877 he was engaged in the manufacture of nest eggs, and for five years met with success. In 1883 he commenced the manufacture of Kemp's balsam, in which he has secured a large trade. He was married to Miss Cora Talmadge.

William Waterman, a substantial farmer, was born January 20, 1819, in Stafford, and is a son of Anthony and Sophia (Bannister) Waterman. He was reared on a farm and received a good common school education. In April, 1846, he married Nancy M., daughter of Thomas and Nancy M.

(Pierson) Hanna, and they have had five children, viz.: Edwin, of Allegan, Mich., Mary E., Charles W., Esther S. (deceased), and George. Mr. Waterman's wife died in May, 1875. After his marriage he moved to Byron, and in 1849 located where he now resides He and his wife are members of the Presbyterian Church. Anthony Waterman and wife came from Windsor, Berkshire County, Mass., in 1816. They had built an ox-shed with which to make the trip, but there being no snow they came with a wagon, and were 17 days on the road. They were accompanied by two other families, his father and a Mr. Miner. They settled in Stafford, Anthony Waterman locating on 97 acres, where he resided until his death. He had 11 children, as follows: Hannah, Thaxter, William, Rollin, Melvina, Harlow, Oscar, Hartwell, Gorden, Elma, and Bennett. He was drafted in the War of 1812, but furnished a substitute. Mr. Waterman was an active member of the Baptist Church, and a son of Jamas Waterman, who was twice married, first to a Miss Bates, who bore him one son, Anthony, the father of our subject, and second to Polly Payson, a native of Massachusetts. He died in Ohio. He had three sons and three daughters.

Wilber Waterman was born September 26, 1858, in Byron, and is a son of Thaxter and Mary (White) Waterman, natives of Stafford. He was twice married, first to Elmira White, by whom he had one daughter, Elmira. By his second wife he had children as follows: Salina, Dorrence, Anthony, Wilber, Fannie (Mrs. Stevens), and Addie (Mrs. Miller). After his marriage he moved to Byron. In 1861 he returned to Stafford, and died in January, 1881, aged 64. His wife survives. They were members of the Christian Church. He was a son of Anthony, who married Sophia Bannister, and came about 1819 from Vermont with cattle and a sled, settling on 100 acres in Stafford. They reared 10 children. He was of English descent. Wilber is a farmer, had a limited education, and married, in October, 1886, Bell, daughter of William and Lizzie (Tapp) Stevens, of Le Roy.

OAKFIELD.

OAKFIELD.—The primitive history of Oakfield, its town officials, its early improvements and societies, must necessarily be incorporated with Elba, because it was a portion of that town during its settlement, and until the growth of the original Elba had called for a division of its territory, and April 11, 1842, this town was set off from the western part. The name "Oakfield" was given it from the large surface of oak timber and oak openings covering the territory. The town is in range 2 of towns, which ranges are numbered from the east Transit line, and in township No. 13, numbering from the Pennsylvania line. · It is one of the northern tier and lies west of the center of the county. Its surface is quite level, gently undulating, and sloping to the north and west. The soil is a deep sandy loam, with a clay subsoil, and very fertile.

The town is well watered by the Oak Orchard Creek, which flows westerly through the northern part, and by one of its tributaries that flows northerly into it, affording ample power for mills and manufacturing ; and pure water is easily obtainable from its many springs and living wells. The Tonawanda Swamp extends across the northern portion, along Oak Orchard Creek, and· this is heavily timbered. It is said that the best and richest land of the town will be found here when it is brought into cultivation.

The western part of the town contains one of the finest plaster beds in the State, extending from the west border of the town east two miles, and is half a mile in width. Salt springs, from which much salt was manufactured at an early day, are found near the center of the town. Oakfield is bounded on the north by Barre, Orleans County, west by Alabama, south by Batavia, and east by Elba. A great portion of its area was embraced in the Tonawanda Reservation, as described in the history of the Holland Purchase title, in preceding pages, the title of which was not obtained from the Indians till 1829. It contains 15,379 acres, being six miles north and south, and four east and west.

In this town are Indian mounds and earthworks that have gone into history as the most remarkable and best preserved of any in the State. The best preserved, according to *Harper's Magazine*, is about half a mile west of Caryville, and is known as the " Old Fort," consisting of a ditch and breastworks, including about 10 acres of land. The ditch is now about six feet in depth, calculating from the top of the embankments, and contains every evidence of artificial grading and engineering skill. In a part of the works, under cultivation, are traced ancient lodges and a supply of broken pottery. The west side of the fort is formed by a ravine, through which flows "Dry Creek." Trees, apparently 300 years old, have grown upon the works, and on the west side are passages with sides built up of stone. A mile to the northeast is " bone fort," which, when the first settlers came, was yet perfect in detail, but scattered fragments of bones only mark the spot now. Rev. Samuel Kirkland in 1788 visited the spot, and says the Senecas called these forts *Te-gat-ai-neaaghgue*, or " double-fortified town "—a town with a fort at each end. The several gateway openings, the way dug to the water near the center, the great age of the works as shown by the forest, and other marked evidences lead to the conclusion that this was the citadel of the ancient Senecas, and was proof against invading tribes. These works are upon what is known as the Armstrong farm, and after a few generations will be preserved only in the written history of the white man. An examina-

36

tion of the fort in 1846 verified Rev. Mr. Kirkland's report of 1788, of a ".double-fortified town," or a town with a fort at each end. This was at that time on the farm owned by John Smith. There was also one on the farm of Moses True, about one mile northeast from the above fort.

Early settlers.—The settlement of the town was begun in 1801, when Aaron White and Erastus Wolcott came in. Mr. White, while serving as a captain in the War of 1812, was killed at the battle of Black Rock. Gideon Dunham also came in 1801, settled in the oak openings, and gave the name to Dunham's Grove. His son, Col. Shubael Dunham, deceased, has left for record the fact that the road along the Tonawanda Creek, from Batavia to Bush's, thence north to the openings, was cut through in 1801–02. Erastus Wolcott, Peter Rice, and Christopher Kenyon also came that year, and Peter Lewis, from Vermont, came the next year and settled near Mr. Dunham. Daniel Ayer and Job Babcock settled in 1802, and in 1803 we find the following persons in the town: Hiram Smith, Silas Pratt, William McGrath, George Lathrop, Darius Ayer, Philip Adkins, Lemuel L. Clark, and James Robinson. In 1804 the following settled: Rufus Hastings, Roraback Robinson, Benjamin Chase, Solomon Baker, Samuel Jerome, Sr., and Samuel Jerome, Jr. The following are reported as having settled in 1806: Micajah Green, Caleb Blodgett, Jr., George Hoge, Eldridge Buntley, George and John Harper, Nicholas Bentley, James Crossett, David Woodworth, David Clark, William Parrish, Ezra Thomas, and Caleb Blodgett, Sr.

Elijah Blodgett, originally from Vermont, came in 1807 from Ontario County, and settled at what is now Mechanicsville. He died in 1839, aged 89 years. William McCrillus came in 1810, and George W., John, and Jeremiah H. Gardner in 1811. George Driggs was one of the first who settled on the north line of the Reservation, in 1811, and he cut the Lewiston road from Alabama to Walsworth's tavern. Russell Nobles, John Orr, Mr. Terrill, Othniel Brown, Laurens Armstrong, Harvey Hubbell, and others, of New England, were early settlers. Aaron Brown, also an early settler who served in the War of 1812, came to Oakfield in 1815, from Chili, and was the first to locate in the north part of the town, on road 4, where his son George now lives. Another settler of that year, and one who was also in the War of 1812, was John Underhill. His son Alfred came with him, and is now living on the old place. Isaac Stringham settled at an early day on the Shultz farm, on road 6. Reuben Norton came from Pennsylvania to Elba, thence to Oakfield, and settled on a farm where Arthur J., a grandson, now lives. David C. Reed came in 1825 and located lots 52 and 53, on road 10, called Temple Hill road, which is owned by Seymour Reed.

The first birth in the town was Calvin Nobles, in 1806, a son of Russell Nobles, who will be remembered by the older residents as the early "fiddler" of the Purchase, and to whose left-handed bowing and scraping many of the pioneers bowed and scraped in the mazes of the dance as he visited from cabin to cabin. He had no competitor. He and his old violin mark the advent of music upon the Holland Purchase. In those times, in sleigh or ox-sled rides, at recreations that followed log-house raisings, logging bees, road cuttings, at Christmas and New Year's frolics, Noble and his fiddle formed an accustomed and necessary part. Gideon Dunham opened the first tavern, and Mr. Davis soon followed in the same business. Oliver Wolcott was also an early tavern-keeper. Christopher Kenyon erected the first mills, in 1811, and Othniel Brown commenced wool-carding and cloth-dressing in 1829. The latter erected a good woolen factory in 1835, which was an important factor of the town for many years. A great portion of the town being included in the Reservation, and the thriving village of Batavia being only a few miles distant, with Elba as the center of the town proper, the opening of a store in this part of the town was not considered practicable; but in 1829, after the sale of the Reservation lands, its settlement followed so rapidly that within a few years this part of the town was fully developed. In 1833 Col. Alfred Cary started the first store at Caryville, now Oakfield postoffice, and for years was successful in business, giving the name to the village, and occupying a prominent position in the county.

The town clerk's office was destroyed by fire June 15, 1866, which swept away the books, records, and papers belonging to the town from its organization to that time; but we here give the first officers as elected: Moses True, supervisor; George Burden, town clerk; William Wolcott, John C. Gardner, John G. Satterlee, assessors; John G. Satterlee, justice; John G. Gardner, Perez Howland, and George E. Martin, commissioners of highways.

The justices for the town from 1842 to the present time have been as follows:

John G. Satterlee, Otis L. Freeman, Henry Howard, Benjamin F. Hawes, John C. Gardner, George E. Martin, Henry Field, Samuel Haxton, John Willard, Perez Howland, Eden McIntyre, Parley V. Ingalsbe, Norman Drake, B. F. Hawes, B. J. Chapman, Charles H. Chamberlain, Philip Capel, Benjamin Carr, Seward A. Ingalsbe, Richard Stevens, William H. Griffin, Everett A. Nash, Richard Stevens, J. J. Stedman, William H. Griffin (1886), Darius Manchester (1887), B. F. Hawes (1888), Irving J. Stedman (1889).

The supervisors have served as follows:

Moses True, four years; William Wolcott, seven years; John G. Gardner, two years; Clitus Wolcott, three years; William C. McCrillus, two years; Addison Armstrong, two years; William Wolcott, one year; Parley V. Ingalsbe, three years; Homer D. Waldo, two years; Charles H. Chamberlain, two years; Asa A. Woodruff, three years; William Wolcott, two years; Darius King, two years; Norman Drake, two years; Julius Reed, one year; J. J. Stedman, one year; A. B. Rathbone, two years; C. H. Chamberlain, since 1886.

The following have served as town clerks

George Burden, James Gibson, George March, Elbridge A. Jaquith, Lorenzo H. Olcott, Solomon H. Parmalee, Samuel March, Charles H. Chamberlain, Asa A. Woodruff, Richard Stevens, John D. Stedman, Eugene I. Chamberlain, Francis A. Griffin, Wilber H. Martin, E. T. Chamberlain, Charles H. Griffin, Fred W. Isaac.

The following statistics were used, as correct, in establishing a new town clerk's office after the fire in 1866:

Population of the town	1,408.
Acres of land in the town	15,379.
Amount of assessed real estate	$495,884.
Amount of assessed personal estate	51,250.

The town officers for 1889 were Charles Chamberlain, supervisor; Charles H. Griffin, town clerk; B. F. Hawes, D. Manchester, and B. Sparr, justices.

CARY (Oakfield p. o.) was settled as soon as the territory could be severed from the Reservation, and at once became the center of the town. It was named in honor of Col. Alfred Cary, who was an early and enterprising business man. It lies south of the center of the town, six miles northwest of Batavia village, on the Lewiston road, and is a thriving place. The West Shore Railroad has a station here, and as a market for grain and produce Oakfield is noted as one of the best on the line of the road. The village contains 700 inhabitants, who have the best of religious and educational advantages, and the places of business keep pace with the rapid development of the rich territory around. There are four churches (Methodist Episcopal, Presbyterian, German, and Episcopal), the Oakfield Seminary, a postoffice, a bank, three dry goods stores, two hardware stores, one foundry, one evaporator and cider-mill, three hotels, one grist-mill, two drug stores, two harness shops, a tailor shop, one furniture store, two barber shops, a grocery store, one jewelry store, a boot and shoe store, three meat markets, one wagon shop, one manufactory of plows and agricultural implements, one lumber yard, one stave and coopering factory, one bank, three firms buying grain, and about 200 dwellings. The name Caryville was changed to Plain Brook in 1837, and soon after called by its present name. The village was incorporated in 1858, under the laws of the State, and August 7th of that year the following were declared the officers of the village by an election at the Olcott House: Andrew Thompson, Virgil C. Calkins, Asa A. Woodruff, Abner C. Dodge, and Seres P. Champlin, trustees; Rice Baldwin, Samuel Fellows, and Horace R. Holt, assessors; Solomon H. Parmalee, clerk; Cyrus Pond, treasurer; Thomas Brown, collector; Dewitt C. Colony, poundmaster; Samuel March, A. A. Woodruff, and S. P. Champlin, inspectors of election. To Oakfield belongs the honor of electing the first Prohibition village president in Western New York, William W. Stevens being elected to that office in March, 1890. The other officers for this year are H. C. Martin, treasurer; James L. Plate, collector; and A. T. Heckroth, A. A. Grinnell, and C. L. Calkins, trustees; A. E. Howland, chief engineer fire department.

EAST OAKFIELD, lying about three miles northeast of Oakfield, contains a postoffice, one store, blacksmith shop, and a feed, saw, and cider-mill.

The first preaching in this town was by Freewill Baptists, and afterwards by the Methodists, about 1830. The services were held in a log school-house, which stood on what is now the green in front of the Seminary.

St. Michael's Episcopal Church was organized June 14, 1858, by Rev. G. C. V. Eastman, who was also the first rector. There were 25 members at the organization. After struggling along for years without any suitable place for worship efforts were made which resulted in the building of a neat and commodious church edifice, which was consecrated in 1885 by Rt Rev. Bishop Coxe. The structure is of wood, of churchly design, and is a credit to the energies of so small a parish. There are at present 48 communicants, with 50 scholars, seven teachers, and three officers in the Sunday-school. Rev. Curtis C. Gove, A. M., is the present rector. He came from North Adams, Mass. The house of worship and grounds cost $6,000.

The Oakfield Presbyterian Church was organized in December, 1833, by Rev. C. Fitch. In 1837 there were 87 members, and Rev. E. H. Stratton was the pastor. The first church edifice was a frame building put up in 1843. In 1848 there were 98 members, and H. Gregg was pastor. There are now 71 members in the society, presided over by Rev. E. N. Manley. The value of the church and grounds is estimated at $6,000. The edifice will comfortably seat 300 persons, and there are 121 members belonging to the Sunday-school.

The Oakfield Methodist Episcopal Church was organized by Rev. Hiram May about 1832, with six members. A church was built in 1839, of wood, and cost $1,600. This society was at first served by ministers from adjoining towns. Their present pastor is Rev. E. C. Dodge The property of the society is valued at $5,000. The edifice will seat 250 persons, and the Sunday-school has about 125 members.

The German Methodist Episcopal Church was organized November 1, 1886, by Carl Stocker, Lewis Shultz, Carl Bloom, John Harloff, Gottleib Wayback, and Fred Harloff, with about 30 members. Rev. Carl Stocker was the pastor. A church was erected, of wood, in 1886, funds to the amount of $1,800 being procured by general subscription. There are now 40 members, and Rev. D. Pape is pastor. L. Meyers is superintendent of the Sabbath-school.

Cary Collegiate Seminary is pleasantly situated in Oakfield, and has ever been favored with a most able and efficient faculty, which has raised the institution to an important rank among the educational institutions of the State. It was founded in 1840, mainly through the liberality and efforts of Col. Alfred Cary, after whom it was named. This gentleman afterwards endowed the institution with $20,000, which, well invested, is a partial support. The buildings were erected during the next three years, and in 1845 the first meeting was held. The school is under the supervision of the Regents of the University of the State, and the property is in the hands of a board of trustees, of which the bishop of Western New York is the head. The first principal was W. Reynolds, with Miss E. A.

Richard as assistant. In 1865 Rev. James R. Coe assumed control of the school, and continued until his death, in March, 1874, leaving a perpetual monument to his name. The school was very successful under the administration of Mr. Coe, and too much credit cannot be accorded to him for his efforts put forth in the interest of the institution. This seminary has for its object the preparation of the young for the duties and business of life, under the influence of Christian principles. The best men of the country have been, and are, among its trustees and patrons. It is now under the auspices of the Protestant Episcopal Church. Its buildings and grounds are ample, and its library and philosophical laboratory adequate to the high standing of the school. It is properly classified according to Regents' examinations, and in every manner is its high educational and moral standard kept up. The present trustees are Rt. Rev. A. Cleveland Coxe, D. D., LL. D., president; Abner C. Dodge, vice president; Arthur B. Rathbone, secretary; Henry Caple, treasurer; Gad B. Worthington, N. S. Godfrey, Hon. Robert W. Nichol, W. C. Simpson, J. L. Macomber, W. C. Dunlap, Dr. Albert P. Jackson, I. J. Stedman, H. Halsey, T. L. Nichol, Rev. W. A. Hitchcock, D. D., John W. Heal, W. D. Olmsted, Rev. A. J. Warner, E. T. Chamberlin, Hon. Safford E. North, F. E. Wright, Rev. Charles F. J. Wrigley, Hon. Herbert P. Bissell, and Rev. Pierre Cushing. The instructors are Rev. Curtis C. Gove, A. M., head-master; Miss Anna M. Thompson, M. A., preceptress; Miss Mary G. Armstrong, assistant; and Miss S. A. Buell, instrumental music.

Newspapers —About two years since a Mr. Van Hoesen started an eight-page story and general newspaper called the *Fireside Journal*, and continued it for nearly two years. The *Oakfield Reporter* was established in 1889, by B. H. James, as an independent, non-partisan journal. It is a four-page paper with seven columns to a page, and is issued on Thursday of each week. In April, 1890, Mr. James disposed of the *Reporter* to E. B. Gregory, who is now conducting it.

The Oakfield cornet band was organized in 1888. It is composed of 15 members, under the leadership of Frank Giese.

Oakfield Lodge, No. 155, E. O. M. A, was instituted in 1880. The present officers are Frank L. Brown, president; Henry E. Stevens, vice-president; Benjamin F. Hawes, corresponding and financial secretary; and Dr. Albert P. Jackson, treasurer.

Industries.—The completion of the West Shore Railroad running through the towns in the northern part of Genesee County caused a material increase and growth of population in the villages through which it passed, and Oakfield has been more benefitted than all others. The produce of the town and parts of adjoining towns, heretofore carted to Batavia, now finds a ready sale through the hands of produce dealers in the village.

The cooperage business is a lively one in the fruit season, and E. S. Thayer, whose shop is located on South street, manages to supply the community with all packages needed in his line. He built the shop in 1888, and manufactures 5,000 barrels each year. He also manufactures woven wire and picket fence to the amount of 5,000 rods annually.

The saw, heading, and stave-mills work up a large amount of native woods ready for their manufacture into barrels and butter tubs. M. B. Tarba's mill, in the northeast part of the town, on road 3, was built in 1886, and burned April 17, 1889, and immediately rebuilt. In 61 days (or June 18th) from the time it was burned the shop was in running order. There are about 60 hands employed, who make 6,000 sets of barrel heads per month. They also turn out about 8,000 bushels of charcoal monthly. The establishment is owned and run by Mr. Tarba, of Rochester.

Harmon Parker also owns a saw and heading-mill, on road 1, which is run by steam-power. He gets out lumber, staves, heading, shingles, etc., manufactures barrels, and employes about 10 men.

Another manufactory of a similar nature is controlled by Olmsted & Staples, at Oakfield. It was built in 1883. They employ 20 hands, and turn out 2,000 sets of heads and 20,000 staves daily. They have recently added a plaster-mill, with a capacity of 50 tons of plaster per day. In 1842 Stephen Olmsted bought the Nobles mill, and in connection with it built a plaster-mill in 1856, with a capacity then of 25 tons per day. There are over 1,000 acres in the town covered with a very superior plaster stone, from which to get a supply.

The Oakfield mills, located on a branch of Oak Orchard Creek, were built in 1842, by Stephen Olmsted, who operated them until 1856, when he sold to Calvin Nobles, who run them until 1883, when his son, N. C. Nobles, bought the property and put in roller machinery, making it a model mill. He grinds about 1,000 bushels of grain per week. The mill is run by steam and water power.

George Drake has a brick and tile yard on road 9, which was started in 1856.

Henry Fishell in 1878 bought the property formerly controlled by the Wiard plow works, and conducted it until 1889, manufacturing all kinds of agricultural machinery. In the latter year Albert Howland came into possession. He rebuilt and still continues the business. He is located on Main street.

Enoch Heal has a cider-mill on road 5, which is run by steam-power. He has two presses and does a large business.

Henry E. Stevens also conducts a cider-mill of large capacity, near the West Shore depot. It was built in 1889, has a hydraulic press, is run by steam, and has a capacity of 60 barrels of cider per day. His mill is fitted up with the latest improved machinery.

E. B Sparr has a saw, cider, and feed-mill at East Oakfield, which does a good business.

J. D. Isaac owns and controls a first-class blacksmith and wagon shop, and employs five hands. He makes a specialty of manufacturing an improved hay rigging, having some novel features of utility combined in it.

Nathan Avery, a native of Groton, Conn , was an ensign in the militia in the war of the Revolution. He was at Fort Griswold, and aided in saving it from destruction by fire. He died at Groton at the age of 77 years. His wife was Lucy Swan, of Stonington, Conn., and their children were Christopher, who was for many years a physician, and died in Windham County, Conn.; Mary, who died young; Lucy, who married Isaac Gallop, of Vermont, where she died; Isaac, who died in Lebanon, Conn.; William, who lived and died in Windham County, after serving in the War of 1812; and Nathan, a native of Groton, Conn., who married Matilda, daughter of James and Margaret Babcock, and had eight children, viz.: Nathan S., Elias B., Phebe, Ardelia, Lucy A., James B., Amos G., and Albert G. Nathan, the father, died at Groton, where he lived. Albert G. Avery came to Elba in 1869, and settled on a farm, where he resided 17 years, when he removed to Oakfield village, where he now resides. He married Emily, daughter of Joseph and Lura (Witter) Gere, of Groton, and his children are Francis G., John F., Lura M. (deceased), and Charles B. Mr. Avery served one term as superintendent of schools in Orleans County, and the oldest son, Francis G., served in the 27th N. Y. V., under Col. Slocum, and participated in the battle of Bull Run. Charles B. Avery came to Elba from Yates, Orleans County, in 1869. He removed in 1884 from Elba to the farm on road 19, in Oakfield, where he still lives. He married Phebe J., daughter of William H. and Jane M. (Edgerton) Baldwin, of Elba. They have one daughter, Fern L.

Bela Armstrong, who served as captain in the war of the Revolution, was a native of Franklin, Conn., and removed from that place to Perry, N. Y., where he remained until his death, at the age of 80 years. His children were Sanford, Fitch, Laurens, and Gates. Laurens, also a native of Connecticut, went first to Wheatland, and afterwards removed to Oakfield and settled on a farm, where he remained until his death, at the age of 75 years. His wife was Fanny Ladd, by whom he had five children: Fanny, Fidelia, Addison, Sheldon, and Herbert E. Sheldon married Ellen M., daughter of Hamilton Gifford, of Oakfield, and their children are Katie B., Mary G., Fitch L., Frank R., Charles, Wilber J., and Bennett S. He is now a resident of Oakfield village. Addison, another son of Laurens Armstrong, was born in Riga, Monroe County, and came to Oakfield in 1882. His first wife was Nancy A., daughter of John and Desire (Wolcott) Smith, of Oakfield. His second wife was Jane A , daughter of Henry and Elizabeth (Asmond) Pask, of Lincolnshire, Eng., and his children are Mary L., John S., Elizabeth, and Fanny N. He is now a resident of Oakfield village, and has served as supervisor two years.

Paul Anthony, of Pamelia, Jefferson County, died at the age of 80 years. He had seven children, viz.: Paul, Isaac, Darius, Matthew, Mark, Isaiah, and Charles. Darius, born at Pamelia, first moved to the town of Shirley, Erie County, thence he removed to Darien, where he now resides, aged 98 years, and draws a pension because of the loss of a son killed in the late war. Rachel, daughter of Joshua and Mary Winner, was his wife, and their children are Joshua, John, Paul, Julius, Collins, Edmond, Charles, Thomas, Margaret, Laura, Martha, Henry, and Mary and Joseph (twins). Henry Anthony, born in Jefferson County, married, in 1864, Eliza, daughter of Burton and Polly (Dodge) Bentley, of Grove, Allegany County. He was a soldier in Co. H, 8th N. Y. H. A., participated in the battle of Cold Harbor, and was a prisoner at Andersonville, Florence, and Libby prisons. He was honorably discharged from the service. In 1878 he came with his family to Oakfield to reside. He has four children, viz.: Charles, Burton D., Alice, and Arthur. They reside on road 1. Edward, who also served in Co. H, 8th N. Y. H. A., with his brothers Thomas and Henry, was killed during the war. Paul Anthony married for his first wife Sophia Burdick, and had four children, Alice, Sophia, Albert (deceased), and Charles. His second wife was Emily Child, of Pembroke. They now reside in Oakfield. His son Charles married Victoria, daughter of William and Elmira (Hotchkiss) Duers, of Alabama. They have one son, Glen D. He resides on road 14, and is a farmer and a school teacher.

Aaron Arnold, a native of Connecticut, came to Genesee County about 1815, being one of the early settlers. He died at the age of 70 years, and his children were Charles, 1st (deceased), Charles, 2d, George, and Orpha. Charles, 2d, who married Irene, daughter of Linus Beecher, of Bergen, settled on the home farm in Bergen, where he died in 1841, aged 34 years. His children were Aaron, Eliza, Rialto, John B., and Seth J. John B. Arnold married Fanny, daughter of John and Fanny Carmel, and they had one child, E. Lena, who married Fred Sutherland. She had one son, John C., and died August 22, 1882; her husband died in 1881. John B. Arnold served in Co. I, 129th N. Y. Inf, and was transferred to the 8th N. Y. H. A. He was two years and 10 months in the service, and is now the proprietor of the Olcott House in Oakfield village.

John Allen came from Otsego County, N. Y., to Oakfield, where he died, aged 75 years. He married Ruth Prandall, of Otsego County, and his children were Lebbeus, Arthur, Eliza, Frank S., Nancy, John, Hiram, and Charles. Lebbeus Allen, a native of Maryland, Otsego County, N. Y., moved in 1815 to Batavia, where he still lives, at the advanced age of 94 years. He married Esther, daughter of Earl Wright, of Ogden, N. Y. Their children were Seneca, William, Jeannette, Walter, Jerome, Jane, and Laura. Seneca was born in Batavia, September 26, 1821, and married Maria, daughter of William and Susan (Lampman) Showerman, of Sharon, N. Y. Their children were Levant M., Clarissa J., Millard F., Loretta, and Walter E. Clarissa married William H. Ware, and died December 3, 1879, leaving one daughter, Clara M. Seneca Allen has lived on road 25 for 41 years. William Allen married Rebecca Carr, of Batavia, and their children are Mary (deceased), Frank, and Jennie (Mrs. E. Clark). Arthur, another son of John Allen, married Rachel, daughter of Fred Kreatsinger, and they have one child, Mary. Arthur served in the late war in Co. H, 8th N. Y. Art., was wounded in the battle of Cold Harbor, and died at Oakfield, June 9, 1882, aged 37 years. His widow, Mrs. Rachel Allen, still lives in Oakfield, where his brother, Charles H., is also a resident. Another brother, John, also served in the war of the Rebellion, in the 28th N. Y. Art.

Chauncey Brooks, son of Thomas, was born in Connecticut in 1765, and died in 1821, aged 56 He married Elizabeth Barnes, and their children were Wealthy, Betsey, 1st, Charles, Frederick, Chauncey, Betsey, 2d, Correl, Ransell, Sylvester, and Celestia. Sylvester, a native of Connecticut, married Prudentia, daughter of Allen Peck, of Burlington, Conn., and moved to Oakfield in 1861, where he still resides. Their children are Chauncey, Almeron, Elizabeth, and Charles.

Samuel Bliss, of Gilboa, N. Y., son of Capt. Samuel and Keziah Bliss, of Rehoboth, Mass., was born in 1761. He served three years in the war of the Revolution under Capt. Coles. He married, September 17, 1790, Anna Mason, who was born September 5, 1768, and died January 10, 1840 He died in Gilboa, March 15, 1837. Their children were Susan, Harvey, Lydia, Anna, Samuel, Calvin H., Barnum, Susan, and Nathaniel F. Barnum Bliss was born March 20, 1805, and married, first, Mary Ann, daughter of Weeden and Hannah (Jones) Tripp, May 15, 1828, and their children were Weeden T., John E., William, Anson T., Hannah L., and Julia A. He is now a retired farmer, and resides in Oakfield, where he has lived over 50 years. He has filled important offices for his townsmen. Mr. Bliss married, second, Eveline, daughter of William and Julia A. (Chatfield) Day, who was the mother of two children by her former husband, viz.: Levi C. and Eveline Dunn. Mr. Bliss is an active man and has been a member of the Masonic Lodge since October 21, 1828.

Joseph Bromsted came from Mecklenburg, Germany, in 1853, and settled on a farm on road 4, where he died October 12, 1879, aged 56 years. He married Mary, daughter of Ernest and Christina (Shoemaker) Fox, of Germany. Their children were William, Theodore, Louise, Annie, Frank, Sarah, Ella, Eddie, and Mary. His widow still lives on the homestead farm. Their daughter Mary married Daniel Ryne, and died July 14, 1865, leaving one child, Joseph Ryne. William married Louise Peters, of Oakfield, where he now resides.

Andrew Balfour, who died in Galston, Ayrshire, Scotland, was a native of Edinburgh. He married Agnes ———, and their children were Robert, James, Christina, Jean, Margaret, and Rachel. Robert came to Oakfield in 1851, and died March 19, 1879, aged 58 years. He married Mrs. Jean Loudan, daughter of William and Jessie (Howison) Symington, of Galston, Scotland, and they had two sons, Andrew and William. Mrs. Balfour had by her first husband, Thomas Loudan, one daughter, Nellie. Andrew married Stella, daughter of Ephraim and Mary (Nash) Vail, of Oakfield. Mrs. Jean Balfour still lives in Oakfield.

Henry J. Bartels's father, John Bartels, was a farmer in the town of Metzendorf, Hanover, Germany, and married Dora M. Beherins, by whom he had nine children. Henry, born September 23, 1818, married Theresa, daughter of Clement and Margaretha (Venneberg) Ulthoff, of Retchwischdorf, Germany, and they came to Oakfield in 1853. Their children were Alfred H., W. Theodore (deceased), Eliza M., Bertha C., Julia J., and Alvina. Julia married Henry Dash, of Elba. Henry Bartels served in the 4th Inf. Regt., of Hanover, at Luneburg, in 1843, and was discharged in 1846. His home is now on road 7, Oakfield, where he has lived 25 years.

James R. Bickle, who came to Oakfield in 1851, was of English parentage. His parents, Richard and Mary (Rockey) Bickle, had five children, viz.: James R., Fanny, Mary, Richard, and Thomas. James R. was born in 1831, and had reached his 20th year when he came to Oakfield. He married Alice, daughter of William and Ann (Watts) Mills, of Oakfield, and their children were William H., Richard R., George M., John W., Charles E., Frank J., and Alfred E. He died in 1884, aged 54 years. His widow occupies the home farm on road 14. John W. married Annie, daughter of John and Mary (Harloff) Sparling. Charles E. married Sarah, daughter of James and Rose (McCabe) Boyce, of Oakfield.

Isaac Brulett, a native of Le Prairie, near Montreal, Canada, and a son of Michael and grandson of Bush Brulett, came to Oakfield in 1852, an orphan boy three years old. He married Ellen, daughter of Daniel and Deborah (Kellogg) Hosselkus, of Oakfield, and has one daughter, Nellie, now Mrs. H. H. Buck, of Brockport, N. Y. Isaac Brulett, still a resident of Oakfield, served three years in the late war in the 25th N. Y. Lt. Art., and now draws a pension.

Edward Britton, a native of Vermont, served in the War of 1812, came to Elba about 1805, and settled on a farm where he remained until his death, at the age of 65 years. He married Caroline Fuller, of Rutland, Vt., who died at the age of 65 years. Their children were Cyrus R., Andrew J., and Spencer H. Andrew J. Britton married Aurelia, daughter of Henry L. and Julia A. (Tripp) Jones, of Oakfield. Their children are Mary C., Major A., Dora A., Harry E., and John G. Andrew J. Britton's grandfather, John Fuller, served in the Revolutionary war.

Christopher Bobsen came from Germany to America in 1865, and located in Oakfield, where he died January 27, 1885, aged 83 years. His wife was Eliza Abbott, of Germany, and they had six children, viz.: Frederick, Christian, John, Joseph, Sophia, and Rachel. Frederick, also a resident of Oakfield, married Mary, daughter of Fred and Mary (Bbroktt) Peters, of Germany. Their children are Ettie, Willie, Eliza, Myrtie, and Fred.

The Chamberlin family have occupied a conspicuous place in the early history of Western New York. Amos Chamberlin, with a family of six sons and two daughters, came from Vermont to Byron in 1813, where

he died about 1830.   His wife was Phebe Alger.   His son Amos came
to Oakfield in 1836, where he died in 1865, at the age of 66.   His wife
was Phebe Shedd, and their children were Charles D., Young, Helen,
and Charles H.   Charles H. married, first, Mary A. Bates, and second,
Abbie Jane Shedd.   He was for many years engaged in the dry goods
business in Oakfield village, and subsequently built a fine block of brick
buildings.

Benjamin Dodge, a native of New Boston, Mass., died in 1781.   His
wife was Esther Perkins, and his children were Joseph and Esther.   Joseph Dodge, also a native of New Boston, was a volunteer in the War of
1812.   He came to Le Roy, where he lived many years, and moved to
Castile, N. Y., where he died at the age of 84 years.   He was a carpenter and joiner, and a farmer, and married Mary, daughter of Joseph and
Elizabeth (Dana) Chase, of Litchfield, N. H.   Their children were Abner C., Eliza, Albert, Benjamin D., in California, Horace, Mark, Joseph,
Jr., Miles, Mary A., Dexter, and Myron L.   Abner C. Dodge married
Polly B. Bouthwell, of Richmond, N. Y., and is now a resident of Oakfield, where he has lived 33 years.   He has been poormaster 14 years,
president of the corporation of Oakfield three years, and vice-president
of the board of trustees of the seminary.

Henry Doerwig, born in Germany, came to America in 1856, and settled in Canajoharie, N. Y.   From thence he removed to Oakfield in
1867, and still occupies a place on road 7.   He married Bertha, daughter of John and Johanna (Haits) Prang, of Charleston, S. C.   They have
two children, Charles and Rose.   Henry Doerwig's parents, Charles and
Henriette Doerwig, lived in Hanover, Bodenfelde, Germany, and Henry
was one of a family of five children.

Gideon Dunham, one of Oakfield's pioneers, settled on 400 acres of
land at what is now known as Dunham's Corners, on road 26, where he
kept tavern for many years, and where he remained until he died, at the
age of 85 years.   He was a soldier in the Revolutionary war.   His children were Solomon, Shubael, Sarah, Phebe, Lucy, Fanny, and Mary.
Solomon married Catharine, daughter of Frederick Shutter, and his children were Chauncy, Gideon. Solomon, Henry, and Frederick.   Chauncy
resides in Oakfield, and his wife was Clarissa, daughter of Lyman Dean,
of Churchville, N. Y., by whom he had three children : John L., Eveline,
and Laura, who died in Chicago in 1879.   Chauncy has been a successful live stock breeder and dealer in horses and cattle.   His son John L.,
a resident of Oakfield and engaged in the jewelry business, married Ellen,
daughter of Thomas J. Kennedy, of Oakfield, and his children are Burt L.
and Frank R.

William Drake, a native of Dutchess County, N. Y., married Eunice
Holmes, and removed to Greene County, where they both died.   Their
children were Jessamine, John, Polly, Susan, Catherine, Samuel, Claudius, Ransom, James, and Joseph.   James Drake was born in Greene
County, N. Y., came to Batavia, and served in the War of 1812.   He

married Hannah, daughter of Cain Blackmore, and their children were Lucinda A., Octavia M., Elisha B., John F., Norman, and Francis. Norman Drake married, first, Keziah, daughter of William and Mahala (Hallock) Stillwell, of Elba, and their children were James W., Albert H., and Julia A. His second wife was Cynthia, daughter of Silas Earl, of Napoli, N. Y. His third wife was Eliza Earl, by whom he had one child, Nina A. He is now a resident of Oakfield, and has held the offices of supervisor two terms, justice of the peace four years, commissioner of highways eight years, assessor 12 years, and overseer of the poor three years.

Henry Fishell was a native of Carlisle, Pa., where he resided 35. years, when he removed to Rush, Monroe County, N. Y., where he died at the age of 93 years. He married Catharine Cooley, of Pennsylvania, who bore him the following children : Polly, Katie, Betsey, Daniel, John, Henry, and Joseph. Joseph Fishell came from Pennsylvania to Genesee County in 1846, and died here in 1868, at the age of 72 years. He married Amelia A., (now 91 years of age, and living in Climax, Mich.,) daughter of Jacob and Katie (Keffer) Lighton, of Rush, N. Y., and his children were John, Mary A., Elizabeth, Eveline, Susan, Lydia, Catharine, Joseph, and Henry J. Henry J. Fishell, a native of Rush, N. Y., came to Oakfield in 1857. He married Sarah, daughter of William and Mary (Howard) Roderick, and his children are Charles, Eugene, Lydia J. (deceased), and Mary (deceased). Charles Fishell married Susan, daughter of Richard and Mary Galliford, of Oakfield, and his children are Harry, Raymond, and Burnie E. He is a resident of Oakfield.

Daniel Hosselkus, a native of Oneida County, N. Y., lived in Herkimer County until he attained manhood, came to Oakfield in 1829, and married Deborah Kellogg, of Herkimer County. There were but two houses in the village of Oakfield when he came here. He gave the site for the Methodist Church, and he and his wife were the first members. Mr. Hosselkus died in the winter of 1890, aged 91 years. They lived together 68 years. He gives us some of the names of the early settlers. Hiram May was the first minister, and E. McIntyre the first justice of the peace. Alfred Cary built the first hotel, Perez Howland was the first druggist, and William B. Beebe and John Foote were the first dry goods merchants.

Nathaniel Fuller commanded a vessel during the Revolutionary war, was taken prisoner by the British, and the ship on which he was being sent to England was lost at sea. His son, James Fuller, a native of Ipswich, Mass., was born in 1770, settled in Bristol, N. H., where he married Hannah Kidder, and removed in 1815 to Elba, this county. His children were Daniel, Hibbard, Joel, John, James, Emily, Holland, and Mary. Holland married Betsey, daughter of George and Sally (Cleaveland) Driggs, of Elba. He was a farmer in Oakfield, and died in 1873, aged 75 years. His children were Sarah C., Franklin J., George D., and Charles H. George D. Fuller married Mary J., daughter of John M.

Catherine and (Page) Sleeper, of Elba (formerly of Grafton, N. H.). They have six children : Minnie C. (who married Clark Parker, now of Elba, and had one child, Alice M.), George M., Holland, John M., Marion, and James E. George D. Fuller is a farmer and has lived 53 years in this town.

Christopher Fisher died in his native town, Mecklenburg, Germany, in 1826. His wife was Dorotha Ridance, who bore him three children : Charles, now a resident of Oakfield, and two sons deceased. Charles married Mary, daughter of John and Rachel (Hank) Castor, of Mecklenburg. In 1833 they left the Fatherland and came to America, and established themselves in Oakfield, where they are yet living. Their children were Charles J., born June 9, 1833, who married Betsey Ultonburg, and is now residing in Batavia; Emma, who died November 26, 1856, aged 10 years ; Theodore S.; Annie R., who married Darius Manchester, now of Oakfield ; Mary, who died January 1, 1867 ; and Viola E., who married Frank L. Brown and had one child, Howard C., who died August 25, 1886, aged 17 months. The latter are now residents of Oakfield.

Herman, son of John Gursslin, a denizen of Lockport, came to the United States from Germany in 1855. His wife was Elizabeth Woulthman, of Germany, and their children were Henry, Rickey, Mary, Herman, Carrie, Rose, Matilda, Minnie, and Ella. Henry was seven years old when he came with his father from Bremen to Lockport. He came to Oakfield in 1882. He married Mary, daughter of Seth and Adaline (Luther) Ransom, of Shelby, N. Y., and their children were Albert (deceased), Nettie E., and Reuben W. Mr. Gursslin has recently removed to Alabama, in this county.

Henry Griffin died in Wales, Erie County, aged 75 years. He was a soldier during the Revolutionary war. His wife was Thirza, and their children were John, Henry, Solomon, Samuel, and Thirza. Henry was born in Onondaga County, was a soldier in the War of 1812, and came to Oakfield in 1840, where he died in 1844, aged 52 years. He married Samantha, daughter of Paul and Eunice (Howlett) Dodge, of Marcellus, Onondoga County. Their children were Helen, Candace, Henry, Samuel B. and Solomon B. (twins), Andrew, Orpha, Thirza, Cordelia O., Lester, Sarah, and Orcelia. Samuel B., a native of Wales, N. Y., was born December 17, 1829. When 11 years old he came with his parents to Oakfield. He married Mrs. Mary G. Macomber, daughter of Richard and Temperance (Everts) Crampton, of Alabama, N. Y., and their children are Francis A., Archibald M., Myrtie A., John A., Charles H., Sarah A., Nancy G., and Annie (deceased). He has lived on the farm which he now occupies since 1850. Charles H. Griffin married Clytie F. Benton, of Oakfield, daughter of Andrew and Libbie (Thomas) Benton, and is engaged in the dry goods business.

Josiah Griffin was a resident of Stanford, Dutchess County, N. Y. One of his sons, Thomas Griffin, born October 27, 1772, left Dutchess County and came to Elba among the pioneers in 1820, where he remained until his death, February 16, 1854, aged 81 years. He married Susanna, daughter of John Ireland, of Dutchess County, and their children were Jacob, John, Thomas, Abigail, Daniel T., and Mary. Daniel T., born in Dutchess County, November 14, 1811, moved to Elba, where he lived 22 years, and thence came, in 1866, to Oakfield, where he has since remained. His first wife was Louisa Warner, of Ypsilanti, Wayne County, Mich., and his second wife was Abigail, daughter of Frederick and Mary (Grovenor) Buck, of Batavia. Thomas Griffin, a brother of Daniel T., also a native of Dutchess County, came to Elba with his father in 1820. He was a farmer and owned a saw-mill. In 1883 he removed to Talbot County, Md., where he remains. He married Emeline, daughter of William and Susanna (Sheffield) Weeks, of Elba, and their children are William H., Elwood, Maria, Susan, John, Cynthia, Hubert, Frank, Edwin, Sarah, Emma, George, and Lewis. William H. was a soldier in Co. H, 8th N. Y. H. A. His home is now in Maryland, and he married Caroline C., daughter of Elijah and Elvira (Staples) Chapman, of Hillsdale County, Mich. Their children are Almond, Elvira, Orie, Earl and Pearl (twins), Jay, and Daniel D.

Thomas Gibson, of Ireland, the father of Thomas Gibson, Jr, John, Nancy, Eliza, Jane, and Mary, died at the age of 75 years. Thomas Gibson, Jr., lived and died in Ireland. He married Mary, daughter of Simon Swayles, and his children were Mary A., Eliza and Jane, twins, Rachel, and John. John Gibson was born in County Down, Ireland, came to America in 1850, and to Oakfield in 1866, settling on a farm. He married Harriet, daughter of Robert and Harriet (Ringland) Newell, of Ireland.

Albert A. Grinnell, born in Shelby, N. Y., in June, 1865, came to Oakfield in September, 1888, and became a dealer in produce. In September, 1889, he began business for Ferrin Brothers. He also deals in carriages, carts, etc.

Watson J. Gardner was born February 2, 1775. He married Freelove ———, and their children were John C., Barshea, Amy, Jaffrey, Mary, William C., Freelove, and Hannah. John C. married three times, first, Atha Field, second, Atha Hoose, and third, Jane, daughter of Claudius and Mary (Turner) Britton, of Michigan. He died May 29, 1882, aged 78 years. Mrs. Gardner lives in Oakfield. Her father and grandfather, both bearing the name of Claudius Britton, were soldiers in the war for independence, and the son was taken prisoner by the British, but succeeded in making his escape.

Daniel Hawes came from Boston to Oakfield in 1832, and settled on a farm, where he died 20 years later, in the 62d year of his age. He married Clara, daughter of Elihu Church, of Riga, N. Y. Their children were Eli, Eliza, Almira, Benjamin F., and Henry L The latter was born in Riga, Monroe County, and came to Oakfield in 1832. He studied law with G. W. Brown, of Oakfield, attended Albany Law School, and was admitted to the bar in 1856. He still owns the homestead of his father. Mr. Hawes has been justice since 1860, justice of Sessions one term, supervisor for many years, and clerk of the board of supervisors since 1867.

Sylvenus Halsey, a native of Long Island, came to Herkimer County, whence, after many years' residence, he came to Alabama, where he remained till his death in 1863, aged 82 years. His son, Edward Halsey, born on Long Island, came to Alabama in 1845, and settled on the farm where he now resides. He married Nancy Goff, of Monroe County, and his children were Alice (Mrs.. Frank Blackman), of Rockford, Ill., and Henry C., who married Lucetta, daughter of Hiram and Rosina (Snell) Tracy. His children are Fred E. and Bruce F., and he resides in Oakfield village.

James Hale, an Englishman by birth, came to the United States in 1851, and located in Oakfield, where he still resides. He married Grace, daughter of Thomas Sanders, of Oakfield. Their children were Susan, Thomas, William, Jay Hugh, and Mary. He served in Co. H, N. Y. H. A. during the late war, and draws a pension on account of wounds received in the service. He now lives on a farm on road·2. His father, James Hale, Sr., was a native of Devonshire, Eng., and followed his son to Oakfield in 1872, where he died June 1, 1880, aged 67 years. His wife was Mary A. Ching, of Devonshire, Eng. Their children were John, William, Robert, Thomas, Enoch, George, Susan, and James.

Henry Heckroth, a native of Germany, removed from that country to Hazleton, Luzerne County, Pa., about 1842. He died there in 1866, aged 71 years. His children were Julia and Henry, and the latter married Julia Crouse, of Hazleton, Pa. In 1859 he was killed in a coal mine, in the 45th year of his age. His children were George and Augustus T. George now resides on the homestead farm, and Augustus T., who married Elizabeth A. Dorf, of Elba, is a resident of Oakfield village. Their mother is living, has married the second time,—Henry Eichler,—and resides in Oakfield.

George Hill, son of George, came from Somersetshire, Eng. (his native place), to Stafford in 1837, and thence, in 1840, to Oakfield, where he died in 1847, at the age of 47 years. He married Grace, daughter·of James and Joan (Cox) Webber, and his children are Mary J., James W., John D , Frances E., George W., and Sarah A. Mrs. Grace Hill, now 76 years of age, is living in Oakfield with her son and daughter, John·D. and Sarah.

William Hutton, a native of Ireland, married Martha McDowell. His children were William, John, Sarah, and Jane. William came to Oakfield, July 11, 1842, and married Jane, daughter of Robert and Isabella (Drake) Galloway. Their children were John, Robert, William T., James, Jane, Hugh, and Samuel. His widow, Jane Hutton, is still living in Oakfield, at the age of 72 years. William Hutton served in Co. G, 129th

N. Y. Inf., was promoted to second sergeant and transferred to the 8th Art., and was killed at Baltimore. His son, John F. Hutton, enlisted in Co. G, 129th N. Y. Art.; and was transferred to the 8th H. A. William T. Hutton served in the 12th N. Y. V.

William Isaac, a native of Swimbridge, Eng., and a butcher, came to Oakfield in 1844, where he remained until his death, in March, 1870, aged 63 years. He married Elizabeth, daughter of John and Elizabeth (Ball) Dunn, of Swimbridge, Eng., and his children were Elizabeth, Mary A., William, Emmanuel, Kate, John D., and Harry I. John D. Isaac came from England with his father and settled in Oakfield, and his wife was Susan, daughter of William and Mary Wieden, of Barnstable, Eng. Their children are William D., Frank, Fred W., Minnie L, and Sidney N. He is still a resident of Oakfield. Kate Isaac married David Stegman, and her children are Frank B., Milton, and Ettie D., now residents of Oakfield. His sister Elizabeth, born November 15, 1801, is still living at the age of 89 years, being the oldest woman in this town. His brother, Emmanuel Isaac, also came to Oakfield with his father. He married Mary, daughter of Anson and Luranda (Ames) Hulett, of Stafford, and his children are Cora B., George A., and Flora L. He is still a resident of Oakfield. His son George, now of Oakfield, married Susan Weeks, of Elba, and Cora married George Crabb, now of Batavia.

Ebenezer Ingalsbe was a captain in the English army. Desiring to visit America he gave up his commission and secured passage on a ship. Arriving here he settled in Massachusetts, where he remained until his death. His son Ebenezer, born in Massachusetts, moved to Scipio, Cayuga County, where he died in the 70th year of his age. He married Phebe Easterbrook, and their children were Elijah, born September 12, 1780; Ebenezer, born December 23, 1781; Phebe, born March 28, 1784; Azel, born February 14, 1786; Huldah, born January 4. 1789; Sally, born August 20, 1790; Adna, born January 11, 1793; Samuel, born August 17 1796; and Emory, born October 24, 1798. Elijah, who was a farmer, came to Alabama in 1832, and remained until his death, which occurred July 9, 1872. His first wife was Polly Mitchell (born February 11, 1781, died in 1813), daughter of Urial Mitchell, and his children by her were born as follows: Elijah. May 2, 1805; Rial E., September 24, 1806; Huldah, September 2, 1808; Parley V., May 29, 1810; and Sally L., April 15, 1812. His second wife was Nancy Mitchell (born May 8, 1797), and his children by her were Philinda, born August 29, 1815; Phebe, born October 1, 1816; Adna, born September 15, 1818; Anda, born October 9, 1821; and Levi, born November 24, 1824. Parley V., born in Wayne County, N. Y., moved to Alabama, thence to Oakfield in 1855, and settled on the farm he now owns. He married Sarah, daughter of William and Harriet (Cutler) Macomber, of Alabama. Their children were William, born January 26, 1847; Edwin J., born October 12, 1852; Judson L., born February 4, 1855, and died in 1858; Seward A., born June 9, 1857; and Frances H., born

37

March 11, 1860, and died in 1863. Seward A. married Ella, daughter of Weeden T. and Jane (Calkins) Bliss, of Oakfield. Their children are Florence, Lewis, and Myrtie. He is a druggist in Oakfield village. Edwin J. married Mary Bliss, a sister of his brother Seward's wife, and their children are Frances, George W., and Edie. He is a farmer in Oakfield. Parley V. Ingalsbe served three years—1863, '64, and '65— as supervisor of this town. He also served as recruiting officer during the late war.

Stephen Martin, a native of Connecticut, was born January 26, 1761, and died December 19, 1834. He, with his twin brother, John, served in the war of the Revolution, and came to North Bloomfield, Ontario County, N. Y., in 1800, engaging in a foundry and furnace, where he remained till his death. John, the brother, settled in West Bloomfield, same county, where he died. Stephen's wife was Bettie Barrows, of Mansfield, Conn., born May 4, 1764, and died March 13, 1841. His children were Stephen, Jr., Robert, Harvey, Alexander, Z. Berthia, Fanny, Hannah, and Lydia. Stephen Martin, Jr., born in Connecticut, settled in Clarendon, N. Y., in 1811, where he died in 1855, aged 67 years. He served in the War of 1812, as a captain, and married Anna, daughter of Constant Balcomb, of Ontario County, February 23, 1814. She was born in 1794 and died in 1870, aged 76 years. Their children were John, born in 1815, died in 1841 ; Dan, born in 1817, died in 1886 ; Eliza A., born in 1821 ; and Henry C., born in 1826. Henry C. Martin, born in Clarendon, Orleans County, came to Oakfield in 1877, and engaged in the dry goods business, which, with his two sons, Frank and Wilber, he still continues. Wilber married Nancy E., daughter of Samuel and Mary (Buck) Shorey, from near Dansville, Steuben County, and their children were Cora E., born in 1856 ; Eloise B , born in 1864, died at the age of seven years ; Wilbur H., born February 7, 1859 ; and Grace, born May 13, 1863. He was appointed postmaster in 1885. Eloise married W. W. Smallwood, of Warsaw, N. Y., and their children are Martin W., Winfield, Merlin, Clarence, Irving H., and Fanny. Wilbur H. married Louise, daughter of James D. and Laura A. (Bemont) Gregory. She was born May 14, 1862. They have a son, Harry G., born in February, 1886. Frank H. Martin married Sarah, daughter of Mortimer and Harriet (Foster) Milliken, of Clarendon, N. Y., and has two children, Grover H., born March 28, 1883, and Millard G., born March 19, 1885.

William McCrillus was born in Colrain, Conn., and came to Oakfield in 1810. He married Eunice Cleaveland, of Connecticut, and their children were William C.; Bailey, a physician, who died in Indiana ; Eunice, who married J. C. Wilford and died in Elba ; Phebe, who married Rice Baldwin and died in Oakfield ; Erastus, a physician, who died in Indiana ; and Sarah, who married a Mr. Hurd and died in Michigan. William C. was born in Madison County, N. Y., and came to Oakfield when four years of age. Here he remained until his death, in the 79th year of his age. He married Sarah, daughter of Jeremiah and Abigail (Hawley) Haxton, of Batavia, and their children were Ann J., Mary A., E. Bailey, Carrie H., W. Clayton, Flora A., Julia J., and Delia E., now residents of Oakfield. Mrs. McCrillus is still living, at the age of 76 years, and occupies the home farm on road 19, where she has lived 34 years. Mr. McCrillus was supervisor and assessor for a number of years.

Among the patriotic soldiers who served under Gen. Washington during the Revolutionary war, and who was a participant in the battle of Ticonderoga, was Benjamin Cowles, of Sheffield, Mass. In 1796 he came to Lima, N. Y., where he died in 1828, aged 84 years His wife was Hannah Bardman, of Massachusetts, and their children were James, Pliny, William, Sylvester, Annie, Cynthia, Pina, and Polly. James, born in Sheffield, Mass., came with his father in 1796 to Lima, from whence, in 1830, he removed to Oakfield, where he died in 1859, aged 73 years. He was colonel in the State militia, and participated in the War of 1812. His first wife was Temperance Brockway, of Lima, by whom he had two children, Emily and Osmer K. His second wife was Elsie, daughter of Ichabod and Mercy (Tripp) Dickinson, and his children by her were Norman B., Harriet L., James A., Temperance E., Mary A., and E. Payson. Harriet L., born in Lima, and at present a resident of Rochester, married William C. Wilford, son of John C and Eunice (McCrillus) Wilford, of Elba. Their children are John C., A. Maud, M. Louise, Cola, and Sarah E.

Abram McIntyre came to Elba about 1820, and to Oakfield about 1850, where he died two years later, aged 82 years. His wife, Lydia Peckham, was born in 1774, and died in Elba in 1840, at the age of 66 years, and was buried by his side at Pine Hill, in Elba. Their children were Jerrah, Lowell, Laura, and Melinda. Jerrah died in Batavia at the age of 31 years. His wife was Alice Willis, also of Batavia, who was born in 1798, and died in 1864. Their children were Loren, William, and Caroline. Loren McIntyre, who resides in Oakfield, married Cynthia, daughter of Sargent and Lydia (Colborn) Blaisdell, of Batavia, and their children were Byron F., residing at Orange, N. J., and doing business at 99 North Moore street, New York city; Clara M. (Mrs. William Glover), of Detroit; Fanny (Mrs. George Craft), of Oakfield; and Metta F.

Eli Moore came from Scotland to America about 1800, and settled in Ridgeway, Orleans County, N. Y., in 1804. He was the first hotelkeeper in town, ran the first stage, and was the first mail carrier in the county. He finally moved to Ohio, where he died. He married a Miss Doolittle, and they had seven children: Uri D., Ori W., Eli B., James, Ardelia, Eclista, and Aurelius. Aurelius, born in Ridgeway, Orleans County, now a resident of Medina, married Delia Timmerman, of Medina, and their children are Lina M. and Joseph T. Joseph T. married Louise, daughter of Charles H. and Harriet Waite, of Buffalo. Their children are Mabel J., Charles H., and Sarah H. He is a resident of Oakfield, and a dealer in general produce. His wife died in 1888.

William Maltby, a citizen of Ontario County, moved to Elba in 1815, and after 40 years' residence in that place moved to Brockport, where he died at the age of 77 years. He was twice married. His first wife was Cynthia Carr, and his second Delia Chapin, of Canandaigua. His children were Cynthia, John C., and William H. The latter, born in Ontario County, came with his father to Elba, and during the late war was a member of Battery B, N. Y. Vols. He died in a hospital near Washington, D. C., in 1864, at the age of 25 years. His wife was Emma C., daughter of Robert and Elizabeth (Locke) Erwin, of Elba. They had one son, William H., who is now a resident of Oakfield, and lives with his widowed mother on a farm on road 15, where they have lived five years.

Sidney A. McCullock was a native of Gainesville, Wyoming County, N. Y., and came to Oakfield in 1878, where he now resides. He marrie Calma Ely, of Gainesville, N. Y., and has one son, Edward A., who married Cora, daughter of William and Martha Galliford, of Fairport, N. Y. They have one son, Lagrande, who is also a resident of Oakfield.

Russel Nobles, a native of Connecticut, was a resident of Oakfield many years, and died in Detroit. Calvin Nobles was the first child born in the town of Oakfield, and was a life-long resident, dying April 1, 1884, at the age of 76 years. He married Harriet Winman, of Rochester, N. Y., and his children were Norton C., Norman L., Newton D., Newman J., Mary E., Laura A., George B., and Frank P. Norton C. Nobles married Martha E., daughter of Whiting C. Wolsey, Jr., of Batavia, and his children are Robert W. and Ralph C. He is a resident of Oakfield village.

Whitman Nash, a citizen of Madison County, removed to Oakfield in 1853, and purchased a farm. He married Elizabeth, daughter of Henry and Mary Beggerly, of Clifton Springs, N. Y. Their children were Mary (deceased) and Amerrisa E. Mary married Ephraim Vail, of Oakfield, and left three children, Carrie, Estelle, and Henry. Amerrisa E., the postmaster at East Oakfield, married Harriet, daughter of George W. and Miriam (Grimes) Gardner, of Oakfield. They have one daughter, Miriam F. He resides on the farm with his father, with whom he has lived 33 years. Alpheus Nash, father of Whitman, was a native of Massachusetts. He moved from that State to Orleans County, N. Y., and finally to Pennsylvania, where he died, aged 60 years. He was a soldier in the War of 1812.

Smith Pugsley, son of David, was born in Dutchess County in 1799. His mother was a daughter of Judge Betz. He was obliged to work hard for a living, and in early manhood lost much property through the carelessness of others. He married, January 2, 1825, Elizabeth V., daughter of George Peterson, of Cayuga County, and in 1831 moved to Clarence,

Erie County. After reaching there he had but 50 cents in money with which to begin housekeeping. Teaching school winters and surveying at times enabled him to get started again. He was the assessor of his town for 20 years. His wife died in 1860. His son, Capt. David E. Pugsley, was born February 7, 1833. In 1861 he enlisted in the 18th Regt. Ky. Vols , and was elected captain. He was in command at Paris when Morgan burnt the government stores there. He was twice taken prisoner, and died in service February 20, 1863. William W. Pugsley enlisted in 1862, served three years, and was honorably discharged. He finally moved to Indian Territory. Dr. Charles S. Pugsley enlisted in the N. Y. S. Guards, and served under Capt. Ransom, at Elmira, during the stay of the 98th Regiment at that place. He now resides in Oakfield, where he is engaged in the practice of medicine. John T. Pugsley is a farmer, and resides on a part of the old homestead. Of the daughters of Smith Pugsley Sarah M. and Libbie reside in Buffalo, Mary E. in Hinsdale, Mass., and Cornelia V. on the old homestead. George E. Pugsley was born February 7, 1833, in Clarence, Erie County. He lived on the old homestead till 1868, and assisted in putting on all the improvements. He received his education at the district school, except two terms of 11 weeks each at the Clarence Classical School and six weeks at the Caryville Seminary. After finishing his education he taught school winters and farmed it summers. He has held the offices of court collector, justice of the peace, and justice of Sessions of Erie County.

Thomas Powell was a native of Wales, where he died at the age of 60 years. His children were David, William, and Thomas. David came to Oakfield in 1850. His wife was Sarah, daughter of William and Hannah Morgan, also of Wales, and his children were William, Elizabeth, David, and Sarah. Mrs. Sarah Powell, who survives her husband, is living at Oakfield at the age of 66 years. David Powell served in Co. E, 150th N. Y. V., and died in December, 1862, aged 30 years.

Jonathan Phillips, a native of New York, came to Oakfield to reside, and married Eliza Owen. Their children were Warren, Charles, George, Harriet, and Anna. Warren, born in Gates in 1825, married Margary, daughter of Aaron and Sally (Dean) Boorom, of Oakfield. Their children were George, Levi, John, Elmer, Addison, Laura, Sarah, and Elizabeth. George married Carrie I., daughter of Willard W. and Clarinda (Foster) Herrick, of Barre, Orleans County, and they have one daughter, Dora M.

Arnold Plate, who was born in Fayette, Seneca County, N. Y., came to Oakfield in the spring of 1852. He married Emily S., daughter of Elliott and Orissa (Brown) Lewis, by whom he has four children, viz.: Mary Ellen (Mrs. Warren Gorton), of East Pembroke ; Emily E. (Mrs H. E. Stevens), of Oakfield; George A.; and James L. He is now a resident of Oakfield, and is a harnessmaker. He has held the office of poormaster two terms.

Daniel Rathbone, a native of Stonington, Conn., moved to Richmond,

Mass., and thence to Milton, Saratoga County, where he died, at the age of 93 years. He married Sarah Higby, of Stonington, Conn., and their children were Daniel, Jr., Dr. John, William, Valentine, Philander, Solomon, Abigail, Sally, Ruby, Huldah, and Lydia. Daniel, Jr., removed to Milton, N. Y., and died in 1808, aged 49 years. He married Anna Reddington, of Stonington, Conn., and their children were Wightman, Ransom, Laurin, Anna, Phœbe, Amanda, Lucy, Melinda, and Julianne. Laurin Rathbone was born May 19, 1806, in Milton, and March 14, 1833, married Elizabeth Barker, of Oakfield. In 1830 he came to Oakfield and purchased the farm formerly owned by Robert Troup and others, and has since followed farming. His children are Arthur B. Rathbone, a hardware merchant of Oakfield, and Miss Augusta Rathbone. Lewis V. R. Rathbone, of Rochester, is a son of Ransom.

Arthur B. Rathbone, son of Laurin Rathbone, was born in Oakfield, December 23, 1837. He was educated at Cary Collegiate Seminary, which he attended in 1852–54, and at Wyoming Seminary in 1855. He then spent four years at the University of Rochester, from 1855 to 1859, graduating as A. B., and in 1863 as A. M. He engaged in the nursery business from 1868 to 1879, since which he has been engaged in the hardware trade. He was president of the village in 1874, 1875, 1877, and 1881, and was supervisor for the town in 1883 and 1884. Mr. Rathbone is one of the trustees of Cary Seminary, and a vestryman of St. Michael's Episcopal Church, of which he is a generous and liberal supporter.

Anton Thie was born in Hanover, Germany, July 24, 1859, and came to America and located in Oakfield in 1882. He married Josephine Stoll, of Bavaria, who died November 17, 1889. He has two children, Mary and Kate. Mr. Thie has a shoe store on Main street, Oakfield, where he began business in 1885.

Jeremiah J. Smith, a native of Troy, N. Y., came to Oakfield in 1830, was a blacksmith for 50 years in town, and died in 1885, at the age of 78 years. He married Louisa Hart, of Troy, and his children were Warner H., Melancton J., Rial, Edward, Wallace, Nancy A., Louisa, Helen, and Emma. Warner H. Smith married Louisa, daughter of Ira and Beattie (Randall)Tripp, of Fort Plain, and his children are Beattie, Frank, and Della. He has been chief engineer of the fire department of Oakfield.

Richard Stevens, a native of Devonshire, Eng., married Ann Creamer, and they had eight children, viz.: Richard, John, William, Samuel, Simon, Grace, Mary, and Ann. William married Frances Kelland, and their children were William, Anna M., Frances, Mary E., Grace, Caroline, Richard, Jane, Matilda, John, and Harriet. John, the subject of this sketch, married, first, Mary A. Rattenburg, of Devonshire, Eng., by whom he had two sons, John A. and William A. His second wife was Ellen, daughter of William and Jane (Webber) Grimshaw, of Devonshire, Eng., and his children by her were Sumner R., Mary E., and

Frederick J.   Mr. Stevens, who is now a resident of Oakfield, came here from Devonshire, Eng., in 1852, and has been town collector one year and trustee of Oakfield corporation four years.

Richard Stevens, a native of Winkleigh, Devonshire, Eng., emigrated to Canada in 1843, and thence to Oakfield in 1844, where he now resides. His first wife was Elizabeth Webber, of Chunleigh, Devonshire, Eng., by whom he had two children, William W. and Richard H.   His second wife was Mrs. Ellen L. Young, of Orwell, Vt., daughter of Stephen W. and Naomi (Root) Brown, of Benson, Vt.   By her first husband Mrs. Ellen Stevens has one son, Darwin S. Young, of Oakfield.   Mr. Stevens resides in Oakfield, in which town he has held many offices of trust. William W. Stevens, son of Richard, was born in Stafford, and married Frances, daughter of William and Almira (Whitney) Wolcott, of Oakfield.   They have two children, Richard H. and William W.   He is a resident of Oakfield.

Richard Stevens, an Englishman by birth, came to Oakfield in 1832, removed to Alabama, and died there at the age of 78 years.   His children were James, Henry, George, Laonia, Fanny, Annie, Jane, Mary, and Thomas.   Henry married Hannah, daughter of William Showerman. Their children were Levant, Nettie, and Henry E.   The latter married Elizabeth, daughter of Arnold and Emily (Lewis) Plate, of Oakfield, and their children were Nellie I. (deceased) and Ellsworth, a resident of Oakfield.

Martin Sparling, a citizen of Mecklenburg, Germany, married Mary Fox, of the same place.   He died in the 65th year of his age.   They had three children: John, Charles, now of Alabama, and Anson, of Pembroke. John, born in Germany, married Mary, daughter of Christopher and Mary (Will) Harloff, of Germany, in 1829.   They emigrated to America in 1853, and first settled in New Jersey.   From that State they removed, in 1855, to Oakfield, and purchased a farm on road 15, where they still reside.   Their children are Sophia, John, Mary, Eliza, Fred, William H., and Anna.

Martin Smith, grandfather of Frank Smith, was a native of New York, but moved to Vernon, Shiawassee County, Mich., where he died in the 92d year of his age.   He had four children, Julia A., Amelia, Peter M., and William I.   Peter M. was born in New York and now lives at West Kendall, this State.   He married Almira, daughter of George and Betsey Acker, and their children are Wesley, Fletcher, William, Frank, Lavina, Eva, Ella, and Sarah M.   Frank, born in Kendall, Orleans County, came to Oakfield in 1879, where he now lives on his farm on road 1. He married Isabella, daughter of William and Isabella (Hermiston) Jaffrey, of Kendall.

William Smith, a farmer, was a native of Berlin, Rensselaer County, N. Y., where he died in 1840, at the age of 70.   He married Esther Godfrey, of Berlin, and his children were John, George, Calvin, Robert, Catharine, Rachel, Ann, Panelpia, William C., and Hannah.   William C.

Smith married Margaret Harris, of London, Eng., and has four children, Mary, Emma, William H., and George. William H. Smith married Anna McCue, daughter of Peter and Mary McLaughlin, formerly of Ireland. They have four children, Raymond, Charles, Carrie, and Florence. He was the proprietor of the Oakfield House. His brother George was a dry goods merchant of Oakfield, and married Laura, daughter of William and Laura (Amsden) Howland.

Benjamin Williams, a native of Langwerne, Eng., was a farmer. His children were Alfred, Mary A., George, Emma, Edward, Henry, and Arthur W. Henry Williams came to Ohio in 1879, and thence, in 1880, to Oakfield, where he now resides, and is engaged in the business of painting and paper hanging. He married Kate Way, daughter of George Brown, of Oakfield.

F. E. Wright came to Oakfield in the spring of 1883. July 1, 1883, he associated himself with A. H. Green, of Byron, under the name of the Exchange Bank, and together they did the banking business of the northern section of the county until July, 1887, when Mr. Wright purchased the interest of Mr. Green, and has since continued the business alone. He was elected president of the village in March, 1889.

John Watts, a native of Norwich, Eng , was a farmer. He married Mary A. Lunnon, of Norfolk, Eng., and their children were John, George, William, Susan, Ann, Jacob, Isaac, and James. Isaac served 10 years in the English army. William came to America, located in Middleport village, town of Royalton, in 1853, and afterwards removed to Hartland, Niagara County, where he now resides. He married Susanna, daughter of John and Julia (Holt) Watson, of London, Eng. Their children were William, Matthew, Mary A., Emma, Susanna, John C., Ella, and George. William served in Co. D, N. Y. H. A., was taken prisoner at the battle of Cold Harbor, and was sent to Salisbury prison, where he, with so many others, suffered untold hardships. Starvation wrought its work and death came to his relief. Matthew, who was born in England in 1849, was four years old when his father settled in Middleport. He came to Oakfield in 1883, and now has a farm on road 1. He married Amelia V., daughter of John W. and Lucinda (Kelsey) Strong, of Hartland, Niagara County.

Sylvester Willis, of Rutland, Vt , settled in Oakfield in 1830. He was a carpenter and built many houses in Genesee County. He died in 1885.

PAVILION.

PAVILION was formed from Covington, Wyoming County, May 19, 1841. A portion from the townships of Le Roy and Stafford was annexed March 22, 1842. The surface is undulating in the north, and in the south hilly. The principal stream is the Oatka Creek, which flows north through the center of the town. The town received its name from Harmon J. Betts in 1825. He was a native of Saratoga, and gave the name from the hotel of the same name in that village. Joseph Ellicott surveyed the first road across the present town of Pavilion, extending in a straight line from Batavia village to Leicester, through the village of Pavilion. About the time Mr. Ellicott made this survey the State surveyed a road from Canawaugus, Indian village, on the Genesee River, at Avon, extending in a straight line to Buffalo, called the new State road; that road centers the town of Pavilion, and passes through what was known as Bradley's Corners, near Pavilion Center.

The following is a list of the early settlers, and is as accurate as can be given at the present time:

The Burgess brothers, James Baker, Stephen Branch, Capt. Betts, George Bidwell, Capt. Daniel Buell, Nathan Bryant, Joseph Chaddock, H. Dodge, Lucius Parks, Jared Miller, Horace Rugg, Thomas Studley, Ashley Townsend, Hon. Townsend, David Snow, and Levi Ward. In 1805, Isaac D. Lyon. In 1807, the Lawrence family and Richard Walkley. In 1809, Peter Crosman, David Filkins, Levi McWethy, James McWethy, Ezra Terrill, Laura Terrill, and Solomon Terrill. In 1810, Reuben Burnham, Dr. Benjamin Hill, William Halbert, Orange Judd, Rowland Perry, Joshua Shumway, Calvin Spring, Erastus Spring, Amos Spring, Elliott Terrill, and Ezra Walker. In 1811, Barber Allen, Amasa Allen, Issachar Allen, William Almy, Leman Bradley, Samuel Bishop, H. B. Elwell, Libbeus Graves, Calvin Lewis, Daniel Lord, Samuel Phelps, Elijah Phelps, Page Russell, Cyril Shumway, Noah Starr, Isaac Storm, Jesse Sprague, Daniel Walker, Isaac Walker, Loomis Walker, and Sylvanus L. Young. In 1812, Harry Conklin, Lovell Cobb, Francis Herrick, Richard Pearson, W. E. Pearson, D. W. Matteson, Isaac Shepard, Hazel Thompson, Dr. Abel Tennant, and Dr. Daniel White (before 1812). In 1813, Isaac Crocker, Ezra Coe, Harry Coe, Francis Ruby, and Aaron Tufts. In 1814, Leonard Anson, Elijah Cheney, J. E. Holcomb, John Hendee, Elijah Olmsted, W. C. Smead, Marshall Smead, and Jesse Snow. In 1815, T. Butler, Naomi Davis, Rufus Glass, William Glass, Darius Howe, Seth Miles, James Nobles, John Reed, Elijah Rogers, Seth Smith, James Tompkins, Daniel Ward, Washington Weld, and Samuel Webb. In 1816, Eli Carr, Joel Crofoot, Chester Hannum, Horace Hannum, Amos Halbert, Daniel Knowlton, Bial Lathrop, and Francis Royce. In 1817, Horace Bates and Erastus Bailey. In 1818, John Ward and Chauncey Tillotson. In 1819, Oswald Bond, Carlton Cooley, Albert Hill, and Charles Hill. In 1820, William Gilmore and George Tubbs. In 1822, Jason Duguid and Asa Higgins. In 1823, Dr. Warren Fay. In 1824, John Doty. In 1825, Alexander Boyd, Horace S. Coe, Simeon Dutton, and George Murray. In 1826, Edward Landerdale. In 1827, Ira Townsend.

In further explanation of the preceding list it must be borne in mind that the settlement of Le Roy and the north half of Pavilion are coincident, and are so connected that our readers will find much valuable material in the sketch of that town (kindly furnished us by D. R. Bacon).

Hence we refer them to that town for matters pertaining to Pavilion of the portion taken from Le Roy in 1842.

Former historians give the name of Peter Crosman, who came in 1809, as being the first settler in the town. Our researches enable us to mention settlements as having been made earlier, viz.: Isaac D. Lyon in 1805, the Lawrence family in 1807, Richard Walkley and the McWethys in 1809, and quite a family of Terrills the same year. We wish here to call attention to the fact that our information is obtained from a personal interview of every resident of the town, a very large proportion of whom are descendants of the first settlers, and whose sources of information ought to be regarded with some degree of confidence, even though some of them are anxious to anticipate, by a year or so, the date of priority of settlement. These earliest pioneers all endured hardships in their journey to the Genesee country, and a continuance of them for many years after, and generally the experience of one is that of all. Therefore it is not necessary to enter into detail the story of each as it has been told to us from their sons and daughters. There were some whose names are difficult to obtain, who made complete failures, and yet some credit is due even them. Of them it can be truly said: "Unreliable and incomplete is any history that fails to notice that numerous, laborious, and unfortunate portion of the population who took up land, cleared and fenced it, failed to perfect their title, and after years of agonizing labor sold for what they could get, or were closed out by the sheriff without getting anything. Farms cleared up and partly paid for by those who were obliged to leave them make up a melancholy and voluminous unwritten record. Frequently the buildings and improvements cost more than the land sold for, to say nothing about the money advanced, which was about one-third the original price."

A brief sketch here of some of the early happenings will be found interesting. Ezra Terrill, who died in 1885, aged 97 years, came from Vermont in 1809, and first went to Byron with Roswell Newell. He later returned to the East and induced his father, Zebulon, to accompany him to the Genesee country. He purchased three-quarters of a section—360 acres—near Union Corners, and built a log house near Edward Cheney's present residence. He married Roxanna Elliott, who made flour sacks of flax with which to purchase glass for windows. His father was a shoemaker. Daniel Lord came in 1811. He was a tailor, and with his wife made clothing for the soldiers who were in the War of 1812. Elijah, father of Ezra Cheney, and who lived where Mr. Hazleton now resides, was a prisoner of the War of 1812. He was taken to Halifax, discharged at Boston, and begged his way home to his family. Capt. James Sprague, one of the prominent business men and farmers of Covington, was born in 1766, near New London, Conn. In 1798 he married Abiah Carpenter, and they lived in Massachusetts, where all their children were born. In 1812 they moved to Covington, and he built a saw-mill on the Oatka in company with Aaron Spaulding, it being the first saw mill in the neighborhood, and a very great convenience to the new settlers. Soon afterwards he erected a carding and cloth-dressing establishment. In 1826 he built the grist-mill now owned by William Crosman. He subsequently established his sons in business in Pavilion—James in cloth-dressing, and William and Daniel as merchants, while Paul took charge of the grist-mill, and Erastus of the farm of 400 acres. William, on retiring from mercantile business, practiced medicine successfully (see chapter on the Medical Society of the county). Capt. Sprague was respected as a man of energy and integrity, and of much public spirit. For a long time he stood first in wealth and enterprise in Covington. He died in Pavilion in 1849 John Nobles, who came in 1817, married Mary, daughter of Capt. Sprague, and attended to his mill. He lived to be over 84 years old. Leman Bradley, of Vermont, came on foot in 1811, with Calvin Lewis, and located one mile northeast of Pavilion on 50 acres. He served in the War of 1812, returned to Vermont, and with his family came about 1816 and located where William S. Bradley now lives. He was a commander of militia. His father, John F. M. Bradley, of Connecticut, was born in 1769, and died in 1868, at the age of 100 years.

Amasa Allen, son of a Revolutionary soldier, married Lucinda Loomis, and settled in 1811 near where Samuel Phelps lived. Their log cabin was covered with elm bark, a blanket was used for a door, and hewed planks of basswood used for a floor. He died in 1834. His sons were Amasa, Chauncey, and Capt. Issachar, the latter a captain of militia. Shoes were a scarce commodity when the Allen boys went to school to Rodema Judd, and they were fortunate enough one winter to kill a deer that could not travel, by reason of the crust upon the snow, and with the skin they made themselves comfortable moccasins, so they were enabled to defy the cold of that winter.

Dr. Daniel White, the first physician in what was Covington, was a surgeon in the War of 1812. He was very skillful, had a large practice over what is now Pavilion, gave calomel and whisky freely as the fashion was, and was more companionable than constant as his wife believed. He was a leading member and champion of the Masonic order. While leading a grand Masonic procession on "St. John's day," at Pavilion, arrayed in royal robes, his wife, who had more temper than self-respect, and who frequently gave her husband the benefit of it, brought up the rear, clad in the most slatternly garments imaginable. Their daughter Volina was the first child born in the town.

During the War of 1812 all able-bodied men were summoned to the frontier, leaving but few male persons at home, who were not all able to get crops in and gathered, so that it devolved upon the women to give their attention to much necessary farming in order to procure the means of sustenance. Planting bees were quite common, as by united effort only were they enabled to get their planting done and crops gathered. We were told that when an engagement was taking place at Buffalo, or Fort Erie, every peal of cannon could be heard, and it was common for dishes

to be jarred by the concussions. The cold year of 1816 proved a hard
one for the farmers of that day, as but little sustenance could be raised
for the pioneers

Money was not to be had ; all kinds of produce was high, and many
derived their food from herbage and from roots found in the forest.
Some of the settlers (in the Scotch settlement, east), having been longer
in the new country, and having raised more crops, were able to supply
the necessities of their less fortunate neighbors, and they came to their
relief.

"In those days there were no pianos nor guitars in the county, and the girls made
music upon the spinning wheel, and the notes practiced upon were flax and wool. The
flax was to be spun into threads of a certain number, and in the evening of a party
each girl was to bring her skein of thread. Those who lived on the direct road came
in wagons. Others lived in the woods, where some of the prettiest girls were found,
and they mounted a horse behind a young man, with a blanket to sit upon, and were
dressed in their every-day apparel, with woolen stockings and strong shoes on their
feet. They would dash through the woods on some trail, through brush, and over
every obstacle in their way, carrying their ball dress and skein of thread in a bundle in
their hand, A few minutes at the toilet put them in a condition for the dance. Others,
living a mile or so away, thought it no great task to come on foot. In the ball room
their rosy cheeks, sparkling eyes, and blooming health gave pleasure to all who beheld
them. The supper was prepared by the hardy pioneer's wife (and well done, too) from
the products of the farm, and with the addition of tea, coffee, sugar, and some light
wine, was all that was thought necessary. As no barn could hold the horses they were
picketed around the wagons and fences. As daylight appeared the girls would doff
their ball dresses, don the homespun, and return to their homes in the woods."

The early school teachers were Laura Terrill, Louis Moon, Daniel
Walker, Mary Hill (who married Leman Bradley), and Rodema Judd.
The latter taught school at Union Corners, and one of her scholars says
he has seen her many a time eat a dinner of pudding and milk brought
in a pail from home. The first death was that of a child of Reuben Burnham in 1812.

Seth Smith opened the first tavern, on the Leicester road, at Pavilion,
in 1815, and Horace Bates the first store at the same place in 1817.
Miller Mills had a tavern at Union Corners quite early. Bial Lathrop
had the first mill, in 1816, on the Oatka. Elliott Terrill was an early
shoemaker, and one Barrett had a tannery and shoe shop at Union Corners. A blacksmith shop was built in Pavilion in 1820, by a Mr. Whitaker, where Mr. Buckingham now holds forth. In 1832 Stephen J.
Branch made chairs.

The pioneers very early gave attention to religious matters, and when
it was announced that a meeting would be held at some school-house or
the cabin of a settler the people would gather from miles around to give
thanks for their protection amidst all the dangers incident to the new settlement. Elder Leonard Anson was probably the first one who held services with any regularity. He was also a prominent Mason, and lived
near Bailey's Mills.

The Baptist Church in Pavilion was organized in 1816, with 14 members, by Elder Leonard Anson. Meetings were often held in the Storms
neighborhood. In 1834 a church was erected, of wood, capable of seat-

ing 400 persons. The society at present has about 126 members, with Rev. W. T. Walton, of London, Eng., pastor. The church property is valued at $4,000. The Sunday school, which is presided over by Darius Covell, has about 100 members. Rev. H. B. Ewell, one of the pastors of this church, was born in Middlebury in 1811, and preached in Pavilion from 1838 until his death in 1884. The cemetery around the church is very old, the first interment, that of Peter Crosman, being made in 1812.

About 1830 a meeting-house was built near the brick school-house and used by the Methodists, but as early as 1810 the Genesee Conference sent its itinerants all through Genesee County, and meetings were held by its missionaries. The preachers were zealous, self denying, and often illiterate, but were never allowed to read their sermons. Single men were allowed $80 per year, and their board cost them nothing, as they were welcome comers. A large share of the settlers were Methodists. Among the preachers who came were Elders Millard, Church, Anson, Badger, Segar, Story, May, Hamilton, Davis, Wait, and Comfort.

The First Methodist Episcopal Church of Pavilion was formed in connection with one at Moscow, Livingston County, N. Y., in connection with the Covington Methodist Episcopal Church, and moved from Covington to Pavilion in 1840, and which is a part of the history of the same. There are now 95 members belonging to the society, presided over by Rev. George H. Van Vradenburg. There are also about 125 members in the Sunday-school. The valuation of the church property is $6,000.

The First Universalist Society of Pavilion was organized October 10, 1831, by James Sprague, who was chosen moderator, and Elijah Olmsted. There were 38 members that composed the first meeting. Rev. L. L. Sadler was the first minister. The present church was erected in 1832, at a cost of $2,100. Capt. James Sprague, Jr., was the leading man of the society in its early days, and foremost in its support. Some of its ministers have been Alfred Peck in 1834, A. Kelsey in 1840, J. Davy, J. S. Brown, N. M. Fisk, Orville Brayton, Charles Cravens, Charles Dutton, and M. D. Shumway. The society is not increasing in numbers, and at present they have no settled minister, but sometimes are supplied from Le Roy. The cemetery adjacent to the Universalist Church was the first used as such in the town, in 1812.

There is a very prosperous, but small, community of Catholics at Pavilion, under the charge of an energetic and much beloved priest, Rev. Father T. B. Milde.

We find that Asbury Church was built in 1832 at Union Corners, and cost $1,500. Rev. Hiram May was on this curcuit, and was very active in obtaining funds for its erection and completion. It was used by the Methodists until 1876, when the Free Methodists undertook to continue meetings, but without success. Isaac Walker was one of the trustees, and meetings were held at his house before the erection of the church.

A union church was built at Pavilion Center at an early day, and was used by all sects. It is now in use as a town hall.

Clarissa Starr, a relative of Noah Starr, has the credit of starting the first Sunday-school organized at Pavilion while it was a part of Covington. She was assisted by Captain Betts, who was a good singer.

The Woman's Christian Temperance Union was organized March 20, 1886. The present officers are Mrs. George Carr, president; Mrs. Heman Terrill, secretary; and Miss Nellie Ewell, treasurer. The society meets semi-monthly in Union Hall, West Main street.

Loyal Legion, auxiliary to the W. C. T. U.; Miss M. Ella Thomas, superintendent; Mrs. George Carr, assistant superintendent. The legion meets semi-monthly in Union Hall.

Woman's Foreign Mission Society, of the Methodist Episcopal Church, was organized in 1884; Mrs. G. H. Van Vradenburg, president; Mrs. Grove D. Whitney, Miss M. Ella Thomas, and Mrs. C. T. Lewis, vice-presidents; Mrs. William Austin, corresponding secretary; Mrs. O. Phelps, secretary; Mrs. James Lawson, treasurer.

Ladies' Aid Society, of the Methodist Episcopal Church, was organized in 1879; Mrs. James Lawson, president; Mrs. C. M. Terrill, vice-president; Mrs. M. Prill, secretary; Mrs. C. A. Paine, treasurer; meets semi-monthly.

Foreign Mission Society, of the Baptist Church, was organized about 1853; Mrs. D. L. Smead, president; Mrs. William Burt, secretary; Mrs. W. T. Walton, treasurer.

Home Mission Society, of the Baptist Church, was organized March 7, 1889; Mrs. James Ward, president; Mrs. A. Reese, secretary; Mrs. Harvey Young, treasurer.

The Epworth League, No. 881, of the young people of the Methodist Episcopal Church; Leslie M. Judson, president; Miss M. Ella Thomas, Mrs. Dora Hubbard, Miss Mary Graves, and George C. Whitney, vice-presidents; Charles W. Wilson, secretary; Miss Edna Sapp, treasurer.

Pavilion Center King's Daughters was organized in August, 1889; Mrs. Louisa Britton, president; Mrs. Ella Reese, secretary and treasurer.

BAILEY'S MILLS is the location of a grist-mill established about 1817, by Erastus Bailey and Bial Lathrop. The present dam was built in 1828. In 1835 the mill was sold to Mr. Bosley, in 1840 to D. W. Olmsted, and to Mr. Bailey again in 1843, who built a stone mill in 1848. In 1879 George Gaugel bought the concern. The present proprietor is Frank Gaugel. A saw mill has also been maintained at the same place, and a heading-mill is now operated there.

The Pavilion grist and saw-mill was erected by Henry Chilson in December, 1888. It is run by steam, and has a capacity of 300 bushels of grain per day. It is located at the depot of the R. & P. Railroad.

The present warehouse was built by John C. Doty, who uses it for the produce and grain trade. Dr. William B. Sprague had previously built two warehouses on the spot, but they were destroyed by fire. He also engaged in the evaporation of apples where Mr. Trescott has his present spacious buildings.

B. F. Trescott, in addition to his evaporator, is the proprietor of a fruit farm of 28 acres. He has seven acres of Niagara grapes, besides many acres in raspberries, and annually raises about 1,200 bushels of a superior variety of pop-corn on about 12 acres of ground, keeping six or more hands busy. He came from Livingston County, has built a nice home in the village, on South Lake street, and is one of the most energetic and active citizens. Mr. Crosby also has a factory.

The Page cooper works were established in 1886 By J. Quincy D. Page, for the purpose of supplying the farmers with apple barrels, butter tubs, and other packages. They have a capacity of 50,000 barrels per season.

Pavilion Grange, No. 423, P. of H., at Pavilion Center, was organized April 11, 1878. William L. Bradley is master; Charles L. Hannum, secretary; Asahel Higgins, treasurer; and E. T. Bradley, purchasing agent. They own a library of 100 volumes and hold their meetings in their own hall.

Equitable Aid Union, No. 404, was chartered February 9, 1882. John C. Doty is chancellor; L. W. Evarts, advocate; D L. Smead, president; Dr. S. M. Thomas, vice-president; Susan E. Doty, secretary; Mrs. Grove D. Whitney, accountant and treasurer; S. M. Burt, warden; W. R. Burt, auxiliary; D. M. Plucker, chaplain; Mrs. Rose Reed, conductor; L. Brownell, watchman; Solomon Reed, sentinel. They meet in Masonic Hall the second and fourth Fridays in each month.

John M. Hutchinson Post, No. 243, *G. A. R.,* was organized November 3, 1881. C. D. Sapp is commander; E. T. Bradley, adjutant; J. W. Dow, quartermaster. The post meets the first and third Friday evenings of each month in Burt's Hall.

A. O. U. W., No. 261, was chartered January 1, 1880. J. P. Hawks, M. W.; Charles E. Bond, foreman; C. D. Sapp, recorder; W. M. Dean, financier; H. N. Chilson, receiver. They meet on the first and third Tuesdays of each month in Burt's Hall.

Oatka Lodge, No. 343, *I. O. O. F.,* was chartered April 23, 1888. Louis Wyeth, N. G.; Edwin Sprague, V. G.; J. W. Dow, treasurer; Grove Dauchy, recording secretary; Fred Chilson, permanent secretary. They meet on Monday evening of each week.

The first known of the Bradley family in the United States was Stephen Bradley, a soldier of Oliver Cromwell's army, who came over from England in 1642, and located in Guilford, Conn. Stephen, the fifth in the order of descent, came to Sunderland, Charlotte County, Province of New York (now Vermont), in 1774, and was great-grandfather to William L. J. F. M. Bradley, his grandfather, lived to be 100 years old. Leman, father of William L., came to Pavilion in 1811, and served in the War of 1812. December 27, 1821, he married Mary Hill, of this town, who was the first school teacher in Pavilion. They had five children, viz.: Mary J., Hermione G., Miles L., Sarah I., and William L. Mary J., Miles L., and Sarah I. are deceased. William L Bradley was born June 17, 1836, in the house which he now owns, and where he resides. He received a common school and academic education, and now holds the position of justice of the peace, is one of the commissioners of the United States Deposit Fund, and is a surveyor, conveyancer, and farmer. December 11, 1866, he married Fanny M., youngest daughter of Horace Bradley, of Pavilion Center, and they have had six children, viz.: Lee, who died in infancy; and Mary I., Etta E., Robert L. and Horace S. (twins), and Bertha E., who survive. Mr. and Mrs. Bradley reside near Pavilion Center.

E. T. Bradley, who was born January 21, 1838, where he now resides, at the age of 16 started in life to earn a livelihood for himself. August 19, 1862, he enlisted in Co. I, 151st N. Y. Vols., was selected as corporal, and participated in the battle of Mine Run, Va., and was wounded in the right elbow. After being in the hospital at Alexandria nine months he was discharged as sergeant. Since his return he has been engaged in farming and coopering, beginning the latter business in 1868. He has served three years as justice, five years as clerk, two terms as deputy sheriff, and now holds the position of constable and collector. He is a son of Horace and Emeline (Bigelow) Bradley, natives respectively of Sunderland, Vt., and New York. Horace Bradley came to Pavilion with his parents in 1814, with an ox-team. He reared four children, Amanda, E. T., Sophia, and Fannie. He died May 22, 1855, aged 58 years. Horace was a son of Benjamin Bradley, who was born in Vermont, married Sally Brunson, reared five sons and two daughters, and died aged 89 years.

James A. Boyd was born September 4, 1820, in Charlton, Saratoga County, N. Y., a son of Alexander and Eleanor (Gibson) Boyd. Alexander was born in 1790, near Glasgow, Scotland, and when 18 years of age came to the United States and settled in Saratoga County. He was a weaver by trade and also a farmer. His wife was born near Belfast, Ireland, in 1781, and when a girl of 15 years came with her parents to Saratoga County. They had six children, namely: Mrs. Margaret McArthur, James A., Samuel, John (deceased), Jane, and Alexander. In 1825 Alexander Boyd and wife came to Covington. He died in 1874, and his wife in 1869. They were United Presbyterians. James A. married, March 19, 1856, Margaret, daughter of Duncan McMillan, of Covington. Mr. McMillan was born in the Highlands of Scotland in 1789, and came to the United States with his parents, John and Margaret (McGregor) McMillan, settling in Johnstown, thence removing to York, Livingston County, prior to 1812. Duncan McMillan located where Mr. Boyd now resides about 1830, and raised three sons and four daughters. James A. Boyd has two children, Ella C. and William J. They are members of the United Presbyterian Church.

William Buckingham, born in Devonshire, Eng. (Bishop's Tawton),

July 15, 1832, is a son of John and Susanna (Joce) Buckingham, who reared two sons. William Buckingham came to the United States in June, 1854, located in Batavia, and engaged at his trade as blacksmith. He worked at various places until May, 1855, when he located in Pavilion and entered the employ of Tompkins & Co., wagon and carriage manufac- turers, for one year, when he began work for Samuel Crosman. In 1860 he purchased the blacksmith shop of Tompkins & Co., which he run for 11 years, when he purchased the entire establishment, and has since oper- ated it alone. This is a business established about 70 years ago by Whitney & Whitaker. He married Maria Fulling, of Gloucester, Eng., and they have two daughters, Lottie and Mary.

Don C. Bond, born May 16, 1830, in Pavilion, was a son of Elias and Abigail (Hutchinson) Bond. Elias Bond was born May 17, 1799, in Grafton, Vt., and his wife in Saratoga County, N. Y., November 1, 1807. In 1810 he came to Middlebury with his parents, and in 1820 he located on 125 acres where the village now is, for which he paid $17 per acre. In early life he served as constable and collector for many years. His chil- dren were Don C., Ellen G, Dewitt C., of Dakota, Albert D., Edward A., Florence L., who died in infancy, and Charles E. He died in February, 1876, and his wife in April, 1870. The grandfather of Don C. Bond, William, who died in 1860, aged 82, was a native of Vermont and a sol- dier of 1812, and married Miss Relief Rugg, of Virginia, raised five sons and six daughters, and spent their last days with Elias Bond. The father of William Bond was William Henry. Don C. Bond was reared on the farm, had a common school education, and at the age of 24 began to learn blacksmithing, which trade he has followed since, except three years in the hotel and three years teaming at Le Roy. He married, March 27, 1855, Sarah J., daughter of Smith and Sarah (Mead) Dauchy. His wife was born in Pavilion. They had one child, George W. (deceased). Charles E. Bond was born September 23, 1850, in Pavilion, and began at an early age as clerk in a store. He opened a store on his own ac- count in 1876, and continued in the business for 11 years. He was for four years postmaster under Cleveland's administration. He was also town clerk for six or seven years. Although a Democrat his popularity was such as to be elected for several terms in a strong Republican town.

A. K. Cobb, born February 10, 1844, where he now resides, is a son of Lovel and Ruth (Kentfield) Cobb, of Canaan, Pa., and Massachusetts, respectively. Lovel Cobb, born in 1792, came to this county in 1812, and settled on 100 acres where his son now lives. He died in 1871. His children were Justus, who died in Michigan ; Ransom L., who died in Kansas ; Darius, who died in Pennsylvania ; Richard W., who died in Canada ; Mary Lull, of Michigan ; Sarah J.; Hanlon; Willard T., of Mich- igan ; Joseph N., of Pennsylvania ; William L., of Michigan ; Rufus C, of Indiana ; Millard F.; and A. K. The mother of Mr. Cobb was a daugh- ter of David Kentfield, who was born in Mansfield, Conn., February 9, 1777, and married Betsey Lyon, who was born in 1775. They came from

38

Massachusetts to Genesee County about 1813. He served in the War
of 1812, and reared seven children. A. K. Cobb, being raised on the
farm, received but a common school education. He owns the old homestead.

J. Lyman Crocker was born in Hamilton, Madison County, N. Y., September 4, 1814. He is an intelligent and well informed farmer. He received a good English education at the common schools and Middlebury
Academy, and in early life he taught considerable in the common schools.
He has served as town superintendent of schools and supervisor, and has
had other honors conferred upon him, but not desiring the positions refused to qualify. He married, June 14, 1843, Lamma McIntyre, of Worcester County, Mass., who bore him two children, Edgar M. and Henry
C., the latter of whom died at Saginaw, Mich. Mr. Crocker is a prominent member of the Presbyterian Church. He is a son of Isaac and Susan
(Emmons) Crocker, who were born in Colchester, New London County,
and East Haddam, Middlesex County, Conn., respectively. They were
married in December, 1812. Mr. Crocker, soon after his marriage, entered the army in the War of 1812, but in a short time furnished a substitute. He came to Hamilton, Madison County, in 1814, and in February, 1816, came to Genesee County, and settled three miles south of
Le Roy village, on 90 acres, which he had purchased in the fall of 1815.
He died July 30, 1859, aged 70 years and 10 months, and his wife January 5, 1862, aged 73 years and 10 months. J. Lyman was their only
child. Isaac was a son of Simeon Crocker, Jr., who was a soldier in the
war for independence, and was connected with the quartermaster department. He married a Miss Swift, and reared a family of four sons and
three daughters. His father was Simeon Crocker, who came from England and settled in Connecticut.

George W. Cook was born November 26, 1833, where he now resides. He is a son of Joseph and Mahala (Kelsey) Cook, who were born
in Eastman, Washington County, and Greenfield, Saratoga County,
respectively. Joseph Cook came to Genesee County in 1830 and located
on 30 or more acres where George W. now resides, to which he continued to add until he owned 175 acres: He was industrious and honest,
was a man of more than ordinary intelligence and ability, and was highly
esteemed by all who knew him. He served his town as assessor for
several terms. In 1853-54 he served as a member of the Assembly
from his county. He had a family of three sons and four daughters, as
follows: John L., Leonora S., George W., Ann O. (Mrs. Shadbolt),
Mary E. (Mrs. Edson), Sarah J., and William J. Joseph Cook died in
1858, aged 56. He was strictly a self-made man. His wife was a
daughter of William Kelsey, who came from Saratoga County to Genesee
County in 1817, and located about one mile south of Le Roy. He was
a soldier in the War of 1812. George W. Cook has always lived on the
farm where he now resides. He received a good common school education, and married Emma E., only daughter of John G. and Harriet

(Taber) Barber. Mr. Barber came from Vermont and was one of the early pioneers of Le Roy. He was a dentist and druggist. Mrs. Cook died in 1882. They had one child, Emma E. William J. Cook, a genial, clever, and hospitable gentleman, and brother of George W., was born in September, 1845, and occupies a portion of the homestead. He is an active politician and has filled a responsible position in the revenue department. He married Lucinda M., daughter of Homer and Lucinda (Buck) Daw, of Dawes Corners, this county. They were born in Connecticut and Vermont respectively, and came to Dawes Corners about 1820.

Homer Cook was born January 14, 1841, where he now resides, on Burleigh Hill. He was a son of Ambrose and Betsie (Beckwith) Cook. Ambrose Cook was born in Onondaga County, N. Y., and came to Pavilion with his parents in 1819. They settled on Burleigh Hill, where he resided during his life, except three years spent in Wyoming County. He had seven children : Harriet, who died in Illinois, Levi, Warren, Esther, Mahala, of Michigan, Ambrose, and Homer. Mahala and Homer only are living. He died in 1859, aged 53. He was a son of Levi and Betsey (Brown) Cook, who came from New Marlboro, Mass., to Vernon, Oneida County, N. Y., and thence to Pavilion. He served as justice for a time, and reared four sons and three daughters. His father was Hezekiah Cook, of Massachusetts, who had five sons and one daughter. Homer Cook received a good English education in the district schools. His father having left a debt of $4,000 on the homestead at the time of his death, young Homer, then but 17, took charge of the farm, and, being energetic and ambitious, he paid off the indebtedness, and now possesses one of the best farms in the county. He has given considerable of his time to fruit growing, and now owns one of the largest pear and quince orchards in the town. His residence is so located that he commands a view of the country for many miles. For the past 14 years he has served as highway commissioner. Mr. Cook married, November 24, 1864, Kate, daughter of James Fisher. Their children are Jennie F., Jay, Mary, and Alice B.

Joel Crofoot, an early pioneer of Genesee County, was a native of Vermont. He moved to Cayuga Lake about 1810, and in 1816 located in Covington, now Pavilion. He entered an article for 50 acres one mile east of the village, where he lived until his death in 1863, aged 77 years. He married Polly Carr, and reared five sons and two daughters. His sons were Richmond R., Gideon W., Leonard, William D., of Michigan, and George W., also of Michigan. The father of Joel was Marcom Crofoot, of Vermont, a general of militia, who moved from Cayuga County to Painesville, Ohio, about 1816, where he resided until his death. His father came from Scotland. He married a Miss Knapp, and they had four sons and five daughters. Richmond R. Crofoot was born in 1820, on the place where he now resides, and was educated at the district schools. In 1840 he was elected captain of militia, which position he re-

tained for seven years.   Leonard Crofoot was born in 1823, raised on a
farm, received an academic education, and at the age of 21 began teaching school.   About 1858 he engaged in the insurance business, remaining in it for 20 years, and was one of the most successful in the business.
He has also been engaged in farming since 21.   Mr Cook has served as
justice of the peace two terms and school commissioner four years.   He
married, September 18, 1854, Lenora E. De Long, of Akron, Erie
County.   They have two sons, George W. and Charles R.   He located
where he now resides in 1855.   They belong to the Universalist Church.

Addison Christman was born in Palatine, Montgomery County, N. Y.,
November 30, 1831, a son of John I. and Sally (Trumbull) Christman,
natives of the same county and Massachusetts respectively.   He was a
farmer and a boatman on the canal, and reared seven sons and one daughter.   He was a soldier in the War of 1812, and was twice married.   Addison was reared upon the farm, received a common school education,
and at the early age of 16 began to learn the carpenters' trade.   At the
age of 18 he married Elizabeth, daughter of Benjamin Lampman, of St.
Johnsville, N Y.   They had five children, of whom four are living, viz :
William C., Menzo A., Anna, and Edwin R.   He has followed farming
since his marriage, until three years ago.   He lived in Wheeler, Steuben
County, four years, and in 1860 located at Bailey's Mills, on 120 acres
of land.   In July, 1885, he came to Pavilion, and has since been a contractor and builder.   He has served as railroad commissioner.   The family
are now members of the Universalist Church, but were formerly members of the Dutch Reformed Church.   Menzo A. Christman, son of Addison, was born in Palatine, December 29, 1855, received a common
school education, and married, January 10, 1883, Cora A., daughter of
James and Sarah (Notnaugle) McDuffie, farmers, of Seneca County,
N. Y.   They are members of the Universalist Church.   He located
where he now resides, near Pavilion Center, in 1878.

Abel Chilson, born in Connecticut, married a Miss Groesbeck.   He
was a native of Holland and came to New York when a young man.
One of his sons, Nicholas, was born in the Mohawk valley, in Dutchess
County, January 23, 1809.   He was educated in the public schools, and
was a farmer.   December 7, 1828, in Manchester, Ontario County, he
married Mareba Corey, of Shortsville, and they had 10 children, of whom
two are deceased, and eight survive, namely : Nathaniel, Chester, Sophia,
Maria, Clara, Henry, Fred, and Frank.   Fred Chilson was born in Covington, Wyoming County, on the farm he now owns, April 1, 1854, and
was educated in the public schools and an academy until he was 20 years
old.   December 9, 1874, he married Jennie, oldest daughter of Horace S.
Coe, of Pavilion Center.   They have two children, namely : Eva M.,
born January 4, 1875, and Howard F., born July 21, 1878.   Mr. Chilson
is a farmer and general dealer, and resides in the village of Pavilion.

Henry N. Chilson, a native of Covington, Wyoming County, was born
May 12, 1848, and is a son of Nicholas and Mareba (Corey) Chilson,

natives of Hartwick, Otsego County, N. Y., and Litchfield, Mass., respectively. They had six sons and four daughters, and came to Wyoming County in 1830. Nicholas was a son of Abel Chilson, who was born in Vermont, married Maria Groesbeck, of Hartwick, and had six sons and four daughters. Henry N. Chilson was educated at the common schools and reared upon a farm. · He was in the coopering business for three years, and has followed threshing for 11 years. He has resided in Pavilion since 1861. August 17, 1867, he married Nancy J., daughter of John and Julia (Stephens) Steward, who came to Pavilion in 1828 from Amsterdam, where he was born in June, 1809. Mr. Chilson has lost three children, and has two, Albert and Ina J., who survive. He is a member of the A. O. U. W.

Eli Carr was born May 25, 1834, one mile east of Pavilion, and is a son of Richmond and Rosanna (Perry) Carr, natives of Rhode Island and Saratoga County. They came to Genesee County in 1816, and took up 157 acres of land. They reared six sons and two daughters, viz.: Livingston, Sylvester, Sallie A., Eli, Wellington, Edwin, of Kansas, Calafornia, and Arvid. They belong to the Baptist Church. Mr. Carr received a common school education, and lived on a farm until April, 1872, when he moved to the village. He married Jane L., daughter of Levi Carr, of Saratoga County, and has one son, George D.

Peter Crosman, born in Morris, N. J., March 14, 1782, when six years of age went to Pennsylvania with his parents, and came to Genesee County in 1809, settling at the foot of Burleigh Hill. About six years later he moved one mile west of Pavilion. He was a soldier of 1812, and married Hannah, daughter of David Bowen, who came from Wales. Their children were William, Samuel, Frances M., and Marion. He died in March, 1864, aged 82 years. The father of Peter was William, who was born in Connecticut, September 24, 1757, of Scotch ancestry. He was a Revolutionary soldier. He married Martha, daughter of Dr. Lewis Workman, who died at the age of 101, and his wife at the age of 96. They had four sons and four daughters. He died in 1813, and was the first person buried in the Pavilion Cemetery. He was a member of the Universalist Church. Mrs. Frances M. Crosman and her brother William are the only surviving members of Peter Crosman's family.

Robert R. Dow was born in Glasgow, Scotland, about 1800, and came to the United States in 1820 with his parents. They located in York, Livingston County, N. Y., and took up 175 acres of land. The father of James W. married Sarah J., daughter of Reuben R. Wooster, of Livingston County, and they had eight children, two of whom died in infancy, and six survive, namely: James W., John R., Marion, Robert R., Margaret A., and Mary J. James W. Dow, born in York, Livingston County, February 7, 1837, was educated in the public schools until he was 16 years old. January 27, 1869, he married Margaret E., youngest daughter of James Copeland, of Covington, Wyoming County. They have two children: William D., born May 22, 1870, who was educated in the public schools and in the Normal school at Geneseo, and graduated from Rochester Business University; and James C., who was born July 25, 1873. Both reside with their parents. November 2, 1861, Mr. Dow enlisted in Co. G, 104th Inf. N. Y. Vols. (Wadsworth Guards), and participated in the battles of Cedar Mountain, August 9, 1862; Rappahannock Station, August 17, 1862; Thoroughfare Gap, August 28, 1862; second Bull Run, August 30, 1862; Chantilly, September 1, 1862; South Mountain, September 14, 1862; Antietam, September 17, 1862; Fredericksburg, December 13, 1862; Chancellorsville seven days' fight, May 2 to 10, 1863; and Gettysburg, in the latter of which he was wounded, in the first day's fight, in his right wrist, with a minie-ball. July 10, 1863, he was granted leave of absence until January 9, 1864, when he reported to his regiment for duty, and remained with them until May 2, 1864. At the organization of his company, November 2, 1861, he was made second sergeant; September 12, 1862, was promoted first sergeant; October 31, 1862, to second lieutenant; and in June, 1863, was made first lieutenant. In May, 1864, he resigned on account of ill health caused by his wound, and applied for a position in the Veteran Reserve Corps, which he received as second lieutenant May 9, 1864, and was assigned to Co. E, 12th Regt. He was on duty at Prince Street prison in Alexander, Old Capital prison, Washington, D. C., and at the prison on Carl street, where he was one of the guards after the capture of Wilkes Booth and his conspirators until they were hung or sent to the Dry Tortugas. Mr. Dow was discharged from this important duty June 30, 1866. He is now a resident of the village of Pavilion, and by occupation a general dealer.

Jason Duguid, of Pompey, Onondaga County, was born March 26, 1803. His father was William, whose father, John, came from Scotland. Jason began life as a teacher at the age of 17 years. He was a leading citizen of Pavilion, where he settled in 1822, and held the office of justice of the peace, and others. He died December 24, 1874. His wife was the daughter of Amos Halbert, who came from Westmoreland, N. Y., and settled near Roanoke very early. He died during the war, aged 84 years. The sons and daughters of Jason Duguid, all of whom are living and have families, are Addison, Sarah A., Maud L., Jeanette L., Melvin D., William H., Nelson A., Henry C., and Manfred. Manfred Duguid was born October 17, 1836, where he now resides, and was educated at the district schools. He enlisted in the 129th N. Y. Inf., and was transferred to the 8th N. Y. H. A., as second sergeant. He was in the battles of the Wilderness, Cold Harbor, Petersburg, and North Anna, and all others in which his regiment participated. He was commissioned second lieutenant in the fall of 1864, and discharged June 22, 1865, at Rochester, since when he has been engaged in farming. Mr. Duguid has held several positions of trust. He married, August 18, 1868, Nancy J., daughter of John Ward, of Pavilion, and their children are Minnie A. and John W.

Calvin Dutton, born February 14, 1806, in Washington, Oneida County, is a son of Calvin and Polly (Edgerton) Dutton, natives of Massachusetts and Connecticut, respectively. Calvin, Sr., was a farmer, came to Oneida in 1812 with his family, and died in Fulton, N. Y. He reared four sons and two daughters. Calvin, Jr.'s, grandfather (Dutton) was born in England, came to the United States after his marriage, settled in Massachusetts, and taught school for 40 years. The maternal grandfather, Zedediah Edgerton, was a farmer, and reared seven sons and eight daughters. Calvin Dutton married, in November, 1834, Mehitable, daughter of Elijah Rogers, and they have one child, Nancy Louisa Sparks. After their marriage they lived in Batavia one year, and in 1837 they settled where they now reside. He has served six years as highway commissioner. He is a member of the Presbyterian Church, and his wife of the Baptist Church.

John Doty, of Connecticut, married Olive E. Walker, of Rutland, Vt., and came to Covington in 1824, settling on 50 acres, which was finally increased to 1,000 acres, one mile south of the village, where he died in 1876, aged 74 years. He was captain of a boat on the Erie Canal and an active citizen. They were of Dutch descent, and had four children, one of whom, John C., is living. John C. Doty, who was born in Covington, September 9, 1841, received a common school education, was reared on the farm, and after 19 years of age pursued that calling for seven years, when he took a contract to build 37 miles of the Buffalo, Rochester & Pittsburg Railroad, between Salamanca and Eagle, and 35 miles of the new four-track road on the N. Y. C. & H. R. Railroad. He has been engaged in speculation for the past six years. He is an F. & A. M. In August, 1871, he married Susan Fay Baker, daughter of Dr. Warren Fay, of Walpole, N. H., who, in 1796, when 21 years of age, came to Avon Springs, studied medicine, graduated at Castleton, Vt., and finally located in Pavilion, where he practiced his profession and was the leading physician for 50 years. Dr. Fay married Freelove Palmer, of Stonington, Conn. They were of English origin, and reared four sons and three daughters Mrs. Doty has one daughter, Blanche, by a former husband. Her brother Casper W. is in Chicago in the insurance business, Joseph is in Hamilton, Neb., engaged in the lumber trade, and another, Lieut · Col. Fay, served in the 151st N. Y. Inf., and is a partner of A. P. Laning, of Buffalo.

Frank Gaugel, born August 16, 1857, in Le Roy, is a son of George and Josephine (Myers) Gaugel, natives of Wittenberg, Germany. They came to the United States in 1855, and settled in Le Roy. He was a miller. They reared eight children, viz.: Frank, Carrie Legg, Barbara, Josephine, George, Emeline, Edward, and Jay. He died in 1885, aged 50 years, where Frank now resides, and to which place he moved in 1869. Frank Gaugel received a common school education. He was taught the business of milling and is now the proprietor of Bailey's Mills. He married, October 11, 1882, Josephine, daughter of Jacob Bernd, of Le Roy, and they are members of the Roman Catholic Church.

Frederick Graves, born in England, was a soldier in the English army in the war of 1776. One of his sons, Frederick Graves, was born in Massachusetts in 1817, and married Margaret Lockrow, of Albany. Her father, Thomas, served in the colonial army in 1776. They had 10 children, namely: Almira, Mary, Sarah, Fannie, Emma, George C., William H., Charles P., Frederick A., and Richard R. C. George C. Graves was born in Albany, March 22, 1832. He was educated in the common schools, and married Rebecca J. Upton, of Quebec, Canada, by whom he has had seven children, viz.: Alice J., Ellen R., Estella J., William and Edwin R. (twins), Marietta, and Julietta. Mr. Graves enlisted in 1861 in Co. I, 151st Inf N. Y. Vols., and after three years' service he was discharged for disability. He is now a pensioner. He has been a resident of Pavilion 30 years. Here his children were born, and here three of them are buried, Alice J., Ellen R., Estella J.

Rev. Henry B. Ewell was born in Middlebury, Wyoming County, N. Y., April 13, 1811. He was educated in the public schools and in Middlebury Academy, graduated from the theological department of Madison University in August, 1836, and was ordained in January, 1837. He married, first, in April, 1838, Amelia Dix, by whom he had two children: Amelia S. and William H. For his second wife he married, February 25, 1845, Fanny Blackmer, and they also had two children, viz.: Helen E., born February 3, 1851, and Jirah B., born March 29, 1853. Rev. Mr. Ewell died in April, 1884, after a faithful and well rounded life of ministerial work. He was pastor of the Baptist Church in the village of Pavilion 44 years, and his earnest work in this part of the State was ably seconded by his estimable wife, who survives him. Their son Jirah B., after his education was completed, entered the ministry at Warsaw, N. Y. He married M. Florine Mallery, of La Grange, and they had two children, Glen B. and Bertha A. Rev. Jirah B. died July 8, 1887.

William H. Gilmore was born in Pavilion, October 23, 1836, a son of William and Mehitable (Smead) Gilmore. William was born at Cambridge, N Y., in 1809, came to Pavilion in 1826, opened a saddler's shop, and conducted the business for 51 years. He was also a general merchant for 18 years. His second wife was Sarah H. Carr. George Gilmore, father of William, was from Pittsfield, Mass., and was a sufferer by the raid of the Hessians during the Revolutionary war. The family are of Scotch descent. William H. Gilmore received a common school education, and is a graduate of the Albion Academy and Pittsburg Commercial College. At the age of 14 he entered a drug store. Two years later he went to school, where he continued for five years, and excepting one year spent in Iowa has always lived in this town, being engaged in the general merchandise and drug trade. In 1883 he organized the Gilmore Aromatic Wine Co., with a capital of $20,000, whose products received the endorsement of the medical profession. In 1886 he sold out his interests in the company and the business was moved to Rochester. Mr.

Gilmore has filled public offices for 17 years, being eight years postmaster of the village. He has been twice married, first to Ellen, daughter of James Wilson, and second to Elva, daughter of Edwin Fellows, of Orleans County. He has four children, Sarah E. and Nellie N. (twins), Clayton N., and Clarence H. The family are members of the Baptist Church, and Mr. Gilmore is a member of the order of A. O. U. W.

John D. Gillett, who was born in Delaware County, N. Y., in January, 1798, came to the Genesee country in 1812. When he was 18 years old he married Cornelia W. Bronson, who was born in 1804, and was only 13 years of age at the time of her marriage. They had 10 children, of whom three daughters are dead, and seven survive, viz.: Thomas, Gideon B., William F., George D., Lucy, Cornelia, and Adeline. William F. Gillett enlisted in July, 1861, in Co. A, 85th Inf. N. Y. Vols., reënlisted in January, 1864, and was in the following battles: Siege of Yorktown, Williamsburg, Fair Oaks,˙ Gaines Mills, Newburn, N. C., Roanoke Island, and Little Washington. He was discharged in July, 1865, and now resides near Pavilion Center. He is a bachelor. His mother is living in Stafford, aged 86 years. George E., son of George D., is station agent at Pavilion, and his daughter Florence A. at Pavilion Center.

William H. Huyck was born in Manlius, N. Y., March 18, 1812. He married Hannah Ferguson, of Orangeville, Wyoming County, and they had four children, one of whom died in infancy, and three are living, viz.: Nellie A., Mary L., and Evelyn P. Nellie A. was born in Le Roy, January 23, 1842. She was educated in the public schools, and early in life became a school teacher. May 27, 1861, she married Charles W. Wallace, M. A., and they had four children, namely: Nina C., Glen A., and L. Claude and Maude (twins). The oldest boy died when he was three years old Mr. Wallace died at Columbus, Ohio, in 1876. Mrs. Wallace then went to New Jersey and taught in the Reform School and the next year she moved to Nashville, Tenn. February 12, 1882, she˙ married Joseph Walmsley, who died in 1887. Mrs. Walmsley is now keeping house for her uncle, Mr. Huyck, in the village of Pavilion. Her son L. Claude resides with them, and is learning the undertaking and furniture business.

R. L. Hutchinson, who was born in Ira, Cayuga County, February 28, 1825, is a son of Timothy B. and Lydia (Farnham) Hutchinson, natives of Saratoga County, N. Y., and Vermont, respectively. Timothy B. reared two sons and two daughters, viz.: R. L., Elias B ,˙ Sarah, and Abigail They settled in Cayuga County in March, 1849, and later located in the town of Pavilion, where he died in 1871, aged 71 years. His father was Elijah Hutchinson, who was born in 1768, married a Miss Bishop, and reared three sons and four daughters. He was a Revolutionary soldier The mother of R. L. Hutchinson was a daughter of Benniah Farnham, of Vermont, and also a Revolutionary soldier. R. L. Hutchinson was reared on a farm and received a common school and

academic education. At the age of 21 he began for himself by cutting
staves, and later engaged in farming, in which he continued for 30 years,
since which he has been engaged in the produce, grain, and stock business. He married, December 28, 1846, Alida, daughter of Derick L.
Van Derheyden, of near Troy. Mr. Van Derheyden was a son of Jacob
V., who was a son of Derick I. Van Derheyden, and they were among
the first settlers of Troy, N. Y. Their descendants number among the
most prominent families of that locality. Mr. Hutchinson and wife are
members of the Baptist Church. They have two children, Rufus and
Grant D.

J. Prescott Hawks, born in Geneva, October 2, 1833, is a son of Porter and Sophia (Prescott)Hawks, natives respectively of Deerfield, Mass.,
and Phelps, N. Y. Porter Hawks was born July 4. 1804, and died
August 7, 1841. He was a merchant in Geneva until his death. He
left four children, viz.: J. Prescott, Caroline Sayre, Henry, of Galva, Ill.,
and Harriet. Mrs. Sophia (Prescott) Hawks married for her second husband James B. Darrow, by whom she had three children, James P.,
George M., and Mary S. Compson. The grandfather of J. Prescott was
a doctor at Phelps, N. Y. J. Prescott Hawks remained in Geneva until
the age of 12 years, when he came to Roanoke, where he was educated,
and removed to Pavilion in 1864. He married, March 8, 1855, Amanda
A., daughter of Marcus and Margaret (Hamilton) Mason. They have
four children, Fred P., Helen H. Pinney, Carrie M. Sampson, and Stella.

James E. Hazleton, a native of Haddam, Conn., was born June 29,
1829, and is a son of Sidney and Jemima (Hill) Hazleton, natives of
Haddam and Killingworth, respectively. Sidney, a stone quarryman,
came to Genesee County in 1846, settled on 100 acres where James
E. now resides, and farmed until his death in 1878. He had five children, viz.: Elizabeth Ensign, of Madison, Ohio; James E.; Sidney S.,
who was second lieutenant in the 4th Ind. Cav., and died at Paint Rock,
Ala.; Frances J. Field; and S. Albert, who served as town clerk. Sidney's father was Simon Hazleton, of Connecticut, also a quarryman and
farmer. He married A. Jedidah Smith, and reared three children, Simon, James, and Sidney S. James was a lieutenant in the War of 1812.
Simon was a son of Capt. James, of Haddam, Conn., a Revolutionary
soldier whose brother Arnold was a captain in the same war. He reared
one son and two daughters. His father, James, was born in 1694, and
was a son of James, of Devonshire, Eng., who settled in Haddam in 1666.
James E. Hazleton was educated at Brainard Academy. He has lived
on the old homestead, and has planted every fruit tree in his orchard of 10
acres. He brought the first thoroughbred Jersey into his community,
in 1876, and also the first Berkshire swine. Mr. Hazleton married Sarah,
daughter of Abel W. Page, of Bethany, and has four children, Fred P.,
Flora E., Grace J., and Ruth. The family are Presbyterians. His
mother is related to Governor Hill's ancestors. Mr. Hazleton has one
of the finest pear orchards in Genesee County. He takes an active in-

terest in introducing new varieties of grains and grasses best calculated for this climate.

Charles J. Hill, born May 4, 1846, on the farm where he now resides, is a son of Charles and Julia A. (Wilcox) Hill, of Killingworth and Middletown, Conn. With his brother Albert he came here in 1819, and located on land bought by their father in 1808, which they improved. The father of Charles J. was a captain of militia. He taught school winters, by which he earned money to pay for clearing land. He died in 1874, aged 74 years. He had two daughters, Hannah A. Husted and Catherine M. Seaver. His father, Benjamin Hill, of Killingworth, born in April, 1765, was a physician of 40 years practice, and married Jemima Stannard. They reared five sons and one daughter, came to Genesee County in 1808, and bought 450 acres of land, and in 1828 located on 160 acres one mile north of where Charles J. now lives, called Hill's Corners. He died in 1849. He was a son of James Hill, who married Hannah Nettleton, by whom he had 12 children, one of whom was Selah, grandfather of Gov. Hill. Charles J. Hill was educated at Le Roy and Valparaiso, Ind., and married, in February, 1887, Jennie W., daughter of William Russell, of Minnesota.

James A. Hamilton, born April 12, 1849, in Pavilion, is a son of William and Margaret (McClause) Hamilton. William Hamilton was born April 12, 1811, in Glasgow, Scotland, came to the United States in 1833, and located first in Fairfield County, Conn., where he remained two years, when he came to Oneida County, N. Y. He also lived two years in New York city. In 1839 he returned to Scotland, where he was married June 2, 1843, and in 1844 came again to the United States and settled in Pavilion, where he engaged in farming. He died in January, 1890. His wife was born in Stirling County, Scotland. They had six children: Mrs. Margaret McSlay (deceased), James A., Elizabeth (deceased), William M., Christina (deceased), and John. William was a son of James and Margaret (Shanks) Hamilton, of Scotland. James A. Hamilton received his education in the common schools and Franklinville Academy. At the age of 18 he went to Rock County, Wis., where he worked by the month four and one-half years, when he leased a farm. In 1884 he returned to Pavilion and purchased 100 acres two miles east of the village. In 1888 he moved to Le Roy, and November 1, 1889, took charge of the Pavilion Hotel. He married Jennie Traynor, who was born in Scotland, and who was a daughter of John and Barbara (McKethan) Traynor, who were born in North Ireland, near Belfast. They moved to Renfrew, Scotland, and had two children, Peter and Jennie. After his death the widow, about 1868, came to the United States and settled in Rock County, Wis. Mr. and Mrs. Hamilton have three children, William J., Mary E., and Maggie May. They are members of the Presbyterian Church.

Rev. David C. Herrell was born in Anderson County, East Tenn., November 1, 1847, a son of John and Sarah (Davis) Herrell, and was reared on a farm. At the age of 19 he entered Oak Grove Academy, which he attended for two years, when he went to Iowa, where he began teaching He entered the Baptist Union Theological Seminary at Chicago in 1871, graduating in the class of 1876. While here he also took instructions at the University of Chicago. His first charge was at Union City, Mich., where he remained for six years, when he took a charge at Hermitage. In 1885 he became pastor of the Baptist Church at Pavilion. He was married, October 25, 1876, to Lois A., daughter of Timothy Botsford, of Medina, and they have one son, George N. Mr. Herrell is a plain, unassuming man, possessing that hospitality and sociability so common with Southern people. His parents, who were born and raised on a farm in East Tennessee, reared nine sons and three daughters, as follows: Rev. Azariah, Riley, Warren, of Missouri, Rufus, John, Delany, Nancy, Frances, Malsfield, William, George, of Iowa, and David C., the latter being the youngest of the family. Four of the older brothers served in the Union army. 'His parents died about 1872 and 1869, respectively. His grandfather, John Herrell, was born in Scotland, came to America in colonial days, and was an officer on Gen. Washington's staff. He first settled in North Carolina, but died in Tennessee.

Thomas Jeary, of Tunstead. County Norfolk, Eng., was born July 9, 1832, a son of William and Charlotte (Coman) Jeary. He came to this country in June, 1854, and worked for Perry Randall, of Stafford, for five years. He was self-educated, and purchased a farm, where he now resides, in 1876. He married, first, in 1862, Aneliza, daughter of Peter Harder, of Monroe County. They have two children, Jessie and Georgia. His second wife was Mrs. Abbey S. Cox, widow of Edward Cox, whom he married in January, 1882. She was a daughter of Ephraim and Fidelia (Wood) Mick, of Carthage, N. Y. Ephraim was a son of Michael Mick, a native of New Jersey, and whose father came from Holland. The father of Thomas Jeary came to the United States in 1857, locating in Stafford. He reared eight children, viz.: Mary Ann Tollman, of England, Thomas, who died in the army, George, Frank, Margaret Hunt, of Illinois, Elijah, Fred C., and Ellen Newcomb. Mr. Jeary has been quite successful in life. He and his wife are members of the Presbyterian Church.

James L. Lawson, who resides one mile east of Pavilion village, was born March 7, 1827, eight miles north of Batavia, and is a son of Benjamin F. and Mary (Griffin) Lawson, respectively from Sullivan and Cayuga counties. Benjamin F., with his parents, came to Alexander in 1814. When of age he moved to Elba, thence to Wheatland, N. Y., and served as overseer of the poor for many years. He reared three children, viz.: James L., Daniel G., and Mrs. Ann Selfridge, of West Superior, Wis. John W., grandfather of James L., was twice married. His second wife was Hannah Timlow, by whom he had four sons and two daughters. James L. Lawson married, January 29, 1852, Jane O., daughter of Rufus Smead, a brickmaker. He has had eight children : Lora, deceased, Frank F., Charles S., Henry M., of Syracuse, Lewis J., Rufus, Eliza, and

John F. John F. Lawson, of Pavilion village, was born in Middlebury, in February, 1857, received an academic education at Le Roy, and at the age of 21 began work on a farm by the month. The past four years he has followed the carpenter and joiner trade. He married, March 26, 1884, Florence, daughter of John Kember, of Henrietta, N. Y. They are members of the Methodist Episcopal Church.

William Marsh was a soldier of the Revolutionary war. Andrew J. Marsh, his father, was born in Castile, Wyoming County, March 28, 1829, was educated in the public schools, and learned the carriagemaking trade. January 20, 1867, he married Amelia B. Whitney, of Pavilion, and they have had three children: Fred H., Charles A., and Glen A., of whom the last two named are deceased. Fred H. Marsh, born December 12, 1867, received a common school and academic education, and is now conducting a meat market on West Main street, Pavilion, with his father. December 31, 1889, he married Carrie E. McNaughton, of Caledonia, Livingston County.

Dugald R. McCall, born December 15, 1832, in York, N. Y., is a son of John R. and Elizabeth (McPherson) McCall, who died in August. 1862, aged 70 years, being killed by a runaway. John R. was born in Argyle, Scotland, and when three years old came with his parents to Johnstown, N. Y. In 1806 they came to York, and took up 100 acres of land, to which John R. afterwards added 100 acres more. Daniel, father of John R., served in the War of 1812. John R. reared seven children, viz.: Dugald R., Duncan R., of Nebraska, Daniel R., Elizabeth Spratt, Christina. Gray, Augusa, of Sweden, N. Y., and Alexander. Mrs. J. R. McCall still survives her husband. She was born in 1812, and was a daughter of Duncan McPherson, of Scotland. Dugald R. McCall received a common school education, and at the age of 22 years began business for himself. He married, in January, 1875, Marion, daughter of William Phillips, of Michigan, who was a soldier during the late war. Mr. McCall located in 1869 where he now resides. His children are Christie, Finley, Mary, John, Jane A., and Emeline. They are members of the United Presbyterian Church. His father went to Scotland in 1851, and brought back 20 of his relatives, paying their passage, in order to settle them in his neighborhood.

George Murray, son of George and Jane (Robb) Murray, was born August 18, 1828, five miles south of where he now resides. He received a common school education, and has lived on the farm he now occupies since 1832. His parents were born in Schenectady County, and came to Genesee County in April, 1825. About 1832 they settled where George now resides. George, Sr., reared two sons and four daughters, viz.: William G., Isabella, Jeanette, Helen, Margaret, and George. He died in 1872, aged 77, and his wife in 1867. He was a son of Alexander Murray, who was born in Wigtonshire, Scotland, and came to the United States when but 12 years of age. He participated in the Revolutionary war, and settled in the eastern past of this State. His wife was Ellen Duguid,

and they reared five sons and three daughters.   He went West with a
daughter and died there.   George Murray, Jr., married, November 6,
1855, Emily, daughter of John and Laney (Van Vleet) Whiteman, natives
of Dutchess and Schenectady counties, respectively.   They have one
son, Charles H.   John Whiteman came from Oneida County to Genesee
County about 1834, and settled in Pavilion.   He was a son of Zachariah
Whiteman, of Dutchess County.   .

Daniel W. Matteson, a native of Vermont, came to Perry in 1813, at
the age of 17, and engaged in farming.   He married, first, Hannah
Waldo, of Vermont, and second, Sarah T., daughter of Levi and Lorinda
(Church) McWethy, also of Vermont, who came here in 1809, and purchased 160 acres one mile southeast of Pavilion, where he resided until
his death in 1812   Mr. Matteson's children were Lyman C., Mary, Harrison, L. Van Rensselaer, Sanders, Sarah, and Jane.   The family were
Baptists.   He served in the War of 1812.   In those days they went to
mill at Perry, and sold their wheat in Rochester.   They came from Onondaga County, where he lived one year, with an ox-team.

Rev. Thomas B. Milde was born in Brooklyn, N. Y., June 8, 1857, a
son of Edward and Ann (O'Reilly) Milde, natives of Jena, Germany,
and County Cavan, Ireland, respectively.   Edward came to the United
States when a young man, about 1850 or 1855, and reared four sons and
two daughters.   Rev. Thomas B. was educated at St. Francis Xaviers's
College, Brooklyn, remaining there nine years from 1872, and was four
years at the Seminary of Our Lady of Angels, Niagara Falls.   He was
ordained May 1, 1885, and sent to Hornellsville.   In June, 1887, he
came to Pavilion and took charge of the Catholic Church here, which,
though small in numbers, is gradually increasing in membership.

Clark Nellis, born March 15, 1851, is a son of John J. and Elizabeth
(Fox) Nellis, both of Montgomery County.   John J. was a farmer,
served as assessor for 40 years, and held other offices.   He reared a
family of five sons and three daughters.   His father was John I. Nellis,
Jr., a soldier of 1812, who married Anna Christman, of Montgomery
County.   They had one son and three daughters.   His father was John
L., who reared four sons and three daughters, and served as captain
in the war of the Revolution.   The father of John L. was Lewis Nellis,
who came from Germany.   The mother of Clark Nellis was a daughter
of John C. and Mary (Myers) Fox.   John C. Fox, who served in the
War of 1812, was a son of Christopher and Margaret (Nellis) Fox.   Chris-
topher was a soldier in the Revolution, and reared four sons.   Clark
Nellis received a common school education.   He married, first, in January, 1876, Jeanette England, and second, Elizabeth, daughter of Henry
Saltsman.   She has one child by her first husband.

J. Quincy D. Page was born April 10, 1859, one mile north of Pavilion.
He was reared in the family of his grandfather (Doty), and received a
common and Normal school education.   At the age of 20 he began the
coopering business, which he has since followed, making from 20,000 to

30,000 barrels per year. He married, March 22, 1887, May, daughter of Shubael Walker, and they have one child, Olive A. The father of Mr. Page was John R., of Bethany, who married Mary Doty, of Middlebury. J. Quincy D. was their only child. He was well educated and taught school until 50 years of age. His wife died in 1863, and he married, second, Mary Kellogg, by whom he had one son, Frank. After the war he moved to Douglass County, Ill., where he accumulated a good property. The grandfather of J. Q. D. Page was John Page, who was one of the earliest settlers in Bethany. He reared five sons and two daughters.

Gideon V. Phelps, born July 20, 1826, has always lived at his present location. He was educated at the public schools, taught school one term, and married Rachel, daughter of Samuel Dodge, of Erie County, May 7, 1851, and they have three children : Ella M., who married Dr. Denton Rugers, of Wyoming County; Emma J., who married Fred Hawks, of Perry; and Clinton G., who married, in November, 1884, Jennie F., daughter of Homer Cook, by whom he has one child, Mabel R. The parents of Gideon V. were Elijah and Anna (Elliott) Phelps. Elijah was a native of Columbia County, and his wife of Otsego County. They settled here October 1, 1811, on 50 acres, which was subsequently increased to 143 acres before his death, in 1881, at the age of 96. He served in the War of 1812, and reared four sons and two daughters. Jonah Phelps, the grandfather of Gideon V., and a native of Hebron, Conn., was born October 11, 1744, and married Sarah Mack. They had eight sons and five daughters. Jonah, son of Noah, was born at Hebron in January, 1694, and married Anna Dyer in 1719, by whom he had six children. Noah, who moved to Hebron in 1701, and who was a son of Timothy, was born in November, 1663, and married Martha Crow in 1686. They had five children. He was a son of Timothy, who was born in 1639, married Mary Griswold in 1661, and had 12 children. Timothy Phelps was a son of William, from Exeter, England, who came to Dorchester, Mass., in 1630.

Abert S. Rogers, M. D., a prominent physician and surgeon of Genesee County, was born in Pavilion, April 6, 1846 He was reared on a farm, and received a common school and academic education. At the age of 17 he left home and spent a few years in New York city, Jersey city, and on Staten Island, and at the age of 19 began the study of medicine with Dr. Warren Fay, of Pavilion. In 1865 he entered the College of Physicians and Surgeons of New York city, graduating therefrom in 1867, and immediately locating in Buffalo, where he sucessfully practiced his profession for five years. He spent one year in Cleveland, Ohio, and has since resided in Pavilion, where he has an extensive practice. The Doctor is a member of the I O. O. F. He married Mary, daughter of J. G. Coats, of Cleveland, by whom he has two children, George C. and Mary N. The father of Dr. A. S. was Matthey Rogers, who was born in Pavilion, and who was twice married, first to Phœbe Almy, of Pavilion, who bore him two children, Frederick and Abert S. His second wife was Elizabeth Simmons, of Connecticut, by whom he had three daughters. He was a son of Elijah and Hannah (Beckwith) Rogers, who were born in Lyme, New London County, Conn. Elijah was a soldier in the War of 1812, and came to Pavilion in 1811, making the trip on foot with a knapsack on his back. He took up 100 acres of land west of Pavilion Center, and in 1812, with a yoke of oxen and one horse, he moved his family here. He improved and added to his farm until he finally owned 300 acres. His father, Matthey, died in Connecticut, and his mother in Genesee County. He reared four children, William E., Mehitable, Josiah B., and Matthey.

Abram Reese was born in Galway, Saratoga County N. Y., May 19, 1834, and soon after his birth his parents moved to the town of Providence. At the age of 10 he left home and hired out to work by the month. In March, 1857, he came to Le Roy, where he remained two years, when he went to Bethany and worked in the county poor-house for two years, when he came to Pavilion, where he worked for Denly Lewis six years for a share of the crops. He then spent two years in Canada in the lumber business, and returned to Pavilion and purchased a farm of 80 acres. In 1871 he located on the farm where he now resides, and purchased the farm known as the James Sprague place in 1875. He has served nine years as supervisor, three years as county superintendent of the poor, and is now overseer of the town. He married Fannie, daughter of Henry Wright, of Ballston Spa, Saratoga County, and they had one child, Wright H. Mr. Reese is a great friend to the poor. He is a son of Martin and Elizabeth (Murray) Reese, of Galway, N. Y., who reared six sons and three daughters. Martin was a son of Daliel Reese, who was born in Schenectady, and reared five sons and two daughters. He was of Dutch parentage. Mr. Reese's grandfather, Peter Murray, was born in Schenectady, of German parents, and was a soldier of the Revolution.

Wright H. Reese, son of Abram and Fannie (Wright) Reese, was born in Galway, Saratoga County, N. Y., August 31, 1867, was reared on a farm, received his education in the common schools and Le Roy Academy, and graduated from Rochester Business University in 1886. Afterwards he spent a year on the farm, and in September, 1887, entered the store of R. O. Holden & Son, of Batavia, as salesman. In November, 1888, he purchased the store of W. I. Chase, of Pavilion, and began business for himself. His is said to be the oldest stand in the village. Mr. Reese is an active, energetic business man, has a neat and well filled store, and takes an active interest in political affairs. January 24, 1889, he married Anna, daughter of Addison and Elizabeth (Lampman) Christman, of Pavilion.

Nicholas J. Rosenburg was born January 27, 1818, in Rhinebeck, Dutchess County. His parents were John and Elizabeth (Van Dewalker) Rosenburg, who moved to Cortland County, and thence to Sullivan

County. The father died aged 72 years. His father (John) came from Holland, and the mother was of Holland Dutch origin. Mr. Rosenburg received a fair education, and married, in October, 1847, Jane S., daughter of Levi McWethy. They have had children as follows : James L. (deceased), Lorena, Elizabeth, Frank E., Jennie, Etta, and Ellen. F. E. Rosenburg came to Pavilion in 1849, located east of the village, and two years later located where he now resides, in one of the first houses built in the village. In September, 1862, he enlisted in Co. I, 151st N. Y. Vols., and participated in the battles of the Wilderness, Cold Harbor, and Petersburg. He was in the last charge in Ewell's corps the day before the surrender of Lee. Mr Rosenburg was discharged June 26, 1865. He is a member of the G. A. R. He owns a fine farm of 51 acres east of the village.

William C. Smead, born April 18, 1853, where he now resides, is a son of William and Caroline L. (Sprague) Smead, natives of Scipio, Cayuga County, and Livingston County, respectively. William came to Pavilion with his parents in 1814, and in time became one of the most enterprising and substantial farmers in the town. His father was Jedediah L. Smead, a native of Vermont, who married Caroline Howe, by whom he had seven children, viz.: Mehitable. Harvey, William C., Morgan J., Selah, Mosley, and Harman B. Caroline L. Smead was a daughter of James Sprague, who was born in Willimantic, Conn., and when but 12 years of age settled in Schoharie County, N. Y. He married Mary Wilkins, and reared one son and four daughters. James was a son of Daniel Sprague, of Connecticut. William C. Smead received his education in the common schools and Le Roy Academic Institute. At the age of 21 he began his career as a farmer, in which business he has since been actively and successfully engaged. In February, 1880, he married Elizabeth, daughter of James Gayton, of Stafford. Their children are Mary Lucy, Morgan J., and Gayton.

William E. Stanley was born November 14, 1825, in Cazenovia, N. Y., a son of Lewis and Betsey (Smith) Stanley. Lewis was born in Hartford, Conn., November 6, 1780, and died in 1857. Mrs Betsey was the mother of 13 children, of whom seven were sons, two of whom were ministers of the Methodist Episcopal Church, one a physician, one an attorney, one a teacher, and two were farmers. The second wife of Lewis Stanley was Maria Dunbar, by whom he had five children, one of whom was a merchant, and one at the head of a collection agency in St. Louis. Lewis Stanley was a son of James, who was born near Hartford, Conn., and who was a captain in the Revolutionary war seven years. He married Miss Gridley, and reared three sons and two daughters. The Stanley family came from England 200 years ago and settled at Hartford. William E. was reared in his native town, was educated at the common schools and the seminary, and taught school two terms. He married, January 13, 1853, Sarah E., daughter of James and Lucy (Lamb) Jackson, and they have had three children, of whom one daugh-

39

ter, Cora A. Osborn, is living. They belong to the Methodist Episcopal Church. He located where he now resides in 1864. His mother was á daughter of Peter Smith, who served as a captain seven years in the Revolution. They were of Dutch ancestry and had 10 children.

Dr. William B. Sprague, son of Dr. William M. and Cynthia (Bishop) Sprague, was born April 6, 1836, in Covington (now Pavilion). He was educated in his native town and at Temple Hill Academy, Geneseo. In 1854 he began to study medicine with his father, teaching school in winter. In 1855 he went to Buffalo and entered the office of the late Dr. Frank H. Hamilton, where he remained until he graduated in 1857, from the Buffalo Medical College. After his graduation he was resident physician at St. Mary's Hospital for one year. In 1858, his health failing, he moved to Oneida County, N. Y., where he practiced three years, when he came to York, Livingston County, where he remained until 1867, when, upon his father's death, he returned to Pavilion and succeeded him in practice. He spent the winter of 1884–85 in Europe in company with a patient, whom he left in Ireland. In the fall of 1887 he was appointed surgeon on the steamship *Rotterdam*, and in the following spring returned home. He is a member of the New York State Medical Association of Central New York, has been president of the Genesee County Medical Society since 1885, and has served as railroad commissioner six years. Having an excellent literary taste he has contributed valuable articles to the press and to medical journals. The mother of Dr. Sprague lives on the old homestead, aged 90 years.

Samuel E. Stevens, born December 4, 1848, in England, is a son of Henry and Mary (Harper) Stevens, who came to the United States in 1853, and located in Stafford. At the age of nine years Samuel E. left home, educated himself, and earned his own living. At the age of 23 he learned the trade of broommaking. He farmed for two years, and then engaged in the cooperage business for nine years at Pavilion, when he came to Pavilion Center, where he has since followed his trade and farming. May 19, 1879, he married Vastia V., daughter of John L. Foster, of Three Rivers, Mich. They have one child, and are members of the Baptist Church.

Noah Starr, a native of Danbury, Conn., and a volunteer of the War of 1812, served at Fort George, and came to Pavilion in 1818, settling on a farm of 200 acres. He reared 13 children. In 1856 he and 10 sons went to the polls and voted. In 1825 he joined the Masons, and at the time of his death, in 1865, was an active member of Olive Branch Lodge. He died aged 83 years. His son Jasper is the only member of the family living in this county.

Hon. Elbert Townsend, a native of Pavilion, was a son of Ashley Townsend, an inventor, of Vermont, and was born in 1842. He married Emily Olmsted in 1861. He was an extensive breeder of fine sheep and blooded cattle and horses, and represented his county in the legislature in 1873–74. Mr. Townsend died in Pavilion, April 21, 1890.

Elijah M. Tillotson was born June 11, 1825, on the farm where he now and has always resided. He received a good common school education, takes an active interest in political affairs, and has served as supervisor and railroad commissioner. His parents, Capt. Chauncey and Emily S. (Miller) Tillotson, were born in Farmington and Hartford, Conn., respectively. In 1817 Capt. Chauncey Tillotson went to Ohio, and on his return to Connecticut he stoped in Pavilion, and in February, 1818, took up 126 acres where Elijah M. now resides. At his death he possessed 250 acres. In early life he was a dealer in clocks, and was the first to introduce wooden clocks in this part of the country. He served in the War of 1812, and died where he located, November 29, 1873' aged 80 years. His widow, who was born in August, 1798, is still living on the old homestead with a grandson. They reared three children, Harriet Halbert, of Grand Ledge, Mich., Chauncey E., and Elijah M. He was a son of Elias Tillotson, of Connecticut, a Revolutionary soldier, who married Betsey Hosford, and had five sons and five daughters.. Three of his sons, Giles, Shubael, and Romanta, settled in Louisiana, where they became extensive and wealthy planters. Chauncey and three of his sisters settled in Genesee County, one in Scottsville, and two in Wyoming County. The father of Elias was supposed to be Elijah Tillotson, who came from England and settled in Connecticut. Elijah M. Tillotson married Mahala, daughter of William and Sallie (Bowen) Shumway, who were natives respectively of Connecticut and Rhode Island, and who came from Saratoga County to Genesee County about 1821. They had two sons and five daughters. William was a son of William Shumway, who came from France, settled in Connecticut, married Sally Turttelot, and had one son and eight daughters. Mr. and Mrs. Tillotson reared four children, Harriet A. McWethy, Frank A., George W., and Ettie M. Higgins.

Chauncey E. Tillotson, son of Chauncey and Emily S. (Miller) Tillotson, was born June 22, 1822, east of Pavilion Center. He received a good English education, and at the age of 21 began business for himself. March 13, 1844, he married Jennette L., daughter of Jason W. Duguid, and they had two children, Florence A., Stanard and Fred D. They are prominent members of the Universalist Church. Mr. Tillotson has taken an active interest in the affairs of his town, and has filled several responsible positions. He served as justice nine years. He is highly respected by all who know him.

James Tompkins was born August 3, 1781, in Cayuga County. His wife, Clarissa, daughter of Joel and Rosanna (Wagner) Stoddard, was born January 29, 1789, in the same place. They came to Genesee County in 1815, and settled on 100 acres one mile north of Pavilion. He served in the War of 1812, and died September 9, 1863, and his wife January 7, 1879. Their children were William, Rosanna, Warren, Mosely, Almond, and Cyrus. The latter was born November 29, 1818, where his son Albert C. now lives, and died August 24, 1875. He married Harriet, daughter of Joshua Shumway, a prominent citizen, who came in 1810 and settled on an adjoining farm. She died January 27, 1889. They had three sons, William H., Henry H., and Albert C. William H. Tompkins, born May 25, 1843, was educated in the district schools and at the academy. He has served as justice of the peace and highway commissioner six years, being elected in 1883. Mr. Tompkins was a captain of the State Guard in 1864. He married, April 6, 1865, Clara J., daughter of Nicholas Chilson, of Covington, N. Y., and they have one child, Daisy M.

Henry H. Tompkins, born March 2, 1845, one mile north of Pavilion, was reared upon a farm, received his education at Middlebury and Lima academies, and at the age of 20 years went to Le Roy as clerk in a clothing and shoe store. He was two years in a store in Toledo. Returning to his native town he acted as agent for the Watertown Fire Insurance Co. for 12 years. He went to Texas for a short time, and returned, and has since followed the mercantile business and buying wool and produce. December 1, 1868, he married Ophelia B., daughter of Gardner Davis, of Wyoming, and they have three children, Ella G., Harriet L., and Claude C. He is active in politics and has served as constable for 20 years.

George R. Van Buren, who was born in Trenton, Oneida County, N. Y., January 11, 1830, came with his parents to Pavilion and settled where he now resides. He received a common school education, and February 28, 1853, married Eliza Ann West. They had three children, Sabrina Ida, Hattie A., and Rumayne Martin. George R. was a son of Martin and Sabrina (Burlingame) Van Buren, who were born in Easton, Washington County, N. Y., July 12, 1805, and Trenton, Oneida County, respectively. Martin Van Buren came to Oneida County with his parents in 1808, and thence to Livingston County, where he lived two or three years, when he returned to Oneida Springs. In 1838 he settled where George R. now resides, on 77 acres. He had 116 acres at the time of his death, April 22, 1849. G. R. Van Buren was his only child. Martin served as an officer in the militia. He was a son of Bernard Van Buren, who was born in Holland, December 1, 1780, and shortly after was brought to the United States by his parents, who settled near Kinderhook Later they located in Washington County. He was a farmer, and a cousin of Martin Van Buren. He married Betsey Wood, who was born January 14, 1781, in New Bedford, Mass. They had 13 children, viz.: Martin, William, Cheney G., Bernard, Jr., Alexander H., Edward, Ocenus, James, Abner, Pliny, Lorany, Betsey Ann, and Lydia. Bernard Van Buren died in 1853, and his wife in April, 1871. The wife of George R. is a daughter of Francis and Phebe (Jewell) West, natives of Montgomery and Milton, N. Y., respectively. At an early day they came to Middlebury, Wyoming County. Francis West was a son of Francis, a brother of Nathaniel West, a distinguished divine. The mother of Francis and Nathaniel West was Sarah, daughter of David

Crandall, who came from Manchester, England. Phebe (Jewell) West was a daughter of Benjamin Jewell, who came from Germany and settled in Eastern New York. His wife was a Miss Ellis.

Grove D. Whitney was born May 8, 1842, in the village of Pavilion, a son of Alvin and Betsey (Cook) Whitney, who were born in Granville, Washington County, in September, 1802, and Vernon, Oneida County, in June, 1812, respectively. Alvin Whitney came to Pavilion in 1823, where he worked at the carpenters' trade and teaching school for the first three winters, after which he taught select school for a number of terms. In 1853 he purchased and located on a farm one mile west of the village, where he resided until his death, in February, 1883. His wife is still living. He had born to him 11 children, two sons and seven daughters of whom attained maturity, the sons being Homer and Grove D. Alvin was a son of James Whitney, who, in 1813, located and cleared a farm where the village of Mexico, Oswego County, now stands. He married Betsey Law, and they had four sons and two daughters. He died early in life, and his widow remarried. The Whitneys are of Welsh stock. They came from Connecticut to Yew York. Grove D. received a common school education, and has taught four terms of school. July 29, 1863, he enlisted in Co. A, 140th N. Y. Regt., joining it at Culpepper Court House, Va., and participated in the battles of Mine Run, Wilderness, Laurel Hill, Spottsylvania Court House, North Anna River, and Cold Harbor. At the latter battle he was wounded in the right side, and still carries the ball. He spent 13 months in the hospital at Alexandria, and was discharged from Sickel Barracks Hospital, July 3, 1865. After his return home he began the study of medicine, taking a course of lectures during the winter of 1865–66, but on account of poor health he was compelled to abandon the studies. He then taught a few terms of school, and later entered a store as clerk, but was compelled to leave for out-door exercise, and took up painting and paper hanging. He is a member of the F. & A. M., has served three terms as town collector, and two years as school trustee. December 23, 1867, he married Rebecca B., daughter of Luther Whitney, of Hadley, Mich. They have had five children, Mary E., George C., Effie A. (deceased), Lutine D., and Bessie A. The family are members of the Methodist Episcopal Church.

Thomas J. Wilson, born in Donegal County, Ireland, August 1, 1842, is a son of Thomas and Elizabeth (Gartly) Wilson, of the same county, who came to County Durham, Canada, in 1843, where he was engaged in farming until 1865, when they came to the United States, settling in Pavilion. Thomas is still living, and has reared five sons and four daughters. His sons are Thomas J.; William G., an M. E. minister in Manitoba; Samuel J., of Orleans County; Robert D., of Medina; and Charles A., of St. Paul. The grandfather of Thomas J. was James Wilson, of Ireland, who married Margaret Wilson, an English lady, and had two sons and four daughters. The old homestead in Ireland has been in the family name since the war of William III. Thomas J. Wilson received a common English education. In 1864 he came to the United States, settling at Pavilion, and in January, 1865, enlisted in Co. I, 116th N. Y. Regt., and in June of the same year was transferred to the 90th Regt. He was discharged in 1866. After his return home he worked at the carpenters' trade for two years, and then spent two years in Canada, engaged in shoemaking. He came to Spencerport, N. Y., where he remained eight years, when he removed to Pavilion, where, in 1883, he engaged in general merchandising, in which business he has since continued. Mr. Wilson is strictly honorable in all his dealings, and has the confidence and esteem of his townsmen. In October, 1869, he married Elizabeth, daughter of James Lyon, of Canada, and they have had nine children, viz.: Charles W., Emma J., Thomas A., Fred L., Elizabeth L., Katie M., Frances N., Rosco C., and Florence L. Mr. and Mrs. Wilson are consistent members of the Methodist Episcopal Church, and he is a member of the I. O. O. F.

Ezra Walker, born July 4, 1824, near Asbury Church, is a son of Loomis and Hannah (Bow) Walker, who were born in Berkshire County, Mass., and Middletown, Conn., respectively. Loomis Walker came to Genesee County with his parents. He served in the War of 1812, was an industrious, hard working man, and improved a farm of 90 acres. He and his wife were active and consistent members of the M. E. Church, to which they were cheerful and liberal givers. He died where his son Ezra now resides. He had a family of two sons and three daughters, Ezra being the only one who lived to rear a family. Loomis was a son of Isaac Walker, who was born in Massachusetts, and who served in the Revolutionary war seven years. He had eight children, all of whom were born in Massachusetts. In 1810 he came with his family to Genesee County, locating south of where Asbury Church now stands. His first purchase was 60 acres east of Asbury Church, in 1814, where he resided at the time of his death. He and his family are buried in the same graveyard at Asbury. He had but two children who reared families, a son and a daughter. Ezra received a common school education, his first teacher being Rebecca Spring. Mr. Walker has resided on the old homestead all his life. He married Rebecca, daughter of Amos and Abigail (Brown) Wells, all of whom came from Colchester, New London County, Conn. He has two children, Charles L. and Jay.

John Webb was born May 11, 1795, in Vermont, and came to Western New York, when a young man. He married Nancy Gillett, of Detroit, Mich., in 1816, and they located in West Bloomfield, Ontario County. They had eight children, of whom Ira and Frances are deceased, and six are living, viz.: Mary, John, Jane, Emma, George, and Homer B. Mary married three times, first, Morgan Filkins, of Pavilion, by whom she had four sons, Daniel J., George B., Frank L , and Charles M. Mr. Filkins died September 11, 1855, and she married, second, in 1863, Robert Butterfield, of Alden, N. Y. They had one son, William R., born June 3, 1864.. Mr. Butterfield died in August, 1866. January 27,

1874, she married, third, William Hollenbeck. She now resides on road 4, in Pavilion, on the farm she owns, and where she has lived for 40 years.

Frederick A. Webb, son of Samuel C. and Elizabeth M. (Hickox) Webb, was born August 10, 1849, in the house where he now resides. He received a common school education, and at the age of 14 began the trade of painter, working summers and attending school winters. For two years he traveled for Schuyler & Co's nursery. In 1873 he went to Ohio, where he remained three years. He lived in Corfu four years, in Cortland one year, where he was connected with the Cortland Wagon Co., four years at Whitney's Point, and in 1887 came to Pavilion, where he has since resided. He is a member of the I. O. O. F. Mr. Webb married, March 3, 1875, Florence, daughter of John C. Augier, of Mentor, O., and they have one son, Percy. Samuel C. Webb was born in Lunenburgh, Essex County, Vt., January 17, 1816, and came to West Bloomfield in 1834, where he workedat his trade (painter) until 1846, when he came to Pavilion, where he has since resided. His wife was born in Salem, O. They have had six children, four of whom grew to maturity, viz.: Walestien C. (deceased), F. A., Josephine E , who died in Battle Creek, Mich., and Estina S., wife of Joseph Maddock, of Wellsville, N. Y , Mr. Webb has served as constable and collector. He is a son of Samuel and Hannah (Carleton) Webb, of Vermont, who were farmers, and who had four sons and three daughters, the sons being Alfred, who died at the age of 14; Samuel C., of Mount Sterling, Ill.; Philo, who died in Vermont; and Bradford, of Cedar Rapids, Ia. Samuel Webb died at Mount Morris, Ill., and his wife at St. Clair, Mich. He was a son of Samuel Webb, who was a Revolutionary soldier, and whose wife was Chloe Chandler. They had seven sons.

John Ward was born September 15, 1809, in Marlborough, N. H., and is a son of Levi and Nancy (Whitney) Ward, both of the same county. His parents came to this county in 1818, settled on a farm of 100 acres, which he improved, and subsequently added 75 acres more, where John now resides. Levi had six children, Emery, Sarah Moore, Mary Coe, Daniel, Nancy Moore, and John. The Wards are of English origin. John Ward received a common school education, and married, March 29, 1835, Mercy, daughter of Cyril Shumway, who was one of the first settlers, about 1815. They had eight children, viz.: Hannah Hutchinson, Nancy Duguid, George, Henry, Elizabeth, Frank, Emma, and William S.

George Wilson, who died in September, 1882, was born in Radford, Nottinghamshire, Eng , February 7, 1824. He was a son of Richard Wilson, who had five sons and two daughters. Mr. Wilson and his brother James came to the United States in 1849, locating at Morgansville. They were millers. George Wilson moved to Roanoke, and thence to Rochester, where he was for 17 years working at his trade. In 1882 he located on Burleigh Hill and engaged in farming. He married Harriet A., daughter of Luther Brown, who was born in Concord, Mass., in 1803.

He came to Le Roy with his parents in 1812, married Parmelia Liely, and had three sons and five daughters.   Mr. Brown was a machinist and cooper by trade.   Mr. Wilson had two children, Izora A., who lives on the homestead, and Henry D., who lives in La Crosse, Wis.

PEMBROKE.

PEMBROKE was formed from Batavia, June 8, 1812.   It is the central town on the west border of the county, and is bounded on the north by Alabama, east by Batavia, south by Darien, and west by Erie County.   Its surface is gently undulating.   The principal streams are the Tonawanda and Murder creeks.   The former flows through the northeast corner, and the latter through the south and southwest part.   The soil is a sandy and gravelly loam.   The Tonawanda Indian Reservation occupies a portion of the north part of the town.

The names of nearly all of the early settlers are given in the sketch of Darien, to which we call the attention of our readers.   The first settlement was made by David Goss in 1804, who located where Mr. Ellinwood now resides, and erected a dwelling which he used for a tavern. Samuel Carr settled at Richville in 1808, and also kept a tavern.   He built the first grist and saw-mills.   John Barr in 1812 kept a store at the same place.   John Long and his father, Dr. David, settled in 1808, at what is now Corfu, and from their settlement the place was for a time called Long's Corners.   John Murray was an early inn-keeper, in 1811. The oldest house in Corfu is that erected by Jonas Kinne, who came in 1812 and soon built a roomy two-story house, and opened it to the public as "Kinne tavern."   He died in 1822, and his widow kept it many years after.   It was headquarters for town meetings, elections, and trainings.   The first school teacher was Anna Horton, in 1811.   The first marriage was that of Ansel Hastings and Polly Long, in 1812.

Among the persons who were former residents of Pembroke may be mentioned Calvin Cummings, who came to Bushville in 1816.   His son John was a shoemaker.   George Dennison was a farmer and cooper.   In 1847 he had in his employ 25 hands.   In 1868 he bought a mill and built another shop, doing an extensive business.   Reuben Millett came about 1827, located at East Pembroke, conducted a wool-carding and cloth dressing-mill, and soon was proprietor of the hotel that was burned in 1854.   He was station agent from 1853 until his death in 1883. Burnham Barber came in 1829, and lived here about 40 years.   He was a carpenter, millwright, and farmer.

The villages in the town are Corfu, Indian Falls, Richville, East Pembroke, and Mogadore, or North Pembroke.

CORFU (p. o.) was incorporated May 1, 1868. The first board of trustees were H. P. Porter, president, Daniel Carter, R. W. Kinne, E. W. Croft, and George Newell. A. Billington was the first clerk, and N. Read, treasurer. The present officers are Dwight Dimock, president, Ira S. Mann, William Crawford, M. Doyle, and Lester Webb. J. W. Safford is clerk, and A. J. Smith, treasurer. There are about 100 houses within the corporation, and a population of 450. The village sprang into existence by the building of the Central Railroad. Corfu contains many new modern built houses, and puts on an air of thrift not often seen in country villages. The main industry is the propagation of cut flowers for the Buffalo and Rochester markets, there being three large greenhouses doing an immense business in this line. One, that of T. A. & L. Webb, is devoted exclusively to carnations, of which they have nearly 10,000 plants, in two houses, 21 feet wide by 50 feet long, with a smaller house 18x50. E. M. Giddings and Mrs. Charles Tyrrell are also engaged in the business of propagating cut flowers.

George and Henry Porter, Seloy Kidder, and Alanson Fisher were early merchants. Among the physicians who have practiced in Corfu may be mentioned Dr. Rumsey, from Bethany, 30 years ago; Dr. Sullings and Dr. McPherson, who were here four years; Dr. Fuller, who went to Buffalo; Dr. Hinman, a pupil of Dr. Hutchins, of Batavia, who is now in Michigan; and Dr. Scott, who was here four years, and returned to Medina. The first minister in Pembroke was the Rev. Joshua Spencer, a Congregationalist, who organized the first church in the town in 1810, at Corfu, or Long's Corners.

The First Presbyterian Church of Pembroke was organized in 1817, by Rev. Hugh Wallis, who moved into town in 1816 with his family, and resided here for many years. He acted as general missionary on the Holland Purchase. In 1825 there were 25 members, and F. B. Reed acted as stated supply. The Rev. L. B. Sullivan came about the year 1828 In 1830 there were 42 members. In 1831 a wood building was erected, capable of seating 100 persons. In 1833 John Sherer was the minister in charge, when Rev. A. C. Page succeeded him, and the society consisted of 161 members. He had charge until 1842. S. C. Brown succeeded him in 1845, and in 1846 there were 114 members. Rev. D. Chichester was the next minister. Others followed, and the church is still prosperous. The present number of members is about 100, under the pastoral charge of Rev. John McK. Brayton. The present house will seat 300, and cost $4,000.

The First Methodist Protestant Church of Pembroke; located in Corfu, was organized in 1845, by Rev. A. C. Paine, M. D., with 15 members. In 1853 they built a brick edifice, which is still in use, and which was repaired and renovated in 1889 at a cost of $200. At present there are 60 members, and Rev. W. T. Edds is the pastor in charge. The original cost of the edifice was $3,000, but it now has a valuation of $4,000, and will seat about 175 persons. The members of the Sunday-school number about 80.

St. Luke's Protestant Episcopal Church of Corfu.—Services were begun in May, 1876, by the Rev. Jay Cooke, and an interest was developed such as warranted a church being erected, the corner-stone of which was laid June 14, 1880. There are now about 35 communicants, and Rev. A. A. Brockway is the pastor. The church cost $3,000, and will seat 125 persons. The members of St James's Church of Batavia first started a mission at this place.

All Souls' Union Church of Corfu was organized in July, 1881, by C. C. Richardson, with about 27 members, and he was its first pastor. The same year a building was erected at a cost of $4,000, which will seat 200 persons

In February, 1819, 20 persons, residents of Alexander and Pembroke, associated themselves as an organization to keep and maintain a public library. They met at the house of Eben North, and called the association the "Franklin Library." Perhaps as an indirect result of this movement the formation of the "Corfu Ladies' Library" may be due. Such a society was organized October 31, 1872, and has been in active operation since. The officers consist of a president, secretary, treasurer, and librarian. An admission fee of $1 is charged, with yearly dues of 60 cents, and by the aid of entertainments the funds of the society are augmented so as to keep up a new supply of books.

The D. W. Kinne Post, No 635, G. A. R., was organized September 10, 1888, and was named in honor of Daniel W. Kinne, son of Royal, who was killed near Petersburg, Va. The post meets in Good Templars Hall. The citizens presented the order on Decoration Day, 1889, with an elegant silk flag.

Corfu Lodge, No. 120, was organized in 1878. There are at present 17 members. The officers are Dwight Dimock, M. W.; A. K. Carrier, O.; W. D Edwards, financial secretary; J. W. Safford, recording secretary; T. A Webb, recorder; and A. K. Carrier, trustee for three years.

The cornet band of Corfu was formed in September, 1886, with 14 pieces W. H. Nehrbos is leader, and H. M. Smith is secretary.

Corfu Grange, No. 142, *P. of H.,* has for its master George W. Thomas, and C. D. Silliman is secretary.

Evergreen Hill Cemetery of Corfu.—About 32 years ago interments were first made in the plat of ground lying north of the village of Corfu. In January, 1878, a movement was agitated towards incorporating a cemetery, which resulted in an organization being formed through the efforts of the citizens, and in February, 1878, the Evergreen Hill Cemetery was started with nine trustees, viz.: James Tyrrell, H. P. Porter, Dr. F. W. Crane, Charles Griffith, E. A. Brown, N. Hartshorn, R. W. Kinne, John Lincoln, and James A. Harrown. The grounds comprise three acres and form a beautiful adjunct to the surrounding country.

Church street steam-mills of Corfu, Henry W. Francis, proprietor, are located on Church street, and are furnished with one run of stones for grinding meal and provender, a set of reduction rollers for making graham, and a bolt for sifting meal. The machinery is run by a 15-horse-power engine, and turns out 250 bushels of feed and meal and eight bar-rels of graham in 10 hours. Mr. Francis does custom work, and deals in flour, feed, and grain.

The Corfu roller-mills are located near the depot, on the New York Central Railroad. The power is supplied by a 50-horse-power steam engine. The mills have two runs of stones, a seven-break roller flouring-mill, and one roller-mill for grinding provender. The proprietor, War-ren Gorton, turns out only work of the best quality. The flour mills have a capacity of grinding 50 barrels per day. Mr. Gorton deals in grain, flour, and feed, and does custom grinding.

RICHVILLE, a small village in the western part of the town, was named in honor of a prominent business man, C B. Rich. He was a clerk for Kimberly and Trumbull Cary, of Batavia, who started him in business un-der the name of C. B. Rich & Co. The firm dissolved in 1832. In early days Benjamin Blodgett was a hotel-keeper at Richville. One evening an extra coach stopped at his door, and a lady with servant maids alighted and entered the house. The lady directed the maids to inspect the house and see if it was fit for her to stop in. After doing so they re-ported "all right"; and her ladyship directed one of the maids to instruct the driver to put up his horses, as they would stop all night Mr. Blod-gett, who had been nervously regarding the proceedings, which he con-sidered an imputation upon his care of the house, here broke in with "No, you won't, madam." "Why not?" said the lady. "Because I own this house." "Do you know who you are talking to?" said she; "I am the Countess of Sligo, and I desire to stop here through the night." "Well, madam," gruffly replied Mr. Blodgett, "I am the Earl of Pem-broke, and you can't stay." That settled it and she went on, and the hotel was often referred to as "Earl of Pembroke's castle." Mr. Blod-gett was at one time the editor of the Batavia *Spirit of the Times.* His "inn" was a high-toned house—the "Astor" House of Western New York. He charged 50 cents for a meal, even in early times, but they were worth it. Ten or a dozen stages passed his house daily, but the advent of the railroad made a great change in the tavern business.

The Genesee roller-mills (Messrs. Lee & Garrett, proprietors) are lo-cated in Richville, on Murder Creek, and are run by water with steam as auxiliary. Their flouring machinery is now the best and latest improved, and the mills have a capacity of 40 barrels of flour per day. Their buck-wheat flour is unsurpassed and has a wide celebrity. They are doing a wholesale and retail business, and their local trade is very extensive. They are dealers in flour, feed, and grain, and do custom grinding and ex-changing.

The Church of the Disciples of Christ was organized at Richville by J. C. Goodrich in 1867. There were at first 75 members, and W. H. Rogers was the first pastor. The nucleus of this church was a small one at Newstead, Erie County, where Mr. Goodrich held services. In 1868 they erected a house of worship, of wood, which they still own, and which is valued at $3,500. They now have 110 members, with J. C. Goodrich as pastor. The Sunday-school has about 125 teachers and scholars.

INDIAN FALLS is a post village located in the north part of Pembroke, on Tonawanda Creek, and has two grist-mills, several stores and churches, an hotel, and a population of about 250.

The model roller-mills of Indian Falls were built by the present proprietors, Gilmore & Co., in 1879. They are located on Tonawanda Creek, which affords an ample power, with a head of 41 feet. The mills are furnished with a full set of rolls, of the Stevens patent, manufactured by J. T. Noyes, of Buffalo, and have a capacity of turning out 50 barrels of flour every 24 hours. They also do custom grinding, and are wholesale and retail dealers in flour, feed, and grain. In connection with the roller-mills the company owns and operates a plaster-mill, which has a capacity of one ton per hour.

Indian Falls grist and flouring-mill, D. K. Chaddock, of Batavia, proprietor, is located about one-quarter of a mile above the falls on Tonawanda Creek. The mills are furnished with four runs of stones, and have a capacity of 80 barrels of flour per day. The proprietor does custom work, and deals in flour, feed, and grain.

Pastor John Siegrist, of the Evangelical Association, was the means of starting a church at Indian Falls in 1865, with 16 members. In 1866 they built a house of worship costing $1,100 A. Getser is the present pastor, and the membership is 40, with about 40 persons in the Sunday-school. Their property has a valuation of $1,500.

In 1868 the Rev. D. M. L. Rollin, of the Freewill Baptist denomination, organized a church with 11 members. They built a church edifice in 1877, of wood, which cost $2,000, and capable of seating 250 persons. Rev. W. W. Holt is the minister in charge.

There is also a Methodist Church at Indian Falls.

EAST PEMBROKE has a population of about 300 inhabitants. It is located on Tonawanda Creek, and on the Batavia and Tonawanda branch of the N. Y. C. & H. R. Railroad, and has three churches, a seminary, an hotel, a grist-mill, saw mill, stave and heading-mill, a wool-carding-mill, and a cheese factory.

The Batavia and Pembroke Baptist Church was organized at East Pembroke, February 18, 1826. The following were the constituent members: Benjamin Wells, Daniel McCracken, Chauncy Wolcott, William Upton, Mary A. McCracken, Lydia Wolcott, and Sally Harrington. Benjamin Wells was moderator. Previous to this organization meetings ware held in private houses and school-houses. Elder Amos Lampson was the first pastor. They built a frame church in 1840, and in 1867 erected a brick building costing $7,000, and capable of seating 400 persons. They have a membership of 70, with about 138 in the Sunday-school. Rev. J. M. Derby is the pastor.

The Presbyterian Church of Pembroke and Batavia was organized

December 24, 1854, by Rev. William Lusk, of Batavia. Daniel C. Houghton was the first pastor, and the number of members was 22. The same year they erected a building, of wood, costing $5,000, and capable of seating 280 persons. They now have an edifice valued at $6,000 and a membership of 100, with Rev. Theron L. Waldo in charge. There are 140 members in the Sabbath-school.

St. Mary's Roman Catholic Church at East Pembroke was organized by Father Cunningham in 1868. The church is increasing in numbers. They now have 200 members under the charge of Rev. T. H. Barrett, and expect to build a new edifice this year.

The East Pembroke Rural Seminary is the result of the forethought of enterprising citizens of the village, and is a credit to the originators of the enterprise It was formed in 1856, Rev. Mr. Horton, a Presbyterian minister, generously donating land for the purpose, the fee in the same being held by trustees so long as used for school purposes. The institution has been exceedingly prosperous in years gone by; but, like all other rural educational institutions, is affected by the larger schools and colleges that have been endowed. The trustees, with a few of the more energetic citizens, raised money enough lately to thoroughly repair the building, and invited Miss Thrall, of Batavia, to occupy the same. The school is now in a flourishing condition, having 30 scholars.

Owen Lodge, No. 432, I. O. O. F. — Pembroke Lodge, No. 353, I. O. O. F., was instituted July 12, 1850, and after a hard struggle surrendered its charter in 1859. May 1, 1890, Owen Lodge, No. 432, was instituted by D D. G. M O. J. Christopherson, of Darien Center. The present officers are as follows: N. G., Jerry Stage; V. G., George Clark; secretary, Frank Fanning; and treasurer, F. A. Clark.

Rural Lodge, No. 395, I. O. G. T., of East Pembroke, has the following officers: C. T., Will Christie; P. C. T., Robert Peard; V. T., Mrs. L. Waterman; C., L. Waterman; S., B. A. Van Horn; A. S., Laura Cook; F. S., —— Little.

The flouring-mill at East Pembroke is owned by W. E. Babcock, and is run by Mr. Nold.

NORTH PEMBROKE, on Tonawanda Creek, contains about 20 dwellings, a saw and grist-mill, and one church.

The First Christian Church of Pembroke, located at North Pembroke, was organized June 30, 1849, by Rev. Joseph Weeks, with 15 members. They built a house of worship in 1850, which was remodeled and enlarged in 1888. They now have 75 members, with Rev. Warren Vreeland as pastor. Their property has a valuation of $2,500.

The North Pembroke Lodge, No. 194, I. O. O. F., was instituted August 22, 1867. There are now 46 members in good standing. Its officers are Charles Loomis, N. G.; Charles Graves, V. G; J. W. Hatch, R. S.; and E. H. Miller, treasurer.

The Excelsior flouring-mills of North Pembroke. Frank Ladd, proprietor, are located on Tonawanda Creek, which furnishes a sufficient power, and on the site of a mill built by Holland Earl about 1836. There has always been a mill on this site. Mr. Ladd has thoroughly remodeled his mills, and has put in new and improved machinery for grinding flour and buckwheat. The capacity of the mills is 50 barrels of flour every 24 hours.

William E. Babcock, born near Troy, N. Y., was one of 10 children. His father, Reuben Babcock, Jr., was captain of a rifle company during the War of 1812, but did not serve as such in that war. His grandfather was in the Revolutionary war. Mr. Babcock's parents removed from Troy to Pembroke in 1833. He had only three months' schooling after he was 13 years old. After attaining his majority he prosecuted his trade as contractor and builder, and gave special attention to bridge building for several years. He has also been engaged in several manufacturing enterprises, and for one year and a half was in mercantile business. In 1880 he became the proprietor of the East Pembroke custom and merchant flouring-mills, to which he has since given his attention. Mr. Babcock possesses good financial abilities, and has been quite successful. He was elected collector of taxes, and performed the duties of that office so acceptably that he was reëlected the ensuing year by an increased majority—the largest on the ticket. He was elected to another town office the ensuing year, but declined to serve.

Joel W. Bates, M. D., was born in Ontario, Canada, in 1852. He received an academic education, and commenced the study of his profession with Drs. Carson and Bogart, of Whitby, was one year with Dr. Floor, of Youngstown, Ohio, and one term at Toronto University. He passed the examination of the medical board of Toronto and graduated from the Eclectic Medical Institute of Cincinnati, Ohio, in January, 1875. He was three years at Kinmount, Victoria County, and in 1879 settled at Indian Falls, this county, where he has built up a good and successful practice. In 1880 he married M. Eugima McWain, of Pembroke.

John Boyce was born in Suffolk County, England, February 2, 1804, and married Mary Mullinger, of his native town. In 1836 he, with his family, emigrated to America in a sailing vessel, was nine weeks in making the passage, and landed in Montreal. He went to Buffalo, where he resided nearly two years, and eventually made a permanent home on a new farm of 50 acres on the town line between Bennington and Sheldon. He first resided in a log house in the town first named. By the aid of their son John, Jr., who worked out among the farmers, money was secured toward making a payment on an additional 90 acres. John Boyce, Sr., died in July, 1876. Mrs. Boyce died some years before. They were parents of seven sons, all of whom are living except the youngest, who died at the age of 14 years. Mr. Boyce was a true Christian worker.

John Boyce, Jr., born in England, March 20, 1825, resided with his father until 21 years of age. Mr. Boyce worked for the farmers until he was 27. In 1851 he married Betsey H. Safford, of Elba, and settled permanently in Pembroke in 1853. They now reside on a fine farm of 250 acres, two and one-half miles northeast of Corfu. They have three sons and nine daughters. Mr. Boyce is a prominent citizen of Pembroke, is a Republican, has served his town six terms, a period of 18 years, as assessor, and has been appointed executor or administrator in settling quite a number of estates. He is a breeder of thoroughbred Jerseys, from which Mrs. Boyce manufactures a gilt-edge quality of butter. Mr. Boyce is a member and elder of the Presbyterian Church of Corfu, and one of its trustees. The Boyce homestead in Sheldon is still in the Boyce family, and is owned by William, brother of John Boyce, of Pembroke.

Thomas Lloyd was born in Wales, educated in England, and became a member of the English Church, but afterwards became a Quaker. About the time William Penn came to America Mr. Lloyd left his native country and settled in Pennsylvania. He occupied the positions of president of the council, chief of the commission, and also deputy governor of the colony under Penn. He finally retired from office in 1694 He married Sarah Ann Nugget, and they had six children.—four sons and two daughters,—whose descendants have scattered over the entire continent. About 1809 three of the sons emigrated to Canada, and settled in the townships of King and Whitchurch, and from them the Canadian branch of the great Lloyd family is descended. In June, 1889, the Lloyd family held a reunion at Aurora, Canada, with 800 in attendance

Sarah Lloyd, daughter of William and granddaughter of Thomas, who emigrated to America, was born near Williamsport, Pa., and married John Bennet, a native of England, born in 1787. A few years later he emigrated to Kings County, Canada, about 30 miles north of Toronto, where he had peaceful possession of his home until the commencement of the War of 1812. Because he refused to bear arms against the United States he was cast into prison in Toronto, where he remained until York (now Toronto) was taken by the United States army. He immediately joined the American army and served to the close of the war. Soon after he removed his family to Batavia, and settled on a new farm. His patriotism cost him a good farm of 100 acres in Canada. Mr. Bennet eventually removed from Genesee County to Michigan, where he died at an advanced age. Mrs. Bennet died at the home of her son, Henry L., in 1848.

Henry L. Bennett was born near Williamsport, Pa , June 26, 1809, was reared in Batavia, and has always been a farmer. He married Jane Simpson in 1836, and they had three sons and five daughters. All of his sons served in the Union army in the late war. James F. Bennett, the oldest, received three gun-shot wounds; William and Hiram escaped unwounded, but returned with impaired health and shattered constitutions. Henry L. Bennett has been a prominent man in Genesee County, where he has resided the past 70 years. He commenced his political career with the old Whig party, and upon the organization of the Republican party he became one of its loyal members.   Mr. Bennett has held many of the offices of his town.   He has served as constable about 50 years, and has been deputy sheriff many years.

Hon. John W. Brown, second son of Cyrus and Milla (Lawrence) Brown, was born in Sharon, N. H., July 7, 1817.   He attended the common school of his district in Pembroke until 16 years old.   Since then he has acquired a good practical education by close study and a course of reading by himself.   January 1, 1838, he married Lorette R., daughter of Winthrop and Ruth Noble, of Batavia, and settled on a portion of the homestead.   He commenced his political life with the "old line Whig" party, and joined the Republican party at its organization.   He has been honored by his town with the office of supervisor five years—1862–64, inclusive, and again in 1866.   He was efficient in filling the quota of Pembroke during the war, and was chairman of the county committee of three appointed for the purpose of raising and paying soldiers' bounties.   In 1865 and 1866 he represented his county in the State legislature, where he did efficient work.   Mr. Brown has also held other prominent town offices.   Mr. and Mrs. Brown have had born to them 11 children, eight of whom are now living.   They celebrated their "golden wedding" in 1887.   In financial matters Mr. Brown has been fairly successful.

John Brown, son of John, came to Alexander early.   He was a carpenter, served in the War of 1812, and married Mary Sheldon, of Canada.   They had 11 children, of whom Mrs. Charles H. Davis is the only one living.   They settled in " Buck House " (built in 1815), which was a noted tavern and place for holding town meetings.

Edward A. Brown was born in South Bristol, Ontario County, N. Y., December 10, 1826.   He acquired a good practical education, and began an active business life with correct habits and a good constitution. January 15, 1853, he married Sue D. Witwer, of Williamsville, Erie County.   Mr. Brown, at the age of 22 years, embarked in the livery and omnibus business in Williamsville, which he conducted for eight years.   He then (1858) removed to Richville, in Pembroke, and engaged in the manufacture and sale of lumber, which he prosecuted until the spring of 1870, when he sold his mills and bought the fine farm where he now resides, near the center of the town.   Mr. Brown still retains much of the push and energy that characterized him in his early life. He has a fine herd of Jersey cows, breeds fine horses, and has erected a good set of buildings.   He is a prominent man in town affairs, has been a staunch Republican since 1860, and has the confidence of his fellow townsmen, who have placed him at the head of the affairs of his town as their supervisor in the years 1869, '70, '72, and '73.   Mr. and Mrs. Brown are parents of two daughters, viz.: Eva (Mrs. W. T. Bunell), whose husband is a farmer in Pembroke, and Esther V. (Mrs. F. V. Brown), whose husband is a Christian minister in Auburn, N. Y.

Lewis Burgess, born in Ovid, N. Y., April 9, 1809, married Effie Mook, and settled at North Pembroke about 1837, on a farm of 50 acres, partly cleared. He had little means, was industrious, and had a fine constitution. He was a constant worker, careful, economical, and finally had a clear title to over 200 acres. He was always a farmer. He died April 30, 1883. Mrs. Burgess still survives, and resides on the homestead. They were parents of four children, all of whom are living. Their oldest son, Abram E. Burgess, born on the homestead, was educated in the common schools, and November 8, 1868, married Mary J. Dickinson, and settled on a portion of the homestead, where he now resides. He is an enterprising business man, a reliable citizen, and an obliging neighbor. Mr and Mrs. Burgess are parents of two sons, Louis E. and Henry M., and one daughter, Effie J.

Andrew F. Clark was reared in Essex County, N Y., was educated in the common schools, and at a very early age learned the nailmaking trade, which he followed about 10 years. In January, 1854, he went to California, and labored in the mines nine and one-half years. September 17, 1863, he came to Pembroke and purchased the farm where he still resides. He married Mrs. Mary Peckham. Mr. Clark has the confidence of his townsmen. He has served as constable eight years, collector one term, and is now serving the 10th consecutive year as justice of the peace. He is a staunch Republican. Mr. and Mrs. Clark are parents of three children, viz.: William F., a graduate of Cornell University, who is now a law student with W. C. Watson. of Batavia ; Tracy E., who is a student in the senior class at Cornell University ; and Lillian, who is a student in the academic department of the Union School in Batavia. Besides these they are raising two other children by adoption, Sherman T. and Mertie May Peckham.

Martin O. Coe, son of Ithamar and Sarah (Ball) Coe, was born in Massachusetts in 1786, and married Clara Hatch, who was born in Pawlet, Vt. They emigrated from Pompey, N. Y., to Le Roy in 1811. He was a farmer, and settled on Oatka Creek, which furnished him a good water-power at that time. He built two saw-mills and an oil-mill, which he successfully conducted. Mr. Coe was overseer of the poor for a long time, county superintendent of the poor 14 years, and loan commissioner about 10 years. In early life he was colonel of a regiment of militia, and was familiarly known as Colonel Coe. He died in Le Roy village, in September, 1861, aged 75 years. Mrs. Coe survived about two years, and also died in Le Roy. They had five children, two of whom are now living. William S. Coe was born in Le Roy, June 29, 1820, received a good English education, and married Sarah A. Covert. He settled in Le Roy, and two years later (1845) removed to Wisconsin. where he engaged in farming. In 1852 he returned to Genesee County, and settled in Pembroke, where he resided 13 years. During this time he was justice of the peace 10 years, and postmaster of Corfu from 1861 to 1865, when he returned to Pembroke and again engaged in mercantile

40

trade. He served in Le Roy as a magistrate eight years, and justice of
Sessions two terms. Mrs. Coe died in January, 1873. Their only surviving child is Clara H. (Mrs. George H. Chadeayne), of Buffalo. In the
fall of 1875 he married Mrs. Laura Covell, of Le Roy, who died in January, 1886. October 12, 1887, he married Mrs. Mary D. Chase, of Pembroke. They reside near the village of Corfu.

Hiram Carrier, son of Josiah and Betsey (Kellogg) Carrier, was born
in Geneseo, N. Y., April 5, 1806. His father emigrated from Connecticut in 1805, and in 1810 returned to that State, where Hiram was reared,
and where he resided until he was 23 years of age. He received an education sufficient to enable him to teach common schools, and after working for the farmers a few seasons after attaining his majority, with $50 in
his pocket, and with a knapsack on his back, he walked to Geneseo and
Le Roy, N. Y., and returned on foot through the southern tier of counties to Connecticut. Two years later he returned and bought and sold
lands with some success, and in 1831 returned again to Connecticut,
married Elizabeth B. West, of Marlborough, and with a team of horses
and wagon brought his wife and her furniture to Geneseo. In 1835
they moved to Newstead, Erie County, where they resided until May,
1847, when they removed to Pembroke, where his son Ansel K. now
lives. Mr. Carrier and his aged wife now reside near his son. He is a
man of more than ordinary ability, a good financier, and a reliable citizen.
Mr. and Mrs. Carrier have had five children, viz.: Milo, a machinist, of
St. Paul, Minn.; Lucy (Mrs. James E. Holmes), who died in 1867, leaving
one son, Edmund W., who married Kate Holmes, and is a farmer adjoining his brothers; Ansel K., who married Phila A. Sumner ; and Loraine,
who resides with her parents.

Barnabas Carrigan, son of James and Bridget Ann Carrigan, was born
in Kingston, Canada, in March, 1844. He was reared a farmer, and educated in the public schools. At about the age of 20 he commenced
farming for himself, and began dealing in horses and cattle. He resided
in Frontenac County until 1869, when he removed to Pembroke, and engaged in farming In the fall of 1876 he married Mrs. Fanny M. Moore,
and settled where he now resides. Mr. Carrigan is an enterprising and
reliable citizen.

Thomas Dimock was born in Norwich, Conn., May 14, 1774. He married Sophia Otis, of his native State, who was born January 24, 1780.
They emigrated in 1817 and spent a year in Wyoming County, and finally
settled in Darien (then Pembroke), where they died. Mr. Dimock died
August 5, 1862, and his wife June 1, 1856. He was one of the substantial pioneer farmers. His son, Col. Otis Dimock, was born in Norwich,
Conn., February 12, 1808, married Helen Fair, and settled in Darien. In
early life he was a captain, and was promoted to the office of colonel of
militia. He spent most of his life on a farm, but conducted a hotel in
Buffalo for two years. He was public-spirited, a genial companion, and
fond of fine horses. He came to an untimely and instant death by be-

ing crushed by a falling tree. Dwight Dimock, of Corfu, his only surviving child, was reared on his father's farm. He married Helen Dodge in
1868, and settled on the homestead. In 1873 he moved to the village of
Corfu, and in 1878 he settled on the farm where he now lives. Mr. Dimock is a genial companion, an outspoken Republican, and holds the responsible positions of county superintendent of the poor and postmaster
of Corfu. He also deals in agricultural implements and is engaged in the
fire insurance business.

Eli Ellinwood, born in Kirkland, N. Y., August 28, 1795, married Sophia M. Gridley, who was born March 8, 1800, and settled on his father's
farm. In 1834 he removed to Pembroke, and bought the farm of
David Goss, where his son Henry P. now lives. Mr. Goss settled there
in 1804, and his was the first family in the town of Pembroke. In 1839
Mr. Ellinwood erected the residence on the opposite side of the road,
which his son has repaired and improved. His " old white tavern " has
been torn down. He was a natural scholar, had a good education, taught
schools, and served his town as supervisor, magistrate, and superintendent of schools, and with J. Green Russell, of Batavia, was a county board
of inspectors of plank roads. For 20 years he was a constant attendant
of the Presbyterian Church at Corfu, and a trustee of the church a part
of the time, and about the last year of that period was a member. In
1854, to aid in forming an infant Presbyterian Church in East Pembroke,
he withdrew from the Corfu church. He aided in erecting their church
edifice, and was elected one of its elders at its organization, which position
he held until nearly the close of his long life. He was a progressive man,
an ardent temperance worker, and gave his influence for the advancement of all the benevolent, educational, and religions interests of his
town. He died April 8, 1880, aged 84 years. Mrs. Ellinwood survived
her husband until March 10, 1881. They had 11 children, of whom
three died in infancy, the others grew to maturity, and six are now living. Henry P. Ellinwood, born in Oneida County, April 3, 1829, prepared for college, but by reason of ill health he was unable to take a
college course. He has spent his life in cultivating the homestead,
except about six years, when he was engaged in the United States mail
service. He began an " old line Whig," and is now a Republican. Mr.
Ellinwood became a member of the East Pembroke Presbyterian Church
very soon after its organization, has been one of its elders since 1856, is
an active member of its board of trustees, and for more than 20 years
has been superintendent of the Sunday-school. June 11, 1863, he married Helen M. Allen, of Honeoye Falls, and they have four sons and an
only daughter. Their oldest son, George A., is engaged in the shoe business with an uncle in Williamsport, Pa. Their daughter Helen S. is a
student at the Boston Conservatory of Music. Henry F. is in the senior
class of Williams College, and Albert G., who is preparing for college,
and Emory A. reside with their parents.

Rev. John S. Flagler, son of Solomon, was born in Dutchess County in 1782. In early life he entered the ministry of the Universalist Church. He came to Livingston County, and preached in all the towns of Genesee County as far as Alexander. In 1833 he settled in Darien, and continued his work in surrounding towns. He was a pioneer of Universalism on the Holland Purchase. He died in Ridgeway in 1860. His son James H. is the only surviving one of his eight children, and now lives in Corfu.

Harry Forward, son of James and Mindwell (Owen) Forward, was born in Granby, Conn., March 27, 1803, and resided in his native town until 1829. November 17, 1825, he married Gratus Winchel, of Granby, and in October, 1829, he moved with his wife and two children to Pembroke, where he had the previous summer cleared a small piece of ground and built a log house. Mrs. Forward spun and clothed her family in "homespun." They lived in the old log cabin until 1851, when they built a fine farm house, where his son, Henry J. Forward, now resides, and where they lived to the close of their lives. He died July 6, 1881, and she January 6, 1888. Mr. Forward was prominent in town and county affairs, held several town offices, and was county superintendent of the poor six years. He was also the agent of the Ogden Land Co., and was engaged in the fire insurance business. Their children were George, born January 5, 1827, married Margaret Moore, October 23, 1852, settled on a farm adjoining the homestead, and died March 19, 1875; Andrew, born July 26, 1828, married Charlotte A. Soule, March 21, 1854, and also settled on a farm adjoining the homestead, where he still resides; Chauncey, born August 31, 1831, married Eliza A. Dunham, August 12, 1855, and is a dealer in butter and eggs in East Pembroke; Henry J., born February 14, 1834, married Emily M. Paul, and resides on the old homestead; and Emily M., born March 8, 1837, married James S. Durham, April 10, 1864, who was the father of her two daughters, Lucy (Mrs. Elijah Phelps), of Pembroke, and Electa S., who resides with her mother. Mr. Durham died March 8, 1872, and Mrs. Durham married Dennis Dibble, January 1, 1879, by whom she has one son, Harry. Mr. and Mrs. Dibble reside on a farm about one mile west of the old homestead. The children of Andrew Forward are Helen (Mrs. E. H. Stone), of Akron; Cora E. (Mrs. H. H. Fountain), of Alabama; and Walter S. Forward, born July 6, 1866, who is a farmer adjoining his father. The wife of George Forward, Margaret Moore, by whom he had two children, now living, died January 17, 1888.

Col. Samuel Huntington was at the head of a regiment in the Revolutionary war. About 1805 he came to the Holland Purchase, and located at Town Line, 15 miles east of Buffalo, and later removed to Pembroke, near the site of East Pembroke village, where he cleared a farm. In his old age he lived with his daughter Philura (Mrs. John W. Marston), and died at the age of 85 years. He was a man of fine physique, an ardent patriot, and was never known to exhibit anger but once, when, about the time of the burning of Buffalo, a neighbor called him the offensive name of ".Old Tory." His children were Mary (deceased), who married Simon Edwards, and went Illinois ; Samuel (deceased), who married Mrs. Polly (Carter) Shaw, and went to Michigan; and Philura, who married John W. Marston, of Pembroke. Mr. Marston was a native of Connecticut, set- tled in the west part of Batavia, and died in June, 1840, aged 36 years. Mrs. Marston died in March, 1867. He was a farmer, was an " old line Whig," and did his party good service.

John W. Marston, son of John W., was born December 5, 1834, received a common school education, and on account of the death of his father he was early obliged to manage the farm. In 1868 he bought his sister's interest in the homestead, and in 1879 sold it and removed to where he now lives, one and one-half miles east of Corfu. He married, January 12, 1860, Mary Shoulters, of Batavia, and they have five children living, viz.: John N., a mechanic, contractor, and builder, who married Ida Pal- mer, and now resides in Corfu ; and Mary E., Clarence U., Orlo G., and Emma E., who live with their parents.

Luther Hart Kitchel, son of Rev. H. D. Kitchel, D. D., was born in Thomaston, Conn., November 6, 1845, prepared for college at Andover, and graduated from Yale College in 1867, and from the Buffalo (N. Y.) Medical University in 1870. He also took a course of lectures in Belle- vue College, New York. He returned to Buffalo, and was appointed to the position of resident physician and surgeon of Buffalo General Hos- pital, and commenced the practice of his profession in that city. He moved to Olean, where he resided six years, and on account of ill health removed to Texas. After a rest of a year and a half he resumed prac- tice in Hamilton, Texas, and in 1886 returned to New York and settled in Corfu.

Henry P. Porter, son of George A., received an academic education, and served an apprenticeship in the store of Wells & Seymour, of Ba- tavia, about 1843. When 21 years of age he settled in Corfu, then known as Long's Corners, and opened a general store in company with his former employers, under the firm name of Porter & Co. The postoffice was established here about 1840 by Robert Miller. In 1854 Wells & Seymour retired, and were succeeded by George A. Porter, a brother of H. P., the firm name being Porter Brothers, which continued as such for 25 years. In 1879 H. P. Porter withdrew, and George A. Porter has since conducted the business alone.

John Long, son of Dr. David and Margaret Long, was born in Ba- tavia, July 29, 1785. He married Martha Brown (born January 16, 1786), January 8, 1807. Mr. Long came from Salem, N. Y., in 1807, and located in Pembroke, about two miles west of Corfu, to which he removed his wife and infant son, William B., in January, 1808. About 10 years later he removed to the present site of Corfu, and occupied the site where Mr. Giddings's house now stands. He was a farmer, was one of the most prominent of the early pioneers, and was always in town office. He was town clerk at the time of his death. His house was opened for town and religious meetings. He was liberal to the poor and needy. Mr. Long died August 14, 1836, aged 52 years, and Mrs. Long January 24, 1858, aged 72 years. They had three sons. William B., one of their sons, was born December 3, 1807, married Eliza M. Lown, March 28, 1858, and settled on the farm where his widow still resides. He was always a farmer, but never enjoyed robust health. He died March 23, 1881. They had two children, one of whom, a son, died in infancy. Their daughter Martha L., born January 22, 1861, married Henry B. Cochran, January 21, 1877, and settled on the homestead, where they still reside. Mrs. John Long, too, experienced many of the hardships and inconveniences of pioneer life. John Long was a lieutenant in the War of 1812.

Benjamin Lawrence, born in Jaffrey, N. H., in December, 1800, marrien Roaney Gowan, of his native town, and came to the Holland Purchase in 1826, settling on the farm where his son, Edwin L. Lawrence, now lives, and where he died in 1868. He was a captain of militia, and had the confidence and esteem of his neighbors. Mrs. Lawrence died in 1880. Edwin L. Lawrence, born in 1831, received a common school education. In 1860 he married, first, Abigail Hoyt, and they had three children. She died in 1868, and in 1870 he married Eliza Reed, who is the mother of eight children. Mr. Lawrence was reared on a farm. His oldest daughter married Frank A. Day and resides in Des Moines, Iowa. He is a Democrat in a Republican town, and has been honored with the office of highway commissioner for three years.

Samuel Pratt, born May 3, 1758, married Abigail Caswell, April 13, 1780, who was born April 28, 1760. He served as a soldier in the Revolutionary army. In 1830 he came to Darien with his youngest son, Harvey, and resided with him until his death, November 23, 1831. His wife survived until October 12, 1844, and died at the home of her daughter Peddy (Mrs. Carruth), of Wyoming County. Harvey Pratt was born December 11, 1796, and in the early part of 1816, with a knapsack on his back, he walked from Oneida County to Bennington, then a part of Genesee County, and located a farm in the woods. He married Orpha Hills, and settled there, where they remained until 1823, when he returned to Oneida County to administer to the wants of his aged parents. In 1830 the entire family settled in Darien, where Harvey Pratt resided until 1855, when he removed to Michigan, and died in February, 1856. Charles P. Pratt, son of Harvey, was born in Bennington, January 16, 1818, and married Ellen M. Humphrey, of Darien, in 1846. He was a manufacturer of and dealer in lumber in Darien from 1839 to 1849, when he engaged in the manufacture of shingles in Alden for six years, and later was a merchant in Alden village for three years. In 1859 he moved to Marilla, and was again a lumberman, until 1864, when he purchased a grist and flouring-mill at Indian Falls, where he removed his family in 1865, and where he now resides (1889). He successfully conducted the mills until May, 1872, since which time he has been a farmer and general merchant. Mr. and Mrs. Pratt have had two sons, Charles T. and William F., who are enterprising farmers.

Daniel Peck, son of Daniel who was a Revolutionary soldier, and a descendant of the Peck family who emigrated from England to America, came from Sand Lake, Rensselaer County, N. Y., in 1830, and settled near East Pembroke. He was always a farmer, and was twice married, first to Hannah, daughter of David Woodward, and second to Bathsheba, daughter of Reuben Gould. By his second wife he had 12 children, of whom four are living. Mr. Peck died July 28, 1886. His eldest son, William, born at Sand Lake, August 19, 1811, came to this town with his parents in 1830. He married Celinda Ryckman, March 5, 1837, and settled on a farm on the Buffalo road, where his widow now resides. He had a son and a daughter, and died September 23, 1885. He was a man of good judgment and accumulated a fair competency. His son, Joel Peck, married Lizzie Crawford, and settled on the Barden farm. He has dealt some in farm produce, and has always been a farmer. His wife died September 13, 1886, leaving an only daughter, Lydia, who married William Cleveland, a farmer near her old home, by whom she has nine children.

E. Chapin Richardson, M. D., son of Rev. C. C. and Eliza (Rabel) Richardson, was born in Sherman, N. Y., May 1, 1862, and commenced the study of his profession under the preceptorship of Dr. I. V. Mullen, in Alexander. He graduated at the University of Buffalo, February 26, 1884, and commenced practice in Warsaw, but settled permanently in the practice of his profession at East Pembroke in the spring of 1886. Dr. Richardson has a high reputation as a physician. September 29, 1887, he married Augusta E. Cummings, of Pembroke, and they have one child, a daughter.

Lewis C Read, born in Batavia, September 24, 1831, married Helen A. Gould in 1858. In 1866 he located on the farm where he now resides, about half a mile south of the village of East Pembroke. Besides cultivating his farm he is an extensive dealer in grain and other produce, agricultural implements, phosphates, and live stock. He has an extensive acquaintance in his large business, and is known as a shrewd buyer and fair dealer. Mr. and Mrs. Read have a daughter, E. Corinne, who married G. H. Dennison, an enterprising merchant of East Pembroke, and a son, Nathaniel M., who is a farmer with his father. Mr. Read has held the offices of assessor, justice 20 years, supervisor, and county superintendent of the poor. He came to this State and taught school two years at Onondaga Hollow.

Herbert M. Smith is a son of Rev. Alonzo Smith, who has been an active itinerant minister in the Methodist Protestant Church for the past 21 years. Herbert M. was born in Amboy, Oswego County, N. Y., November 24, 1868, and came to Corfu with his father in September, 1885. June 15, 1887, they formed a copartnership in the jewelry business, which he is successfully conducting.

Col. Jesse Safford, a pioneer of Pembroke, was born in Hartwick, Mass., in 1755, and married Abigail Damon, who was born in 1763. They settled where their grandson Fred M. now lives, in the cold season of 1816. He was a Revolutionary soldier and a colonel in the army. Mr. Safford died in 1834, aged 80 years. He had seven children. John D., a son, was a lawyer in Allegany County, was a justice for 30 years, a supervisor for several terms, and died in 1875.

George B. Seamans, son of Benjamin and Abigail (Brown) Seamans, was born in Connecticut in 1812, and married Matilda Howard in 1836. In 1840, with his father, he came to Pembroke. Charles Seamans, son of Benjamin, of Connecticut, was born June 30, 1815, came to Pembroke in 1840, and settled adjoining his brother George. He learned the trade of shoemaker, and served as poormaster of the town. He married Hannah Howard, of Connecticut, a sister of Mrs. George B. Seamans, and they had six children, four of whom lived to mature age. He died in 1888, and his wife a few years earlier.

Ezra A. Seamans, son of Charles and Hannah (Howard) Seamans, was born in East Pembroke, July 12, 1849, and was reared on his father's farm, where he continued until about 25 years of age, when he learned the trade of tinsmith. He soon engaged in the general hardware business, and now has a lucrative trade. December 29, 1875, he married Esther, daughter of Edward Smith, and they have three children. Mr. Seamans is a Republican, has served as postmaster six years, and has just received a commission for another term.

Joel Sutherland, son of Joshua and Sarah (Wolcott) Sutherland, was born in Batavia, September 5, 1811. His father came from Dutchess County, N. Y., in 1800, and followed an Indian trail through the Holland Purchase to Canada. The next year (1801) Mr. Ellicott, the agent of the Holland Land Co., located an office in Batavia, and Mr. Sutherland and his brother Isaac returned to Genesee County, and were residents of Batavia the remainder of their lives. Joel Sutherland was reared on his father's farm, and received such an education as the primitive schools of that early day afforded. In 1841 he married Phebe M. Perkins, in Bushville. He was a carpenter and millwright until 1848, when he purchased a farm and engaged in farming until 1865, when he removed to East Pembroke, where he still resides (1889). Mr. Sutherland has seen about two generations come and go. He gives a vivid description of the event of filling the Erie Canal with water for the first time. The men in charge of the feeders, from Buffalo to Albany, were signalled to open the gates, beginning at Buffalo, by the booming of cannon along the entire waterway. He and all others in early days were clad in homespun, and he well remembers when the luxury of " cotton factory " (cloth) was introduced at 50 cents per yard. Mr Sutherland is an honorable representative of one of the prominent pioneer families of Genesee County. He is the father of two sons : Homer J., born in 1843, who died in 1873, and Herbert, born in 1850, who died at the age of 11 years.

George W. Thayer, born in Alabama, this county, September 23, 1839, was reared upon a farm and educated in the log school-house, supplemented by an attendance at Cary Academy in Oakfield. In 1860 he cast his first vote for Abraham Lincoln. May 26, 1861, he enlisted in Co. F, 28th N. Y. Vols., and was mustered out in 1863. He reënlisted January 2, 1864, in Co. M, 2d N. Y. Mounted Rifles, and remained with his regiment until August 10, 1865, when he was honorably discharged as a lieutenant. He participated in 17 general engagements and 20 cavalry skirmishes, and was once captured by the enemy. He remained a prisoner about one hour, was taken by guards to a camping-place, and while his captors were forming the camp he mounted his own horse and escaped to the Union lines. Two sabre wounds were all that he received just before he was captured. He participated in the battles of Winchester, Cedar Mountain, second Bull Run, South Mountain, Antietam, Chancellorsville, Spotsylvania, North Anna River, Petersburg, June 17, 1864, and July 30th, Pegram Farm, Stony Creek, Dinwiddie Court House, High Bridge, and Appomattox. He returned home, disabled by being thrown from his saddle, for which he receives a small pension. In 1865 he settled at Indian Falls, and in 1866 he built a plaster and shingle-mill on Tonawanda Creek. In the fall of 1867 his right arm was cut off by the saw in his shingle-mill. He is now engaged in the business of fire insurance, auctioneer, and dealing in agricultural implements. In 1858 he married Mira E. Van Buren, of Alabama, a native of St. Lawrence County, N. Y.

Samuel Van Alstine, son of Peter Van Alstine, was born in Oakfield, July 4, 1844, and received a good education. August 22, 1862, he was mustered into the U. S. service in Co. H, 8th N. Y. H. A., and served three years. He was in the battles of Cold Harbor, Wilderness, and several others. He suffered from an attack of small-pox, and received a gun-shot wound in his left arm, which is badly crippled. Mr. Van Alstine returned to his home with an honorable discharge. He is now the postmaster of North Pembroke, and is the proprietor of a country store. In 1865 he married Anna M. Martin, and they have two sons.

Daniel Ward, son of Levi and Nancy (Whitney) Ward, was born in Keene, N. H., February 1, 1818, and came to Pavilion with his parents in 1819. At that time good wheat sold for two shillings and sixpence per bushel in Rochester (the nearest market), and a pair of coarse boots cost from $6 to $7. He was educated in the old log school-house with the old Dutch fire-place and stick chimney. Sometimes the scholars carried raw meat (sausage) for their dinner, and roasted it, Indian-style, over the roaring fire, on a long, sharpened stick. Mr. Ward remained on the homestead with his parents until 26 years of age. In 1844 he removed to Pembroke and settled on the Indian Reservation, but was warned off by the Indian chiefs. A few weeks later he met the " chief" at a feast and dance, and told him that he should return to his claim. Mr. Ward's facetious remarks so amused the chief that when he did return he was never seriously molested by his redskin neighbors. He was an ambitious, hard working young man, and soon made for himself a good home, where he remained until the fall of 1883, when he removed to his present home in the village of Indian Falls. Mr. Ward married, first, in 1840, Catherine Phelps, who bore him a son and a daughter, and died in 1847. In 1848 he married, second, Harriet Wilcox, who was the mother of six children. Mrs. Ward died in 1871, and in 1872 he married for his third wife Mrs. Caroline N. (Bibbins) Phelps. Mr. Ward is a man of sterling integrity. In politics he is a Republican, and in religion is a worthy member of the Methodist Episcopal Church, being one of the first in its organization.

Oliver Wakeman was born in Vermont, January 30, 1797, and came to Batavia with his parents when young. He married Lucinda Reed, of Batavia. In 1860 he moved to East Pembroke, where he died March 7, 1876. Mrs. Wakeman survives her husband, and is in her 86th year. They were parents of 12 children. She resides with her youngest son, Orsemus Wakeman, in the village. He married Demaris Burdick, August 12, 1871, and they have two sons. Mr. Wakeman is a painter and farmer.

Rev. Hugh Wallis, of Massachusetts, came to Pembroke about 1816, and settled on 200 acres which he purchased of John Long. He was pastor of the Presbyterian Church at Corfu, and late in life moved to Rochester. He died in Gates, over 80 years of age. He was a graduate of Yale, and was a sound and acceptable preacher. His oldest son, Hugh, lived on the old homestead until his death in 1881.

Seth Wakeman, at one time a prominent lawyer of Batavia, resided in Pembroke. He attended the district school. The family were very poor, the father dying in 1813. Seth removed to Batavia in 1837, and began the study of law. He was county treasurer at one time, and also a member of Assembly.

STAFFORD.

STAFFORD has the best claim, we think, of being the locality of the earliest settlement on the Holland Purchase. James Brisbane, the first merchant on the Purchase, came here in 1798, with a load of goods, or supplies, for the surveyors employed by Mr. Ellicott, and opened a store-house or station at this place, from which event it was called Transit store-house. The location of the store-house cannot now be clearly defined, but it is believed to be on the west side of the creek, and north of the present bridge, in the village of Stafford. In the spring of 1799 James Dewey, one of the surveyors, was waiting there with a gang of hands to start upon an expedition as soon as the weather would permit.   At the request of Mr. Brisbane he cleared 10 acres of land west of the Transit, which was mainly sowed with oats.   This is supposed to be a portion of the land now owned by I. M. Peck, whose father, Richard, bought the property from Joseph Ellicott.

Upon an old map made by Joseph Ellicott in 1800, for the Holland Land Company, we find the name " Walther," as indicating a settlement at this place.   Walther was induced to settle here by reason of a proposition made to him by Mr. Ellicott for the Holland Land Company, who appreciated the importance of places of entertainment for the early land seekers and settlers.   Mr. Busti, the agent, gave authority "to contract with six reputable individuals to locate themselves on the road from the Transit line to Buffalo Creek, about 10 miles apart, and open houses of entertainment for travelers; in consideration for which they are to have from 50 to 150 acres of land each, at a liberal time for payment, without interest, at the lowest price per acre."   Three persons accepted the offer, one being Frederick Walther, who was then residing on the land, who took 150 acres west of and adjoining the eastern Transit, including the company's store-house.   Because of his officiousness he proved to be an undesirable settler for those days, and soon left the county.   Thus was begun the actual settlement of the town and village of Stafford, but the name "Transit" was retained and a postoffice of that name kept until 1841.   It is said that Ira Gilbert was the first postmaster.   Orin De Wolf was his deputy.   Gilbert also at one time kept the old Churchill tavern, long known as the temperance tavern, on the road to Batavia.

The town was formed March 24, 1820, being taken from parts of Le Roy and Batavia.   It contains 20,000 acres of land, is undulating in character, and has a very productive soil, upon which good crops of wheat, beans, potatoes, and general farm produce are always grown.   Portions of the town are underlaid with limestone, much of which is used for building purposes.   The town is well watered by Black Creek, flowing north through the central portion, and Bigelow Creek, which flows through the west portion into Byron.   Horseshoe Lake is situated on the latter creek, and has become a pleasant summer resort.

In 1802 Col. William Rumsey, from Hubbardton, Vt., came and settled on " Stafford Hill," the highest point of land in the town.   He was a surveyor in the employ of Joseph Ellicott, and a colonel of militia, and represented the county in the legislature.   Joseph E. Rumsey also came with his father the same year, and eventually moved to Chicago.   Nathan Marvin bought a large tract of land at Transit (Stafford) in 1803, comprising farms now owned by Mrs. Bagot, the former proprietor being Richard Radley, who bought the property in 1831.   Marvin moved to and died in Ohio.   John Debow settled on the Webber farm in 1804.   General Worthy Lovell Churchill located near Rumsey.   His wife died in 1803, and soon after occurred the birth of a child, being respectively the first death and birth in the town.   Gen. Churchill was in the War of

1812, was in command of the 164th Regt. of State militia, and was sheriff
of the county from 1820 to 1825. In 1836 he owned the place (now the
Mead estate) near Horseshoe Pond, and died there. Zenas Bigelow, in
1804, located the farm now owned by the Dowd estate, near the creek
that bears his name. Other settlers came in the years following, among
whom were D. Hall in 1808, and in 1809 Eben Eggleston, who kept tavern on the Big Tree or Leicester road. The same year Leonard King,
who settled in the east part of the town, came in, as did also Josiah
Churchill and H. Rumsey, the latter of whom located on lot 5, where Arthur Prole now lives. In 1810 we note the advent of Malachai Tyler,
Phineas White (who married Polly Beswick), and John Bean. Mr. Tyler
settled east of Beech Creek. He had a wood turning shop, and made
chairs, bowls, and spinning-wheels, and was a blacksmith. In 1811
Amos Stow built a saw-mill on Bigelow Creek, and Seymour Ensign a
grist mill. He also carried on wool-carding and cloth-dressing, being
assisted in the latter work by a Scotchman, named Falconer, who afterwards was taken prisoner in the War of 1812. The same year (1811) came
Nathan Bannister and Betsey Bigelow, the latter locating on lot 11, near
school-house No. 2. In 1812 came Elisha Prentice and Capt. Nathan
Cash, and in 1813 Merritt King. Peter Stage, in 1814, located on lot 7,
where John Webber now lives. In 1815 Eden Foster and Noble Daniels came in. The latter located where Perry Randall now resides. In
1816 came Adget Lathrop and David McCracken. Abel Cross came in
1817. In 1818 came Chester Scott, who also located land in Elba, and
as late as 1833 kept a distillery. B. Clark, Joel Philleo, J. J. Reynolds,
and John S. Blair came in 1819. On the old Genesee road, neighbors to
the Rumseys and Churchills, were B. Bristol and Mr. Van Alst, who came
in 1821.

Upon the Craigie tract, in the southeast portion, of the town, the persons who first took up land were J. Bushnell, in 1815, and D. Biddle-
cum. Following them were C. Sweetland in 1817, D. Laid in 1821, E.
Wright in 1823, S Plant in 1824, E. W. Cobb in 1827, E. Northrop in
1820, Mr. Sweetland and Mr. Lent in 1825, and Mr. Bannister and Mr.
Coon in 1826 Others from 1827 to 1835 were Tanner, Snow, Tomlin-
son, Beckley, Pratt, and Lewis. On the old Genesee road east of the vil-
lage the early settlers were as follows: In 1823, J. Reynolds; 1824, Z.
Terry, Otis Drury, A. Hubbard, and A. Bangs; 1825, J. Stage; 1826,
C. Kelsey; 1827, J. Ellis; 1829, Ira Danolds; and 1830, O. H. Kendall,
T. Judd, R. Blish, J. Iden, Mr. Stutterd, Moses Smith, and Hinsdale and
Smith Kellogg.

Settlements upon the Pultney lands of the Connecticut tract were delayed, and the earliest we can get any trace of are Nathaniel Watson and
Daniel Prentice in 1812, and the family of Stephen Randall, who came in
1815. Mr. Randall had nine children to help him maintain a home in
the wilderness. They started from New Hampshire in the winter, were
on the road three weeks, and reached Le Roy February 2d. He bought

the farm now occupied by Perry Randall, upon which he moved within 24 hours after their arrival. There were 15 acres, of which only three acres had been cleared, but happily a log house had already been built. There was no road to the place, so they left their teams and luggage one and a half miles away. Clark Daniels also came in 1815, as did also John, the father of Jay Lathrop. The Mosses located here in 1826, and others scattered along in the years following, until about 1831, when the settlements were rapidly made by Englishmen who were attracted to the lands in this section.

Three separate tracts, or large original divisions of land, are represented in the town. The first in order of settlement is the Holland Purchase, forming the western part; the Craigie tract, of 46 lots, varying from 87 to 115 acres each, in the southeast portion; and the Pultney lands of the Connecticut tract, in all 80 lots, from 100 to 120 acres each, located in the northern and eastern portions of the town.

The town is well laid out, the drainage good, and the death rate for 1888 only seven per 1,000. Two physicians are located in the town, but are not kept very busy, owing to its healthful location. Since 1803, and to within a few years, the village has been quite prosperous. It is mainly settled by English people, and partakes of the character of an English village. Most of the village residents are farmers, and with their nearness to each other form a happy society of their own entirely unlike that of any other village in the county. The first English settler was John Webber, who came in 1817. He was followed by a Mr. Stutterd in 1830, and soon a large and influential colony of Devonshire people were congregated in the town, thousands of miles from their native land, to make new homes for themselves and families. A fair business is transacted in the village. The buying and shipping of grain and produce of all kinds is extensively carried on, assisted by excellent railroad facilities, there being two depots for that purpose. During the busy season it is not uncommon to ship 1,000 car loads of the products of the soil from this village.

The first school was kept and taught by Esther Sprout in 1806. At one time Richard Radley kept a private school in the building east of the Episcopal Church, which was very prosperous, and of great utility to the English settlers in carrying out their ideas of instruction to the young. The district schools are generally well built, and the educational facilities for teaching the young are of a good and practical order. There are 10 district schools, with a school population of 612, employing 14 teachers. The site of school No. 8, on lot 124, in the north part of the town, was deeded in 1822 to "Walter Campbell and others, in trust," for school purposes. Upon the same lot, in 1824, a small portion was set apart for a burying ground. The old cobblestone school-house, in the northwestern part of the town, was built over 50 years ago.

Early merchants.—As has already been stated the first settlement of the county was made in Stafford, and with it was the advent of trade. Mr.

Brisbane seems to be the first merchant, coming in 1799 from Williams-
burgh, on the Genesee River.   His clerk was John Thompson.   He dealt
in all kinds of goods necessary for the new settlement.   Mr. Brisbane removed to Batavia in 1802, it being decided to establish the county seat
there.   Settlement in the village progressed on the opening up of the
adjoining lands, making it a center for trade, and an inducement for mechanics, merchants, and tavern-keepers to pursue their callings.   In 1820
Samuel A Bigelow opened a store, and remained until 1826.   Ira Danolds came in 1827 and engaged in trade, and in connection with his
brother operated a distillery.   They built the stone structure (still standing) in 1827, which they used as a store, and later added a third story
to be used as a lodge room.   It was so used by Olive Branch Lodge,
and it was here that David C. Miller, editor of a Batavia paper, was
taken, when arrested, and rescued by his friends.   Robert Stage followed
in 1829, and others in succession until 1843.   That year came the March
family, consisting of three brothers—William, Samuel, and Isaac.   C. W.
March, another brother, came in 1869.   In 1864 Stephen Crocker and
his brother George and Dr. L. M. Haynes came in, and they were all
engaged in trade.   John Burden and J. & E. B. Sanders were also early
merchants

The entertainment of travelers in early times caused the erection of
many taverns.   Jonathan Bemis was a landlord as early as 1804.   David
Danolds was among the earliest, and he kept the old log tavern where
Walther first opened.   The building stood just west of the stone store-
house.   Henry Peck had a place of entertainment in 1827.   Isaac Newton Stage kept for 30 years where Mr. Heal now owns.   He died in
1858.   Others who preceded Mr. Heal were Wolfe, White, Fisk, and
Odell.   Ira Gilbert, who was the first postmaster, also kept tavern in the
western part of the town, at a place once called " Churchill tavern," and
for some time after " Temperance tavern."   A Mr. Heacock married Gilbert's widow, and the Temperance House was continued by them.
Churchill had for a sign a plow, which was fastened upon the stump of a
tree, 25 feet from the ground.

Besides the hotels kept at Morganville, when it was a prosperous village, was one opened by a Mr. Eggleston in 1809, on the Big Tree road,
in the southwestern part of the town.   This was afterwards kept by Mr.
Lee, and later by Mr. Bartholf, and retained the name of Checkered tavern (being painted in checker style) for a long time.   It was finally purchased by Mr. Wemple.

Present industries.—John Passmore is engaged in making a superior
quality of cider at his mill on road 46.   He manufactures 50 barrels per
day, having a 16-horse-power engine and all the latest improvements.
His cider has attained a wide reputation for purity, and shipments are
made all over the country.   The mill was built in 1876.

The cider-mill at Stafford village is owned by E. M. Pamphilon and
Charles and Alonzo Dezendorf.   It was built in 1883, has a capacity of
30 barrels per day, and is run by steam.

An evaporator for drying fruit is located near the depot, and is a source of employment to many hands in the fruit season.

One of the principal industries of Stafford village is the finely equipped storage warehouse and feed-mill owned and operated by Sanders & Son, who are also extensive grain and produce buyers.

MORGANVILLE, so-named from Morgan of Masonic notoriety, is situated about one and one-half miles north of the village of Stafford, on Black Creek, and has a population of over 100. Twenty years ago considerable business was transacted here, there being several mills and machine shops. The fall of the creek in that locality is 30 feet, which affords valuable water-power. The location of the new Geneva and Buffalo Railroad, just south of the village, and the new depot contemplated, will undoubtedly cause business to revive in that section.

The Christian Church, located on the main street, was built in 1833, by a union of Christians and Universalists. The latter all died or moved away, and since 1870 the church has been termed Christian. The same denomination built a church in the eastern part of the town in 1836, which was sold in 1867. The church was organized in 1816 by Rev. Joseph Badger, with 40 members. The first pastor was H. Thompson. The present number of members is 70, under the pastoral charge of Rev. John B. Clark, and there are about 70 Sunday-school scholars. The church will seat about 250 persons, and is valued at about $4,000.

Charles Lathrop built a brick hotel in 1835, and kept it several years. The house is now owned by H. Stone, but not used as an hotel. There was an hotel nearly opposite, kept in 1833 by Jerome Randall, in the house now owned by Edwin Ross.

The present grist-mill in Morganville was built about 1878, by John Simmons. It is of stone, 40x60 feet, three stories high, has two runs of stone, and does a custom and flouring business. It is now run by Robert M. Parkerson. The first mill on the present site was built by Adget Lathrop about 1820. R Fisher built an addition afterwards. This mill was burned in 1874. The wagon shop, built about 1853, is now owned by Albert H. White, who bought it in 1886, and has since carried on the business. He manufactures wagons, carriages, sleighs, potato diggers, etc. Besides these Morganville has a postoffice, store, harness shop, blacksmith shop, and a pottery.

It is said the first postoffice in Morganville was established about 1838, with Germain Lathrop as postmaster. The building used as such was built in 1820, and is now used for the same purpose. The old Remington harness shop is one of the few existing landmarks of the locality, being built by Hazen Moss in 1825. Another interesting building is the stone school-house, built previous to 1830, which was arranged for holding religious exercises, having a pulpit in one end. Robert Fisher is to be credited for his efforts in establishing business at Morganville. He it was who built the stone mill and set on foot various enterprises that caused it to be a busy place from 20 to 40 years ago. He was the post-

master in 1869. David Rogers, a mechanic, about 1820, made the first
cultivator with a wheel. His shop was in the old stone building erected
by Mr. Bronson.

ROANOKE is a hamlet in the extreme southeast part of the town, near
the Pavilion line. It was named by Major John Ganson in honor of
John Randolph, of Virginia, whose residence in that State was so-called.
The main branch of Oatka Creek skirts the southern part of the village,
affording excellent power for grist and saw mills. A store, cooper shop,
blacksmith shop, and about 25 houses make a good locality for business.
J. H. Ganson and Jonathan Lay were prominent men in early times.
They operated the old furnace.

The Methodist Episcopal Church at Roanoke was organized as a
union church in 1840, with about 50 members, and with Rev. Daniel
Burke as pastor. A church edifice was built in 1843, costing $1,500,
and capable of seating about 170 persons. Services are only held occasionally.

The Roanoke roller-mills, located on the Oatka, have a full set of rolls
and three runs of stones, and are operated by H. C. Duguid & Son, who
have operated them since 1887. They were built in 1835 by Lay, Ganson & Co.

In 1840 S. Pierce operated the old (Northrop) woolen factory.
Knowlton, Rich & Co. were there in 1845, and Shaffer & Hardy in 1853,
when it was burned.

During the war of the Rebellion the town contributed nobly its share
of clothing, money, and men for upholding the cause of the Union,
and the heavy demands were readily responded to by each and every
citizen. In all 50 men left the town for the field of battle, 23 of whom
gave up their lives for the cause of their country. The return of those
who survived was the occasion of great rejoicing, and public homage
was accorded them; while for the martyrs a beautiful monument was
erected, in a conspicuous place in Rural Cemetery, where yearly the
citizens vie with each other in honoring the memory of the names given
herewith, and which are inscribed upon the shaft: John Ball, Martin R.
Bowan, Christ Cooper, Mortimore M. Cummings, Thomas Gayton, David Greening, John Folk, George Jerry, Francis Lander, William F.
Lewis, William F. Mills, George Merlin, Alonzo Nichols, Thomas Passmore, Jr., Isaac Page, Thomas Phelps, William Rudd, Riley Stevens,
Dewitt Van Alst, John T. Twamley, William Webber, F. B. Wright,
and Charles Willmore.

Religion has always had a strong hold upon the residents of this town,
and manifested itself as early as 1810, when services were conducted at
the house of Col. Rumsey by the Rev. William Green. From this inspiration the Baptist Church was started, and a stone structure, a part of
which is now in existence, was erected in 1815, nearly one half a mile
west of the Transit, on the road to Batavia. The building is now used
as a tenement. The Rev. Amos Lampson was the first minister of this

church. In 1821 a Congregational Church was organized, which afterwards adopted the Presbyterian form of government. Rev. Mr. Huxley was the minister until about 1825, when L. Judson, until 1836, officiated under the patronage of the Missionary Society. Then followed Louis Mills, and afterwards H. G. Ward. A union church was kept up for some time, but dissatisfaction arose as to occupancy of the building, and separation was the result.

Owing to the influx of so many Church of England families about the year 1830 a movement was made towards the formation of an Episcopal Church. Previous to this the adherents of that church were compelled to go to Batavia or Le Roy. As early, however, as February 16, 1823, E. Mix, Lucius Smith, and Richard Smith, of Batavia, organized St. Phillips's Protestant Episcopal Church, but no records exist concerning it. In February, 1833, a parish was organized at Stafford village, under the name of Trinity parish, with the Rev. John P. Robinson in charge In October, 1834, there were 40 communicants. Services were held in the old stone (or union) church for want of an edifice of their own. In 1841, through the activity of the members, a church was built and consecrated in 1842 by Rt. Rev. Bishop Delancey, under the title of St. Paul's Protestant Episcopal Church. Richard and John Warren, Sr., were chosen wardens. Rev. George D. Gillespie, now bishop of Western Michigan, was the rector. In 1843 Rev. Stephen C. Millett was rector. He resigned in 1845, and John P. Calhoun succeeded him in 1846 He was followed by Rev. Milton Ward, and he by Rev. Philemon E. Coe in 1850. Rev. Richard Radley took charge in 1851, and served for 19 years, or until 1870. He died in 1879. Other rectors followed until 1882, when the Rev. Mr. Edson came, and in 1888 the Rev. E. R. Armstrong, the present rector. The present house of worship is a substantial structure, built of wood on a stone foundation, and is capable of seating 300 persons. It cost $2,500. The present value of church property is $3,500. The membership of the church is 200, and the Sunday school has over 80 children.

Stafford Rural Cemetery Association.—Soon after the Holland Purchase was opened for settlement Col. Nathan Marvin purchased the lands now owned by Mrs Mary E. Bagot and Mrs. E. S. Wood. The early burials on these grounds, where Mrs. Bagot's small orchard now is, were Col. Marvin and Peter Stage. Four acres of land was set apart for town purposes : one acre for burial purposes, one acre for a town house on the Clipknock road, and two acres for church and school purposes, the whole forming a square of four acres. The land for burials was found unfit for the purpose, and Col. Marvin exchanged for an acre lying west of the Transit road, the location of the present cemetery. Burials were made on that plat thereafter, and an enclosure was made by. Maj. Harvey Sweetland. In 1831 Mr. Marvin sold his lands to Richard Radley, reserving the acre for a cemetery, the school-house site, and ground where his children were buried. These reservations were afterward con-

41

veyed to Isaac N. Stage and the town of Stafford. The grounds were soon neglected and grew up to weeds and brush, and disorder generally prevailed. In August, 1865, the ladies of Stafford exhibited the usual energy of the sex by agitating the subject, and calling attention to the necessity of a reform in cemetery matters, which resulted in an entertainment, from which $65 was realized. From this time the subject was thoroughly ventilated, committees were appointed, and the above associa· tion was duly organized under the law of the State pertaining to cemeteries. Israel M. Peck was chosen president; Stephen Crocker, vice-president; C. W. March, secretary; and J. I. Stutterd, treasurer. After this the title to the land was vested in the corporation, additional land bought, and by a systematic plan lots and walks were laid out, the energy of its officers being met by the usual amount of prejudice and opposition, but the general good of the community triumphed. At a town meeting in 1868 $900 was taxed and voted to be expended for a soldiers' monument. One was finally erected at a cost of $950, containing names of 23 soldiers, former residents who gave up their lives in the Rebellion. The association has a fund of nearly $2,000, the interest of which is spent in caring for the grounds, the fund being augmented constantly by the sale of lots. The people of the town are justly proud of the few persons who gave their time and energies to the accomplishment of so beneficent an object. The present officers are Israel M. Peck, president; John H. Drury, vice-president; and John Sanders, secretary.

Stafford Benefit Association was originally organized in 1870, and the rules by which it is now governed were adopted at its reörganization in 1877. It was incorporated in 1881. The society is one of the most prosperous of its kind in the State. Its present officers are I. M. Peck, president (who has served as such for 11 years); O. J. De Wolf, vice-president; E. M. Pamphilon, secretary; and Archie D. Sanders, treasurer. In 19 years there have been 37 deaths. There were 100 applications for membership in 1888. The standing for 1887 was as follows: total income from fees, dues, and assessments, $1,612; disbursements for losses, claims, salaries, etc., $1,445; policies in force, 415; policies for the year, 68.

Stafford Lodge, No. 222, *I. O. O. F.*, was organized in 1867, with the following charter members: ·William Barnett, John Sanders, John Passmore, I. M. Peck, and A. Keller. It has been a flourishing organization, having at one time 85 members. It numbers now about 40. A large fund amounting now to $1,400 has been accumulated for the benefit of its members.

Transit Lodge, No. 363, was organized in October, 1823, with Dr. Samuel S. Butler as master; Eden Foster, S. W.; and Jacob Wade, J. W. It was dedicated in September, 1825, and Rev. Lucius Smith, of Batavia, preached a sermon on the occasion. It survived only a few years.

Mrs. Elizabeth Bagot, only daughter of George and Mary (Radley)

Bagot, was born in 1833. Her father was among the first of a party of Englishmen to settle in the town, in 1831. She was baptized in Trinity Church by Rev. John Robertson. Her grandfather was one of the first wardens, remaining as such till his death in 1862. She received her education at the school of her uncle, Rev. Richard Radley, and completed her studies in Le Roy. During a visit to Elk City, Mich., in 1879, she married Richard Bagot, a prominent merchant and citizen, and at one time county clerk and treasurer. Mrs. Bagot's father and mother died the next year, and she returned to Stafford to settle the estate. She still carries on the 180-acre farm left her, besides spending much time in travel, passing her winters in Florida with her husband, whose interests in that State and Michigan are extensive.

Stephen Crocker, son of George and Sarah, was born in Bishop's Tawton, Devonshire, Eng., February 26, 1808. His father was a prominent farmer, holding 200 acres. He died in 1850. Mr. Crocker was educated at the public schools, finishing his studies at Barnstable. On leaving school he remained with his father until 1831, when he, with a party of Devonshire Englishmen, came to America, being among the first English settlers in this town. In July of that year he bought the Anson Bristol farm on the "Clipknock road." In September, 1832, he married Susanna, eldest daughter of Richard and Elizabeth Radley. In 1836, with two others, he went to St. Louis, and in 1839 returned to England, where he remained until 1841, when he returned to the United States with his parents and family. He was assessor of the town for six years, and during the Rebellion enrolled the citizens who went to war. Later he was one of the "war committee," doing efficient service, has been road commissioner for six years, and held the office of poormaster for about 20 years. He has also been elected town clerk, and during the administration of President Cleveland was appointed postmaster. Although a staunch Democrat his Republican friends have given him their suffrage. Mrs. Crocker died in 1879. They had one child, Elizabeth, born in 1833, who was the first one baptized in Trinity Episcopal Church at Stafford, by the then rector, John Robertson. She received her education at Mrs. Bryan's school in Batavia, and at the Ingham University of Le Roy. In 1855 she married Dr. Thomas, son of Rev. B. King, D. D., who was pastor of the church at Rockaway, N. J., for 50 years. Mr. King died in 1867, and two years later she married William Wood, son of Leonard, of Devonshire, Eng., by whom she had two children, Leonard and Gertrude. Mr. Wood died in 1884. In 1885 Mrs. Wood removed from "Wood's farm," Morganville, to the rectory in Stafford, and is now living with her father.

Miss Carrie Douglass, fifth child of Leander and Isabella Douglass, was born in Byron. She was educated at Stafford and Le Roy. Her ability as an artist is of no common order. Her paintings of scenery and fruit are excellent, and for some time she carried on a studio in New York. She studied with Col. P. Staunton, of the Le Roy Art School, and later with Frost Johnson, of New York. She is a niece of A. Hart Norris, and spends most of her winters at Spring Garden, Florida, where she has the management of the Norris Spring Garden silk farm. The father of Miss Douglass died on the Douglass homestead in 1872, and her mother in 1882. Besides attending to the duties of her 100-acre farm, and keeping up her artistic studies, she gives much of her attention to the Episcopal Church, of which she is a member, and attends to the wants of the deserving sick and poor in her section of the town.

John De Wolf, born near Hartford, Conn., married Lucy Jackson, and they had 12 children. In April, 1805, he moved to Batavia, when there were but two framed houses there—James Cochran's and William Keyes's. He was a cabinetmaker, and carried on that business there. In 1814 he located in Stafford, on road 29, on the farm now owned by John Mullen. He died in 1868, aged 86 years. Five of his children are living: Harlow and Peter reside in Michigan; Zorada (Mrs. James Manning) resides in Batavia; and John and Orin reside in Stafford. Orin was born April 6, 1804, in East Bloomfield, and came to Batavia in 1805. He has resided here since 1814. He married Zobede Perkins, and they have had 14 children, of whom 11 are living. Mr. De Wolf is a blacksmith, and settled on the place where he now lives in 1830, carrying on the business since. He was deputy postmaster under Mr. Gilbert, at Transit (now Stafford), and served as constable in 1835 and '36. He was elected justice of the peace in 1852, and has held the office ever since, being elected six times without opposition. John, his brother, was born October 10, 1805, married Eliza Fales, and had a family of 10 children. He is a farmer.

Clark Daniels, born in Danville, Vt., in 1794, was the seventh child of Solomon Daniels. Only a common school education was afforded him. Entering the army at an early age he fought in the War of 1812, and is one of the few surviving pensioners of that struggle. He came to Stafford in 1815, when all around was a forest, and well remembers the cold summer of 1816, when wheat and corn could not grow, the latter being sold for $3 per bushel, and frozen at that. That year he bought the "Alfred Fisk" farm. He was burned out in 1818, and the same year married Laura Beswick, of Massachusetts. In 1827 he moved to Allegany County, where he lived until 1832, when he returned and bought the farm where Francis Darbee now resides. In 1835 his wife died, leaving seven children. He then sold his place and bought the "Beswick farm," and in 1836 married Mrs. Hannah Powers, by whom he had one child, Charles Daniels. In 1849 the "Beswick" farm was sold, and the "Allen" farm purchased. His second wife died in 1848, and he married, later, Huldah, daughter of James Courer, who died in 1862. The "Allen" place was then sold and the "Watson" farm bought. His son Charles entered the army in 1862 and fought under Gen. Dix. In 1864 Mr. Daniels married, fourth, Sarah Ware, widow of Jacob Bushman. She, at the age of 84, is still living. In 1875 the "Watson" farm was sold and the old " Lathrop " place purchased, which Mr. Daniels still owns. He cast his first vote for James Monroe in 1817, and has always voted the Republican ticket. He has been a member of the Christian Church for 50 years.

Thomas Waldron, son of Abraham and Sarah Waldron, was born in Devonshire, Eng., in 1853, was educated at the village school, and at the age of 15 was apprenticed to the coopers' trade, serving five years. April 7, 1872, he married Mary, eldest daughter of John and Jane Darch, and came to Monroe County. In 1875 he came to Stafford and engaged in business with his brother-in-law, John Darch. Two of his four children survive, viz.: John H. T., born in June, 1873, and Rosa Maud, born in May, 1886.

Henry A Fiske came from Jefferson County, N. Y., in 1810, when he was seven years of age. He married Eliza Parker, of Batavia, and had five children. He died in 1863, and his wife in 1874. His father, Sylvanus, located on road 24, and had eight sons, of whom two are now living, viz.: Frederick in Indiana, and William in the State of Washington. Sylvanus W., son of Henry A., was born October 8, 1829. He attended school at Morganville until the age of 15, and taught until he was 20 years old, when he worked upon his father's farm, which he purchased. In 1851 he married Jeanette, daughter of Aaron and Electa Beswick, and they had one child, Henry, who died in 1879. In 1874 Mr. Fiske went to the Rocky Mountains. In 1880 his wife died from cancer, and February 28, 1881, he married Louisa, daughter of Tobias Hufletine, and spent some years in travel in this country and in Europe. Upon his return he again occupied his farm, to which he has since devoted all his energies He was highway commissioner for two years.

Byron Farley came to Le Roy from Vermont. He was a cooper by trade, and had a family of nine children, five of whom are living, and two in this county. Maria, wife of Norman Stevens, resides in Le Roy. Abiathar, born in 1839, married Mary, daughter of Ephraim Niles, who came to Stafford in 1816, from Vermont. and settled on road 37. He married Polly Hill, and they had five children. He died in 1877, aged 97 years. His son Eben resided on the old farm until he died about 1851. Two other sons, Edwin and Ephraim, reside in Le Roy. The daughter Mary (Mrs. A. Farley) occupies the homestead. They have three children, De Forest, Fenton, and Estelle (Mrs. H. D. McCall), of Pavilion. Mr. Farley is a musician and leader of Farley's orchestra.

Michael Linsler, born in Steuben County, in December, 1849, married Margaret Coogan, of Wyoming County, and they have three children. He has been superintendent of C. F. Prentice's farm for the last four years, and a resident of the county since 1864. His father, Simon, came from Germany about 1837, and settled in Schenectady, and afterwards in Steuben County.

Dr. Newton Graves, a native of Herkimer County, was born in 1828, and graduated from Western Reserve College, of Ohio, in 1852. He resided in Oneida County 20 years, and removed to St. Lawrence County, where he practiced for five years, and came to Stafford in 1884. He married Caroline Pierce, of Livonia, N. Y.

Abial Gardiner, son of Abial, came to Pennsylvania from Fngland. He married Amanda Smith, of Middlebury, N. Y. John Smith, her father, was in the War of 1812. Mr. Gardiner settled in Elba in 1851, where he resided seven years, when he moved to Stafford and settled on the farm now owned by his son Enos J. He died July 13, 1879. He was born April 1, 1812, in Durham, N. Y. His wife died April 6, 1884. They had two children, viz.: Lydia A., who resides in Michigan, and Enos J., who was born June 24, 1845, and is a stock dealer and farmer. The latter married Olive E , daughter of Charles M. Hoyt, who was born in Florida, N. Y. Mr. Hoyt married Mary Galentine, of Rush, N. Y., and they had four children, three of whom are living, viz.: Eveline Goodenough, Sarah Jackson, and Olive E. He settled in Elba, where he resided until 1843, when he came to Stafford. He was a farmer, and died in June, 1889. His wife died July 15, 1881.

F. C. Miller, born in Germany, came to this country when he was 16 months old, with his father, Charles, in 1864. He married Addie Waterman. In 1888 he opened a general store at Morganville, and September 12, 1889, was appointed postmaster at that place.

John Heywood, son of William, of Devonshire, Eng., was born in November, 1809, and came to this country in 1835. He received his naturalization papers in 1848. The same year he purchased the Heywood farm, and married Sarah, daughter of George Shapland, also from Devonshire Seven children were born to them, of whom five are living, viz : John, Elizabeth Radley, Anna Sutterby, Mary, and William. Mr. Heywood is considered one of the richest farmers in this section of the county.

Edward William C. Pamphilon, born at Stoke-on-Trent, Eng., in 1854, is the eldest son of Edward Pamphilon. He was educated at Owen's College, Manchester. In 1879 he came to Stafford, and in 1883 purchased the Radley farm. In 1886 he married Sarah M., daughter of E. E. Allen, of Corfu. Their child, Edward, was born September 12, 1888. Mr. Pamphilon is an enterprising farmer, and has the respect of his townsmen. His wife has filled the position of organist of the Episcopal Church for several years.

Edward M. Pamphilon was born in this town November 9, 1858. His father, Henry, was the leading physician here for 30 years, and was well known in all parts of the county. For a few years Edward Pamphilon attended a select school here, and later went to a public school, and in 1873 completed his education at the Batavia Union School. In 1876 he began clerking for E. B. Sanders & Son, with whom he remained two years, when he went to New York to assist his brother in his store on Bond street. Later he removed to Batavia and engaged as clerk for Shaw & Stiles, druggists. Returning to Stafford he worked for J. Sanders & Son until 1882, when he became a partner, the firm name being Sanders & Pamphilon. In 1886 he married Amy A., granddaughter of H. B. Booth. She was born in 1863, and received her education at Batavia. Upon the death of E B. Sanders, in 1887, Mr. Pamphilon bought the interests of his partners, and has since carried on the business alone He has been deputy postmaster since 1887, and is now postmaster, town clerk, and secretary of the Stafford Benefit Association, besides holding other positions of trust.

Matthew W. Heal, one of the 13 children of John and Mary Heal, was born in Devonshire, Eng., in 1827. At the age of nine years, with his parents, he came to Stafford, and after leaving school he worked on a farm. In 1849 he married Harriet, daughter of John and Mandy March. She was born in Ohio. After his marriage he pursued farming, purchasing the Richardson place. Selling that farm he bought the Babbage property, and later the Crocker place. In 1865 he became the possessor of the old stage tavern, formerly owned by Henry Wolf, and which is now the well known Heal Hotel. Of their seven children six are still living, viz.: William H., Hattie A., John M., Frank C., who is in business in Batavia, Minnie P., and Georgie Anna. In 1860 he was elected constable, which office he still holds. He served as collector for eight years. In 1887 he was appointed deputy sheriff, and in 1869–70 he took the census of Byron, Stafford, and Pavilion. He is a Mason, belonging to Olive Branch Lodge, of Le Roy, and a member of Lodge No. 222, I. O. O. F. Mr. Heal manages a farm of 60 acres, upon which is a valuable stone quarry, the stone from which was used in the bridge of the D., L. & W. Railroad.

The Houseman family are of German ancestry. Mr. Houseman's great-grandfather and his brother were killed in battle under General Wolff, at Quebec. His two sons, John and William, afterwards resided in New York city, where they were in trade, the former as a painter and glazier, and the latter as a tailor. John Houseman, son of William, was born in Fulton County, N. Y., in 1797, and about 1820 married Ann Scribner, of the same county. Their children were George, James, William W., John M., and Emmitt. William W. was born in Fulton County, May 12, 1827. He was educated in the common schools, and came to Stafford when 21 years old. He married, first, December 31, 1849, Harriet A. Lighthall, of Brockport, N. Y., and resided in Le Roy four years, when he removed to Illinois, and returned after four years to Stafford. They had two children: Mary, who died at the age of six years, and Jay, who is now in California. His wife died in 1858, and March 18, 1863, he married, second, Sarah E. Filkins, of Bethany. They have one daughter, Cora I., born October 26, 1866. Mr. and Mrs. Houseman reside in the southwestern corner of the town of Stafford.

John V. Horn, born in Took, of Hesse Cassel, Germany, in 1819, married Catherine Derbaker, and came to America in 1855. For the last seven years he has been manufacturing proprietary medicines. He has seven children. He owns a distillery, and distils his own peppermint and spearmint, which he raises on his farm. Adam Horn was born in Batavia, and is a distiller of peppermint and spearmint. He has five acres of willows, which he ships to different cities, besides manufacturing willow baskets. He also manufactures "Horn's German balm," a pain destroyer. He married Mary Benning, and they have one child, Rosa. Henry Horn is an Evangelical minister in Syracuse. Albert resides in Buffalo, John in Michigan, Herman in Walworth, N. Y., and Alice (Mrs. William Green) at Roanoke Elizabeth (Mrs. Rev. C. F. Stube) resides at Little Valley, N. Y.

Jay Lathrop, born in Stafford in 1840, was the eldest son of John and Elizabeth Lathrop, who settled in 1814, coming from Rutland County, Vt. They did much towards the settlement of the town. Mr. Lathrop received a good, practical, common school education, and at the age of 24, with his brother Howard, worked the home farm on shares. Five years later he became the sole owner of the homestead. In 1883 Mr. Lathrop was elected town supervisor by a very large majority, and again in 1888 and 1889 he filled the same office. He married, in 1872, Mina, third daughter of Abram Warner, by whom he has a daughter, Florence, who was born in 1875. Mr. Lathrop's father lived to the age of 92 years.

John Mullen, born in Devonshire, Eng., in 1844, is a son of Philip Mullen, and came to America in 1867 and settled in Stafford. He married Mary Engall, and they have three children, Gilbert, Levi, and Arthur. He is a farmer on road 29, where he has resided since 1875.

Francis Darbee, son of Lafayette, was born in Bethany in 1841, and has lived in this county most of his life-time. He married Sarah Moore, and they had three children, of whom one, Floy, is now living. His second wife was Louise Schwab, of Bethany. He is a large farmer, cultivating 280 acres, and makes a specialty of seed grain and potatoes.

A. Hart Norris, youngest son of Deacon Abijah Norris, from Ridgebury, Conn., came to Stafford in 1835 from Orange County. He was born in Sullivan County in 1814, and was partly educated there and partly in Orange County, finishing his education at Troy and Williamstown, Mass. He worked on his father's farm a few years, when he began for himself by setting out a peach orchard, and later engaged in the nursery business, carrying on an extensive trade as far west as California. In 1851, acting upon the advice of his brother, he bought a section (640 acres) of land in La Salle County, Ill., which has proved a profitable investment. A few years later he leased his nursery business to a nephew, and went to Iowa, where he engaged in a similar trade, and also conducted a real estate and mortgage office. Soon after 1857 he went to Dade County, Mo., and purchased several thousand acres of improved land, a portion of which he still holds. In 1859 he located a quantity of land in Northern Iowa and in Nebraska, and engaged in the cattle business. Later, through the efforts of a brother in Florida, he became interested in the Spring Garden orange plantation in Volusia County, and built a steamer to run from the lake to Jacksonville. He also engaged in the growing of oranges, pears, persimmons, and the mulberry, and passes his winters in that section.

John Passmore, a native of Devonshire, Eng., was born December 14, 1824. His parents were Richard and Susanna Passmore. His father came here in 1832, and purchased a farm in the eastern part of the town. He died in 1875, and his wife in 1865. John Passmore married Elizabeth, daughter of George and Sarah Shapland, who was born in 1829. They had 13 children, of whom 10 are living, namely: Susan, Mary Elizabeth, Thomas, Richard, Charles, Sarah Ann, John, Eliza Jane, Henrietta, and James. In 1850 he bought the Warren farm, upon which he now lives, and the Chapell property in 1858. He is a member of the I. O. O. F. Lodge, No. 222.

Edgar G. Rugg, son of Horace and Elvira Rugg, was born in Pavilion, November 17, 1842. His father came from Vermont and was one of the early settlers of this county. Edgar A. was educated at Pavilion and at Lima Seminary, and during 1863–64 he taught school, besides carrying on a farm. He went to Le Roy in 1866, and in 1872 purchased the farm where he now resides. He married Ada L., daughter of Chauncy and Lucy Allen. In 1880 he was elected justice of the peace, holding the office five years, and in 1884 was elected to the office of supervisor, which he held for three years, and was chairman of the board one year.

John W. Perry, a native of Galesburg, Mich., the eldest son of Elton W. and Mary Perry, was born February 18, 1855, and received his education at the Union School at Batavia. He went to Bushville to learn the millers' trade, where he remained until 1874, when he returned to Batavia. In 1878 he worked in the West mill in this town. He married Ella E., youngest daughter of Anthony J. and Emeline Gallagher, of Philadelphia, in 1879. Her father was a well-known rectifier and distiller of high wines. Their children are John, born March 26, 1881; Harry W., born April 8, 1884; and Frank G., born July 19, 1887. In 1885 he returned to Stafford and settled upon the farm of 100 acres where they now reside, it having been inherited by his wife from an aunt.

Israel M. Peck is the third son of Richard and Catherine Peck, who settled in Bethany in 1808. Richard was a lieutenant in William Rumsey's regiment, doing duty at Chestnut Ridge and Black Rock, in the War of 1812. Israel M. was born in 1823, received his education at the district schools and at Clarkson Academy, in Monroe County, and taught school in Orleans County, and in Little Rock, Ill., in 1847. In 1848 he was a clerk in Mr. Prindle's store, East Bethany, and in 1852 he came to Stafford, locating upon the farm where he now lives, and which was bought by his father in 1811. In 1853 he married Frances C., daughter of Lyman Fargo, of Bethany, and they have three children living, viz.: Elizabeth, Junius M., and W. Scott. At the age of 21 Mr. Peck was school collector; in 1850 school superintendent; in 1856 school commissioner of the six eastern towns of the county, serving two years; and in 1859 inspector of elections, serving for 16 years. He has been justice of the peace since 1871, has served four times as Sessions justice, and was supervisor for three years, serving as chairman. At the age of 47 he again taught school for three winters. To him is due much credit for the organization and final development of the plans for beautifying the present attractive cemetery in the village. It was also through his management that the present Stafford Benefit Association has been placed upon so firm a foundation. He has been secretary of the I. O. O. F., No. 222, for 16 years, was district deputy grand master for three years, and has installed officers of many lodges in Genesee and Wyoming counties. He has also represented the Grand Lodge, and attained the degree of past grand.

Cyrus P. Bell, eldest son of Prosper and Emeline Bell, was born in September, 1836. His father was an early settler, coming to Batavia in 1825. In 1837 he purchased the F. Fisk farm, where he remained until 1852, when he bought the Crocker farm in the south part of the town, and in 1857 the William Burden place. Prosper Bell died in 1867, aged 71, and his wife in 1873, aged 69. C. P. Bell was educated at the seminary in Alexander, leaving that institution in 1858. He taught school 12 terms. During a visit to the West he married, October 5, 1864, Alantha, third daughter of John E. Adams, of Cuyahoga County, Ohio, and their children are Clara, born August 5, 1865; Howard and Hattie, born January 29, 1868; and Flora, born December 2, 1869. In 1870, and again in 1873, Mr. Bell, by a large majority, was elected assessor by the Republicans. In 1885 he was elected justice of the peace, which position he still holds.

M. W. Oderkirk, only son of F. R. and Ann Oderkirk, was born in Rensselaer County, N. Y., July 4, 1829. His grandfather, Isaac, was the first white child baptized in Albany. The family are of Dutch origin. Mr. Oderkirk's education was limited, being obliged in early life to assist in the support of his mother and sisters. His youth was spent at Johnstown, N. Y., where he was engaged in the express business. From 1868 to 1874 he was a wholesale and retail dealer in flour, feed, and grain in Gloversville, N. Y. He was also supervisor of that town in 1874–77. In 1851 he married Caroline, eldest daughter of John D. and Desire Haggart. She was born in 1829. Four children were born to them, viz.: Anna C., who died in 1879; Frank J., born in 1855; John H., born in 1858; and Watts, born in 1863. In 1877 Mr. Oderkirk came to Stafford and purchased the farm known as the Gillett place, where he now resides.

T. O. Parminter is the youngest son of James and Elizabeth Parminter, from Devonshire, Eng. They came to this town in 1839, and purchased the farm which Edward Hill now owns. He was a prominent farmer, and being a strong churchman was instrumental in building the Episcopal Church. He died in 1864, aged 74 years, and his wife in 1873, aged 84. T. O. Parminter was born in Devonshire, July 6, 1836. His principal education was obtained at Cazenovia and Lockport, and after assisting his father on the farm. for five years he went West, where he remained four years. Returning home he was in the produce business four years. In the spring of 1872 he purchased his present farm of 200 acres, which he devoted to fruit and grain growing. In 1879 he married Florence, eldest daughter of Stephen and Fanny De Bow, of Bethany. Her education was received at Le Roy Institute. They have had two children, viz.: Carrie Louisa, born September 28, 1884, and Ethel Gertrude, born January 11, 1886, who died April 29, 1887.

Robert M. Parkerson, born in Onondaga County, N. Y., in 1835, learned the millers' trade at Suspension Bridge, where he resided eight years, and finished at Rochester in 1856. He came to Alexander, and had charge of the Rix flouring-mill for eight years. He also resided in Scottsville three years and in Elba two and one-half years. He is the inventor of the hand flour-sack packer. Mr. Parkerson owned and run the Folsomdale mills one year, and has resided at Morganville since August, 1888. He married Mary A., daughter of Alpheus Waite, of Alexander, and they have one son, George W., who is a jeweler in Westfield, N. Y.

Harry White, a native of Massachusetts, settled on road 5, on the farm owned by B. H. Bean. He was a soldier in the War of 1812, and his widow, Orpha, now draws a pension. She lives with her son Albert H., who is a wagonmaker, and carries on that business in Morganville. Albert H. married Fannie Cash, of Stafford, by whom he has one child, Fannie.

Joseph Remington, of Morganville, was born in Auburn, N. Y., April 8, 1820. His father, Martin, was sheriff of Cayuga County. When seven years of age he came to Stafford, and lived with his uncle, Noble Daniels. At the age of 15 years he was apprenticed to the trade of harnessmaking, with Hazen Moss, in the shop now occupied by him, and where he has always worked. He married Jane C. Joyce, and they had three children, two of whom are living. He has been justice of the peace since 1856, and was postmaster for 16 years. One son, F. J. Remington, is express agent from Attica to Sandusky. His daughter Frances is the wife of Wallace Wade, who is postmaster at Arcade.

Stephen Randall, born in Nottingham, N. H., in 1782, married Rachel Fifield, and they emigrated to this county, reaching Le Roy, after a three weeks' journey, February 2, 1815, with a family of nine children, a span of horses, two yokes of oxen, and three cows. They also brought $1,400 in gold. They reared a family of 14 children, all of whom were living at the death of Mr. Randall in 1859. Mrs. Randall died at the age of 91 years. Of their descendants six are living. Three grandsons have become officers in the U. S. army, one was sent on a tour of inspection around the globe, and another is a minister of the gospel. Gen. Brewster Randall moved to Wisconsin, as did also Ruth, widow of F. Finch, and Edward F. Sallie, wife of Joseph Dodge, resides in Michigan. Betsey married Mark Watson. Rachel, widow of J. D. Stafford, and Perry live in Stafford. The latter now occupies the homestead and lives in the house built by his father. He was born July 16, 1822, married Mary E. Bachelder, of Le Roy, and they have had seven children, six of whom are living. Mr. Randall was supervisor in 1859, holding the office four years, and has always followed farming.

Warren J. Tyler, son of Joel, was born in Byron, July 28, 1828. He married Cassandra Tyler, of Stafford, and has four children living. He is a farmer and breeder of registered Merino sheep.

George A. Constable was born in Hawley, Orleans County, N. Y., and married Mary L. Cole, of Elba. They have three children. He is a farmer, and has resided in Stafford since 1882.

August Rody was born in Mecklenburg, Germany, March 17, 1851. When 17 years of age he came to Batavia. He married Hannah Bromsted, and they have five children. In 1878 he located on the farm where he now resides. His brother Charles came to America with him, but died the following year. Their mother died in 1888.

Nathaniel Watson came from Vermont in 1812, and settled on road 38, on the farm now owned by Michael Buckley. He cleared the land and built the house now standing. He married Sallie Sevey, and eight children were born to them, only two of whom are now living. He kept a diary from 1816 until 1856, the year of his death. Ira, a son, was born in 1834, and married Harriet Allen, by whom he had three children, two of whom are living. He was a farmer, and died June 2, 1875. His widow still resides in this town. Gordon T, son of Ira, was born May 23, 1851. He married, first, Laura C. Drury, and second, Hattie L. Drury, by whom he has three children. Mr. Watson was elected assessor in 1889.

John H. Webber, second son of John and Sophia Webber, was born in this town April 15, 1837. He is the grandson of Gen. Worthy L. Churchill, a very old settler, and a soldier of 1812. Mr. Webber's mother was a daughter of Gen. Churchill, and was the first child born in this town. John Webber, Sr., came from Somersetshire, Eng., in 1817. He married Gen. Churchill's daughter in 1827, and settled on the Debow farm, which was located in 1804. John H. Webber was educated at Batavia and at Alexander and Oakfield seminaries, and lived on the homestead until 1866. December 19, 1867, he married Mary Jane, eldest child of William and Elizabeth Radley, who were early settlers. Their children are Nellie Churchill, born September 30, 1872; Charles Radley, born September 19, 1874; and Clara Elizabeth, born April 2, 1881.

Giles Miner, born in 1805, came to Stafford in 1826, and settled on the farm now owned by his sons H. C. and C. J. He built the stone house, in 1840, now occupied by them. Henry Clay Miner, son of Giles, was born on the farm where he now lives in 1848. He married Lizzie L. Maxom, and they had three children, Bessie M. and Reuben R. (deceased), and Raymond C. He is the inventor of Miner's patent automatic stanchion for cattle.

Luther Brown was born in Concord, N. H., in 1802, and came to Le Roy in 1811, where he married Pamelia Lilly, of Pompey, N. Y., February 12, 1824. In 1835 he removed to Roanoke, and died August 17, 1876, aged 74 years. He was a millwright and built the grist-mill, now standing, and the Methodist Church. He had eight children, seven of whom are living. James E. Brown, born August 13, 1834, married Mary Foster, and their two children reside in St. Louis, Mo. He is a carpenter, is also highway commissioner, and has been a correspondent of the *Le Roy Times* since that paper was started.

John Wakley, son of Samuel and Grace Wakley, is a native of Devonshire, parish of Parkham, Eng., and was born July 13, 1823. He received the usual training common to English youth, and learned the trade of carpenter. September 9, 1849, he married Mary Anna, daughter of John Webber, of Devonshire. Mercy, his daughter, was born in May, 1848. In 1855 Mr. Wakley came to Stafford, where Samuel was born November 9, 1855, and Dora September 3, 1860. The latter died in 1887. Mrs. Wakley died the same year, aged 56. Their youngest child, Flora, was born September 10, 1863. Mr. Wakley has been sexton of the Episcopal Church since 1864. He received his naturalization papers in 1860. Samuel Wakley has been station agent of the N. Y. C. & H. R. Railroad since June 24, 1880. He married Sarah Bolt.

Louis Bauer, son of Jacob, was born in Batavia in 1845, married Mary E. Wilson, and has six daughters. He is a farmer. Mr. Bauer's father was six years of age when he came to America with his father, Louis, who was born in Alsace, France. With the exception of about three years spent in Ohio Jacob has always lived in Genesee County. He married Catherine Rupp, and they had two sons, Charles and Louis, both of whom reside in Stafford.

Anthony Waterman came from Cummington, Mass., where he was born in 1791. He married Sophia Bannister in 1816, and settled in Stafford, on road 22, on the farm now owned by his son Oscar. In 1834 he built the brick house now used as a residence by Oscar. Mr. Waterman had 11 children, five of whom are living. He died in 1882, and his wife in 1873. Oscar F. Waterman was born in Stafford, July 13, 1827, and has always resided on the homestead. His brother Bennett, born December 21, 1837, married Isabella Cash, and they have one son. Florence, William, and Harlow Waterman reside in Le Roy, and Hartwell in Michigan.

Hon. John Sanders, born in Devonshire, Eng., in 1822, where he was educated, came to Stafford in 1841, and settled upon a farm which he carried on for years. He then opened a store in the village, and pursued the mercantile business until his death, February 2, 1882. He was a member of Assembly for 1879 and '80, and held the office of supervisor several years. He married Elizabeth Dovell, and had seven children, of whom three are living. Edwin B. Sanders, brother of John, and also a native of Devonshire, was born October 8, 1841, and was a son of Henry.

who came here in 1841.   He entered his brother's store when young,
and became a partner in 1864.   He took sole charge of the business in
1874, carrying it on until 1884, when E. M. Pamphilon became a partner.   Mr. Sanders was postmaster for 22 years and town clerk 19 years.
He died April 25, 1887.   Mrs. Ann Sanders, the widow of Henry, is
still living in Stafford, aged 92 years.

Maj. Harvey Sweetland, a native of Connecticut, settled in Stafford in
1810, on the farm now owned by Robert Call.   He was one of the most
enterprising of settlers, was ever ready to lend a helping hand to his
neighbors, was foremost in every enterprise for the benefit of the town,
and held various offices, among them being that of supervisor.   He built
the old stone church, and died in 1849.   He received his title of major
from being the organizer of a band.   His brother John came to this
county with him, and both served in the War of 1812.   John was a
brave man, was appointed a captain of militia, and lost his life in the
cause.   Another brother, Caleb, lived here until 1840, when he moved
to Michigan.   A son of Harvey Sweetland, Charles J., resides in Stafford.

Otis Drury came here in 1810.   In 1839 he built the stone house
where J. H. Drury now lives.

SUMMER VACATIONS.

FOR the general health and enjoyment of people who have the leisure and opportunity a summer tour or vacation has come to be regarded almost a necessity. It is our purpose in this sketch to remind the people of Genesee County that one of the pleasantest and cheapest outings may be had by purchasing of the Rome, Watertown & Ogdensburg Railroad Company an excursion ticket, at reduced rates, from Rochester to the Thousand Islands, where a few weeks or a few days may be enjoyed among the labyrinths of that wonderful archipelago, with headquarters at Clayton or Alexandria Bay, or at Round Island, Thousand Island, Central, Westminster, or Grand View parks, from any of which points excursions to Kingston, Brockville, Ogdensburg, and among the islands are of daily occurrence, and where fishing and picnic parties find ample opportunities for enjoyment. If one desires the route may be continued to Ottawa, the Dominion capital, or to Montreal, Quebec, and up the Saguenay, from where one's steps may be retraced; or extended to the seaboard, *via* Lake Champlain, Portland, or Boston, and thence home by either of the several routes.

By sending 10 cents in stamps to Theodore Butterfield, general passenger agent of the R., W. & O. Railroad, at Oswego, N. Y., a guide book of tours, containing also several fine maps, will be mailed to the applicant.

By the way what a wonderful road the R., W. & O. has become! stretching more than 650 miles in length through the counties of Oneida, Lewis, Jefferson, St. Lawrence, Oswego, Cayuga, Wayne, Monroe, Orleans, and Niagara, and has terminal stations at Utica, Rome, Syracuse, Rochester, Niagara Falls, Suspension Bridge, Oswego, Sackets Harbor, Cape Vincent, Clayton, Ogdensburg, Norwood, and Massena, connecting in all with more than 20 other roads, and has besides more than 15 junctions and crossings with its own branches and with other roads. The aforesaid book of tourists' routes contains a map of the railroad, one of the Thousand Island region, one of the Adriondack region, another of the White Mountain region, a general map of all eastern resorts, and nine other maps of great value to tourists. The company will sell excursion tickets over all the routes mentioned in their lists.

This great railroad, under its present progressive management, has become one of the most important railways in the country. No effort has been spared to make it the greatest tourist route in America.   The road has been practically rebuilt in the last five years, the track having been relaid with heavy steel rails and thoroughly ballasted with gravel and stone.   New, heavy, and powerful locomotives, specially designed to haul heavy passenger trains at a high rate of speed, have been placed in service ; and the passenger equipment has been raised to the highest standard.   New coaches recently purchased are of the most magnificent style, with vestibules and all the latest modern improvements.   Fast limited express trains are run between Niagara Falls, Syracuse, and Clayton, to the Thousand Islands, and also between New York, Albany, Utica, and Clayton.   Wagner buffet sleeping cars are run between Chicago, Niagara Falls, Rochester, and the Adirondack Mountains, White Mountains, Portland, Me., and the sea coast resorts in Maine.   Through sleeping cars are also run from New York and Albany to Clayton, Thousand Islands, and the Adirondack region   These limited express trains are run particularly for tourist travel, and make quick time, avoiding stops, and performing the same service as that of the great trunk lines of the country.

PART SECOND.

BUSINESS DIRECTORY

— OF —

GENESEE COUNTY, N. Y.

1890.

COMPILED AND PUBLISHED

— BY —

J. W. VOSE & CO.

PERMANENT OFFICE,　-　-　SYRACUSE, N. Y.

"He that hath much to do, will do something wrong, and of that wrong must suffer the consequences; and if it were possible that he should always act rightly, yet when such numbers are to judge of his conduct, the bad will censure and obstruct him by malevolence, and the good sometimes by mistake."—SAMUEL JOHNSON.

SYRACUSE, N. Y.:
D. MASON & CO., PRINTERS.

CENSUS TABLE.

POPULATION OF THE SEVERAL TOWNS IN GENESEE COUNTY, NEW YORK, AT EACH CENSUS SINCE 1810, INCLUSIVE, SHOWING THE LOSS AND GAIN IN EACH TOWN.

TOWNS.	1810.	1820.	1830.	1840.	1850.	1860.	1870.	1880.
ALABAMA	.....	.....	819	1,798	2,054	2,061	1,805	1,975
ALEXANDER	.....	1,496	2,331	2,242	1,927	1,801	1,605	1,608
BATAVIA	3,610	2,597	4,264	4,219	4,461	5,876	6,485	7,516
BERGEN	.....	2,438	1,508	1,832	1,897	2,008	1,997	2,002
BETHANY	.....	1,691	2,374	2,286	1,904	1,897	1,652	1,671
BYRON	.....	1,767	1,936	1,907	1,566	1,864	1,734	1,754
DARIEN	.....	.....	.....	2,406	2,084	2,143	2,054	2,046
ELBA	.....	1,333	2,678	3,161	1,772	2,040	1,905	1,968
LE ROY*	.....	2,611	3,902	4,323	3,473	4,247	4,627	4,469
OAKFIELD	.....	.....	.....	.....	1,457	1,597	1,471	1,495
PAVILION	.....	.....	.....	.....	1,640	1,723	1,614	1,649
PEMBROKE	.....	2,576	3,828	1,970	2,279	2,855	2,810	2,815
STAFFORD	.....	2,069	2,368	2,561	1,974	2,077	1,847	1,808
TOTAL	3,610	18,578	26,008	28,705	28,488	32,189	31,606	32,776

* Le Roy was, until 1812, in *Caledonia*, which town in 1810 had 2,355 inhabitants.

BUSINESS DIRECTORY

—OF—

GENESEE COUNTY, N. Y.

EXPLANATIONS.

Directory is arranged as follows:—

1—Name of individual or firm.

2—Postoffice ad lress in parenthesis if different from the name of town.

3—The figures following the letter r indicate the number of the road on which the party resides, and will be found by reference to the map in the back part of this work. Where no road number is given the party is supposed to reside in the village.

4—Business or occupation.

5—The figures placed after the occupation of a farmer indicate the number of acres owned or leased.

6—Names in CAPITALS are those who have kindly given their patronage to the work, and without whose aid its publication would have been impossible.

☞ *For additional names, corrections, and changes, see Errata.*

ABBREVIATIONS —Ab., above; ave., avenue; bds., boards; bet., between; cor., corner; E , east; emp., employee; fac. op , factory operative; h., house; manuf., manufacturer; Mfg., manufacturing; N., north; n., near; opp., opposite; prop., proprietor; reg., registered as applied to live stock; regt., regiment; com., commercial; ins., insurance; S., south; W., west.

The word *street* is implied.

ALABAMA.

(Postoffice address is Alabama, unless otherwise designated in parenthesis.)

Aberdeen George E., (S. Alabama) postmaster, notary public, and general merchant.

Aberdeen John H., (S. Alabama) r 48, station agent W. S. R. R.

Ackerson John, r 54, 100 apple trees, farmer 47.

Ackerson Oren, farm laborer.

Ackerson Orrin, (Basom) r 56, farmer.

Ackerson Sheldon, r 40, laborer and farmer 2.

Adair John, (Indian Falls) r 80, farmer 2.

Addis Daniel H., r 20, prop. heading-mill.

Ahrens Joseph, r 33, farm laborer.

Allen Gideon, r 21, refused to give information.

Allen Russell, locomotive engineer W. S. R. R., h and lot.

Ames Alphonzo, (N. Pembroke) r 86, farmer 84.

Ames George, (Wheatville) r 11, mason and farmer 48½.
Ames Theron, (N. Pembroke) r 86, farmer.
Amsden William A., (Wheatville) r 25, 100 apple trees, 150 high grade Merino sheep, farmer 175.
Antis Jacob E., r 14, emp. in mill.
Appleton ———, r 20, widow of Thomas.
Baird Gustavus J., r 17, 300 apple trees, farmer 136.
Baker John, (S. Alabama) r 43, laborer.
Barber Alden S., (Wheatville) r 11, shoemaker and farmer 48½.
Barber Lewis A., (Wheatville) r 11, farmer with his father, Alden S.
Barrett Elvin A., (S. Alabama) r 44, farmer 200.
Barrett Joseph B., (S. Alabama) r 44, retired farmer 187.
Bartz Charles, r 4, farmer 50.
BASOM HARRISON S., (Basom) r 52, town assessor and farmer 114.
BASOM SABERT H., (Basom) r 52, notary public and farmer 111.
Basom Charles W., (Indian Falls) r 76, farmer 83.
Bateman Sylvester, r 19, farm laborer.
Beals Albert G., r 14, farmer, leases of Mrs. J. S. 130.
BEALS JAMES A., r 15, 200 apple trees, farmer 75.
BEALS JEREMIAH S., r 8, 100 apple trees, farmer 40.
Becker Peter, (S. Alabama) r 43, blacksmith.
Beckman Fred, r 18, farmer 80.
Bell Thomas C., r 23, pastor M. E. Church.
Bell William F., physician and surgeon, Church, h do.
BEMENT ALPHA E., (Basom) r 53, justice of the peace, carpenter, and builder, 100 apple trees, farmer 104.
Benson Edward, r 8, laborer.
Bertz Julius, off r 4, farmer 100.
Bickell George, (Wheatville) r 12, laborer.
Bickford John M., com. traveler, lot Pleasant.
Bloomingdale Charles, r 17, farmer 65.
Bloomingdale Fay F., r 17, 200 apple trees, farmer 73.
Bloomingdale John, r 17, apiarist 40 colonies, farmer 2.
Board Clinton O., r 40, farm laborer, h and lot.
Boice Reuben, r 23, laborer.
Boice Wilbert, r 23, laborer.
Bonvemoyer Jonas, r 7, farmer, leases of Spring House 748.
Bootz John, (Wolcottville, Niagara Co.) r 3, farmer.
Bootz William, (Wolcottville, Niagara Co.) r 3, farmer 17.
Bootz William, Jr., r 18, farmer 90.
Boyce James, 1st, (Wheatville) r 27, 400 apple trees, 100 grade Leicester sheep, farmer. [Died Dec., 1889.]
Boyce James, (Wheatville) r 27, farm laborer.
Brackett Welcome M., prop. meat market, h and lot Main.
Bradburn John, (S. Alabama) r 48, farmer 6.
Bradburn William, (S. Alabama) r 48, laborer.
Brown John, (S. Alabama) r 43, butcher.
Brownell Frank, (S. Alabama) r 44, laborer.
Buchanan Peter, (S. Alabama) retired.
Buckle Augustus, (Indian Falls) r 76, farmer 250.
Buckle Charles L., (Indian Falls) r 76, farmer with Augustus.
Burlingame Warren, r 23, gunsmith.
Burnett Daniel, r 35, farmer 75.
Cain Peter, r 33, farmer 50.
Caine Gideon, farmer, leases of Almina Duers 73.
Caleb Harrison, r 8, farmer 47.
Caleb Harrison W., (Shelby Center, Orleans Co.) r 8, farmer 50.
Call Edward, (Basom) laborer.
Callahan William, (S. Alabama) clerk.

Canvert William, r 5, farmer 40.
Carney Eliza, (Oakfield) r 46, farmer 89..
Carney Michael, (Oakfield) r 46, farmer.
Carney Thomas, (Oakfield) r 46, farmer.
Casey Arthur, r 16, farmer with his father, Thomas.
Casey Bartley, r 16, farmer with his father, Thomas.
Casey Owen, r 16, farmer with his father, Thomas.
Casey Thomas, r 16, farmer 156.
Casper Benjamin, (S. Alabama) r 46, laborer.
Cassidy James, (Wheatville) r 14, farmer 62.
Castelo James, (S. Alabama) r 46, farmer 4.
CEDER HENRY, (Basom) prop. Ceder House and livery stable.
CEDER HOUSE, (Basom) Henry Ceder, prop., livery stable connected.
Chamberlain Charles P., (S. Alabama) r 44, farmer 136.
Chamberlain George, (Wheatville) r 66, gardener and laborer, h and lot.
Chamberlain Sarah, (S. Alabama) r 44, widow of John.
Chamberlain Wade, (S. Alabama) r 44, farmer 68.
Champion Eliza A., (N. Pembroke) r 84, widow of Ezra, farmer 100.
Charlau Augustus, r 18, farmer 95.
Cheney Dudley, (Akron, Erie Co.) r 60, farmer 10.
Child Increase, Baptist clergyman, h Church.
Childs Robert, (S. Alabama) r 42, laborer.
CLARK ALICE, owns Clark House, Main.
Clark Enos, (Wheatville) r 12, laborer and farmer 5.
Clark House. Louis Miller, prop., Main.
Clark Susan, (Indian Falls) r 80, widow of William, farmer 10.
Clark William, (Indian Falls) r 80, laborer.
CLOSEN FRED J., r 23, 300 apple trees, farmer, leases of H. Frary, of Oakfield, 210.
Closen John, r 18, farmer 80.
Clossen William, (Wheatville) r 14, farmer 170.
Colten Charles, r 4, farmer 72.
Cook William D., r 19, farmer 55.
Cottingham William, r 23, laborer.
Craft James, farm laborer and farmer 3.
Crook Freeman H., (S. Alabama) r 44, farmer for Amanda R. 20.
Cross Ira, (Wheatville) laborer, h and lot.
Curray Henry, (S. Alabama) r 42, laborer.
Daniels George, (S. Alabama) r 42, farmer 55.
Debbage Fred, r 4, farmer 50.
Derr Charles, (Indian Falls) r 51, farmer 104.
Dewolf Caroline, (S. Alabama) r 42, widow of Anson, farmer 3.
Direne Augustus, r 23, laborer.
Dolan Thomas, (Basom) r 34, trackwalker W. S. R. R.
Donnan Samuel, (S. Alabama) r 48, farmer 93.
Donnan William, retired farmer 125.
Drake Charles, carpenter and farmer 10, h Church.
Drake Joel, carpenter and joiner, h Church.
Dual Florrilla, r 19, widow of Isaac P., farm 50. [Died 1889.]
Dual Freeman, r 23, laborer.
DUAL GEORGE W., wagonmaker and blacksmith, Main, h do.
Dual Wellington, r 23, farmer 61.
Duers Almina, r 40, widow of William, farm 73.
Dugan Charles, (Wheatville) r 26, farmer with Patrick 80.
Dugan Patrick, (Wheatville) r 26, farmer with Charles 80.
Dunn Nicholas, (S. Alabama) r 32, farm laborer.
Eaton Lyman T., r 19, farmer 53.
Elliott George L., (S. Alabama) r 44, mason, h. and lot.
ELLIS JOSEPH, (S. Alabama) r 33, 200 apple trees, farmer, leases of Israel Kurts, of Alexander, 140.

Evans S. R., (Wheatville) Freewill Baptist clergyman.
Farnsworth Frank, (Basom) r 53, farmer with Philip.
FARNSWORTH PHILIP, (Basom) r 53, 350 apple trees. 10 horses, farmer 90.
Feeley Michael, (Basom) r 34, section foreman W. S. R. R.
Fennell John, (S. Alabama) r 42, laborer.
FENNER NATHANIEL C., (Indian Falls) r 52, 100 apple trees, farmer 52.
Filkins Abigail, r 19, widow of James, 500 apple trees, 1,000 pear trees, farmer 125.
Filkins Marion A., r 19, farmer with his mother, Abigail.
Filkins Philander, (S. Alabama) r 40, 100 apple trees, farmer 80.
Finger William, r 23, farmer 6.
Fink Fred, (W. Shelby, Orleans Co.) r 4, assessor and farmer 229.
Fisher Charles, (Wheatville) farm laborer, h Main.
Fisher Edmond, (S. Alabama) r 43, laborer.
Fisher Horace P., (S. Alabama) r 32, 300 apple trees, farmer 161½.
Fisk Levi, r 23, formerly farmer.
Fisk Levi B., r 23, 300 apple trees, farmer 70.
Forward John D., (Basom) r 34, general merchant and farmer 110.
Fountain Howard, (Oakfield) r 46, com. traveler.
Fountain Norton D., (Oakfield) r 46, owns with Paulina farm 217.
Fountain Paulina, (Oakfield) r 46, widow of Charles, owns with Norton D. farm 217.
Fox Charles, (Wheatville) r 27, farmer, leases of Robert Nichol, of Medina, Orleans
    Co., 175.
Garnham George, com. traveler, h Pleasant.
Garnham Henry, mason, h Pleasant.
Gibson Robert, (S. Alabama) r 48, retired.
Gibson William, (S. Alabama) r 48, retired farmer 140.
Gilbert Harrison, (W. Shelby, Orleans Co.) r 1, farmer 62.
Gilbert Jeremiah, (W. Shelby, Orleans Co.) r 1, farmer 40.
Goatrick Thomas, (Wheatville) r 11, farmer 123.
Goodwin Edwin, (S. Alabama) r 42, carpenter.
Goorko Harmon, r 18, farmer 52.
Goorko William, r 18, farmer 4.
Gray Charles W., r 4, farmer 60.
Green Aaron, (S. Alabama) r 49, farmer 50.
Green Julius, (Basom) r 51, farmer for his mother, Maria, 98.
Green Maria, (Basom) r 51, widow of Lester, farm 98.
Gregory Frank, (Wheatville) farmer 40.
Grice James G., (Wheatville) r 26, blacksmith and farm 10.
Griffin John, (Basom) r 38, farmer 53.
Griffin U. S. Grant, (Basom) r 38, farmer 23.
Guiteau Resoloo, r 23, painter.
Guwaer Emma, dressmaker, Main.
GUWAER JAMES, r 16, 100 apple trees, farmer 299.
Haack Augustus, laborer.
Hale George, (S. Alabama) r 71, farmer 104.
Hale John, (Wheatville) laborer, bds. Main.
Hale Robert, (S. Alabama) off r 47, farmer 50.
Hale Thomas, (Wheatville) r 12, farmer 51.
HALSEY EDWARD, (S. Alabama) r 42, retired farmer 52.
Hammu Philip, (Wheatville) r 27, 100 apple trees, farmer 80.
Harloff Henry, (S. Alabama) r 43, farmer 10.
Hartwick Charles, off r 18, farmer 16.
Harvey Henry, (S. Alabama) r 42, laborer.
Haskell Deforest, r 34, farmer, leases of the H. Norton estate 107.
Haskell Elmer, r 16, farmer, leases of the Bloomingdale estate 76.
Haskell Jane, r 17, widow, farm 10.
Herr George, r 6, farmer for Mary 49.
Herrick Dyer, (Wheatville) r 12, farmer.
Herrick Eli W., (Wheatville) r 12, 400 apple trees, farmer with Martha 220.

Herrick Martha, (Wheatville) r 12, farmer 220.
Hescock David, (Basom) r 52, 100 apple trees, farmer 68.
HESTON LEWIS E., (S. Alabama) r 73, breeder of Jersey cattle, reg., farmer 175.
Hirschfeld Frances, (Basom) r 34, (Mrs. P.) prop. boarding-house.
Hiscock Charles, (Basom) r 52, farmer 49.
Hitchcock George, (Basom) r 39, 400 apple trees, farmer 250.
Hitchcock Lyman, (S. Alabama) r 50, retired farmer.
HITCHCOCK WILLIAM Q., (S. Alabama) r 40, farmer 130.
Hodgins William Henry, (Basom) r 39, farmer, leases of W. Ingalsbee 120.
Hodgon Henry, r 18, farmer 1.
Holmes Catharine, r 35, (Mrs. Nathan T.) farm 100.
Holmes Nathan T., r 35, farmer for Catharine 100.
Holmes Lydia G., (Wheatville) r 23, resident.
Hopkins Mary, (Wheatville) r 23, widow of Isaac N., resident.
HOTCHKISS ANNA, (S. Alabama) r 40, widow of.Sterling, farm 72.
HOTCHKISS GEORGE E., (Basom) r 52, general ins. agent, represents the Continental and American Fire Ins. Companies, farmer 30.
Houseknecht Charles, (Indian Falls) r 67, farmer 132.
Houseknecht John, (Indian Falls) off r 68, farmer 36.
Houseknecht Philip, (S. Alabama) r 73, M. E. clergymen, farmer 236.
Howitt Samuel C., (S. Alabama) farmer, leases of P. Filkins 80.
Howland Aria, (Wheatville) r 23, farmer, leases of Darius White 100.
HOWLAND CHAUNCY, (Wheatville) r 27, retired farmer, h and lot.
Howland David, r 33, 100 apple trees, farmer 63.
HOWLAND IRA P., r 21, farmer 91.
Hudson Charles, (S. Alabama) r 42, widow of John.
Hunt Angeline, (S. Alabama) r 40, widow of Rev. Benjamin.
Hutton Hugh (S. Alabama) r 49, laborer.
Ingalsbe Alpheus, (S. Alabama) r 49, farmer 112.
Ingalsbe Junius M., (Basom) r 56, farmer with W. L. 134.
Ingalsbe Levi, (Basom) r 39, 100 apple trees, farmer 234.
Ingalsbe Marion R., (Basom) r 40, farmer with his father, Rial E.
INGALSBE RIAL E., (Basom) r 40, 100 apple trees, farmer 193.
Ingalsbe Slocum B., (Basom) r 56, farmer, leases of Levi 100.
Ingalsbe Whitman L., (Basom) r 56, farmer with Junius M. 134.
Ingalsbee Harman C., (Basom) r 40, farmer, leases of R. E. Ingalsbe 96.
Ingalsbee Julius, (Basom) r 52, postmaster, dealer in groceries and meats, agent for fertilizers and agricultural implements.
Ingalsbee Whitman, (Basom) r 56, farmer.
Ingalsbee William, (Basom) r 39, farmer 120.
Inglasbee Edmond A., (S. Alabama) r 43, jeweler, engineer, and musician.
Inglasbee Lucretia, (S. Alabama) r 43, widow of Elijah B.
INGLESBE EBENEZER, (S. Alabama) r 49, 300 apple trees, farmer 231.
Inglesbe Mary, (Indian Falls) r 79, widow of Enos, farmer 28.
Inglesbe Solomus, (Indian Falls) r 79, farmer.
Irek John, (S. Alabama) r 30, laborer.
Johnson William, (Wheatville) r 12, carpenter and farmer 4.
Jones Abiah M., r 17, farmer with his father, John A.
Jones John A., r 17, farmer 119.
Jones William R., r 17, farmer with his father, John A.
Joslyn Henry, (Wheatville) farmer 1.
Joslyn John, (Wheatville) r 12, farmer, leases of Mrs. C. Hale 90.
Kannack John, (Wheatville) r 23, 100 apple trees, 100 pear trees, farmer, leases of J. W. Holmes, of Batavia, 107.
Keegan Lawrence, (S. Alabama) r 46, farmer 280.
Kelsey Elizabeth S., (N. Pembroke) r 85, (Mrs. Norman) farmer 86.
Kenwood George, r 5, farmer 41.
Kenyon Orson, (Basom) r 51, farmer 93.
Kenyon Orville, (Basom) r 51, laborer.

KESSLER JOSEPH, farm laborer, h and lot Main.
Kigdom Philip, (Wheatville) r 26, laborer and farmer 7.
Kiser John N., farm laborer, h Railroad.
Kiser William, laborer, h and lot Railroad.
Klasen William, (Wheatville) r 27, 1,500 apple trees, 125 grade Southdown sheep, farmer, leases of J. W. Hael 160.
Klotzbach Peter, (Indian Falls) r 76, farmer 50.
Knic Charles, r 18, farmer 21.
Korkow Herman, r 18, farmer 54.
Korkow William, r 18, farmer 2½.
Kotzbach John, (S. Alabama) r 68, farmer, leases of Calvin Wheeler 240.
Krautz Ferdinand, (Wolcottville, Niagara Co.) r 3, farmer 88.
Krautz Lewis, (Wolcottville, Niagara Co.) r 3, farmer 274.
Lambert John, r 16, farmer 50.
Lamkin John, (Basom) r 62, farmer 82.
Lanckton Aaron S., (Wheatville) retired farmer and currier, born in 1799, h and lot Main.
Landers Patrick, (Wheatville) r 11, farmer 160.
Landers Patrick, Jr., (Wheatville) r 11, farmer 50.
Lawrence Charles, (Akron, Erie Co.) r 77, farmer 150.
Leno Henry, (Wheatville) r 23, farmer, leases of George Rhodes.
Lester Peter, (Indian Falls) r 76, farmer 15.
Lintner Christopher, r 33, farm laborer.
Lumley Rolla, r 17, farmer 275.
Lund Frank L., r 15, farmer, leases of his father, Franklin F.
Lund Franklin F., r 15, 200 apple trees, farmer 102.
Lyday Frank N., r 40, farm laborer.
MACOMBER JOHN L., (Oakfield) r 45, breeder of Shropshiredown sheep, 1,300 apple trees, 750 pear trees, farmer 177½, and on the W. J. Macomber estate 114.
Manchester Eugenia A., (E. Shelbv, Orleans Co.) r 11, widow of Sanford E., farm 100.
Marble Alonzo, (Indian Falls) r 64, farmer.
Marble George, (Indian Falls) r 64, farmer 140.
Marble Pamelia, (Basom) r 53, widow of Samuel, farmer 8.
Marry John, (S. Alabama) r 42, laborer.
Martin Abram, (N. Pembroke) r 84, retired farmer.
MARTIN DANIEL, (S. Alabama) r 71, farmer 100.
Martin George W., (N. Pembroke) r 72, farmer 100.
Martin Hannah, (S. Alabama) r 49, widow of Elijah, farmer 89.
Martin Henry, (N. Pembroke) r 85, farmer 40.
Martin Jacob, (N. Pembroke) r 85, farmer 225.
MARTIN WALLACE H., (S. Alabama) r 71, farmer with Daniel.
Mason Eliza, (S. Alabama) r 43, widow of Collius T.
Maxwell David A., (Wheatville) r 12, farmer 83.
McAlister James, (Basom) r 52, farm laborer.
McAlpin Samuel, (Indian Falls) r 62, farmer, leases of E. Diver, of Pembroke, 300.
McAlpine John, (Indian Falls) r 80, farmer 106.
McCormick Michael, (Wheatville) r 26, farm laborer.
McCracken ———, r 16, laborer and farmer 4.
McInter John, (S. Alabama) r 49, farmer, leases of B. Chapman, of Oakfield, 250.
McGinn Thomas, (Basom) blacksmith.
McGuire Daniel, (Wheatville) r 26, laborer and shoemaker, h and lot.
McMannus John, (Wheatville) r 26, mason, h and lot.
McPartland Bridget, (Wheatville) r 25, widow of Patrick, 100 apple trees, farmer 144.
McPartland John, (Wheatville) r 25, farmer with Bridget.
McPartland Thomas, (Wheatville) r 25, farm laborer, h and lot Main.
MEAD CHARLES M., (Basom) r 53, agent for Rowley & Eddy, dealers in lumber, lath, shingles, fence posts, sash, doors, blinds, coal, etc.
Merkle Albert, r 36, farmer 95.
Merry John, (S. Alabama) r 42, laborer.

Miller Eugene H., (N. Pembroke) r 72, farmer for Jacob Shoemaker 94½.
Miller Fred, (N. Pembroke) r 83, farmer, leases of Edward Halsey 107.
Miller Lewis, r 33, farm laborer.
Miller Louis, prop. Clark House.
Miller Michael, (N. Pembroke) r 83, farmer 181.
Monohan John, (S. Alabama) r 42, farmer 5.
Mook Catharine, (N. Pembroke) r 85, widow of Anthony.
Mook Daniel D., (N. Pembroke) r 85, farmer.
Mook Vienna, (N. Pembroke) r 85, resident.
Moore Dennis, r 23, laborer,
Moore Osro, r 20, prop. stage from Alabama to Medina.
Moore Walter, r 35, farm laborer.
Morse Nelson, (Basom) r 53, farm laborer and farmer 2.
Muier Alexander, (Wolcottville, Niagara Co.) r 3, farmer 100.
Newman J. C., (S. Alabama) pastor Baptist Church.
Newton Ara R., (W. Shelby, Orleans Co.) r 1, farmer, leases of Franklin 150.
Newton Arie, r 2, farmer.
Newton Franklin, (W. Shelby, Orleans Co.) r 2, 600 apple trees, farmer 150.
Nichol Harry, r 19, laborer.
Nichol Thomas L., (Wheatville) r 27, 600 apple trees, 100 fine wool sheep, farmer 175.
Nichol William A., (Wheatville) student Batavia Union School.
Noble Charles B., r 23, harnessmaker.
Noble Judson, r 23, harnessmaker with Charles B.
Norris Abraham, (N. Pembroke) r 72, farmer for Elizabeth 108.
Norris John C., (N. Pembroke) r 84, farmer 100, and for Eliza A. Champion 100.
NORTON ALLEN E., r 34, breeder of thoroughbred poultry, Wyandotte, Light Brahmas, and Plymouth Rock fowls, farmer with his father, Frank.
Norton Daniel, r 34, produce dealer and farmer 362.
NORTON FRANK, r 34, 650 apple trees, 16 horses and mules, farmer 200.
Norton Halsey, r 34, deputy sheriff and farmer.
NORTON HARMON J., (Wheatville) r 37, postmaster, overseer of the poor, farmer 115.
NORTON HEMAN, r 34, farmer 107. [Died in 1889.]
Norton Medad, r 33, farmer 182.
O'Haron John, (Basom) r 34, laborer.
O'Reily Thomas, (Wheatville) r 13, teacher.
Ostrander Arthur J., (S. Alabama) r 40, farmer, leases of Anna Hotchkiss 72.
Ostrander John, r 4, farmer 2.
Paile Nicholas, (Wheatville) r 31, farmer 15.
Palmer Edmund E., (Wheatville) deputy postmaster and general merchant, Main.
Palmer Jane, (Wheatville) r 27, widow of Joseph. farm 10.
Parker Isaac, (Wheatville) r 11, formerly farmer.
Parker Raymond J., r 15, farmer with his father, Wesley J.
Parker Sherman S., r 34, prop. creamery, manuf. of butter and cheese, farmer 80.
Parker Wesley J., r 15, 200 apple trees, farmer 78.
Parker Willard E., (Wheatville) r 11, farmer 200.
Pask Edward, r 34, farmer, leases of Frank Norton 200.
Patterson Hiram B., r 36, farmer, owns with Westley 40.
Patterson James, r 36, 100 apple trees, farmer 100.
Patterson James, (S. Alabama) r 42, laborer.
Patterson James, Jr., r 34, laborer.
Patterson Westley, r 36, farmer, owns with Hiram B. 40.
Pender James, r 16, teamster and farm laborer.
Peters Herman, (S. Alabama) r 43, farmer 1½.
PHILLIPS CHARLES R., farmer, owns in Erie Co. 105, h and 2 acres Railroad.
PHILLIPS WILLIAM J., farmer with his father, Charles R.
Pickworth William, r 39, 200 grade sheep, farmer 254.
Pierce Emma J., (Basom) r 39, widow of Charles R., dressmaker.
Pierce James, (Wheatville) r 11, laborer, h and 2 acres.

PIXLEY ARA, (Wheatville) 200 apple trees, 90 sheep, 6 horses, farmer, leases of Harmon J. Norton 113.
Pixley Frank A., general merchant and dealer in agricultural implements.
Pixley Jay, r 20, farmer with his father, Joseph.
Pixley Joseph, r 20, 150 apple trees, 12 cows, farmer 197.
Pixley Theodore, r 20, farmer with his father, Joseph.
Poodry Barnum, r 38, farmer with his father, E. M.
POODRY E. M., r 38, 1,000 apple trees, 12 horses, 12 head other stock, farmer 350.
Post Jessee F., (S. Alabama) r 49, farmer, leases of E. Inglesbe 138.
Potter Charlotte L., widow of George H., h and 1 acre.
Potter Cora C., r 39, widow of Abel J.
POTTER EUGENE D., r 17, 200 apple trees, farmer, leases of Donnin 125, and of Jacob 225.
POTTER JACOB, r 39, 150 apple trees, farmer 215.
Pratt Dexter, r 23, deputy postmaster and grafter.
Price George B., (S. Alabama) r 73, farmer, leases of Lewis E. Heston 175.
Price William, r 19, prop. steam saw and heading-mills, farmer 4.
Quible Benjamin, (Wheatville) r 20, farmer, leases of G. Allen 100.
Quigley John, laborer.
Rapp Charles S., (Indian Falls) r 62, farmer for Sarah 112.
Rapp Ephraim F., (Basom) r 39 cor. 52, farm laborer.
Rapp William, (Indian Falls) r 79, farmer 14.
Reak Charles, (Wolcottville, Niagara Co.) r 3, farmer 33.
Reak Fred, r 18, farmer 60.
Reed Elmer E., (S. Alabama) r 32, farmer 189.
Reed Loren, (S. Alabama) r 30, 200 apple trees, 100 grade Merino sheep, 14 horses, farmer, leases of his father.
Reed William, (Wheatville) r 26, salesman for E. E. Palmer.
Rheimer Augustus, (S. Alabama) r 43, farmer, leases of Mrs. T. Gordon 125.
Rhodes George, (Wheatville) r 25, 100 apple trees, farmer 150.
Rhodes Joseph, r 4, farmer for Eliza 50.
Roatch Sabert E., (S. Alabama) r 48, farmer 212.
Roberts Charlie.D., (Wheatville) r 13, 200 apple trees, farmer 100.
ROBERTS CHARLES W., (Wheatville) r 11, 400 apple trees, 70 Shropshire sheep, farmer 125.
Roberts Rudell R., (Wheatville) r 13, 200 apple trees, farmer 102.
Roggo Christian, off r 4, farmer 54.
Roggow Christopher, (W. Shelby, Orleans Co.) off r 4, farmer for Caroline 30.
Rood Joseph, r 4, farmer 60.
Royce Gilmore D., town clerk and school teacher, h Church.
Sanders Elon, (S. Alabama) r 47, farmer 5.
SAXTON EMILY A., (S. Alabama) widow of Orimel W., farm 190.
Saxton Ray, (S. Alabama) r 43, farmer, leases of Orpha Wolcott 100.
Scharlau August, r 18, farmer 95.
Scharlau Godfred, (Wolcottville, Niagara Co.) r 3, farmer 26.
Scharlau William, (Wolcottville, Niagara Co.) r 3, farmer 5.
Schoal Charles, r 17, 100 apple trees, farmer 123.
Scroger Anson, (S. Alabama) r 30, farm laborer.
Scroger John, (Wheatville) r 27, laborer.
SHOEMAKER JACOB, (N. Pembroke) r 72, retired farmer 94½.
Shugarts Ann E., (S. Alabama) r 47, widow of William.
Shugarts Clinton, (S. Alabama) r 47, farmer, leases of W. C. Pond, of Climax, Mich., 92.
Shultz Lewis, (Wheatville) r 27, 200 apple trees, 120 grade Southdown sheep, 17 head cattle, farmer 154.
Shultz William, (Wheatville) farm laborer, h and lot Main.
Siebert Augustus, (Wolcottville, Niagara Co.) r 35, farmer 57.
Siebert John, off r 4, farmer 75.
Singer Solomon, r 16, farmer, leases of F. Vosburgh.
Slimmer John, (Basom) r 53, laborer.

Slimmer John, r 53, farm laborer and farmer 3.
Smith Christopher, (Wheatville) r 8, farmer 50.
Smith Leighton, (Wheatville) r 11, laborer.
Smith William, r 3, farmer 100.
Snyder Henry, (Basom) r 63, farmer, leases of the Norton sisters, of Batavia, 193.
Southlin Amel, (Wheatville) r 8, laborer.
Southlin Joseph, r 8, laborer, h and lot.
Sparling Charles. (Akron, Erie Co.) r 77, farmer 128.
Stafford Frank, (Basom) r 53, carpenter and joiner, h and lot.
Stafford Theodore, r 21, peddler and farmer 5.
Starkweather Morrell, r 17, laborer.
Steinhorst Augustus, r 3, farmer 30.
STEVENS GEORGE E., (Wheatville) r 25, 100 apple trees, farmer 50.
Stevens James, r 23, laborer.
Stevens John, (Wheatville) r 12, laborer, h and lot.
Stickney Harriet R., (S. Alabama) r 44, widow of Addison.
Taber Frank, (Basom) r 40, farm laborer.
Taber Willie M., r 39, salesman for F. A. Pixley, h and lot.
Tabor Lovina, (Basom) r 39, widow of W. G., h and lot.
Tank Augustus, (S. Alabama) r 43, laborer, h and lot.
Taylor Bryant W., (Oakfield) r 86, farmer, leases of Daniel R. 150.
Taylor Daniel R., (Oakfield) r 86, farm 150.
Tesno Christian, (Akron, Erie Co.) r 77, farmer 376.
Thayer Olive, (Basom) r 39, dressmaker, daughter of Riley.
Thayer Riley, (Basom) r 39, cooper and farmer.
Thompson Adelbert, (Basom) r 34, produce dealer and farmer 80.
Thomson William, (Basom) farmer, leases of Adelbert 80.
Town Elijah, (S. Alabama) r 33, 100 apple trees, farmer 106.
Tumalty Arthur, (S. Alabama) r 42, farmer.
Tumalty John H., blacksmith, Medina, h and 3 acres do.
Tumalty Seward E., farm laborer.
Tuttle Albert, r 5, farmer 270.
TUTTLE EDWARD, (Basom) r 40, farmer 103.
Tuttle Elizabeth, (Wheatville) widow of Earl, h and lot Main.
Underhill Alva W., (Wheatville) r 12, farmer with his father.
Underhill Eleazer R., (Wheatville) apiarist 31 colonies, 100 apple trees, farmer 93.
Underhill John, (Wheatville) r 13, farmer 41.
VAIL CHARLES A., r 20, (E. P. Vail & Sons) farmer 15.
VAIL E. P. & SONS, r 34, (Frank D. and Charles A.) fruit evaporators and dealers.
VAIL ELI P., r 34, (E. P. Vail & Sons) 400 apple trees, 100 pear trees, farmer 150.
VAIL FRANK D., r 20, (E. P. Vail & Sons) 100 apple trees, farmer 6.
Vail Henry, (Basom) r 39, farmer, leases of A. E. Bement 104.
Vaughn Freeman S., r 20, house, ornamental, and carriage painter, h and lot.
Vaughn Nelson, r 14, 300 apple trees, farmer 55.
Vaughn Oscar D., r 20, carpenter.
VAUGHN WESLEY F., r 14, farmer, leases of his father, Nelson, 55.
Vincent Julius, (Wheatville) r 27, laborer, h and lot.
VOSBURGH FRANK E., r 6, postmaster, prop. Alabama stave and heading-mill. 600 apple trees, farmer 112.
Wade William M., (Basom) r 53, laborer and farmer 10.
Wakeman George W., (Wheatville) 100 apple trees, farmer 111½
Wakeman John P., (Wheatville) r 28, 100 apple trees, farmer 99.
Walker Ira, (Indian Falls) r 62, laborer.
Waterstreet Henry, (Wheatville) r 25, farmer, leases of W. A. Amsden 168.
WEBB GEORGE W., (Basom) station and National Express agent W. S. R. R.
Webb John T., (Basom) telegraph operator W. S. R. R.
Webster C. Eugene, r 17, farmer with his mother, Maria.
Webster Maria, r 17, widow of Porter, 100 apple trees, farmer 67.
Webster Squire, laborer and prop. steam thresher.

West Richard, (Wheatville) blacksmith, Main.
Westfall T. Dewitt, r 17, laborer.
Wheeler Calvin, (S. Alabama) r 68, 100 apple trees, 315 grade sheep, 14 head cattle, farmer 240.
White Arthur P., r 17, farmer, leases of his father, Phineas B.
White Cornelius, produce dealer, h Church.
White Hale, (S. Alabama) r 43, farmer, leases of ——— Hitchcock 96.
WHITE LAURA A., r 17, h and lot.
White Michael, (S. Alabama) r 30, farmer 50.
WHITE PHINEAS B., 100 apple trees, farmer 99.
WIGHT ABBOTT, (S. Alabama) r 50, farmer 165.
WIGHT ABEL, (S. Alabama) r 50, 200 apple trees, farmer 160.
Wight Bruce, (S. Alabama) r 50, school teacher and farmer 32.
Wight Fay, (S. Alabama) teacher, son of Abel.
Wight George, (S. Alabama) r 50, 200 apple trees, farmer 200, and in Pembroke 78.
Wight Hale, (S. Alabama) r 43, carpenter and farmer, leases of ——— Hitchcock 50.
Wight Miles, (S. Alabama) r 50, farm laborer, h and lot.
Wight Noah, (S. Alabama) r 40, 100 apple trees, farmer, leases of J. Ackerson 50.
Wight P. Hewit, (S. Alabama) r 50, farmer with his father, Abbott.
Wight Perry H , (S. Alabama) r 50, farm laborer.
Willis Dorr D., (Basom) r 52, farmer 26.
Willis Elizabeth, r 23, widow of John.
Willis John E., r 23, laborer.
Winchell Albert, r 14, laborer.
WINCHELL LYMAN W., teamster, served in 19th N. Y. Bat. 3 years, h and lot Medina st.
Winegar Theresa, (Oakfield) r 46, widow of Philip, farm 18.
Winslow Edward J., (S. Alabama) r 42, carpenter.
Winslow Norman H., (Indian Falls) r 76, farmer 52, and leases of C. Brooks, of Akron, Erie Co., 130.
WOLCOTT ORPHA, (S. Alabama) r 43, widow of Thomas, farmer 100.
Woodstroke Augustus, r 18, farmer 75.
Woolston George, (Shelby Center, Orleans Co.) r 8, farmer 30.
Woolston Jerry, r 8, laborer.
Worthington Alfred, (Indian Falls) r 67, farmer, leases of Philip Housekneck 130.
Worthington Jonathan, (Indian Falls) r 64 cor. 66, farmer 50.
Wright John, (Akron, Erie Co.) r 77, farmer 136.
Yargo Charles, (W. Shelby, Orleans Co.) off r 4, farmer 49.
ZURHORST AUGUSTUS T. G., supervisor, physician, and surgeon, Railroad, h do.

ALEXANDER.

(*For explanations, etc., see page 3, part second.*)

(Postoffice address is Alexander, unless otherwise designated in parenthesis.)

Adams George, Jr., (Attica, Wyoming Co.) r 50, tinker.
Adams James, r 43, farmer 6½.
Adams Sarah, (Attica, Wyoming Co.) r 50, widow of George, resident.
Ahl Charles, (Linden) r 63, farmer 168.
Ahl George, r 60, farmer 230.
Alexander Hotel, George Fancher, prop.
Allen Edgar M., r 14, farmer with his father, James.
Allen James, r 14, 10 grade Durham cows, farmer 92.
Allen Walter, (Linden) r 64, farmer, leases of J. Mowrer 60.

Allworth Charles, r 33, farmer, leases with Horace of J. G. Shepard 236.
Allworth Horace, r 33, farmer, leases with Charles of J. G. Shepard 236.
Andrews Almond, retired carriagemaker and farmer 12, h State.
ANDREWS AUGUSTA V., r 62, widow of Charles D., farmer 112.
Andrews Betsey G., widow of Dr. David, h Buffalo st.
Andrews Harvey A., r 62, farmer, leases of Augusta B. 112.
Andrews Judson, r 21, carpenter, builder, and contractor, farmer 20.
Atwood Brigham, farmer, h Buffalo st.
AVERY GEORGE E., r 44, served in Co. M, 9th N. Y. H. A., retired farmer, owns a
    farm in the West.
AVERY RUFUS G., r 59, 20 cows, 7 Jersey, full blood Holstein, and grade Dur-
    ham cattle, farmer 233, and leases of W. H. Locke 133.
Bacon Charles, pastor Free Methodist Church, bds. Church.
Balch H. Celestia, resident, h Buffalo st.
Baldof Martus. r 16, farmer 49.
BALDWIN IRWIN N., r 60, dealer in hay and grain, farmer, leases of Allen Lin-
    coln, of Bethany, 47.
BARNETT WILLIAM H., painter and farmer, served in Co. D, 14th Inf., and in Co.
    M, 2d Mounted Rifles N. Y. Vols., h and 7 acres Main.
Beam Fredrica, r 54, widow of William C.
Beaver William, r 28, farmer 50.
Beideck William, laborer, h Buffalo st.
Bellsmith Harrold S., emp. East & Co., of Rochester, h Main.
Benedict Henry, r 35, farmer 51.
Benson Patrick, (W. Batavia) r 2, farmer 32.
Bentley Elizabeth, widow of William, resident, aged 95, bds. Church.
Bentley Norman, (Pollard & Bentley) postmaster.
Bidlack Earl, (Batavia) r 17, farm laborer.
Bishop Betsey, widow of Abraham.
Blood Luman, (Batavia) r 4, farmer 70.
Blooman Clarence, (Batavia) r 14, farmer, leases of O. Moulton.
Bogart Nettie, clerk and deputy postmaster, h Main.
Bogart William C., dealer in nursery stock, h Allegany st.
Boothe Ambrose, (Linden) r 64, farmer 60.
Bowen Dwight, (Attica, Wyoming Co.) r 47; farmer, leases of David 214.
Bower Philip, r 65, farmer 20.
Bradfield Frank, r 45, laborer.
Brainard Sebe B., r 53, 25 cows, 60 Spanish Merino sheep, farmer 222.
Bratt James, (Batavia) r 7, farmer 101.
Brice Richard, (Batavia) r 11, farmer 5.
Brldof Mrtrs, r 26, farmer 50.
Brookins Marvin W., (Batavia) r 3, farmer 10.
Brown Belle, r 44, school teacher.
Brown Fanny A., widow of Melangtin W.
Brown John B., laborer, h Main.
BROWN JOHN H., r 44, served in Co. D, 14th N. Y. Inf. Vols., farmer 40.
Brown Lyman, r 60, farmer 127.
Brown Olive, widow of Walter, resident, h Main.
Brown Royal M., carpenter, h and lot.
Brown William, carpenter, h State.
Buck Amasa M., r 41, laborer and dealer in live stock.
Bullock Galan, r 59, farmer 3.
Burgler George, laborer, h Church.
Burk Walter, (Batavia) r 36, farmer 22.
BURR FRED E., r 31, farmer, leases the Russell farm 170.
Burt Delia J., (Batavia) r 14 cor. 10, widow of Myron A., farmer 50.
Burt Roderick O., (Batavia) r 14 cor. 10, farmer for his mother, Delia J.
Buterman Fred, (Attica, Wyoming Co.) laborer.
Burton Lyman B., retired, h Buffalo st.

Cady Arthur D., h Main.

Cady Clark S., r 20, 15 grade Durham cows, farmer 77.

Cady Franklin D., (Batavia) r 17, agent nursery stock.

Cady Milo E., r 20, farmer, owns in Batavia 40.

Cady Return B., (Batavia) r 17, 7 grade Durham and Jersey cows, farmer 63.

Carroll Newton A., contractor and builder, h Church.

Carter Betsey, widow, h Church.

Carter Lewis, 'bus driver Parker House, Batavia.

Chadbolt Edwin, farmer, h Buffalo st.

Chaddock Edwin, farmer 8, h Buffalo st.

Chaddock Joseph, (Linden) r 64, farmer 400.

CHADDOCK LEWIS, r 68, 6 cows, 110 grade Merino sheep, farmer 220.

Chaddock Sewell, farmer, h Buffalo st.

Chaddock Suel, farmer. owns in Bethany 300, h Buffalo st.

Chaddock William, r 68, laborer.

Chamberlain Alfred, laborer, h Buffalo st.

Chamberlain Alvin, paper hanger, h Buffalo st.

Chamberlain ———, (Batavia) r 3, farmer 80.

Champlin James, (Batavia) r 7, cheesemaker, emp. Winchester & Willson.

Chapin Benjamin T., off r 13, engineer.

Chapple Thomas, (Attica, Wyoming Co.) r 49, 10 cows, farmer, leases of James Dunbar 90.

Churchill Charles, (Batavia) r 7, 50 sheep, farmer 105.

Churchill Fred J., r 59, laborer.

Churchill John, (Batavia) r 7, farmer with his father, Charles.

Clark Calvin, r 35, farmer 100.

Clemont Emeline L., r 35, widow of Royal M.

Colby Fred C., r 19, farmer, leases of Henry Sprague 95.

Coleman Augustus, (Batavia) r 9, farmer 20.

Comre Peter, laborer, h Main.

Comrie Peter, r 39, farmer, leases of C. Loomis 160.

Comue Peter J., farmer, h Main cor. Buffalo sts.

Conrad Jacob, laborer, h Buffalo st.

Cooley Nial, r 28, farmer 46.

CORNWELL HENRY C., r 52, farmer 48.

Cornwell Mary A., r 52, widow of Chancey, resident, aged 88.

Craig Hamilton, r 34, laborer.

Crosman Cortland C., r 24, county supt. of the poor, farmer 400.

Crossman Edson, (Batavia) r 18, farmer 10.

Curtis George R., r 46, farmer 55.

Curtis J. Milton, r 46, 10 cows, farmer, leases of Roswell C. 144.

Curtis Joseph, r 55, farmer 10.

CURTIS MARCUS L., wagonmaker, Main, h do.

Curtis Roswell C., r 46, farmer 144.

Cuthburt Thomas, r 39, retired soldier.

Dart George, r 60, farm laborer.

Dart James, r 38, farmer 20.

David Egerton C., allo. physician and surgeon, h Main.

Day Elmer, r 2, farmer, leases of Hannah H. Lawton 96.

Day James H., farmer 100, h Buffalo st.

Dean Charles H., r 27, assessor and farmer 4, and leases of C. F. Seward 45.

Delura Timothy, laborer, h Buffalo st.

Demara Sylvester, r 52, laborer. owns 5 acres.

Denslow Laura, widow of Ira, farmer 80.

De Vinna ———, (Attica, Wyoming Co.) r 50, foundryman.

De Wolf Charles, (Batavia) r 8, 9 cows, farmer, leases of G. W. Furguson 142'.

DICKINSON AMY, r 67, widow of Moses H., 8 cows, farmer 128.

Dickinson Hannah, widow of Jerome, resident, aged 82.

Dickinson Harriet, school teacher.

Dickinson William L., general merchant, Main, h do.
Dirstine Pallas, widow of John, aged 70.
Dunbar Henry, (Attica, Wyoming Co.) farmer 120.
Dunbar James, r 47, farmer 89.
Dunham George, r 52, farmer, leases of James Dotey 130.
Dunton Samuel F., r 17, farmer, leases of O. M. 112.
Durfee L. Emery, r 18, farmer 79.
Dye Reuben, (Batavia) r 16, farmer, leases of J. R. Day 100.
Earll Mahlon, r 51, farmer, leases of Orlando 50.
Earll Orlando, r 51, farm 50.
Eddy Herbert W., house painter and paper hanger, h Allegany st.
Egleston Ann E., widow of Alexander, resident, aged 79, h Buffalo st.
EGLESTON CHARLES R., carriage and house painter, president of the village and
    cemetery association, h Buffalo st.
Elliott Thomas, r 42, blacksmith, State.
Ellis Jonas, (Attica, Wyoming Co.) r 57, 10 grade Durham cows, 50 Spanish Merino
    sheep, farmer 95.
Enos Mathew V. B., r 31, farmer, leases of David Cosad 120.
Enos Sherman A., r 31, thresher.
Fairfield Charles, r 35, laborer.
Falker Fred, (Attica, Wyoming Co.) r 56, laborer.
Fancher George, prop. Alexander Hotel.
Fargo Adelbert, r 57, farmer, leases of S. Riddle 165.
Fincher John A., r 40, 10 cows, farmer 76.
Flemming L. J., r 45, widow.
Fraser Donald G., r 14, dealer in coal and salt, station agent and telegraph operator
    D., L. & W. R. R.
Fridsche Hermann, r 43, farmer 25¼.
Frink Frederick C., r 59, farmer, leases of R. G. Avery 233.
Frink Wilber C., r 21, farmer 10, and in Darien 50.
Fuller William, r 57, laborer.
Gardner Annie, widow of George J.
Gardner Cora J., r 35, school teacher.
Gardner Flynt M., r 66, farmer 88.
Gardner John C., r 35, farmer 126.
Gardner Luther W., r 35, farmer with his father, John C.
Gardner Moulton, r 35, farmer 20.
Garrett George T., (Batavia) r 14, laborer.
GARRETT SAMUEL L., (Batavia) r 14, farmer 48.
Geise John, r 25, farm laborer.
Geise Philip, r 43, 10 cows, farmer 60.
GERE ZAXIE C., widow of William, resident, aged 70, h Church.
Gihuly Michael, r 38, farmer 75.
Gillett Thomas, r 45, 20 cows, farmer.
Good Edwin, r 57, laborer.
Gould Josiah, r 43, retired farmer, h Buffalo st.
Gray Marcus, (Batavia) r 11, prop. stave-mill, farmer 12.
Gray Martin, (Batavia) r 11, farmer with his father, Marcus.
Green Arion, r 14, farmer with his father, Francis.
Green Francis, r 14, 6 cows, 70 grade Spanish Merino sheep, farmer 109
Greene Dora Z., r 19, school teacher.
Greene Edith O., r 19, school teacher.
Greene Joseph O., r 19, 8 cows, farmer 90.
Greene Lucian, r 19, student.
Greene Walter, r 19, student.
Greene ———, widow of Thomas, r 7, farmer 48.
Grow Jacob, r 55, farmer 26.
Hall James C., r 53, farmer 135.
Hallman August, (Batavia) r 9, farmer 29.

Halstead Hiram, (Batavia) r 3, farmer 120.
Halstead William, (Batavia) r 22, farmer 210.
Harloff John, (Attica, Wyoming Co.) r 56, laborer.
Harman George, r 65, farmer 20.
Harman James, (Batavia) r 4, farmer 120.
Harrington Andrew B., life and accident ins. agent, h Allegany st.
Harrington William H., dentist, Buffalo st., h do.
Hastings John C., r 14, 112 grade Spanish Merino sheep, farmer 140.
Hawkins Charles J., r 43, 9 cows, 60 grade Merino sheep, farmer 107.
Hawkins Ira T., r 43, farmer, leases of Charles J. 107.
Hawkins Jessie A., r 32, farmer, leases of Van Rensselaer 290, h Main.
Hawkins Van Rensselaer, retired farmer 290, h Main.
Hawley James, r 45, laborer.
Hay Ewin, r 59, deputy postal clerk on railroad.
Hick James, (Linden) r 64, farmer 6.
Hickox Charles. r 23, 18 Durham, Jersey, and Devonshire cows, farmer 105.
Hickox Edwin, r 23, 12 grade Holstein and Jersey cows, farmer 75.
Hickox Irvin, r 23, farmer, leases of his father, Edwin, 75.
Higgins Harlo, (Batavia) r 76, farmer 36.
Hill Thomas, laborer, h Buffalo st.
HINDRICK BENJAMIN F., r 32, 5 cows, farmer 112.
Hindrick Lewis M., r 32, farmer, leases of Benjamin F. 112.
Hinsdale George A., (Batavia) r 7, 8 grade Durham and Jersey cows, farmer 92.
Hinsdale Jennie A., (Batavia) r 7, school teacher.
Hinsdale Jessie D., (Batavia) r 27, school teacher.
Hinsdale Martha E., (Batavia) r 7, school teacher.
Hopkins Chandler R., retired farmer, h Main.
Hudson Henry, (Batavia) r 17, farmer with his father, Joel.
Hudson Joel, (Batavia) r 17, farmer 67, and in Pavilion 94.
Hunn Maro W., (Batavia) r 10, farmer 90.
Hunn Milo, (Batavia) r 11, farmer 5.
Hurd Darwin M., r 39, farmer leases of Harriet M. 275.
Hurd Harriet M., r 39, widow of Charles B., 15 cows, farm 275.
Hyde Benjamin F., r 38, farmer 25.
Isaac Louis, (Attica, Wyoming Co.) r 56, laborer.
Isaac Thomas, (Attica, Wyoming Co.) r 56, blacksmith.
Jemmerson Andrew, r 46, laborer.
Jemmerson David, r 46, laborer.
Jewel Stephen, laborer, h State.
Jewel William, laborer, h State.
Johncox Ezra, r 21, laborer and farmer 6.
Karan Hugh, r 14, laborer.
Karan John, r 14, farmer 10.
Karan Philip, r 14, farmer 19½.
Karcher Jacob H., (Attica, Wyoming Co.) r 50, clerk.
Karcher John, (Attica, Wyoming Co.) r 50, clothier, Market st., Attica, owns 9 acres.
KARNES JULIA, r 61, daughter of Michael.
Karnes Michael, r 61, farmer 14.
Kearn John, (Batavia) r 14, farmer 10.
Kearn Philip, r 14, farmer 19.
Kelsey Albertus, teamster, h Church.
Kelsey Charles, farmer for his mother, Lucy.
Kelsey Charles D., r 14, farm laborer.
Kelsey Deforest, r 62, farmer 198.
Kelsey Duwain, r 42, farmer 4.
KELSEY LUCY, widow of Theodore, resident, owns 11 acres Church.
Kelsey Sally, widow of Daniel, farmer 160.
Kibler Joseph, (Batavia) r 8, farmer, leases of Jerome Gallup 160.
Kidder Albert D., r 43, farmer with his father, Oel S.

Kidder Earl, r 43, farmer.
Kidder Oel S., 20 cows, r 43, 50 Spanish Merino sheep, farmer 257.
Kidder Perry, r 43, farmer and student.
King Alice, r 26, widow of Uriah.
King Isaac, r 26, farmer 40, and leases of B. R. Sannard 100.
Knight Eddie, r 44, farmer for his father, Silas W.
KNIGHT SILAS W., r 44, 7 grade Jersey cows, served in Co. H, 78th N. Y. Vol.
     Inf., farmer 100.
Knight Theron H., r 44, farmer, leases of M. E Simpson.
Krauss Jacob, (Attica, Wyoming Co.) r 48, farmer, leases of R. Bowen 125.
Kreger Augustus, r 28, laborer and farmer 14.
Kufahel Christopher, (Attica, Wyoming Co.) r 56, laborer.
Kufahel Joseph, (Attica, Wyoming Co.) r 56, laborer.
Kurtz Arthur H., farmer for his father, Isaac.
Kurtz Byron R., r 14, farmer for his father, Isaac.
Kurtz Isaac, r 14, 55 sheep, farmer 122.
Lapp Byron, r 12, farmer, leases of David 112.
Lapp Hibbard, r 35, farmer.
Lapp John, r 35, farmer.
LAWRENCE CHARLES, farmer, leases of L. Moulton 185.
Lawton George W., r 27, farmer 25.
LAWTON HANNAH H., r 27, 9 Durham cows, farmer 96.
Leonard James, (Batavia) r 10, 6 grade Jersey cows, farmer 70.
Leonard Walter J., (Batavia) r 10, farmer with his father, James.
LEWIS ANSON, r 40, 13 cows, farmer 115.
Lewis Charles F., r 40, 13 cows, farmer 3, and leases of Anson 115.
Lewis Ezekiel P., r 40, 15 cows, farmer 110.
Lewis Jasper B., ticket agent and telegraph operator N. Y., L. E. & W. R. R., h Allegany st.
Lewis Willard, r 40, farmer.
LINCOLN ARIAL B., r 46, 7 cows, 180 Spanish Merino sheep, reg., farmer 182.
Lincoln Charles, teamster, h and lot.
Lincoln Emory, r 27, student.
Lincoln Emory P., r 27, student.
Lincoln Eunice A., dealer in millinery, h Allegany st.
LINCOLN FLAVILLA, r 27, widow of Fisher, 28 fine wool sheep, farmer 44.
Lincoln Janette, widow of Emory F.
Lincoln Lucius, r 27, carpenter.
LINCOLN MERRILL F., r 25, 6 grade Durham cows, 100 American Spanish Merino
     sheep, reg., farmer 155½.
Lincoln Miles W., r 27, farmer.
Long Lewis, (Attica, Wyoming Co.) r 56, laborer.
LOOMIS FRANCIS, r 38, veterinary surgeon, owns 4 acres.
Love Martha, (Attica, Wyoming Co.) r 49, widow of Leonard, farmer 30.
LOVERIDGE FRED B., r 45, 4 cows, farmer 81.
Loveridge George L., r 46, farmer 82.
Lyon Cyrus R., r 44, farm laborer.
Lyon Elias, (Attica, Wyoming Co.) r 47, farmer 20.
Manson Charles, station and ticket agent N. Y. C. & H. R. R. R., bds. Alexander Hotel.
Marsh Mary, resident, h Allegany st.
Martin James, r 35, laborer, owns 4 acres.
Mayne Joseph, r 21, farmer, leases of D. L. Dodgson 125.
McCormick Andrew, r 14, farmer 8.
McCuen John, retired Methodist clergyman, h Church.
McGrath James, (Batavia) r 10, farmer 40.
Menzie Robert, r 29, farmer 70.
Menzie Robert A., r 27, 6 cows, farmer 115.
Meredith Adelpha, r 35, farmer 48.
Merritt Clark, r 62, laborer.

2*

Merritt Clinton, r 62, farmer, leases of H. Chaddock 125.
MILLER ANN E., (Attica, Wyoming Co.) r 48, (Mrs. John A.).
Miller Frank, r 65, farmer 30.
Miller George L., (Attica, Wyoming Co.) r 48, carpenter.
Miller Gustavus, (Linden) r 65, farmer 70.
Miller John A., (Attica, Wyoming Co.) r 48, carpenter and farmer 37.
Miller Leroy, (Attica, Wyoming Co.) r 48, carpenter.
MILLER LEROY Mrs., resident.
Miller Tracy R., r 60, 10 cows, 250 sheep, farmer, leases of C. C. Newton 120, and of
    L. Brown 128.
Millington Calvin, house painter, h Church.
MILLINGTON MARTHA J., (Mrs. Calvin) h and lot Church.
Mitche Arville N., widow of William.
Mooers Clara, widow of Alonzo, resident.
Moore William L., pastor M. E. Church, h Allegany st.
Morgan Adaline C., r 67, widow of John, resident.
Mots Barbara, r 48, widow, resident, owns 5 acres.
Mots Henry, (Attica, Wyoming Co.) r 49, farmer, leases of B. Mots 50.
Moulton Allen, r 14, farmer 120.
MOULTON ALLEN J., r 14, farmer 100.
MOULTON BYRAM, iron bridge contractor and builder, breeder of American Span-
    ish Merino sheep, reg., 500 head, farmer 415, h Buffalo st.
Moulton Byram, Jr., r 12, 15 cows, 45 Spanish Merino sheep, reg., farmer, leases of
    Byram 400.
MOULTON ELBRIDGE G, justice of the peace, retired merchant and farmer, h Buf-
    falo st.
Moulton Lewis, r 33, farmer 100, and leases of Mrs. Denslow 100.
MOULTON MARY, (Mrs. Elbridge G.) farm 18, h Buffalo st.
Moulton Oran, (Batavia) r 14, farmer 60.
MOULTON OSSMAND B., r 14, 100 grade Spanish Merino sheep, farmer 140.
Moulton Warren E., r 59, 13 Jersey, Holstein, and grade Durham cows, farmer 121.
Muhs Frank, r 52, laborer.
MUHS WILLIAM, r 52, farmer 10.
Mullen John R., allo. physician and surgeon, Main, h do.
Muxworthy Emily, r 19, school teacher.
MUXWORTHY FREDERICK, r 19, 5 grade Jersey and Durham cows, farmer 65.
Muxworthy George, r 19, farmer with his father, Frederick.
Myers Jacob, r 47, farmer 84.
Nash Homer D., r 32, 7 cows, farmer 346.
Neadler Augustus, (Attica, Wyoming Co.) r 56, laborer.
Newell Morris B., r 26, farmer, leases of Isaac King 40.
NEWTON CLARK C., r 60, breeder of grade Merino sheep, farmer 125.
Nichols Edward, (Batavia) r 12, 75 sheep, farmer 52.
Nichols Frank, (Batavia) r 12, farmer for his father, Edward, 52.
Nichols Frederick, (Batavia) r 7, farmer 22.
Nichols Nancy A., widow of Asher, farm 60. h Church.
North Edgar, r 20, 18 grade Durham cows, farmer 117.
North Ralph E., r 20, farmer 70.
Osgood John W., (Linden) r 65, farmer 40.
Page Albert, retired farmer, h Allegany st.
Page Andrew, retired farmer, h Allegany st.
Paige Ann Eliza, widow of Dr. Joel S., resident, h Buffalo st.
Palmer Seymour J., r 59, laborer.
Parish George B., r 57, 27 cows, farmer 165.
Parker Zilphia E., (Attica, Wyoming Co.) r 49, widow of Harry J., farmer 18.
Parmenter Thomas, mail carrier, h Main.
Parsons Addison, (Attica, Wyoming Co.) r 50, cooper and farmer 10.
Parsons Addison D. J., (Attica, Wyoming Co.) r 50, laborer and cooper.
PECK ASA, r 19, farmer 86.

Peck Charles E., r 19, farmer, leases of Miss L. Emeroy Durfee 79.
Pelton Allen, r 52, 8 cows, farmer 65.
Perkins C. Ione, widow of Rev. T. H., h Buffalo st.
Perry George W., r 43, farmer 22½.
Pestaline Charles, r 62, farmer 130.
Pierce Loren W., miller, h and lot.
Pollard William G., (Pollard & Bentley) justice of the peace and justice of Sessions, h Main.
Pollard & Bentley, (William G. P. and Norman B.) general merchants, Main.
Porter James, r 39, laborer.
Post William, (Batavia) r 14, farmer 193.
Prue John F., general merchant, Main, h Buffalo st.
Putney Frederick, r 43, farmer, leases of John Kiefer 122.
Quillins Joseph, r 42, farmer, leases of S. Riddle 110.
Radder Joseph, (Attica, Wyoming Co.) r 48, farmer 70.
Rawp William T., r 57, laborer.
Renager Martin H., cheesemaker.
Reynolds James, (Batavia) r 14, farmer 74.
Rice Fred, (Attica, Wyoming Co.) r 56, laborer.
Rice John, r 52, laborer.
Richards Frank M., town clerk and miller, h Church.
Richards Jerry D., miller, owns farm in Bethany 100, h Main.
Richmond Elvira, widow of Austin, resident, aged 71, h Buffalo st.
Riddle Jerome, r 58, 40 cows, 100 Spanish Merino sheep, farmer 360.
Riddle Sanford, r 57, 20 cows, 50 Spanish Merino sheep, reg., farmer 277.
Ridge A., r 42, farmer, leases of Mrs. G. Moulton 118.
Ridge William, r 53, farmer, leases of the Phelps estate 200.
Roberts John W., r 52, farmer.
Roth Adam I., r 66, 15 cows, 100 grade Merino sheep, farmer 157.
ROTH ALBERT, r 66, farmer.
Roth Fred, r 66, laborer.
Roth Hammond, r 66, laborer.
Roth Louis, r 66, farmer, leases of Mrs. Kopke 80.
Rowe Albert, r 62, laborer.
Rundel Malinda, widow of Willis S., resident, h Allegany st.
Sanderson Jay, (Attica, Wyoming Co.) r 4, farmer 7.
Scheer Fred, (Batavia) r 7, farmer for S. B. Thompson 115.
Scheller Anthony, r 15, laborer.
Scheller Toney, r 15, laborer.
Schlenker Martin, (Attica, Wyoming Co.) farmer 98.
SCHNEIDER FRED, (Attica, Wyoming Co.) r 67, florist, prop. greenhouses, farmer 6½.
Schriber Charles, r 67, farmer.
Schriber Jacob, r 67, farmer 70.
Schriber Jacob, Jr., r 67, farmer.
Schriber Julius, r 67, farmer.
Schriber Lewie, r 67, farmer.
Schrnan John, r 52, laborer.
Scoville Whiting T., r 53, 16 cows, farmer 165.
Seward Charles F., r 27, farmer 45.
Seward Ora, r 27, school teacher.
Seward Victor M., (Batavia) r 7, farmer 53.
Seward Winfield, (Batavia) r 7, farmer 53.
Shadbolt Edwin, farmer 8.
Sharrick Charles, laborer.
Shaw Clark, r 41, farmer 93.
Shears George, (Batavia) r 8, farmer 1½.
SHEPARD JAMES G., (Attica, Wyoming Co.) r 33, 30 cows, farmer 436, resides in Attica.

Shug Charles, r 15, farmer 55.
Shug Christopher, (Batavia) r 11, laborer.
Simmons John, r 43, 7 cows, farmer, leases of M. I. Andrews 135.
SIMPSON MARY E., r 44, widow of Samuel A., farmer 70.
Slater Benjamin, r 51, tanner.
Smith Archillus, r 37, farmer 75.
Smith George L., r 29, farmer 104.
Smith Howard P., carpenter and joiner, h Allegany st.
Smith Wallace M., blacksmith, h Buffalo st.
Smith William J., r 46, farmer, leases of N. Bentley 50.
Sodeman Charles, r 52, laborer and farmer 3.
Spink Winfield, (Batavia) r 9, farmer 100.
Spink Winfield S., (Batavia) r 9, 7 cows, farmer 80.
Sprague Carl D., r 40, farmer, leases of Drayton 225.
Sprague Charlie, (W. Batavia) r 21, farmer, leases of Daniel 50.
Sprague Daniel, (W. Batavia) r 21, farmer 50.
Sprague Drayton, r 40, farmer 225.
Sprague Edward, r 28, farmer 20.
Sprague Mary M., r 14, widow of Charles A., resident.
Sprague Solomon, r 28, farmer 90.
SPRING DAVID S., r 55, 20 cows, served in Co. M, 9th N. Y. H. A., farmer 140.
Springer Oscar F., com. traveler, h Main.
Spurgle George, r 55, farmer 12.
Spurr James R., r 18, farm laborer.
Squires George A., r 14, 60 Spanish Merino sheep, farmer 89.
STANARD BUTLER R., r 25 cor. 26, 7 Durham cows, 2 road horses, farmer 65.
Stanard Horace A., r 29, farmer, leases of John P. 190.
Stanard John P., r 29, 18 grade Durham cows, 2 reg., prop. stock horse "Don Goth-
    ard," farmer 190.
Stewart James, r 38, farmer 25.
Stimers Minervia, r 14, widow of John, resident.
Stowe William, r 54, laborer and farmer 4.
Straub John, r 57, 12 cows, farmer, leases of Samuel Wright 130.
Stringham Charles, r 62, farm laborer.
Strong Calvin, r 38, farmer 100.
Strong Orlo, miller, h Buffalo st
Sweathammer Jacob, r 52, laborer.
Sweathammer Jacob, Jr., r 52, laborer.
TALLMAN ADELBERT C., r 14 cor. 15, prop. Railroad saloon and boarding-house.
Thomas David G., r 41, cheesemaker.
Timm Frederick, (Attica, Wyoming Co.) r 49, farmer 22.
Tinney James, r 34, laborer.
Toomey Patrick W., r 14 cor. 15, section foreman D., L. & W. R. R.
Triftshauser George, r 65, farmer with his father, John.
Triftshauser John, r 65, farmer 120.
Van De Bogart John A., r 19, farmer with his father, Joseph E.
VAN DE BOGART JOSEPH E., r 19, 7 cows, 57 Spanish Merino sheep, farmer 110.
Van De Bogart Josephus W., r 19, carriage painter.
Van De Bogart Miles H., r 19, farmer with his father, Joseph E.
Van De Bogart Pattie, widow of Charles, aged 70, h Allegany cor. Church sts.
Van De Bogart Wolcott, (Batavia) r 12, farmer 180.
Vickory Albert E., r 53, farmer, leases of A. A. Waldo 51.
Voelker Augustus, r 46, farmer.
Voelker Fred, r 46, farmer 175.
Vroman Clarence, r 14, farmer, leases of O. B. Moulton 80.
Waite Richard L., r 53, retired, presiding elder M. E. Church, farmer 61.
WALDO ALLEN A., r 53, farmer 51.
Walker Frederick, 15 grade Holstein cows, farmer 117.
Walton Henry C., (Attica, Wyoming Co.) r 50, ice dealer.

Walton Sarah, (Attica, Wyoming Co.) r 50, widow of Girden, resident, aged 78.
Warner John, r 52, farmer 33.
Warner John, Jr., r 52, laborer.
Warren Jay, r 32, farm laborer.
Webber John, pensioner, bds. Main.
Weekman Charles, r 52, laborer.
Wells Aurelia N., widow of Harlow A., resident, aged 72, h Church.
Welsh Henry, (W. Batavia) r 3, farmer, leases of D. Finch, of Pembroke, 92.
Wheetman Joseph, (Attica, Wyoming Co.) r 56, laborer.
Whiteside Robert, r 43, farmer 13½.
Whiteside Robert, Jr., barber, Main. h Buffalo st.
Whiteside Robert G., barber, farm 13, h Buffalo st.
Whitney Anson S., (Batavia) r 18, farmer 37.
Whitney Charles, (Batavia) r 18, farmer 125.
Wickens John, r 15, laborer.
Wilkinson Daniel L., (W. Batavia) r 1, farmer 20.
Wilkinson Henry, (Batavia) r 1, farmer 100.
WILLIAMS DAVID, retired farmer, h Church.
Williams Henry, r 34, laborer.
Williams John H., r 68, farmer, leases of H. E. Osborn 151.
Winchester Cost, (Attica, Wyoming Co.) r 50, cheesemaker.
Wing Eunice, clerk and deputy postmaster, h Main.
Wing George S., dealer in coal, fertilizers, and agricultural implements, h Main.
Wing Phebe Ann, r 57, widow of George W., farmer 130.
Wolfley Conrad, r 32, farmer, leases of Homer Nash 200.
Wyman Peter, laborer, h Main.
Wyman Winfield, (W. Batavia) r 21, farmer 3½.
Zwetsch Charles, prop. meat market, Main, h Allegany st.
Zwetsch Frank, retired farmer, h and 8 acres Main.
Zwetsch Frederick, teamster, h and 3 acres Main.
Zwetsch George, laborer, h Allegany st.
Zwetsch James, butcher, h Allegany st.
Zwetsch John, laborer, h Buffalo st.
Zwetsch Peter, shoemaker, Main, h Buffalo st.
ZWETSCH PHILIP, farmer, h Allegany st.
Zwetsch Philip, Jr., laborer, h Allegany st.
Zwetsch William E., school teacher.

BATAVIA VILLAGE.

TOWN OF BATAVIA.

(For explanations, etc., see page 3, part second.)

Aberdeen Henry, clerk for G. P. Bowen, bds. Hotel Richmond.
Acker George, engineer N. Y. C. & H. R. R. R., h 26 Maple.
Acker George H., fireman, h 29 S. Main.
Acker William, engineer N. Y. C. & H. R. R. R., h 20 Walnut.
Adams Amos H., farmer 86, h 446 Ellicott.
Adams Augustus F., book keeper, h 162 State.
Adams Fitch, feather renovator, h 19 Evans.
ADAMS MILES B., dealer in wood and coal, 16 School, h 133 Bank.
Adar John, carpenter, h 46 Church.
AGAR HENRY, carriage painter, rear Parker House, h 34 State.

Agar James Demotte, foreman *News* office, bds. 34 State.
Ahl Henry, laborer, h Ross.
Akes Joseph, tinsmith, h 114 W. Main.
Aldridge Alfred, laborer, h 210 Ellicott.
Alexander Eugene, carpenter, h 110 North.
Allen Jennie M., (Mrs. Dexter) prop. boarding-house, 113 Jackson.
Allen Marion, artist, bds. 12 Chestnut.
Allen Mary, widow of Hiram, h 12 Chestnut.
Allen Sarah E., h 5 Chestnut.
ALLEN WILLIAM, farmer in Oakfield 150, h 30 Ellicott ave.
Allis Henry S., sec'y Schad Wheel Co., bds. 49 Ellicott ave.
Allis Selden C., retired, h 49 Ellicott ave.
American Express Co., J. H. Napier agent, 10 Jackson.
American Hotel, John Fix, prop., 122 E. Main.
Anderson Susan, asst. matron Institution for the Blind.
ANDREWS ANDREW J., prop. livery stable, Court, h 32 Ellicott.
Andrus Frederick M., com. traveler, h 129 Bank.
Ansel John, farmer 28, h S. Main.
Arnold Peter, carpenter, h 443 Ellicott.
Ashley Mary E., matron Institution for the Blind.
ATWATER EDWARD W., manager of the Dean Richmond estate, 212 E. Main,
    h do.
Atwater Lucius, Baptist clergyman, h Prospect ave.
Atwood Amasa, laborer, h 20 Maple.
Austin Clarence B., clerk, bds. 142 State.
Austin George G., (Austin & Prescott) h 142 State.
Austin Susan, widow of Fayette, h 142 State.
Austin and Prescott, (George G. A. and Charles F. P.) watchmakers, jewelers, and op-
    ticians, 90 E. Main.
Averill George W., (Welch & Averill) bds. Park Hotel.
Ayers Thomas H., laborer, h 31 Cherry.
Bacon Allie, widow of T. T., h 114 State.
BADGEROW ISAAC B., prop. meat market, 49 Jackson, h do.
Bailey Bridget, widow of John, h 138 Summit.
Bailey J. Patrick, mason, h 49 Maple.
Bailey Thomas M., carpenter, h 138 Summit.
Baker Arthur C., painter, h 5 Chestnut.
Baker Arthur J., machinist, bds. 21 Liberty.
Baker Charles F., machinist, bds. 21 Liberty.
Baker Charles J., clerk, bds. 103 W. Main.
BAKER ELLIS L. DR., pres. Syracuse Forging and Gun Co., h 36 Center.
Baker Jacob, retired, h 103 W. Main.
BAKER JOHN F., M. D., homeo. physician and surgeon, 5 Bank, h do.
BAKER JOHN W., M. D., homeo. physician, 5 Bank, h do.
Baker Lucius, (Baker & Walkinshaw) h 132 State.
BAKER WILLIAM H., general supt. Syracuse Forging and Gun Co., h 21 Liberty.
    [Died October 10, 1889.]
BAKER & WALKINSHAW, (Lucius B. and James M. W.) bakers, 63 E. Main.
Baldwin Frank A., agent, h Central ave.
BALDWIN JANE M., (Mrs. W. H.) h 15 Summit.
BALDWIN WILLIAM H., farmer 109, and in Elba 104, h 15 Summit.
Ball Joseph, laborer, h 8 S. Swan.
Ballard Elbert F., clerk, bds. 124 Jackson.
BALLARD FRANK W., (Tyrrell & Ballard) bds. 124 Jackson.
Ballard John D., retired farmer, h 124 Jackson.
Ballard Margaret, widow of Norton, h 15 Liberty.
Balle Joseph A., beer bottler, h 110 S. Main.
Bank John, retired pastor St. Paul's German Evangelical Church, h 7 Robinson.
BANK OF BATAVIA, D. W. Tomlinson, pres.; H. F. Tarbox, vice-pres.; H. T.
    Miller, cashier, 71 E. Main.

BANK OF GENESEE, A. N. Cowdin, pres.; T. Cary, cashier, 98 E. Main.
Bannister Frank, bds. 18 Church.
Bannister Grant, laborer, h 45 Tracy Place.
Bannister Maggie, widow of John, h 18 Church.
Barber Carlos M., carpenter and farmer 8½, h River.
Barber Daniel, carpenter, h 110 Ross.
Barber Henry R., agent, bds. 9 Otis.
Barber Robert E., engineer, h 23 S Liberty.
Barker Charles A., com. traveler, h 26 Summit.
Barnard James, laborer, h 18 Wiard.
Barnes Isaac M., retired farmer, h 304 E. Main.
BARNES JOSEPH C., merchant tailor, 96 E. Main, h 25 Summit.
Barrett Thomas, retired, h 43 Hutchins.
Barrows John, retired, h 325 Ellicott.
Batavia Brewing Co., W. Hooker, pres.; W. Gamble, supt., brewers of ale and porter, Elm.
BATAVIA BUSINESS UNIVERSITY AND STENOGRAPHIC INSTITUTE, established in 1867, W. W. Whitcomb, pres.; John McKenzie, sec'y, over 89 E. Main.
Batavia Cemetery Association, John B. Crosby, sec'y.
Batavia Club, Henry Todd, pres.; Frank S. Wood, sec'y and treas., 201 E. Main.
Batavia Gas and Electric Light Co., Alexander Wyness, Jr., supt., 27 Ellicott.
BATAVIA PRESERVING CO., Sprague, Warner & Co, of Chicago, props.; W. E. Flynn, supt., Mill.
Batavia Steam Laundry, Mrs. Nettie Showerman, prop., 202 E. Main.
Batavia Union Free School, Gardner Fuller, A. M., supt. and prin., Ross.
Batavia Water Works, W. Main.
BATAVIA WHEEL CO., Frank Richardson, pres.; W. C. Gardner, vice-pres.; W. W. Leavenworth, sec'y; A. M. Colt, treas.; J. M. Sweet, supt., Walnut.
Batcheller Isaac W., dealer in furniture (installment plan), 7 Jackson, bds. 113 do.
Bateman Merritt, peddler, h 22 Thorp.
Bates Frank, machinist, h 37 S. Main.
Beachel Eva, widow of Anthony, h Pearl.
Beachel John, teamster, h 88 S. Main.
Beachel William, butcher, h William.
Beals Francis, retired, h 150 Jackson.
BEAN CLARENCE J., (Underhill & Bean) bds. Liberty.
BECK WILLIAM, (Beck & Salway) h 335 E. Main.
BECK & SALWAY, (William B. and John E. S.) dealers in flour, feed, grain, hay, and phosphates, Exchange building, Court.
Becker Peter, molder, h 5 S. Liberty.
Beecher Augustus, laborer, h Otis.
Beecher John, teamster, h 88 S. Main.
Beekman Samuel, barber, Hotel Richmond, resides in Buffalo.
Bellows Jennie M., laundress, h 16 Seaver Place.
Bender Alfred, painter, h 45 Washington ave.
Bender Josephine, widow of William, h 10 Church.
Benedict Daniel B., clerk, bds. 53 Jackson.
BENEDICT ELMINA H., widow of Dr. H. S., physician and surgeon, female diseases a specialty, h 53 Jackson.
Benedict Frank H., clerk, bds. 53 Jackson.
Benedict George B., baggagemaster N. Y., L. E. & W. R. R., bds. 53 Jackson.
Benham Le'Roy, sewing machine agent, h 115 State.
BENJAMIN HILAND H., dentist, over 68 E. Main, h 31 Center.
Bennett Maria, dressmaker, h 103 Main.
Bennett Thomas H., barber, bds. 9 S. Liberty.
Bennington Edward, carpenter, h 40 South.
Bently Gorton, ins. agent, 38 Jackson, h 31 Maple.
Benton Edwin J., mail carrier, h 21 Pearl.

Bergen Anna M., h 6 Tracy Place.
Bergen Emily A., h 6 Tracy Place.
Bergher Kiern, retired, h 340 Ellicott.
BERGMAN MICHAEL C., prop. Parker House barber shop, E. Main, h 110 W.
    Main.
Berkhart Martin, mason, h 23 School.
Bermingham John, waiter, bds. 49 Main.
Bermingham Mary, widow, h 104 Oak.
Bermingham Simon, laborer, h 205 Bank.
Bernard John, carpenter, h 14 Evans.
Bernd Frank J., carpenter, bds. 90 S. Main.
Beswick Andrew, retired, h 10 Walker.
Beuchley Albert, carpenter, h 130 W. Main.
Beuchley Clarence A., printer, bds. 130 W. Main.
Bidlack Jasper P., carpenter, h rear 29 Harvester ave.
Bidwell Cyrus H., carpenter, h 9 North.
Bierce Manley S., clerk, bds. 219 E. Main.
Bierce Miles H., dealer in dry goods, boots, and shoes, 75 E. Main, h 219 do.
Bigelow Jerome L., cashier First National Bank, h 306 Washington ave.
Birmingham David, mason, h 63 Oak.
Birmingham Michael, laborer, h 34 Main.
Birmingham Simon, laborer, h 205 Bank.
Bisbee Dwight M., peddler, h 138 W. Main.
Blair Cordelia J., dressmaker, h 5 Pearl.
Blake John, h 23 Maple.
BLAKE JOHN H., resident, bds. 23 Maple.
Blatt Augustus, laborer. h 12 Ganson ave.
Blenker Anna G., teacher, bds. South.
Bleyler Elizabeth, (Elizabeth Bleyler & Co.) h W. Main.
Bleyler Elizabeth & Co., (G. Scheuing) florists, W. Main.
Bleyler Peter, florist, h W. Main.
Blighton Polly P., widow of William, h 21 Seaver Place.
Bliss Anson T., painter, h 11 Trumbull Place.
Bliss Weden, laborer, h 25 Harvester ave.
Block John, cooper, Railroad ave., h Cedar.
Blodgett Azubia, h 433 E. Main.
Blodgett Edmond, horse trainer, h E. Main.
Blodgett Norman, horse trainer, h 121 State.
BLOOMFIELD ALBERT E., merchant tailor and dealer in gents' furnishing goods,
    50 E. Main, h 125 State.
Bloomfield Skinner, tailor, Main, h 131 State.
Bloss Erwin L., Singer sewing machine agent, 80 E. Main, h do.
Blount Sarah M., stenographer, Walker block, bds. 106 E. Main.
Blumrick Charles, prop. saloon, 148 Ellicott.
Board Frank W., foreman, h 12 Vine.
Bodmer Urban, carpenter, h 34 Cedar.
Boles John, laborer, h 28 Harvester ave.
Bolt George, canmaker, h 29 Seaver Place.
Bolt Michael, clerk, bds. 107 Harvester ave.
BOLTON WILLIAM T., M. D., physician and surgeon, 200 E. Main, h do.
Booth Christina, widow of William, bds. 19 Center.
Booth Ellen E., dealer in millinery and fancy goods, 68 E. Main, bds. 202 Washing-
    ton ave.
Booth Fred, carpenter, h 142 Harvester ave.
BOOTH HERBERT B., overseer of the poor, h 211 W. Main.
Booth Herbert T., asst. book-keeper Bank of Batavia, bds. 211 W. Main.
Booth Laura E., widow of Joseph, h 109 Bank.
Booth Phineas, teamster, h 19 Center.
Bostwick Henry O., dealer in phosphate, agent for agricultural implements, buggies,
    etc., 9 Jackson, h 9 Vine.

Bostwick Homer, (Dodgson, Bostwick & Co.) h 11 Bank.
BOSWORTH CHARLES M., manager for William R., h 9 Swan.
BOSWORTH WILLIAM R., dealer in boots and shoes, 69 E. Main, h 11 Swan.
Boucher Catharine, widow of William, h 47 Oak.
Boucher Hannah, widow of Andrew, h 27 Lyon.
Boucher William D., postoffice clerk, bds. Oak.
Bowden Thomas, laborer, h Wiard.
Bowe Edwin A., canvasser, h 128 State.
BOWEN GEORGE, lawyer, 2 and 3 Walker block, h 210 E. Main.
BOWEN GEORGE P., dealer in crockery, wall paper, etc., 107 E. Main, bds. Parker
  House.
Bowman Olive L., h 8 Tracy Place.
Boyd John, flagman, h 5 Central ave.
Boyd Owen, laborer, h 224 Ellicott.
Boylan Edward, painter, h 23 Tracy Place.
Boylan George B., (Boylan & Locke) h 48 Tracy Place.
Boylan & Locke, (George B. B. and William H. L.) painters and paper hangers, 2
  Seaver Place.
Boyle Fred, barber, bds. 224 Ellicott.
Boyle Patrick, laborer, h 62 Swan.
Boynton Henry P., engineer N. Y. C. & H. R. R. R., h 6 Maple.
Bradfield William H., laborer, h 52 South.
Bradish John H., (G. B. Worthington, Son & Co.) bds. 217 E. Main.
Bradish Philander P., pres. board of education, bds. 203 Washington ave.
Bradley C. Clifton, (Caney & Bradley) bds. 28 Bank.
Bradley Clarissa, widow of Bradford D., h 28 Bank.
Bradley William E., retired, h Clifton ave.
Braman Edward, carpenter, h 132 Harvester ave.
Bramble Theodore E., (Webster & Bramble) h 210 W. Main.
Brant D. Wood, dealer in drugs, medicines, books. stationery,etc., 99 E. Main, h 435 do.
Brickman William, mechanic, h 84 Hutchins.
Brill John, retired, h 17 Harvester ave.
BRISBANE GEORGE, retired, h 8'W. Main.
BROADBOOKS PETER, manuf. of carriages, 27 and 29 Ellicott, h 47 do.
Brockway Charles, laborer, h 15 Center.
Brockway Frank U., carpenter, h 132 Summit.
Brockway James, agent Eureka wind-mill, farmer in Byron 70. h 571 E. Main.
BROCKWAY MARY J., (Mrs. Charles) prop. Center Street Laundry, 15 Center.
Broombach Fred, laborer, h 72 Hutchins.
Broomstad Anna, widow of Lewis, h 29 Cherry.
Brougham Thomas P., priest St. Joseph's Roman Catholic Church, h 303 E. Main.
BROWN ALBERT E., dealer in boots and shoes, 82 E. Main, h 117 State.
Brown Almon C., carpenter, h 7 Ganson ave.
Brown Delia, teacher of music in Institution for the Blind.
Brown George W., laborer, h 29 Harvester ave.
Brown Henry W., expressman on railroad, h 13 Maple.
Brown Hiram, laborer, h 21 Harvester ave.
Brown John, farmer 10, h 40 Cedar.
Brown John S., dealer in groceries and provisions, 30 E. Main, h do.
BROWN MARTIN A., lawyer, 8 Walker building, h 33 Bank.
Brown Nicholas, machinist and apiarist, h 546 E. Main.
BROWN STEPHEN W., prop. West End Hotel and dealer in horses, W. Main.
Brown William H., upholsterer, h 10 Swan.
Brumber Lewis, laborer, h 86 Hutchins.
Brusie Cornelius, molder, h 117 Jackson.
Buchanan Daniel, laborer, h 25 Pearl.
Buchanan John, blacksmith, h 9 Trumbull Place.
Bucher Orpha, widow of Julius C., bds. 105 Summit.
Buckholtz Christina, widow of William, bds. 204 W. Main.

Buckholtz Fred, carpenter, r 53 Hutchins.
Buckholtz John, carpenter, h 8 Otis.
Buckholtz Lewis M., teamster, h 114 Vine.
Buckholtz William, laborer, h 337 Ellicott.
Buckley James, fireman, h 57 Walnut.
Buckley Margaret, widow of James, h 136 Ellicott.
Buckley Michael, prop. saloon, 40 E. Main, h do.
Buell Columbus, h 533 E. Main.
Buell Edward G., (E. N. Rowell & Co.) h 533 E. Main.
Buell Melvin, carpenter, h 308 Ellicott.
Buisch Henry G., barber, 45 E. Main, h 38 Walnut.
Bull Edward, drug clerk, h 40 State.
Bull Maria C., widow of Miles I., h 40 State.
Bulley John B., musician, h 3 S. Main.
BULLOCK WATSON, manuf. of People's liquid bluing, dyer and scourer, 39 Liberty, h 14 do.
Bunn Sidney, machinist, h 13 Spruce.
Burke Martin, maltster, h 318 W. Main.
Burke Patrick, section boss N. Y. C. & H. R. R. R., h off Franklin.
Burns Benjamin, engineer, h 142 Bank.
Burns George, fireman N. Y. C. & H. R. R.. R., bds. 14 Swan.
Burns Martin, laborer, h 23 Hitchins.
Burns William, laborer, h 119 Summit.
BURNS WILLIAM H., roadmaster N. Y. C. & H. R. R. R., h 14 Swan.
BURNS WILLIAM R., asst. roadmaster N. Y. C. & H. R. R. R., h 119 Summit.
Burt George, live stock dealer and farmer 204, h 1 Tracy Place.
Butler Henry, laborer, h Oak.
Butler Jane, widow of Calvin, bds. 82 S. Main.
Buxton Charles H., glazier, h Otis.
Buxton Emily A., h 51 Ellicott.
Buxton Frances J., h 51 Ellicott.
Buxton Fred, carpenter, bds. 139 Summit.
Buxton Joseph T., constable, h 139 Summit.
Byam David, teamster, h 7 Central ave.
Cady ——, widow of Austin, h 5 Wood.
Calbick John, (C. A. Kibble's real estate agency) h 36 Bank.
CALDWELL CHARLES H., (Craft & Caldwell) sec'y Consumers' Electric Light and Power Co., h 114 Jackson.
Caldwell Harry C., painter and decorator, h 12 North.
Caldwell William, clerk, bds. 108 Jackson.
Call Frank, teamster, h 113 W. Main.
Call John, fireman, Hotel Richmond, bds. do.
Callan Michael D., dealer in wines, liquors, and cigars, 12 State, h 16 Evans.
Callen Byron, laborer, bds. 125 Summit.
Callen William W., book-keeper, bds. 132 State.
Callender Benjamin F., crayon manuf., 128 Jackson.
Campbell Cordelia, widow of Henry, bds. 7 North.
CANEY ASHTON W., (Caney & Bradley) h 16 Ross.
CANEY & BRADLEY, (Ashton W. C. and C. Clifton B.) opticians and jewelers, E. Main cor. Jackson.
Canty William, laborer, h 10 S. Swan.
Carey James W., mason, h Otis.
Carey Thomas J., pres. board of health, mason, h 13 Ross.
Carmody George, laborer, h 103 Oak.
Carmody Michael, retired, h Oak.
Caroll Catharine, widow of James, h 509 E. Main.
Carpenter Charles, laborer, h 430 E. Main.
Carpenter William, retired, h 434 E. Main.
Carson Fred, teamster, h 15 Wiard.

Carson John, mason, h 102 Ross.
Carter Myron B., painter and paper hanger, h 38 Center.
CARY TRUMBULL, cashier Bank of Genesee, h 209 E. Main.
Casazza George, dealer in fruit, Jackson, h 30 Seaver Place.
Casey Bridget, widow of William, h 160 State.
Casey Brothers, (John P. and William C.) dealers in groceries and provisions, 117 E. Main.
Casey John P., (Casey Brothers) h 158 State.
Casey Margaret, widow of Thomas, h 17 South.
Casey Simon R., blacksmith and horseshoer, Clark Place, bds. Genesee House.
Casey William C., (Casey Brothers) h 16 Center.
Cashman John. retired. h Franklin.
Cashman John H., fireman, h Franklin.
Caswell Susan, widow, h 110 Summit.
Caton Thomas, laborer, h 37 S. Liberty.
CENTER STREET LAUNDRY, Mrs. Mary J. Brockway, prop., 15 Center.
Central House, J. J. Ryan, prop., 100 Jackson.
Chaddock Calvin, retired, h 10 Mix Place.
CHADDOCK DENNIS K., prop. livery and sales stable, dealer in horses, owns Pratt's mills at Indian Falls, farmer 214, 8 State, h 27 Ellicott ave.
CHADDOCK HIRAM, retired, h 1 Prospect ave.
CHADDOCK JOHN B., (Chaddock & Hickox) h 123 Bank.
CHADDOCK & HICKOX, (John B. C. and George W. H.) dealers in grain, seed, produce, wool, etc., Ellicott.
Chamberlain Carl, h 12 Center.
Chamberlain Eugene, clerk, h 6 East ave.
Champlin Henry G., painter, h 201 W. Main.
CHAPIN JAMES M., wholesale and retail dealer in lumber and coal, 20 and 22 Evans, office 237 Broadway, New York city.
Charlton Earl C., (Charlton & Stein).
Charlton & Stein, (Earl C. C. and John L. S.) dealers in house furnishing goods, 48 Main.
Chick·Sarah, asst. matron Institution for the Blind.
Childs Frank, bartender, bds. 1 State.
Chittenden John E., laborer, h 140 State.
Chittenden O. E., h Wood.
Chittenden Oscar, h 4 Wood.
hittenden William, laborer, h 42 Walnut.
Choate Carey H., machinist and repairer, Clark Place, h Pearl.
Churchil. Richard, carpenter, bds. 13 Swan.
Clancey Caroline, widow of Peter, h 103 Main.
Clancey Patrick, laborer. h 39 S. Liberty.
Clark Adel, dressmaker, h 24 S. Main.'
Clark Adelbert B., reaper inspector, h 43 S. Main.
Clark Ann, widow of John, h 28 Liberty.
CLARK ARTHUR E., lawyer, over 84 E. Main, h 410 do.
Clark Eliza, widow of Jerome, h 410 Bank.
Clark Elizabeth, (Mrs. L.) dressmaker, h 59 Jackson.
Clark Frank, laborer, h 7 Thorp.
Clark Grace B., widow of Norris G., bds. 410 E. Main.
Clark High, waiter Batavia Club.
Clark John H., market gardener and farmer 30, h 1 Chestnut.
CLARK MARY, h 221 W. Main.
Clark Mary, widow of Timothy, h 34 Liberty
CLARK ORLO R., general ins., real estate, and loan agent, 110 E. Main, h 121 Bank.
Clark Thomas, barber, State, h 219 Ellicott.
Clarke Libbie, teacher, bds. 105 Washington ave.
Clarke Myrtie L., teacher, bds. 105 Washington ave.
Clarke Sarah, widow of Orville, h 14 Ross.

Cleghorn Edward, laborer, h 4 Cherry.
CLEMENT ARTHUR G., A. M., supt. Institution for the Blind, h do.
Cleveland Herbert A., farmer 102, h 109 North.
Cline James, laborer, h 20 Hewitt Place.
Clune Simon, laborer, h Union.
Cobb John H., printer, h South.
Coddington Charles A., laborer, h 13 S. Liberty.
Coddington William F., laborer and thresher, h 138 Harvester ave.
Cohen Marcus, dealer in variety and fancy goods, 55 E. Main, bds. Genesee House.
Colby Junius J., miller, h 27 Seaver Place.
Colby Wellington, bds. 36 State.
Cole George, retired farmer, h 120 State.
Coleman Frank T., carpenter, h 307 Ellicott.
Collins Euphenia C., widow of Lewis D , h 28 Center.
Collins Lewis D., book-keeper, bds. 28 Center.
Collins Lucinda, widow of M. L., h 115 Jackson.
Colt Alva M., treas. Batavia Wheel Co., h 4 Central ave.
Colt James R., (Batavia Wheel Co.) h 6 Central ave.
Colt Joseph R., blacksmith, Russell Place, h 103 Bank.
Combs Thomas H., agent for Combs & Co., h 4 Bank.
Combs & Co., (John S. C., of Stafford, and W. W. Britt, of Le Roy) props. meat market,
     5 Jackson.
COMISKEY FRANCIS B., merchant tailor and dealer in gents' furnishing goods,
     110 E. Main, h 326 Ellicott.
Condon John, laborer, h 8 Pearl.
Condon John, Jr., dealer in hides and tallow, h 8 Pearl.
Condon William, lineman, emp. Western Union Telegraph Co., h 8 Pearl.
Cone Hobart B., lawyer, 98 E. Main, h 159 Jackson.
Connor Mary, widow of John, h Union.
Connor James, mason, h 142 Ellicott.
Conrad Paul, (Kibler & Conrad) h 22 Main.
Considine Michael, laborer, h 46 Walnut.
Consumers' Electric Light and Power Co., Henry Craft, pres.; C. H. Caldwell, sec'y ;
     R. L. Kinsey, treas., off Evans.
Continental Hotel, Kibler & Conrad, props., 22 E. Main.
Conway James, laborer, h 25 Oak.
Cook Helen, widow of Thomas, h 132 Jackson.
Cooley Ann, widow of William A., h 15 Washington ave.
Cooley Charles A., drug clerk, bds. 15 Bank.
Cooley Orville, (Dudley & Cooley) bds. Hotel Richmond.
Cooley Thomas, machinist, bds. 15 Washington ave.
Coon May, widow of James, h 26 Center.
COOPER SAMUEL, harnessmaker, 9 State, h 51 Washington ave.
Cooper Sarah E., dressmaker, 119 E. Main.
Cope Orville G., (Cope & Son) bds. 18 Harvester ave.
Cope Philip, (Cope & Son) h 18 Harvester ave.
Cope & Son, (Philip and Orville G.) manufs. of and dealers in wood and iron pumps, and
     dealers in wind-mills, tanks, and iron pipe, 113 Harvester ave.
Copp Thomas, sexton Elmwood Cemetery, h 12 East ave.
Corb William, laborer, h 363 Ellicott.
Corbett Thomas, laborer, h 56 Walnut.
Corey Hattie, clerk in county clerk's office, bds. 121 Summit.
Corey William B., clerk, bds. 121 Summit.
Corey William G., retired, h 121 Summit.
Cosgriff James, laborer, h 58 Walnut.
Costelle Ellen, widow of Thomas, h 29 Central ave.
Cotes Fannie T., widow of Dr. J. R., h 208 E. Main.
Cottrell Thomas F., produce buyer, h 37 S. Main.
Courtney Timothy, laborer, h 15 Lyon.

COWDIN AUGUSTUS N., pres. Bank of Genesee, h 402 E. Main.
Cox Edwin, ins. agent, Walker block, h 31 Bank.
Coy Thomas, shoemaker, h Lafayette ave.
Crabb Charles J., prop. saloon, 50 Ellicott, h do.
Crabb Estella, widow of Pepworth, h 16 Pearl.
Crabb George, engineer, h 14 Pearl.
CRAFT HENRY, (Craft & Caldwell) pres. Consumers' Electric Light Co., farmer 160,
   h 26 Bank.
CRAFT & CALDWELL, (Henry C. and Charles H. C.) maltsters, dealers in coal,
   agents for Armour & Co., 61 Jackson.
Cramer Alfred, blacksmith, h 6 Hutchins Place.
Crampton Mary, widow, h 107 Summit.
CRARY ALBERT B., foreman for H. M. Lay, h 14 Maple.
Crayon Simon, laborer, h 57 S. Liberty.
Crego Henry C., clerk Tibbitts House, h 28 State.
Crego Sarah, widow of Lester, h 7 East ave.
Crehan Simon, laborer, h 57 Liberty.
Crocker Walter M., carpenter, h 82 S. Main.
Crofoot Mary A., widow of A. D., h 6 East ave.
CROSBY LAWRENCE L., lawyer and police justice, 3 Postoffice block, h 7 Park
   ave.
Crosby Theodore W., bds. 34 Bank.
Crosman Maria, (Mrs. James) h 32 S. Liberty.
Crosman Maria, widow of Amos, h 13 Pearl.
Cross Henry T., agent for second-hand furniture, Ellicott hall, h 29 Summit.
Crouse Charles, com. traveler, h 112 North
Crowley Frank, laborer, h 126 Harvester ave.
Culp Martha J., widow of Jerry, h 24 S. Main.
Culp Metta, dressmaker, bds. 24 S. Main.
Cummerford Thomas, laborer, h 58 Hutchins.
Cummings James, mason, h 22 Central ave.
Cummings James C., carpenter, h 12 Tracy Place.
Cummings John, laborer, h Franklin.
Cummings John, Jr., baggagemaster N. Y. C. & H. R. R. R., h 152 Jackson.
Cummings Michael D., molder, h 7 Hewitt Place.
Cunningham Martha W., widow of Alfred C., h 7 Harvester ave.
Curry Michael, laborer, h rear 43 Maple.
Curtin Michael, carpenter, 159 Summit.
Curtis Henry, laborer, h 19 Hutchins.
Curtis Samuel, farmer in Bethany 152, h 12 Bank.
Curtiss George H., prop. Parker House, E. Main.
Curtiss Henry J., laborer, h 566 E. Main.
Cutlan Fred J., engineer Batavia water works, h Ellicott.
Cutler Angeline, teacher of music in Institution for the Blind.
Dagg David, butcher, h 117 Oak.
DAILEY ANNA, widow of Michael, undertaker, upholsterer, and dealer in furniture,
   8 to 15 State, h 307 E. Main.
DAILY NEWS, Griswold & McWain, editors and props., 10 State.
Dale Asbury, waiter Batavia Club.
Darrow Lydia A., widow of Edwin, h 7 Maple.
Davidson Sidney, laborer, h 15 Oak.
Davis Elmer W., carpenter, h 49 Buell.
Dawson William E., carpenter, h 12 Walker.
Day William H., lawyer, 58 E. Main, h 20 Summit.
Dean Lack, teamster, h 31 Lyon.
Dean Roger, mason, bds. 31 Lyon.
Dean Thomas, prop. saloon, 10 E. Main, bds. do.
Defenbach John, tailor, bds. Continental Hotel.
Defner Christopher, laborer, h 48 Buell.

Delaney Joseph P., cutter, emp. O. Town & Son, h 507 E. Main.
Delaney Richard, manager for Mrs. Anna Daily, 8-15 State, bds. State.
Delano Addie, (Mrs. H. J.) dressmaker, 106 Main.
Delano Harvey J., agent for organs, 106 Main.
Delano Henry, grocer, 58 Jackson, h do.
Delano Jesse S., book agent, h 24 Seaver Place.
Delbridge Charles J., printer, h Summit place.
Delbridge George, molder, h 135 Summit.
Delbridge James, laborer, h 136 Summit.
Delbridge Thomas, shoemaker, 108 Main, h 131 Summit.
Delbridge Walter, carpenter, h Summit Place.
DELLINGER JOHN, (Dellinger & Glade) (Haitz & Dellinger) (Schad, Dellinger & Glade) prop. Dellinger opera house, h 25 Bank.
DELLINGER & GLADE, (John D. and John G.) contractors and builders, 30 W. Main.
Deming William H., milk peddler and farmer 25, h 9 Chestnut.
Demund John, barber, h 4 Willow.
Dennis Merton O., ins. adjuster, over 96 E. Main, h 31 Summit.
Dennison Floens, house-keeper Institution for the Blind.
Denton Francis G., carpenter, h 6 William.
Derrick Frank, teamster, h 26 Swan.
De Shou Joseph C., policeman, h Swan cor. Ellicott.
Dewey Alvern, telegraph operator, h 132 Ellicott.
Dewey Alvern C., agent Wells, Fargo & Co. Express, and manager Postal Cable Telegraph Co., 2 Jackson, h 132 Ellicott.
Dewey Charles D., dealer in real estate, h 437 E. Main.
DEWEY CHARLES E., (Houghton & Dewey) h 209 Washington ave.
DEWEY JAMES H., contractor and builder, h 10 Walker Place.
Dewey R. Dwight, h 413 E. Main.
Dibble Isaac, foreman, h 36 Maple.
DIBBLE ISAAC C. V., contractor at Wiard plow works, h 36 Maple.
Dibble William S., painter, h 125 Jackson.
Dickinson Dwight, painter, h 15 East ave.
Dickson Cornelia, widow of Hezekiah, h 6 Liberty.
Diem Eugene, com. traveler, h 55 Ellicott ave.
Dimmick Charles, laborer, h 26 Walnut.
Dippold John, butcher, h 34 S. Liberty.
Diskin Thomas, laborer, h Union.
Ditzel John P., butcher, h 112 W. Main.
Ditzel Philip, mason, h 19 Oak.
Dixon John C., barber and hair-dresser, 44 E. Main, h do.
Dobbs William, plumber, h Main.
Dobney Josiah W., jeweler, 57 E. Main, h Clifton ave.
Dodge Caroline, widow of Erastus, h 310 E. Main.
Dodgson, Bostwick & Co., (Deloss L. D., Homer B., and C. W. Van Valkenburgh) general ins. agents, over 96 E. Main.
Dodgson Deloss L., (Dodgson, Bostwick & Co.) h 29 Ellicott ave.
Dodgson Earl A., (Dodgson & Wilder) h 21 Ellicott ave.
Dodgson & Wilder, (Earl A. D. and Elmon S. W.) dealers in agricultural implements, buggies, and harnesses, Evans.
Doherty Felix R., clerk Parker House, bds. do.
Donhuge John, retired, h 216 Ellicott.
Donoghue Daniel, car inspector, h 50 Washington ave.
Donoghue Margaret, clerk, h 26 Main.
Donohue John, shoemaker, 47 Jackson, h do.
Donohue Kate, widow of John, h 19 Lyon.
Donohue Patrick, brakeman, h 16 Hutchins.
Donohue Patrick, conductor, bds. 24 Center.
Donohue Patrick, section boss N. Y. C. & H. R. R. R, h 6 S. Swan.

Donohue Patsey, harnessmaker, bds. Jackson.
Donohue Rosa, widow of Coleman, h 24 Center.
Donohue Sylvester, laborer, h 23 Swan.
DORF FRANK, dealer in dry goods, carpets, etc., 107 Main, h 17 Ellicott ave.
Dotzauer John, laborer, h Mill.
Dougherty Patrick, laborer, h 58 Swan.
DOUGLASS MARY L., h 10 Tracy Place.
Dow Frank L., machinist, h 121 Harvester ave.
Dow George E., foreman, h 451 Ellicott.
Dowd Margaret, widow of Thomas, h 49 Ellicott.
Dowd Thomas, night telegraph operator and ticket agent N. Y. C. & H. R. R. R., bds. 49 Ellicott.
Downing Spencer, engineer, h 14 Thorp.
Doyle Michael, laborer, h 54 Hutchins.
Doyle William H., blacksmith, h 18 Central ave.
DRAPER ALLAN D., pastor First Presby. Church, h 11 Liberty.
Driker Edward C., blacksmith, h 9 School.
Driscoll James, retired, h 37 Liberty.
Dudley Frank T., (Dudley & Cooley) bds. Hotel Richmond.
DUDLEY & COOLEY, (Frank T. D. and Orville C.) dealers in drugs, books, stationery, etc., 92 Main.
Duffy John, laborer, h Franklin.
Duffy Mary, widow of Owen, h 136 State.
Duffy William H., laborer, h 40 Hutchins.
Dufour Joseph, foreman, h 2 Prune.
Dunfee Margaret, widow of Dennis, h 40 Maple.
DUNHAM FRANK, (Dunham & Howe) lawyer, 64 E. Main, bds. 32 Bank.
Dunham George, laborer, h 21 Central ave.
Dunham & Howe, (Frank D. and Frank A. H.) ins. agents, 64 E. Main.
Dunlap Gordon, lawyer, Uebele block, 16 Main, bds. European Hotel.
Durfee Samuel B., sailor, h 10 Vine.
DURKEE JACOB H., pastor Freewill Baptist Church, h 159 Bank.
Dustin Asa D., tinsmith, h 23 S. Liberty.
Dustin Jonah, laborer, h 26 S. Liberty.
DUSTIN STEPHEN A., dealer in drugs, medicines, fancy goods, school books, etc., 57 E. Main, h 5 Ellicott ave.
Dustin Stephen C., cartman, h 24 S. Liberty.
Dustin William H., engineer, h 3 Central ave.
DWIGHT CLARENCE N., manager for J. M. Chapin, bds. 113 Summit.
Dwight William C., salesman for J. M. Chapin, h 113 Summit.
Dye Daniel B., owns farm in Oakfield 65, h 55 Ellicott ave.
Dyer Bessie, widow, h 5 Walker.
DYER EDNA V., clairvoyant physician, h 12 North.
Eager Herbert B., (Eager & Co.) h 200 W. Main.
Eager John F. V., (Eager & Co.) h 200 W. Main.
Eager Wellington T., (Eager & Co.) h 200 W. Main.
Eager & Co., (John F. V., H. B., and W. T. Eager, and Emily M. Whitcomb) wholesale dealers in wines, liquors, beer, ales, etc., W. Main.
Earl Allen, laborer, h 18 Hewitt Place.
East End Hotel, Peter Werner, prop., 508 E. Main.
Ebling Charles M., prop. meat market, 200 Ellicott, h do.
Eccleston William, foreman, h 518 E. Main.
Eckerman Herman, laborer, h 118 North.
Eckert Charles, carpenter, h 217 W. Main.
Edgerton Alanson, farmer in Elba 230, h 200 State.
Edgerton Henry G., retired, h 8 North.
Edmonds James A., carpenter, h 3 Fisher Park.
Eggleston Dwight A., laborer, bds. 11 Summit.
EGGLESTON JOHN A., magnetic healer, h 11 Summit.

Eggleston William, laborer, h Colorado ave.
Eighmy Ira, laborer, h 11 Spruce
Eipper Augustus H., prop. Eipper House, 103 Harvester ave.
Eipper House, A. H. Eipper, prop., 103 Harvester ave.
Eldridge William H., foreman job department *News* office, h 101 State.
Ellicott House, Fred. J. Stakel, prop., Jackson cor. Ellicott.
Ellicott John, retired, bds. 114 State.
Ellicott Street Roller Mills, Frank G. Moulton, owner ; Parsons & Co., props., dealers
    in flour, feed, and grain, Ellicott.
Elliott Arthur, laborer, h 9 Ross.
Elliott John O., laborer, h 15 Swan.
Emerick Cornelius M., maltster, Elm, h in Jordan, Onondaga Co.
Emerson Harrison, carpenter, h 117 W. Main.
Emery R. Arthur, ins. agent, h 108 North.
Emka Henry, shoemaker, 503 E. Main, bds. 152 Vine.
Emka Henry, carpenter, h 150 Vine.
Engelhart Charles, clerk, h 215 Washington ave.
Engle Frank, wood worker, bds. 108 Jackson.
Englehart Jacobbina E., widow of John, h 120 W. Main.
English Marian, widow of Alden C., h 19 Maple.
ENSIGN ELIZABETH L., widow of Henry J., h 9 Bank.
Escritt Henry, machinist, h 19 Buell.
European Hotel, Philip Perfield, prop., 36 E. Main.
Evans Evan W., carriage painter, h 305 Ellicott.
Everingham Thomas K., wood worker, h 339 Ellicott.
Fargo Robert S., retired, h 16 Ellicott ave.
FARMERS' BANK OF BATAVIA, C. W. Stickle, teller; J. H. Ward, cashier and
    manager, E. Main cor. Jackson.
FARRAR ALONZO H. Hon., (Farrar & Farrar) bds. Hotel Richmond.
FARRAR ELBERT O. Hon., (Farrar & Farrar) bds. Hotel Richmond.
FARRAR & FARRAR, (Alonzo H. and Elbert O.) attorneys and counselors at law,
    1 Postoffice building, Jackson.
Farrell George A., foreman, h 358 Ellicott.
Farrell Patrick, laborer, h 222 Ellicott.
Farrell Susana, milliner and dressmaker, over 78 E. Main, h do.
Fay Michael, laborer, h 29 Hutchins.
Fellows Mary, widow of Orlando, h 318 E. Main.
Felsinger Harry, barber, bds. Genesee House.
Feltis Fred, upholsterer, h 108 Oak.
Feltz Joseph, machinist, h 15 S. Swan.
Ferdun John, machinist, h 118 Ross.
Ferrien Grove H., teamster, h 112 Jackson.
Ferrin Charles, coal dealer in Lockport, h 24 Ross.
Ferrin Brothers Co., (incorporated) dealers in grain, produce, fruit, etc., Ellicott.
Ferrin Frank G., (Ferrin Brothers Co.) h 18 Bank.
Ferrin Louise, widow of Horace, h 101 Jackson.
Ferris Arthur, dealer in coal and wood, 45 Center, h 72 S. Liberty.
Ferris Michael, retired, h 70 S. Liberty.
Field Judson, machinist and farmer 37, h 316 Ellicott.
Fillmore Henry, janitor South Side school, h 162 Jackson.
Fillmore Jennie B., dress and cloakmaker, h 162 Jackson.
Finch Laverne, mechanic, h 20 Cedar.
Fines Christopher, laborer, h Colorado ave.
FINKELSTEIN HENRY S., prop. Batavia dying and cleaning works, ladies' and
    gents' clothing cleaned, dyed, and pressed, 150 Ellicott, h do.
FIRST NATIONAL BANK, L. C. McIntyre, pres.; G. B. Worthington, vice-pres.;
    J. L. Bigelow, cashier, 84 E. Main.
Fisher Henry B., lawyer, h 26 Ross.
Fisher Kate, h 429 E. Main.

Fisk George W., laborer, h 34 Church.
Fitzgerald Joseph, brick mason, h 155 Summit.
Fix George, laborer, bds. 122 Main.
Fix John, prop. American Hotel, 122 E. Main.
Flannery Michael, laborer, h 219 Bank.
Flinn Michael, section boss, h 118 Ellicott.
Flinn Patrick, laborer, h 30 Hutchins.
Flint Charles, painter, h 214 Ellicott.
FLYNN WILLIAM E., supt. Batavia Preserving Co., h 105 Jackson.
Foley Timothy, hackman. h 12 S. Liberty.
Foley Timothy, laborer, h Union.
Folger Timothy, machinist, h 8 Wiard.
Folk John, farmer 4, h 30 Cedar.
Follett Herman, shoemaker, h 156 Jackson.
Fonda Brinton P., retired, h 28 S. Liberty.
FONDA JOHN B., dealer in hardware, stoves, ranges, and furnaces, 70 E. Main, h
    15 North.
Fonda William H., candy manuf., bds. 28 S. Liberty.
Ford Chester, clerk, h 24 Summit.
Ford George, h 106 Summit.
Ford Orrin B., dealer in tobacco and cigars, 118 E. Main, h 107 Summit.
Ford Wesley, painter, h 13 Tracy Place.
Forsyth Israel E., laborer, h 44 Buell.
Fortier William, bartender Parker House, bds. do.
Forward Charles G., agent, h 7 Vine.
Foster Henry, engineer, h 144 State.
Fowler Robert, retired, bds. 8 W. Main.
Fox Edward, blacksmith, h 27 State.
Fox James A., constable and blacksmith, h 449 Ellicott.
Fox Joseph F., (Ott & Fox) h 30 Cedar.
Fox Wilbur, carriage painter, h 36 Walnut.
Fox William, bartender Hotel Richmond, bds. do.
Francis John, laborer, h 34 Hutchins.
Frank Catharine, widow of Nicholas, h 7 Wiard.
Frank John, carpenter, h 32 State.
Frank John, carpenter, h 117 Ross.
Franklin Mary, widow of Daniel, h 51 S. Liberty.
Frederick Carl, prop. saloon, 40 Jackson, h do.
Fredley Charles, fireman N. Y. C. & H. R. R. R., h 110 Evans.
Friedley Mary, widow of John, h 34 Liberty.
Friedley William, fireman, h 225 Ellicott.
Frum Alfred, carpenter, h 441 Ellicott.
Fuller Edwin J., conductor, h 38 Ellicott ave.
FULLER GARDNER, supt. and prin. public schools, bds. 101 Summit.
Fuller Theodore B., ticket agent N. Y. C. & H. R. R. R., h 141 State.
Fuller Willis H., retired farmer, h 38 W. Main.
Gaffney Michael, laborer, h 38 Hutchins.
Gage Adin G., (Gage & Seaver) h 29 Ellicott ave.
Gage & Seaver, (Adin G. G. and Charles A. S.) life and accident ins. agents, 108 E.
    Main.
Galligher John, laborer, h 41 Lyon.
Galligher Thomas, ins. agent, Masse block, h 71 Oak.
Gallup Jerome J., farmer 350, h 22 South.
Galvin John, prop. saloon, 112 E. Main, h do.
Gamble Annie music teacher, bds. 23 Vine.
Gamble Edward H, book-keeper, bds. 23 Vine.
Gamble William, (Batavia Brewing Co.) brewer and maltster, h 23 Vine.
Gardiner Abbey, widow of Josiah, h 12 Bank.
Gardiner Charles W., medical student, bds. 92 E. Main.

Gardiner William C., dentist and vice-pres. Batavia Wheel Co., 92 E. Main, h do.
Gardner Fred G., law student with F. S. Wood.
Gardner Jefferson, prop. pool room, 28 E. Main, h W. Main.
Garen James P., asst. pastor St. Joseph's Church, bds. 303 E. Main.
Garner Joseph F., cigar manuf., over 90 E. Main, h 32 W. Main.
Gartland Hannah, teacher Institution for the Blind.
Gaskin Owen, laborer, h 125 Ross.
Gast H. P. & J. E., dealers in groceries, 80 Main.
Gast Henry, retired, h W. Main.
GAST HENRY P., (H. P. & J. E. Gast) h 217 Washington ave.
Gast Joseph, baker, h 15 Jackson.
Gast Joseph E., (H. P. & J. E. Gast).
Gay Lucy, widow of Norris, h 161 Bank.
Gear William, laborer, h 351 Ellicott.
Gehm Jacob, blacksmith, h 29 Harvester ave.
Gehm John, barber, bds. Genesee House.
Geiger Andrew F., carpenter, h 153 Bank.
Gelser George H., pastor Evangelical Association, h 25 Center.
GENESEE COUNTY BANK, R. T. Howard, pres.; William C. Watson, vice-pres.;
    John W. Smith, cashier, 103 E. Main.
GENESEE HOUSE, T. Lynch, prop., 18 Jackson.
Getter Henry, book-keeper, bds. 7 North.
Getz Andrew, laborer, h 32 Buell.
Gibbs Arthur, dealer in millinery and ladies' furnishing goods, 59 E. Main, h 108 Bank.
Gibbs Elizabeth, dressmaker, h Cherry cor. S. Liberty.
Gibbs Horace, harnessmaker, h 2 Wiard.
Gibbs James, laborer, h 48 S. Liberty.
Gibson Charles M., (Guiteau & Gibson) h 25 Ellicott ave.
Giddings Albert, carpenter, h 13 Vine.
Giddings John K., manuf. of cigars and dealer in tobacco, 42 Main, h 34 Walnut.
GLADE JOHN, (Dellinger & Glade) (May & Glade) h 30 W. Main.
GLASS ALBERT J., pres. and treas. Johnston Harvester Co., h 428 E. Main.
Glass Joseph J., invoice clerk Johnston Harvester Co., bds. 428 E. Main.
Gleason David, retired farmer, h 33 Tracy Place.
Gleason Fred B., dealer in groceries and provisions, 100 E. Main, h 42 State.
Gleason John B., retired, h 42 State.
Glosser Lottie, prop. bakery, 38½ Jackson, h 32 do.
GLOWACKI HENRY I., retired, h 16 Summit.
Goade Frank H., harnessmaker, bds. 210 Bank.
Goade William, laborer, h 210 Bank.
Goade William J., painter, bds. 210 Bank.
Godfrey Charlotte, widow of Lebbeus, born in 1797, bds. 103 State.
Godfrey William, prop. saloon, 114 E. Main, h do.
Gold James, carpenter, h 20 Walker Place.
Gonyer Mary, tailoress, h 103 Main.
Goodenbery Theodore, teamster, h 23 Buell.
Goodson John, machinist, h 4 Prune.
Gordon John, cigar manuf., State, h 16 Maple.
Gould Albert, fireman, h 14 Robinson.
Gould Charles R., h 10 Maple.
Gould Claud C., electrician, h 1 Central ave.
Gould William W., dealer in produce, wool, grain, etc., 52 Ellicott, h 34 Ellicott ave.
Graham George W., carpenter, h 122 State.
Graham John, blacksmith, h 59 Swan.
Graves Edward L., photographer, over 63 E. Main, h 16 Harvester ave.
Green Andrew, mason, h 26 Hutchins.
Green George F., prop. restaurant, 115 E. Main, h do.
Green George S., tanner, h 138 Bank.
Green Harry J., prop. saloon, 50 Jackson.

Green James, blacksmith, h 8 Walker Place.
Green Lucy, widow of Newton, h 16 Harvester ave.
GREENE JOHN C., real estate dealer, loan and ins. agent, 61 E. Main, h 132 Bank.
Greene Maryette, widow of Edwin, bds. 7 Vine.
GRIFFIS ANN A., widow of George W., h 19 Pearl.
Griffis Daniel W., dealer in flour and feed, farmer 40, 39 Jackson, h 57 S. Main.
Griffis Frank, molder, bds. 19 Pearl.
Griffis Guy E., clerk, bds. 57 S. Main.
Griffis John, policeman, h 17 Pearl.
Griswold Edwin, clerk, h 44 S. Main.
GRISWOLD GERRIT S., (Griswold & McWain) h 7 Tracy Place.
Griswold Lucius D., com. traveler, h 3 Tracy Place.
Griswold Ralph A., clerk, h 115 Washington ave.
GRISWOLD & McWAIN, (Gerrit S. G. and Andrew J. McW.) props. *Daily News* and job printers, 10 State.
Gruger August, carpenter, h 14 Cedar.
Guiteau George, stenographer. bds. 105 Bank.
Guiteau Jerome C., (Guiteau & Gibson) h 105 Bank.
Guiteau Sarah, widow of L. M., h 22 Bank.
Guiteau & Gibson, (Jerome C. G. and Charles M. G.) real estate agents, 38 Jackson.
Guymer Elizabeth, dressmaker, h 4 Wiard.
Haines Hobert H., carpenter, h rear 37 State.
HAITZ WILLIAM F., (Haitz & Dellinger) manager Dellinger opera house, h 1 Ellicott ave. cor. Main.
HAITZ & DELLINGER, (William F. H. and John D.) dealers in musical instruments, sewing machines, artists' materials, wall paper, etc., 105 E. Main.
Hale John C., laborer, h 7 Ross.
Hall Edward, patternmaker, h 56 Buell.
Hall Edward F., h 10 Fisher Park.
HALL JOSEPH F., (Thomas & Hall) editor *Spirit of the Times*, bds. Hotel Richmond.
Haller George, laborer, h 27 Harvester ave.
Halsted Eunice, widow of J. B., bds. 34 Bank.
Hamilton David, M. D., physician, 117 E. Main, h 123 do.
Hamilton Fred W., retired farmer, h 11 Prospect ave.
Hamilton James M., foreman, h 151 Jackson.
HAMILTON JOHN M., (Joseph Hamilton & Son) h 24 Pearl.
HAMILTON JOSEPH, (Joseph Hamilton & Son) h 18 Ellicott.
HAMILTON JOSEPH & SON, (John M.) marble and granite dealers, 24 E. Main.
Hamilton Lucy, teacher, bds. 24 Ross.
Hamilton Thomas, machinist, h 8 Hutchins.
HAMMOND LEON W., (Hammond & Son) penman. bds. 126 Ellicott.
HAMMOND OSCAR D., (Hammond & Son) h 126 Ellicott.
HAMMOND & SON, (Oscar D. and Leon W.) manufs. of and dealers in harnesses, horse furnishing goods, etc., 108 Main.
Hampton Herbert D., machinist, h 18 Chestnut.
Hampton Philo S., machinist, h 409 Ellicott.
Hanley John, laborer, h 9 Harvester ave.
Hanshaw George E., laborer, h Union
Hanson Edmond, laborer, h off Buell.
Harding William E., teacher Institution for the Blind.
Harmon Carrie M., h 433 E. Main.
Harmon Emma C, h 433 E. Main.
Harmon Harriet E., widow of Eugene. h 137 State.
Harmon Israel, carpenter, h 20 Swan.
Harmon Ors D., architect and job carpenter, rear Court, h Swan.
Harper Charles W., carpenter, h 312 Ellicott.
Harrington Charles H., general sec'y Y. M. C. A., 7 Jackson, bds. 306 Washington ave.
Harrington Thomas, laborer. h 6 Thorp.
Harris Charles, painter, h 43 Maple.

Harris Eva, (Mrs. F. B.) prop. boarding-house, 37 State.
Harris Henry S., carriagemaker, h 26 Cherry.
Harrison Willard C., prop. billiard parlor, E. Main cor. State, h 36 Jackson.
Hart Daniel, h 210 W. Main.
Hart Frederick, machinist, h 550 E. Main.
Hart Thaddeus, carriage builder, h 6 S. Liberty.
Hartley Ann, h 10 Seaver Place.
Hartshorn Eugene G., clerk, bds. 307 Washington ave.
Hartshorn Mary, widow of Russell, h 10 Liberty.
HARTSHORN NELSON, farmer in Darien 284, h 307 Washington ave.
Harvey Andrew J., laborer, h 18 Swan.
Hass William, farmer 14, h Pearl.
Hawes Silas, laborer, h 49 S. Main.
Hawkins Ernest C., prop. Troy Laundry, 32 Jackson, h 3 School.
Hawkins John, laborer, h 32 S. Main.
Hawley Alfred, clerk, bds. 25 Vine.
HAY MICHAEL W., street supt., h 37 Center.
Hayden Charles, laborer, h South.
Hayes Thomas, tinsmith, h 47 State.
Hays Alexander, freight and station agent N. Y. C. &. H. R. R. R., h 34 Ellicott.
Haywood John H., h 217 E. Main.
Hazel Ernest, cabinetmaker, h 100 Harvester ave.
Heal Frank C., wholesale dealer in liquor, tobacco, and cigars, 36¼ E. Main, h Ellicott cor. Evans.
Heal Frederick, laborer, h 30 Harvester ave.
Hedden William, mechanic, h 8 Wood.
Heidkner George, bartender Ellicott House, bds. do.
Henderson Anson W., machinist, h 6 Fisher Park.
Henderson Sarah A., (Mrs. R. R.) h 63 Hutchins.
Henion Tunis, laborer, bds. 20 Harvester ave.
Hensner Philip, painter, h 15 Vine.
Hermance Frank, laborer, h South.
Hermance George, laborer, h 25 Hutchins.
Herrick Anna, teacher.
Herrick Joshua G., carpenter, h 12 Ross.
Herrick Mattie, teacher.
Hess Fred, laborer, h 119 Ross.
Hess John, ins. agent, h 3 Walker.
Hewitt Henry, (J. B. & H. Hewitt) h Hewitt Place.
Hewitt J. B. & H., dealers in dry goods, carpets, etc., 72 E. Main.
Hewitt John B., (J. B. & H. Hewitt) h E. Main.
BICKOX GEORGE W., (Chaddock & Hickox) h 6 Vine.
Hide Joseph, mason, h 48 Walnut.
Higgins Heman W., sexton M. E. Church, h 6 Washington ave.
Higgins Thomas, retired, h 553 E. Main.
HIGLEY ANSON, retired farmer, h 305 Washington ave.
Hill William, molder, h 336 Ellicott.
Hiller Andrew, laborer, h 30 S. Liberty.
Hilton Frank, prop. Brunswick billiard parlor, 11 Jackson, h do.
Hinds John, farmer 130, h 137 Bank.
Hinkston Elizabeth, widow of Dows, h 10 Ellicott ave.
Hinkston Fred P., com. traveler, h 10 Ellicott ave.
Hodges Gerry O., carpenter, h 41 W. Main.
Hoffman Martha, widow of Peter, h 7 Oak.
Hoffman William, tailor, h 32 Pearl.
Hogan James H., cigarmaker, bds. 33 Lyon.
Hogan John, laborer, h 34 Pearl.
Hogan Mary, widow of James, h 35 Lyon.
Hogancamp Charles W., marble worker, h 211 Bank.

Hohn Edward, machinist, h 162 Vine.
Holahan John, laborer, h 30 Church.
Holden Frank, com. traveler, bds. 422 E. Main.
Holden George H., deputy county clerk, h 206 E. Main.
Holden Hannah, widow of R. O., h 424 E. Main.
HOLDEN HINMAN, (R. O. Holden & Son) h 422 E. Main.
Holden William, carpenter, h 120 Main.
HOLDEN R. O. & SON, (Hinman H. and C. M. Robson) dealers in dry goods, 83 and 85 E. Main.
Holdridge George W., hackman, h 37 Jackson.
Holihan John, blacksmith, h 55 Oak.
HOLMES JOSEPH W., civil engineer, manuf. of engineers', surveyors', and astronomical instruments, owns farm in Alabama 105, 7 Prospect ave., h do.
Homelius Frances, widow of Frank B., h 24 Walnut.
Homelius Henry B., carpenter, h 24 Walnut.
HOMELIUS HENRY W., architect, contractor, and builder, 39 Walnut.
HONECK CHARLES H., supt. New York Lumber and Wood Working Co., h 12 Swan.
Hooker William, (Batavia Brewing Co.) h 218 Washington ave.
Hooper David, prop. boarding-house, 104 Jackson.
Hopkins Charles, laborer, bds. 31 Tracy Place.
Hopkins Dewitt C., carpenter, h 205 Washington ave.
Hopkins Mary G., widow of Fones, h 31 Tracy Place.
Hopp William, jeweler, bds. 15 Bank.
Horsch Anthony, mason, h 144 Harvester ave.
Hosmer Harriet, widow of Simeon, h 536 E. Main.
Hosmer Walker W., teamster, h 529 E. Main.
HOTEL RICHMOND, William J. Mann, prop., E. Main.
HOUGH CHARLES W., treas. Wiard Plow Co., h 432 E. Main.
Hough George, book-keeper, h 318 E. Main.
Hough William H., laborer, h 128 Ellicott.
HOUGHTON CHARLES, (Houghton & Dewey) h 139 State.
HOUGHTON & DEWEY, (Charles H. and Charles E. D.) dentists, 108 E. Main.
Houlihan Simon, laborer, h Oak.
House Jacob, manuf. of ginger ale, soda, and mineral waters, 108 W. Main, h do.
HOUSEKNECHT PHILOS B., artist and photographer, ink, crayon, and pastel work a specialty, 106 Main, h rear 37 State.
Hovey Luke S., carriage trimmer, Ellicott, h 139 Summit.
Hovey Spencer, carriage trimmer, h 6 School.
HOWARD HAYDEN U., negotiates loans, etc., 1 Walker block, h 220 E. Main.
HOWARD ROYAL T., pres. Genesee County Bank, h 104 Bank.
Howard Stephen D., laborer, h 334 Ellicott.
Howe David, retired farmer 23, h 11 Maple.
Howe Frank A., (Dunham & Howe) h 538 E. Main.
Howe Frank E., student, bds. 538 E. Main.
Howe Ira, teamster, h 532 E. Main.
Howe Phineas, retired, aged 95, bds. 538 E. Main.
Howe William, engineer N. Y. C. & H. R. R. R., h 11 Maple.
Hoyl John, carpenter, bds. 28 State.
Hoyt John, laborer, h 17 William.
Hubbard Henry C., teamster, h 455 Ellicott.
Huber John, laborer, h 8 Robinson.
Huggins Charles W., clerk, h 15 Pearl.
HULL CARLOS A., county clerk, bds. Hotel Richmond.
HUMPHREYS HANNAH M., widow of Hector, h 35 Bank.
Hunn Julia, h 62 S. Main.
Hunter Mary W., (Mrs. Dr. D. C.) h 146 Jackson.
HUNTLEY BYRON E., vice-pres. Johnston Harvester Co., h 212 E. Main.
Hurbolt Charles, clerk, h 56 S. Liberty.

Hurd Chester P., carpenter, h 157 Bank.
Hurlburt Truman, retired, h 33 State.
HUTCHINS HORACE S., M. D., homeo. physician, 89 E. Main, h 215 do.
Hutchinson John, laborer, h Clifton ave.
Hyde Walter, laborer, h 36 Pearl.
INSTITUTION FOR THE BLIND, A. G. Clement, A. M., supt., Richmond ave.
Irvine Robert, engineer, h 164 State.
Ives Henry A., dealer in patent rights, h 322 Ellicott.
Jackson Henry, laborer, h 20 Cedar.
Jackson John A., spoke finisher, bds. Continental Hotel.
Jameson Frank M., accountant at Institution for the Blind, h 8 Mix Place.
Jaquith Henry, shoemaker, h 6 Wiard.
Jarvis Will O., teacher at the Rectory School, Hamden, Conn., h 10 Tracy Place.
Jasper Fred, laborer, h 61 S. Liberty.
Jaynes William, molder, h 4 Otis.
Jerome Mary R., widow, h 16 Bank.
Jewel Frank, laborer, h 15 William.
Johnson Cyrus A., pastor First Baptist Church, h 116 State.
Johnson Harvey, butcher, h 4 Oak.
Johnson Homer, com. traveler, h 364 Ellicott.
Johnson George T., piano tuner, bds. 112 State.
Johnson Horace E., machinist, h 9 Wood.
JOHNSON JOHN G., lawyer, 74 Main, h 143 W. Main.
Johnson Martha E., h 105 State.
Johnson Peter, laborer, h 23 Lyon.
Johnson Sarah, widow of William, h 9 S. Liberty.
Johnson Thomas, teamster, h 321 Ellicott.
JOHNSTON HARVESTER CO., A. J. Glass, pres.; B. E. Huntley, vice-pres.; E. J.
    Mockford, sec'y and supt., Harvester ave.
JONES AMELIA C., widow of Alva, h 203 Washington ave.
Jones David C., prop. Park Hotel and dealer in horses, Court cor. Ellicott.
Jones James B., (Jones & Son) h 21 Oak.
Jones James H., (Jones & Son) h 45 Ellicott ave.
Jones & Son, (James H. and James B.) dealers in groceries and meat, 19 Jackson.
Joslyn Almarin, retired, h 407 E. Main.
Josllyn Amanda, widow of Samuel B., bds. 115 Bank.
Kane James, blacksmith, h 11 William.
Kane John J., (Shults & Kane) town clerk, h 41 Liberty.
Kane Mary, widow of Timothy, h 41 Liberty.
Kane William F., cutter, emp. C. W. Luckel, bds. 41 Liberty.
Karlson Frans L., tailor, h 310 Ellicott.
Kearney Thomas, laborer, h 47 Buell.
Keefe John, laborer, h Union.
Keehn John, retired, bds. 28 State.
Keehn William, carpenter, h 1 Pearl.
Kellar Fred M., patternmaker, h 32 Maple.
Kellar Moses F., machinist, h 137 Summit.
Kelley Jerry, laborer, h Union.
Kelley John, laborer, h Union.
Kelley John, laborer, h 154 Bank.
Kelley John, laborer, h 8 S. Liberty.
Kelly James, laborer, h 19 School.
Kelsey Homer N., agent, h 27 Walnut.
Kelsey Jerome, teamster, h 105 W. Main.
Kempton John A., carpenter, h rear 29 Harvester ave.
KEMPTON MARTIN L., manuf. of wire and picket fence, 117 Harvester ave, h 15
    Vine.
Kendall Cory, telegraph operator, bds. 312 Washington ave.
Kendall Solomon B., retired, h 312 Washington ave.

Kendall William H., carpenter, h 23 Harvester ave.
Kennedy Daniel, laborer; h 16 S. Swan.
Kennedy Edward, laborer, h 48 Swan.
Kennedy John, laborer, h 2 Thorp.
Kennedy Michael, laborer, h 18 East ave.
Kenney John, cartman, h 26 South.
Kenney Joseph, laborer, h 45 Hutchins.
KENNY ADELAIDE R., widow of Dr. William J. C., h 311 E. Main.
KENNY MICHAEL, (Kenny & Rourke) h 152 Ellicott.
KENNY & ROURKE, (Michael K. and John R.) dealers in groceries and provisions, wholesale and retail dealers in wines and liquors, 152 Ellicott.
Kent Frederick, wheelmaker, bds. Jackson.
KENYON E. PORTER, formerly dealer in groceries, provisions, and ice, 80 Main, h 149 Bank.
Kenyon Edward L., com. traveler, h 107 Bank.
Kenyon Enoch, carpenter, h 2 James.
Kerslake James, tailor and prop. meat market, 113 Main, h 17 Center.
Kerslake William E., clerk, bds. 8 Center.
Keyes William, carpenter, h 531 E. Main.
Keystone Mfg. Co., A. W. Preston, prop., manufs. of picture frames, and dealers in picture and art goods, 55 E. Main.
KIBBE CHARLES A., farm agency and real estate dealer, 94 E. Main, h 13 Bank.
Kibbe Chauncy S., glove manuf., h 36 Ellicott ave.
Kibler George, (Kibler & Conrad) h 22 Main.
Kibler & Conrad, (George K. and Paul C.) props. Continental Hotel, 22 E. Main.
Kies Gottlieb, book binder, 57 E. Main, h 55 W. Main.
KING ALBERT H., bds. Hotel Richmond.
King Asa, (King & Redshaw) h 218 Ellicott.
King Cornelia, widow of Darius, bds. 16 Spruce.
KING FRANCIS D., contractor and builder, h 11 Vine.
King Harry, laborer, h 330 Ellicott.
King Walter E., building mover, h 16 Spruce.
KING & REDSHAW, (Asa K. and John R.) contractors and builders, Church.
Kinne Charles A., deputy internal revenue collector, h 111 Jackson.
Kinney Dennis, laborer, h Pearl.
Kinney William V., painter, h 38 Church.
Kinsella James, molder, h 19 Hewitt Place.
Kinsella Milo, molder, h 41 Center.
KINSEY RUSSELL L., lawyer, 5 Postoffice block, bds. Parker House.
Kinsley Theresa, widow of C. P., h 33 Ellicott ave.
Kirsch Nicholas J., carpenter, bds. Continental Hotel.
Klimitz Charles, leader Batavia Cornet Band, music teacher, and gun and locksmith, 4 Center, h 12 Robinson.
KLIMITZ CHARLES A. Prof., piano tuner and teacher of instrumental music, h 18 Walnut.
Klimitz Edward W., laborer, bds. 18 Walnut.
Klimitz Emil, gunsmith, bds. 18 Walnut.
Klug William, teamster, h 110 Ellicott.
Knapp Lynn E. D, widow of Volney, owns in Alabama farm 275, h 17 North.
Knickerbocker Frank E., book-keeper N. Y. C. & H. R. R. R. freight office, h Franklin.
Knickerbocker James, retired farmer, owns in Elba 130, h 104 Ross.
Knill Charles A., mason, h 147 Bank.
Knowles John W., machinist, h 217 Ellicott.
Knowlton Hattie, teacher, h 16 East ave.
KNOWLTON THADDEUS J., farmer in Pavilion 69, h 24 Wood.
Koons George W., auctioneer, bds. Park Hotel.
Krause Henry, blacksmith, h 55 S. Liberty.
Kritz Peter, cooper, bds. Jackson.
Kuhn Joseph, farmer, h 534 E. Main.

Kunard Julius, wood carver, h 342 Ellicott.
Kurtz Frank, prop. saloon, 14 E. Main, h do.
Kurtz Frank, Jr., bartender, bds. 14 E. Main.
Kurtz John F., dealer in groceries and provisions, 57 Jackson, h Ellicott.
Kyre Martin, laborer, h 20 Evans.
Lacy Charles E., millwright, h 21 Swan.
La Fountain Charles H., dealer in blue stone flagging, h 26 Walnut.
Lake Jerry, laborer, h 13 Wiard.
Lake Richard, carpenter, h 1 James.
Lamberton Ruby M., widow of John, dressmaker, h 10 State.
Land George, carpenter, h Oak.
Landers William, laborer, h 14 Liberty.
Lane Cyrus D., com. traveler, h 539 E. Main.
LANE LOUIS B, (Lawrence & Lane) h 153 Summit.
Lannigan John, laborer, h 58 S. Liberty.
LAPE JOSEPH, constable and prop. restaurant, 45 Jackson, h 17 School.
Larigo Almina, widow of Charles F., bds. 203 Washington ave.
Lathrop Harry E., laborer, h 1 Prune.
Lathrop Sarah E., widow of Charles A., h 13 Swan.
LATHROP SARAH E., widow of Samuel, h 9 East ave.
Lawless Bridget, widow of Stephen, h 44 Walnut.
Lawrence Asa F., manuf. and designer of fine or art furniture, 110 Jackson, h do.
Lawrence Charles, laborer, h 73 Hutchins.
Lawrence Henry, laborer, h 75 Hutchins.
Lawrence Reuben, com. traveler, h 39 W. Main.
LAWRENCE SPENCER J., (Lawrence & Lane) bds. 9 Swan.
LAWRENCE & LANE, (Spencer J. H. and Louis B. L.) lawyers, 69 E. Main.
Lawson Thomas N., blacksmith, h Otis.
Lay Catharine, (Mrs. J. L.) h 30 Tracy Place.
LAY GEORGE W., lawyer, h 420 E. Main.
LAY HARRY M., prop. planing-mill, dealer in coal, lumber, and baled hay, 29 Liberty, h 30 Tracy Place.
LAY JOHN F., retired, h 420 E. Main.
Lay Pauline, widow of Gustavus A., h 16 Bank.
Leavenworth Edward E., book-keeper, bds. 32 Bank.
LEAVENWORTH WILLIAM W., sec'y Batavia Wheel Co., h 23 Ellicott ave.
Lee Marion, widow of C. W., agent Fleischman Yeast Co., h 514 E. Main.
LEFLER GEORGE W., veterinary surgeon, Exchange Place, h do.
Legett Pulaski, clerk, h 20 Ganson ave.
Lehmann John, laborer, h 352 Ellicott.
Lennon Edward, laborer, h 41 S. Liberty.
Lent David, att'y at law, Postoffice block, Jackson, h 127 Bank.
Leonard John, laborer, h Otis.
Leonard John A., prop. Leonard's baggage express, h 5 Robinson.
Leonard John B., manager for Ferrin Brothers Co., h 19 Otis.
Leonard Lawn, truckman, h 6 S. Liberty.
Leonard Richard B., musician, h 120 Jackson.
Lerch John, laborer, h 125 Summit.
Le Seur James A., clerk Surrogate's Court, h Wiard.
Le SEUR JOHN W., M. D., homeo. physician, over 89 E. Main, bds. 215 do.
Lewis Alva W., printer, h 134 Summit.
Lewis Frank H., carpenter, h 5 Cherry.
Lewis Fred A., (North & Lewis) bds. 130 State.
Lewis James, farmer in Bethany 70, h 114 Ross.
Lewis Miles, gunmaker, h 15 School.
LEWIS ROBERT S., editor and prop. *Progressive Batavian*, 64 Main, h 130 State.
Lewis Sarah, widow of Walter S., h 127 State.
Lewis Walter W., station agent N. Y., L. E. & W. R. R., h 309 Washington ave.
Lightsinger Jacob, laborer, bds. 508 E. Main.

Lincoln Allen D., farmer in Alexander 47, h 125 Jackson.
Lincoln Mary J., widow of F. W., h 16 Swan.
Lincoln Sarah F. Miss, h 16 Swan.
Lloyd Sylvester W., pastor M. E. Church, h 8 Bank.
Lochnicht John, mason, h 7 Pearl.
Lochnicht Joseph, carpenter, h Pearl.
Locke Charles, laborer, h 131 Ross.
Locke Edward S., painter, h 127 Harvester ave.
Locke Sarah D., widow of David, h 514 E. Main.
Locke Walter G., painter, h 18 Pearl.
Locke William H., (Boyden & Locke) h 204 Ellicott.
Loftus Mary, widow of Patrick, h 212 Ellicott.
Long Edwin C., lawyer, h 150 Bank.
Long George, laborer, h Oak.
Long Lewis, carpenter, h Webster.
Loomis Calvin, farmer, h 135 Bank.
Loomis Jane, widow of Washington, h 35 Center.
Loomis Loren, laborer, h 71 Swan.
Loomis Reuben H., carpenter, h 22 Vine.
Looney George, gas fitter, h 5 Chase Park.
Lord Leonora V., widow of Oscar W., h 211 Washington ave.
Lorish Charles H., clerk, bds. Central ave.
Lorish J. & L. C., dealers in groceries and provisions, 21 and 23 Jackson.
Lorish Josiah, (J. & L. C. Lorish) h 21 and 23 Jackson.
Lorish Lester H., laborer, h 23 Central ave.
Lorish Luellan C., (J. & L. C. Lorish) h 21 and 23 Jackson.
Lounsberry Florilla M., widow of Dr. Earl B., h 111 Summit.
Lowe Alexander B., molder, h 121 Ross.
Lown Benjamin F., carpenter, h 11 East ave.
Lown Irving J., laborer, h 11 Wood.
LUCKEL CHARLES W., merchant tailor, 30 Jackson, bds. 4 Cedar.
Luckel Philip, tailor, Main cor. Jackson, h 4 Cedar.
Luf Charles, cabinetmaker, h 100 Harvester ave.
Luppert George, carpenter, h 38 S. Swan.
Lusk Lucinda P., widow of R. S., h 100 Bank.
Lynch James, laborer, h 48 Hutchins.
Lynch Nellie M., music teacher at Institution for the Blind, bds. Genesee House.
Lynch Thomas, agent for shirts and gents' furnishing goods, bds. Genesee House.
LYNCH TIMOTHY, prop. Genesee House, 18 Jackson, h do.
Lyseght John, gardener, emp. Mrs. D. Richmond, h 29 Ross.
Mackey David S., millwright, h 42 Ellicott.
Mackey James, clerk, h 32 Ellicott.
Mackey John, laborer, bds. 221 W. Main.
Mackey Margaret, prop. variety store, 38 Main, h 32 Ellicott.
Mackie James G., dealer in dry and fancy goods, 61 E. Main, h 12 Ellicott ave.
Macy Louise J., widow of George, h 320 E. Main.
MADDOCK HUMPHERY P., teacher industrial department Institution for the Blind, h 213 Bank.
Mahaney Kate, dressmaker, Main, h 13 Wood.
Mahoney James, laborer, h 44 Church.
MAIN SIDNEY U., retired, h 431 E. Main.
Malley Joseph, laborer, h 7 S. Swan.
Maloney Michael, dealer in groceries, crockery, etc., 34 Main, h 119 Bank.
Maloney Michael, mail agent, h 107 State.
Maney James, coachman, h 122 Ross.
Mann Charles A., clerk Hotel Richmond, bds. do.
Mann Eunice, widow of Chester, born in 1803, bds. 11 Summit.
Mann George G., mason, 5 Howard.
Mann Harry, laborer, h Thorp.

Mann William B., retired, bds. Hotel Richmond.
MANN WILLIAM J., prop. Hotel Richmond, resides do.
Manning James, laborer, h 11 S. Main.
Manning James, laborer, h 127 W. Main.
Manning John, mason, h 61 Oak.
Manning Peter, manager billiard room, Hotel Richmond, bds. do.
Manning Redmond, laborer, h 129 W. Main.
Manning Thomas, mason, h 40 Lyon.
Marble Gardner, section boss N. Y. C. & H. R. R. R., bds. 108 Jackson.
Marble Henry, laborer, h 39 Jackson.
Maroney John, emp. on N. Y. C. & H. R. R. R., h Central ave.
Maroney Mary, widow of Michael, h 24 Cherry.
Marse Solomon, ins. agent, 10 E. Main, h 418 do.
Marshall George, machinist, h 3 Chase Park.
Marshall Henry, machinist. bds. 3 Chase Park.
Marshall Thomas H., machinist, bds. 3 Chase Park.
Martelle Theophilus, laborer. h 6 Walker.
Martin Isaac, carpenter, h Ross.
Martin Margaret, widow of John, tailoress, bds. 114 State.
Martin Rose, dressmaker, h 27 State.
Mattice Michael, carpenter, h 35 S. Main.
Mansnest John, barber, 4 Jackson, h 57 Ellicott.
MAXWELL ROBERT A., State supt. of insurance, h 37 Ellicott ave.
May Herman, (May & Glade) h 123 Ellicott.
May & Glade, (Herman M. and John G) dealers in groceries and provisions, 13
    Jackson.
McAllister Frank, owner and late prop. Ellicott House, Jackson cor. Ellicott.
McBride Arthur, engineer, h 15 Hewitt Place.
McBride James, laborer, h 14 Trumbull Place.
McBride John, mason, h 4 S. Swan.
McBride Thomas, mason, h 6 Hutchins.
McCann Kate, visitors' attendant Institution for the Blind.
McCann Minnie, (Mrs. William) dressmaker, 103 Main.
McCann William H., clerk, bds. 43 State.
McCarthy Michael, laborer, h 24 Walker Place.
McCory Robert, machinist, h 43 Liberty.
McCully Andrew, constable, h 60 Swan.
McCully James, laborer, h 23 Cherry.
McDonald Alexander, molder, h 25 Otis.
McDonald John, retired, h 13 Center.
McDonald Margaret, widow of Callahan, h 26 Main.
McEllven Carrie M., widow of William, h 15 Wood.
McElus Isabella, widow of John, h 116 State.
McEuty Patrick, laborer, h Franklin.
McFarlan Owen, laborer, h Pearl.
McGowan Thomas, laborer, h 39 Maple.
McGrath Michael J., engineer N. Y. C. & H. R. R. R., h 104 Summit.
McGuirk Owen, farmer, h Cone Place.
McIntire Martin, conductor, h 14 Center.
McIntire Nellie G., teacher, bds. 27 Bank.
McINTYRE LEVANT C., pres. First National Bank, h 27 Bank.
McKaon Michael, laborer, h 365 Ellicott.
McKelvey William, machinist, h 109 State.
McKENZIE JOHN M. Hon., (McKenzie, Ryan & Storms) bds. 15 Bank.
McKENZIE, RYAN & STORMS, (John M. McK., John F. R., and John C. S.) dealers
    in clothing and gents' furnishing goods, 87 E. Main.
McKeon Grace, teacher of vocal music.
McKEOWN DAVID, successor to F. J. Gast, baker and confectioner, candies and ice
    cream a specialty, 119 E. Main.

McLaughlin Charles D., com. traveler, h 140 Ellicott.
McLaughlin James, prop. saloon, 140 Ellicott, h do.
McLaughlin James R., com. traveler, 140 Ellicott.
McLaughlin Peter, carpenter, h 14 Vine.
McLean Lewis H., clerk Bank of Genesee, h 14 Bank.
McMahon John, brakeman, h 130 Ellicott.
McMann Hugh, laborer, h 48 Swan.
McNeeley Henry, waiter, bds. 49 Main.
McNish John, hay dealer, bds. 132 Jackson.
McVean Daniel, farmer in Darien 200, h 310 Washington ave.
McWAIN ANDREW J., (Griswold & McWain) h 5 Ross.
Mead Eda, widow of Charles, h 17 Ross.
Menkle George, laborer, h 50 South.
Merrihew William P., com. traveler, h 52 Washington ave.
Merrill John, clerk, h 11 Jackson.
Merrill Joseph C., laborer, h 17 Washington ave.
Merritt Emma, widow of Salem, h 204 W. Main.
Meserve Charles W., railroad contractor, h 457 Ellicott.
Metcalf Joseph, prop. National Hotel, off Jackson.
Metzger Jacob, laborer, h 32 Vine.
Metzger Michael, omnibus driver Hotel Richmond, bds. do.
Metzker William, painter, h 153 Jackson.
Metzler Lizzie, widow of Peter, h 30 Cherry.
Michal George, laborer. h 154 Vine.
Millen John, carpenter, h 155 Jackson.
Miller Andrew T., asst. cashier Bank of Batavia, h 22 Ross.
MILLER HOLDEN T., cashier Bank of Batavia, h 404 E. Main.
Miller Jacob, sexton St. James's Church, h 48 S. Main.
Miller William F., mason, h 31 Walker.
Mills Orlin, laborer, h 3 Willow.
Minahan Cornelius, laborer, h off Franklin.
Minahan Julia, tailoress, h 221 Bank.
Miner William, laborer, h 11 Otis.
Minges Lewis, machinist, h 4 Chase Park.
Minges Pulaski, painter, h 133 State.
MIX DAVID E. E., civil engineer, Uebele block, h 4 Mix Place.
Mix George, pattern fitter, h 10 Center.
Mix Nancy, widow of Joseph B., h 9 Bank.
MOCKFORD EDWARD J., sec'y and supt. Johnston Harvester Co., h 20 Bank.
Mockford Henry. lumber inspector, emp. Johnston Harvester Co., h 128 Harvester ave.
Mockford John E., supt. Johnston Harvester Co., farmer 156, h 20 Bank.
Mockford Milton J., machinist, bds. 128 Harvester ave.
Mockford William H., foreman, h 5 Harvester ave.
MOGRIDGE THOMAS, blacksmith, manuf. of wagons, carriages, and sleighs, 2 Seaver Place, h 100 Ross.
Moiles John, laborer, h off Buell.
Moll Morris, molder, h 116 Vine.
Monnell Henry C., laborer, h 50 Walker.
Monroe Amos H., varnisher, h 111 State.
Moore Joseph H., teamster, h off Jackson.
Moran Mary, widow of John, h 16 S. Liberty.
Moreau Frank A., laborer, h 108 Jackson.
Moreau George W, express messenger, h 25 Central ave.
Moreau Pauline, (Mrs. Frank) prop. boarding-house, 108 Jackson.
Moreau Wilber C., wagonmaker, h 45 State.
MORGAN GEORGE E., clerk, h 13 S. Main.
Morgan Lucius J., carpenter, h 38 Maple.
Morgan Sarah B., widow of Ebenezer B., h 69 S. Main.

Morgan William E., h 36 State.
Morris George B., peddler, h 170 State.
Morrison Wesley, carpenter, rear 34 Cedar.
Morse Charles G., milk peddler, h 6 Walker Place.
Morse Edward P., founder Elmwood Cemetery, dealer in gravel, farmer 15, h 530 E. Main
Morse Henry L., laborer, h 4 Robinson.
Morse Herbert A., physician and surgeon, Main cor. Bank, h 17 Summit.
Mosier William. retired, h 16 Vine.
Moss Philip, laborer, h 46 Washington ave.
Moule Levi, retired farmer 116, h 53 Ellicott ave.
MOULTON BURT, manager Cottage restaurant and bar, 1 State, h do.
Moulton Edward T., ex-mail agent, h 1 State.
Moulton Frank G., (Parsons & Co.) dealer in hay, straw, etc., h 129 Jackson.
Moulton Orson, dealer in horses, h 122 Bank.
Mower Benjamin F., carpenter, h Walnut.
MOYNIHAN MICHAEL, merchant tailor, dealer in clothing and gents' furnishing goods, 47 E. Main, h do.
Mullen Charles, laborer, h 3 Prune.
Mullen Eliza, widow of James. h 8 Chase Park.
Mullen Joseph, clerk, bds. 32 Bank.
Muller Eugene R., watchmaker, emp. Caney & Bradley, bds. 37 State.
Munger Luman, gunsmith, h Jackson.
Munn Fred C., clerk, bds. 15 Bank.
Muntz Conrod, laborer, h rear 34 Cedar.
Muntz John, cabinetmaker, h 103 Evans.
Murphy Daniel, prop. saloon, 25 Evans.
Murphy Martin, switchman, h 22 Cherry.
Murray Peter, laborer, h 11 Trumbull Place.
Myers Adam, laborer, h Elm.
Myers Charles, dealer in groceries, 59 S. Liberty, h 50 do.
Myers Fred, overseer of the poor, h 38 Ellicott.
MYLCRANE W. T., sec'y and treas. Syracuse Forging and Gun Co., bds. Hotel Richmond.
Napier John H., agent American Express Co., 10 Jackson, bds. Genesee Hotel.
Narey Kate, dressmaker, h Wiard.
Nash Willard, retired, h 12 Pearl.
Neasmith John B., member board of health, h 9 Walker.
Negus Addison G., barber, h 13 Chestnut:
Neil Charles, mason, h 147 Bank.
Nelson William C., canvasser, h 128 State.
Netzen Oscar, tailor, h 20 Tracy Place.
New Mary E., widow of Jacob, h 3 Harvester ave.
NEW YORK LUMBER AND WOOD WORKING CO., Charles H. Honeck, supt., capital $100,000, offices in New York city, Elizabeth.
Newell Albert C., retired clergyman, h 108 State.
Nichols Charles, prop. meat market, h 115 W. Main.
Nichols Marion, inventor Nichols's binder, h 15 Tracy Place.
Nichols Raymond, machinist, h 138 Bank.
Nims Louisa, widow of W. W., h 11 Wiard.
Nobles Newton D., prop. roller-mills, 23 Evans, h 18 Ellicott.
Nolan Thomas, laborer, h 108 S. Main.
Norcutt Alphonzo, section master N. Y. C. & H. R. R. R., h 65 Ellicott ave.
NORTH SAFFORD E., (North & Lewis) county judge, surrogate. and attorney at law, 84 Main, h 13 Summit.
North & Lewis, (Safford E. N. and Fred A. L.) attorneys and counselors at law, 84 Main.
Northrop Julia A., widow of Charles A., h 315 E. Main.
NORTON ANN, widow of Moses, h 38 Ellicott ave.

Norton Jacob, blacksmith, h 357 Ellicott.
Norton Minnie, dressmaker, h 13 Jackson.
Nott Ebert, laborer, h 64 S. Liberty.
NOYES EBENEZER B., retired, h 15 Bank.
NOYES EVA L., (Mrs. E. B.) prop. boarding-house, 15 Bank.
Nugent James, mason, h 12 Hutchins.
Nugent Michael, laborer, h 130 Harvester ave.
Nugent Michael, engineer, h 121 Jackson.
Nugent Perry, teamster, h 32 Seaver Place.
Nugent Thomas, laborer, h 27 Walker.
O'Brian Michael, dealer in groceries and provisions, 106 Main and 107 Harvester ave,
    h 107 Harvester ave.
O'Connor Bridget, widow of James, h 327 Ellicott.
O'Connor Daniel, laborer, h 34 Pearl.
O'Connor Edward, laborer, h 44 Church.
O'Connor James, brakeman, h 41 Central ave.
O'Connor John, laborer, h 46 Walnut.
Odion Robert C., carpenter, h 68 S. Liberty.
O'Donnell John, retired, h 61 Swan.
O'Donnell Patrick, laborer, h 15 Central ave.
Ogden George, teacher of music Institution for the Blind.
O'Hara James A., conductor, h 18 Robinson.
O'Hara Owen, laborer, h 33 Hutchins.
Oliver Kittie, widow of Robert, h 16 Ellicott.
Oliver William H., carpenter, h 13 Hutchins.
OLMSTED ALBERT C., dealer in coal and lumber, 43 Center, h 423 E. Main.
ONDERDONK HENRY L., dealer in harnesses and horse furnishing goods, 65 Main,
    h 103 State.
Onderdonk Ralph W., harnessmaker, h State.
O'Neil Martin, laborer, h 6 Robinson.
Osborne Charles R., book-keeper, bds. 22 Center.
Osborne Sarah C., widow of E. N., h 22 Center.
Osborne William E., clerk, bds. 22 Center.
Ostrander Delbert, doorman N. Y. C. & H. R. R. R., h 106 Evans.
Ott Frank A., (Ott & Fox) h 16 Walnut.
Ott George, blacksmith, h 48 Washington ave.
Ott & Fox, (Frank A. O. and Joseph F. F.) horseshoers and blacksmiths, Echange Place.
Page Eliphas B., musician and dealer in musical instruments, 66 Main, h 127 Summit.
Page Orris, clerk, bds. 127 Summit.
Page William, molder, h 112 Vine.
Palmer Damon, retired physician, h 14 Wood.
Palmer G. Welton medical student, bds. 14 Wood.
Palmer George, engineer, h 42 Church.
Palmer Samuel, retired, h 124 State.
Palmer William T., manuf. of paper boxes, 56–60 Main, h 216 Washington ave.
Pardee George, retired, bds. Tibbitts House.
Park Hotel, D. C. Jones, prop , Court cor. Ellicott.
PARK PLACE SCHOOL, Mary J. Wilkins, prin.; Prof. H. D. Wilkins, musical di-
    rector; Prof. A. M. Hill, linguist; Miss Gertrude Wilson, mathematics and nat-
    ural science; Miss Louise Kellogg, musical assistant; Miss Helen Cox, history
    and art, Park Place.
PARKER HOUSE, formerly Purdy's Hotel, George H. Curtis, prop., E. Main.
Parker Le Roy, lawyer in Buffalo, bds. 16 Summit.
PARKER ORRIN C., bds. Parker House.
Parkin William, supt. cemetery, 108 Ross.
Parmele E. Steven, agent Wiard Plow Co., h 151 Summit.
PARMELE LUCIUS B., M.D., physician and surgeon, 38 State, h do.
Parmelee Fred, mechanic, h 12 Hewitt Place.
Parmelee Harry W., clerk, h 130 Summit.

Parson Martin, laborer, h 25 Harvester ave.
PARSONS JAMES P., with Parsons & Co., h 46 S. Main.
Parsons James R., (Parsons & Co.) h 4 Liberty.
Parsons & Co.. (Frank G. Moulton and James R. Parsons) props. Ellicott Street rol-
    ler-mills, manufs. and dealers in flour, feed, and grain.
PATTEN HENRY J., M. D., physician and surgeon, 64 E. Main, h 41 State.
PATTERSON JEROME J., (W. S. & J. J. Patterson) h Prospect ave.
PATTERSON W. S. & J. J., dealers in drugs, medicines, books, etc., 102 E. Main.
PATTERSON WILLIAM S., (W. S. & J. J. Patterson) h Prospect ave.
Pattridge William B., Free Methodist clergyman, h 5 Spruce.
Peabody Watkins J., laborer, h 10 Chase Park.
Peard Robert, laborer, h 3 Willow.
Pease Alvin, retired, h 119 Summit.
PEASE ROBERT B., dealer in hardware, 54 E. Main, h 32 Ellicott ave.
Peck Charles B., com. traveler, h 117 Bank.
Peck Edward C., bartender, bds. 10 Main.
PECK MYRON H., lawyer and ex-county judge, residence in Buffalo.
PECK MYRON H., JR., lawyer and ex-postmaster, 5 Postoffice block, h 213 Wash-
    ington ave.
PECKES JOHN B., prop. saloon and restaurant, and dealer in wines and liquors,
    504 E. Main.
Peet George, prop. saloon, 43 Swan.
Peet William, laborer, h 431 Ellicott.
Pember Alfred J., canvasser, h 119 State.
Pember Leander U., retired, bds. Parker House.
Perfield Philip, prop. European Hotel and restaurant, 36 Main.
Perfield Thomas J., prop. restaurant, 56 Main.
Perkins Edwin, fireman, h 311 Ellicott.
Perkins Samuel F., engineer, h 313 Ellicott.
Perrin Charles N., postoffice clerk.
Perrin Edward A., laborer, h 1 Mill.
Perrin George E., dealer in cigars and tobacco, 8 Jackson, h 1 Mill.
Perry Albert R., bill poster, bds. 41 Jackson.
Perry Alton W., retired, h 41 Jackson.
Perry George G., cartman, h 31 S. Main.
Perry Simon, laborer, h 11 S. Swan.
Peshong Elizabeth, widow of John, h 27 Buell.
Peters Phil Gen., dealer in tobacco and cigars, prop. restaurant and saloon, Jackson,
    h do.
Peters William, cabinet finisher, h 227 W. Main.
Phelan Cornelia, teacher Institution for the Blind.
Phelps George, clerk, h 57 Jackson.
Phelps Henry, cabinetmaker, h 54 Buell.
Phelps Walter G., case hardener and blower, h 2 Wiard.
Pickard John, carpenter, h 15 S. Main.
Pierce Charles, emp. in gun works, h 332 Ellicott.
Pierson J. Marsden, miller, bds. Tibbitts House.
Pillsbury George N., agent, h 34 Maple.
Pither John, clerk, h 7 Tracy Place.
Plato Walter H., machinist, bds. 113 Bank.
Plato William J., machinist, bds. 113 Bank.
Plato William W., policeman, h 113 Bank.
Plock Henry, cooper, h 577 E. Main.
Plock John, cooper, Railroad ave., h 5 Cedar.
Plow William H., clerk, bds. 104 Jackson.
Pomeroy Lovicey B., h 24 Maple.
Pomeroy Lucy J., h 24 Maple.
Pomeroy Mary E., h 24 Maple.
Pond ———, widow of Cyrus, h 19 Swan.

Pond Mary, widow of Stillman, h W. Main.
Pond William, laborer, h 19 Swan
Porschet John, farmer 157, h 548 E. Main.
Porter George, laborer, h Ross.
Porter James, retired, h 160 Vine.
Porter Thomas, laborer, h 164 Vine.
Post Catharine A., widow of Abraham, h 69 S. Main.
POSTENS EDWARD, prop. livery, feed, and sales stable, Exchange Place, bds. Parker House.
Potter Nelson R., night watchman, h James.
Poultridge John G., tailor, bds. 127 Summit.
Poultridge Mary A., widow of George, h 128 Summit.
POWERS CHARLES, stationary engineer N. Y. C. & H. R. R. R. since 1861, h 4 Mill.
Powers Edward, laborer, h 104 North.
Powers Edward F., fireman, h 107 Oak.
Powers John R., baggagemaster N. Y. C. & H. R. R. R., h 25 Jackson.
Pratt Frank, laborer, h 5 Wiard.
Pratt George W., carpenter, h 29 Bank.
Pratt Gery, prop. cider-mill, h 59 S. Main.
Pratt John W., book-keeper, h 39 State.
Pratt Mary, widow of Nelson H., h 5 Pearl.
Pratt Victor, laborer, h 19 South.
PRENTICE WILLIAM E., lawyer, Walker block, h 547 E. Main.
Prescott Charles F.. (Austin & Prescott) h 542 E. Main.
Prescott Frank, blacksmith, h 343 Ellicott.
Prescott John, carpenter, h 542 E. Main.
Prescott Lizzie J., teacher, bds. 542 E. Main.
Preston Augustus W., prop. Keystone Mfg. Co., h 302 Washington ave.
Preston Mary A., widow of William H., h 302 Washington ave.
Pridmore Edward, patternmaker, h 3 Spruce.
Priester Henry, laborer, h 146 Vine.
Prill John, laborer, h Franklin.
Prill Nicholas, prop. saloon, 6 Jackson, h do.
Prindle Martha U., widow of B. R, h 32 Bank.
PROGRESSIVE BATAVIAN, R. S. Lewis, editor and prop.. 64 Main.
PURDY CHARLES G., formerly prop. Purdy House, bds. Parker House.
Putnam John H., carpenter, h 12 Walker Place.
Putnam Phebe C., widow of Charles, h 130 Bank.
Putnam Vannie, widow of Newel, h 130 Bank.
Quance James M., retired farmer, h 461 Ellicott.
Quirk James, florist, h 24 Church.
Quirk John, prop. meat market, 120 Main, h 136 Bank.
Radley William, shoemaker, h 108 Washington ave.
Ramsdell Frank, mail carrier. bds. 6 Otis.
Ramsdell Fred, com. traveler, h 6 Otis.
Ramsdell Fred C., book-keeper, bds. 6 Otis.
Ramsey Richard, machinist, h 28 Vine.
RAND CHARLES F., M. D., physician, 1228 Fifteenth st., Washington, D. C.
Rapp Andrew, laborer, bds. 112 Main.
Rapp Emeline, widow of Fedel, h 112 Main.
Rapp Henry, laborer, h 8 East ave.
Ray S. Margaret, h 3 Pearl.
Reagor Jacob, laborer, h 212 Bank.
Real Herbert F., market gardener, h 539 E. Main.
Redmond William, brakeman, h 14 Hutchins.
Redshaw Charles F., carpenter, bds. 48 State.
Redshaw George, retired builder, h 48 State.
Redshaw George, hay presser, h 7 Chestnut.

Redshaw George E., dealer in groceries and provisions, 16 Jackson, bds. 48 State.
REDSHAW JOHN, (King & Redshaw) h 19 Walnut.
Reed John E., engineer, h 23 Pearl.
REEDY WILLIAM J., sheriff, court-house, h 101 W. Main.
Reeves Edwin D., pharmacist, bds. Hotel Richmond.
Regar Peter, shoemaker, h 217 Bank.
Reynolds Edwin D., laborer, h Pearl.
Reynolds James, mason, h Vine cor. Chase Park.
Rial Edward A., laborer, h 2 Watson.
Rice Anna E., widow of Rev. Milton H., h 103 Bank.
Rice George W., laborer, h 39 W. Main.
Richardson Anna H., widow of John, h 150 State.
RICHARDSON FRANK, pres. Batavia Wheel Co., bds. 32 Ellicott.
Richardson Hannah, widow of Phineas, h Jackson.
Richardson Rebecca, widow of Thomas, 93 years old, bds. 15 Wood.
RICHARDSON WILLIAM E., dentist, 101 E. Main, h do.
RICHMOND LIBRARY, Agnes Wiard and Elizabeth Wood, librarians, Ross.
RICHMOND MARY E., widow of Dean, h 311 E. Main.
Rider Charles, laborer, h 30 Buell.
Riker Peter, shoemaker, 9 State, h 217 Bank.
Riley John, laborer, h 21 Evans.
Rimmer Peter, laborer, h 4 School.
Roach John, laborer, h 73 S. Liberty.
Robbins Clarence A., butcher, h 20 Walker.
Roberts Frank, laborer, h Colorado ave.
Robinson Arthur, laborer, h Chase.
Robinson Edward, mason, h 11 Harvester ave.
Robinson Frederick D., blacksmith, 42 Jackson, h 47 do.
Robinson George, laborer, h 30 Liberty.
Robinson Joseph, ex-sheriff, h 36 Seaver Place.
Robinson Matthew, laborer, h 314 Ellicott.
Robinson Moses E., shipping clerk Johnston Harvester Co., h 34 Seaver Place.
Robinson Walter, melter, h 71 Swan.
Robinson ———, mason, h 4 James.
Rogers Abiga, widow of Isaac B., h 11 Tracy Place.
Rogers Arthur, fireman N. Y. C. &. H. R. R. R., bds. 11 Tracy Place.
Rolfe Lucius F., served in 105th N. Y. Vols., mail carrier, h 149 Jackson.
ROLFE WALTER P., retired farmer, h 149 Jackson.
ROOT MARGARET C., widow of Dr. John, h 161 Bank.
Rosecrance Martha P., widow of Daniel, bds. 111 Bank.
Rosenkranz Frederick, laborer, h 24 Harvester ave.
Rosenkranz Katie E., teacher, bds. 24 Harvester ave.
ROSS BROTHERS, (George H. and Edward H.) carriage manufs., painters, and iron-ers, rear Parker House.
ROSS EDWARD H., (Ross Brothers) h 14 School.
ROSS GEORGE H., (Ross Brothers) bds. 14 School.
ROSS MEREDITH, wholesale dealer in tobacco, cigars, groceries, and sundries, Park Place, h 57 Ellicott ave.
Roth Charles, cooper, h Pearl.
Roth George, (Short & Roth) h 26 State.
Roth John, cooper, S. Main, h do.
Roth Joseph, cooper and farmer 12½, h 91 S. Main.
Roth Joseph S., laborer, h 2 Pearl.
Rourke Daniel, laborer, h Ross.
Rourke John, (Kenny & Rourke) h 152 Ellicott.
Rowan Jerome, retired, h 101 Bank.
Rowell E N. & Co., (E. G. Buell) manufs. of box novelties for druggists, 66 E. Main.
Rowell E. Newton, (E. N. Rowell & Co.) bds. Hotel Richmond.
Rowlan William H., machinist, h 338 Ellicott.

Rowley Chauncy, laborer, h 27 Vine.
Rowley Fred J., machinist, h 8 Fisher Park.
Rowley Hiram S., machinist, h 6 Chase Park.
Rowley Myron, laborer, bds. 27 Vine.
Royce Rachel M., widow of Henry P., h 45 and 47 W. Main.
Roylander Edward, tailor, bds. Continental Hotel.
Rudd Frank, laborer, h 162 Bank.
Rudd Freeman J., doorman N. Y. C. & H. R. R. R. depot, h 18 Ganson ave.
Rumsey Addie, widow of Dr. Rumsey, h 108 Summit.
RUPP ANDREW, tinsmith and dealer in real estate, h 225 W. Main.
Rupp Charles, shoemaker, h 45 Ellicott.
RUPP ERNST, formerly shoe dealer, h 125 W. Main.
Rupp Fred, laborer, h Oak.
Rupp Henry, h 40 Main.
Rupp Julia, h 225 W. Main.
Rupprecht Charles H., teller First National Bank, bds. 206 Washington ave.
Rupprecht George, retired, h Ellicott cor. Evans.
Rupprecht Soloma, widow of Fred, h 206 Washington ave.
Russell Carlos M., harnessmaker, 129 Summit.
Russell Edward, (Skelley & Russell) h 128 W. Main.
Russell Henry, carpenter, h 14 Chestnut.
Russell John G., retired, h 114 Bank.
Russell John J., (Schlenker & Russell) h 8 School.
Russell Stephen H., clerk, h 10 Liberty.
Russell William G., clerk, h 25 Vine.
Russell William J., milk peddler, h 301 Ellicott.
Ryan Catharine, widow of Michael, h 210 Washington ave.
Ryan Dennis, laborer, h 317 Ellicott.
Ryan James, laborer, h State.
Ryan James J., prop. Central House, 100 Jackson.
RYAN JOHN F., (McKenzie, Ryan & Storms) h 210 Washington ave.
Ryan Julia, cook Institution for the Blind.
Ryan Patrick, laborer, h 26 Liberty.
Ryan Thomas, clerk, bds. 210 Washington ave.
Ryan William S., mail agent, bds. 210 Washington ave.
Rykert Charles M., carpenter, h 10 Wood.
Rykert Minerva, widow of Charles, h 10 Wood.
Sackett Fred B., manager White Sewing Machine Co., 57 Main, bds. Parker House.
Safford Frank H., clerk, h 14 North.
Sager Fred L., barber, 4 Jackson, bds. 13 Oak.
Sager Nicholas, formerly mail carrier, h 13 Oak.
Salway Edward, (Beck & Salway) h 435 Ellicott.
SALWAY JOHN E., (Beck & Salway) h Ellicott.
Sanford Lamont H., engineer and tinsmith, 146 Ellicott, residence in Buffalo.
Sanford Orin D., com. traveler, h 113 State.
SANFORD WILLIS D., dealer in hats, caps, furs, trunks, etc., 76 E. Main, h 50 State.
Sawday George, laborer, h 15 Walker.
Sawday John, painter, h 14 Ellicott.
Sawyer Charles F., com. traveler, h 28 Ellicott ave.
Scanlan Michael, section foreman E. R. R., h 24 Evans.
Scarff Mary E., teacher Institution for the Blind.
SCHAD BARNARD, (Schad, Dellinger & Glade) vice-pres. Schad Wheel Co., inventor Schad's broom-holder, bicycle and wood carriage wheel, 19 Jackson, h 6 Wood.
SCHAD, DELLINGER & GLADE, (Barnard S., John D., and John G.) manufs. of Schad's patent elastic bicycle, carriage, and hose-cart wheel, and agents for wheels, rear Jackson.
Schad Wheel Co., J. J. Ellis, pres.; B. Schad, vice-pres.; Henry S. Allis, sec'y; F. J. Shults, treas., manufs. of the Schad and other carriage and wagon wheels.
SCHAEFER JOHN, mason and contractor, h 3 Dellinger ave.

Schaefer John, Jr., mason, bds. 3 Dellinger ave.
Schafer Augustus, wood carver, h 3 Buell.
Schafer George, engineer, h 359 Ellicott.
Schafer George, foreman, h 23 School.
SCHAFER HERMAN, wholesale and retail dealer in imported and domestic wines,
    liquors, cigars, tobacco, etc., 15 Jackson, h 35 State.
SCHEER GEORGE, dealer in groceries and provisions, 202 Ellicott, h do.
Schellenger George, bartender, bds. 49 Main.
SCHELLENGER WILLIAM L., prop. oyster house and first-class restaurant, oysters
    in every style, meals at all hours, Moynihan block, 49 E. Main.
Schendelmyre Joseph, machinist, h 4 Walker Place.
SCHEUING GOTTLIEB, (E. Bleyler & Co.) h 224 W. Main.
Schisler Adolph, mason, h 7 Trumbull Place.
Schlenker Jacob, clerk, h 32 Center.
Schlenker John, (Schlenker & Russell) h 11 School.
Schlenker & Russell, (John S. and John J. R.) plumbers and dealers in house fur-
    nishing hardware, 7 State.
Schneidler Fred, tailor, h 12 Spruce.
Schofield George H., machinist, h 552 E. Main.
Schooley John, molder, h 82 Hutchins.
Schrader Michael, carpenter, h 306 Ellicott.
Schwartz Lee, (agent) dealer in dry and fancy goods, 64 E. Main, h 146 State.
Scott Charles L., clerk, h 15 Liberty.
Scott George W., steward Batavia Club, 201 E. Main.
Scott Olivia J., widow of Graham, h 20 Harvester ave.
Scotland James, molder, h 45 Central ave.
Scoville Lyman E., farmer 5, h 124 W. Main.
Scripter Cora, (Mrs. Dorson) prop. boarding-house, 28 State.
Scripter Dorson, laborer, h 28 State.
Seacord John M., (Seacord & Weeks) h 16 Tracy Place.
Seacord & Weeks, (John M. S. and George D. W.) manufs. of steam pipe and boiler
    covering, 34 Bank.
Seargent William, laborer, h 121 W. Main.
Sears Benjamin L., telegraph operator, h 105 Washington ave.
Seaver Charles A., (Gage & Seaver) h 105 Summit.
Sellon P. R., Christian clergyman, h 303 Ellicott.
Senate Robert, laborer, h 18 S. Swan.
Sergeant Charles, teamster, h 112 W. Main.
Sergeant William, laborer, h off Ross.
Serve Nicholas, cartman, h 32 Liberty.
Serve William, coachman, h 6 Swan.
Sexton Patrick. laborer, h 12 Evans.
Shadbolt Emery, retired, h 64 S. Main.
Shafer Charles, molder, h 14 Spruce.
Shafer Jacob, carpenter, h River.
Sharrock Joseph, blacksmith, h 15 Seaver Place.
Shaul Nathan, patternmaker, h 20 Vine.
Shay Mary, widow of Daniel, h Union.
Shebish Frank, laborer, h 35 S. Swan.
Shedd Charles, carpenter, h 17 Wiard.
Shedd Clayton N., clerk, h 8 Trumbull Place.
Sheffield Robert A., book-keeper, bds. Hotel Richmond.
Sheldon ———, widow, h 104 State.
Shepard David, teamster, h 32 South.
Shepard Dwight D., laborer, h 7 Chase Park.
Shepard George B., patternmaker, h 3 Fisher Park.
Sherman Addison, rector St. James's Episcopal Church, h 524 E. Main.
Sherwin Edgar M., carpenter and ins. agent, h 17 Swan.
Sherwin Sidney A., (Tarbox & Sherwin) h 415 E. Main.

Sherwin Susie Grace, teacher, bds. 17 Swan.
Shetter Mary E., widow of Charles, h 10 School.
Shetter William, clerk, bds. 10 School.
Shore William, laborer, h 10 Wiard.
Short Edward F., (Youngers & Short) h W. Main.
SHORT JAMES, (Short & Roth) pres. board of excise, h 320 W. Main.
Short Marcus W., harnessmaker, bds. 320 W. Main.
Short Margaret, widow of James, h 320 W. Main.
SHORT & ROTH, (James S. and George R.) manufs. and dealers in harnesses, 64 E.
  Main.
Shotwell Isaac M., retired, bds. 32 Bank.
SHOWERMAN B. F., M. D., physician, E. Main, h 128 Bank.
SHOWERMAN J. M., M. D., physician, h 128 Bank.
Showerman Jennie, music teacher Institution for the Blind.
SHOWERMAN NETTIE, (Mrs. Stephen) prop. Batavia Steam Laundry, 202 E. Main,
  h do.
Showerman Stephen, tinsmith, h 202 E. Main.
Shults Eugene D., clerk, bds. 61 Ellicott ave.
Shults Frank J., (Shults & Kane) treas. Schad Wheel Co., h 61 Ellicott ave.
SHULTS JOSEPH C., dealer in tea, coffee, spices, etc., and importer of choice teas,
  43 Main, h 61 Ellicott ave.
Shults & Kane, (Frank J. S. and John J. K.) dealers in groceries and provisions, 87
  Main.
SIDWAY WILLIAM H., financial clerk New York Lumber and Wood Working Co.,
  h 522 E. Main.
Silbie Frank, carpenter, h 16 Cedar.
Sillesky John M., dealer in groceries, provisions, meats, etc., 500 and 502 E. Main.
Simons Alfred B., prop. farmers' sheds, 23 State, h do.
Simpson Laura, widow of Gardner, h 21 Hutchins.
Simpson Warren, com. traveler, h 26 S. Main.
Simpson William C., dealer in dry goods, 101 Main, h 124 Bank.
Skahen John, clerk, bds. 163 Summit.
Skelley Andrew W., (Skelley & Russell) h 143 State.
Skelley & Russell, (Andrew W. S. and Edward R.) dealers in groceries and provis-
  ions, 58 E. Main.
Smedle Stephen, butcher, h 33 S. Liberty.
Smith Anna A., teacher, bds. Hotel Richmond.
SMITH BRADLEY S., news and subscription agent, dealer in books, stationery, mu-
  sic, etc., 67 E. Main, h 46 Ellicott.
Smith Carl, laborer, h 16 Trumbull Place.
Smith Celia A., widow of Alvah, h 117 Washington ave.
Smith Edwin C., jeweler, 9 Jackson, h 11 Chestnut.
Smith Herbert, electrician, h 117 Washington ave.
SMITH HORACE K., teacher piano tuning at Institution for the Blind, h 209 Bank.
Smith James, blacksmith and horseshoer, rear Hotel Richmond, h 18 Maple.
Smith John, laborer, h 329 Ellicott.
Smith John, laborer, h 68 Hutchins.
Smith John C., laborer, h 10 State.
SMITH JOHN W., cashier Genesee County Bank, h 112 Ellicott.
Smith Julia, h 101 Summit.
Smith Lorenzo R., retired, h 11 Chestnut.
Smith Louis, cooper, h 46 Ellicott.
SMITH LOUIS E., with Bradley S., h 46 Ellicott.
Smith Lydia, h 101 Summit.
Smith Martha, widow of Julius A., h 18 W. Main.
Smith Martha E., teacher, bds. 18 W. Main.
Smith Mary A., widow of Philander H., h 107 Evans.
Smith Mary A., widow of George, bds. 112 Ellicott.
SMITH MARY J., widow of Nathan T., h 4 Tracy Place.

Smith Russell, telegraph operator, bds. 11 Chestnut.
Smith Silas H., retired, h 107 Evans.
SMITH WILBER, pres. Batavia Gas and Electric Light Co., dealer in hardware, 52 E. Main, h 417 do.
Smith William D., clerk, bds. 419 E. Main.
Snedler Frederick H., tailor, h 12 Spruce.
SNELL CHARLES A., ins. agent, real estate dealer, and loans negotiated, farm 23, 53 E. Main, h Lewiston road.
Snell Frank A., with Charles A.
Snyder John L., retired, h 134 State.
Southworth Cornelia E., widow of Gardner T., h 312 E. Main.
SOUTHWORTH IRVING D., h 110 Bank.
SOUTHWORTH SAMUEL, bds. 110 Bank.
Spafford Mary J., widow, h 6 Hewitt Place.
Spafford Rossanna, widow of B. J., h 22 Wood.
Spalding Albert B., carriagemaker, Ellicott, h 9 Otis.
Spalding Sanford E., jeweler, 110 E. Main, h 9 Otis.
Spann Robert, clerk, h 103 Main.
Sparling Alexander, mason, h 53 S. Liberty.
Spellman Thomas, laborer, h 17 School.
Spencer Amanda, widow of Christopher, h 4 Hewitt Place.
Spencer Herman A., clerk, h 21 Vine.
Spencer Wallace F., laborer, h 1 Watson.
Spengler John, life ins. agent, h 304 Washington ave.
SPIRIT OF THE TIMES, Democratic, issued every Friday, established in 1818, Thomas & Hall, publishers, Times building, Jackson.
Sprague Alvin, laborer, h 46 South.
Sprague Frank, mechanic, h Otis.
Springer Albert, shoemaker, h 58 S. Swan.
Springer Robert, shoemaker, 19 Liberty, h 58 Grant.
Squires Edward T., foreman New York Lumber and Wood Working Co., h 104 Washington ave.
Squires Frank W., with George P. Bowen, h 21 Tracy Place.
Stackal George, retired, h 71 Hutchins.
Stafford Fred, laborer, h 29 Vine.
Stakel Fred J., prop. Ellicott House, Jackson cor. Ellicott.
Stanley Charles J., mechanic, h 7 Wood.
Stanley Luther, carpenter, h 20 Wood.
Stannard Willis, laborer, h 103 Washington ave.
Stapleton John, carpenter, h 10 Cedar.
Stark Cyrus F., auctioneer, bds. Tibbitts House.
Stark David, teamster, h 60 S. Liberty.
Stebbins Almon, binder expert, h 31 Vine.
Steel Orin C., clerk, h 123 State.
Steele Clara, prop. select primary school, 311 Washington ave., bds. do.
Steele Sarah E., widow of L. G., h 311 Washington ave.
Stein John, laborer, h 20 Hutchins.
Stein John L., (Charlton & Stein) bds. 15 Bank.
STEPHENS MARY J., prin. Park Place School for girls, Park Place.
Stephens Simon P., machinist, h 217 Washington ave.
Stevens Clarence M., mechanic, h 40 S. Swan.
Stevens G. Willis, (Suttell & Stevens) h 28 S. Liberty.
Stevens Jane, (Mrs. James) h 23 Liberty.
Stevens Sarah K., h 218 E. Main.
Steves Milan D., laborer, h 115 Summit.
Stewart Celia F., widow of Allen, h 26 Evans.
Stewart Harriet D , widow of R. N., h 152 State. [Died Oct. 8, 1889.]
STEWART JAMES S., retired, h 403 E. Main.
Stewart William H., fireman, bds. 26 Evans.

STICKLE CHARLES W., teller Farmers' Bank of Batavia, h 112 State.
Stickney Adelbert, mechanic, h 16 Wood.
Stickney Charles, printer, h. 30 State.
Stickney Eugene A., clerk, h 18 Wood.
Stickney Nelson, teamster, h 110 Summit.
St. John George, barber, h 118 W. Main.
St. Joseph's Convent of Mercy, 1 Summit.
Stone Charles, engineer, b 9 S. Swan.
STONE ELONZO N., dealer in dry goods, 94 Main, h 43 State.
Stone Eugene, prop. West End Hotel, W. Main.
Stone Julia, teacher Institution for the Blind.
STORMS JOHN C., (McKenzie, Ryan & Storms) h in Elba.
Strever Emma, widow of Frank, h 4 Hewitt Place.
Stroh Louis C., cooper, manuf. of cisterns, barrels, etc., Railroad ave., h 12 School.
Stuffings George, farmer, h 40 S. Main.
Sullivan Daniel, laborer, h 14 S. Swan.
Sullivan John V., clerk, bds. 589 E. Main.
Sullivan Mary, widow of Cornelius, h Union.
Sullivan Michael, laborer, h 22 Harvester ave.
Sullivan Patrick, brakeman, h 23 Oak.
Sulwah Owen, laborer, h 22 Walker.
Sunderland Abbey R., h 5 Tracy Place.
Susat Fred, laborer, h 13 Trumbull Place.
Susat William, baker, h 13 Trumbull Place.
Suttell George, (Suttell & Stevens) bds. Summit.
Suttell Joseph, painter, h 215 Bank.
Suttell & Stevens, (George S. and G. Willis S.) painters and paper hangers, 8 Center.
Sutter Jacob, laborer, h off Jackson.
SUTTERBY HARRY, veterinary surgeon, farmer in Oakfield 150, 20 W. Main, h 14 do.
Suttle Benjamin, ice dealer, h 36 South.
Swanson A. Eugene, tailor, h 125 Bank.
Swarthout Cornelius, carpenter, h 112 Ross.
SWEET JOHN M., supt. Batavia Wheel Co., bds. 115 Washington ave.
SWEZEY HIRAM, 23 high grade Holstein cows, 1 Holstein bull, farmer 111, h 567 E. Main.
Swift Henry, wagonmaker, h Walnut.
SYRACUSE FORGING AND GUN CO., Dr. E. L. Baker, pres.; Ralph Helm, vice-pres.; W. T. Mylcrane, sec'y and treas.; W. H. Baker, general supt., 18 to 22 Liberty.
TAGGART EARL W., (Taggart & Son) farmer 96, and in Pembroke 53, h Russell Place.
Taggart Fred E., (Taggart & Son) h Russell Place.
TAGGART & SON, (Earl W. and Fred E.) props. livery and boarding stable, Russell Place.
Tallman Buell G., com. traveler, bds. 212 Washington ave.
TALLMAN CHARLES W., photographer, over 80 and 82 E. Main, h 212 Washington ave.
Tallman Clarence B., book-keeper, bds. 212 Washington ave.
Tanner James H., clerk, h 8 Vine.
Tarbox Henry F., (Tarbox & Sherwin) postmaster, vice-pres. Bank of Batavia, h 400 E. Main.
Tarbox & Sherwin, (Henry F. T. and Sidney A. S.) lawyers and ins. agents, 71 E. Main.
Taylor Edward, farmer, leases of C. F. Bissell, of Le Roy, 40, h Pearl.
Taylor Edwin W., blacksmith, h 146 Bank.
Taylor Judson A., printer, h 126 State.
Taylor Mary, widow of Randall, bds. 1 Watson.
Taylor Melancton, molder, h 1 Wiard.

Taylor Thomas, night watchman at Institution for the Blind, h 19 Washington ave.

Teford ———, laborer, h 43 Walker.

Tefner Jacob, carpenter, h 62 S. Swan.

Telfair Louise, widow, h 25 Swan.

Templeman John B., tinsmith, h 22 S. Main.

Terry Charles E., compositor, bds. 37 State.

Terry Frank E., com. traveler, h 51 Buell.

Terry Sarah E., (Mrs. Frank) h 207 Washington ave.

Thayer Sarah, widow of Augustus, h 32 S. Main.

Thayer George, laborer, h Mill.

THOMAS A. HOSEA, (Thomas & Hall) editor and publisher *Spirit of the Times*, bds. Parker House.

Thomas Benjamin F., laborer, h 1 Hutchins Place.

Thomas Charles W., com. traveler, h 18 Vine.

Thomas Dorothy, widow of Peter P., bds. 111 Washington ave.

Thomas Edward R., machinist, h 3 Hutchins Place.

Thomas Henry, retired, h rear 5 Dellinger ave.

THOMAS JOHN, county treasurer, dealer in hats, caps, trunks, robes, gloves, etc., 66 E. Main, h 111 Washington ave.

Thomas Nathan, harnessmaker, farm 17, h 14 Central ave.

Thomas Peter, mail agent, h 5 Dellinger ave.

Thomas Sophia, widow of Frederick, h 140 Bank.

Thomas William, laborer, h 145 Vine.

THOMAS & HALL, (A. Hosea T. and Joseph F. H.) publishers *Spirit of the Times* and job printers, *Times* building, Jackson.

Thompson Arthur, laborer, h 14 Ganson ave.

Thompson Charles A., carpenter, h 5 Prune.

Thompson George, com. traveler, h 44 South.

Thompson Rockwell, engineer, bds. 539 E. Main.

Thorp Wilbur, stationary engineer N. Y. C. & H. R. R. R., bds. 26 Evans.

THROOP ORANGE S., dealer in gravel and sand, farmer 10, h 33 South.

Thwing Almira, widow of John, h 314 Washington ave.

Tibbitts House, S. C. Tibbitts, prop., 46 E. Main.

Tibbitts Samuel C , prop. Tibbitts House, 46 E. Main.

Tibbits Walter C., com. traveler and farmer 9, h 428 Ellicott.

Tillinghast R. Clark, (Johnston Harvester Co.) h 8 Swan.

Tobin James, laborer, (h 28 Church.

Tock Abraham, teamster, h 13 North.

Todd Charles E., foreman *Times* office, h 208 Washington ave.

TODD HENRY, retired publisher and editor, h 41 Ellicott ave.

TOMLINSON DANIEL W., pres. Bank of Batavia, h 412 E. Main.

Tomlinson Susan E., widow of D. W., h 409 E. Main.

Tompkins Lavinia J. Miss, dressmaker, dealer in millinery, fancy goods, hair work, etc., 124 E. Main, h 118 do.

Tompkins Peter, gas fitter, bds. Warren House.

Tompkins Richard G., engineer Batavia Gas Co., h 118 Main.

TOMPKINS SARAH, widow of William M., h 144 Jackson.

Tompkins Walter H., student Cornell University, bds. 144 Jackson.

Torrey Anna, widow of Samuel P., h 101 Summit.

TOWN FRED D., (O. Town & Son) bds. 411 E. Main.

TOWN O. & SON, (Fred D.) merchant tailors, clothiers, and dealers in gents' furnishing goods, 51 and 53 E. Main.

TOWN ORLANDO, (O. Town & Son) h 411 E. Main.

Town William A., book-keeper, bds. 411 E. Main.

TOZER WILLIAM, manuf. and dealer in brick, rear 538 E. Main, h do.

TOZIER LEMUEL L., M. D., physician and surgeon, 406 E. Main, h do.

Tracy Peter, laborer, h Colorado ave.

Train Richard, painter, h 7 Walker.

Trainor James, prop. saloon, 35 Liberty.

Trick Willis, teacher, h 160 Bank.
Tricker John, laborer, h 49 Hutchins.
Trietley Charles, truckman, h 25 S. Liberty.
Trietley Henry, coachman, h 12 Trumbull Place.
Troy Laundry, E. C. Hawkins, prop., 32 Jackson.
True Minerva, widow of Luther, h 107 Washington ave.
TRUE MOSES E., inventor True's shell band, dealer in and repairer of Star bicycles, saw gummer and filer, h 107 Washington ave.
True William F., broommaker, bds. 140 Ellicott.
Trumball Charles, clerk, h 30 Jackson.
Trumball E. A., widow of George, h 34 Jackson.
Tryon Anderson, h 435 E. Main.
Turner Anna, widow of John, h 10 State.
Turner George, laborer, h 5 James.
Tuttle William M., carriage trimmer, 5 Seaver Place, h 20 Center.
Twichell William, foreman, h Mill.
Tyler Philetus S., dealer in musical instruments, h 10 Fisher Park.
TYRRELL WILLIAM, (Tyrrell & Ballard) farm 52, h 131 Jackson.
TYRRELL & BALLARD (William T. and Frank W. B.) lawyers, 9 Postoffice block.
UEBELE LOUIS, baker and confectioner, Uebele block, 16 Main, h do.
UEBELE WILLIAM C., clerk Parker House, bds. 16 E. Main.
Uhlrich Fritz, clerk, h 109 Evans.
Underhill Orrin, farmer, leases 50, h 9 William.
UNDERHILL WILLIAM C., (Underhill & Bean) bds. 105 Bank.
UNDERHILL & BEAN, (William C. U. and Clarence J. B.) dealers in ready-made clothing and gents' furnishing goods, 88 E. Main.
UNION COAL CO., (George D. Weaver & Co., props.) dealers in coal and wood, 28 Swan.
Usinger Augustus, teamster, h 39½ Center.
Usinger Philip, truckman, h 39 Center.
Valentine Joseph S., com. traveler, h 14 Ellicott ave.
Vallett Charles F., carpenter, h 17 Seaver Place.
Van Dusen Nancy E., widow of Sylvenus, h 108 State.
Van Etten Edwin, mechanic, h 20 Hutchins.
Vanalsh Isaac, farmer, h 28 Seaver Place.
Van Schaick Levi, machinist, h Masse Place,
VanValkenburgh Charles W., (Dodgson, Bostwick & Co.) h 132 W. Main.
Vanzault J. B., artist, bds. Parker House.
Volz Albert, retired, h 7 S. Main.
Volz George O., book-keeper Johnston Harvester Co., h 9 S. Main.
Volz Henry, tinsmith, h 123 Summit.
Vrooman Nicholas Y., laborer, h 549 E. Main.
Wagoner Frank, laborer, h 69 S. Liberty.
Wakeman Bryon E., com. traveler, bds. 13 School.
Wakeman Edgar A., engineer, h 75 Main.
Wakeman Laura, widow of Seth, h 13 School.
Wakeman Libbie, (Mrs. E. A.) dressmaker, 75 Main.
Wakeman Nathan, carpenter, h 5 Hutchins Place.
Wakeman William S., mail carrier, bds. 13 School.
Walbridge Charles E., (F. E. & C. L. Walbridge) h 21 State.
Walbridge F. E. & C. E., props. meat market, 21 State.
Walbridge Frank E., (F. E. & C. E. Walbridge) h 21 State.
Waldo Amasa D., auctioneer, bds. 112 State.
Waldo Charles, laborer, h 9 Ward.
WALKER EDWARD C. Hon., lawyer, Walker block, h 20 Ross.
Walker Edward C., Jr., att'y at law, Walker block, bds. 20 Ross.
Walker Frank, laborer, h 120 Ross.
Walker Jesse I., engineer, h 55 Buell.
Walker Richard, wagonmaker, Russell Place, h 31 Seaver Place.

Walkinshaw Adaline, widow of Dr. Maxwell, h 24 Walnut.
WALKINSHAW JAMES M., (Baker & Walkinshaw) druggist, 63 E. Main, h 142 Jackson.
Wallace Anna, widow of Ira, h 9 Tracy Place.
Wallace David, machinist, h 9 Fisher Park.
Wallace William, machinist, h 1 Richmond ave.
Walter Charles, dealer in ice, h 18 South.
Walworth Truman J., retired farmer, h 31 Ellicott ave.
Ward George, laborer, h 32 Cherry.
WARD JOHN H., manager and cashier Farmers' Bank of Batavia, h 39 Ellicott ave
Ward Owen, laborer, h 505 E. Main.
Ward Patrick, carpenter, 129 Harvester ave.
Ward Patrick, blacksmith, Jackson, bds. 27 Jackson.
Ward William H., carpenter, bds. 32 Cherry.
Ware Mary, milliner and agent Staten Island Dye Works, 90 E. Main, h 435 do.
Ware Thomas B., manuf. of pills, h 526 E. Main.
Warner Christopher, prop. Warner House, 116 Main.
Warner House, C. Warner, prop., 116 Main.
Warren Alfred, painter, owns in Bethany farm 130, h 33 Center.
Warren Anna, music teacher, h Wiard.
Warren Henry, book-binder, 58 Main, h 37 Lyon.
Warren Joseph, fireman, h 3 James.
Warren Mary J., widow of Thomas, h 37 Lyon.
Warren Susan M., widow of Horace N., h 20 Ellicott.
Washburn George C., dealer in coal and lumber, 62 Jackson, h 43 Ellicott ave.
Washburn John, retired, h 425 E. Main.
WASHBURN JULIAN J., sec'y Wiard Plow Co., h 18 Ross.
Washington Elijah W., expressman, h 38 E. Main.
Wassink Gebhard, carpenter, h 19 Seaver Place.
Watrous Alexander, retired, h 125 Harvester ave.
Watson Albert M., com. traveler, h 48 S Main.
Watson Malona M., widow of Alonzo M., h 48 S. Main.
WATSON WILLIAM C., lawyer and vice-pres. Genesee County Bank, 69 E. Main, h 6 Ellicott.
Waugh William A., manuf. of patent medicines, h 4 Fisher Park.
Way George, carpenter, h 26 Walker.
Way Mary, widow of George, h 17 East ave.
WEAVER CHARLES A., dealer in boots and shoes, 104 Main, bds. 103 Bank.
WEAVER GEORGE D., (George D. Weaver & Co.) h W.Main.
WEAVER GEORGE D. & CO., (Union Coal Co.) (Charles R. Winslow) dealers in coal and wood, and agents for Stewart's ready roofing, 28 Swan.
Weaver Mary J., widow of Jesse, h 103 Bank.
Weber Albert, deputy postmaster, h Lowe ave.
WEBSTER WILLIAM E., (Webster & Bramble) justice of the peace, 59 Main, h 37 State.
WEBSTER & BRAMBLE, (William E. W. and Theodore E. B.) attorneys at law, 59 Main.
Weed Anson M., laborer, h 12 Wiard.
Weeks George D., (Seacord & Weeks) h 134 Bank.
Weigel Jacob, carpenter, h 148 Vine.
Welch Richard E., (Welch & Averill) h 116 State.
Welch & Averill, (Richard E. W. and George W. A.) horseshoers, Ellicott.
WELLS ANDREW J., prop. Park Place restaurant.
Wells, Fargo & Co. Express Co., A. C. Dewey, agent, 2 Jackson.
Welsh Michael, lineman, h 8 Central ave.
Werner Peter, prop. East End Hotel, 508 E. Main.
WEST END HOTEL, S. W. Brown, prop., W. Main.
West Isaiah W., carpenter, h 339 Ellicott.
Westacott Charles, plumber, h 430 E. Main.

Westacott William, janitor Batavia Union School, h 106 Ross.
Westacott William G., painter, emp. Wiard Plow Co., h 152 Bank.
Westcott Charles A., plumber, h 19 Harvester ave.
Westcott Minnie, widow of Rufus, h 8 Hewitt Place.
Wested Bridget, widow of Michael, h 19 Cherry.
WESTERN HOTEL, Eugene Stone, prop., W. Main.
Whalen Emma F., teacher, h 3 Ellicott ave.
Whalen Sarah, teacher Institution for the Blind.
Wheat Samuel S., retired, h 74 S. Main.
Whimple Peter, laborer, h 3 Wiard.
Whitcher Charles B., machinist, h 41 Vine.
Whitcomb Josiah T., clerk, bds 26 Center.
Whitcomb Orrin, carpenter, h 137 Jackson.
WHITCOMB WARD BEECHER, M. D., physician, 124 E. Main, h 200 W. Main.
White James L., dealer in baled shavings, h 6 School.
White John, laborer, h Franklin.
Whiteside John F., clerk, bds. Ellicott.
Whiteside William, laborer, h 4 Hutchins Place.
WHITNEY ORLANDO, h Walker.
Wiard Agnes, librarian Richmond Library, h 17 Vine.
Wiard Elizabeth, (Mrs. Norman) h 17 Vine.
Wiard Frederick. emp. Wiard Plow Co., bds. 17 Vine.
WIARD GEORGE, pres. Wiard Plow Co., h 213 E. Main.
WIARD PLOW CO., George Wiard, pres.; C. W. Hough, treas.; J. J. Washburn, sec'y, Swan.
Widler Andrew, painter, h 19 North.
Wildrich Henry, fireman, h 12 Wood.
Wilber Ogden, carpenter, h 111 W. Main.
Wilbur Cornelia, widow of David, h 137 Jackson.
Wilbur David, carpenter, h 111 W. Main.
Wilcox Mark, retired, h off Trumbull Place.
Wilder Elmon S., (Dodgson & Wilder) h 52 S. Main.
Wilford Sarah M., widow of Dr. J. B., h 19 Vine.
Will John F., prop. saloon, 8 Main, h do.
Willett Janette, widow of Reuben, h 13 Walker.
Williams C. A. & Co., (J. M. Williams) prop. livery, sale, and boarding stable, State, rear Tibbitts House.
Williams Charles, laborer, bds. 32 Walnut.
Williams Charles A., (C. A. Williams & Co.) h 58 S. Main.
Williams David F., clerk, bds. Tibbitts House.
Williams Frank C., book-keeper, bds. 32 Walnut.
Williams Henry L., well driver, h 445 Ellicott.
Williams Homer, broker, h 401 E. Main.
Williams James M., (C. A. Williams & Co.) h 51 S. Main.
Williams Louisa, widow of Cyrus, h 32 Walnut.
Williams Robert, gardener and farmer 21, h Pearl.
WILLIAMSON GEORGE D., furniture dealer and undertaker, 111 E. Main, h 131 Bank.
Williamson William H., clerk, h 138 State.
Wilson Harvey, bds. 19 Bank.
Wilson Lochlin M., carpenter, h 436 E. Main.
Wilson William, painter and grainer, h 15 Spruce.
Winling Joseph, prop. saloon, 12 Main, h do.
Winne Isaac, laborer, h 41 S. Swan.
WINSLOW CHARLES R., (George D. Weaver & Co.) h W. Main.
Winters George, tailor, h 133 Jackson.
Wise George, laborer, h 101 Harvester ave.
Wise Philip, laborer, h 39 Central ave.
Wisner John M., teamster, h 215 W. Main.

Wolfram Henry, cabinetmaker, h 46 S. Swan.
WOOD EDWARD F., farmer 70, h 145 Jackson.
Wood Edwin H., engineer, h 215 Ellicott.
Wood Elizabeth, librarian Richmond Library, bds 145 Jackson.
WOOD FRANK S., lawyer and district attorney, 74 E. Main, h 314 do.
Wood Grace A., teacher, bds. 101 Summit.
Wood John H., chief clerk post office, bds. 145 Jackson.
Woodard William H., machinist, h 10 Hutchins.
Woodcock Helen M., teacher, bds. 101 Summit.
WOODWARD CHARLES H., M. D., physician, 1 Postoffice block, h 21 Liberty.
Woodward Grace A., teacher, bds. 17 Liberty.
WOODWARD NATHAN A., lawyer, 58 E. Main, h 118 Bank.
WOODWARD THERON F., dealer in boots and shoes, 74 E. Main, h 17 Liberty.
Woodworth William, wood finisher, h 123 Ross.
Woolsey Alvilana, widow of W. R., h 125 W. Main.
WOOLSEY WHITNEY C., contractor and builder, president of village, 126 W. Main.
Wormuth Selmser, dealer in hides and pelts, 57 Jackson, bds. Genesee House.
Wortendyke Phebe R., widow of John, farm 65, h. 54 S. Main.
WORTHINGTON G. B., SON & CO, (Gad D. and John H. Bradish) dealers in hard-
    ware, stoves, etc., 86 E. Main.
Worthington Gad B. (G. B. Worthington, Son & Co.) vice-pres. First National Bank,
    h 214 E. Main.
Worthington Gad D., (G. B. Worthington, Son & Co.), bds. 214 E. Main.
Wright Charles M., clerk freight office, h 111 Bank.
Wright Franc, teacher, bds. 316 E. Main.
Wright Horatio, retired, h 316 E. Main.
Wright Samuel, canvasser, h 119 State.
Wyman Cyrus, painter, 32 Jackson.
Wyness Alexander, silver plater, cutter, and grinder, 11 State, h 35 Tracy Place.
Wyness Alexander, Jr., supt. Batavia Gas and Electric Light Co., silver plater, h 38 Vine.
Wynn Catharine, widow of Patrick, h 18 S. Main.
Wynn George W., clerk, bds. 18 S. Main.
Yates Arthur C., compositor, bds. 100 State.
Yates Charles, laborer, h 113 Washington ave.
YATES JOHN H., local editor *Progressive Batavian*, h 100 State.
Yates Thomas, retired, h 113 Washington ave.
Young James C., ticket agent and telegragh operator N. Y., L. E. & W. R. R., bds. 432
    E. Main.
Young Men's Christian Association, C. H. Harrington, general sec'y, 7 Jackson.
Youngers Emily, widow of Peter, h 48 Church.
Youngers John M., (Youngers & Short) h 48 Church.
Youngers & Short, (John M. Y. and Edward F. S.) book and job printers, 55 and 57 Main.
Youngers Peter, laborer, bds. 48 Church.

BATAVIA.

TOWN OUTSIDE OF CORPORATION.

(For explanations, etc., see page 3, part second.)

(Postoffice address is Batavia, unless otherwise designated in parenthesis.)

Adelman Edward, r 46, laborer.
Adelman Francis A., r 46, cigarmaker, h and 10 acres.
Adelman Henry B., r 46, laborer.
Allen John, (E. Pembroke) r 38, ins. agent.

Ames David, r 63, farmer, leases of S. N. Royce 130.
Ames Edward, r 54, farmer, leases of L. Hitchcock 60.
Amidon Cyrus, (W. Batavia) laborer.
Amidon Nellie, (W. Batavia) r 56, deputy postmaster.
ARMSTRONG RUTH A., r 13, widow of Ira, resident, aged 72.
Babcock Eaton, (E. Pembroke) r 38, prop. grist-mill.
Bailey Frank W., r 13, carpenter, h and 2 acres.
Baker John, r 26, laborer.
Ballsmith Emery, r 13 cor. 29, laborer.
Ballsmith William, r 13 cor. 29, laborer.
Barnette Jessie, r 63, school teacher.
Barrett Edward, r 51, farmer 112.
Barrey James, (E. Pembroke) r 38, butcher.
Bateman Clark A., farm laborer, h and 3½ acres Park.
Bausch Charles, r 5, farmer 3.
Beecher Adam, r 46, retired.
Beecher Philip, r 46, switchman N. Y. C. & H. R. R. R., and house painter.
Belle George A., r 19, farmer 100.
Bennett Hiram, (E. Pembroke) r 38 carpenter.
Bezona Jacob, carpenter and farmer 8.
BIGELOW EGBERT A., r 76, farmer, leases of Mrs. A. Higgins 80.
Bigelow Florence J., r 76, school teacher.
Bigelow Gertrude S., r 76, formerly missionary in Japan.
Bigelow William R., r 76, farmer 80.
Black Hugh, r 14, farmer 10.
Blatter Fred, r 29, farmer, leases of George Bowen 300.
Bliss Helen L., r 46, widow of Weeden T.
Bogue Nathan, r 6, prop. Batavia nurseries, 100 acres.
Bowden William, (W. Batavia) r 54, farmer 180.
Bowden William, Jr., (W. Batavia) r 54, farmer 20.
Bowen William H., r 65, farmer, leases of the Mariah E. Brown estate 89.
Boyd John B., r 58, farmer 20.
Boyle Owen, r 7, farmer 50.
Boynton Abbie, (W. Batavia) r 74, farmer 50.
Bradley William T., r 20, farmer 126.
Branton Augustus, r 61, 20 cows, farmer, leases of George Kellogg 260.
Bratt Emory O., r 13, farmer 147.
Brayton Augustus, r 61, farmer, leases of George Kellogg.
BRIGGS GEORGE A., r 20, 4 grade Jersey and Durham cows, 40 sheep, 1 brood
    mare, breeder of Patchin horses, farmer 123.
Briggs William J., r 21, farmer 75.
Brinckerhoff Garry R., r 48, farmer, leases of Olive A. 40.
BRINCKERHOFF OLIVE A., r 48, (Mrs. G. R.) farmer 40.
Brown Charles W., (W. Batavia) r 56, agent and telegraph operator N. Y. C. & H. R.
    R. R.
Brown John, r 26, farm laborer.
Brown John, (Oakfield) r 2, laborer.
BROWN JOSEPH, (W. Batavia) r 56, ex-postmaster and general merchant, farmer 14.
Brown Michael, off r 7, farmer 33.
Brown William, r 15, farmer 80.
Brownell William, r 15, farmer 80.
Brumstead Louis, r 69, farmer 60.
Brumstead William, r 69, farmer 50.
Brumsted Charles, r 02, farmer, leases of S. H. Russel 150.
Buckholtz Herman, r 69, farmer 180.
Buckholtz Lewis, r 46, carpenter.
Buckholtz William C., r 46, carpenter, h and lot.
Burgot George, r 26, laborer.
Burke Stephen, r 30, laborer.

Burke Thomas, r 30, laborer.
BURR NORRIS T., (Oakfield) r 2, 3 Holstein cows, 200 sheep, farmer 88.
Burt Charles, r 46, laborer.
Burt George, r 13, farmer 80.
Burtus Warfield C., iron molder and farmer, leases of Michael Kennedy 14.
Buxton Martha C., r 30, widow, resident.
Campbell Alexander, r 61, retired farmer.
Campbell Charles, r 61, farmer in Bergen 60, and leases of Mary F. Palmer 77.
Campbell Glen O., r 28, farmer with his father, Levi O.
CAMPBELL JOHN J., r 76, 14 grade Holstein and Durham cows, farmer, leases of.
    C. S. Bissill 275.
Campbell Levi O., r 28, farmer 10, and leases of E. C. Holbrook 60.
Campbell Peter C., r 76, farmer with his brother John J. 275.
Carey Julia, r 47, widow of Bernard.
Carey Michael J., r 47, laborer.
Carey William J., r 47, emp. on railroad.
Carlisle George, (W. Batavia) r 54, laborer.
Carmody John, r 7, laborer.
Carroll Nicholas, r 7, laborer.
Carson James H., r 50, farmer 52.
Cary Martin, r 6, farmer 133.
Case Lois, (E. Pembroke) r 39, produce dealer.
Case Melinda, (E. Pembroke) widow of Ichabod.
Cash Jacob, r 26, farmer on the estate of John Welker 136.
Chaddock Walter H., r 29, dealer in and feeder of sheep, 200 head, farmer 167.
Chapin Charles, (E. Pembroke) r 35, farmer 40.
Chine John, r 46, laborer.
Church Edward, r 71, farmer 37.
Churchill Darius D., r 10, 300 sheep, farmer 334.
Churchill Robert S., r 10, farmer with his father, Darius D.
Clark Howard M., r 10, farmer for Hart Baldwin.
Clase Peter, r 49, farmer 14.
Classe Michael, r 28, laborer.
Cole James, r 29, farmer, leases of R. T. Howard 83.
Collins Albert G., r 34, farmer 152.
Collins John, r 13, farmer 30.
Conover George, r 20, farmer 50.
Coon John A., r 9, farmer 125.
Cooper James, r 57, farmer 20.
Copeland Edward, r 11, farmer 126.
CORNWELL CHARLES B., r 63, brickmaker, h and 8½ acres.
Coupland John W., r 66, farm laborer.
COUPLAND JOSEPH, r 66, 2 cows, 24 grade Merino sheep, 1 brood mare, farmer 56..
COVERT JAMES H., (E. Pembroke) r 38, general merchant.
Cramer Henry, r 7, farmer 5.
Cramer John, r 7, laborer.
Craran Simon P., r 62, milk peddler, 17 cows, farmer 90.
Crowsway Frederick, r 6, laborer.
Curry James, (E. Pembroke) r 40, laborer.
Curry William, r 59, farmer 33.
Dailey Dennis, (W. Batavia) r 41, laborer and farmer 11.
Dailey Dennis, r 7, laborer.
Dailey John, r 49, farmer 40.
Daley Timothy, r 45, laborer.
Dargish Herman, r 62, laborer, h and 3 acres.
Darnell John, r 15, farmer 39.
Dascumbe Lewis, r 63, 5 grade Jersey cows, farmer 62½.
Davis A., r 13, engineer, h and 3 acres.
Davis G., r 54, laborer.

Davis John, r 50, farmer 110.
Day Elisha, r 18, farmer 111, and in Darien 80.
.DEAN FORDYCE O., r 10, dealer in granite monuments, 32 grade Merino sheep, 6' Jersey, Holstein, and Durham cows, prop. stock horse " Stranger," grandson of " Harold," sire of " Maud S.," farmer 102½.
Dean William L., r 31, rector Friends Church.
.Derby J. M., (E. Pembroke) r 40, pastor Baptist Church.
Dewey Grotius, r 10, farmer 57.
Didget George, r 66, farmer 6.
DIDGET JAMIMA, r 66, (Mrs. John) farmer 10.
Didget John, r 66, farm laborer.
Didget William, r 65, farmer 15.
Ditzel John, r 29, farm laborer and farmer 10.
Ditzel Louis H., r 29, mason and farmer.
Ditzel Mary, r 7, widow of Philip.
Ditzel Rose C., r 29, dressmaker.
Donahew Roger, r 49, farmer 30.
Dorman Carlton G., r 62 cor. 70, 16 Ayrshire, Jersey, and Durham cows, 6 full blood Jersey cattle, 200 grade Merino and thoroughbred Southdown sheep, 20 horses, farmer for his mother. Caroline L., 263.
Dorman Caroline L., r 62 cor. 70, widow of John, farm 263.
.Dorman Clark, r 70, farmer 50.
Dorman Cleveland W., r 62 cor. 70, farmer.
Douglass George, r 12, fruit grower and farmer, leases of H. Norris 100.
Downey George H., (Oakfield) r 3 cor. 16, farmer with his father, James.
Downey James, (Oakfield) r 15, 50 grade Shropshire sheep, farmer 124½.
DRAKE SAMUEL O., r 6, 5 grade Durham cows, farmer 98½.
Duane James, r 6, farmer for his mother, Margaret.
Duane Joseph, r 6, farmer for his mother, Margaret.
Duane Margaret, r 6, widow of Patrick, farmer 25.
Dumphey Michael, r 45, laborer.
Dunham Henry, r 14, farmer 20.
Dunn Joel B., r 9, laborer.
Dunnahai James, (E. Pembroke) r 40, produce dealer.
Dusing Frederick, r 65, laborer.
Dymond Charles, (N. Pembroke) r 17, farmer 20.
Earll Robert, r 61, 30 grade Jersey, Devon, and Durham cows, apiarist 70 colonies, milk peddler, farmer 144.
Edwards George, r 73, farmer 50.
Eldred Benjamin J., r 50, farmer 101.
Eldred Charles, (W. Batavia) r 54, farmer, leases of Mrs. Wortendyke 50.
Eldred Ira, r 52, farmer 87.
Fargette Frank, farmer 36.
Fargo Arthur W., r 65, farmer with his father, Fred H.
Fargo Elmer L., r 65, student.
Fargo Fred H., r 65, apiarist 100 colonies, farmer.
Fargo Henry D., r 65, farmer 117.
Fargo Warren, r 65, book-keeper and salesman.
Farnsworth Nathan T., (Oakfield) r 4, farmer 150.
Fifer John, r 13 cor. 29, farm laborer.
Finch John, (E. Pembroke) r 38, laborer.
Fish Elizabeth, r 7, widow of Eli H., resident.
Fisher Charley, r 13, farmer, leases of George Burt 92.
Fitzpatrick Michael, r 45, laborer.
Flaherty Michael, r 59 cor. 58, farmer 40.
Flaherty Timothy, r 59 cor. 58, farmer for his father, Michael.
Flaherty Timothy, r 51, farmer 30.
Flanders Hiram, r 29, blacksmith.
Flarita Frank, (W. Batavia) r 56, flagman N. Y. C. & H.R. R.R.

Flarita Frank Jr., (W. Batavia) r 56, laborer.
Follett Edward, r 62, farmer 8.
Forsyth James, r 12, farmer 96.
Foster Heklie L., farmer 70.
Foster William, r 70, farmer 72.
Fotch John G., r 12, harnessmaker, hop grower, prop. stone quarry, farmer 130.
Fotch Walter W., r 12, market gardener 35.
Galliger Daniel, r 14, farmer, leases of N. W. Kelsey 45.
Galloway Brothers, (James and Robert) 46 sheep,farmers,lease of the estate of John 286.
Galloway James, (Galloway Brothers).
Galloway Mary J., (Oakfield) r 16, widow of John, farmer 286.
Galloway Robert, (Galloway Brothers).
Galloway William, (Oakfield) r 16, farmer 300.
Gamble Robert, (E. Pembroke) r 21, laborer.
Ganson Rosa, r 72, widow, farmer 110.
Garey David, r 9, farmer 158.
Garrett James, r 69, farmer 18.
Garrett Penrose, r 69, farmer 14.
Garwood John, r 32, prop. grist-mill, farmer 13.
Garwood William, r 50, farmer 133.
Gates Isaac P., r 9, farmer 116.
Gates Joseph, r 26, farmer 56.
German George, r 50, farmer 80.
Gibson John A., (Oakfield) r 2, farmer 95.
Gill Daniel J., (Oakfield) r 3, retired farmer 2.
Gillett Charles L., r 34, farmer 133.
Gillett John, r 34, farmer with his father, Charles L.
Gillette Harry, r 45, laborer.
Gillons Albert T., r 7, farm laborer.
Gillons Eddie L., r 7, farmer, leases of William 170.
Gillons William, r 7, 7 cows, farmer 170.
Gillons William Jr., r 6, farmer 6.
GODEY E. WARD, r 23, farmer 125.
Godey Marian, r 23, iron machinist.
Godey Maynard A., r 23,10 grade Durham cows, breeder of and dealer in Clydesdale
     and Percheron horses, farmer 100.
Godnow Talmage, (East Pembroke) r 35, farmer, leases of John Merrill 100.
Goodrich Louisa, r 29, widow of Isaac, farm 12.
Goodridge Albert M., r 76, 100 sheep, farmer 80.
Gorton Warren, (E. Pembroke) r 38, farmer 47.
Gould George C., (E. Pembroke) r 37, retired farmer.
Gould George R., (E. Pembroke) r 37, 140 sheep, farmer 135.
Gould John H., r 34, farmer 90.
Gould Susan, r 34, widow of William.
GOWING JOSEPH M., (E. Pembroke) r 37, farmer 71.
Gowing Willis C., (E. Pembroke) r 37, farmer, leases of Joseph M. 71.
Graham Benjamin F., r 64, farmer 100.
Grame George, r 46, laborer.
GREEN JONATHAN, r 52, 1 thoroughbred Durhambull, 38 Merino sheep, reg.,
     farmer 103.
Green Nathaniel, r 52, house painter.
Green Olive A., r 65, widow of Joseph C., farmer 46.
Grice Eugene, r 30, farmer, leases of Margaret 50.
GRICE MARGARET, r 30, widow of Richard, farmer 50.
Grice Richard S., r 30, farmer, leases of N. A. Woodard, executor, 110.
Griffin John, (W. Batavia) farmer 12.
Griffin Patrick, (W. Batavia) farm 36.
Groat Frank, (W. Batavia) r 53, laborer.
Groat William, (W. Batavia) r 53, farmer 80.

Gubb William, r 6, farmer leases of Henry Craft 200.
Gunshaw William, r 15, farm laborer and farmer 2.
Hackley Ezekiel, r 6, retired farmer.
Hackley Francis A., r 6, student.
Hackley Levant M., r 6, laborer.
Hackley Orlando D., r 6, 7 cows, farmer 163.
Hale Fred, r 65, farmer 35.
Haller John H., r 72, farmer 105.
Hamilton Eugene, r 66, laborer.
Hamilton John C., r 66, farmer 70.
Hammer Augustus, r 65, farmer.
Hammond Elizabeth, r 72, farmer 125.
Hampton Frank, r 46, junk dealer.
Hancock John, r 65, thresher and farmer 15.
Hancock Samuel, r 65, farmer 4.
Hanrahan John, r 50, farmer 63.
Hardfile Frank, r 62, gardener.
Harmen John, r 6, laborer.
Harris Frank J., r 7, farmer 110, and leases of M. E. 130.
Harris Mary, r 28, widow of L. P.
Harris Mary E., r 7, widow of James W., farmer 176.
Harris Nancy, (W. Batavia) r 54, widow of John, farmer 18.
Harris Oscar P., r 28, 75 grade Merino sheep, farmer 95.
Hart Elliott, r 42, farmer, leases of John Heintz 78.
Hart John, r 52, farmer, leases of John Heintz 86¾.
Hartnell Philip, r 46, laborer.
Hartnell Philip, Jr., r 46, house painter.
HARTSHORN ANDREW, (W. Batavia) r 41, postmaster, 9 grade Jersey, Durham, and Holstein cows, farmer 143.
Hatch Jarvis M., r 7, farmer 176.
Hawker Fred, r 30, farmer, leases of T. F. Woodard 103.
Hayes Edgar, r 24, farmer 20.
Hayes Michael, r 7, retired.
Haynes Haynes, r 26, market gardener 8.
Hemmer Louis, r 70, farmer 4.
Henryhan John, r 30, farmer 70.
Herbold Edward, r 34, farm laborer.
Herbold George, r 34, farm laborer.
Herbold Martin, r 34, prop. saw-mill and farmer 5.
Hersch Frederick, r 69, farm laborer.
Hickey Charita, r 13, widow of William.
Higley John O., r 10, 5 Jersey and Holstein cows, 146 grade Merino and Shropshire sheep, farmer 97.
Hill Israel, Jr., (N. Pembroke) r 17, farmer 100.
Hirsch Charles, (Oakfield) r 16, farmer 200.
Hofer Levi, r 31, farmer with his father, Samuel.
Hofer Samuel, r 31, 10 grade Durham and Holstein cows, 60 sheep, farmer 166.
Holland Martin, (W. Batavia) r 55, farmer 20.
Hollen George, (Oakfield) r 16, laborer.
Holler Frank, r 72, farmer 23.
Holler John, r 72, farmer 120.
Holleran Morris, r 29, farmer 25.
Holly Therzy, r 65, widow of William.
Hood Isaac, r 65, farmer 65.
Hood Jesse R., r 65, school teacher.
HOPKINS ROBERT N., r 63, farmer 95.
Hopkins Thomas M., r 63, farmer with his father, Robert N.
Hosmer Philo S., r 12, 8 grade Durham cows, 55 sheep, farmer 211.
Houghmaster Ernest, r 26, laborer.

Houghmaster Joseph, r 62, laborer, h and 2 acres.
Houston Charles, r 26, farmer 12.
Howe Fred, r 23, laborer.
Howe Phebe A., r 9, farm 155.
Hubbard Lydia, r 58, farmer 160.
Huddleson James, r 13, laborer, h and lot.
Huffer Samuel, r 34, farmer 163.
Huirsch William, r 28, 12 cows. 100 sheep, farmer, leases of John Mockfort 155.
Huntington Henry, r 69, farmer 100.
Huntington Henry A., r 69, 6 grade Durham cows, farmer 55.
Huntzeman George, r 9, laborer.
Hursh Frederick, r 69, laborer.
Hussey Thomas F., r 65, dealer in buggies and cutters, farmer 14.
Idema George, r 9, laborer.
Ike Charles, (Oakfield) r 16, laborer.
Jacks J. Corwin, r 13, farmer 40.
JACKS JAMES C., r 13, 15 grade Durham cows, 1 Holstein bull, reg., 35 grade Me-
    rino sheep, farmer 185.
Jacks Samuel, (E. Pembroke) r 35, farmer 160.
Janson Eliza, r 48, farmer 51.
Jefford Morris, (W. Batavia) r 55, farmer 49.
Jerge Casper, r 7, farm laborer.
Johncox Henry, r 72, farmer 93.
Johnson Charles, (E. Pembroke) r 35, farmer, leases of S. Jacks 160.
Johnson George, r 5, farmer with his father, Uri.
JOHNSON HORACE, r 13, farmer.
Johnson Lewis M., r 13, 9 grade Durham and Jersey cows, farmer, leases of E. S. Wil-
    fred 282½.
Johnson Morace W., r 13, farm laborer.
Johnson Robert, r 46, painter.
Johnson Uri, r 5, 6 grade Jersey, Durham, and Holstein cows, farmer 80.
Johnson William H., r 13, farm laborer
Jones Brothers, r 26, (John E. and George W.) farmers, lease of S. Shepard 223.
Jones George W., r 26, (Jones Brothers).
Jones James, r 61, farmer 160.
Jones John E., r 26, (Jones Brothers).
Jorden Thomas, r 9, engineer at Institution for the Blind.
Joslyn Charles, r 23, laborer.
Joslyn George, r 15, farm laborer and farmer 2½.
Kane Michael, r 45, blacksmith.
Kapp Nathaniel P., r 28, dealer in boots and shoes.
Kearnes Phelix, (W. Batavia) r 56, farmer 20.
Kellogg Charles A., r 7, farmer for his father, Silas.
Kellogg Elmer, r 61, farm laborer.
Kellogg George, r 61, 10 cows, farmer 260.
Kellogg Herbert, r 61, machinist.
Kellogg Silas, r 7, farmer 200.
Kellogg Smith A., r 7, farmer with his father, Silas.
Kelsey Fred, r 60, laborer.
Kelsey Oscar B., r 76, farmer, leases of H. Higgins 36.
Kershner John, (E. Pembroke) r 40, farmer, leases of the Calkins estate 100.
Kemp B. George, r 30, farmer 12.
Kemp George B., r 30, farmer 72.
Keting Michael, r 41, farmer 7.
Kidder Alvin, (E. Pembroke) r 39, farmer 10.
Kilborn Hector, r 71, farmer 36.
Kinner Albert, r 46, farmer 7½.
Kinney Richard, r 11, farmer 80, and in Byron 87.
Kirk James, r 50, laborer.

Lampson Nathaniel, (Oakfield) r 2, farmer 100.
Lapp David, r 30, farmer 30, and in Alexander 110.
Lapp George, r 30, collector and dealer in horses.
Laring Philip, r 11, farmer 125.
Latrope Charles, r 30, laborer.
Lavis Robert, r 6, foreman Batavia nurseries.
Lawrence Charles, (Oakfield) r 15, farmer 106.
Lear William, (W. Batavia) r 57, farmer, leases of B. Grimes 130.
Lewis George, r 58, farm laborer.
Leyden Orson, r 19, farmer 6.
Lincoln Frank, r 78, farmer 28.
Lincoln Jennie, r 63, school teacher.
Linsey Anthony, r 50, farmer 58.
Long David, Sr., r 60, farmer 100.
Long David, Jr., r 60, 10 grade Durham cows, farmer 140, and leases of David, Sr., 100.
Lortz William, (Oakfield) r 2, farmer 97.
Lowe John, r 45, farmer 40.
Lown Benjamin, (E. Pembroke) r 21, farmer 20.
Lown Royal, r 54, farmer 25.
Lusk Marcus, r 46, retired farmer.
LUSK SALMON B., r 46, 3 cows, 100 American Merino sheep, reg., farmer 82.
Lusk William B., r 46, farmer with his father, Salmon B.
Lynch Daniel, r 7, farmer 70.
Mahana John, r 26, laborer.
Mahony Cain, farmer 20.
Mahony John, r 9, laborer.
Maine William, (E. Pembroke) r 4, farmer 5.
Mallery Harry, r 20, farmer, leases of Charles Day 128.
Manley Grorge, r 29, milk peddler, 14 cows, farmer, leases of Mrs. S. Passmore 18.
Mann Locke, r 14, farmer 5.
Marsh Almond C., r 46, farmer 85.
Martin Andrew, r 5, farmer, leases of J. Mercer 94.
Martin Andrew, r 26, 200 sheep, farmer 375.
MARTIN CHARLES T , r 7, 4 cows, farmer 100.
Martin Patrick, (W. Batavia) r 56, farmer 21.
Maynard Robert, r 26, laborer.
McCabe John, (W. Batavia) r 56, farmer 15.
McCally James, r 45, laborer.
McCarthy Patrick, r 9, laborer.
McCarty Daniel, r 47, laborer.
McCarty Jane, r 47, widow of Timothy.
McClerey Martha, r 18, farmer 128.
McCulley John H., r 7, milk dealer, 20 Durham, Jersey, and Holstein cows, farmer 82.
McDonald Mack, r 7, laborer.
McDonald Patrick, r 9, laborer.
McIntyre Erskine, r 13, farmer with his brother George 41.
McIntyre George, r 13, farmer 41.
McLaffin Thomas, r 45, laborer.
McMann Thomas, r 26, laborer.
McMannis Matthew, (W. Batavia) r 56, farmer 80.
McWain Sarah E., r 34, widow of Alonzo, farmer 134.
McWain T. Pratt, r 34, farmer for his mother, Sarah E.
Melius William, r 45, farmer 7.
Mercer Alexander, r 4, farmer 172.
Mercer Ellic, (Oakfield) r 4, farmer 100.
Mercer John, r 4, farmer 94.
Merrill John P., r 34, farmer 100.
Merrill Leman, (E. Pembroke) r 35, farmer 100.

5*

Messing William, r 50, laborer.
Miley John, r 7, farmer 18.
Miller John, r 30, farmer, leases of Sarah Morgan 220.
Miller John, r 33, farmer 100.
Miller John, r 15, laborer and farmer 5.
Millspaugh John R., r 6, clerk Batavia nurseries.
Minor Austin T., r 46, 40 grade Merino sheep, farmer 95.
Minor John A.; r 28, farmer 100.
Minor Seward H., r 46, 15 Merino sheep, farmer 72.
Mitchell Robert, r 47, wood worker.
Monagan James, r 46, laborer
Moore John, r 20, 15 grade Durham and Holstein cows, farmer 146.
Moore John, r 13, laborer.
MOORE MICHAEL, (E. Pembroke) r 38, retired farmer.
Moore Newton, r 41, laborer.
Morris Edgar C., r 47, maltster.
Mott William, (E. Pembroke) r 38, prop. saw-mill.
Moule Levi, r 26, farmer 100.
Myer John, r 18, laborer and farmer 2.
Myers Alonzo, r 24, farm laborer.
Myers Herman H., r 48, farmer with his father, Peter.
Myers John, r 76, farmer 5.
Myers John, Jr., r 29, farmer 3.
Myers John S., r 29 cor. 24, farm laborer.
Myers Julius, r 76, laborer.
MYERS PETER, r 48, 13 cows, 1 full blood and 4 reg. Jersey bulls, farmer, leases of J. Tozer 150.
Near George M., r 65, laborer.
NESTELL HOMER, r 61, served in Co. F, 2d N. Y. H. A., 3 years.
Nevilles Daniel, r 7, laborer.
Nevilles John, r 7, carpenter and farmer 8.
Newkirk John O., r 11, blacksmith, h and 3 acres.
Nole Isaac, (E. Pembroke) r 38, miller, emp. E. Babcock.
Northrup Mary E , r 13, widow of James, farmer 12¼.
Norton Frank W., r 65, farmer 272.
Nown John J., r 52, farmer 36.
Nown Joseph, r 42, laborer.
Nown William, r 52, carpenter.
O'BRINE DENNIS, r 46, 3 cows, farmer 50.
O'Brine William, r 46, farmer with his father, Dennis.
Odell William S., (W. Batavia) r 56, farmer 53.
O'Neal John, r 41, laborer.
Orcutt Charles E., r 12, farmer with his father, Chester E.
ORCUTT CHESTER E., r 12, 5 grade Durham cows, 50 grade Merino sheep, farmer 165.
Orcutt George, r 12, farmer with his father, Chester E.
Osborn Nehemiah, r 13, supervisor, 100 sheep, farmer 119.
Palmer Ara, r 71, farmer 38.
Palmer George, r 12, farmer 60.
Palmer William D., (W. Batavia) r 52, farmer 40.
Pardee Ann, (E. Pembroke) r 39, widow of R. D., farmer 38.
Pardee Charles T., r 13, 65 grade Merino sheep, farmer 100, and in Pembroke 50.
Parker Frank A., r 15, farmer, leases of Franklin J. 116.
Parker Franklin J., r 15, farm 116.
Parkhurst John, (E. Pembroke) r 40, retired farmer.
Parsons Charles F., r 7, farmer with his father, Thomas G.
PARSONS THOMAS G., r 7, 7 Durham and Jersey cows, 1 full blood Jersey bull, farmer 106.
Patterson John, r 69, farmer 24.

Patterson Thomas, (Oakfield) off r 15, farmer 43½.
Pease Edward, r 10, farmer 95.
Pember Ralph, (E. Pembroke) r 31, farmer 6.
Pember William, (E. Pembroke) r 21, farmer 16.
Perry Edward, r 52, farmer 30.
PERRY FRANK D., r 46, 5 grade Durham cows, 200 sheep, farmer 160.
Pflug Frederick, Sr., r 28, farmer, leases of Kirk P. White 150.
Pflug Frederick, Jr., r 28, farmer with his father, Frederick.
Phelps Luman, r 6, laborer.
Pinder Francis, r 70, farmer 17.
Plant Robert, r 64, retired farmer.
Plato Albert, r 62, farmer 150.
Plato George W., r 70, laborer, h and 5 acres.
Plock Henry, r 47, gunsmith.
Plock John, r 47, cooper.
Pluck Matthew, r 15, farmer 50.
Pomter Jack, r 13, laborer.
Poorholtz Herman, r 69, farmer 160.
Porter George, r 73, farmer, leases of the estate of James L. Smith 100.
Post Grant, r 50, farmer for his father, William H.
Post Seward R., farmer for his father, William H.
Post William, r 50, farmer.
Post William H. G., r 50, 18 grade Durham cows, farmer 245.
Potter Joseph H., r 23, breeder of and dealer in horses, farmer 200.
Potter William H., r 23, farmer 140.
Powers Menzo E., r 19, 6 cows, 64 sheep, farmer 125.
Pratt Charles, r 20. (Pratt & Sisters) assessor.
Pratt Charles, r 62, farmer.
Pratt Harry K., r 10, farmer for his father, Kirk W., 15.
Pratt Jane, r 62, widow of A. S.
Pratt Kirk W., r 10, 5 Durham and Holstein cows, farmer 113.
Pratt Martha J., r 20, (Pratt & Sisters).
Pratt Mary A., r 20, (Pratt & Sisters).
Pratt & Sisters, r 20, (Charles, Mary A., and Martha J.) 20 grade Jersey and Devon
   cows, 100 grade Cotswold sheep, farmers 325.
Putnam Monroe H., r 67, farmer 50.
Putnam Warren, r 68, farmer 75.
Quance Israel, farmer 60.
QUANCE JAMES M., r 63, farmer.
Quance Willard, r 6, laborer.
Radmore William, r 64, laborer.
Raid James, r 29, farmer 98, and leases of Holdenaud 120.
Raid John, r 29, farmer for his father James.
Raid Patrick, r 29, blacksmith.
Raid Roger, r 29, farmer for his father James.
REDFIELD FRANK B., r 29, breeder of horses, farmer 250.
Redman Mary, r 49, farmer 30.
Redshaw George, r 71, farmer 38.
Reinholtz Harman, r 70, farmer 40.
Rich Frank F., (W. Batavia) r 55, farmer, leases of Ellen Conners 44.
Ricks Mark, r 13, farmer, leases of the W. Wolsey estate 60.
Rigney Herbert, (Oakfield) r 2, farmer, leases of Joseph 90.
Roach Aaron, r 20, farmer 92.
Robson George, r 69, laborer and farmer, leases of William Plato 18.
Rose Morton, r 59, farmer 165.
Rose Seth M., r 59, farmer 44.
Rose Walter, r 47, laborer.
Ross Berney, r 12, farmer 90.
Royce Samuel N., r 63, farmer 130.

Rumsey Edward, r 13, farmer 120.
Russel John, r 11, farmer 20.
Ryan James, r 9, market gardener 4.
Ryan Michael, r 7, farmer, leases of the Hatch estate 176.
Safford Burton, r 58, farmer 30.
Saile Joseph, r 42, farmer, leases of Mrs. Sarah Hopkins 40.
Saulsbury Nelson L., r 29, fruit grower and farmer 17¼.
Savacool Albert T., (W. Batavia) r 57, carpenter.
Savacool Eugene, (W. Batavia) r 52, carpenter.
Savacool George M., (W. Batavia) r 57, laborer.
Savacool Merritt P., (W. Batavia) r 57, farmer 32½.
Sawens Severence, (W. Batavia) r 74, farmer 80.
Scanlin Charles, r 28, farmer, leases of R. Terry 41½.
Scott George, r 46, 50 sheep, farmer 80.
Seamens Ezra, (E. Pembroke) r 40, postmaster and dealer in hardware.
Seymour Henry, r 61, retired farmer.
Seymour James H, r 61, 7 cows, farmer 83.
Shadbolt Vern C., r 10, student.
Shaw Mary, r 73, widow of Anthony, farmer 50.
Sheflin James, (Oakfield) r 16, farmer leases of Ann Daily 89.
Shepard Charles, r 66, farmer with his father, John.
Shepard Charles E., r 66, farmer 76, and leases of John 124.
Shepard John, r 66, 200 grade Merino sheep, farmer 124.
SHEPARD THOMAS B., r 6, farmer 75.
Sherwin Francis L., r 76, (O. G. & F. L. Sherwin).
Sherwin O. G. & F. L., r 76, farmers 67.
Sherwin Orra G , r 76, (O. G. & F. L. Sherwin).
Showerman William, r 6, laborer.
Shrader Augustus, r 26, laborer.
Shultz August, r 5, laborer.
Sinskey Joseph, r 62, laborer.
Skeet George, r 13, laborer.
Skelton Philip, r 13, farmer, leases of Mary A. Northrup 12¼.
Smith Herman, r 61, farmer 30.
Smith Jacob, r 7, gardener 3.
Smith John, r 62, carpenter.
Smith Rando, r 29, farmer 25.
Smith Sarah, r 73, widow of James L., farmer 100.
SNELL CHARLES A., r 13, real estate, loan, and ins. agent, W. Main, farmer 23.
Snell Charles I., r 13, school teacher.
Snell Frank A., r 13, real estate and ins. agent with his father, Charles A.
Snell Nettie L., school teacher.
Sougler Peter, r 7, laborer.
Speed Henry, r 6, laborer.
SPEYER CONRAD, (Daws) r 7 cor. 6, postmaster and farmer 18.
Spicer Derrick W., r 50, farmer 41.
Spicer Dwight, r 50, farmer with his father Derrick W.
Sprague Henry, r 61, retired farmer, owns in Alexander 90.
Spring Alpheus, r 61, farmer 50.
Squires John, r 28, farmer, leases of H. L. Terry 126.
Squires William, r 27, farmer, leases of John 61.
St. Claire Lyman, r 58 cor. 73, farmer 20, and leases of E. K. Warner 60.
Steinberger John, r 70, farmer.
Storms Isaac, r 29 cor. 24, wagon repairer, h and 2 acres.
STRINGHAM ALONZO, r 63, emp. in planing-mill.
STRONG SYLVESTER F., r 7, 6 cows, 2 Jersey cattle, reg., farmer 136
Sullings David, r 24, farmer 60.
SULLINGS DAVID, r 24, farmer 100.
Sullivan John, r 46, emp. on railroad.

Sutherland Homer, (W. Batavia) r 74, farmer 25.
Sutherland Myron, (W. Batavia) r 74, farmer 90.
Sutherland William, r 24, laborer.
Sweney Daniel, r 70, farmer 70.
Tabor Willard, r 32, farmer 105.
Taylor John, (E. Pembroke) r 41, farmer 24.
Terry Hattie L., r 28, 76 grade Merino sheep, 17 head cattle, farmer 126.
Terry John W., r 28, farmer 95.
Terry Van Rensselaer, r 46, farmer 42½.
Thoma Magnus, r 52, farmer with his father, Mattba
Thoma Mattha, r 52, farmer 17.
Thomas William, r 7, farmer 20.
Thompson George, r 29, laborer.
Thompson Joseph, r 62, carpenter.
Thomson Ann, r 46, widow of Jerome.
Thomson Charlie, r 13, student.
Thomson Seymour B., r 131, farmer.
THOMSON SYLVANUS B., r 13, retired merchant, prop. Almonarch s'ock farm and
    trotting stock horse " Almonarch," No. 3234, record 2:24¾, sire of " Elmonarch,"
    2:17¼, owns farm in Alexander 115.
Thorp Charles, (Oakfield) r 15, farmer 6.
Timan Charles, r 47, laborer.
TORRANCE EUNICE S., r 63, widow of Charles G., 6 cows, 50 Shropshire sheep,
    farmer 150.
Torrance William M., r 63, farmer for his mother, Eunice S., 150.
Townsend Luther H., r 2, farmer, leases of Norris Burr 88.
Tryon Jerome, r 54, farmer 4.
Tryon Lemuel J., r 45, laborer.
Underhill George F., (Oakfield) r 4, farmer 100.
Uphill Benjamin, r 57, farmer 60.
Uphill George, r 57, farmer, leases of O. W. Dewey 56.
Uphill Oliver C., (E. Pembroke) r 41, carpenter and farmer 2.
Uphill William, r 73, farmer 99.
Vallett John, r 29, horse breaker, prop. stock horse "Leader," farmer 3.
Vallett William, r 12, laborer, h and 3 acres.
Van Horn Tennis, (W. Batavia) r 55, farmer, with his father.
Van Horn Tunis, (W. Batavia) r 55, farmer 71.
Vedder Eugene G., (W. Batavia) r 55, laborer.
Vedder John G., (W. Batavia) r 55, farmer 4.
Votary Ezra, r 61, farmer 26.
VOTARY MARY, r 61, widow of Joseph, farmer 9½.
Votrey Edward, r 61, farm laborer.
Votrey John, r 61, farm laborer.
Wade Hannah, r 46, widow of Harris, farmer 53.
Wade James, r 46, farmer for his mother, Hannah.
Wade John, r 46, farmer for his mother, Hannah.
Wagner Charles, r 7, laborer.
Wagner George, r 5, laborer and farmer 5.
Waldron Edward, r 13, farmer, leases of George Burt 105.
Wall John, (E. Pembroke) r 40, laborer.
Walsh George, r 76, farmer, leases of A. G. & F. Sherwin 67.
Waltham Joseph, r 52, farmer 30.
Ward Adelbert, off r 20, farmer, leases of Aaron Roach 66.
Ward Delbert, (E. Pembroke) r 21, farmer, leases of Aaron Roach 60.
Ward Edward, (W. Batavia) r 55, farmer 125.
WARD WILLIAM, r 65, 4 cows, farmer 97.
Ware Walter W., r 63, 175 sheep, farmer 155.
Ware William, r 47, farmer 90.
Warner Thomas, r 45, farmer 25.

WEED HARVEY, r 31, farmer 96.
Weisseit Christopher, r 34, farmer 48.
Weisseit George, r 34, laborer.
Wescott George, r 13, coachman.
WESCOTT JAMES R., r 13, farmer 4.
West Carlos, r 67, laborer.
West Warren, r 67, farmer 40.
Wewrich Charles, r 4, laborer.
Wheeler George, r 33, farmer 98.
Wheeler Harrison, r 33 cor. 34, farmer 98.
WHITCOMB WILLIAM W., r 52, pres. Batavia Business University and Steno-
    graphic Institute, farmer 28.
White Alva B., r 7, farmer 100.
White Cornelia M., r 13, farmer 12.
White Darius, r 13, farmer, owns in Alabama 99.
White Kirk, r 11, farmer 127.
WHITNEY NELSON, r 30, 3 cows, 16 grade Merino sheep, farmer 60.
Whitney Sylvester, r 30, retired farmer.
Wickham Herbert, farm laborer, h and 3 acres Park.
Wicks John, r 9, laborer.
Wiggins Samual, r 31, tin canmaker, h and lot.
Wilber Ada, r 7, widow of George, farmer 100.
Wilber Dewaine W., r 7, 65 Merino sheep, farmer, leases of Ada 100.
Wilber Sanford, r 7, farmer 170.
Wilkie Mary, r 66, widow of James, farm 4.
Williams Burt C., r 7, farmer with his father, Myron A.
Williams Edward, r 2, farmer 42.
Williams Elwyn A., r 7, student.
Williams George, r 41, farmer, leases of A. Hartshorn 143.
Williams Myron A., r 7, farmer 130.
Wilson James, (E Pembroke) r 40, retired farmer.
Wolf William, r 47, laborer.
Worthington John, off r 30, 50 sheep, farmer 120.
Wrigley Joseph, (Oakfield) r 3, farmer 95.
Young William, r 65, retired farmer 4½.
YOUNG JOHN E., r 65, 180 grade Merino sheep, farmer 147.
Young William H., r 67, 85 grade Merino sheep, farmer 90.
Zehler Peter, (W. Batavia) r 55, prop. hotel.
Zimmerman Daniel F., r 62, farmer 13.

BERGEN.

(For explanations, etc., see page 3, part second.)

(Postoffice address is Bergen, unless otherwise designated in parenthesis.)

Abell Charles A., (N. Bergen) r 4, farmer 99.
Adams Chester, (W. Bergen) r 26, farmer 50.
Akin Ambrose, r 33, farmer, leases of Horace Knapp 130.
ANDREWS ROBERT, physician and surgeon, Lake cor. McKenzie, h do.
Apthorp Edward, butcher, h Rochester st.
Apthorp Ida, (Mrs. J. Ira) milliner, h Rochester st.
Apthorp J. Ira, com. traveler, h Rochester st.
Aradine James, (N. Bergen) r 5, blacksmith.

Aradine William, r 8, farmer 35.
Armstrong Richard, gardener and laborer, h Gibson.
Arnold Aaron, farmer and ins. agent, h Lake.
Arnold Cassius, laborer, h Buffalo st.
Arnold Charles, carpenter, h Le Roy st.
Arnold Clarence H., general merchant, Lake, h Clinton.
Arnold Ebenezer, r 32, retired farmer 87.
ARNOLD GEORGE W., prop. boarding-house, Clinton.
Arnold H. Windsor, retired farmer, h Clinton.
Arnold Irving W., r 32, farmer 90.
ARNOLD LINDEN D., r 32, farmer 120.
Arnold Mary A., widow of David, h Buffalo st.
Avery Richardson, r 10, farmer 79.
Avery Seeley, (N. Bergen) r 1, laborer.
Babcock Fred P., (Edgerton & Co.) h Clinton.
Bailey Brothers, (Henry and Charles) wholesale butchers, Spring.
Bailey Charles, (Bailey Brothers) h Spring.
Bailey Henry, (Bailey Brothers) h Spring.
BAIRD JOHN, manuf., h Rochester st.
Baker Emily M., widow of James F., h Lake.
Baker John W., r 34, laborer.
Barnaby Asahel, r 32, farmer.
Barnaby Asel, farmer, h Lake road.
Barnaby Betsey, r 32, invalid, aged 86.
Barr James, r 25, farmer 525.
Barr William, r 20, farmer, leases of James 175.
Barringer Frank, laborer, h 1 Buffalo st.
Barton William, butcher, h Rochester st.
Bassett George, laborer, h Clinton.
BASSETT PHILO B., funeral furnisher and director, dealer in artistic materials, pictures, frames, stationery, etc., Carpenter & McKenzie block, h Lake.
Bassett Richard, painter, h Clinton.
Bater John, r 34, laborer, h and 2 acres.
Beardsley Joseph, farmer, h Lake road.
Beedham Jonathan, (N. Bergen) farmer 20.
Bergin John, baggagemaster N. Y. C. & H. R. R. R., h Church.
BERGIN MICHAEL F., dealer in groceries and liquors, Lake, h do.
Berry Jane, r 7, widow of Moses, farmer 120.
Beswick Frank, (W. Bergen) r 27, farmer with Fred 70.
Beswick Fred, (W. Bergen) r 27, farmer with Frank 70.
Beswick Wesley F., (W. Bergen) r 27, farmer 50.
Beswick William H., (W. Bergen) r 27, farmer 73.
Bissell Adaline, widow of Jerry, farm 135, h Lake road.
BISSELL BROTHERS, (George A. and William A.) shippers of grain and produce, dealers in coal, etc., farmers 218, West Shore freight-house.
Bissell Calvin, r 33, farmer 24.
BISSELL FRED M., professor of music and house painter, h Rochester st.
BISSELL GEORGE A., r 21, (Bissell Brothers) farmer 90.
Bissell James, r 33, farmer 77.
BISSELL JAMES A., milk dealer, farmer 77.
BISSELL WILLIAM A., (Bissell Brothers) h Lake road.
Bitteridge Harry, (Stone Church) r 39, laborer.
Bodell William, (N. Bergen) r 2, blacksmith.
Bovanizer James A., (N. Bergen) r 3, farmer, leases of Bellona Bissell, of Le Roy, 170.
Bovee Elihu C., (Stone Church) r 40, laborer.
Bower Abner, (W. Bergen) r 26, farmer 180.
Bower Francis, retired farmer, h McKenzie.
BOWER MICHAEL, farmer 80, h Clinton.
Bower Rosannah, (W. Bergen) r 26, widow of Jacob.

Bower Samuel E., (W. Bergen) r 26, town supervisor, thresher, and farmer, leases of Michael 80.

BOWER WILLIAM A., breeder of Holstein cattle, farmer 100, h Buffalo st. [Died April 17, 1889.]

Boyce Stephen, farmer, h Gibson.

Brennon James. emp. N. Y. C. & H. R. R. R., h Le Roy st.

Bristol Isaac, (N. Bergen) r 2, farmer 2½.

Brodie Christie, r 37, widow.

Brodie James C., r 37, farmer 200.

Brodie ———, (W. Bergen) widow of Peter, h Dibble.

Brown Celia, widow of David, h Lake.

Brown Charles, laborer, h Clinton.

Brown James, clerk, bds. Lake.

Brown Parley W., r 21, farmer 10.

Buell Gilbert N., dealer in groceries and provisions, Rochester st., h Lake.

Buell J. Burchard, r 33, farmer 60.

Burns Francis, shoemaker, h Clinton.

Burns James, r 29, laborer.

Burns William E., tonsorial artist, Morton block, h Clinton.

Byrne John. carpenter, h Rochester st.

Cain Peter, emp. N. Y. C. & H. R. R. R., h Lake.

Callister William, farmer, leases of Mrs. Charles Field.

Campbell John, r 21, farmer 98.

Campbell Sarah A., r 1, widow.

CARPENTER CARLOS N., (Carpenter & Sons) h Lake.

CARPENTER GEORGE A., (Carpenter & Sons) h Lake.

Carpenter John, (N. Bergen) r 5, farmer, leases of Mrs. ——— Hickey, of Batavia, 12½.

CARPENTER SAMUEL, (Carpenter & Sons) h Lake.

CARPENTER& SONS, (Samuel, George A., and Carlos N.) dealers in clothing, boots, shoes, hats, caps, gents' furnishing goods, wall paper, Domestic sewing machines, trunks, and traveling bags, Lake.

Carroll Philip, r 29, farmer 100.

Carruthers Dow L., r 8, farmer 20.

Carruthers Thomas A., r 8, farmer 80.

Caswell William, r 19, farmer, leases of Andrew Southworth 65.

Caulkins Virgil C., apothecary and jeweler, Lake, h do.

Cavanaugh James, (Stone Church) r 33, farmer, leases of Mrs. Brewer.

Cavanaugh John, r 33, farmer 21.

Cavanaugh Thomas, r 32, laborer.

Chipman Charles J., r 11, farmer 106.

Church George H., prop. planing, saw, and feed-mill, and dealer in lumber, Lake ave., h Buffalo st.

CHURCH HARRIET A., widow of Samuel, h Buffalo st.

Clark Thomas, (N. Bergen) r 1, laborer.

Collins Andrew, r 7, farmer 3.

Collins Earl S., r 9, farmer, leases of Alexander Campbell, of Batavia, 60.

Collins Jane E. Mrs., h McKenzie cor. Clinton.

Collins John, constable, h Lake.

Collister William H., (W. Bergen) r 25, farmer, leases of Charles Field 90.

Congdon George H., r 11, farmer 60.

Conlin Thomas, r 29, farmer 5.

CONNERY H. H., pastor St. Bridget's Church, h Gibson.

Converse Melvin C., (N. Bergen) r 2, laborer.

Conway William G., liquor dealer and farmer 71, Lake, h Buffalo st.

Cook John, r 21, laborer.

Cook Walter, r 25, farmer 55.

Cooper Henry, (N. Bergen) r 1, farmer 8.

Corcoran John, r 34, farmer 58.

Corcoran Margaret, r 29, widow of Patrick.
Cornwell Altemont, r 20, farmer 190.
Cowles Ann, r 32, widow of Robert.
Cox Benjamin, laborer, bds. Spring.
Cox George, (N. Bergen) r 1, farmer 35.
Crampton James G., (Stone Church) r 33, farmer 80½.
Crampton Jerry H., r 32, farmer 18.
Cramton Amon G., (Stone Church) r 33, farmer 67.
Cramton James, (Stone Church) r 33, farmer 20.
Crittenden Josiah T., laborer, h Rochester st.
Dart Charles, r 9, farmer 33.
Davis Asher, (Stone Church) r 40, farmer.
Davis George, r 31, laborer.
Davis George T., real estate dealer, h Clinton.
Davis Jonathan L., laborer, h Rochester st.
Davis Newell J., dentist, Lake, h Le Roy st.
Davis Porter, (Stone Church) r 40, retired farmer.
Davis Porter M., com. traveler, h Clinton.
Davis Porter S., (Stone Church) r 49, farmer 90.
Davy George, (N. Bergen) r 5, farmer, leases of Daniel Barker, of Clarendon, Orleans Co., 70.
DAVY JOHN W., blacksmith, horseshoer, carriage ironer, and woodworker, h Rochester st.
Dawes Jonathan, laborer, h Rochester st.
Deacon Andrew, laborer, h Church.
Dean Alden, r 24, retired farmer.
DEAN THOMAS J., (N. Bergen) r 2, thresher and farmer 11½.
Decker Mary, emp. Carpenter & Sons, h Gibson.
Dettman Christian, r 8, farmer, leases of D. S. Morgan, of Brockport, Monroe Co., 140
Dettman Fred, r 8, farmer with Christian.
Dewey Cynthia E., (Mrs. Jesse) farm 60, h Buffalo st.
Dewey Jesse, broker and retired farmer, h Lake.
Dibble Edwin C., (Stone Church) r 37, farmer 56.
Dibble Emily, (Stone Church) r 37, widow of Henry D.
Dibble Fayette M., r 37, farmer 90.
Dibble Irena, r 37, widow of Marvin.
Doran John, r 35, farmer 80.
Doran Michael, street commissioner, prop. cider-mill, h Munger.
Doran Miles, r 19, farmer 60.
Dowling Ann, widow of William, h Richmond.
Drury Patrick, (W. Bergen) r 29, switchman.
Eddy David U., farmer 4, h Rochester st.
Edgerton & Co., (Charles E. E. and F. P. Babcock) general merchants.
Edgerton Charles E., (Edgerton & Co) bds. Rochester st.
Elliott John, (W. Bergen) r 27, laborer.
Elmer Orrin, r 19, laborer.
Elmer Sedgwick, r 11, farmer 120.
Elmore Jonathan, general fire ins. agent, h Lake.
Emerson George, retired farmer, h Buffalo st.
Emerson George O., lawyer, h Buffalo st.
EMERSON JOHN R., clerk, h at Riga, Monroe Co.
Erwin William, (W. Bergen) r 28, farmer 93.
Evart John, r 7, farmer 10.
Evarts Richard, retired farmer 43, h Lake road.
Fansom Francis W., r 7, farmer, leases of Jane Berry 120.
Farnham Chester, farmer.
FARNHAM JOSEPH N., (Stone Church) r 36, farmer 50.
Farnham Stephen L., (W. Bergen) r 36, farmer 50.
Feathers Jerry, r 32, farmer, leases of Halsey Wilcox 200.

FEEZLEAR JEROME T., teacher for 29 years, dealer in horses, farmer 7, h Rochester st.
Fields Amanda, widow of Timothy, farm 46½.
FIELD CHARLES, r 24, farmer 75, and with Amanda F. 88.
Field Emily J., r 25, widow, farmer 72.
Fisher Adelbert, town clerk, bds. with Amos S.
Fisher Amos S., dealer in drugs, medicines, chemicals, etc., Lake, h Clinton.
Fitzsimmons Ann, (W. Bergen) r 27, widow.
Fitzsimmons John, (W. Bergen) r 27, farmer 87.
Fitzsimmons John W., (W. Bergen) r 36, farmer, leases of Mrs. Fitzsimmons 100.
Flarherty John, telegraph operator, h Munger.
Fodge Michael, r 29, farmer 15.
FORDHAM HARLAN F., r 33, farmer 125.
Fuller Ezra N., r 7, general ins. agent and farmer 50.
Furnace Robert, (N. Bergen) r 1, laborer.
Gage Homer L., (Oathout & Gage) h Munger.
Ganiard Henry O , r 33, farmer 160.
Gapp Joseph, r 9, farmer 108.
GAY G. ROWLEY, (N. Bergen) r 1, farmer 105.
German Christopher, r 7, farmer 70.
Gibbons Moses C., r 20, farmer 168.
Gifford A. B. & J. D. (N. Bergen) r 1, general merchants.
Gifford Aaron B., (N. Bergen) r 2, (A. B. & J. D. Gifford) postmaster and farmer 76.
Gifford Andrew H., retired liveryman, h Lake.
Gifford John D., (N. Bergen) r 1 cor. 2, (A. B. & J. D., Gifford).
Gifford Susan M., widow of Morris, h Buffalo st.
Gilbert Thomas, blacksmith, h Rochester st.
Gillette George, r 17, farmer, leases the Sylvester Gillette estate 210.
Gillette Harmon, r 8, laborer.
Gillette Henry W., r 87, farmer 25.
Gillette Joel, r 87, farmer 80.
Gillette M. James, r 7, farmer 100.
Gillette Miles S., r 7, aged 84.
GILLETTE SYLVESTER, r 17, farmer 148½.
Gilman James, off r 9, farmer 218.
Gleason John, r 7, buttermaker and farmer 70.
Goff James, (N. Bergen) r 1, farmer, leases of G. Rowley Gay 105.
Gordon James, emp. N. Y. C. & H. R. R. R., h Richmond.
Gorton William, r 25, farmer 60, and leases on shares of Mrs. Jesse Dewey 60.
Graham Elmer, r 37, laborer.
Green Alonzo L., r 15, farmer 47.
Green Amos J., (N. Bergen) r 1, farmer 95.
GREEN ELIAS P., r 32, farmer 5½.
Green Horace, cartman, h Rochester st.
Green Orlando M., (N. Bergen) r 1, farmer 115.
Green Randall, (N. Bergen) r 1, farmer 108.
Growney Edward P., (W. Bergen) r 27, clerk.
Growney James, (W. Bergen) r 27, farmer 110.
Gunn Chauncey C., com. traveler, h Lake.
Haley John (W. Bergen) r 27, section hand on railroad.
Haley Richard, manuf. and repairer of boots and shoes, Lake, h Le Roy st.
Haley Timothy, (W. Bergen) r 29, railroad track hand.
Hall Eugene D., (Stone Church) r 38, farmer 100.
Hall William W., (N. Bergen) r 1, peddler.
Halsey Catherine, widow of Patrick, h Le Roy st.
Hammond Frank, resident, h Buffalo st.
Hammond Henry E., (N. Bergen) r 13, farmer 36.
Hanley Edward, carpenter and joiner, h Gibson.
Harford Benedict, prop. Harford House and livery stable, Lake cor. Rochester sts.

Harford House, B. Harford, prop., Lake cor. Rochester sts.
Harrington Con., (W. Bergen) r 27, farmer 25.
Harris George W., (N. Bergen) r 1, painter.
Hatch Charles, r 32, farmer, leases of Jamin B. 38.
Hatch James B., r 32, prop. meat market, Lake.
Hatch Jamin B., r 32, farmer 38.
Hawes Joseph, (N. Bergen) r 1, laborer.
Henderson Benjamin F., (N. Bergen) r 2, farmer 16.
Hendrick Moses B., clerk, h Le Roy st.
Hendricks Dennis J., emp. N. Y. C. & H. R. R. R., h Richmond.
Hendricks Michael, farmer 6, h Munger.
Herbert Henry E., r 16, farmer 69.
Hermance James, (N. Bergen) r 1, laborer.
Herrick Edward P., (W. Bergen) r 27, farmer, leases of Abner Bower 100.
Herrick Margaret, r 17, farmer 62.
Herrick Sebastian, r 17, farmer for Margaret.
HEWES DAYTON, r 14, farmer with Marcena B.
Hewes George, (Stone Church) r 37, farmer, leases of Mary Wilcox 86, and owns in
    Le Roy 50.
Hewes Marcena B., r 14, farmer 289, and in Riga, Monroe Co., 130.
Hewes Otis M., r 14, farmer with Marcena B.
Hickey Ann, (N. Bergen) widow of Patrick.
Hiscock Robert E., carpenter and joiner, h Buffalo st.
Hiscock John, butcher, h Clinton.
Hiscock Sarah, widow of William, h Buffalo st.
Hoag Henry, r 30, farmer 8.
Hodges George, (N. Bergen) r 1, farmer 5.
Hoffman Frederick, r 20, farmer 126.
Holden Mary J., widow of Joseph, h Lake.
Holdridge Gershom B., r 16, farmer 60.
Hollenbeck Effie C., r 32, widow of Edward J.
Holt Minerva, widow, h Lake.
Hopkins ———, (Stone Church) r 40, widow of Bruce.
HOPKINS BRUCE, (Stone Church) teacher and farmer 1¼. [Deceased.]
Horiz Sebastian, farmer 32, h Lake road.
Hough Mark, section foreman N. Y. C. & H. R. R. R., bds. Richmond.
Hough Patrick, section foreman N. Y. C. & H. R. R. R., h Buffalo st.
Houston Sally, (N. Bergen) r 2, h and lot.
Howell David W., farmer 25½, h Gibson.
Howell Edwin P., r 24, farmer, leases of the Samuel Richmond estate 90.
Howell Henry W., r 11, farmer 84.
Hoyt Charles, r 23, cooper.
Hubbard Ezra, retired, bds. Harford House.
Hughson David, (N. Bergen) cooper and laborer.
Hull Eugene D., (Stone Church) r 33, farmer 110.
Hull Newton M., (Stone Church) r 33, laborer.
Hunsberger Joseph, (Stone Church) r 40, pastor Presbyterian Church.
IDE BROTHERS, (Dorwin A. and Irwin) harnessmakers, Lake.
IDE DORWIN A., (Ide Brothers) h Lake.
Ide Irwin, (Ide Brothers) h Lake.
Irwin James, (W. Bergen) r 27, track hand.
Irwin John, (W. Bergen) r 27, farmer with William.
Irwin William, (W. Bergen) r 27, farmer 100.
Irwin William J., (W. Bergen) r 27, farmer with his father 50.
Jenkins Edward, r 20, farmer 103.
Jenkins Thomas, (N. Bergen) r 1, farmer 20.
Johnson John L., (N. Bergen) r 3, farmer 95.
Johnson Porter H., (N. Bergen) r 3, farmer 1, and leases on shares of John L. 95.
Johnson Winfield S., carpenter, h Munger.

Jones G. B., professor of penmanship.
Jonrowe Benjamin F., r 32, laborer.
Joslyn Elias P., prop. billiard room, bds. Lake.
Kavien John, r 33, farmer 80.
Kearney Patrick, laborer, h Lake.
Kelehar Jerry, retired, h Le Roy st.
Keller Andrew, (W. Bergen) r 35 cor. 28, farm 100.
Keller Wilbur, (W. Bergen) r 27, farmer, leases of Andrew 100.
Kelly Francis, (W. Bergen) r 36, farmer with James.
Kelly Hugh, mason, h State road.
Kelly James, (W. Bergen) r 36, farmer 150.
Kenny Thomas, (W. Bergen) r 27, flagman.
Keaiven Patrick, r 30, farmer 15.
Kersh Charles, (W. Bergen) r 36, farmer, leases of J. O. Wilsey, of Geneva, 100.
Kerwin John, (Stone Church) farmer 81.
Kingman Theodosia, widow of Franklin D., h Lake.
Kinney Thomas, (W. Bergen) flagman N. Y. C. & H. R. R. R.
Kirk Patrick, r 33, laborer.
Kirkpatrick Samuel r 9, laborer.
Kirsh Charles, (W. Bergen) farmer, leases of S. L. Farnham and C. Wilson.
Knapp Horace, r 33, farmer 130.
KNICKERBOCKER HIRAM, r 32, retired farmer.
La Due George W., (N. Bergen) r 1, farmer 100.
La Due H. Augustus, (N. Bergen) r 6, farmer 37.
La Due Maria, (N. Bergen) r 1, farmer 60.
Lake William, r 20, farmer 5.
Langham William C., r 8, farmer 60.
Lawrence Kate L., (W. Bergen) postmistress.
Lawrence Laura Miss, (N. Bergen) r 1, resident.
Lawrence William A., (W. Byron) r 27, ticket agent and general merchant.
Leonard Alexander, farmer in Byron 100, h McKenzie.
Lefler John A., r 33, laborer.
Lewellyn Clarence, r 29, farmer 90.
Lewellyn Decatur C., r 15½, farmer 57, and leases on shares of Myron H., of Olean, Cattaraugus Co., 100.
LEWELLYN FRED, farmer 100, h McKenzie.
Lewellyn Levi, r 25, farmer 220.
Lewis John R., pastor Presbyterian Church, h McKenzie.
Lipe James, carpenter and farmer 2, h Buffalo st.
Long John, (Stone Church) r 33, laborer.
Loomis Effie A., r 24, widow of Elijah, farmer 60.
Loring Bridge, r 8, farmer 90.
Loring Charles, r 8, laborer.
Ludlow Frank M., r 35, farmer 60¾.
Lyle Abraham C., r 29, farmer 103.
Lyman Melville W., carpenter, h Rochester st.
Lynch James, laborer, h Buffalo st.
Maher John, (Stone Church) r 40, farmer 200.
Maley James, laborer.
Mann Amos, flagman N. Y. C. & H. R. R. R., h Church.
Mansfield George, r 32, laborer.
MANSFIELD GEORGE W., farmer 8, h Lake.
Marion Barnard, (Stone Church) r 40, blacksmith.
Marion Edward T., (W. Bergen) r 27, blacksmith.
Marion Thomas, blacksmith, Lake, h Rochester st.
Marshall Mary Ann, (Stone Church) r 33, widow of D. Bishop.
Marshall Robert, butcher, h Rochester st.
Matthewson Perry J., painter, h Clinton.
McCall Alexander, (N. Bergen) r 1, farmer 60.

McConnell Joseph D., r 17, farmer with Joseph L.
McConnell Joseph L., r 17, farmer 170.
McConnell Judson, r 14, farmer 153.
McDonald Laughlin, r 7, buttermaker.
McGuire James, r 11, farmer 60.
McGuire John, (W. Bergen) r 27.
McKENZIE JAMES R., contractor and builder, owns in Riga, Monroe Co., farm 104, h Clinton.
McLean Laughlin, r 7, farmer 5.
McPartland Peter, section boss West Shore R. R., h Rochester st.
McPartland Philip, laborer, h Rochester st.
McPhail John, (Stone Church) r 40, carpenter.
McPHERSON D. & SON, (Daniel J.) dealers in grain, produce, and coal, Lake cor. Yates.
McPHERSON DANIEL J., (D. McPherson & Son) h McKenzie.
McPHERSON DONALD, (D. McPherson & Son) h Lake.
McShaen James, r 32, mason.
McShaen John, r 32, laborer.
McVean Margaret, (Stone Church) r 40, widow of John, resident.
Meek Martin, r 7, farmer 85.
MERRILL FRANK M., printer and ex-postmaster, h Lake.
Meyers De Witt C., r 19, farmer, leases of Horace Southworth 114.
Miller Daniel S., r 8, farmer 40.
Miller Edwin S., r 20, dealer in produce, h Main.
Miller Ella S., (Mrs. Lewis J.) dressmaker, h Lake.
MILLER JAMES, farmer 46½, h Lake.
MILLER JAMES A., carriage manuf., h Rochester st.
MILLER LEWIS J., manuf. of carriages, sleighs, cutters, etc., h Lake.
MILLER ORVILLE J., prop. brass foundry, machinist, manuf. of small stationary engines, brass force-pumps, engine supplies, etc., bds. Rochester st.
Miller Sarah, widow of William H., h Le Roy st.
Miller Willard, r 7, farmer 45½.
Moore Matthew, r 33, farmer 57.
MORTON BROTHERS, (William and Thomas) merchant tailors and dealers in ready-made clothing, Lake.
MORTON THOMAS, (Morton Brothers) bds. Rochester st.
MORTON WILLIAM, (Morton Brothers) h Rochester st.
MOSELY CHARLES F., station agent N. Y. C. & H. R. R. R., h Clinton.
Mull Gilbert C., farmer, h Rochester st.
Mullen Eugenia, widow of Harvey, h Lake.
Mullen George H., carpenter and joiner, h Lake.
Mulroney Michael, switchman N. Y. C. & H. R. R. R. R., h Le Roy st.
Munger Charles M., draughtsman and paperhanger, h Lake.
Munger Elbert Mrs., r 33, farmer 50.
Munger James B., r 17, farmer, leases the estate of Elbert 50.
Munger Palmer W., (N. Bergen) r 1, retired lumber dealer.
Munger William P., broker and retired farmer 65, h Lake.
Murray Elwood D., physician and surgeon, h Rochester st.
Neal William, (N. Bergen) r 12, farmer 51½.
Neal William C., (N. Bergen) r 12, farmer 90.
Nolan John, laborer, h Gibson.
Oathout Charles E., r 32, (Oathout & Gage).
Oathout & Gage, (Charles E. O. and Howard L. G.) dealers in hardware, tinware, stoves, paints, oils, glass, etc., Lake.
O'Brian Catharine, widow of Patrick, h Clinton.
O'Brian Joanna, widow of James, h Rochester st.
O'Brian William, laborer, h Rochester st.
O'Brien John, prop. saloon, Tully block, h Lake.
Osgood Lorenzo, laborer, h Church.

O'Hara John, laborer, h Lake.
Palmer Robert, r 21, farmer for James Miller.
Palmer William, r 21, farmer 12.
Parish George, farmer, h McKenzie.
Parish Hudson B., farmer in Monroe Co. 26, h Buffalo st.
PARKER SYLVESTER E., justice of the peace farmer 150, h Lake.
PARMELEE BROTHERS, (Edward H. and Myron H.) dealers in flour and feed,
     Lake.
PARMELEE EDWARD H., (Parmelee Brothers) justice of the peace and asst.
     postmaster, h Main.
Pamelee Elbert W., (Stone Church) r 33, carpenter.
PAMELEE MYRON H., (Parmelee Brothers) postmaster, h Lake.
Peachey James, r 9, farmer 101.
Peachy James, off r 11, farmer 60.
Peck Daniel G., stock broker and farmer in Bergen 26, and in Pembroke 106, h.
     Clinton.
Peck Elmer, tinsmith, h Buffalo st.
Peck George W., r 25, farmer 80.
Peters John W., r 8, farmer with Marion.
Peters Marion, r 8, farmer 45.
Phelps Truman J., (N. Bergen) r 1, mail carrier.
Pierce George A., r 9, farmer, leases of George Loveridge, of Rochester, 96.
Potter Reuben J., (N. Bergen) r 1, carpenter.
Pridmore Thomas, (N. Bergen) r 3, farmer 83.
Pridmore Thomas E., (N. Bergen) r 2, laborer.
Primmer Elizabeth, (Mr. G. C.) dealer in confectionery, bread, etc., Lake, h Buffalo st.
Randall Howard, r 9, farmer 21.
RANDALL WILLIAM A., r 8, dealer in Bradley's standard fertilizer, farmer 160.
Randolph William H., cooper and florist, Gibson cor. Lake, h Gibson.
Reardon Edward, baggagemaster N. Y. C. & H. R. R. R., h Richmond.
Reardon Mary, widow of James, h Richmond.
Reardon Michael, laborer, h Le Roy st.
REED CHARLES N., (N. Bergen) r 1, farmer 125.
Reed Sarah, (N. Bergen) r 1, widow of S. Hale, farmer 50.
Reynolds George, r 29, farmer 33.
Reynolds William H., r 31, carpenter and joiner, farmer 36.
Richards Ira D., retired physician, h Lake.
Richards John H., retired farmer, h Lake.
Richardson Avery, r 10, farmer 60.
Richmond Cynthia, widow of Samuel, h Rochester st.
Richmond Loren, (W. Bergen) r 35, farmer 30.
Richmond Van R., painter, h Rochester st.
Riley Daniel, retired, h Rochester st.
Robbins Robert, farmer, h Gibson.
Roberts Achsah Miss, r 32, resident.
Roberts Joseph, (N. Bergen) carpenter and joiner.
Rogers Arthur P., r 24, farmer, leases of Cynthia Parish 120.
Rohr Charles, r 14, laborer.
Ross John A., wagonmaker, Davy block, h Clinton.
Rutter Lindley C., (N. Bergen) r 1½, clergyman.
Ryan Michael, laborer, h Richmond.
Sackett Alonzo, r 18, farmer 65.
Sackett Burt A., r 10, farmer with Edmund.
Sackett Edmund, r 10, farmer 65.
Sackett George W., engineer, h Buffalo st.
Sage Monroe W., professor of music, h Lake.
Sands Addison, prop. meat market and farm 115, h Buffalo st.
Sands George, r 18, farmer 87.
Sands Mary, r 12, widow of Thomas, farmer 200.

Sands William, r 14, farmer 65, and leases of Addison 160.
Sands William, Jr., (N. Bergen) farmer 40.
Sanford Marquis L., (N. Bergen) r 2, farmer 3.
Sawtelle Martha, (N. Bergen) r 2, widow of Hulburt, h and 1¼ acres.
Seely Chester, r 33, farmer 5.
Seely Eugene, r 33, laborer.
SEELY HOMER, r 33, farmer 105.
Seely Josiah W., r 33, farmer 10½.
SEELY MAURICE, (Stone Church) r 40, postmaster and dealer in groceries.
Shamp Cyrenus, (W. Bergen) r 25, laborer.
Shamp Lewellyn, r 33, laborer.
Shattuck Eugene, (N. Bergen) r 5, farmer 13.
Shaw Charles, r 9, farmer, leases of William Dart, of Keysport, Pa., 33.
Shepard Sophia C., widow of Ezra S., h Lake.
Sheriden James, r 30, laborer.
Sheriden John, r 31, farmer 10.
Shultz John, (W. Bergen) r 29, laborer, h and lot.
Shultz William, r 8, laborer.
Smith Frank, farmer, leases the Samuel Smith estate, 102.
Smith George D., r 31, farmer 30.
Smith J. Albert, pastor M. E. Church, h Lake.
Smith John R., r 20, farmer 60.
Smith Mary, r 18, widow of Samuel, farmer 100.
Snyder David, r 31, farmer.
Snyder Edward, farmer, leases of Mrs. ——— Field 71½.
Snyder Eugene D., r 21, farmer with Philip.
Snyder George, hop grower and farmer 49.
Snyder Harriet, r 31, farmer 15.
Snyder John J., carriage painter, Davy block, h Munger.
Snyder Philip, r 21, farmer 166.
SOUTHWORTH ANDREW T., prop. Southworth block, erected in 1881, h Buffalo st.
Southworth Horace, retired farmer 137, h Lake.
Southworth Wheaton, r 19, farmer 42.
Spafford Jerome H., r 16, farmer 90.
Speed George, (W. Bergen) r 25, farmer, leases of Frank Weeks 180.
Spencer Seymour E., retired, h Buffalo st.
Steedman James, r 35, laborer.
Stevens Albertus, (Stone Church) r 40, laborer.
Stevens Alvah, (Stone Church) r 38, farmer 114.
Stevens Ellsworth, farmer 112, h Dibble.
Stevens Ellsworth T., r 39, farmer 220.
Stevens Harmon L., retired farmer, h Rochester st.
Stevens Orson, (Stone Church) farmer 2.
Stevens Millard, (Stone Church) r 39, farmer 50.
Steves Caleb L., r 32, mason.
St. George Michael, farmer 4, h Church.
STOVER DANFORD, r 32, retired farmer.
Stratton Edward, station agent W. S. R. R., bds. Munger.
STRATTON JAY W., justice of the peace, real estate, ins., and collecting agent., h Munger.
Stuart Adam M., r 23, butcher.
Templeton James M., (N. Bergen) r 2, farmer 75.
Thomas Charles, r 19, farmer 67.
Thompson Orange, laborer, h Munger.
TONE THOMAS J., grain and coal dealer, prop. elevator, Church, h Lake.
Townsend E., physician and surgeon, bds. Clinton.
TOWNSEND M. W., physician and surgeon, h Clinton.
TULLEY SAMUEL C., prop. Tully block, erected in 1886, dealer in hardware, stoves, tin, sheet iron, paints, oils, glass, etc., Lake cor. Buffalo sts., h Rochester st.

Van Sickle Fayette, r 24, farmer, leases of Effie A. Loomis 60.
Van Sickle Gerritt, farmer 52, h Munger.
Walker Benjamin N., r 7, manager Cold Spring creamery, farmer 40.
WALKER HOUSE, William C. Walker, prop. Lake cor. Rochester sts.
Walker Uriah, r 7, farmer 60.
WALKER WILLIAM C., prop. Walker House and livery stable, Lake cor. Roches-
    ter sts.
WARD DIANTHA S., widow of Abner, bds. Lake.
Ward Edward, (Stone Church) r 33, carpenter.
Ward Howard, r 24, farmer, leases of Mrs. Amanda F. Field 60.
Warren Alva Nathaniel, (N. Bergen) r 5, farmer 70.
Warren Charles E., (N. Bergen) r 5, farmer with Nathaniel.
Weber Peter, basket manuf., Buffalo st., h do.
Weeks Frank S., r 27, farmer 180.
Welch John F., r 33, farmer 52¾.
Whalen James, track hand.
Whelden James, mason, h Richmond.
Whitaker George E., dealer in produce, h Lake.
Whitaker Wealthy Ann, widow of Thomas, h Lake.
White Herbert S., r 21, farmer with Morse.
White Morse, r 21, farmer 105.
White Shipman, r 21, painter and farmer 20.
Wiard Charles T., r 32, butcher.
Wilbur Albert E., laborer, h Rochester st.
Wilcox Charles S., (Stone Church) r 39, farmer 50.
WILCOX EDWIN M., r 33, farmer 144.
WILCOX ELEANOR, widow of Thomas J., dressmaker, h Lake.
Wilcox Eliphalet, r 24, farmer, leases of George B. Parish 150.
WILCOX HALSEY H., r 33, breeder of thoroughbred Merino sheep, farmer 200.
WILCOX J. SPENCER, r 33, farmer 84.
Wilcox Mary Miss, (Stone Church) r 39 farmer 86.
Wilkinson John O., (N. Bergen) laborer, h and ½ acre.
Wilson James, r 10, farmer, leases of John Mulholland 120.
Wilson John, r 11, farmer 60.
Wilson John, Jr., farmer 58.
Winegar William, upholsterer, h Lake.
Wingard Cornelia, (N. Byron) r 5, widow, farmer 20.
Wood Edwards, (Stone Church) r 33, farmer 74.
Wood Frank D., r 24, farmer, leases of L. D. Arnold 90.
Wood George, r 33, laborer, h and 2 acres.
Wood Isaac, r 11, farmer 100.
Wood James S., retired farmer.
Wood Mary, widow of Nathan S., h Clinton.
Woods Frank, farmer, leases of L. D. Arnold.
Woods George, laborer.
Woodworth John, dealer in reapers and mowers, h Rochester st.
Worboys Fred, (N. Bergen) machinist and machine agent.
WRIGHT NELSON D., retired farmer, h Rochester st.
Wright Selah, (W. Bergen) r 35, farmer 50.
Youngers Frank, (N. Bergen) r 1, farmer 44.

BETHANY.

(For explanations, etc., see page 3, part second.)

(Postoffice address is Bethany, unless otherwise designated in parenthesis.)

Agar Arthur, (W. Linden) r 41, farmer with his father, William.
Agar William, (Linden) r 41, farmer, leases of Jared D. Richards, of Alexander, 100.
Albright Charles, (Linden) r 30, laborer and farmer 16.
Andrews Herbert, (Pavilion) r 36 cor. 37, 500 apple trees, farmer 80.
Andrews Herbert, Jr., (Pavilion) r 36 cor. 37, farmer with his father, Herbert.
Annabel Russel H., (Linden) r 40, farmer 100.
Annabel Mercy P., (Linden) widow of Charles B., bds. W. Main.
Armbrewster Ezra, (Linden) r 4, section hand D., L. & W. R.R., hand lot.
Armbrewster Frances H., (Linden) r 31, widow of Martin, farmer 31¼.
ARMBREWSTER FRANK, (Linden) r 31, farmer with his mother, Frances.
Armbrewster Fred, (Linden) r 31, farmer with his mother, Frances.
Avery Spencer C., (Linden) r 31, retired farmer, 109.
Bacon Charles W. Rev., (E. Bethany) r 6, pastor Free Methodist Church.
BAKER THOMAS S., (Pavilion) r 36, 500 pear trees, 300 apple trees, farmer 120.
Baldwin Alta M., (W. Bethany) r 29, widow of William D., aged 78.
Baldwin John S., (W. Bethany) r 29, breeder of grade Cotswold sheep, farmer 104.
Barross James C., (Linden) r 43, breeder of grade Merino sheep, farmer 74.
BARROWS CHARLES C., (Linden) r 32, carpenter, breeder of Percheron horses, farmer 71.
Barrows George N., (Linden) r 32, farmer 32.
BARROWS SEXTURS T., (Linden) farmer 25, h Batavia st.
Bassert Louis, (E. Bethany) r 22, laborer.
BASSERT MARK, (E. Bethany) r 22, retired farmer, served in Co. G, 8th H. A. N. Y. Vols., h and lot.
Beckwith Charles, r 26 cor. 27¼, 800 pear trees, farmer 136.
Beckwith Esther M., (Batavia) r 5, widow of Henry J., farm 130.
Bednark George, (E. Bethany) off r 23, laborer.
BENINGTON JOHN R., (Batavia) r 2, farmer, supt. of the James H. Hume farm, 411.
Berry Ernest C., (Linden) r 31½, laborer, h and lot.
Bigelow Fayette S., (Linden) notary public and farmer 93, h and 4 acres E. Main.
Blair William J., (Linden) section hand N. Y., L. E. & W. R. R., h and lot W. Main.
Blood Ella M. Miss, (Linden) r 42, school teacher.
Blood Eunice E. Miss, (Linden) r 43, school teacher.
BLOOD OSCAR W., (Linden) r 45, breeder of thoroughbred Merino sheep, 500 apple and pear trees, farmer 135.
Blood Sally, (Linden) r 42, widow of Nelson.
Blood N. Wallace, (Linden) r 42, farmer for his mother, Sally.
Bolt Nicholas R., (Stafford) r 9, retired farmer 40, and in Stafford 152.
Bolt Thomas, (Stafford) r 9, farmer for his father, Nicholas R.
BOOTH FRED A., (Linden) r 45, farmer, leases of John Conway 63.
Bower Henry P., (Linden) r 30, farmer, leases on shares of J. C. Shepard 100.
Bower Philip, (Linden) r 30 cor. 47, foreman for Sewell Chaddock, farmer 241, and in Wyoming Co. 59.
BOYLE JOHN, r 15 cor. 15½, fruit grower and farmer for his wife 23.
Bradfield Andrew, (Batavia) r 1, laborer.
Bradfield Emra, (Batavia) r 1 cor. 1½, foreman for Hobert B. Cone, of Batavia, farmer 125.
Brainard Seymour, r 35, resident.
Brest Henry, (E. Bethany) r 23, laborer and farmer, leases on shares of Jerome French 40.

6*

Brice James, (Batavia) r 1½, carpenter and laborer, h and 3 acres.
Brierley Charles S., (E. Bethany) r 16, breeder of pure blood Poland China swine, farmer 96.
Brown Benjamin R., (W. Bethany) r 19 cor. 27, farmer 72.
BROWN SOPHIA A., (W. Bethany) r 19 cor. 27, widow of Heman, Jr., aged 80, pensioner of the War of 1812.
BROWN WALTER, (W. Bethany) r 19, dealer and farmer 81.
BROWN WILDER, (W. Bethany) r 19, carpenter and farmer 80.
Budd William, r 34 cor. 26, blacksmith and farmer 82½.
Budge John S., (W. Bethany) r 28 retired farmer, h and 1 acre.
BURPEL JOHN, (Batavia) r 6, fruit grower, breeder of Jersey cattle, farmer 20.
Burks Philip G., (Wyoming, Wyoming Co.) r 37, breeder of grade sheep, farmer 130.
Burks Wakefield, (Wyoming, Wyoming Co.) r 37, farmer with his father, Philip G.
BURNS JAMES, (E. Bethany) r 14, section hand D., L. & W. R. R., h and lot.
Burns Patrick, (E. Bethany) r 15, laborer, 2 houses and lots.
Burst Irving J., (Linden) r 31, laborer, farm 30.
Burst Jacob, (Linden) r 31, shoemaker and butcher, h and lot.
Burt George C., r 21, farmer 102.
Burt Lettice, r 21, widow of Benjamin.
CACNER GEORGE, r 20, butcher and farmer 35.
Camp James M., (Linden) r 40, farmer 14.
CANNON PATRICK H., Sr, (E. Bethany) r 22, farmer, leases of Issaber Cameron 105.
Cannon Patrick H., Jr., (E. Bethany) r 22, laborer.
Carson George G., (W. Bethany) r 18, farmer with his father, William.
Carson James A., r 34, laborer, h and 7½ acres.
Carson Robert C., r 34, laborer.
Carson William, (W. Bethany) r 18, 9 cows, farmer 166.
Chaddock Ira J., r 16, 1,000 dwarf pear trees, 400 apple trees, farmer 64.
CHADWICK J. EDWARD, r 34, ins. agent.
Chadwick Joseph H., r 34, farmer 67.
Chapman Harvey M., r 41, farmer 37½.
Churchill Alice N. Miss, (Linden) r 35, school teacher.
Churchill Catherine, (E. Bethany) r 7, widow of George L., fruit grower, farmer 60, and in Stafford 20.
Churchill Frank C., (Linden) r 35, farmer, leases of Alma Stevens 100.
Churchill George, (E. Bethany) r 7, farmer for his mother, Catherine.
Churchill Nathaniel H., (E. Bethany) r 7, farmer for his mother, Catherine.
Churchill William C., (Linden) r 25, retired farmer.
Clapsaddle John F., (Batavia) r 7½, 530 pear, plum, and apple trees, 450 grape vines, farmer 40.
Clark Michael, (Stafford) r 8, 200 pear trees, 900 apple trees, farmer 110.
Clark Milo, (Stafford) r 9, prop. Percheron stock horse "Emmitt," No. 870, reg., breeder of Durham cattle and Southdown sheep, fruit grower, farmer 106¾.
Clark Stephen, (Stafford) r 8, school teacher and farmer.
Clark Walter, (E. Bethany) off r 22½ cor. 22, blacksmith and farmer 25½.
Clement Fred W., (W. Bethany) r 19, breeder of grade Merino sheep and Percheron horses, farmer 84.
COLTAX JOHN, (Batavia) r 14, laborer.
Cone Charles H., r 5, farmer 27, and for his wife, Mary Ann, 35.
Cone Charles S., r 34, retired farmer, aged 91, h and 2 acres.
Cone Charles W., r 34, poormaster and farmer 70.
Cone Melvin H., r 5, laborer.
Considine Larry, (Batavia) r 4, retired farmer.
Considine Patrick, (Batavia) r 4, farmer 61.
Considine Thomas, (Batavia) off r 4, farmer 30.
Conway James, (Linden) r 45, section boss N. Y., L. E. & W. R. R., farmer 63.
COPELAND JOHN, r 34, breeder of grade Jersey cattle and Hambletonian horses, farmer 111½.

Copeland Stewart, r 34, retired farmer.

COPELAND STEWART, Jr., r 34, 3,000 apple trees, breeder of Henry Clay and Black Hawk horses, farmer 103.

Cotton John P., (Batavia) r 4½ cor. 4, laborer.

COVEY FRANK H., (Batavia) r 5, 1,000 apple trees, 1,000 pear trees, 200 peach trees, breeder of grade Jersey cattle, farmer 186.

CRAWFORD JOSEPH, (W. Bethany) r 29, postmaster, prop. grist-mill, grocer, and farmer 13.

Crawford William M., (W. Bethany) r 17 cor. 19, small fruit grower, apiarist, and farmer 77.

Crocker Angeline, (E. Bethany) r 14 cor. 22, widow of Charles, prop. East Bethany Hotel.

Croff Ganson W., r 21 cor. 26, physician and surgeon, farm 72.

CROFF ORLANDO R., r 34 cor. 25, postmaster, physician and surgeon, farmer 437, in Attica, Wyoming Co., 80, and in Nebraska 320, h and 1 acre.

Croff Orlando R., r 21 cor. 26, school teacher.

Curren John, r 27½, laborer.

CURTIS DANIEL S., (E. Bethany) r 14, miller and sawyer, prop. grist-mill, h and lot.

Cutcliffe Edward, (E. Bethany) r 13, blacksmith, patentee of a cultivator tooth, h and lot.

Darrow Henry F., (E. Bethany) r 11 cor. 10, farmer, leases of the Deshon estate 150.

Dauchy George, (Pavilion) r 36, breeder of grade Merino sheep and Durham cattle, 500 dwarf Dutchess pear trees, farmer 120.

Dauchy Grove W., (Pavilion) r 36, farmer with his father, George.

Deming William H., r 21, farmer 25.

Dixon Charles A., (E. Bethany) r 14 cor. 15, laborer.

DIXON SOPHIA, (E. Bethany) r 23, widow of William R., farmer on the Dixon estate 254.

Dixon W. Walter, (E. Bethany) r 23, farmer for his mother, Sophia.

Dohse Charles, (Linden) r 30, farmer with his father, Loies.

Dohse John C., (Linden) r 30, laborer.

Dohse Loies, (Linden) r 30, farmer 105.

Downing Philetus R., (W. Bethany) r 26, farmer 37.

Durgy Lucius C., (Linden) retired merchant, h and lot E. Main.

Dutton Walter H., (E. Bethany) r 24, farmer 100.

Dye George E., (W. Bethany) r 19 cor. 27, laborer.

DYE SAMUEL H., (W. Bethany) r 20, small fruit grower and farmer 22½.

Dye Sarah, (W. Bethany) r 20, widow of Samuel.

East Bethany Hotel, (E. Bethany) r 14 cor. 22, Angeline Crocker, prop.

Eastland Lewis, r 40, farmer, leases on shares of R. 90.

EDWARDS CHARLES D., (Batavia) r 3, 20 cows, 500 apple trees, farmer 183¾.

Edwards Sheridan, (Batavia) r 3, farmer with his father, Charles D.

Elliott Mary W., (Batavia) r 6, widow of Rev. Jesse.

ELLIOTT S. WILLIS, (Batavia) r 6, school teacher and farmer on the Elliott estate 70.

ELLISON NELSON C., (W. Bethany) r 28, breeder of Jersey cattle, farmer, leases of J. H. Campbell 103½.

Elsaser John E., (E. Bethany) r 22½, farmer 9¼.

Empie Jacob F., (E. Bethany) r 36¼, retired farmer.

Empie John C., (E. Bethany) r 36½, breeder of Leicester and Cotswold sheep, dealer in horses, farmer 106.

Fales Eunice, r 5, widow of Anson, aged 72.

Fancher Albert, (Linden) r 35, breeder of grade Merino sheep, farmer, leases on shares of James Stewart 120.

Farnsworth Abbie, (E. Bethany) r 14, widow of David, h and lot.

Fellows Cynthia, (Linden) r 27½, widow of Horatio D., h and lot.

FILKINS JEROME H., r 21, constable and farmer 4½.

Fleming George A., (Wyoming, Wyoming Co.) r 35, farmer with his father, Loren.

Fleming Loren, (Wyoming, Wyoming Co.) r 35, breeder of grade Merino sheep, farmer 160.

FOLK CASPER, (E. Bethany) r 14 cor. 13, farmer 96, and leases of F. C. Bissell, of Le Roy, 300.

Ford Charles H., (E Bethany) r 12, farmer, leases on shares of George 116.

Ford George, (E. Bethany) r 12, retired farmer 116.

Ford John, (E. Bethany) r 7, carpenter and farmer 160.

Ford William, (E. Bethany) r 15, farmer, leases of Aba Paul, of Le Roy, 200.

Fox Dominick, r 22, farmer, h and 2 acres.

Francis Dennis J., (Batavia) r 11, farmer.

Francis Patrick, (Batavia) r 4, farmer 130.

Francis Patrick, Jr., (Batavia) r 4, section hand D., L. & W. R. R., farmer 20.

FRENCH W. CARY, r 35, 115 pear trees, farmer 125.

Frolicker Catherine, (E. Bethany) r 15 cor. 16, h and 6 acres.

Fuller Hannah, (Linden) r 44½ cor. 43, widow of Thomas, h and lot.

Furse James J., (Linden) blacksmith and horseshoer, E. Main, h do.

Gardner Edmund P., (W. Bethany) r 20, farmer, leases of his father, Rolland, 55.

Gardner Rolland, (W. Bethany) r 20, retired farmer 55.

GARTNER JACOB, (Linden) r 31, farmer 40.

Genesee County Alms-House, (Linden) r 41 cor. 40, capacity 100 inmates, farm 300; supts.: Cortland Crossman, Alexander; Dwight Dimmock, Pembroke; Henry O. Bostwick, Batavia; keeper, Benjamin W. Hartwell, Pavilion; physician, Ganson W. Croff, Bethany.

Gibbons Miles, (Batavia) r 4, farmer 100.

Gifford Caleb T., (E. Bethany) r 22 cor. 22½, retired farmer.

GIFFORD JAMES H., (E. Bethany) r 22 cor. 22⅞, supervisor, 150 pear trees, farmer 75.

GILLARD WALTER A., (E. Bethany) r 7 cor. 6, farmer 30.

Glasser John, (E. Bethany) r 10, farmer, leases of John Simmons 100.

GRANGER BYRON, (E. Bethany) r 5, carpenter and farmer, served in Co. A, 1st Dist. Columbia Cav. Vols., h and 5 acres.

Granger Sanford B., (E. Bethany) r 5, laborer.

Gray Martin, (Batavia) r 1½, (M. Gray & Son, of Alexander) manuf. of headings, staves, etc., h and 4½ acres.

Grile John, (Linden) r 31, farmer 70.

Grover Hiram A., r 34, laborer.

Guymer Robert, (E. Bethany) r 22, harnessmaker and repairer, apiarist 60 colonies, h and lot.

Haffley Fred, (Batavia) r 3, laborer, h and lot.

Hamilton Benjamin F., (Batavia) r 4, 400 pear trees, 1,000 apple trees, farmer 70.

Hamilton Fred W., r 5, 700 pear trees, 200 apple trees, breeder of grade Merino sheep, farmer 100.

Harding Achsah Miss, r 21, (Achsah & Julia M. Harding).

Harding Achsah & Julia M., r 21, farmers on the Harding estate 134.

HARDING ERASTUS D., r 21, retired farmer 118.

Harding Herbert H., r 21, farmer, leases of his father, Erastus D., 118.

Harding Julia M., r 21, (Achsah & Julia M. Harding).

Harding Thomas J., r 21, (old Huggins's hotel) farmer 184.

HARPER CHARLES W., (E. Bethany) r 24, carpenter and joiner, owns h and lot 150 Bank st., Batavia.

Harrington Ezekiel B., (Linden) r 45 cor. 30, blacksmith and farmer 40.

Harris Calvin J., (W. Bethany) r 18, breeder of Hambletonian and Percheron horses, farmer, leases of Daniel 260.

Harris Daniel, (W. Bethany) retired farmer 180.

Harris Mary E., (W. Bethany) (Mrs. Daniel) farmer 80.

Hart Charles E., (Linden) r 40, locomotive engineer and farmer 78½.

Hart Thurman A., (Linden) r 40, farmer, leases of Dr. O. R. Croff 108.

Harttle Joseph, (Stafford) r 8, laborer.

Hartwell Benjamin W., (Linden) r 41 cor. 40, farmer and keeper Genesee County Alms-House.

Heal Ephraim, (Batavia) r 4, farmer 100.
Hebel Henry, (Batavia) r 2, laborer.
Hill Homer H., r 34, farmer 84.
Hill Peletiah, r 34, farmer 64.
Hill Rolla H., r 34, student Genesee Normal School.
Hillman Thomas, (E. Bethany) r 12, fruit grower and farmer 81.
Hockey John, (Linden) section hand N. Y., L. E. & W. R. R., h and lot E. Main.
Holly Mary C. Miss, (W. Bethany) r 29, h and lot.
Howard Aaron E., (Linden) dealer in dry goods, groceries, crockery, hardware, boots,
    and shoes, owns farm in Attica, Wyoming Co., 55, h and lot Main.
Howard Jonathan, M. D., (Linden) eclectic physician, E. Main, h and lot do.
Howden Judson, (Linden) r 44½, farmer, leases of the Cornell estate 80·
Howes George M., r 34, breeder of pure blood Merino sheep, farmer, leases of C. G.
    Jenne 116.
Hoxie Cary E., (W. Bethany) r 20, school teacher, apiarist 35 colonies, farmer 34.
Hoxie Joseph, (W. Bethany) off r 20, farmer 34.
HOYLE CORDELIA, (W. Bethany) r 29, widow of Thomas, owns the Lounsbury es-
    tate 73.
Huggins Carlos A., r 21 cor. 25, deputy postmaster, dealer in dry goods, groceries, boots,
    and shoes, h and lot.
Huggins Harvey H., r 16, 200 pear trees, 110 apple trees, farmer 90.
Hunt Charles, (E. Bethany) r 36½, farmer, h and 9 acres.
Huntington Charles A., (Linden) retired farmer and dealer in fertilizers, h and 14 acres,
    W. Main.
HYDE EDWIN J., (W. Bethany) r 28, teacher of vocal music, farmer 175.
Jasper John C., (E. Bethany) r 15 cor. 16, laborer, leases of Catherine Frolicker h and
    6 acres.
Jeislar Joseph, (Batavia) r 2, laborer.
Jenne Charles G., r 34, speculator and farmer 118.
JENNE WILLIAM N., r 34, farmer 100.
Jensen Nesse C., (Linden) r 30, farmer 12½, and in Alexander 6½.
Jolls Mary, (Linden) widow of Simeon L., aged 81, h and lot W. Main.
JONES JOSEPH T., (E. Bethany) r 14, laborer.
JUDD FRANKLIN I., r 21, live stock dealer, farmer 153, and leases of his father, Is-
    rael E., 216.
Judd Israel E., r 21, retired farmer 216.
Judd Oscar D., (W. Bethany) farmer, leases on shares of George South 109.
Kelley John, (W. Bethany) r 4, section boss D., L. & W. R. R.
Kelly Mary, (W. Bethany) r 4, widow of John.
Kelly Mary A., (E. Bethany) r 14, widow of Michael L., farmer for her son 96½.
Kelly Thomas M., (E. Bethany) r 14, farmer.
Kelsey De Forrest, (Alexander) r 4, farmer, leases of the Ashel Shepard estate 100.
Kemp John B., (E. Bethany) r 6, laborer.
KEMP MYRON J., (Linden) retired farmer, owns in Wyoming Co. 178, h and 3 acres
    E. Main.
Kemp William E., (Linden) produce dealer, W. Main, h and lot do.
Kendall Dwight B., (E. Bethany) r 14, horse trainer, h and lot.
Kimball Charles N., (Linden) carpenter and builder, h and lot Batavia st.
Kimball Charles W., (Linden) r 43, farmer 56.
Kimball Willis, (Linden) laborer, bds. E. Main.
Kinney Stephen, r 26, farmer, leases of Dr. O. R. Croff 135.
Knowlton Harriet L., r 5, widow of David K., 300 pear trees, 250 apple trees, farmer
    70.
Lacy Morris, (Pavilion) off r 38, fruit grower and farmer 45.
Lacy Patrick, (Pavilion) off r 38, resident, aged 75.
Lambkins John, (Batavia) r 18, farmer, leases of Dr. O. R. Croff 100.
Lawrey John, (Linden) blacksmith, E. Main, h and lot do.
Lawton Joseph F., (Batavia) r 3, farmer 107.
Lawton William H., (Batavia) r 1, laborer.

Legg Cassius C., (Batavia) r 5, invalid, farm foreman for James Lewis, of Batavia, 60.
LEITZ FREDERICK, (Linden) r 35, pensioner and farmer, served in Co. E, 136th Inf.
    N. Y. Vols., h and 3 acres.
LENT GEORGE V. N., r 16, 1,700 dwarf pear trees, farmer, leases of the Henry
    Dixon estate 124½.
Lincoln Florence M. Miss, (W. Bethany) off r 20, school teacher.
LINCOLN HARRY T., (W. Bethany) off r 20, farmer with his mother, M. Jennie.
Lincoln John S. Prof., (W. Bethany) off r 20, school teacher.
Lincoln M. Jennie, (W. Bethany) off r 20, widow of Charles, 300 pear trees, farmer
    145.
Lincoln Theron L., (Stafford) r 9, breeder of Clydesdale horses, farmer 54.
LORD HATTIE C. Miss, (Linden) h and lot W. Main.
LORD J. S. Mrs., (Linden) r 27½, breeder of Wyandotte and Java fowls, apiarist 33
    colonies.
Lord James S., (Linden) r 27½, fruit tree jobber, breeder of Jersey cattle, farmer 15.
Lord Mary W., (W. Bethany) r 28, widow of Alanson D.
LOUNSBURY EDWIN, (W. Bethany) breeder of grade Cotswold sheep, farmer 124.
Lounsbury Thomas E., (W. Bethany) farmer with his father, Edwin.
Lowell Daniel, (Linden) r 45, laborer, h and lot.
Lyon Asa J., r 20, laborer, h and 4 acres.
Lyon George W., r 20, with his son, Asa J.
Markley John, r 27½, retired farmer 102½.
Marsh Almira, r 30, farmer 25.
Marsh Delos, (Batavia) r 4, breeder of Clydesdale horses, farmer 96.
Marsh Orlando, (Batavia) r 4, 100 pear trees, 150 apple trees, farmer 100.
Marsh Rose D., (E. Bethany) r 23 cor. 25, widow of Lewis J., asst. postmaster and
    general merchant.
Marsh Truman P., r 30, prop. steam thresher, farmer 40.
Martin Alva A., r 34, laborer.
Martin Norman B., (E. Bethany) r 6 cor. 7, local preacher and laborer, h and lot.
Mayne Thomas, (Stafford) r 5, breeder of grade Cotswold sheep, fruit grower, farmer
    109.
McCumber Austin, r 21 cor. 22, fruit grower, farmer, leases of Charles Rumsey 112.
McIntyre James P., (Linden) r 41, laborer.
McLernon John, (E. Bethany) r 14, section boss D., L. & W. R. R.
McPherson Fred P., (Linden) r 27½, farmer 44.
McTarnaghan Alexander, (Batavia) r 5, fruit grower, farmer 55.
Merritt Daniel B., (Linden) cooper, prop. cider-mill, h and 6 acres Batavia st.
Merritt David, r 21. breeder of Jersey cattle and dealer in horses, farmer 79½.
Merritt George T., (Linden) farmer 74, and in Alexander timber land 10
Metcalf John, (Linden) r 31, ropemaker and farmer 16½.
Metzler William, (E. Bethany) r 5, farmer, leases of Willis Trick 69½.
Michael George, (Linden) section hand N. Y., L. E. & W. R. R.,h and lot W. Main.
MILLERICK ANN, r 34, widow of James, farmer, leases of W. R. Odell 125.
Millerick Richard, r 34, farmer for his mother, Ann.
Mills Thomas W., (E. Bethany) off r 23, laborer.
Mitchel George E., (Batavia) r 5, farmer, leases on shares of Sophronia F. 51¼.
Mitchel Sophronia F., (Batavia) r 5, widow of Daniel W.
Mix George J., r 25, mail carrier from Batavia to W. Bethany and Bethany Center.
Moran Henry, (Batavia) r 5, retired farmer 40.
Morford Polly, (Linden) widow of William, h and lot E. Main.
Morford William H., (Batavia) r 2, laborer.
Morris George A., (W. Bethany) r 4. farmer, leases of Mrs. Alvin Chaddock 130.
Mortimer William H., r 26, farmer, leases of Joseph Kuhn 86.
Mott Henry, (E. Bethany) r 22, thresher and farmer with his father, John.
Mott John, (E. Bethany) r 22, breeder of grade Merino sheep, prop. steam thresher,
    farmer 114.
Mott Lemuel I., (Linden) r 31, prop. steam thresher.
Mulcahy Richard, (Linden) r 31, farmer for his father, Thomas.

Mulcahy Thomas, (Linden) r 31, blind, retired farmer 30.
MULLEN ISAAC V., M. D., (Alexander) r 29, also office in Alexander village.
MUNGER LUIN L., (W. Bethany) r 28, retired farmer and pensioner, h and 3 acres, served in Co. E, 105th Inf. N. Y. Vols.
Muntz Anthony, (E. Bethany) r 7, section hand D., L. & W. R. R.
Nelan Maurice, (Wyoming, Wyoming Co.) r 39, dealer in agricultural implements and phosphate, farmer 127 and in Wyoming Co. 98.
Nelan Maurice, Jr., (Wyoming, Wyoming Co.) r 39, farmer with his father, Maurice.
Nichols Cyrus J., Sr., r 25, farmer with his son, Cyrus J., Jr.
Nichols Cyrus J., Jr., r 25, farmer, leases of F. I. Judd 97.
Nichols Freeling H., (E. Bethany) r 6, farmer 2½.
Nichols George W., (E. Bethany) r 11, farmer, leases on shares of P. L. Ashley 137.
Nichols Letty M., (E. Bethany) r 23, widow of Robert C., h and lot.
Norton Azro M., (W. Bethany) r 19, farmer 31.
Norton Charles A., r 25, fruit grower and farmer, leases of Elizabeth 110.
Norton Clarence J., (W. Bethany) r 19, farmer with his father, Azro M.
Norton Cyena, (Linden) widow of Ira, farm 11, and in Wyoming Co. 34, h E. Main.
Norton Elizabeth, r 21, widow of Benjamin F., farm 110, h and lot.
Norton Eugene B., (W. Bethany) r 19, laborer.
Norton Nancy P., (W. Bethany) r 4, widow of Tichnor P.
Norton Walter F., 2d, (Batavia) r 1, breeder of grade Southdown and Cotswold sheep, farmer 100.
NORTON WALTER FRANK, r 27, 310 pear trees, farmer 124.
Nott Francis E., r 21 cor. 20, farmer 18.
Nott Franklin J., r 5, carpenter, breeder of grade Jersey cattle, 400 apple trees, farmer on the J. W. Nott estate 60.
Nott Harriet B., r 5, widow of John W.
Odiorne Ella J. Miss. r 21, dressmaker.
O'Donnell Thomas, (Pavilion) r 38, fruit grower and farmer 45.
Page George A., (E. Bethany) off r 15, (George A. & Ransom I. Page).
Page George A. & Ransom I., (E. Bethany) off r 15, speculators, breeders of thoroughbred Merino sheep, farmers 176.
Page Ira J., r 5, 700 apple trees, farmer, leases of Esther M. Beckwith 130.
Page Ransom I., (E. Bethany) off r 15 (George A. & Ransom I. Page).
Page William S., r 25. live stock dealer, 3,500 pear trees, farmer 220.
Parish Melvin, (Linden) r 31, farmer, leases on shares of John Grile 70.
Parmenter Emel R., (Linden) house painter, h Batavia st.
Patous Christopher, (W. Bethany) r 28, farmer 18.
Patous Fred C., (W. Bethany) r 28, breeder of Percheron horses, farmer 70.
Patridge William A., (Pavilion) r 36, farmer, leases of Mrs. E. Wright 80.
Pearson Arthur, (E. Bethany) r 36, farmer with his father, Richard.
Pearson George, (E. Bethany) r 36, farmer with his father, Richard.
Pearson Richard, (E. Bethany) r 36, apple orchard 30 acres, farmer 269, and in Pavilion 10.
PECK BENJAMIN F., (E. Bethany) r 23, manuf. of drain tile, breeder of reg. Devon cattle and pure blood Merino sheep, fruit grower, apple orchard 30 acres, farmer 390.
Peck Esther C. Miss, (E. Bethany) r 14, farmer 12.
Peck Gilbert M., (E. Bethany) r 14, justice of the peace, retired farmer 223.
Peck Ida C., (E. Bethany) r 13, widow of William G., h and lot.
Peck Mary Miss, (E. Bethany) r 14, farmer 21.
Peck Richard, (E. Bethany) r 23, farmer for his father, Benjamin F.
Peck Robert C., r 25, farmer, leases on shares of S. Marvin 112.
PECK S. MARVIN, r 24 cor. 35, farmer 164.
Peck William G., (E. Bethany) r 13, postal clerk.
Peggs John C., r 34, farmer, leases of Dr. Ganson W. Croff 70.
Pelton Albin, r 21, farmer 97½.
Perry Alexander G., (Linden) prop. grist and saw-mill, off Batavia st., h and lot do.
Perry George, (Linden) miller and sawyer for his father, Alexander G.

Perry John F., (E. Bethany) r 22, shoemaker and prop. cider-mill, h and lot.
Perry Milford, (Linden) miller for his father, Alexander G., bds. Batavia st.
Perry William, (Linden) blacksmith, W. Main, h and lot do.
Pervorse Henry D., (Linden) sheep shearer and laborer, h and 2 acres Batavia st.
PERVORSE LESTER A., (Linden) laborer, bds. Batavia st.
Pervorse Orville H., (Linden) r 31, laborer, h and lot.
Phillips William, (E. Bethany) off r 13, stationary engineer, emp. D., L. & W. R. R. Co.
Pixley Charles B., (Linden) postmaster, dealer in groceries, candy, tobacco, and cigars,
    E. Main, h and lot do.
Pixley Edgar, (Linden) r 35, retired farmer 64.
Pixley Ellen A., (Linden) r 33 cor. 44½, widow of Willard J., h and lot.
Pixley Merritt E., (Linden) r 33 cor. 44, farmer 50.
Plucker Daniel M., (Pavilion) r 37, breeder of grade Merino sheep, farmer, leases on
    shares of the Wells estate 123½.
Porter Phebe G., (E. Bethany) r 7 cor. 6, widow of Hiram.
Powers Charles M., (Batavia) r 4, 150 apple trees, farmer 58.
Powers James H., (Pavilion) r 37, farmer for his mother, Julia A.
Powers Julia A., (Pavilion) r 37, widow of John, h and 10 acres.
PRESCOTT THOMAS, (E. Bethany) r 7, 600 pear and apple trees, farmer 100.
Price William, (Stafford) r 6, 350 pear and apple trees, farmer 30.
PUTNAM HARTSON O., (Batavia) r 1, farmer, leases of his father, Orrin, 100.
Putnam Julius D., (Batavia) r 3, farmer 47.
Putnam Lydia, (Batavia) r 3, widow of Josiah.
Putnam Merritt F., (Batavia) r 3, farmer, leases of the Josiah Putnam estate 97.
Putnam Orrin, (Batavia) r 3, retired farmer 100.
Radley George, (Stafford) r 9, farmer 55.
Ragan Elhanan L., (Batavia) r 1, 500 pear and apple trees, 15 cows, farmer 108.
Ramsey Daniel, (W. Bethany) r 4, farmer, leases of Nancy P. Norton 137½.
Ray Julius E., (E. Bethany) r 7, laborer.
Rich Mortimer J., (E. Bethany) r 22, section hand Lackawanna R. R., h and lot.
Richardson Elmer W., (Linden) clerk, bds. E. Main.
Richardson William H., (Linden) traveling dentist, h and lot Batavia st.
Richardson Henry, (Linden) dealer in dry goods, groceries, boots, shoes, proprietary
    medicines, tobacco, cigars, and coal, farm 40, W. Main, h and lot E. Main.
Rienholz Herman C., (Batavia) r 2, farmer 3, in Alexander 123, and in Batavia 40.
Riley John W., (E. Bethany) r 22½, laborer.
Robbins Frank J., r 35, apiarist 50 colonies, farmer 94.
Robinson Arnold B., (Batavia) r 4½, farmer, leases on shares of James M. Showerman
    90.
Rockwell Frederick, r 27 cor. 20, laborer.
Rockwell George, r 27 cor. 20, farmer, leases of Cynthia Jackson 35.
Rockwood Sarah E., r 21, widow of Alvin, farmer 46.
Roderick James M., (Linden) cooper and carpenter, h E. Main.
Rogers Byron J., r 25 cor. 22, breeder of grade Merino sheep, fruit grower, farmer
    105.
Rogers Matthew, (E. Bethany) r 24, fruit grower, farmer 24, and in Pavilion 100.
ROGERS WILLIAM E., r 24 retired farmer, aged 81.
Rudolph Daniel C., (E. Bethany) r 10, farmer, leases of Frank Prescott 116.
Rumsey Albert J., r 31, fruit grower, speculator, and farmer 96.
Russell C. Arthur, (Batavia) r 4, farmer for his mother, Mary A.
Russell Mary A., (Batavia) r 4, widow of Charles A., farm 61.
Sammis Collis H., (Pavilion) r 36, 1,600 pear trees, 600 apple trees, farmer 130.
Sanders William, (E. Bethany) r 8, farmer 12.
Scarff Frank E., r 35, farmer 41, and leases of Rev. J. M. 100.
Scarff James M., r 35, pastor Baptist Church at Bethany Center, farmer 100.
Schoonover Hiram G., (W. Bethany) r 29, pastor Freewill Baptist Church.
Schwab Edwin C., (E. Bethany) r 23, laborer, leases of John G. h and 10 acres.
Schwab John G., (E. Bethany) r 23, carpet weaver, h and 10 acres.
Schwucho Herman L., (E. Bethany) r 23, farmer, leases of Bart Kelley 47.

SHEPARD DANIEL, (Batavia) r 4, 300 apple trees, farmer 75½.

Shore Samuel C., r 34, cooper.

Showerman Charles L., (E. Bethany) r 23, laborer.

SHOWERMAN FRANK C., (Linden) station agent and telegraph operator N. Y., L. E. & W. R. R., agent Wells-Fargo Express Co., W. Main, bds. do.

Skeels Fred W., (E. Bethany) r 23 cor. 12, agent D., L. & W. R. R. and United States Express Co., telegraph operator.

Skeels Ray M., (E. Bethany) r 23 cor. 12, night operator D., L. & W. R. R.

SMILEY FRANK J., (Linden) farmer, leases of A. J. Lorish 135.

Smith August, (E. Bethany) off r 23, laborer.

Smith Hale M., (Linden) carriagemaker, E. Main, h and lot do.

Smith Solomon, (E. Bethany) r 23, laborer.

Snell Elizabeth, (W. Bethany) r 19, widow of Charles.

Snow Emily N., (E. Bethany) r 22, widow of William.

SOUTH GEORGE, (W. Bethany) r 19, carpenter and builder, apple orchard 5 acres, 225 plum and peach trees, 100 pear trees, farmer 109.

Sperry Emeline, (E. Bethany) widow of Platt E.

Sprague Della Miss, r 25, dressmaker.

Sprague Frank B., (E. Bethany) r 22, carriage painter.

Sprague Harriet M., r 25, widow of Barney, h and lot.

SQUIRES GEORGE, (W. Bethany) r 28, prop. saw. feed, and cider-mills, farmer 29¾.

Stakel George, Jr., (E. Bethany) r 14, farmer, leases on shares of George, Sr., 120.

Starkweather Frank E., (Pavilion) off r 36, farmer 120.

STAUB JOHN, (E. Bethany) r 35, farmer for his wife 10.

STAVELY JONATHAN, (E. Bethany) r 14, brickmaker, served in Co. E, 1st Vet. Cav. N. Y. Vols., h and lot.

Stebbins Charles M., r 21, cooper, carpenter, and farmer 17.

Stebbins Lyman S., r 34, farmer 57.

Stephens Alma, (Linden) widow of Luman, farm 100.

Stevens Frank H., r 21, laborer.

STEVENS HENRY, (W. Bethany) r 28, farmer, leases of John Ford 120.

Stevens Henry, (E. Bethany) r 13, retired farmer, h and lot.

Stewart John W., (Linden) produce dealer, apiarist 35 colonies, h and 3 acres Batavia st.

Stewart William H., r 34, farmer 50.

Stickney William A., r 33, farmer, leases of Rose D. Marsh 30.

Stine Martin, (Linden) r 41, farmer, leases on shares of S. T. Curtis 152.

Stringham Ida, r 21, widow of Isaac W., h and lot.

Strong Wilber O., (W. Bethany) r 27, laborer, h and 1 acre.

Sulzmann Martin, (Linden) r 35, laborer.

Swan Henry A., (Batavia) r 4, breeder of grade Jersey and Durham cattle and pure blood Shropshire sheep, farmer 272.

Taylor Emily Miss, r 21, h and lot.

Taylor Sally, (Batavia) r 6, widow of Rodney; aged 90.

Taylor William P., (Batavia) r 6, farmer 206.

Thomas Charles E., (E. Bethany) r 10, laborer.

Thomas George N., (E. Bethany) r 14, house painter.

Thomas George R., (E. Bethany) r 14, dealer in dry goods, groceries. boots, and shoes, h and lot.

Thomas Heman S., (E. Bethany) r 14, clerk for his father, George R.

THOMAS LUCY E., (E. Bethany) r 14, widow of Norman G., h and lot.

Thomson Frank D., r 21, carpenter and builder, h and lot.

Thomson Joseph R., r 21, carpenter and builder, h and lot.

Tisdale Mary E., r 34, widow of William C.

TOLL SIMON J., (E. Bethany) r 12½, breeder of grade Merino sheep, served in Co. A, 6th Cav. Iowa Vols., farmer 102.

Torrey Daniel W., (Stafford) r 8, farmer for his father, Mulford S.

Torrey George H., (Stafford) r 8, school teacher and farmer with his father, Hamilton H.

Torrey Hamilton H., (Stafford) r 8, assessor, fruit grower, breeder of Clydesdale horses, farmer 57.

Torrey Mulford S., (Stafford) r 8, retired farmer 53.
Underhill Theodore R., (E. Bethany) r 24, carpenter and farmer for M. Rogers.
Vader Cornelius, (Linden) r 30, farmer for his wife 61.
Voorhees J. Abraham, (Linden) retired merchant, h Main.
Wagner Henry F., (Batavia) r 2, laborer.
Wait Ira, (Linden) r 31 cor. 47, retired farmer 32.
Wait Madenette M., r 35, widow of Obed.
Wales Oliver, (E. Bethany) r 22½, farmer, leases of Hiram Chaddock 225.
Walker Robert, r 35, farmer with his father, William M.
Walker Shubael, r 35, retired farmer 150.
WALKER WILLIAM M., r 35, breeder of grade Holstein and Durham cattle, farmer
    100, served in Co. H, 8th H. A. N. Y. Vols.
Walker William N., r 35, farmer with his father, William M.
Ward Charles F., (E. Bethany) r 35, breeder of grade Merino and Cotswold sheep,
    farmer, leases of Oliver D. Farnsworth.
Ward Lodowick C., (E. Bethany) r 16, carpenter and thresher.
Warren Franklin, (W. Bethany) r 28, laborer, h and 1 acre.
Warren Morris, r 25, laborer, h and 2½ acres.
WEBER GEORGE P., (Linden) off r 31, farmer 28.
WEBSTER JOHN M., r 34, justice of the peace, retired farmer 24, and in Wyoming
    Co. 130.
Webster P. Henry, r 35, farmer, leases on shares of Shubael Walker 150.
Wellert Joseph, (Stafford) r 8, laborer, h and lot.
WELLERT LEWIS, (Stafford) r 8, laborer.
Westacott Henry, (E. Bethany) laborer, h and lot.
Whalen James J., (Pavilion) off r 36, farmer 47.
Whalen Johana, (Pavilion) off r 36, widow of Matthew.
Wheeler Guy E., (Linden) r 31, truck gardener and small fruit grower, leases of Morris
    Smith 46.
WHEELER NORA G., (Linden) r 31, school teacher.
Wilkinson Elizabeth, (E. Bethany) r 12, widow of Amon.
WILSON GEORGE, (W. Bethany) r 29, blacksmith and horseshoer, fine shoeing a
    specialty, h and lot.
Wood Erastus, (E. Bethany) off r 14, retired miller, owns grist and saw-mill, aged 86,
    farm 40.
Wood Leonard, (E. Bethany) r 14, carpenter.
WOOD WILLIAM J., (E. Bethany) r 14, carriage and sleigh manuf., blacksmith and
    repairer, prop. saw-mill, h and lot.
WOOLF HARRY, r 21, dealer in dry goods, groceries, boots, and shoes, h and lot.
Worthington Dan L., (E. Bethany) r 23 cor. 13, postmaster, retired merchant, h and
    lot.
Ziegler John, (E. Bethany) r 6, cooper, h and 2½ acres.

BYRON.

(For explanations, etc., see page 3, part second.)

(Postoffice address is Byron, unless otherwise designated in parenthesis.)

Adams W. Henry, dealer in lumber, farmer 90, h Main.
Alcott Clara Miss, r 39, resident.
Alcott Nancy Miss, r 39, resident.
Allen Milton, (N. Bergen) r 8, farmer 155.
Ames Clarrisena, (S. Byron) r 60, widow of Samuel, farmer 114.

ANDREWS L. B., physician and surgeon, Main, h do.
Arnold James B., (S. Byron) r 68, school teacher and farmer 106.
Austin Thomas J., r 5, farmer 55.
Bain Janet, r 5, widow of John, farmer about 150.
Barker Eugene, r 17, dealer in pianos, organs, and musical merchandise, farmer 150.
Barnard Uri, r 19, farmer 5.
BAWER CELINDA M., r 35, widow of James M., 5 cows, 50 sheep, 6 horses, farmer 255.
Bean Bert H., (S. Byron) r 65, (Boynton, Prentice & Co.) farmer 125.
Bean Edward F., (S. Byron) baggagemaster, bds. Gillett House.
Bean James, (S. Byron) station agent N. Y. C. & H. R. R. R., farmer 172, h and lot.
Bean James L , r 37, salesman.
Bean Marshall D., (S. Byron) farmer 28, and in Stafford 150.
Beebe Lyman, (S. Byron) r 76, carpenter and joiner.
Beebe Thomas, (E. Elba) r 44, farmer 128.
Benham Caroline Mrs., (S. Byron) r 78, resident.
Benham Howard C., (S. Byron) postal clerk.
Benham Martha J. Mrs., r 54, farmer 140.
Benham Martin C., (S. Byron) r 78, dealer in grain at S. Byron and Byron Center, farmer 200.
Benham Mary L., widow of James D., farm 55.
BENHAM MILTON. r 39, farmer 1.
Bennett Albert F., (McKenzie & Bennett) practical miller.
Billings Appleton W., (S. Byron) r 65, retired physician.
Billings Charles, (S. Byron) r 78, laborer.
Bird Brothers, (N. Bergen) r 6, (Frederick and James) 6 cows, farmers, lease of their father, William, 150.
Bird Frederick, (N. Bergen) r 6, (Bird Brothers).
Bird James, (N. Bergen) r 6, (Bird Brothers).
Birge Clarence W., (S. Byron) r 71, farmer 70.
Blair Caroline, r 19, widow of John L., farmer 5.
Blair Charles L., (S. Byron) r 62, farmer 69.
Blair Eli, (S. Byron) r 60, farmer 121.
Bonnette Frederick J., (N. Bergen) r 11, 6 cows, breeder of grade Holstein cattle, farmer, leases on shares of William S. Peckham, of Brockport, 100.
BOYCE JAMES A., dealer in stoves, hardware, and tinware, Rochester st.
Boynton Emily T., (S. Byron) r 66, widow of James, farmer 90.
Boynton, Prentice & Co., (S. Byron) (J. T. B., deceased, George W. P., and Bert H. Bean) produce dealers.
Bradley Sally. (S. Byron) r 65, widow of Miner, owns farm in Stafford 80, h and lot.
Bratt Albert M., (S. Byron) r 76, farmer 65.
Brockway William, (S. Byron) r 62, farmer, leases on shares of J. C., of Batavia, 70.
Brodie William B., (S. Byron) r 63, farmer, leases on shares of James Bean 150.
Brown Ann Mrs., (S. Byron) resident, h and lot.
Brown Charles D., r 18, laborer.
Brown Edwin B., r 2½, farmer 75.
BROWN MELVILLE B. C., r 2, farmer 125.
Brown Moses, (S. Byron) r 71, invalid.
Brown Seth C., r 2, farmer, son of M. B. C.
BROWN WILLIAM F., r 2½, 60 sheep, 5 cows, fruit grower, farmer 170, and timber land 25.
Brown William W., (N. Bergen) r 17, farmer 50.
Browning Fred, r 49, laborer.
Browning Louisa, r 49, (Mrs William) milliner.
Browning Richard, r 31, farmer 12.
Browning Richard, Jr., off r 32, farmer 25.
Browning William, r 37, laborer.
BULL REBECCA W. Miss, r 3, farmer 150.
Burgot John, r 5, farmer 96.

Burling John, (S. Byron) r 57, farmer, leases of Terry Brothers 230.
Burns James M., r 3, painter and farmer 61.
Bushman Andrew, (S. Byron) r 65, carpenter.
BUSHMAN HENRY, (S. Byron) farmer 193, h Main.
Bushman Sherman, (S. Byron) r 76, trackman.
BYRON CENTER HOTEL, Charles Leonard, prop.
Calkins Cherbury M., r 16, dealer in furs, hides, and pelts, h and 3 acres.
Campbell Oliver M., (S. Byron) r 73, wagonmaker and farmer 5.
Carpenter Marquis D. L., r 18, farmer 32.
Carruthers Robert, r 2, farmer 126.
Cash William, (S. Byron) r 77, farmer 50.
Caswell Will, (S. Byron) r 63, farmer, leases on shares of H. S. Peckham 165.
Chadwick Leander J., r 18, wagonmaker and farmer 4.
Chaple Morris, r 45, farm laborer.
Chase Charles O., r 35, farmer 77.
CHASE H. BURDETT, (N. Bergen) r 8, farmer 100.
CHICK GEORGE G., (S. Byron) r 66, farmer 65.
Child J. Ray, (S. Byron) r 66, breeder of horses and grade Holstein cattle, milk dealer, 8 cows, farmer 164.
CLARK LIVILLA, (S. Byron) r 53 cor. 50, widow of Edward B., farm 115.
Cline George, (S. Byron) r 72, farmer with Joseph.
Cline Joseph, (S. Byron) r 74, farmer 85.
CLOSE THOMAS, r 14, mason, farmer, leases of Abigail Shedd 38, served in 94th N. Y. Vols. about 3 years.
Cockram Albert E., r 45, farmer, leases on shares of his father, William, 133.
Cockram William, r 45, fruit grower, farmer 133.
Cole George W., r 30½, farmer 376.
Cole John, r 5, farmer 135.
Cole William, r 28, laborer.
Collister Edward J., (S. Byron) r 67, farmer 120.
Collister Elsbie, (W. Bergen) r 51, resident.
Collister Jeanette, (W. Bergen) r 51, resident.
Collister Richard B., (W. Bergen) farmer with Susan Morton 114.
Colston Edward R., r 37, farmer 100.
Colston Everett, r 37, farmer with his father, Edward R.
Conant Dewey, r 49, (Conant & Surgenor).
Conant & Surgenor, (Dewey C. and William K. S.) dealers in dry goods, groceries, etc.
COOK CHARLES E., r 65 cor. 63, fruit grower, 2,000 apple trees, about 200 pear trees, 250 quince trees, 1 acre grapes, inventor and prop. Cook's fruit gatherer, farmer 170.
Cook Edwin J., (S. Byron) r 64, mail agent.
Cook Fred, r 35, breeder of Merino sheep, 60 head, farmer, leases on shares of Mrs. Diantha Ward, of Bergen, 150.
COOK IRVING D., (S. Byron) r 64, breeder of grade polled cattle, fruit grower, farmer 140.
Cook Marshall N. Capt., (S. Byron) r 78, fruit grower and farmer 5.
Cook William, r 17, farmer 56.
Cook William, (S. Byron) ticket agent and telegraph operator N. Y. C. & H. R. R. R., h Main.
Corcoran Philip, (S. Byron) r 71, farmer 30.
Cory Emerson, r 35, laborer, h and lot.
Coward Charles H., r 41, farmer 90.
Coward Frank P., (S. Byron) postmaster and general merchant.
Coward William H., (S. Byron) r 65, invalid.
Cowley John, (W. Bergen) r 52, farmer 53.
Crandall Ruth B., r 49, widow of John T., h and lot.
Crocker Edwin M., r 39, farmer, leases of Maria 110.
Crocker Maria, r 39, widow of Hollis, farmer 110.
Crook Clarence S., station agent W. S. R. R., and agent National Express Co., h Terry

Curan James C., harnessmaker.
Daniels Frank, laborer.
Darch Charles, r 2½, farmer 50.
Darch James, r 39, farmer.
DE KAY CHARLES W., ex-postmaster, justice of the peace, carpenter, and joiner, Main cor. Holley.
De Lapp Amelia Mrs., (S. Byron) h Mechanic.
Deming William H., r 39, farmer 129. [Died May 3, 1889.]
DEMMING HENRY D., r 35, breeder and dealer in horses, 40 sheep, farmer 180.
Dibble Charles J., r 36, farmer 4.
Dibble Joseph D., r 36, farmer 110.
Dibble Lavant A., r 36, carpenter, contractor, and builder.
Dibble Merriman C., r 2, farmer 130.
Dibble William D., r 36, carpenter and thresher, h and lot.
DILLINGHAM ISAAC, r 43, supervisor, sheep feeder for market, fruit grower, farmer 160.
Donnoghue Patsey, journeyman harnessmaker.
Donoghu ——— Mrs., (S. Byron) widow of Patrick, h and lot Mechanic.
Dowd Charles V., r 39, 9 cows, fruit grower, farmer, leases of the estate of William H. Deming 90.
Doudes Thomas, (S. Byron) r 78, track hand.
Dusen Chauncey J., (S. Byron) dealer in lumber, reapers, mowers, pumps, etc., Main.
Dunning Orin, r 19, mason and farmer 12.
Durfee Isaac S., (S. Byron) r 69, farmer 7, and in Stafford 20.
Durfee W. Ray, (S. Byron) r 69, formerly merchant.
Eaton Albert, r 22, farmer 15.
Egglet Martin, r 21, farmer, leases on shares of Leo A. Bibble, of Clarendon, Orleans Co., 70.
Ernst Christ, (S. Byron) r 66, farm laborer.
Ernst John, r 14, farmer, leases of Henry Adams 90.
Fairly Thomas, (S. Byron) r 60, cooper and farmer 7.
Faley Garrett, (S. Byron) r 60, farmer 5. [Died Jan. 2, 1889.]
Faley John, (S. Byron) laborer.
Faley William, (S. Byron) r 65, track hand.
Farnham William, (S. Byron) r 14, farmer, leases on shares of Henry Adams 90.
Farrant John, r 35, laborer.
Farrington Horatio, r 47, farmer 10.
Ferguson James W., r 36, farmer, leases of Mrs. Hammond, of Bergen, 88.
Ferrant Peter, r 49 cor. 54, farmer 54.
Fisher George, r 31, farmer about 40.
Fisher William, r 15, farmer 9.
FISK JOHN S., r 49, retired farmer.
Fisk Levi W., r 49, farmer 225.
Fisk Pliny B., r 49, farmer about 75, and owns farm in Bergen.
Fitzpatrick — Mrs., (S. Byron) r 68, widow of Edward, farm 50.
Flaherty Frank, (S. Byron) r 76, section boss.
Follett Edgar A., (S. Byron) r 60, farmer with Hiram.
Follett Hiram, (S. Byron) r 60, farmer 50.
Ford Adelaide, r 2½, widow of David, farmer 12.
Ford Edward, r 26, mason and farmer, leases of Josiah Gardner 22.
Foreman Thomas, r 37, laborer.
Fuller Charles M., (S. Byron) r 65, wagonmaker, h and lot.
Gaines Clarence B., r 15, farmer with Leiel B.
Gaines Leiel B., r 15, farmer 126.
Gaines Solomon D., r 30, dealer in country produce, live stock, etc., farm 1½.
Garry James, (S. Byron) r 52, farmer 9.
Gartley Charles, r 18, mason, farmer with John.
Gartley John, r 18, farmer, leases of Mrs. Elizabeth Larkin 87.
Genesee Mills, r 30½, McKenzie & Bennett, props., custom grinding, dealers in flour, meal, feed, and grain.

Gibbs J. Milton, resident, h Terry ave.

GILBERT GALETTE B., physician and surgeon, Rochester st.

GILBERT MARY M., (Mrs. G. B.) farm 80.

Gillam Chandler B., r 20, farmer 50.

Gillam Chandler P., r 20, farmer with Chandler B.

Gillett Cleveland, (S. Byron) farmer with his father, Jerome.

GILLETT HOUSE, (S. Byron) Jerome Gillett, prop., livery stable connected.

GILLETT JEROME, (S. Byron) prop. Gillett House, farmer with B. F. Graham, of Batavia, 143.

Gillum Henry A., off r 29, farmer 147.

GLOBE MILLS, r 24 cor. 26, A. W. Graves, prop., manuf. of flour, feed, lumber, etc.

Goodliff George, r 1, farmer 14. [Deceased.]

Goodliff William, r 30, farmer h and lot.

Goodliffe John, (S. Byron) r 78, constable, carpenter, and joiner, manuf. of cider and cider vinegar.

Goodwin Charles T., r 24, farmer with his father, James M.

GOODWIN JAMES M., r 24, breeder of Henry Clay horses, 10 head, 3 brood mares, 50 thoroughbred Poland China swine, 8 cows, farmer 400.

Gould George, (S. Byron) r 78, laborer.

Grant John, r 16, blacksmith, h and 2 acres.

GRAVES ADIN W., r 24 cor. 26, prop. Globe mills.

Gray James, (S. Byron) track hand, h Main.

Green Abigail F., r 49, widow of Loren.

Green Arthur H., (S. Byron) r 66, farmer 226.

Green Herbert L., r 49, farmer 100.

Green Newton H., (S. Byron) r 46 cor. 45, farmer 396.

Green William, r 24, farmer 165.

Green William W., (N. Bergen) r 12, farmer 50.

Gross Leo, clergyman.

Gurnett Charles, r 2, laborer.

Hager Charles, r 17, farmer, leases on shares of E. Barker 160.

Hair Robert W., carpenter, joiner, contractor, and builder, bds. Byron Center Hotel.

Haley Daniel, (S. Byron) r 76, track hand.

HALL ANDREW J., (S. Byron) r 72, prop. grist-mill at Rochester, machinist and farmer 120.

Hall Joseph E., (S. Byron) r 72, son of Andrew J.

Hall William T., (S. Byron) r 72, farmer with Andrew J.

Harnel Edward W., (S. Byron) r 78, pastor of M. E. Church.

Harris George, r 32, farmer, son of Jedediah.

Harris Jedediah, r 32, farmer 140.

Hayes David O., r 24, farmer 95.

Hayward George E., (S. Byron) r 71, laborer.

Higham William S., r 24, farmer, leases of Arthur Green about 200.

Hines Burt, (S. Byron) r 76, track hand.

Hochschuls Fred, farmer 9.

Holt Harrison C., r 16, carpenter and joiner, sexton Free Baptist Church cemetery.

Holt Mary, r 16, (Mrs. Harrison C.) h and lot.

Holt Oliver D., r 18, jeweler.

Humphrey Erastus, (S. Byron) r 78, breeder of thoroughbred Shropshire sheep, reg., and full blood Jersey cattle, farmer 97.

Humphrey George, (S. Byron) r 78, farmer, leases on shares of Erastus 97.

Hunt Charles, (S. Byron) r 70, farmer with Ralph.

Hunt Ralph, (S. Byron) r 70, farmer, leases of N. Y. C. & H. R. R. R. Co. 30.

Hunt Ralph, Jr., (S. Byron) r 72, laborer.

Hunt Sylvester, (S. Byron) r 70, farm laborer.

Huyck Isaac, (S. Byron) r 64, farmer 86.

Ivison Thomas, (S. Byron) r 69, farmer 64.

James Charles P., r 30, carpenter.

Johnson William, r 1, farmer for Mrs. Mariette Peckham, h and lot.

Jones Charles, r 30½, carpenter and farmer 9.
Joslyn Charles, laborer, h Terry ave.
KELLOGG CHARLES R., (S. Byron) r 77, commissioner of highways, farmer 188.
Kelly George, (S. Byron) r 53 cor. 50, farmer, leases the Reuben Mann estate 115.
Kelly Richard, (E. Elba) r 57½, laborer.
Kenney Brothers, (S. Byron) r 62, (John and Joseph) farmers 89.
Kenney John, (S. Byron) r 62, (Kenney Brothers).
Kenney Joseph, (S. Byron) r 62, (Kenney Brothers).
King J. Henry, r 14, painter and manager for Gillett & Graham, farm 140.
Knapp Henry H., r 18, farmer 3.
Kreger William, (W. Bergen) r 51, laborer.
Ladue Augustus, (S. Byron) prop. meat market, h Mechanic.
LANGDON GORDON, (N. Bergen) r 8, farmer 82.
Langdon Herbert E., (N. Bergen) r 8, carpenter and builder.
Langdon William H., (N. Bergen) r 8, farmer, leases on shares of his father, Gordon,
    82, and of Ruth Osborn 20.
LARKIN ELIZABETH, r 18, widow of Colvin, farmer 125.
Lathrop Whitman, r 49, farmer 45.
Leanen Fred, r 46, farmer 4.
LEONARD CHARLES, prop. Byron Center Hotel.
Leonard George, r 36, farmer 112.
Lewis George W., r 37, carriage painter.
Lindsey John, (S. Byron) r 76, farmer 2.
Logal Nicholas. r 39, emp. F. T. & E. H. Miller.
Logle Joseph, r 49, thresher.
Louer Ellen, widow of George B., h and lot.
Lyman Dwight, (S. Byron) r 71, farmer 107.
Lyman Orville D., (S. Byron) r 71, farmer with Dwight.
Macartney James, r 32, farmer, leases on shares of J. Harris 140.
Macartney Samuel, r 32, farmer, son of James.
Macartney William H., r 32, farmer with his father, James.
MANN ALFRED, (S. Byron) r 54, breeder of horses, 7 head, 5 cows, farmer 120.
Mann Charles, (S. Byron) r 54, farmer with Alfred.
Mann Earl W., (S. Byron) teamster, horse trainer, and hay presser, h Main.
Mann Ezro, r 16, farm laborer, h and 1 acre.
Mann Lucius, (S. Byron) laborer, h Mechanic.
Mann Willie E., (S. Byron) r 54, farmer, son of Alfred.
MANN AZUBA, (S. Byron) widow of William, h Mechanic.
Marble Alphonzo, r 18, manuf. of and dealer in Golden oil and Green Mountain salve,
    agent for pillow inhaler, farmer 93.
Marshall Adaline, (S. Byron) r 65, widow of John B., h and lot.
MAYBACK CHARLES W., (N. Bergen) r 6, farmer 54.
McDaniels George, r 16, resident.
McDaniels Sarah, r 16, (Mrs. George) farmer 230.
McDermott Frank, r 31, section boss.
McElver Burt, (McElver & Radley) postmaster, h Furnace.
McElver Edwin L., clerk for McElver & Radley.
McElver James, (McElver & Sons).
McElver James H., (McElver & Sons) molder.
McElver William, r 39, (McElver & Sons) molder.
McElver & Sons, (James, James H., and William) manufs. of agricultural implements
    and props. iron foundry.
McElver & Radley, (Burt McE. and George H. R.) general merchants, Main.
McKenzie & Bennett, (Hon. John McK., of Batavia, and Albert F. B.) props. Genesee
    grist-mills, dealers in flour, feed, and grain.
McLaury John Frederick, pastor Presbyterian Church.
Meehan Joseph, blacksmith, manuf. of light carriages and sleighs, h Main.
Merrill Abner J., (N. Bergen) r 13, farmer 56.
MERRILL MAJOR H. W., r 53, farmer, leases of T. Benton, of Clarendon, Orleans
    Co., 115.

Merrill Nelson J., r 16, breeder of horses, 50 grade Southdown sheep, 12 cows, farmer 160.

Merrill Otto C., r 16, son of Nelson J., farmer.

MERRIMAN HARRY, r 2, dealer in agricultural implements, farmer 140.

Merriman Henry W., r 34, breeder of Hambletonian horses and full blood Merino sheep, 65 head, 6 cows, farmer 282.

Merriman Robert E., r 23, 60 sheep, farmer 163.

Metcalfe Thomas, (S. Byron) r 66, blacksmith.

Metcalfe William, (S. Byron) r 67, laborer.

Miller Albert D., (N. Bergen) r 13, farmer 50.

MILLER ELISHA H., (F. T. & E. H. Miller) justice of the peace and farmer in Barre, Orleans Co., 112, h Holly.

MILLER F. T. & E. H., wholesale dealers in grain, wool, dressed hogs, and coal, agents Pennsylvania and New York ins. companies, Holly.

MILLER FRANCIS T. Hon., assemblyman, farmer 280, h Holly.

Miller John G., (N. Bergen) r 15, small fruit grower, farmer 12.

Miller Lincoln C., (N. Bergen) r 15, farmer with John G. 12.

Miller William, r 26, horse trainer.

Mills Albert, (N. Bergen) r 15, farmer 15.

Mills James E., r 15, farmer 90.

Mills William R., r 4, farmer 87, and in Clarendon, Orleans Co., 146.

Mitcham Ezro, r 4, farmer. leases on shares of Hiram Butcher 100.

Moore John E., (Moore & Seaver).

Moore Michael, (S. Byron) track hand, h Mechanic.

Moore & Seaver, (John E. M. and James W. S.) general merchants, Main.

Morton Susan Mrs., (W. Bergen) r 51, farmer 115.

Moshier Ayden A., r 34, farmer 50, and timber lot 5.

Mullen Albert, (S. Byron) r 54, farmer, leases of Martha J. Benham 140.

Munger Henry M., (N. Bergen) r 10, farmer 71, and leases on shares of his father, Martin D., 150.

Munger Martin D., (N. Bergen) r 10, farmer 150.

Newell John. r 48, farmer in Sheldon, Wyoming Co., 54½, and leases of E. S. Miller 73.

Newton William, r 61, laborer.

NICKERSON EMILY, r 18, widow of David, h and lot.

Nightingale Charlie R., r 3, farmer 4.

Nightingale Frank A., r 3, farmer, leases of John about 70.

Nightingale George H., r 27, miller, emp. A. W. Graves.

Nightingale John, r 3, farmer, leases of Rebecca W. Bull 150.

Norton Charles A., r—, farmer 54.

Norton Erastus H., r 38, farmer 210.

Norton Harry C., r 48, farmer, leases on shares of Erastus H. 210.

Oatway Harry, r 30, miller.

Oatway James, r 30½, laborer, h and lot.

Oatway James, Jr., r 30½, flagman W. S. R. R.

Oatway Thomas, emp. Charles Leonard, bds. do.

O'Brien Thomas, (S. Byron) r 76, farmer 2.

Oderkirk John, r 49, farmer, leases of John Fisk 150.

O'Keefe William, blacksmith, Main, h do.

Olmsted Alfred, r 18, dealer in agricultural implements, farmer 3.

O'Neill Hugh, (S. Byron) r 71, farmer 18.

O'Rourke Thomas, (S. Byron) flagman N. Y. C. & H. R. R. R., h Mechanic.

OSBORN BYRON E., night operator, h at Churchville, Monroe Co.

Osborn John, (E. Elba) r 44, blacksmith and farmer 3.

Paige Alonzo, r 3, carpenter and joiner, farmer 10.

Parker Jacob L., r 30½, carpenter and joiner, dealer in horses, h and lot.

Pasal Chris, (S. Byron) r 58, farmer 120.

Passmore Thomas, (S. Byron) r 53, farmer, leases of John 100.

Peckham Francis I., (N. Bergen) r 11, farmer.

Peckham Henry S., r 49, fruit grower, 50 sheep, farmer 165

Perkins Dwight W., r 43, 4 cows, farmer, leases of Mrs. Julia Judd, of Bath, N. Y., 75.
Perry Charles, r 3, farmer, son of James G.
PERRY JAMES G., r 3, farmer 100.
Petherbridge Ann, r 24, widow of Manuel, farmer 90.
Petherbridge Richard, r 4, farmer 100.
Petherbridge Willie W., r 4, farmer with his father, Richard.
Philleo C. Eddie, (S. Byron) r 78, farmer with his father, Henry S.
PHILLEO HENRY S., (S. Byron) r 78, breeder of grade Shropshire sheep, 30 head, farmer 103.
Phillips George, (W. Bergen) r 70, farmer for Hannah Waterman 52.
Phillips Mercy B., r 22, widow of Albert, farmer 38.
Post George G., r 28, farmer 86.
Powell James, r 29, farmer 5.
Pratt Silas C., r 2, farmer with Robert Carruthers.
Prentice Adelbert C., (S. Byron) civil engineer.
PRENTICE CYRUS, (S. Byron) retired farmer, owns in Stafford about 200.
Prentice George W., (S. Byron) (Boynton, Prentice & Co.) farmer in Stafford 225.
Pridmore Frank, r 19, laborer.
Pugh Hugh, (W. Bergen) r 52, farmer 40.
Putnam James, (S. Byron) blacksmith, Main, h do.
Radley George M., (McElver & Radley) h Main.
RAMBO JOHN, (S. Byron) dealer in hardware, stoves, tin, sheet iron ware, etc., Main.
Rapp Andrew, (S. Byron) r 73, breeder of horses, 16 head, 125 sheep, farmer, leases on shares of the Erastus Cash estate 345.
Rapp Anna Mrs., (S. Byron) r 73, farm 130.
Rapp Hart, (S. Byron) r 73, farmer.
Roach Thomas, r 61, farmer, leases of W. C. Rowley 123.
Rollin Cary, r 22, farmer 70.
ROLLIN D. M. L., (Byron) r 20, Free Baptist clergyman, farmer 50.
Rose J. Fred, (S. Byron) r 65, cooper and dealer in fruit.
Roth Fred, laborer.
Rowley Lavant B., cooper.
ROWLEY WARREN C., retired farmer 120, h Holly.
Sage George, r 49, blacksmith.
Sanderson Anson P., (N. Bergen) r 12, farmer 51.
Sanderson Levi L., r 12, farmer 140.
Schaffer Herbert, (S. Byron) r 65, telegraph operator.
Scott William, r 23, farmer 18.
Searls Charles C., r 25, farmer with his father, Isaiah.
Searls Horace H., r 25, farmer 100.
SEARLS ISAIAH, r 25, 100 sheep, 20 head swine, stock and fruit grower, farmer 255.
SEAVER JAMES W., (Moore & Seaver) h Rochester st.
Shedd Abigail, r 14, widow of Milo W., farm 38.
Shedd Charles, r 39, laborer.
Shelt Frederick, r 20, farmer 70.
Shelt Kate H., r 18, widow of Henry, dressmaker.
Shelt Philip, (N. Bergen) r 12, farmer 58.
Shelt William F., (N. Bergen) r 12, son of Philip.
Sherwood Alice G., r 20, widow of James H., farmer 67.
Shilling Christ, r 29, farmer 2.
Shipley Fred A., (S. Byron) r 66, shoemaker.
Smith Eugene L., r 49, clerk for Moore & Seaver.
Smith John, (S. Byron) r 76, track hand
Smith Joseph, r 5, farmer, leases of Mrs. Elizabeth 60.
Soules William, r 19, carpenter.
Spear John, r 47, farmer, leases of Louisa A. Terry 130.
Stafford John, (S. Byron) laborer.

7*

Stanton Benjamin W., r 4, farmer 72.
Steele John N., (N. Bergen) r 10, breeder of swine, 35 head, farmer 150.
Stevens Alma, painter and laborer, bds. Byron Center Hotel.
Stevens Charles S., teacher, h Main.
Stevens Fred, r 38, cheesemaker.
Stevens Fred, (S. Byron) r 69, laborer.
Stiles Porter, (South Byron) r 76, track hand.
Studley Horace, (S. Byron) r 66, farmer 23.
Studley Jerome, (S. Byron) r 66, thresher, farmer with Horace 23.
Studley Lorenzo, (S. Byron) r 66, resident.
Suiter George, r 23, farmer, leases of Mrs. Lettie Godfrey 100.
Sullivan Dennis, (S. Byron) r 73, farmer 36.
Surgenor William K., r 49, (Conant & Surgenor).
Swan George W., r 3, farmer 50.
Taggart Benjamin F., (W. Bergen) r 52, farmer 68.   [Died March 21, 1890.]
Taggart Frank J., (W. Bergen) r 52, farmer.
Taggart Irving D., (S. Byron) r 78, butcher.
Taggart Sarah, (S. Byron) r 65, widow of John.
Tehan Bridget, (S. Byron) widow of Timothy, h Mechanic.
Terry Addison, r 55 cor. 66, farmer 164.
TERRY JAMES Z., r 47, dealer in agricultural implements and phosphates, farmer 200.
Terry Lawton A., r 55 cor. 66, farmer with Addison.
Terry Louisa A., r 47, widow of Zerva, farmer 120.
Thomas Franklin L., (S. Byron) r 75, farmer, leases of Alexander Leonard, of Bergen,
    109.
Thomas James, (S. Byron) r 78, laborer.
Thomas James, r 32, farmer about 40.
Thomas John, r 32, farmer with his father, James.
Tompkins Delina D., r 39, widow of Daniel D., h and lot.
Thompson Merinda, (S. Byron) r 65, widow of Spencer, h and lot.
TODD ISAAC A, r 43, 40 sheep, feeder of lambs for market, breeder of horses and
    Chester White and Berkshire swine, 5 brood mares, farmer 300.
Todd J. Grandison, r 49, produce dealer.
Todd John, r 43, farmer with Isaac A.
Torpy Asenath, (S. Byron) r 78, farmer with Mrs. Alta Gould 120.
Tripp Byron L., r 35, fruit grower and nurseryman, farmer 10.
Tripp Horace, r 35, retired nurseryman, aged 87.
Tuttle Horace, r 23, resident.
Tuttle Waity, r 23, (Mrs. Horace) farmer 46.
Voigt Fred, r 39, shoemaker.
Walker Charles A., r 16, teacher and farmer 110.
Walker Edgar, r 61, 60 sheep, 8 cows, farmer 137.
Walker George H., farmer; leases on shares of Mrs. Sarah McDaniels 120.
Walker Harry C., (S. Byron) r 61 cor. 69, farmer with his father, John C.
Walker John C., (S. Byron) r 61, farmer 265.
Walker Joseph C., r 21, resident.
Walker William A., r 61, breeder of thoroughbred Merino sheep and horses, farmer
    137.
Warboys John, (N. Bergen) r 14, breeder of horses, 12 cows, 100 sheep, farmer 190,
    and in Bergen 52.
Warboys Loren, (N. Bergen) r 14, breeder of horses, 10 cows, farmer, leases of Levi
    Sanderson 141.
Ward Frank D., (S. Byron) r 76, breeder of Shropshire and Cotswold sheep, farmer,
    leases of David Gleason 85.
Warn Carlie L., (N. Bergen) r 6, farmer with his father, Horatio.
Warn Frank G., (N. Bergen) r 6, farmer with his father, Horatio.
WARN HORATIO, (N. Bergen) r 6, breeder of thoroughbred Chester White swine,
    farmer 115.
Warner Charles, (S. Byron) r 76, laborer.

Warren Henry, (N. Bergen) r 13, farmer 20.
Waterman Hannah, (W. Bergen) r 70, widow of Rollin, farmer 52.
Watson Clifton, r 33, farmer 168.
Watson John, r 33, farmer, son of Clifton.
Watson Samuel, r 33, farmer with his father, Clifton.
Wells Caleb, r 49, retired farmer, owns farm in Elba.
Westbrook Frederick, (S. Byron) retired farmer, h Mechanic.
White Iverson W., r 17, breeder of Shropshire sheep, full blood Chester White swine, and grade Jersey and Durham cattle, farmer 150.
WHITON ALPHA M., (S. Byron) physician and surgeon.
Whittaker Richard, (S. Byron) emp. N. Y. C. & H. R. R. R.
Weldgen Frank, (S. Byron) r 68, emp. M. C. Benham.
Wilson Charles, (E. Elba) r 44, farmer 9.
Winter Calvin D., r 19, laborer.
Wood David, (S. Byron) farmer 5, h Mechanic.
Wood Robert W., r 24, farmer with Ann Petherbridge.
Wood Samuel, (N. Bergen) r 7, farmer 15.
Woodbine Thomas H., r 55, farmer, leases of Mary Gilbert 85.
Woodbine William, r 39, invalid.
Woodward Edwin C., r 30½, painter.

DARIEN.

(For explanations, etc., see page 3, part second.)

(Postoffice address is Darien, unless otherwise designated in parenthesis.)

Abel Albert, 100 sheep, farmer 105.
Acquard Joseph, (Darien Center) prop. saloon and restaurant, R. R. depot.
Adair William, (Corfu) r 5, farmer, leases on shares of John Diver 73.
Adams Mary S., r 60, widow of Robert, resident.
Adams Michael, (Darien Center) r 73, farmer 50.
Allen Charles D., (Sawens) r 35, 8 cows, farmer 71.
Allen Chauncey, (Fargo) r 4 cor. 25, dealer in bees and honey, apiarist 49 colonies, 18 cows, farmer 166.
Allen Martin L., (Darien Center) r 62, blacksmith.
Allen Millard, (Corfu) off r 79 in Pembroke, fruit grower, 14 cows, farmer 96.
Amedick George, (Attica, Wyoming Co.) r 80, farmer with his father, John.
Amedick John, (Attica, Wyoming Co.) r 80, 16 cows, farmer 121.
Ames Leslie, r 56, farm laborer.
Anthony Darius, r 59, retired mason, aged 94.
Anthony Julius, r 59, farm laborer, h and 1½ acres.
Ashley Chauncey T., (Corfu) r 2, 11 cows, farmer 130.
Bachelder Christian, (Darien Center) r 64, laborer.
Bahringer George, r 45, farmer 35.
Bahringer George, Jr., r 45, farmer with his father, George.
Bailey William, (Darien Center) r 52, 16 cows, farmer 70, and leases on shares of Sylvanus Humphrey 200.
Baird Jacob, (Darien Center) retired farmer, aged 88.
Baker Anson, (W. Batavia) r 17, farmer 59.
Baker George, (Alexander) r 38, 6 cows, farmer on the estate of his father, Wilson.
Baker George M., (Darien Center) r 62, com. traveler.
Baker Thomas, (Darien Center) hostler, emp. A. J. Richardson.
Baker William H., (Darien Center) r 62, 400 apple trees, farmer 25.
Barber Esther, (Sawens) r 34, widow of Joshua, resident, aged 95.

Barber Henry I., (Alexander) r 38, teacher.
Barber James, (Alexander) r 38, 6 cows, farmer 77.
Barlow Lewis, r 57, 16 cows, farmer 99.
Barry John, (Corfu) r 2, breeder of horses, farmer 26.
Barry Michael, (Corfu) r 2, farmer with his father, John.
Bartell Theodore, (Darien Center) r 73, farmer 115.
Barth W. Fred, (Darien Center) r 62, 6 cows, farmer 100.
BAUER EDWARD C., (Darien Center) r 51, farmer, emp. P. Hutchinson.
Bauer Francis Joseph, (Darien Center) r 47, broommaker, farmer 42.
Bauer Frank J., (Darien Center) r 47, huckster.
Bearlin Adam, r 77, farmer 45.
Beattie Margaret, (Darien Center) r 62, widow of David, h and lot.
Beck John, r 32, 15 cows, farmer 148.
Beck John, Jr., r 32, farmer, leases on shares of his father, John, 148.
Bennett Helen M., (Sawens) r 34, widow of James O., farm 60.
Bennett Thomas, (Corfu) r 4, fruit grower, 10 cows, farmer 63.
Bertchey Jacob, (Alden, Erie Co.) r 51, farmer, leases of Mrs. Caroline Hall 115, and
    owns in Alden, Erie Co., 20.
Bieser Frederic, (Alden, Erie Co.) r 67, carriage painter and farmer 9.
Bijers Jacob, (Darien Center) r 73, farmer 51.
Blair David, (Crittenden, Erie Co.) r 3, farm laborer.
Blair James, (Fargo) r 49, farmer.
Blair Thomas, (Fargo) r 49, farmer 86.
BORDWELL AARON, (Corfu) r 26, importer and breeder or pure blood Oxford-
    down sheep, reg., 100 head, and high grade Holstein cattle, fruit grower, farmer144.
Bowen Charles B., (Attica, Wyoming Co.) r 85, farmer with his father, Richard.
BOWEN RICHARD, (Attica, Wyoming Co.) r 85, breeder of pure blood Durham
    cattle and Oxforddown sheep, 200 head, 50 head reg., 20 cows, farmer 500.
Boyers Charles, (Corfu) r 6, farm laborer.
Brickman Christian, (Darien Center) r 73, farmer 50.
Brown Alexander, retired.
Brown William H., (Darien Center) r 30, 9 cows, farmer 52.
Browning Lucy A., (Darien C-nter) r 52, farm 4½.
Bruner John, r 61, farmer 13.
Brush Henry R., (Darien Center) laborer, h n depot.
Bucknum Helen, (Alexander) r 36, resident.
Burke Mary, (Darien Center) widow of Michael, h and lot.
Burr Lorenzo, (Darien Center) r 61, farmer 60.
Bushell Thomas, (Alden, Erie Co.) r 67, 6 cows, farmer 80.
Bushell William, (Alden, Erie Co.) r 51, farmer 16.
Butler John H., (Darien Center) r 61, breeder of grade Morgan-Hambletonian horses,
    farmer 72, and wood lot 5.
Buttolph Hiram, (Sawens) r 13, 45 high blood Merino sheep, farmer 74.
Buttolph Larnard D., (Sawens) r 13, farmer.
Canfield David, (Darien Center) r 52, farmer 100.
Canfield Burroughs P., (Darien Center) r 52, farmer 12½.
Carpenter Duane J., r 42, mason and farmer 12.
Carter Burton D., (Sawens) r 19, apiarist 15 colonies, farmer 20.
Carter Frank W., (Sawens) r 13, dealer in agricultural implements and fertilizers, 80
    sheep, farmer 50.
Carter Harriet F., r 60, widow of Joseph, owns 4 acres.
Carter Javan, (Sawens) r 15, farmer 30.
CARTER RILEY S., (Sawens) r 15, 8 cows, 100 sheep, farmer 136.
CHAPIN ALBERT F., (Darien Center) r 54, 8 cows, 150 sheep, farmer, leases of his
    mother, Mary Ann, 150.
Chapin Horace H., retired merchant, 79 full blood Merino sheep, farm 65, h and lot.
Chapin Joseph O., (Darien Center) mason, h and lot.
CHAPIN MARY ANN, (Darien Center) r 54, widow of Frank, farm 150.
CHICK CHARLES F., (Attica, Wyoming Co.) r 62, 35 cows, milk sold in Buffalo,
    dealer in horses, cows, and fertilizers, farmer 247.

Chick William, (Attica, Wyoming Co.) r 82, 10 cows, farmer 82.

Choate Elizabeth, (Corfu) r 23, (W. C. Choate & Co.) prop. Cloverfield cheese factory, h and lot in Batavia.

Choate Henry M., (Corfu) r 23, farmer 200.

Choate W. C. &. Co., (Corfu) r 23, (Mrs. Elizabeth Choate) conductors of Cloverfield cheese factory at Fargo, farmers, lease of Henry M. 200.

Choate Wilbur C., (Corfu) r 23, (W. C. Choate & Co.) dealer in Crocker's phosphate.

Christopherson Andrew O., (Darien Center) r 47, house painter and paper hanger, apiarist 10 colonies, farmer 31.

Christopherson Otto J., (Darien Center) r 47, painter, agent for pumps, wind-mills, manure spreaders, etc.

Clafquin Joseph, dealer in tobacco and cigars, h and 2 acres.

Clark Elisha W., (Alden, Erie Co.) r 69, farmer 5.

Clark Frank W., (Alden, Erie Co.) r 67, musician and band teacher, farmer 25.

Clark Fred C., (Alden, Erie Co) r 67, musician and farmer with his father, James C.

Clark Ira, (Darien Center) r 47, mason and farmer 13.

Clark James C., (Alden, Erie Co.) r 67, carpenter, apiarist 34 colonies, farmer 26.

Clark Rufus, (Sawens) r 19, breeder of horses, 11 cows. 100 sheep, farmer 171.

Cloverfield Cheese Factory, (Fargo) r 26, Elizabeth Choate, prop., W. C. Choate & Co., managers.

Cochrane Hamilton, (Alden, Erie Co.) r 51, 8 cows, farmer 125.

Cochrane James, (Alden, Erie Co.) r 51, farmer with his father, Hamilton.

Cochrane Robert, (Alden, Erie Co.) r 51, farmer, leases of his father, Hamilton, 125.

Cofran Elmer M., (Fargo) r 30, farmer, leases of W. E. Sumner 88.

Cofran Milo, (Fargo) r 29, farmer with his father, Thomas.

Cofran Thomas, (Fargo) r 29, 12 cows, farmer 100.

Colby Aaron H., (Corfu) r 21, mason and farmer, aged 77.

Colby Albert, (Corfu) r 10, (Joshua Colby & Son).

Colby Birdie A. Miss, (Sawens) r 21, teacher, daughter of Jerome L.

Colby Daniel, (Corfu) r 10, breeder of high grade Jersey cattle, 14 cows, fruit grower, farmer 183.

Colby Darius H., (Corfu) r 21, apiarist 10 colonies, farmer 50.

Colby David A., (Corfu) r 10, prop. cider-mill, dealer in cider and vinegar, farmer, leases of his father, Daniel, 100.

Colby Jerome L., (Sawens) r 21, 6 cows, farmer 53.

Colby Joshua, (Corfu) r 10, (Joshua Colby & Son).

Colby Joshua & Son, (Corfu) r 10, (Albert) breeders of Jersey cattle, reg., fruit growers, farmers 66.

COLBY LEVI H., (Corfu) r 10, 500 sugar trees, 9 cows, apiarist 29 colonies, farmer 150.

Cole Charles, (Darien Center) r 47, laborer.

Cole Hiram, (Crittenden, Erie Co.) r 1, laborer.

Cole William A., r 56, 6 cows, farmer 55.

Corp Charles E., (Darien Center) r 52, 10 cows, farmer 50.

Corp Henry, (Corfu) r 22, 6 cows, farmer 52.

Corp Justus B., (Darien Center) r 53, 30 cows, farmer 223.

Craft Adelbert, (Darien Center) r 30, 100 sheep, farmer, leases on shares of Elijah Gay 106.

Crosby Fred S., (Sawens) r 15, laborer.

Culing John, (Crittenden, Erie Co.) r 3, farmer 3.

CURTIS MELESON Mrs., widow of Thurman, owns h and lot with her sister, Mrs. Norman Matteson.

Curtis Wilbur A., (Colesville, Wyoming Co.) r 70, farmer 66.

Curtiss Clarence E., (Sawens) r 15, job printer, publisher *The Fireside Friend*, issued monthly, dealer in general mail merchandise.

Curtiss Ira A., (Sawens) r 15, 112 sheep, farmer 128.

Damradski Gustavus, (Darien Center) r 61, farmer 49.

Dan Augustus, (Alden, Erie Co.) r 51, farmer leases of Miss Hattie Slosson 12.

Darien Center Cheese Factory, (Darien Center) Bernhard Huver, of Buffalo, prop., manuf. of Swiss cheese.

Darien Center Hotel, (Darien Center) A. J. Richardson, prop., livery stable connected.
Davison Charles C., (Fargo) r 26, telegraph operator.
Davison John, (Fargo) r 26, blacksmith, prop. Percheron stock horse, farmer 40.
De Temple Alexander, (Darien Center) r 53, farmer with his father, Nicholas.
De Temple Nicholas, (Darien Center) r 53, 12 cows, fruit grower and wine manuf., farmer 128.
Devens John, (Sawens) r 21, section boss D., L. & W. R. R
Devens Margaret Mrs., (Sawens) r 21, h and 2 acres.
Dignan Charles (Corfu) r 23, farmer with his father, Michael.
Dignan Michael, (Corfu) r 23, 22 cows, breeder of horses, farmer 141.
Dillon Peter, (Sawens) r 13, farmer 65.
Dimock Charles O., (Darien Center) farm laborer.
Diver Ward, (Corfu) r 23, 25 cows, owns half interest in grist-mill, farmer 154.
Dodge Austin M., (Darien Center) blacksmith, carriagemaker, and dealer in carriages and sleighs, h and lot.
Dodge Guy B., (Darien Center) barber, prop. pool room, dealer in cigars and tobacco, bds. with Austin M.
Doolittle Albert, (Corfu) r 31, farmer 50, and leases on shares of Earl W. Sumner 125.
Dunham Frank B., (Attica, Wyoming Co.) r 82, 10 cows, farmer, leases on shares of his father, George, 80.
Dunham George, (Attica, Wyoming Co.) r 82, 10 cows, farmer 80.
Durbon Edgar M., (Darien Center) r 62, night telegraph operator at Alden, Erie Co.
Durbon William S., (Darien Center) r 62, retired blacksmith, aged 80, h and 2 acres.
Dyer Frank, r 42, fruit grower and gardener 8.
Eastland George, (Darien Center) tanner, emp. in Alden, Erie Co.
Eastland Sheldon, (Fargo) r 29, retired farmer.
Eddy Delos, (Darien Center) r 47, prop. Morgan stock horse "Green Mountain," farmer 5.
Edgerton Jacob, r 60, laborer.
Ellis James E., farm laborer.
ELLIS JOHN J., (Darien Center) (Ellis & Kinsey) station agent, dealer in agricultural implements, coal, and lumber, h and lot Railroad.
Ellis & Kinsey, (Darien Center) (John J. E. and William E. K.) millers and dealers in country produce.
Erhart Jacob, (Darien Center) r 62, dealer in fruit and potatoes, farmer 101.
Ernest John, (Darien Center) r 45, farmer 18½.
Evans George A., (Alden, Erie Co.) r 67, tanner, emp. Moffat Brothers, of Alden, Erie Co., 8 cows, farmer 50.
Evans John, (Alexander) r 36, 6 cows, farmer, leases on shares of E. A. Dodgson, of Batavia, 77.
Evans Joseph W., (Alden, Erie Co.) r 67, farmer with his father, George A.
Excelsior Cheese Factory, No. 1, (Attica, Wyoming Co.) r 86, M. D. Winchester, of Attica, Wyoming Co., prop; Eugene Spink, cheesemaker.
Excelsior Cheese Factory, No. 2, (Sawens) r 13, M. D. Winchester, of Attica, Wyoming Co., prop.; W. G. Thomas, cheesemaker.
Farnsworth Ervin, (Fargo) r 29, 7 cows, farmer with his father, Melvin.
Farnsworth Melvin, (Fargo) r 29, 7 cows, farmer 150.
Fellows Lorenzo D., (Corfu) r 24, 15 cows, farmer 103.
Ferner J. Adam, (Alden, Erie Co.) r 51, 12 cows, breeder of horses, farmer 130.
Fess Benjamin, (Fargo) r 26, cheesemaker.
Fess Levi, (Alden, Erie Co.) r 51, laborer.
Finlay Julane, (W. Batavia) r 17, widow of Robert, farm 84.
Fisher James, (Crittenden, Erie Co.) book agent and laborer, bds. with H. Cole.
Fisher Monroe L., (Darien Center) dealer in horses.
FISHER SOPHIA M., resident.
Fix Jocob, (Fargo) r 29, 12 cows, farmer 110.
Folts Elizabeth, (Darien Center) r 52, widow of John, 6 cows, farm 60.
Forward Riley A., (Darien Center) r 31, laborer.
Foster Elizabeth W., (Crittenden, Erie Co.) widow of William, farm 65.

Foster Lucy, (Darien Center) widow of Lyman B., h and lot.
Foster Oscar, (Darien Center) farm laborer.
Foster William, (Darien Center) r 66, 7 cows, farmer 95.
Freeman Edward C., (Alexander) r 36, blacksmith, h and 1½ acres.
FRINK EARL, (Sawens) r 17, telegraph operator.
FRINK WILSON, (Sawens) r 17, farmer, leases on shares of Anson Baker 57.
Fritsch Peter, (Darien Center) r 31, farmer 57.
Frost Henry W., (Sawens) r 3, 55 cows, farmer 68.
Gagear George J., (Alden, Erie Co.) r 66, farmer 86.
Galley Henry C, (Darien Center) r 61, 8 cows, farmer 112.
Gardner John, (Crittenden, Erie Co.) r 3, farmer 16.
Garigen Frank N., r 45, farmer, son of Nicholas.
Garigen John, r 45, farmer with his father, Nicholas.
Garigen Nicholas, r 45, carriagemaker, 14 cows, farmer 160.
Gay James, (Fargo) r 26, farm laborer.
Gay Myron, (Alden, Erie Co.) r 51, laborer.
Getman Lucius F., (Darien Center) farmer 2.
Getman Otis, (Darien Center) laborer, h and lot.
Gilbert Frank D., (Darien Center) r 73, 10 cows, farmer 111.
Gowan Albert J, (Corfu) r 21, railroad engineer.
Gowan Albert J. Mrs., (Corfu) r 21. farm 50.
Grannis George S., (Darien Center) with his father, Timothy G.
Grannis Timothy G., (Darien Center) dealer in hardware and agricultural implements, farmer 126.
Grant Eliza, r 60, widow of Thomas, apiarist 24 colonies, h and lot.
Grant Henry V., sexton and laborer, h and lot.
Grant Jonathan, (Sawens) r 18, laborer.
Grant William, r 42, 7 cows, farmer 40.
Greene Elmer, (Sawens) r 34, farmer.
Greene Hannah E., (Sawens) r 34, widow of Stephen V. R., resident.
Griffith Julius, (Sawens) r 19, carpenter, 8 cows, farmer 68.
Grim Nicholas, (Sawens) r 19, laborer.
GRISWOLD BENAJAH, r 60, 15 cows, farmer 118.
Griswold Charles C., r 60, 15 cows, farmer, leases of Benajah 118.
Griswold Eugene, r 60, farmer.
GRISWOLD JOHN, r 59, farmer 20.
Griswold Zeno, (Sawens) r 13, prop. grist, saw, and cider-mills and steam threshing machine, dealer in grain and feed, farmer 29.
Groat William, (Corfu) r 4, farmer 7½, and leases on shares of Thompson Maxwell 20.
Groff Hugh O., r 60, carpenter, contractor, and builder, h and lot.
Gruner Christian, (Attica, Wyoming Co.) r 58, farmer 2.
Hagen John C., r 60, laborer, h and lot.
Haley Ann R., (Darien Center) widow of Patrick, h and lot.
Haley Martin, (Darien Center) r 47, farmer 50.
Haley Michael, (Darien Center) r 51, 12 cows, farmer 130.
Hall Henry W., (Corfu) r 6, farm laborer.
Hall Langford, (Attica, Wyoming Co.) r 86, farmer 33.
Hamill Alec, (Corfu) r 8, farmer 83.
Hamill Hugh, (Corfu) r 8, carpenter.
Hamill John, (Corfu) r 8, farmer with his father, Alec.
Harlow Henry L., (Alden, Erie Co.) r 51, (Henry L. Harlow & Sons).
Harlow Henry L. & Sons, (Alden, Erie Co.) r 5, (Peark K. and Robert L.) fruit growers, breeders of pure blood Holstein cattle, reg., and draft and trotting horses, manufs. of creamery butter, and props. fruit evaporator, farmers 236.
Harlow Peark K., (Alden, Erie Co.) r 51, (Henry L. Harlow & Sons).
Harlow Robert L., (Alden, Eric Co.) r 51, (Henry L. Harlow & Sons).
Harmon Albert W., (Corfu) r 24, 12 acres Niagara grapes, breeder of horses, 14 cows, farmer 44, and leases of L. D. Fellows 103.
HARMON HENRY W., r 20, station agent and dealer in coal.

Harnden Barnum. (Darien Center) retired farmer.

Harper Lampson G., r 42, 12 cows, farmer 91.

Harper Nelson A., (Sawens) r 20, 15 cows, 125 sheep, 500 pear trees, farmer 142½.

Harrington George, (Fargo) r 26, teamster, emp. Buffalo Storage and Carting Co.

Harris Martin, (Corfu) r 8, laborer, farmer 18.

Harris Michael, (Corfu) r 8, brakeman N. Y. C. & H. R. R. R.

HARROUN GILBERT K., (Corfu) breeder of thoroughbred Jersey cattle, farmer 50.

Hartrich John, r 57, 8 cows, farmer, leases on shares of Andrew Krause, of Attica, Wyoming Co., 73.

Hartrich Nicholas, r 57, 14 cows, farmer, leases on shares of Michael Sunricher 100.

Hays William, (Corfu) r 7, laborer, h and 1 acre.

Hemline Michael, (Darien Center) r 66, farmer 65.

Herbert B., (Alden, Erie Co.) r 66, farmer 50.

Hewitt Jared, shoemaker and mail carrier.

Hewitt Jared Mrs., seamstress.

HIGGINS ROBERT S., (Corfu) r 24, 7 cows, 15 grade Oxforddown sheep, farmer 20, and with his father, Samuel C., 59.

HIGGINS SAMUEL C., (Corfu) r 24, farm 59.

Hills Byron E., (Corfu) r 6, 9 cows, farmer 60, and leases on shares of his father, James L., 100.

Hint Charles, (Colesville, Wyoming Co.) r 73, breeder of horses, 6 cows, farmer 170.

Hitchcock Moses, (Darien Center) r 47, 6 cows, farmer, leases of George Patridge, of Buffalo, 175.

Holmes Asher C., (W. Batavia) r 16, farmer 37.

Holmes David C., r 34, 30 cows, farmer 180.

Holmes Delia Mrs., (Darien Center) r 62, resident.

Holmes Sylvester, r 34, farmer 113.

Hopkins Nicholas, (Darien Center) carpenter.

Howie James, (Darien Center) r 61, 6 cows, farmer 96.

Huebel Ferdinand, (Darien.Center) shoemaker.

Hugunin Anne C. Miss, (Darien Center) h and lot.

Huhn Frederic, (Darien Center) r 62, farmer 4.

Hume James, (Corfu) r 24, 10 cows, farmer, leases on shares of Nelson Hartshorn 160.

Hume William, (Corfu) r 24, canvasser and farmer.

Humphrey Amos B., (Darien Center) r 52, 10 cows, farmer 110.

Humphrey Arthur M., (Darien Center) farmer with his father, Amos B.

Humphrey H. Levant, (Darien Center) grade Ayershire cows, farmer 31.

Humphrey Horace L., (Darien Center) farmer 31.

Humphrey Sylvanus, (Darien Center) r 52, 16 cows, farmer 200.

Humphrey Wallace W., (Darien Center) r 52, 300 sugar trees, breeder of Holstein cattle, reg., 10 cows, farmer 100.

Huntley Allen J., (Darien Center) r 31, carpenter and joiner, 300 sugar trees, farmer 85.

Huntley Hugh E., (Darien Center) r 31, carpenter and farmer with his father, Allen J.

Hutchinson Aaron P., (Alden, Erie Co.) r 51, breeder of horses, 14 head, 20 cows, farmer 285.

Hutchinson Henry P., (Alden, Erie Co.) r 51, farmer, owns in Michigan 130, and leases on shares 285.

Ingraham George S., (Sawens) r 35, (George S. Ingraham & Son).

Ingraham George S. & Son, (Sawens) r 35, (Harmon) 15 cows, 100 sheep, farmer 200.

Ingraham Harmon, (Sawens) r 35, (George S. Ingraham & Son).

Irving Helen, (Darien Center) r 21, widow of Ira, farm 10.

Irving Henry, (Darien Center) r 21, carpenter.

Jameson William, (Darien Center) r 74, 6 cows, farmer 50.

Johncox Frank, r 42, farm laborer.

Johncox George, (Sawens) r 36, laborer and farmer 10.

Johncox Henry, (Corfu) r 21, small fruit grower 4 acres.

Johncox James. (Darien Center) r 21, farmer and laborer.

Johncox James Mrs., (Darien Center) r 21, carpet weaver.

Johncox Thomas, (Darien Center) r 21, farmer 6.

Johncox William, (Corfu) r 14, farm manager for Nelson Hartshorn, of Batavia, 150.
Johnson Carrie Mrs., (Corfu) r 24, farm 28.
Johnson Charles, (Corfu) r 24, farmer.
Johnson Myron, (Corfu) r 24, farm manager 28.
Jones Dana Mrs., (Darien Center) r 62, farm 50.
Jones David, (Darien Center) r 62, 10 cows, farmer 62.
Jones Frank B., (Corfu) r 21, 8 cows, farmer 87.
Jones Horace, (Darien Center) r 62, farmer with his father, David.
Jones Irving, (Darien Center) r 51, farm manager for B. N. Hopkins, of Buffalo.
Jones Jacob, (Darien Center) r 52, laborer and farmer 13.
Jones Lawson D., (Corfu) r 21, 8 cows, farmer 87.
Jones Preston, (Darien Center) r 62, carpenter and joiner.
Joslin Hannah, (Darien Center) r 53, widow of Square, farm 73.
Joslin Ira B., (Darien Center) r 53, apiarist 8 colonies, farmer 5, and leases of Hannah 73.
Keibler John, (Sawens) r 13, 7 cows, breeder of grade Durham cattle and Hambletonian horses, farmer 80.
Kelley Arthur, (Fargo) r 29, farm laborer.
Kelley George, (Alexander) r 35, farmer, leases on shares of J. J. Gallup, of Batavia, 84.
Kemp Edward, (Darien Center) r 61, carpenter, jobber, and builder.
Kemp George, (Darien Center) r 61, 8 cows, farmer 114.
Kenline John, (Darien Center) r 75, farmer with his father, Michael.
Kenline Michael, (Darien Center) r 75, 9 cows, farmer 67.
Kennedy Emet, (Fargo) r 29, laborer.
Kennedy Frank, (Fargo) r 29, 12 cows, farmer 59.
Kenney George W., (Darien Center) r 75, farmer with his grandfather, Seymour F.
Kenney Seymour F., (Darien Center) r 75, farmer 35.
Kidder Herschel, (Alden, Erie Co.) r 51, 16 cows, farmer 150.
King Bissel L., (Darien Center) teamster, dealer in maple sugar, poultry, and eggs.
Kinney Timothy, (Corfu) r 8, farmer 32.
KINSEY JAMES, (Darien Center) r —, farmer.
Kinsey Stephen, (Darien Center) 12 cows, fruit grower, dealer in cattle and agricultural implements, farmer 100.
Kinsey William K., (Darien Center) (Ellis & Kinsey).
Kirtland Benjamin C., (Corfu) r 2, farmer 80.
Knapp Adam, (Sawens) r 13, blacksmith, farmer 13.
Krauss Andrew, (Attica, Wyoming Co.) r 85, 10 cows, farmer, leases on shares of Mrs. Amanda Reynolds, of Attica, 100.
Kreutz Daniel, (Colesville, Wyoming Co.) r 70, farmer 100.
Lamb Elijah, (Darien Center) r 62, farmer with his father, John E.
Lamb John E., (Darien Center) r 62, breeder of horses, 28 cows, fruit grower, farmer 320.
LANGWORTHY JAMES R., (Alexander) r 36, 100 sheep, farmer 118.
LANGWORTHY JAMES R. Mrs., (Alexander) r 36, resident.
LATHROP ANDREW J., (Darien Center) r 54, farmer with his brother James C. on the estate of his father, Elisha H.
Lathrop Anson, (Attica, Wyoming Co.) r 59 cor. 82, farmer 105.
LATHROP EUSEBA, (Darien Center) r 54, widow of Elisha H., executor and administratrix estate of her husband, 200 sugar trees, 60 Merino sheep, reg., breeder of thoroughbred Ayrshire cattle, 30 cows, farm 300.
LATHROP JAMES C., (Darien Center) r 54, farmer on the estate of his father, Elisha H.
Lawrence David, r 59, farmer, owns with his son Orville 85.
Lee Aurelia, widow of David, h and lot.
Leopoldt Henry, (Attica, Wyoming Co.) r 84, farmer 40.
Leverett Richard, (Crittenden, Erie Co.) r 3, farm laborer.
Lincoln Fred E., r 33, 10 cows, farmer, leases on shares of Milton 83.
Lincoln Jones, (Sawens) r 10, 9 cows, farmer 65.
Lincoln Milton W., 9 cows, farmer 79, h and lot.

Lindley George, (Alexander) r 39, 10 cows, 350 sugar trees, farmer 80.
Lindley George W., (Alexander) r 39, farmer with his father, George.
Lombard Hiram A., (Darien Center) laborer, h and lot,
Lombard Orville W., (Darien Center) laborer.
Losee Frank D., r 32, breeder of Hambletonian horses, 8 cows, and farmer 77.
Losee Frank E , r 56, 400 sugar trees, 100 sheep, farmer 111.
Losee Frederick R , r 56, farmer.
LOSEE RICHARD R., r —, breeder of Merino sheep, reg., 150 head, and Holstein
    cattle, reg., 12 cows, farmer 125.
Magry Charles C., (Darien Center) r 52 cor. 63, 9 cows, breeder of horses, farmer 71.
Maloney John, (Darien Center) r 47, farmer, leases of Martin Haley 50.
Mansell John, (Crittenden, Erie Co.) r 3, section boss, farmer 10.
Mapes George (Darien Center) r 62, 8 cows, farmer, leases on shares of Stephen
    Kinsey 100.
Marsh Alfred, (Sawens) r 11, 50 sheep, farmer 70.
Matteson George, r 55, 15 cows, farmer, leases of Norman 95.
Matteson Louisa, (Darien Center) r 63, widow of Samuel, farm 27.
MATTESON NORMAN, 15 cows, breeder of grade Holstein cattle and Percheron
    horses, farmer 94.
Maxwell Thompson, (Fargo) r 25, 24 cows, farmer 144.
May Earl H., (Alden, Erie Co.) r 69, farmer with his father, Harvey W.
May Harvey W., (Alden, Erie Co.) r 69. 8 cows, farmer 112.
McDiarmid James, (Darien Center) r 45, fruit grower, farmer 20.
McKay Ann Miss, daughter of Andrew, resident.
McKay M. Adele Miss, daughter of Andrew, resident.
McKay Mary Miss, daughter of Andrew, resident.
McLean John, r 55, 10 cows, farmer 100.
McLean Laura Miss, r 55, teacher, daughter of John.
McNally ———, (Corfu) r 8, widow of William, farm 7.
McNally William, (Corfu) r 8, laborer, emp. N. Y. C. & H. R. R. R. Co.
McVean Daniel, (Corfu) r 22 cor. 8, 800 sugar trees, breeder of high grade Holstein
    cattle, 12 cows, fruit grower, farmer 200.
Meinweiser Andrew, r — farmer, leases on shares of R. R. Losee 125.
Meinweiser Jacob, (Bennington Center, Wyoming Co.) r 77, 6 cows, farmer 65.
Meisner George, (Colesville, Wyoming Co.) r 73, farmer 20.
Meisner John, (Bennington Center, Wyoming Co.) r 62, 18 cows, farmer and mana-
    ger for Mrs. Mary King, of Bennington, Wyoming Co., 212.
Miller Emma A. Miss, teacher.
Miller John G., r 42, dealer in poultry and fruit.
Miller Ruth R. Miss, teacher.
Miller Samuel, (Darien Center) r 61, farmer 25.
Moissenac Eugene H., (Darien Center) r 63, 7 cows, farmer 57.
Moore Bradford, r 59, grower of strawberries, raspberries, currents, and vegetables,
    farmer 15¼.
Moore John, (Attica, Wyoming Co.) r 86, farmer, refused to give information.
Morgan Julia F., r 60, widow of Endell, resident.
Morgan Malony Mrs., (Darien Center) r 75, resident.
Morgan Michael, (Darien Center) r 75, farmer 45.
MORGAN PHILIP W., r 42, veterinary surgeon, fruit grower, 12 cows, farmer 92.
Murphy Willard, r 60, carpenter, emp. N. Y., L. E. & W. R. R. Co.
Myers Charles, r 57, 20 cows, fruit grower, farmer 145.
Myers Fred, r 42, 20 cows, farmer 144.
Myers George, r 57, farm laborer.
Newton Charles J., (Fargo) r 29, farmer 98.
Newton George, (Fargo) r 26, postmaster and general merchant.
Newton Ira, (Fargo) r 29, breeder of grade Percheron and French coach horses, mem-
    ber of Genesee County Breeders Association, farmer 140.
Newton John H., (Fargo) r 29, farmer with his father, Ira.
Ney Mary S., widow of Leander, h and lot.

Nichols Jacob, (Darien Center) retired merchant, h and lot, and real estate in Florida, h Main cor. Allegany sts.

Nolan Marks, (Corfu) r 23, farmer 11.

Noonen Charles E., (Corfu) r 6, pension, fire, and life ins. agent.

Nye Eugene, (Darien Center) r 61, farmer 66.

Nye Harriet, (Darien Center) widow of Freeman J., resident, h and lot.

Nye Thomas, r 55, retired carpenter, farmer 30, aged 82.

Oleir Fred, (Darien Center) r 47, laborer, h and 1½ acres.

Ortner Antoine, (Attica, Wyoming Co.) r 83, prop. threshing machine, farmer, leases on shares of his father, Mattis, 75.

Ortner Mattis, (Attica, Wyoming Co,) r 83, 6 cows, farmer 75.

Ostertag Edward, (Darien Center) r 53, farmer with his father, Sebastian.

Ostertag Emil A., (Darien Center) clerk for H. J. Raynor.

Ostertag Sebastian, (Darien Center) r 53, 12 cows, farmer 136.

Packer George, (Corfu) r 6, 190 sheep, farmer 100.

Patterson Fred M., r 59, 11 cows, farmer 106.

Peacock Frederick W., (Darien Center) r 30, 9 cows, farmer 98.

Perry Albert H., (Darien Center) r 62, justice of the peace 20 consecutive years, 3,000 apple trees, 2 acres small fruits, farmer 142.

Petrie Alexander, (Darien Center) wheelwright.

Pettibone Chauncey S., (Attica, Wyoming Co.) r 57, (Sumner & Pettibone).

Pettibone James A., (Attica, Wyoming Co.) r 57, 30 cows, prop. stock horse "Logan," farmer 295.

Pettibone Willis A., (Attica, Wyoming Co.) r 57, 400 sugar trees. 20 cows, 50 sheep, farmer 170.

Pfalzer Michael. r 32, 12 cows, farmer 100.

PHILLIPS ELMER A., r 60, physician and surgeon.

Phillips Thomas, (Darien Center) retired. h and lot.

Pixley Lucius, (Fargo) r 29, 12 cows, farmer 75.

Pope Edward, (Corfu) r 8, laborer, farmer 20.

Prime Hannah Miss, (Darien Center) r 47, farm 59.

RANGER GILES, r 60, (Ranger & Sutherland).

Ranger John, (Attica, Wyoming Co.) r 82. farm laborer.

Ranger Margaret Mrs., h and 5 acres.

Ranger Walter W., r 60, carpenter.

RANGER & SUTHERLAND, r 60, (Giles R. and James H. S.) dealers in coal, grain, and lumber, manufs. of heading, small fruit growers, farmers 33.

Raynor Henry J., (Darien Center) town clerk, dealer in drugs, medicines, dry goods, boots, shoes, and notions.

Reber John, r 21, farmer, leases of Caroline Riser 67.

Reling Michael, (Crittenden, Erie Co.) r 1, 7 cows, farmer, leases of Prince Waldo 75.

Reynolds William, (Corfu) r 4, farmer, leases of Jerome Allen 75.

Rheinhart Charles, (Alden, Erie Co.) r 62, farmer, owns with his brother Michael 7 cows and farm 113.

Rheinhart Joseph, (Alden, Erie Co.) r 72, 6 cows, farmer 75.

Rheinhart Joseph, Jr., (Alden, Erie Co.) r 72, farmer with his father, Joseph.

Rheinhart Michael, (Alden, Erie Co.) r 72, farmer with his father, Joseph,.

Rheinhart Michael, (Alden, Erie Co.) r 62, farmer, owns with his brother Charles 7 cows and farm 113.

Rhinesmith August, (Darien Center) farm 30, h and 1 acre.

Rice Mary, (Alden, Erie Co.) r 51, widow of Eviro, resident.

Richardson Annie J.. (Darien Center) prop. Darien Center Hotel and livery stable.

Richley Alexander F., (Sawens) r 13, dealer in agricultural implements and fertilizers, 6 cows, farmer, leases of his father, Florin, 60.

Richley Florin, (Sawens) r 13, 6 cows, farmer 135.

Richley Florin, Jr., (Sawens) r 13, farmer, leases on shares of his father 75.

Riddle Thomas, retired merchant, aged 85.

Roach Michael, (Crittenden, Erie Co.) r 3, farmer 4.

Roberts James, (Alden, Erie Co.) r 51, tanner, emp. in Alden.

Robinson Alva J., blacksmith.
Robinson Laban H., carpenter, prop. saw-mill and custom feed-mill.
Rogers Elijah P., r 60, 14 cows, farmer 143.
Rogers Frank M., r 60, prop. fruit evaporator and dealer in agricultural implements, farmer, leases on shares of his father 143.
Rogers James E., (Corfu) r 2, grower of small fruits, farmer 4.
Rudd Charles, (Sawens) r 21, laborer.
Rudd Adelia, (Sawens) r 34, widow of Edgar S., resident.
Rudd Lorinda, (Sawens) r 34, widow of Bradley, farm. 42.
Rudy Henrietta, (Sawens) r 12 cor. 11, widow of Martin, farm.6.
Rudy Julius, (Sawens) r 12 cor 11, farm laborer.
Russ George J., (Corfu) r 2, 16 cows, farmer, leases on shares of Emett Sumner 100.
Ryker James L., (Corfu) r 5, farmer 60.
Safford Elisha, (Darien Center) r 30, 9 cows, farmer 98.
Sagers Fred, (Sawens) r 11, farmer 5.
Sagers Hattan, (Sawens) r 11, resident.
Sagers John, (Sawens) r 11, laborer.
Sattler John, (Darien Center) r 61, farmer 50.
SAULSBURY CHARLES F., r 59, grower of small fruits, apiarist, farmer with his father, John, 12.
SAULSBURY JOHN, r 59, retired farmer 12.
Sawens Hiram, (Sawens) r 15 cor. 16, farmer 43.
SAWENS WILLIAM, (Sawens) r 15, 8 cows, 100 Merino sheep, farmer 110.
Sawtell Eliza A., (Sawens) r 14, (Harriet, Eliza A. & Mary Sawtell).
Sawtell Harriet, (Sawens) r 14, (Harriet, Eliza A. & Mary Sawtell).
Sawtell Harriet, Eliza A. & Mary, (Sawens) r 14, 6 cows, 85 sheep, farm 130.
Sawtell Mary, (Sawens) r 14, (Harriet, Eliza A. & Mary Sawtell).
Scanlon John, (Darien Center) r 47, section foreman and farmer 15.
Scanlon Nora Mrs., (Darien Center) r 47, farm 20.
Scanlon Thomas, (Darien Center) track walker.
Schad Charles, (Bennington, Wyoming Co.) r 75, farmer 41.
Schad Michael, (Darien Center) h and lot.
Schenck Charles, (Darien Center) telegraph operator.
SCHRADER FRED A., (Alden, Erie Co.) r 67, 150 sugar trees, 9 cows, farmer 80.
Schriver William, (Attica, Wyoming Co.) r 58, laborer.
Schwartz Charles, (Corfu) r 2, laborer, leases of John Taylor h and 6 acres.
Seagors Joseph, (Attica, Wyoming Co.) r 80, 12 cows, farmer 114.
Shaffer Lewis, (Darien Center) r 65, 6 cows, farmer 57.
Shaffer Samuel T., (Darien Center) r 64, farmer 45.
Sharick Frank, breeder of grade Holstein cattle and Hambletonian horses, 16 head, prop. stock horse "Gov. Cleveland," 20 cows, 108 Merino sheep, 20 swine, farmer 223½.
Sharrick Isaac, (Corfu) r 9, farmer 37.
Sharrick Isaac, (Corfu) r 9. carpet weaver and spinner.
Sharrick William, (Corfu) r 9, grower of small fruits and onions.
Shaw Charles F., (Darien Center) r 54, farmer 78.
Shaw Charles W., (Darien Center) r 63, 8 cows, farmer 100.
Shaw George W., (Darien Center) r 63, farmer with his father, Charles W.
Shaw John P., (Darien Center) r 63, aged 89.
Shaw William H., (Corfu) r 24, farmer, leases of Ezra Chapman, of Bethany, 81½.
Shear Henry D., (Sawens) r 32, 300 sugar trees, 12 cows, farmer 113.
Shear Luther P., (Sawens) r 13, postmaster, general merchant, subscription agent for papers and periodicals with C. E. Curtis, owns 3½ acres.
Shirm George, (Darien Center) laborer, h and lot N. depot.
Silliman Charles D., (Corfu) r 2, teacher, 10 cows, breeder of horses, farmer 77.
SIMONDS BENJAMIN C., (Sawens) r 19, breeder of horses, 12 head, 125 sheep, 12 cows, farmer 166.
Simonds Chauncey C., (Sawens) r 19, student.
Simonds Frank W., (Sawens) r 19, 6 cows, farmer 40.

Simonds Meritt D., (Sawens) r 19, farmer, leases on shares of his father, Benjamin C., 166.

Skeet John, (Sawens) r 11 cor. 20, farmer 48.

Slingerland Henry A., pastor M. E. churches of Darien and Darien Center.

Smith Frank H., r 56, 9 grade Jersey cows, breeder of French coach horses, 300 Merino sheep, farmer 270.

Smith J. Craig, (Darien Center) general merchant, h and lot.

Snider Benjamin P., (Fargo) r 49, blacksmith and farmer, leases of J. A. Eddy, of Alden, Erie Co., 62.

Sodeman Charles, r 78, 15 cows, farmer 171.

Soper Bradford. r 54, carpenter, jobber. and builder.

Spink Eugene, (Attica, Wyoming Co.) r 86, cheesemaker Excelsior cheese factory, No. 1.

Staebell George, (Alden, Erie Co.) r 28, farmer 25.

Staebell John, (Fargo) r 29, farmer 36.

Staebell Joseph, (Alden, Erie Co.) r 29, farmer 50.

Staebell Martin, (Crittenden, Erie Co.) r 3, 30 cows, farmer 164.

Steigler Michael, (Darien Center) r 54, 11 cows, farmer, leases of Charles Fisher.

Steigler Wilhelm, (Darien Center) r 66, farmer 4½.

Stevens Franklin E., (Darien Center) r 52, 10 cows, farmer, leases the Elias Humphrey estate 96.

Stickney A. McCall, (Fargo) r 26, mail carrier and farmer 11.

Stickney Amos, (Fargo) r 49, resident.

STICKNEY CAROLINE Mrs., (Fargo) r 26, resident.

Stickney Nelon, (Fargo) r 49, farmer 60.

Stickney Norman C., (Fargo) r 29, laborer and farmer 6.

STILES JOHN F., (Corfu) r 2, breeder of horses, manuf. of creamery butter, fruit. grower, 10 cows, farmer 95, served in 8th N. Y. H. A.

Streeter George A., (Sawens) r 19, pastor Church of God (Second Advent).

Strong Anna L., (W. Batavia) r 18, widow of Miner, 60 sheep, farm 104.

Strong Elizabeth. (Corfu) r 21, widow of Henry, aged 89.

Strong George, (W. Batavia) r 17 cor. 15, 60 sheep, farmer 97.

Strong Milo, (W. Batavia) r 18, 50 sheep, farmer 74.

Strong Perry V., (W. Batavia) farmer with his father, George.

SUMNER CHARLES, (Fargo) r 30, 100 sugar trees, breeder of Percheron and French coach horses, part owner of stock horses "Volcan" and "Houghton," 14 cows, farmer 85.

SUMNER DALLAS A., (Fargo) r 30, 200 sugar trees, 10 cows, 75 Merino sheep, fruit grower, farmer with his father, Winslow, 154.

Sumner Earl W., (Darien Center) r 31, fire ins. agent, 130 sheep, farmer 126.

SUMNER EPHRAIM, (Fargo) r 30, 12 cows, breeder of Percheron horses and grade Holstein cattle, farmer 117.

SUMNER JEROME, (Fargo) r 30, 150 sugar trees, breeder of French coach and Percheron horses, part owner of stock horses "Volcan" and "Houghton," 15 cows, farmer 115½.

Sumner John, r 57, (Sumner & Pettibone).

SUMNER JOHN W., (Fargo) r 26, 75 sheep, breeder of horses, member Genesee County Breeders Association, farmer 116.

Sumner Lewis, (Fargo) r 26, 6 cows, farmer 62.

SUMNER WINSLOW, (Fargo) r 30, farmer, owns the John Sumner homestead 154.

Sumner & Pettibone, (Attica, Wyoming Co.) r 57, (John S. and Chauncey S. P.) 400 sugar trees, 15 cows, fruit growers, farmers 120.

SUTHERLAND JAMES H., r 60, (Ranger & Sutherland) justice of the peace.

Suttle George, (Darien Center) r 30, farmer for Miss M. Wright.

Taylor Aaron P., (Alden, Erie Co.) r 68, mechanic and farmer 12.

Taylor George E., (Corfu) r 3, 23 cows, farmer, leases on shares of his father, William H., 138.

Taylor John A., (Corfu) r 2, resident.

Taylor Marcellus E., (Darien Center) r 62, carriagemaker and musician.

Taylor William H., (Corfu) r 3, 23 cows, farmer 138.

Terrey Lewis, (Darien Center) farmer 73.
Thayer William, (Corfu) r 23, 6 cows, farmer 82.
Thayer William H., (Corfu) r 23, prop. grist-mill, farmer with his father, h and lot.
Thomas Abram. (Corfu) r 2, farmer 30.
THOMAS GEORGE W., (Corfu) r 2, manuf. of creamery butter, 9 cows, farmer 54.
Thomas William G., (Sawens) r 13, cheesemaker Excelsior cheese factory, No. 2.
Thorne Minard R., (Colesville, Wyoming Co.) r 71, farmer, leases on shares of F. M.
    Cummings, of Marilla, Erie Co., 60.
TIFFANY DELIEU, (Darien Center) retired farmer, resides with his son, Henry C.
TIFFANY HENRY C. (Darien Center) postmaster and general merchant, Main, h do.
Timms Fred, (Attica, Wyoming Co.) r 58, 20 cows, prop. milk route, farmer 153.
Timms William M., (Attica, Wyoming Co.) r 58, farmer with his father, Fred.
TISDALE BERTHA R., r 60, dressmaker.
TISDALE IRA J., r 60, retired farmer.
Tompkins Julia Mrs., resident.
Tracy Harriet, (Alden, Erie Co.) r 51, widow of Orsemus, winter residence in Buffalo.
Tullar Hiram O., (Darien Center) r 52, 9 cows, breeder of horses, farmer, leases of H.
    J. Weston 140.
Turner Eleazer, (Corfu) r 2, 12 cows, farmer, leases of Thatcher B. 85, and owns in
    Pembroke 20.
Turner Thatcher B., (Corfu) r 2, 16 cows, farmer 85.
Tuttle Samantna, widow of Milo, farm 179, h and lot.
Tyrrell Amos, (Corfu) r 6, farmer 65.
Tyrrell Charles, (Corfu) r 6, florist.
Tyrrell Charles Mrs., (Corfu) r 6, wholesale and retail florist, farm 4.
Tyrrell James, (Corfu) r 6, farmer 75.
Tyrrell John, (Corfu) r 6, retired farmer.
Ulrich Frederic J., (Darien Center) r 75, farmer 70.
Vader Flora E. Mrs., dealer in dry goods and groceries, n depot, h do.
Vader Frank J., station agent and telegraph operator, h n depot.
Van Cran William Wallace, (Alden, Erie Co.) r 65, laborer.
Van Curean William, (Darien Center) r 65, dealer in horses, 8 cows, farmer, leases on
    shares of Bently 201½.
Van Curen Edward, (Corfu) r 24, 6 cows, farmer 50.
Van Curen William W., (Darien Center) r 65, farm laborer.
Van Devort Ten Eyck, (Corfu) r 8, farm manager for W. H. Grimes, of Lancaster,
    Erie Co., 126.
Van Ocker Dwight, (Darien Center) com. traveler.
Vellacott William J., (Crittenden, Erie Co.) r 3, 6 cows, farmer 41.
Vianger Jacob, r 46, 8 cows, farmer 50.
Vianger Rudolph, r 46, farmer wi h bis father, Jacob.
Vickery Howard H., (Darien Center) r 47, farmer with his father, Samuel N.
Vickery Howard W., (Darien Center) physician and surgeon, owns 30 acres Main.
Vickery Julia Miss, (Darien Center) prop. laundry.
Vickery Mary, (Darien Center) widow of William.
VICKERY SAMUEL N., (Darien Center) r 47, eclectic physician, apiarist 6 colonies,
    6 cows, fruit grower, farmer 68.
Vickery W. Frank, (Darien Center) farm laborer.
Wagner Catherine Mrs., (Corfu) r 7, farm 120.
Wagner Joseph, (Fargo) r 30. 20 cows, farmer 104.
Wagner Leonard, (Corfu) r 7, resident.
Wagner Leonard, Jr., (Corfu) r 7, 16 cows, farmer, leases of his mother, Catherine, 120.
Wagner Louis, (Crittenden, Erie Co.) r 28, farmer 16.
Wait Horace, 8 cows, farmer 73.
Walker Edward C., r 59, 7 cows, farmer 40
Walker John, r 39, breeder of horses, 9 head, 170 sheep, farmer 52, and on the estate
    of his father, Robert, 93.
Walker Matthew, r 39, 65 sheep, farmer 90.
Ward Benjamin F., (Sawens) r 39, farmer with his father, Jehiel.

Ward Jehiel, (Sawens) r 39, 900 sugar trees, 16 cows, farmer 128.

Warner George, (Darien Center) r 63, farm laborer.

Warner James N., (Darien Center) retired apiarist, aged 76.

WARNER PETER, (Darien Center) r 63, 300 sugar trees, 25 cows, farmer 250.

Weatherston James, (Crittenden, Erie Co.) r 3, farmer with his father, Nicholas.

Weatherston Nicholas, (Crittenden, Erie Co.) r 3, farmer 49.

Weaver Oliver, (Darien Center) r 61, laborer.

Welch Samuel G., r 47 cor. 30, farmer, leases of Rev. J. V. Lowell, of Franklinville, Cattaraugus Co., 130.

Welker August, r 59, 18 cows, farmer, leases on shares of Mrs. Samantha Tuttle 178.

Wertinan Noa, r 33, farmer 60.

Weston Henry J.. (Darien Center) retired farmer 140.

WHITING FLAVIUS J., r 60, supervisor, 8 cows, farmer 45.

Whitman George, (Fargo) r 27, 20 cows, farmer 150.

Whitman George, Jr., (Fargo) r 49, farmer 25.

Whitman William, (Fargo) r 27, dealer in carriages and agricultural implements, farmer with his father, George.

Wicker Jonah C., (Darien Center) r 75, farmer 65.

Wilbur Stephen, (Sawens) r 19, farmer 35.

Wilcox Almon W.. (Darien Center) carpenter.

Wilcox Fred D., (Darien Center) hay presser.

Williams Alonzo C., (Darien Center) r 62, fruit grower, farmer 50.

Williams Chester E., (Darien Center) r 62, farmer 7, and with his father, Alonzo C., 50.

Winans Elisha L., (Corfu) r 10, dealer in horses, boards horses in winter, farmer 126

Winans Frank, (Darien Center) laborer.

Wing John, (Corfu) r 21, farmer 50.

Wood George S., (Alden, Erie Co.) r 51, 15 cows, farmer with his brother Simeon M. 150.

Wood Simeon M., (Alden, Erie Co.) r 51, farmer with his brother George S. 150.

Woodard Albert H. T., (Darien Center) tin peddler, h and lot.

Woodworth Jehiel D., (Darien Center) carpenter.

Wotton Fairman L., r 56. reporter *Progressive Batavian* and farm laborer.

Wright George W., (Corfu) r 6, retired farmer 35.

Wright Melinda Miss, (Darien Center) r 30, farm 98.

Wright Orlo W., (Corfu) r 6, farmer 55, and leases on shares of George W. 35.

Wyckoff Calvin, r 56, farm manager for Horace Wait 72.

Wyman Ralph, (Sawens) r 18, 10 cows, 100 sheep, farmer, leases on shares of Cyrus Wait, of Corfu, 141.

Yates Alson E., r 60, 18 cows, farmer, leases on shares of his mother, Helen, 170.

Yates Helen, r 60, widow of Eugene R., 18 cows, farm 170.

Yates Lucius L., r 56, farmer with his father, Orlando B.

Yates Orlando B., r 56, dealer in farm produce, 400 sugar trees, 7 cows, horse breeder, grower of strawberries, farmer 80.

Young Jacob, (Darien Center) r 61, retired farmer, aged 75.

Young Jacob, Jr.. (Darien Center) r 61, 10 cows, farmer 102.

YOUNG THEODORE, postmaster, general merchant, breeder of pure blood Holstein cattle, reg., and Merino sheep, reg., prop. Hambletonian stock horse, 12 cows, 300 sheep, farmer 324.

ELBA.

(For explanations, etc., see page 3, part second.)

(Postoffice address is Elba, unless otherwise designated in parenthesis.)

Acker John, r 12, farmer 15.
Allen Orrin B., r 30, farmer 41.
Ames Almond A., (S. Byron) r 53, laborer.
Ames Israel D., (S. Byron) r 53, laborer, h and lot.
Andrews Charles, retired wagonmaker, h and lot. West ave. cor Cemetery.
Andrews W. Almon, school teacher, bds. West ave.
Arnold Lincoln. r 26, breeder of and dealer in Hambletonian horses, farmer, leases of
    Anson Torpy 100.
Atwater Lucius C., off r 21, farmer.
Austin Albert, r 24, small fruit grower and farmer 28.
Baba Henry, r 6 cor. 7, charcoal burner and laborer, h and 4 acres.
Babcock Alva, farmer 90, h Main.
Bacon William J., (Batavia) r 48, machinist, h and 1 acre.
Bailey D. Judson, pastor Baptist Church, parsonage Maple.
Balfour Andrew, r 18, farmer, leases on shares of Alva W. Slater 78.
Balfour William, r 14, farmer, leases of Elmer Willis, h and 4 acres.
Bamm Charles, (Dawes) r 60, laborer.
Barber Coryden J., r 38. farmer 20.
Barber Isaac S., r 38, farmer 142.
Barber Lincoln G., r 38, farmer with his father, Isaac S.
Barber Martin F., (E. Elba) r 54, farmer 130.
Barber Raymond L., (E. Elba) r 54, farmer with his father, Martin F.
Barber Thomas L., (E. Elba) r 53, prop. steam threshing machine, h and 3 acres.
Barber William A., (E. Elba) r 41, farmer 25.
Barber Arthur, r 35, farmer 107.
Barr Julius J., off r 32, breeder of Clydesdale horses, farmer 80.
Barr Mary M., widow of Frank E., h and lot Main.
Barr Phineas, r 26, machinist and farmer, h and 5 acres.
Barr Truman P., off r 32, farmer with his father, Julius J.
BARR WILLIAM J., (Batavia and Elba) off r 32, school commissioner.
Barton Elliot P., notary public, village clerk, and retired merchant, h and lot Mechanic.
Bauba Mary, r 2, widow of Louis.
Bell C. Stanley, (Dawes) r 59, laborer.
Benham Augustus C., (Batavia) r 60, 16 cows, milk dealer, breeder of draft horses,
    farmer 127½.
Benham Willis, (E. Elba) r 49, laborer.
Bennett Nancy Miss, r 26, farm 47.
Berg Albert, off r 20, laborer.
Berg August, r 9, farmer 32.
Berg Frederick C., r 1, laborer and farmer 15.
BERK FREDERICK, r 9, farmer 50.
Bert Fred, r 36, laborer.
Bignall Frank M., off r 45, breeder of draft horses, farmer 69.
Bignall Hiram, r 45, farmer 150.
Black John C., butcher and meat dealer, Main, h and lot do.
Blood Albert E., r 24, farmer, leases on shares of Robert 148.
Blood Robert, retired farmer 148, h and lot Main.
Bloom Charles, off r 20, farmer 113.
Bloom Sophia, off r 20, widow of Louis.
Bogue Anson W., (Batavia) r 60, book-keeper for Nelson.

Bolton Thomas, (E. Elba) r 43, laborer.
BOOTH JOEL A., (Batavia) r 56, retired wagonmaker, h and lot.
Bougher Henry, r 23, laborer.
Boyce Edward W., carpenter and builder, h Main.
Boyle Frank, laborer, h Mechanic.
Boylen Matthew, r 23, laborer.
Bradley Gardner, r 44, farmer with his father, William.
Bradley Jefferson W., r 43, horse dealer and farmer 45.
Bradley William, off r 44, deacon Presby. Church, farmer 60.
Bradway Frederick, (E. Elba) r 53, carpenter and joiner.
BRADWAY GEORGE W., (E. Elba) r 53, farmer 8.
Brailey Emily B. Mrs., dressmaker, Main, h do.
Brailey William, engineer, emp. B. B French, h and lot Main.
Bray James, (E. Elba) r 53, retired woolen manuf.
Bridge Bertha, r 27, widow of Joseph, house-keeper for her son Henry.
Bridge Frail, r 26, mason, h and lot.
Bridge Henry, r 27, mason and farmer 10.
Bridge John, r 27, invalid.
Bridge Joseph, r 27, highway commissioner and farmer 34.
Britton Alva S., street commissioner, carpenter, and joiner, h Main.
Britton Susan, r 35, widow of Cyrus R, h and 4 acres.
Brockway Henry, carpenter and builder, h and lot Mechanic.
Brockway Walter A., carpenter, h and lot Maple ave.
Brown Ann Mrs., r 30 cor. 27, farm 42.
Brown Arthur, r 32, farmer 24½.
Brown James A. J., r 30 cor. 27, farmer 92.
Brown John N., (E. Elba) r 42, pastor M. E. Church.
Brown Merton T., r 2, farmer 75.
Buck Cyrus, r 44, laborer.
Buckley Daniel, (Batavia) r 60, laborer.
Buckley Stephen, Sr., (Batavia) r 60, farmer 16.
Buckley Stephen, Jr., (Batavia) r 60, laborer.
Bullock Alva N., (Dawes) r 47, carpenter and farmer 40.
Bullock Silas E., (Dawes) r 47, carpenter and joiner.
BURGESS SEYMOUR G., r 34, farmer 42½, and in Orleans Co. 30.
Burling Jackson A., (S. Byron) r 53, laborer.
Burmaster John, r 9, farmer 50.
Burns Joseph, (Dawes) r 48, farmer 14.
Burr Henry, r 4, farmer 82½, and leases of W. J. Crawford 50.
Burr John, r 5, farmer, leases of Addison Wilder 125.
Burr Louis C., r 4, farmer 50.
Burr William, r 4, farmer with his father, Henry.
Burton Harry S., r 23, laborer.
BUTCHER EUNICE L., r 16, farmer 53.
Butcher William, r 16, breeder of horses, farmer in Byron 122.
CAPLE EMMA L. Miss, dressmaker, Maple, h do.
Caple Martha, dressmaker with her sister Emma, Maple.
Caple Mary A., dressmaker with her sister Emma, Maple.
Caple Robert, retired tailor, h and lot Maple.
CHAPELL FRANK, r 30, farmer, leases of M. Nelson Moulthrop 125.
Chapell Morris D., (S. Byron) r 53, laborer, h and lot.
Churchill George B., (Batavia) r 50, farmer, leases of Darius D. 70.
Churchill Howard D., (Batavia) r 59, farmer, leases of Darius D. 124.
Clark Abram E., r 35, laborer.
Cochran Alexander, r 35, laborer, h and 3 acres.
COLBY JEROME B., (E. Elba) r 52, farmer 15¾.
Cole William H., clerk, h Chapel.
Coleman Albert G., (Dawes) r 60, laborer.
Coleman Thomas, (Dawes) laborer, h and 9 acres.

8*

Conner Garrett, boot and shoemaker, h and lot West ave.
Cook Lewis L., r 5, laborer.
Corcoran Kate, (Batavia) r 60, widow of Patrick, h and 2 acres.
Corcoran Patrick, (Batavia) r 60, laborer.
Corcoran Richard, (Batavia) r 60, resides with his mother, Kate.
Cosway John F., r 10, farmer 152, and leases on shares of James M. Sleeper 18.
Crabb Ann M., r 18, widow of Christopher, h and 10 acres.
Crabb Charles W., (Dawes) r 59, laborer.
Craft Charles F., engineer, h and lot Chapel.
Craft Edgar R., emp. J. A. Staples & Son, h and lot Chapel.
Craft George H., (Oakfield) r 46, farmer, leases on shares of J. D. 94.
Craft Joseph B., (Oakfield) r 46, retired farmer 94, aged 88.
Craven Richard C., (Dawes) r 48, farmer 15.
CRAWFORD WILLIAM J., r 24, retired farmer 50.
Crocker Amanda, (E. Elba) r 42, postmaster, boot and shoemaker, aged 81, h and 6
    acres.
Crosby Russell, stage driver, h Main.
Crosby Zebulon R., r 23, farmer, leases on shares of Gilbert Shelley 112.
Dampier James, r 6, farmer 47.
Daniels Frank A., (E. Elba) r 29, laborer.
Dash Charles, r 35, farmer 34, and leases of J. E. Wilford 250.
Dash Henry, r 36, farmer 18, and leases of Lorinda Phelps 42.
Dash John, r 36, laborer.
Davidson Dewitt, (Dawes) laborer, leases of Frank Walter h and 10 acres.
Davis Charles E., r 23, laborer.
Davis Cicero D., town clerk and jeweler, Willis block, Main, h do.
Davis M. Eugene, r 11, laborer.
Davis Roy, off r 17, laborer.
Davis Henry, r 9, laborer.
DEIS HENRY, 1st, r 9, farmer, leases of the Doly estate 160.
Deis Henry, 2d, r 9, laborer.
Dersom Frank, blacksmith and horseshoer, Mechanic, h do.
Dersom George, blacksmith, horseshoer, and carriage ironer with his father, Frank, h
    and lot Mechanic.
Dersom William, house painter, h Mechanic.
De Shon Joseph C., (Dawes) r 48 cor. 60, farmer and grocer, h and 11 acres.
Dewey William E., (Byron) r 40, farmer 50.
Dillingham Oscar, r 29 cor. 39, breeder of grade Durham and Holstein cattle, farmer
    110.
Doody Rodolphus, r 34, peddler.
Dorf George, r 23, painter.
DORMAN GEORGE E., (E. Elba) r 42, farmer, leases of A. I. Hulett 140.
Dorman John H., r 41, dealer in grain, farm produce, agricultural implements, evapo-
    rators, dried fruits, coal, etc., farmer 140, S. Main.
Dorman Sarah, (E. Elba) r 58, widow of Amasa E.
Douglass Eliza J., r 19, widow of Ambrose, farmer 54½.
Downey Mary, (Dawes) r 60, widow of Dennis, h and 3 acres.
Downey Michael, (Dawes) r 60, laborer.
DRAKE AARON, (Oakfield) r 46, retired farmer 72.
Drigg Charles W., r 46, farmer 64.
Driggs Frank E., r 24, laborer.
Dryer John, (Dawes) r 60, laborer, h and 5 acres.
Dunn A. B. & Brother, (S. Byron) r 55, (George M.) farmers, lease of J. J. Gallup 88.
Dunn Arthur B., (S. Byron) r 55, (A. B. Dunn & Brother).
Dunn George M., (S. Byron) r 55, (A. B. Dunn & Brother).
Eckert Frank C., r 26, farmer with his father, Lewis.
Eckert Frederick, r 26, farmer with his father, Lewis.
Eckert George A., r 26, farmer with his father, Lewis.
ECKERT LEWIS, r 26, shoemaker and farmer 30, and leases of Nancy Bennett 47.

Eckert Lewis, Jr., r 26, laborer.
Edds Polly, r 24, widow of James, aged 84.
EDDS THOMAS, r 24, farmer, h and 4¼ acres.
Edgerton Freeman, (E. Elba) r 49, breeder of grade Cotswold sheep and draft horses, farmer 60, and leases of Alanson 177⅔.
Edgerton John C., r 44, farmer, leases of his father, Philo, 128.
Edgerton Philo, r 44, farmer 160.
Edgerton Rodney R., r 48 cor. 49, farmer 111¼.
Elba High School, organized in 1883 by Miss Mary H. Hollister, Chapel.
Elba Hotel, Anna A. Swartz prop., livery stable connected, Main.
Engel John, (Dawes) r 47, farmer 33.
Ess Adam, (E. Elba) r 42, laborer.
Fisher Matthew, W., r 11 cor. 7, farmer 50.
Fisher Theodore S., laborer, h Church.
Ford Alfred W., retired farmer 120, h Main.
Ford Elmer L., r 43, (Ford & Johnson).
Ford George W., r 43 cor. 44, blacksmith, h and lot.
Ford Manly F., r 43, breeder of Percheron and coach horses, farmer, leases on shares of Alfred W. 120.
Ford Philetus G., justice of the peace and farmer, h and 18 acres Chapel.
Ford Sylvanus, r 43, 350 pear trees, farmer 100.
Ford & Johnson, r 43, (Elmer L. F. and Marion J.) small fruit growers, h and 10 acres.
Foster Addison, (Batavia) r 57, under sheriff, breeder of and dealer in Hambletonian horses, farmer 230½.
Fowles Alexander, r 34, farmer 57.
Fowles William H., r 34, laborer.
Free John, r 19, laborer, h and lot.
French Benson B., dealer in and manuf. of staves, heading, and barrels, prop. cider-mill, Main, h and lot do.
Fromm August W., carriage manuf. and repairer, Mechanic, h and lot Main.
Fromm John C., r 12 cor. 18, carriagemaker and repairer, apiarist 90 colonies, h and 7 acres.
Fromm Loui, r 18, laborer.
Fromm Theodore, r 12 cor. 18, carpenter.
Fuller Edgar K., (S. Byron) r 54 cor. 55, woolen manuf. with his father, Mason B.
Fuller George W., r 11, farmer 30.
Fuller Lois B., r 8, widow of John, aged 76.
Fuller Mason B., (S. Byron) r 54 cor. 55, prop. woolen factory and saw-mill, h and 9 acres.
Gancho John, r 1 cor. 8, farmer 31½.
GARDNER MARTHA M., off r 21, widow of Jeffery W., retired farmer 238, and in Oakfield 72.
Garvey Patrick, (Batavia) r 59, farmer 20.
Gebhart Christian, off r 8, farmer 51.
Godfrey Nathan S., retired farmer, h and lot Chapel.
Godfrey Andrew B., r 49, breeder of grade Holstein cattle, farmer 127½.
Godfrey Charles A., r 49, farmer with his father, Eli N., and leases on shares of B. A. Griswold 63.
GODFREY ELI N., r 49, farmer 120.
GODFREY OSCAR E., r 33, breeder of grade cattle, farmer 203.
Goodliff Elizabeth, r 14, widow of George.
Gould Ozro A., (Batavia) r 41, breeder of grade Jersey and Durham cattle and Hambletonian horses, farmer 75.
Gourley James, r 23 cor. 19, blacksmith, wood worker, horseshoer, and repairer, h and lot.
GRAHAM GEORGE W., (Batavia) r 56, laborer, h and lot.
Graham George W. Mrs., (Batavia) r 56, carpet weaver.
Graham James, r 22 cor. 34, farmer, h and 5 acres.

Graham Lizzie M., r 22 cor. 34, dressmaker.
Graham Robert C., r 21, farmer, leases of Theodore and Jonas Halstead 102, and of Ann E. Holmes 42½.
Graham Thomas N., r 24, laborer.
Gray Clarence V., allo. physician, graduate Buffalo Medical University, Main, h do.
Green Orlo D., r 8, laborer.
Green William, r 21, farmer, leases of Lewis J. Hundredmark 30.
Griffin Almond, r 14, school teacher.
Griffin Archibald M., (Dawes) r 60, breeder of Hambletonian and Messenger horses, farmer, leases on shares of James Gregory, of Oakfield, 114.
Griffin Thomas C., retired stone mason, h and lot Main.
Griswold Benajah A., (E. Elba) r 49, retired farmer.
Hahn Charles, (Batavia) r 47, laborer, h and 8 acres.
Hall William T., (E. Elba) r 50, laborer.
Halstead Henry J., r 12, (William Halstead & Son).
Halstead Jonas, retired farmer, h and lot Main.
Halstead William, (William Halstead & Son) h and lot Main.
Halstead William & Son, (Henry J.) painters, paper hangers, and house decorators.
Hardegan George, r 43, emp. L. Harris & Son, h and lot.
Harkness Daniel R., r 11, breeder of draft Percheron horses, farmer 60.
Harkness George N., r 11, farmer with his father, Daniel R.
Harkness Westel E., r 11, farmer with his father, Daniel R.
Harris Charles D., r 23, (L. Harris & Son).
Harris David, retired farmer, h and lot Main.
Harris L. & Son, (Charles D.) dealers in coal, hay, produce, and lumber, S. Main.
Harris Lanckton, (L. Harris & Son) h and lot Main.
Harris Wesley J., r 18, farmer 31.
Harrod Edward, r 14, farmer 18½.
Hassett Mary E. Mrs., dealer in millinery and fancy goods, Main.
HASSETT WILLIAM H., molder, h and lot Main.
Hayes Edwin, r 59, laborer.
Height Morris J., r 10, laborer.
Henderson James, r 43, laborer
Hicks George B., r 18, laborer.
Higley Isaac A., (Batavia) r 59, breeder of grade Holstein cattle, farmer 144.
Hitzelburg Frank J., (E. Elba) r 58, laborer.
Hitzelburg William, (E. Elba) r 41, farmer 20.
HOFFMAN ELIAS, (Dawes) r 59, market gardener and farmer 10.
Hoffman Henry, r 43, farmer 97.
Hoffman Robert, r 29, laborer.
Hollister Marcus W., retired carpenter, h and lot Chapel.
Hollister Mary H. Miss, school teacher Elba High School, bds. Chapel.
Holmes Ann E., r 23, widow of Jonas H.
Holmes Ralph H., r 10, laborer.
Holmes Roxana O., r 11, widow of Westel G.
Hood Charles, (E. Elba) r 39, laborer.
Horn John, farmer 95, h West ave.
Hosmer Simeon W., (E. Elba) r 58, farmer 293.
Howland Dallas A., r 7, farmer 95.
Howland Daniel J., r 7, breeder of horses and grade Merino sheep, farmer 82.
Howland John N., r 7, farmer 114.
Hoyt Charles L., r 5, clerk.
Hoyt Mary J., widow of Philander, h and lot Main.
Hoyt Orlando T., r 5, breeder of grade Jersey and Holstein cattle, farmer 82.
Hoyt Sylvester O., laborer.
Hudson George L., (Dawes) r 48 cor. 59, farmer 20.
Hudson Julia M., (Dawes) r 48 cor. 59, widow of William R.
Hudson William S., r 35, retired farmer 47.
Hundredmark Lewis J., clerk, h and lot Mechanic.

HUNDREDMARK WILLIAM A., postmaster and general merchant, Main, h do.
Hunn Oliver T., (Batavia) r 41, painter, h and 3 acres.
Hunn Wells, r 26, laborer, h and lot.
Hunn William H., painter, paper hanger, and house decorator, h and lot Main.
Hunt Rinnear, (E. Elba) r 56, laborer, h and 4 acres.
Irwin Charlotte M. Miss, r 34, (Misses Irwin).
Irwin Margaret Miss, r 34, (Misses Irwin).
Irwin Misses, r 34, (Charlotte M., Margaret, and Rebecca) retired farmers 80.
Irwin Rebecca Miss, r 34, (Misses Irwin).
Ivison Charles, retired farmer, h and lot Main.
Ivison Charles H., r 32, laborer.
Johnson Jacob, retired stone mason, aged 82, h and lot Cemetery.
Johnson Marion, r 43, (Ford & Johnson).
Johnson Stephen, (Batavia) r 60, farmer 111½.
Jones Andrew E., r 25, (Andrew E. & Charles W. Jones) farmer for his mother, Roxania S.
Jones Andrew E. & Charles W., r 25, farmers 60.
Jones Charles W., r 25, (Andrew E. & Charles W. Jones) h and 10 acres.
JONES JOHN, (Dawes) r 60, breeder of grade Durham cattle and Chester White swine, farmer 64½, and leases of Cordelia Wilber 113.
JONES ROXANIA S., r 25, widow of Eli M., farmer 128.
JOSLIN ROBERT, (Batavia) r 59, breeder of Cheshire White swine, farmer 109.
Kearn Hugh, clerk Elba Hotel, bds. do.
Kellogg John H., (Dawes) r 48, farmer, h and 3 acres.
Kellogg Silas F., (Dawes) r 48, laborer.
Kelly Samuel, (E. Elba) r 56, laborer.
KERN GEORGE, laborer, h and lot Mechanic.
Knickerbocker Charles H., r 14, carpenter and farmer with his father, George.
Knickerbocker George, r 14, carpenter and builder, farmer 65.
Knickerbocker Hiram, r 16 cor. 14, farmer 65.
Knickerbocker Jay B., r 16 cor. 14, farmer with his father, Hiram.
Knulk Christian, r 13, farmer 10.
Kreeger Fred, r 9, farmer 27.
Kreer William H., (E. Elba) r 49, laborer.
Kulp Charles W., mason, h Main.
Lamb Elizabeth Mrs., dressmaker, bds. Cemetery.
Lamb Isaac, laborer, h West ave.
Lamka William, r 9, farmer 50.
Lampson Elias P., (E. Elba) r 51, farmer, h and 15 acres.
Larkin Christopher G., r 18, cooper, h and lot.
Larkin Porter J., clerk, bds. Main.
Le Shander John B., cooper, h and lot Mechanic.
LEWIS JOSEPH M. DR., physician, Chapel, h and lot do.
Lilley Charles, r 43, farmer 57.
Lintner Henry, (Dawes) r 48, laborer.
Little Charles M., r 5, breeder of grade Merino sheep, farmer, leases on shares of John Laborn 120.
Loomis Allen S., (Dawes) r 48, (Seymour evaporator) grower of and dealer in small fruits and vegetables, farmer 25.
Loomis William H., r 32, breeder of Clydesdale horses, farmer 22¼.
Lord John, r 34, breeder of half blood Percheron horses, farmer 52.
Lum Edgar A., r 8, farmer 62½.
Lum John H., r 17, peddler.
Lynch Humphry, (Batavia) r 59, farmer 76.
Maltby Delia E., r 48, school teacher.
Maltby Delia W., r 44, widow of William, aged 75.
MALTBY JOHN C., r 44, farmer 75.
Maltby Mary S., r 48, school teacher.
Manchester Robert, r 21, retired farmer 140.

Mark Calvin, r 18, laborer.
Mark Calvin A., r 18, laborer.
Mark Sarah A., r 18, widow of Joseph, farmer 34½.
Marsh Joseph F., r 33, laborer.
Martin Hiram N., r 49, farmer, leases of Anson Higley 152.
McAvoy William A., (E. Elba) r 50, retired tobacconist.
McCalla William, r 33, laborer, h and 3 acres.
McClouth Lydia A., r 21, widow of Joseph, h and lot.
McCrary John, retired farmer, owns in Stafford 174, h and lot Main.
McElveen David, retired farmer, h Chapel.
McGowen William, r 21, farmer 10.
McIntyre Hattie Miss, h and lot Mechanic.
McKurth Elmer E., (E. Elba) r 41, cooper and laborer, h and 2 acres.
McMarra Henry C., (Dawes) r 47, painter.
McMarra Michael, (Dawes) r 47, farmer, h and 17 acres.
McNarney Patrick, r 43, section boss W. S. R. R.
Merrill James K.. r 23, stage driver for Russell Crosby, h and lot.
MERRIMAN JOSIAH, r 15, farmer 216½.
Merriman Sheldon J., (Byron) r 15, farmer with his father, Josiah.
Middlestate Louis, (Dawes) r 47, farmer, h and 9 acres.
Millis Charles V., r 27, farmer with Eleazer T. Wood.
Mills Ansel D., (E. Elba) r 42, retired farmer.
MILLS OLIN J., (E. Elba) r 42, farmer 133.
Mirch Hiram, laborer, h and lot Mechanic.
Moore Charles, r 7, laborer.
MOORE CHARLES W., r 37, station agent W. S. R. R., W. U. telegraph operator,
    and agent National Express Co.
Moore Frank, r 7, laborer.
Moore John M., r 7, laborer.
Moore Sanford, r 7, laborer, h and 3½ acres.
Moore Thomas, drayman.
Morris James P., custom harnessmaker and repairer, Willis block, h and lot Main.
Morris Mary J. Miss, school teacher, bds. Main.
Moses Carlton W., laborer, h Main.
Moss John, r 13, laborer.
Moss Leonard, r 32, farmer, h and 7 acres.
Motz George, r 43, laborer, h and 4 acres.
Moulthrop M. Nelson, r 37, retired farmer and merchant, pres. of the village, justice
    Court of Sessions, and justice of the peace, farm 120, h Main.
Munce George, off r 46, retired farmer.
Munce William R., off r 46, farmer, leases of George 80.
Munn Charles, r 1, farmer, leases of O. F. Williams 220.
Muntz Charles W., r 26, laborer, h and lot.
Murdock Alfred A., r 18, breeder of Poland China swine, prop. boar "Billy Murdock,"
    No. 7283, and sow "Murdock Betsie," No. 17306, dealer in horses, farmer, leases
    on shares of Ellen C. Dersom 150.
Murphy Patrick, r 43, farmer 20.
Nelson George, (E. Elba) r 50 cor. 51, farmer 27.
Niendorf John H., r 26, laborer.
Norton Fidelia C., (E. Elba) r 42, widow of Horace B.
Norton Frances A. Miss, (E. Elba) r 42, school teacher.
Norton John R., (Batavia) r 59, farmer 67½.
Norton Myron W., (E. Elba) r 42, breeder of grade Merino, Cotswold, and Southdown
    sheep, farmer 120.
Noyes Philo E., r 22, farmer, leases of Stephen Shepard 122.
Nulty Elizabeth, widow of Henry, owns h and lot in Alabama, h and lot Mechanic.
Pardee Cordelia A., widow of Philo, bds. Mechanic.
Pardee M. & N., (Batavia) r 60, breeders of English coach horses, farmers 130.
Pardee Morrison, (Batavia) r 60, (M. & N. Pardee).

Pardee Nelson, (Batavia) r 60, (M. & N. Pardee).
Parker B. Clark, r 23, farmer, leases on shares of Samuel 300.
Parker Edwin, r 48, farmer 275.
PARKER FRED B., r 12, farmer, leases of Edwin 240.
Parker Harlow E., r 23, farmer 195, h Main.
Parker Jay D., breeder of Holstein cattle and Southdown sheep, farmer 104, and leases of Libbie 36, h Main.
Parker Joseph N., r 23, farmer 210, and swamp land 40.
Parker Libbie, widow of Albert, 2 houses and 36 acres Main.
PARKER SAMUEL, r 23, breeder of grade Merino sheep and horses, farmer 325.
Parker Will H., farmer with his father, Harlow E.
Parnell John W., r 38 cor. 41, farmer 131.
Peattie Rachel, r 11, retired farmer 120.
Perry Nelson H., r 2, farmer 132½.
Pettibone Augustus E., gardener, h Mechanic.
Pettibone Elias J. Col., retired farmer 380, aged 90, h Main.
Pfann Fred, r 16, farmer 50.
Pfann John, r 26, farmer 9.
Phelps Laurinda, widow of Chester, farm 39, h and lot West ave.
Phillips William R., carpenter, h and lot Chapel.
Pingrey Nelson, (Dawes) r 48, farmer, leases of E. B. & E. J. Wilford 100.
Pingrey Thomas S., (Dawes) r 48, farmer with his father, Nelson.
Piper John, r 12, retired farmer 50.
Piper John D., r 12, farmer 40, and leases on shares of John 50.
Porter George W., r 39, farmer 41½.
Porter John W., r 24, veterinary surgeon and farmer 15.
Porter Lyman, r 5, laborer, h and 1 acre.
Porter Ralph, r 10, farmer, leases of Stephen A. Wicks 140.
Pratt William, r 13, farmer, leases of Sylvester Wait 145.
Ransier Henry, peddler, h and lot West ave.
Ratca Fred, r 20, laborer.
Rath Fred, (E. Elba) r 40, farmer, leases on shares of Mary 100.
Rath Mary, (E. Elba) r 40, widow of Henry, retired farmer.
Raymond W. H. & W. H., general merchants, Main.
Raymond Walter H., (W. H. & W. H. Raymond) h Main.
RAYMOND WILLIAM H., (W. H. & W. H. Raymond) served in Co. H, 8th H. A., h Main.
Reynolds Columbia H., r 28, farmer 52, and in Byron 30.
REYNOLDS MARTIN, r 24, farmer 10.
Ries John, peddler, h and lot Mechanic.
Ries John C., r 12, breeder of grade Durham and Holstein cattle and Cotswold sheep, farmer 16, and leases of his mother, Mrs. John Acker, 15.
Ritter Amelia M. Miss, dressmaker, bds. Mechanic.
Ritter Christiana, widow of William, h and 3 acres Mechanic.
Ritter William C., painter, bds. Mechanic.
Roach Michael, (S. Byron) r 53, laborer, h and lot.
Robe William K., r 36, supervisor and farmer 110.
Rollings Thomas, r 6, farmer 29, and wood lot 10.
Root Erastus, r 17, laborer.
Rowcliffe Charles H., r 43, farmer with his father, John.
Rowcliffe John, r 43, farmer, leases of Charles Iverson 114.
Rowcliffe William, r 43, farmer with his father, John.
Sackett Loren N., r 30, farmer 61.
Salisbury Abraham, (Turner & Salisbury).
Seamans Charles H., 25 cows, milk dealer, farmer, leases of A. U. Willis 238, h Church.
Schlick Hollis N., laborer, h West ave.
SCHURZ GEORGE F., r 34, farmer with Alexander Fowles.
Shamp Amos A., r 23, laborer.
Shamp Joseph, r 23, lost right arm in threshing machine.

Shedd Sally A., r 16, widow of George W., farm 40.
Shelley Frank, r 23, farmer, leases on shares of Gilbert 125.
SHELLEY GILBERT, r 23, retired farmer.
Shelley Harvey W., r 20, farmer with his father, William B.
Shelley Josiah, r 23, farmer, leases on shares of Gilbert 125.
SHELLEY WILLIAM B., r 20, breeder of Berkshire swine, farmer 80, and wood lot 20.
SHEPARD STEPHEN A., farmer 127½, and in Batavia 223, h and 10½ acres Church.
Sherwood Charles G., retired harnessmaker, h Main.
Shieke August, r 8, laborer.
Shotwell Hugh P., r 20, breeder of grade Durham cattle, farmer 167½.
Shotwell Murray A., off r 20, farmer 90.
Shoultz Louis, r 44, laborer.
Shuknett Christopher, r 20, farmer 105.
Shultz Fred, r 9, laborer.
Shultz George, r 9 cor. 10, retired farmer, aged 76.
Simons Alvah E., journeyman blacksmith, emp. John Weber, bds. Mechanic.
Slater Alva W., r 18, retired farmer.
Slater Orville L., r 12, breeder of Holstein and Durham cattle and English coach horses. farmer 56.
Slater W. Henry, r 12, school teacher.
Slater William H., r 12, breeder of Percheron horses, farmer 127.
Sleeper Catherine, r 20, widow of John.
Sleeper James M., r 20, farmer 170.
SMITH ALONZO, pastor Methodist Protestant Church, parsonage Chapel.
Smith Wesley J., r 6, laborer, h and 1 acre.
Smith William H., r 3, farmer 52, and leases of James Knickerbocker 128.
SNYDER ELLIS, (E. Elba) r 50 cor. 51, farmer.
Snyder William, (E. Elba) r 49, farmer 22.
Snyder William, Jr., r 12 cor. 19, farmer, leases on shares of L. Harris & Son 255½.
Sparling John, Jr., r 22, farmer, leases of Robert Manchester 140.
Speed Alva, r 47 cor. 46, farmer, leases of Aaron Drake 70.
Speed Charles, (E. Elba) r 42, farmer 40.
Speed John, r 47 cor. 46, farmer 50.
Spencer Frederick, r 18, farmer and thresher, h and 10 acres.
STAPLES HENRY M., retired farmer and teamster, h and lot Mechanic.
Staples J. A. & Son, (N. Elmer) manufs. of and dealers in staves, headings, hoops, barrels, and lumber, props. saw and grist-mills, dealers in Akron cement, sewer-pipe, groceries. provisions, flour, and feed, Mechanic.
Staples Job A., (J. A. Staples & Son) h and lot Chapel.
Staples Loren M., student Buffalo Medical University, bds. Mechanic.
Staples N. Elmer, (J. A. Staples & Son) h and lot Chapel.
Staples Ruth H. Miss, (Misses Sunricker & Staples) bds. Mechanic.
STEELE HERBERT J., r 8, farmer, owns ¾ and leases ¼ of Lois Fuller 130, silo, 10 x 14, built after Prof. Mill's plan.
Steigman Sophia, r 23, widow of John.
Stephens Andrew J., (S. Byron) r 55, laborer, h and lot.
Stewart Robert, (Dawes) r 47, market gardener and farmer 40.
Stickney Alva, (Dawes) r 47, farmer. h and 9 acres.
Storer Eliza, (Dawes) r 59, widow, farmer 20.
Storms John C., (Dawes) r 57, farmer, leases of William H. Baldwin 100.
Stroable Antoine, laborer, h and lot Church.
Stroable John, teamster, h Church.
Strouts Edward J., r 12, school teacher and farmer with his father, William E.
STROUTS WILLIAM E., r 12, breeder of thoroughbred Percheron horses, prop. Percheron stock horse "Hector," reg. No. 1717, weight 1,400 lbs., farmer 131.
Suits Richard J., r 21, mason. h and 3 acres.
Sunricker Mary Miss, (Misses Sunricker & Staples) h and lot Mechanic.
Sunricker Michael, retired farmer, h Mechanic.

Sunricker & Staples Misses, (Mary S. and Ruth H. S.) dressmakers, h Mechanic.
SWARTZ ANNA A., widow of John, prop. Elba Hotel and livery stable, Main.
Sweet Charles W., r 23, pastor Friends Church.
Talbot Edwin R., r 7, laborer.
Talbot Henry, r 7, farmer 20.
Tansley James, r 36, farmer for Mrs. Luceba M.
Tansley Luceba M. Mrs., r 36, farmer 76.
Tansley Lucian S., r 36, hay presser and farmer.
Taylor Eli Hon., (E. Elba) r 29, farmer 200.
Taylor Erastus, (E. Elba) r 29, farmer 130.
Thomas Mary E., widow of Isaiah, h and lot Main.
Thompson Melvin W., laborer, h and lot Church.
Tilney Charles H., manuf. of harnesses and extras, dealer in robes, whips, trunks, etc., Main, h do.
Todd William G., (Byron) r 28, breeder of Chester White swine, farmer, leases of Caleb Wells 100, and owns in Byron 30.
Torpy Anson, r 26, retired farmer 110, aged 88.
Torpy Charles H., r 16, farmer with his father, Reuben.
Torpy Daniel, r 16, breeder of grade Durham cattle, farmer 180, and leases of Sally A. Shedd 40.
Torpy Eli A., (Rochester) r 16, book-keeper and school teacher.
Torpy Reuben, r 16, live stock dealer, farmer 147.
Turner Albert L., (Turner & Salisbury) resides in Holly, Orleans Co., 2 houses and lots West ave.
Turner & Salisbury, (Albert L. T. and Abraham S.) dealers in hardware and builders supplies, Main.
Vagg George J., r 7, farmer 24.
Vail Stephen, off r 21, farmer 225.
Wager George A., general merchant, Main, h Mechanic.
Wait Lutecia E., widow of Thompson, farm 45, h and lot Chapel.
Wait Sylvester, retired farmer, h and lot Chapel.
Waldo Amasa D., (Dawes) r 48, auctioneer and farmer 17.
Warneking Frederick, r 2, farmer, h and 7 acres.
Warner George E., emp. on W. S. R. R., h and lot Church.
Warner Israel W., allo. physician, apiarist 50 colonies, owns 16 acres on Maple ave., h and 20 acres Main.
Warner Will I., graduate Carey Seminary, bds. Main.
WATSON DAVID, r 4, breeder of grade Merino sheep and Holstein cattle, farmer 160.
Watson David J., r 4, farmer with his father, David.
Watson Ellen, r 4, widow of James, aged 89.
Watt John, off r 21, 1 full blood Jersey bull and Morgan horses, farmer, leases on shares of Martha M. Gardner 300.
Watt Samuel J., off r 21, laborer.
Weber John, blacksmith and machinist, Mechanic, h do.
Weiland Edward W., carpenter and joiner with Henry Brockway, bds. Mechanic.
Walker Peter, laborer, h and 2¾ acres West ave.
Wentz Charles, (E. Elba) r 43, laborer.
Wetzel Henry, r 27, laborer.
WHEAT ELIAS A., retired Methodist Protestant clergyman, h Mechanic.
Whipple Orrell, r 24, farmer, leases of Mrs. Laura E. Scofield 25.
White Edwin A., r 38, farmer with his father, Milo F.
White Isaac, r 47, laborer.
White James, Sr., r 47, farmer 118.
White James, Jr., r 47, farmer with his father, James, Sr.
White Milo F., r 38, gardener and farmer 43½.
White William D., r 38, farmer with his father, Milo F.
White William R., (Oakfield) r 46, farmer 88½.
Wicks Frank J., r 45, laborer.
Wicks Hersey E., r 2, mason, leases of John Shulah h and 4 acres.

Wicks Isaac L., r 2, laborer.
Wicks James H., r 8, farmer 119.
Wicks Walter, r 2, laborer.
Wiedrich Charles L., laborer, bds. Chapel.
Wiedrich Henry F., butcher and clerk, h and lot Main.
Wiedrich Jacob, Sr., laborer, h and 5 acres Mechanic.
Wiedrich Jacob, Jr., r 33, emp. on W. S. R. R., h and lot.
Wiedrich Peter, teamster, h and lot Chapel.
Wigton John, r 34, farmer, leases on shares of the Misses Irwin 80.
Wigton Thomas J., r 5 cor. 6, laborer.
Wilber George W., laborer and gardener, h and lot Mechanic.
Wilcox Dey E., druggist and bookseller, Sherwood block, h Main.
Wilder Eliza, widow of John, h and lot Mechanic.
Wilder Lucy, widow of Addison, h and lot Main.
Wilder Sarah A., widow of Sumner, h Mechanic.
Wilford Charles C., r 45, farmer with his father, Eugene B.
Wilford E. B. & J. E., r 45 cor. 44, breeders of and dealers in grade and pure blood
    stock, farmers 330.
WILFORD EUGENE B., r 45, (E. B. & J. E. Wilford).
Wilford Joseph E., r 44, (E. B. & J. E. Wilford).
Wilford Joseph S., r 45, farmer with his father, Eugene B.
Will Charles, (E. Elba) r 50, thresher, h and 6 acres.
Will Christiana, (E. Elba) r 50, widow of John.
Will Frank E., (E. Elba) r 41 cor. 39, laborer and carpenter.
Williams Anson P., (Dawes) r 48, breeder of grade Durham cattle, farmer 114.
Willis A G. & G. N., r 3, farmers 57½, and lease on shares of the Willis estate 179.
Willis Alonzo G., r 3, (A. G. & G. N. Willis).
Willis Alva U., farmer 200, h Main.
Willis Charles J., farmer with his father, Alva, h and 3 acres Chapel.
Willis Frank G., r 12, breeder of Poland China swine, farmer 100.
Willis George N., r 3, (A. G. & G. N. Willis).
Willis Lovina, r 3 cor. 4, widow of Alanson.
Wilson Frank B., (E. Elba) r 58, laborer.
Wilson James M., (E. Elba) r 50, veterinary surgeon and farmer 17.
Wolf Caroline, r 9, widow of William, farmer 17.
Wood Eleazer T., r 27, farmer 13¼, and swamp land 17½.
Woodbine John, (E. Elba) r 41 cor. 39, farmer 15.

LE ROY.

(For explanations, etc., see page 3, part second.)

(Postoffice address is Le Roy, unless otherwise designated in parenthesis.)

Abbe Mary M. Mrs., h 57 Main.
Acker Charles W., farmer, h 5 Maple ave.
Acres Margaret Mrs., h 24 E. Main.
Acres Mary A. Mrs., h 9 Pleasant.
Acres Margaret Mrs., h 23 Pleasant.
Adams John H., laborer, h 68 Lake.
Adams William H., gardener, h 68 Lake.
Aiken Grace Mrs., h 14 Myrtle.
Albee Horace, contractor and builder, h 58 E. Main.
ALBEE ELIAS O., contractor and builder, farm 40, h 8 South.
Alexander Allen, r 40, resident.

Allen Catharine, widow of Timothy, h 40 North.
Allen Charles J., laborer, h 61 Church.
Allen Fannie E. Mrs., milliner, h 36 Clay.
Allen James, laborer, h 61 Church.
Allen Michael, laborer, h 39 North.
Allen Oliver, Jr., woolen manuf. at Mumford, Monroe Co., farmer 58, h 7 E. Main.
Allis Emma Miss, h 27 Myrtle.
American Express Co., L. G. Paul, agent, 20 Main.
Anderson Albert, h 29 Church.
ANDERSON JAMES A., pastor Presbyterian Church, h 7 Clay.
Anderson John, book-keeper, h 34 Clay.
Anderson John, r 12, farmer 20.
Anderson John B., law student, h 99 Lake.
Anderson John R., retired, h 99 Lake.
Anderson Lucy, widow of Seneca, h 13 South.
Anderson Mary Ann, r 12, widow of James, farmer 176.
ANNIN JAMES, jeweler and watchmaker, Lampson House block, h 44 Myrtle.
Annin William L., retired teacher, h 44 Myrtle.
Arnold Asa, retired merchant, h 81 Lake.
Arnold Ella M. Miss, teacher Ingham University, bds. do.
Arnold Henry A., (Stone Church) r 7, farmer, owns one-half of 155.
Artman Arthur M., r 56, fruit grower and farmer 121.
Atchison Edward J., drug clerk, bds. 7 Lake.
Atchison Frederick, agent patent rights, h 7 Lake.
Atchison William, retired, h 7 Lake.
Atwater Allen, (Stone Church) r 7, mason and farmer 4.
Atwater Lawrence, r 26, farmer 70.
Avery John, laborer, h 43 Myrtle.
Avery Samuel, carriagemaker, h Lincoln ave.
Ayers Charles W., laborer, h 11 Pleasant.
Bacon Byron H., furniture dealer, 35 Main, h 13 Clay.
Bacon Charles E., laborer, bds. 72 Myrtle.
BACON DAVID R., retired, h 7 E. Main.
Bacon Seth P., street com., h 72 Myrtle.
Bader August, laborer, h 55 Church.
Bailey Erastus W., dealer in coal, h 21 Lake.
Baldwin G. M., widow of David E., h 3 Myrtle.
Ball Falla M., widow of Samuel A., h 40 Myrtle.
BALL FRANK W., dealer in groceries and provisions, 30 Main, h 16 Craigie.
Ball James M., r 32, farmer 15.
Ballard Randolph, retired lawyer, h 1 W. Main.
Ballintine Eveline P., physician and teacher Ingham University, h 48 Myrtle.
Ballintine H. Miss, teacher Ingham University, h Myrtle.
Ballintine James, Presbyterian clergyman, h 48 Myrtle.
Bank of Le Roy, William Lampson, pres.; Butler Ward, cashier, Main cor. Bank.
BANNISTER ADOLPHUS D., r 4, farmer with his father, Luther, 128.
Bannister Carl L., teacher and farmer.
Bannister Dwight N., teacher and farmer.
BANNISTER ELLEN M., r 17, farmer with Mary 47.
BANNISTER ERVILLE, r 60, farmer.
Bannister James F., att'y at law, h Lincoln ave.
Bannister Jay A., artist, over 38 E. Main, bds. Eagle Hotel.
Bannister Luther, r 4, farmer 128.
BANNISTER MARY, r 17, farmer with Ellen M, 47.
Bannister Myron A., r 16, farmer 9.
Barker Jared P., retired, h 33 Lake.
Barlow Arthur, r 44, farmer with his father, Charles.
Barlow Charles, r 44, farmer, leases of H. H. Falkner 30.
Barnes Richard, stone cutter, h 46 Lake.

Barrett Angelica B., widow of Solomon, h 61 Main.
Barrett Edwin Victor, h 61 Main.
Barrows W. Henry, book-keeper, h 37 Clay.
Bartlett Rufus, poormaster, h 74 Gilbert.
Bartlett Sophia, widow of Jonas, h 86 Gilbert.
Bartolf Stephen Mrs., h Clay.
Barton Harry, (Stone Church) farmer.
Barton James, (Stone Church) r 9, farmer 8.
Barton Mary L. Mrs.. h 18 North.
Bassendoff Frank M., harnessmaker, bds. Eagle Hotel.
Bater Joseph, r 57, farmer and mason.
BAXTER MARY, widow ef Alexander, florist, h 59 Wolcott.
Baxter William H., florist, h 59 Wolcott.
Beach Florence L. Mrs., teacher Ingham University.
Beaver Frederick J., grocer, 37 Main, h do.
Beckwith Lewis W., retired, h 43 Church.
Beer William, laborer, h 84 South.
Beierlein George, laborer, h 59 South.
Bell Emeline Mrs., h 16 Exchange.
Bell John M., clerk, h 16 Exchange.
Bellamy R. W. Mrs., teacher Ingham University. bds. do.
Bernd Charles F., r 62, farmer with his father, Jacob.
Bernd Edward, r 62, carpenter.
Bernd George S., r 62, farmer with his father, Jacob.
Bernd Jacob, r 62, breeder of Shorthorn cattle, farmer 200.
Bernd John J., carpenter, h 57 Wolcott.
Bidwell Anna M., widow of George, h 55 Wolcott.
Bishop Edwin, carriage painter, bds. Eagle Hotel.
Bishop Henry A., painter, h 53 Wolcott.
Bishop Lemon C., retired farmer, h 83 Lake.
Bishop Theron C., r 41, farmer with his father, William L.
BISHOP WILLIAM L., r 41, fruit grower. breeder of Wilkes horses, farmer 160.
BISSELL BELLONA A., widow of Levi, h 13 South.
Bissell C. Fitch, att'y at law, 33 Main, h 104 W. Main.
Bissell David J., att'y at law, 33 Main, h Gilbert.
Bissell Francis E., r 39, farmer with his father, Frank J.
BISSELL FRANK J., r 39, farmer 123.
Bissell John C., supt. gas works, h 36 Lake.
Bissell Livingston J.. h 109 W. Main.
Black Catharine Mrs., h off Maple Place.
Blackmer Emma R., h 12 South.
Blackmer Salvira H., widow of Abner, h 12 South.
Blair Alexander, laborer, h 52 North.
Blair Ruth D., widow of Alexander, h 7 St. Mark.
Blood Charles, laborer, h 37 North.
Blood Daniel, laborer, h 37 North.
Blood Eugene, mason, h 4 Bacon.
Blood Felix T., dentist, 14 Main, bds. Eagle Hotel.
Blood William J., laborer, h 46 Church..
Boak Charles, dealer in poultry, h 7 South.
Boak William C., mail agent, bds. 7 South.
Boatfield James, r 47, farmer, leases of Leland Taft 100.
Bovee Lorenzo J., r 28, manuf. of and wholesale dealer in lumber, farmer 60.
BOWDEN SAMUEL, clergyman, h 93 W. Main.
BOWEN CAROLINE, (Bowen & Robinson) widow of Daniel V., h 18 Church.
Bowen Emma Mrs., h 42 North.
Bowen Julius F., painter and decorator, h 42 North.
Bowen Lewie C., painter, h 42 North.
Bowen & Robinson, (Caroline B. and John E. R.) dealers in groceries and crockery,
    58 W. Main.

Brown John S., salt packer, h 52 Myrtle.
Brown M. Filmore, att'y at law, 366 Main st., Buffalo, h E. Main.
Bull James, h 98 Myrtle.
Burbridge Robert, r 32, gardener.
Burdoff George, r 54, farmer.
Burke Martin, laborer, h 27 South.
Burke Martin J., laborer, h 27 South.
Burns Mary, widow of Christopher, h 61 South.

Brown Thomas W., saltmaker, h 32 Clay.
Brown William S., printer, h 12 Craigie.
BROWN WILLIAM S., dealer in lime and all kinds of rough and cut stone, manuf.
    of buggies, carriages, wagons, and sleighs, 60 Main, h 6 Myrtle.
Bryant Clarence, prop. meat market, h 82 Lake.
Buckley John, butcher, Mill.
Buell E. H., widow of David H., h Wolcott.

Cameron Elizabeth Miss, dressmaker, h 36 Myrtle.
Cameron Isabella, widow of Hugh, farm in Bethany 112, h 14 Craigie.
CAMPBELL ARCHIBALD D., (Bergen) r 9, farmer with Peter D. 105.
Campbell Duncan, r 12, farmer 60.
Campbell John, Sr., r 69, farmer 92.
Campbell John, Jr., r 69, farmer with his father, John, Sr.
Campbell Peter D., (Bergen) r 9, farmer with Archibald B. 105.
Campbell Nancy, r 12, resident.
Carey David, r 61, miller and farmer 27.
Carey Mary, h 61 Myrtle.
Carlin John, r 48, farmer 2.
Carlisle Etta Miss, dressmaker, h Summit.
Carlisle Fannie, h 36 Clay.
Carlisle George, r 50, farmer.
Carlisle Joseph Mrs., h Summit.
CARLTON CHARLES L., wagonmaker, Mill, h 28 Summit.
Carney John, foreman at salt works, bds. Wiss House.
Carney Patrick, r 48, farmer 80.
Carney William, r 36, farmer 160.
Carpenter Elizabeth, r 44, widow of Jesse E.
Carragher Benjamin, laborer, h 13 Maple ave.
Carroll Michael, laborer, h 36 North.
Carson William, laborer, bds. Summit.

Carson William A., clerk, bds. Summit.
Cary James, r 52, farmer with his father, John.
Cary John, r 52, farmer 48.
Cassidy Patrick J., dealer in boots and shoes, 17 W. Main, h 96 do.
Caswell Florence M., with Martha R., hair worker, bds. 50 E. Main.
Caswell John P., millwright, h 50 E. Main.
Caswell Martha R., with Florance M., hair worker, bds. 50 E. Main.
Cater Frederick, carpenter and joiner, h 37 Clay.
Cater John W., dealer in fruit and ornamental trees, farmer 2½, h North.
Cavanaugh Arthur, prop. saloon, 14 Main, bds Eagle Hotel.
Cavanaugh James J., r 27, farmer, leases of William Huyck 160.
Chaddock Frank E., dealer in phosphate, h 38 Clay.
CHADDOCK GEORGE W., blacksmith, h 15 Craigie.
Chaddock Suel, retired farmer, h 46 Clay.
Chafer Fred, emp. in salt works, h 92 Myrtle.
CHAMPION JOHN N., prop. livery and sale stables, 3 North.
CHAPMAN WILLARD M., real estate agent, 41 W. Main, h 21 Summit.
Church William I., painter, h 23 Myrtle.
Cissan Charles H., r 72, farmer, leases of Mrs. Elsia Harris 80.
CLARK ALEXANDER, (Stone Church) r 4, farmer 160.
Clark Alvin, retired farmer, h 4 Union.
Clark Frank, (Frank & Mike Clark) h 111 W. Main.
Clark Frank & Mike, dealers in dry goods and notions, Lampson House block.
Clark Margaret, widow of Henry T., h 65 Wolcott.
Clark Martin L., r 66, farmer 70.
Clark Mike, (Frank & Mike Clark) h 111 W. Main.
Clark Perry, gardener, leases of F. C. Bissell 15, h W. Main.
Clark Samuel G., manuf. of lumber and farmer, h 69 Wolcott.
Clark Walter H., molder, h 65 Wolcott.
Clasly Hannah Mrs., h 46 North.
Clemens Robert, retired, h 19 Myrtle.
CLEVELAND J. FRED., physician and surgeon, 21 Main, h do.
Clifford Andrew, laborer, h 106 Gilbert.
Clubine Genevieve, teacher Ingham University.
Cochran Elliott P., (S. M. Cochran & Son) bds. Lampson House.
Cochran S. M. & Son, (Elliott P.) props. Lampson House.
Cochran Sarah M., widow of Joseph, (S. M. Cochran & Son).
Coe Albert, r 48, farmer 150.
Coe Ransom, retired farmer, h 37 E. Main.
Coffey Eben, (Stone Church) r 7, farmer, leases of Dennis D. Barker, of Brooklyn, 60.
Cole Elias, (Stone Church) r 7, farmer.
Cole Frank W., (H. Cole & Son) h 7 North.
Cole H. & Son, (Frank W.) dealers in boots, shoes, etc., 23 W. Main.
Cole Harman, (H. Cole & Son) h 7 North.
Cole William W., miller, h 15 North.
Coleman John, r 40, veterinary surgeon and farmer.
Coleman Julia & Harriet, 75 South.
Coleman Libbie, dressmaker, bds. 10 Lake.
Coleman Mary, dressmaker, bds. 10 Lake.
Coleman Peter J., r 17, farmer, leases of Edgar Crocker 75.
Coleman Thomas H., off r 22, farmer 23.
Coleman Timothy, r 23, farmer 5.
Collins Albert H., r 18, farmer 95.
COLLINS JAMES A., h 41 Church.
COMSTOCK ASAHEL O., retired, h 9 E. Main.
Comstock Frank M., teacher, h 19 Wolcott.
COMSTOCK SAMUEL F., ins. and real estate agent, 7 Main, h Clay.
CONLIN MATTHEW, r 14, breeder of Jersey cattle, farmer 130.
Conlin Michael, r 14, farmer, leases of the Angus McPherson estate 120.

Conlin William, r 14, farmer with his father, Matthew.
Conlon Patrick, r 50, farmer 19.
Conner John, laborer, h 6 Bacon.
Connor Catharine, widow of Thomas, h 87 Myrtle.
Connor James A., carpenter, h 33 South.
Convery John H., h 24 Summit.
Convery Mary, widow of Francis, h 24 Summit.
Cook Henry, laborer, h 55 Myrtle.
Cook John H., printer, h 55 Myrtle.
Cook John L., farmer in Pavilion 50, h 54 Lake.
Coon John, r 19, farmer, leases of O. C. Thwing 130.
Coop Sarah Mrs.. r 48, resident.
Cooper John W., (Stone Church) r 7, farmer 50.
Cooper Neil, r 50, teamster.
Copeland George I., laborer, h 49 Wolcott.
Cora Anthony, r 50, farmer.
Corolan John, r 50, laborer and farmer 2.
Corcoran James, r 38, farmer 10.
Cory Joseph, r 50, farmer 21.
Costolo Bridget Mrs., r 23, farm 3.
Cottage Hotel, James Prendergast. prop., 56 Lake.
Cowan Hugh O., tailor, 39 Main, h 34 Clay.
Coyle Hugh, laborer, h 10 Maple ave.
Crittenden Sheltem, r 27, farmer 2.
Crocker Henry, agent Atlantic and Pacific Tea Co., h 34 Church.
Crocker Lucy Mrs., h 16 Park Place.
Crocker Phebe A., widow of James, h 47 E. Main.
Crofoot Frank M., r 54, farmer with his father, Gideon D.
Crofoot Gideon D., r 54, breeder of Hambletonian horses and Jersey cattle, farmer 210.
Crofoot William R., att'y at law, over 21 W. Main, bds. Lampson House.
Crow John, bds. Wiss House.
Cullen James, laborer, h 18 Gilbert.
Cullen Mary Mrs., h 22 North.
Cunningham Sarah Miss, seamstress, h 14 Gilbert.
Curren Ann Mrs., h 16 Bank.
Currey William, r 27, farmer 18.
CURTIS DAVID E., r 23, farmer 80.
Curtis William E., r 23, farmer.
Curtiss Charles E., clerk, h 11 Craigie.
Curtiss Horace P., laborer, h 15 Summit.
Curtiss John B., laborer, h 41 South.
Curtiss Solomon, h 11 Craigie.
Curtiss Stephen F., retired, h 4 Craigie.
CUSHING PIERRE, rector St. Mark's Episcopal Church, h 30 Church.
Cutler James E, retired, h 98 W. Main.
Cutler Miriam S. Miss, h 98 W. Main.
Dagg Charles H., butcher, h 16 Bank.
Dailey Jennie, (Mary A. & Jennie Dailey) h 88 W. Main.
Dailey Mary A., (Mary A. & Jennie Dailey) h 88 W. Main.
Dailey Mary A. & Jennie, dressmakers, 88 W. Main.
Dailey Thomas, laborer, h 46 North.
Daniels Hannah L., h 12 Park Place.
Darby Mary A. Mrs., h 54 North.
Darrow Frank, cooper, h W. Main.
Darrow Jacob W., farmer, leases of M. G. Bissell 220, h W. Main.
Darrow Nancy, widow of William, h W. Main.
Dauman Jennie Miss, teacher Ingham University, bds. do.
Davis Calvin C., r 56, fruit grower and farmer 85.
DAVIS IRA C., r 48, farmer 28.

Davis Jonathan F., clerk, h Lake.
Davis Mary Ann Mrs., r 27, resident.
Davis Monroe, r 27, fruit grower and farmer 35.
Davy Charles, laborer, h 43 Summit.
Davy James H., (S. Byron) r 2, farmer 87.
DECKER MORRIS C., wholesale and retail dealer in liquors and cigars, 37 Main, h 3 Myrtle.
Dechon Frederick H., engineer at malt houses, h 80 Lake.
Delavan Henry William, cartman, h rear 3 Lake.
Dennis William, laborer, h 23 Exchange.
De Shon Henry G., retired, bds. Lampson House.
Despard John, shoemaker, 77 E. Main, h do.
DIBBLE CHRISTOPHER N., (Stone Church) r 7, farmer 91.
Dickens George B., r 66, carpenter and farmer 6.
Dickinson Champion, brushmaker, h 21 Union.
Dielschent Charles, (Bergen) r 3, farmer.
Dillon Edward, laborer, bds. 87 Gilbert.
Dillon John, Sr., retired, h 87 Gilbert.
Dillon John, Jr., carpenter and machinist, h 91 Gilbert.
Dillon Richard, stonecutter, h 22 North.
Dillon William, retired farmer, h 8 Maple Place.
Disbrow George, teamster, h 3 Lake.
Diskin Patrick, laborer, h 18 Maple ave.
Dix Isabella Mrs., (Stone Church) r 16, farmer 10.
DIX JULIA A., widow of Samuel L., h 18 Myrtle.
Dix M. A. Mrs., h 14 Myrtle.
Doble Charles P., horse trainer, h 61 E. Main.
Dodge Horace, dealer in hardware, 12 W. Main, h 40 Church.
Dolan William, laborer, h 17 Mill.
Donald John, (Stone Church) r 8, farmer 24.
Donnan William C., asst. cashier Bank of Le Roy, h 29 Main.
Donohue Michael, off r 36, farmer 10.
Dorey Lawrence, laborer, h 22 Gilbert.
Dorn George, r 72, farmer 24.
Dornbrock Carl, r 68, farmer, leases of Frank Lawrence 150.
Dossenbach Herman, teacher of violin Ingham University.
Doty S. Bryan, r 23, mason.
Douglas Margaret C. Mrs., r 30, farmer 100.
DOUGLAS SANFORD C., r 30, farmer with Margaret C. 100.
Dowdle Kate Mrs., h 5 Pleasant.
Dowdle William, butcher, h 5 Pleasant.
Dowdle William J., butcher, Bank, h Myrtle.
Dowling James, r 22, farmer 22.
Dowling John J., laborer, h 91 North.
Dowling Michael, r 46, laborer.
Drengeman August, agent Bartholomay Brewing Co., of Rochester, h 55 Church.
Drury Albert K., photographer, bds. Lampson House.
Duncan Richard, emp. on railroad, h 62 Lake.
Dunn Amelia J., widow of John, h 3 St. Mark.
Dutton George W., r 53, farmer 55, and in Pavilion 45.
EAGLE HOTEL, W. C. Reed, prop., 11 Main.
Eaton Morris B., druggist, 38 W. Main, h 63 Myrtle.
Eberhardt Frederic, tailor, h Pleasant.
Eddy Matilda I., widow of Joseph R., h and 3 acres 74 North.
Eddy Fidellio, shoemaker, bds. Union.
EDSON CHARLES E., gardener and farmer 30, h 80 Wolcott.
Edson Frank C., carpenter, breeder of Brown Leghorn and Plymouth Rock fowls, h 80 Wolcott.
Edson Galen K., ratired physician, farm 60, h 74 Wolcott.

Ellingham Freeman, (S. Byron) r 2, farmer 100.
Elliott Andrew, retired, h 9 Bacon.
Elliott Catharine, milliner, h.9 Bacon.
Ellison John, (Mumford, Monroe Co.) r 34, farmer with his father, Robert.
Ellison Robert, (Mumford, Monroe Co.) r 34, farmer, leases of the R. Brown estate 400.
Elmore Emory, com. traveler, h 14 Park Place.
Elmore George G., dealer in groceries and provisions, 11 W. Main, h 14 Park Place.
ELMORE WILLIAM, foreman N. Y. C. & H. R. R. R., h 71 Lake.
Elston Isaac, retired farmer, h 38 Church.
Elston William, retired farmer, h 38 Church.
Ely Enoch, Jr., r 51, farmer 9.
Etter Christover, r 47, farmer.
Evans Henry, r 60, farmer 42.
Evans Henry, Jr., r 60, farmer, leases of Charles Simons 20.
Evans William H., r 60, farmer with his father, Henry.
Ewell Emerson, retired farmer, h 3 South.
EYRES JOHN, supt. Kidd salt works, h 1 Myrtle.
Falkner Harry H., ins. and real estate agent, h 81 W. Main.
Farnham Margaret J. Mrs., owns 3 farms, h 10 Clay.
Farnham Nathaniel, (Stone Church) r 16, farmer 100.
FARNSWORTH HARRIET J. Mrs., h 17 Summit.
Faughey Owen, laborer, h 40 Gilbert.
Faunce George E., prop. livery, sale, and boarding stable, Clay.
FAUNCE WILLIAM W., prop. livery, sale, and boarding stable, Bank, h 6 Clay.
Fay John, prop. livery stable, h 22 Bacon.
Fay Matthew, laborer, h 7 Maple Place.
Fitzgerald Mary Mrs., r 23, resident.
Flanigan John, engineer in planing-mill, h 105 Myrtle.
Flanigan Owen, laborer, h 63 South.
Foley Michael, laborer, h 89 North.
Fonda Catharine, widow of Adam, h 75 Wolcott.
Fonda Charles, laborer, h 75 Wolcott.
Fonda Frank, laborer, h 87 South.
Fonda Nellie M. Mrs., h 28 Myrtle.
Fondy Adam, laborer, h 43 Gilbert.
Foote Ely, r 49, farmer 56.
Forbes Orson C., farmer, h 12 Bacon.
Ford Catharine T. Mrs., h 16 Bacon.
Ford George W., patent att'y at Batavia, h Church.
Ford Thomas, laborer, h 15 Pleasant.
Ford Thomas, laborer, h 5 Gilbert.
Fordam Adelaide Miss, (Stone Church) r 7, resident.
Fordam Rachel, (Stone Church) r 7, widow of Milton.
Fordham Caroline, widow of Francis, h 112 Lake.
Fordham Gideon, mechanic, h 38 Lake.
Foreman J. M., retired merchant, h 84 W. Main.
Fox Michael, blacksmith, bds. Eagle Hotel.
Fox Michael J., blacksmith, bds. Wiss House.
FRANKLIN HOUSE, Hubart Ponce, prop., 40 W. Main.
Freeman Caroline M. Mrs., h 18 E. Main.
Freeman Michael, blacksmith, h 18 Union.
FRENCH JEROME, manuf. of and dealer in brooms, farmer 51, h 6 Union.
Frigheit Caroline, r 39, resident.
Frigheit Kooghan, r 39, farmer, leases of J. Ostow, of Buffalo, 5.
Frigheit Louis, quarryman 1½ acres, h North.
Frost Edward, h 44 North.
Frost Susan, widow of William, h North.
FULLER BENJAMIN A., physician and surgeon, h 3 Main.
Gage Wesson, r 56, farmer, leases of R. L. Hutchinson, of Pavilion, 110.

9*

Gall Henry, (S. Byron) r 2, farmer 107.
Gallaghar Owen, emp. on L. E. & W. R. R., h rear 1 Lake.
Gallagher Kate, h 8 North.
Gallagher Patrick, laborer, h 15 Maple ave.
Gallagher Peter H., broommaker, h 24 Lake.
Gallagher Thomas, broommaker, h 10 Exchange.
Gardner James, laborer, South ave.
Garvey Jacob, r 42, farmer 13.
Garvin Nancy Mrs., h 5 North.
Gavin James, cartman, h 24 North.
Gavin Patrick E., foreman railway construction, h 9 St. Mark.
Gayton James, carpenter and joiner, h 35 Gilbert.
Gayton John R., r 40, farmer 135.
Geddes John, (Mumford, Monroe Co.) r 32, farmer.
Geer Oscar F., clerk, h 79 Myrtle.
GENESEE COURIER, George M. Howe, editor and prop., weekly, 29 and 31 Main.
Genesee House, W. S. Howard, prop., 60 Lake.
Genesee Steam Laundry, Edward A. Robbins, prop., 4 W. Main.
Gibbons R. John, blacksmith, h 30 Myrtle.
Gibson John, r 67, farmer 12.
Gibson William, r 67, farmer 11.
Gilbert Harriet B. D., widow of William, h 7 Summit.
Gilbert Sephrine D., justice of the peace and village clerk, 27 W. Main, bds. 7 Church.
Giles John, cooper, h 89 Myrtle.
Giles Peter M., cooper, bds. 89 Myrtle.
GILLETT JAMES B., (James B. Gillett & Co) h 29 E. Main.
GILLETT JAMES B & CO., dealers in hardware, 54 Main.
Gillett S. Frank, r 21, farmer 150.
GILLETT SAMUEL, r 46, farmer 60.
Gillett Watson C., molder and apiarist, h W. Main.
Gilmore George, salesman, h 14 Clay.
GILMORE WILLIAM H., mechanic, h 8 St. Mark.
Glass Frank C., carpenter and joiner, h 10 Gilbert.
Glass Reuben, carpenter and joiner, h 13 North.
GLEASON PATRICK, dealer in produce and coal, 78 W. Main, h 39 Gilbert.
Gleason Thomas, laborer and farmer 7, h 100 Gilbert.
Gleed Caroline, r 42, resident.
Gleed True, r 42, farmer 3.
GOODING MATTHEW S., dentist, over 45 W. Main, bds. Lampson House.
GRAHAM WILLIAM H., veterinary surgeon, 9 South, h 97 W. Main.
Granger Ann F. Mrs., h 86 Myrtle.
Granger Charles, laborer, h 9 South.
Graves Clemintena Mrs., h N. Lake.
Graves Edward J., (Steuber & Graves) h 26 Myrtle.
Graves Sarah W. Mrs., h 26 Myrtle.
Greehem Fred, printer, h 51 Myrtle.
Greehem Richard, h 51 Myrtle.
Greehem Thomas D., tinner, h 51 Myrtle.
Green Peter, (Stone Church) r 16, farmer 70.
Greenham Thomas, porter, emp. E. Bannister, bds. 14 Bank.
Greig James M., (Greig & Olson) h E. Main.
Greig & Olson, (James M. G. and George S. O.) dealers in dry goods, carpets, and millinery, 26 Main.
Griswold Frank, r 16, carpenter.
Griswold William, r 2, farmer 100.
Grogan Thomas, r 51, farmer 4.
Grover David, engineer, h 116 W. Main.
GROWNEY BERNARD, r 27, farmer 57.

Grumiaux Augustin L., barber, h North cor. St. Mark.
GRUMIAUX JOHN N., dealer in newspapers, stationery, and tobacco, 34 Main, h 21 North.
Grumiaux Lewis, retired, h 21 North.
Gushurst Lazarus, (Bergen) r 9, farmer 126.
Gustin Walter G., (Mumford, Monroe Co.) r 11, farmer 100.
Hager John F., farmer 146, h 38 Clay.
Halbert Emma C., h 53 Myrtle.
Halbert Nancy M. Mrs., h 53 Myrtle.
HALBERT WILLIAM R., r 39, farmer 133.
Halsted James B., book-keeper, b Lake.
Hamilton John D., school teacher, bds. Eagle Hotel.
Hammond Amanda Mrs., h 33 Myrtle.
Harcourt Augustie Mrs., teacher Ingham University, bds. do.
Hardey George, laborer, h 45 North.
Harmon Edwin M., ins. agent, over 32 W. Main, h Myrtle.
Harris Elijah, r 72, farmer with his mother, Elsie.
HARRIS ELSIE, r 72, widow of Seth, farm 245.
HARRIS WILLIAM, r 68, farmer 190.
Harris William H., r 68, farmer 100.
HARSCH ANDREW, manuf. of and wholesale and retail dealer in cigars, 70 W. Main, h 14 Pleasant.
Hart C. W., widow of Chester, h 11 South.
Hart Daniel F., r 54, farmer
Hart Edward, h 32 E. Main.
Hart James, r 56, laborer and farmer 4.
Hart John, r 11, farmer 100.
Harvey Catharine Mrs., h Lake.
HASCALL HIRAM W., att'y at law, 8 Main, h 19 E. Main.
Haskell C. L., Universalist clergyman, h N. Lake.
Haskins Ida, bds. 10 Lake.
HASKINS JOHN H., r 57, prop. grist-mill, 8 cows, farmer 65.
Haskins Mary L., widow of George W., h 24 E. Main.
Haskins William, painter, h 94½ Myrtle.
Hawkins Edward, blacksmith, Mill, h 22 Summit.
Heal William H. agent, h 94 W. Main.
HEAMAN THOMAS, blacksmith, horseshoeing a specialty, Mill, h Wolcott.
HEAMAN WILLIAM, manuf. and repairer of boots and shoes, 15 Main, h E. Main.
Heddon Leonard, r 53, farmer 10.
Heddon Lewis P., ins. agent, 27 W. Main, h 45 Myrtle.
HEDDON THOMAS P., att'y at law, over 27 W. Main, h 35 Myrtle.
Heimlech John, r 48, teamster.
Heller Charles, laborer, h 55 Church.
Heman William, shoemaker, h 52 E. Main.
Hewitt James, carpenter, h 51 South.
Hibbard Delbert C., (Mumford, Monroe Co.) r 31, farmer.
Hibbard Lewis B., (Mumford, Monroe Co.) r 31, farmer 200.
Higgans Henry L., painter, h 77 Wolcott.
Higgans Thomas, r 48, quarryman and farmer 16.
Hiland Edward, h 40 North.
Hill Eliza Mrs., r 32, resident.
Hill John, r 32, farmer 16.
Hill Orphana, widow of William, h 19 South.
Hill William, r 32, farmer.
Himmelman Ernest, baker, h 44 Wolcott.
Himmelman John H., retired, h 44 Wolcott.
Hoffman Frank A., barber, h 14 Bank.
Hoffman Martin, jeweler, watchmaker, and repairer, 94 Lake, h do.
Hoffman Ransom, r 25, gardener.

Hoffmann Wesley, farmer, h 19 Exchange.
HOGAN CHARLES, section forman N. Y. C. & H. R. R. R., h 75 Myrtle.
Hogan Margaret, milliner and dressmaker, 49 W. Main.
Holbrook Louisa Mrs., r 7, farmer 40.
Holdridge Gershom C., retired farmer, h 13 Summit.
Holdridge Lincoln, carpenter, bds. 13 Summit.
Holland Catharine, widow of John, h 43 North.
Holland Richard, r 46, laborer and farmer 6.
Hollister Milo, produce dealer, h 47 Lake.
Holmes Fred H., with his father, George H.
HOLMES GEORGE H., r 48, stone and lime contractor, farmer 36.
Holmes Harriet N., widow of John T., h North.
Holmes Henry, laborer, h 11 Pleasant.
Holmes Parley M., r 48, with his father, George H.
Homes Sylvester P., r 44, farmer, leases of J. F. Husted 97.
Hookers Percy, book-keeper, h 1 W. Main.
Horrigan James, r 23, farmer.
Hoskins Sarah Miss., h 12 Park Place.
Housten Walter, laborer, h 18 Erie.
Houston Frank, engineer, h 42 Gilbert.
HOUSTON FRANK H., (Lawson & Houston) overseer Le Roy salt works, h Gilbert.
Houston Henry, farmer, h 16 Summit.
Howard Anna A., dressmaker, h 82 Lake.
Howard Hannah, widow of George, h 82 Lake.
Howard Samuel T., (Howard & Lampson) h 69 Myrtle.
Howard Walter S., prop. Genesee House, 60 Lake.
Howard & Lampson, (S. T. H. and William L.) dealers in hardware, 10 Main.
HOWE GEORGE M., editor and prop. *Genesee Courier*, 29 and 31 Main, h 31 North.
Howe Orton W., invalid, h 33 Church.
Howell Elizabeth A. Mrs., r 48, resident.
HOWELL LIVINGSTON D., r 48, prop. blast furnace, quarrier and shipper of lime rock for Elmira, farmer 200.
Hoy James L., laborer, h 23 South.
Hoy John, laborer, h 23 South.
Hoyt Frank G., laborer, h 9 Maple ave.
Hoyt George R., clerk, h 9 Maple ave.
HUBBELL HULDAH, widow of James, h 17 North.
Hubbs Darwin, farmer, h 19 Gilbert.
Huftelen Elijah, r 25, grower of lilies, 6 acres.
Hughes John, h rear Maple Place.
Humelbaugh William E., h 9 North.
Husted Charles F., r 44, book-keeper.
Husted Frank S., r 44, civil engineer.
Husted J. Fletcher, r 44, farmer 87.
Huyck William, farmer 150, h 72 Lake.
Huyck William F., law student, bds. 72 Lake.
Ingham University, Charles F. Prentice, sec'y; Butler Ward, treas.; Miss R. N. Webster, prin., Main cor. Wolcott.
Innis Edith M. Miss, teacher Ingham University.
Innis Sarah A., matron Ingham University.
Ives Mary A., h 8 Clay.
JAMES EZRA S., r 44, 10 cows, farmer 130.
Jenks Christine Mrs., r 48, resident.
Jenks Jacob, r 48, farmer 175.
Jenks John, r 48, farmer.
Jennett John, r 52, farmer.
Jerry Frank, r 33, farmer, leases of H. H. Falkner 250.
Johnson Isaac, r 48, farmer, leases of S. Loucks 200.
Johnson James L., r 60, farmer 130.

JOHNSON JOHN, (Stone Church) r 8, farmer 256.
Johnson Robert, farmer, leases of R. McArthur, of Mumford, Monroe Co., 147.
Johnson William, (Mumford, Monroe Co.) r 11, farmer, leases of George P Davis 165.
Johnson William, Jr., (Mumford, Monroe Co.) r 11, farmer with his father, William.
JONES ALBERT W., novelty seed grower, h 102 Lake.
Jones Charles, (Stone Church) r 7, farmer.
Jones Cylus, (Stone Church) r 7, farmer, leases of H. Parmaley 45.
Jones William S., farmer, h 102 Lake.
Kanaley Thomas, laborer, h 100 Myrtle.
Kane Peter, laborer, h 38 North.
Kane Thomas, baggageman N. Y. C. & H. R. R. R., h 64 Lake.
Kaneen Daniel, clerk Lampson House, bds. do.
Karslake James, book-keeper and produce dealer, h 92 W. Main.
Karslake William J., student, h 92 W. Main.
Kavanaugh A. J., (Kavanaugh & O'Mealia).
Kavanaugh Part, teamster, h 15 Gilbert.
Kavanaugh Thomas J., stone cutter, h 43 North.
Kavanaugh & O'Mealia, (A. J. K. and A. J. O'M) dealers in liquor and tobacco, 14 Main.
Kavenaugh Patrick, (Stone Church) r 5, farmer 50.
Keenan Elizabeth Miss, h 46 Wolcott.
Keenan Henry, laborer, h Mill.
Keenan John, laborer, h 55 South.
Keenan John, r 57, farmer 14.
Keeney Allen, r 44, farmer 700.
Keeney Allen, Jr., r 44, farmer 10.
KEENEY CALVIN N., (N. B. Keeney & Son) h W. Main.
Keeney N. B. & Son, (Calvin N.) produce dealers, Lake.
Keeney Nicholas B., (N. B. Keeney & Son) h 40 Lake.
KELLOGG FRANCES A., widow of Richard, h 8 Craigie.
Kellogg Hannah M., widow of Julius C., h 3 Gilbert.
Kellogg Mariette, widow of Seth, h 15 St. Mark.
Kellogg Minnie, music teacher, bds. 15 St. Mark.
Kelly James, mason, h 29 South.
Kelly James, Jr., clerk, h 31 South.
Kelly John, r 36, farmer.
KELLY JOHN M., supt. Machpelah Cemetery, h 87 North.
Kelsey George W., (Stone Church) r 7, farmer.
Kelsey James, r 53, farmer 105.
Kelsey Lewis, (Stone Church) r 7, farmer 180.
Kelsue George W., (Stone Church) r 7, farmer, leases of his father, Lewis, 150.
Kelty James, r 54, laborer and farmer 13.
Kelty John J., butcher, h 12 Exchange.
Kelty Martin, maltster, h 12 Exchange.
Kemp Ada J., widow of Lewis, h 41 Clay.
Kemp Frank, h 5 Pleasant.
Kemp Margaret Mrs., h 5 Pleasant.
Kendall Elmina H. Mrs., h 16 North.
Kendall Oorator, laborer, h 16 North.
Kenney Fred G., book-keeper, bds. 32 Myrtle.
Kenny George. carpenter, h 30 Myrtle.
Kenny James H., cashier Lathrop's Bank, h 32 Myrtle.
Kerney John, r 36, farmer.
Kilburn John, r 61, farmer.
King Abner W., supt. Dreamland stock farm, h E. Main.
King Frank M., drayman, h 14 Bacon.
KING MELVIN N., deputy sheriff and constable, h 70 Myrtle.
Kinne Frank, painter, h 44 South.
Kinne George, carpenter, h 44 South.

Kinne Jacob, carpenter, h 46 South.
Kinne Nelson, carpenter, h 44 South.
Kinney James, r 54, farmer.
Kinney Jerome B., r 44, farmer 20.
Kinney Luther Mrs., h 19 St. Mark.
Kinney Rebecca Mrs., h 21 Clay.
KIRKHAM ORVILLE C., Baptist clergyman, h 12 Church.
Kirkham Walter A., chemist, bds. 12 Church.
Knowles Jennie, widow of Benjamin, h 53 South.
Koehler Michael, r 54, farmer 33.
Koehler William, r 54, farmer with his father, Michael.
Kroner Augusta, tailoress, h 31 Mill.
Kroner Barbara P., widow of Michael, h 31 Mill.
Kroner George M., mechanic, h Lincoln ave.
Kufman John, laborer, h Munson.
Kurtz Jacob, maltster, h 16 Maple ave.
Ladd Miles A., wagon and carriage manuf., h 112 W. Main.
Lambert Augustus, stone cutter, h 65 South.
Lampson House, S. M. Cochran & Son, props.
Lampson Miles P., Jr., vice-pres. Bank of Le Roy, h W. Main.
Lampson William, (Howard & Lampson) pres. Bank of Le Roy, h 85 W. Main.
Lane Lucinda G., widow of Peter, h 58 Gilbert.
Lane Samantha A., h 58 Gilbert.
Lapp Charles, laborer, h 65 Church.
Lapp Joseph, carpenter, h 65 Church.
Lapp William, carpenter, h 65 Church.
Larkin Thomas W., dealer in boots and shoes, 26 W. Main, h 10 St. Mark.
Lathrop's Bank, F. C. Lathrop, pres.; J. H. Kenny, cashier, 5 Main.
Lathrop Francis C., pres. Lathrop's Bank, h E. Main.
Lathrop Ruth W. Miss, h 18 North.
Latour Pascal V., barber, 24 Main, h do.
Lawrence Abbie Mrs., h South ave.
Lawrence Addison W., r 53, auctioneer and farmer 44.
Lawrence Alida J., r 53, widow of James, farmer 150.
Lawrence Charles R., r 68, farmer 150.
Lawrence Rosman, r 68, farmer 145.
LAWSON MAC, (Lawson & Houston) h 9 Gilbert.
LAWSON & HOUSTON, (Mac L. and Frank H. H.) props. livery, boarding, and sale
    stables, new rigs, hacks, carriages, and careful drivers furnished for weddings
    and funerals, rear 37 Main.
Le Baron Irving, r 16, farmer.
Legg Dwight, laborer, h off Maple Place.
Lehy Cornelius, confectioner, 2 Main, h 66 Lake.
Lehy Jerry P., produce buyer, h 49 Main.
Lenk Mades, r 17, farmer.
Lenty John, engineer, h 44 Gilbert.
Lenty Mary, widow of Thomas, h 44 Gilbert.
Lenty William, quarryman, h 44 Gilbert.
Lepp Henry J., engineer at salt works, h 17 Maple ave.
Le Roy Academic Institute, F. M. Comstock, prin., E. Main.
Le Roy Gas Co., D. J. Bissell, pres.: John C. Bissell, supt., foot of Mill.
LE ROY GAZETTE, George E. Marcellus, editor and prop., 39, 41, and 43 Main.
Le Roy Salt Co., C. F. Prentice, pres.; C. N. Keeney, sec'y; A. E. Miller, treas., W. of
    depot.
LE ROY TIMES CO., F. H. Morgan, manager, publishers Le Roy Times, weekly,
    30 and 32 W. Main.
Lester Adaline A., artist, h 49 Myrtle.
Lester Matilda A., widow of William H., h 49 Myrtle.
Lewis Fred W., car inspector, h 8 Erie.

Lewis Thomas, gardener, h 76 Myrtle.
Lindley Thomas, r 58, farmer.
Lindsler John, laborer, h 45 South.
Lippman Ernest, r 54, laborer and farmer 3.
Lochriedg George, r 57, miller and farmer.
Lock Henry, retired merchant and dealer in real estate, h 32 Lake.
Logan Patrick, r 58, cooper.
Long John. r 27, laborer.
Loucks F. Bruce, r 47, farmer.
LOUCKS STEPHEN, general merchant, farmer 340, h Lake.
Loucks Walter F., dealer in dry goods, 16 Main, h do.
Lowe George F., r 50, farmer 165.
Lucas Thomas T., laborer, h 2 Mill.
Luscher Augustus, (Bergen) r 9, farmer 154.
Lutton Eliza, r 58, widow of Samuel.
Lutton Joseph, laborer, h W. Main.
Luttrell George T., carpenter and cooper, h 49 Gilbert.
Luttrell William H., stone cutter, h 50 Myrtle.
Lynch Barney, r 48, farmer 6.
Lynch Morris, h Mill.
Lynch Philip, r 48, laborer and farmer 4.
Lynch William, r 27, farmer, leases of E. Alby 40.
Maher John, (Stone Church) r —, farmer 64.
Mahoney William G., barber, Main, h Myrtle.
Maier Charles A., stone cutter, h 26 North.
Maish Charlotte Mrs., h 47 Clay.
Maish Theodore S., photographer, h 47 Clay.
Mallock Daniel, r 40, carpenter.
Mallock Edwin, r 40, carpenter.
Mallock Moses P., r 40, farmer 4.
Malone Patrick, r 36, farmer 20.
MALONEY JOHN, dealer in groceries and provisions, 25 W. Main, h 90 do.
Maloy Michael S., farmer and teamster, h North.
Maloy Patrick, miller, h 32 North.
Maloy Patrick, laborer and farmer 20, h North.
Manwaring Emra H. Miss, h 82 Gilbert.
MARCELLUS GEORGE E., editor and prop. of *Le Roy Gazette*, 39, 41, and 43 Main, h 6 Craigie.
March James L., shipping clerk and yard foreman for W. D. Matthews & Co., h 100 Lake.
March John D., musician and music teacher, h 30 E. Main.
Marion Edward P., (Stone Church) r 8, farmer.
MARION PATRICK, (Stone Church) r 8, farmer 116.
Marsh Edward, r 25, farmer 70.
Marshall Albert, laborer, h 23 Union.
Martin Edward H., news agent, etc., h 16 Clay.
Martin James, shoemaker, h 65 E. Main.
Martin W. L., retired farmer 182, h 3 St. Mark.
Martin William H., r 51, farmer with W. L. 182.
Marvin Lydia Mrs., h 26 Gilbert.
Mason Isaac G., carpenter and joiner, h 118 W. Main.
Maston William, laborer, h 11 Maple ave.
Matice Abraham, r 48, farmer.
Matthews ———, widow of W. D., h Main.
Matthews Frank, laborer, h 6 Pleasant.
Matthews John, mason, h 6 Pleasant.
Matthews John, Jr., laborer, h 6 Pleasant.
MATTHEWS W. D. & CO., E. Rogerson, manager, maltsters and dealers in Canada barley, Church.

Mattice William E., r 47, farmer.
Maud Joseph, mason, h 4 Pleasant.
Mavis William, shoemaker, bds. Church.
McBride James A., prop. livery stable, h 30 Myrtle.
McBride Stephen, laborer, h 60 North.
McBurney John, (Stone Church) r 8, farmer 6.
McCann David, r 36, farmer 40.
McCarg John H., (S. Byron) r 2, farmer.
McCarg John C., (S. Byron) farmer 50.
McCarrick Patrick, carpenter, h 50 Church.
McCauley Anastasia, dressmaker, bds. 33 North.
McCauley Augusta, dressmaker, bds. 33 North.
McCauley C. Miss, teacher Ingham University, bds. do.
McCauley John, r 56, section boss and farmer 4.
McCauley Patrick, laborer, h 33 North.
McCauley Thomas, r 56, laborer and farmer 10.
McConnon John, r 51, farmer.
McCormick Henry, r 22, farmer 10.
McCormick James, r 22, farmer 3.
McCuley James, stone cutter, h North.
McDermott Bridget, widow of Owen, h 68 E. Main.
McDonald Angus, off r 48, farmer.
McDonald James, r 32, farmer 13.
McDonald Patrick, carpenter, h North.
McDowell David, carpenter, h 16 Union.
McEntee Eugene, r 23, farmer.
McEntee Owen, r 23, farmer 7.
McEwen Daniel, r 69, farmer 150.
McEwen Duncan D., r 69, farmer with his father, Daniel.
McEwen George S., shoemaker, h 14 Craigie.
McEwen James, r 50, farmer with his father, Thomas.
McEwen James D., r 69, farmer with his father, Daniel.
McEwen John W., r 52, farmer with his mother, Margaret J.
McEWEN MARGARET J., r 52, widow of Archibald, farmer 135.
McEwen Thomas, r 50, farmer 100.
McFarland John, r 56, laborer and farmer 17.
McGrady James, carriagemaker, h 41 Gilbert.
McIntosh John, r 60, artist.
McKanna James, stone cutter, h 34 North.
McKeary John, laborer, h 17 Pleasant.
McKeary Thomas, mason, h 35 South.
McKechnie John, cooper, h Mill.
McKenzie James, retired, h 23 Bank.
McKeon Alexander, r 51, farmer with his father, George, Sr.
McKeon Ann Mrs., off r 37, farmer 10.
McKeon George, Sr., r 51, farmer 40.
McKeon George, Jr., r 51, farmer with his father, George.
McKeon Thomas, r 56, farmer, leases of John Kinny, of Geneseo, 110.
McLachen Daniel D., constable, h 27 Lake.
McManus William, cooper, h 18 Bacon.
McMartin Charles, farmer, h 8 Maple.
McMartin Daniel, laborer, h 8 Maple.
McNalley Ellen R. Mrs., h 9 Pleasant.
McPherson Alexander J., r 30, farmer 120.
McPHERSON ALEXANDER, Jr., r 29, farmer 165.
McPherson Alexander, 2d., r 16, farmer 100.
McPherson Ann Eliza Mis., (Mumford, Monroe Co.) r 32, farmer 220.
McPherson August B., farmer, h 47 E. Main.
McPherson Donald H., r 30, farmer with his father, Alexander J.

McPherson Homer, r 16, farmer with John, Jr.
McPherson James B., r 16, farmer with his father, Alexander, 2d.
McPherson Jane, r 29, widow of Alexander, farm 100.
McPherson John, r 16, farmer 40.
McPherson John, Jr., r 16, farmer with Homer.
McPHERSON JOHN A., r 28, breeder of Percheron horses and Poland China swine,
    farmer 50, and leases of his mother, Jane, 100.
McPherson John B., (Mumford, Monroe Co.) r 32, teacher and carpenter.
McPherson Sarah Mrs., (Stone Church) r 16, resident.
McPhillips Felix, laborer, h opposite Erie depot.
McPhillips James, r 50, farmer 2.
McQuillen Thomas, r 70, farmer 5.
McSeeney Joseph, laborer, h 70 E. Main.
McVane Archibald, (Mumford, Monroe Co.) r 9, farmer 125.
McVean Archibald, (Stone Church) r 16, farmer.
McVean James D., r 30, farmer 90.
Merritt Mial A., carpenter, h 76 Lake.
Meyers Martin, r 16, farmer.
MEYETTE NELSON, painter and decorator, h 74 North.
Michel Andrew W., r 50, (George & Andrew W. Michel).
Michel George, r 50, (George & Andrew W. Michel).
Michel George & Andrew W., r 50, farmers 60.
Michel Julia, r 50, widow of Andrew J , farmer 60.
Miggin Michael, laborer, h 14 Erie.
MILLER AUGUSTUS E., treas. and general supt. Le Roy Salt Co., h 21 Church.
Miller Clarissa, r 56, widow of Lewis.
Miller David, cooper, h 25 Pleasant.
Miller Edgar L., r 56, fruit grower and farmer 75.
Miller Henry, butcher, h Pleasant.
Miller John H., cooper, h 40 Wolcott.
Miller Lucia C., h 92 Lake.
MILLINER FREDERICK J., ticket agent, telegraph operator N.Y., L. E. & W. R. R.,
    h 5 Myrtle.
Mills Harriet, r 68, widow of Henry S., farm 60.
Mills William H., r 68, farmer.
Mire Leonard, laborer, h 42 South.
Moe Alfred L., r 47, farmer.
Moffit James, laborer, h 11 Gilbert.
Monroe Frank, r 35, farmer 600.
Mont Frank, r 42, carpenter and farmer, leases of H. Norton 12.
Montroy Harry, painter, h 29 Exchange.
Montroy Henry, painter, h. 38 Summit.
Moody Bridget, widow of Robert, h 39 Gilbert.
Moody Frank T., clerk, h 20 Gilbert.
MOODY HENRY, builder, h 90 Myrtle.
Moody John L., prop. livery stable, h 34 Gilbert.
Moody Joseph R., laborer, h 39 Gilbert.
Moody Mary A., dressmaker, h 20 Gilbert.
Moody Mary B. Miss, dressmaker, h 31 Gilbert.
Moody Sarah J., house-keeper, 20 Gilbert.
Moody William, tailor, h 20 Gilbert.
MOORE AURELIA W., widow of Oliver, h 40 E. Main.
Moore George, cooper, h 7 Maple Place.
Morgan Charles, retired, h 98 W. Main.
MORGAN FRANK H , editor Le Roy Times, h 98 W. Main.
Morris Daniel, tailor, h 35 Church.
Morris Frank L., stone cutter, h North.
Morris James L., (Morris & Strobel) h North.
Morris & Strobel, (James L. M. and Gottlieb S.) props. stone quarry and dealers in
    railroad and building stone.

Mortimer Charles B., laborer, h 19 Maple ave.
Mott F. H., (T. B. Tuttle & Co.).
Muller John D., retired, h 62 Wolcott.
MULLER MATHIAS, dealer in groceries, crockery, woodenware, paints, and oils, 66 Main.
Munro Frank, r 35, breeder of horses and mules, 25 Jersey cows, farmer 523.
Munson Henry, carpenter and joiner, h and 4 acres 96 Gilbert.
Munson Marriette A., carpenter and joiner, h 52 E. Main.
MUNT JOHN, r 19, farmer 125.
MURDOCH SAMUEL H., prop. planing-mill, manuf. of house building materials, Mill, h St. Mark.
Murdoch William J., with Samuel H., h 20 Union.
Murnan John, bartender, bds. Wiss House.
Murnan Michael, r 52, farmer 47.
MURNAN THOMAS H., wholesale and retail dealer in California wines and brandies. Kentucky whisky, and tobacco and cigars, 52 Main, bds. Eagle Hotel.
Murphy John, laborer, h 1 Gilbert.
Murphy Mary, farm 80, h E. Main.
Murphy Matthew J., salesman, h 7 South.
Murran Thomas, wholesale liquor dealer, Main, bds. Eagle Hotel.
Murray Anna Mrs., h 101 Myrtle.
Murray Francis P., printer, h 68 North.
Murray Jerry R., (Jerry R. & Roger W. Murray) h 101 Myrtle.
Murray Jerry R. & Roger W., farmers, 101 Myrtle.
Murray John A., (Bergen) farmer with his father, Robert.
Murray Matthew, r 37, farmer 100.
MURRAY MICHAEL, stone cutter. h and 3 acres 64 North.
Murray Patrick H., stone cutter and contractor, h 64 North.
Murray Robert, (Bergen) r 9, farmer 123.
Murray Roger W., (Jerry R. & Roger W. Murray) h 101 Myrtle.
Murray Thomas, section boss N. Y. C. & St. Louis R. R., stone cutter, and mason, h 68 North.
Murrey Alice Mrs., h 46 Wolcott.
Murrey James, r 36, farmer 10.
Naid Thomas, off r 36, farmer 50.
Nash Frank J., r 47, farmer.
Netson Otto, r 57, farmer.
Newton William, book agent, h South ave.
NILES EDWIN J., carpenter and farmer, h 20 South.
Niles Ephraim, r 57, laborer.
Noon James, peddler, h 22 North.
Noonen William, laborer, h 9 Maple Place.
Northrop Celia Miss., h 14 Craigie.
Norton Harley, r 55, farmer 26.
Nosker John C., wagonmaker, h 9 Myrtle.
Oatka Restaurant, Edwin Bannister, prop., 14 Bank.
O'Brien John J, clerk Wiss House.
O'Connor Lawrence, r 56, stone mason.
Oelschlegel Robert, laborer, h 83 South.
Olmsted Albert H., r 47, farmer with his father, Henry H.
Olmsted Allen S, manuf., h 41 E. Main.
OLMSTED CHARLES L., r 40, farmer 50.
Olmsted Egbert S., r 40, farmer 30.
Olmsted Henry H., r 47, breeder of Jersey cattle, farmer 150.
Olmsted John R., att'y at law, h 41 E. Main.
Olmsted Maryette L., widow of Chauncy L., h 24 Lake.
Olson George S., (Greig & Olson) bds. E. Main.
O'Mealia N. J., (Kavanaugh & O'Mealia).
O'Neal Patrick, r 51, farmer 14.

O'Reiley Miles, r 16, farmer 8.
O'Reiley Patrick, r 16, farmer.
O'Rilley Miles B., teamster, h 115 W. Main.
O'Rilley Patrick, signal and flagman at junction, h 115 W. Main.
Osborn Sylvester, r 44, farmer 100.
Oshea Daniel, r 23, teacher.
Oshea Michael, r 23, laborer and 4 acres.
Palliser Alfred H., carpenter and joiner, h 56 E. Main.
Palmer Delia A., h 42 Clay.
Palmer Elisha, retired farmer, h 42 Clay.
Pangrazie Anthony, r 50, quarryman.
Pangrazie John, r 49, quarryman and farmer 4.
Pangrazie Joseph, r 50, quarryman.
Pangrazie Modesto, r 50, quarryman and farmer 5.
Park Francis M., (Pavilion) farmer 5.
Parks Caroline M., h 18 Bank.
Parks Elizabeth, h 18 Bank.
Parks Mary J. Miss, h 8 Craigie.
Parmala Alvin, (Stone Church) r 7, mechanic.
Parmala Mariah Miss, (Stone Church) r 7, resident.
Parmelee Byron G., r 61, laborer.
Parmelee John H., r 16, farmer 106.
Parmelee William G., (Stone Church) r 16, farmer 28.
Parmely Albert, r 29, farmer, leases of L. J. Bower 60.
Parsons B. K., widow of Marshfield, h 22 E. Main.
Parsons Lucy A. S. Mrs., teacher Ingham University, bds. do.
Passmore Thomas T., carpenter, h 8 Maple Place.
Paul Alba, farmer in Bethany 192, h 90 Gilbert.
Paul Dean R., salesman, h 77 Lake.
Paul Frank, r 44, farmer.
Paul Henry C., r 44, farmer 175.
PAUL LYMAN G., station agent B., R. & P. R. R. and agent American Express Co.,
    h 77 Lake.
Peck George W., mason, h 66 Wolcott.
Peck James, r 60, farmer 56.
Peck William A., r 57, mason and farmer 17.
Peoth Frank, (Trousdell & Peoth) h 44 Clay.
Peoth Mary A. Mrs., h 44 Clay.
Perhamus John H., agent N. Y. C. & H. R. R. R., h 14 Lake.
Perry Alfred, carpenter, h 5 Maple.
Petherbridge Thomas, gardener, h 68 Myrtle.
Pfeisterer Christopher, tinsmith, h Church.
Pfister John, painter, h 72 South.
Philipene Sarah Mrs., h 18 Simmit.
Phillips Delia A., h 80 Myrtle.
Phillips John J., r 29, farmer 1.
Pierson Angeline C., h 79 E. Main.
Pierson Daniel M., r 29, farmer 30.
PIERSON DWIGHT H., r 16, farmer 100.
Pierson Maria B., widow of J. P., h 17 Wolcott.
Pinder Ann, widow of Francis, h 8 South.
Pipton Thomas, mechanic, h 10 Maple Place.
Pither Mary Mrs., h 25 Myrtle.
Platts Henry, retired farmer, owns in Pavilion 103, h 74 E. Main.
PONCE HUBART, prop. Franklin House, 40 W. Main.
Potter Mary A. Miss, bds. 69 E. Main.
Pratt Josephine E. Mrs., teacher, h 34 Church.
PRATT MELVIN D., r 47, farmer 95.
Prendergast James, prop. Cottage Hotel, 56 Lake.

Prentice Charles, prop. Le Roy roller flouring-mills, owns farm in Stafford 400.
Price Richard, (Stone Church) r 9, farmer 2.
Pritchett Henry J., laborer, h 94 Myrtle.
Quackenbush James P., farmer 14, h 112 Lake.
Quance Arthur E., baker, h 73 Wolcott.
Radband George, mason, h 20 Pleasant.
Radcliff Benjamin, h 42 Church.
Ramsay David, r 4, farmer, leases of John Brodie 75.
Randall C. E. Mrs., h 10 St. Mark.
RANDALL ORANGE F., r 24, farmer 250.
Randall William P., clerk, h 27 Wolcott.
Rantz Frederick C., tinsmith and plumber, h University Cottage.
Raplee Rebecca Mrs., h 30 Church.
RAWSON EDWARD B., retired, h 51 Wolcott.
Rawson Safford, retired, h 51 Wolcott.
Raymond Frank, stone cutter, h 35 North.
Raymond Vetal J., stone cutter, h 35 North.
Raymond William Mrs., h 35 North.
Reed Louise E. Miss, teacher Ingham University.
Reed Lucina B., widow of Daniel L., h 5 Summit.
REED WILLIAM C., prop. Eagle Hotel and breeder of Wilkes horses, 11 Main.
Reilley George, retired, h 37 South.
Reimer Fred, r 18, farmer 75.
RENNER CASPAR, clothier and merchant tailor, 29 W. Main, h 23 Clay.
Rich Eugene, r 17, farmer.
Rich William H., 'bus driver, h 9 South. +
Richardson Mary E. Miss, h and 6 acres W. Main.
RICHMOND ALBION D., r 25, prop. stone quarry, farmer 145.
Ridd James, (Stone Church) r 8, breeder of draft and coach horses, farmer 60.
Rider Frank, laborer, h 18 South.
Rider Philip, laborer, h 18 South.
Rider Philip, salt sifter, h 19 East ave.
Riley Patrick, farmer 6, h Munson.
Ripton John L., barber, h 68 E. Main.
Ripton Margaret Mrs., h Mill.
Ripton Thomas, laborer, h Lake.
Robb Margaret, r 16, farm 84.
ROBBINS EDWARD A., prop. Genesee Steam Laundry and agent Rochester Dyeing Co., 4 Main, h r 55.
Robbins Russell, r 55, 25 cows, farmer 130.
Robbins William H., r 55, farmer 17.
Roberts Caroline, widow of George, h 33 Wolcott.
Roberts Eurania E., h 31 Fulton.
Robertson Francis, (Mumford, Monroe Co.) r 37, farmer.
Robertson Lucretia A., h 33 E. Main.
Robertson Sarah Ann, h 33 E. Main.
Robertson William, (Mumford, Monroe Co.) r 37, farmer 70.
Robinson John E., (Bowen & Robinson) h 18 Church.
Roe William H., r 56, farmer.
Roger Altnea N., h 65 Myrtle.
Roger Fred C., lumber dealer, h 12 St. Mark.
Rogers Charles B., laborer, h 14 St. Mark.
Rogers Charles W., r 65, farmer 95.
Rogers Fred C., manuf. of sash, doors, and blinds, h 14 St. Mark.
Rogers George E., r 65, carpenter and farmer.
Rogers James O., r 65, farmer 36.
Rogers Nathaniel M., dealer in groceries and lumber, h 14 St. Mark.
Rogers Peter, off r 36, farmer.
Rogers Richard, off r 36, farmer 70.

Rogerson Edward, supt. malt works, h E. Main.
Rooney Michael, r 30, farmer 57.
Rooney Thomas, r 30, farmer with his father, Michael.
Rose Livora S., widow of George, h 69 E. Main.
Rosman Zundal, dealer in clothing and gents' furnishing goods, 22 Main, bds. Lampson House.
Ross Thomas H., tailor, W. Main, h 15 North.
Rugg John A., r 47, farmer.
Rumsey Azra J., teacher, h 73 Wolcott.
Rumsey Eveline A., r 56, widow of George W., farm 37.
Ryan Cornelius, gardener 3, h Munson.
Ryan John, laborer, h 21 Exchange.
Ryan Michael, r 46, farmer 5.
Samson John P., book-keeper, h 22 E. Main.
Samson Mary E. Miss, teacher Ingham University.
Samson Mary E., widow of R. L., h 22 E. Main.
SANDERSON ANDREW J., r 39, farmer 115.
Scanlan Ann Mrs., h 47 South.
SCANLAN DENNIS, dealer in boots, shoes, and clothing, Lampson block, W. Main, h 12 Clay.
Scanlan Edward, r 17, farmer 10.
Scanlan John B., r 53, farmer 8.
Scanlan Michael, clerk, h 9 Erie.
Scanlan Michael B., clerk, h 12 Lake.
Scanlan Thomas F., r 53, farmer.
Scanlin Josephine Miss, seamstress, h 10 Erie.
Scanlin Margaret Mrs., h 10 Erie.
Schlick Peter K., miller, h 17 St. Mark.
Schober Mike, maltster, h 23 Pleasant.
Scott Isaac C., r 4, farmer 85.
Scott Seneca L., retired farmer, owns in Stafford 125, h 76 Gilbert.
Scyffer Ed G., clerk, h 15 St. Mark.
Seeley George, mason, h 16 Erie.
Seiz Frank, blacksmith, bds. Eagle Hotel.
Sekins Adelbert, (Mumford, Monroe Co.) r 37, resident.
Selden C. Hubert, r 17, farmer 31.
SELDEN RICHARD L., r 17, breeder of thoroughbred Jersey cattle and Berkshire swine, farmer 36.
SELDEN STEPHEN M., r 17, farmer 105.
Selden William A., r 17, farmer with his father, Richard L.
Sellinger Loring, molder, h Myrtle.
Service John M., r 44, farmer with his father, Malcomb.
Service Malcomb, r 44, farmer 110.
Seward Myron N., (Stone Church) r 7, farmer.
Seward Wellington, (Stone Church) r 7, farmer 77.
Seyffer George, baggageman Erie R. R. depot, h 29 North.
Seyffer Gottlieb F., tinsmith, h 29 North.
Shanon Frank, (Pavilion) r 82, farmer, leases of James Hamilton 100.
Shave Rose M. Miss, teacher Ingham University.
Shaw Alexander H., marble polisher, h 27 North.
Shaw Anna M. Mrs., h 16 North.
Shaw Charles T., prop. livery stable, bds. Eagle Hotel.
Shaw Mary J., (Mary J. & Sarah I. Shaw) bds. 63 Wolcott.
Shaw Mary J. & Sarah I., dressmakers, 63 Wolcott.
Shaw Sarah I., (Mary J. & Sarah I. Shaw) bds. 63 Wolcott.
Shaw Susan, widow of Samuel, h 63 Wolcott.
Shaw William H., molder, h 63 Wolcott.
Sheffer Newell M., r 49, farmer, leases of H. Chaddock 350.
Shelden Luther, r 36, resident.

Sheldon William H., retired, b 15 E. Main.
Shepard C. Albert, r 61, farmer 60.
Shepard Edwin D., teacher, h 31 Clay.
Shepard Charles W., r 56, farmer, leases of Mary Harris, of Buffalo, 16.
Shepard John, r 36, farmer 20.
Shepard Norman G., r 61, farmer 58.
Sherman Cornelia Mrs., h 87 South.
Sherman Elisha, mason, h 85 South.
Sherman William, mason, contractor, and builder, h 21 Pleasant.
Sherwood Fred H., h 13 Craigie.
Sherwood Nathan, dealer in ready-made clothing, boots, shoes, and gents' furnishing
    goods, 32 Main, h 13 Craigie.
SHILOH'S FAMILY REMEDIES, S. G. Wells & Co., props., 3 Church.
Shimley Anthony, blacksmith, h 54 Church.
Shimley Anthony, farmer 10, h 54 Church.
Shimley George, laborer, h 54 Church.
Shirley Matthew, r 58, farmer 46.
SHUMWAY MONTE DELLA, Universalist clergyman, h 65 Myrtle.
Shumway Solomon, r 56, farmer 20, and in Pavilion 65.
Simmons Arthur W., ice dealer, bds. Lake.
Simmons Elmore, clerk Franklin House.
Simmons Thomas, laborer, h 42 Wolcott.
Simpson Anna Mrs., r 41, resident.
Simpson James, r 41, laborer.
Simpson William, farmer, h 84 Lake.
Sisson Julia M., farm 160, h 59 E. Main.
Shellay William J., laborer, h 75 Lake.
Skelly Amelia, widow of John, h 20 Bacon.
Skinner Charlotte M., widow of Dewitt C., h 17 Myrtle.
Skinner Scott W., M. D., physician, h 12 Myrtle.
Slader John, r 57, laborer.
Slader John, r 23, farmer 40.
Slader John, Jr., r 23, farmer with his father, John.
Slader William, r 57, farmer 14.
Smith Alson W., (Stone Church) r 7, farmer 62.
Smith Barney, r 23, farmer 25.
Smith Bernard, prop. saloon, 2 Bank, h School Place.
Smith Charles, painter, h 96 Myrtle.
Smith Charles H., (Stone Church) r 7, farmer with his father, Alson W.
Smith Charles L., r 52, farmer 70.
Smith Christian, laborer, h 96 Myrtle.
Smith Cornelia A., widow of Chauncey, h 86 W. Main.
Smith Daniel J., r 12, farmer with George J. 102.
Smith George J., r 12, farmer with Daniel J. 102.
Smith Hannon, r 67, farmer.
Smith Henry, r 67, farmer 25.
Smith James, retired harnessmaker, h 41 Myrtle.
Smith James, laborer, bds Wiss House.
Smith John, r 40, engineer.
Smith John, r 66, farmer 6.
Smith Jonathan, r 28, farmer 4.
Smith Jonathan, r 29, farmer.
Smith Leonard, laborer, h 38 Gilbert.
Smith Lucy P., widow of Algeray, h 10 Lake.
Smith Peter, stone cutter, h 28 North.
Smith Stanley M., druggist, h 86 W. Main.
SMITH WALTER H., att'y at law, 22 W. Main, h 31 E. Main.
Smith Warren C., r 52, farmer with his father, Charles L.
Smith William, laborer, h 49 South.

SMITH WILLIAM H., manuf. of harnesses and dealer in harnesses, whips, etc., 70 Main, h 54 Myrtle.
SNOW EPHRAIM L., postmaster and produce dealer, h 13 Lake.
Snow Homer, produce buyer, h 86 Lake.
Sperry Cyrus, retired farmer, h 38 Myrtle.
SPERRY PHILO J., r 47, farmer 152.
Spittal John, farmer, leases of Clara Torrey, of Brooklyn, 100, h Main.
Sprague Edwin B., r 54, farmer 100.
SPRAGUE GEORGE F., r 57, farmer 100.
SPRING ERASTUS, retired farmer, h 19 South.
Squires Isaac, r 42, farmer.
Stage John C., r 23, farmer 50.
Stalker Alexander, h 31 Myrtle.
Stalker John S., grocer, 66 W. Main, h 31 Myrtle.
Stamp Clarinda J., h 14 Exchange.
Stamp Hubert G., laborer, h 14 Exchange.
Stanard Edwin G., ins. agent and com. traveler for Warsaw Salt Co., h 8 Clay.
Stanard Egbert E., r 44, farmer 95.
Stanard Nancy F., r 44, widow of Eldridge.
Stanley Elliott L., joiner, h 71 Myrtle.
Stanley Emily A., widow of H. M., h 17 Wolcott.
Stanley Hiram P., clerk Erie R. R., h 90 Lake.
Stanley M. E. Miss, h 17 Wolcott.
Starr Henry K., r 56, farmer 10.
St. Clair Archibald, town assessor, h 5 North.
STEINER SAMUEL, r 19, breeder of Percheron horses, farmer 281.
Steinnetz Philip, baker and confectioner, 62 Main, h do.
Steuber Elizabeth, (Stone Church) r 7, resident.
Steuber Frank G., with his father, Henry, bds. 49 Clay.
Steuber Frederick A., (Steuber & Graves) h 102 W. Main.
Steuber G. G., undertaker, 35 Main, h 11 Clay.
Steuber George G., furniture dealer, h 11 Clay.
STEUBER HENRY, furniture dealer, undertaker, and manuf. of picture frames, 8 Main, h 49 Clay.
Steuber & Graves, (F. A. S. and E. J. G.) dealers in jewelry, books, and stationery, Lampson block, W. Main.
Steuber L. W., (Vicary & Steuber).
Stevens Charles S., carpenter and joiner, h W. Main.
Stevens Ebert H., r 23, farmer.
Stevens Emory, (Stone Church) r 7, weaver and agent.
Stevens James, laborer, h 13 Mill.
Stevens John, r 61, laborer.
Stevens Mary A., widow of Peabody S., h 43 Lake.
STEVENS MATTHIAS M., r 61, carpenter and joiner.
Stevens Norman, r 42, farmer 5.
Stevens Samuel H., r 23, farmer 42.
Stevens Wilber C., carpenter, h 49 Clay.
Stevens William, farmer, h 49 Clay.
Stevens William J., carpenter, h 51 Clay.
Stewart Albert, (Mumford, Monroe Co.) r 37, farmer 37.
Stewart Archibald W., carpenter, h 51 Summit.
Stone Ada Mrs., widow of Newton A., h 113 W. Main.
STONE FRANK L., physician and surgeon, 38 W. Main, h 100 do.
Stoppelbine George, r 22, farmer 30.
STOWELL LUTHER K., r 47, farmer 40.
Strong Daniel R., retired, h 34 Myrtle.
Stripp Abisha L., r 48, farmer 92.
Strobel Andrew, laborer, h 94 W. Main.
Strobel Christian, marble cutter, h 10 Craigie.

Strobel Frank H., barber, h 10 Craigie.
STROBEL GOTTLIEB, (Morris & Strobel) stone cutter, h 48 South.
Strouse Edward G., laborer, h 13 Main.
Styles Laura Mrs., h 30 Gilbert.
Sullivan Cornelius N., barber, 28 Main, bds. Eagle Hotel.
Sullivan Michael, r 23, quarryman and farmer 4.
Sullivan Morris, h 23 Lake.
Sullivan Patrick, laborer, h 16 Exchange.
Sullivan Timothy, laborer, h n salt works.
Sunderland Gust, r 52, farmer.
SUTTERBY JOSEPH, veterinary surgeon, bds. 4 Lake.
Swartz Jacob, night watchman at malt works, h 12 Maple ave.
Sweney Patrick, laborer, h 7 Maple ave.
Sweeney Thomas, foreman on N. Y. C. & H. R. R. R., h 63 Lake.
Swift Isabell Mrs., h 34 Clay.
Taber Benjamin F., blacksmith, 15 Bank, h do.
Taft Fred L. B., clerk, bds. 49 Lake.
Taft Leland, retired farmer 107, h 49 Lake.
Taft Royal W., farmer, h 48 E. Main.
Tarplee Caleb, r 40, contractor and builder, farmer, leases of William Lampson 80.
Taylor Edmond C., physician, h 41 Wolcott.
Thayer Mary H., r 57, widow of Nelson.
Thomas Charles C., laborer, h 15 Pleasant.
Thomas George, r 57, laborer.
Thomas Henry, engineer, h 55 E. Main.
Thomas Jacob, r 47, farmer, leases of ———— Hascall 120.
Thomas William, h 101 W. Main.
Thomas William V., r 64. farmer.
Thompkins Eliza M., h 39 Church.
Thompson Isaac, agent, h 13 Wolcott.
Thompson Mary Mrs., h 25 Myrtle.
Thompson Rhoda Mrs., h 47 Lake.
Thompson Rhoda J. Miss, h 8 North.
Thorn Lewis, tailor, h 12 Park Place.
Thornton Mary E. Miss, r 44.
Thwing Orton C., dealer in produce and agricultural implements, farmer 123, Main cor. Lake, h 7 E. Main.
Tierney Jennie, (Mary & Jennie Tierney) bds. 45 Lake.
Tierney Lucy E, music teacher, h 45 Lake.
Tierney Mary, (Mary & Jennie Tierney) widow of Patrick, bds. 45 Lake.
Tierney Mary & Jennie, milliners, over S. A. Ball's.
Tillou Albert, carpenter and joiner, h 103 Gilbert.
Tillou Charles M., carpenter, h 10 Clay.
Tillou James M., r 58, farmer 60.
Tillou William H., r 54, farmer 15.
Toal George E., r 54, farmer, leases of Alvin Clark 27.
TOMPKINS ANGUS L., private sec'y to A. Maxwell, h 39 Church.
Tompkins Fannie Mrs., h 10 Bank.
Toomay Mary, widow of Timothy, farm 41, h 11 East ave.
Toomay Timothy, h 11 East ave.
TOOMEY TIM., farmer 41, h East ave.
Toulsey Peter, r 44, farmer.
Tracy Peter, r 32, farmer 6.
Tregea Thomas E., foreman salt works, h 82 Myrtle.
Tremaine Albert W., clerk, h 66 Myrtle.
Trousdell William, (Trousdell & Peoth) bds. Eagle Hotel.
Trousdell & Peoth, (William T. and Frank P.) butchers.
Tryon Augustus S., farmer, leases of Helen M. 30, h North.
Tufts Thomas B., printer, h 5 North.

Tulley John, hostler, h 25 East ave.
Tulley Joseph, stone cutter, h 58 North.
Tulley Patrick, stone mason and farmer 10, h 31 East ave.
Tulley Philip, laborer, h 25 East ave.
Tuttle T. B. & Co., (F. H. Mott) dealers in drugs and stationery, 20 Main.
TUTTLE THOMAS B., (T. B. Tuttle & Co.) h 16 Park Place.
Tyrrell Cristia, r 12, widow of John.
Valentine Henry, mason, h 24 Bacon.
Vanallen Lucas W., carpenter, h 27 Lake.
VANDEPOEL LAMBERT W. REV., pastor St. Peter's Roman Catholic Church, h 42 Lake.
Van Deusen Frank, r 67, farmer 102.
Van Deusen William H., r 48, farmer 102.
Van Lien Adaline Mrs., h 52 Lake.
Van Lien Lewis, telegraph operator B., R. & P. R'y, h 52 Lake.
Van Valkenburgh Abraham, r 47, farmer 134.
VAN VALKENBURGH JOHN H., r 59, 20 cows, farmer 147.
Van Wormer E., horse trainer, h Church.
Varley Patrick, laborer, h 63 Church.
Vary George P., r 47, farmer 100.
VARY PELEG G., retired farmer 100, h 39 Myrtle.
Vaughn Alexander H., saw filer, h 20 Church.
VICARY CHARLES N., (Vicary & Steuber) h 36 Church.
Vicary & Steuber, (C. N. V. and L. W. S.) merchant tailors, dealers in boots, shoes, gents' furnishing goods, trunks, satchels, etc., 18 Main.
Wadd John, farmer, h 13 E. Main.
Wait Anna M. Miss, r 44, resident.
Wait George W., carpenter, h and lot and 7 acres W. Main.
Wait Helen M. Miss, r 44, farmer 60.
Walker Adelaide A., widow of Horace, h and 6 acres W. Main.
Walker Charles E., machinist new salt works, h 102 W. Main.
Walker Jesse B., retired farmer, h 2 Craigie.
Walkley Frank L., r —, farmer with his father, Rosman L.
Walkley Juliet, widow of Richard, h 88 South.
WALKLEY ROSMAN L., r 68, farmer 200.
Walkley William, r 53, farmer 4.
Wallace Patrick, maltster, h 75 North.
Walsikoski John, r 19, farmer.
Walter Fred, gardener, h 25 North.
WALTON CHARLES A., r 72, farmer 91.
Wansor Nellie, r 56, widow of William.
Ward Butler, cashier Bank of Le Roy, h 95 W. Main.
Ward Charles K., retired farmer, h 16 Church.
Ward Eunice, r 58, farmer 14.
Warren Jabez, machinist, h 53 E. Main.
Warren Jabez T., machinist, 35 Mill, h 53 E. Main.
Waterman Dorance, r 42, carpenter.
Waterman George A., (S. Byron) r 42, carpenter.
Waterman James H., r 23, farmer 50.
Waterman Mary Mrs., h 49 Clay.
Waterman Wilber, r 42, farmer 15.
WATERMAN WILLIAM, (S. Byron) r 2, farmer 120.
Watherwax John H., r 18, farmer.
WATTLES WALDO M., prop. monumental works, 77 W. Main, h 7 South.
Webb Alton J., carpenter, h 20 Church.
Webb Jerome, carpenter, h Church.
Webber Lewis, r 40, farmer, leases of John Haskins 155.
Webber William, engineer, h 13 South.
Webster R. N. Miss, lady principal Ingham University.

10*

Weigel Frank, h 82 South.
Weigel George, h 82 South.
Weigel John, h 82 South.
Weigel Joseph, clerk, h 82 South.
Weigel Lewis, dealer in eggs, h 82 South.
Weigel Margaret, widow of Simon, h 82 South.
Weinman Christ, teamster, h 24 Pleasant.
Weld Emeline Miss, r 72, resident.
Wells Ellen L., r 53, farmer with Frances C. 4.
Wells, Fargo & Co. Express Co., J. P. Wheeler, agent, Erie depot.
Wells Frances C., r 53, farmer with Ellen L. 4.
WELLS GEORGE H., (S. C. Wells & Co.) h 14 Church.
WELLS S. C. & CO., (George H. Wells) manufs. of Shiloh's family remedies and
    Wells's Persian perfume "Hackmetack," Church.
WELLS SCHUYLER C., (S. C. Wells & Co.) breeder of thoroughbred trotting Ham-
    bletonian horses, h 80 E. Main.
Wester Charles, r 49, laborer.
WESTLAKE ALBERT S., dentist, 26 W. Main, h 98 Lake.
Westtacott William, r 56, laborer.
Wetherwax Stephen, r 23, farmer 47.
Wetherwax William, r 16, blacksmith.
Whalen William J., cigar manuf., h 78 Myrtle.
Wheeler Joseph P., express agent, h 9 Myrtle.
Whitcher Clarence T., r 22, farmer.
Whitcher Juliana Mrs., r 22, farmer 50.
Whitcher Melvin, r 42, farmer 6.
White George W., r 42, farmer with his father, Nathan.
WHITE JAMES, r 41, farmer 80.
White John W., laborer, h 94 Myrtle.
White Nathan, r 42, farmer 62.
Whiteman John N., com. traveler, h 74 Gilbert.
Whiting Burt, cooper, h 50 South.
Whiting Elizabeth Comstock, widow of Joel, farm 95, h 52 Summit.
Whitman Joseph, off r 49, farmer, leases of John Williams.
Whitney Amanda M., widow of B. Franklin.
Wicks Heppie E. Miss, artist, h 43 South.
Wicks Mary A., widow of John G., h 43 South.
Wier John W., miller, h 81 Gilbert.
Wilbor William C., pastor M. E. Church.
Wilcox Clarence, (Stone Church) r 12, farmer 133.
WILCOX FREDERICK T., druggist, 56 W. Main, h 99 do.
Wilcox George, r 40, farmer.
Wilcox Heman, r 61, farmer 5.
Wilcox Horace B., r 33, farmer with his father, L. F.
Wilcox Lucius F., r 33, farmer 90.
Wilcox Mark S., r 33, farmer.
Wilder Frank, r 25, farmer with his father, John.
Wilder John, r 25, farmer 123.
Willard Frank H., sewing machine agent, h 13 St. Mark.
WILLIAMS CASEY, r 72, breeder of Jersey cattle, farmer 28.
Williams Frank, r 72, farmer.
Williams George E., carpenter, h 26 Summit.
Williams Horatio C., carpenter, h 8 Union.
Williams John, off r 49, farmer 176.
Williams Joseph C., r 48, butcher and farmer 115.
Williams Lucian T., carpenter, h 69 Wolcott.
Williams Mariah Mrs., h 80 Myrtle.
Williams Peter H. W., r 61, painter.
Williams Randall, M. D., physician, 25 Church.

Williams Sarah, h 80 Myrtle.
Willis Susan Mrs., h 18 E. Main.
Wilson James, r 70, farmer 10.
Wilson James, (Stone Church) r 4, farmer.
Wilson Robert, r 48, laborer.
Wilson Thomas, r 70, farmer.
Winans Christopher, laborer, h 37 Mill.
WINGATE HENRY LENT, painter, grainer, and paper hanger, h 74 Myrtle.
WISS ANNA K., widow of John, prop. Wiss House, Main cor. Lake.
Wiss George G., harnessmaker and carriage trimmer, bds. Wiss House.
WISS HOUSE, Mrs. Anna K. Wiss, prop., Main cor. Lake.
Wiss John, dealer in groceries and crockery. 24 Main, h 82 W. Main.
Witter Alvin R., retired farmer, h 6 Maple Place.
Witter Caroline C. Miss, h 5 Summit.
Wolcott Albert W., r 22, farmer 104.
Wolcott Ann Miss, h Wolcott.
Wolcott Mary M., r 22.
WOODARD BETSEY, r 40, farm 150.
Wooding Frank E., dealer in dry goods, 45 Main, h 23 E. Main.
Woodruff John W., retired marble and stone cutter, h 78 Lake.
WOODWARD ORATOR F., manuf. of Kemp's balsam, 17 Main.
Woodward Phebe J. Mrs., h 14 North.
Wright Abbey Mrs., h Munson.
Yawman Joseph, cooper, h 37 Gilbert.
Young Myron K., com. traveler, h 39 E. Main.

OAKFIELD.

(For explanations, etc., see page 3, part second.)

•

(Postoffice address is Oakfield, unless otherwise designated in parenthesis.)

ALLEN CHARLES H., laborer, h South.
Allen Frank, r 26, farmer for William 150.
ALLEN RACHEL, widow of Arthur, who served in Co. H, 8th N. Y. V. Art., h South.
ALLEN SENECA, r 25, farmer 108.
Altenburg Barney, (E. Oakfield) r 3, farmer 20.
Altenburg Henry, (E. Oakfield) r 8 cor. 6, laborer.
Anthony Burton, r 1, farmer with his father, Henry.
Anthony Charles, r 1, farmer with his father, Henry.
ANTHONY CHARLES, r 14, school teacher and farmer 44.
Anthony Henry, r 1, farmer 60.
Anthony Paul, r 15, farmer 67.
Armstrong Addison, r 11, farmer 76.
Armstrong Fitch L., carpenter, h Pearl.
Armstrong John, r 13, farmer with Mary L. 250.
Armstrong Mary G. Miss., school teacher, bds. Pearl.
Armstrong Mary L., music teacher, owns with John farm 250.
Armstrong Sheldon, retired farmer, h Pearl.
ARNOLD JOHN B., prop. Olcott House, Main.
Ash Lyman, r 28, farmer 14.
AVERY ALBERT G., farmer in Elba 125, h Main.
Avery Charles B., r 19, breeder of Durham cattle and dealer in live stock, farmer 123.
Balfour Andrew, (E. Oakfield) r 7, farmer.

BALFOUR JEAN, (E. Oakfield) r 7, widow of Robert, farmer 11.
Bartels Alfred, (E. Oakfield) r 7, farmer.
BARTELS HENRY J., (E. Oakfield) r 7, farmer 153.
Bauer Fred, r 5, farmer 60.
Beecher Elmer L., telegraph operator and ticket agent W. S. R. R., h South.
Bennett Jasper G., (E. Oakfield) r 7, farmer 18.
Benton Andrew J., carpenter, h Main.
Benton Lizzie T. Mrs., dealer in millinery and fancy goods, Main.
Berry Charles, r 12½, laborer.
BICKLE ALICE, r 14, widow of James R., farmer 50.
BICKLE JOHN W., r 14, farmer.
BLISS BARNUM, retired farmer 50, h Main.
Blodgett Alva J., r 18, farmer 100.
Blodgett Harry, r 18, farmer with A. J.
Blodgett Julia B. Miss, r 18, school teacher.
Bobsen Fred, (E. Oakfield) off r 3, laborer.
POBSEN FREDERICK, (E. Oakfield) r 6, farmer, h and lot.
Bond George, r 18, farmer 60.
Boorom Addison, r 4, farmer 50.
Boorom George, r 4, farmer 148.
Bower Charles, r 14, farmer 1¾.
Bower John, r 11, farmer, leases the R. Stevens estate 237.
Braley Edward, r 12, farm laborer.
Braley Elizabeth, widow of James, h Chapel.
Braley James, laborer, h Chapel.
Braley Lineaus, laborer, h Chapel.
Bridge Bartley, r 14, laborer.
BRITTON ANDREW J., laborer, h Main.
BRITTON AURELIA O., Mrs., dressmaker, h Main.
BROMSTED MARY, r 4, widow of Joseph, farmer 77½.
Bromsted Theodore, r 4, farmer with his mother, Mary.
Bromsted William, r 4, farmer.
BROOKS SYLVESTER, retired farmer, h Chapel.
Brown George, book-keeper, h Water.
Brown Harriet A., widow of George S., h Water.
Brown Jackson, r 25, farmer 1.
BRULETT ISAAC, boot and shoemaker, served 3 years in the 25th N. Y. Lt. Art., Mill, h do.
Bullock Homer D., clerk for C. H. Griffin, h Main.
Bullock Levant A., carpenter and joiner, h South.
Burns Charlotte B., widow of John, h Drake.
Burr Albert, (E. Oakfield) r 3, laborer.
Burr Frederick, (E. Oakfield) r 3, farmer 122.
Burr John, r 9, farmer 5.
Burr Minnie, widow of Henry, h Chapel.
Busmire Lewis, r 16, farmer 16.
Calkins Beecher, laborer, h Gibson.
Calkins Sidney, laborer, h Gibson.
CAPLE ALFRED, merchant tailor, owns farm 120, h Main.
Caple Henry, retired merchant tailor, farm 93, h Main.
Carr Benjamin P., r 1, justice of the peace and retired farmer.
Cary Collegiate Seminary, Rev. C. C. Gove, prin.
Case Charles P., prop. meat market, Main, h do.
Chaffee Sarah, widow of William, h Main.
Chamberlain Charles, town supervisor, dealer in flour, feed, etc., Main, h do.
Chamberlin Eugene T., (Chamberlin & Wiedrich) h Chapel.
Chamberlin & Wiedrich, (Eugene T. C. and George D. W.) dealers in dry goods and groceries, Main.
Chapin Ralph E., (Harris & Chapin) h Gibson.

Chapman Bradley J., retired farmer, owns in Alabama 250, h Main.
Chapple Thomas, r 6, farmer 112.
Coe Susan, widow of Whitman, h Drake.
Cooper James, farmer 10, h Pearl.
Cope Ella L. Miss, (E. Oakfield) r 7, artist.
Cope Isaac, (E. Oakfield) r 6, farmer 50.
Cope Susanna, (E. Oakfield) r 7, widow of Simon, farm 17.
Corlet Stephen, laborer, h Water.
Cosway George C., r 13, farmer.
Cosway John I., r 27, farmer with his father, William.
Cosway John I., market gardener and farmer 6, h Drake.
Cosway Nettie Mrs., r 21, dressmaker.
Cosway William, r 27, farmer 26.
Curtis Sheldon, r 6, farmer 50.
Davis Joshua C., retired, h Main.
Decker Henry A., butcher, h South.
Decker Jesse R., house painter, h South.
Decker Levi J., laborer.
Dice George, (E. Oakfield) r 8 cor. 6, laborer.
Dillingham Stephen, r 5, farmer 107.
Dillingham William, r 4, school teacher and farmer.
DODGE ABNER C., dealer in harnesses and trunks, Main.
Dodge E. Clair Rev., pastor M. E Church, h Main.
DOERWIG HENRY, (E. Oakfield) r 7, cigarmaker, h and lot.
Dolan Martin, r 11, retired.
Doss John H., (E. Oakfield) r 6, farm laborer.
Douglass William, laborer, h Main.
Drake George, r 9, manuf. of brick and tile, farmer 24.
Drake James W., laborer, h Drake.
DRAKE NORMAN, book-keeper, h Gibson.
Dryer Charles, r 14, farmer.
DUNHAM CHAUNCY, r 19, live stock breeder and dealer, 20 head Durham cattle, farmer 120.
DUNHAM JOHN L., jeweler and watch repairer, Main, h Gibson.
Dunham William, r 21, laborer.
Dunlap Andrew, r 19, farmer with his father, William C.
Dunlap Merritt S., dealer in cattle, h Gibson.
Dunlap William, r 19, farmer with his father, William C.
Dunlap William C., r 19, farmer 283.
Dunn Patrick, laborer.
Dutcher Sylvester, laborer.
Dutcher William, r 1, farmer 70.
Eichler Henry, r 21, tailor and farmer 90.
Eighmy John, r 28, farmer 60.
Ellis Francis, r 15, farmer 68.
Ellis William, r 15, farmer with his father, Francis.
Exchange Bank, Frank E. Wright, prop., Main.
Farnsworth Ebenezer B., r 11, farmer, leases of L. Rathbone 136.
Farnsworth Edward N., r 21, farmer 130.
Farnsworth Shubael, (E. Oakfield) r 7, laborer.
Fidinger Charles, r 5, farmer 65.
Fidinger Charles, r 5, laborer.
Fidinger William, r 9, farmer 72.
Field Joseph, r 4 cor. 5, farmer 16.
Fishell Charles, machinist, h Mill.
FISHELL HENRY J., formerly manuf. of agricultural implements, machinist, h Mill.
Fisher Agnes, r 16, widow of Samuel, farm 16.
FISHER CHARLES, (E. Oakfield) r 2, farmer 226.
Fisher Frank W., (E. Oakfield) farmer with his father, Charles.

FISHER THEODORE S., r 1, farmer 113.
Fletcher Ervilla, widow of Lyman, h Main.
Frank Isaac J., prop. meat market, Water.
Frary Hiram, (Frary & Halsey) retired hay presser and farmer, owns in Alabama 210.
Frary & Halsey, (Hiram F. and H. C. H.) dealers in hay, Main.
Frenz Frederick. (E. Oakfield) r 6, mason.
Frenz Henry, (E. Oakfield) r 6, laborer.
Fuhrer George H., r 5, farmer 94.
Fuller Charles H., farm laborer, h Main.
FULLER GEORGE D., 10 head cattle, farmer 125, h Mill.
FULLER GEORGE M., farmer with his father, George D., bds. Mill.
Fuller Holland, farmer with his father, George D., bds. Mill.
Gann George, r 4, farmer 18.
Gann William, r 11, laborer.
GARDNER JANE, widow of John C., h Drake.
Gardner Harriet B., (E. Oakfield) r 7, widow of William R.
Gardner John W., (E. Oakfield) r 7, farmer and mill sawyer.
Geartz August, (W. Barre, Orleans Co.) r 2, farmer for S. Bodine.
GIBSON JOHN, retired farmer, h Pearl.
Gilse Frank, musician and leader Oakfield cornet band, bds. West Shore Hotel.
Goffe Charles, r 18, farmer 400.
Gorton Charlotte, widow of Thomas, farm 140, h Drake.
Gove Curtis C. Rev., rector St. Michael's Church and prin. Cary Seminary, h Main.
Grant Susan, widow of Daniel, h Mill.
Gray Andrew, laborer, h Main.
Gregory James D., farmer, owns in Elba 112, h Mill.
Grey Herbert, barber, Main, h Gibson.
GRIFFIN CHARLES H., dealer in ready-made clothing, boots, shoes, groceries, etc., Main.
GRIFFIN DANIEL T., (E. Oakfield) r 8, carpenter and farmer 32.
GRIFFIN FRANCIS A., house painter and joiner, owns Griffin block, Main.
Griffin John, r 20, farmer, leases of S. B. 135.
GRIFFIN SAMUEL B., retired farmer 135, h Mill.
GRINNELL ALBERT A., agent for Ferrin Brothers Co., and dealer in carriages, carts, wagons, cutters, farm implements, etc., South, h do.
Grover Lewis, r 4, farmer 16.
Gurding Carl, r 24, laborer.
Habicust Rachel, r 14, widow of Frederick, farm 60.
Hackley Francis S., overseer of the poor, retired farmer, h Main.
Hale Fanny, widow of William, h Main.
Hale ——, widow of Curtis, h Main.
Hale George, r 4, farmer 15.
HALE JAMES, r 2, served in Co. H, N. Y. H. A., owns h and lot in Alabama, farmer 314.
Hale Jane, r 9, widow of William, farmer.
Hale Robert, r 4, farmer 1½.
Hale William, r 23, farmer.
Hale William, r 2, farmer with his father, James.
Halsey Fred, (Haxton & Halsey) h Church.
HALSEY HENRY C., r 18, hay packer and dealer, farmer 73, h Church.
Hardwick Henry, r 11, laborer.
Harloff Charles, r 15, farmer, leases of A. Caple 80.
Harloff Christ, r 17, farmer 16.
Harloff John, r 16, farmer 56.
Harris & Chapin, (Frank L. H. and Ralph E. C.) dealers in stoves and hardware, Main.
Harris Frank L., (Harris & Chapin) h Gibson.
Hartwick Henry, r 20, laborer.
HAWES BENJAMIN F., justice of the peace and att'y at law, Main.
Hawes Henry L., r 22, farmer 44, h South.

Hawkins Sidney, building mover, h Gibson.
Haxton George W., (Haxton & Halsey) general ins. agent, evaporator of fruits, farm 63, h Pearl.
Haxton John H., r 6, farmer for J. Field, of Batavia, 37.
Haxton & Halsey, (George W. H. and Fred H.) dealers in beans, Main.
Haywood Robert, r 4, farmer 50.
Haywood William H., r 5, farmer 5.
Heal Enoch, r 5, prop. cider-mill and farmer 5.
Heal James, r 5, farmer 85.
Heal John W., dealer in coal and grain, farmer 240, h Main.
Heal Thomas, r 5, farmer 3.
HECKROTH AUGUSTUS T., clerk for A. B. Rathbone, h Mill.
Hentz William, r 17, carpenter and farmer 12.
Hepner William H., teamster, h Water.
Hickey Eugene F., barber, Main, bds. West Shore Hotel.
HILL GRACE, widow of George, h Pearl.
Hill John D., carpenter, h Pearl.
Hill Sarah, carpet weaver, h Pearl.
Hopkins Smith, laborer, h South.
Hosselkus Daniel, retired shoemaker, h Chapel.
Howland Adelbert, prop. machine shops and foundry, manuf. of agricultural implements, Main, h Mill.
Hundredmark George, (E. Oakfield) r 6, farmer, h and lot.
Hundredmark John, (E. Oakfield) r 3, farmer, h and lot.
Hutton Hugh, laborer, h Chapel.
HUTTON JANE, widow of William, who served in Co. G, 129, N. Y. Inf., promoted to 2d sergeant, and transferred to 8th Art., h Chapel.
Hutton Robert, r 23, farmer 80.
Hutton Samuel, r 18, laborer.
Ingalsbe & Hoffman, (Seward A. I. and Henry M. H.) druggists and agents Bell Telephone Co., Main.
Ingalsbe Edwin J., r 12, live stock breeder and dealer, farmer, leases of Parley V. 216.
INGALSBE PARLEY V., r 12, farmer 257.
INGALSBE SEWARD A., (Ingalsbe & Hoffman) h Main.
Isaac Elizabeth, widow of William, h South.
Isaac Emanuel, wagonmaker and blacksmith, Water cor. Main.
Isaac Fred W., clerk, h South.
Isaac George A., carriage painter and trimmer, h Water.
ISAAC JOHN D., blacksmith, Main, h South.
Isaacs Abner, laborer, bds. West Shore Hotel.
Isaacs Frank, prop. meat market, Main, h do.
Jackson Albert P., allo. physician and surgeon, Main.
Jackson Andrew, r 1, farmer 31.
JACKSON HARRIET S. Mrs., r 1, farmer 12.
Jackson Ralph, r 1, carpenter.
James Burt H., editor and prop. *Oakfield Reporter*, job printer, h Main.
Jaquith Franklin H., carpenter and joiner, h South.
Jarvis George, (E. Oakfield) r 7, teamster.
Johnson George, r 1, farmer 50.
Johnson Samuel, r 4, laborer.
Jones Julia A., widow of Henry L., h Main.
Jones Major A., laborer, h Main.
Kennedy Thomas J., r 28, retired.
Kingdon William, (E. Oakfield) r 6 cor. 3, blacksmith.
Knickerbocker James, farm laborer, h Mill.
Lehmann Fred, r 14, farmer 16.
Leschander Nicholas, cooper.
Leschander Peter H., cooper, bds. West Shore Hotel.
Ludlum Herbert H., r 25, farmer 105.

Lynch Edward, section foreman W. S. R. R.
Macumber ———, widow of Nathan C., h Water.
MALTBY EMMA C., r 15, widow of William H.
Maltby William H., r 15, farmer 120.
Manchester Darius J., justice of the peace, farmer 42, h Mill.
Manley Elezur N., pastor Presbyterian Church. h Chapel.
Martin Frank H., (H. C. Martin and Sons) h Mill.
Martin H. C. & Sons, (Frank H. and Wilbur H.) general merchants, Main.
MARTIN HENRY C., (H. C. Martin & Sons) h Main.
Martin Wilbur H., (H. C. Martin & Sons) h Pearl.
Mayback Gottlieb, r 4, farmer 27.
MAYBACK JACOB H., (E. Oakfield) r 7 cor. 3, mail carrier and general merchant.
McCrillus Delia E.,•r 19, school teacher and farmer 46.
McCrillus Julia J., r 19, school teacher and farmer 40.
McCRILLUS SARAH, r 19, widow of William C., farmer 61.
McCrillus W. Clayton, r 19, farmer 61.
McCulloch Edward A., (S. A. McCulloch & Son) h Drake.
McCULLOCH S. A. & SON, (Edward A.) general merchants, Main.
McCULLOCH SIDNEY A., (S. A. McCulloch &Son) owns farm in Batavia, h Drake.
McDonald Nancy, widow of Thomas J., h Pearl.
McGann Michael, r 9, farmer 9.
McGuire Matthew, r 23, farmer 178.
McHugh Henry, r 1, farmer 33.
McHugh James W., (E. Oakfield) off r 3, carpenter.
McINTYRE LOREN, house, sign, and ornamental painter, Main, h Chapel.
McMurray William, r 25, laborer.
McPartlain William, r 25, farmer, leases of Ann Stannard 80.
McVea John, r 27, farmer 12.
McVea Robert, r 22, farmer 44.
McVea Robert B., clerk, bds. Drake.
McVea William, r 25, farmer 37.
McVey Albert, miller, h Mill.
Mead Henry, r 1½, farmer 21.
Merry Frank, r 11, laborer.
Michels Joseph, r 14, retired.
Millard Charles, blacksmith, h South.
Miller Joseph, r 10, farmer, leases of J. M. Heal 230.
Mills James, laborer, h Pearl.
MOORE JOSEPH T., dealer in grain, produce, flour, feed, bailed hay, and straw, South, h Mill.
Morgan Sidney, farm laborer, h Pearl.
Moulton Elizabeth, widow of Martin, h Main.
Moulton Nathaniel, retired, h Chapel.
Mullen Joe V., drug clerk.
Murray Hugh, r 11, laborer.
NASH AMERRISSA E.. (E. Oakfield) r 7, postmaster and live stock breeder, farmer 345.
Nash John, (E. Oakfield) r 3, farmer.
Nash Whitman, (E. Oakfield) r 8, retired.
Needham Charles, r 2, farmer, leases of Samuel Sprout 100.
Nichols Arthur, freight and National Express agent W. S. R. R., h Main.
Nicholson Alexander G., farmer 102, h South.
Nicholson Frank, r 1, farmer 46.
Nicholson Mary, widow of Alexander, h South.
Nobles Harriet, r 28, widow of Calvin.
NOBLES NORTON C., prop. Oakfield mills, dealer in flour, feed, grain, and plaster, Mill, h do.
Norton Arthur A. J., r 19, farmer.
Norton Caroline, r 19, widow of Lorenzo, farmer 105.

OAKFIELD HOUSE, William C. Smith, prop., near W. S. R. R. depot, South.
OAKFIELD REPORTER, B. H. James, editor and prop., Main.
OLCOTT HOUSE, J. B. Arnold, prop., Main.
Olcott Lorenzo, r 19, farmer 2.
Olmsted Carlos P., book-keeper Exchange Bank, h Chapel.
Olmsted Francis A., (Olmsted & Staples) h Chapel.
Olmsted & Staples, (Francis A. O. and Job A. S.) dealers in staves, heading, and lumber.
Ott Judson, r 10, farmer, leases of B. Bliss 50.
Parker Alanson, r 1, farmer.
Parker Albert, r 2, farmer.
Shoemaker Henry, r 1, laborer.
Parker Eugene, farmer, leases of D. J. Manchester 42.
Parker Ezekiel, r 2, farmer with John.
Parker Harmon, r 1, prop. saw and stave-mill.
Parker John, r 2, farmer on the estate of S. C. 73.
Parker Willis, r 1, fireman in saw and stave-mill, h and lot.
Parks Sarah, r 1, widow of David, farmer 50.
Parsons Don F., off r 1, farmer 30.
Parsons James, r 1, laborer.
Pasel Carl, (E. Oakfield) r 3, farmer, leases of J. Pratt, of Gaines, Orleans Co., 50.
Pearce Ann, widow of Emery, h Main.
Pearce George W., dealer in carriages and carriage trimmer, h Main.
Peo Frederick, r 9, farmer 9.
Phillips Charles, r 6, farmer 50.
PHILLIPS GEORGE, (W. Barre, Orleans Co.) r 2, farmer, leases of N. D. Ensign 165.
Phillips Levi, r 4, stone mason and farmer 2.
Phillips Martha, widow of Joseph, h Gibson.
Philips Warren, r 2, farmer 150.
Pierson Augustus, carpenter and joiner, h Drake.
Plate Arnold, harnessmaker, h Mill.
POWELL SARAH, widow of David, who served in Co. E, 150th N. Y. V., h Pearl.
Prince Alpheus, physician and surgeon, Main.
PUGSLEY CHARLES S., M. D., druggist and dealer in books, Main, h Chapel.
Ransier Lewis A., mason, h South.
Rapp George, clerk Olcott House, bds. do.
RATHBONE ARTHUR B., dealer in hardware and building material, Main.
RATHBONE LAURENS, retired farmer 136.
Reed Amanda M., r 11, widow of Julius W.
Reed George W., live stock breeder and dealer, farmer 180½.
Reed Julia W., r 11, farmer 106.
Reed Seymour, r 9, live stock breeder and dealer, farmer 224.
Reed Sherman, retired farmer, owns in Alabama 385, and in Michigan 195, h Mill.
Reed Wilbur, r 12, farmer 350.
Relyea Jacob H., telegraph operator, bds. West Shore Hotel.
Richmond George H., wagonmaker, h Main.
Rigley Joseph, retired, h Drake.
Robbins Charles, (E. Oakfield) r 6, farmer.
Root Charles, h Main.
Root Elmer, r 22, teamster.
Root Frank, r 22, farmer for Oliver 95.
Root Oliver, retired farmer 95, h Main.
Russell Robert, r 26, farmer 2.
Safford Allen B., school teacher, h Main.
Safford Charles F., (Safford & Craft) h Main.
Safford Edward, laborer, h South.
Safford Lucy, r 9, widow of Chellus.
Safford & Craft, (C. F. S. and George C.) dealers in coal and produce, South.

Sanderson Wilbur, clerk West Shore Hotel, bds. do.
Sanderson William W., prop. West Shore Hotel, n W. S. R. R. depot, South.
Sawdey Edson, (E. Oakfield) r 3, carpenter.
Sawdey Henry, (E. Oakfield) r 3, laborer.
Sawdey Peleg, (E. Oakfield) r 3, wagonmaker.
Schroger John, r 9, farmer 5.
Schurz Charles, r 14, laborer.
Schurz Sebastian, r 14, farmer 20.
Scuffman Michael, r 14, farmer 31.
Seetor John, (E. Oakfield) r 7, laborer.
Shoemaker Fanny, r 1, widow of Nathaniel, farmer 68.
Showerman William, r 26, laborer.
Shultz Albert, (E. Oakfield) r 7, farmer, leases of Hale & Caple 188.
Shultz Charles, r 4, farmer with his father.
Shultz Christopher, r 6, farmer 109.
Shultz John, r 4, farmer 10.
Shultz John C., thresher, h Chapel.
Sleeper George, painter, h Mill.
Stegman Frank, r 28, farmer 4.
SMITH FRANK, r 1, farmer 1½.
SMITH GEORGE A., clerk Oakfield House.
Smith Nicholas, prop. Oakfield stage line, h Main.
SMITH WARNER H., blacksmith, Main, h Mill.
SMITH WILLIAM C., prop. Oakfield House, South.
Smith William F., clerk, h Main.
SMITH WILLIAM H., r 12, laborer, h South.
SPARLING JOHN, r 14, farmer 187.
Sparling William H., r 15, farmer with his father.
Sparr Eliphaz B., (E. Oakfield) r 6, prop. feed, saw and cider-mills, farmer 14.
Sparr Jane B. Mrs., (E. Oakfield) r 6, h and 10 acres.
Stannard Ann E., r 22 cor. 25, widow of Franklin, farmer 80.
Staples Job A., (Olmsted & Staples) h in Elba.
Stedman Irving J., justice of the peace and collection agency, Main, h Chapel.
Stedman Kate, widow, h South.
Stevens Henry, teamster, h Main.
STEVENS HENRY E., expressman, constable, and prop. cider-mill, h South.
Stevens John, prop. meat market, Main.
Stevens Levant J., hay packer, h Main.
Stevens Nettie S., school teacher, h Main.
STEVENS RICHARD, JR., book-keeper for J. W. Heal, bds. Oakfield House.
Stevens Sumner R., butcher, h Main.
Stevens William W., farmer 237, h Main.
Stringham Albert M., (E. Oakfield) r 6, farmer 100.
Taft Mary G., widow of Josiah C.
Taylor Daniel, farmer 150, h Gibson.
Taylor Evander W., r 2, farmer for Sarah E. 160.
Taylor Sarah E., widow of Elliot W., farm 160.
THAYER ELI S, manuf. of barrels and woven wire and picket fence, agent for
    Allen's patent gate, South, h do.
Thayer Syrene, widow of Daniel, bds. Chapel.
THIE ANTON, boot and shoemaker, h Main.
Tilley James F., postmaster and auctioneer, h Main.
Tripp Anson J., (E. Oakfield) r 7, farmer 26.
Tripp Charles, laborer, h Mill.
Tripp Frederick, (E. Oakfield) r 7, retired farmer 16.
Trippensee Ferdinand A., (W. Barre, Orleans Co.) r 2, farmer 110.
Tubbs Samuel, blacksmith, South, h Main.
Turner Lewis, r 1, carpenter and farmer 40.
Underhill Alfred, r 19, farmer 120.

Underhill Sidney G., r 19, farmer 53.
Vail Ephraim M., (E. Oakfield) r 8, farmer 129½.
Vail Stephen, (E. Oakfield) r 7, farmer 108.
WATTS MATTHEW, r 1, farmer 52.
Way Mary, widow of George, h Water.
Weaver Lyman A., undertaker and dealer in furniture, Main.
Welch Peter, r 24, farmer 94.
Wells George, farm laborer.
Wells Norman, carpenter, h Main.
West Shore Hotel, W. W. Sanderson, prop., livery stable connected, n W. S. R. R.
    depot, South.
Whitman Anna E., teacher, h South.
Whitney Alonzo, r 25, farmer 55.
Wicks Steven A., farmer in Elba 140, h Pearl.
Wiedrich George D., (Chamberlin & Wiedrich) h Chapel.
Wigdon James, r 15, carpenter.
Wigdon Mary, r 14, widow of James, farm 12.
Wigdon Melvin, (E. Oakfield) r 8, mason and farmer 10.
Wigdon William, r 16, farmer.
Wigton George, (E. Oakfield) r 7, farmer.
WILLIAMS HENRY, painter and paper hanger, h Pearl.
Williams Henry C., r 25, farmer 55.
Willis Smith, r 1, farmer 20, and in Alabama 50.
Winans Elizabeth, widow of Elisha, h South.
Winnegar Edwin R., h Main.
Wolcott Gilson L., r 28, farmer 40.
Wolcott William L., r 21, 10 head cattle, 140 sheep, farmer on the estate of William 230.
Wright Frank, (E. Oakfield) r 6, farmer 160.
WRIGHT FRANK E., prop. Exchange Bank, h Main.

PAVILION.

(For explanations, etc., see page 3, part second.)

(Postoffice address is Pavilion, unless otherwise designated in parenthesis.)

Abbey Emeline L., (Le Roy) r 17, farmer 21.
Acker Adelbert F., (E. Bethany) r 1, farmer 82.
Acker Adelbert S., (E. Bethany) r 1, farmer 86.
Adams Ezekiel H., (Pavilion Center) r 25, farmer.
Adams William H., (Pavilion Center) r 25, farmer, leases of Le Roy Salt Co. 97.
Allen Daniel, (Linwood, Livingston Co.) r 62, farmer 98.
Annis Joshua C., laborer.
Armstrong Cicero O., r 76, farmer 130.
Armstrong Frederick D., r 76, farmer with his father, Cicero O.
Armstrong Obadiah, (Le Roy) r 6, freight clerk and telegraph operator at D., L. & W.
    R. R. junction.
Austin William M., farmer.
Baker James P., r 55, farmer 205.
Baker John A., r 54, farmer 54.
Baker Joseph R., r 71, fruit grower and farmer 150.
Baker Lloyd C., (Pavilion Center) r 29, farmer 54.
Balfour Alexander, (Linwood, Livingston Co.) r 86, farmer 98.
Balfour James, (Linwood, Livingston Co.) r 86, farmer with his father, Alexander.
Balmer John P., farmer 2.

Balmer Thomas, laborer.
Barnett Emma C., widow of De Witt.
Beaver John, (Le Roy) r 20, farmer for Miller Walkley.
Beedle Walter D., (Le Roy) r 14, farmer 196.
Bezent Edward, boot and shoemaker.
Bicknell James, resident.
Bicknell Squire, resident.
Biggard William J., r 72, farm 168.
Biggart James, r 71, farmer 50.
Bishop Samuel J., (Le Roy) r 8, farmer 81.
Bishop Eliza, widow of Osher.
Bishop Martha E., (Le Roy) r 8, widow of Samuel.
Bliss James R., (Le Roy) r 8, farmer 68.
Bloodgood Dwight C., (Linwood, Livingston Co.) r 45, farmer 47.
Bloodgood Lucy Mrs., (Le Roy) r 41, lives with O. J. Hill.
Bloodgood Seth C., (Linwood, Livingston Co.) r 45.
Boatfield Samuel, r 54, farmer.
BOND CHARLES E., ex-postmaster.
Bond Charlotte H., (Pavilion Center) r 50, widow of Oswald, fruit grower and farmer
        127.
BOND DON C., blacksmith.
Bond Edwin A., (Pavilion Center) postmaster and general merchant, agent for farm
        implements and phosphates.
Botts Peter, (Pavilion Center) r 26, farmer.
Bowden James, (Pavilion Center) r 38, farmer 120.
BOYD JAMES A., r 84, breeder of Durham cattle and Merino sheep, famrer 150.
Boyd William J., r 84, farmer with his father, James A.
Bradley Ella E., r 68, music teacher.
BRADLEY ETHAN T., (Pavilion Center) r 39, cooper and farmer 7.
Bradley Hermie G. Miss, r 80, resident.
Bradley Mary J., r 68, school teacher.
Bradley William B., (Pavilion Center) r 39, cooper and farmer.
BRADLEY WILLIAM S., r 68, justice of the peace, fruit grower, and farmer 96, and
        owns with W. M. Austin, in Covington, Wyoming Co., 275.
Branch Thomas J., (Pavilion Center) r 49, farmer 30.
Bridgeman Harry, r 57, farmer, leases of Mrs. H. A. Wilson 128.
Britton Edmond M., (Pavilion Center) r 25, farmer 14.
Bryand Janet, (Le Roy) r 6, farmer 110.
Bryant Asa, (Le Roy) r 8, breeder of Southdown sheep, farmer 80.
Bryce William G., (Linwood, Livingston Co.) r 47, farmer 75.
Buchanan Alexander, (Linwood, Livingston Co.) r 63, farmer 70.
BUCKINGHAM WILLIAM, manuf. and repairer of wagons and carriages, h Broad-
        way.
Buckman Walter, r 65, laborer.
Burns John, r 80, farmer 49.
Burt Eliza, widow of William.
Burt George H., farmer.
Burt William R., farmer.
Calhan Pat, (Le Roy) r 22, section foreman and farmer 43.
Campbell Alexander H., (Le Roy) r 16, farmer 155.
Campbell Fred, (Pavilion Center) r 3, farmer.
Campbell George, (Le Roy) r 16, farmer with his father, Alexander H.
Cane Charles, r 75, farmer 106.
Cane Charles, Jr., r 75, farmer.
Cane Pat, r 75, farmer with his father, Charles.
Cane Timothy, r 75, farmer with his father, Charles.
Cannon James, blacksmith.
Carl Michael, (Pavilion Center) r 26, farmer 3.
Carmichael Alexander, (Le Roy) r 16, farmer with his father, John J.

Carmichael Daniel D.; (Le Roy) r 17, farmer 63.
Carmichael John J.. (Le Loy) r 16, farmer 100.
CARR ELI, retired farmer, owns with Sylvester 50.
Carr George I., (Carr & Graves).
Carr Herbert, farmer with S..L. Young.
CARR SYLVESTER, retired farmer, owns with Eli 150.
*Carr & Graves, (George I. C. and Edwin R. G.) general merchants.
Cheney Edward, r 61, farmer 250.
CHILSON FRED, r 77, farmer 150, general dealer in Covington, Wyoming Co.
CHILSON HENRY N., r 68, miller and farmer 25.
Chilson Marile, resident, h Maple.
CHRISTMAN ADDISON, contractor and builder. [Died January 20, 1890.]
Christman Edwin R., r 78, dealer in hardware, seeds, paints, oils, agricultural implements.
CHRISTMAN MENZO A., (Pavilion Center) r 25, fruit grower and farmer 130.
Christman William C., carpenter and builder, h and lot Lake.
Christner Peter, (Pavilion Center) r 25, farmer.
Church Mary, r 81, widow of Alden.
Clemens Frank W., r 58, farmer 93.
COBB ALANSON K., r 59, farmer 112.
Cobb Millard F., r 59, farmer.
Coe Emory, (Le Roy) r 47, farmer 101.
Coe Henry W., r 66, farmer, leases of his father, Horace, 60.
Coe Horace S., (Pavilion Center) r 40, farmer 100.
Cole John T., retired.
Conde Carrie C., milliner.
Conde Ophelia, widow of Albert O.
Conner Arthur, (Le Roy) r 24, farmer.
Connor John, (Pavilion Center) r 36, farmer, leases of Matthew Rogers 88.
Conrad Peter, r —, resident.
COOK GEORGE W., (Le Roy) r 12, farmer 75.
COOK HOMER, r 51, fruit grower and farmer 140.
Cook William J., (Le Roy) r 12, farmer 50.
Cooley Carlton, farmer 12.
Copeland William W., (Pavilion Center) farmer, leases of C. Rogers 125.
Corry Carlos E., (Le Roy) r 10, farmer.
Cosway Abraham L., (Le Roy) r 10, farmer, leases of William Huyck, of Le Roy, 99.
Courts John, r 69, farmer 7.
Cox John, laborer.
Coxon Fred W., barber, h and lot Lake.
Crocker Edgar M., (Le Roy) r 12, farmer with his father, J. Lyman.
CROCKER J. LYMAN, (Le Roy) r 12, farmer 112.
Crofoot Charles R., r 80, farmer.
CROFOOT LEONARD, r 80, farmer 124.
CROFOOT RICHMOND A., r 78, farmer 220.
CROSMAN FRANCES M., r 75, farm 100.
Crosman Hannah, r 75, widow of Peter.
Cudney George, carpenter.
Culver Willis L., postmaster, dealer in drugs and proprietary medicines.
Davis Jay B., (Le Roy) r 7, station agent D., L. & W. R. R. junction, telegraph operator and U. S. Express agent.
Dean William M., carpenter, h S. Lake.
Dickenson Edward W., (Linwood, Livingston Co.) r 86, farmer with his father, Eli.
Dickenson Eli, (Linwood, Livingston Co.) r 86, farmer, leases of John D. Hamilton 106.
Dinan Patrick, (Le Roy) r 47, farmer 90.
Dinan Patrick, (Linwood, Livingston Co.) r 47, farmer 87.
Dobson George, (Pavilion Center) r 48, farmer 5.
Dobson William E., (Pavilion Center) r 50, carpenter.
Donahue John, section foreman of B., R. & P. R. R., lives in Pavilion.

Donnelly Thomas E., (Le Roy) r 7, laborer.
Donovan Daniel, (Le Roy) r 22, laborer.
Donovan Mary Mrs., (Le Roy) r 22, farmer 13.
Doran James, r 74, farmer.
Doran John, r 74, farmer with his father, Patrick.
Doran Patrick, r 74, farmer 97.
DOTY JOHN C., dealer in grain and wood.
DOW JAMES W., dealer in wool, stock, and produce, farmer in Covington, Wyoming Co., 115, h E. Main.
Duffy Edward. emp. on railroad.
Duffy Julia, resident.
Duguid Homer S., (Le Roy) r 3, farmer with his father, Nelson A.
DUGUID MANFRED, (Le Roy) r 5, farmer 143.
Duguid Nelson A., (Le Roy) r 3, farmer 108.
DUTTON CALVIN, r 57, farmer 122.
Dutton La Fayette, r 54, farmer 78.
Dutton William F., r 54, farmer with his father, La Fayette.
Elliott Montgomery H., (Pavilion Center) r 26, farmer 39.
Elliott William, (Bethany) r 34, farmer 12.
Emerson Ira E., (Pavilion Center) r 26, farmer 16.
Evarts Loren W., r 78, dealer in coal. lumber, and phosphates.
Evarts Merriam W., dealer in coal and lumber, h and lot Lake.
EWELL FANNY B., widow of Rev. Henry B.
Ewell M. Florence, widow of Rev. Jirah B., h Hutchinson ave. cor. Maple.
Fagan R. John. (Le Roy) r 21, farmer, leases of Mrs. Alice Warren 130.
Farley Peter, (Le Roy) r 17, farmer 20.
Farnsworth Oliver D., (Pavilion Center) r 53, farmer.
Ferris James C., laborer.
Fisher Wellington W., harness manuf.
Fitz Simons George, (Linwood, Livingston Co.) r 65. farmer 48.
Found George, (Le Roy) r 27, blacksmith and farmer 50.
Friend James, (Linwood, Livingston Co.) r 62, farmer.
Gage Ebenezer, (Le Roy) r 8, farmer, leases of T. L. Hitchcock, of Wyoming, 50.
GANGEL FRANK, (Le Roy) r 3, prop. saw and grist-mill, and heading factory.
Gangel Josephine, (Le Roy) r 3, widow of George.
Gayton Charles A., (Pavilion Center) farmer.
Gayton Frederick, (Le Roy) r 6, farmer, leases of Mrs. C. F. Bissell 95.
Gayton James, (Pavillion Center) r 50, farmer.
Gayton James P., (Pavilion Center) r 25, farmer.
Gayton Marlin, (Pavilion Center) r 50, carpenter, prop. portable steam saw-mill.
Gillett Flora A. Miss, (Pavilion Center) r 38. station agent.
Gillett George D., (Pavilion Center) r 38, express messenger, gardener, and farmer.
Gillett George E., telegraph operator and agent American Express Co.
GILLETT WILLIAM F, (Pavilion Center) r 38, farmer.
Gilmore Charles, (Linwood, Livingston Co.) r 43, farmer, leases of Rev. T. E. Bell, of Bath, Steuben Co.. 20.
GILMORE WILLIAM H., druggist and mfg. chemist.
Gleber Daniel, (Le Roy) r 20, farmer 5.
Gleeson Patrick, (Pavilion Center) r 28, farmer 35.
Gould Charles E., (Le Roy) r 47, farmer with Charles J. Hill.
Graham Alexander, (Le Roy) r 20, farmer 1.
Graham Hugh, r 57, farmer 19.
Graves Edwin R., (Carr & Graves).
GRAVES GEORGE C., painter.
Green Anna, (E. Bethany) r 1, widow of Charles.
Green Charles R., (Le Roy) r 28. farmer 60.
Green John, (E. Bethany) r 30, farmer 10.
Grogan Patrick, (Le Roy) r 24, farmer.
Guymer George, harnessmaker, farm 27.

Hackett William H., r 81, farmer 36.
HAMILTON JAMES A., r 82, prop. Pavilion Hotel and Clydesdale stock horse, farmer 100.
Hamilton William, r 84, farmer 100.
Hamilton William M., r 84, farmer with his father, William.
Hannum Charles S., (Pavilion Center) apple grower and farmer 200.
Hannum Horace S., (Pavilion Center) r 50, farmer with his son Charles S.
Hannum Lottie C. Mrs., r 78, resident.
Harding Thomas, (Pavilion Center) laborer.
HAWKS J. PRESCOTT, (Pavilion Center) r 1, farmer 132.
Hayward David L., (Linwood, Livingston Co.) r 47, mason.
Haywood David, (Linwood, Livingston Co.) r 62 cor. 47, resident.
Hazleton Abert S., (Pavilion Center) r 24, farmer 96.
Hazleton Fréd P., (Le Roy) r12, farmer with his father, James E.
HAZLETON JAMES E., (Le Roy) r 12, breeder of Jersey cattle, fruit grower, and farmer 100.
Heaman John, (Le Roy) r 21, farmer with his brother Robert.
Heaman Robert, (Le Roy) r 21, farmer, leases of Henry Platt 103.
Henderson George, blacksmith.
Henry Lewis, (Linwood, Livingston Co.) r 41, farmer, leases of Henry Lock, of Le Roy, 105.
Henry Theodore, real estate dealer.
Henrys John, 69, farmer 25.
HERRELL DAVID C. Rev., Baptist clergyman. [Removed to Perry, Wyoming Co.]
Hewett William, r 76, farmer.
Higgins Asahel, (Pavilion Center) r 25, fruit grower and farmer 50.
Higgins Charles A., (Pavilion Center) r 25 cor. 38, farmer 120.
Hill Adelbert, (Le Roy) r 17, farmer.
HILL CHARLES J., r 41, farmer 185.
Hill Harriet, (Linwood, Livingston Co.) r 42, widow of Lyman.
Hines Jacob, (Le Roy) r 15, farmer 7.
Holcomb Antoinett, (Pavilion Center) r 40, resident.
Holcomb Ellen, (Pavilion Center) r 40, farmer 65.
Holcomb Eudocia, (Pavilion Center) r 40, resident.
HOLLENBECK MARY, (Le Roy) r 4, widow of William, farmer 72.
Hooper George, (Le Roy) r 15, farmer ½.
Howard John M., (Le Roy) r 8, farmer 150.
Howe Julia M., r 58, widow of Harlow.
Hoyt Edson W., r 65, teacher and farmer 4.
Hoyt Fred M., (Pavilion Center) r 26, farmer.
Hoyt Nathan, (Pavilion Center) r 26, farmer 4.
Hoyt William, (Pavilion Center) r 26, farmer.
Hubbard Alfred J., (Le Roy) r 12, farmer 80.
Hubbard Henry, farmer.
Hubbard Sheridan O., farmer 50.
Hudson Mary, (Wyoming, Wyoming Co.) r 73, widow of James, farmer 92.
Hudson William G., (Wyoming, Wyoming Co.) r 73, farmer with his mother, Mary.
Hunt Thomas, (Le Roy) farmer 85.
Husted Arabella, (Le Roy) r 14, widow of H. S., lives with R. A. Tanner.
Hutchinson Elias B., r 58, fruit grower and farmer 60.
Hutchinson Grant D., coal dealer and farmer.
Hutchinson Orville, r75, breeder of thoroughbred Holstein cattle, farmer 30.
HUTCHINSON RENSSELAER L., dealer in produce and fertilizers, farm 20, and in Le Roy 100.
Hutchinson Rufus, com. traveler, owns in Wyoming Co. 2 farms 125.
Hutchinson Thomas, (Linwood, Livingston Co.) r 20, farmer 85.
Hutton Jane, (Linwood, Livingston Co) r 43, widow of Thomas.
Hutton John, (Linwood, Livingston Co.) r 43, farmer 80.
Huyck Wilber H., furniture dealer and undertaker.

Jeary Elijah, (Le Roy) r 21, farmer with his brother Thomas.
JEARY THOMAS, (Le Roy) r 21, farmer 98.
Johnston Mary, (Linwood, Livingston Co.) r 43, widow of Alexander, farmer 95.
Johnston Thomas F., (Linwood Livingston Co.) r 43, farmer with his mother, Mary.
Jones Levi, mail carrier.
Karcher Samuel M., (Le Roy) r 47, farmer 2.
Karcher Sophia Miss, (Le Roy) r 47.
Keller William J., (E. Bethany) r 29, farmer.
Kingdon Thomas, (Pavilion Center) r 39, farmer 35.
Kingdon Thomas L., (Pavilion Center) r 40, farmer 50.
Lauderdal John, r 82, farmer 100.
Laurish Richard, (Le Roy) r 3, farmer 4.
Lawrence George W., (Pavilion Center) teacher and farmer 60.
Lawrence Hiram, (Linwood, Livingston Co.) r 42, farmer 150.
LAWSON JAMES L., r 82, farmer 150, and leases of S. & E. Carr 150.
LAWSON JOHN F., carpenter and joiner.
Legg Ann, (Le Roy) widow of John, farmer 5.
Legg Henry F., (Pavilion Center) r 27, farmer, leases of Benjamin Hartwell 105.
Legg William W., (Pavilion Center) r 27, farmer with his son Henry F.
Lewis Frank S., r 75, farmer for Eunice 66.
Lewis Mary, (Pavilion Center) resident.
Logan James L., (Le Roy) r 20, farmer.
Logan John, (Le Roy) r 20, farmer 120.
Lord Ervin D., r 57, farmer 145.
Lord Melvin P., (Pavilion Center) off r 25, farmer.
Lord Perry E., (Pavilion Center) off r 25, farmer.
Lord Sarah C. Mrs., r 57, resident.
Loudin Daniel, (Pavilion Center) r 36, resident.
Loudin David, (Pavilion Center) r 36, farmer, leases of Charles Rogers 97.
Maier Anton (Le Roy) r 10, farmer 12.
Mallory Phebe, widow, resident.
Mannix William E., (Le Roy) r 3, farmer, leases of Mrs. Nancy Stannard 100.
Marsh Andrew J., (Andrew J. Marsh & Son) h Main.
Marsh Andrew J. & Son, (Fred) butchers, Main.
MARSH FRED, (Andrew J. Marsh & Son) h Main.
Marsh Peter, r 71, farmer 60.
Martin John B., r 65, farmer 100.
MATTESON SARAH L., r 81, widow of Daniel, farm 48.
Maud Henry J., (Le Roy) r 22, farmer.
Maud Jane, (Le Roy) r 22, widow of James, farm 60.
McCarrick Barney, (Pavilion Center) blacksmith.
McCarrick Bernard, (Pavilion Center) blacksmith.
McCaughan Thomas, (Linwood, Livingston Co.) r 45, farmer, leases of James A. Boyd 25.
McCauley Mark, r 74, farmer 27.
McClelland Archibald, r 11, farmer.
McColl Dougald J., (Le Roy) r 18, farmer 13.
McCOLL DOUGALD R., (Le Roy) r 15, farmer 95.
McColl Hugh, (Le Roy) r 19, farmer 203.
McColl Hugh D., (Le Roy) r 19, farmer 10.
McColl James D., (Le Roy) r 18, carpenter.
McColl John, (Linwood, Livingston Co.) r 86, farmer 16.
McColl Malcolm D., (Le Roy) r 19, farmer with his father, Hugh.
McColl Niel C., (Le Roy) r 20, farmer 38.
McDowell Robert, (Linwood, Livingston Co.) r 42, farmer 15.
McDowell Robert, Jr., (Linwood, Livingston Co.) r 42, carpenter and farmer.
McEwen Thomas, (Le Roy) r 47, farmer 50.
McGrath Jeremiah, (Le Roy) r 24, farmer with his father, John.
McGrath John, (Le Roy) r 24, farmer 140.

McLean James, r 80, farmer, leases of Walace Mason, of Geneseo, 80.
McLean Jennett, (Linwood, Livingston Co.) r 42, farmer 50.
McMillan Catharine, (Le Roy) r 65, widow of Duncan, farm 160.
McMillan Catharine Miss, (Le Roy) r 65, resident.
McMillan Charles, (Le Roy) r 47, farmer 17.
McNaughton John R., (Linwood, Livingston Co.) r 86, farmer 75.
McVean William J., (Linwood, Livingston Co.) r 18, farmer, leases the Henry Chase estate 90.
McWethy Elmer E., (Pavilion Center) r 37, farmer and Indian relic hunter.
McWethy John E., r 51, farmer 125.
McWethy Sidney A., laborer.
McWethy Warren S., (Pavilion Center) r 37, farmer 92.
McWorthy Kneeland S., r 65, clerk.
McWorthy William H., r 65, retired farmer.
Mercer Edward D., r 75, farm laborer.
MILDE THOMAS B. Rev., Catholic clergyman.
Mills Charles J., produce and coal dealer, h S. Lake.
Mills John, r 35, farmer.
Mills Thomas, r 45, farmer 6.
Morgan Charles, carpenter.
Morgan Michael, r 83, farmer 49.
Moyles Patrick, (Le Roy) r 21, farmer 8.
Murnan Michael, (Le Roy) r 18, farmer 3.
Murray Charles H., (Linwood, Livingston Co.) r 46, farmer 52.
MURRAY GEORGE, (Linwood, Livingston Co.) r 45, farmer 42.
Murphey Eliza, resident, h Maple.
Murphey Henry, r 81, laborer on railroad.
Myers Anthony, (Le Roy) r 10, farmer 12.
Nagle Charles E., (Le Roy) r 21, breeder of Brown Leghorn fowls, farmer, leases of J. L. Cook 50.
NELLIS CLARK, (E. Bethany) farmer 76.
Nelson Nielson, (Pavilion Center) r 51, farmer 70.
Niebch Charles K., (Le Roy) r 22, farmer 54.
Niebch George, (Le Roy) r 24, farmer 147.
Niebch George L., (Le Roy) r 24, farmer with his father, George.
Niebch John, (Le Roy) r 24, farmer with his father, George.
Noble George, (Linwood, Livingston Co.) r 45, farmer with his father, James.
Noble James, (Linwood, Livingston Co.) r 45, farmer 50.
Noble Samuel, (York, Livingston Co.) r 86, farmer with his father, William.
Noble Thomas, (Linwood, Livingston Co.) r 43, farmer 130.
Noble William, (York, Livingston Co.) r 86, farmer 50.
Noble William T., (Linwood, Livingston Co.) r 45, farmer.
O'Brien Frank, resident.
O'Brien Martin, (Pavilion Center) r 3, laborer.
O'Conner Michael, laborer.
O'Connor Arthur, (Le Roy) r 11. farmer 44.
PAGE J. QUINCY D., r 69, manuf. of barrels.
Papke Charles, (Le Roy) r 17, farmer 40.
Park F. M., retired farmer 6.
Parkhouse George H., r 71, farmer with James 40.
Parkhouse Grace Mrs., r 71, resident.
Parkhouse James, r 71, farmer with George H. 40.
Parkhouse John, r 69, farmer 10.
Partlon James H., r 85, farmer 50.
Partlon John, r 74, farmer 54.
Partlon Mary, r 74, widow of Luke.
Pattridge Byram W., (Le Roy) r 20, farmer 71.
PAVILION HOTEL, J. C. Hamilton, prop.
Peddels George, r 80, farmer 40.

11*

Peddels Hugh, medical student, son of George.
Peddels John, r 70, farmer 4.
Perfield Mary, r 74, widow of James, farmer.
Perfield Philip, r 74, farmer 95.
Perry Frank C., r 71, farmer.
Pestol Frank, r 84, farmer, leases of G. Phillips 75.
Pestol John, r 84, laborer.
Petrie Frederick, (Le Roy) r 18, farmer 12½.
Phelps Clinton G., r 65, farmer 143.
Phelps Edgar E., (Le Roy) r 65, farmer with Myron 98.
PHELPS GIDEON V., r 65, farmer 76.
Phelps Myron A., (Le Roy) r 65, farmer with Edgar 98.
Phelps Oliver W., r 65, farmer 83.
Phelps Samuel, r 65, farmer 60.
Phillips Henry, r 51, farmer, leases of George Bowen, of Batavia, 102.
Phillips John, r 54, farmer 57.
Pierson Myron P., (Le Roy) r 18, farmer 84.
Pierson Reuben R., (E. Bethany) r 32 and 31, fruit grower, 68 acres apple trees apiarist, farmer 132.
Pixley George W., r 54, farmer 70.
Prill Michael, carpenter and farmer 5.
Quinlan William A., jeweler and watchmaker, Lake.
Quinlin Patrick, r 77, farmer 114.
Rawson Safford, (Le Roy) r 10, farmer 83.
Raymond Adelbert, r 55, farmer, leases of J. Hudson, of Alexander, 67.
Reed Nathan, (E. Bethany) r 29, farmer 128.
Reed Solomon D., farm laborer.
Reed W. A., r 65, farmer, leases on shares of W. E. Shepard 100.
Reed William A., (E. Bethany) r 30, farmer 160.
REESE ABRAM, r 69, farmer 200.
Reese Alfred H., (Pavilion Center) r 50, laborer.
Reese Edward, r 32, farm laborer.
REESE WRIGHT H., general merchant.
Reichard Peter, (Le Roy) r 21, farmer.
Reiter Charles, r 35, farmer 50.
Reiter Charles, Jr., r 35, farmer with his father, Charles.
Riggs Christopher, (Pavilion Center) r 38, mason and farmer 10.
Riley Catharine, (Pavilion Center) r 26, resident.
Riley Cornelius, r 74, emp. on railroad.
Riley Michael, r 74, farmer 10.
Robertson William W., (Le Roy) r 20, farmer 108.
Robinson Barzilla B., r 65, carpenter.
Robinson Edgar, r 65, carpenter.
ROGERS ALBERT S., physician and surgeon.
Rogers Champion E., (Pavilion Center) r 53, farmer 258.
Rogers Charles, (Le Roy) r 27, farmer 75.
Rogers Fannie, (Pavilion Center) r 53, widow of E.
Rogers Josiah B., retired farmer 72.
ROSENBURG FRANK E., farmer 51, h E. Main.
Rosenburg Nicholas J., retired, h E. Main.
Russell James M., (Le Roy) r 15, agent.
Russell Lydia, (Le Roy) r 15, farmer 40.
Sandles George, (Pavilion Center) r 53, farmer 17.
Sapp Columbus D., r 68, clerk, h and lot.
Severson Charles H., (Le Roy) r 41, farmer.
Sinnot Miles, (Le Roy) r 4, farmer 12.
Shannon Frank, r 82, farmer, leases of James Hamilton, of Le Roy, 100.
Shay Mary, r 75, widow of Levi, farmer 40.
Shay Myron S., r 75, farmer 10, and leases of Eunice Lewis 66.
Shumway George, (Linwood, Livingston Co.) r 62, farmer 1.

Shumway Harrison, (Linwood, Livingston Co.) r 65, farmer 31.
Shumway Laura, resident.
Shumway Melissa B., r 58, widow of Luther.
Shumway Orville B., r 58, farmer 30.
Shumway Solomon, (Le Roy) r 6, farmer 63.
Shumway Sophia, r 75, resident.
Shepard Frank J., r 80, breeder of sheep and farmer with his father, John.
Shepard John, r 82, farmer 200.
Shepard W. Edward, r 65, farmer 100.
Shephard Eliza, (Pavilion Center) r 53, resident.
Shephard William J., (Pavilion Center) r 53, farmer.
Shirley John, r 76, farmer 69.
Smead Caroline S., (Pavilion Center) r 34, widow of William C.
Smead De Lamont, r 58, farmer 70.
SMEAD WILLIAM C., (Pavilion Center) r 34, farmer 227.
Smith James, (Linwood, Livingston Co.) r 65, farmer.
Smith Julia T., resident.
Snow Mary E. Mrs., r 65, resident.
Sparks Irvin, r 57, farmer.
Sparks Wells C., r 56, fruit grower and farmer 90.
Sperry Emeline R., (Le Roy) r 47, widow of Platt T.
Sperry George W., (Le Roy) r 47, farmer 100.
Sperry Harvey, (Le Roy) r 47, farmer 75.
Sponable Irvin D., r 69, farmer, leases of George Guymer 20.
SPRAGUE WILLIAM B., physician and surgeon, farm 10.
Stanb John, (Pavilion Center) r 27, farmer, leases of Luke Van Allen, of Le Roy, 34.
STANLEY WILLIAM E., (Le Roy) r 14, farmer 70.
Stannard Nancy, (Le Roy) r 3, widow of Eldred, farmer 97.
Starr Clarissa, r 69, resident.
Starr Jasper, r 75, fruit grower and farmer 125.
Stephens Royal, (Le Roy) r 23, farmer.
Stevens Rollin L., (Le Roy) r 23, farmer 50.
STEVENS SAMUEL E., (Pavilion Center) r 39, farmer 90.
Stevens Wilber H., (Le Roy) r 9, farmer 110.
Stewart Daniel, r 68, retired farmer.
Stewart John, r 68, retired.
Strouts Felix C., (Le Roy) r 14, farmer 165.
Swan George W., retired.
Tanner Rufus A., (Le Roy) r 14, farmer 80.
Tapp George, (Pavilion Center) r 29, farmer 120, and leases of Michael Braugh 30.
Tapp John, (Le Roy) r 2, farmer 52.
Tapp William, (Pavilion Center) farmer with his father, George.
Tapp William E., (Pavilion Center) r 36, farmer, leases of J. Rogers 75.
Terrill Polly Mrs., resident.
Thomas Charles H., (Le Roy) r 21, breeder of Henry Clay horses, farmer 300.
Thomas Henry H., (Le Roy) r 21, farmer with his father, Charles H.
Thomas Samuel N., manuf. of Ozone oil.
Thornton Hugh, (Pavilion Center) r 27, farmer 16.
TILLOTSON CHAUNCEY E., (Le Roy) r 3½, breeder of Durham cattle, farmer 200.
TILLOTSON ELIJAH M., (Pavilion Center) r 40, agent farm implements and phos-
    phates, farmer 200.
Tillotson Emelia S., (Pavilion Center) r 40, lives with George W.
Tillotson Frank A., r 51, farmer 120.
Tillotson Fred D., (Le Roy) r 26, farmer with his father, Chauncey E.
Tillotson George W., (Pavilion Center) r 40, farmer 60.
Tillou Jane, (Le Roy) r 10, widow of Adney, farmer 18.
Tompkins Albert C., r 68, farmer with W. H. and H. H. 110.
TOMPKINS HENRY H., dealer in produce and wool, farmer with W. H. and A. C. 110.
TOMPKINS WILLIAM H., r 68, fruit grower and farmer with H. H. and A. C. 110.
Toomey Timothy, (Le Roy) r 11, farmer 39.

Townsend Arthur, dealer in agricultural implements, lime, and cement, h Maple.
Townsend Elbert, (Pavilion Center) r 25, breeder of Holstein cattle, Percheron horses, American Merino sheep, and Berkshire swine, farmer 200.
Townsend Ernest, (Pavilion Center) r 25, farmer with his father, Elbert.
Townsend Horace, (Pavilion Center) r 25, farmer with his father, Elbert.
TOWNSEND IRA, retired farmer, owns farm in Covington, Wyoming Co.
Tracy Peter, laborer.
Tremble James, (Pavilion Center) r 26, farmer, leases of H. N. Kinney, of Le Roy.
TRESCOTT B. F., fruit grower, prop. evaporator, dealer in dried fruits and pop corn, farmer 28.
Tubbs George, (E. Bethany) r 30, farmer 105.
Tubbs Sidney L., (E. Bethany) farmer with his father, George.
Tufts Charles A., r 74, farmer 40.
Tufts Eli P., r 74, farmer 108.
Tulley Catharine Mrs., (Le Roy) r 18, farmer 29.
Tulley Hugh, (Le Roy) r 22, laborer.
Tulley John, (Le Roy) r 22, farmer.
Tulley William, (Le Roy) r 22, farmer 2.
Usher Levi, laborer.
VAN BUREN GEORGE R., r 66, farmer 116.
VAN BUREN ROMAYNE M., r 66, breeder of Cleveland Bay horses, farmer with his father, George R.
Van Duser Thomas, resident.
Van Valkenburgh Nicholas, (Le Roy) r 18, farmer 2.
Van Vradenburg George H., M. E. clergyman.
Vishian Henry W., (Pavilion Center) r 26, farmer 16.
Walker Charles, (Le Roy) r 15, farmer 112.
WALKER EZRA, (Le Roy) r 20, farmer 122.
Walker James, (Le Roy) r 16, farmer 4.
Walker William, (Linwood, Livingston Co.) r 63, farmer 100.
Walkley Miller, (Le Roy) r 20, farmer 150.
WALMSLEY NELLIE A. Mrs., housekeeper.
Ward Frank, (Pavilion Center) r 58 cor. 60, farmer with his father, John.
Ward George N., (Le Roy) r 47, farmer 106.
Ward Henry C., (Pavilion Center) r 49, farmer 83.
WARD JOHN, (Pavilion Center) r 58 cor. 60, farmer 160.
Ward William S., (Pavilion Center) r 25, farmer 98.
WEBB FREDERICK A., painter.
Webb Samuel C., painter.
Webster John H., (Wyoming, Wyoming Co.) r 73, farmer, leases of his father, James H., 155.
Wellington James, r 45, farmer 4.
Wellington James. (Bethany) r 35, farmer.
Wells Lewis H. com. traveler.
Wentworth Levi B., (Pavilion Center) r 25, shoemaker.
Wheeler James H., r 57, farmer 9.
White Alfonzo E., laborer.
Whiteman Romey E., (Linwood, Livingston Co.) r 42, farmer 100.
Whiteman Samantha A., (Le Roy) r 42, lives with her son, Romey E.
WHITNEY GROVE D., painter and paper hanger.
Williamson Moses, carpenter and joiner, h E. Main.
WILSON HARRIET A., r 57, widow of George, farm 128.
WILSON IZORA A. Miss., r 57, resident.
Wilson Moses, (Le Roy) r 21, farmer, leases of C. F. Bissell 200.
WILSON THOMAS J., general merchant.
Woodworth Henry A., (Linwood, Livingston Co.) r 45, farmer 140.
Wyeth Louis, dealer in drugs, dry goods, and groceries.
Young Harvey I., carpenter and joiner.
Young Sylvanus L., farmer 70.
Youngs George W., (Le Roy) r 22, farmer.

PEMBROKE.

(For explanations, etc., see page 3, part second.)

(Postoffice address is Pembroke, unless otherwise designated in parenthesis.)

Ackerson Claud, (Indian Falls) mason, h and 1 acre.

Ackerson Emory, (Indian Falls) mason, h and 4 acres.

Adams George W., (Corfu) carpenter, h Main.

Adams William H., (Corfu and Buffalo) life ins. agent (office 263 Main st., Buffalo), h Main.

Alexander Eugene, r 52, carpenter and joiner.

Alexander Rodney, laborer.

Allen Homer E., (Corfu) r 68, 20 cows, grower of fruit and potatoes, farmer 144.

Altenburg Gaius, (Corfu) farmer 9.

Amidon George, (E. Pembroke) r 26, farmer, leases of Ellen Goodrich 78.

Amidon Marvin, (Corfu) r 53, breeder of horses, farmer 92.

Anderson Frank, laborer, h and lot.

Anderson Herbert, r 49, laborer, h and lot.

Andrews William A., r 67, farmer for his daughter, Mrs. Charles F. Tabor, 30.

Anger Philip, (E. Pembroke) r 22 cor. 43, farmer 80.

Annon Martin, (Corfu) r 53, farmer, leases on shares of Charles Swartz 67.

Arnold Arthur J., (Indian Falls) carpenter and joiner.

Arnold Charles W., (Indian Falls) postmaster and butcher.

Arnold Lyman E., (Indian Falls) dealer in hardware, groceries, boots, shoes, and meats.

Arras Peter, (Indian Falls) r 31, painter and farmer 7.

Austin Martha, (N. Pembroke) r 24, widow of Robert S., farm 24.

BABCOCK WILLIAM E., (E. Pembroke) prop. East Pembroke flouring-mills, contractor and builder.

Backus John, (Indian Falls) r 31, machinist.

Ball Caroline A., (Corfu) widow of William, h Main.

Banton Jonas, (Corfu) farmer 74, h and lot Main.

Barber George W., (W. Batavia) r 71, farmer 6.

Bard William, (N. Pembroke) laborer.

Barden Alvah O., (Corfu) prop. Barden hall, farm 160, h Main.

Barlow William, (E. Pembroke) 12 Cotswold sheep, farm 60.

Barlow William, Jr., (E. Pembroke) r 56, farmer 55.

Barnham Peter T., r 52, farmer 23.

Barrett Thomas H., (E. Pembroke) pastor The Holy Name of Mary Church.

Bartholf Wilbur P., (Corfu) r 48, farmer, leases on shares of Joel Peck 138.

Bartlett Alfred, (E. Pembroke) r 48, farmer 35.

BATES JOEL W., (Indian Falls) eclectic physician and surgeon.

Bauer John, (Corfu) r 63, farmer 15.

Baum Henry, (Corfu) r 61, laborer.

Beckwith Harris, (N. Pembroke) r 21, 8 cows, 100 sheep, grower of potatoes and fruit, farmer 260.

Bennet Thomas, (Corfu) r 49, farmer 40.

Bennett Fred T., (Corfu) 13 cows, farmer, leases on shares of James Farnham 211.

Bennett Henry L., (E. Pembroke) r 41, farmer 155.

Bennett Henry W., (Corfu) dealer in horses, farmer 50.

BENNETT JAMES F., (E. Pembroke) r 41, farmer, leases on shares of his father, Henry L. 155, served in Co. F, 28th N. Y. Vols., from April, 1861, to May 22, 1863.

Bennett John D., (Corfu) (Bennett & Sumner) bds. Main, owns h and lot.

Bennett & Sumner, (Corfu) (John D. B. and Emmett E. S.) dealers in fresh, salt, and smoked meats, fish, and oysters, Main.

Bentley George, (Indian Falls) laborer, h and lot.
Berg Frank, r 52, farmer 10.
Bland ————, (Corfu) r 63, widow of Henry, h and 3 acres.
Blood John H., (E. Pembroke) r 42, laborer.
Board Irving, (Corfu) r 48, laborer.
Booth James L., (Corfu) r 74, 6 cows, farmer 33.
Booth Seymour, (W. Batavia) r 73, laborer.
Boughton Martha M., (E. Pembroke) r 46, widow of Leander, music teacher.
Boughton Willis E., (E. Pembroke) r 46, farmer, leases on shares of G. B. Seamans
      117.
Bower John, (Corfu) r 63, farmer 15.
Bowie Thomas, (Corfu) r 79, retired carpenter, h and 1 acre.
Boyce Enoch S., (Corfu) r 55, farmer with his father, John.
Boyce Helen Miss, (Corfu) r 55, teacher, daughter of John.
Boyce James, (Corfu) r 55, farmer with his father, John.
Boyce James C., (Corfu) r 55, farmer with his father, John.
BOYCE JOHN, (Corfu) r 55, assessor, breeder of and dealer in thoroughbred Jersey
      cattle, reg., and McGee Poland China swine, 20 cows, 32 sheep, farmer 250.
Boyce John, Jr., (W. Batavia) r 72, 6 cows, farmer, leases on shares of John Lown,
      of Batavia, 80.
Boyce Keziah Miss, (Corfu) r 55, teacher, daughter of John.
Bramstadt John H., (Akron, Erie Co.) r 50, farmer with his father, Louis.
Bramstadt Louis, (Akron, Erie Co.) r 50, farmer 77.
Bramstadt Louis, Jr., (Akron, Erie Co.) r 50, laborer.
Brayton John McK., (Corfu) pastor Presbyterian Church, h Railroad ave.
Breman Edward, (E. Pembroke) r 48, farmer 118.
Breman Edward, Jr., (E. Pembroke) r 48, farmer with his father.
Briggs Leander C., (E. Pembroke) shoemaker.
Brill John, (Indian Falls) r 7, shoemaker.
Bronson James, r 50, breeder of horses, farmer 78.
Brown Alexander, r 48, farmer 160.
Brown Almira C., (Corfu) r 67, widow of John, 6 cows, farmer 65.
Brown Anthon H., (W. Batavia) r 72, farmer with his father, John W.
BROWN EDWARD A., (Corfu) r 49 cor. 30, breeder of thoroughbred Jersey cattle
      and fine horses, 25 cows, farmer 196.
Brown Henry I., (Corfu) cartman, h Main.
Brown Henry J., (Corfu) dealer in butter, eggs, fruit, and vegetables, h Main.
Brown Henry M., r 49 cor. 30, farmer.
Brown J. Worth, (N. Pembroke) r 40, breeder of Chester White swine and White
      Rose fowls, farmer, leases of Mary Burgess 25.
BROWN JOHN W. Hon., (W. Batavia) r 72, 200 Merino sheep, fruit grower, farmer
      220.
Brown Nelson A., (Corfu) dealer in tin, Main cor. Railroad ave., h Main.
Brown Robert, (Corfu) r 67, laborer.
Buckley Charles, (Corfu) teamster, h Main.
Buckley Edward, r 52, peddler.
Buckley Patrick, r 52, farmer 6.
Buckman Fred, (Corfu) r 68, farm laborer.
Buckston Rice W., r 38, retired farmer, h and 2½ acres.
Bullard William A., (Corfu) 12 cows, farmer 88.
Bunell William T., r 67, blacksmith and farmer 77.
BURGESS ABRAM E., (N. Pembroke) r 21, 5 cows, breeder of Clydesdale horses,
      grower of strawberries and apples, farmer 131.
Burgler Frederick, (E. Pembroke) section foreman.
Burke John, (Corfu) r 61, farmer 15.
Burnette Andrew, r 52, carpenter,
Burns Alexander, r 50, 250 sheep, farmer 220.
Burns Frank M., r 50, invalid.
Burrill Amasa, r 51, farmer 7½, and leases on shares with his brother Marcius 89.

Burrill Arba F., r 51, farmer 89.
Burrill Marcious, farmer 23, and leases on shares with his brother Amasa 89.
Burroughs William, (E. Pembroke) r 41, farmer 5.
Butler Byron W., (N. Pembroke) r 24, laborer and saw-filer.
Cain Frank, (E. Pembroke) farmer 14.
Calnan Daniel, farmer, leases on shares of his father, John, 140.
Calnan John, r 33, farmer 140.
Carl Mary A., r 34 cor. 35, widow of Edward B., farm 25.
Carrier Ansel K., (Corfu) r 79, pres. Genesee County Horse Breeders Association, breeder of horses, 27 cows, fruit grower, farmer 170.
Carrier Edmund W., (Corfu) r 79, 20 cows, fruit grower, farmer 130.
CARRIER HIRAM, (Corfu) r 79, retired farmer, aged 83.
Carrier Media K. Miss, (Corfu) r 79, teacher, daughter of Edmund W.
CARRIGAN BARNABAS, (Indian Falls) r 27, farmer 53.
CARTER DANIEL, (Corfu) retired farmer.
Case Harlow, (Corfu) r 63, 20 cows, farmer 165, and in Wyoming Co. 160.
Cathcart Brothers, (Corfu) r 61, (Cyrus D. and Daniel) 6 cows, farmers 70.
Cathcart Cyrus D., (Corfu) r 61, (Cathcart Brothers).
Cathcart Daniel, (Corfu) r 61, (Cathcart Brothers).
Central Hotel, (Corfu) M. M. Fleming, prop., livery stable connected, Main.
Chadeayne Daniel, (Corfu) retired carpenter and undertaker, h Main.
Chadwell James, (E. Pembroke) r 57, painter, h and lot.
Chapman Henry, (Corfu) laborer.
Chase Lyman, (Corfu) farmer 5.
Childs Albert S., (Corfu) carpenter and cooper, h Main.
Childs Clark, (Corfu) cooper and farmer 30, h Main.
Childs George F., (E. Pembroke) r 45, farmer 6, and leases of Naomi Post 28.
Childs Richard, (Indian Falls) r 4, farmer 15.
Childs Sarah, (E. Pembroke) r 42, widow of William, owns with her son George S. h and 6 acres.
Childs Thomas A., (Indian Falls) r 4, life ins. agent and photographer.
Childs Wilbur J., general merchant.
Childs William, (Indian Falls) r 27, 70 sheep, farmer, leases on shares of John D. Forward 110.
Childs William Eaton, (Corfu) r 55, farmer 46.
Clidds Jesse R., (Indian Falls) r 4, teacher.
Christie Clinton, (E. Pembroke) r 15, farmer 96.
Christie Daniel H., (E. Pembroke) r 24, breeder of May Duke coach horses, 8 cows, farmer 160.
Clanson Sophia, r 51, widow of August, farm 78.
CLARK A. FRANK, r 49, justice of the peace and farmer 105.
Clark David, (Indian Falls) blacksmith and horseshoer.
Clark Edward H., (E. Pembroke) r 45, 60 sheep, farmer 80.
Clark George B., r 49, foreman railroad construction.
Clark James B., (N. Pembroke) r 18 cor. 19, carpenter, breeder of horses, 50 sheep, farmer, leases of Jacob Martin 89.
Clark James J., (E. Pembroke) r 44, farmer, leases on shares of his mother 59.
Clark John, (Indian Falls) r —, farmer 38.
Clarkston Stephen, (Corfu) retired farmer, h Main.
Clemons Maria, r 50, widow of Artemas L., farm 92.
Cleveland John, (E. Pembroke) r 71, farmer 254.
Cleveland William Nelson, (E. Pembroke) r 48 cor. 39, farmer with his father, William H.
Cleveland William H., (E. Pembroke) r 48 cor. 39, 10 cows, 100 sheep, fruit grower, farmer 254.
Cobb Isaac, (Indian Falls) r 11, carpenter.
COCHRAN HENRY, (Corfu) r 48, 5 cows, farmer on the estate of William B. Long 75.
COE WILLIAM S., (Corfu) r 79, farmer 63.
Coffey James, (W. Batavia) r 71, laborer.

Coffey John, (W. Batavia) r 71, laborer,
Coffey Mary, (W. Batavia) r 71, widow of John, farm 4.
Coffey William J., (E. Pembroke) postmaster, dealer in tobacco, cigars, stationery, and confectionery, Main, h Railroad.
Colby Aaron H., (Corfu) r 69, breeder of high grade Durham cattle, 20 cows, fruit grower, farmer 156.
Colby Alexander, (Indian Falls) r 49, farmer, leases of E. Taggart, of Batavia, 50.
Colby Elmer, (Corfu) r 49, farmer, leases of Paulina Stanley 85.
Colby Francis H., (Corfu) r 69, farmer with his father, Aaron H.
Colby Garrett, (Corfu) laborer, h Church.
Colby Henry, (Corfu) r 69, laborer.
Colby Louisa, (Corfu) widow of Samuel, h and lot Church.
Colby William H., (E. Pembroke) truckman.
Colby William H. Mrs., (E. Pembroke) milliner.
Cole Anson, (N. Pembroke) resident.
Cole Horace M., (North Pembroke) farmer, leases of Abram Burgess 24
Coleman Adelphia T., (Akron, Erie Co.) r 37, widow of Ezra, farm 50.
Coleman Henry, r 49, farmer 57.
Collins Charles, (Corfu) painter.
Coniber George, (N. Pembroke) shoemaker and farmer 20.
Coniber Henry, (N. Pembroke) r 17, farmer 61.
Cook Anna, (E. Pembroke) widow of James, dressmaker.
Cook Charles, (Akron, Erie Co.) r 3, farmer 20.
Cook George, (E. Pembroke) r 42, farmer 60.
Cook Otto, (Indian Falls) r 29 cor. 30, farmer 86.
Corsett Edmund, (Indian Falls) r 15, farmer 4½.
Corsett Grant, (Indian Falls) r 15, laborer.
Cowell Edward, (Corfu) r 69, laborer.
Crane Frank W., (Corfu) physician and surgeon.
Crawford John. (Corfu) r 55. farmer 57.
Crawford John, Jr., (Corfu) r 55, farmer with his father.
Crawford William, (Corfu) farmer 140, h and lot Main.
Crawford Willie H., (Corfu) r 68, 26 cows, farmer, leases on shares of his father, William, 140.
Crocker John, (Indian Falls) farmer.
Crocker Lucy A., (Indian Falls) widow of Oscar W., farm 10.
Crossen J. Ward, r 35, farmer 50.
Croxton Jesse, (Corfu) laborer.
Cummings Calvin, (E. Pembroke) r 60, carpenter and farmer 15.
Cummings John, (E. Pembroke) retired farmer.
Cummings William, (Indian Falls) farmer 7.
Cunshafter August, undertaker, dealer in furniture, and prop. cider-mill.
Currier John, (Indian Falls) r 7. student and laborer.
Currier Mary, (Indian Falls) r 7, widow of William, h and 4 acres.
Curtis Caroline P. (Nichols), (Corfu) widow of Amos O., h Railroad ave.
Cutler Sarah, widow of Rev. Harvey H., farm 10.
Dailey James, (E. Pembroke) r 47, farmer on the estate of his father, Thomas, 65.
Danahay James D., (E. Pembroke) r 57, laborer.
Darrow Asa K., (Corfu) banker in Kansas, h Main.
Davis Charles H., (Corfu) r 48 cor. 54, farmer 53.
Day Emory L., (N. Pembroke) r 20, 50 sheep, farmer 160.
Day William, r 33, farmer 8.
Deinhart Nicholas, (Crittenden, Erie Co.) r 66, farmer 44.
Dennison George H., (E. Pembroke) (Dennison & Moore).
Dennison John, (E. Pembroke) r 45, farmer, leases on shares of John Gould, of Batavia, 110.
Dennison Otis G., (E. Pembroke) resident.
Dennison & Moore, (E. Pembroke) (George H. D. and Herbert B. M.) druggists and general merchants, Main.

Denton Henry C., (N. Pembroke) r 21, carpenter.
Derby J. M., (E. Pembroke) Baptist clergyman.
Derrick Edward, laborer, h and lot.
Dibble Dennis, (Indian Falls) r 27, highway commissioner, fruit grower, farmer 100.
Dickinson John H., (E. Pembroke) r 40, deputy sheriff, assessor, and farmer 54.
Dietschler Caspar, blacksmith.
Dillon Frank, (Corfu) r 69, farmer with his father, Michael.
Dillon Michael, (Corfu) r 69, 60 sheep, farmer 100.
Dillree William H., r 52, laborer.
DIMOCK DWIGHT, (Corfu) r —, county supt. of the poor, postmaster, general ins. agent, breeder of coach and trotting horses, 27 head, and high grade Durham cattle, 16 cows, fruit grower, farmer 130.
Diver Edward, (E. Pembroke) 75 sheep, breeder of horses, fruit grower, farmer 290, and in Alabama 305.
Doane Dan, retired farmer.
Doane Willis, r 65, farmer 6.
Dodge Caroline, (Corfu) r 54, 12 cows, farmer 107.
Dodge Catherine, (Corfu) widow of Caleb, h Main.
Dodge David, (E. Pembroke) r 41, laborer and farmer 3.
Dodge Ezra, (Corfu) r 54, resident.
Donovan Cornelius, r 49, wool grower, farmer 166.
Donavan Daniel, r 49, farmer.
Donovan John, r 49, farmer with his father, Cornelius.
Donovan Patrick, r 38, laborer and farmer 6½.
Dorschild Nicholas, (Corfu) r 55, laborer, h and 4 acres.
Donit George, r 66, farmer 38.
Downing Catherine, (E. Pembroke) r 43, widow of C. Downing, h and 5 acres.
Doyle Barnard, (Corfu) r 76, laborer.
Doyle James, (Corfu) r 76, brakeman.
Doyle John, (Corfu) r 76, laborer.
Doyle Matthew, (Corfu) r 77, section hand.
Doyle Michael, (Corfu) baggagemaster N. Y. C. & H. R. R. R., h Railroad ave.
Drake Edward, (Corfu) retired, aged 80, h Main.
Duggan Cornelius, (E. Pembroke) r 70, farmer 50.
DUGUID WILLIAM H., (Corfu) r 79, breeder of grade Holstein cattle and fine horses, prop. St. Lawrence stock horse "Prince," 14 cows, farmer 140.
Dunn Elmer, laborer, h and lot.
Dunn William, (Corfu) laborer, h Main.
Durham Cash M., (E. Pembroke) farmer, leases on shares with his father, Edwin.
Durham Edwin, (E. Pembroke) dealer in agricultural implements and farm produce.
Durham Frank R., (E. Pembroke) emp. American Express Co.
Durham George, (E. Pembroke) r 59, farmer, leases on shares of his father, James, 180.
Durham James, (E. Pembroke) r 59, farmer 180.
Durham John, (N. Pembroke) laborer.
Durham John, Sr., (E. Pembroke) retired farmer.
Durham John, Jr., (Corfu) r 14, farmer 37.
Dutton Simeon E., (Corfu) fire ins. agent, wholesale dealer in farmer produce and coal, h Railroad ave.
Dwyer John, (E. Pembroke) blacksmith.
Dwyer Patrick, (N. Pembroke) blacksmith and farmer 10.
Dymond Charles, (N. Pembroke) r 20, carpenter and farmer 7.
Dymond Chester, (N. Pembroke) laborer.
Dymond Eugene, (N. Pembroke) blacksmith, h and 1 acre.
Dymond Frank, (N. Pembroke) r 25, prop. steam threshing machine, farm 2.
Dymond Lincoln, (N. Pembroke) r 25 cor. 15, 8 cows, farmer 150.
Dymond Sherman, (N. Pembroke) r 22, laborer.
Eagau Mary E., r 50, farm 92.
Eagan Thomas, r 50, farmer, manages the estate of Artemas L. Clemens 92.
East Pembroke Hotel, (E. Pembroke) G. G. Elliott, prop.

Edds William T., (Corfu) pastor M. P. Church, parsonage Main.
Eddy George W., (N. Pembroke) harnessmaker, h and lot.
Eddy Lucian, (Corfu) r 69, laborer.
Edsoll John, off r 51, farm 52.
Edwards Anna Miss, milliner, h Main.
Edwards William D., (Corfu) dealer in drugs, stationery, and confectionery, Main, h do.
Eggleston Charles L., (E. Pembroke) r 71, farmer 54.
Egloff John, (Crittenden, Erie Co.) r 80, h and 2 acres.
ELLINWOOD HENRY P., (E. Pembroke) r 48, 10 cows, 100 sheep, breeder of horses, farmer 145.
Elliott Edward, (E. Pembroke) r 47, farm laborer.
Elliott Edwin R., (E. Pembroke) r 59, fruit grower, farmer 118.
Elliott George G., (E. Pembroke) prop. East Pembroke Hotel, breeder of Blue Danube horses, 6 head, farmer 112.
Elmore Thomas, (W. Batavia) r 71, section boss.
Ensign Willard E., (E. Pembroke) school teacher.
Etzold John, r 66, farmer 52.
Etzold Julius, (Crittenden, Erie Co.) r 66, laborer.
Eustace John, (Corfu) laborer, h Allegany st.
Eustace Mary Miss, (Corfu) h Allegany st.
Falker Adam, (Corfu) r 64, farmer 27.
Fanning Frank, postmaster and general merchant, h and 2 acres.
Farnham James, (Corfu) dealer in farm produce, 16 cows, farmer 212.
Ferger Francesca, (Corfu) r 64, widow of Daniel, farm 5.
Fincher Charles C., (Corfu) r —, 10 cows, farmer 72.
Finlay Alexander, (E. Pembroke) r 41, farmer 82.
Firman Fred, (Indian Falls) r 7, stone mason, farmer 4.
Firman Jacob, (Indian Falls) r 7, laborer,
Fishell Abner, (N. Pembroke) r 16, farmer 72.
Fishell Ira B., prop. Pembroke Hotel.
Fisher Herman, r 52, farmer 30.
Flagler James H., (Corfu) retired farmer, h Main.
Fleming Melvin M., (Corfu) prop. Central Hotel and livery stable, Main.
Flint J. Monroe, (Akron, Erie Co.) r 37, farmer 71, and n Richville 150.
Flint Milo, (Akron, Erie Co.) r 37, farmer 125.
Ford Ann, (E. Pembroke) r 24 cor. 25, widow of William, farm 71.
Forward Andrew, (N. Pembroke) r 27, breeder of Chester White swine, farmer 50.
Forward Chauncey, (E. Pembroke) dealer in butter and eggs.
Forward Henry J., (E. Pembroke) r 26, fire and life ins. agent, fruit grower, farmer 25,
FORWARD WALTER S., (N. Pembroke) r 27, breeder of horses, 10 head, 38 sheep, farmer 67.
Fosdick Miner, (E. Pembroke) r 47, farmer 50.
Foss Fred, r 33, farmer 85.
Foss John, r 33, farmer with his father, Fred.
Foster Daniel, (N. Pembroke) r 23, horse trainer and laborer.
Foster Myron, (N. Pembroke) r 23, prop. threshing machine, h and 4 acres.
Foster Vina, (N. Pembroke) conducts saw-mill on shares owned by William Gillins, of Batavia.
Fotel Charles, (Indian Falls) farmer with his father, Otto.
Fotel Otto, (Indian Falls) blacksmith and farmer 28.
Francis Albert, (Corfu) r 79, farmer 11.
Francis Henry W., (Corfu) prop. grist-mill, dealer in grain, flour, and feed, Church, h do.
Francis John, (N. Pembroke) farmer 25.
Frisbey Albert, r 52, farm laborer.
Fuhrmann John C., (Indian Falls) r 31, farmer 6.
Fuller John A., (Corfu) r 49, farmer 50.
Fuller Libbie Miss, (Corfu) r 48, teacher, daughter of John A.
Funkey C. W. & L. A., (Indian Falls) r 15, 90 sheep, farmers, lease on shares of the estate of Robert Brown 308.

Funkey Charles H., (Indian Falls) r 31, farmer 13.
Funkey Charles W., (Indian Falls) r 15, (C. W. & L. A. Funkey).
Funkey Christian, (Indian Falls) r 6, farmer 10.
Funkey George, (Indian Falls) r 6, farmer with his father, Christian.
Funkey Louis A., (Indian Falls) r 15, (C. W. & L. A. Funkey).
Furman Fred, (Indian Falls) farmer 4½.
Furman John, (Indian Falls) mason and farmer 6.
Gabbey James C., r 33, farmer, owns with his brother Robert 100, and a share in the
    estate of his father, James, 150.
Gabbey Jane, r 33, widow of James, 10 cows, 110 sheep, farm 150.
Gabbey John, r 33, student and farmer on the estate of James 150.
Gabbey Robert, r 33, breeder of thoroughbred Shorthorn Durham cattle, reg., 10 cows,
    farmer 110.
Gabbey Thomas, r 33, farmer.
Gardner Richard, (N. Pembroke) r 23, laborer, owns 2 acres.
Garrett Eugene, r 52, grower of raspberries, blackberries, strawberries, apples, and
    pears, farmer 30.
Garrett Frank, laborer.
Garrett George H., miller.
Garrett James, (Lee & Garrett).
Garrett James, r 52, 7 cows, farmer 82.
Garvin Jeremiah A., (Corfu) station and American Express agent, dealer in coal, h
    Railroad ave.
Gates Clark E., (Indian Falls) r 6, laborer.
Gates Judson, (Indian Falls) r —, farmer 12½.
Gates Moses F., (Indian Falls) r 6, farmer 6.
Gay Charles, r 52, laborer.
Gay Charles, Jr., stationary engineer, emp. Lee & Garrett.
Gay Walter, laborer, h and lot.
Gay William, r 52, carpenter, h and 1 acre.
Geiger John, (Corfu) r 60 cor. 63, farmer 33.
Gibson Cora A. Miss, (Corfu) r 48, teacher, daughter of William.
Gibson William, Jr., (Corfu) r 48, 60 sheep, farmer, leases of his father 160.
Giddings Edwin, retired lawyer, h Main cor. Allegany sts.
Giddings Edwin M., (Corfu) wholesale and retail florist, Allegany st, h do.
Gilmore Charles D., (Indian Falls) miller, emp. Gilmore & Co.
Gilmore Lyman E., (Indian Falls) miller, emp. Gilmore & Co.
Gilmore Miner A., (Indian Falls) miller, emp. Gilmore & Co.
Gilmore Samuel, (Indian Falls) (Gilmore & Co.) manager roller grist-mills, wholesale
    and retail dealer in flour, feed, and grain.
Gilmore & Co., (Indian Falls) (Samuel G. and William Carpenter, of Batavia) props.
    roller grist-mills.
Goodrich Joshua C., pastor Church of the Disciples.
Goodridge Emeline, (Indian Falls) r 8, widow of William, farm 35.
Gorham Mary E., (E. Pembroke) r 46, widow of Damon H., resident.
GORTON WARREN, (Corfu and E. Pembroke) prop. Corfu roller-mills, wholesale
    and retail dealer in flour and feed, breeder of Patchin trotting horses, farmer 47, h
    at E. Pembroke.
Gould Francis A., (Corfu) pilot on N. Y. C. steamboat line, h Main.
Gourdenier Mary, (E. Pembroke) r 41, widow of Henry, h and lot.
Gourdenier Thomas J., (E. Pembroke) r 41, mason.
Gowdy John, (Indian Falls) r 7, laborer.
Gowin Fred A., (Corfu) teacher, apiarist 22 colonies, farmer 40, h Main.
Granger John, (Corfu) retired farmer.
Gratinger Levi, (N. Pembroke) r 23, farmer.
Gratinger Matie Miss, (N. Pembroke) r 23, farm 15.
Graves Charles, (Indian Falls) carriagemaker.
Greenan Thomas, (E. Pembroke) r 70, 11 cows, 140 sheep, farmer 57, and leases of
    John Cleveland 165.

Griswold Cora E. Miss, (Indian Falls) (Mrs. W. H. & Miss Cora E. Griswold).
Griswold Samuel, (Corfu) breeder of pure blood Merino sheep, 100 head, fruit grower, and farmer on the "Griswold homestead," in Alexander, 150, h Main.
Griswold W. H. Mrs., (Indian Falls) (Mrs. W. H. & Miss Cora E. Griswold).
Griswold W. H. Mrs. & Cora E. Miss, (Indian Falls) dressmakers.
Griswold Willis H., (Indian Falls) mason, h and lot.
Grout Horace, r 67, breeder of grade Jersey cattle, 13 cows, farmer 80.
Hair Margery, (Corfu) r 67, widow of John, farmer, owns with her daughters the estate of her husband 91.
Hall Adelbert, (E. Pembroke) r 59, laborer.
Hall George W., (Corfu) r 77, section hand and farmer 15.
Hall Henry, (Corfu) farmer 40, h n railroad depot.
Hall Wilber, r 50, breeder of Jersey Red swine, farmer 62.
Hall William, (Corfu) farmer 10, h n railroad.
Hamilton Albert L., (E. Pembroke) r 47, farmer 80.
Hardwick Thomas K., widow, h and lot.
Harmon Henry P., (Corfu) r 55, farmer 60.
Harmon St. Clair, (Corfu) r 55, farmer 143.
Harrington Althea Mrs., r 52, h and 2 acres.
Harrington Eugene, (Indian Falls) r 11, hay presser and farmer 40.
Harrington Mary, r 49, widow of Peter Y., h and lot.
HARROWN G. K., (Corfu) farmer.
Hart Alciba, r 49, widow of William, h and lot.
Hart J. L. Mrs., r 67 cor. 65, h and 1¼ acres.
Hart John L., r 67 cor. 65, clerk.
Hascock Effie Mrs., (N. Pembroke) r 18, farm 30.
Hatch Joseph, (N. Pembroke) r 20, laborer.
Hatch Wallace, (N. Pembroke) r 25, laborer.
Hathaway Eleazer, (Corfu) pastor Universalist Church, bds. Main.
Hatling John, (Crittenden, Erie Co.) r 66, blacksmith, owns 10 acres.
Hendricks Louisa, (Akron, Erie Co.) r 10, widow of John, farm 40.
Hibbard Charles, r 35 cor. 36, farmer 50.
High George, r 52, dealer in butter, eggs, poultry, fruit, and potatoes.
Hill Hosea, (N. Pembroke) r 20, farmer, leases on shares of his father, Israel, 100.
Hill Israel, (N. Pembroke) r 20, grower of fruit and potatoes, farmer 100.
Hill Oliver, (N. Pembroke) r 20, teacher and farmer.
Hills James L., (Corfu) farmer 102, h and lot Main.
Hint Augustus, (N. Pembroke) r 16, farmer, leases of George White, of Alabama, 74.
Hint Frederick, r 67, member Genesee County, Horse Breeders' Association, farmer 122.
Holahan Martin, (Corfu) r 61, farmer 40.
Holdfeller Conrad, r 66, farmer 52.
Holt Walter W., (Indian Falls) r —, pastor Free Baptist Church.
Hopkins William B., (Indian Falls) r 5, farmer 65.
Houlehan Brothers, r 48, (Thomas & John) 8 cows, breeders of Durham cattle and Jersey Red swine, farmers 75.
Houlehan John, r 48, (Houlehan Brothers).
Houlehan Thomas, r 48, (Houlehan Brothers).
Houseknecht Hiram S., (Indian Falls) r 27, 60 sheep, farmer 74.
Houseknecht Philip, (Indian Falls) r 13, farmer 17.
Houseknecht Reuben, (Indian Falls) r 29, farmer 30.
Houseknecht Samuel L., (E. Pembroke) r 24, 99 sheep, farmer 75, and leases on shares of H. J. Forward 30.
Hoyt Betsey A., (E. Pembroke) r 41, widow of Daniel, h and lot.
Huff John C., r 48, farmer 76.
Hunn John E., (Corfu) r 54, 10 cows, farmer 111.
Hunt George W., (Corfu) retired farmer, h Main.
Hunt Orrin, (Corfu) laborer, h Main.
Hussy Michael, r 52, farmer 30.

Hutton William, (Corfu) r 48, laborer.
Indian Falls House, (Indian Falls) A. J. Layton, prop.
Ingraham Lucinda, (E. Pembroke) r 58, widow of Isaac, farmer 63.
Innes George W., (E. Pembroke) r 45, prop. threshing machine and manuf. of land-plaster.
Innes John H., (E. Pembroke) r 45, retired merchant, prop. land-plaster-mill, h and 10 acres.
Jaycott Alonzo, r 52, farmer, leases of George Bowen, of Batavia, 37.
Johncox Albert E., (Corfu) farm laborer.
Johns Newton, (Corfu) r 54, farmer on shares with Charles Jones.
Johnson William, (E. Pembroke) r 41, laborer.
Jones Antoinette, (Corfu) widow of Harley.
Jones Charles, (Corfu) r 54, 24 cows, breeder of horses and cattle, fruit grower, farmer 272.
Jones Elizabeth, (Corfu) widow of George, h Main.
Judge Thomas, (W. Batavia) railroad track hand, farmer 50.
Judge Mark, (W. Batavia) r 70, 7 cows, farmer 58.
Judge Michael, (W. Batavia) r 71, railroad track hand.
Kane Francis, (E. Pembroke) r 42, laborer.
Karchner John, (E. Pembroke) r 57, farmer, leases the estate of Bradley and Samuel Calkins.
Kellaher Hugh, r 49, resides with John.
Kellaher John, r 49, 7 cows, farmer 100.
Kellaher John, laborer.
Kelleher John, (W. Batavia) r 71, teacher and laborer.
Kelleher Patrick J., (Corfu) r 61, farmer 65.
Kennedy Dennis, (E. Pembroke) r 56, section boss, h and lot.
Kepner William, r 32, laborer.
Kern Burton, r 52, farmer with his father, Ezra.
Kern Ezra, r 52, farmer 20.
Kern Sadie Miss, r 52, teacher, daughter of Ezra.
King Albert, (E. Pembroke) r 22, 60 sheep, farmer, leases on shares of Sarah A. Amidon 115.
King George, r 52, laborer.
King Oscar, r 50, farmer, leases on shares.
Kinne Jonas W., r 50, breeder of Percheron horses, farmer 87.
Kinne Robert L., r 35, prop. Hambletonian stock horse " Garrison," farmer 50.
Kinne Royal W., (Corfu) 9 cows, farmer 70.
Kinsalow Michael, (Corfu) laborer, h Prospect.
Kinsella Luke, (Corfu) forman section 15 N. Y. C. & H. R. R. R.
Kinsella Terrey, (Corfu) r 77, laborer and farmer 8.
Kirtland Frank C., (Corfu) r 79, telegraph operator.
Kirtland Fred S., (Corfu) r 79, brakeman.
Kirtland Orlando N., (Corfu) r 79, farm laborer.
Kitchel Luther H., (Corfu) physician and surgeon, Main, h do.
Klotchbach Caspar, (Indian Falls) r 31, farmer 21.
Klower William, (Crittenden, Erie Co.) r 65, farmer 20.
Knapp Leonard, (Corfu) r 54, farmer 40.
Knapp Mason, (Corfu) r 54, farmer 66.
Knoop Catherine M., (N. Pembroke) widow of John, resident.
Kraatz Henry, (Akron, Erie Co.) r 2, laborer.
Kraatz Louis, (Akron, Erie Co.) r 36, farmer 121.
Krisher Philip, r 52, mason and farmer, leases on shares of Monroe Flint 150.
Ladd Frank, (N. Pembroke) prop. Excelsior flouring-mills, wholesale and retail dealer in flour, feed, and grain, farmer 6.
Ladd Frank H., (E. Pembroke) dealer in farm produce, bds. E. Pembroke Hotel.
Ladd Giles W., (N. Pembroke) miller, emp. Frank.
Lake Charles D., r 52, farmer 120.
Lake Ira, r 52 cor. 65, carpenter and farmer 34.

Langworthy Frank W., (N. Pembroke) r 25, farmer 24.
Langworthy Milo B., (E. Pembroke) r 47, farmer, leases of Cordelia Van Curen 90.
Lanning Helen, (E. Pembroke) r 46, widow of David B., house-keeper for her father, George Shaw.
Lawrence Anson, (Corfu) r 74, farmer 133.
Lawrence Charles, (Akron, Erie Co.) r 3, farmer 125.
LAWRENCE EDWIN L., (Corfu) r 73, 50 high blood Merino sheep, 6 cows, farmer 112.
Lawrence Fred, (Corfu) r 73, (Fred & Morris Lawrence) farmer, leases on shares with his father, Edwin L., 112.
Lawrence Fred & Morris, (Corfu) r 73, farmers 68½.
Lawrence Morris, (Corfu) r 73, (Fred & Morris Lawrence) prop. steam. threshing machine.
Lawrence William, (Corfu) off r 60, farmer 59.
Layton Andrew J., (Indian Falls) prop. Indian Falls House and cider-mill, dealer in cider and cider vinegar.
Lear William S., (Corfu) teacher intermediate department graded school, bds. Main.
LEE GEORGE H., (Lee & Garrett).
LEE & GARRETT, (George H. L. and James G.) props. Genesee roller-mills, dealers in flour, feed, buckwheat flour, and grain.
Leiter Eck, (N. Pembroke) prop. steam threshing and wood sawing machines.
Lemley Leonard W., (Corfu) carriagemaker and general jobber, Main.
Lerch Andrew, (Corfu) r 76, laborer.
Lester James, carpenter.
Lester Warren, (Indian Falls) r 4, farmer 30.
Leveque Theodore, (E. Pembroke) shoemaker, Railroad, h do.
Lincoln John, (Corfu) dealer in agricultural implements, h Main.
Long Charles W., r 38, farmer, leases on shares 132.
Long Edward, r 38, farmer 132.
LONG ELIZA M., (Corfu) r 48, widow of William B.
Long John, farmer 145.
Long Romeyn S., (Corfu) r 79, 18 cows, farmer 85.
Long Sterling, farmer 47.
Loomis Charles R., (E. Pembroke) r 46, teacher.
Loomis Clara V. Miss, (E. Pembroke) r 46, dressmaker.
Loomis Samuel, (E. Pembroke) r 46, cooper and farmer 25.
Louttit Joseph, (Indian Falls) r 29, farmer 29.
Lovell William H., r 50, farmer 86.
Lovell William H., Jr., r 50, farmer with his father.
Loveridge Joel A., (Corfu) r 49, teacher and farmer 67.
Lowrence Anson, (Corfu) r 74, 12 cows, farmer 138.
Lowrence Fred, (Corfu) r 73, laborer and prop. threshing machine.
Lowrence Henry, (Dick) (Corfu) r 73, farmer 50.
Lowrence William, (Corfu) r 60, prop. steam threshing machine and steam bean thresher, dealer in fertilizers, farmer 59.
Lyman Leonard F., (E. Pembroke) teacher, grower of small fruits, farmer 7.
Lyons Robert, (E. Pembroke) laborer.
Mahoney James, (Akron, Erie Co.) r 2, prop. Akron Falls Hotel, breeder of horses, farmer 92.
Mahoney John, (Akron, Erie Co.) r 2, farmer with his father, James.
Mallison Jefferson H., (Corfu) farmer 50.
Mann Hattie L. Miss., (Corfu) teacher primary department graded school, bds. Main.
Mann Ira S., (Corfu) farmer 35, h Main.
Mann Ira S. Mrs., (Corfu) prop. boarding-house, Main.
Marble Almenzo, (Indian Falls) r 13, farmer 6.
Marsh Jennette, (E. Pembroke) r 57, widow of Amos N., farm 30.
Marston Clarence U., (Corfu) r 68, farmer with his father, John W.
Marston John N., (Corfu) carpenter and builder, dealer in lumber, Main, h do.
MARSTON JOHN W., (Corfu) r 68, 18 cows, fruit grower. farmer 126.

Martin John S., (Indian Falls) r 29, 100 sheep, farmer 142.
Mayne John, (Corfu) section foreman N. Y. C. & H. R. R. R., h Allegany st.
Mayne Richard, (Corfu) farm manager for Mrs. Read.
McDermot Duncan, r 5, farmer 25.
McDonald Charles A., (Corfu) r 76, fruit grower, farmer 89.
McDonald James M., (Corfu) r 69, fruit grower, farmer 52.
McDonald Melvin, (Corfu) r 76, fruit grower, farmer 74.
McDonald Nellie L. Mrs., (Corfu) h Main.
McGee S. Mrs., h and lot.
McGee Orange S., painter.
McGee William, house painter and paper hanger.
McGregor William W., (Corfu) notary public, fire ins. agent, dealer in and repairer of
    harnesses, Main, h do.
McJury James, carpenter, millwright, and farmer 25.
McKenzie William J., (Corfu) r 49, (McKenzie & Peck) manuf. of fine butter, 6 cows.
McKenzie & Peck, (Corfu) r 49, (William J. McK. and J. Fremont P.) breeders of
    Hereford cattle, dealers in beef cattle, farmers 106.
McManis James J., (Indian Falls) r 27, farmer, leases on shares of the Dr. Norton
    estate 170.
McMurphy Ruth, (N. Pembroke) widow of Webster, h and lot.
McNally Ann, (E. Pembroke) widow of Peter, farm 12.
McNelley Patrick, (E. Pembroke) farmer 50, h and 2 acres in village.
McNulty Patrick, (E. Pembroke) r 56, farmer 82.
McSimons Sarah Miss, r 34, h and 5 acres.
Meiser Andrew, (Indian Falls) r 29, farmer 17.
Meiser August, (Indian Falls) r 29, laborer.
Meiser George, (Indian Falls) r 29, laborer and farmer.
Merkt Lawrence, (N. Pembroke) wagonmaker.
Miller Lines B., (Indian Falls) retired blacksmith; aged 82.
Miller Mary, r 52, widow of Chris John, farm 10.
Mills Alva, r 50, sawyer.
Mook Abram, (E. Pembroke) r 24, 8 cows, fruit grower, farmer 112.
Mook Seba, (E. Pembroke) r 46, 11 cows, farmer 100.
Moon Frank E., (Indian Falls) r 31, farmer 11.
Moore Charles E., (Indian Falls) r 27, farmer with B. Carrigan 53.
Moore Cyren, (Indian Falls) farmer 4.
Moore George R., (Indian Falls) r 27, farm laborer.
Moore Herbert B., (E. Pembroke) (Dennison & Moore).
Moore Isaac, (Indian Falls) r 27, carpenter and farmer 70.
Morse David, (Indian Falls) laborer.
Morse William, (N. Pembroke) laborer.
Moynahan Ambrose, (E. Pembroke) r 56, section hand.
Moynahan Julia, (E. Pembroke) r 56, teacher, daughter of Thomas.
Moynahan Thomas, (E. Pembroke) r 56, farmer 6.
Mullaney Bernard, (E. Pembroke) r 56, laborer.
Mullaney John, (E. Pembroke) r 56, baggagemaster, farmer 6.
Mullaney Michael, (E. Pembroke) r 56, section hand.
Muller Mary, r 52, widow of John Christian, owns 10 acres.
Munsie James, r 49, farmer 50.
Myres Joseph, (Crittenden, Erie Co.) r 66, farmer, leases on shares of Daniel Bates, of
    Akron, Erie Co., 78.
Newell Alvin D., (Corfu) r 79, farmer 9, aged 83.
Newell George W., (Corfu and Buffalo) r 55, cashier L. S. & M. S. R. R., farmer 78.
Newell Seymour, (Corfu and Buffalo) r 55, collector L. S. & M. S. R. R.
Newland William, r 36, farmer 71.
Newton Nelson, (Akron, Erie Co.) r 3, farmer 26.
Newton George, r 38, laborer.
Nighthart Anson, (Indian Falls) r 22, farmer 65.
Nighthart Enos, (Indian Falls) r 32, farmer with his father, Anson.

Nobes Samuel, (Corfu) section hand N. Y. C. & H. R. R. R., h Railroad ave.
Norton Julius, (Corfu) r 61, retired farmer.
Norton William H., (Corfu) r 39, farmer, leases on shares of Julia T. Reid 39.
Ogden Alfred E., (Corfu) dealer in groceries, dry goods, boots, and shoes, Main, h do.
O'Reilly Ann, (E. Pembroke) r 24 cor. 25, widow of Isaac.
Ostheimer Josephine L. Mrs., (Corfu) dressmaker.
Ott Fred, (Indian Falls) r 15, laborer.
Ott George, (Indian Falls) r 15, butcher and laborer.
Ott George, Jr., (Indian Falls) laborer.
Ovenden Road, (Corfu) railroad track hand.
Owen John D., station agent, h and 10 acres.
Palmer Cyrus O., (Corfu) tinsmith, emp. C. E. Whittlesey, h Prospect.
Palmer David, (Crittenden, Erie Co.) r 66, farm laborer.
Palmer Hiram, (Crittenden, Erie Co.) r 66, farmer, leases on shares of his father, **Levi,** 124.
Palmer Levi, (Crittenden, Erie Co.) r 66, farmer 124¾.
Pardee Isaac D., r 50, farm manager for Mary J. Griswold, of Michigan, 64.
Pargel Charles, r 34, farmer 61.
Parker Adelbert D., (E. Pembroke) r 46, cheesemaker in factory No. 8.
Parker G. G. Mrs., (E. Pembroke) r 46, dressmaker.
Parker George G., (E. Pembroke) r 46, blacksmith, horseshoer, and repairer.
Parker John W., (Corfu) r 49, farmer 43.
Parker Merton, (E. Pembroke) r 22, farmer, leases on shares of A. Whitney 41.
Passago John, (E. Pembroke) r 56, laborer.
Peachry Sarah, (Corfu) widow of James, farm 38, h Main.
Pearce Frank N., (E. Pembroke) r 59, farmer 71.
Pearce Richard, (E. Pembroke) r 59, 6 cows, farmer 105.
Peard Robert, (E. Pembroke) r 56, dealer in farm produce, farmer 7.
PECK CELINDA, (E. Pembroke) r 48, widow of William, farm 50.
Peck J. Fremont, (Corfu) r 49, (McKenzie & Peck).
PECK JOEL, (E. Pembroke) r 48, farmer 138.
Peck Nathan, (E. Pembroke) farmer 70.
Peckham Gurdon, r 49, farmer, leases of the estate of his father, Elisha, 1.
Pembroke Hotel, Ira B. Fishell, prop.
Phelps Elijah, (Indian Falls) r 15, farmer 62.
Phelps Enoch, (Indian Falls) r 6, farmer 80.
Phelps Harvey B., (Corfu) street commissioner, h off Main.
Phelps Robert, (Corfu) r 64, laborer.
Phillips Charles, (Indian Falls) r 15, farmer 11.
Phillips Elihu, (E. Pembroke) r 47, 6 cows, farmer 120.
Porter George A., (Corfu) (George A. Porter & Co.) notary public, h Main.
Porter George A. & Co., (Corfu) (William H. Taylor) general merchants, Main.
Porter George W., (Corfu) r 54, retired farmer 50.
Porter Henry P., (Corfu) retired merchant, farmer 6, h Main.
Porter Nathan, (Corfu) r —, farmer 31, and leases of George W. 50.
Porter Nathan C., (Corfu) r 69, farmer 48.
Porter William H., (Indian Falls) r 7, farmer 17.
Post Elias G., (Corfu) carpenter, contractor, and builder, dealer in lumber.
Post Naomi, (E. Pembroke) r 45, widow of Cornelius, farm 28.
Pratt C. T. & W. F., (Indian Falls) 13 cows, breeders of Holstein cattle, farmers, lease of their father, Charles P., 102, and own in Batavia 106.
PRATT CHARLES P., (Indian Falls) general merchant and farmer 102.
Pratt Charles T., (Indian Falls) (C. T. & W. F. Pratt) farmer.
Pratt Luther, r 49, overseer of the poor, farmer.
Prevorce Alice, widow of Henry P., h and lot.
Price John M., (Corfu) mason and bricklayer, h Main.
Puls Charles, (Akron, Erie Co.) r 3, farmer 25.
Puls Charles, Jr., (Akron, Erie Co.) r 3, farm laborer.
Putnam James E., r 49, carpenter and farmer 21.

Putnam Lewis, r 49, farmer 31.
Quackenbush Alonzo, r 51, farmer, leases of M. Long 52.
Quackenbush Nelson, (Indian Falls) r 29, breeder of horses, farmer 74.
Read Amanda, (Corfu) widow of Nathaniel, farmer 100.
READ LEWIS C., (E. Pembroke) r 57, dealer in agricultural implements, phos_
    phate, horses, cattle, and sheep, breeder of high grade Jersey cattle, fruit grower,
    farmer 80.
READ NATHANIEL M., (E. Pembroke) r 57, farmer with his father, Lewis C.
Redman Abram, r 50. farmer 53.
Redman Frank A., r 50, carpenter.
Redman Lafayette, r 65, farmer 35.
Redman Ossian, r 65, laborer.
Redmond James E., r 52, farmer 22.
Reed George, laborer.
Reid Julia T., (Corfu) r 61, widow of Andrew M., farm 39.
Reid Orlando W., (Corfu) r 54, farmer on shares with Charles Jones.
Reily John, r 48, 7 cows, farmer, leases of Alexander Brown 160.
Remsen William, r 38, farmer 96.
Reynolds Austin, (Indian Falls) dentist and jeweler.
Ribby Lovinia, (N. Pembroke) r 17, widow of John, farm 30.
Rich Calvin, (E. Pembroke) laborer and prop. threshing machine.
Richards John W., (Indian Falls) r 9, miller.
RICHARDSON E. CHAPIN, (E. Pembroke) physician and surgeon, Main, h do.
Roberts Charles D., r 67, farmer 15.
Robinson Charles, (Indian Falls) r 6, laborer.
Robinson Harriet, (Indian Falls) r 6, widow of J. R., farm 20.
Rockwell Ann L., widow of Alexander, h and lot.
Rogers Sarah A., (W. Batavia) r 71, widow of Aaron farm 95.
Rohr Fred, (Indian Falls) laborer.
Rohr John, (Indian Falls) r 7, mail carrier, h and 4 acres.
Ross Frederick D., (Corfu) r 69, breeder of Percheron horses, 15 cows, farmer 152.
Ross Stephen, (Corfu) r —, resident.
Russell George, (E. Pembroke) r 45 cor. 42, prop. saw and feed-mills.
Russell James S., r 49, farmer 76.
Russell William, r 35, farmer on the estate of his father, John, 75.
Rutter Margaret Mrs., (E. Pembroke) r 41, laundress.
Safford Abigail R., (E. Pembroke) r 59, widow of John D.. farm 72.
Safford Fred M.. (E. Pembroke) r 59, farmer on the estate of his father, John D., 72.
Safford Joseph W., (Corfu) justice of the peace, h Main cor. Railroad ave
Sager John, (Corfu) laborer, h Main.
Sawens Fred L., (W. Batavia) r 72, farmer with Hon. John W. Brown.
Sawyer Elmer, r 33, farmer 48.
Sawyer Henry, r 33, dealer in live stock and farm produce, farmer 96.
Schieb Louis, r 52, farmer.
Scheip Edward, r 52, laborer.
Scheip Louis, r 52, laborer.
Schelt Daniel, (Corfu) shoemaker, Niagara st., h Allegany st.
Schlageinhan Gottleib, (Indian Falls) r 30, farmer 110.
Schumlein Andrew, (Corfu) r 64, farmer 64.
Schuyler Henry, (Indian Falls) r 31, laborer.
Seamans Asa, (E. Pembroke) r 46, farmer 20.
SEAMANS EZRA A., (E. Pembroke) postmaster and manager Union Hardware Co.
Seamans George B., (E. Pembroke) r 46, 6 cows, farmer 117.
Searls Clayton, (E. Pembroke) r 40, farmer with his father, John.
Searls John, (E. Pembroke) r 40, 6 Durham cows, fruit grower, farmer 110.
Seits John E., (Corfu) r 69, confectioner and laborer.
Shaw Belle, (Corfu) r 48, teacher.
Shaw George, (E. Pembroke) r 46, carpenter and farmer, leases of H. Gillette 20.

12*

Shaw John A., (E. Pembroke) r 59, 190 sheep, farmer, leases on shares of George P. Packer 100.
Shaw Walter, (E. Pembroke) r 42, farmer, leases on shares of George Cook 12.
Shaw Warren, (Corfu) r 48, carpenter and farmer 50.
Sheets Merritt N., (Corfu) prop. Union Hotel and livery stable.
Shelt William H., (E. Pembroke) farmer with his mother, Ann Ford.
Shultz Albert, (Indian Falls) r 31, laborer.
Shultz John, (Indian Falls) r 31, laborer and farmer 4.
Shumway De Bonville, (E. Pembroke) r 41, (William Shumway & Son).
Shumway William, (E. Pembroke) r 41, (William Shumway & Son) farmer 4.
Shumway William & Son, (E. Pembroke) r 41, (De Bonville) coopers.
Simington William, (Corfu) jeweler, telegraph operator N. Y. C. & H. R. R. R., h Allegany st.
Singleton Daniel, off r 38, laborer.
Sisson Alonzo, (Corfu) r 69, farmer 53.
Sisson Frank W., (Corfu) farm manager for G. K. Harroun, h Main.
Sisson H. Nelson, (Corfu) r 55, farmer 24.
Sisson Louisa A. Mrs., (Corfu) r 69, farm 73.
Sliker John, (Indian Falls) r 29, laborer.
Sliker Peter, (Indian Falls) r 29, farmer 12.
Sliker Peter, Jr., (Indian Falls) r 29, carpenter.
Slusser Alonzo, (N. Pembroke) r 19 cor. 20, (Alonzo & Frank E. Slusser).
Slusser Alonzo & Frank E., (N. Pembroke) r 19 cor. 20, farmers, lease on shares of their father, Henry, 150.
Slusser Edward, (N. Pembroke) laborer.
Slusser Frank E., (E. Pembroke) r 19 cor. 20, (Alonzo & Frank E. Slusser).
Slusser Henry, (N. Pembroke) r 19 cor. 20, farmer 150.
Slusser John, (N. Pembroke) laborer, h and 2 acres.
SMITH A., (Corfu) (A. Smith & Son).
SMITH A. & SON, (Corfu) (Herbert M.) dealers in watches, clocks, jewelry, and stationery, Main, h do.
Smith Andrew J., (Corfu) general merchant, Main, h do.
Smith Austin D., (E. Pembroke) physician and surgeon, Railroad, h do.
Smith Daniel, (Indian Falls) justice of the peace and carpenter.
Smith Edward, (E. Pembroke) r 39, breeder of high grade Jersey cattle, farmer 63.
Smith Elliott C., (Corfu) physician and surgeon, Main, h do.
Smith George, (Corfu) blacksmith, Main, bds. do.
Smith George U., (Corfu) 60 sheep, farmer, leases on shares of Jennette Main, of Michigan, 132.
SMITH HERBERT M., (Corfu) (A. Smith & Son) bds. Main.
Smith Lorenzo, (Corfu) breeder of grade Durham cattle, 20 cows, fruit grower, farmer 153.
Smith Reid, (E. Pembroke) r 40, farmer, leases of Nathan Peck, 50.
Smith Sarah, (Indian Falls) r 8, widow of Eli, h and lot.
Smock Nelson, (Indian Falls) r 7, laborer, h and 1 acre.
Sneider Elizabeth, (Indian Falls) r 8, widow of George, farm 4.
Snell Charles I., (Indian Falls) r 8 cor. 30, teacher.
Snider George, (Indian Falls) r —, farmer, leases on shares of Mary Marble 18.
Soper John, (Corfu) r 69, retired farmer, owns in Alexander 52½.
Sparling Anson, (Akron, Erie Co.) r 3, farmer 140.
Sparling Fred, (Akron, Erie Co.) r 3, farmer 100.
Spencer Charles E., (E. Pembroke) wagonmaker, h and lot.
Stafford Gardner, r 52, farmer 60.
Stage Hiram, (Corfu) retired farmer, h Main.
Stage Jerry, farmer, h and lot.
Stang Charles, (N. Pembroke) r 16, farmer on the estate of his father, George.
Stang Elizabeth, (N. Pembroke) r 16, widow of George, wool grower, farmer 121.
Stang Frank, (N. Pembroke) r 16, farmer on the estate of his father, George.
Stanley Paulina, (Corfu) r 49, widow of Adna, farm 85.

Starks Abram, r 36, laborer.
Starks George, (Corfu) r 53, farmer 1¼.
Starks William, (Corfu) r 53, farmer 18.
Stevens Charles, (Corfu) prin. Corfu graded school, bds. Main.
Stickney Jonas, (Corfu) capitalist, bds. Railroad ave.
Stimer William, r 67, farmer 40.
Stoddard Abijah W., (Corfu) r 68, farmer 33.
Stone Eltham, (N. Pembroke) dealer in dry goods and groceries, farmer 11.
Stone Guernsey E., (N. Pembroke) clerk.
Stone Harry, (N. Pembroke) retired merchant, h and 9 acres.
Sturdevant Hannah, widow of Alfred, h and lot.
SUMNER CLARISSA, (Corfu) widow of Jerome, h and 8 acres, tenement to rent.
Sumner Emmett E., (Corfu) (Bennett & Sumner) farm in Darien 100, h Main.
Sumner Wilder E., (Corfu) town clerk, member Genesee County Horse Breeders' Association, dealer in farm produce and agricultural implements, owns farm in Darien.
Sumeriski Healy, r 51, farmer 37.
Sumeriski Isaac, r 67, mason and farmer 30.
SUTHERLAND JOEL, (E. Pembroke) farm 2¼.
Sutter Matilda, (N. Pembroke) r 24, widow of John, farm 16.
Swan Amelia Mrs., (N. Pembroke) seamstress, h and ⅓ acre.
Swan Henry F., (N. Pembroke) constable and laborer.
Swartz Charles, (Corfu) r 64 cor. 53, 6 cows, farmer 67.
Taggart Adaline, r 48, widow of George O., resides on the estate of her husband 76.
Taggart Ella, r 48, dressmaker, daughter of the late George O.
TAYLOR CHARLES, (E. Pembroke) r 48, 4 cows, 2 horses, farmer 55.
Taylor William H., (Corfu) (George A. Porter & Co.) bds. Main.
Taylor William J., (Corfu) r 80, farmer, leases of Mrs. Sarah 38.
Tenner Roselle, (Indian Falls) laborer, h and lot.
THAYER GEORGE W., (Indian Falls) fire ins. agent, auctioneer, and dealer in agricultural implements, enlisted as private May 2, 1861, discharged August 10, 1865, as 1st lieut. of Cav.
Tice Frank, (Indian Falls) r 6, laborer.
Tice George, (Indian Falls) r 6, farmer 14.
Tiffany Frances, (Indian Falls) r 15, widow of Edward, h and 3 acres.
Toon Fred, r 34, farmer 50.
Toon John, r 34, laborer.
Travers Thomas, (E. Pembroke) r 27, farmer 11.
Tubbs Frank, (Corfu) musician, h Main.
Tubbs Ira, (Corfu) laborer, h Allegany st.
Tupper Charles, (Indian Falls) r 15, farmer, leases on shares of his father, Sheldon C., 74.
Tupper Sheldon C., (Indian Falls) r 15, farmer 74.
Turner Edgar E., stationary engineer.
Turner Edward, laborer.
Tuttle Nathan J., (N. Pembroke) laborer.
Underhill Arza, r 50, retired farmer.
Underhill Mary Miss, teacher, daughter of Arza.
UNION HARDWARE CO., (E. Pembroke) Ezra A. Seamans, manager, dealers in general hardware, flour, and feed.
Union Hotel, (Corfu) M. N. Sheets, prop., livery stable connected.
Van Alstine Peter, (E. Pembroke) r 41, laborer and farmer 3.
VAN ALSTINE SAMUEL, (N. Pembroke) postmaster, general merchant, and farmer 4, served in Co. H, N. Y. H. A.
Van Buren Edwin, (N. Pembroke) r 15, farmer, leases on shares of E. Diver 95¼.
Van Buren Hiram, (N. Pembroke) r 17, farmer 15.
Van Buren Horace, (Corfu) r 67 cor. 80, farmer 52½.
Van Curen Cordelia Mrs., (E. Pembroke) r 47, farm 90.
Van Curen Thompson, (E. Pembroke) r 47, farmer.

Van De Bogart Henry D., (Corfu) tobacconist, confectioner, and barber, Main, h do_
Van Norman John, r 52, farmer 30.
Vile John, (Indian Falls) r 31, farmer 16.
Wade Amos, (E. Pembroke) r 41, carpenter, contractor, and builder.
Wade W. Wallace, (E. Pembroke) r 41, carpenter.
Wagener Philip, (Corfu) r 48, farmer 30.
WAIT CYRUS, (Corfu) wool dealer and farmer, owns the Wait homestead in Dariem 141, h E. Main.
Waite Erwin J., (E. Pembroke) r 47, painter and farmer with his father, Jerome B.
Waite Jerome B., (E. Pembroke) r 47, painter and farmer 62.
Wakeman Henry T., (Indian Falls) r 4 n cor. 34, 8 cows, 65 sheep, farmer 191.
WAKEMAN ORSEMUS, (E. Pembroke) r 57, painter and farmer 9¼.
Waldo Theron L., (E. Pembroke) pastor Presbyterian Church of Pembroke and Batavia, h Main.
Waldron Adelia S., (Indian Falls) widow of John W., h and lot.
Waldron Herman, (N. Pembroke) r 20, laborer.
Waldron Willett, (N. Pembroke) r 20 cor. 21, painter.
Wallis Amelia Miss, (Corfu) r 79, daughter of Hugh, farm, estate of her father, 87.
Wallis Mary, (Corfu) r 79, widow of Hugh, 6 cows, resides on the estate of her husband 87.
Waltz ———, (Corfu) r 48, widow of Michael, farm 14.
Waltz Jacob, (Corfu) r 48, laborer.
Walworth Samuel, (Indian Falls) r 31, 11 horses, farmer 188.
Ward Addison, (Indian Falls) r 6, farmer 30.
Ward Albert, (Indian Falls) r 27, breeder of grade Shropshire sheep, 32 head, farmer 70_
WARD DANIEL, (Indian Falls) r 9, retired farmer 14.
Ward Emory, (Indian Falls) r 9 cor. 13, farmer 3.
Ward Merton R., (Indian Falls) r 27, teacher, son of Albert.
Ward Warren, r 49, farmer 144.
Ward Washington, (Corfu) r 55, farmer, leases on shares of Alvah Barden 165.
Warren George D., (N. Pembroke) r 23, merchant and farmer 12.
Warren Reuben, stationary engineer,
Waterman Clifford H., (Corfu) r 61, farmer on the estate of Solomon Hastings 100_
Waterman Loren T., (E. Pembroke) r 71, farmer 60.
Waterman Truman C., (Corfu) r 61, farmer 57, h and lot in Corfu.
Waterstraw Fred, r 3, farmer 18.
Webb Alexander, (Corfu) r —, farmer 100.
Webb Jerome B., (Corfu) r —, farmer with his father, Alexander.
Webb Lester, (Corfu), (T. A. & L. Webb) h Main.
Webb T. A. Mrs., W. U. telegraph operator.
Webb T. A. & L., (Corfu) wholesale and retail florists, Main.
Webb Thomas A., (Corfu), (T. A. & L. Webb) h Main.
Weiser John, (E. Pembroke) r 12. laborer.
Wells Charles H., (W. Batavia) r 73, 100 sheep, farmer 120.
Wells George R., (W. Batavia) r 73, 100 sheep, farmer, leases on shares of his father, Charles H., 120.
Werron William, (Crittenden, Erie Co.) r 80 cor. 66, laborer and farmer 8.
Whimple John, (E. Pembroke) r 45, blacksmith.
White Zadoc, r 48, laborer.
Whittlesey Curtis E., (Corfu) dealer in hardware, tinware, paints, and oils, Main. h do
Wiedrich Henry, (Indian Falls) r 29, breeder of horses, farmer 75.
Wiedrich John, (Indian Falls) r 29, farmer with his father, Henry.
Wight Fred, (Indian Falls) r 6, laborer.
Wight Guy, (W. Batavia) r 71 cor. 57, farmer with his father, Levi.
Wight Levi, (W. Batavia) r 71 cor. 57, farmer 48.
Wight Samuel, r 49, farmer 6.
Wiley James W , (N. Pembroke) r 17, farmer, leases on shares of E. Diver 111.
Willett Edward R., (E. Pembroke) station agent N. Y. C. & H. R. R. R., h Railroad_ ave.

Wilson Theodore F., r 50, farmer 25.
Winchell Fred, (E. Pembroke) r 24, farmer, leases of Abram Mook 55.
Wolf Herman, r 50, shoemaker.
Wood Albert W., (Corfu) r 54, farmer, leases on shares of Caroline Dodge 107.
Wood Ransom, r 51, farmer 20.
Wooley Frank E., (Indian Falls) (E. E. Hescock & Co.).
Wyman Albert, (Indian Falls) r 4, farmer 18.
Wyman John, (Indian Falls) r 15, farmer, leases on shares of Samuel Walworth 38.
Wyman Levi, carpenter, contractor, and builder, h and 2 acres.

STAFFORD.

(For explanations, etc., see page 3, part second.)

(Postoffice address is Stafford, unless otherwise designated in parenthesis.)

Adams Charles W., (Batavia) r 3, dealer in live stock and produce, farmer 180
Adams John, retired farmer.
Adams John, Jr., r 50, farmer 3.
Alford Fred, laborer, h Main.
Alford Irwin, laborer, h Main.
Alford John, laborer, h Main.
Alford Will.am, laborer, h Main.
Alice Arnold Z., (Bativia) r 19. farmer 65.
Alworth Henry, (S. Byron) r 9, farmer, leases of H. U. Howard 111.
Armstrong J. W., rector Episcopal Church.
Atchinson Joseph, (Morganville) farmer 2.
Avery Mary, (Morganville) resident.
Bage George, r 39, farmer 75.
BAGOT MARY E., (Mrs. R. W.) farmer 170.
BAGOT RICHARD W., retired.
Baker Willis, (E. Bethany) r 43, laborer.
Barneck Frank, (Batavia) r 28, laborer.
Barnes Samuel, (Morganville) laborer.
Bartholf Lewis, r 35, farmer, leases of Sophia Hunt 44.
Batar James, (Morganville) r 10, farmer, leases of John 35.
Batar John, (Morganville) r 10, farmer 35.
Batchelder E. J., pastor M. E. Church, h Main.
Bateman John, (Morganville) r 27, farmer 4.
Bauer Charles, (Batavia) r 10, farmer, leases of Jacob 125.
Bauer Jacob, (Batavia) off r 10, farmer 125.
BAUER LOUIS, (Batavia) r 43, farmer 100.
Bean Jay J., (S. Byron) r 9, farmer, leases of Michael D. 150.
BELL CYRUS P., r 47, farmer 100.
Bennet William N., farmer 100.
Beswick Frank, (Morganville) r 19, farmer 55.
Bissell Russell, r 39, farmer 190.
Blumerleck William, r 38, laborer.
Boatfield James, r 38, laborer.
Bold Richard, laborer.
Bolt Christ, (Morganville) r 24, farmer 75.
Bolt Fred, blacksmith.

Bolt George, r 39, laborer.
Bolt John, (Morganville) laborer.
Bolt Keziah, (Morganville) r 19, widow of John.
Bolt Richard, (Morganville) r 14, farmer for Helen 23.
Bolt Samuel, r 26, farmer, leases of Stephen Crocker 40.
Bolt Thomas, (Morganville) r 19, laborer.
Booth Everett T., (S. Byron) r 4, farmer for Hezekiah B. 178.
Booth Hezekiah B., r 41, farmer 178.
Bowen George, (S. Byron) r 2, farmer, leases of Caroline Blair, of Byron, 96.
Bradley Minor N., (S. Byron) r 9, farmer 74.
Bridges Samuel, r 50, farmer, leases of Robert Call 120.
Bridges Samuel, Jr., r 50, farmer 83.
Bridges Thomas, r 50, farmer, son of Samuel.
Brierly Jennie, widow of James, dressmaker.
Broe Thomas, (Batavia) r 31, farmer 120.
BROWN JAMES E., (Le Roy) r 57, highway commissioner, carpenter, and farmer 22.
Buckingham George C., (Le Roy) r 58, farmer 135.
Buckland Charles, (S. Byron) r 6, farmer, leases of the M. M. Bradley estate 80.
Buckland Henry S., (S. Byron) r 7, farmer for Smith 65.
Buckland Smith, (S. Byron) r 7, farmer 65.
Buckley Michael, (Le Roy) r 38, farmer 100.
Burling James, (S. Byron) r 5, farmer, leases of G. Prentice, of Byron, 175.
Burns Albert J., clerk Heal's Hotel.
Call Albert H., (Morganville) r 34, farmer 108.
Call Elbert, r 34, farmer 107.
Call Robert, r 40, farmer 320.
Campbell Lucien, (S. Byron) r 4, farmer 76.
Cash Andrew, (Morganville) r 26, retired.
Cehler John, (S. Byron) r 37, laborer.
Chandler Henry, (Morganville) r 25 laborer.
Chandler Horace, (Morganville) r 37, laborer.
Christman Silas, (Le Roy) r 58, farmer 85.
Clace Peter, r 39, laborer.
Clancy Milton M., (Batavia) r 17, farmer 148.
Clancy Pierre R.. (Batavia) r 17, farmer.
Clancy William B., (Batavia) r 7, farmer, leases 116.
Clark John, (Batavia) r 31, farmer 98¼.
Clark John B., (Morganville) pastor Christian Church.
Colson William, (Batavia) r 14, farmer, leases of Sarah Vallet 125.
Combs Henry M., r 26, farmer with John S.
Combs John S., r 26, farmer 128.
CONSTABLE GEORGE A., (Batavia) r 13, dealer in sheep, farmer, leases of S. J. Merriman, of Elba, 150.
Corry Emerson, (Batavia) r 11, carpenter and joiner.
Courtney James, farmer 10, h Main.
Covell Darius, (Le Roy) r 59, farmer 100.
Coyne Peter, (Batavia) r 13, laborer.
Coyne Peter, (Batavia) r 11, farmer, leases of J. Purcell, of Buffalo, 50.
Crocker Stephen, retired farmer.
Danapier Eli, laborer.
DANIELS CLARK, (Morganville) r 26, farmer 119.
Daniels Eben L., (S. Byron) r 3, farmer 5.
Daniels Walter, (Morganville) r 26, farmer, leases of Clark 119.
DARBEE FRANCIS M., (Batavia) r 32, stock grower and grower of choice varieties of potatoes, wheat, and barley, farmer 280.
Darch John, cooper.
Darch Philip, r 52, farmer 70.
Davis Burt, r 50, farmer.
Davis Frank, r 50, farmer, leases of C. D. Sweetland 130.

Delaney Edward, (Batavia) r 12, farmer.
Demar William, (Le Roy) r 55, laborer.
Demarfe William, (Le Roy) r 55, laborer.
Dennis Eli, r 49, farmer for Thomas 57.
Dennis John, (Le Loy) r 39, farmer 50.
Dennis Thomas, r 49, farmer 57.
De Wolf Fred, clerk.
De Wolf John, (Batavia) r 29, farmer 27.
De Wolf Oren J., blacksmith, Main.
DE WOLF ORIN, (Batavia) r 17, justice of the peace, blacksmith, farmer 3.
De Wolf Sandford, (Batavia) r 12, farmer 25.
Diefendorf Alonzo, well driller.
Diefendorf Charles, farmer 15.
Donahue John, (Morganville) r 21, farmer, leases of Mrs. E. W. Wood 227.
DOUGLASS CARRIE, r 33, farmer 100.
Douglass Hart, r 33, farmer 40, and leases of A. Hart Norris 85.
Doyle John, (S. Byron) r 4, farmer with Owen.
Doyle Owen, (S. Byron) r 4, farmer 93.
Drury Frank C., r 40, farmer with John H.
Drury John H., r 40, farmer 142.
Duguid Charles H., (Le Roy) r 57, miller.
Duguid Henry C., (Le Roy) r 57, prop. Roanoke mills
Duguid Melvin D., (Le Roy) r 57, painter.
Durfee George, (Le Roy) r 5, laborer.
Elderkin Royal A., (Le Roy) r 54, farmer 103.
Empie Eli, (Le Roy) r 58, farmer for S. Christman 85.
Empie Jacob, (Le Roy) r 56, farmer 120.
Ernest Fred, (S. Byron) r 5, laborer.
Evans Angeline, (Batavia) r 12, widow of John, farmer 21.
Evans Fred, emp. on railroad, h Main.
Evans James, r 41, farmer 10.
Ewell Foster C., (Le Roy) r 52, farmer 148.
Fargo John G., (Batavia) r 45, 10 cows, fruit grower, farmer 150.
FARLEY ABIATHA, (Le Roy) r 37, leader Farley's orchestra, farmer 30, and for
    Mary 36.
Farley De Forest, (Le Roy) r 38, musician and farmer.
Fay William, r 41, laborer.
Finch John, (Batavia) r 45, farmer 7.
Fisher Charles J., (Batavia) r 31, miller and farmer 40.
Fisher Joseph, (Batavia) r 31, farmer 84.
Fisk Abby, (S. Byron) r 24, widow of Alfred, farm 114.
Fisk Wallace. (Morganville) manuf. of corn planters.
FISKE SYLVANUS W., (Morganville) r 24, farmer 127.
Fogerty Thomas, (Bethany) r 56, farmer 1½.
Ford Charles, (Morganville) manuf. of flower pots.
Forsyth James, (Batavia) r 1, farmer 100, and leases of J. McCory, of Elba, 150.
Freelove Frank, (S. Byron) r 13, laborer.
Gardiner James, (Batavia) r 30, farmer 50.
GARDINER ENOS J., (S. Byron) r 4, live stock grower and dealer, farmer 145.
Gill James, r 51, farmer 79.
Gellard John, mason, h Main.
Getton Thomas, r 40, farmer 95.
Glasscock Herbert, r 41, laborer.
Good George, (S. Byron) r 6, carpenter.
Graves Newton, physician and surgeon, h Main.
Green William, (Le Roy) r 57, blacksmith.
Greening Frank, (Batavia) r 14, laborer.
Grentzinger George, (S. Byron) r 43, laborer.
Grentzinger John, (S. Byron) r 7, laborer.
Grentzinger Peter, (Batavia) r 43, farmer 16.

Griswold Carr L., (Morganville) farmer 14.
Hallock Frank, (Le Roy) r 56, farmer 130.
Hammett Henry, (Morganville) mason.
Harding John, farmer for Mary E. Bagot 170.
Harding Thomas, laborer, h Main.
Harper Charles, (Morganville) laborer.
Harper George, (Morganville) laborer.
Harrigan John, (Le Roy) r 54, farmer 25.
Harris John, (Bethany) r 57, retired.
Haws A. Lincoln, (Batavia) r 44, farmer.
Haws Sarah, (Batavia) r 44, (Mrs William) farmer 60.
HEAL'S HOTEL, Matthew W Heal, prop., Main.
HEAL MATTHEW W., prop. Heal's Hotel, stone quarry, and farmer 60, h Main.
Heal William, laborer, h Main.
Heart Charles, (S. Byron) r 5, farmer, leases of B. Bean, of Byron, 123.
Heddon Benjamin, (Le Roy) r 55, farmer.
Heddon John P., (Le Roy) r 58, farmer 60.
Heddon Thomas J., r 51, farmer 107.
Heddon William, (Le Roy) off r 55, farmer 100.
Heddon William P., (Le Roy) r 58, farmer 60.
Hennesey Patrick, (Le Roy) r 37, farmer 10.
Hermance James B., (Batavia) r 43, farmer 55.
Hess Alice,(Le Roy) widow of Alexander.
Hess Dolan, (Le Roy) r 55, mechanic.
Hess Peter, (Le Roy) r 55, farmer 15.
HEYWOOD JOHN, r 33, farmer 156.
Heywood John, 2d, r 46, farmer 195.
Heywood John, Jr., r 33, farmer with John.
Heywood John C., r 46, farmer.
Heywood William, r 33, farmer.
Hill Edward, r 34, farmer, leases of E. D. 130.
Hill Edward D., r 42, farmer 218.
Hill James, r 42, farmer.
Hill John, r 42, farmer.
Hill William, (Batavia) r 43, farmer 48, and leases of William Bosworth, of Batavia, 102.
Hodges Charles O., (Batavia) r 16, prop. Horse Shoe Lake.
Hodges Linell, (S. Byron) r 6, farmer 50.
Holland James, r 46, farmer.
HORN ADAM, (Batavia) r 15, manuf. of and dealer in Horn's German balm, dealer in willow and willow baskets, farmer 51.
Horn John V., (Batavia) r 15, with Adam.
Hough Christopher, (Batavia) r 16, farmer 1.
House John B., (Batavia) r 14½, farmer for E. F. 90.
HOUSEMAN WILLIAM W., (Batavia) r —, breeder of Jersey cattle, one Jersey bull, " Ko-Ko, of St. Lambert," No. 22,617, reg., farmer 116.
Howe William, laborer, h Main.
Hunt Sophia, r 35, widow of James, farmer 44.
Johnson Seymore, (Le Roy) r 58, farmer 135.
Johnson William G., (Batavia) r 10, collector and farmer.
Jones Walter, r 42, mason.
Kaneen William, shoemaker, h Main.
Keffler Jacob, (Morganville) r 27, farmer 45.
Keller George, (Batavia) r 31, laborer.
Kelleg Edward, (S. Byron) r 7, farmer 3.
KELLNER C., manuf. of willow, ratan, and reed chairs, etc.
Kellogg William, (Morganville) laborer.
Kelly Patrick, (Morganville) laborer.
Kendell Charles F., (Le Roy) r 59, farmer 90.

Kenny John, r 40, farmer 40.
Kiley Patrick, (Morganville) laborer.
Kingdon William, (Morganville) r 18, farmer 134.
Kingdon William E., (Morganville) r 18, farmer, leases of William 134.
Kingdon William G., (Morganville) r 18, farmer 6.
Lambie Fred, r 53, laborer.
Lathrop Elizabeth, (Morganville) r 25, widow of John.
LATHROP JAY, (Morganville) r 25, town supervisor, farmer 197.
Law Clarence, (Morganville) laborer.
Law Walter, (Morganville) laborer.
Law Wesley, (Morganville) laborer.
Leeplow Fred, (Morganville) r 26, farmer.
Legg Ellsworth. (Le Roy) r 57, laborer.
Legg George, (Le Roy) r 55, laborer.
Legg Jerome, r 42, laborer.
Legg Winfield, (Le Roy) r 58, laborer.
Lembke Fred, (S. Byron) r 21, farmer 75.
Lembke William, (S. Byron) farmer with Fred.
LINSTER MICHAEL, (Le Roy) r 36, farm supt. for Charles F. Prentice 400.
Luplow Frank, r 34, farmer with Joseph.
Luplow Fred, (Morganville) r 24, farmer, leases of the McCormick estate 60.
Luplow Joseph, r 34, farmer 210.
Luplow William, r 34, farmer with Joseph.
Maidment John, r 31, farmer 4.
Mann Emily J., (Batavia) r 17, widow of Dwight.
March John, retired, h Main.
Mason Eli P., (Le Roy) r 55, farmer with Mark 64.
Mason Mark, (Le Roy) r 55, farmer with Eli P. 64.
Mason Margaret, (Le Roy) r 55, widow of M. C.
Mason William H., (Le Roy) r 57, farmer 2.
Mayne John W., (Morganville) blacksmith.
Mayne Richard, r 45, farmer for George Prole 105.
McNuliff Mary, (Bavtaia) r 12, widow of Thomas, farm 8.
McNulty William, (Batavia) r 12, farmer 10.
McVean Peter J., (Morganville) r 25, farms O. Bassett estate 75 acres.
Mest George, (Morganville) laborer.
Mest Matthias, (Morganville) laborer.
Mest Mott, (Morganville) laborer.
MILLER FERDINAND C., (Morganville) general merchant and postmaster.
Miner Bradford, (Batavia) r 43, farmer with Stephen.
Miner Christopher J., (Batavia) r 45, farmer 133.
MINER HENRY CLAY, (Batavia) r 45, inventor and manuf. of Miner's automatic stanchion, and farmer 133.
Miner Lydia A., (Batavia) widow of Giles.
Miner Stephen, (Batavia) r 43, farmer 100.
Mortimore John, r 42, laborer.
Mortimore John, Jr., r 42, laborer.
Moulthrop Edwin N., (Batavia) r 13, farmer 216.
MULLEN I. T., M. D., coroner, physician, and surgeon.
MULLEN JOHN, (Morganville) r 29, farmer 76.
Mullen John W., (Batavia) r 18, carpenter.
Mullen William, (Batavia) r 18, farmer 96.
Murnan William, (Le Roy) r 39, farmer 5.
Newcomb Arthur, (Morganville) r 19, farmer, leases 114.
Newcomb Edgar, r 16, farmer 3.
Newcomb Edward, r 9, farmer 13.
Noel John, (Batavia) r 15, carpenter.
Nolan Bridget, (Morganville) r 19, widow of Peter, farmer 11.
Nolan John, (Le Roy) r 38, farmer 6.

NORRIS A. HART, (Morganville) r 27, farmer 600.
North James, r 50, school teacher, farmer 80.
O'Brian Martin, (Le Roy) r 57, laborer.
ODERKIRK MOSES W., (Batavia) r 10, fruit grower and breeder of American
    Merino sheep, reg., farmer 144.
Oderkirk Watts, (Batavia) r 10, farmer 1.
Page ———, widow of William, h Main.
Page Harry, laborer, h Main.
Page John, laborer, h Main.
Page Thomas, laborer.
Page William, shoemaker, h Main.
PAMPHILON EDWARD W. C., r 40, farmer 100.
PAMPHILON E. M., general merchant.
PARKERSON ROBERT M., (Morganville) prop. Union mills and dealer in flour,
    feed, etc.
PARMINTER THOMAS O., (Morganville) r 19, fruit grower and farmer 200.
PASSMORE JOHN, r 46, manuf. of and dealer in pure cider and cider vinegar, farmer
    171, and in Byron 116.
Passmore John, Jr., r 46, farmer with John.
Passmore William H., r 52, farmer.
Payne Harriet, widow of William.
PECK ISRAEL M., r 47, farmer 178.
Peck June, r 47, farmer.
PERRY JOHN W., (Batavia) r 29, farmer 100.
Peters William A., (Batavia) r 31, farmer 2, and leases of G. W. Scott 110.
Petherbridge Anthony, r 53, farmer 35.
Phelps George A., (Le Roy) r 57, laborer.
Pinney Frank, (Le Roy) r 57, farmer 75.
Plant Eliza, (Le Roy) r 58, widow of Columbus, h and 4 acres.
Porschet George, r 33, farmer, leases of John, of Batavia, 100.
Presticott George, tailor, Main.
Printice William, (Morganville) harnessmaker.
Prole Arthur, (Batavia) r 31, farmer 80.
Prole George, (Morganville) r 41, farmer 56.
Prole Henry, (Morganville) r 41, farmer 140.
Prole William H., (Morganville) r 41, farmer for Henry 140.
Quadley James, r 33, farmer 20.
Quadley James, Jr., r 33, laborer.
Quadley John, r 33, laborer.
Quadley William, r 33, laborer.
Radley Albert, laborer.
Radley Henry, r 24, farmer for J. Heywood 50.
Radley James, r 48, farmer 200.
Radley James S., r 49, farmer 140.
Radley Leonard, r 40, laborer.
Radley William E., (Morganville) r 24, resident.
Randall Frederick S., (Morganville) r 25, farmer with Perry.
Randall George M., (Morganville) r 25, farmer, leases of Nancy 250.
Randall Nancy, (Morganville) r 25, widow of Hiram, farm 250.
RANDALL PERRY, (Morganville) r 25, farmer 750.
Reed Mary, (Morganville) r 19, widow of Peter.
REMINGTON JOSEPH (Morganville) justice of the peace and harness manuf.
Rickard Patrick, (Batavia) r 15, laborer.
RODY AUGUST, (S. Byron) r 5, dealer in sheep, farmer 120.
Rody Fred, (Batavia) r 3, farmer 90.
Roman George, (Morganville) laborer.
Ross Edwin, (Morganville) laborer.
Roth Henry, (Morganville) laborer.
Roth Joseph, (Batavia) r 29, farmer, leases 120.

Ruben Harry, (Le Roy) r 55, general merchant.
Ruben John, (Le Roy) r 55, carpenter.
Rudolph Charles J., (Batavia) r 16, farmer, leases the J. Stone estate 130.
RUGG EDGAR G., (Batavia) r 32, farmer 50.
Russell Sherman, (Morganville) laborer.
Ryers William, r 42, laborer.
Sanders Ann, widow of Henry.
Sanders Archie D., (J. Sanders & Sons).
Sanders Elizabeth, widow of John.
Sanders Henry R., (J. Sanders & Sons) farmer 108.
Sanders Isabell, widow of E. B.
SANDERS J. & SON, (Archie D. and Henry R.) country produce dealers.
Sayers Robert, (Batavia) r 12, farmer 10.
Schram Guster, (Morganville) laborer.
Schram Christ, (Morganville) laborer.
Scions Mary, (Morganville) r 9, widow of John, farmer 35.
Scott George R., (Le Roy) r 54, farmer 125.
Scott George W., (Batavia) r 31, farmer 100.
Seldon Mira, widow of Robert, h Main.
Sellhorst Henry, r 19, chairmaker and farmer 10.
Shulters Leonard, (Batavia) r 15, farmer 50.
Simmons Harris, r 42, laborer.
Simmons John, (Morganville) r 41, highway commissioner, farmer 400.
Simmons Richard, laborer.
Smith Edward, r 39, farmer 82.
Smith Henry, (Morganville) laborer.
Smith Mason, r 40, farmer 55.
Smith Peter, (S. Byron) r 6, farmer 5.
Snider Walter, (S. Byron) r 4, laborer.
Squires Frank W., r 52, laborer.
Squires Thomas, laborer, h Main.
Squires William, r 50, farmer 18.
Stafford Rachel, (Morganville) r 25, widow of W. J.
Stephenson Robert, (Le Roy) r 57, cooper and farmer 25.
Stephenson William, (Le Roy) r 55, cooper.
Stevens Orrin, (Morganville) r 37, farmer.
Stickney Frank I., (Morganville) r 19, telephone operator and station agent Erie R. R.
Stone Harmon, (Morganville) ex-postmaster.
Strong Wells G., (E. Bethany) r 45, farmer 46.
STUTTERD JOSEPH F., r 40, farmer 112.
Sweetland Charles D., r 50, farmer 131.
Tellson Jerome, (S. Byron) r 4, farmer 3.
Terger Wendell, (Batavia) r 27, farmer 4.
TERRY JOHN W., (Batavia) r 13, farmer 163.
Thomas John, r 42, farmer 90.
Thomas Thomas, r 42, blacksmith.
Thompson Charles, (Le Roy) r 56, farmer.
Thompson Leonard, (Batavia) r 44, farmer 13.
Tillotson Fenimore, (Batavia) r 29, farmer 4.
Toger John, r 48, farmer, leases of J. Simmons 90.
Totterdale George, r 41, farmer 110.
Totterdale John W., farmer with George.
Travis Leonard, (Batavia) r 15, fruit grower, farmer 10.
Trick Thomas H., butcher, h Main.
Trick Wilber J., r 46, farmer with William.
TRICK WILLIAM, r 40, farmer 183.
Trick William I., farmer, h Main.
Trick Willis S., school teacher.
Tucker David N., (Morganville) peddler.

Tucker Emanuel, r 33, farmer 150.
Tucker Thomas, r 42, farmer 50.
Tyler Albert, (S. Byron) r 8, farmer with Warren J.
Tyler Martin C., (S. Byron) r 20, farmer for Sallie A. 100.
Tyler Sallie A., (Batavia) r 19, farm 100.
TYLER WARREN J., (S. Byron) r 8, breeder of Merino sheep, reg., farmer 260.
Vallett Bertie, (Batavia) r 29, laborer.
Vallett Henry, (Batavia) r 17, painter and farmer 3.
Vallett Sarah, (Batavia) r 16, widow of Joseph, farmer 125.
Vickery George, r 40, farmer.
Vickary William N.. r 40, farmer 55. [Died April 7, 1889.]
Wade Louisa, (Batavia) r 15, widow of Louis.
WAKLEY JOHN, carpenter, h Main.
WAKLEY SAMUEL J., station agent N. Y. C. & H. R. R. R. h Main.
Waldron Abraham, laborer.
WALDRON THOMAS, stone mason and cooper, h Main.
Walker Frank C., (S. Byron) r 9, farmer 140.
Ward William, r 4, carpenter.
Waterman Anthony J., (S. Byron) r 19, farmer with Selma 75.
Waterman Bennet, (Morganville) r 21, farmer 72.
Waterman Charles W., (S. Byron) r 6, farmer 83.
WATERMAN OSCAR F..(S. Byron) r 22, farmer 100.
Waterman Selma, (S. Byron) r 19, farmer with Anthony J. 75.
WATSON GORDON T., r 40, farmer 46.
Watson Harriet M., (Le Roy) r 38, widow of Ira, farm 62.
WEBBER JOHN H., r 42, farmer 141.
Weller Addison, r 40, farmer 30.
Weller Charles, r 41, wagonmaker.
Weller William, r 40, farmer 111,
Westacott George, (Le Roy) r 54, breeder of Southdown sheep, farmer 70.
Westacutt James, r 35, farmer 17, and leases of G. Tutterdale 40.
Westacutt John, r 41, farmer 9.
Westtrook John A., (Morganville) r 19, farmer 70.
WHITE ALBERT H., (Morganville) manuf. of wagons, carriages, and potato diggers.
WHITE ORPHA, (Morganville) widow of Henry, pensioner of the War of 1812.
Whiting Jane, (Morganville) widow of Amos, weaver.
Williams Peter, dealer in bed springs, h Main.
Wilson William W., (S. Byron) farmer for D. C., of Rochester, 160.
WOOD ELIZABETH S., widow of William, farmer 350, h Main.
Woodbine Samuel, (Batavia) r 11, farmer 50
Wright James H., (Morganville) r 24, farmer 108.
Yerger Wendall, (Morganville) r 27, farmer 4.
Young Ann, (Morganville) widow of William.
Young Julia, (Morganville) teacher of elocution.
Zastrow John, r 31, laborer.

TONAWANDA RESERVATION.

(For explanations, etc., see page 3, part second.)

(Postoffice address in parenthesis.)

Abrams Chauncy H., (Akron, Erie Co.) r 37, chief.
Abrams Milton, (Akron, Erie Co.) off r 37, chief.
Allick William, (Akron, Erie Co.) r 37.
Bigfire Jane, (Akron. Erie Co.) r 37, widow.
Billy John, (Akron. Erie Co.) off r 37.
Blackchief Charles, (Akron, Erie Co.) r 37.
Bluesky Samuel, (Akron, Erie Co.) off r 37, chief.
Carpenter Harvey, (Akron, Erie Co.) r 37.
Carpenter Moses, (Akron, Erie Co.) r 37.
Charles John, (Basom) r 57.
Charles Joseph, (Basom) r 57.
Clute Charles, (Indian Falls) off r 62.
Doctor Charles W., (Akron, Erie Co.) r 60, chief.
Doctor Frank A., (Akron, Erie Co.) r 37.
Doctor Frederick, (Akron, Erie Co.) r 59.
Doctor Isaac, (Akron, Erie Co.) r 37, chief.
Doctor Jacob, (Akron, Erie Co.) r 61, chief.
Doxtater James, (Akron, Erie Co.) r 61.
Fish Daniel, (Indian Falls) r 61.
Fish John, (Akron, Erie Co.) r 60.
Fish William, (Akron, Erie Co.) r 37.
George James, (Akron, Erie Co.) r 61.
Griffin John, (Basom) r 38, Baptist clergyman and Indian doctor, farmer 50.
Ground Andrew, (Basom) r 55.
Ground Benjamin, (Akron, Erie Co.) off r 37.
Ground Moses, (Akron, Erie Co.) r 37.
Hatch Howard, (Akron, Erie Co.) r 37, chief.
Hatch James, (Akron, Erie Co.) off r 37.
Hill Isaac, (Akron, Erie Co.) r 61.
Hill James, (Akron, Erie Co.) r 37.
Hill William, (Akron, Erie Co.) r 61.
Hotbread Lewis, (Akron, Erie Co.) r 37, chief.
Infirst Henry, (Indian Falls) r 62.
Jimason George, (Akron, Erie Co.) r 37, chief.
Jimason John, (Akron, Erie Co.) r 59.
Jimason Jonathan, (Basom) off r 57.
Jimason Wallace, (Basom) r 57, chief.
Johnson Charles, (Akron, Erie Co.) r 37.
Johnson Eli, (Akron, Erie Co.) r 61, chief.
Johnson Herbert, (Basom) off r 62, chief.
Johnson James, (Akron, Erie Co.) off r 61.
Jones John, (Akron, Erie Co.) off r 37.
Jones Mariah, (Akron, Erie Co.) r 37, widow of William.
Kennedy Charles C., (Akron, Erie Co.) off r 61.
Lone Chauncy, (Akron, Erie Co.) off r 37, chief.
Miller Jacob, (Basom) r 62.
Milten George, (Basom) r 62, farmer.
Milten James, (Basom) r 62, retired.

Moses Clinton, (Akron, Erie Co.) r 59.
Moses David, (Akron, Erie Co.) r 60.
Moses William H., (Akron, Erie Co.) r 37, farmer.
Parker Levi, (Basom) r 62.
Parker Otto W., (Basom) r 37.
Poodry E. M., (Basom) r 38, chief.
Poodry William, (Akron, Erie Co.) r 37.
Pordry Sampson, (Basom) r 62.
Pordry Edward M., (Basom) r 38.
Pordry Thomas, (Basom) r 38.
Printup Erastus, (Basom) r 57, chief.
Printup John, (Basom) r 55.
Printup John, (Basom) r 37.
Ruben Jacob, (Akron, Erie Co.) r 61.
Scrogg Carlo, (Akron, Erie Co.) r 37.
Shanks Eliza, (Akron, Erie Co.) r 57, widow of Isaac.
Skye Robert, (Akron, Erie Co.) r 37, chief.
Skye Stephen, (Akron, Erie Co.) r 37.
Skye Thomas, (Akron, Erie Co.) r 37, chief.
Skye Warren, (Akron, Erie Co.) r 37.
Smith Julia A., (Akron, Erie Co.) r 37, widow of Abram.
Snow George, (Akron, Erie Co.) r 37.
Snyder Alexander, (Akron, Erie Co.) r 37.
Snyder Amos, (Akron, Erie Co.) r 37.
Snyder Gilson, (Akron, Erie Co.) r 37.
Snyder Peter H., (Akron, Erie Co.) r 37.
Spring Jesse (Basom) r 53, chief.
Spring Solomon, (Basom) r 53, chief.
Stone Charles, (Akron, Erie Co.) r 59.
Strong William, (Basom) r 38, chief.
Sundown Newton, (Akron, Erie Co.) r 59.
White Eliza, (Basom) r 55, widow of Thomas.
Wilson Mary, (Akron, Erie Co.) r 61, widow of John.

CONTENTS.

INDEX TO ILLUSTRATIONS.

COURTS.

AT BATAVIA.

Genesee County Circuit Courts, special terms of the Supreme Court, and Courts of Oyer and Terminer:

Second Monday in March, Lambert; third Monday in June, Lewis; and second Monday in November, Childs.

County Court and Court of Sessions:

Third Monday in April, second Monday in September, and second Monday in December.

INDEX TO BIOGRAPHIES.

13*

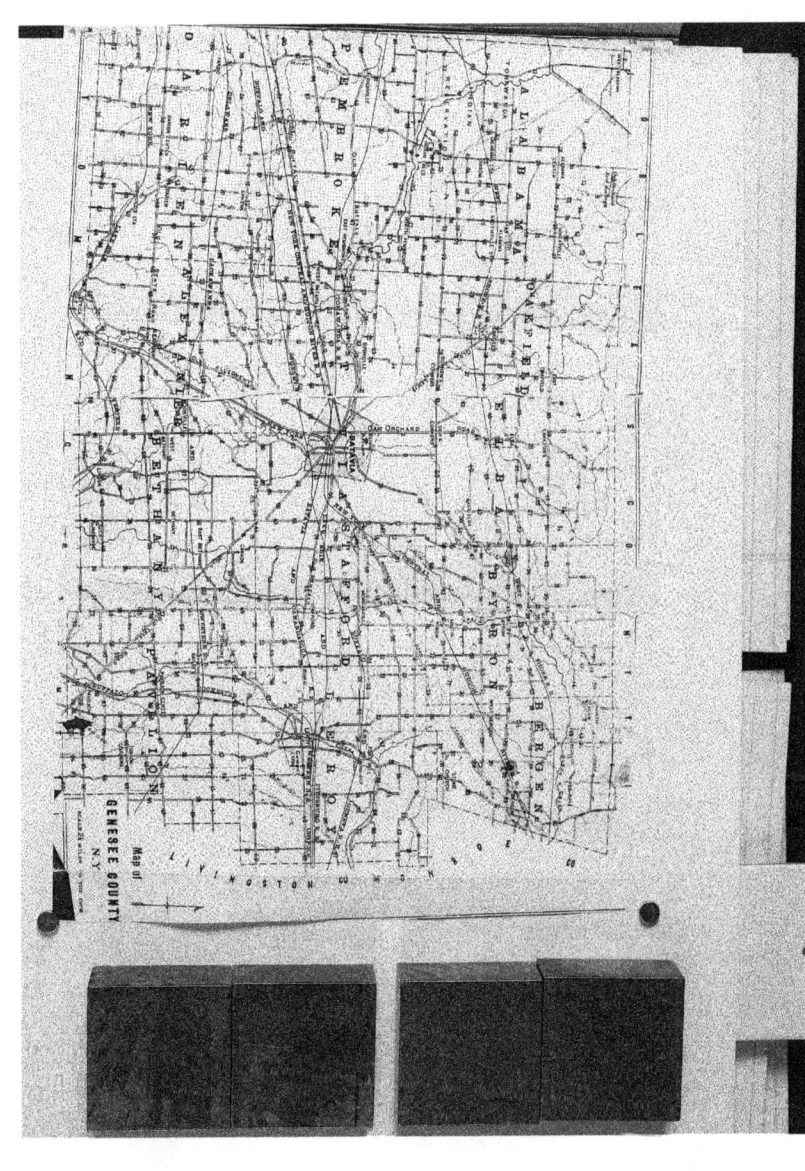

Map of
GENESEE COUNTY
N.Y.

CPSIA information can be obtained
at www.ICGtesting.com
Printed in the USA
BVHW04*1726060818
523683BV00018B/1435/P